GREAT THINKERS
OF THE
WESTERN WORLD

GREAT THINKERS
OF THE
WESTERN WORLD

*The major ideas and classic works of more than
100 outstanding Western philosophers, physical and
social scientists, psychologists, religious writers,
and theologians*

EDITED BY IAN P. McGREAL

HarperCollins*Publishers*

HarperCollins books may be purchased for educational, business, or sales promotional use. For information, please call or write: Special Markets Department, HarperCollins Publishers, Inc., 10 East 53rd Street, New York, NY 10022. Telephone (212) 207-7528; Fax: (212) 207-7222.

FIRST EDITION

Designed by Irving Perkins Associates

Library of Congress Cataloging-in-Publication Data

Great thinkers of the Western world : guide to the principal theories
and major works of more than 100 famous thinkers in philosophy, the
physical sciences, the social sciences, psychology, and religion /
edited by Ian P. McGreal. — 1st ed.
p.   cm.
Includes bibliographical references and index.
ISBN 0-06-270026-X
1. Philosophy.   2. Theology.   3. Science.   I. McGreal,
Ian Philip, 1919–
B72.G74   1992
190—dc20   91-38362

93 94 95 96 PS/RRD 10 9 8 7 6 5 4 3

CONTENTS

PREFACE

This book has been designed to make as clear as possible the principal theoretical ideas of more than one hundred great thinkers of the Western world—thinkers from philosophy, theology, the physical sciences, the social sciences, psychology, and religion.

The descriptive and explanatory ideas generated by these creative thinkers have profoundly affected the character and course of world history and have definitively influenced the Western perspective, mind, and spirit. The ideas may not all be true—certainly many of them are inadequate, if not false or misleading—but they have all been influential, and they have all contributed to the building of the modern mind.

However, the concentration on Western thinkers is not intended to suggest that the thinking of the *Eastern* world—particularly the contributions of China, India, and Japan—is not also of profound importance because of its distinctively creative contributions to philosophical, scientific, and ethical thought. But the editorial decision was made to concentrate on the Western thinkers in this book, partly because we were not sure we could competently do both East and West in a single volume and partly because we think that for Western readers it is especially helpful if we first of all understand and appreciate the Western ways of thinking. Unless we know what the great thinkers of the West, with their reliance on experience, reason, and logic, have produced, we are hardly in a position to grasp and appraise ways of thought that involve for their understanding an appreciation of Oriental cultures and the recognition of ways of understanding—intuitive, paradoxical, and aesthetic—that are in many respects different, at least in emphasis and the manner of their employment, from our own.

No one can be knowledgeable in every field or even, to any significant degree of thoroughness, in any one. But we would all like to grasp as a matter of general knowledge the fundamental theories—explanatory or descriptive ideas—that have advanced human understanding and the appreciation of the human condition and its creative possibilities. By drawing upon scholars from the various areas in which the great thinkers have exercised their genius and by making the effort to explain the major lines of thought without being superficial or pedantic, we have worked to provide a substantial guide for the general reader.

The articles are arranged chronologically, from Parmenides to Albert Camus, so that readers who choose to browse through the book can to some degree recognize and appreciate the development of ideas from the early Greeks through the first half of the twentieth century. The book also provides an alphabetical index of thinkers, making it a ready reference to the ideas of thinkers about whom the reader is especially inquisitive at any given time.

Great Thinkers of the Western World, then, is a *guide* and, for some readers, an *introduction* to the great ideas and works that the most creative and influential thinkers of the Western world have produced. Our book cannot make anyone an expert in any of the fields the book covers, but it can, we hope, provide a foothold on—or a mind-grasp of—the illuminating theories and perspectives that have shaped the modern mind and left their traces in the history of human accomplishments.

In closing, I want to thank my fellow contributors not only for their enthusiasm, cooperation, and careful work but also for their invaluable suggestions during the early phases of the project when we had to decide which thinkers to include and which to leave out. We have tried to include the most original, creative, and influential thinkers, of course, but we have also recognized the importance of representing the diversity of significant Western thought, even though the result may be that some thinkers that deserve to be regarded as great have been left out, while others that might not be universally regarded as "great" have been included.

As usual, Jean H. Faurot, Professor of Philosophy Emeritus, my colleague in the Department of Philosophy at California State University, Sacramento, has been an informed and conscientious adviser to me, and his suggestions have certainly influenced the book for the better. My only regret is

that ill health prevented him from joining our staff of contributors; his articles surely would have been like the many others he has written—scholarly, lively, and perceptive.

I appreciate also the very helpful suggestions given me by Professor Gene Barnes of the Department of Physics, California State University, Sacramento; he was particularly resourceful in commenting on and adding to the list of scientific thinkers to be included.

Ian P. McGreal

CONTRIBUTORS

W. Loyd Allen (*Ph.D., Southern Baptist Theological Seminary*). Associate Professor of Church History, Southern Baptist Theological Seminary, Louisville, Kentucky.

D. Brian Austin (*Ph.D., Southern Baptist Theology Seminary*). Assistant Professor of Philosophy, Cumberland College, Williamsburg, Kentucky.

Harry James Cargas (*Ph.D., St. Louis University*). Professor of Literature and Religion, Webster University, St. Louis, Missouri.

Bowman L. Clarke (*Ph.D., Emory University*). Professor of Philosophy, University of Chicago, Chicago, Illinois.

Constance Creede (*M.Div., Union Theological Seminary*). Department of English Literature, Rutgers University, New Brunswick, New Jersey.

John Cronquist (*Ph.D., Stanford University*). Professor of Philosophy, California State University, Fullerton, California.

Don Thomas Dugi (*Ph.D., Purdue University*). Professor of Political Science, Transylvania College, Lexington, Kentucky.

Frederick Ferré (*Ph.D., University of St. Andrews, Scotland*). Professor of Philosophy, University of Georgia, Athens, Georgia.

Robert D. Frye (*Ph.D., University of Illinois*). Professor of French, Regis College, Weston, Massachusetts.

Mary E. Giles (*Ph.D., University of California, Berkeley*). Professor of Humanities, California State University, Sacramento, California.

Donald E. Hall (*Ph.D., Stanford University*). Professor of Physics, California State University, Sacramento, California.

Thomas E. Helm (*Ph.D., University of Chicago*). Professor of Philosophy and Religious Studies, Western Illinois University, Macomb, Illinois.

E. Glenn Hinson (*D.Phil., Oxford University; Th.D., Southern Seminary, Louisville*). Professor of Church History, Southern Baptist Theological Seminary, Louisville, Kentucky.

Lawrence F. Hundersmarck (*Ph.D., Fordham University*). Professor of Philosophy and Religious Studies, Pace University, White Plains, New York.

Paul E. Hurley (*Ph.D., University of Pittsburgh*). Assistant Professor of Philosophy, Pomona College, Claremont, California.

Oliver A. Johnson (*Ph.D., Yale University*). Professor of Philosophy Emeritus, University of California, Riverside, California.

Terry Kershaw (*Ph.D., Washington State University*). Assistant Professor of Sociology, College of Wooster, Wooster, Ohio.

Clark A. Kucheman (*Ph.D., The University of Chicago*). Professor of Philosophy, Claremont McKenna College, Claremont, California.

Burton M. Leiser (*Ph.D., Brown University*). Professor of Philosophy, Pace University, New York, New York.

Ian P. McGreal (*Ph.D., Brown University*). Professor of Philosophy Emeritus, California State University, Sacramento, California.

Robert J. Meindl (*Ph.D., Tulane University*). Professor of English, California State University, Sacramento, California.

M. E. Moss (*Ph.D., The Johns Hopkins University*). Professor of Philosophy, Claremont McKenna College, Claremont, California.

Richard A. Muller (*Ph.D., Duke University*). Professor of Historical Theology, Fuller Theological Seminary, Pasadena, California.

M. Basil Pennington, O.C.S.O. (*S.T.L., Pontifical University of Saint Thomas Aquinas; J.C.L., Pontifical University of Gregoriana, Rome, Italy*). School of Theology and Institute of Monastic Studies, St. Joseph's Abbey, Spencer, Massachusetts.

Richard H. Popkin (*Ph.D., Columbia University*). Professor of Philosophy Emeritus, Washington University, St. Louis, Missouri, and Adjunct Professor of History and Philosophy at the University of California, Los Angeles, California.

Marjean D. Purinton (*Ph.D., Texas A & M University*). Professor of English, Texas A & M University, College Station, Texas.

Mark T. Riley (*Ph.D., Stanford University*). Professor of Classics, California State University, Sacramento, California.

John K. Roth (*Ph.D., Yale University*). Professor of Philosophy, Claremont McKenna College, Claremont, California.

Gary R. Sattler (*Dr. Theol., University of Marburg*). Assistant Professor of Christian Formation and Discipleship. Fuller Theological Seminary, Pasadena, California.

Dion Scott-Kakures (*Ph.D., University of Michigan*). Professor of Philosophy, Scripps College, Claremont, California.

Rowland A. Sherrill (*Ph.D., University of Chicago*). Professor of Religious Studies, Indiana University, Indianapolis, Indiana.

Frederick Sontag (*Ph.D., Yale University*). Professor of Philosophy, Pomona College, Claremont, California.

Eric O. Springsted (*Ph.D., Princeton Theological Seminary*). Associate Professor of Philosophy and Religion, Illinois College, Jackson, Illinois.

Dan R. Stiver (*Ph.D., Southern Baptist Theological Seminary*). Associate Professor of Christian Philosophy, Southern Baptist Theological Seminary, Louisville, Kentucky.

Susan Williamson (*Ph.D., Brandeis University*). Professor of Mathematics, Regis College, Weston, Massachusetts.

GREAT THINKERS
OF THE
WESTERN WORLD

PARMENIDES

Born: C. 515 B.C., Elea, Italy
Died: After 450 B.C.
Major Work: Poem, extant only in fragments, on the "One Being"

Major Ideas

A contrast must be made by philosophy between "the way of truth," concerning the oneness and changelessness of being, and "the way of seeming," concerning our perception of change.
Being, or "it is," is the fullness of all that exists; not-being, or "it is not," cannot exist.
Being cannot come from not-being or be reduced to not-being.
Cosmology, the presentation of the world order as becoming, is false and self-contradictory.

Although it is certain that Parmenides was born in Magna Graecia, in the city-state of Elea, sometime toward the end of the sixth century B.C., the precise dates of his birth and death are unknown. Plato tells us in his dialogue *Parmenides* that the great Eleatic philosopher visited Athens with Zeno and met Socrates. Parmenides, Plato tells us, was about sixty-five, Zeno about forty, and Socrates "very young." Socrates was born in 470 B.C. and the date of the meeting, granting the youthfulness of Socrates, is assumed to have been c. 450 B.C. yielding 515 B.C. for the birth of Parmenides. Although several ancient writers report that Parmenides was a Pythagorean, at least for a time, he is usually thought to have been the pupil of Xenophanes, the founder of the Eleatic school of philosophy. His teaching, in any case, directly reflects Xenophanes's critique of polytheism in the name of the "one god . . . [who] . . . abides in the selfsame place, moving not at all" and who is identical with the whole world.

Like Xenophanes, Parmenides chose to elaborate his thought in the form of a poem. We may surmise that Parmenides was somewhat younger than Heraclitus (fl. 504–501 B.C.) inasmuch as Heraclitus attacks the monism of Xenophanes but gives no evidence of knowing Parmenides's thought, whereas Parmenides appears to argue directly against the cosmological theory of Heraclitus. We also know from the comments of later writers that Parmenides, like many of the early Greek philosophers, took an active role in the poli-

tics of his native city and that he even formulated the basic law code of Elea.

However vague the biographical data concerning Parmenides, it is quite clear that his thought marks a watershed in pre-Socratic philosophy. Parmenides's thought, coming at the close of the sixth century B.C., was influenced by both the worldly, scientific, and cosmological views of early Greek philosophical inquiry and the Orphic religious revival of the early sixth century, with its focus on ecstasy, the reality of the soul as divine, the ultimate reality of "the One God who dwells in all," and the bliss of release from the body. The Orphic religion, moreover, tended to organize itself into small communities and to emphasize the cultivation of a way of life under the instruction of a revealed knowledge—a model for life and teaching very much like that adopted by later Greek philosophers and their schools.

Contrary to what is commonly assumed, the earliest Greek philosophers hardly eschewed observation in favor of rational speculation about the cosmos. Thus, Xenophanes's view that "all things are earth and water" and that these two fundamental elements mingle and separate was based at least in part on his examination of fossilized seashells found in the hills. Similarly, Anaximander argued the development or evolution of man from other animals on the basis of observations of the natural order and the inability of infants to find food for themselves. Anaximander appears to have viewed the shark, which cares briefly for its young as at a midpoint in the development of higher forms of life.

The question raised concerning early Greek philosophy (though certainly not solved) by the sixth-century religious revival was surely a question of the nature of reality: Was reality to be found in the observed many or in the ultimate One? To a certain extent, this question had already been posed from the philosophical side by Xenophanes, who, after studying the world in its multiplicity, had endeavored to identify an ultimate principle or principles and had spoken of the whole of the world as "the One" and as "God" in a scientific and philosophical polemic against polytheism. Even more important to the way in which Parmenides's philosophy is constructed was Heraclitus's attempt to resolve the problem: Heraclitus taught that the world is both the many and the One and that the unity of all things as the One consists in the movement of the many in their separation out of the One and their resolution into it. The ultimate unity Heraclitus identified as "Fire," presumably because of the way in which living fire both disperses smoke and consumes fuel, continually changing and continually remaining the same.

The poem in which Parmenides presented his philosophical alternative to these earlier views of the world is preserved in a set of eighteen fragments quoted in Simplicius's commentary on Aristotle's *Physics*, written in the sixth century A.D. Simplicius still had the great library of the Academy at his disposal and he serves as the primary source for the fragments of pre-Socratic philosophy. Scholars have estimated on the basis both of the fragments themselves and of other ancient comments on the philosophy of Parmenides that we possess the prologue and most of the first portion of Parmenides's poem, "The Way of Truth," but very little of the second part, "The Way of Opinion" (or "of Seeming").

The prologue to the poem describes Parmenides's sudden insight into truth as a religious experience guided by divine hands. A chariot is described as bearing Parmenides toward "the gates of the ways of Night and Day." Guided by maidens, he passes through into the realm of the goddess Diké or Justice. He there is taught "the

way of truth" and encouraged to "judge" or "examine" truth through "reason" or "rational discourse" (*logos*).

The prologue to Parmenides's discussion of the two ways reveals much about Parmenides's thought and about the foundations and direction of Greek philosophy. First of all, the close relationship both in form and in inspiration between early Greek philosophy and Greek religion is quite apparent. Parmenides not only associates the knowledge of truth with the knowledge accessible primarily to the gods, he also understands human access to that truth as a matter of revelation rather than of mortal investigation. The very form of his prologue has suggested an Orphic revelation or "apocalypse" as his model. Of course, what Parmenides develops in his "way of truth" is not religion but philosophy, and no mention of the divine or of the need for divine assistance is mentioned beyond the mythic or allegorical language of the prologue. Nonetheless, if only in a formal sense, the perception of truth is, for Parmenides (as it would be for Socrates and Plato), a matter of penetration beyond the realm of fallible human perceptions and, indeed, a matter that must often be presented in the form of myth rather than in forms dictated by the native powers of human observation.

Second, and equally important, Parmenides's prologue contains the first known use of *logos* as the term for rational discourse or argument, as it would be taken over by Socrates and Plato. One sees, surely, the acknowledgment of this indebtedness in Plato's dialogue the *Parmenides*, where the young Socrates fails in argument before the older master and is instructed by him in the intricacies of dialectical argumentation—albeit in a place where the Socratic doctrine of the participation of sensible things in the Forms is being posed against the Eleatic view of the illusory nature of the world of sense. Plato appears not so much to argue with the use of logic by the school of Parmenides as to conclude, in defense of Socrates's views, that their thought was not as strictly logical and rational as it ought to have been.

There is some justice, then, in the judgment that

Parmenides's philosophy of being stood in the way of the development of empirical science and, to the extent that Parmenides determined the course of Greek philosophy, it contributed to the rational investigation of the problem of the really real, the changeless reality behind phenomena, carried forward by Socrates and Plato. Like his teacher Xenophanes and Alcmaeon, the Pythagorean, Parmenides could draw a distinction between the certainty of ultimate or divine knowledge and the uncertainty of sense experience, but it was the burden of Parmenides's philosophy to adopt the standpoint of what Alcmaeon and others would have identified as divine knowing. The uncertainty and apparent knowing characteristic of human beings who examine the world of variety, distinction, and flux is set aside by Parmenides's identification of true knowledge as a certainty concerning the changelessness of the One. Rather than find knowledge in and through the examination of externals, Parmenides rests knowledge on the divine revelation of truth. In his poetic philosophical manifesto, he is conducted by "the daughters of the Sun" from the "abode of Night" and instructed by the goddess in the distinction between "well-rounded truth" and "the opinions of mortals, in which there is no true belief."

The "well-rounded truth" concerning changeless being is a truth of the pure intellect, which cannot be known through sense experience and cannot be reached by a process of logical progression or regression from the world of change to the realm of Being. By Parmenides's own account, "the way of truth" is revealed in a moment to the intellect alone, from beyond the grasp of sensuous human knowing, and consists in a meditation on the nature and character of the realization that "it is" rather than "it is not." Aristotle, whose emphasis on the senses as the genuine avenues of knowledge led him in precisely the opposite direction from Parmenides, saw that Parmenides assumed two ways of knowing: the one resting on reason or intellect and recognizing that "all things are one," and the other resting on sense perception and falling into the assumption that reality is diverse or "plural."

Parmenides not only offered a trenchant critique of the cosmological tendencies of previous Greek philosophy, he also posed the critique in such a way as to redirect the course of Greek thought. His view of reality took as its point of departure the logical flaw in earlier theories of cosmological becoming, particularly the view of Heraclitus that the universal fire transforms into the varieties of things and then returns again to itself. Not only was it a truism in this earlier philosophy that nothing can be generated from nonexistence, it was also the case that the earlier philosophy could not explain why or how the ultimate principle transforms itself. In other words, Parmenides recognized that the philosophies of change could find no genuine explanation for the change that was so fundamental to their conception of reality. Parmenides, therefore, argued the opposite view: Rather than identifying reality with change or becoming and the stability of being with semblance or illusion, he referred all change to the problems inherent in sense perception and identified reality as changeless existence.

Parmenides assumed that, logically, there could be only two ways of understanding reality—and a third way caused by confused thinking. Thus either something exists and must exist or nothing exists: Reality is to be conceived either as being ("it is") or as not-being ("it is not"). The second logical option is, of course, an impossibility that defies the very process of knowing: "For you could never learn what is not; that is impossible; nor could you describe it." The third way assumes, in Parmenides's own cryptic phrasing, that "to be and not to be are thought the same and not the same" or that "things that are not *are*"—in other words, that what is and what is not are somehow convertible and interchangeable, much after the pattern of Heraclitus's philosophy. After excluding this third way as a result of confusion, Parmenides considers the two ways of approaching the world and reality: "the way of truth" and "the way of opinion."

In Parmenides's way of thinking, the impossible and unknowable approach to reality as not-being or what is not, "the way of opinion," is precisely the approach of previous philosophy, granting that it has concentrated on the changing world of human sense perception and has refused to contemplate that which simply *is*—that which "is" and is, therefore, "without beginning, indestructible, entire, single, unshakable, endless. . . ."

Parmenides's view of reality is not, as might be inferred from subsequent discussions of being and not-being, a form of idealism that identifies reality as a supersensible or intelligible Form, distinct and separate from matter. Rather, Parmenides's philosophy appears to have been a thoroughgoing materialism that dwelt on the truth that something "is" and that, therefore, "it is" constitutes the ground of philosophical meditation, not "it is not."

This unity of what *is*, Parmenides viewed as finite, indivisible, immovable, and spherical. Since all that *is* simply *is*, and since "it is not" cannot be said to be without contradiction, there can be nothing apart from what is and no empty space. What simply *is* cannot come into or pass out of existence. By the same logic, what *is* must be complete in itself and have nothing beyond it—and it must be equally complete in all directions.

Far from being a consideration of the opposite side of the problem of the world, therefore, the second half of Parmenides's poem, "the way of seeming," is nothing other than a recitation of the conclusions reached by the erroneous examination of the world by the senses. Here Parmenides speaks of "the substance of the sky," and "the wandering motions of the round-faced moon." Indeed, Parmenides discusses these conclusions in order that "no opinion of mortals will ever surpass" him or his followers. The value of this second part of the poem, therefore, must be restricted to what it tells us of the cosmology of Parmenides's contemporaries, most probably the Pythagoreans.

The importance of Parmenides derives from his application and elaboration of the Eleatic assumption of the ultimate reality of the One, inherited from Xenophanes. Parmenides recognized that the great issue of Greek philosophy was the problem of the One and the many, of being and becoming, which he expressed in his radical dichotomy, "either *it is* or *it is not*." He is the father in a direct sense of later materialism and, in an indirect sense, as witnessed by Plato's *Parmenides*, of the Socratic and Platonic attempt to reestablish a relationship between the One and the many on idealist grounds, with the One considered as Form and the many as its embodiments.

RICHARD A. MULLER

Further Reading

Guthrie, W. K. C. *A History of Greek Philosophy*. 6 vols. Cambridge: Cambridge University Press, 1962–81. The definitive modern study, excelling all other works on the subject in detail and grasp of the materials. The treatment of Parmenides is found in vol. 2, pp. 1–80.

Nahm, Milton C. *Selections from Early Greek Philosophy*. 4th ed. New York: Appleton-Century-Crofts, 1964. A good modern translation of the major fragments and collateral testimonies.

Snell, Bruno. *The Discovery of the Mind in Greek Philosophy and Literature*. Trans. T. G. Rosenmeyer, 1953; reprinted New York: Dover, 1982. A superb study of Greek language and thought that documents the development of the concept of a self-conscious intellect out of the more or less descriptive language of early Greek thought.

Zeller, Eduard. *A History of Greek Philosophy from the Earliest period to the Time of Socrates*. 2 vols. Trans. S. F. Alleyne. London: Longmans, 1881. A classic work that offers useful discussion of the various pre-Socratic philosophers together with an excellent sense of the development and movement of early Greek philosophy.

ZENO OF ELEA

Born: C. 490 B.C., Elea, Italy
Died: C. 430 B.C.
Major Works: No extant works, but the following famous paradoxes are attributed to Zeno: *Paradox of Achilles and the Tortoise, Paradox of the Arrow, Paradox of the Race Course, Paradox of the Stadium, Paradox of Plurality*

Major Ideas

The Paradox of the Race Course *argues that motion would require a process of infinite division.*
The Paradox of Achilles and the Tortoise *concludes that a swifter runner cannot overtake a slower.*
The Paradox of the Arrow *argues that an arrow cannot move in flight.*
The Paradox of the Stadium *maintains that double the time is sometimes equal to half the time.*
The Paradox of Plurality *argues that if space and time are composed of discrete units, the number of such units is both finite and infinite.*

Zeno of Elea was a disciple of Parmenides, who argued that Reality is One—an unmoving, solid, homogeneous sphere. In his support of Parmenides and against the Pythagoreans, Zeno composed a number of paradoxes designed to show that if one accepts a pluralistic account of space and time, a view that space is made up of discrete and divisible units of space, and time of discrete and divisible units of time, then one runs into difficulties, if not contradictions.

Very little is known of Zeno's life. He was born about 490 B.C. in Elea (now Velia, southern Italy). His father was Teleutagoras. It is reported (in Plato's *Parmenides*) that Zeno was "tall and fair to look upon," and that at the time of a purported discussion involving Zeno, Socrates, and Parmenides, Zeno was forty years old and Parmenides sixty-five. Zeno appears to have been politically active and to have been critical of a Sicilian tyrant and to have refused, even under torture, to reveal the name of his political associates. (One account tells us that, rather than reveal anything that might be damaging to his associates, Zeno bit off part of his tongue and threw it at his torturers.)

In various ancient works, reference is made to Zeno's "writings," but unfortunately none of Zeno's works is extant. However, in a discussion of the continuity of motion, space, and time, Aristotle (in his *Physics*) gives an account of four paradoxes of

motion attributed to Zeno and comments critically on them.

A fifth paradox—which has been called the Paradox of Plurality—may be found in the *Physics* of Simplicius.

The Paradox of the Race Course

The first of Zeno's arguments against the possibility of motion is given by Aristotle in these words (translation by W. D. Ross in the *Oxford Translation of Aristotle*):

> The first [of the arguments about motion] asserts the non-existence of motion on the ground that that which is in locomotion must arrive at the halfway stage before it arrives at the goal.

The paradox becomes clearer if one attends to John Burnet's rendering of the argument in his *Early Greek Philosophy*:

> You cannot cross a race-course. You cannot traverse an infinite number of points in a finite time. You must traverse the half of any given distance before you can traverse the whole, and the half of that again before you can traverse it. This goes on *ad infinitum* . . .

There are two ways of considering this paradox dramatically, both of them mind-challenging. According to Zeno, any attempt to cover any finite distance (say, to make a trip or to run a race) is frustrated by the circumstance that before finishing the whole distance, there is still half the remaining distance to go. Even if that half were covered, there would still be half the remaining distance. There is always half the remaining distance to go, no matter how many halves one manages to cover. So it appears that a trip or a race (or any passage from one place to another) can never be finished.

Another way of looking at it is this: One cannot even get started in the effort to move from one place to another. For before covering the first half of the distance, one would have to cover half of that first half. But before covering *that* half, one would have to cover half of it. But there is never a first half by covering which one could get started. The frustration is complete before the trip (or race) even gets started!

Aristotle criticizes this paradox by contending that anything continuous (such as motion from one place to another) is infinitely divisible. (A half is itself divisible, and the quarters are divisible, and so forth, *ad infinitum*.) But to say that a distance is "infinite" in that it is infinitely divisible, he explains, does not mean that it is *composed* of an infinite number of points that would have to be covered one by one. "Accordingly," Aristotle writes, "Zeno's argument makes a false assumption in asserting that it is impossible for a thing to pass over or severally to come in contact with infinite things in a finite time" (since anyone in motion traverses a course that is infinitely divisible and can do so in a finite time). After all, Aristotle points out, if space is "infinite" in that it is infinitely divisible, then so is time.

One notes that the adverse criticism of the paradox is not after all a criticism of Zeno. For Zeno was apparently attempting to show, by way of his paradox, that if a distance is *composed* of an infinite "many," it could never be covered in a finite amount of time by covering that infinite many *one by one*. His argument against the conception of a distance as composed of discrete units of space,

either finite or infinite, is sound. Zeno's argument is a *reduction ad absurdum* (a bringing-out of the inconsistencies) in the Pythagorean conception of space as composed of a plurality of discrete units.

The Paradox of Achilles and the Tortoise

The second of the arguments is the famous paradox known as *The Paradox of Achilles and the Tortoise* (as translated from Aristotle's *Physics*, book 6, chapter 9, by Philip H. Wicksteed and Francis M. Cornford):

> The second [of Zeno's paradoxes of motion] is what is known as "the Achilles," which purports to show that the slowest will never be overtaken in its course by the swiftest, inasmuch as, reckoning from any given instant, the pursuer, before he can catch the pursued, must reach the point from which the pursued started at that instant, and so the slower will always be some distance in advance of the swifter.

Imagine the race between Achilles and the tortoise as follows: The tortoise has taken the lead. By the time Achilles starts, the tortoise has reached a point we'll call A. By the time Achilles reaches point A, then (no matter how fast Achilles runs—since the tortoise is moving steadily forward toward the goal) the tortoise has reached point B. But by the time Achilles reaches B, the tortoise has reached C. Even if Achilles comes closer and closer to the tortoise, it appears that since Achilles is forever reaching points (and there is an infinite number of such points) where the tortoise *was*, the tortoise is forever moving some distance ahead. Achilles (the swifter runner) cannot overtake the tortoise (the slower)!

Aristotle's criticism here is that the Achilles argument depends, like the previous bisection argument, on a mode of division that never terminates. Although the tortoise is never overtaken *while it holds a lead*, it does not follow, of course, that it is never overtaken. In other words, although the process of division (concentrating on successive cases of Achilles's reaching points at which the tortoise *was*) is never terminated, the race (or the overtaking of the tortoise by Achilles) certainly can be.

If one now drops the mode of analysis that is interminable (a concentration on points where the tortoise *was*) and turns to a consideration of what happens when Achilles reaches a point where the tortoise *is*, one realizes that once Achilles has covered *all* the points at which the tortoise *was*, Achilles has succeeded in overtaking the tortoise (at which point Achilles can take the lead, if he wishes, since he is the swifter).

But *how* can Achilles cover all the points at which the tortoise *was* if the number of such points is infinite? By simply closing the gap between himself and the tortoise, of course. As Aristotle points out, it is a fallacy to suppose that one cannot cover an infinite number of points in a finite number of time. After all, the points are *not* units of space but are simply what might be called nondimensionless "cuts," envisaged by a mode of analysis, of a conceived line.

The Paradox of the Arrow

The third argument is *The Paradox of the Arrow* (Burnet's translation):

> The arrow in flight is at rest. For, if everything is at rest when it occupies a space equal to itself, and what is in flight at any given moment always occupies a space equal to itself, it cannot move.

The force of the argument comes from the assumption that at any point in its flight, an arrow is somewhere. To be somewhere is to occupy a space, and to occupy a space is to be at rest. Hence, at any point in its flight, an arrow is at rest. But motion could hardly be a sequence of rests. Therefore, the arrow cannot move.

Aristotle argues that the *Paradox of the Arrow* depends on the assumption that time is composed of moments, and he contends that if the assumption is not granted, the argument collapses.

This criticism is perhaps correct, but it is vague. The argument involves the premise that the arrow "at any given moment . . . occupies a space equal to itself." If we are not willing to grant that at an *instant* (that is, at some "cut" in time—like high noon, which has no duration) the arrow "occupies" a space, that is, is *for some time in* a space defined by its dimensions, then we need not grant that the arrow is "resting" there, even for an instant. To "occupy" a space, to be at rest, involves being somewhere for *some time*, that is, for some duration of time; since an instant is not a duration, an arrow cannot rest anywhere in an instant.

(We are not disputing the premise that "at any point in its flight, an arrow is somewhere." At a given instant, the arrow is, indeed, somewhere: Its coordinates could be determined. But it does not "occupy" that space; it does not rest there. And we cannot say where the arrow is in "the next instant," for there is *no* next instant even though, after the given instant, there are any number of instants.)

The Paradox of the Stadium

The fourth argument is *The Paradox of the Stadium* (as given by Burnet):

> Half the time may be equal to double the time. Let us suppose three rows of bodies, one of which (A) is at rest while the other two (B, C) are moving with equal velocity in opposite directions. By the time they are all in the same part of the course, B will have passed twice as many of the bodies in C as in A. Therefore the time which it takes to pass C is twice as long as the time it takes to pass A. But the time which B and C take to reach the position of A is the same. Therefore double the time is equal to the half.

According to Aristotle (Ross translation), "The fallacy of the reasoning lies in the assumption that a body occupies an equal time in passing with equal velocity a body that is in motion and a body of equal size which is not; which is false."

Aristotle's point is, of course, well taken: It would

take longer to pass a line of standing horses (or chariots) than it would take at the same rate to pass the same number of bodies moving in the opposite direction. It is because of our realization of this point that Zeno's paradox does not strike us as being paradoxical. It might very well take only half the time to pass a moving object as it would take to pass that object were it not moving; we would not *say*, on that account, that half the time is equal to twice the time (which, taken out of context, is nonsense).

However, if one understands Zeno to be making the point that if the Pythagoreans are right in maintaining that there are units of space and time, and if a unit of time is relative to a unit of space, then if while passing, say, two stationary objects, one is passing four objects moving in the opposite direction, then two units of time (relative to the two objects) are equal to four units of time (relative to the four objects); hence (on the Pythagorean assumption) half the time is equal to twice the time.

Zeno's argument is effective and interesting only in relation to the Pythagorean conception of space and time as made up of discrete units.

The Paradox of Plurality

The Paradox of Plurality was briefly stated by Simplicius in his *Physics* (as translated by Burnet):

> If things are a many, they must be just as many as they are, and neither more nor less. Now, if they are as many as they are, they will be finite in number.
>
> If things are a many, they will be infinite in number; for there will always be other things between them, and others again between these. And so things are infinite in number.

The conclusion, then, is that "if things are a many," they will be both finite and infinite in number, which is impossible.

Zeno may appear to make two mistakes in this argument. In the first place, a set consisting of an infinite number of entities would have "just as many as they are," namely, an infinite number: Hence, the set, although having just as many as there are,

would not necessarily be finite in number. Second, even if a set were finite in number and each of the units were infinitely divisible, it would not follow that "things are infinite in number" if one restricted the use of the term "thing" to the units.

However, if the argument is related to the Pythagorean conception of space and time, the difficulties that follow from assuming that space and time are *composed* of *units* of some magnitude are brought out. If points and instants are of no magnitude, they are nothing, and space and time are illusions. If, on the other hand, points and instants are of some magnitude, the above paradox would seem to apply (if one regards the parts of units as themselves units). The paradox calls into question the very conception of a "unit." In Simplicius's *Physics*, Eudemos, referring to Zeno, reports (as translated by Burnet): ". . . If anyone could tell him what the unit was, he would be able to say what things are."

Zeno's Accomplishment

Critics differ as to what Zeno attempted and what he accomplished with his paradoxes. Some have maintained that Zeno was indirectly defending Parmenides by simply arguing against the Pythagoreans, who maintained that there are "many" units of time and space, not a single continuity; Zeno constructed his paradoxes by assuming his opponents' premises and showing that they led to contradictions. Other critics say that Zeno directly defended Parmenides by showing that the idea of a reality of space, time, and motion is absurd.

As far as the accomplishments are concerned, most critics agree in thinking that Zeno failed to show that motion is impossible or that time and space are unreal. Some critics, however, think that Zeno did succeed in bringing out the contradictions that are generated by assuming the Pythagorean idea of discrete units of time and space. Bertrand Russell wrote (in *Our Knowledge of the External World*) that "Zeno's arguments, in some form, have afforded grounds for almost all the theories of space and time and infinity which have been constructed from his day to our own." Zeno's principal accomplishment, according to Russell, was to show that if one assumes that covering an infinite number of points would take an infinite amount of time, paradoxes result that suggest that motion is impossible. The remedy, Russell goes on to say, is not to deny motion but to realize that covering an infinite number of nondimensional points can be accomplished in a finite amount of time.

Some critics have insisted that Zeno's arguments are valid, given the assumptions that Zeno set out to undermine; others have judged the arguments to be fallacious, either in the assumptions or in the lines of reasoning involved. Anyone interested in pursuing the history of the criticism of Zeno's arguments will find a great deal of material for intensive consideration, some of it involving technical mathematical and physical theory, but most of it challenging and all of it, either directly or indirectly, a tribute to Zeno.

IAN P. MCGREAL

Further Reading

Burnet, John. *Early Greek Philosophy*. 4th ed. London: Adam & Charles Black, 1930, reprinted 1963. The Zeno material is in chapter 8, "The Younger Eleatics." Burnet not only presents the sources but also elucidates the texts, places Zeno's work in context, and credits Zeno with establishing continuity by discrediting the Pythagorean idea that spatial and temporal quantities are discrete.

McGreal, Ian P. *Analyzing Philosophical Arguments*. San Francisco: Chandler, 1967. In Chapter 4, McGreal analyzes Zeno's *Paradox of Achilles and the Tortoise*. The argument is reconstructed and analyzed line by line.

Ross, W. D. *Aristotle Selections*. New York: Charles Scribner's Sons, 1927, 1938. Section 32 contains Aristotle's accounts and criticisms of Zeno's paradoxes of motion. The translation used is the Oxford Translation.

Salmon, Wesley C., ed. *Zeno's Paradoxes*. Indianapolis and New York: Bobbs-Merrill, 1970. An excellent collection of some of the most illuminating and provocative criticisms of Zeno's paradoxes, with essays by Salmon, Bertrand Russell, Henri Bergson, Max Black, J. O. Wisdom, James Thomson, Paul Bencerraf, G. E. L. Owen, and Adolf Grunbaum. Contains a very useful bibliography.

Wicksteed, Philip H., and Francis M. Cornford, trans. *The Physics*. Cambridge, Mass. and London: Harvard University Press and William Heinemann, 1932. A clear, accurate, and lively translation of Aristotle's text that contains his version of Zeno's arguments.

PROTAGORAS OF ABDERA

Born: C. 490 B.C., possibly in Abdera, Greece
Died: C. 420 B.C., possibly by drowning at sea
Major Works: *On Truth, On the Gods* (only fragments remain)

Major Ideas

Educated persons are skilled in the art of rhetoric, which enables them to articulate thought with clarity and superior argumentation.

What enables one to lead others can be taught.

No one is absolutely self-sufficient, for human survival depends on mutual cooperation in society—hence the importance of values, communication, and laws.

Because all have a basic need for self-preservation, all have the obligation to participate in the governance of the community.

Man is the measure of all things: Perception and truth are related to the experience and judgment of the individual.

One cannot with certainty either affirm or reject the existence of the gods.

Protagoras is the first and the greatest of a group of educators referred to as the Sophists. The term, from the Greek word *sophos*, or *sophia*, means "wise" or "wisdom." The Sophists were those who taught and wrote, offering a special knowledge, a wisdom to their students. They were individualistic, often rivals with one another to gain public attention and favor. They did not constitute a school teaching the same doctrine, although there were themes shared by them all. The most important theme was a skeptical attitude regarding the possibility of attaining certain knowledge. According to the Sophists, we come to know only through the experience of our senses; the mind is unable to grasp a permanent and eternal reality.

Protagoras and other Sophists are pictured by Plato as filled with ideas and charm, often receiving invitations to be guests at the homes of the richest men of Athens. The Sophists, as a group, did not so much seek to educate the masses as to focus on those who would be the future leaders of the people. For a fee, sometimes very large, they instructed young men or offered to entertain them with public displays of eloquence. Plato informs us in the *Meno* that Protagoras was so successful in his art that he earned more from his teaching than the great Greek sculptor Phidias and ten other sculptors put together.

The exchange of wisdom for money was often the object of scorn in the Platonic *Dialogues*. Nevertheless, the Sophists had little difficulty in finding students to pay their high fees or to attend their public lectures. Even Plato, in his portrait of Protagoras, speaks of the first Sophist in tones of respect because of his superb skills. Protagoras, and those who follow in his tradition, represent the Greek attention to things that are human. The Sophists are not preoccupied with the essential nature either of the gods or of nature itself. They represent, in essence, a humanism. They embodied a culture that could be transmitted through the vehicle of education.

Rhetoric

Leadership required a talent in the art of public presence. This meant the ability to express oneself with clarity, precision, and force. In an age of Athenian democracy, there were numerous opportunities for those with ambition and talent to rise solely on the basis of their rhetorical skills. The Sophists catered to this career-oriented education. Protagoras, it is said, was the first to divide discourse according to the intention of the speaker, be it the expression of a wish, a question, an answer, a command, or a narrative. He also distinguished among the genders of names (masculine, feminine, and those referring to inanimate objects). In all of this he sought to correct common Greek usage and formulate a system of rational morphology, thus seeking to offer his students a clarity of thought that would enable them to convey lines of argumentation superior to others.

As far back as Homer, Greeks had recognized the power of rhetoric. With the Sophists, we find a systematic reflection on its nature and a concerted effort to teach its principles. Protagoras, who said that "there are two opposing arguments on every subject," would have taught the art of understanding the various lines of argumentation and if it were necessary, to seek to make the weaker argument the stronger. Some Sophists were so good at this art that they were condemned for a cleverness that sought always to triumph over the opponent; indeed, this is one of the meanings in the English language of the word "sophistry," relating to specious reasoning employed in arguments with the intention of deceiving others.

Sophists thus embodied the power of persuasive speech. Protagoras, as the first in this tradition, offered his students the promise of political and worldly success. His students would have been trained to see all sides of an issue, to have realized the weakness of an opponent's position and the strength of one's own. This, for Protagoras, would have been wisdom. The clarity by which one articulates words would itself express the content of the intellect as it molded the intellect. This is the way to have power and influence over the minds of others.

Society's Values

Protagoras was particularly attentive to the value of social life. He represented the typical Greek view that no one is absolutely self-sufficient; all are members of a society, the existence of which is itself a great gift from the gods. In the Platonic dialogue the *Protagoras*, Plato has the first Sophist articulate what scholars refer to as the Protagoras myth regarding the beginnings of things. The focus of his speech is on the question of what is necessary for

survival. The gods, he tells us, have offered to some animals strength to defend themselves; to others, smallness, so that they can escape, while to birds the ability to fly is given. The gods ordained that some animals would feed upon others, while all species together would form a *cosmos*, a well-balanced order. Turning to mankind, the gods remained attentive to the problem of their survival. To this end they offered to humanity two great gifts; first, fire—in broad terms, technical power over nature. This gift of Prometheus was, however, not enough. According to Protagoras, earliest man remained alone and unrelated to his neighbor and even with this power would not be able to survive the onslaught of nature and the attacks of wild animals. Thus, Zeus, fearing that our race would utterly perish, offered to human beings the social impulse that binds them and the whole of civilization. This is the greatest gift offered to humanity, the gift of social community, the bonds of social interrelationship that give rise to feelings of solidarity with other human beings.

Here is the secret of human survival, that all members of the community, although they have different roles, work together for the good of the whole. This is why Protagoras thought that virtue—and for the Greeks this meant human excellence—could be taught. He argued that all should participate in the political life, for all are motivated by self-preservation. In this line of thought we find the first theoretical justification for democracy. For Protagoras, in participatory democracy all enter into discussion concerning those things that pertain to righteousness and temperance and, with reason, offer counsel on what constitutes the good of the community.

Law itself is an educator and one ought to have respect for it. Law is instituted by human beings and is altered by their consent; it is fundamentally an agreement that members of the society make with one another. Laws are not grounded in the inalterable will of the divine, nor in the unchanging dynamics of the natural order. Rather, laws are human customs that serve as a restraint on the individual wills of members of the society, a restraint necessary for human survival. The law thus guides and teaches its citizens the limits within which they can act. The Protagorean myth of the origins of human community celebrates the triumph of reason over nature. For law and order were not in our nature from the beginnings of our existence but, rather, grounded in the agreement each member of the society made with each other as was necessary for the society's self-preservation.

We know from tradition that Protagoras was friends with Pericles (c. 495–429 B.C.), the great Athenian statesman who, it is said, asked the Sophist to draft a constitution for the Greek colony of Thurii in southern Italy.

Theory of Knowledge

Protagoras was aware, as were many Greeks of his day, of the wide variety of customs and laws found among different peoples. He lived in an age of increasing travel, a widening of horizons due to enhanced contacts with other peoples. He also lived in an age when the Greek people demonstrated enhanced mastery over the natural world, as seen in the arts of medicine, astronomy, shipbuilding, navigation, and farming. In an age that saw the growth of democracy, every person had the right to express an opinion, and all opinions were given consideration. These tendencies enhanced pluralism and grounded knowledge in experience. The axiom of Protagoras, "There are two contradictory arguments about everything," typified the age.

The most famous quotation attributed to Protagoras, by which he may have opened his work *On Truth*, is the following: "Of all things the measure is man, of the things that are, that they are, and of the things that are not, that they are not." The focus of the quotation is on the individual person, not the whole human race. In Plato's *Theaetetus*, this quotation is discussed with the example of wind, which feels cold to one person but not cold to another. Protagoras and the Sophist movement in general focused on how objects are perceived by individuals. The focus was on the subject, who measured truth in his or her own experience. The Greek word for measure, *metron*, in fact implies a standard of judgment. For the

individual, what is true is what is true in his or her judgment. Sextus Empiricus, the codifier of Greek skepticism, who lived in the last half of the second century A.D., tells us that for Protagoras, truth is something relative. (Protagoras's focus on the experience of the one who is experiencing would enjoy a long and honored history in a great many philosophical "isms"—relativism, individualism, empiricism, humanism, positivism, skepticism, pragmatism, and so forth.)

Behind this view is the influence of the pre-Socratic philosopher Heraclitus (c. 500 B.C.), who understood all things to be constantly changing like a flowing river. Protagoras seems to adopt the position that there is no reality behind, or independent of, experiences by which the mind itself can be measured. The wise person is the one who is able to grasp more of experience than the less well-informed. The product of Sophist education would be able to see more clearly the consequences of his or her actions and thus be able to produce better effects in the future. The product of Sophist education would know how to make the strongest argument by marshaling the greatest number of experiences and seeking to enumerate their meaning.

This Protagorean subjectivism should not be taken to an absolute extreme relativism. It is clear that Protagoras would have been opposed to a total individual egoism that would destroy the unity and cohesion of society. His claim is that persons in societies differ widely concerning what for them constitutes the good, but every society at least affirms what is necessary for its continued existence. There is no evidence to indicate that Protagoras thought it possible to prescribe a universal good for all societies.

It would also seem fair to Protagoras not to interpret the doctrine that man is the measure of all things to imply that there exists nothing except insofar as it is perceived by the human person. For it is clear in the examples given by Plato and Aristotle that Protagoras affirms that we are the measure of the properties or characteristics of things rather than of their very being, and we are the ones who decide what is useful and good.

On the Gods

History has judged Protagoras to be an agnostic. A sentence said to have belonged to his work *On the Gods* reads as follows: "Concerning the gods, I am not able to discover whether they exist or do not exist, nor what they are like in form; for the factors preventing knowledge are many: the obscurity of the subject and the shortness of human life." This view would follow from Protagoras's theory of knowledge, tied as it was to the realm of experience. It is important to note that Protagoras was not, as is sometimes charged, an atheist. For, in accord with the "man as the measure" principle, the gods would exist for those who believed them to exist, but not for others. Nor can it be said that Protagoras repudiated all religious activity. In the Protagorean myth, we hear him saying, "Now man, having been made a partaker of the divine lot, by reason of his kinship with the godhead, alone among living creatures believed in gods, and began to take it in hand to set up altars unto them and make graven images of them." In Protagoras's agnosticism we see the influence of a long tradition in pre-Socratic philosophy that substituted natural for supernatural causes. The naturalistic cosmologies, which tended to be evolutionary, moved away from the idea of divine causality.

Protagoras's agnosticism is expressed by the claim that he is suspending judgment regarding the existence of the gods, for what is clear is not the gods but the flow of natural experience, a flow that one can neither get behind nor above. This line of interpretation has led many scholars to see the words of Protagoras's myth regarding the origins of human society as expressed in the common form of a popular mythology rather than as a personal confession of his own belief in the existence and activities of the Greek pantheon. Regarding the existence of the gods, Protagoras could only suspend judgment.

LAWRENCE F. HUNDERSMARCK

Further Reading

Kerferd, George B. *The Sophistic Movement.* London: Cambridge University Press, 1981. A solid, readable introduction to the major themes that emerge from Greek Sophists.

————. ed. *Sophists and Their Legacy: Proceedings of the Fourth International Colloquium on Ancient Philosophy.* Deerfield, Ill. Coronet Books, 1981. Here noted scholars examine the impact of Sophism on a wide variety of issues in the history of Western thought.

Loenen, Dirk. *Protagoras and the Greek Community.* Amsterdam: Noord-Hollandsche Uitgevers Maatschappij, 1940. Situates Protagoras in the context of Greek opinion on the nature of community.

Nill, Michael. *Morality and Self-Interest in Protagoras, Antiphon and Democritus.* Leiden: E. J. Brill, 1985. His doctoral dissertation, yet very accessible to the general reader. The focus of the work addresses the interplay of three key ideas: society, self-interest, and the good.

HIPPOCRATES

Born: C. 460 B.C., on Cos, an island in the Aegean Sea
Died: C. 370 B.C., Larissa, in northern Greece
Major Works: *Nature of Man, Prognostic, Regimen in Acute Diseases; Airs, Waters, Places; Epidemics I and III*

Major Ideas

Diseases have natural origins: They do not arise from divine action; the course of diseases and their critical days can be found from observation and experience.

Good health results from a balance of fluids (humors) in the body; disease results from an imbalance.

The balance of fluids—hence the occurrence of disease—is governed by environmental factors: heat, cold, water, winds; close observation of these factors enables the physician to predict the frequency of disease in any given locality.

Nature itself accomplishes all healing by attempting to blend harmoniously the body's humors; a physician's task is to remove any obstacles to nature's healing action and to foresee the course of the disease.

Little is known about the life of Hippocrates of Cos, the most famous physician of antiquity. In his own lifetime, he was known to Plato as a prominent physician who accepted pupils and wrote books. He is said to have been the son of a doctor, Heraclides; to have studied with his father, and to have traveled widely in Greece, meeting the contemporary philosophers. Legend elaborated on his career: He saved Athens from the plague; he was invited by King Artaxerxes of the Persians to heal a plague that had fallen on his army; he averted an Athenian attack on his home island of Cos by an impassioned plea to the Athenian assembly; during his travels he met the philosopher Democritus and rescued him from being certified insane. This last story, even if fictional, certainly symbolizes the close ties between fifth-century medicine and contemporary pre-Socratic philosophy.

About seventy medical treatises attributed to Hippocrates have survived. Unfortunately, no criterion allows us to attribute with certainty any individual treatise to the master himself, although several (particularly *Epidemics* I and III) show a talent for accurate observation and description and seem to be from the same hand. One would like to believe that these works show Hippocrates at his best. *Regimen* is mentioned in Plato's *Phaedrus* and may also be from the master's hand. Difficulties in attributing authorship arise for several reasons: The

various treatises expound contradictory theories about the nature of health and disease, and among all these theories it is always difficult to distinguish Hippocrates from his contemporaries and from the more developed theories of later physicians like Galen (second century A.D.), who considered that all developments in medicine were in fact implicit in Hippocrates's work. For the sake of convenience in this survey, I will attribute significant theories and methods to "Hippocrates" or "the Hippocratic physician."

To most readers, the major treatises seem divided into two distinct categories: those like the *Epidemics*, which report in graphic detail episodes of disease and the specific environment in which they occurred, and the theoretical works (*Prognostic, Regimen in Acute Diseases, Nature of Man*), which attempt to give the causes for disease. An example of the first sort from *Epidemics* I:

Philiscus lived near the city wall of Thasos. He took to his bed and the first day he had an acute fever, sweating, a miserable night. Second day: generally worse . . . a calm night. Third day: in the morning and until the middle of the day, he seemed without fever; then in the evening, acute fever, sweating, thirst, black urine; a miserable night . . . Fourth day: worse, black urine, a better night. Fifth day:

around midday, a slight nosebleed; irregular urination with floating particles in suspension . . . a miserable night, delirium, extremities cold, brief drowsiness towards dawn, no voice, cold sweats . . . He died around the middle of the sixth day. Toward the end, deep, infrequent breathing . . . The spleen stuck out . . . ; cold sweats until the end.

(The unfortunate Philiscus was suffering from a particularly malignant form of malaria.)

These clinical observations have served as models for generations of physicians because of their standard terminology, orderly analytic procedures, and attempt to avoid hasty or *a priori* judgments. No name is given to Philiscus's disease, not because it had none (the physician would have called it a *kausos*, an ardent fever), but because the observer does not wish to prejudice the observation by a premature labeling. This starkly phenomenological approach is one of the noteworthy traits of the *Epidemics*.

In addition to these case histories, the *Epidemics* presents "constitutions," which describe environmental conditions in a given season at a given locality (generally the north Aegean around 400 B.C.) and the syndromes that followed throughout the entire population. The constitutions attempt to give the data from which the environmental causes of epidemics might be deduced. These sketches were apparently written as generalizations derived from individual clinical histories, as detailed study shows. Indeed, Philiscus's case is cited in the third constitution of Thasos (*Epidemics* I).

The delightful *Airs, Waters, Places* also combines acute observation with generalization about the influence of the environment, specifically on the physique and character of the inhabitants of various nations. This treatise asks the physician to evaluate the effects of the seasons, the winds, the quality of the water, and the nature of the soil on the inhabitants of the town he is visiting. If he does this, he will not be ignorant of the prevailing diseases: He will be able to forecast their attacks, will know the remedies in advance, and—last but not least—he will "achieve the greatest triumphs in the practice of his art." This last phrase reveals the conditions under which the itinerant physician practiced, ever in competition with his fellow physicians, not to mention local healers and medicine men. *Airs, Waters, Places* outlines how each environmental factor, for example, north winds vs. south winds, dry seasons vs. wet seasons, affects the health of cities and regions. In a further sweep of generalization, Hippocrates then describes the nature of the various nationalities, Egyptians, Libyans, Scythians, Greeks, and so forth, and attempts to show how the environment of each nation has molded the character of the inhabitants: Asiatics (inhabitants of the Near East) are less warlike than Europeans—and therefore feeble and tyrannized by kings—because of the uniformity and mildness of the seasons in Asia; the Scythians (steppe dwellers of the Ukraine) have a moist and cold nature from the fogs and cold wind of their northern home and they are fat, ruddy, relatively infertile, and so on. The ethnography of *Airs, Waters, Places* can be compared to passages in the history of the contemporary historian Herodotus, particularly in their common interest in the Scythians.

In contrast to the *Epidemics* and *Airs, Waters, Places*, the treatises *Prognostic*, *Regimen in Acute Diseases*, and *Nature of Man* present the theoretical structure for medical practice. Earlier Greek literature portrayed disease as originally external to mankind: Disease, or sudden death not from violence, was symbolized by the arrows of Apollo (in Homer) or by the plagues that flew from Pandora's jar (in Hesiod; both authors seventh to eighth centuries B.C.). In either event, they are not part of the natural order, but are autonomous, striking where they will. In contrast, Hippocrates and all of later Greek medicine considered disease to be a disturbance of man's natural equilibrium. In 500 B.C., Alcmaeon of Croton used a political metaphor: "Health results from equal rights of the qualities, wet, dry, cold, hot, bitter, sweet, etc. A dictatorship among the qualities produces disease." The pre-Socratic philosophers systematized this concept: Empedocles (490–430 B.C.) taught that love and strife brought about opposite effects on the four elements of life: earth, air, fire, and water. Anaxagoras (500–428 B.C.) taught that the original mixture of things consisted of pairs of opposite qualities: wet/dry, hot/cold, light/dark. The Hippocratic physicians applied these theories to health and disease, attempting to establish a logical foundation for medicine. Thinkers differed widely in the proposals they offered, but all had in common a preference for reason over authority, experience over tradition. Typical is the statement that begins *On the Sacred Disease* (sacred disease: epilepsy): "The disease which is called sacred is no more sacred than the rest, but has natural causes."

Hippocrates's explanation for disease was based on the theory of *humors*: An originally undetermined number of these fluids occur in the human body and they combine with air to create an individual's state of health. A balance of humors produces good health; excessive air, water, or an imbalance of a given humor causes disease. When the humors are proportioned correctly with one another, a person enjoys the most perfect health. Illness arises when one humor is in deficit or excess, or is isolated in the body without being compounded with all the others. In time, the number of humors was reduced to four, although *which* four remained in doubt. The treatise *Diseases* names water, bile, blood, and phlegm: water from the spleen, bile from the gallbladder, phlegm from the head, and blood from the heart. *Nature of Man*, which best describes humor theory, proposes a new humor in place of water: black bile, causing diseases of the kidneys, spleen, liver, quartan fever, headaches, and epilepsy. Black bile is visible in black feces (from ulcers), and black urine (in the malignant form of malaria experienced by Philiscus). The following table shows the relationships among these humors:

Humor	Element	Season
Yellow bile	Fire	Summer
Black bile	Earth	Autumn
Phlegm	Water	Winter
Blood	Air	Spring

Combinations	Qualities
Yellow bile + blood	Hot
Yellow + black bile	Dry
Blood + phlegm	Wet
Phlegm + black bile	Cold

The relation of the humors to the four elements and to the four human temperaments—the melancholic, sanguine, bilious, and phlegmatic—is not fully developed in the Hippocratic corpus, but was of great scientific and literary importance in later centuries.

An example: *phthisis*, or "consumption" (which often means tuberculosis), is said to arise from a flow of excess phlegm from the head to the lungs, where it festers and forms abscesses (masses of pus), which may then be evacuated by coughing or may remain and continue to plague the organism. Note that the concept of contagion, the transmission of disease from one person to another, does not occur in Hippocrates. He considered that epidemics occur because of similar environmental factors affecting all inhabitants at the same time. Since the concept of contagion was so close to the magico-religious concept of pollution, and since all explicitly magical concepts were rejected by the rational physician, the (to us) obvious occurrence of disease transmission was not noticed.

The remedies mentioned in these treatises (drugs, herbs, exercises, plain living) operate by helping the body counteract the excess humor and restore the natural harmony; this state of harmony is called a "blending," or *krasis*. The process of restoration was viewed as a "cooking out," or *pepsis*, by the body of the excess humor. Sudden expulsion of the excess brings a *crisis*, a sudden turn in the disease; a long cooking-out is a *lysis*, a slower recovery. The expulsion may take the form of vomiting, sweating, and so forth, or the morbid excess may be isolated in an abscess, tumor, or gangrene. The physician's function is to aid this restoration. Some physicians went to extremes: Herodicus, mentioned by Plato, killed patients by prescribing excessive exercise; for others, "plain living" meant a starvation diet. As often happened in Greek theorizing, a common-sense rule was subjected to pathological overelaboration. Other than explaining the theory behind the restoration process, the Hippocratic treatises give little attention to specific remedies for specific diseases. One must remember that the Hippocratic writings do not offer recipes for the everyday healer; they offer theories for the thinking physician. The writers could assume that any healer would know the appropriate remedy for a given case.

In addition to the theory of humors, Hippocrates used a system of *critical days* to structure his observations: Fevers recur on the odd days or the even days, and a crisis on other than the expected day will probably be fatal. This system of critical days may owe something to Pythagorean numerology, but it also satisfied the scientific impulses of the physician. Just as astronomers or engineers used numbers to solve problems, so too could the physician predict the outcome of disease with numbers. Very important was the reality behind the critical days: The fevers of malaria, the single most important disease in the ancient Mediterranean, recur at two-, three-, and four-day intervals, depending on the strain of the disease. Sufferers from pneumonia, also common, suffer a crisis after a week of fever.

Using the theory of humors and critical days, Hippocrates required the physician to attempt a *prognosis*, a forecast of the outcome, for all cases presented to him. Successful prognosis—in addition to impressing the client and confounding the physician's rivals—served as the equivalent of the modern diagnosis, since the physician, in order to forecast accurately, must recognize the syndrome in question and classify it by outcome. The correct prognosis, as the touchstone of the skilled physician, was valued for its own sake, even if the prognosis was inevitable death.

The theoretical underpinnings of Hippocratic medicine have been described. Many treatises in the corpus fall neither in the clinical nor the theoretical categories but instead can be called practical handbooks. These include *Anatomy*, *Nature of Bones*, *Surgery*, and a dozen treatises on childbirth, premature infants, and gynecology. Miscellaneous works include the *Oath*, today perhaps the best-known work of Hippocrates. It has two parts; the first of which commands the candidate to show gratitude toward the person who taught him the art. The second lists the obligations resting on the physician: (1) do no harm, (2) assist in no suicide, (3) cause no abortion, (4) perform no surgery, (5) maintain professional confidentiality. Several of the provisions are strange, particularly (3) and (4), since abortions and surgery were in fact frequent in antiquity; surgery is mentioned without prejudice in many Hippocratic treatises. Consequently, the *Oath* has been considered to be of Pythagorean origin, since that sect did prohibit these actions. In late antiquity the *Oath* became the standard of medical conduct: Surgery was separated from general medicine, and measures were taken against suicide and abortion. It remained the standard until modern times.

The Hippocratic writings display two characteristics of early scientific texts: The theories are wrong, but the attitude toward research is correct. The theory of humors and the system of critical days were both derived from observations of the medical realities of ancient Greece, then wrongly applied as universal principles. On the other hand, Hippocrates's insistence that (1) there is a natural origin for disease, discoverable by rational investigation, (2) close observation, unprejudiced by *a priori* theorizing, is necessary for an accurate appreciation of the facts, and (3) environment and health are correlated, made future progress in medicine and the other sciences possible.

MARK T. RILEY

Further Reading

Edelstein, Ludwig. *Ancient Medicine*. Baltimore: Johns Hopkins, 1967. A collection of papers by one of the foremost researchers in ancient philosophy and medicine; topics include the role of the physician in ancient society, the origin of the Hippocratic oath, and later Greek medicine.

Grmec, Mirko D. *Diseases in the Ancient World*. Translated by M. and L. Muellner. Baltimore: Johns Hopkins, 1989. Originally published in France as *Les maladies à l' aube de la civilisation occidentale* (Paris: Payot, 1983), this landmark text studies the medical reality behind the Hippocratic treatises.

Lloyd, G. E. R. *The Revolutions of Wisdom*. Berkeley: University of California Press, 1987. The first chapter of this text, a study of the transition from myth to quasi-science, discusses Hippocrates and puts him in the pre-Socratic context. Other chapters discuss the position of science, including medicine, in ancient Greece.

Potter, Paul. *Short Handbook of Hippocratic Medicine*. Quebec: Editions du Sphinx, 1988. An excellent overview of the subject, this text contains short synopses of sixty-eight important Hippocratic treatises, with a list of available translations.

Smith, Wesley D. *The Hippocratic Tradition*. Ithaca, N.Y.: Cornell University Press, 1979. This study investigates the origin of the Hippocratic corpus and the attitude of later physicians toward Hippocrates, with particular attention to Galen, the chief medical theorist of Roman times.

PLATO

Born: C. 429 B.C., in either Athens or Aegina
Died: 347 B.C., probably in Athens
Major Works: *Laches, Charmides, Ion, Protagoras, Euthyphro, Euthydemus, Apology, Crito, Gorgias, Meno, Symposium, Phaedo, Republic, Parmenides, Theaetetus, Phaedrus, Sophist, Laws, Timaeus, Statesman, Philebus*

Major Ideas

The goal of intellectual inquiry is to discover the eternal immutable forms or "ideas," which serve as the essence and ideal of all things; in this way a true philosopher seeks wisdom.

These eternal truths, already in the mind, can be recalled by the immaterial and immortal intellect; they cannot be grasped by the bodily senses.

Education consists in perfecting the whole person in order to achieve self-mastery and self-realization.

Education has as its goal, as should all human acts, knowledge of the good, for ignorance of the good leads to evil.

A perfect society is but the external reflection of a harmoniously integrated soul where appetite and desire are under the command of reason.

Only the Philosopher who has achieved true knowledge is fit to rule; democracy, the rule of the majority, is usually rooted in mere opinions.

Plato in his writings, referred to collectively as the dialogues, sought to discover the unity within the diversity of experience. He wanted to abstract from the chaos and flux of the empirical world a cosmos where all is ordered, arranged, and organized. The highest good consists in contemplating this ideal realm. To be in contact with what is perfectly ordered is to bring to the self harmony and peace. Platonism is, in no small measure, an attempt to find this unity. Most of Plato is concerned with "the ascent of the soul to the intelligible realm" (*Republic*), the restless tendency to grasp the eternal so that the temporal may be understood. This is how Plato sought to fulfill the mandate found in the inscription on the wall of the Delphic sanctuary, *Gnothi Seauton* (Know thyself).

At the core of Plato's philosophical enterprise is the conviction derived from Socrates (c. 469–399 B.C.) that the point of intellectual inquiry is to search after the essence of things. Plato presents Socrates as actively engaged in this inquiry through dialogue with others. To find the stable and permanent behind the flux of human experience is Plato's attempt to find unity and purpose in this world. He would decisively influence subsequent thought in its attempts to deal with the complexities occasioned by the interplay of the invisible and the visible, spirit and matter.

Plato was one of the most prolific authors of classical antiquity. His works have come to us in their entirety. Plato's dialogues may have been written to appeal to the educated at large and to interest them in philosophy. Plato was also one of the greatest literary artists of antiquity. In him, myth, metaphor, humor, irony, pathos, and a rich Greek vocabulary captivate the reader's attention as it is led to the most pressing issues of the mind and reality.

The Dialogues

The exact sequence and dating of the dialogues have been the object of intense scholarly scrutiny and debate. Some general consensus has been formed by situating certain dialogues in Plato's early manhood, in his midlife, or in his old age. The early dialogues offer a dramatic portrayal of Socrates as he seeks to articulate the fundamental ethical issues. These texts do not elaborate a sophisticated theory of Forms or Ideas. In this category we may place the *Apology,* the *Crito, Laches, Charmides, Euthydemus, Euthyphro, Protagoras*, and *Gorgias.* Second are the major Platonic dialogues, which present Plato's theory of Forms and the idea of knowledge as recollection. Here scholars situate the *Meno, Phaedo, Symposium, Republic*, and *Phaedrus.* Third, in an anticipation of Aristotle (384–322 B.C.), Plato offers dialogues (*Theaetetus, Parmenides, Sophist*) that consider the ways in which the human mind organizes experience under such terms as likeness, beauty, difference, ugliness, being, negation, error, and definition. Finally, we have the last dialogues wherein Plato offers his mature views on ethics (*Philebus*), physics and cosmology (*Timaeus*), and society (*Laws*).

Plato is the author of some twenty-five dialogues. His name is also attached to thirteen letters whose authenticity, however, with the exception of the *Seventh Letter*, is much debated. All of Plato's writings articulate the two great passions of his life: a faith in the supremacy and power of the mind, and a never-ending concern for human improvement.

The Influence of Socrates

In Plato, Socrates found his greatest disciple; in Socrates, Plato found the model, the ideal, and the spokesperson for philosophy. From Socrates, Plato learned that the goal of philosophy is to understand the general concept; from Socrates he also learned the use of the inductive method, from particular to universal. It was Socrates who was always asking about universals: What is justice? What is piety? What is self-control? What is courage?

For Socrates, the great business of life was conversation. He sought out everyone, and seizing upon some trivial issue would pass easily and quickly to a discussion of the deepest problems of human life. This discourse became a pattern for what we call today the Socratic dialogue. To the end, Socrates maintained that he was but a humble searcher for truth, not one filled with pride and arrogance. So it is ascribed to him the adage, "The unexamined life is not worth living." That is to say, a life without dialogue, without cross-examination, without conversation, a life where the intellect does not pursue truth is, for him, a life not worth living.

In Plato's *Apology,* we hear Socrates preaching that every person must "care for his soul." With this focus, Socrates gives the conduct of life the central place in his thinking. The soul is that which is able to be foolish or wise, good or evil; the soul is the seat of personal intelligence and character. This is why Socrates saw his mission as tending to the soul and seeking to make it as good as possible. The Socratic focus is on introspection and self-realization. Happiness does not depend so much on physical or external goods, but on knowing how to act rightly. Socrates is presented as most wise because he alone knows how much he does not know. Wisdom begins with the knowledge of one's ignorance; wisdom grows only with the knowledge of one's soul.

The civilization of the soul is a fundamental duty of every human being. The essence of education is to enable one to reach his or her true aim in life. This is but another way of speaking of a knowledge of the good. Socrates, with his focus on the soul, became antiquity's great champion of the inner life. For Socrates, life is meaningful because it can be understood and ordered toward known goals. His attention was focused on the good. Thus, pleasures were examined with an eye as to whether or not they were good, for some pleasures can lead to harm. The good always benefits the person, and thus Socrates sought to ascertain the nature of the benefit to the self and to others. This implies that the real self is rational and moral: rational, for the person can distinguish what is good from what is merely pleasurable; moral, because when the good is known, it is also, according to Socrates, sought. Thus we have the famous Socratic dictum, "Virtue is knowledge." This orientation toward the good would leave a lasting impression on Plato.

Later, Christianity would find echoes of Greece in the biblical question, "What shall it profit a man if he gain the whole world and lose his soul?" Gaining the soul is accomplished through the exercise of virtues or excellences, that is, appropriate powers developed for the particular parts of the soul. Thus piety and justice, courage and prudence, as well as beauty and health are all virtues that ought to be pursued; each in its way helps human nature to fulfill itself.

In Socrates and Plato, Greek civilization celebrates the inner life where qualities of the spirit, happiness and virtue, become primary. The impact of this turning to the soul on later Greco-Roman and Christian thought would be decisive and overwhelming. Henceforth the human person would be seen not as a mere collection of environmental influences but, rather, as a unity that can be known and directed to deliberately shaped ends and goals. All questions regarding the good of this or that act imply the question, "What is the purpose of life?" Until this great question is answered, it is not possible to offer a standard of choice among competing goods. The key to much of the Socratic-Platonic enterprise lies in this effort to ground the objectivity of moral values.

It was also through Socrates that self-control became a central conception in our moral thinking. In the age of the Sophists (teachers of the arts of persuasion), where much external authority of law broke down, the ideal of self-mastery became most important. Plato learned from Socrates the value of the mastery of the spirit over the passions, the mastery of the intellect over animal impulse. The goal is not only self-control but a harmonious agreement within one's own soul of all the multiple impulses of the soul. This type of self-control implies freedom, a freedom that comes from the rule of reason over human desires. The loss of such freedom would leave one a slave to one's own passions. What becomes important then, in the eyes of Socrates, is that a person become a master of himself. This self-mastery is beautifully portrayed in Plato's *Phaedo*, where, freely accepting the laws of his own society even though the charges against him are false, Socrates accepts the sentence of death.

Aristotle, Plato's famous student, tells us in his *Metaphysics* that Socrates occupied himself with ethical questions, neglecting the world of nature as a whole. He was concerned with universals in ethical matters, and thus he focused his thinking on definitions. That is why he spent so much effort attempting to find the full and essential characteristics of any matter under discussion by considering, indeed by testing, every definition by contradictory instances and by constantly bringing forth new cases and examples. Thus, for every true thinker, everything must be examined. Socrates taught Plato and the entire Western world that one ought not to take action grounded on mere belief without attempting to ascertain the basis for this belief through the use of critical intelligence. For Plato, Socrates preached self-mastery and the self-sufficiency of the moral character. It can be said that in no small measure Socrates embodied the Greek attempt to articulate the essence and the fullness of the human soul. Socrates set out to explore the moral cosmos within the human person. For Socrates and for Plato the essential question was, "What is the nature of the good that can be found within the self and within all things?"

Plato's Theory of Knowledge

Plato developed this Socratic legacy at a time when the Athenian city-state was in a period of decline. Athens had suffered humiliating military defeats and unsuccessful political leadership while many, like the Sophists, questioned the validity of any attempt to find permanent and abiding knowledge. Epistemology, discourse about the nature of knowledge, was of critical importance for Socrates's greatest student, for unless one can distinguish true from false knowledge, it is impossible to further the Socratic attention to values and the soul. Plato, in no small measure, sought to create social and political stability by grounding them on moral and spiritual absolutes.

Plato was in dialogue with his age and with his predecessors, and some of his most important ideas resulted from attempts to solve the epistemological problems bequeathed to him by the great minds of the past. From Heraclitus (c. 500 B.C.), Plato took the view that the sensible world is in a state of constant flux and thus cannot be the object of stable and true knowledge. Plato stood with the Pythagoreans in his passion for mathematics as a way to glimpse the eternal truths, as well as in his view of the interrelationship of all parts of nature. Like the Pythagoreans, he saw the way to salvation as the purification of the soul from the limitations of matter. The Pythagorean theory of reincarnation also exercised an influence on Plato (see *Meno* and *Phaedrus*).

The single greatest influence on Plato after Socrates was Parmenides (c. 450 B.C.). Parmenides was the first to focus attention on the essential question of Greek metaphysics, that is, What is the nature of real being? To answer this question, Parmenides focused his attention on the nature of change, development, and growth. He concluded that there can be no change despite the evidence of our senses; our reason tells us that everything which is, *is*, and that which is not, *is not*. For Parmenides, then, there were only two basic categories of reality, being and nonbeing.

In his reflections on Parmenides and Heraclitus, Plato interrelated the categories of permanence and impermanence, unity and diversity—that which never changes and that which changes. All of this is referred to as the problem of the one and the many. Thus, what in the world of change is changeless? Or, put in other words, what in the mutable is immutable? For Plato, reason looked to the world of unchanging ideas. For him, the model was mathematics, which set before one's eyes a truth outside the empirical world. The Form (or Idea) of triangularity remains constant, although it may be manifested in this or that triangle. Being, for Plato, that is, all of reality, has a dimension that is always changing, like a flowing river; at the same time, being has a stable dimension, like the riverbed that supports the changing river.

In the *Theaetetus*, Plato sets about refuting false theories regarding the nature of knowledge. Here, as in the *Phaedo*, he critiques the view of the Sophists, who claimed that knowledge is only perception. He repudiates the highly individualized view that what appears to an individual as true is, thus, true. If this were so, Plato argued, no man could be judged wiser than any other. If this were so—that each person measured his own wisdom—then how could the traveling teachers, the Sophists, claim to teach wisdom? For Plato, our senses do not give us the whole of reality. What is needed is rational reflection, judgment that corrects deceptive sense experiences (as in the case of a stick appearing to be bent in water although we know that it is not). Plato argued that the mind judges the similarity or lack of similarity between two sense experiences. The ability to judge something as more or less equal, or more or less beautiful, implies a basic standard of equality and of beauty. Thus what we see, hear, taste, feel, or smell is subject to constant change, while true knowledge for Plato is knowledge of what is stable and unchanging. To have true knowledge is to have an infallible knowledge of the real, and the real can be grasped only in a clear, universal definition.

In a famous discussion in the *Republic*, Plato sets forth the simile of the line by which he divides all knowledge into the realm of opinion and the realm of true knowledge. Opinion relates to particulars (for example, a particular expression of justice), whereas knowledge relates to universals (as in knowing the essence of justice that is applicable in all cases, the norm of the particulars). For Plato, opinions can be shaken by criticism or by conflicting evidence, while true knowledge cannot. In the *Republic*, he seeks to illustrate his meaning by distinguishing four grades of cognition, each with its own class of objects. The lowest grade is that of mere guesswork, which has as its objects the images of dreams or the reflections in water. A higher state of cognition is that of belief, where one has learned to distinguish physical things from their mere shadows. Here a person has a conviction about the experience of the world as known through the senses. It is only when we move higher, to understanding, that we have knowledge—when we move, so to speak, from a particular horse to the essence, "horseness," that which makes all horses alike as horses but different from human beings and other animals. There is, however, one more step needed to ascend to the supreme first principle. Each step in the ascent to knowledge moves to a higher level of abstraction, farther and farther from the particular and more and more toward the universal; from the shadow of a horse to a specific horse to horseness to the basic and fundamental principles characteristic of all biological life.

For Plato, a universal concept is not subjective but, rather, an objective essence of things. These universals are objects of thought; horseness and triangularity are discovered, not created, by the thinking mind. Thus, the Form of the good is what makes all things good.

The difficulty of locating these forms began with Plato's pupil Aristotle, who criticized the view that the Forms are separate from sense particulars, somewhere "out there" apart from things and the mind of any thinking subject. Aristotle severely criticized his teacher, for he could not understand how humanity or triangularity could be "things" that exist apart from and outside actual existing human persons or triangles. Perhaps Aristotle's difficulty stemmed from the fact that his paradigm of knowledge was often biology, while for Plato it was mathematics. Plato's own language tends to reinforce Aristotle's critique. In the *Phaedo*, to emphasize conceptual objectivity, Plato affirms that the Forms exist in a sphere apart from the sensible world; while in the later *Timaeus*, things are said to be "copies" of Ideas. This language of separation, however, cannot be forced into spatial language, for the Ideas cannot be in "some place"; they are incorporeal. To be situated in time and space is a state reserved only for bodies.

According to the common interpretation of Plato, the Forms are other than sense particulars. They are what the mind knows as an object of thought, while that which is in the sensible world is an object only of sense experience. Again, in the *Timaeus*, Plato imaginatively portrays the Demiurge as shaping the physical universe on the model of the Ideas portrayed as objects set apart and independent of the creative molder of the physical world. Thus, time is the moving image of eternity.

Turning to the *Meno*, one can find Plato's well-known doctrine of recollection. The key issue centers on the question of how one knows that one knows or, in other words, how can anyone inquire about what he does not know, for it seems that he must have some knowledge about that about which

he is inquiring to begin inquiry at all. This question occasions the famous scene in the *Meno* where a young uneducated slave in response to Socrates's questions is able to move from the sensible phenomena of the world to the Forms of abstract mathematics. Since for the Greeks knowledge is always knowledge of an object, it is assumed that the boy must have known the truths of mathematics in a previous existence. The soul, when it is in contact with the sensible world, becomes aware of what it already knows, its recollection of the essences of things, which it had seen from all of eternity. Here Socrates is pictured as an intellectual midwife who helps others realize explicitly what is already present in the depths of their being.

Here the Greek mind is in a dynamic longing for completion; Plato refers to this in the *Symposium* as eros. Eros stands midway between ignorance and wisdom, between ugliness and beauty. It is that longing for perfection grounded in an awareness of imperfection; it is the thirst for immortality as it reaches beyond mortality. Eros is presented as a dynamic spirit in the *Symposium*, one who closes the gap between the earthly and the celestial, that which binds together the whole of the universe. Here is the driving power that unites lover with beloved; here is the craving of philosophers to achieve wisdom. A philosopher is (literally) one who loves wisdom—that is to say, one who is absorbed in a constant yearning and striving for completion. Thus eros is all human striving to attain the good; eros is the force that carries the lover from lower to higher; eros is the dynamic thrust of the soul like an arrow shot in the air, for the target of all inquiry is the realm of Ideas.

All this is illustrated most powerfully in the beginning of book 7 of the *Republic*, the famous "Myth of the Cave," where chained prisoners think reality consists of the passing shadows they see cast onto the wall by a fire that blazes behind them. One of them finally escapes the world of darkness and shadows and moves out of the cave and sees with perfect clarity under the light of the sun. For Plato, this is akin to the journey from ignorance to knowledge, from the world of the senses to the world of the Forms, from passing shadows caught up in the flux of things to the permanent truths known only by the intellect. It is only in the light of the intellect that reality can be seen for what it is, and he who escapes from the cave returns to help those who live in darkness.

For Plato the Idea of the good is, like the sun, the source of light by which the eye of the mind sees everything; it is what the intellect seeks to grasp in all of its inquiry. Put another way, to recognize the good as the supreme source from which all Ideas derive their being is but another way to say that all things form an organic unity wherein all truths are connected one to another, a cosmos rather than chaos. Plato's entire discussion is grounded in the claim that there are degrees of reality discoverable by the mind. For Plato, the goal of philosophy is the ultimate integration of all truths to find the unity and purpose of all human life.

Political and Social Thought

The social and political program set forth in the *Republic* is nothing but the application of this theory of Forms to the problem of determining the ideal state. The unity and interrelationship of all sensible things stems from the unity and interrelationship of all Forms; here the many conform to the eternal law.

Plato always showed a keen interest in the interrelationship among political, social, and philosophical issues. His two longest works, the *Republic* and the *Laws*, are devoted to this topic. Like other Greeks of his day, Plato saw the political life as an essential part of human existence, and not to participate in the society of his own time would have been to deny himself an essential dimension of human fulfillment. Plato, writing late in his life, in his midseventies, tells us in his *Seventh Letter* that he had hoped when he was young to enter into a life of public service, but the trial and death of Socrates, who was falsely accused of impiety, exemplified the rampant injustice that was characteristic of the society of his own day. Plato set about to build his life on a different foundation from that which he saw around him, a situation that he considered one of complete disintegration and lack of attention to the

just and the virtuous. Plato, in following Socrates, sought to understand the meaning of virtue and the meaning of justice and to ground society on that knowledge. In the fate of Socrates, Plato saw the disintegration of Athens. If there were any hope for Athens, indeed for any society at all, it was imperative that it be grounded on the unchanging and eternal values of truth, goodness, and justice. This idea comes to full flower in the *Republic*, Plato's description for an ideal society.

For Plato, political activity is but an external expression of the various activities of the human soul. So the question "What is justice?" leads Plato to discourse on the various parts of the soul. For him the problem of the soul, its parts and functions, is fundamental for all questions of the state. Thus, education of the soul, discovering its dynamics and cultivating it, is of the greatest importance. Indeed, Plato often pictures Socrates as seeking to move the art of politics from the dynamic of self-serving cravings for power to the proper shaping of the soul. With a focus on the issue of justice, Plato rejected the claim that justice consists in mere adherence to the laws, for justice is based on the inner nature of the human spirit; nor can justice be the triumph of the stronger over the weaker.

A just state, Plato argues, is achieved in a situation in which everyone does one's own job, where each part functions properly with an eye to the good of the whole. In a just society, the rulers, the military, the working-class persons, all do what they ought to do. In a just society, the rulers are wise, the soldiers are brave, and the producers of material goods exercise self-control and are not overwhelmed by their desires for gain.

The key to the *Republic* is the dynamic nature of the soul, which has the three aspects of reason, spirit, and desire (corresponding to the rulers, the soldiers, and the workers in the state). The *Republic* is thus a work about the molding of the human soul where proper order is grounded in the rule of reason, the obedience of desire to rational ends. The tripartite nature of the soul in the *Republic*, a theme probably taken over by Plato from the Pythagoreans, saw the human person as having a rational part, a spirited part, and an appetitive part.

These three aspects of ourselves ought to work in harmony under the rule of reason. So in the *Phaedrus* Plato offers the image of the rational part as that of a charioteer, while the spirited and the appetitive parts are like two horses that remain under the rule of reason.

We read in the *Republic*:

Until philosophers are kings, or the kings and princes of this world have the spirit and power of philosophy, and political greatness and wisdom meet in one, . . . cities will never have rest from their evils,—no, nor the human race, as I believe,—and then only will this our state have a possibility of life and behold the light of day.

The theme of the *Republic*, then, is that philosophy alone offers true power; it alone is the way to genuine knowledge. The philosopher knows the Forms, the ideal standards by which all ought to mold their lives. The philosopher is not caught up like others in the flow of opinions. Thus for Plato the great issue is to determine who shall set the standards. He had little confidence in the majority acting together, as in democracy, for the majority often falls into the hands of the few, who use their persuasive powers to manipulate the mobs. Thus, the ultimate problem for all states is to understand the right standard: It is the problem of true knowledge. The philosopher alone is fit to rule. The foundation of the whole republic rests on knowledge of the true standards of life, for only the navigator who knows the art of navigation is capable of guiding the ship of state.

This is the idea at the heart of all of Plato's suggestions regarding education. One way in which the soul is educated is through music—sounds, rhythms, and the spoken word. What is taught to children by way of stories has a profound impact on the child's soul. Children should be offered only what is edifying; they are to be nourished by what is good, not evil. Plato thus offers in the *Republic* a critique of some Greek poetry that, in his view, failed to live up to a high moral standard. Behind this is Plato's belief that if one imitates the heroes and the gods of the Greek poetic tradition, this continuous imitation cannot help but influence for the better the character of the imitator. Thus, present only what is good and noble. Education is a lifelong process whereby one becomes more and more the end toward which one is striving. Just as the body needs exercise, so the soul needs nourishment—good literature, beautiful music, and above all, philosophical truth.

Platonism

Plato is regarded as one of the most comprehensive philosophers of antiquity. His mind gave full attention to the complexities of being as expressed in the interplay of permanence and change, unity and diversity, spirit and matter. In this interplay he offered a hierarchical universe. Such a universe is well described by the poet Shelley (1792–1822) in his celebrated *Adonais*:

The One remains, the many change and pass;
Heaven's light forever shines, Earth's shadows fly;
Life, like a dome of many-colored glass,
Stains the white radiance of Eternity,
Until Death tramples it to fragments.

Elsewhere, in art, the Renaissance painter Raphael (1483–1520) would try to capture Platonism in his *School of Athens* with a single gesture by depicting the Athenian philosopher with a raised arm pointing upward.

Throughout the history of Western thought, Platonism was understood to be that dynamic orientation of the intellect that goes beyond what is limited and finite in its longing for the realm of the eternal. Plato thus stands as the great enemy of all those forms of materialism that see the most basic stuff of reality as emerging from and returning to matter. This is why Hegel (1770–1831) would write in the second volume of his *History of Philosophy*:

The peculiarity of the Platonic philosophy is precisely this direction toward the supersensuous world,—it seeks the elevation of consciousness into the realm of spirit.

This attention to the unseen, as Saint Paul put it in 2 Corinthians 4:18, would prove very appealing to later authors who looked to Plato as the noble guide out of the cave. In the first two centuries of the Common Era, an interest in the value of Plato can be seen in Judaism (Philo) and Christianity (Clement of Alexandria and Origen). The *Enneads* of Plotinus (c. 205–270) would present a very influential select reading of Plato which has become known as Neoplatonism. This tradition is characterized by a mysticism that seeks in acts of abstraction and contemplation to move from the particular to the universal and thus discover the ultimate One that lies behind all appearances. The tension between the biblical tradition with its respect for the created order and this Neoplatonism would find expression in Saint Augustine of Hippo (354–430) and, through him, to the entire Middle Ages. Augustine would follow the tradition, already common in his day, to situate Plato's intelligible Forms as the fundamental characteristic of the mind of God.

It is ironic that Platonism would become so identified with the flight of the soul toward the eternal. Plato, in his attempt to overcome Sophistic relativism, sought to distinguish real from apparent goods in this world. Throughout history, there have been many positive and negative evaluations of Plato's ideal society. The fundamental basis of the *Republic*, however, remains vital. That is, all laws and social arrangements must be grounded in real goods. A society needs spiritual values that produce unity and happiness. Thus, philosophy is also to be a legislative science. Plato never forgot the unjust death of Socrates. The Socratic legacy of "care for the soul," as preserved and developed by Plato, would leave a profound impression on history. The soul as the seat of the moral personality capable of self-direction toward the good would be fundamental to all subsequent discussions of conversion and reform. Here is the Hellenic tradition that the quality of human life comes down to what one thinks and what one does. Life carries with it the obligation to leave the cave as well as the duty to participate harmoniously in communal life. This Plato sought to do in a lifetime of service to his students and to society as founder of one of the earliest Greek universities, the Academy.

The dialogues are not only masterpieces of philosophy; they are also masterpieces of literature. And the hero is not only Plato; it is also Socrates. The genius of Plato led him to use the figure of Socrates as the concrete image of the Form of the philosopher: Socrates—the persistent questioner, the tireless critic of the pretenders to wisdom, the ironic commentator on human follies—becomes the dynamic exemplar of the philosopher as the relentless examiner of ideas. Furthermore, Socrates emerges as more than a brilliant dialectician: He is a moral hero as well. In Plato's *Apology*, Socrates, in defending himself against charges of impiety and of corrupting the youth of Athens, describes himself as a "gadfly," stinging the great steed of the state to life, unmasking the pretenders to wisdom by his tactics in dialogue with them. But the image that emerges is not simply that of a skillful philosopher; it is also the image of a person dedicated to the value of inquiry, the examination of values, and the commitment to the good. Socrates could have escaped from Athens—his friends urged him to do so—but as one who regarded a society of law and obedience as necessary to the good, Socrates could not have justified escaping from its judgment. Socrates is the moral hero of the dialogues because he not only sought the ideal; he exemplified it.

Accordingly, there is no substitute for reading the dialogues themselves. Since the philosophical discussions to be found there are in dialogue form, they are dramatically alive. Philosophy is seen to be an activity of inquiry, a matter of framing ideas and then challenging them, a persistent and unending effort to achieve clarity, order, and—when all goes well—wisdom. In the dialogues, the issues are alive because they are propounded and explored by living persons, of various types but always recognizably human; the problems and the answers framed in the course of inquiry matter to the reader because they are recognized as being at the very heart of the human condition.

Lawrence F. Hundersmarck

Further Reading

Crombie, I. M. *Plato, The Midwife's Apprentice.* New York: Barnes & Noble, 1965. An easy-to-read short introduction.

Field, G. C. *The Philosophy of Plato.* London: Oxford University Press, 1949. Summary of Plato's thoughts around key themes.

Friedlander, P. *Plato.* Translated by H. Meyerhoff. 3 vols. Princeton: Princeton University Press, 1970. This is a very important survey of the development of Plato's thought.

Guthrie, W. K. C. *A History of Greek Philosophy.* Vols. 4 and 5. London: Cambridge University Press, 1978. This is the standard work in the field with excellent bibliographies.

Jordan, N. *The Wisdom of Plato: An Attempt at an Outline.* 2 vols. Lanham, Md.: University Press of America, 1981. Another helpful and substantial summary.

Navia, L. E., and Katz, E. *Socrates: An Annotated Bibliography.* New York: Garland, 1988. A bibliographic survey of scholarship on Socrates.

Ritter, C. *Bibliographies on Plato.* New York: Garland, 1980. A bibliographic survey of scholarship on Plato.

Taylor, A. E. *Plato: The Man and His Work.* New York: Routledge, Chapman and Hall, 1960. This famous work discusses the major themes of each dialogue and is a great help in alerting the reader of Plato to the key philosophical moves throughout the text.

Vlastos, Gregory, ed. *Plato: Metaphysics and Epistemology*, vol. 1, and *Plato: Ethics, Politics, Philosophy of Art and Religion*, vol. 2. South Bend, Ind.: University of Notre Dame Press, 1978. These two volumes are collections of critical essays on various aspects of Platonic thought.

ARISTOTLE

Born: 384 B.C., Stageira, in Thrace

Died: 322 B.C., Chalcis, in Euboea

Major Works: (1) First period (before 348 B.C.): *Physics*, books I, II and VII; *On the Soul*, book I; (2) Second period (347–336 B.C.): *On Philosophy* (fragmentary); *Eudemian Ethics*; *On the Heavens*; *On Generation and Corruption*; (3) Third period (335–322 B.C.): the logical *Organon*, consisting of the *Categories*, *On Interpretation*, the *Prior* and *Posterior Analytics*, the *Topics*, and the *Sophistical Fallacies*; the *Metaphysics*; *Physics*, books III–VI, VIII; *Meteorology*; the *Histories of Animals*; *On the Generation of Animals*; *On the Soul*; treatises on perception, memory, life and death, breathing, and related subjects: the *Parva Naturalia*; the *Nicomachean Ethics*; the *Politics*; the *Rhetoric*; the *Poetics*. (Not all of these works were written solely by Aristotle: Some probably were written under his direction by followers and associates like Meno, Theophrastus, and Eudemus, at the Lyceum.)

Major Ideas

Ideas do not have an independent, extra-mental subsistence, but exist in things.

The material substratum, which is the potential for the existence of finite things, must be distinguished from absolute nonbeing or privation.

The substances of things are a union of form and matter.

Body and soul are conjoined as matter and form.

The existence of all finite and transitory things can be understood as a movement from potential to actual existence.

The world exists eternally, and movement of all things is an unceasing movement.

The source of this movement is the unmoved or eternally actual First Mover, the actuality of which draws finite things from potential into actual existence.

The empirical order is a suitable realm for inquiry based on sense perception.

Whereas in the logical order, demonstration proceeds deductively from general principles to particular conclusions, discussion of the natural order proceeds inductively from the observed particular to general conclusions.

The "good" is "that at which all things aim."

All human inquiry and behavior is, therefore, guided by its end or goal, which is a particular good.

The most eminent pupil and the eventual rival of Plato, Aristotle was simply called "the Philosopher" during the Middle Ages and is still thought of by many as the greatest philosopher of all time, both on account of the keenness of his insight into the fundamental philosophical problems of knowing and being and on account of the encyclopedic character of his work. He was born in Stageira, in Thrace, the son of Nichomachus, the personal physician of Amyntas II, the king of Macedon. Early in his life he acquired an interest in medicine and in biological study in general. It is believed that he was trained in dissection and may actually have practiced medicine. At the age of seventeen (367 B.C.),

Aristotle journeyed to Athens, where he studied closely with Plato until the latter's death in 347 B.C. We have no reason to believe that Aristotle either disagreed radically with Plato's teaching during his student years or that Aristotle's expressions of admiration for Plato are anything less than genuine.

Rather than remain in the Academy after Plato's death when the headship passed to Plato's nephew, Speusippus, Aristotle left Athens for Assos and there founded his own school. After three years in Assos, he left for Mitylene on the island of Lesbos. Many of his biological works were based on the examination of species living in these places. He was invited in 343 by Philip of Macedon to become the tutor of Philip's son and heir, Alexander, known to history as Alexander the Great. Aristotle remained in Macedon until 336, when Alexander succeeded to the throne.

In 335, Aristotle returned to Athens and founded a new school at the Lyceum. The style of Aristotle's school was different from that of the Academy, inasmuch as it functioned more as a research institute in which the scholarly members lectured than simply as a school. Lectures and discussions appear to have been presented in a covered walkway—perhaps with the lecturer moving freely among his hearers—leading to the identification of the school of Aristotle as the Peripatos and his followers as Peripatetics. After Alexander the Great died in 323 and his protection was removed from his teacher, Aristotle was charged, as Socrates had been before him, with "atheism." He is reported to have left Athens with the comment that he would not permit the Athenians to sin against philosophy a second time. He died of natural causes in the following year.

Logic, Metaphysics, and Cosmology

Aristotle's development of a theoretical, formal logic sets him apart from all his predecessors. Whereas previous Greek philosophy, including that of Socrates and Plato, had made only a preliminary effort to explain and elucidate the nature of knowledge or "science" prior to undertaking the exposition of science, Aristotle provided the world with a full-scale and thoroughly self-conscious discussion of the forms and rules of scientific thinking as a prolegomenon to his discussions of other branches of knowledge.

The logical treatises gathered together as the *Organon* present a series of rules and techniques, such as the proper patterns of syllogistic argumentation, the identification and refutation of fallacies, and the basic categories used for the identification and description of all things—substance and incidental properties like quantity, quality, and relation. It can, of course, easily be shown that previous philosophers had used these or similar patterns of argumentation and predication, and Aristotle himself

believed that his logical work was based on an examination of the way in which argument actually functioned. What he contributed was the first formal discussion and analysis of these patterns. Had Aristotle done nothing else, his future reputation—indeed, his domination of the field of logic for some two thousand years, both for debate and for the construction of deductive system—would have been assured.

Like Plato, Aristotle assumed the reality of the universal or the general, and he assumed that it could be known. Where he differed from Plato was in his assumption of the reality of particulars and, more fundamentally, in his assumption of an immediate real relation between the universal and the particular. Thus, for Aristotle, the ideas or forms of things cannot be understood as realities independent of their embodiment or actuality. Not only Aristotle's logic but also his cosmology builds on these assumptions: Both assume the dependence of the particular upon the universal. In logic, the particular is deduced from the universal—the syllogism being the perfect example of such deduction. In cosmology, physics, and metaphysics, the general or universal is found by inference or induction that begins in the particular.

This perception of the relation of universal to particular represents, in the case of cosmology, the solution to the fundamental problem of Greek philosophy—the dichotomization of form and matter, of the One and the many. As noted earlier, Plato, for the sake of finding truth beyond fallible perception of mutable phenomena, had argued for the real existence of ideas or forms apart from matter, but had nowhere proved the point. In fact, he resolved the problem of the separation only by recourse to myth.

Aristotle accepts the reality of ideas or forms—the universal—but argues for the existence of the universal in the particular and never apart from it. Aristotle also dispenses with the Platonic assumption of the unreality or nonbeing of corporeal particulars and argues the real existence of both form and matter. Thus, Aristotle distinguishes between nonbeing (*me on*), which is nothingness or space, and which cannot produce anything, and the material substratum of things, which is nothing or nothing in and of itself (*me po on*), but which exists in the sense of material potential, the capability of receiving form and moving toward the actualization of form or idea in a completed particular.

Aristotle recognized with great clarity that the idea or essence of any thing is, quite simply, the "what" of a thing, the answer to the question "What is it?" Aristotle also recognized that if this "what" is reified—considered in itself as a "thing"—then we are forced to ask the question again and determine the "what" of the "what," the essence of the essence, the idea of the idea; and having done that, we still have no answer but must ask all over again the question of essence, the idea of the idea of the idea, the "what" of the "what" of the "what"—and that is absurd (*Metaphysics*, 7:6, 1031b–1032a). The only philosophically responsible solution is to refuse to separate essence from the thing of which it is the essence.

What Aristotle has done in this argument, with characteristic clarity, is solve the Platonic problem of a dualism of form and matter by beginning the argument where, in his estimation, it should have begun in the first place—with the concrete reality of individual things. The Platonic problem of mediating between eternal ideas and their corporeal embodiments is here turned on its head: Instead of trying to get from a changeless incorporeal idea to a corporeal individual by means of either a mythological mediating deity or an infinite series of graduated emanations, Aristotle begins with the corporeal thing and shows that it is impossible and therefore unnecessary to ascend to a pure essence beyond which there is no further idea.

The union of form and matter, the relation of the universal to the particular, is achieved logically and explained naturally by Aristotle's view of development or process in things as a movement from potency to actuality. Aristotle, in other words, understood the life of the cosmos as a process in which the essences or forms of things, the universals, are realized in the particular, in the phenomenal order. This development or realization is explained by Aristotle in terms of the ideas or principles of matter and form, with form being considered both as cause and as goal or end. Although form and matter are inseparable, we experience a world in process: Seeds grow into trees, calves and colts grow into cows and horses. The seed, the calf, and the colt are neither matter without form nor form without matter, but they are also productive of other embodiments of form, trees, cows, and horses. The actuality of the seed, the realization of form in a material particular, is potency as regards the tree. Form appears both as cause and as result or goal. The form Aristotle calls entelechy (*entelechia*) or inner *telos*; the motion or development that moves a thing from potency to actuality (from *dynamis* to *energeia*) is *kinesis*.

This approach to form also allowed Aristotle both to distinguish between nonliving things, plants, animals, and human beings on metaphysical grounds and to argue a hierarchy or ranking of beings on the basis of their forms, or in the case of living beings, their souls. The form of living things is superior to that of the nonliving inasmuch as the form of the living is a soul or principle of life, relating to the growth and reproduction of the species. The animal soul, in addition to being the principle of life, is also the principle of motion and sensation, in that animals, unlike plants, must seek out their food. To the life, movement, and sensation characteristic of these lower souls, the human adds the faculty of reason. This series, Aristotle assumes, is cumulative and in a sense, evolutionary: The higher forms presuppose the lower.

This view of form and of soul as the entelechy avoids the fundamentally dualistic character of the Platonic theory of the relation of soul and body. Aristotle does not, in other words, conceive of the soul as inhabiting the body but rather assumes that the substantial reality of human beings is a composite of form (soul) and matter, with the particular character of the human body resulting from the impress of the soul upon the materiality. Without the soul, there is also no "body" in the normal sense of the word—and neither soul nor body can exist separately. Aristotle, therefore, argues a genuine unity of the human individual, paralleling the unity of other substantial beings in the physical world, both living and nonliving.

On the larger metaphysical scale or, as Aristotle himself termed it, the scale of "first philosophy" or "theology," Aristotle's model assumes the eternity of form and matter, neither of which is created or destroyed and presupposes also some absolutely necessary, independent, and self-existent being as the first mover of things, the source of all *kinesis*, motion or development. This, too, represents a considerable advance upon Plato's mythical Demiurge, since the idea of a first mover represents a logically or scientifically deduced first principle, the knowledge of which rests upon analysis of the system of the cosmos. Aristotle's First Mover or First Being stands in the place of Plato's Idea of the Good as a rationally defined pure actuality (*actus purus*) over the pure potency of primary matter (*me po on*). In a logical sense, the First Mover is simply the realization of the motion of the whole universe from potency to actuality: Matter is that which is moved but cannot move anything; pure actuality is that which moves without being moved.

It is crucial to note that the motion or *kinesis* so fundamental to Aristotle's philosophy is not a movement from place to place but a development from potential existence toward full realization made possible in a teleological sense by the full reality of the First Mover. The First Mover does not act on the material order the way in which a sculptor acts upon marble: This would imply a change or motion in the First Mover, which to Aristotle's mind would itself require a prior act to set it in motion—and would result in the impossibility of arriving at the origin of the movement. The First Mover is a final cause who moves all things not as a point or act of origin but as a final, unmoved goal, as the pure actuality toward which all that is potential tends.

Aristotle thus understood "physics" as the theory of the motion or movement of things from potential to actual existence and, therefore, as an inclusive approach to the real and natural order, from the divine First Mover and immovable principle, to the imperishable motions and movers of the heavens, to the perishable order of our world, the sublunary sphere, in which things come into existence, develop, decay, and pass out of existence. Aristotle's philosophy of nature, then, is the perfect refutation of the frequently heard generalization that Greek philosophy tended to deal with the static and the abstract. The focus of Aristotle's thought was upon motion, change, development, and the understanding of the goal-directedness of things, of the movement of things from potential to actual existence.

Ethical and Political Thought

The ethical thought of Aristotle carries forward this goal-directed or teleological principle into the realm of human inquiry and behavior. The presupposition of this teleological perspective is Aristotle's conception of the soul as the form or *entelechia* of the human being. The soul, therefore, is not a static principle, but an inward, telic principle that is the goal or actuality toward which the human being strives. The human soul, moreover, is both animal, having sense perception and memory, and intellective, having reason akin to that of the divine. Together, these aspects of the soul point to the identity of the human being as an ethical or moral being. Indeed, for Aristotle, morality is the unique attribute of human beings.

Granting Aristotle's teleological premise, all conduct, whether related to purely intellectual pursuit, to moral choice, or to physical activity, is guided by its end or goal, which is a particular good. This underlying assumption led Aristotle to chart a broad course for his ethical thought, including a discussion of the various forms of knowing, such as science, prudence, and art, each of which is to be understood in terms of its goal. Even so, Aristotle's ethical thought has both its individual and its corporate dimensions, with the category of prudence or discretionary conduct extending to the ethical theory of the state.

Very much in accord with the more inductive and empirical approach taken in his thought on the natural order, Aristotle's ethical and political thought stands in contrast to the idealistic and generally utopian approach of Plato. Rather than define the unreachable ideal as the goal of ethics and politics, Aristotle rests his arguments on experience and example. The good of human beings cannot be understood, therefore, as capable of deduction or of precise determination like the solution to a logical or mathematical problem. Ethics does not begin with a set of general principles but with an examination of the results of human actions. The general principles of ethics are inferred by the comparison of results. Similarly, both in his politics proper, in his analyses of the histories and constitutional documents of some 158 cities, and in the constitution that he drew up for Athens, Aristotle recognized that different states and different historical circumstances dictated different forms of government, and he searched for an "ideal state" only on the basis of his extensive consideration of the problems and virtues of actual governments. Even so, Aristotle could identify monarchy as the best form of government and its abuse, tyranny, as the worst. Both ethics and politics, thus, are matters of discretionary judgment, arising out of the natural propensities of human beings.

From the relationship of morality to responsibility, Aristotle inferred also that ethics implies the freedom of the individual moral agent in choosing and seeking out goals. Aristotle assumed, therefore, that both vice and virtue are capable of being chosen by human beings. Typically, he understood vice as the result of excessive or defective activity, and he regarded virtue as the attainment of a judicious balance or mean between excess and defect, a state good or excellent in itself and suitable as a goal of conduct. (For example, courage is the mean between cowardice and rashness; temperance is the mean between "insensibility" and self-indulgence.)

On the most general level, Aristotle argued that happiness (well-being) is the goal of human life. This basic principle of conduct only serves, however, to underscore Aristotle's point about the discretionary nature of ethics: Human beings differ in their views about happiness. For some, happiness is wealth; for others, pleasure; for others, honor.

Nonetheless, Aristotle believed that he could construct a reliable account of happiness based on the intellectual nature of human beings. Nourishment and growth are goods common to all living beings, including those not endowed with reason. But because of their unique nature, human beings cannot be truly happy simply with these animal pleasures. Happiness must relate to an activity capable of attaining the good of the individual, to a pattern of life that is uniquely human. On the analogy of the ancient definition of the health of the body in terms of a balance of its humors, Aristotle argues that the health or happiness of the soul is the attainment of a moral equilibrium through training and the cultivation of good habits or dispositions. Thus, only the actively virtuous life, in which a stable or balanced rule of conduct is followed, is conformable with true happiness.

The significance of Aristotle's thought, both in its own time and in subsequent ages, lies to a large extent in its distinction from the philosophy of Plato. Although Aristotle retained from his training under Plato an ultimately idealistic definition of reality in his conception of the First Mover, and although he lodged the identity of things in the more spiritual concept of form, he stood outside the fundamentally dualistic path of Greek philosophy that can be traced from the Orphic religious revival of the early sixth century B.C., to Parmenides, through Socrates and Plato, to middle- and Neoplatonism. His thought, for all of its reliance on certain of the insights of idealism, returned philosophy at a new and more scientific level to the work of observation begun by the Ionian or Milesian philosophers, Thales, Anaximander, and Anaximenes. Granting that Platonism in its later forms was the dominant philosophy of the classical world, this scientific, inductive dimension of Aristotle's thought was less appreciated and less influential in ancient times than it would become with the rediscovery of the Aristotelian corpus for the Latin West in the thirteenth century. From that point onward, as evidenced in the work of Albertus Magnus (Albert the Great), Saint Thomas Aquinas, and to a certain extent, Robert Grosseteste and Roger Bacon, the strongly empirical bent of Aristotle's work in the

Physics and in the various books examining the natural order bore abundant fruit in philosophy and science. If Plato was the philosopher par excellence of the ancient world, it was Aristotle who was, as the medieval philosophers and theologians called him, "the Philosopher" for the West from the thirteenth to the seventeenth centuries.

RICHARD A. MULLER

Further Reading

Aristotle. *The Basic Works of Aristotle*. Edited with an introduction by Richard McKeon. New York: Random House, 1941. A standard collection of all the most important philosophical works, with major excerpts from the natural histories; it contains an excellent general introduction and a fine annotated bibliography.

Cherniss, H. *Aristotle's Criticism of Presocratic Philosophy*. Baltimore: Octagon Books, 1935. A useful introduction to an important issue in the background of Aristotle's thought.

Copleston, Frederick C. *A History of Philosophy*. 9 vols. Garden City, N.Y.: Doubleday, 1946–74; reprinted, 1985. Vol. 1, pp. 266–378, contains a very helpful account of Aristotle's thought.

Jaeger, Werner. *Aristotle: Fundamentals of the History of His Development*. Translated by R. Robinson. Oxford: Oxford University Press, 1934. Still the basic study of the development of Aristotle's thought.

Ross, Sir W. D. *Aristotle*. 2d ed. London: Methuen, 1930. A superb introduction to the whole of Aristotle's thought by one of the greatest modern Aristotle scholars.

————. *Aristotle's Metaphysics*. 2 vols. Oxford: Oxford University Press, 1924. A commentary on the *Metaphysics*, indispensable to the careful and detailed study of Aristotle's thought.

Taylor, A. E. *Aristotle*. London: Nelson, 1943. A significant brief study of Aristotle's thought by a convinced Platonist.

Zeller, Eduard. *Aristotle and the Earlier Peripatetics*. 2 vols. London: Longmans, 1897. A useful study.

EUCLID

Born: 350–325 B.C., place unknown
Died: C. 275 B.C., probably in Alexandria, Egypt
Major Work: The *Elements* (*Stoicheiai*)

Major Ideas

A rigorous, systematic treatment of mathematics requires the statement of all assumptions and the proof of all propositions by means of a uniform methodology.
All mathematical quantities can be expressed by geometrical figures, either lines, areas, or solids.
Physical events can be modeled using mathematical expressions.
Space is infinite in extent, but not infinitely divisible.

Euclid was the author of history's longest-lived textbook, the *Elements*, which forms to this day the basis of instruction in plane geometry, the chief mathematical achievement of ancient Greek civilization. In addition to the familiar theorems of geometry, the thirteen books (long chapters) of the *Elements* also cover number theory, incommensurable or irrational quantities, solid geometry and the properties of polyhedra (regular solids, from the tetrahedron—a four-sided solid—to the icosahedron, the twenty-sided solid), and a type of "geometrical algebra."

Nothing definite can be said about Euclid's life, although two anecdotes circulated in antiquity. One relates that the king of Egypt, Ptolemy, who was the first of the Greek dynasty that ruled Egypt from 323 B.C. to 30 B.C., asked Euclid if there was any easier way to geometry than that of the *Elements*. Euclid replied, "There is no royal road to geometry," meaning that there is no specially smoothed and easy road to learning. The second anecdote records Euclid's answer to a student who asked him, "How shall I benefit if I learn these theorems?" Euclid told his assistant to give the student an obol (a small coin), "Since he must profit from whatever he learns."

From these stories we can deduce that Euclid taught geometry in Alexandria around 300 B.C., during the reign of Ptolemy I. He may have been born or lived as a youth in Athens, and he may have studied at Plato's Academy, since that institution was the center of mathematical research in the fourth century B.C. At any rate, he spent his later life in Alexandria, where Ptolemy was setting up the scholarly institute known as the Museum (Center for the Muses), and taught geometry there. The famous mathematician Archimedes (born c. 287 B.C.) studied with some of Euclid's students, not with Euclid himself, so we may be sure that Euclid had died before the mid-third century B.C..

Euclid can best be seen as a talented collector and systematizer of all then-existing mathematical knowledge. He collected the work of the earlier mathematicians Eudoxus, Theaetetus, and Pythagoras, and presented this work in a uniform format, with many additions of his own. The success of his systematization insured that geometry and geometrical proofs would dominate mathematics until modern times. Even a work as late as Newton's *Principia* (first edition 1687) has the same outward appearance as the *Elements*, with geometrical diagrams and proofs filling each page, even though Newton had by then developed the calculus, which would have better served his purpose.

The Elements

Since the *Elements* describes a complete mathematical universe, Euclid begins with the basic task: to define this universe. To do so, he lists the *definitions*, the *postulates*, and the *axioms* on which this universe is based. He lists twenty-three *definitions*; for example,

1. A point is that which has no length.
2. A line is a length without breadth.

down to

23. Parallel straight lines are straight lines which, being in the same plane and being extended indefinitely in both directions, do not meet one another in either direction.

This last definition establishes that the universe of Euclidean geometry is infinite. It would not be true in closed-space geometries.

Next Euclid lists five *postulates*, that is, statements that are not proven, but simply demonstrated. For example, postulate 1 says:

1. It is possible to draw a straight line from any point to any other point.

The most controversial of these postulates is 5:

5. If a straight line falls on two straight lines in such a way as to make the interior angles on the same side *less* than two right angles, then the two straight lines, if extended indefinitely, will meet on that side on which the angles less than two right angles occur.

(In non-Euclidean, curved-space geometries this postulate does not hold true.)

As his final preliminary step, Euclid lists five *axioms*, or *common notions*, which must be accepted as the basis of this geometry, but which cannot be proven. For example, axiom 1 says:

1. Things which are equal to the same thing are also equal to each other.

These are all common-sense observations about normal space, but they are difficult to prove in any rigorous sense. If other axioms are adopted, non-Euclidean geometry results.

After listing the definitions, postulates, and axioms, Euclid begins his thirteen books of propositions, which may be *theorems* (in which something is proven) or *problems* (in which something is constructed). Every proposition, unless it is abbreviated, exhibits the same method of proof:

1. the statement of the problem;
2. the setting-out of the materials for the proof—usually a geometric figure;
3. the definition or statement of the conditions under which the proposition may be satisfied;
4. the construction or drawing of the figure;
5. the proof;
6. the conclusion, which usually ends with Q.E.D., the Latin for "what had to be proven."

Take as an example of Euclid's procedure his proof of the Pythagorean theorem (book 1, proposition 47). The *statement* is as follows:

In right triangles, the square on the side subtending the right angle is equal to the squares on the sides containing the right angle.

Then follows the *setting-out*:

Let *ABC* be a right triangle having the angle *BAC* right.

Then the *definition*:

I say that the square on *BC* is equal to the squares on *BA* and *AC*.

Next the *construction*, which in this proposition is two pages long.

Finally, the *proof*:

Therefore the whole square, *BDEC*, is equal to the two squares, *GB* and *HC* . . . Therefore the square on the side *BC* is equal to the squares on the sides *BA* and *AC*. and the *conclusion*, which repeats the original statement, Q.E.D.

The *Elements* is the first such systematic treatment of the entire mathematical universe, beginning with fundamental definitions and employing a standard method of proof throughout. By no means did Euclid consider this book an elementary text, and he gives no hint as to how the truth of these propositions was discovered or why they are presented in this particular sequence. The propositions have leaped like Athena, fully formed from the brow of the mathematician. Thomas Hobbes, when he first read the example given above is said to have exclaimed, "By God, this is impossible!" Such is the impression of the majesty of the propositions and the inexorability of their march through the text.

Books 1 through 4 of the *Elements* deal with the geometry of points, lines, areas, and rectilinear and circular figures. Books 5 and 6 deal with ratios and proportions, a topic first treated by the mathematician Eudoxus a century earlier. For Euclid, a *ratio* is a relationship according to size of two magnitudes, whether numbers, lengths, or areas. For example, 6 has a certain ratio to 10, in modern terms, 6/10. Two pairs of magnitudes that have the same ratio are *proportional*. For example, 12 has the same ratio to 20 as 6 has to 10; therefore the two pairs, 6 and 10, 12 and 20, are proportional to each other. The manipulation of ratios and proportions is fundamental to Greek mathematics and to a large extent takes over the function of modern algebra. For example, in book 6, proposition 13, finding of a mean proportional between two lines, using geometrical figures, is the equivalent of finding the square root of the length of one of the lines. It is precisely this combination of geometry with ratios and proportion to solve problems for which modern mathematics uses arithmetic or algebra that gives ancient Greek mathematics its peculiar character.

In book 5, definition 4, Euclid states that any magnitude/quantity can, when multiplied by a factor, exceed any other magnitude. This means that infinitely small or infinitely large magnitudes are impossible. (For instance, one could not find a number bigger than an infinitely large number, if such an infinitely large number could exist—but it cannot, according to definition 4.)

Books 7 through 9 of the *Elements* deal with "arithmetic" and numbers, beginning with the usual definitions: the (to us) familiar—even, odd, prime, composite (nonprime), squares, cubes; and the unfamiliar—the even-times-even numbers (products of two even numbers, for example $12 = 6 \times 2$), the even-times-odd numbers (the product of an even and an odd number, for example, $18 = 6 \times 3$), perfect numbers (which are equal to the sum of their factors, for example, $6 = 3 + 2 + 1$). It must be remembered that "arithmetic" in ancient texts means the study of numbers and their properties,

not the techniques of calculation, which was called "logistic." Much of the material in books 7–9 is attributable to the semilegendary Pythagoras and his school.

In the course of his long book 10, often considered his masterpiece, Euclid develops the theory of *incommensurability*, a topic that had previously been treated by the mathematician Theaetetus. Two magnitudes are *commensurable* if they have a common measure/factor that divides into each an exact integral number of times. *Incommensurable* magnitudes are those which have no such common measure: "If the lesser of two quantities is continually subtracted from the greater, and the remainder never measures (is a factor of) the quantity which precedes it, then the quantities will be incommensurable" (book 10, proposition 2). In modern terms, incommensurable quantities are those which cannot be expressed by a common fraction (such as $1/3$) and which, if put in decimal notation, are expressed by an infinite decimal. The most commonly cited example of incommensurability is the hypotenuse of a right triangle with sides equal to one. By the Pythagorean theorem, the hypotenuse of this triangle is $1^2 + 1^2 = 2^2$, therefore the hypotenuse is $\sqrt{2}$, quantity that is incommensurable with the sides. (In modern notation, this means that $\sqrt{2}$ is an infinite decimal. Euclid's reliance on geometrical means of expression means that he avoids the problem of how to represent incommensurable quantities; he does not, for example, have to find a numerical approximation to $\sqrt{2}$.) The theorems of book 10 were closely studied by the developers of algebra, Paciuolo, Cardano, and Stevin.

Books 11 through 13 deal with solid geometry: the construction and relationships between circumscribed and enclosed figures, the volumes of pyramids and other solid figures, and the construction of the five "Platonic" solids, the regular tetrahedron, the cube, the octahedron, the dodecahedron, and the icosahedron. These figures were given quasimystical importance by the school of Plato. In these books Euclid employs the *method of exhaustion*: by taking smaller and smaller areas, he shows that the area of a circle can be "exhausted," that is, reduced to an amount smaller than any given quantity. Less than a century later, Archimedes refined this method to find an approximation to $\pi = 3.14+$.

Euclid wrote other books, the most significant of which is the *Optics*, a treatise on sight and perspective. It assumes that vision is produced by rays that are emitted from the eyes and "touch" the object that is seen. These rays are straight and their behavior can be modeled by the straight lines of plane geometry. For example, things that are farther away are seen less distinctly because fewer of these eye-rays hit them; the rays diverge like lines from a point. This book on optics was the only treatment of the topic until Ptolemy wrote his *Optics* in the second century A.D.

MARK T. RILEY

Further Reading

Euclid. *The Thirteen Books of the Elements*. Translated with introduction and commentary by Sir Thomas L. Heath. Cambridge University Press, 1926. Reprint, New York: Dover Publications, 1956. This is the essential work for a study of Euclid: It includes not only a translation but also an extensive commentary on the text with many citations from the history of mathematics.

Greenberg, Marvin. *Euclidean and Non-Euclidean Geometries: Development and History*. San Francisco: W. H. Freeman, 1980. Greenberg outlines the essence of Euclidean geometry and shows how the hyperbolic and elliptic, non-Euclidean, geometries have developed in modern times.

Heath, Sir Thomas L. *A History of Greek Mathematics*. Oxford: Clarendon Press, 1921. Reprint, New York: Dover Publications, 1981. The best overall history of Greek mathematics, this text puts Euclid in context.

Knorr, Wilbur R. *The Evolution of the Euclidean Elements*. Dordrecht and Boston: D. Reidel, 1975. Not a text for beginners, this book discusses pre-Euclidean theories, particularly the development of the concept of incommensurability.

EPICURUS

Born: C. 341 B.C., Samos, Greece
Died: C. 270 B.C., Athens, Greece
Major Works: Fragments: "To Herodotus," "To Menoeceus," "To Pythocles," "Cardinal Principles," "On Nature"

Major Ideas

All sensation is true; sensation is the primary source of knowledge.

The two criteria of knowledge are a "clear view" and noncontradiction.

The universe is wholly material; it consists of matter and void.

Nothing is created out of nothing, and nothing is destroyed: The universe is neither increasing nor decreasing.

It is in the nature of human beings to pursue pleasure and avoid pain; therefore, the good or virtuous life consists in the pursuit of pleasure and the avoidance of pain.

True pleasure is found in imperturbability.

The swerve of the atoms accounts for the presence of freedom of will in an otherwise causally determined universe.

Epicurus lived during a time of great change in early Greece, change that influenced his philosophy. In 323 B.C., Alexander the Great died. Epicurus was living in Athens at the time. He was eighteen years old and his family was living on the island colony of Samos. In Athens, Alexander's death brought the suppression of democracy. On Samos, it brought the expulsion of the Greeks. The family moved to Asia Minor, and Epicurus soon left Athens to join them.

In Asia Minor, Epicurus continued his study of philosophy and, in particular, he encountered Nausiphanes, a student of Democritus's atomistic theory. By 311, he had started his own school, teaching first in Mitylene and and later in Lampsacus. He attracted followers. In 307, he returned with them to Athens and founded the Garden, the first Epicurean community. The community provided a sharp contrast to the unsettled nature of the times. In defiance of convention, the group included both men and women, courtesans and slaves. Under Epicurus's leadership, this unusual and diverse collection of people built a simple life, bound by friendship and secluded from the world. Epicurus lived in this community of friends, writing and studying, until his death.

Epicurus was a materialist. Although he did not like to admit it, he was deeply influenced by Democritus's early theory of atomism. Epicurus argued that everything, the soul as well as the body, is composed of atoms. His reliance on sensation is the center of his theory; it links his metaphysics with his ethics. For Epicurus, all sensation is true. Sensation is, therefore, the source of all knowledge.

The Ethical Theory

The sensations of pleasure and pain form the basis of Epicurus's ethical program. For it is obvious, he thought, that by nature we pursue pleasure and avoid pain. In other words, the natural goal or end of life is the pursuit of pleasure and avoidance of pain. In agreement with traditional Greek philosophy, Epicurus accepted the view that the good life consisted in the fulfillment of nature. Therefore, the good life must consist in the pursuit of pleasure.

Epicurus's own contemporaries misunderstood and ridiculed his ethical theory. Both the misunderstanding and criticism have continued throughout history. The word "epicure" is even now associated primarily with a connoisseur of food and wine, a devotee of subtle pleasures. While most

Greek philosophers agreed that the natural goal of life is the pursuit of happiness, they generally claimed that true happiness is found only when the mind, or reason, regulates or orders the body's appetites. Thus they drew a distinction between the pursuit of pleasure and the pursuit of virtue, a distinction that seems necessary to even a common-sense view of ethics. Because of his materialism, such a solution was not available to Epicurus. He could not, for example argue that the mind is of a higher order of reality than the body, and so, by nature, meant to govern it. For this reason, it has seemed to many that by "pursuit of pleasure" Epicurus must have meant "satisfaction of the appetites." But, as many scholars have pointed out, this is not the case.

Although Epicurus wrote diligently throughout his career, only fragments of his work survive. The major sources are three letters ("To Herodotus," "To Pythocles," and "To Menoeceus") and a list of forty cardinal principles in Diogenes Laertius's *Lives*. Parts of Epicurus's essay "On Nature" have been recovered from the remains of an Epicurean library destroyed by Vesuvius in A.D. 79. Finally, there are the writings of his followers, principally Lucretius's poem *De Rerum Natura*.

The decline of the city-state of Athens brought with it broad changes in philosophy that help explain Epicurus's views. In contrast to Socrates, who described the ideal republic as ruled by a philosopher-king, later Greek philosophy is concerned with the private life of the individual. This is true of both major schools of the period, Epicureanism and Stoicism. Stated as "the pursuit of pleasure" versus "forbearance," the ethical goals of the two schools seem directly opposed to each other. But once it is understood that Epicurus thought that the highest pleasure is "imperturbability," his conception of the good life is clearly quite similar to that of Stoic "self-sufficiency." It is less the goals than the explanations behind them that mark the difference in the two schools of thought.

For early Greek philosophers, physical and ethical theories were directly related. To understand the nature of human beings, and so also the end they should seek, one must understand the nature of the world. Epicurus's response to the question "What is the nature of the world?" grew out of a long tradition. One of the central problems of this tradition was how to explain change and persistence. If, as some philosophers thought, the world is made up of distinct substances, how does one thing become another, as, for instance, it does when water becomes vapor or grass becomes a cow. On the other hand, if the world is made up of one essential substance, why does it appear in so many different forms?

Epicurus's Atomism

For Epicurus, the only satisfactory explanation was by reference to atomism. As with all his thinking, the truth of sensation forms the basis of his argument. We perceive change in the world. Therefore change must be real; it cannot be an illusion. We perceive that everything in the universe can change, and as, according to Epicurus, only bodies can change, everything must be material. Change occurs only by direct contact, that is, only when bodies collide with each other, moving and displacing one another. But this means that in addition to bodies there must be space—the empty void or place into which a body moves. Thus, Epicurus concluded, the universe is made up entirely of bodies and the void.

The theory explains change, but it must also account for persistence. Persistence requires that there be something that does not change. That something is the atoms. Atoms are very small, hard, durable bodies. They move in response to collision, decomposing or rearranging larger, perceptible objects. But atoms themselves do not decompose into infinitely smaller and smaller parts. Instead, they form new aggregates. The different configurations of atoms, then, produce the variety of objects in the world. Thus, while the universe is constantly changing, nothing is created out of nothing and nothing is destroyed. The universe is neither increasing nor diminishing.

While the atomistic theory succeeds in addressing the traditional problem of change and persistence, it also created major difficulties for

Epicurus. For if, as Epicurus insisted, all knowledge is based on sensation, then how can one demonstrate the existence of atoms? Clearly we have no direct sensory experience of them. Moreover, if all change, and so all experience, is the result of bodies acting on bodies, how does one explain sensation itself?

Epicurus outlined his theory of knowledge in a canon. There, along with sensation as the primary arbiter of knowledge, he cites a second, negative principle of reasoning that together with sensation can guide knowledge of the nature of the world. The principle states that everything that does not contradict sense experience must be true.

Epicurus's explanation of how sensation occurs provides the ground for his claim that it is true. Sensation, like all change, is the result of bodies acting on bodies. Ordinary objects give off "idols"—images or airy replicas of themselves. The atoms that make up these idols collide with the body of the perceiver. Repeated encounters with idols result in what Epicurus called "preconceptions." A preconception is simply the registered impact of similarities and differences between idols. The similar impacts of different goats, for instance, build the preconception of a goat in general. Preconceptions are thus also the foundation of language.

Sensation is true because it merely registers the idols. Error arises when we compare a preconception with a new sensation. The new sensation is true; however faint, it reproduces the object. But we may be mistaken in assigning it to this or that preconception, confusing a stranger in the distance with a friend, perhaps. Epicurus's solution to such errors of opinion is the "clear view." A clear view of an object yields truth.

The two criteria of knowledge, a "clear view" and "noncontradiction" dictate Epicurus's division of the world into three kinds of objects: objects that can directly be perceived by a clear view, objects that could be perceived directly but where a clear view is blocked (for instance, the planets, because they are too far away), and imperceptible objects, like the atoms or gods.

While the theory as a whole is admirable, there are problems with Epicurus's explanation of our knowledge of the world. As to the first kind of case, there seem to be undeniable exceptions to the claim that sensation, even a clear view, is always true: A common example of an exception is an oar that appears bent in the water. And in the third kind of case, Epicurus is forced to invoke a kind of mental perception analogous to ordinary sensation. He argues that with respect to the gods, mental perception somehow "senses" the idols of the gods directly; with respect to the atoms, a certain clarity of thought (again analogous to the clear view of sensation), together with the noncontradiction principle, confirms the atomistic, material theory of the universe as the only true explanation of its nature.

Ultimately, Epicurus's physical theories are meant to serve his ethical ones. He prided himself on giving an explanation of the universe for the common person. It can be argued that the primary motive of his philosophy was his desire to rid his contemporaries of the myths and superstitions he believed enslaved their lives. In particular, Epicurus fought against the idea that the gods control or manipulate the world. These motivations may lie behind some of the peculiarities in Epicurus's argument. According to Epicurus, the gods exist, but they do not interact with the world. In a wholly material world, where the gods are indifferent, an individual can begin to take control of his or her life without fear of arbitrary interference.

Just as sensation provides knowledge of the world, it provides knowledge of the good life through the feelings of pleasure and pain. Pleasure and pain are both conceived as functions of the movement of atoms. Epicurus's argument against debauchery depends on his distinction between kinetic and static pleasure. Static pleasure is a state of equilibrium; in contrast to the momentary, if sharper, kinetic pleasure, it offers stability. Kinetic pleasure, on the other hand, is often accompanied by pain. Thus, overindulgence in rich foods leads to indigestion, while a simple diet avoids both the pain of hunger and the pain of excess. Similarly, the warmth of friendship is to be preferred to the upsets of passion and romance, and a private life is preferable to a public one.

The pursuit of pleasure, then, is more accurately described as avoidance of pain. In the end, the goal is to preserve as much control over one's own well-being as possible by maintaining imperturbability. But the materialism that frees individuals from the whims of the gods also presents a problem, for a thoroughgoing materialism implies a world that is wholly causally determined. Causal determinism, however, is no more attractive in Epicurus's view than is divine manipulation. To avoid determinism, Epicurus produced the "swerve," a tiny, uncaused, spontaneous deviation in the movement of the atoms. From the fragments we possess, it is clear that Epicurus believed that the swerve somehow allows for freedom of the will; what is not clear is how it does so.

CONSTANCE CREEDE

Further Reading

Bailey, C. *The Greek Atomists and Epicurus.* Oxford: Clarendon Press, 1928. A fundamental and thorough review of Epicurus's work.

Farrington, Benjamin. *The Faith of Epicurus.* New York: Basic Books, 1967. A positive interpretation of Epicurus's ethics.

Panichas, George A. *Epicurus.* New York: Twayne Publishers, 1967. A scholar explores the various facets of Epicurus's thought.

Zellar, Eduard. *The Stoics, Epicureans, and Sceptics.* Translated by O. J. Reichel. 1870 ed. rev. New York: Russell & Russell, 1962. Still a very useful source on the period.

ARCHIMEDES

Born: C. 287 B.C., Syracuse in Sicily
Died: 212 B.C., Syracuse
Major Works: (1) Works on the areas and volumes of figures: *On the Sphere and the Cylinder, On the Measurement of the Circle*; (2) Works on statics and hydrostatics: *On the Equilibrium of Planes, On Floating Bodies, On the Method of Mechanical Theorems*; (3) Numerical methods: *The Sandreckoner*

Major Ideas

Convergence methods, in which a curvilinear figure is bounded inside and out by similar rectilinear figures, can approximate the area of the curved figure to any degree of accuracy: Using convergence methods, the value of π is found to be greater than $3^{10}/71$ and less than $3^{1}/7$.

Objects have a center of gravity and for mathematical purposes can be treated as if they were composed of parallel lines (plane figures) or parallel planes (solid figures).

Mechanical methods can suggest the truth of mathematical propositions, which must then be rigorously proven by mathematical methods.

Numbers of any size can be expressed using a suitable system of notation.

Magnitudes cannot be infinitely small.

Archimedes, the most famous mathematician of antiquity, was born to a distinguished family of Syracuse in Sicily. His father was the astronomer Phidias, and he was on close terms with King Hieron II of Syracuse. After study in Alexandria with students of the geometer Euclid, Archimedes returned to Syracuse, where he pursued his mathematical researches until he was killed during the capture of Syracuse by the Romans in 212 B.C. The traditional story is that Archimedes, seeing an enemy soldier invading his chambers and interrupting his studies, exclaimed, "Don't disturb my diagrams!" The soldier, enraged, slaughtered the mathematician.

In antiquity, Archimedes was best known as a deviser of ingenious machines. To him were attributed the Archimedean screw (a machine for raising water) and various pulleys and levers—in fact, he once said, with reference to his levers, "Give me a place to stand on, and I will move the earth." He also built a planetarium or orrery in the shape of a sphere which represented the motion of the sun, moon, and planets; he wrote a book, *On Sphere-making* (now lost), about the construction of this instrument. His last efforts were devoted to designing war machines (catapults and cranes) to repel the Romans. The ancient biographer Plutarch reports that the Roman soldiers were so impressed with these machines that as soon as they saw a rope or a piece of wood projecting from the walls, they would flee in terror, shouting that Archimedes had invented another machine to destroy them.

"Eureka! Eureka!"

The best known of Archimedes's discoveries in physics is his recognition that different materials have different *specific gravities*. King Hieron had given a quantity of gold to a goldsmith and ordered him to make a gold crown as a dedication to the gods. After the crown was dedicated, the king began to suspect that the goldsmith had substituted base metal for some of the gold and had pocketed the difference. Unable to wring the truth out of the smith, he asked Archimedes to look into the problem. The mathematician, pondering the problem one day in his bath, noticed that the deeper he descended into the tub, the more water flowed over the edge. Overjoyed at this insight, he ran naked down the street shouting, "*Eureka! Eureka!*" ("I have found it!"). He then procured a lump of gold that weighed the same as the crown. He submerged the lump in a container full of water and observed how much water overflowed; he did the same with the crown and noted that more water overflowed. He knew then that the crown was not of pure gold, because, although it weighed the same as the lump of gold, it was physically larger and therefore must have been alloyed with a lighter metal.

Many of Archimedes's later writings show his interest in applying mathematical methods to physical phenomena. His earlier books *On the Sphere and Cylinder* and *On the Measurement of the Circle* closely follow Greek mathematical tradition. The first of these begins with a list of the axioms and postulates necessary to prove the propositions. The most important of these is the fifth, in which Archimedes states that the difference between two unequal quantities is not infinitesimal, but can be expressed by ratios: Lines, planes, and solids can be continuously subdivided into smaller magnitudes, but such magnitudes cannot be infinitely small. This denial of infinitesimal magnitudes is characteristic of Greek mathematics as a whole.

Convergence and the Reductio ad Absurdum

The propositions of *On the Sphere and the Cylinder* illustrate two of Archimedes's characteristic methods: the method of convergence, often called exhaustion, and the *reductio ad absurdum*, or the reduction to a contradiction. For example, proposition 34 says, "The volume of any sphere is equal to 4 times the cone whose base is equal to the circumference of the sphere and whose height is equal to the radius of the sphere." The proof is along the following lines: Let S be a sphere and X be a cone with the base equal to the circumference of S and the height equal to the radius of S. Prove that volume S = 4 times volume X.

1. Assume that volume S is *less than* 4 times volume X. Polyhedral solids are constructed circumscribing and inscribing the sphere, with the ratio of the side of one solid to the side of the other less than the ratio of two given lines to each other. A contradiction (*reductio ad absurdum*) is shown to follow from this construction; therefore it is impossible that the sides of the solids have such a ratio.

2. A similar line of reasoning is used to show that volume S cannot be *greater than* 4 times volume X. Therefore they must be equal. A figure illustrating the corollary to this proposition was carved on Archimedes's tomb: It showed a sphere circumscribed by a cylinder having the circumference of the sphere as its base and the height of the sphere as its diameter; the volume of such a cylinder equals $3/2$ the volume of the sphere.

Using these same methods in his work *On the Measurement of the Circle*, Archimedes shows that the area of a circle is equal to that of a right triangle ABC where A is the right angle, side AB equals the radius of the circle, and side AC the diameter of the circle. He proves this by circumscribing a polygon about the circle and inscribing another inside the circle (as in proposition 33 above), then proving that the circumscribed polygon is greater than the triangle ABC and the inscribed polygon is less. Therefore the circle must be equal to the triangle. Proposition 3 of this same work goes on to prove that the circumference of a circle is greater than $3^{10}/_{71}$ times and less than $3^{1}/_{7}$ times the diameter $(3.141 < \pi < 3.142)$. In both examples, the areas of the circumscribed and the inscribed polygons converge on, or approach, the area of the circle as closely as one wishes.

These methods (convergence and *reductio ad absurdum*) appear throughout Archimedes's strictly mathematical works. In addition to the two discussed above, these include *On Conoids and Spheroids*, *On Spirals*, and *On the Quadrature of the Parabola*. They are also used in the treatises that apply mathematical analysis to the physical world, specifically to problems in statics and hydrostatics. These treatises include *On the Equilibrium of Planes*, *On Floating Bodies*, and *On the Method of Mechanical Theorems*. In addition, these last-named treatises use the concepts of "center of gravity" (which is nowhere defined and was perhaps treated in a now-lost work) and equilibrium: "Magnitudes balance at distances inversely proportional"; for example, $2x$ will balance x at one-half the distance from the fulcrum.

On Floating Bodies deals with hydrostatics; several propositions are relevant to the problem of King Hieron's crown, although such an application is never mentioned. For instance, proposition 5 states, "When a solid which is lighter than the fluid is thrown into the fluid, it will sink down until a volume of the fluid equal in weight to the whole solid is displaced." The action underlying the proof of this proposition seems to be this: The solid pushes a volume of fluid down toward the center of the sphere formed by the fluid (as, for example, a ship would push ocean water down toward the center of the earth); this pressure is then retransmitted upward to the region of the fluid adjacent to the solid and balances the original downward force. Thus the propositions dealing with center of gravity and equilibrium can be applied to these problems in hydrostatics. This simplification of what is now called hydrostatic pressure, which states that the fluid's pressure is exerted uniformly in every direction on a body immersed in the fluid, suited Archimedes's techniques.

This same simplified view of hydraulic action can be seen in *On Floating Bodies*, book 2. Here Archimedes investigates the different positions in which a parabolic solid (the solid formed by the rotation of a parabola) can float. By an ingenious mathematical proof, he shows that in the stable equilibrium for such a figure, the axis of the solid is vertical; in other words, the solid will not float in a tipped position. Such investigations might well have been applicable to the design of ships, but no hint of practicality can be found in the text.

Archimedes, like Euclid and the other Greek mathematicians, normally gives no clue as to how he discovered his propositions; he gives instead a rigorous geometrical proof of their validity, leaving the student to wonder how he thought of the proposition in the first place. Only in *On the Method of Mechanical Theorems* does he give a glimpse into his workshop. He "proves" proposition 1 (if a triangle is inscribed in a segment of a parabola, the segment is one-third larger than the triangle) by assuming that the figures are balanced on a lever and by determining the conditions under which the figures are in equilibrium. In the course of deter-

mining the equilibrium, he assumes that the area of the figures, and hence their "weight," is the sum of all the parallel line segments contained in the figure. He then balances the figures on the ends of his lever to determine the ratio between them. Now, Archimedes did not consider this method to be a real geometrical proof, but successful results may be grounds for supposing that the proposition is true and that a rigorous geometrical proof is possible, a proof which he would then proceed to discover.

In addition to his work with geometrically based propositions, Archimedes developed numerical methods. An example was given above from *On the Measurement of the Circle*, the value of π; the same work gives an approximation of $\sqrt{3}$. Archimedes's most striking work with numbers is found in *The Sandreckoner*, in which he calculates how many grains of sand could fill the universe! The real purpose of this treatise is not the calculation of the size of the universe, but the demonstration of a unique method for expressing large numbers. His numerical system is based on units of 10,000, because 10,000 in ancient Greek is "myriad," the biggest number word. (No words for million, billion, etc., existed.)

1,2,3 . . . 10,000 times 10,000 (10^8, or in Greek, "a myriad myriads") are the "first-order numbers."

10^8 . . . $(10^8)^8$ (10^{64}, or "a myriad myriad of first order numbers") are the second-order numbers.

The system continues to $(10^8)^{10^8}$ ("a myriad myriads to the myriad myriad-th power" or 1 followed by 800 million zeros). This large number becomes in turn the basic unit for the next series, although Archimedes did not in fact need numbers of greater magnitude to express his result, which is only 10^{63} in our notation. Archimedes's scheme for large numbers was never used, since ancient science had no need for such magnitudes. By modern times, when the need arose, Arabic notation had replaced the Greek system. *The Sandreckoner* is best known for Archimedes's adoption of a heliocentric cosmos: The sun is stationary at the center of the universe, with the earth revolving about it, and the sphere of the fixed stars surrounding the whole at a distance of about 1.2 billion miles. Archimedes attributes this theory to Aristarchus of Samos, who thus anticipated Copernicus by 2,000 years.

Archimedes's mathematical work was not widely known in antiquity despite his fame as an engineer of marvelous machines. His works were translated into Arabic in the ninth and tenth centuries A.D. and from Arabic into Latin in the twelfth century. The noted mathematician Leonardo Fibonacci worked on several of Archimedes's propositions in the thirteenth century. In 1450, improved translations became available, and knowledge of Archimedes's work spread during the next century. Simon Stevin, Kepler, Torricelli, and Galileo, who mentions Archimedes more than 100 times, are only a few of the scientists influenced by the mathematics and mechanics of this man who has been called the most modern of ancient mathematicians.

MARK T. RILEY

Further Reading

Dijksterhuis, E. J. *Archimedes*. Princeton: Princeton University Press, 1987. Originally published in 1938, and reissued with a concluding essay by Wilbur Knorr summarizing work since 1938, this text is the standard—and best—approach to Archimedes. Not strictly speaking a translation, the book recasts the original text in a notation that attempts to show the thought behind each proposition. This approach avoids the difficulties arising from a literal translation of the Greek: Ancient mathematical authors wrote out in narrative form expressions for which we use equations or formulas, such as $A = \pi r^2$. A modern reader finds the original Greek unbearably prolix.

Heath, T. L. *Works of Archimedes*. Cambridge: Cambridge University Press, 1897, 1912. Like Dijksterhuis, Heath paraphrases rather than translating literally, but he went too far in putting Archimedes in entirely modern notation.

Schneider, I. *Archimedes: Ingenieur, Naturwissenschaftler und Mathematiker*. Darmstadt: Wissenschaftliche Buchgesellschaft, 1979. This is the standard survey of the scholarship on Archimedes in this century. Many items cited are in English.

EPICTETUS

Born: C. A.D. 50, in Hierapolis, Phrygia
Died: C. A.D. 125, in Nicopolis, Epirus
Major Works: *Discourses, Enchiridion*

Major Ideas

Only bodies exist, but bodies are combinations of two fundamental principles, logos, *a rational principle, and* physis, *a creative principle.*

God is nature: Logos, *the rational principle, accounts for the order and unity of the universe; nature is thus intelligent and intelligible.*

Because God is nature, the universe as a whole is the best possible.

Human beings, as opposed to plants and animals, have logos *as their individual governing principle.*

Logos *also defines the goal of life as virtue; the life of virtue is a life lived according to reason: It is the life of a philosopher.*

Reason distinguishes between things that are and things that are not under one's control; externals, like reputation, wealth, and power are not under one's control; desire, aversion, and opinion are.

The virtuous individual finds freedom in limiting his or her desires to those things under one's control and accepting all other externals as indifferent.

Epictetus was born a slave in Hierapolis in Phrygia. At some point in his early life, he was brought to Rome. His master, Epaphroditus, was Nero's administrative secretary. Epaphroditus apparently recognized Epictetus's talent because he sent him to study with a celebrated teacher, Musonius Rufus. Musonius Rufus was a Stoic and Epictetus became his most famous student, surpassing the fame of his teacher.

Epictetus was eventually freed from slavery, perhaps on the death of his master. In A.D. 94, the emperor Domitian ordered all philosophers to leave Rome, and Epictetus went into exile in Nicopolis, a somewhat barren and isolated place, where he lived simply, in a hut with only a mattress for furniture. He formed a school and spent his days lecturing young men from Rome and elsewhere in the empire on the art of living. It is reported that late in life he adopted a child that was about to be abandoned by its parents.

The purpose of philosophy for Epictetus, as for most Greek philosophers, was to teach the nature of the world and virtue. But Epictetus, more than most, focused on the moral life. One of his favorite exemplars was Socrates.

The teaching of Epictetus has been described, on the one hand, as warm and noble, and, on the other hand, as harsh and cold. There is a story told of Epictetus, which, while it may or may not be authentic, may help to illustrate his reputation as a man and teacher. Epictetus was lame. As the story goes, his master one day took hold of Epictetus's leg and began to twist it. Epictetus said: "You're going to break it"; the master persisted in twisting and the leg broke. Epictetus commented simply: "I told you so."

Stoicism was one of the most influential schools of thought in the Hellenistic world. The school takes its name from the Greek word for the Porch, the place in Athens where Zeno, the founder of the school, first began to teach around 300 B.C. Cleanthes and then Chrysippus succeeded Zeno as head of the school. Chrysippus is famous as a logician and credited with developing and systematizing the Stoic philosophy. But while Chrysippus and his successors, Panetius and Posidonius among them, wrote prodigiously and reportedly with great sophistication, we possess almost none of their work. Our understanding of Stoicism relies therefore on the secondhand references of other philosophers and historians and the writings of three men who lived almost 400 years after the school began:

Seneca, whom Nero ordered to kill himself while Epictetus was in Rome, Epictetus, and Epictetus's student, Marcus Aurelius.

Epictetus was primarily a lecturer, not a writer. One of his students, Arrian, made copious notes of Epictetus's lectures for a friend. He claimed to have transcribed the teacher "word for word." Four of Arrian's eight books of notes survive in the *Discourses*. The *Enchiridion* is a manual of excerpts from the *Discourses* compiled by Arrian.

The need to distinguish between what is and what is not within an individual's control is the central feature of Stoic philosophy. It is also the main object of Epictetus's teaching. Epictetus saw himself as educating young men to live a life of virtue. For Epictetus, the virtuous life combines knowledge and practice, truth and freedom. One understands what is in one's control by understanding the nature of the world and the human individual. Then, by training one's desires and aversions to accommodate that truth, one achieves freedom. Freedom is not the power to do anything one pleases; freedom is found in understanding the limits of one's power and accepting them. Accepting limits is what preserves choice; in yielding to desire for things not in one's control, one gives up freedom.

The Stoics, like most Greek philosophers, saw the universe as an ordered whole. But they differed from other philosophers in their claim that God and nature are one. Because they claimed that only bodies exist, at first it seems that the Stoics were materialists. But bodies, for the Stoics, are not simply material objects. Instead they are combinations of *logos*, a rational principle, and *physis*, or nature. These two concepts represent aspects of a fundamental unity. They also describe a kind of hierarchy in nature. Nature as a whole is rationally ordered, but not everything in nature is rational. As the rational principle permeating the world, *logos* refers to its intelligibility. The universe is intelligible because it is governed by laws. Plants and animals, for example, exhibit the order and coherence of an intelligible world; in other words, they exhibit a governing principle; they have distinctive natures. But as individuals they do not have rationality as their governing principle.

Human beings, by contrast, do have rationality as their governing principle.

Logos, then, refers to the rational principle governing the universe and it also refers to the governing principle in human individuals, that is, in particular, to their power to see connections, understand laws, and use language.

Like most Greek philosophers, the Stoics divided philosophy into three parts: logic, physics, and ethics. The Stoics in particular were concerned to show that each of the disciplines follows from and supports the other two. The *logos* that governs the physical world is the same as that which orders speech and thought, the subject matter of logic. The rational governing principle in each human individual allows him or her to achieve knowledge of the physical world and of the life of virtue. And this individual rational principle is also what each individual shares with God. The world is intelligent and intelligible. As such, it is God. And, as such, it is the best world possible.

Epictetus is generally acknowledged as the most orthodox of the later Stoics. At times he speaks as if God could be above or beyond nature—but this is also true of earlier writers and does not necessarily indicate a departure from the Stoic view of God and the world as one. More importantly, Epictetus is not concerned with elaborating physical or logical theories. His focus is entirely practical; he is important to the tradition because in Epictetus philosophy comes to life.

For the Stoic, the life of virtue is the life of the philosopher. Epictetus is often cited as the individual who came closest to realizing the Stoic ideal, an ideal many criticized as impossible to achieve. He lived simply, eschewing those things that are "not under our control," as he described them—body, property, reputation, command. He chose Nicopolis as the site of his school in order that his students, too, might have few temptations and distractions. His innovation was to change the emphasis of moral teaching from achievement of the ideal to progress toward the life of virtue.

The rational principle in the person determines the first requirement of a virtuous life: The *ability* to understand the nature of the world requires the individual to *exercise* his understanding, that is, his rationality. The point of understanding is twofold. First, in common with most Greeks, the Stoics saw the perfection of nature as the life of virtue: To be virtuous, the individual must let reason be her guide. But secondly, understanding nature as a whole is to understand the world as the best possible world. From this point of view, to wish things were otherwise represents a failure of reason that sets the individual against the *logos* of the universe, rather than bringing him or her into harmony with it.

It is this sense of the world as the best possible, together with the individual's rational nature, that defines the Stoic sense of value. To be rational is to understand the difference between things that are in one's power and things that are not. Only those things in one's power affect an individual's moral worth, that is, whether he or she is good or bad. Everything else is indifferent. In particular, the individual cannot choose external circumstances; he or she can only choose a response to them. The life of virtue is therefore open to everyone, rich or poor, slave or free. It is the only life that is prosperous.

The point is that what counts for the Stoic is the individual's choice or intent, not the result of an action. It is this distinction that perhaps accounts for the differing evaluations of Stoic ethics in general and Epictetus in particular. The virtuous individual will pursue the good actively in the world. She will, thus, try to save a child's life. However, if her efforts fail, she will also accept the result. She will not regret or mourn the loss. This may strike us as strange, unnatural, or lacking in compassion. But it is consistent with the Stoic conviction that the world as a whole is rational and the best possible. Moreover, it is consistent with the acceptance of reason as sovereign. For, after the event, the only thing in one's power is one's attitude toward it, that is, acceptance or rejection. Epictetus emphasized that what really frightens and dismays people is not external events themselves, but rather the way we think about them. How we think about something after the fact, for instance the loss of a loved one, is in our power, but changing the fact is not.

The life of virtue is finally the life of freedom. It is achieved by forming good habits. Epictetus himself impressed his contemporaries with his humor and serenity. He was not vain or condescending. On his death, he was described as a "friend of the immortals."

CONSTANCE CREEDE

Further Reading

Long, A. A. *Hellenistic Philosophy,* London: Duckworth, 1974; New York: Scribner, 1974. A survey of the three main schools of Hellenistic thought: Epicureanism, Skepticism, and Stoicism. The chapters on Stoicism contain a thorough and sophisticated discussion of fundamental Stoic ideas, with frequent references to Epictetus.

Meredith, Anthony. "Later Philosophy." In *The Oxford History of the Classical World.* Edited by John Boardman, Jasper Griffin, and Oswyn Murray. Oxford and New York: Oxford University Press, 1986. Includes a short but very clear introduction to Epictetus's thought and places him in the context of his contemporaries.

Xenakis, Iason. *Epictetus, Philosopher-Therapist.* The Hague: Martinus Nijhoff, 1969. The first book-length study of Epictetus in English. Xenakis reviews in detail the major elements of Epictetus's ethical teachings.

PTOLEMY

Born: C. A.D. 100, near Alexandria, Egypt
Died: C. A.D. 175, near Alexandria, Egypt
Major Works: *Almagest, Handy Tables, Planetary Hypotheses, Tetrabiblos, Geography, Optics*

Major Ideas

The position of the celestial bodies can be determined with the help of a kinematic model: These bodies move on eccentric and epicyclic circles with uniform velocities, even though their velocities are not uniform when viewed from the earth; these circles lie inside the sphere of the fixed stars; carefully made observations allow the velocities to be calculated.

The distance and size of the celestial bodies can be found by determining the size of their eccentric and epicyclic circles relative to the earth's radius.

The spherical earth can be projected onto a plane map using geometrical techniques; localities can be plotted on a standard grid of latitude and longitude lines.

Problems in plane and spherical trigonometry can be solved with the help of a table of the chords subtending the arcs from 0° to 90°.

The data derived from experiments can be represented by mathematical equations and can be presented in tabular form.

Little is known about the life of Claudius Ptolemaeus (usually called Ptolemy), antiquity's most famous astronomer. His observations recorded in the *Almagest*, his earliest work, date between March A.D. 127 and February A.D. 141. One ancient source states that he "flourished"—reached his full powers—under the emperor Marcus Aurelius (A.D. 161–180). From these few facts, Ptolemy's dates are deduced. He records that he made his observations in Alexandria, and he had the parameters of his astronomical theory carved on a stele in Canopus, near Alexandria, perhaps the location of his family's estates. These are the only certain data about Ptolemy. Later writers often considered him a member of the Ptolemy family who ruled Egypt from 323 to 30 B.C.; indeed, in several medieval illustrations he is pictured wearing a crown. The royal family, however, had vanished long before the astronomer Ptolemy's lifetime.

Ptolemy's best known work is in astronomy: his *Almagest* (an Arabic title meaning *The Greatest*; original title, *Syntaxis Mathematica*, or *Systematic Mathematical Treatise*) became the standard textbook for astronomy for more than 1,000 years. Even Copernicus's *De Revolutionibus* (published 1543), in which heliocentric astronomy was first systematically presented, was entirely dominated by the procedures and the concepts of the *Almagest*. Ptolemy also wrote pioneering works in geography and optics. In his works he developed modern techniques: the presentation of mathematical data in tables like our modern tables of logs, squares, and sines; the presentation of geographic information by means of maps with localities identified by latitude and longitude; and experimentation aimed at collecting new data—in his case, data on the phenomena of vision.

It must be remembered that the "Ptolemaic" universe was not the creation of Ptolemy, but was the universally accepted view of antiquity, certainly after Aristotle. However, the superiority of Ptolemy's presentation of this theory forever linked his name to it. At the beginning of the *Almagest*, Ptolemy reviews the nature of this universe from the point of view of a professional astronomer: The spherical earth is motionless at the center of the cosmos; it is immensely far from the sphere of the fixed stars, the outermost limit of the cosmos; there are two primary motions in the cosmos, the motion of the whole from east to west in the plane of the earth's equator, and the contrary motion of the seven celestial bodies (moon, Mercury, Venus,

Sun, Mars, Jupiter, and Saturn in order of increasing distance from the earth) from west to east in the plane of the ecliptic (the path of the sun).

In the remainder of the *Almagest*, Ptolemy presents all the parameters (factors basic to the calculations) and explains all the procedures necessary to calculate the position at any date of these celestial bodies. Book 1 describes the trigonometry necessary for doing astronomical calculations; books 2 and 3 treat the sun and its apparent yearly motion; books 4 and 5, the moon; book 6, eclipses; books 7 and 8, the fixed stars; books 9 through 13, the planets. The entire exposition is 1,152 pages in Greek, 647 in English translation.

The chief problem in determining the position of the seven celestial bodies is to account for their variations in velocity, known as the *anomaly*. If they moved at the same speed at all times, the calculation of position would be simple: Distance = Rate × Time, but they do not. For example, we see that the sun's velocity varies, since the time between the winter solstice and the spring equinox (winter) is longer than the time between the summer solstice and the fall equinox (summer). The planets Mars, Jupiter, and Saturn at times even seem to move backwards in their orbits.

In order to provide a kinematic model that allows for these variable motions, Ptolemy proposed that the motion of these bodies be viewed as a composite of a number of different circular motions in a plane. He then assigned certain velocities to each of these motions. Two motions are fundamental: (1) the *mean motion* and (2) the *motion in anomaly*.

A planet is carried on an *epicycle*, a circle whose center moves on the circumference of a larger circle called a *deferent*. The earth, although in the center of the universe, is not in the center of the deferent, which is therefore *eccentric* by a determinable amount with respect to the earth. The motion of the epicycle's center on the deferent is the *mean motion* of the object, or the *average* position at which it will be found. The correction applied to the mean motion in order to find the *true* position is represented by the planet's position on the epicycle (the true position may be ahead of or behind the center of the

epicycle as shown in the mean position) and is called the *motion in anomaly*.

Much of the *Almagest* is devoted to providing Ptolemy's model with numerical parameters: the radius of the deferent, the radius of the epicycle, the direction of the apogee, the distance from the deferent to the earth, among others. Ptolemy first finds observations (some dating from Babylonian times, some made by himself) when a planet is on the line between the deferent and the center of the planet's epicycle; these enable him to determine the mean motion. Next he finds observations that give a position for the object that differs from the mean motion; the point of greatest difference must equal the radius of the epicycle. He finally compiles all the data into tables of *mean motion* and of *motion in anomaly*, with which the astronomer can calculate any object's position at any date.

For the extremely complex motions of the moon, another model involving additional circles is needed. The center of the moon's epicycle moves on the circumference of a deferent, as before, but the deferent in turn is carried on a small circle having earth as its center, and the motion of the deferent around the earth-circle depends on the position of the sun. Several tables must be constructed to calculate the moon's position. With this model, Ptolemy accounted for a subtle influence of the sun's gravitation on the moon's motion, now called *evection*. The discovery of this influence and the development of the techniques necessary to calculate it was one of Ptolemy's major achievements.

In transferring celestial observations to positions on the epicycles and deferents of his kinematic model, Ptolemy uses trigonometry, performing countless numerical calculations. His trigonometry is based on the *chord* subtended by the angle in question. Some of the chord values are easily derived: Assuming a circle of radius 1, the chord of 60° is 1.0 (found from the equilateral triangle), the chord of 36° is 0.618, of 72°, 1.174. (These decimal values are converted from Ptolemy's sexagesimal number system.) Ptolemy derived a table of chords for the arcs from 0° to 90° in $1/2$° increments, and in so doing made the first surviving trigonometric table. The *chord* function is the equivalent of our *sine* function (chord = twice the sine of one-half the angle; for example, chord 60° = 2 × sine 30°). Therefore with the help of this table all trigonometric calculations can be done, although the lack of cosine and tangent functions makes calculation laborious.

The practicing astronomer or astrologer used the tables of the *Almagest* to find planetary positions: He consulted the tables of *mean motion* to discover how far the object had moved from the hypothetical starting point (the *epoch*) to the date in question. He then consulted the tables for the *motion in anomaly* to adjust the calculated mean motion. He would then have the *true position* of the object. The *Almagest* contains all the tables necessary for doing this, inconveniently scattered, however, among pages of explanation. Sometime after the publication of the *Almagest*, Ptolemy made a separate edition of the tables, with a brief explanatory preface. These are the *Handy Tables*, the most widely used set of astronomical tables ever compiled. Dozens of updated editions are known from the Arab world, the Byzantine Empire, and medieval and Renaissance Europe. All maintain Ptolemy's layout, changing his original figures in only minor ways to correct for small errors found in the centuries since his time.

In the *Planetary Hypotheses*, Ptolemy assumes the physical reality of the deferents and epicycles of the *Almagest* and draws some conclusions: The planets move in a band of space at a certain average distance from the earth; the depth of this band is equal to the diameter of the planet's epicycle; the maximum distance of each planet is equal to the minimum distance of the planet next farthest from the earth. For example, the outer limit of the moon's band is the inner limit of Mercury's; the outer limit of Mercury's band is the inner limit of Venus's. The distance of the moon is set at approximately 230,000 miles (this relatively accurate figure had long been known); the outer limit of Saturn's band, which is also the distance of the fixed stars and therefore the outer limit of the universe, is set at approximately 71 million miles.

The only work of Ptolemy commonly available in libraries is the *Tetrabiblos* (*The Four Books*), the most influential manual of astrology ever written. Ptolemy regarded the basic claims of astrology— that the stars influence human affairs—as obvious: The sun warms the earth when it is in certain signs; the moon rules the tides. He goes on to discuss the influence of the other celestial bodies and their mutual configurations on the earth's different zones and on the weather (books 1 and 2) and on human life (books 3 and 4). He claims in his introduction that the prediction of planetary positions (astronomy) is an exact science, whereas prediction by means of astrology is only a matter of probabilities. During the first four centuries A.D., astrology was almost universally accepted as a scientific and dispassionate method of viewing one's fate. Ptolemy could not escape its influence, but he tried to put it on a scientific basis, with sometimes incongruous results.

Ptolemy attempted to systematize geography as he had astronomy. In book 2 of his *Geography*, he described two methods for mapping a spherical surface on a plane without excessive distortion: Both are conic projections that avoid the distortion inherent in simple rectangular projections (such as the familiar Mercator maps, on which Greenland is the size of South America), and preserve the appearance of a partial globe. Ptolemy's world map extends over 180° of longitude and from 16° south to 63° north latitude (the then-known world), and so avoids the problems of mapping an entire sphere. He also drew maps of smaller areas, using the same conic projections. (Copies of these maps are extant in the beautiful manuscripts of the *Geography*.) In books 2–7, Ptolemy made lists of the latitudes and longitudes of the chief cities and physical features of the known world so that the maps could be redrawn if lost. His longitudes begin at "the Blessed Isles," probably the Canary Islands in the Atlantic, and extend 180° to China. His latitudes begin at the equator. The latitudes are accurate, since they depend only on the observation of the elevation of the sun at the solstice. The longitudes, on the other hand, are inaccurate, since it was only in the eighteenth century that precise time measurement, the prerequisite for determining longitudes, became possible. Ptolemy had only dead reckoning estimates for the east-west distance between localities.

The phenomena related to vision were of importance to the practicing astronomer. The *Optics* is Ptolemy's contribution to the study of these phenomena. In books 1 and 2, he described the mechanism of vision as understood in antiquity (the eye projects a visual ray that senses objects by sight in the way a hand senses objects by touch). In books 3 and 4, he recounts his experiments in binocular vision, which include ingenious demonstrations using black-and-white sticks, of the different field of vision of each eye. In book 5, he presents his study of refraction, the bending of light waves as they pass through different materials. He made a disk that was suspended half in water and through which the experimenter sighted to determine the amount of refraction at varying angles. (Refraction is zero when the eye looks straight down into the water; it increases as the angle from the vertical increases.) He showed that the amount of refraction changes in a regular pattern as the angle of vision increases and he presented this information in a table, as follows:

1. Angle of Vision	2. Angle of refraction	3. Amount of Change (*not in Ptolemy*)
0°	0°	—
10°	8°	8°
20°	15½°	7½°
30°	22½°	7°
40°	29°	6½°

And so on to 80°. His figures show a constant decrease in the rate of change (column 3), and while not entirely accurate, are reasonable for naked-eye observations. Their regularity, however, raises the suspicion that the observations were "adjusted" to fit the formula. Ptolemy investigated refraction in water, glass, and air, the latter being of obvious concern to astronomers, although we do not know what practical use, if any, he made of his data.

Ptolemy brought order to the confusion of ancient astronomy and geography, and his order survived for 1,500 years. His *Almagest* and *Handy Tables* dominated astronomy until Kepler, in the sixteenth century, developed new techniques and new tables based on heliocentric theory. The fate of the *Geography* was somewhat different. Geographical knowledge deteriorated with the decline of the Roman Empire. Only in the sixteenth century, with the boom in exploration, were Ptolemy's procedures for mapping appreciated, reapplied, and improved. His *Tetrabiblos*, which systematized a pseudoscience of great cultural influence, whatever we may think of its validity, legitimized astrology and perfected the arguments with which it has been defended to this day. His experimental methods, moreover, and his organization of data in tables set a pattern for experimental science in the Renaissance and later. The closer one studies his work, the more remarkable it seems.

MARK T. RILEY

Further Reading

Neugebauer, Otto. *The Exact Sciences in Antiquity*. Providence, R.I.: Brown University, 1957. Reprint. New York: Dover Publications, 1969. The best introduction to the methods and techniques of ancient mathematics and astronomy, with stress on the discoveries made by the Babylonians and on the Ptolemaic system.

————. *A History of Ancient Mathematical Astronomy*. 3 vols. Berlin, Heidelberg, and New York: Springer-Verlag, 1975. A compilation of the life work of the scholar who has dominated the study of the history of ancient science. These volumes discuss in detail Babylonian and Greek astronomy; they also cover mathematical geography, optics, the astrolabe, and a host of other topics. The first volume is devoted primarily to Ptolemy.

Pedersen, Olaf. *A Survey of the Almagest*. Odense: Odense University Press, 1974. More accessible to the beginner than Neugebauer, *A History . . .* , this text walks the reader through the *Almagest*.

Ptolemy. *Ptolemy's Almagest*. London: Duckworth, 1984. A complete translation with an introduction outlining what Ptolemy expects his readers to know: the number system, basic astronomical facts, basic spherical trigonometry. This book is indispensible for the study of Ptolemy.

————. *Tetrabiblos*. Edited and translated by F. E. Robbins. Cambridge: Harvard University Press, 1940, reprint 1980. Translation with a few notes. The two books just listed are the only texts of Ptolemy available in English.

MARCUS AURELIUS

Born: 121, Rome, Italy
Died: 180, on the battlefront in Eastern Europe, the exact location unknown
Major Work: *Meditations*

Major Ideas

The universe is governed by reason, which is God.
In a rational universe, everything that happens is not only necessitated but good.
Human happiness consists in a life lived in accordance with nature and reason.
Though his actions are necessitated, an individual becomes free by acting rationally.
The bad acts of others do not harm us; rather we are harmed by our own opinions about those acts.
All rational beings are subject to natural law and so are citizens of a world community.
The rational individual should have no fear of death because it is a natural event of life.

Marcus Aurelius was a Stoic philosopher. To understand his philosophy, therefore, it is necessary to have some background in Stoic thought. Stoicism was one of the major philosophical schools during the Hellenistic and Roman periods. Although it had its roots in earlier thinkers—particularly Heraclitus and Socrates—it originated as a distinct philosophy around 300 B.C. when a man by the name of Zeno (c. 336–264 B.C.) arrived in Athens from his native Cyprus and began teaching in the Stoa, or covered marketplace.

Zeno and his successors developed a total system of philosophy, including an epistemology, a metaphysics, a logic, an ethics, a political philosophy, and a philosophy of religion. At the heart of this system was a metaphysical materialism that, although not so intellectually sophisticated as the atomism of Democritus, allowed the Stoics nevertheless to describe the universe as a purely natural entity functioning according to law and also to find ontological room for God. Though this combination may not have been completely viable logically, it provided them the framework around which they constructed their entire philosophy.

Stoicism came to Rome soon after Roman arms had subjugated the Greeks, around the middle of the second century B.C. It attained its dominant influence over Roman intellectual life in the early period of the empire. The two most important Roman Stoics were Marcus Aurelius (A.D.

121–180), emperor, and Epictetus (c. A.D. 50– c. 125), slave.

Marcus Aurelius was born in Rome of a wealthy patrician family. He was educated at home and while still a young boy came under the influence of a teacher who was a Stoic. Marcus embraced the philosophy and remained its disciple throughout his life. His unusual abilities were soon recognized and the reigning emperor, Antoninus Pius, believing that he did not have many years to live, adopted Marcus, who was his nephew, gave him the family name of Antoninus, and began to groom him to take over the reins of state on his own death. However, Antoninus actually lived for several more years, so it was only in 161 that Marcus succeeded him.

The nineteen years of Marcus's reign were difficult ones for the empire. There were major natural disasters, a plague from the East came and decimated the population, and there was constant warfare, mainly against barbaric tribes who kept threatening the borders of Roman territory, particularly along the Danube River in Eastern Europe. Marcus spent nearly half of his reign on the front lines with his soldiers and parts of his *Meditations* were written in his tent, probably at night while the rest of his army was asleep. The constant strain and the rigors of military life finally broke his health and Marcus died in his fifty-ninth year, while campaigning on the frontier, somewhere in the vicinity of modern Vienna.

Meditations

The *Meditations* is not a standard philosophical treatise. Rather, it can perhaps be described best as a combination of intellectual memoir and a series of admonitions addressed by the author to himself on how he should conduct himself not only in his daily affairs but also in his life as a whole. Indeed, the title that Marcus himself gave to his work was not *Meditations* but rather a Greek phrase that can be translated as "thoughts addressed to oneself." Because it was addressed to himself and presumably never meant for public consumption, the *Meditations* lacks the finish of a formal philosophical work. It is fragmented in its thought, unduly repetitious, and highly personal in tone. As a result it is difficult sometimes to extract the author's views from the text or to follow the line of argument that leads him to a particular conclusion. Nevertheless, the *Meditations* contains a philosophy, which is Marcus's version of Stoicism.

Perhaps because of their more practical approach to life, the Roman Stoics did not concentrate their attention on the abstruse problems of logic and metaphysics to the extent that their Greek predecessors had done. Rather they tended to take over this basic framework pretty much as it had come to them and to devote themselves to the ethical and social side of the Stoic philosophy. This is certainly true of Marcus, as it had been for Epictetus in the preceding century. In the case of Marcus, however, one addition needs to be made. He was also very much concerned with religion, and the *Meditations* is liberally sprinkled with passages that emphasize the theological aspects of Stoic ontology.

To comprehend Marcus's version of Stoicism in its entirety, it is necessary to begin with his metaphysics. Here he was generally orthodox: The universe is a material entity, composed of four basic elements. Everything that happens is necessitated, hence there is no room for chance. Another way of putting this, and one that Marcus emphasized, is to say that the universe is governed by law, or that the order of things is the revelation of reason. This, he believed, implies a rational lawgiver who governs the universe, or God. Marcus did not, however, conceive of God as a transcendent being having a personal relationship with humans, as does the Judeo-Christian tradition. Rather, God, for him, is simply the indwelling reason that orders the course of universal history. Because the universe is throughout rational, Marcus concluded, it is also good. Therefore, to think that anything that occurs in the natural order of things is bad is a fundamental mistake. We have, thus, at the center of Marcus's thinking a form of cosmic optimism.

The Stoicism of Marcus Aurelius

Many, but not all, of Marcus's ethical conclusions follow directly from his metaphysics and theology. Perhaps the most important of these is his admonition, which he reiterates throughout the *Meditations*, to keep one's will in harmony with nature. This is the famous Stoic doctrine of acceptance. The doctrine of acceptance operates on two levels. The first relates to the occurrences of everyday life. When someone treats you badly, Marcus advised, you should accept the ill treatment because it cannot harm you if you do not let it do so. This view is similar to, but not quite the same as, the Christian admonition to "turn the other cheek." When Jesus said of his tormentors, "Forgive them for they know not what they do," his statement was one that Marcus could have accepted in part. Like Jesus, he believed that people who engaged in wrongful acts did so in ignorance; like him, as well, he maintained that their doing so should not be attributed to some viciousness of their character. Rather they did what they thought to be the right thing and so erred only in their judgment. But, unlike Jesus, Marcus did not stress the importance of forgiveness. Instead he concentrated on the inner response of the victim of wrongdoing, emphasizing that no harm could come to him against his will. Whatever might happen to his possessions and even to his body, he, in his inner and true self, would remain unscathed as long as he refused to acknowledge that the harm had affected him.

The second aspect of the doctrine of acceptance concerns the individual's life and place in the world. It seems clear from the *Meditations* that

Marcus did not relish his exalted role as Roman emperor. He would almost surely have preferred to spend his life as a teacher and scholar. But it was his destiny to be emperor just as it was that of Epictetus to be a slave. Therefore, it was his duty to accept his post in life and perform the functions required by it to the best of his abilities.

The concept of destiny raised a problem for Stoic philosophy. If, as Marcus acknowledges, the universe is governed by reason and, therefore, everything that happens is determined to occur just as it does occur, can there be any possibility of human freedom? Marcus resolves this problem by drawing a distinction. If one means by freedom making choices between open alternatives, this clearly cannot exist. But there is another meaning of freedom: to accept whatever happens as being a part of a benign world order and to respond to events in a rational rather than an emotional manner. The individual who lives in this way, Marcus contends, is the truly free person. Not only is such a person free but he or she is living the good life as well. Since the rationality of the universe is the foundation for its goodness, whatever happens in the universe must contribute to that goodness. Thus the rational person, in the acceptance of events, is not only responding to an external goodness but making a personal contribution to the value of the whole.

The Stoic conception of reason as the governor of the universe is ambiguous, and this ambiguity is repeatedly revealed in the *Meditations*. On the one hand, reason refers simply to the fact that the universe, which is totally material, operates according to inviolable law. On the other hand, reason is construed as universal intelligence, which suggests a mind. This concept introduces the notion of God. It is clear that Marcus was in some sense a theist, for he repeatedly speaks of God in a way that implies the existence of a cosmic intelligence that is good. So we are left with a basic problem of theology: How could he reconcile his materialism with his theism?

Another theological issue to which Marcus devotes many passages concerns death and immorality. For the rational human being, death is nothing to be feared. Since death is an event of nature, it cannot be bad; on the contrary, it shares in the goodness of every natural event. At death we simply cease to exist. There is nothing any more negative about the ages we shall spend in nonbeing after our death than there was in the ages we spent in similar nonbeing before we were born. Yet this is not the full story. Marcus accepted the Stoic theory of immortality. According to this view, cosmic history is not linear but cyclical. (This doctrine is often called "eternal recurrence.") After aeons the universe will come to the end of its present epoch and lapse into a state of primordial fire. From this fire a new universe will emerge, which will repeat the history of the present universe. And so on, *ad infinitum*. Hence we shall live again the same lives that we are living now.

This life, though it has its intensely personal side, is nevertheless primarily a social life. Each of us lives in a particular society and is governed by its laws. But as rational beings we are also governed by a higher law—the law of nature. This law applies to each of us, whatever the particular society to which we belong may be. Under the law of nature we are all equals, whether we be an emperor, a slave, or anything else. Thus we can say that, as rational beings, all human beings are members of one society operating under the ame set of laws. As Marcus proclaimed in his famous declaration: "My city and my country, as I am Antoninus, is Rome; as I am a man, it is the world" (*Meditations*, book VI, section 44).

It has often been said that the "pagan" world produced two "saints." The first is Socrates. The second is Marcus Aurelius. The claim of Marcus to our enduring memory and respect is due not so much to the ethical content of the *Meditations*, lofty as that undoubtedly is, but even more to the fact that Marcus himself successfully modeled his life, often under the most trying circumstances, on the precepts contained in his little book of "thoughts to himself."

OLIVER A. JOHNSON

Further Reading

Arnold, E. V. *Roman Stoicism*. Cambridge: At the University Press, 1911. This is a standard text devoted to the thought of the Roman Stoics. It includes a substantial discussion of the philosophy of Marcus.

Blanshard, Brand. *Four Reasonable Men*. Middletown: Wesleyan University Press, 1984. Chap. 1. In this highly readable account, the author, an eminent American philosopher, describes the life and thought of Marcus as the embodiment of reason.

Rist, J. M. *The Stoics*. Berkeley, Los Angeles, London: University of California Press, 1978. This book contains a number of essays by scholars from various countries who are devoted to different aspects of Stoic philosophy.

Zeller, Eduard. *The Stoics, Epicureans, and Sceptics*. Translated by O. J. Reichel. New ed. New York: Russell & Russell, 1962. This is a classic work on the main philosophical schools of the Hellenistic period, written by a nineteenth-century German scholar. Part 2 is devoted to the Stoics.

SEXTUS EMPIRICUS

Born: Middle of second century A.D.
Died: First quarter of third century A.D.
Major Works: *Outlines of Pyrrhonism, Against the Mathematicians*

Major Ideas

It is futile to attempt to determine external realities (the nonevident) by appeal to appearances (the evident).
We have access only to appearances and no reason to prefer one appearance to another.
Appearances vary according to the condition of the observer and the nature of what is judged.
Any claim about the nonevident can be opposed by an equally compelling contrary claim.
Any effort to argue for the priority of some one appearance will involve circular reasoning or infinite regress.
The skeptic, unlike the dogmatist, withholds judgment on all matters of external fact and, as a result, achieves the state of unperturbedness.
Practical action will be taken, however, because of the involuntary promptings of nature.

Next to nothing is known of the life of Sextus Empiricus. This is perhaps appropriate in the case of the thinker who gives us the richest, most subtle, and most developed picture of ancient skepticism. What is known amounts to the following: Sextus was a doctor, a skeptic, and in all likelihood a Greek. It appears that he spent at least some of his life at Alexandria in Egypt.

Not all of Sextus's works have survived. *Outlines of Pyrrhonism* (the work with which we shall be chiefly concerned) contains in book 1 an introduction to the fundamental skeptical methods and arguments. Books 2 and 3 are devoted to a skeptical appraisal of the three traditional parts of philosophy: Logic, Physics, and Ethics. *Against the Mathematicians* (the last term might be better translated "Professors" or "Dogmatists") contains eleven books. Books 1–6 are a skeptical attack on the various fields of learning, while books 7–11 contain what amounts to an elaboration of books 2 and 3 of the *Outlines*.

The Greek word *skeptikos* means roughly "inquirer." The proper contrast here is with the dogmatist. The skeptic, according to Sextus, has not ceased his investigations because he has not yet reached a settled opinion regarding the truth or falsity of a particular claim of interest. So in his present state of uncertainty, he suspends judgment about the truth or falsity of the claim. The

dogmatist, on the other hand, claims to have settled matters. He makes positive assertions of fact. There is, as well, another way of being a dogmatist. One might claim that it is definitely the case that one cannot know a particular matter. This is, according to Sextus, a nonskeptical, or at least a Nonpyrrhonian position. The true skeptic neither believes nor disbelieves.

Sextus draws very deeply from a long tradition of Greek skepticism. Indeed, Sextus himself writes very near the end of this tradition. This makes it difficult to ascertain when Sextus is merely repeating existing skeptical materials and when he is extending those arguments in a novel fashion. At times Sextus draws on disparate skeptical traditions with unhappy results.

We can say with some certainty that Sextus, like his intellectual forefather Pyrrho (c. 360–270 B.C.), conceives of skepticism not as a theoretical intellectual enterprise but as a way of life. Skeptical inquiry makes for the good human life. Like much philosophy of the Hellenistic period, skepticism might be called "eudaimonistic," from the Greek word for "happiness." The aim of skepticism is *ataraxia*, unperturbedness.

Skeptical Inquiry

Skepticism, says Sextus, is "an ability, or mental attitude, which opposes appearances to judgments in any way whatsoever, with the result that, owing to the equipollence of the objects and reasons thus opposed, we are brought to a state of mental suspense and finally to a state of 'unperturbedness' or quietude."

Consider some claim, X, in which we have an interest. Imagine that we wish to know whether X is true or false. To ask such a question is to initiate inquiry on some subject or issue about which we are presently uncertain. To know whether X is true or false is to know how things stand in the world quite independently of how I take the world to be. X purports to record some objective fact about the independently existing world. The dogmatist will claim that X is true or that X is false; the dogmatist, writes Sextus, "posits the matter of his dogma as substantial truth," a truth about "external realities."

In hopes, no doubt, of gaining unperturbedness by means of settling questions once and for all, the skeptic, Sextus suggests, begins inquiry by seeking answers. Things seem or appear to the skeptic a particular way, and he begins inquiry by seeking to vindicate some particular appearance. Thus, initially, at least, investigation takes the form of attempting to demonstrate on the basis of how things appear that things are objectively some way or other. Yet the skeptic discovers that this cannot be done. On any investigative venture, the skeptic finds himself "involved in contradictions of equal weight." There is no reason to conclude on the basis of how things appear that things are in fact so. All that the skeptic does is this: "He states what appears to himself and announces his own impression in an undogmatic way, without making any positive assertion regarding external realities."

Thus the skeptic discovers that with respect to any question there are appearances, judgments, and objects of equal weight on both sides of the question. As a result, the skeptic suspends judgment on the question. He neither affirms nor denies that things are in fact one way rather than another. This is the famous "epoche" of the sceptic, "a state of mental rest [a paralysis of the intellect] owing to which we neither deny nor affirm anything." As a consequence of withholding judgment, unperturbedness results. That unperturbedness results from

suspension of judgment is an empirical psychological discovery. Sextus likens it to the painter Apelles's effort to paint the foam on a horse's mouth. In frustration over his many failures he threw a paint-soaked sponge at his painting, producing the desired likeness. In this way "unperturbedness" is produced by suspension of judgment.

Three points should be emphasized. First, when Sextus speaks of "appearances," he does not mean only sensory appearances. Sextus uses "appearance" in such a way that not only can honey appear sweet but arguments can "appear" sound. Sextus is pointing to a distinction between how things seem to us or strike us and how things in the world are as a matter of fact. This distinction is completely general. Second, and this is a matter of some controversy, Sextus's skepticism is global in the sense that all statements of external fact are greeted by the skeptic with suspension of judgment. Third, in rejecting dogmatism, Sextus rejects belief. To believe X is to believe that X is true. And this is to be a dogmatist.

Two questions about skeptical inquiry are of special interest for an understanding of Sextus. First, what are the ways in which the skeptic discovers that appearances and judgments can, in all cases, be equally opposed to each other? And second, why is it that there is no way to adjudicate between conflicting claims, appearances, and arguments?

The Tropes

The most visible resource in Sextus's skeptical armamentarium are the tropes or modes of skepticism. There are many differing versions of the tropes. Sextus devotes nearly half of book 1 of the *Outlines* to the most famous of these, the ten tropes of Aenesidemus (first century B.C.). In general, the tropes are a series of arguments or procedures whereby the skeptic can bring about the oppositions that result in a suspension of judgment.

The fourth trope, of "Circumstances," is reasonably typical. Consider any faculty of sense, for example, vision or taste. Sextus notes that the psychological or physical condition of the perceiving subject can dramatically alter the character of appearances. Some examples from Sextus: "The same coat which seems of a bright yellow color to men with blood-shot eyes does not appear so to me. And the same honey seems to me sweet, but bitter to men with jaundice." Sextus mentions many such conditions that affect appearances: youth and age, health and illness, loving something and hating that thing. In all cases the point is the same. Any one appearance can be opposed to some conflicting appearance in virtue of the different condition of the perceiver.

This is the point of the tropes in general: to oppose one appearance or judgment to another. We ask, "Is the coat *really* of a bright yellow color?" No answer can satisfy us since the appearances and the judgments cancel out each other.

The skeptic cannot rest with a mere conflict of appearances. The dogmatist will respond that we can have good reasons for preferring one appearance to another as a guide to how things stand in the world. What the skeptic must show is that the choice between appearances is undecidable—that there is no criterion by means of which we have a basis for our choice between conflicting appearances or judgments.

Sextus has two principal lines of response to this dogmatist challenge. In the first, Sextus points out that whenever we prefer one judgment or appearance to another, we must be in some condition or other. As a result, our judgment will be biased and infected. That is, given what we know about the way in which appearances vary with circumstances, so does our own preference hinge on our own circumstances.

The second response is of greater interest and substance. It is itself one of the chief tools of ancient skepticism. Sextus begins: "For he who prefers one impression to another, or one circumstance to another does so either uncritically and without proof or critically and with proof." This consideration initiates a series of dilemmas for the dogmatist: If the dogmatist takes one appearance rather than another as a guide to truth, and he does so without proof, then he does not need to be taken seriously. So he must presumably be making use of some criterion; but if he is to be taken seriously, he must

judge this criterion to be sound. But why does he do this? Either he does so with proof or argument or without. And presumably he must judge *this* very argument to be sound, and so again he must have some reason for *this* preference. Sextus suggests that this will involve the dogmatist in circular reasoning—perhaps because Sextus thinks that the dogmatist will appeal, in defending his criterion, to considerations already adduced earlier in preferring one appearance to another. It is, however, clear that the real problem here is one of infinite regress. According to Sextus, the lesson is straightforward: The dogmatist cannot provide reasons for preferring one appearance to another.

Concluding Remarks

Let us assume that the skeptical arguments succeed. This means that in consequence of discovering that one appearance can always be opposed to another we will suspend judgment. We will be quite unable to choose between conflicting judgments of fact. As we know, Sextus claims that this results in "unperturbedness." This may seem odd. We must ask how it is that the skeptic can get on with living while suspending judgment about external facts. For example, is food really good for a human being? Is it, in fact, the case that water quenches thirst? These are matters about which the skeptic claims to have suspended judgment.

This concern about the practical consequences of skepticism gives rise to a serious problem. David Hume (1711–76), himself profoundly influenced by Sextus, writes of the skeptic that "he must acknowledge . . . that all human life must perish, were his principles universally and steadily to prevail. All discourse, all action would immediately cease, and men remain in total lethargy till the necessities of nature, unsatisfied, put an end to their miserable existence."

Sextus would claim to have an answer to this criticism. The skeptic leads a life "in accordance with appearances." He is pointed "to a life conformable to the customs of [his or her] country . . . and to [his or her] own instinctive feelings." Thus Sextus urges a life in accord with nature's guidance. It is important to note, however, that such a life is not a matter of choice. It is a matter of "involuntary affection." The point is that honey's appearing sweet to me, or pain's appearing evil to me, is not open to question. We are constrained to lead our lives in accord with how things appear to us. But we are not constrained to agree that any particular appearance is a guide to external reality.

In closing, we must note that we have only just commenced to recount the riches of Sextus's skepticism. Though his writings are of uneven quality, Sextus has profoundly altered the course of the history of philosophical investigation. Indeed, the publication—in 1562—of the first modern edition of the *Outlines* has lastingly changed the history of philosophy in the West. The centrality of the theory of knowledge—where this is understood to require an answer to the skeptic—which characterizes so much of the philosophical work of the modern epoch is, in large part, the legacy of Sextus Empiricus.

DION SCOTT-KAKURES

Further Reading

Annas, Julia, and Barnes, Jonathan. *The Modes of Scepticism*. Cambridge: Cambridge University Press, 1985. A clear and compelling account of the history and significance of the tropes of skepticism.

Burnyeat, M. F., ed. *The Sceptical Tradition*. Berkeley: University of California Press, 1983. Contains some of the best contemporary scholarship on the history of skepticism.

Long, A. A. *Hellenistic Philosophy*. 2d ed. Berkeley: University of California Press, 1986. A history of the philosophy of the Hellenistic period, including a discussion of skepticism and the dogmatic schools.

Popkin, Richard. *The History of Scepticism from Erasmus to Descartes*. New York: Harper and Row, 1964. The now-classic account of the reappropriation of ancient skepticism during the modern period.

Schoefield, M., M. F. Burnyeat, and J. Barnes, eds. *Doubt and Dogmatism*. Oxford: Oxford University Press, 1980. An outstanding collection of essays concerning the development of ancient skepticism.

Stough, C. L. *Greek Scepticism*. Berkeley: University of California Press, 1969. A very useful book-length treatment of the history of Greek skepticism.

ORIGEN

Born: C. A.D. 185, Alexandria, Egypt
Died: C. A.D. 254, Caesarea Maritima, Palestine
Major Works: *Treatise on First Principles* (c. 220–225), *Against Celsus* (c. 246–249)

Major Ideas

God as the Ground of Being ("the First God") is unknowable except to the Logos-Son and Spirit eternally generated by God.

God, however, has communicated through the Logos-Son (Christ: Wisdom, Power) not only in the incarnation in Jesus but in Moses and the prophets and, in a qualified way, in Greek greats.

All rational creatures, and to some degree even the natural order, have free will and therefore are responsible to God.

Although a "fall" shattered an original unity, the entire universe will ultimately have its unity restored along with all creation.

Scriptures, every jot and tittle of which is inspired, provide the key to understanding the mysteries of life.

The most prolific and original Christian thinker of the third century, Origen was born at Alexandria about 185 A.D., probably of Christian parents. His father, Leonidas, schooled him in Scripture and secular subjects from a very early age. When the latter was martyred during the persecution of Septimius Severus in 202, Origen tried to accompany him, but his mother prevented that by hiding his clothes. He studied in the Christian school at Alexandria under Clement. When Clement fled, Origen became a teacher and then head of the school, a position he held until 232, attracting a great many students.

At Alexandria, Origen initially taught preparatory subjects—dialectics, physics, mathematics, geometry, and astronomy—as well as philosophy and theology. When burgeoning classes made this impossible, he assigned preparatory instruction to his pupil Heraclas and concentrated on philosophy, theology, and interpretation of scriptures. Meantime, he attended lectures by Ammonius Saccas, father of Neoplatonism. He also traveled extensively—to Rome in 212, to Arabia in 215, to Antioch at the invitation of Julia Mamaea, mother of the Emperor Alexander Severus, and to Palestine in 216.

On this initial visit to Palestine, the bishops of Caesarea, Jerusalem, and other cities generated friction for Origen with Bishop Demetrius of Alexandria by asking him, a layman, to preach. Origen meekly acceded to Demetrius's command to return immediately to Alexandria. Fifteen years later, however, Alexander of Jerusalem and Theoctistus of Caesarea created an irreparable breach when they ordained Origen as he passed through Caesarea on his way to Greece. Demetrius then, contending that Origen's self-castration as a youth prevented him from being ordained, proceeded to convene a synod, which excommunicated Origen from the church at Alexandria. A year later, in 231, a second synod rescinded his ordination. When Origen returned to Alexandria following the death of Demetrius, however, Heraclas, Origen's former assistant who had succeeded Demetrius as bishop, repeated the excommunication. Consequently Origen quickly returned to Palestine and took up residence in Caesarea.

Ignoring the censure of Origen in Alexandria, the Bishop of Caesarea induced Origen to found a new school at Caesarea. Once again, he attracted students from far and wide. One of these, who became the fabled missionary in Cappadocia, Gregory Thaumaturgus, delivered an insightful if somewhat overblown address on Origen's gifts as a teacher. Imprisoned during the persecution under Decius (250–252), Origen suffered severe tortures. His health impaired by persecution, he died around 254.

Aided by stenographers hired by an admiring layperson, Origen wrote prolifically during his Caesarean period. Although well-grounded in the classical tradition, he conceived his role chiefly as that of an expositor of scriptures, reveling in finding the "spiritual" or allegorical meaning of texts. His major writings consisted of textual criticism, scholia and commentaries and sermons, and his reply to Celsus's *True Discourse* as well as theological treatises. To reply to those who objected to the use of the Greek Old Testament, he produced the *Hexapla*, a six-column version of the Old Testament giving the Hebrew, a Greek transliteration, and four translations arranged from most to least literal—Aquila, Symmachus, the Septuagint, and Theodotion. For the Septuagint he employed diacritical marks to indicate deviations from the Hebrew. Although not all of his expository materials have survived, Origen wrote notes on difficult passages, sermons, or commentaries on all books of the Old and New Testaments. Pamphilus reported in his biography that Origen preached every day, but only a third of the 574 recorded sermons have survived. Similarly, only portions of commentaries on Matthew, John, Romans, and the Song of Songs are extant; those on other books of the Old and New Testaments have perished in their entirety. *Against Celsus* (*Contra Celsus*), Origen's reply to Celsus's *True Discourse* (a work now dated about 177–180) entailed a point-by-point refutation of charges framed by Celsus.

Treatise on First Principles

The writing in which Origen laid bare most of his philosophical views, entitled in Greek *Peri Archon* ("On Beginnings") and in Latin *De Principiis* ("On First Things"), belongs to his Alexandrian period and is now dated around 220–225. Unfortunately, only fragments of the Greek original have survived, and the Latin translator, Rufinus, Bishop of Aquileia, took considerable liberty to edit the text in such a way that the reader "would find in them nothing out of harmony with our faith." He also omitted some difficult passages or "clarified" them by adding his own interpolations. Consequently readers can never be certain when they are hearing Origen and when Rufinus.

Origen made it clear from the start that he wanted to be recognized as an "orthodox" Christian, but Platonism of the late Middle or Neoplatonist variety so saturated his thought that he can be best interpreted as "discovering" in scriptures the best of that philosophy. Writing in the context of somewhat strained relations with his bishop, Demetrius, Origen prefaced his treatise with an assertion of his conviction that "that only is to be believed as the truth which in no way conflicts with the tradition of the church and the apostles." Beyond the elements included there—a Trinitarian confession, the immortality of the soul, the resurrection, human free will, the existence of the Devil and his angels, the creation of the world in time and its dissolution because of its corruptible nature, the inspiration of the Scriptures by the Spirit, and the existence of angels—Origen felt free to seek truth, especially with the aid of Scriptures.

Origen divided the main body of his *Treatise on First Principles* into four books: God, the world, humankind, and the Scriptures. Reflective of his Platonism, he repudiated vigorously those who thought of God as corporeal. God the Father is "incomprehensible and immeasurable," far removed from human ability to conceive, and characterized by absolute *oneness*. God the Son, Christ (called Wisdom, Firstborn, and Power of God in the Scriptures), is the Word of God who always existed, coeternal, with the Father. In him God the Father created all things. The Holy Spirit, who shares the divine nature, functions as the inspirer of Scriptures and indweller of saints. The Spirit, too, coexisted eternally with the Father and the Son and thus receives knowledge of the Father independent of the Son. The Father, however, is superior to both Son and Spirit. According to the Greek text, "the Son, being less than the Father, is superior to rational creatures alone (for he is second to the Father); and the Holy Spirit is still less, and dwells within the saints alone." The Father creates, the Son bestows reason, the Spirit sanctifies. But through the action of all three, humankind may attain the beatific vision.

Continuous Creation

Origen espoused a theory of continuous creation. The plan of creation existed in the wisdom of God from the beginning. In the beginning, nothing was essentially good or essentially bad. All rational creatures—angels, demons, and human beings—possessed free will (a central and often-repeated concern of Origen). Origen backed up his emphasis on free will with Scripture. Even the sun, moon, and stars, he argued, undergo change and receive commands from God. They probably have souls inserted into them by God, just as human beings do. Certainly angels operate on instructions from God and receive rewards according to their merits.

Origen's cosmology reflects the Platonic theory of a "fall" from unity into multiplicity. Though diverse, however, the world is not dominated by discord and contradiction, for God holds the entire universe together and directs it toward the unity of God's self. Matter has not always existed; it was created by God. Rational beings require bodies suitable to their natures; only God is incorporeal. At some future time, however, they will relinquish their bodily state, as God "becomes all in all." Although Rufinus had Origen deny it, Origen seems to have propounded a theory of successive worlds and the transmigration of souls.

Like most of his predecessors, Origen repudiated Marcion's distinguishing of the God of the Old Testament from God the Father of Jesus Christ. Marcion argued that the God who is the Father of Jesus is good but not just, whereas the God of the Old Testament was just but not good. Origen blamed Marcion's error on his literalistic interpretation and contended that God is both just and good.

In his effort to interpret the incarnation, Origen theorized that Jesus' soul acted as a "medium" for the union of the Logos-Son with humanity. Predictably, Origen underscored the claim that Jesus had free will but was without susceptibility to sin because of the indwelling Logos-Son. Whereas the prophets and apostles possessed the Logos in part, Christ possessed the whole Logos, and his rational soul acted as a "shadow" of the Logos. Before the incarnation, the Holy Spirit was given only to the prophets, but now it is given to all believers.

Although he debated whether angels have souls, Origen concluded from the fact that Christ had a soul that all rational creatures have souls. When saved, souls become something like fire and light. If they sin, they forfeit their rational condition, though their downward course varies, and they can be restored if they direct their course toward God. If the saints persevere, they will eventually see things more clearly and their bodies become pure mind.

Free Will

Throughout, Origen underscored free will. Rational animals have the ability to choose between good and evil. The fact that God requires a good life of human beings proves they have free will. The fact that demonic powers oppose and try to thwart them does not disprove free will; it proves, rather, the need for God's help. Some souls contracted guilt in their preexistence, but with divine help all can rise above their limitations.

At this place in his discourse Origen introduces his idea of the eventual restoration (*apokatastasis*) of all things, even the Devil. To sustain this, he invokes his doctrine of successive worlds. As the present world, which "fell," hastened toward its end, God intervened directly in the Son. As Paul contended in 1 Corinthians 15, the Son will eventually submit to the Father in order to restore the whole human race to unity in God. The final goal is "to become as far as possible like God." When God is "all in all," corporeality will cease and mind will no longer be conscious of anything but God, so that evil will no longer exist. It will require ages, but ultimately all things will be restored.

In what should probably have been his prologue, Origen presented his case for inspiration and interpretation of the Scriptures. Proving the divine nature of Scriptures, he argued, are both the rapid spread of Christianity in fulfillment of Jesus' predictions and the fulfillment of Old Testament prophecies through Jesus. Both the Jews and heretical sects, as well as many simple folk, fail to understand the Scriptures, however, because they try to interpret them literally. Proper interpretation will take into account their spiritual nature and recognize different levels of meaning: the literal for simple persons, the moral for those who have "made some progress," and the spiritual for the "mature." Yet not all Scriptures have a literal meaning; taken literally, as a matter of fact, some will be highly offensive. But all will have a spiritual meaning. Although not incognizant of the dangers posed by his approach, Origen concluded that piety demanded its use in uncovering the depth of God's wisdom and knowledge.

E. GLENN HINSON

Further Reading

Berchman, Robert W. *From Philo to Origen: Middle Platonism in Transition*. Chico, Calif.: Scholars Press, 1984. Helpful in locating Origen within the Platonist tradition.

Chadwick, Henry. *Early Christian Thought and the Classical Tradition*. Oxford: Clarendon Press, 1966. Chadwick establishes Origen's critical stance toward Platonism and intense desire to be considered orthodox.

Crouzel, Henri. *Origen*. Translated by A. S. Worrall. Edinburgh: T. & T. Clark, 1989. The most recent critical biography of Origen, based on a lifetime of research.

Danielou, Jean. *Origen*. Translated by Walter Mitchell. New York: Sheed & Ward, 1955. A sympathetic biography stressing Origen's orthodoxy in his context and deemphasizing allegorical method.

Dechow, Jon F. *Dogma and Mysticism in Early Christianity: Epiphanius of Cyprus and the Legacy of Origen*. Macon, Ga.: Mercer University Press, 1988. A careful critical study of the Origenist debates during the late fourth and early fifth centuries.

Trigg, Joseph Wilson. *Origen: The Bible and Philosophy in the Third Century*. Atlanta: John Knox, 1983. A balanced assessment of the impact of the Bible and Platonism on Origen.

PLOTINUS

Born: C. A.D. 204, perhaps in Lycopolis (now Asyūt), Egypt
Died: A.D. 270, in the Campania region of Italy
Major Works: The *Enneads*, written between 253 and 270

Major Ideas

The Soul is more important and real than the body or any other material object.
In its pure state, the World-Soul is the same as the Intellect (or Mind).
The Intellect is a system of Platonic ideas that exists simultaneously in all individual souls.
Above the Intellect is the One, the absolute unity from which all things come.
The One is beyond being and is indescribable.
The three principal levels of reality, in descending order, are the One, the Intellect, and the Soul.
The goal of human life is to return to the One through developing a good moral character, cultivating reason, and experiencing a mystical unity in which body, soul, and intellect are left behind.

Plotinus, the great rational mystic, was one of several famous pupils of a little-known Egyptian teacher called Ammonius Saccas. It is hard to guess at the teachings of Ammonius (which were supposed to be secret anyway), but one speculation is that he tried to harmonize Plato with Aristotle, and both with Indian philosophy. (The alternative would have been to emphasize the differences between the schools of thought, and repudiate the others where they disagreed with Plato.) In any case, we know that Plotinus tried other teachers and did not like them, heard Ammonius and said, "This is the man I was looking for," and studied with him for eleven years. After that, Plotinus joined a Roman army that was marching east, because he wanted to reach a place where he could study Persian or Indian philosophy. The army, however, was defeated, and Plotinus never got to Persia or India.

In the year A.D. 244, Plotinus began to give seminars in Rome, using the Greek language. In his own opinion he was a loyal Platonist, teaching the same thing as Plato, who had lived 600 years before. Modern scholars, however, think that the views of Plotinus show major differences from those of Plato, and accordingly it is customary nowadays to call the philosophy of Plotinus not Platonism but *Neoplatonism*. There were no Neoplatonists before Plotinus, unless Ammonius was one, but for 250 years after Plotinus almost all Western philosophers were Neoplatonists.

In 263, Plotinus was joined by his most important pupil, a man from Lebanon whose name in his own language (Aramaic) was "Malka." In Greek, however, he called himself "Porphyrios," so he is known in English as "Porphyry." Porphyry collected the essays of Plotinus and arranged them into six groups of nine, which he called simply *Enneads* (an ennead is a group of nine). Porphyry also wrote the *Life of Plotinus*, one of the most vivid character portrayals of a real person in all of ancient literature. The *Life of Plotinus* is found in modern libraries at the beginning of each complete edition of the *Enneads*. Porphyry is also known for his work in Aristotelian logic. In addition, he wrote a treatise denouncing Christianity, which was fifteen books long and was later suppressed.

Plotinus was noted for his personal honesty and integrity, even though his philosophy claimed that worldly goods and activities were unimportant. People who were approaching death used to name him as guardian of their children. Several of these orphans were raised in Plotinus's household. Plotinus's comment was that as long as they had not yet become philosophers, their property had to be kept safe for them.

Although Plotinus was a mystic, and experienced reunion with the One on several occasions, he was unlike many other mystics in that he liked to give straightforward, logical answers to theoretical questions. One time Porphyry kept pressing him for three days with problems about the connection of the soul to the body. Plotinus gave thoughtful, responsive answers. A visitor to the seminar complained that he wanted to hear Plotinus's lecture and not Porphyry's questions. Plotinus replied that if he couldn't answer Porphyry's questions, there wouldn't be anything to put in the lecture. Most philosophers would applaud that answer heartily. That attitude makes Plotinus count as a philosopher, and not as a mystic only. The ancient Greek cultural tradition valued reason more than many other cultures have done, so it is not too surprising that the combination of mysticism with philosophical analysis was achieved by someone from that tradition.

Some incidents are recorded that bear on Plotinus's attitude toward the body. Porphyry said that Plotinus seemed to be ashamed even to *have* one. He would not sit for a portrait, saying, "Isn't it enough that I have to carry around this image that nature has put around us [the body], without also having to allow an even longer-lasting image of the image [a painting]?"

In Rome, he lived sociably in the house of a widowed woman, and the household was filled with his friends, including married men and women. He himself never married. His overall attitude appears to have been one of moderation and inwardness, not one of total revulsion from the world (as is sometimes supposed).

Plotinus speaks of philosophers as "lovers" of invisible, nonsensory beauty. When saying this, Plotinus uses word forms related to the word *erōs*, meaning passionate longing, especially sexual. Only those who feel such "erotic" longing for nonphysical things will make progress in philosophy, he thought. Examples of such objects of longing are good moral character, rational insight, and reunion with the One. To a naturalistic modern critic, it could appear that this was a redirection of sexuality away from its natural objects. A follower of Plotinus, however, would say that longing directed at another person is itself a redirection, onto a not very appropriate object, of our natural urge to return to our transcendent source. It is important to see that these two opposing theories are quite symmetrical with each other. Neither one can be

assumed at the outset to be more profound. Each one has an explanation of why someone would believe the other, and each also explains many other things. The connection between mysticism and sexuality is a well-known theme; the issue between the mystic and the modern critic is not whether the two are connected, but which is prior.

Although Plotinus's philosophy held that each soul ascends alone if it ascends at all, so that society plays no role in salvation, he had at least some interest in forms of social organization. He petitioned the emperor Gallienus, who favored him, to establish or reestablish a city of philosophers in southern Italy, to be ruled according to Plato's *Laws*. Nothing came of this proposal, however.

In his sixties, Plotinus was affected by a loathsome disease, possibly a form of leprosy, and people started to shun him. He then retired to a country estate, where he died in the year 270. As he died, he admonished his doctor (who was also a pupil and friend) to try to bring back (or bring up) the god in himself to the divinity in the all.

Theory of the Divine Mind or Intellectual Principle

Plotinus believed that the "Ideas" of Plato (that is, the logical patterns that manifest themselves in the constitution of material objects) do not exist independently of one another but form an interpenetrating system. To this system of ideas Plotinus gave the name of "Intellect" (another translation would be "Mind"; the Greek word is *nous*). When we study geometry, we are exploring a small part of this realm. Theorems of geometry refer not to the imperfect diagrams we draw but to such things as a perfect circle, or a completely straight line without width. These ideal mathematical objects are certainly not material things. What they are, according to Plotinus, is ideas in the Intellect or Mind. By calling them "ideas," he is not saying that they are subjective. They are Platonic Ideas, that is, real patterns that exist independently of what anyone thinks about them. If we make a mistake about these Ideas, they are not affected by our mistake; they remain unchanged.

According to Plotinus, the unchanging nature of the Ideas—we could say, the fact that they are outside of time—is a sign of their greater reality and importance. Things that undergo change (states of the soul and material objects) are of less value. No historical event could ever be of much importance, according to the philosophy of Plotinus.

Plotinus, like many other ancient, medieval, and early modern thinkers, assumed that the other sciences would turn out to be much like geometry once they were better understood. It is therefore implicit in the philosophy of Plotinus that we should be able to make progress in, for example, physics or biology by cultivating the ability to pay attention to ideas that are already timelessly present in the intellect. The fact that scientific progress outside of mathematics has hardly ever happened in this way is probably the single most powerful objection to Neoplatonism.

According to Plotinus, all of the Ideas are in principle available to each individual human being who desires (and, by self-discipline, becomes able) to pay attention to them, instead of paying attention to the objects of the senses. We do this by turning our attention toward them, which is to say, inward, since the intellect is at the center of the soul. Turning around in this way, from looking out to looking in, is the root meaning of the religious expression "to convert." It is the first main step on the usual path of mysticism: outward, then inward, then upward.

Plotinus's account is not the same as the medieval and early modern doctrine of "innate ideas." According to that doctrine, we have knowledge of important truths because all of us have, inside us, innate ideas that are reliable copies of real things or facts. According to Plotinus, however, we do not have copies. *We have the originals.*

An Idea, to Plotinus, is not a representation of something else (except in the sense that each Idea is an imperfect expression of the One). An Idea is a real thing, at the level of the intellect. Far from representing things in the material world, the Ideas are actually archetypes that cause the production of bad copies of themselves, and it is these bad copies that make up the material world. Causation moves in this way from higher to lower, and never in the other direction, according to Plotinus.

The Levels of Reality: One, Intellect, Soul

According to Plotinus, if we ask for the cause of a thing, we are asking for something that it resembles but is higher than it. "Higher" means more unified, and therefore more real. Plotinus recognized three principal levels of reality. Each of these is called a *hypostasis*, meaning something solid, something real. Each hypostasis gives rise to the next lower level by an automatic process of diffusion of its own reality called *emanation*. The emanation of a lower level from a higher one is a necessary consequence of the abundance of reality possessed by the higher one, and it takes place without in any way diminishing, or even affecting, the higher one.

In descending order, the three hypostases are the One, the Intellect, and the Soul. At each successively lower level, there is more disunity. The One has no internal divisions at all. The Intellect has logical distinctions. The Soul has these plus time order. Material objects have both of these plus spatial separation. This means that physical objects are so strongly divided from each other that they actually exclude each other from their respective spaces. So, there is hardly any unity left by the time we reach the material world; material objects as perceived by the senses are on the very borderline of nonexistence. Therefore the material world does not count as a hypostasis, and is too feeble to generate anything below itself.

That the Soul is higher than matter is shown, according to Plotinus, by the fact that even though symmetry contributes to beauty, a living, asymmetrical face is more beautiful than a statue's symmetrical one. The Soul, according to Plotinus, actually lights up the face that it animates. Being higher, it confers beauty on it. Beauty, incidentally, is objective, according to Plotinus. We do not need any indoctrination from society to find a crushed animal carcass ugly. It is ugly not because our cultural tradition says so but because it has lost all of the unity conferred by the soul, and most of that confer by symmetry. Our soul notices this and recoils, without having to be told.

Plotinus's views may seem strange to us today. Hardly anyone nowadays rejects the saying that beauty is in the eye of the beholder. Hardly any modern philosopher could use the familiar phenomenon of someone's face "lighting up" as a central example of anything. Philosophies differ, most irreducibly, in which features of experience they regard as easy to explain, and which they regard as complex and obscure. These examples suggest that Neoplatonism is far indeed from the philosophies that are now usual. Nevertheless, to its followers it seemed plainly true. Almost any philosophy comes to seem obvious to those who hold it. This is partly because each philosophy trains people to direct their attention and imagination onto just those examples that it takes to be easiest to explain. Then whoever starts from those examples is already aimed toward that philosophy, or one like it.

Such unity as material objects have is conferred upon them, according to Plotinus, by the Soul. The reason why a living body heals when injured is that an offshoot of the Soul has looked far enough down to take care of it. Were the body inanimate (unsouled), this would not happen. On a larger scale, if there were not a World-Soul, the material world would fall apart. (Strictly speaking, the World-Soul is the whole of soul; the individual souls are in it.)

The body, then, is unified by the soul, but from the soul's point of view it is better and more congenial to turn away from the body and toward the intellect. Then instead of becoming distracted (disunited) by matter, it returns to its truest (most united) self. If the soul then lingers long in contemplation of the intellect, becoming entirely identified with it, it may occasionally experience reunion with the One. This is what the soul has really wanted all along; its yearning is built into it by its manner of creation, namely, exile from its source. Since the One is the object of our deep desire, we also call it the Good.

The One does not return our love. Unlike ourselves, it has no desires, no needs, and no knowledge.

JOHN CRONQUIST

Further Reading

Armstrong, A. H. [Arthur Hilary]. *The Architecture of the Intelligible Universe in the Philosophy of Plotinus.* Amsterdam: Adolf M. Hakkert, 1967. An advanced treatment by the author of the following book.

Armstrong, A. H., ed. *The Cambridge History of Later Greek and Early Medieval Philosophy.* London: Cambridge University Press, 1967. The section on Plotinus is probably the best introduction for beginners.

Atkinson, Michael. *Plotinus: Ennead V.1, On the Three Principal Hypostases: A Commentary with Translation.* New York: Oxford University Press, 1983. A detailed, line-by-line explanation of one of Plotinus's more important essays. This book takes you as close to the actual words of Plotinus as you can get without reading Greek.

Dodds, E. R. [Eric Robertson]. *Pagan and Christian in an Age of Anxiety: Some Aspects of Religious Experience from Marcus Aurelius to Constantine.* Cambridge, England: Cambridge University Press, 1965. Treats only some aspects of Plotinus's work, but is reliable and insightful on those aspects. Perhaps the most interesting work for the nonspecialist.

Irwin, Terence, *Classical Thought.* (A History of Western Philosophy, Vol. 1.) New York: Oxford University Press, 1989, pp. 185–201. A highly condensed interpretive summary.

Wallis, R. T. *Neoplatonism.* London: Duckworth, 1972. A reference work, filled with insights and information, masterfully compressed. Parts of the book cover predecessors and followers of Plotinus. This is the best comprehensive work on Neoplatonism.

SAINT AUGUSTINE

Born: A.D. 354, Thagaste, Numidia (North Africa)
Died: A.D. 430, Hippo Regius, Numidia
Major Works: *Confessions* (c. 397), *The Trinity* (c. 397–401), *The City of God* (c. 413–426)

Major Ideas

Faith and understanding go hand in hand: "Understand that you may believe; believe that you may understand."

True happiness consists in knowledge of God.

Father, Son, and Spirit coinhere in the Godhead as the faculties of memory, intellect, and will coinhere in the human mind.

Individual beings in the empirical world have developed out of the primeval matter God created ex nihilo *with the help of seminal powers implanted in it.*

Not only sin but also guilt has been transmitted from Adam as a consequence of the "Fall" by way of concupiscence, which Christ alone has avoided.

As a consequence of Adam's sin, humankind was condemned, but God has chosen to predestine some to salvation as an act of grace while permitting others to be lost.

The Church on earth is a mixed body of saints and sinners outside of which there is no salvation.

So long as human civilization lasts, there will be two "cities," one composed of those who desire to serve themselves and to grasp worldly power, the other of those who desire to serve God and who would forfeit power.

The most influential figure in Western history, Augustine was born in Thagaste, a small town in the Roman province of Numidia in North Africa, on November 13, 354. His mother, Monica, a devout and puritanical Christian, did her best to rear him in the Catholic faith, but his father, Patricius, not yet converted, placed before him a quite different example. Both parents had lofty ambitions for him. After educating him in schools at Thagaste and Madaurus, the neighboring village, they scraped to find money to send him to Carthage, where he found love as well as learning, entering into a long-term liaison with a woman who bore him a son named Adeodatus.

At age nineteen, Augustine experienced his first "conversion" through the reading of Cicero's *Hortensius*, a work known only in fragments today. "This book changed my desires," he wrote in the *Confessions*; "I began to arise and return to you." Burdened with guilt and troubled by the teachings of the Church, however, Augustine joined the Manichaean sect. Manichaeism helped momentarily to assuage his conscience regarding his sexual liaisons and led him to dispense with the

Old Testament. The death of a dear friend whom he had persuaded to join the sect, however, generated a profound personal crisis and proved to him how superficial Manichaean theology was. After nine years he broke with the Manichaeans and turned to Neoplatonism.

Neoplatonism offered Augustine a more satisfactory solution to the problem of evil. Whereas Manichaeism explained evil as a corporeal reality, Neoplatonism denied its very existence. Only good exists; evil, therefore, is the absence or the perversion of the good. Now Augustine knew he did what he did because he wanted to, not because he had to. At the same time, nevertheless, he realized that he could not take the decisive step away from the evil which he hated without the aid of divine grace. The conversion of the noted Neoplatonist philosopher Victorinus made him realize that he could be both a Christian and a philosopher.

The last decisive step in his conversion took place at Cassiciacum in July 386, in the presence of friends who had followed him from Carthage to Rome and to Milan. Ponticianus narrated the story of the conversion of two young Roman noblemen on hearing the story of Anthony's conversion in response to hearing Jesus' challenge to the rich youth. The story, as Augustine himself described its impact, took him "from behind his own back" and made him look at how "defiled and deformed" he was. Exasperated, he withdrew to another part of the garden to sulk. After a time a child's voice cried out, "Take up, read." The book he had hurled to the ground fell open at Romans 13:14, which urged him to "put on the Lord Jesus Christ and no longer take thought for the flesh and its concupiscences." On April 24, 387, he received baptism at the hands of Ambrose, Bishop of Milan.

Already thirty-two, Augustine's reputation spread rapidly on his return to North Africa. Immediately he formed around himself a monastic community at Thagaste. In 391, on a visit to Hippo Regius, however, Bishop Valerius conscripted him for the priesthood. Four years later, he installed Augustine as his coadjustor. Augustine served as Bishop of Hippo from that time until his death on August 28, 430, the beginning of the siege of the city by the Vandal king Genseric.

The Controversialist

Although bishop of a relatively small see, Augustine became the recognized leader of the Catholic Church in North Africa. He wrote as a controversialist rather than as a systematic theologian, replying by turns to his one-time comrades the Manichaeans, then to the Donatists and Pelagians, and then, after the fall of Rome to the Goths in 410, to pagans.

Augustine's debate with the Manichaeans (389–405) focused on the relationship between faith and knowledge, the origin and nature of evil, free will, and revelation through the Scriptures. His most effective response was the *Confessions*, composed between 397 and 400.

His reply to the Donatists (405–412) had to answer two basic questions they raised: (1) whether the guilt of ministers invalidates the sacramental acts they perform, and (2) whether toleration of such ministers by churches in North Africa defiles the whole Church. In response to the first, he distinguished between validity and efficacy. Christ alone, he argued, determines whether an act is valid; the faith of the recipient determines whether it is effective for salvation; the character of the minister does not affect the sacrament at all. In response to the second, he contended that the surrender of Scriptures by certain clergy in North Africa cannot have invalidated the Church everywhere. The Church is a *corpus permixtum*, whose holiness depends on Christ and not on the personal worthiness of each member.

Augustine's answer to Pelagianism (412–418) was deeply rooted in his own experience of grace. Pelagius, a British monk, picked up on Augustine's emphasis on free will in the anti-Manichaean writings and thought an emphasis on natural grace represented Augustine faithfully. Augustine, however, underscored *super*-natural grace.

In 418, Augustine initiated his critique of Arianism, a matter of increasing concern as the barbarians, most of whom were Arian, pressed farther and farther southwards.

The City of God

The City of God, composed serially between 413 and 426, was Augustine's reply to pagan criticism of Christianity after the sack of Rome in 410 and is his most significant contribution to Western thought. In the first ten books, he examined critically pagan charges that Christianity, by undermining the devotion of Romans to the gods that had made Rome great, was responsible for the fall of Rome. In books 11 through 22 he constructed his grand scheme for the operation of divine providence in history.

In books 1 through 5, Augustine answered two questions: (1) Was Christianity responsible for Rome's fall or paganism for its rise? (2) If not the gods of Rome, then what spiritual power made Rome great? To the first he answered a resounding no. Christianity had mitigated, not exacerbated the fury of the Goths. Moreover, it offered consolation in its constant reminder that we have no enduring habitation here. The eternal City remains for the righteous who turn to Christ. Quite clearly, on the other side, preposterous pagan religion could offer little support. Rome suffered wars and disasters long before Christianity appeared on the scene. What, then, accounted for Rome's rise to power? Neither the gods nor Roman devotion to them but God's providential purpose in history. God raised up the Empire to give Roman laws and literature and civilization. So Rome's greatness has not been due to fate but to God's foreknowledge and providence.

In books 6 through 10, Augustine disputed the claims of all pagan systems to authenticity. He recounted facts taken chiefly from Varro to point up the folly of polytheism and cited Socrates and Plato in support of monotheism. Although not an exposition of philosophy, books 8–10 clearly reflect Augustine's struggle to define his stance against Neoplatonism, especially concerning the incorporation of popular paganism into its system. He contrasted the Christian cult of martyrs, despite its similarities, with the worship of wandering spirits. Platonists vainly seek to mediate between God and humankind through their demons; Christians have a true mediator in Jesus Christ. They offer true sacrifices to God through the Eucharist.

In books 11–22, Augustine spun out his philosophy of history in terms of the struggle between two "cities"—two types of human beings and societies. The story begins in prehistory with "the holy and faithful angels who never were nor ever will be deserters from God" and "those who rejected the eternal light and were turned toward darkness." What happened there was replicated in the human creation and fall. Created good, humankind fell by disobedience and became subject to death of both body and soul. Hereafter there are two cities—one of those who live according to the flesh under and like the Devil, the other of those who love God and other human beings. The former will perish, the latter will reach their immortal home. "What we see, then, is that two societies have issued from two kinds of love. Worldly society has issued from selfish love, which dared to despise even God, whereas the communion of saints is rooted in a love of God that is ready to trample on self."

In the next four books (15–18) Augustine sketched the tale of twos: Cain and Abel, Sarah and Hagar, Remus and Romulus. Evidences of the City of God are slim from Noah to Abraham. With Abraham, however, began its clear history, in which one can see promises eventually fulfilled in Christ. The Old Testament supplies "types." Paralleling the story of the City of God is that of the earthly city characterized by constant conflict because humankind did not adhere to Absolute Being. God chose through Rome "to subdue the whole world, to bring it into the single society of a republic under law, and to bestow upon it a widespread and enduring peace." But at what great price—bloodshed and war! Meantime, in difficult times, the Church learns by tears to hope. Spreading under the power of the Spirit and in fulfillment of prophecy, she perseveres as the pilgrim City of God until the Second Coming.

In book 19, Augustine arrived at his own time and presented his case for Christian rather than Platonist ethics. Christians hold that eternal life is the supreme good and that virtues are real only when one believes in God. Philosophers fail because they seek the temporal rather than the eternal. Christians too desire peace and recognize its limitations until mortality ceases, but they seek it in obedience to God and possess it already by faith. Philosophers lack such faith.

In the last three books, Augustine looked to the future. He repudiated millenarianism. The Millenium applies either to what remains of the thousand years since Christ or to the entire time the world still has to go. The Devil has been bound since the day the Church began its expansion from Judea into the whole world. The two cities, of God and of the Devil, will reach their consummation at the final judgment, the subject of book 21. Unlike Origen, Augustine held out no hope for the redemption of all, even the Devil. Even faithful Catholics must beware; salvation depends on *living* an upright life and not merely on baptism or Eucharist or almsgiving. Neither heretics nor schismatics nor evil Catholics will escape punishment if they do not repent. In book 22, Augustine delineated the eternal blessedness of the City of God, but spent much of his space sustaining the doctrine of resurrection and miracles. He contended that there was no dearth of miracles in his own day. Although pagan philosophers deny resurrection, Augustine wrote, they agree with Christians about rewards after death; both Plato and Porphyry, moreover, believed God could do the impossible. In the eternal City, Christians will attain perfect freedom, and their wills will be in perfect harmony with God's in the promised Sabbath Rest.

E. GLENN HINSON

Further Reading

Battenhouse, Roy W., ed. *A Companion to the Study of St. Augustine.* New York: Oxford University Press, 1955. Essays on different facets of Augustine's thought.

Bonner, Gerald. *St. Augustine of Hippo: Life and Controversies.* London: SCM Press, 1963. An excellent sketch of Augustine's life and writing as a controversialist.

Brown, Peter R. L. *Augustine of Hippo, A Biography.* Berkeley: University of California Press, 1967. The best current biography.

Chadwick, Henry. *Augustine.* New York: Oxford University Press, 1986. A brief but competent interpretation of Augustine in his context.

Gilson, Etienne. *The Christian Philosophy of Saint Augustine.* Translated by L. E. M. Lynch. New York: Random House, 1960. A classic study of Augustine and Neoplatonism.

Kirwan, Christopher. *Augustine.* London and New York: Routledge, 1989. A fine summary of Augustine's thought as evolved in the North African context.

O'Meara, John J. *Charter of Christendom.* New York: Macmillan, 1961. A brief introduction to *The City of God.*

ANICIUS MANLIUS SEVERINUS BOETHIUS

Born: C. A.D. 480, perhaps in Rome, Italy
Died: C. A.D. 525, Pavia, Italy
Major Work: *The Consolation of Philosophy* (c. 524)

Major Ideas

True happiness is found in pursuit of the highest good, which is God.

Temporal possessions, honor, fame, pleasure, and power are inadequate and disappointing goals; only the happiness that comes from loving God cannot be taken away by misfortune.

Even though God foresees the free acts of the human will, freedom of choice remains, for God sees all times concurrently and through eternity.

Upon the death of his father, the Consul Aurelius Manlius Boethius (c. 488), young Boethius became the ward of Quintus Aurelius Memmius Symmachus, one of the most prominent and influential of those surviving members of the Roman aristocracy who had chosen to cooperate with the Gothic conquerors of Italy. During his early years, he received a magnificent education in Greek, at least partially in Athens, according to a popular tradition, that was to determine the course of his intellectual destiny.

Entering service to Theodoric, the Ostrogothic king, Boethius occupied and distinguished himself in a number of important positions, rising by the end of his life to that of Master of the Offices. He himself was most proud of his sons' achievement in becoming joint consuls in 522 (Boethius had been consul in 510, his father in 487). Accused of treason for causes that are not altogether clear (although it seems likely that he was working toward the doctrinal and ecclesiastical union of Rome and Constantinople), Boethius was tried, imprisoned, and eventually executed. His foster father (who had become as well his father-in-law), Symmachus, was put to death in the course of the same train of events.

Boethius's written works fall into two unequal halves: the translations, commentaries, textbooks, logical, and theological works (the *opuscula*), and *The Consolation of Philosophy*.

At the start, Boethius intended to translate, comment upon, and reconcile the total works of Plato and Aristotle. However, this plan proved to be too ambitious and he completed work only on Aristotle's *Categories*, *Topics*, *Prior and Posterior Analytics*, *Sophistical Arguments*, and *On Interpretation*. He also completed a translation and commentary upon Porphyry's *Isagoge*, textbooks on music, arithmetic, and geometry (perhaps also one on astronomy), a host of logical discussions, and a treatise on the Trinity.

In all this, the greatest contribution Boethius made to subsequent developments was the preservation of Aristotle for the Middle Ages. Not until the recovery of the twelfth century would the remainder of the canon be forthcoming, largely from Arabic sources.

Boethius also provided, in his discussion of Porphyry, the starting point for the great medieval debate of the nominalists and realists on the subject of universals that was to preoccupy scholastic philosophers. Plato had held universals to be real and incorporeal (realism), whereas Aristotle had proclaimed them merely mental concepts (nominalism). Boethius denied that a universal can be a specific thing because it must be common to at least several things. Yet, if it completely lacked substance, it would be a thought about nothing. Boethius tried to reconcile the two positions by suggesting that the mind is able to distinguish qualities common to a group of objects, thus recognizing that the immaterial universal subsists in matter.

The Consolation of Philosophy

Written in alternating prose and verse, the *Consolation* attempts to answer the age-old question

of why bad things happen to good people. It concludes that the inability of most persons to perceive
ultimate and true realities results in persistently
inaccurate perceptions of events and their meanings. In effect, Boethius concludes, finite minds are
incapable of understanding God's infinite intention.
All that happens in the world, therefore, must be to
a good end despite appearances to the contrary.

The *Consolation* opens with the imprisoned
Boethius (a heavy chain around his neck), venting
his sorrows, in particular his loss of the youth and
wealth that he has misidentified as the sources of his
happiness, in the presence of the muses of poetry.
Suddenly he becomes aware of a woman, Lady
Philosophy, standing over him.

Her appearance is highly symbolic of philosophy
and its workings: She has piercing eyes, a young/old
face, a height that varies from normal to towering,
and a dress, covered with dust and roughly torn by
violent hands, which depicts on its front the progress of philosophy from the letter pi up a series of
steps to theta. These letters are symbolic in a complex and compact manner, representing, in the first
instance, the lesser fields of study associated with
this world, and, in the second, the higher thinking
that pursues the nature of higher reality (and suggesting also the symbolic theta—for *thanatos*—
worn by condemned prisoners).

Blinded by tears and so unable to see Philosophy
clearly, Boethius is dumbfounded when the appari-
tion imperiously orders the muses of poetry, the
sources of emotional excess, to leave. Sitting on the
edge of his bed, she wipes the tears from his eyes
and begins a lengthy Socratic dialogue with the
distraught man.

If you wish my help, begins Lady Philosophy,
ignoring Boethius's reproaches that she has neglected him, you must first tell me what has happened. Book 1, therefore, is devoted largely to
Boethius's perceptions of why he has been unjustly
imprisoned and sentenced to death. The charges are
four: desiring the safety of the Senate, hindering the
use of perjured testimony against the Senate, desiring the freedom of Rome, and sacrilege. With a few
deft questions, Philosophy determines the source of
Boethius's misery: He has forgotten what it means

to be human, a part of the creation that, along with
all matter, will find its true end and fulfillment when
it returns to the creator, who controls all to his own
ends and to whom slavish obedience is the source of
true liberty.

Book 2 is essentially an analysis of Boethius's
losses with reference to the concept of Fortune,
whom he has blamed for his misfortunes. Philosophy, however, absolves Fortune, whose very nature,
she points out, is change. Those who feel they have
risen upon her wheel should not complain when they
fall. In any case, Fortune and her gifts—wealth,
power, and fame—cannot lead to happiness if it is
true that happiness is the highest good and that anything that can be taken away cannot be the highest
good. Paradoxically, bad fortune often teaches the
valuable truth that a man's life is far better spent in
the pursuit of more lasting values. The final poem of
book 2, a hymn of praise to the love that binds the
cosmos, concludes, "O felix hominum genus / Si
vestros animos amor / Quo caelum regitur regat"
("O happy race of men, / If love, by whom the
sky / Is ruled, governs your spirits").

Book 3 begins by recapitulating the Stoic arguments that predominated in book 2. The pleasures
and possessions of this world are simply not the
source of true happiness, not if happiness is the
state made perfect by the presence of all that is
good. The former lead merely to false felicity, but
true felicity is that which makes a man self-
sufficient, strong, worthy of respect, glorious, and
joyful.

Lady Philosophy has now brought Boethius to
the major turning point of the *Consolation*. Having
learned the errors of his past conduct, he is ready
for an exposition of the truths he has neglected. At
this point the *Consolation* also reaches its literary
climax in the poem *O qui perpetua*, a literary prayer
that Philosophy offers to the Father of all by way of
laying a proper foundation for what is to follow, the
delineation of the way to true happiness. Heavily
dependent upon Plato's *Timaeus* for both thought
and expression, the hymn turns the work's attention
from this world and its things to their Author, who
is the true object of our life's search, its end, source,
maker, lord, path, and goal.

Having earlier identified happiness as the goal of life, Philosophy goes on to show where perfect happiness is to be found. The answer is in God, the author of all things, who is also to be equated with the highest good. Since God and happiness are the same thing, it follows that God is found in goodness and nowhere else. Since all things desire unity and since unity is good, the end of all things is in the good.

At the end of book 3, Boethius quickly sketches evil's role in the created universe. Since God is the highest good and therefore incapable of evil, it follows that evil is, in itself, nothing, merely the absence of good. (This topic is developed further in the beginning of book 4.) Book 3 concludes with a famous poem that sees in the ancient myth of Orpheus and his visit to the underworld an image of humanity ascending the stairs from darkness and death to light and life.

Where then does evil, demonstrably a presence in the world, come from? Book 4 in its beginning takes up the topic in greater detail and then progresses to the ideas of Providence and Fate, which can be seen to grow out of it. All persons, both good and evil, desire the good—as Lady Philosophy established early in the argument. Only the good, however, achieve the good, which they do by the exercise of their virtues. The wicked strive to acquire good by the exercise of their various desires, which is an unnatural method of obtaining the good. Good persons, explains Philosophy by way of clarification, walk (so to speak) on their feet; the wicked, on their hands.

If evil men do have power, therefore, that power comes from weakness and not from strength and only makes it more clear that they can do nothing. Because they are evil, their power is evil; since evil is nothing, their power is nothing. Therefore, the ability to do evil is not a form of power. Those who follow their base desires, forgetting that goodness is happiness, descend to the level of beasts, there to wallow in nonhuman behavior.

The rest of book 4 is devoted to an account of how God governs the creation through Providence and Fate to bring about good. Providence is divine reason itself, whereas Fate is the planned order inherent in things. Fate is subordinate to Providence, which also controls other areas that do not involve Fate. Fate is a sort of aspect of Providence, which governs the details of this creation, and Providence no doubt has many such aspects about which we know nothing. Because of their limited mental abilities, human beings think everything confused and upset in the realm of Fate, when in actuality pure and unchanging order originating in the divine mind governs all.

That the order of divine control does govern the creation provides another argument to refute the notion that there is such a thing as evil and that it often prevails. If we could see the plan of Providence, we would recognize how all apparent evil serves an ultimate purpose in the cause of good. When the wicked seem to be prospering, when evil deeds afflict us, we must recognize that we see but darkly, within the limitations of circumscribed time, the true workings of Providence's plan.

It therefore follows, continues Lady Philosophy, that all fortune is good despite its appearance, since it is meant to reward or discipline the good and to punish or correct the bad. The wise person, seeking the path of virtue, will avoid falling victim to Fortune when she is adverse or being corrupted by her when she is favorable. The virtuous person will hold with unshakable strength to the middle way. It is in our own hands, concludes Philosophy, what fortune we wish to shape for ourselves.

Book 5 returns to the subject of divine foreknowledge and human free will and comprises Boethius's most complete handling of the topic. Asked by Boethius to discuss the notion of chance, Lady Philosophy responds that there is no such thing, if by "chance" is meant random occurrence with no causal nexus. God's imposition of order does not allow for random events. There are unexpected consequences to actions that may seem to us random, but all endure the rule of God's law.

Is there then, pursues Boethius, room in God's close-knit chain of control for freedom of the will? Yes, answers Philosophy, for without it rational natures would be impossible. The more one contemplates the mind of God, the freer one is; the more one descends to the flesh, the more enslaved. God looks out from eternity upon all persons and arranges predestined rewards according to their merit.

Boethius is perplexed and confused by this answer and, speaking throughout Prose 3, desires to know how human beings can have free will if God has foreknowledge. The coming to pass of things foreknown is necessary, whatever the order of causes, and that alone seems to Boethius to make freedom of the will impossible. How can human thoughts and actions have freedom if the divine mind, in foreseeing all things, binds them? Even wickedness must be derived from the author of all.

Yes, answers Philosophy, that is an old charge against Providence and no one has yet answered it correctly, because human reason cannot begin to approach the immediacy of divine foreknowledge. However, she patiently explains, just as knowledge of present events imposes no necessity on what is happening, so foreknowledge imposes no necessity on what is going to happen. People get confused because they comprehend according to their own ability to know, not according to a thing's own nature, not according to its ability to be known. Small wonder then that we are generally in error.

Continuing, Philosophy points out that true intelligence belongs only to God and must not be confused with the powers of reason that belong to the human race. Such being the case, it is fitting for human reason to bow to divine wisdom. For God, existing in eternity, the world and time are perpetual. We should think of God's foreknowledge, therefore, not as a prevision of the future but as knowledge of a never-ending presence.

If it is argued that those events preknown by God must happen of necessity, then one must learn to distinguish two kinds of necessity: simple and conditional. It is true by simple necessity that all human beings are mortal. It is, however, true by conditional necessity when we know that someone is walking. This conditional necessity does not imply simple necessity, however, for those who walk do so of their own free wills. All things that are present to God will happen, some from the necessity of things, others from the power and choices of those who do them. God with his knowledge of all times remains a spectator of all things from on high.

Since human beings live in the sight of the judge who sees all things, concludes Lady Philosophy, it behooves everyone to avoid vice and cultivate virtue, to lift up their minds in hope, and to pray humbly. It is necessary that all be good.

Thus ends *The Consolation of Philosophy*, a philosophical synthesis drawn from, among others, Plato, Seneca, Cicero, the Neoplatonists, and the church fathers, especially Augustine. Presumably Boethius's execution ensued soon after its completion, putting to the ultimate test the strength of the philosophical convictions so lastingly argued that the work became for over a thousand years an indispensable *vade mecum* of Western education. Despite the qualms of some medieval men about the pagan nature of the *Consolation*, there are few who would deny its deep-seated Christianity. Faced with the supreme challenge of his beliefs, beliefs nurtured by a lifelong study of Plato and Aristotle, Boethius affirms in his last work the value of the human mind as a means of discovering God and insists that free exercise of the will and the consequent responsibility for events are at the same time man's glory and his burden.

ROBERT J. MEINDL

Further Reading

Chadwick, Henry. *Boethius: The Consolations of Music, Logic, Theology, and Philosophy.* Oxford: Clarendon Press, 1981. An attempt to see Boethius in the setting of his age and to integrate the various constituent elements in his intellectual achievement.

Rand, E. K. *Founders of the Middle Ages.* Cambridge, Mass.: Harvard University Press, 1929. Contains a classic essay, "Boethius, the First of the Scholastics."

Reiss, Edmund. *Boethius.* Boston: Twayne Publishers, 1982. An introduction for the student and general reader that focuses on the interrelationship of Boethius's various writings and on the literary merit of the *Consolation*.

Stewart, H. F., and E. K. Rand. *Boethius: The Theological Tractates and The Consolation of Philosophy.* The Loeb Classical Library. Cambridge, Mass.: Harvard University Press, 1918. An authoritative Latin text and translation.

SAINT ANSELM OF CANTERBURY

Born: 1033, Aosta, Kingdom of Burgundy (now Italy)
Died: 1109, Canterbury, England
Major Works: *Monologion* (c. 1077), *Proslogion* (1078), *Cur Deus Homo* (1098)

Major Ideas

God exists, for there is goodness in the world, and goodness can be good only through a supreme good that is good through itself, and only God is good through himself.

God exists, for since whatever exists does so only through something, there must be a supremely great being that exists through itself and through which all other things exist.

God exists, for there are degrees of worth in the world, and degrees of worth are understandable only by reference to a being of supreme worth, the highest of all existing beings.

God necessarily exists, for he is the being than whom none greater can be thought, and it is greater for such a being to exist than not to exist, and to exist necessarily.

God freely became a human being because to secure man's happiness (for which man was created) man had to be punished for his sin and no one but God could make such satisfaction: God became man in order to make the offering necessary for redemption.

Saint Anselm of Canterbury is one of that limited number of great theologians of the Church who, secure in faith, nevertheless sought to bring reason to bear on the problems of faith so as to give understanding not only to believers but also to those who, lacking the incentive to believe, might eventually be willing to give assent to what reason without faith reveals. If the task were beyond his powers, then one must be ready to say that it was also beyond the powers of Aristotle, Saint Augustine, Saint Thomas Aquinas, Pascal, and a host of other brilliant and dedicated philosophers and theologians.

Furthermore, one must acknowledge that Anselm himself, as a believer rejoicing in the degree to which God had strengthened and directed his reason in the defense of the great truths of his faith and convinced that reason can give understanding to faith, realized that something more than reason is needed when unbelievers cannot be moved even by the best of reasons.

In the preface to the *Monologion*, Anselm describes his treatise as a "meditation," written, with some reluctance, to satisfy certain brothers who had asked him to defend various central propositions of faith, not by reference to Scripture, but through the use of reason alone. He confesses that he was reluctant to do this "because of the

difficulty of the assignment and the weakness of my intellectual power." He hoped that his writings would be made available only to those who had asked him to write, and he frankly states that, as far as the product of his labors was concerned, he fully expected "that after a while they would overwhelm it with contempt, scorning it as a thing of little value."

Anselm was born in 1033 in Aosta, in what was then the kingdom of Champagne, now northwestern Italy. When he was about twenty-three years old, he left his native village; his mother had died, and he was not on good terms with his father, with whom he was temperamentally and in faith at odds. He became a disciple of the great churchman and theologian Lanfranc, who in 1043 had become prior of the Benedictine abbey of Bec in Normandy. Anselm's interest was that of a scholar—he originally had no intention of becoming a monk—and he went to Bec in 1059 because, under the influence of Lanfranc, the abbey had become a center of learning.

In 1062, only three years after his arrival at Bec, Anselm was appointed prior of Bec when Lanfranc left to become abbot of Saint Stephen's in Caen.

While at Bec, after having written a considerable number of meditations and prayers, Anselm finally found time to write his monumental "meditations" (in this case, philosophical works): the *Monologion* (c. 1077) and the *Proslogion* (1078).

In 1078, Anselm was appointed abbot of Bec. In the following year he made his first visit to England, where he became acquainted with the young monk Eadmer, who was to become Anselm's close associate and biographer.

In 1089, Lanfranc died (at the age of 84); and in 1093 Anselm, despite his reluctance, was made archbishop of Canterbury by the King of England, William II (Rufus). Much of Anselm's time and effort during his remaining years were spent in attempting to preserve the freedom of the church from political intrusions by Rufus and his successor, Henry I. However, he did manage to complete his most ambitious theological work, *Cur Deus Homo*, during a period of self-imposed exile from England in 1098.

Anselm died in Canterbury on April 21, 1109, and was buried in the cathedral there.

The Monologion

In his writings, Anselm was concerned with demonstrating reason's support of faith. He was convinced that by reason alone, without appeal to the Scriptures, much that the believer adopts on faith can be made evident to those who, lacking understanding, also lack faith. Furthermore, by the use of reason, those who have faith may come to understand. When Anselm wrote in the *Proslogion* that "I do not seek to understand in order to believe, but I believe in order to understand," he was reflecting the position of Saint Augustine (whose work specifically influenced him) and emphasizing the power of faith to illuminate the rational basis of faith.

Anselm's efforts to prove the existence of God through the use of reason alone, without any appeal to authority or the Scriptures, were not designed to show that faith is not necessary, only that understanding, although achievable through faith, can be reached through the use of reason alone.

The *Monologion* begins with a proof of God's existence based on the contention that goods—all

things that in various ways and to various degrees are good—are good through a supreme good that is good "through itself."

By a similar line of reasoning, Anselm argued that whatever is "great," that is, worthy and excellent, must be so through something supremely great that is great through itself.

Accordingly, Anselm maintained, there is that which is both supremely good and supremely great, "the highest of all existing things."

A third argument rests on the assumption, presumably evident to reason, that whatever *is*, that is, *exists*, must derive its existence from some one thing that exists "through itself" and, accordingly, is greater than anything that exists only through another.

Anselm then develops his idea of a "Supreme Nature" to account for the creation of all things. The Supreme Nature could not have been caused, nor could it have come from nothing. Therefore, the Supreme Nature must exist through and from itself. But everything that has been created must have been created by the Supreme Nature from nothing (and not from some material, which itself would have to have an origin). It must be, then, that all things were created from nothing, *ex nihilo*, in that they once were nothing but now are something: Once they were not, and now they are. (Anselm went to great lengths to make it clear that he is not maintaining that created things were made from "nothing" as if "nothing" were the material, a "something," from which they were made: an impossibility—since nothing cannot be something.)

Carefully constructed arguments are advanced by Anselm to support the claims that the Supreme Being is just in that it is justice (as it is good in that it is goodness, it is great in that it is greatness, and so forth). The Supreme Being is simple in that "whatever the Supreme Being in some respect essentially is, it is as a whole."

Anselm argues that the Supreme Being is without beginning or end; it exists at all places and at all times. But it is also true that the Supreme Being exists "in no place at no time." How can this apparent contradiction be resolved? Anselm explains (in a long, drawn-out but carefully composed argument) that the Supreme Being exists at all places and at all times in that the Supreme Being is absent from no place or time; however, the Supreme Being "does not receive into itself distinctions of space and time" (it is not a thing somewhere at some time). Accordingly, both claims are true in that what is being said in each is not the contradictory of the other.

The Supreme Being can be called a "substance," Anselm argues, but it is a unique substance in that this being has "from itself . . . its being whatever it is." Also, this being is uniquely an individual spirit. Finally, one may talk about Father, Son, and Spirit, for the Supreme Being, a unity, is also in a unique sense three "persons" (or substances): The Father begets the Word, who is the Son; the Spirit "proceeds" from Father and Son. The three persons are all God, and to talk of the three is to distinguish certain relationships of God to God without in any way suggesting that there are differences among the persons of nature, existence, or worth.

Anselm's demonstration of the triune unity of God is not so much a purely logical proof as it is a rational attempt to understand the unique nature of the Supreme Being. Anselm's approach to the problem follows the pattern of Augustine's reasoning in *De Trinitate* (*On the Trinity*).

The Ontological Proof of God's Existence

In the *Proslogion*, Anselm presents a proof of God's existence that stems from a consideration of God's nature or essence. The basic device of the proof is that of conceiving (thinking) of a *kind* of being such that there *must be* a being of that kind. It is as if Anselm asked, "Can you think of a kind of thing—whether or not initially you believe there are things of that kind—such that it is clear to you from your thinking of that kind of thing that there *must* be a thing of that kind?"

Anselm's answer is that the nature of God is such that it is evident from an understanding of that nature that a being of that kind *must* exist. It is further evident that there is one and only one being of that kind. Therefore, God, as the exemplification

or instance of the divine kind of being, must exist and must exist *necessarily*; that is, not only must it be that God exists, but it must be that God's existence must be. (Or, put another way, Anselm is arguing not only that it is necessarily true, given other truths, that the proposition "God exists" is true, but also that the proposition "God exists" is itself necessarily true, that its truth is evident from its meaning alone.)

Anselm's "ontological" argument (derived from a consideration of a "nature," that is, of a *kind* of being) is especially fascinating (and continues to intrigue scholars) because it does not rest on factual assumptions of the kinds involved in other proofs (attempted proofs) of God's existence. The argument that God must exist because whatever exists must have a cause and God is that cause, for example, rests on the factual assumptions that there are existents and that "whatever exists must have a cause." The latter proposition, it has been argued, would be false if whatever exists (say, energy) were without beginning. The ontological argument begins with a reference to a "nature," a "kind" of being (what we might loosely call the "definition" of a descriptive term) and *not* with the assumption of any fact and, in particular, *not* with the assumption Anselm sought to prove true: There is God; that God (in fact) exists.

Thus, although Anselm begins his argument in chapter 2 of the *Proslogion* by addressing God: "Lord, do thou, who dost give understanding to faith, give me . . . to understand that thou art as we believe," he was certainly not assuming what he was setting out to prove: that there is a God. He was simply appealing to God to give him the power to show, through the use of reason alone, that God exists, just as faith affirms.

The proof itself, pared down to its essentials (and its basic parts numbered), runs as follows:

1. The Lord is the greatest conceivable (thinkable) being.
2. Even the Fool (of Psalms 14:1) who says in his heart that there is no such being understands what he hears when he hears the words "greatest conceivable being."

3. So, the Fool understands what he conceives when he thinks of God, the greatest conceivable being.
4. Whatever is understood is in the understanding.
5. So, even though the Fool does not understand God to exist—that is, does not realize that God exists—God is (so to speak) in the understanding of the Fool.
6. But if God existed only in the understanding, he would not be as great as he would be were he to exist in reality as well as in the understanding.
7. So, if God exists only in the understanding of the Fool, he is not the greatest conceivable being.
8. But since God *is* the greatest conceivable being, he could not exist only in the understanding.
9. Therefore, God exists in reality.

The above argument, presented in chapter 2 of the *Proslogion*, is supplemented by a further argument in chapter 3, in which Anselm attempts to show that not only must it be that God exists in reality; it must be that God *must* exist in reality.

Anselm begins his second argument—designed to show that God cannot be conceived *not* to exist—by arguing that it is possible to conceive of a being that cannot be conceived not to exist. Such a being would be greater than a being that *can* be conceived not to exist. "Hence," Anselm writes, "if that, than which nothing greater can be conceived, can be conceived not to exist, it is not that than which nothing greater can be conceived. But this is an irreconcilable contradiction." Since God cannot even be conceived not to exist, he must be conceived (and hence understood) to exist, Anselm concludes. (For Anselm, in this context, to "understand" something to be the case is, through understanding, to *know* that it is the case.)

A brilliant critic of Anselm's ontological argument, the monk Gaunilo, who was Anselm's contemporary, argued that Anselm failed, in the first place, to show that the Fool could conceive the idea

of God (because of the uniqueness of God, God is inconceivable). In the second place, Gaunilo argued, Anselm failed to show, even if the Fool could conceive the idea of God, that the Fool must, if he follows Anselm's line of argument, come to realize that God exists in reality.

The monk composed a striking example to illustrate his point: Suppose one conceives of an island that is without qualification excellent—an island none better than which could be conceived. If one reasons as Anselm proposes, then one would have to conclude that the island really existed since, as the greatest of all islands, it could not fail to exist.

Such an argument, Gaunilo argues, is not persuasive. For even if someone came to believe, on the basis of the argument, that such an island exists, he would have no basis for claiming to *know* that it exists. If someone argued in this way, Gaunilo writes, "I would think he were jesting or else I would not know whom I ought to regard as the more foolish—either myself, were I to grant his argument, or him, were he to suppose that he had proved to any extent the existence of the island."

Anselm's reply is careful and lengthy but adds nothing substantially new to his original argument. As for Gaunilo's island, Anselm replies, in effect, that although the being who is the greatest that can be thought must exist (or not be great—a contradiction), an island, no matter how beautiful and idyllic it may be conceived to be, is not itself *the* being than which none greater can be thought; hence, the logic of the argument does not apply to the hypothetical island or to anything other than God.

Critics generally have not been kind in their criticism of Anselm's argument, although most of them have admired the brilliance of the argument's author. Saint Thomas Aquinas rejected the argument on the ground that although God's essence involves his existence, we cannot deduce God's existence from the conceiving of his essence since we cannot know that some being corresponding to the essence exists; Thomas Hume argued that the term "necessary existence" is meaningless; and Immanuel Kant, besides rejecting the argument for much the same reason that prompted Saint Thomas, insisted that the argument is faulty since "existence" is not a predicate (not a descriptive term) that can be part of a definition.

Some critics have given considerable weight to Anselm's supposing that if one conceives of God, God *exists* in the understanding. One conceives what has been called an "essence," and since God's essence includes the feature of necessary existence, if God exists in the understanding, he exists, and if he exists, he exists necessarily.

But whatever Anselm's conception of the intellectual process, he could hardly have supposed that the Fool had *God* literally "in mind" and that therefore God existed at least in the Fool's mind. (After all, Anselm himself wrote that before a painter makes a painting, the painter has the painting in mind, "in his understanding," but only after making it does the painter "understand it to exist"—that is, know that it exists.) In any case, the argument depends primarily on the connection between the idea (concept) of God and the prescribed feature of the necessary existence of God, and that connection, being merely one of stipulated definition, cannot be appealed to as the basis of a proof of God's existence.

In the course of the remaining chapters of the *Proslogion*, Anselm assumes that he has demonstrated that God, as the greatest conceivable being, surely exists. Since God is the greatest being, then he *is* whatever it is better to be than not to be. Accordingly, God is perceptive, omnipotent, merciful, just, unlimited, eternal, and the one supreme good: Father, Son, and Holy Spirit.

Why God Became Man

In *Cur Deus Homo* (*Why God Became Man*), Anselm reached what many notable critics regard as the height of his powers as a theologian. The argument of the book, although carefully developed with the same rigorous relating of ideas to one another as is evident in the *Monologion* and the *Proslogion*, can briefly be summarized:

Human beings were created by God to live and be happy. But man (human beings), through Adam, sinned. For that sin man must adequately be punished: Only man could render satisfaction for the offense against God of deliberate disobedience. But only God could possibly render satisfaction for all humanity. Hence, only a God-man could by his death render appropriate and sufficient satisfaction to save humanity. Therefore, God freely took on human nature and died on the cross.

The problem, as Anselm defines it at the outset of *Cur Deus Homo*, is that of explaining why God, who could have restored life to the world by means of some other person, "angelic or human," or simply by willing it, chose to become human and to die for man—to pay for man's sins and to restore eternal life to all mankind.

The argument is given in the form of a dialogue between Anselm and the monk Boso. Since Boso is a man of Christian faith, the dialogue can be seen as Anselm's attempt to give understanding to faith; the primary intent is not to convert the nonbeliever but to enlighten and satisfy the believer. However, those who scoff at the Christian faith and regard it as a "foolish simplicity," Anselm writes, can also learn from the discussion of the problem.

Boso asks the question in these words: ". . . For what reason and on the basis of what necessity did God—although He is omnipotent—assume the lowliness and the weakness of human nature in order to restore it?"

Boso takes the role of the unbeliever to prompt Anselm by presenting the objections and queries that unbelievers express concerning the Incarnation. To the unbelievers, it seems that the Christian insistence upon the Incarnation dishonors and affronts God—that he descended to the womb of a woman, was fed as a human being, suffered, was weary, was scourged, and finally, with thieves, was crucified and killed.

Anselm replies that it is entirely fitting that God, out of his mercy and lovingkindness, would be willing to die on the cross as a human being freely choosing to pay for man's disobedience.

In the course of the dialogue—which is detailed, sensitive, and thorough—Anselm provides reasons in support of the claims that man could not be saved without being punished for his sins, that satisfaction in the form of punishment and suffering had to be in proportion to the sin, and that only a God-man could possibly render satisfaction for the whole of humanity.

To give himself for all human beings, God had to be fully God and fully human, Anselm argues. It would be impossible for either the divine person or the human person alone to accomplish the salvation of all human persons: ". . . The one who is divine will not do it, because He will not be under obligation to do it; and the one who is human will not do it, because he will not be able to do it." Hence, only a God-man, an individual at once fully divine and fully human, could make satisfaction for man's sin. "For only one who is truly divine can make satisfaction." Anselm explains to Boso, "and only one who is truly human ought to make it."

In all his writings Anselm sought to give credence to the central claims of faith through the persuasive powers of reason. Not all critics agree that he accomplished what he set out to do. But no fair-minded person can fail to acknowledge the intelligence and patient reasonableness of Anselm. If he did not prove his faith, he made it far more appealing than faith alone, without the light of reason, could hope to make it.

IAN P. MCGREAL

Further Reading

Evans, G. R. *Anselm and a New Generation.* Oxford: Clarendon Press, 1980. A notable scholar's effort to make Anselm's accomplishments more understandable and more recognizably remarkable by placing them in the challenging and creative context of the twelfth century.

————. *Anselm and Talking About God.* Oxford: Clarendon Press, 1978. A careful examination of the course of Anselm's thought, proceeding on the assumption that Anselm was exploring what it is we do when we talk about God, and bringing out Anselm's faith that when we talk about God, God is talking to us: the Word determines our language.

Hopkins, Jasper. *A Companion to the Study of St. Anselm.* Minneapolis: University of Minnesota Press, 1972. What Hopkins modestly calls "a handbook for students" is in fact a thorough, serious, scholarly, and effective explication of the content, spirit, and direction of Anselm's works.

McGreal, Ian Philip. *Analyzing Philosophical Arguments.* San Francisco: Chandler, 1967. Anselm's ontological argument is among the ten famous arguments analyzed in this book. The analysis subjects each premise to linguistical analysis and diagrams the argument's logical structure.

Southern, R. W., ed. *The Life of St. Anselm, Archbishop of Canterbury, by Eadmer.* Nelson's Medieval Texts. London, Edinburgh, Paris, Melbourne, Toronto, and New York: Thomas Nelson and Sons, 1962. The Latin text of the monk Eadmer's biography, written from personal knowledge of Anselm because of Eadmer's close association with him, together with an introduction, English translation, and notes by R. W. Southern, author of the companion volume *Saint Anselm and His Biographer.*

————. *Saint Anselm and His Biographer: A Study of Monastic Life and Thought 1059–c. 1130.* Cambridge: Cambridge University Press, 1963. Southern undertakes a detailed examination of Anglo-Norman monastic life and thought by concentrating on the life and intellectual and spiritual growth of Anselm, together with that of Anselm's biographer, Eadmer.

PETER ABELARD

Born: 1079, Le Pallet, near Nantes, France
Died: 1142, Saint Marcel Monastery, near Chalon, France
Major Works: *The Story of My Misfortunes* (1132), *Letters* (1132–1135), *Sic et Non* (1136), *Ethica* (1136), *Theologia* (1140)

Major Ideas

Universals, while not real in and of themselves, have a linguistic and intellectual reality that derives from their participation in particulars.

Authority, while essential, is by itself insufficient to an understanding of dogma; reason must understand dogma by analogies from the material world.

The classics of pre-Christian philosophy are informed by God and contain mystical prefigurations of Christian teaching.

Seemingly opposed views within the authoritative deposit of the faith can often be reconciled by observing the development of a thought throughout the works of the authors in question, by the establishment of best texts, and by the application of hermeneutical dialectic.

Intentions, not deeds, count before God; human works are morally indifferent and do nothing to secure either merit or blame.

The power to bind and loose sins is held only by those discreet and holy bishops who are worthy successors of the apostles.

The life of Peter Abelard has been perceived by many scholars, for all its unpleasant aspects—perhaps because of them—as his most important work. While his scholarship was of great significance and perhaps even looked ahead to the humanism and linguistic logic of later times, it is the often spectacular nature of his life that has captured the modern imagination and made *The Story of My Misfortunes* (actually the first of the *Letters*) by far his most-read work as well as the main fount of information, corroborated to a surprising extent by other sources, about his life.

Not content to be a scholar in the old monastic tradition (in which the transmission of received authoritative opinion dominated scholarship), Abelard played a substantial role in establishing a new intellectual atmosphere in Europe and a new institution for its development and nurturing: the university. Unlike his monkish opponents, he reveled in his intellectual abilities and achievements, to the extent that he himself came later in life to a recognition of his own arrogance. He demanded for himself as well a sensual fulfillment that played a large role in his downfall.

Yet in the end Abelard saw his own life as a patterned repetition of the common Christian experience of the prodigal son, and to explain himself to the world he wrote a celebrated autobiography, the greatest of the twelfth century and arguably the most significant since the *Confessions* of Saint Augustine (upon which it is loosely patterned). (Boethius's *Consolation of Philosophy*, while autobiographical, can hardly be considered an autobiography.)

Abelard was born in rugged pastoral Brittany, into an aristocratic family whose holdings were not far from Nantes. Although the eldest of his father's sons and heir to the vassal rights, in the exercise of which he probably received his earliest training, Abelard renounced the aristocratic life in favor of the scholarly, at which he apparently showed great promise at a young age.

Although it is possible that Abelard studied with Marbod, master of the cathedral school of Angers, and with Roscelin of Compiègne, a well-known dialectician at Loches, little is known of his training before he appeared in Paris about 1100, a student of William of Champeaux, the foremost teacher of his day. According to his own (doubtless colored) account in *The Story of My Misfortunes*, he soon challenged the master, overcame him in dialectical combat, and was forced by the strong negative reaction to his arrogance and presumption to leave Paris. Abelard's conduct in this, the first of his many contentious appearances on the intellectual stage of the twelfth century, set the pattern for his subsequent professional life.

Striking out on his own, Abelard opened a school, first in Melun and then Corbeil, from which he continued his assault on William. Stricken by ill health (perhaps in 1105), Abelard was soon forced to close his school and return home for a convalescence, which apparently lasted until 1108, when he once again appeared in Paris. By then William had left his office at Notre Dame to found a monastery at Saint Victor, just up the Seine from the cathedral that was to achieve great fame in later years and become a center for the study of Abelard's own writings (with an eye in part to their improvement).

Not yet finished with William, Abelard soon entered into renewed contention with him and forced William to abandon his position on universals (characteristics or properties), which William regarded as having a reality above and independent of the individuals within a category. Abelard's position on the problem was developed independently, but along the lines that his studies of the available texts of Aristotle had suggested to him. Adopting the middle ground, essentially that universals have a linguistic reality and are therefore useful, he routed William and his naive realism. As a consequence, William's pupils began to go over to Abelard en masse and the young upstart achieved the first of his great academic triumphs, although he was forced once again by an embittered William to leave Paris for Melun. Soon, however, he returned, and established his school on Mont Sainte Geneviève, just outside the city and the jurisdiction of the Bishop of Paris.

Having ruined William of Champeaux's standing as a teacher (although William was appointed Bishop of Chalons in 1113), Abelard next turned his attention to the venerable Anselm of Laon, Wil-

liam's own teacher and perhaps the most famous master of scriptural studies of the time, whose lectures he began to attend after a brief return home occasioned by his parents' decision to enter the religious life. Rebuked by Anselm's disciples for neglecting the master's lectures, which he soon came to view with contempt, Abelard was challenged to give a lecture himself. Choosing a difficult text from Ezekiel, he spoke the following day with such skill that he was urged by his fellow students to continue along the same lines, which he did to enthusiastic reception.

His success soon boomeranged, however, for an indignant Anselm, master of the schools in Laon, forbade Abelard to teach there. Forced to leave, Abelard returned to Paris, where he acquired the prestigious and profitable position of *magister scholarum* at Notre Dame. Arrogant as always, he soon established himself as one of the greatest teachers of dialectic and theology in France. At this juncture in his life, around 1118, secure in his profession and perhaps even modestly well-to-do, Abelard became private tutor to Heloise, the niece of a certain Canon Fulbert.

The Story of My Misfortunes

The story of the subsequent affair between Abelard and Heloise, a disastrous phase of his life for him personally and as a philosopher, is told in *The Story of My Misfortunes* and expanded in later correspondence between the two lovers. (The authenticity of the letters has been questioned—at the very least, they were subsequently edited and reworked, perhaps by both Abelard and Heloise.) The tutor cynically set out to seduce his seventeen-year-old charge and entered into a physical relationship with her that soon became known to all, including, eventually, Fulbert. That the affair could have remained a secret seems impossible, especially in light of the poems and songs that Abelard himself says he wrote to celebrate their love (these works, which were apparently sung in the streets, have not survived). A son, Astrolabius, was born to the couple and a wedding, celebrated secretly so as not to weaken Abelard's position as a philosopher, did occur. Fulbert, however, humiliated and angered by the course of events, desired knowledge of the marriage to be made public. Thwarted in his wishes by his niece's public denial that a marriage had occurred and by Abelard's sequestering of his wife in the convent at Argenteuil, Fulbert avenged himself upon his new nephew-in-law by hiring a gang of thugs to castrate him.

Disgraced before the world, Abelard retreated, probably in 1119, to the Benedictine monastery at Saint Denis, where he promptly offended his fellow monks by assailing their lax conduct. Soon, however, his students pursued and convinced him to teach again and he began a new chapter in his spectacular career, concentrating now specifically upon theology (to which word he largely gave its modern meaning). The first task he set himself was to explain the nature of the Trinity by logic and reason, by analogies and similes, and not by appeal to authority (the standard method of the day). He developed, for example, the famous explanation of the Trinity by analogy with a piece of brass, from which is begotten the seal, from which proceeds the act of sealing.

The resulting work, *De unitate et trinitate divina*, created an enormous uproar that led to its condemnation and burning without prior discussion by the assembled authorities, at the Synod of Soissons in 1121, where Abelard, denied a defense, was himself obligated to throw the offending work upon the fire. (This study was reworked and retitled several times during the course of Abelard's life, appearing also as the *Theologia "summi boni,"* the *Theologia christiana*, and the first part of the *Theologia*, his major theological text. Most of Abelard's works underwent constant revision and expansion throughout his career and are consequently difficult to date. Dates given above are approximate and refer to final versions.)

Abelard's insistence upon the role of reason in reaffirming authority and in clarifying truth is the central tenet in his teaching and is directly responsible for both his condemnations. It is precisely this feature of his scholarship that has given him a special position in the history of philosophy, for he was working well in advance of the recovery of the "lost" works of Aristotle, which were to substantiate his approach. It must be kept in mind that Abelard never developed a consistent, systematic body of thought or a unique contribution. His concern was methodological.

The conduct of the synod was clearly not in accord with the standards for church investigations, but such was the scandalous nature of Abelard's reputation that its judgment was allowed to stand. From the perspective of the present, it is clear that Abelard was condemned for his style and for the threat to the study of received authority that his writings and teachings were perceived to be, especially by the followers of Anselm of Laon, two of whom (Alberic of Rheims and Lotulf of Novara) were instrumental in calling the synod.

The judgment of Soissons also called for Abelard's incarceration in the monastery at Saint Medard, but after a very short time he was reprieved by the papal legate and allowed to return to Saint Denis. There he immediately angered his fellow monks yet again, this time by attacking the foundation legend of the monastery. Eventually Abelard was allowed by Abbot Suger, newly installed at Saint Denis, to live a solitary life in a suitable place of his own choice. Near Troyes, on a plot of ground that had been presented to him, he built a small chapel out of reeds and straw, named it the Paraclete—the Comforter—and began the next controversial episode in his life.

Sic et Non

Once again the disciples flocked eagerly to hear the voice of the master and Abelard found himself at the head of a sizable school. The students constructed suitable buildings and soon Abelard was complaining that the tasks of administering such a large establishment were taking away time from more important intellectual tasks. Nevertheless, this period (c. 1121–26) appears to have been very fruitful, apparently producing an early version of the *Sic et Non*, the *Theologia christiana*, parts of the *Theology*, and other works.

The *Sic et Non* is the work for which Abelard is best remembered. The idea of the book is novel, although not as revolutionary as modern critics have sometimes perceived it to be. Certainly Abelard's contemporaries seem not to have been perturbed by either the content or the method (which was different and anticipated subsequent scholastic practice). The text comprises opposing views on the same subject by different church authorities, prefaced by an introduction in which Abelard suggests ways in which the apparent inconsistencies and contradictions can be reconciled. We would call these methods (word study, consideration of context, concern for the best text, comparison of texts) "philological" today.

Abelard's enemies had not, however, forgotten him. Recognizing that their adversary still prospered, they put him in desperate fear of another assault upon his theories, another judgment of anathema, another possible imprisonment—or worse. Receiving an invitation to become abbot of the monastery of Saint Gildas de Ruys in Brittany, Abelard therefore dissolved the school at the Paraclete and departed for what he hoped would be the safety of obscurity.

Although he did find temporary refuge from his theological foes, Abelard found himself now confronted by yet another type of deadly enemy: the monks of Saint Gildas. Apparently having become accustomed to a slothful and brutal version of unreformed monkhood, these reacted viciously to their new abbot. During his tenure, which lasted into the mid-1130s, Abelard's monks threatened him with death upon at least two occasions, once inadvertently killing a companion who ate poisoned food that Abelard, not feeling hungry, had declined.

During this same period, the monastery at Saint Denis reasserted its rights to the property of the convent at Argenteuil, where Heloise was then abbess. Abelard thus donated the establishment of the Paraclete to her order; the gift was confirmed in 1131. For a time, Abelard seems to have enjoyed a renewed acquaintance with Heloise until, the threat of scandal looming over their heads, the relationship was again broken off. During his tenure at Saint Gildas, Abelard composed the correspondence to Heloise, which, after having discussed autobiographical materials, dealt with a number of such

monkish issues as a rule for the nuns and a history of their order (the correspondence was gathered after his death into a single volume, probably by Heloise, and apparently was used as a history of the order and its founder). He also wrote for the nuns at Argenteuil some one hundred Latin hymns, perhaps thirty-five sermons, and numbers of tracts on theological issues brought up by Heloise in her letters. It was a fruitful if difficult time in Abelard's life.

Bitterly dissatisfied with the abbacy and in danger of his life from the recalcitrant monks, Abelard was allowed to leave Saint Gildas, while retaining the title of abbot, sometime in the middle 1130s.

Ethica

Little is known of Abelard's next few years until he reappeared in Paris in 1136, having completed the *Sic et Non* and possibly the *Ethica*. The latter, also known as *Scito te ipsum,* caused a degree of furor. Developing the idea that the conduct of good men is generally motivated by error and ignorance, he concluded that human goodness is quite apart from human intention. All that is necessary is that men act with good intentions, for thus they show that they do not hold God in contempt (such being the true basis of sin). Therefore it follows that even the crucifiers of Christ cannot be considered evil men, as they were simply carrying out their orders in support of what they considered to be a just system of government.

Needless to say, Abelard's contemporaries had no little trouble with the argument concerning intentions, although they ultimately accepted it. The early versions of the *Ethica* also consider the notion that only good servants of God have the power to administer the sacraments efficaciously. This notion Abelard abandoned in the final text, having no doubt experienced considerable pressure from advocates of the church's view that the sacraments have power apart from the moral qualities of the person administering them.

About 1136, Abelard began teaching in Paris again, at least off and on (his student John of Salisbury provides the information), which led to the last of the great misfortunes in his life, the condemnation at Sens that was orchestrated by Bernard of

Clairvaux in 1140. His extraordinary popularity as a teacher continued to attract large numbers of students, among them such future luminaries as John of Salisbury, Otto von Freising, Arnold of Brescia, and Roland Bandinelli, who would later become Pope Alexander III. During this time, he wrote a commentary on Saint Paul, a discussion of various scriptural problems for Heloise, and several glosses on Porphyry, Aristotle, and Boethius.

Bernard, abbot of the Cistercian monastery at Clairvaux, proved to be the most deadly of all Abelard's enemies. A leading proponent of reform, Bernard had set the Cistercians on a collision course with the monastic establishment by his criticisms of their lax conduct (in particular, he was dismayed by the abolition of labor from Benedictine practice) and by the threat he posed to the notion of monastic stability (monks flocked to the Cistercians from other orders). Along with such other reformers as Saint Norbert of Xanten and William of Thierry, Bernard set out to return monasticism to a purer model, which he perceived not only in the original Rule of Saint Benedict but also in the practices of the hermit monks of the third and fourth centuries as they had come to be celebrated in hagiographical tradition. In 1136, dismayed by the renewed popular success of Abelard's teaching, Bernard set out to discredit once and for all one whom he perceived as a scandalous and arrogant nuisance who had done great damage to the Church.

Alerted to Abelard's latest teaching by a letter from William of Thierry that contained a refutation of thirteen alleged errors (drawn, apparently, from the *Theologia* and an unidentified work by one of Abelard's disciples), Bernard read the *Theologia*, the strange title of which he found especially repugnant (before Abelard, the word referred to the Greco-Roman pantheon, what we call classical mythology). Bernard's mystical approach to the knowledge of God represented a tradition of ecclesiastical living premised upon the renunciation of the world and all it contains, including human intellectual pretension.

Confronted by Bernard, Abelard was apparently willing to adjust his ideas to a considerable extent. The final version of the *Theologia* is a response to Bernard's criticisms and an attempt to defuse them. Bernard, however, was intent on finishing off Abelard once and for all, to which end he brought about the Synod of Sens, where Abelard was badly outmaneuvered and again condemned. Deciding to go to Rome and appeal the judgment to Pope Innocent II, Abelard was met en route by Peter the Venerable (the abbot of Cluny who had had his own problems with Bernard) and was informed that the pope had confirmed the condemnation. Peter urged him to accept events and offered him refuge in a daughter-house of Cluny at Saint Marcel, where, having been reconciled with Bernard, Abelard died, probably on April 21, 1142. During this last period, he may have composed the *Hexaemeron* for Heloise and her nuns and the *Dialogue between a Philosopher, a Jew and a Christian*, although some consider these works productions of the last sojourn in Paris.

ROBERT J. MEINDL

Further Reading

Gilson, Étienne. *Heloise and Abelard*. Translated by L. K. Shook. Ann Arbor: University of Michigan Press, 1960. The most famous scholarly account of the affair.

Grane, Leif. *Peter Abelard: Philosophy and Christianity in the Middle Ages*. Translated by Frederick and Christine Crowley. New York: Harcourt, Brace & World, 1970. An excellent survey of the man and his time.

Luscombe, D. E. *The School of Peter Abelard*. Cambridge: Cambridge University Press, 1969.

A solid study of Abelard's influence on early Scholasticism.

Robertson, D. W., Jr. *Abelard and Heloise*. New York: Dial Press, 1972. A vigorous and interesting account that shows at great length how later ages perceived the pair.

Southern, R. W. "The Letters of Abelard and Heloise," in *Medieval Humanism*. New York: Harper & Row, 1970. Places the famous correspondence in the context of twelfth-century letter-writing.

SAINT BERNARD OF CLAIRVAUX

Born: 1090, Fontaines-les-Dijon, France
Died: 1153, Abbey of Our Lady of Clairvaux, Burgundy, France
Major Works: *On Loving God* (1123), *On Grace and Free Will* (1128), *Sermons on the Song of Songs* (1136–53), *On Consideration* (1148–52)

Major Ideas

There is a natural simplicity in the very substance of the soul; for the soul, it is the same to be as to live, but it is not the same thing to be as to live well or to live happily; nevertheless the soul can ascend to this.

For God, to be is to live happily.

The soul is simple, immortal, and free; these cannot be lost but can be covered over.

The soul becomes like what it desires—the simple soul becomes dispersed by its multiple desires; the immortal soul desiring changeable and perishing things becomes vascillating and fearful of losing what it desires, and its essential freedom is chained by its desires.

Perhaps no one man has had such a great influence on his age as Saint Bernard of Clairvaux. Though Bernard's views remained faithful to those of the early Christian fathers, his powerful personality and electrifying style left an unforgettable impact on his own and future generations. His standards and concepts of the goal and purpose of the just society and the individual's relation to it have greatly influenced all subsequent Christian thinking.

At the age of twenty-two, Bernard came to Citeaux with thirty followers. Three years later he founded Clairvaux. The rest of his life as well as his personal identity were forged by his new and preferred title: abbot.

Bernard made Clairvaux the motherhouse of nearly half of the houses of the Cistercian order. He wrote, preached, and infected with his ardent zeal both those within and outside his cloister. He shaped the spirituality of the new monastic movement. At the same time, he was a leader of Christendom in the twelfth century in so many aspects that it would be difficult to find a parallel in any other similar period.

In 1228, he inspired the writing of the rule for the newly established military order of the Knights of the Temple. In 1130, Bernard entered the conflict concerning the election of the pope and determined the legitimate one. In 1140, he faced Abelard and brought about his condemnation at the Council of Sens. In 1146, he preached the Second Crusade, convincing both Louis VII of France and Conrad III of Germany to join with their nobles in the holy war.

Bernard left a voluminous correspondence in which he reminded popes of their duties, exhorted cardinals, patriarchs, and bishops, and admonished kings and princes.

Bernard first spelled out the goal of human life in his treatise (actually an amplified letter) *On Loving God*. He struggled more deeply with the interplay of human nature and divine grace in a more mature work, *On Grace and Free Will*. But it is in the later *Sermons on the Song of Songs*, written in the last decade of his life (especially sermons 81 and 82) and in his ultimate work, *On Consideration*, that he most clearly set forth his Christian anthropology.

Faith Seeking Understanding

Bernard begins with a Biblical perspective, the text that so profoundly formed his mind and even his vocabulary. His task was always *fides quaerens intellectum* (faith seeking understanding). Human persons were first made in the image and likeness of God. They were made not in the very image of God as is the Son of God, but *to* the image of God, dependently participating in the divinity. When the primogenitors of the human race sought to be like God in their own right, they lost not the indelible image of God that is of our very nature but their

93

likeness to him, their rectitude. The tragic result, human unhappiness, lies in this: The image within us, which consists in simplicity, immortality, and freedom of will, is constantly confronted with the disfigurement of our duplicity and our servitude to sin and death.

The whole aim of the human life is to free oneself from false ambitions and unnecessary pursuits so that we may be purified and brought to perfect union with God by the recovery of our lost likeness to him. When we seek things that are below ourselves because of their mutability and corruptibility, we ourselves become unsettled, restless, seeking change, unsatisfied, and unhappy. The many exercises and observances of Christian life are to make us keenly aware of such a miserable state of division and to lead us to seek the divine and immutable and to open ourselves to the action of the divine. As we are healed by our presence to the divine presence and freed from our unlikeness and all the fear that goes with seeking the illusive and ephemeral, confidence and love grows and the image of the divine in us is more and more fully restored. Bernard does not hesitate to promise, as the *normal term* of a life of simplicity, a perfect union of wills with God by love, which he calls the mystical marriage.

The human person is made in the resemblance of God but is not equal to God. For God, to be (*esse*) is to live happily (*beatum vivere*)—the highest and most pure simplicity. For the human, to be (*esse*) is to live (*vivere*). And this makes it possible for the human to ascend, by God's action, to participate in the divine's *beatum vivere*.

The primogenitors of the human race did not want to accept their complete dependence on the divine. Seeking to establish themselves as the source of their being and of their being happily, they suffered inhibiting consequences, which they passed on to their progeny. The simplicity of the human soul remains truly unimpaired in its essence. It is covered over only by duplicity, deceit, simulation, and hypocrisy. The resulting contradiction between our essential simplicity and the duplicity engendered by sin confront each other, causing confusion and pain. Desire for the earthly, rather than

for the mutable and mortal, makes us like what we desire: darksome and unstable. We have put on the mortality of sin and death.

What we desire to possess, we fear to lose. This fear has "discolored" our liberty, covered it over and concealed it. Our liberty is held in the bonds of our fear. If we desired nothing—simply loved God whom we possess—we would fear nothing, we would be filled with confidence and remain free, strong, and beautiful.

Everything has been "reduplicated": our simplicity by duplicity, our immortality by the death of sin and of the body, our freedom by the desire of material things, our likeness to God by unlikeness. Our essential goodness has been defiled, but not destroyed, by accidentals, making us not only unlike God but unlike our true selves. In this, Bernard vindicates the perduring essential goodness of human nature.

The Return to God

The first step in our return to God and to our true selves is to know ourselves. The labor of our lives is to be our true selves, returning to the simplicity, immortality, and freedom that belong to us. Bernard goes on to develop the steps: First we come to know the truth about ourselves—sincerity; then we accept it—meekness, self-effacement, humility; then we rid ourselves of all that is useless—mortification: mortification of the lower appetites through external simplicity, of the internal sense and intellect through study and methods of prayer, and of the will (which is most important) through obedience or concurrence with the divine will and integration into the common will.

We are capable of a twofold ignorance: of ourselves and of God. If we truly know ourselves, we will be humble and fear God. This is the beginning of wisdom, the opposite of pride. If we know God, we will be filled with love and hope, possess him, and come to the perfection of wisdom. Without this knowledge of God, in knowing ourselves we could despair. Intellectual simplicity allows us to be taught by God. Contemplation, the highest and most complete form of intellectual simplicity and the realization of our potential divinization, is the "extreme simplicity of an intuition," beyond all concepts, images and pictures, phantasms and discursive acts of the mind. There is no figure, there is the direct contact of love, the created effect of love: *facies formans*. The fact that intellectual simplicity is brought to its fullness through the unity brought about by love leads naturally to the consideration of the simplification of the will.

Bernard notes in his "Third Sermon for the Eastertime" that there is a twofold leprosy that can infect the human heart: attachment to one's own will and attachment to one's own judgment. There can and should be a good self-love that seeks one's own perfection according to the will of God. The self-will that is leprous is the intention simply to please the self ("intention" here understood as the actual movement of the will toward the object of its selfish desires). This self-will is healed by concurrence with the divine plan made evident through the nature of the human. Such concurrence seeks the common good through love. It abandons all internal argument. The will of the individual becomes one with the common will.

Attachment to one's own judgment is the more pernicious. The more strongly we are so attached, the more we can be deceived, setting up our own standard, and unable to see our self-deception. We are freed from this by following the example of Christ, who submitted his human will, however good, to the will of his Father. For Bernard, the will is the highest faculty, hence unity of wills (love) produces the highest and most perfect simplicity. It is ultimately the work of the Divine Spirit and it will be realized perfectly only in heaven.

The restoration of human dignity in reestablishing in us the divine likeness begins in self-knowledge and humility and climbs through obedience to the divine plan for the perfection of human solidarity in love to produce that unity and peace by which the divine blessedness is reflected not only in the individual soul but also in the community, in the human family as a whole. Once a certain degree of perfection in this social simplicity is arrived at on earth, God is pleased to bend down and raise up the individuals who most further this unity by their humility and love to a closer and far more intimate union with him. Thus humanity is crowned in its mystics.

According to Bernard in his treatise *On Loving God*, we are first caught up in self-love. Then we begin to love God because we perceive how good he is to us. As we become more and more aware of his goodness, we begin to love him in himself. Finally, we come to be so unified with God in love that we love even ourselves only because he loves us. This complete unity of will with God is the consummation of the human journey back to its true self.

It may seem a bit paradoxical that we attain a more perfect self-identity when we are more fully absorbed in this union. But the essence of the human soul is to be like God. We are most truly ourselves when we are identified with him, when we lose our own will and are one will, one spirit with him. We come to forget ourselves, all our own wishes and desires, and come to have only the wishes and desires of God. This, then, is the ultimate realization of human potential, Bernard avers: becoming one spirit with the God of infinite love.

M. BASIL PENNINGTON, O.C.S.O.

Further Reading

Gilson, Étienne. *The Mystical Theology of Saint Bernard*. Kalamazoo, Mich.: Cistercian Publications, 1990. One of the best studies of the theology of Bernard of Clairvaux, Gilson's book also does a good job of identifying the author's sources.

Leclercq, Jean. *Bernard of Clairvaux and the Cistercian Spirit*. Kalamazoo, Mich.: Cistercian Publications, 1973. A concise study by the editor of the critical edition of Bernard's works.

Leclercq places Bernard in historical, social, and philosophical context and indicates his ongoing impact.

Pennington, M. Basil, *Saint Bernard: Studies Commemorating the Eighth Centenary of His Canonization*. Kalamazoo, Mich.: Cistercian Publications, 1974. Some of the best scholars in Bernard studies collaborate to give an up-to-date perspective on the saint in light of recent scholarship.

MOSES MAIMONIDES

Born: 1135, Córdova, Spain
Died: 1204, Cairo, Egypt
Major Works: *Commentary on the Mishneh* (1158–68), *Mishneh Torah* (1178), *Guide of the Perplexed* (1185–90)

Major Ideas

The study of philosophy and traditional Jewish law can be brought into harmony.
The existence of God is subject to rational demonstration.
Unity, incorporeality, and priority are qualities of God.
Prophecy is a degree of mental and moral perfection to which all may aspire.
The entire Torah is a divine revelation.
The highest faculty of the soul is the intellect, and its highest function is to discern the true and the false.
Kindness, righteousness, and judgment should motivate the moral life.
The purpose of life is to convert the potentiality of perfection into the actuality of it.

Responding to the challenges posed by the widespread rationalism of the twelfth century, Moses Maimonides sought to do for Judaism what Muslim philosophers and Christian scholastics were to accomplish for their religions. He confirmed rationally the beliefs of Judaism, submitting them to the rigors of philosophical methodology while at the same time insisting on the centrality of divine wisdom.

Maimonides could not have failed to be influenced by Muslim philosophy; he was born in 1135 in Córdova, Spain, which since the eighth century had been the capital of the Umayyad emirs and caliphs of Spain and was a brilliant cultural center for Jews, Christians, and Muslims. Known as Maimonides by Latin authors and as Musa ibn Maimun by speakers of Arabic, he had been given the Jewish name of Mosheh ben Maimon. He was born into a family that for eight generations had been rabbis and rabbinical judges. Although Spain offered a degree of tolerance for Jews that did not prevail elsewhere in Europe, the advent of the Almoravid movement in Islam meant persecution for both Jews and Christians. In 1148, the Almohads conquered Córdova, imposing on Jews and Christians restrictions that prohibited them from public worship. As a result, many non-Muslims died as martyrs, or professed Islam on the surface while

secretly practicing their own religion, or went into exile.

Among those who fled persecution was the family of Maimonides, wandering in Spain and North Africa before settling in Fez in 1160, where they remained for five years. During this time, Maimonides cultivated the intellectual life, showing a marked propensity for science, mathematics, and logic as well as engaging in study of the Talmud and even writing a commentary on the Mishneh, the code of Jewish law. From Fez the family sailed for Palestine, where Maimonides traveled to Jerusalem and Hebron. Life in Palestine was less than congenial for Jews; hence the family moved on to Egypt, where, in spite of the father's death soon thereafter, they found a home in the large Jewish community.

Commentary on the Mishneh and the Mishneh Torah

Continuing his scholarship, Maimonides completed the *Commentary on the Mishneh* in 1168; he also was appointed judge of the rabbinical court. In support of rabbinic authority over individual interpretation, Maimonides sided with the Rabbanite party in Cairo, and in the rabbinic tradition of the Talmud he earned a living not from interpreting the Talmud but from the practice of medicine. It is thought that Maimonides had learned medicine from the texts of Hippocrates, Galen, Razi, Avenzoar, and Avicenna, among others in both the Greek and Roman and the Arabic and Persian traditions, and that he had clinical experience in Cairo. More certain is his position as a physician at court. Maimonides was famed not only as a physician but also as a philosopher. With the completion of his code of Jewish law, the *Mishneh Torah*, in 1178, his legal opinions were sought widely; as a noted Jewish jurist, he answered hundreds of queries from around the world, including Yemen, Baghdad, Aleppo, Damascus, Jerusalem, Alexandria, and Marseilles.

Maimonides's writings reveal his preoccupation with approaching rationally a religion that was based largely on law and tradition: the study of Torah and its interpretation as formalized in the Talmud, the tradition of law, or *halakah*, and nonlegal matters, which form the *aggadah*. The *Commentary on the Mishneh*, started in 1158 when Maimonides was only twenty-two years old, is a rabbinic commentary on parts of the Talmud. Originally written in Arabic and translated into Hebrew during the following two centuries, the work is constituted of three main parts. The first part is an introduction to the study of oral law, its origin in the revelation at Sinai, and its subsequent transmission with interpretation. The second, a treatise on the tenth chapter of the Tractate Sanhedrin (*Perek Helek*), contains thirteen principles of faith, which Maimonides believed all Israelites should accept. The commentary on "Sayings of the Fathers" (*Pirke Avot*), commonly known as the "Eight Chapters," is the third part, a psychological and ethical treatise that in its analysis of the soul and its faculties recognizes free will and the need to honor the golden mean.

Following the conventions of rabbinic literature, Maimonides wrote the *Book of the Commandments* as a summary and classification of the 613 divine commandments referred to in the Talmud. He makes the interesting distinction between rabbinic and biblical law, maintaining that, since the former are the result of scriptural exegesis, they ought not

be included in the enumeration. His concern for law is consummately demonstrated in the *Mishneh Torah*, a fourteen-volume codification of Jewish law written in Hebrew. Maimonides's extraordinary talent for codification enabled him to give a concise form to material that was confusing and complex. Throughout the work is seen his desire to fuse practical and theoretical concerns and to employ the rational tools of philosophy to understand traditional law at its deepest level of meaning.

Guide of the Perplexed

Maimonides's reputation as a philosopher rests in large part on the *Guide of the Perplexed*, written in Arabic between 1185 and 1190 and translated into Hebrew by Samuel ibn Tibbon shortly before his death in 1204. This translation as well as another done after the author's death were the basis for the Latin translations that made Maimonides familiar to the Christian community of philosophers. Although composed for one of Maimonides's students, the *Guide* was intended for religious intellectuals whose dedication to philosophy on the one hand and belief in Jewish law on the other seemed contradictory. Maimonides's purpose was to prove that reason and revelation were compatible and that the person who believes in the heart need not sacrifice intellectual rigor. On the contrary, Maimonides demonstrated in his own exegetical methodology that reason can illumine meanings that remain hidden from the untrained mind. In this endeavor he was indebted to Greek philosophy, especially that of Aristotle.

In addition to the major works, Maimonides wrote responsa, letters, several treatises, such as that on martyrdom directed to the persecuted Jews in Morocco, as well as ten tracts on medicine.

The Thirteen Principles

The thirteen principles that Maimonides set down in the *Commentary on the Mishneh* are an appropriate framework for his philosophical edifice, expressive of themes and issues that appear throughout his writings. The principles can be arranged thematically in three groups: the first concerns God in his existence and essence; the second, the law; the third, beliefs about divine providence and eschatology.

With respect to the first group, Maimonides states that the first principle of faith is the existence of God, which, like other principles, is subject to rational proof. In the twenty-six propositions that appear in the *Guide* to support five main proofs of God's existence, Maimonides reveals his indebtedness to Greek philosophy, as when he posits the existence of a Prime Mover that is indivisible and unchangeable, moving neither of its own accord nor accidentally. In related discussions, he affirms that God created the universe *ex nihilo*; that he is the cause of everything that exists; that the universe had a beginning and is not eternal; that creation is divided into the pure intelligences, the spheres, and transient earthly beings.

Maimonides's belief in God as the cause of everything that exists led inevitably to questions about the nature and cause of evil. God, he argues, is not responsible for the three kinds of evils that affect human beings. The first kind of evil, which is that the body has deficiencies and degenerates, has its source in the nature of change, without which the human species would not continue to exist. Evil also originates within human beings, as when they inflict harm on one another. The greatest number of evils, however, are those that an individual brings upon himself when he indulges in excessive behavior, such as overeating and drinking, bringing injury not only to the body but also to the soul, which, residing in the body, is necessarily affected by bodily changes.

Moving from the question of God's existence to that of his essence, Maimonides shows the impossibility of describing divine attributes except by way of negating them; hence, the more one knows of God, the less can be affirmed of him. Nonetheless, Maimonides speaks to the unity, incorporeality, and priority of God in the second, third, and fourth principles of faith. To support belief in the unity of God, Maimonides advances several proofs, among which is the argument from the fact that the universe is one whole. The incorporeality of

God follows from his unity; that is, since every corporeal object is composed of matter and form, God, as absolute unity, cannot be corporeal. The priority of God means that he is timeless and spaceless; there can be no relation between God and time or space, for both are accidents connected with motion, a condition to which material bodies are subject but which does not affect God, who is immaterial.

Having rationally established the existence of God and addressed his essence, Maimonides declares as the fifth principle of faith that God alone is to be worshipped, implying, in the spirit and letter of the Torah, the prohibition of idolatry. Worship is primarily prayer, which ranges from the petitions of vocal prayer to the loving communion of man and God in ecstasy. Ecstatic union admits no intermediary whatsoever, the presence of which, in such form as an image of wood or stone, would be idolatry. Related to idolatry is superstition, which asserts that phenomena like stars and amulets can affect human destiny.

The sixth principle of faith is entry into the second group of principles, that which treats prophecy. Maimonides believed that prophecy was not a gift that God bestowed on a few individuals but rather a degree of mental and moral perfection that is open to all and for which all may strive. By their own will, human beings create the gift of prophecy as potentiality; God converts the potential prophecy into actuality. Rejecting the views that God selects any person to prophesy and that prophecy is a supernatural faculty, Maimonides maintains both that prophecy is a natural faculty and that the will of God makes real the possibility of prophecy. The prophet, perfected in moral virtues and intellectual discipline, is recognized by his ability to tell the future in detail rather than by an ability to work miracles.

The greatest of the prophets was Moses, a belief that Maimonides formulated as the seventh principle and which he supported with four reasons. First, whereas God spoke with other prophets by an intermediary, with Moses he communed directly; second, whereas other prophets were inspired in a state of sleep, Moses received God's word in the daytime when he was awake; third, whereas other prophets were struck down physically and with terror when they were inspired, Moses experienced neither terror nor confusion; fourth, whereas other prophets were inspired only when God so willed it, Moses was able to set the time for God to inspire him.

The belief in prophecy leads logically to the belief in the Torah as divine revelation, which Maimonides stated as the eighth principle. Aware of the Muslim claim that the Koran was the unchanged, original word of God, Maimonides stressed that the whole of the Torah was revelation and, in the ninth principle, that it was immutable. The divine origin of the Torah and its immutability necessitate study of the Torah, specifically an exegesis that is sensitive to language, such that one can move from the literal meaning of the text to the allegorical one. Explaining the kinds of commandments in the Torah, Maimonides shows that as a complete guide to life, their purpose is to ensure the well-being of the mind and soul and to bring joy to human beings.

In the third group of principles, Maimonides considers the relationship of God and human beings in terms of divine providence, reward and punishment, and eschatology. In the tenth principle of faith, he states that divine providence extends only to rational creation and that each person has an individual share of divine providence in proportion to his perfection. According to the eleventh principle of faith, reward and punishment are temporary expedients to motivate people until such time as, advanced in perfection, they are motivated purely by love.

The final state of human beings is the theme of the twelfth and thirteenth principles of faith: Maimonides posits belief in the coming of the Messiah and in the resurrection of the dead. The Messiah will be a prophet, greater than all the prophets except for Moses; appearing first in Israel, he will be recognized as such by the fact that all earthly kings and their kingdoms will be stirred by the news of his coming. One proof of his identity as messiah is that he will rebuild the temple on its site and bring together again the dispersed Jews. Maimonides also believed in the resurrection of the dead, but he appears not to refer to the body.

Although Maimonides clarified the specific and practical application of laws, he was careful to counsel that their larger purpose was to train and guide a person to perfection. With respect to perfection, he asserted the need for perfection of possessions, bodily constitution, and moral virtues, but the ultimate end for human beings is the perfection of rational virtues, that is, the conception of intelligibles that teach true opinions about the divine things. Thus perfected, a human being fulfills the purpose of life, which is to convert the potentiality of perfection into the actuality of it, directing his energies to the imitation of God's ways by knowing and loving God and by keeping in view the moral virtues of lovingkindness, righteousness, and judgment.

The influence of Maimonides on his contemporaries was enormous, as it has been for subsequent generations of thinkers, among them Aquinas and Spinoza. It is said that Aquinas systematized the syntheses of Maimonides, thus providing a solid foundation for Catholic Scholasticism, while Spinoza, carrying to the limits the implications of synthesis, revealed the vulnerability of the links joining philosophy and scripture, thus imperiling the reconciliation of reason and revelation that Maimonides had accomplished through a lifetime of study and discipline.

MARY E. GILES

Further Reading

Bujis, Joseph A., ed. *Maimonides. A Collection of Critical Essays.* Notre Dame, Ind.: University of Notre Dame Press, 1988. The essays treat issues of interpretation, epistemology, metaphysics, ethics, law, and politics.

Cohen, Rev. A., *The Teachings of Maimonides.* New York: KTAV, 1968. Arranged thematically, the selections are drawn from a variety of Maimonides's writings.

Goodman, Lenn Evan. *Rambam: Readings in the Philosophy of Moses Maimonides.* New York: Viking Press, 1976. The general introduction as well as the introductions to selections and analyses of them make this volume helpful.

Leaman, Oliver. *Moses Maimonides.* New York and London: Routledge, 1990. In this new study, Maimonides emerges as the outstanding figure in Islamic civilization.

Twersky, Isadore, ed. *A Maimonides Reader.* New York: Behrman House, 1972. A major scholar of Maimonides brings together commentary, interpretation, and text in an invaluable volume.

SAINT BONAVENTURE

Born: 1217 (not 1221 as formerly believed), Bagnorea (now Bagnoregio), near Orvieto, Italy
Died: 1274, Lyons, France
Major Works: *Commentaries on the Four Books of Sentences of Master Peter Lombard* (1250–52), *Breviloquium* (1257), *The Journey of the Mind into God* (1259), *On the Reduction of the Arts to Theology* (date uncertain), *The Legend of St. Francis* (*Legenda Major*, 1261), *Conferences on the Hexaëmeron* (1273)

Major Ideas

Traditional Christian doctrines are correct, and innovations are erroneous.

The wish to introduce new doctrines is the expression of a bad moral character, and so is curiosity (the wish to find things out independently of their relevance to salvation).

People need discipline not only of their conduct but also of their intellect, including submission to proper authority and extending even to mortification of the intellect.

All truth is in Christ: There can be no truths that are unrelated to Christ, and nothing can ever be correctly understood, even about the natural world, if Christ is left out.

Christ contains all truth because Christ contains the creative archetypes (called "exemplars" or "exemplary ideas") of all real things.

The natural world is a mirror of God, and by looking in this mirror we can see God, or, more precisely, we can see some of the exemplars, all of which are in God.

The soul's journey to God begins by looking in this way into the mirror of nature, and then proceeds by turning first inward into our own souls, and then upward into God.

To prove the existence of God, we do not have to finish the ascent; a complete proof is available at every level, even the lowest.

In the Franciscan friary in Bagnorea, Italy, around the year 1230, an oblate boy called "Giovanni di Fidanza" began his primary education. Later on in the 1230s, this Giovanni was a student at the University of Paris, and having become a master of arts, he joined the Franciscan order in 1243 or 1244, taking the name "Bonaventura." He made rapid progress in the university, the order, and the Church, becoming a theology master, apparently in 1253, the head of the Franciscan order in 1257, and a bishop and cardinal in 1273. He was regarded by many as a model of good conduct, though he did not practice mortification of the body, because, as he explained, his health was precarious. He died in 1274, was canonized as a saint in 1482, and was named a doctor of the Church in 1587.

Saint Bonaventure and the Three Obnoxious Doctrines

When Saint Bonaventure was a student, and later a master, in the University of Paris, there was a pre-requisite for the theology course called the "arts course." The arts course began with grammar, logic, and rhetoric, and took six years (students could begin at fourteen). From the point of view of the faculty of theology, the arts course was just a preparation for the theology course. Some students and masters in the faculty of arts, however, were becoming interested in arts subjects for their own sake. One reason was that more and more previously unavailable works of Aristotle, commentaries on Aristotle, and works influenced by Aristotle were reaching western Europe. These books seemed to relate to the arts course more than to the theology course, where the main nonbiblical author was Saint Augustine. However, they were more advanced and more interesting than the basic subjects that the faculty of arts had covered before.

Like most theologians of his generation, Saint Bonaventure himself made extensive use of Aristotle. It has been estimated that he makes over a thousand references to Aristotle in his *Commentary on the Sentences.* Nevertheless, he was worried about the influence of Aristotle on undisciplined minds. In his view, members of the faculty of theology were obliged to correct members of the faculty of arts where they deviated from the truth. A sign of something's being true was that Saint Augustine had said it; for, Saint Bonaventure says, it is absurd to suppose so great a church doctor (teacher) to have been mistaken.

Sometimes the masters in the faculty of arts attempted to escape chastisement by saying that they were only historians finding out what Aristotle thought, not followers of Aristotle who agreed with him. An alternative, more ambitious defense was to assert that there were two different subjects: faith, which tells us what is *true* and is the province of the faculty of theology; and reason, which tells us what is *necessary* and is the province of the faculty of arts. (The people who said this seem to have assumed that a sign of something's being necessary was that Aristotle had said it. Emancipation from dependence on authority is not an easy goal.) Then, if only it could be made out that what was necessary could be different from what was true, there would be no occasion for conflict between the two subjects. Outraged conservatives like Saint Bonaventure referred to this as the "double-truth" theory.

Saint Bonaventure identified three particularly pernicious opinions that were beginning to be heard:

1. *That the world is eternal.*

2. *That God knows only universals, and not particulars.*

3. *That there is only one intellect for all human beings.*

In this context, of course, the word "eternal" cannot have its usual theological meaning, "outside of time"; it simply means "everlasting" (without beginning or end in time). As it happens, the first two views were really held by Aristotle, while the third, which was Neoplatonic, can be found in Aristotle only by means of dedicated interpretation.

The reasons for Saint Bonaventure's special horror of the first view are a little obscure; apparently he was unable to conceive of creation except as conferring upon the creature a beginning point in time, so that a world that had lasted forever could not have a creator. His great contemporary, Saint Thomas Aquinas, could have explained to him that this need not follow. As Bible-believing Christians, both men had to accept that the world was only a finite number of years old, but to Saint Thomas this was a simple factual point, while to Saint Bonaventure it was an urgent logical necessity. He tells us that when he was a student, and heard that Aristotle had said that the world was eternal, and heard reasons given for this view, his heart began to pound and he began to think, "How can this be?" Since then, Saint Bonaventure complains, the doctrine has become public! Clearly, his own peace of mind required that it be publicly denounced.

The reasons for objecting to the other two views are easier to identify. If God knows only universal truths (that is, himself, since he supposedly consists of them), then although he knows all about what it is to be a human being, and knows, no doubt, that at any given time there are a lot of them, he knows nothing about any *individual* human being as distinct from any other. So, he cannot watch over individuals, or care for them, or separate those who should be rewarded from those who should be punished, or bring about any particular historical event. In short, there is no such thing as divine providence. If, moreover, there is only one intellect for all men, it could follow that there is no moral responsibility, since moral responsibility requires that people make choices, and know, as individuals, what they are doing. (Note, here, that Saint Bonaventure seems to take the "intellect" to be the part of the soul that has conscious awareness. This may explain why in his most famous work he speaks of the *mind's* journey into God, rather than, as we might have expected, the *soul's*.) A related error, he thought, was to suppose that there is no afterlife. (Saint Bonaventure's way of blocking this error was to claim that the soul does not need the body to serve as its matter, since it has its own incorporeal matter.) Lack of moral responsibility, and also (if people thought of it) lack of an afterlife, could undermine the possibility of influencing people's behavior by rewards and punishments, and in that case, as Saint Bonaventure puts it, there is no governance of the world.

Saint Bonaventure's Way of Unifying His Message

Saint Bonaventure tended to put all three of the detestable doctrines, and several of their consequences, together in his mind, as amounting to virtually the same odious blunder. When he lists errors of this type he likes to list three, but they are not always the same three; he makes rearrangements and substitutions. There is, as it happens, a philosophical basis for considering these views as a unit, namely, that he thinks they all come from a single root, the denial of exemplarism. If there are creative exemplars (archetypes or active patterns) in Christ, then the things in the world can come from them. In that way the world is related to God in an intimate way, *as his creature* and not just as something made out of independent matter and yearning for God from afar. Through exemplars, too, Christ can know each creature individually, and apply standards to it. Finally, creatures are not condemned to languish in a pointless material wasteland but can rise up toward God by coming to know the exemplars, all of which are in Christ. Thus, the three detested doctrines are unified philosophically, by coming from the same source. Elsewhere, however, Saint Bonaventure unifies or amalgamates his message *without* using a philosophical rationale.

Saint Bonaventure was a traditionalist and he started from the manifold details that make up a tradition. His works are thickly filled with allusions and quotations. It is hard for us now to appreciate it, but much of what Saint Bonaventure wrote on speculative topics would have seemed familiar to an educated reader in the thirteenth century the first time it was read. This was likely, and no doubt intended, to produce an effect of rightness and completion, as if one were coming home.

The method of unifying by continually returning to what is familiar reaches a particularly high pitch in the exceedingly concentrated short work, *The Journey of the Mind into God*. So many allusions are made to things scholars would have heard of before that reading it must have been like having a symphony played in one's mind. The sense of wholeness and correctness in such a work is not really given by its logical structure but by the familiarity of the details and the charm of the presentation. So, for instance, when he asks us to move up from the fifth illumination, our knowledge of God as One, to the sixth illumination, our knowledge of God as Good, he contrasts the two by reciting several pairs of contrasting adjectives that could be applied to God's diffusiveness (creativity): "Actualis et intrinseca, substantialis et hypostatica, naturalis et voluntaria, liberalis et necessaria, indeficiens et perfecta." One adjective of each pair considers God as One, and the other considers God as Good. Which is which? A philosopher might expect to find the one that applies to God as One put first each time, and the other second, or else the other way around; but Saint Bonaventure does not do this. He puts now one first and now the other. He imposes a pattern, but it is not one of logic; it is one of sound. The first adjective in each pair is the one that ends in "s" (in the feminine nominative singular), and the second is the one that ends in "a." This is music. The passage is unified not as an argument, but as a chant.

In the speculative works of Saint Bonaventure, the paragraphs *seem* to set forth elaborate logical structures (with special fondness for dividing up topics into threes), but really the structures are not there for the sake of the analysis that they appear to give. They are there for the sake of redirecting our attention onto higher things. What unifies the message of Saint Bonaventure is this fervent aim.

It is in his mystical passages, and nowhere else, that Saint Bonaventure occasionally departs from tradition. For example, in the *Journey of the Mind into God* and elsewhere, he sometimes appears to say that we can have knowledge of God, face to face, *in this life*. It is quite tricky to reconcile this with the requirements of Catholic theology. Indeed, an unfortunate Belgian professor named Gérard Casimir Ubaghs was condemned in 1866 by the Holy Office (the successor of the Inquisition) for failing to do so.

The Work of Saint Bonaventure

It is often remarked that Saint Bonaventure's philosophy is at the service of his theology, and indeed, according to most but not all interpreters, inseparable from it. What is not so often appreciated is that his theological writings are, in turn, to some extent at the service of his political projects within the Church. The subordination is not so radical in this case, since one of his main goals in Church politics was to preserve traditional theology. Nevertheless it is there.

When he became the head of the Franciscan order, Saint Bonaventure faced a quite difficult administrative challenge. The order was in danger of falling apart because of strife between the "spirituals," who regarded themselves as closest to the outlook of Saint Francis (the founder of the order), and the less strict party ("*relaxati*"), who regarded themselves as more practical. The former insisted on absolute poverty; the latter thought that the order needed dormitories at the least. The former, though producing some important literature of their own, basically despised book-learning; the latter sometimes liked books and accumulated them. The former were often attracted to the prophecies of Joachim of Fiore; the latter wished to distance themselves from enthusiasts who might be heretical.

Saint Bonaventure moved decisively to establish his authority and to keep as many members as possible in the order, while allowing as little dissension as possible. He conciliated both factions, while at the same time striking hard against some factional leaders as individuals. For example, he appears to have arranged for the prosecution of the previous head of the order, Blessed John of Parma (a spiritual and Joachimite who had had to resign by command of the pope), on heresy charges.

On a theoretical level, Saint Bonaventure showed (or had already shown; the date of writing is not certain), in his work *On the Reduction of the Arts to Theology*, that book-learning and the practical arts are themselves at bottom spiritual exercises, and are subordinate to spiritual concerns. This was a master stroke, as it implies on the one hand that the spirituals need not fear these arts nor be ashamed if they do not possess them, and on the other hand that the less-strict party need not give them up. He went to Mount La Verna, where Saint Francis had had a vision of a seraph, and there he, too, had a vision of a seraph. He published a report of this experience (*The Journey of the Mind into God*) in which he emphasized its relation to the experience of Saint Francis. He wrote a new *Legend of St. Francis*, mentioning with gratitude that Saint Francis had miraculously cured him of an illness as a child. (This must have been one of Saint Francis's earlier miracles, as he was still on the earth until Saint Bonaventure was about nine.) He then commanded that all copies of previous lives of Saint Francis be destroyed. (Luckily, some survived.) The *Catholic Encyclopaedia* of 1907 defends this decree on the ground that the contentious members of the order were always quoting the words of Saint Francis as given in the earlier reports. Plainly, the aim here is political, not scholarly.

Saint Bonaventure vindicated the rights of scholars within the Franciscan order and of Franciscan friars within the university. He reconciled the factions within the order and postponed the breakup of the order for as long as he lived. These things, more than philosophy or theology, were his life's work, and his famous mystical treatises must be understood in this context.

JOHN CRONQUIST

Further Reading

Bougerol, J. Guy, O.F.M., *Introduction to the Works of Bonaventure*. Translated by José de Vinck. Paterson, N.J.: St. Anthony Guild Press, 1964. A collection of background information and analysis of themes, suitable for readers who already know something of the thought of Saint Bonaventure.

Brady, Ignatius C., O.F.M., "Bonaventure, St.," *New Catholic Encyclopedia*, 1967, Vol. 2, pp. 658–664. A shrewd and trustworthy introduction, suitable for serious-minded beginners.

Copleston, F. C. [Frederick Charles], S.J., *A History of Medieval Philosophy*. New York: Harper & Row, 1972, pp. 160–170. A reworked brief synopsis by the judicious author of several standard textbooks on the history of philosophy.

Gilson, Étienne, *The Philosophy of St. Bonaventure*. Translated by (Dom) Illtyd Trethowan and Frank J. Sheed. London: Sheed & Ward, 1938. Reprinted, with new pagination, Paterson, N.J.: St. Anthony Guild Press, 1965. A book-length treatment in which the subordination of philosophy to theology in the thought of Saint Bonaventure is particularly emphasized.

Healy, Emma Thérèse, C.S.J., *Woman According to Saint Bonaventure*. Erie, Pa.: Villa Maria College, 1956. Saint Bonaventure says that woman is a beast living in man's quarters, but Sister Emma Thérèse explains that he had an exalted view of women and was a nice person.

McInerny, Ralph M., *A History of Western Philosophy*, Vol. 2, *Philosophy from St. Augustine to Ockham*. Notre Dame, IN: University of Notre Dame Press, 1970, pp. 255–286. Not a digest of previous accounts, but an original rethinking of philosophical positions taken by Saint Bonaventure in the course of his theological work.

Pegis, Anton Charles, *St. Thomas and the Problem of the Soul in the Thirteenth Century*. Ch. 2, "St. Bonaventure and the Problem of the Soul as Substance." Toronto: St. Michael's College, 1934; reprinted, Toronto: Pontifical Institute of Mediaeval Studies, 1976. Shows how Saint Bonaventure's theory of the soul contrasts with that of Saint Thomas Aquinas. One of the most lucid modern discussions of a topic in medieval philosophy; a classic.

Ratzinger, Joseph (Cardinal), *The Theology of History in St. Bonaventure*. Translated by Zachary Hayes, O.F.M. Chicago: Franciscan Herald Press, 1971. A perspicacious study, focusing on the *Conferences on the Hexaëmeron*, and treating several subjects that are often overlooked or misjudged by other writers, such as Saint Bonaventure's numerology.

SAINT THOMAS AQUINAS

Born: 1224 or 1225, Roccasecca, Italy (near Naples)
Died: 1274, at Fossanuova
Major Works: *Summa contra gentiles* (c. 1259–67); *Summa theologiae* (1265–73); *De Veritate* [*On Truth*] (1256–59); *De Anima* [*On the Soul*] (c. 1259–67)

Major Ideas

The existence of God is not self-evident to reason, but it is demonstrable.

In God, essence and existence are inseparable, indeed, identical: It belongs to "what" God is "that" God is.

The essence of finite things is separable from their existence.

The finite order receives its existence by "participation" in the divine.

God is not only the first cause of all motion in the finite order, he is also the concurrent cause of all the operations of the natural order.

The substances of finite things consist in a union of matter and form.

The forms or ideas of things, therefore, subsist primarily in things rather than as independent extra-mental forms or as mental abstractions resting on examination of things.

Human knowledge arises as a result of the intellectual analysis of the forms of things as they are accessible to sense perception.

Thomas Aquinas is the greatest of the medieval Scholastics or Schoolmen and one of the foremost philosophers and theologians in the Western tradition. He was born in late 1224 or early 1225 in the castle of Roccasecca near Naples, the son of the Count of Aquino. When Thomas reached the age of five, his father placed him in the Benedictine abbey of Monte Cassino. After some nine years of monastic training and study, Thomas matriculated at the University of Naples. Not only did Thomas encounter there the standard medieval arts curriculum of grammar, rhetoric, and logic (the *trivium*) and arithmetic, geometry, astronomy, and music (the *quadrivium*), he also encountered, most probably, some of the works of Aristotle, newly brought to the West and translated in to Latin, together with the Arabian commentaries on them. The University of Naples, under the patronage of the cosmopolitan emperor Frederick II of Hohenstaufen, was a center of this new learning, and Thomas's instructor in natural philosophy, Peter of Ireland, was strongly Aristotelian.

At Naples, in 1244, against the wishes of his family, the young Thomas Aquinas entered the Dominican order. Not to be deterred in their efforts to lead him into the Benedictine order, Thomas's family had him kidnapped and brought back to Aquino. Thomas is said to have spent the year studying the Bible and Peter Lombard's *Sentences*. Two of his early works may actually date from his year of confinement—a treatise on fallacies and another on modal propositions.

In 1245, after being released by his family, the young Aquinas was sent to Paris and began his studies at the University, most probably under the tutelage of the eminent Dominican teacher, Albert the Great. He studied in Paris until 1248, when he accompanied Albert to Cologne, where the latter had been commissioned by the Dominican order to open a house of studies. Here Aquinas functioned, most probably, as *cursor biblicus*, the lecturer in the basic course of biblical studies. It is to these early years of study with Albert that Aquinas owed, if not his basic acquaintance with the new Aristotelian philosophy, certainly the program of incorporation of Aristotle's wisdom into the study of philosophy and theology. In addition, Albert evidenced a broad interest in many Platonic themes from Augustine, Pseudo-Dionysius, the *Book of Causes*, and the *Enneads* of Plotinus (available in part in a book called, ironically, *The Theology of Aristotle*)—all of which would have their impact on Thomas.

In 1252, Aquinas parted company with Albert and returned to Paris to study and to teach as the *baccalaureus Sententiarum* or lecturer in the University of Paris (for the Dominican order) in the basic theological course in the *Sentences* of Peter Lombard (1252–56). We have, from this period in his life, the commentary on Lombard's *Sentences*, a massive theological work that provides an index to Thomas's genius as a young scholar. The conclusion of this course of study and lecturing brought Aquinas the license of the university to teach, together with the rank of *magister*, master or doctor. He remained in Paris in the Dominican chair of theology until 1259.

From 1259 to 1268, Aquinas taught theology at the papal court in Italy. When he returned to the university of Paris in 1268, probably to assist in the defense of his order's right to preach and to teach in the university, Aquinas found himself embroiled in the debate over the suitability of Aristotelian philosophy in the Christian university, a debate that not only entailed defending and elaborating his own and Albert's approach to Aristotle but also arguing against the so-called "Latin Averroists," who had advocated a radical Aristotelianism sometimes at odds with received Christian theology and philosophy.

In 1272, Aquinas was called from Paris to found a Dominican house of study in Naples. He taught at Naples until 1274 when he was called by Pope Gregory X to the council of Lyons, where he would have worked with Bonaventure to explain the Western, Latin theology to representatives sent from the Greek Orthodox church in Byzantium. Aquinas died on his way to the council at the monastery of Fossanuova.

The chronology of Aquinas's teaching career provides a significant index and guide to his philosophical and theological writings. His early teaching as *baccalaureus* led to the production of his massive commentary on Lombard's *Sentences*. Between 1255 and 1259, when Aquinas solidified his intellectual relationship to Albert the Great and to Aristotelian philosophy, he produced the treatises *On*

Being and Essence and *On Truth*. His first stay in Italy included the composition of the *Summa contra gentiles* and a series of commentaries on treatises of Aristotle, several of them newly translated into Latin by William of Moerbeke. Back in Paris, in debate with the Averroists, he composed the treatises *On the Eternity of the World* and *On the Soul*, together with another series of commentaries on works of Aristotle. His final years, beginning about 1265, saw the development of the incomplete *Summa theologiae*. It is important to note that all of these works, including those on specifically theological themes, are important to philosophy. For although Aquinas recognized the difference between theology and philosophy, they are not easily separated in his writings, granting his fundamental assumption concerning the necessary coherence of faith and reason.

The Summa contra gentiles and Summa theologiae

Aquinas's *Summa contra gentiles*, also known by the title *On the Truth of the Catholic Faith*, is a lengthy philosophical and theological system cast in the form of a rational apologetics and probably intended by Aquinas as a handbook for Dominicans in debate with "gentile" Islamic philosophers and theologians over the right interpretation, use, and theological implication, Christian or Islamic, of Aristotle. The work was probably commissioned by Raymond of Penyafort, master-general of the Dominican order in the mid-thirteenth century, himself of Spanish origins and deeply troubled by the powerful presence of Islam in Spain.

Aquinas's approach is to occupy the perspective of the wise teacher in search of truth and knowledge, precisely the philosophical stance of Aristotle, but to argue that this truth can be most rightly and rationally argued from his own perspective. In accord with Thomas's purpose, the work draws heavily not only on Aristotle but also on Avicenna, the more Platonizing of the two great Islamic exponents of the teaching of "the Philosopher." Perhaps because of its congeniality to the thought of Avicenna as well as because of the influence of Albert the Great, the ordering principle of the *Contra gentiles* is not so much Aristotelian as Neoplatonic, on the model of Pseudo-Dionysius: Books 1 through 3 of this *summa* offer a doctrine of God, of the emanation of all things from God, and of the return of all things to God.

The *Summa theologiae* or, as it is frequently called, the *Summa theologica*, is, justly, Aquinas's most famous and most influential work. In it he offers his most cohesive and finely argued attempt to draw Aristotelian philosophy into the service of Christian theology and philosophy and into company of the already-recognized authorities in teaching, principally Augustine, Dionysius the Pseudo-Areopagite, and Boethius.

The *Summa theologiae* is perhaps best known for its balance of the categories of faith and reason, for its related thesis that the truths known to the faith, even when given from beyond reason, are "not unreasonable," and for its consequent ability to draw its readers into the doctrine of God by way of a consideration of the problem of the knowledge of God and the "five ways" or proofs of the existence of God. In direct opposition to Anselm's "ontological argument," which indicated that the existence of God was evident from the idea of God and that, conversely, anyone who understood the idea of God but denied God's existence was involved in a contradiction, Aquinas argued that the average person may have some rudimentary apprehension of God, but that this apprehension implied so little grasp of the essence of God that it could not lead to a demonstration such as proposed by Anselm.

Although the existence of God is not self-evident, it is demonstrable, Thomas claimed, not from the idea of God but from the evident effects of the existent God noted in our world. In the *Summa theologiae*, Aquinas offers five interrelated "ways" or proofs.

The "first and more manifest way" that Aquinas offers as a proof of God's existence is the argument from finite "motion" to the existence of the first and "unmoved mover." It is crucial to an understanding of the argument that "motion" not be defined in the modern, colloquial sense of action or activity, but rather as the "movement," Aristotle's *kinesis*, from potential to actual existence. Something that is purely potential cannot move itself to actuality: It must be moved by something else. In order to explain existence or actuality, we must either assume an infinite sequence of movers or posit an ultimate unmoved mover. But, argues Aquinas, the infinite sequence of contingent beings is impossible granting that the sequence, taken as a whole, does not provide the basis for its own existence. (The infinite regress that Aquinas denies, in other words, is not a temporal but an ontological one.) There must be something outside of the sequence that accounts for its existence: Therefore, there must be an unmoved mover and this being can be none other than God.

The second and third proofs are directly related to the first. All three rest on Aristotelian philosophy. In the second proof, Aquinas notes that, since nothing can exist prior to and as cause of itself, there must be an order of efficient causes in the world. But, as in the case of the basic argument from motion, there cannot be an infinite series of efficient causes. A first efficient cause must therefore be assumed—and this is to be identified as God. Similarly, it can be recognized from the world that beings come into and pass out of existence. In other words, they are not necessary but contingent. But this recognition of the contingent nature of the world order calls its very existence into question if there were not a necessarily existent or noncontingent being on which the existence of the world order rests. This being can only be God. (It can be argued, moreover, that this third proof is not only related to the proofs from motion and causality but also contains the concept fundamental to all three: Namely, the existence of the necessary Being in relation to the order of contingent being.)

A fourth proof is drawn more from Augustine than from Aristotle and rests on the observation of degrees of perfection or goodness in the world and asks by what standards such comparative judgments are made. Notions of good and better, or of the relatively more perfect, imply a best or most perfect being. Indeed, Aquinas argues, there must be a highest Being whose absolute perfection and goodness are the cause of the relative perfection and goodness of other beings. Once again, such a being can only be God.

The fifth and final proof is a teleological argument. As before, our experience of the world leads to the postulation of the existence of God, now because of the order that is observably present even in inanimate things—things incapable of ordering themselves. Such an order presumes the existence of an intelligent ordering principle. Such a being must be God. In this, as in the preceding arguments, Aquinas does not contend that he has offered an entire doctrine of God, but rather that he has arrived at concepts or attributes that can be predicated only of God.

At least as important as the proofs themselves is the place that they occupy in Aquinas's approach to the problem of the relationship of God and the world. Once Aquinas had established rationally the existence of the necessary or self-existent Being, he was then in a position to argue, drawing on the highly developed Aristotelian theism of Avicenna and Maimonides, that in God essence (*essentia*), or *what* God is, is identical to and inseparable from existence (*esse*), or *that* God is: It is the essence of God to be.

For Aquinas, this conclusion not only distinguishes God from creatures, whose existence and essence are distinct and separable, it also establishes the relationship between God and creatures. If creatures do not necessarily exist or, more precisely, if their essence or *what* they are is not necessarily given individual existence, how do they receive their capability of being? It is hardly enough to say that they are created out of nothing, because "nothing," understood absolutely, contains neither essence nor existence. And it is unacceptable to Aquinas to claim that God created finite beings out of preexistent matter. Rather God has first created a primary, unformed matter and then has proceeded to bring individual species into being by informing this material.

How then does the necessary Being provide the *existence*, literally, the "to be," both of the primary matter of all things and of those creatures that he conceives? Aquinas's answer is that contingent creatures exist because of the divine *esse*: They do not have in themselves the possibility "to be" but receive it from God. God is Existence itself and has the power to confer existence upon other beings. In Aquinas's words, "God is being (*ens*) through his own essence . . . all other being is being by participation." This conclusion is central to the Thomistic approach to the relationship of God and world.

There is, therefore, no possibility in Aquinas's teaching of a view approaching that of the seventeenth- and eighteenth-century Deists, according to which God resembles a watchmaker who made the world, set it running, and subsequently allowed it an independent existence. This *Deus otiosus* or "God on vacation" is totally foreign to Aquinas's world-view, which assumes both the initial creative act and its continuance in the ongoing ontological support of the world order. Granting, moreover, the eternity of God and its corollary, the simultaneity and unity of the divine knowing and willing of all that exists, the divine work that human beings distinguish (from a temporal perspective) into creation and providence is in actuality a single divine act that both calls the world into being and sustains it in being.

Aquinas's view of the finite order is defined by his view of the location of ideas or forms, or as the medieval teachers often called them, "universals," primarily in things, and also by the resultant "hylomorphic" theory of substance. Whereas Platonic philosophy has assumed the independent, extramental existence of ideas as the ground of both the reality of individual things and of our knowledge of them, Aristotelian philosophy as understood by Aquinas allowed no such independent extra-mental existence to ideas, and consequently offered a fundamentally different view of finite reality and of knowledge. Aquinas, from his Christian theistic perspective, which identified God as the first mover, could argue that universals exist "prior to things," not as independent existences, but in the mind of God. Universals exist "in things" as the form and as the principle of individuation that is impressed upon the unformed material: This union of matter (*hyle*) and form (*morphe*) is substance. Universals also exist "after things" in the form of concepts held in the mind of the human knower. The one case in which the universal is "real," that is, has an existence independent of the mind, is "in things." In the act of creation, God understands in his mind all of the possibilities that could be actualized in the finite order, knows which of those possibilities he will in fact bring into being, and then wills their existence by freely willing the good that he knows, conferring upon them the good of being. From the perspective of the created order itself, the act of creation can be understood as the impressing of form upon matter. The result is not only "hylomorphic" substance, but also individual things.

Aquinas viewed this theory as conformable with the traditional, Augustinian view of the goodness of the created order and of the existence of evil as a privation or defect. Since God both conceives of the forms and creates the material substratum of things, there is no ground of any existence outside of the divine willing. Since, moreover, the creation of the substantial order is understood as the conferring of the good of being upon things, there can be no such thing as *substantial evil*. Evil, in short, cannot belong to the basic "stuff" of the created order.

In addition, since Aquinas's Aristotelian approach to creation understands God as the first mover who draws things from purely potential into actual existence and whose willing of the existence of things is an aspect of his willing of his own goodness, existence itself must be understood as a good that tends toward its goal in God. There is, in other words, a strong teleological implication in Aquinas's teaching on creation that parallels the arguments found in his proofs of God's existence. Insofar as things exist, they are good and they participate in the divine goodness. Evil appears not only as a defect or privation but as an assault upon the goodness of being and as a tendency toward nonbeing. Aquinas, thus, denies dualism at the highest level, just as he denied it in his hylomorphic conception of substance and in his assumption of the real existence of universals only *in things*. There cannot be an ultimate or absolute principle of evil: Evil must have a parasitic existence in things.

Aquinas's fundamentally anti- or nondualistic view of the cosmic order carries over, finally, into his view of human nature, where his Aristotelian philosophy provides an important alternative to the Platonic view of soul and body and to its various intellectual descendants. The language of soul and body does not indicate to Aquinas a dualism in human beings or a notion of the soul as what later writers called "a ghost in the machine." Rather the soul is to be understood, in all of its functions, as the entelechy, the form and inward goal of the body, and in such a way that the material "body" could not be a body without the soul.

Hylomorphism, in other words, guides Aquinas's conception of human nature. The "body" indicates the material individualization of the person, while "soul" is the term for the basic form, the life, and the rational functions, both intellective and volitional, of the person. As in Aristotle's teaching concerning the soul, so also in Aquinas's view, the soul is understood in terms of an ascending order of actualization beginning with the formal aspect of all existence, moving on to the "vegetative" life principle identifiable in plants, to the animating principle present in forms of life both capable of movement and of sense perception, and finally to the rational soul of human beings that combines all of the former aspects of form and soul with the faculties of intellect and will.

When he turns to the theory of knowledge, Aquinas holds consistently to his Aristotelian view of ideas or forms as subsisting primarily in things and rejects the more Platonic theory of the illumination of the mind by eternal ideas. We do not know of an idea or form before we encounter it in one of its embodiments or individualization—and we know, therefore, primarily through our senses. Aquinas assumes an analogy between the mind prior to its having knowledge and the created but as yet unformed material substratum of the universe: Both are capable of receiving forms. Just as material things are substantial individuals by reason of the union of form with matter, so too do we know these things by the impress of the form, elicited by the intellect from our perception of the thing, on the mind. The process of learning, therefore, rests on the susceptibility of the mind for the forms or universals residing in things; and knowledge of our world arises neither out of an innate cognizance of ideas or out of an inward illumination. Rather, knowledge arises out of the experience and perception of our world. The categories that frame our knowing, therefore, correspond with the categories that belong to the perceptible order—categories such as time, space, and cause and effect. We have, in fact, come full circle: The proofs of God's existence, noted previously, rise out of the world order and rest on the perceived categories belonging to that order, so that knowledge of God, although not a self-evidencing knowledge like our knowledge of finite things, is nonetheless a knowledge that belongs to the normal patterns of human knowing.

Although, as noted, Thomas Aquinas's thought is important in the context of medieval Scholasticism, his significance is, of course, far broader and his thought continues to be both a subject of study and a primary point of reference for many present-day philosophers. The pattern that he gave to the proofs

of the existence of God, for example, continues to be reflected in works on theistic philosophy and natural theology. And not a few contemporary thinkers would retain Aquinas's approach to our knowledge of the world and of the fundamental categories of perception as a useful alternative to the Kantian theory of transcendental categories as belonging to the mind alone. The clarity and depth of Aquinas's approach to virtually all of the traditional problems of philosophical theism—the existence of God, the identity of the good with being, the relation of God to the finite order, the problem of evil, the nature of human beings, and so forth—has guaranteed his reputation both as the chief of the medieval Scholastics, the most cogent synthesizer of Christian theism with classical philosophy, and author of a fundamental and perennially important vision of the universal order.

RICHARD A. MULLER

Further Reading

Burrell, David B. *Knowing the Unknowable God: Ibn-Sina, Maimonides, Aquinas.* Notre Dame: University of Notre Dame Press, 1986. An excellent discussion of Thomas Aquinas's contribution to the discussion of the relationship of God and the world in the light of the contributions of two of his most outstanding predecessors.

Chenu, Marie-Dominique. *Toward Understanding St. Thomas.* Translated by A.-M. Landry and D. Hughes. Chicago: Henry Regnery, 1964. The standard critical introduction to the thought and the works of Aquinas. Chenu analyzes the intellectual context, the forms of expression and statement, the language and the sources of Aquinas's thought, and then surveys analytically each major work, giving references to texts, editions, translations, as well as a detailed bibliography of studies on Aquinas, aspects of his thought, and the many individual works.

Copleston, Frederick C. *Aquinas.* Baltimore: Penguin, 1970. A balanced and useful introduction to Aquinas's thought.

Gilson, Étienne. *The Christian Philosophy of St.*

Thomas Aquinas. Translated by L. K. Shook. New York: Random House, 1956. A classic study by one of this century's foremost medievalists and greatest exponents of Aquinas's thought; perhaps a bit difficult for the beginner, but well worth the effort.

Gratsch, Edward J. *Aquinas' Summa: An Introduction and Interpretation.* New York: Alba House, 1985. A well-balanced survey and analysis of the teaching of the entire *Summa*.

McInerny, Ralph. *St. Thomas Aquinas.* Notre Dame: University of Notre Dame Press, 1982. A superb introduction to the thought of Aquinas by the incredibly versatile historian of philosophy and author of the Father Dowling mysteries. Includes an annotated bibliography.

Owens, Joseph. *St. Thomas Aquinas on the Existence of God: Collected Papers of Joseph Owens, C. Ss. R.* Edited by John R. Catan. Albany: State University of New York Press, 1980. A set of related essays on Aquinas's Aristotelianism, his concept of being, and the famous "five ways," all written with a profound knowledge of

Aquinas's philosophy and with a high ability to present its fundamental issues to the reader.

Pegis, Anton C. *Saint Thomas and the Greeks.* The Aquinas Lecture, 3 (1939). Milwaukee: Marquette University Press, 4th printing, 1980. A significant short study of Aquinas's relationship to and appropriation of Greek philosophy.

Thomas Aquinas. *On the Truth of the Catholic Faith: Summa Contra Gentiles.* Translated by Anton C. Pegis et al. 4 vols. Garden City, N.Y.: Doubleday Image Books, 1955.

————. *Summa theologica.* Translated by the Fathers of the English Dominican Province. 5 vols. 1911; reprint, Westminster, Md.: 1981. (Although the original title of this work was *Summa theologiae*, it has also come to be called the *Summa theologica*, as in the edition cited here).

Weisheipl, James A. *Friar Thomas D'Aquino: His Life, Thought, and Work.* Garden City, N.Y.: Doubleday, 1974. The standard biography; contains a useful descriptive bibliography of all of Aquinas's genuine works, noting manuscript sources, editions, and translations.

MEISTER ECKHART

Born: C. 1260, Hochheim, Thuringia, Germany
Died: C. 1327, Köln, Germany or, more likely, Avignon, France
Major Works: *Sermons, Commentaries on Genesis and the Gospel of John* (from the unfinished *Opus tripartitum*), *Discourses on Discernment* (before 1298), *The Book of Divine Consolations* and *On the Nobleman* (c. 1315), *On Detachment* (c. 1315)

Major Ideas

Beyond "God" lies the Godhead; that is, "God" as Father, Son, and Spirit is merely representation of the true God, or Godhead.

The ground of God and the ground of the human soul are the same; thus God, or union with God, is to be sought within oneself: Here occurs "the birth of God's Son in the soul."

God cannot be "known" rationally, but only through immediate experience, normally as the result of disinterest and detachment and usually, but not necessarily, arrived at through ascetic practices.

The spiritual and interior are superior to the material and exterior.

Johannes Eckhart, or "Meister" Eckhart, was a dominant force representing Neoplatonic mysticism within the medieval church. As a Dominican monk trained at the Universities of Paris and Köln (hence the title "Meister" or "Master"), prior of Erfurt and vicar of Thuringia, and finally superior-general for all of Germany, a popular preacher and spiritual director, he was widely known and exerted a strong influence, particularly on the church along the Rhine. Due to his popularity and influence, he naturally came under the scrutiny of the Church, and was found wanting in certain areas. He pled his innocence in Köln, and in 1327 he went to Avignon to defend himself against the charges of heresy brought against him in Köln. Eckhart died before the final verdict could be reached (Avignon supported the charges).

Eckhart's thought not only influenced those immediately after him, such as Heinrich Seuse, Johann Tauler (whose sermons were so highly valued by Martin Luther) and Nicholas of Cusa, but were received with what may correctly be called glee by the German idealists. Hegel, for example, introduced to the mystic's works by Franz von Baader, allegedly finished a lecture on Eckhart with the words, "*Da haben wir es ja, was wir wollen*" ("Here we have indeed just what we want").

In this century, Eckhart has been heaped together with numerous other mystics by the "creation

spirituality" school, although with much less intellectual justification than can be found in Baader and his contemporaries. The most common threads of Eckhart's speculation that have run through the various renewals of idealism, romanticism, and mysticism seem to be the utter unity of God, or the Absolute, and the elevation of the human to actual participation in the creative and redemptive life of God.

We must bear in mind that Eckhart's thought was conditioned by mystical and hence ineffable experience involving union with God, or the Absolute. The mystical experience was interpreted within a metaphysical Neoplatonic framework that affirmed the accuracy of the experience. Thus, some sort of synthesis between two conceptions of reality was required: reality as experienced Neoplatonically, on the one hand, and reality as prescribed within the orthodox tradition to be Trinitarian, on the other.

To accomplish such a synthesis, Eckhart faced several problems: that of reconciling the God as understood within Neoplatonism to be Pure Being (eternal Form) with the God who is Three Persons; that of reconciling the Neoplatonic conception of creation as having its true existence and origin in the corresponding idea (eternal Form) with the orthodox conception of creation as finding its origin in God's creative act; that of reconciling the Neoplatonic idea that the ground of the soul is the same as the ground of God (and hence that the soul is uncreated) with the orthodox belief that the soul is God's creation; and that of preaching what is ineffable and hence indescribable in comprehensible and orthodox terms.

It is easily seen that Eckhart's task was almost, if not completely, insurmountable. It is not surprising that his efforts to reconcile Neoplatonism with the orthodox faith led to charges of heresy. Eckhart claimed his innocence of heresy on the ground that heresy requires intention, a deliberate act of will, while he always intended to be orthodox. (We must also bear in mind that Eckhart, like many mystics and preachers, tended to write and preach in terms of the ultimate. For example, even though he claimed that the just person is not merely similar to but is the *same* as Christ, he would not go so far as to claim such a thing of any actual individual.)

Eckhart argues that behind or beyond God (*Deus*) as Father, Son, and Holy Spirit, there is the Godhead (*Deitas*), or God as the ground of God. It is with this God as ground of all that one hopes to attain unity. While at times Eckhart conceives of God as *intelligere* (understanding), he most often uses the word *esse* (Being). This God is not simply a being, or one being among others, but uncreated being in which there are no distinctions.

Such a view raised the question of Eckhart's faithfulness to Trinitarianism. While Eckhart's defenders have taken pains to point out that he maintains that the Father, Son, and Holy Spirit are indeed somehow identical with the divine essence, the majority of his statements make it abundantly clear that for Eckhart what is essential is, after all, the undivided and indivisible unity of God.

God and the Human Soul

In emphasizing the absolute unity of God, Eckhart asserts the unity of God with creation, particularly with the human soul, in that the ground of God and the ground of the soul are one. While maintaining that the creator and the creature are indeed distinct, Eckhart cannot avoid returning to the Neoplatonic position that from God all things come, and to God all things eventually return. In and of itself this does not sound particularly problematic, but in the assumption that in the fall into matter or numbers, any emanations (a word Eckhart uses, albeit sparingly) contain something essential of the prior emanations lies the implication that God and creature are in fact one. Eckhart is careful to distinguish between creator and creature and yet transcendence of distinction and union with God are to be found through mystical experience. It is by turning to the ground of one's soul that one comes across God. Here Eckhart uses terms such as "spark of the soul" (*Seelenfünklein, scintilla animae*) and "ground of the soul." It is in this soul's ground, held in common with God's ground, that the "birth of God's Son in the soul" occurs. Here alone is God known as God.

In fact, God alone is worthy of desire; union with, or knowledge of, God is the ultimate purpose of the human being. Any person must become detached from everything else, even from the idea of becoming detached, if he or she is to gain the immediate experience of God. The person must turn away from everything but his or her own soul, what is within, "For creatures are only God's footprints, but by nature the soul is patterned after God." This means that the soul simply *is*, without self-knowledge, senses, or ideas. Thus God, who simply *is*, can unite with the soul. In detachment the soul receives not the correct concept of God, or even the true experience of God, but God. Eckhart says, "In the eternal birth, the soul becomes pure and one. Thus, its existence is the same as God's." As the Son is born in the person, the person is born in God and thus, now one with God, participates in the creation of all that is in the eternal now. The person who has had God, or God's Son, born in his or her soul actually participates in his or her own creation. (This is one area in which Eckhart encountered considerable suspicion. Even with qualifications, the following kind of statement is puzzling: ". . . I am the cause of myself according to my being which is eternal, but not according to my becoming, which is temporal; and because of that, I am unborn (*ungeboren*)—a being which was never born—and thus I can never die.")

Union with God

Not only a philosopher but also as pastor and preacher, Eckhart was ever concerned to communicate to those in his care the necessity of union with God. The birth of the Son of God in the soul is of absolute importance to Eckhart, and he inserted the idea in numerous sermons. The key to this, as we have seen, is disinterest, or detachment (*Abgeschiedenheit*). Detachment does not indicate rejection of material things as evil but, rather, as inadequate. Thus one must let go, in one way or another, of external things: "If you want the kernel, you must break the shell." The usual way to detachment was through ascetic practices, although Eckhart pointed out that one can become attached even to the practices, thereby defeating the purpose of the practices in the first place. Note that detachment does not preclude activity. It only precludes any attachment to the object of the action, or the activity *per se*.

The point of detachment is not the experience of, but oneness with, God, but one must get beyond even awareness of a goal if one is to attain the goal. Thus the person must mortify the flesh and its desires so that he or she can get to the kernel, the common, disinterested ground of God and the soul. Here the person can be busy or still, either in prayer or in acts of charity—it simply does not matter, for the person "is" one with God, and thus beyond identification with the externals of his or her life. In a sermon on Mary and Martha (Luke 10:38ff), Eckhart stands on its head the usual interpretation of Mary as the contemplative one and Martha as the (too) active one, thus holding Mary up as the model for Christians. He describes Martha as the role model, sufficiently one with God that she is appropriately active in the world, and at the same time sufficiently detached that she is not "attached" even to the teachings of Jesus.

The Spiritual and Interior

As has become clear, the spiritual and interior (because that is where purity or unalloyed being is) is superior to the material and external. Eckhart wrote, "There is no physical or fleshly pleasure without some spiritual harm, for the desires of the flesh are contrary to those of the spirit, and the desires of the spirit are contrary to those of the flesh." He even goes so far as to say that "the pleasure we take in the physical form of Christ diminishes our sensitivity to the Holy Spirit." This priority of the spiritual over the material is evident in Eckhart's interpretation of Scripture. Like a number of early church fathers and virtually all the mystics, he finds an outer and inner meaning in Scripture. Again we have the shell/kernel differentiation that runs through Eckhart's understanding of things in general.

Eckhart, then, is a true forerunner and, we dare say, a progenitor of romanticism and idealism. Even in his strong emphasis on the unity of all things in God, he nonetheless attempts not only to leave room for but even to elevate the individual person. He simultaneously stresses the need for utter detachment and for loving actions; the individual's inherent unity with God (the soul's ground and God's ground being one ground) and, at the same time, the individual's distinction from God, God as the creative source, or cause, and the person (in God) as one who "was the cause of myself."

As noted above, Eckhart attempted to capture the essence of mystical experience in formulations which would not stray too far from orthodox and acceptable language. Rudolf Otto has compared Eckhart favorably with Acarya ("Meister") Shankara, the Indian mystic, indicating, perhaps, not that Eckhart was heretical but that mystical experience *per se* is one of unity, and that, like any experience, its articulation depends upon the mystic's theological and cultural framework. In Eckhart's case, it landed him in trouble.

Part of Eckhart's influence came from his formidable skills in preaching and writing. His insistence that the rites of the Church were not as crucial as the inner appropriation of God (although he never rejected or attacked the practices of the Church) and his emphatic assertion that "God is a God of presence" gave him a wide appeal. His influence appears again and again throughout the history of Western civilization.

GARY R. SATTLER

Further Reading

Clark, James M. *The Great German Mystics.* New York: Russell & Russell, 1949, 1970. A helpful introduction to the lives and thought of Eckhart and other Rhenish mystics, with a discussion of the various critical reactions to Eckhart.

———. *Meister Eckhart: An Introduction to the Study of His Works with an Anthology of His Sermons.* Edinburgh: Nelson, 1957. The introduction is quite solid and contributes significantly to the rest of the book.

Eckhart, Meister. *The Essential Sermons, Commentaries, Treatises and Defense.* Translated by Edmund Colledge, O.S.A. and Bernard McGinn. Ramsey, N.J.: Paulist Press, 1981. A good source of some of Eckhart's central writings, with a useful introduction.

DANTE ALIGHIERI

Born: 1265, Florence, Italy
Died: 1321, Ravenna, Italy
Major Works: *Vita Nuova* (1292), *Convivio* (c. 1304), *De Vulgari Eloquentia* (c. 1304), *De Monarchia* (c. 1312), *The Divine Comedy* (c. 1307)

Major Ideas

Love is the movement of the spirit and the primordial energy of the universe.
The energy of love is manifested in three actions.
In romantic love, the psyche moves toward the object of its erotic affections.
In philosophical love, the psyche contemplates the world of nature through the exercise of reason.
In mystical love, the psyche desires union with God, which is the harmony of the will of the soul and the will of God.
Poetry reveals the movement of the spirit, or love, through its literal sense.
The literal sense of poetry contains the manifestations of love in terms of the poem's allegorical, moral, and anagogical meanings.

Dante's master work, *The Divine Comedy*, is said to bear comparison with the Gothic cathedral in that both are a compendium of medieval knowledge. The claim may be exaggerated, but in Dante's case it strikes close to the mark. *The Divine Comedy* culminates a process whereby Dante mastered a great deal of knowledge that was transmitted through literature, originally written in Latin or translated from Greek into Latin, and including the works of Plato, Aristotle, Cicero, and Virgil, as well as the church fathers, Thomas Aquinas, and the medieval mystics. The significance of *The Divine Comedy*, however, does not rest in its encyclopedic nature alone, for there is, more importantly, the grander vision of the world that takes shape from the fusing of rational understandings acquired through study and the deeply personal, interior understandings engendered in the fact of life itself. For Dante was no recluse. Fully engaged in the drama of living, he was beset now by the tempest of romantic love, now by the incalculable forces of politics.

The *Vita Nuova* tells the story of Dante's love for the Florentine lady, Beatrice Portinari. A combination of thirty-one lyric poems and prose narrative, the text expresses Dante's love for Beatrice in three movements: at the age of nine, when he sees and falls in love with the maid; at eighteen, when the power of a maturing love sweeps through him; at twenty-seven, when he suffers the death of Beatrice, already foretold him in a dream.

The desire to discern the movement of the spirit, which will be an abiding theme in all of Dante's writings, is unmistakable in the *Vita Nuova*. Not only does Dante evoke poetically the ennobling effects of love upon him, the pain of love disdained, and his own longing for death when Beatrice dies, but he explores in prose the deeper meaning of the literal sense of the verse. Already in this early work is heard the voice of the mature Dante who explains in the letter to the Can Grande della Scala, to whom he would dedicate the "Paradiso," that the literal includes allegory, moral, and anagogy.

Another theme of the *Vita Nuova* that will appear in subsequent works is Dante's love of reason. After Dante expresses his sorrow at the death of Beatrice, he writes a sonnet in praise of another lady; interpreting the woman as the figure of philosophy, critics explicate the poet's attraction to her as his propensity to depend on natural reason to the exclusion of faith.

The works that constitute the middle phase of Dante's writing—the *Convivio*, the *De Vulgari Eloquentia*, and the *De Monarchia*—demonstrate the truth of Dante's reliance on human reason. Moreover, these works reflect Dante's preoccupation with politics, in which he himself was involved from 1295 to 1302, the year when he was forced into exile.

Dante's Florence had inherited a bloody political past. At the beginning of the thirteenth century, political life was factionalized into the Ghibellines, who represented the old imperial aristocracy, and the Guelphs, a party that was originally bourgeois and looked to the pope as a political power rather than a spiritual leader. Violent conflicts between the two parties erupted in 1248, 1251, 1258, and 1260; by 1266, one year after Dante's birth, the Guelphs gained control of Florence, ushering in thirty years of prosperity and relative peace. Then the Guelphs split into the so-called Blacks and Whites, the latter being the party of Dante. By 1299, Dante was serving as an ambassador for Florence, and in the spring of 1300 he was elected one of the six consulates governing the city. The effort to insure peace by eliminating factions and banishing party chiefs did not succeed, and continuing conflict resulted in the intervention by Boniface VIII on the side of the Blacks. Having overthrown their enemy, the Blacks purged the political offices by bringing the Whites to trial on false charges of graft and corruption. Dante, who had been sent to Rome as ambassador, was absent during the proceedings; convicted, he was permanently exiled from Florence and spent the remainder of his life with a series of patrons in the courts of Italy.

Dante's political experiences convinced him of the need to train the faculty of reason for the purpose of ordering society in a rational fashion. In the *Convivio* and the *De Monarchia*, Dante manifests his love of the truths that reason yields. Extolling the high mission of reason within society, Dante brings to fruition the theme that he had seeded in the sonnet in praise of the lady in the *Vita Nuova*, the woman who personifies philosophy.

The *Convivio*, or *Banquet*, consists of four treatises inspired by the *canzoni*, which as lyrical philosophical poems of a set pattern were for Dante the premier poetic form in Italian. He employs the term *convivio* in the sense that he is inviting men to a banquet of true knowledge, the purpose of which is to satisfy the fundamental need of rational beings.

After the first treatise, which is an apologia for his life and work up to that time, Dante explores in the second treatise the architecture of the cosmos and the sciences of the heavens, while in the third he pursues the theme of love in Aristotelian terms and in the fourth turns his philosophizing to the political realm, advocating the primacy of reason for the sake of a well-governed society.

This political significance of the love of reason Dante also elaborates in the three books of the *De Monarchia*. Aristotelian politics informs the first book as Dante insists on the separation of church and state and the need for a monarch who serves reason and law. The second book develops the view that God willed ancient Rome to its position of power and designated the emperor to rule all mankind. For Dante, who sought the revelation of God's will through history, Rome represented all that human reason could do before and aside from revelation. His reading of history led him to discern destiny in the fact that the Incarnation occurred during the Pax Romana of Augustus; that is, when Christ chose to be born and die under the authority of Rome, he sanctioned its preeminence as well as that of reason in human affairs. Thus, in the third book, Dante claims for the emperor supreme authority in secular matters, noting that in order to attain happiness in this life, reason and the emperor must prevail.

As Dante was moving toward a nuanced concept of love, so also was he intent on creating a literary form of comparable complexity. In the *De Vulgari Eloquentia* (*Concerning Vernacular Speech*), Dante devotes the first book to the genesis and nature of Italian and the second to a technical discussion of the rules for composing the *canzone*. More importantly, he suggests through his praise of poetry that the form itself is appropriate for expressing love, not merely as erotic passion but as the movement of the spirit that is motivated and informed by reason. The meaning or truth that reason discloses is allegory. Poetry, therefore, is a uniquely effective mode of expressing the life of the spirit because its literal sense, which seems to appeal only to the sensual, passionate nature, in fact contains the truth of reason.

The Divine Comedy

By the time Dante commenced work on *The Divine Comedy*, perhaps around 1307, he had formulated a theory of poetry consonant with his vision of the spiritual life as one that expresses not only erotic and philosophical love but also mystical. Deepening the allegorical meaning discloses the moral and anagogical as well. Dante herewith acknowledges that love in its erotic and rational manifestations alone cannot confer happiness on human beings; ultimately happiness depends on the love for God that opens up the possibility of everlasting blessedness, which is the destiny of humankind.

The *letter* teaches events; *allegory* suggests what one believes; the *moral* indicates what one ought to do; *analogy* reveals the ultimate end of life. So wrote Dante in the letter to the Can Grande della Scala as he explained the form, content, and purpose of his poem. Although it is possible to separate one level of meaning from another, just as it is to classify knowledge into categories like Aristotelian cosmology, to identify characters as biblical, mythological, historical, fictional, and to sort out moral instruction on the relative functions of church and state, such an approach may falter before the larger vision of the poem. *The Divine Comedy* is more than and other than a composite of Dante's previous writings. When Dante said at the conclusion of the *Vita Nuova* that he would write no more about Beatrice until such time as he could do so in a more noble way, his words might have been appended as well to the *Convivio* and the *De Monarchia*. The subjects on which he wrote in those treatises would have to await an entirely new treatment before they would come to life in the mind of the reader. In *The Divine Comedy*, the material of the earlier writings is not merely handled in a different way but rather undergoes a transformation at the hands of a man who himself has been transformed from seeing life in bits and pieces to seeing out of a vision of unity. Whereas Dante previously seemed to be building an understanding of the world through a process of selection and analysis, he now writes out of a vision that is essentially different from intellectual synthesis.

The radical shift in perspective relates to a radical transformation in Dante's life of the spirit and his experience of love. The lover of Beatrice and the lover of philosophy emerge now as the lover of God. Dante's mystical love is not an added dimension of the life of the spirit, but it is that which gives meaning to every other experience of love. Dante's love for God is that within which all manifestations of love come to life. To appreciate *The Divine Comedy* thus necessitates viewing the work as the expression of a man who wakes up—like Dante, the everyman protagonist of his poem—to the primordial fact of human existence: that he is a creature destined to love his creator. All his desires, thoughts, and actions are good insofar as they serve that destiny. What Dante understands about himself with respect to God and his personal destiny is applicable to every human being. By extension, every aspect of human life, from sexual love to political activity, is measured by the criterion of mystical love. Insofar as love for another person or service in the church and state serve love for God and ultimately further one on the journey to everlasting blessedness, they are good.

The insights of mystical theology are helpful in understanding Dante's journey through hell, purgatory, and paradise as a vision of human destiny fulfilled. Traditionally, mystical theology divides the spiritual journey into three stages of consciousness. In the first, a person disciplines reason in order to learn about himself, purging imperfections and endeavoring to love God by imitating Jesus Christ. This stage, called the Way of Purgation, is described as "active" because the individual is primarily aware of the effort he is making to become pleasing to God. In *The Divine Comedy*, the journey through hell is comparable to the purgative way as Dante, and every person who accompanies him spiritually through the poem learns about himself through the negative examples of the condemned souls he meets in the descent through the circles of hell to the frozen pit that holds Lucifer. Appropriately, Dante's guide through hell is the Latin poet Virgil, who, as the voice of reason, instructs Dante in the life of the spirit and helps him form the moral conscience that is needed to live according to God's will.

In mystical theology, the second stage in the journey is the Way of Illumination, wherein the soul continues the active cleansing of the exterior senses and the interior faculties of memory, intellect, and will and at the same time is given moments of illumination that clarify the meaning of life and its place in the cosmos. At this stage the person experiences himself as "passive," for he is aware that the understandings are being infused by the Holy Spirit rather than acquired through the use of reason. Dante's "Purgatory" corresponds to the illuminative way in that the active purgation of the soul continues as Dante and Virgil climb the mountain where the saved souls complete a cleansing of the seven major sins, after which Dante undergoes a final purgation and is given visions of the earthly paradise, the corruption of the Church, and Jesus Christ. Dante thus is illumined by the Holy Spirit with understandings that exceed human reason. Appropriately, Virgil as the voice of reason cedes his place as guide to Beatrice, who in Dante's matured and mystical vision has been transformed from the objective of erotic love to the bearer of God's grace.

The third stage of the mystical journey is the Way of Union, in which the soul experiences itself as utterly passive, the recipient of increasingly intense, delicate, and sublime manifestations of God's love and thus ever more intimately drawn to God in the divine embrace. Clearly there is no place for the workings of human reason in unitive love, which mystics treasure as a foretaste of celestial happiness. The "Paradise" corresponds to the unitive way as Dante, in the company of Beatrice, ascends through the heavenly spheres to the Empyrean, where Beatrice assumes her place among the beatified in the mystic rose and Saint Bernard leads Dante into the presence of the Virgin Mary who, at the request of Bernard, beseeches her Son to grant the mortal Dante the vision of God, which is reserved for the blessed souls. The structure of the heavens suggests the nature of unitive love: just as mystics experience God's love as perfection upon perfection, so are the beatified souls perfected, each according to its capacity to love. Thus there is a hierarchy of souls, each, however, complete and absolutely happy in love. Similarly, in mystical love each experience of unitive love is complete and satisfying in itself, with no remembrance of what has preceded it nor desire for anything more.

Mystical union is described as a marriage of wills, the human and the divine, which is brought about by God's grace. Thus the soul labors to imitate Jesus Christ and make itself pleasing to God through the exercise of reason and discipline of the senses and higher faculties, but it is God who perfects the soul, transforming it so that the soul feels the will as being conformed to the will of God. Thus does Dante sing in the final lines of his magnificent poem that he feels himself, instinct and intellect, perfectly harmonized by the love that moves harmoniously the sun and the other stars. Harmonized within himself, Dante feels himself harmonized with the universe and with God, by whom all harmony is made possible. Thus the movement of the spirit, which is love, is brought to perfection, or completion, in the vision of God and there is brought to fulfillment the destiny for which human beings are created. If a lifetime is needed to move and be moved toward that destiny, then Dante spent his lifetime in the quest to realize his destiny, intellectually, poetically, and above all, spiritually.

MARY E. GILES

Further Reading

Bloom, Harold, ed. *Dante's "The Divine Comedy."* New York: Chelsea House Publishers, 1987. The inclusion of essays by major Dante scholars such as Ernst Robert Curtius, Charles S. Singleton, and Erich Auerbach is a major virtue of this small volume.

Boyde, Patrick. *Dante, Philomythes and Philosopher: Man in the Cosmos.* Cambridge: Cambridge University Press, 1981. A challenging inquiry into Dante's views on cosmology and anthropology and how Dante transmuted them into poetic language.

Caesar, Michael, ed. *Dante. The Critical Heritage 1314 (?)–1870.* London and New York: Routledge, 1989. An invaluable reference, the book includes a history of critical responses to Dante as well as selections, in chronological order, from the immense bibliography about him.

Ferguson, Francis. *Dante.* New York: Collier Books, 1966. A concise introduction to the life and works of Dante, with insightful analysis of the theme of love.

Foster, Kenelm. *The Two Dantes and Other Studies.* Berkeley: University of California Press, 1977. Dante's thought and his "humanism" are the subjects of this solid study.

Freccero, John, ed. *Dante. A Collection of Critical Essays.* Englewood Cliffs, N.J.: Prentice-Hall, 1965. Leo Spitzer, Georges Poulet, Luigi Pirandello, and T. S. Eliot are among the authors of more than a dozen excellent essays.

Gilbert, Allan H. *Dante and His "Comedy".* New York: New York University Press, 1963. A helpful companion for interpreting *The Divine Comedy.*

Singleton, Charles S. *An Essay on the "Vita Nuova."* Cambridge: Harvard University Press, 1949. A fine essay from a noted Dante scholar.

WILLIAM OF OCKHAM

Born: C. 1285, probably in the village of Ockham in the county of Surrey, near London
Died: C. 1347, Munich (probably of the Black Death)
Major Works: The exact chronological order of Ockham's works is not known. His works on logic, physics, and theology written before 1324 are: *The Sum of All Logic, Exposition on the Book of Porphyry's Introduction to Aristotle's Categories, Exposition on the Book of Predicates, Compendium of Logic, Exposition on the Eight Books of the Physics of Aristotle, Commentary on the Sentences of Peter Lombard* (referred to as *Ordinatio* [Book 1] and *Reportatio* [Books 2–4], *Seven Discussions on Anything and Everything (Quodlibeta), On the Sacrament of the Altar, Predestination, God's Foreknowledge, Future Contingents.* Works written after 1324: *The Work of Ninety Days, Compendium of Errors of Pope John XXII, Eight Questions Concerning the Power and Dignity of the Pope, Dialogues Between Master and Disciples upon the Power of Emperors and Popes.*

Major Ideas

Nominalism rejects the view that there are universals (essences) in things; it emphasizes the experienced world of contingent beings.

The name used for a thing does not capture the essence of the thing but is simply a conventional sign used to refer to the thing.

Logic seeks to organize and clarify human thought.

Intuitive cognition is a certain grasp by sense and judgment of any particular being, while abstractive cognition based on intuitive cognition organizes many similar things under universal terms (names).

Ockham's razor is the principle of economy in theorizing; it calls for the least number of assumptions in the construction of an explanation.

God is known by faith in his revelation, not by reason examining his creation.

Creation and salvation are the manifestations of the divine will that call each person to a covenant partnership.

The claim of the papacy to be supreme over the secular realm is to be rejected.

The gospel law is the law of freedom.

William of Ockham (Occam) as a member of the Franciscan order studied and taught at Oxford from 1309 to 1323. He remained a "beginner" in theology; hence, Ockham is called the "Venerabilis Inceptor." He was prevented from occupying an official chair of theology probably by the chancellor of the university, who saw dangerous tendencies in Ockham's thought. The chancellor petitioned Pope John XXII (d. 1334) to examine the writings of his Oxford professor and Ockham was summoned to Avignon. There, while waiting three years for a theological commission to examine his *Commentary on the Sentences*, Ockham found himself embroiled in a controversy with the pope that would affect the remainder of his life. William argued that Jesus and Saint Francis of Assisi (d. 1226) taught by

their lives that spiritual perfection could be achieved only by the complete renunciation of all worldly property. This view, taken by the so-called spiritual Franciscans, was condemned by John XXII. Ockham believed that in this condemnation the pope demonstrated himself to be a heretic. Fleeing certain imprisonment and possible execution, Ockham sought the protection of the German emperor, Louis of Bavaria (d. 1347). Excommunicated, Ockham never left Munich, where he spent the remaining nineteen years of his life.

In his lifetime, Ockham, as a philosopher and theologian, was at the center of the major intellectual and political controversies of the fourteenth century. He remains controversial to the present day. He has been accused of bringing down the entire Scholastic synthesis of faith and reason. Some have seen him as the skeptic who denied causality and the universality of moral norms—in effect, the David Hume of the late Middle Ages. These characterizations are extreme. Blessed with a gift for the observation of facts and the dynamics of logic, Ockham was above all a theologian of the Middle Ages who accepted the basic tenets of the medieval world-view. He lived, however, at a time when the security of that world-view, so well represented by the order and harmony of the *Summa theologica* of Saint Thomas Aquinas (d. 1274) and the great Gothic cathedrals, was clearly breaking down. As paradoxical as it seems, it appears correct that the philosophy associated with the *Venerabilis Inceptor*, nominalism, represented a quest for certainty at a moment in Western history that experienced widespread anxiety about the essentials. At the same time, his philosophy contributed greatly to that loss of cosmic security so characteristic of our modern age.

Nominalism

The Middle Ages inherited from the philosophers of antiquity a theory of knowledge that sought to identify what one knows and how one knows it. This epistemology focused on the universal as it was found in the particular, for example, humanity as it is expressed in the individual human being. To understand nominalism, a brief description of this focus on the universals is necessary, for it is this epistemology against which Ockham's nominalism is reacting.

Saint Augustine (d. 430), who sought to integrate Platonic philosophy with the biblical heritage, taught that the Forms are the exemplars of all created things and in the mind of God before they exist in matter. God gave all created things an identity that stems from the universal form contained in the particular; hence, all horses share a common characteristic of *horseness* that distinguishes them from trees, which all share the universal, *treeness*. To know anything, the human mind needs to grasp the spiritual form in the matter, the universal in the particular, the one in the many. Centuries later,

Saint Thomas Aquinas, under the influence of Aristotelian philosophy, would understand the form in a particular thing to be actualizing itself as the created being strives for perfection. Both authors argued in different ways that the spiritual mind of human beings struggles to grasp from the limitations of matter the intelligible universal form that explains the core of being. In knowing the universal and by ordering all things in accord with a set of integrated and comprehensive ideas, the person moves from the creation to the creator, from the effect to the cause. Reason, as it strives to reach the essence of things, is in harmony with a faith that accepts the revelation of God, for both the creation and the Bible have the same source. The mind by its ascent from the material to the immaterial achieves a closeness to God, the source of all truth and the end of all human longings. Ideas that offer coherence and intelligibility were thought to be truly in touch with the real common element in all the individuals that form any particular class of being. Hence, this tradition is often referred to as realism.

Standing in a tradition that can be traced back to the Stoics and to some early Scholastics, notably Peter Abelard (1079–1142), William of Ockham claimed that universals are simply signs or names the mind employs to organize and represent several objects. Hence the label, *nominalism*, from the Latin *nomen*, meaning name. The universals are not in things but in the mind. With this claim Ockham shifted the orientation of the mind from the problem of being to that of language and logic, from the diversity of being to the diversity of terms used to describe being. Universal names (such as humanness, horseness, treeness) are simply devices by which a person organizes beings that are similar, rather than expressions of what is grasped by the knowing mind. Here is the repudiation of the ontological status of the universals.

Universals are not expressed by divine intelligence nor do they constitute the formative principle at the core of the creation, Ockham argues. The reason for the similarity of things is not that they all participate in a universal idea but, rather, that each thing is known and created by God as a single reality to be similar to other beings in the same class (as a builder uses the plans of one house to build another similar to it). In this nominalism, we see a shift from the view of the creation as a shadow and reflection of a higher level of being to the full reality of the experienced world of beings.

This shift to the world of real beings is basic to Ockham's views on what constitutes knowledge. He claims that our knowledge is grounded in an "intuitive cognition" of a particular aspect of reality. We know through our senses and by making judgments on what is directly experienced in the world or in ourselves. The singular is the immediate object of perception. The mind is in contact with reality and a sign (any name) stands for a real event in the world. The name for a thing represents the thing. When ideas organize many particulars in acts of induction (or as Ockham puts it, "abstractive cognition") they prompt the recognition of similarities among things. Logic is the arrangement of these ideas in order to obtain clarity of thought and an organized body of truths. Ockham's nominalism accepts the classical definition of truth as a correspondence between what one thinks and what is actually the case. The key difference between Ockham and many of his predecessors is that he claimed that what is known is the concrete particular, not the abstracted universal. In this Ockham stands in the tradition of another famous Franciscan, Duns Scotus (d. 1308), in that both sought to repudiate the dangers involved in a false hypostatization of abstraction.

Ockham's Razor

The cutting away of an elaborate hierarchy of ideas and concepts in the attempt to grasp the truth is popularly known as Ockham's razor. Ockham's parsimonious use of explanation stands in the tradition of Saint Francis, who taught his order to avoid "vain curiosity," and for centuries philosophers had tried to use as few principles as possible to explain the essence of reality. However, it was Ockham's nominalism that sought above all to shave away the multiple abstractions that others thought necessary to explain things. Thus we read in his *Quodlibeta Septem* that "when a proposition comes out true for things, if two things suffice for

its truth, it is superfluous to assume a third." This same idea is expressed elsewhere in the *Ordinatio* in the words "plurality should not be assumed without necessity."

God

In his thinking about God, Ockham limited reason to what could be directly experienced. Hence, truths about God could not be demonstrated by reason but rather must be held by faith. For Ockham, the universe does not flow out of the eternal structures of God, as various versions of medieval Neoplatonism claim, but rather from divine decree. Since the creation and the creator have no common ontological ground, the doctrine of analogy, which holds that one can see in the creation reflections of the creator, cannot be used as justification for statements about the divine. What is needed to know God is a faith in his words as revealed in the Bible. In this separation of reason from faith, the harmony of faith and reason so dear to Scholastics is rent by an epistemology that sees these as two separate ways of knowing. They form the basis of a twofold truth, one relating to the sacred, the other to the secular. Reason cannot demonstrate the certainty of revelation. It is able only to elucidate the implications, meaning, and value of revelation.

Ockham, along with Scotus, shifted the focus from the Thomistic emphasis on divine intelligibility worked out throughout the creation to the divine will that called humanity to, above all, love God and obey his commandments. Rejecting the God of metaphysics who as the primary cause empowers and acts through a series of secondary causes, Ockham affirmed the God of the covenant who invites humanity to act as a free partner in the building of the creation.

Society and Papal Power

In the midst of his controversy with Pope John XXII, Ockham wrote in a letter to his Franciscan brothers that against this "pseudo-pope I have set my face like flint." The hostility generated over the question of spiritual poverty and Ockham's own experience of papal power occasioned a series of political writings that sought to define the limit of that power in relationship to the individual and to secular society as a whole. His political views are complex and cannot be reduced to any single principle of nominalism. While the assumptions of nominalism are present, what emerges in the work of the last third of his life are key ecclesiological themes that would be more fully and systematically developed by later writers. The Inceptor was the first great medieval Christian theologian to engage in a sustained and elaborate intellectual attack upon a reigning pope. In this he would anticipate a long and significant tradition in later Western thought.

In 1302, Pope Boniface VIII (d. 1303) issued his most famous papal bull, *Unam Sanctam*, in which he argued that the Church has power over the two swords (Luke 22:38), the spiritual and the temporal. Since the eternal is higher than the temporal and the spiritual greater than the material, the pope thus has jurisdiction over all creatures. This claim, the zenith of a long process of medieval papal assertions to primacy over the creation, emerged from the same hierarchical participation view of being that was being directly attacked by nominalism.

Ockham, while not rejecting the commission to Peter (Matthew 16:18) and the spiritual authority of the Church, rejects the idea of the subordination of the secular society to the sacred one. Worldly kingdoms exist to aid individuals to achieve the common good and to help sinful humanity through the use of just laws. Empires exist as a direct result of God's will, not through the power invested in God's holy people. Thus, Ockham notes that the Bible accepts the existence of Egypt and Babylon, while Jesus and his apostles respected and obeyed the laws of the Roman Empire. The command "render to Caesar" (Matthew 22:21) is the obligation to recognize in the very existence of non-Christian societies the will of God. All persons, no matter what their creed, are given by God the right to life, health, and dominion over the creation (Genesis 1:28). In this, Ockham affirms the radical contingency of all secular societies directly on the will of God as opposed to the power of the Church. Also, this line of thought articulates his attempt to desecrate secular

society and governmental powers while at the same time maintaining their value.

In the claims of Boniface and his successors, Ockham saw a contradiction to the witness of Jesus, who came to serve, not to be served (Luke 22:27). This assertion of papal authority over temporal affairs was also, to one who experienced excommunication, the source of oppression. For Ockham, the basic principle set forth in his *Dialogus* was "Lex Evangelica est lex libertatis." This law of freedom at the core of the gospel means that individuals will find in their faith liberation from ignorance and sin in a partnership with God that alone brings harmony and peace. In the Franciscan ideal, only the knowledge derived from this faith offers to the individual freedom from the oppression of sinful men.

Ockham's Influence

Some scholars have seen in Ockham all the key themes that would later form the core of the Reformation. While it is well known that through later theologians, such as Gabriel Biel (d. 1495), nominalism would be communicated to the sixteenth century, it would not be correct to identify the principle of "Sola Scriptura" as Ockham's own. Although many passages seem to lead to that principle, comprehensive studies of Ockham's writings have resulted in the conclusion that he was more in line with the "two-source" view of the Council of Trent (1545–63), in which both revelation and tradition serve as avenues of divine truth. Jesus had promised to be with the Church until the end of time (Matthew 28:20) and thus, by rejecting the true faith, John XXII, in Ockham's eyes, became a heretic and so ceased to be the true earthly leader of the Christian community. Nevertheless, parallels with the later reformers of the fifteenth and sixteenth centuries can be noted in the following Ockhamite themes: that the visible structures are to be at the service of the spiritual life of faith, that clergy are called to minister not to rule, that secular power has its own independent sphere of influence, that the Christian in the faith that comes from baptism can repudiate a pope who is in heresy, and that no human institution is final or absolute.

The reformers would stand with Ockham in the repudiation of the God of the metaphysicians in favor of the biblical God of the covenant whose will is expressed in word and deed. Although there are many rationalistic elements in Ockham's writings, later ages would develop his voluntarism. Although there are many arguments for the value of institutions, later ages would champion his focus on the individual just as Ockham embodied the rising individuality of the late Middle Ages.

Ockham did not form a school or gather disciples around himself. Nevertheless, the main lines of his nominalism would influence numerous scholars in the intellectual centers of the fourteenth century, notably at the universities at Oxford and Paris. His thought became known as the "modern way" (*via moderna*) as opposed to the "old way" (*via antiqua*) of thirteenth-century Scholasticism. This title proved to be prophetic. Later science would find in nominalistic epistemology an empirical and inductive method that grounded verification in the full reality of the experienced world. Nominalism would clearly delineate, and at the same time reduce, the realm of the knowable. In the loss of coherence, purpose, and hierarchical metaphysical order, life and reality seemed much more complex. William of Ockham stands at the beginning of a long modern tradition where the mind in its struggle with the contingent order of being seeks to overcome the gap between itself and reality.

LAWRENCE F. HUNDERSMARCK

Further Reading

Adams, Marilyn McCord. *William Ockham*. 2 vols. Notre Dame, Ind.: University of Notre Dame Press, 1987. This is an encyclopedic 1,400-page work in which many of the most important passages from Ockham are identified and clearly translated. This study seeks to situate the Inceptor's thought in the context of the intellectual traditions of the late thirteenth and early fourteenth centuries. This study will be difficult for beginners but for the more seasoned reader of Ockham, it yields many insights.

Boehner, Philotheus. *Collected Articles on Ockham*. St. Bonaventure, N.Y.: Franciscan Institute Publications, 1958. This is a collection of twenty-four articles on a wide range of topics from text studies to the metaphysics, epistemology, and politics of William. Boehner was one of the most important twentieth-century interpreters of Ockham. His careful work with the primary sources has greatly helped modern scholars appreciate the complexities and nuances in the texts.

Carré, Meyrick H. *Realists and Nominalists*. London: Oxford University Press, 1946. This work is an easy-to-read, straightforward account of the realist–nominalist debate in the Middle Ages through a consideration of the positions of Augustine, Abelard, Aquinas, and Ockham.

Leff, Gordon. *The Dissolution of the Medieval Outlook: An Essay on the Intellectual and Spiritual Change in the Fourteenth Century*. New York: Harper & Row, 1976. A short, sweeping overview of the fourteenth century that offers the reader a general introduction to the problems, the tensions, and the pluralism of the age.

Leff, Gordon. *William of Ockham: The Metamorphosis of Scholastic Discourse*. Manchester: Manchester University Press, 1975. This is Leff's magisterial study of Ockham, which attempts to set forth in a comprehensive manner all of William's positions on the most important issues relating to the cognitive, the theological, and the created order. This study is accessible to the novice; however, its sheer volume requires discipline and patience.

McGrade, Arthur Steven. *The Political Thought of William of Ockham: Personal and Institutional Principles*. London: Cambridge University Press, 1974. This work seeks to situate Ockham within the political institutions of the age; the study identifies the controlling motives in the Inceptor's social philosophy while offering a positive assessment of his efforts at Church reform.

Oberman, Heiko Augustinus. *The Harvest of Medieval Theology: Gabriel Biel and Late Medieval Nominalism.* Cambridge, Mass.: Harvard University Press, 1963. This important study in the history of Christian theology clearly demonstrates the influence of Ockham and the impact of nominalistic ideas as they were transmitted and developed throughout the fifteenth century.

Trinkaus, Charles, with Heiko A. Oberman. *The Pursuit of Holiness in Late Medieval and Renaissance Religion: Papers from the University of Michigan Conference.* Leiden: E. J. Brill, 1974. This is a collection of learned papers addressing a wide range of topics in theology, lay piety, humanism, and the arts. The first five studies, which directly relate to Ockham, are especially valuable for the identification of the key religious implications that emerge from nominalism.

DESIDERIUS ERASMUS

Born: 1466, Rotterdam, the Netherlands

Died: 1536, Basel, Switzerland

Major Works: *Adages* (1500), *Enchiridion* (1504), *Praise of Folly* (1509), *The Education of a Christian Prince* (1516), *Novum Instrumentum* (1506)

Major Ideas

Perfectability is intrinsic in human beings.

Intrinsic perfectability implies the power of self-determination and moral achievement.

The exemplar of moral achievement is Jesus Christ, whose life of humility, patience, and love is open for all Christians to imitate.

Interior piety, scriptural exegesis, and study of classical and patristic writings are necessary in the imitation of Christ.

Imitating the life of Jesus Christ is a philosophy, the "philosophia Christi," which ought to inspire secular and religious leaders to govern with compassion for the well-being of all Christian people.

Desiderius Erasmus was a man for his times in his humanistic interest in ancient writers and concern for revitalizing Christianity in the spirit of *devotio moderna*. Ultimately, however, he proved to be outside of his time; his call for moderation and compassion was drowned out by the raucous cries of reformers and rebels who regarded the middle path as cowardly.

Erasmus dedicated his life to cultivating the mind for a rational program of action and the heart for generosity and tolerance. His abiding compassion was nurtured early in his studies; from 1478 to 1483, Erasmus attended the school at Deventer that Gerard Groote had founded, establishing there the *devotio moderna* that encouraged inner piety, a personal relationship with God, and reliance on the Bible for moral and spiritual guidance. Groote had also founded the Brethren of the Common Life, a lay congregation that was committed to education and living out the ideals of *devotio moderna*. The years that Erasmus spent at Deventer, which is known as the seedbed of Dutch humanism, obviously left their mark; throughout his life Erasmus remained true to the ideal of a simple, interiorized Christianity in the face of religious practices that fomented superstition, bigotry, and fanaticism, and a church that gave high marks to blind adherence to doctrine and empty exterior piety. These early years also introduced Erasmus to Latin, whetting his ap-

petite for the study of classical literature that he would pursue in the monastery of the Augustinian Canons at Steyn, where he entered in 1487.

The life of the monk did not attract Erasmus, but for a young man who could not afford to go to a university, the monastery had its advantages. Erasmus was not to remain enclosed, however; the year following his ordination in 1492, he left the monastery to accept the post of secretary to the Bishop of Cambray, Henry of Bergen.

With his departure from monastic life, Erasmus embarked on the career of a Peripatetic humanist in search of a patron, which took him to the most celebrated universities of Europe and England. Change of patronage was not necessarily Erasmus's preferred course, and he often bemoaned the financial uncertainties that forced him to seek yet another protector. Frail of constitution and emotionally vulnerable, Erasmus's life was one of hardship.

Yet in one respect he did not waver; his commitment to evangelical humanism was his polestar. His comprehensive knowledge of the classics as well as familiarity with classical languages, which enabled him to develop as a stylist in Latin such as to rival the eminent writers among the ancients, always served the larger goal of encouraging growth in the moral life and interiorized Christianity.

The spirit of evangelical humanism informs all of

Erasmus's writings, beginning with the popular *Adages*, the number of some 800 proverbs in the first edition eventually being increased to more than 5,000. Drawn from Greek and Latin texts, and to a lesser extent from the Bible, the proverbs collected by Erasmus probe the human condition, providing a basis on which to build the edifice of self-knowledge that is necessary for the Christian in search of moral excellence.

Erasmus's humanism extended to the study of the church fathers as well as to the ancients. In the *Enchiridion*, the Greek word for a poniard and a manual, Erasmus adds the authority of Jerome, Ambrose, Augustine, and Origen to that of classical orators, poets, and philosophers in order to fashion a program for a Christian life centered on the example of Jesus Christ. In a letter to the humanist John Colet, Erasmus explained that he had written the *Enchiridion* to persuade followers of external ceremonies and observances to true inner piety; he regarded his work as an act of piety. Not only does Erasmus advocate interiorized Christianity on the individual level but he expands his evangelical message to include nations, whose foremost concern ought to be social harmony and peace among themselves. In his admiration for Origen, Erasmus was influenced by the Greek Father's Neoplatonism, and his program of interior piety was further indebted to the Neoplatonism that he encountered among such humanists as Pico della Mirandola and John Vitrier.

Praise of Folly

The note of Neoplatonism rings true in the evangelical humanism of Erasmus's most famous work, *Praise of Folly*. Although Erasmus himself did not regard the work as his masterpiece, its popularity in his time and the fact that in the large corpus of Erasmian writings it is the only text that has survived with its appeal intact secures for it first place. The hallmarks of Erasmus the humanist are instantly recognizable: mastery of the ancients, scriptural exegesis, criticism of contemporary religious practices, call to the inner life. There is the additional attraction of the satirical mode, probably inspired by the second-century Greek wit Lucian, by

which Erasmus mediates the themes of Christian piety.

Praise of Folly is no exercise in satire. The text is a complex interfacing of at least four voices, rather like a Bach fugue, each identifiable in turn and deftly played one against the other. Were the explicit mockery of the first voice (Folly's as she introduces herself as humanity's principal benefactor along with such attendants as Self-Love and Flattery) to remain in the same key, Erasmus would have exhausted his parody in brief time and fallen short of the spiritual heights he exhorts Christians to attain.

The light-hearted tone gives way suddenly when, less than midway through the text, Erasmus shows not the fun of folly in the illusions that allow society to function but its cruelty, as old men and women, shorn of their illusions, are depicted in grotesque, aging bodies, pursuing the pleasures of the young. These voices play in counterpoint until gaity and cruelty are stilled by Erasmus's serious pronouncements against the abuses and pretensions of those in positions of authority, both secular and religious. No one is safe from Erasmus's attack: theologian and monk, cardinal, pontiff, king and courtier—none escapes criticism. The theologians he contrasts with the apostles, who made no such stupid distinctions as between infused and acquired charity or actual and sanctifying grace but who taught charity and grace through the example of their lives. Theologians waste their time in the schools with such nonsense, although "they believe that just as in the poets Atlas holds up the sky on his shoulders, they support the entire Church on the props of their syllogisms and without them it would collapse."

If Christ is the positive example for pious Christians, the monks are the negative ones, for their concern is not to be like Christ but only to be unlike each other. Nor do bishops, cardinals, and pontiffs offer better models for the Christian who would turn inward to cultivate the virtues of humility and charity. Bishops play the overseer only with respect to their revenues; cardinals put ambition for wealth and prestige above inner riches; and pontiffs glory in war rather than the cross.

The picture that Erasmus paints of the Church is

dreary at best. He does nothing to soften the blows of his frontal attack on the corruption of religion, nor does he hide behind the skirts of Folly. Indeed, the figure of Folly serves his criticism well. As a parody of herself, Folly entices the reader with bantering humor to scrutinize himself and society, setting up the reader, as it were, for the harshness of Erasmus's voice when he summons Christian leaders to an accounting of their ways.

Were *Praise of Folly* to end on this note of harsh criticism, Erasmus's program of Christian human-ism would be incomplete. Satire is the material with which he constructs his edifice of Christian human-ism, but the spirit that lights and warms the build-ing is revealed only in the concluding pages as Erasmus evokes for our moral and spiritual edifica-tion the person of the good fool.

In the little people—children, women, sim-pletons, fishermen—Erasmus seeks his good fool, the one who embraces the cross and who, like Jesus Christ, submits to its folly. For who in their right mind—the mind in accord with the values of worldly wealth, power, and prestige—would choose poverty, suffering, and self-sacrifice? Yet, Erasmus reminds his audience, if men and women are to embrace Christianity, they must do so with heart rather than mind, becoming foolish in the eyes of the world. Like Jesus who suffered the ignominy of crucifixion, Christians are to clasp the cross, imitating their Lord in patience, humility, and com-passion. Prizes for the Christian do not come in the form of money or high office, but there is in this lifetime a supreme reward, which is a kind of mad-ness.

In describing divine madness in the last chapter of *Praise of Folly*, Erasmus raises the vision of the Christian life far above the dirt and stench of the fools of hypocrisy and self-love. In a Neoplatonic flight of the spirit, he shows the soul absorbed in the supreme Mind, delighting in the ineffable goodness of God, and savoring a foretaste of the eternal re-ward. The souls who taste spiritual delights experi-ence a kind of madness. Fools for Christ, they taste divine folly. In an ingenious play on the meaning of folly, Erasmus thus strips the worldly of their illu-sions, exposing them for the bad fools they are and

pleads eloquently for the life of the good fool, the person who embraces the folly of the cross.

The scholarly apparatus that supports the mes-sage of Christian piety in *Praise of Folly* is clearly visible in subsequent works, notably in Erasmus's Greek version of the New Testament and the edition of Saint Jerome's letters. Erasmus shared the con-cern of contemporary humanists that ordinary Christians have access to the New Testament so as to avoid the superstition that corrupted the ignorant masses. Applying modern exegetical techniques, Erasmus produced a text in Greek that pointed up the errors in the Latin Vulgate, which had been the official text of Scripture since the fourth century. The effect of the Greek text was to call into question the authority of the Church as mediator of the rela-tionship of God and human beings; Erasmus envi-sioned a literate Christian populace who would derive immediate guidance from Scripture, thus taking upon themselves responsibility for their moral perfectability and, to a great extent, salvation of their souls.

A similar intent informs his work on Saint Jer-ome, whom the Brethren of the Common Life rev-ered as their patron. As Erasmus sought to reform Christian life through study of ancient literature and Scripture, so he saw in Jerome a precursor in his dedication to learning and interior piety.

By 1516, when both the *Novum Testamentum* and Jerome's letters were published, Erasmus was at the height of his popularity. The most acclaimed hu-manist of the day, he was honored by monarch and pope; Charles V, whose education was based on Erasmian principles, was eager to claim the cele-brated humanist, but to no avail. Invited to the newly established but already brilliant university at Alcalá de Henares, Erasmus confided to his friend, Thomas More, that Spain held no attraction for him. The invitation was, however, a pledge of distinction for Erasmus, and had the ensuing years been as beneficent as the emperor who proferred the invita-tion, Erasmus's later years would have been less painful.

Events were not to grace Erasmus with the peace for which he longed. Added to the continuing uncer-tainties about money was the threat of schism in the

Christian world. Even though he continued to compose masterly commentaries on the Christian life, inspired by the classics and Scripture, his spirit was unsettled and his mind distracted by the religious controversies that erupted around him. Against his will, he was drawn into the arena, answering Luther's position on grace and free will with a disquisition on free will in 1524. Relying on the combined authority of Scripture, tradition, and reason, Erasmus defended his stance on free will, reaffirming his belief in moral autonomy for the individual as well as his fidelity to the Catholic church.

Erasmus could neither find a place for himself in the Europe of his day nor make one, for he was both within his age and outside of it. True to the humanistic impulse of the sixteenth century, Erasmus believed in the power of rational persuasion, but his very commitment to reason rendered him powerless against the forces of intolerance, fear, and dissension that ultimately ruled the day. Although his plea for moderation and enlightened piety was stilled by voices competing for power at the expense of charity, to those who value rational discourse refined in the crucible of learning and compassion, Erasmus was then and remains today an exemplary human being.

MARY E. GILES

Further Reading

Bainton, Roland H. *Erasmus of Christendom*. New York: Charles Scribner's Sons, 1969. A classic study on Erasmus's life and work, the author's account is comprehensive and insightful.

DeMolen, Richard L., ed. *Essays on the Works of Erasmus*. New Haven and London: Yale University Press, 1978. The variety of emphases in the essays reflects the range and depth of Erasmian thought.

Huizinga, John A. *Erasmus and the Age of Reformation*. New York: Harper & Row, 1957. A thoroughly readable portrait of Erasmus the humanist beleaguered by religious controversy.

Levi, A. H. T. "Introduction" to *Praise of Folly*. Translated by Betty Radice. New York: Penguin Books, 1971. The author concisely explains Erasmus's humanism within a complex of tradition and innovation in philosophy.

Spitz, Lewis W. *The Religious Renaissance of the German Humanists*. Cambridge, Mass.: Harvard University Press, 1963. A fine study of Erasmus, Neoplatonism, and the *devotio moderna*.

NICCOLÒ MACHIAVELLI

Born: 1469, Florence, Italy
Died: 1527, Florence, Italy
Major Works: *The Prince* (1513), *Discourses on the First Ten Books of Titus Livius* (1513–17), *The Art of War* (1521), *The History of Florence* (1525)

Major Ideas

Wisdom in the ways of the world can be achieved by careful observation of how people act and a study of history.

Human nature is such that individuals will seek gratification of their lusting for power, pleasures, and profit.

The essential feature of all society is struggle and intense competitiveness.

The wise prince ought to do whatever is expedient to achieve and maintain power.

Consideration of the dictates of traditional morality and religion are not relevant unless they aid in the enhancement of the goods of a well-ordered society.

Human excellence is measured in terms of virtù, *the capacity of intellect and will to act with dynamic vitality.*

The most vital states are those republics where their citizens enjoy the maximum freedom to be masters of their own destiny.

Niccolò Machiavelli was educated in the tradition of Greek and Roman writers, in accord with the prevailing custom of the Renaissance. Machiavelli's father, a lawyer in Florence, saw to it that his son received the best possible grounding in the humanities. This excellent education bore fruit, for at the age of twenty-nine, Machiavelli entered the service of the Florentine Republic, where as a secretary to the Chancellor he was responsible for the foreign and diplomatic relations of the Republic. He served the government for fourteen years on numerous difficult and delicate diplomatic missions throughout France, Germany, and Italy.

Machiavelli had opportunities to observe first-hand some of the leading powers of the day, King Louis XII of France (1462–1515), Pope Alexander VI (1431–1503), Cesare Borgia (1476–1507), Pope Julius II (1443–1513), and Maximilian I, the Holy Roman Emperor (1459–1519). He watched and noted carefully the political intrigues of his time. He would later write with admiration about the cunning designs of Cesare Borgia, the conqueror of Romagna, an area south of Ravena on the Adriatic Sea. Machiavelli was greatly impressed with Cesare, thinking him superhuman in courage and grand designs, one who would control everything and was capable of governing with extreme secrecy, in essence, the very ideal of Machiavelli's later, most famous work, *The Prince*. For this young diplomat, Cesare Borgia was the embodiment of one who ruled with power and glory while laying the foundation for future power.

As a keen observer of political events, Machiavelli realized that they who keep power were those able to accommodate their actions and personalities to the shifting circumstances of their situation. For him, the shrewdest rulers were those who acted when the moment required action and withdrew when withdrawal was mandated. Thus even his hero, Cesare Borgia, made the fatal mistake of backing Julius II for the papacy, failing to realize the well-concealed hatred of the new pope toward him—in essence, failing to keep his judgments firmly rooted in reality. One needs, as Machiavelli put it in the eighteenth chapter of his *Prince*, "to turn and turn about as the winds and the variations of fortune dictate."

Machiavelli's own fortunes also fell before Julius, who ordered his armies of the Holy League to suppress the Florentine Republic and thus restored the power of the Medici. This they accomplished in 1512, leaving Machiavelli, who sought to defend the city with a citizen army, in disgrace and without employment. He returned to his country home and began a long period of reflection, which resulted in the works on political philosophy that have made his name immortal.

Machiavelli's two most important works, *The Prince* and *The Discourses on the First Ten Books of Titus Livius*, both deal with the rise and decline of states and the measures by which a leader can insure the states' continued existence. This issue is approached from different angles in the two works. *The Prince*, Machiavelli's most well-known work, focuses on the activity of the individual ruler, while *The Discourses* considers the constitutive elements that accounted for the success of the ancient Roman Empire. His approach in these works, which was carried on in his later *Art of War* and *The History of Florence*, was not to start from an assumption about the nature of a perfectly good society but, rather, to focus on how societies actually work. His method was experiential and pragmatic. Thus, in the preface to *The Prince*, a work written in an attempt to gain employment with the new masters of Florence, the Medici, he writes that he bases his thoughts on his own "lengthy experience" over "many years" and with "many troubles and perils" as well as his "continual reading" of ancient history.

Machiavelli's works thus inaugurate a new development in the West's reflection on the key issues of political philosophy. He thought that no longer should such discussions depend on the doctrine of theology or moral philosophy. Here is modern political science looking to what has happened and seeing in the interplay of natural forces reasons for events. Personal experience and a careful reading of history were for him indispensable tools for knowing the things of this world.

With the writings of Machiavelli, politics establishes itself as an autonomous field of study, namely, the art of creating, perfecting, and enhancing the power of the state. Thus, the true prince seeks to establish a government that will bring honor to himself and benefit the whole body of his subjects.

Corruption as the Key to Power

Machiavelli's observations of the behavior of the rich and the powerful led him to the view that humanity is corrupt. Men and women will when given the chance, always turn toward evil and self-gratification. His writings were especially preoccupied with what one might call the pathology of states. He was interested in the reasons for the decline and fall of states. He gives careful attention to the tragedies of life because for him the wise student of history has much to learn from what has failed to work.

Machiavelli always insisted on the uniformity of humanity. This theme that human beings are always the same in their nature was reiterated hundreds of times in his works. Standard was the formula "all men are born, live and die in the same way, and therefore resemble each other." All are animated by the same passions, the same desires, and the same impulses.

The corruption of human nature was not a new idea, for many theologians and philosophers had made the same point when discussing the effects of Original Sin. Machiavelli, however, rarely thought in abstract theological terms. For him, the claim that humanity is ruthless, blindly abandoning itself to a lust for pleasures, power, and profit was a plain, observable fact. In *The Discourses* he cautions anyone who wishes to found a state and to give it laws to begin with the basic presupposition that everyone is evil and will show their vicious nature. Even if this evil disposition remains concealed for a time, the wise prince must never be deceived into thinking that his subjects will not, at the earliest opportunity, seek their own self-interest.

For Machiavelli this acquisitiveness was normal, a natural fact. He, unlike innumerable medieval writers, accepted this as the human lot. On this point we find little of the preacher in him. He often notes throughout his *History of Florence* the many times Florentine rulers, like those throughout the history of Rome, were so enamored with their lives of wealth and comfort that they failed in the defense of their own city and thus hastened their own destruction. So Machiavelli's famous cynical remark that a man would more readily forgive the murder of his father than the confiscation of his patrimony. Thus the prudent ruler may kill, but ought not to plunder.

The natural feature of all societies is struggle and intense competitiveness. Men, he writes, always commit the error of not knowing when to limit their hopes. For him, our passions are endless, our desires bottomless. So we read in the fifteenth chapter of *The Prince*:

> My intention being to write something of use to those who understand, it appears to me more proper to go to the real truth of the matter than to its imagination; . . . for how we live is so far removed from how we ought to live, that he who abandons what is done for what ought to be done will rather learn to bring about his own ruin than his preservation. A man who wishes to make a profession of goodness in everything must necessarily come to grief among so many who are not good.

Previous to Machiavelli, there was a long discussion beginning with Plato (c. 429–347 B.C.) and carried throughout the Middle Ages that affirmed that the ruler ought to embody noble ideals and values. This tradition focused on the virtues of justice and mercy as essential for good government. Machiavelli turns away from this tradition and considers in *The Prince* what is necessary to be successful in a corrupt world. It is the situation at the moment that determines which actions are necessary. For Machiavelli, the goal is success, not the virtue or vice of the act. He does not advocate that the successful prince should always violate the rights of others but, rather, calculate what course of action will enhance the strength and vitality of the state.

The Prince is, in essence, a technical book about how to grasp and hold power, rather than one focused on the issues of morality or immorality. Machiavelli saw it as quite enough to offer his advice on what worked and what did not work in advancing a political career. Like a skilled physician, a skilled politician must be able to make an accurate diagnosis and then proceed with a proper course of treatment. Thus Machiavelli's works aim at offering an analysis of the ills of a state and the best possible corrective that should be prescribed. He does not let traditional questions of morality deter the ruler from proper action. Just as, in the hands of a skilled physician, poison may save the life of a patient, so force in the hands of a skilled ruler may eventuate in the health of the whole community. Or, to use another image, for Machiavelli political activity is like a game of chess with its rules, its proven gambits, and its successful strategies. The master player knows how to exploit the weaknesses and blunders of his opponents to maximum advantage. The goal is finding the best move, the move that wins. The qualities needed to win may be judged as vices by others, but, as Machiavelli puts it in *The Prince*, they are "the vices by which you are able to rule." The crimes committed in order to preserve one's country are "glorious crimes." Thus, in the fifth chapter of his *History of Florence* we read, "No good man will ever reproach another who endeavors to defend his country whatever be his mode of doing so."

It is much safer that the prince be feared than loved. Machiavelli advises princes not to be troubled if they are called cruel, for to be cruel is often necessary, especially if one is a commander of an army. Although in the *Discourses* he notes that "a multitude is more easily governed by humanity and gentleness than by haughtiness and cruelty," the point is that a wise ruler does whatever is necessary. What is unnecessary is for the prince actually to have good qualities; all that is necessary is for the prince to *appear* to have them in order to win the confidence of the people. We find in the seventeenth chapter of *The Prince* Machiavelli's use of the example of Pope Alexander VI, who did nothing else but deceive men, always finding victims, by successfully disguising his intentions. He, like his son Cesare Borgia, was as wise as a fox and as terrifying as a lion. All this is clearly summarized in the following passage from the second chapter of *The Discourses*:

Government consists mainly in so keeping your subjects that they shall be neither able nor disposed to injure you; and this is done by depriving them of all means of injuring you, or by bestowing such benefits upon them that it would not be reasonable for them to desire any change of fortune.

Religion and the State

According to *The Discourses*, religion, in terms of its rituals and ceremonies, was "the instrument necessary above all others for the maintenance of a civilized state." The religion of ancient Rome, Machiavelli thought, helped to maintain the strength of the army, binding it by loyalty to an oath. Also, all Roman legislators had recourse to the gods when they introduced laws to the people. For Machiavelli, a source of strength for a country lay in its uncorrupted ceremonies and its veneration of the gods because they instilled bravery and upheld the common good.

This vitality was lost when Christianity began to preach an ethic of humility and docility. In his *Discourses* Machiavelli notes that Christ did not redeem humanity but through Christianity hastened its decline. Christianity glorified the meek, leaving the world to the domination of the arrogant and the wicked. Machiavelli preferred a Roman ethic, which elevated self-preservation, to a Christian one of sacrifice. The necessities of war to maintain and enhance security makes Christian pacifism treasonable and dangerous. If the world were different, if the Church had retained the purity of its ideals, then men would certainly be far happier than they are at present. He writes in *The Discourses*: "And whoever examines the principles on which that religion is founded, and sees how widely different from those principles its present practice and application are, will judge that her ruin or chastisement is at hand."

This contemporary of Luther condemns the Roman Church not out of a religious zeal but rather from the perspective of a thoroughgoing secularism. In Machiavelli's writings the sacred side of the human soul disappears and only its secular elements

(instinct, desire, appetite, emotions, and power) remain. Here is animality guided by intelligence. Religion has value not because it elevates and ennobles humanity but because it can serve as a vehicle of political order. For Machiavelli the focus is on the state; religion is useful if it inspires loyalty rather than salvation. We see here the challenge of a revived paganism to an aging Christianity.

Virtù

The Italian word *virtù* means "virtue," and was a very important term for Machiavelli. It represented a most basic quality for a successful leader. Early in *The Discourses* he declares that the fortunes of a city depend on the *virtù* of its founder. The term sometimes refers to the traditional moral and intellectual virtues emphasized in the writers of antiquity. Often, however, it becomes a key term for Machiavelli expressing the capacity for effective action, a vitality. Therefore we find the use of the term not so much in the medieval sense of a set of virtues but, rather, in the Roman sense of activity—activity that brings honor and glory to the one who acts. With this in mind, Machiavelli often describes as virtuosi those military leaders like Hannibal (247–c. 182 B.C.) who exhibit prowess in war.

The men (*vir*) who exhibited *virtù* were alone able to bend fortune to their side. Machiavelli believed that only half of our lives is under our own control. The other half is under the sway of forces and factors beyond us. This is why history teaches that exactly the same acts at different times yield different results. For the Secretary of Florence, the success of every act depended on the relationship between it and its times. It was good fortune if such a harmonious relationship existed, bad fortune if it did not. As Virgil (70–19 B.C.) put it in his tenth book of *The Aeneid*, "Fortune befriends the bold." Machiavelli was sure that princes become great only when they overcome difficulties and obstacles. Here the Renaissance rediscovers the classical idea of fortune as a woman who looks kindly on men who exhibit the manly virtues of self-reliance and self-affirmation even in the worst of times.

Self-determination

The absolutistic and despotic features of Machiavelli's *Prince* have overshadowed another important dimension of his thought, the value of freedom as an essential element of a good state. Falsely read as a writer who advocated only the absolute will of one dictator at the expense of the free wills of his subjects, Machiavelli is often not credited for his attention to the value of self-determination as a general feature of a healthy state. Indeed, it was his lifelong dream that Italy would unite as one state to overcome her many foreign oppressors. Interestingly, one source of Machiavelli's hostility toward the Church of Rome stemmed from his belief that she stood in the way of complete Italian unity because of her intense preoccupation with control over the papal states. It was his view that the Church was too weak to control the whole of the peninsula, but too strong to permit anyone else from unifying all of Italy.

Unity can be achieved only if people awake to their heritage of republican liberty. This, Machiavelli thought, was the secret of Greek and Roman glory. For Greece and Rome grew only when they were able to sustain themselves in liberty. These ancient states and the old Florentine Republic had as their aim the good of the whole. In strong states, all men freely seek the common good.

The belief in the importance of freedom lies behind Machiavelli's advocacy that the people themselves defend their own territories. The entire population ought to be filled with that intense fervor, that *virtù*, to affirm their own rights. In *The Art of War*, Machiavelli, reflecting on why in 1494 the French had so easily triumphed over the Italians, concludes that it was due in large part to the dependence of the Italians on unreliable mercenary soldiers rather than, as ought to be the case, an army of patriots led courageously by their own prince.

The key to power in the state is unity in diversity. In a healthy state all members would, in their diversity, be oriented toward the same noble ends. Here Cicero (106–43 B.C.) becomes Machiavelli's guide, for both saw in nature a model of diversity that acts as a vast interrelated system. It is in this vein that the Secretary of Florence looked with admiration on the Roman Republic and its practice of keeping a delicate balance between the opposing forces of rich and poor. This is why the Romans gave the nobles control of the Senate while assigning the Tribunate to the plebes. In this way, each faction could prevent the other from pushing to total dominance its own interests. Good laws emerge from that delicate equilibrium between competing groups who seek to affirm their own selfish aims while being kept in check by another equally powerful force. Here human societies can learn from the witness of nature.

Machiavelli's sincere enthusiasm for Roman self-governance led him to consider the value of law and custom as a guarantor of free action. He looked upon his present age with its divisions, disorder, and corruption as helpless before foreign invaders and noted, as did Cicero, that nature instills in humanity the hunger for independence. Cities grow and acquire greatness, he writes, only if "the people are in control of them." This explains why cities under monarchical governments seldom go forward as do those that live in freedom. Therefore, the whole citizen body must keep the quality of *virtù*, while the prince most of all seeks to overcome all threats to the self-preservation and self-determination of a state. The great lawgivers of the past knew, as did Lycurgus, the traditional founder of Sparta, that good laws ensure civil greatness. We read in *The Discourses*, "Just as hunger and poverty make men industrious, it is the laws that make them good."

Machiavellianism

Machiavelli was laid to rest in the Church of Santa Croce. Over his remains there stands a stately monument bearing the words "Tanto nomini nullum par elogium" (No eulogy would do justice to so great a name). His name was so great that it quickly became an adjective and the focus of controversy. Before the end of the sixteenth century, "Machiavellian" came to mean a preference for expediency over morality, a practice of duplicity, cunning, and intrigue in statecraft. The Church did not take kindly to Machiavelli's separation of morality from politics, nor to his critical remarks about the institutions of religion. They placed his works on the Index in 1559. *The Prince*, nevertheless, was widely read, and it overshadowed his comments in *The Discourses* about the value of human freedom and the common good. It became popular to identify the name for the devil, "Old Nick," as an abbreviation for Machiavelli's first name. In a famous scene from Christopher Marlow's work *The Jew of Malta*, penned about 1589, Machiavelli enters in the prologue with the line, "I count religion but a childish toy and hold there is no sin but ignorance." Shakespeare (1564–1616) would later enhance the dramatic use of the Machiavellian image with his portraits of Iago in *Othello* and of Richard III.

In an age that saw the rise of absolute monarchs, many thought that their grab for power was nothing but an action foretold by Machiavelli. The most famous literary condemnation of Machiavelli was offered by Frederick the Great (1712–86) in his work *Anti-Machiavel* (1740), where he writes:

> I venture now to take up the defense of humanity against this monster who wants to destroy it; with reason and justice I dare to oppose Sophistry and crime; and I put forth these reflections on *The Prince* of Machiavelli, chapter by chapter, so that the antidote may be found immediately following the poison.

Considering the later career of Frederick, many would note that by appearing to repudiate Ma-

chiavelli he was behaving in true Machiavellian fashion.

Today the term "Machiavellian" has entered the common lexicon of words that seem capable of a very wide range of diverse meanings. For some, the term is used to describe clever political maneuverings in every conceivable social context, while for others it implies a system of ethics where the ends justify the means. It is a label that seeks to characterize familiar uses of power, whether in the office politics of the modern corporation or in the ruthless tactics of dictators.

This great name to which "No eulogy would do justice" marked an important moment in the creation of the secular world view. In Machiavelli we see a definite break with the concerns of a Saint Augustine preoccupied with the City of God. Machiavelli's entire attention is given to the City of Man (literally: Machiavelli was certainly no feminist). One of the first to develop what we now call modern political science, with its focus on the utility and maintenance of power, Machiavelli, the keen observer of contemporary events, looked to the interplay of natural causes and effects rather than to transcendent religious influences. This is why his portrait of Cesare Borgia in *The Prince* is the forerunner of the "modern man" who frees himself from the conventional morality by the power of his own intellect and will—in essence, by the force of his own *virtù*.

LAWRENCE F. HUNDERSMARCK

Further Reading

Bonadeo, Alfredo. *Corruption, Conflict, and Power in the Works and Times of Niccolò Machiavelli*. Berkeley, Calif.: University of California Press, 1973. This is a very positive reappraisal of Machiavelli with careful attention to the sources of corruption and conflict, which *The Prince* and *Discourses* sought to control.

Burckhardt, Jacob. *The Civilization of the Renaissance in Italy*. New York: Modern Library, 1954. While not directly focused on Machiavelli, this most influential nineteenth-century study offers the reader a sweeping overview of the period.

Gilbert, F. *Machiavelli and Guicciardini: Politics and History in Sixteenth Century Florence*. New York: Norton, 1984. This is an outstanding study of Machiavelli's political thought wherein his views are compared with the Italian historian and political theorist Francisco Guicciardini (1483–1540).

Meineche, Friedrich. *Machiavellianism: The Doctrine of Raison d'Etat and Its Place in Modern History*. Translated by D. Scott. New Haven: Yale University Press, 1954. This is a translation of the 1924 classic study of the history of Machiavellianism.

Pitkin, Hanna. *Fortune Is a Woman: Gender and Politics in the Thought of Niccolò Machiavelli*. Berkeley, Calif.: University of California Press, 1984. A discussion of Machiavelli's focus on machismo as it emerges in his writings on authority, family life, the relationship between the sexes, and politics.

Schmitt, Charles B. and Quentin Skinner, eds. *The Cambridge History of Renaissance Philosophy*. Cambridge: Cambridge University Press, 1988. This text is a comprehensive and exhaustive study of the key philosophical ideas to emerge from the Renaissance.

Skinner, Quentin. *Machiavelli*. New York: Farrar, Straus, Giroux, 1981. A short and very readable overview of the Secretary's life and thought.

NICHOLAS COPERNICUS

Born: 1473, Toruń, Poland
Died: 1543, Frauenberg, East Prussia (now in Poland)
Major Works: *Commentariolus* (1540), *On the Revolutions of the Heavenly Spheres* (1543)

Major Ideas

Motion is relative.

The earth is not at the center of the universe.

The sun, the planets, and the stars do not revolve around the earth; rather, the earth is one of the planets, and it revolves around the sun, as do the other planets.

The apparent "loops" that the planets make in their motions across the heavens are not real motions; they are mere appearances, caused by our position on the earth and the earth's motion around the sun relative to the other planets.

The appearance of the heavens' rotation about the earth is due to the fact that we are on the earth's surface and the earth is rotating about its axis once every twenty-four hours.

It is imprudent for a government to allow two different currencies to circulate at the same time; if bad money circulates along with the good, the good money will soon disappear and only the bad will be left.

Nicolas Copernicus (in Polish, Nicolaus Koppernigk) was born in Toruń, a town in a part of Prussia that was then a part of the kingdom of Poland. Though it has changed hands from time to time, Toruń is once again a part of Poland.

Copernicus's father died when Nicolaus was ten years old. Fortunately, the boy's uncle, a prosperous clergyman, assumed responsibility for his general well-being and for his education. As bishop of Varmia, the uncle was also responsible for Copernicus's acceptance as one of the canons in his cathedral, thus assuring Nicolaus of an adequate income for the rest of his life. Young Copernicus studied at the University of Cracow, then enrolled at the University of Bologna to study law. After a visit to Rome, he decided, with his chapter's consent, to study medicine at the University of Padua. After studying there for two years—not enough to earn his medical degree—he went to the University of Ferrara, where he earned his doctorate in canon law. Evidently he chose not to take the doctorates in law or medicine that he could have earned at Bologna or Padua because he did not have enough money for the elaborate ceremonies connected with the awarding of diplomas at those universities.

Like many clergymen of his day and ours, he was inclined to be somewhat skeptical about the Church's doctrines and rules. There is considerable evidence that he was inclined to fudge a bit on his vows of chastity. A certain woman who had worked as his housekeeper married a man who turned out to be impotent. Soon afterward, she and the woman who was her new employer happened to be passing through Copernicus's town after attending a fair. The young canon was hospitable enough to invite the women to stay the night with him, causing his bishop to raise serious questions about the propriety of his behavior. Well into his sixties, Copernicus was frequently chastised for his liaisons with various women, including one Anna Schilling, who was called his "mistress" in a letter written to the bishop. The bishop, for his part, was so distressed that he ordered certain "prostitutes," many of them housekeepers who served the local clergy, expelled from his diocese. Even after Copernicus's death, the bishop was unrelenting and refused to allow Anna Schilling to return to her home, because she could spread the "contagion" of her "disease" among other clergymen in the region.

The Copernican Theory

Anyone who lies on the ground on a summer's night, watching the heavens, cannot help but be struck by the sensation that the heavens are rotating around the earth. The stars appear to move swiftly enough that their motions are rather easily perceptible. Those that remain above the horizon describe circles around the Pole Star (the North Star), while others rise in the east and set in the west. We say that the sun and the moon rise in the east and set in the west, for that is the most natural way to describe their apparent movements. These movements are quite regular, and unless fairly long-term observations are made and careful records maintained, it is natural to assume that they are perfectly circular. The so-called fixed stars maintain certain positions relative to one another with no perceptible changes whatever. The pattern of fixed stars remains the same, night after night, generation after generation.

The planets, however, are obviously different. It takes no more than a few nights to notice that the planets shift their positions against the pattern of fixed stars that dominates the heavens. Mercury and Venus oscillate against the background of stars so rapidly that their motions are readily observable. The other planets' motions are less rapid, but are nevertheless unmistakable.

Nothing could be more natural than to assume that the heavenly bodies are moving and that the earth is stationary. Everyone knows what it feels like to be in motion. No one has that sensation when lying in a hammock watching the sun or the stars. Indeed, it is quite unnatural to suppose that the earth is rotating on its axis. We all know what it is like to whirl about or to be on the edge of a spinning wheel like a merry-go-round. Ordinarily, we have no such sensation. Nor do we see things flying off into space, as we might expect them to do if the earth were rotating.

The most respected thinkers of antiquity believed that the earth was at the center of the universe with the heavenly bodies revolving around it. In the Bible, Joshua is reported to have stopped the sun in its tracks, with some help from God, so that he could complete a furious battle with Israel's enemies. Aristotle and most of the important Greek philosophers believed that the earth was composed of a heavy substance that tended naturally to move toward the center of the universe, while the heavenly bodies were composed of lighter substances whose natural motions were either upward or circular.

The Greek astronomers, puzzled by the strange motions of the planets and by other astronomical phenomena, sought rational explanations for them. Aristotle concluded, for example, that the earth must be round because its shadow on the moon during lunar eclipses was round. He also inferred that the moon is closer to the earth than Mars because Mars disappeared, from time to time, behind the darkened lunar sphere. Some of the Greek astronomers found that they could explain the seasons and changes in the lengths of days and nights by assuming that the sun's orbit around the earth is an eccentric circle. They assumed that the earth is at the center of the universe, but not at the center of the circle that describes the sun's orbit. Consequently, at various times of the year, the sun's distance from the earth is greater than at other times. Hence, the days are longer or shorter, colder or warmer.

The strange motions of the planets, however, caused the greatest difficulty. The planets appear to move against the background of the stars. For a number of months, a given planet (for example, Jupiter) appears to be moving in an easterly direction. It then slows down and gradually shifts to a westerly motion, which it maintains for some time. The process is then reversed, with the planet slowing down once again and appearing to shift back to its easterly path. These motions are in loops rather than straight lines. Ancient and medieval astronomers devoted considerable effort to the search for an explanation of this phenomenon. Because the loops described by the planets are so complex, the explanations required considerable mathematical sophistication and had to be based upon a multitude of observations collected over long periods of time.

In the second century, Ptolemy (Claudius Ptolemaus) developed an explanation for the motions of the heavenly bodies that formed the foundation for virtually all astronomical work through the next thirteen centuries. The gist of Ptolemy's theory is that the earth is at the very center of the universe with a crystalline sphere containing the stars circling around it once every day. The sun, the moon, and the planets revolve around the earth as well, each in its own orbit. In order to explain the variations that were observed in their motions, the Ptolemaic theory (which was polished and refined over many centuries) concluded that the orbits were somewhat off-center (eccentric). Since this did not fully explain the observed motions, the theory further postulated the existence of smaller spheres, called epicycles, on the large spheres that carried the planets around the earth. A planet (for example, Mars) was thought to be attached to a transparent sphere or wheel, an epicycle, which was in turn attached to the outer rim of the principal sphere or wheel that revolved around the earth from west to east. This epicycle was carried around the rim of the larger sphere in a great circle. At the same time, it had its own motion. Thus, while Mars circled around its epicycle, the epicycle and Mars were borne eastward together on the larger sphere. An observer on the earth, near the center of the system, would see Mars moving in an easterly direction while it was on the far side of the epicycle. But as it crossed the outer rim of the larger sphere it would appear to an earthbound observer to slow down and reverse course, even though it was continuing to travel eastward along with its epicycle. Not until it crossed the larger sphere's outer rim once more would Mars appear to resume its eastward motion.

As the centuries passed and astronomical observations became more reliable and more detailed, refinements in the Ptolemaic theory led to extraordinary complications, with epicycles on the epicycles, each of them necessary to account for all of the phenomena that had been recorded.

Scientific theories serve many purposes. One of them, accounting for observed phenomena and gathering them under a single theoretical framework, was admirably fulfilled by the Ptolemaic system. Another, enabling scientists to make accurate predictions of future events, was also fulfilled by the Ptolemaic system; for using the charts and tables developed by astronomers utilizing the Ptolemaic approach, it was possible to predict the motions of the heavenly bodies with considerable accuracy.

Scientific theories are often expected to fill still another need: to add to the sense of comfort, security, and familiarity that people have in relation to the universe as a whole, to God, and to one another—or at least not to detract from it. The Ptolemaic theory admirably fulfilled all of these functions. It comported well with common sense and with the images people derived from their reading of ancient books. Nothing in it seemed in any way inconsistent with the Bible or any of the received traditions of the Western religions. The earth, the home of mankind, was at the very center of the universe, precisely where one would have expected God to have placed it when he created the universe and crowned it with his proudest creation, humanity. More than that, Ptolemaic astronomy was not at all inconsistent with widespread belief in astrology, the "science" of predicting terrestrial events (and especially those affecting people) by the motions of the heavenly bodies. In itself, the Ptolemaic system did not *support* astrological speculations. But no one who had faith in the ability of astrologers to foretell good fortune or disaster by planetary motions would have been disappointed to learn that the latest scientific theory placed the earth at the center of the universe with all the planets reeling around it, exercising mysterious influences through unknown powers that penetrated all of the heavenly spheres to keep the entire system in motion.

Now came Copernicus. Dissatisfied with the Ptolemaic system, which he saw as a patchwork of *ad hoc* remedies for constantly recurring defects, he sought a new approach that might be more fruitful in explaining the phenomena that had been observed and in predicting those that had not yet been recorded. Although it may not have been first in the sequence of conclusions that he arrived at, certainly one of the central principles of his system was the relativity of motion. Quoting Virgil, who had observed that to a sailor whose ship is sailing out from port, it appears that "the land and the cities slip backward," Copernicus wrote: "When a ship is floating calmly along, the sailors see its motion mirrored in everything outside, while on the other hand they suppose that they are stationary, together with everything on board."

In the same way, he added, "the motion of the earth can unquestionably produce the impression that the entire universe is rotating."

Thus, the stage was set for a revolution in the way people would thereafter see the earth's position in the universe.

Copernicus's early astronomical essay, the *Commentariolus* ("Little Commentary," written some time between 1502 and 1514 but not published until much later), was the first systematic argument for the proposition that the earth is a planet of the sun. There had been other speculations to the same effect, but none of them had been as thoroughly systematic or grounded upon a careful scientific analysis of the available data. More importantly, he argued for the first time in history that the planetary loops were not real—that the planets did not in fact move as they appeared to do. Rather, he said, the planetary motions that we observe result from the motion of the *earth*. The other planets do not stop in their tracks or reverse direction, but appear to do so because of the motion "of the earth as it changes its observational position on the Grand Orb. For since the earth's speed surpasses the motion of the planet, the line of sight directed toward the firmament regresses, and the earth more than neutralizes the planet's motion."

These theories were elaborated and refined over the years, and were finally published not long before Copernicus's death in his epoch-making book, *On the Revolutions of the Heavenly Spheres*.

The Copernican Revolution

There is no clear evidence that Copernicus was aware of the revolutionary impact his *Revolutions* would have upon all subsequent human thought. Nevertheless, it is not inappropriate to say that Copernicus's theory was truly earth-shaking, literally and figuratively. So far as astronomy was concerned, it ushered in a new era of exploration of the heavens and speculations about them. It soon became clear that Copernicus's heliocentric theory was far more elegant and more powerful than the Ptolemaic geocentric system. The Copernican system needed considerable refinement before it would satisfy the scientific need for precision both in accounting for the phenomena that had thus far been observed and in predicting those that would take

place in the future. Those refinements were soon forthcoming with the discovery, for example, that planetary orbits are elliptical rather than circular, and with the development of such instruments as the telescope, which enabled astronomers to make minute observations that proved the existence of parallactic shifts that were predicted by Copernicus and his followers.

Copernicus set the stage for developments in physics that could not have been anticipated in his time: Galileo's discoveries about falling bodies, for example, and Newton's theories of mechanics, optics, and gravitation, all of which led to extraordinary advances that continue to this day.

The new perspectives that some scientists adopted as a result of Copernicus's theory flew in the face of what had been long accepted as common sense and as verified scientific and philosophical truth. As has happened so often in history, such revolutionary ideas are not readily accepted by those who have a vested interest in the intellectual *status quo*. It is not surprising, therefore, that church leaders, both Catholic and Protestant, soon become extremely hostile toward Copernicanism. Some of Copernicus's followers, like Galileo, were warned by the Inquisition that their views were heretical and they were tried and punished for publishing them. Some, like Giordano Bruno, were even less fortunate and were burned at the stake for their temerity. Copernicus had upset the entire world-view of Christian authority. The earth, and the human beings on it, were no longer the center of the universe. The human being was now depicted as a relatively insignificant creature on a speck of dust floating around a relatively minor star in a vast, potentially infinite universe. Those who could extrapolate to the future implications of this heretical theory could see that it would lead to the conclusion that the earth and its inhabitants were formed by impersonal physical forces rather than by an act of divine creation, and that this was tantamount to an assault on the divine throne itself.

Copernicanism thus became the central focus of a colossal battle between the forces of intellectual and scientific progress on the one hand, and those of conservative religious and philosophical dogmas on the other. It set the stage for what came to be called the Copernican Revolution—one of the most momentous intellectual and cultural revolutions in history.

But its creator, blithely unaware of the convulsions his still-unpublished work would bring about, carried on with his duties as canon and served his king by developing a program for the minting of coins that would discourage counterfeiting and the debasement of official currencies. He wrote several essays on money and coinage and was appointed delegate to various royal commissions on coinage.

His essays were the first to proclaim what later became known as Gresham's law, that bad money drives out good. To this day, this principle is recognized as an important one, and no doubt Copernicus's bishop and his colleagues in Varmia thought his work on the problems of Polish and Prussian currency of far greater importance than his stargazing. But he will forever be remembered as the man who shook the universe and banished the earth and all its creatures from its center, relegating them forever to a far less exalted place in the scheme of things.

Burton M. Leiser

Further Reading

Blumenberg, Hans. *The Genesis of the Copernican World*. Translated by Robert M. Wallace. Cambridge: MIT Press, 1987. A lengthy but extremely valuable volume. The author has carefully analyzed most of the important documents, not only of Copernicus's own time but those that preceded and followed him as well, and has put them in historical perspective. He paints the world as it existed before Copernicus on a broad canvas, places the characters who played leading roles in the changes that occurred in context, and provides a good survey of the intellectual implications of the changes wrought by Copernicus and his followers.

Kesten, Hermann. *Copernicus and His World*. New York: Roy Publishers, 1945. More than most, this book puts a very human face on Copernicus and the other persons involved in the Copernican Revolution. The author has gathered considerable biographical information about Copernicus and put it together in an interesting, readable fashion. At the same time, he offers considerable information about the substance of the debates and theories that are at the heart of the issue.

Kuhn, Thomas S. *The Copernican Revolution: Planetary Astronomy in the Development of Western Thought*. Cambridge: Harvard University Press, 1957. A superb, scholarly account of the development of astronomy from the ancient two-sphere universe through the Copernican Revolution. Diagrams throughout the book are immensely helpful as the reader attempts to visualize the solar system from the viewpoints of the various theories discussed. In addition, there is a "technical appendix" that will slake the thirst of the curious for further information on such matters as the precession of the equinoxes, the phases of the moon, eclipses, ancient measurements of the universe, and the like.

Rosen, Edward. *Copernicus and the Scientific Revolution*. Malabar, Fl.: Robert E. Krieger, 1984. A brief, readable account of Copernicus's life and work, with excerpts from important letters, diaries, and books. This small book includes helpful diagrams as well, and a good, concise review of the theories that came before Copernicus.

THOMAS MORE

Born: 1478, London, England
Died: 1535, Tower Hill, London, England
Major Works: *Utopia* (1516), *History of Richard III* (between 1514 and 1518), *Dialogue Concerning Heresies* (1529), *Dialogue of Comfort Against Tribulation* (1534–35)

Major Ideas

A program of education grounded on ethics, the study of Greek and Latin, and the imitation of ancient pagan and Christian writers is the soundest plan for spiritual renewal and reform of the church and society.

Nature teaches that the best society is one whose aim is the temporal well-being or happiness of all its citizens, an aim achieved through the elimination of private property.

The essential life and the fullness of power of any society resides in its members and no legitimate authority exists apart from the common consent of its members.

The surest comfort in this life comes from the knowledge that the Catholic Church's authority, sacraments, and practices are assured by God's promise and his continuing presence through the inspiration of the Holy Spirit.

The greatest pleasure in this world is the meditation on the four last things—on how sin, death, and judgment end in the happiness of eternal life.

Robert Bolt's *A Man for All Seasons* created for twentieth-century audiences a Thomas More more modern than sixteenth century—the very image of a contemporary man with a commanding range of interests, a zest for living, and a heroic integrity in the face of an age riddled with paradoxes and contradictions. Of course, it is true More's age was one of arresting contrast and wrenching change. He was born during the reign of King Richard III, whom he later memorialized in the *History of Richard III*, a work regarded as significant for the development of modern history and biography. Some scholars also see in More's use of perspective, the dramatic monologue, and other novelistic techniques in his biography the anticipation of the novel and modern fiction.

The years following Henry Plantagenet's defeat of Richard at Bosworth Field ended a period of violent civil war in England's history and initiated a period of political stability, peace, and economic prosperity. The reign of Henry VII was also the harbinger of England's great literary renaissance, in which More was to play so central a role. During these years, More began his career in the law, was married to Jane Colt, began his family, and launched his career in government. Of significance

for More and the English Renaissance that commenced with the coronation of Henry's son, Henry VIII (1509), More gave evidence of his inclination to be a player in the international literary movement known as humanism. Following a characteristic humanist program, More steadily gained proficiency in both Latin and Greek; he translated several pieces from Lucian, the second-century Greek satirist; and he prepared an English translation of the *Life of John Picus*—the Italian humanist Pico della Mirandola. In these early endeavors, More collaborated with and was encouraged in his writing by the most famous humanist and scholar of the time, Desiderius Erasmus, who visited England twice during these years.

The prospect of a golden age was bright when Henry Tudor succeeded his father to England's throne. So too did the prospect of More's political fortunes increase with the new king. More had opportunity to demonstrate his legal and diplomatic ability, and Henry resolved to make use of More's talent in royal service on a diplomatic mission to Flanders. The next decade and a half would see More drawn deeper into the king's service and royal politics. In rapid succession, he became under-treasurer, speaker of the House of Commons, high steward of Oxford University and then of Cambridge, and chancellor of the Duchy of Lancaster. Then, with the fall of Cardinal Wolsey, More became Henry's lord chancellor. Yet, in spite of the demands of public office on his time and energy, the years between 1509 and 1520 were exceptionally important ones for More's contribution to literature and the general cause of international humanism. It was during these years that he wrote the *History of Richard III*, and it was this period that saw More emerge as a humanist of international stature. He also found himself cast in the part of the defender of Erasmus's Greek New Testament and *Praise of Folly* against Erasmus's conservative critics. Of all his literary achievements during this humanist phase of his career, the greatest and most famous in his own day and in ours was the *Utopia*.

It is with a certain irony that just when the world seemed for More most certain and promising, just when his literary star was rising and his political future seemed brightest, an obscure German Bible professor published ninety-five Latin theses questioning the Church's doctrine of indulgences. In March of 1518, Erasmus sent More a copy of Luther's theses, but there is no reason to think that More took them seriously. Like the rest of Europe, he seemed unaware of the sea change that was in the making. Yet, in less than two years, Luther's books were in general circulation in England, Lutheran ideas had spread to Oxford, and England's first generation of Protestant thinkers began assembling at the White Horse Inn at Cambridge. The spark that ignited England's controversy with Protestantism, however, was the publication in 1520 of Luther's *Babylonian Captivity of the Church*. Henry VIII rallied to the Church's cause with the *Defense of the Seven Sacraments*. More may have been its author; certainly, he had a hand in its preparation. But it was not until the publication of the *Response to Luther* (1523) that he was personally committed to the Church's cause.

Against Luther, More argued that the Church is a visible, institutional reality on earth, that its teachings and practices are confirmed by the continued inspiration of the Holy Spirit, and that its sacra-

ments were instituted by Christ. And, since Christ did not write a book but established a church, More held that sacred tradition takes precedence over sacred Scripture. The *Responsio* reveals More's conservative turn of mind; his abusive language and *ad hominum* attack on Luther disclose a surprising degree of raw anger beneath his almost stoical public image. Yet, even in the genre of polemical writing, More produced the *Dialogue Concerning Heresies*, a book that is notable for its vigorous dialogue, its lively character portraits, good humor, and the "merry tale" for which More was famous.

Retirement, the charge of treason, and imprisonment defined the last chapter in More's life and in a sense brought his story full circle. It is a reasonable inference that More had given thought to a religious vocation when still a young man. Not only had he gone to study at Oxford, where one might expect to go in preparation for an ecclesiastical career, but while preparing for and practicing law, he had lived in the Carthusian monastery adjoining Lincoln's Inn and shared the discipline and common life of its monks. And, while he pursued his legal studies, he continued a program of reading in Scripture and the Greek and Latin Christian and ancient pagan writers. Even after he had decided for a secular career, the monastic impulse stayed with him, though camouflaged beneath his public persona much as the hair shirt he wore nearest his skin hidden from public view. It was only during the period following his resignation as lord chancellor in 1532 and his imprisonment thereafter that he had the leisure to give himself openly and unreservedly to the monastic devotion to which he had been drawn early in life. In the writing of the Tower period, the mystical strain in his thought and personality surfaced in his reflection on his own death in the light of the suffering humanity of Christ. Still, even at this period of personal trial, More did not lose his humor or that special balance that was so much a part of his charm. Even as he mounted the scaffold More was capable of one last jest. "See me safe up," he counseled the lieutenant, "and for my coming down let me shift for myself."

Utopia

When More invented his imaginary island and named it Utopia, punning on the Greek words for "happy place" and "nowhere," he spawned a whole new literary genre that was to include Francis Bacon's *New Atlantis*, Jonathan Swift's *Gulliver's Travels*, Samuel Butler's *Erewhon*, William Morris's *News from Nowhere*, and Edward Bellamy's *Looking Backward*. This unexpected fruit of More's holiday diversion at Antwerp where book 2 was written was no small literary achievement, yet the weight to be given this little Renaissance masterpiece has been much debated. Many of More's contemporaries and some modern scholars have thought it to be only a literary diversion, the *jeu d'esprit* of a literary humanist; others discover in it earnest proposals for social, political, and economic reform. What has not been questioned, however, was the seriousness of More's identification with the international circle of Christian humanists or his hope that *Utopia* would win their approval. And, when he sent its manuscript to Erasmus in September of 1516, he had cause to hope that his position in that circle would be secure. Not only was his Latin style elegant and his capacity for imaginative invention apparent; he had created an effective instrument for expressing Christian humanism's ideal and spirit.

Using a mixture of dialogue and narrative to create his fiction, More described how his friend Peter Giles introduced him to Raphael Hythloday and how the traveling philosopher drew him into a conversation on the usefulness of counseling kings. The topic was an important one for the humanists of the Renaissance. Many of them earned their keep as advisers to magistrates and princes, and most of them subscribed to the view that the best life was one of civic service. The question of state service may also have been very much on More's own mind at this time, for in a year after the completion and publication of *Utopia* he joined the king's council as a royal adviser. Whatever More's personal reason for agreeing to service in Henry's court, More as a character in *Utopia* exhibits the humanist's optimism about politics, arguing that philosophers must become kings and kings must turn to philosophy if the common good is to be best served. A Platonic truism to which More may or may not have personally subscribed, this opinion nevertheless gives to *Utopia* an old-fashioned feel next to a contemporary work like *The Prince* (1513) by Machiavelli.

Though the question of counseling kings is a prominent element in book 1, the transition to book 2 of *Utopia* makes it clear that More's real concern was not political theory in any narrow sense of the word. With an objective more like that of Erasmus in *The Praise of Folly* than like Machiavelli's, he was committed to giving form to humanist values in the interest of social reformation and religious renewal. Making use of his inventive powers, More thus has his fictive Hythloday narrate the story of an imaginary island and its republic of virtuous pagans who live in a state of nature and have the advantage of reason alone to guide their affairs. Yet, as More's contemporaries surely recognized, these pagans without the aid of revelation have views on religion, ethics, education, work, the family, the state, and warfare that are in many ways superior to those of Christian Europe. Without the benefit of revelation, the Utopians believe in a supreme God who providentially guides human affairs and rewards or punishes virtue and wickedness in a future life. And, against the skepticism of a Renaissance philosopher like Pomponazzi, More's Utopians find in reason cause to affirm the soul's immortality.

Perhaps even more striking was the fact that reason seems to have guided the Utopians to a philosophy of economic communism, a philosophy that has caused More to be heralded in this century as a sixteenth-century socialist far ahead of his time. The likelihood of discovering the spirit of *Utopia*'s communism in the present, however, is less probable than if we look for its source in his reading of ancient Christian writers. From the Greek and Latin church fathers, for example, he would have learned that private property is a principal cause of human vice. And from his letter to a monk (1519) we learn that More believed that God instituted all things in common, that Christ sought to recall humans to this divine institution, and that private property exists because of the corruption of human nature. What he also believed, and what differentiated his attitude from the Anabaptists whom he later opposed, was that Christ summoned only the few to the perfection of communal poverty.

Hythloday's advocacy of communism provided More's contemporaries with a wonderful mirror of Christian perfection, but we need to remember that the Utopians were not Christians. The acceptance of the principle of common property was based on their conviction that nature taught that pleasure is the highest human good. In a philosophy very similar to that of the Roman philosopher Epicurus, the Utopians argued that all pleasures are good, consistent with nature and reason, and are desirable in promoting human happiness, though not all pleasures are equally good. The Utopians hold that pleasures are to be avoided if they are the cause of pain, or if they are won at the sacrifice of a greater pleasure, or if they result in social harm. And Utopian society was carefully planned to prevent such false or spurious pleasures from arising. As a hedge against spurious pleasures, the Utopians, like Calvin's Genevans, tolerated "no wine shops, no alehouses, no brothels anywhere, no opportunity for corruption, no lurking hole, no secret meeting place." And, as an antidote to pride, that greatest of sins according to Augustine, the Utopians adopted a monasticlike style of life and discipline for the discouragement of the false pleasure citizens might take in personal possessions or position. Within the world of Hythloday's narrative, false and spurious pleasures are forbidden because of the Utopians' belief that the greatest social pleasure is the happiness of all citizens, and the greatest spiritual pleasure is the contemplation of the truth and the hope of eternal life.

Dialogue Concerning Heresies

The major themes of More's polemical writing were already evident in his *Response to Luther* (1520). Writing against Luther in this work, More affirmed the unity and permanence of the church. He argued, as he would repeatedly in his books against heresy, that the Catholic church is a divine foundation resting on the authority of Christ and secure in its faith, teaching, and practices because of the living presence of the Spirit. Of More's most remembered controversial writings, however, none compares with his *Dialogue Concerning Heresies*, a book written in obedience to Bishop Cuthbert Tunstall's commission to refute heresy in English so that the "simple and unlearned" might be fortified in their faith.

C. S. Lewis regarded the *Dialogue* as the best example in English of the Platonic dialogue, and another of More's modern interpreters believes that it is spiritual heir to Chaucer. There is no doubt that More enlivened his fiction with vivid characterization, good humor, carefully placed irony, and the folk exempla calculated to amuse and divert when the theological discourse became too dense and wearisome. His seriousness of purpose, however, is never in question. Right from the opening scene in which persona More engages his young sparring partner, the issues central to the Protestant attacks on the Catholic church are before the reader. The student, it should be emphasized, is not a Protestant but is only one who inclines to the Protestant heresy.

The young man objects to the veneration of saints, images, and miracles and remarks that these attitudes of popular piety are not found in Scripture. More's answer is always lively and amiable but also unbending in his defense of traditional Catholic piety and practice. Not only does he maintain, as he had in earlier writing, that the Church cannot permanently err but also in a vein that is strikingly modern, he holds that the Church is prior to Scripture. Against the Protestant elevation of Scripture and individual conscience, More trusts rather in consensus and community and in living voice of tradition.

Dialogue of Comfort Against Tribulation

Written in the Tower and under the cloud of his own impending death, the *Dialogue of Comfort Against Tribulation* is a devotional work that takes the form of an imaginary conversation between two Hungarians who are faced with the prospect of persecution and even martyrdom as the armies of Suleiman threaten conquest of their city. The *Dialogue* is divided into three books and turns on the question of consolation in the face of tribulation and temptation, a question very much on More's own mind at the time of his writing this meditation. On the nature of tribulation, Anthony, the older of the two and More's persona, tells his nephew that suffering need not be an evil before which one flees. For Christians it can be a good to be welcomed as a thing prompting spiritual health and well-being. The suffering that accompanies tribulation, Anthony maintains, can be spiritually "medicinal" if it is payment for past sins or the means of preventing sins that might otherwise have been. And, if unrelated to sin, tribulation can be "more than medicinal," contributing to the Christian's merit and to the Christian hope of future glory.

More once again revived the themes central to his polemical writings, and he cast Anthony as a defender of the Catholic faith which, like the Budapest of Anthony and his young nephew, is besieged on all sides. In particular, he is keen to refute the Protestant belief that salvation is by faith without works. He has Anthony say that he would that the Lutheran teaching were true, but the truth resides in the inspired tradition of the Church, whose authority must be embraced if the Christian is to enjoy the consolation that Christ promised his disciples. And, with this familiar defense, More reaffirms those Catholic doctrines, practices, and sacraments to which the Protestants objected and toward which his king appeared to be drifting. Yet the *Dialogue* revolves on suffering and the thought of death, and its mood is devotional and meditative and not polemical. It is for this reason too that theological controversy is not so much the issue as is the larger, more directly personal preoccupation with persecution and martyrdom. The comfort and remedy for these greatest of temptations, More believes, is Christ's own exemplary Passion and death. In a vein reminiscent of the early Christian literature of martyrdom, More holds that this last and greatest temptation is overcome through the mystical identification of the Christian's suffering with Christ's own.

THOMAS E. HELM

Further Reading

Chambers, R. W. *Thomas More*. London: Jonathan Cape, 1935. A definitive biography that gives a traditional portrait of More with an emphasis on his last years.

Harpsfield, Nicholas. *The Life and Death of Sir Thomas More*. Edited by Elsie Vaughan Hitchcock. Early English Text Society, O.S. No. 186. London: Oxford University Press, 1932. Written by a family friend in 1557 or 1558, this hagiographic treatment is the first full-scale biography of More. It includes recollections of many people who knew More.

Marius, Richard. *Thomas More. A Biography*. New York: Alfred A. Knopf, 1984. An excellent recent biography by one of the editors of the Yale edition of More's collected work. It is especially useful in placing More's thought in relation to theology and philosophy.

_____. *Selected Letters*. Edited by Elizabeth Frances Rogers. New Haven and London: Yale University Press, 1961. Containing sixty-six of More's letters over a period of nearly thirty-five years, this volume reveals the range of More's interest and talent.

Roper, William. *The Lyfe of Sir Thomas More, knighte*. Edited by Elise Vaughan Hitchcock. Early English Text Society. O.S. No. 197. London: Oxford University Press, 1935. Written in 1557 as a brief sketch of his revered father-in-law, this work is a masterpiece of English prose in its own right. It includes valuable personal recollections and is the foundation on which all English biographies of More are based.

Surtz, Edward, S.J. *The Praise of Pleasure*. Cambridge, Mass.: Harvard University Press, 1957. An invaluable analysis of the religious and philosophical ideas found in *Utopia*.

Sylvester, Richard S., ed. *Thomas More: Action and Contemplation*. New Haven and London: Yale University Press, 1972. Written by the executive editor of the Yale edition of More's work, this volume contains four essays on important phases in More's life and career, including his relation to the law, royal service, the Tower works, and his spirituality.

MARTIN LUTHER

Born: 1483, Eisleben, Saxony
Died: 1546, Eisleben, Saxony
Major Works: *Lectures on Romans* (1515–16), *The Ninety-five Theses* (1517), *An Address to the Nobility of the German Nation* (1520), *The Babylonian Captivity of the Church* (1520), *On the Liberty of a Christian Man* (1520), *On Good Works* (1520), *On the Bondage of the Will* (1525)

Major Ideas

Human nature is corrupt, weak, self-centered, and in a state of rebellion from God; the fruit of the fall from grace is death.

God's laws show sinners their distance from God and arouse a desire for redemption.

Although God in his justice could condemn humanity, he chooses out of love to redeem sinners; this love is most fully manifest on the cross.

In the process of redemption one can do nothing but have faith, an absolute trust and response to God's words; human merit and good works are rejected.

The foremost vehicle of God's saving word is the Bible, which presents the whole of the good news for human salvation.

The Catholic priesthood, monasticism, and canon law are rejected as human institutions that make the false claim to control the spirit of God.

The sacraments are signs that communicate God's saving word.

Martin Luther was at the center of the storm that named the sixteenth century the period of Reformation. His views changed Western Christianity to such an extent that by the end of his life there existed competing conceptions as to how a person ought to respond to the divine. Scenes from his life such as the nailing of ninety-five theses on the door of the castle church at Wittenburg on the eve of All Saints, 1517, or his dramatic affirmation of Scripture and conscience before the emperor and the assembled nobility of Germany at the Diet of Worms, 1521, have become the stuff of Western historical memory. Very few in history have been the object of more intense condemnation and praise. To the Catholics of the day he was, in the words of the papal bull of excommunication, *Domine Exsurge* (1520), the "wild boar" that had invaded the vineyards of the Lord. By publicly burning that papal document at Wittenburg, Luther affirmed that he was, as one Protestant cartoon of the day portrayed him, "the German Hercules," the great leader of national and religious liberation. Philipp Melanchthon (1497–1560) in his funeral sermon preached on the death of Luther called him "the

very instrument of God for the propaganda of the Gospel"; while Pope Gregory XV in 1622 wrote in a bull canonizing Ignatius Loyola (c. 1495–1556), the founder of the Jesuits, that Luther was "the foulest of monsters." Polemic works from both sides have appeared over the past 400 years as have recent psychoanalytic and Marxist interpretations of the reformer. However, in all of the discussions on Luther what remains basic is the way he conceptualized Christianity as the personal response of sinful humanity to a loving God known through the Bible by faith.

Sinful Humanity and Death

The Reformation has its origin in the question recorded in the New Testament, "What shall I do to inherit eternal life?" (Luke 10:25). Martin Luther's writings present us with the portrait of a person in a state of profound struggle with exactly that issue; a struggle between two worlds: goodness and evil, the divine and the demonic, light and darkness. At the core of Luther's passionate and melancholy personality was an intense anxiety about his own salvation. He grew up in the piety of the late Middle Ages, which often emphasized an image of God as an awesome judge whose all-knowing frown struck awe and terror in the hearts of sinners.

In the midst of a violent thunderstorm in 1505 when he thought he saw the very wrath of God in the bolts of lightning, Luther vowed that if spared he would enter the monastery of the Augustinian Hermits at Erfurt. Luther experienced the same terror in another context when he said his first Mass in 1507. At that event he was completely humbled at the thought that with his words the bread became the very body of Christ and the wine Christ's own blood. He said that he felt himself to be nothing but sinful dust and ashes daring to address the eternal God.

Luther would write of God's majesty in a later work, *On the Bondage of the Will*, as an all-consuming devouring fire, a God who is beyond all control and manipulation by human will and reason. Nevertheless, humanity, in his view, is always trying by multiple pious, moral, and religious acts to earn its own salvation. These acts, often referred to as good works, were seen by many in his day as guaranteed to merit God's favor. For the reformer all this was nothing but the essence of sin, for its root was in the desire to make the self, not God, the center of the universe.

Adam's fall left humanity in a permanent rebellion from God, a state of enduring wickedness. Humanity, Luther writes in his *Commentary on Genesis*, is "utterly leprous and unclean." Original Sin is humankind's permanent state of weakness and self-absorption. The result of this sinful condition is death, as Paul teaches in his Epistle to the Romans (chapters 5–7).

The laws in the Bible reveal the Lawgiver's desire to be God alone and to have no strange gods before him (Exodus 20, Deuteronomy 5). This first and greatest of commandments not only makes a command but also condemns. It condemns the sinner by pointing out a person's self-absorption, and false gods. Thus, atheism is at the core an idolatry, a sinful egotism that refuses to love God alone.

Justification by Faith

As Luther studied Scripture in preparation for his lectures at the University of Wittenburg, his conception of God gradually changed. The more his thoughts turned to the life and sacrifice of Christ, especially as it was revealed on the cross, the more he saw not only the awesome God but also the all-merciful One who gave his son for human salvation. The inscrutable God who shows himself through the foolishness of the cross reveals that the measure of his mercy is that it is mercy without measure. This compassion for sinners can neither be captured by reason nor manipulated by human actions. This love brings humanity into a right relationship with God. This standing before God (*Coram Deo*) is known as justification. This *Coram* relationship implies that God turns his presence toward the sinner and thus the sinner has a place before God. All this was for Luther fully understood by Paul in his epistle to the Romans:

> . . . God showed His love for us in that while we were yet sinners, Christ died for us. Since, therefore, we are now justified by His blood, much more shall we be saved by Him from the wrath of God. For if while we were sinners we were reconciled to God by the death of His son, much more, now that we are reconciled shall we be saved by His life. (Romans 5:8–10)

Toward the end of his life Luther would recall that as he struggled in the tower of the monastery at Wittenburg to grasp the meaning of the Bible, he came to understand the words of Paul, "the just live by faith" (Romans 1:17). This famous Tower Experience (Turmerlebnis) was a decisive moment in his life; human faith's response to God's grace is a faithfulness to God whereby one puts one's whole trust in God alone.

Faith is seen by Luther not as a human power or attribute but, rather, as that which is received from God. He took seriously the words of Jesus from the Gospel of John ". . . apart from me you can do nothing" (15:5). Contrary to the view of Desiderius Erasmus (1466–1536), Luther affirmed that the human will contributed nothing to the salvation dynamic. Faith as a gift repudiates all forms of merit, for humanity remains, although justified, in sin. Faith as an obedient reception of God's word repudiates all forms of reason. With reason we place what is known under our own control. Again, the reformer was profoundly influenced by the words of Paul: "What have you that you did not receive? If then you receive it, why do you boast as if it were not a gift?" (1 Corinthians 4:7).

The Christian remains simultaneously a sinner and a righteous person. Righteousness comes from God while human corruption remains. This idea is referred to as "imputed righteousness," whereby God no longer looks upon the believer as deserving damnation but as one whose sins are cloaked over by the merits of Christ. As Luther put it in his *Commentary on the Letter to the Galatians*: "It pleases one to call this righteousness (*Justitiam*) of faith or Christian righteousness passive righteousness."

In all this we see Luther's Augustinian reaction against Pelagius (d. 418), William of Ockham (d.c. 1347), and Gabriel Biel (d. 1495), all of whom affirm in various ways the nobility and capacity of the human will to do good. The last two mentioned authors are often linked with a philosophical tendency influential in Luther's education, nominalism. This tendency rejects attempts to ground faith on reason while emphasizing the sovereignty of God's will to predestine whomever he chooses.

The Catholic view defended at the Council of Trent (1545–63) would understand grace to be that which heals and elevates human nature. In this tradition, the person is justified not by the extrinsic imputation of Christ's merits but through the actions of the Holy Spirit within the human soul according to God's good pleasure and each person's free cooperation. This divine indwelling offers to the individual the three supernatural virtues of faith, hope, and charity. Here the soul has a supernatural gift, a habit (*habitus*), which is actualized by good works and, as such, God's free gifts become human merit.

Luther, on the other hand, saw divine grace as that which alters the person's situation in respect to his or her standing before God, not in his or her inner essence. He rejects the substance language of Aristotle and the ordered universe of the Neoplatonists. For Luther the only good work is faith, which is the work of God. Faith alone turns one's attention away from the idolatry of self-absorption and gives a person freedom to love. In this sense, faith is the source of love, the good tree that produces the good fruit, to use Luther's favorite image. Here is the meaning of the reformer's well-known line: "A Christian is free and independent in every respect, a bond servant to none. A Christian is a dutiful servant in every respect, owing a duty to everyone" (*On the Liberty of a Christian Man*).

The Word of God

For some thirty-five years, Martin Luther understood his vocation to be that of a professor of sacred Scripture. His greatest literary achievement was the translation of the Bible into German. This effort established the national language and would have the same prestige and effect in Germany as did the King James Bible in England (the "Authorized Version" of 1611). In his own lifetime it sold over 100,000 copies. His goal, to offer the living word of God to every person, would be the driving passion behind all his writings, lectures, sermons, and hymns. If the new Protestant movement could be summed up in an image, it would be that of Luther in the tower struggling with, and finding comfort in, the biblical text.

The Roman Church of Luther's day repudiated this claim of *sola scriptura*, for the complexity of Scripture demanded an infallible interpreter. Luther, however, argued that the text interpreted itself and that a humble Christian in contact with the word of God was closer to God than any pope without a Bible. The pope and the Councils could and did err, Luther believed, for the only norm for religion was the canonical Scriptures. The problems of interpretation do remain. It was the job of the exegete armed with a knowledge of the biblical languages and the whole of Scripture to dig out the kernel hidden in the shell, to find the baby in the straw of the manger. When a passage proved difficult it was to be interpreted in light of an easier one (*Scriptura Scriptura Interpretatur*). Also, Luther's own hermeneutics would be that of many before him, Christocentric, seeing the New Testament hidden in the Old. For him the psalms spoke of the gospel.

He also stood in the common piety of the age with his attention to the imaginative encounter with the text. The events of the Bible were experienced as if they were happening now. Luther encouraged in his preaching an emotional response of joy or sorrow as occasioned by the scene. By fully encountering the Word with intellect, will, and emotions, time and distance were eradicated. It is no wonder that Luther writes that Christ commanded the apostles to preach.

The Protestant Movement

The Protestant movement, which began as a protest against the selling of indulgences, was, in essence, a systematic reformulation of the ways in which a person can achieve and sustain a relationship with God. Luther's basic principles of *sola fide*, *sola gratia*, and *sola scriptura* would repudiate the medieval idea of the Church institution as the exclusive vehicle for the divine–human encounter. His attention to a personal decision and his religion of conscience would have far-reaching implications for the emerging modern world. For Luther, each person stands alone in the personal encounter with God.

Although he spent fifteen years as a priest and a monk, Luther rejected the ordained priesthood and the special status accorded to monastic life. Both institutions were seen as laying a claim to control the Holy Spirit of God. Even worse, he thought, they served to prevent the Spirit from acting. So to think that true poverty was the unique call of the monastic orders was to ignore the true poverty of spirit as a demand placed on everyone. Luther also noted that greatly lacking in all monastic education was the study of the biblical and classical languages essential for a proper exegesis of Scripture. He argued in his treatise *The Babylonian Captivity of the Church* that especially onerous was the oppression

of the laity by the clergy, who substituted juridical authority for ministry to the people of God.

All baptized Christians are by virtue of their baptism priests, Luther maintained. This "priesthood of all believers" means that every Christian has the obligation not only to accept God's word in faith, but also to minister to the neighbor. The "keys to the kingdom" (Matthew 16:19) belong not to the Roman pontiff but to the whole community of believers. It is true that some, chosen by the whole community, would minister, that is, offer the word of God. This is the essential core of the church for, as Jesus put it, "Man shall not live by bread alone, but by every word that proceeds from the mouth of God" (Matthew 4:4). Thus the head of a family could maintain a church in the home by means of the Bible and baptism. After all, noted Luther, Jesus promised that where two or three are gathered together in His name, there He would be in their midst (Matthew 18:19–20).

The Roman Catholic church had built its legal and juridical structures on the commands of Jesus to Peter to bind and to loose on earth (Matthew 16:19). This gave rise to an extensive system of canon law and human traditions. To many in the sixteenth century, this establishment of ecclesiastical ordinance above the commands of God resulted in oppression and tyranny, which destroyed the liberty of the Christian believer. Luther constantly drew attention to this by making a sharp division between the command of God and the command invented by men. By doing so he undercut the Catholic idea of human tradition, which sought to probe and understand Scripture through centuries of councils, theologians, and saints. Divine law was not, however, to be repudiated, for it remained as a stimulus to penance, humility, and obedience, as well as providing an opportunity to deepen one's longing for the gospel. Human traditions also had a value in preserving human tranquillity and social order. However, for Luther, both had no place in the redemptive process if placed over and above the Bible, grace, and faith.

Sacraments were essential to medieval Catholicism as the vehicle by which God continued His work throughout all of history. In this view the actions of Christ as mediated through a hierarchical–sacramental impartation of grace would produce the power to do good works, acquire merit, and achieve sanctity. Luther, by denying the evolution of tradition as a legitimate expression of divine will, saw the sacramental system as a human invention created by the Roman Church to enhance clerical power. For him the only sacrament was the word of God. This word of command and promise is, however, communicated through three signs: baptism, penance, and the Eucharist, which call for a response of faith. Thus, the Lutheran focus is on the sermon, prayers, and hymns in public worship. Later Protestants would divide over the value of penance, the necessity of infant baptism, and the nature of Eucharistic bread. For Luther, all that mattered was that Jesus came preaching the gospel of God. In this way the true Christian congregation would be the priesthood of all believers who profess the gospel with hands and mouth, by action, and by the proclamation of their faith.

LAWRENCE F. HUNDERSMARCK

Further Reading

Bainton, Roland. *Here I Stand: A Life of Martin Luther.* New York: Abingdon-Cokesbury Press, 1950. The text, which is liberally illustrated with reproductions of woodcuts and illustrations of the age, traces the struggles and triumphs of the reformer. This is a very readable and dramatic biography.

Ebiling, Gerhard. *Luther: An Introduction to His Thought.* Translated by R. A. Wilson. Philadelphia: Fortress Press, 1970. An excellent summary of the fundamental tensions in the theology of Luther. The study goes to the heart of Luther's views on grace and nature by one of the greatest Lutheran scholars of the twentieth century.

Grimm, Harold J. *The Reformation Era, 1500–1650.* 2d ed. New York: Macmillan, 1973. This is a standard summary of the major events and consequences of the whole Reformation movement with a comprehensive bibliography.

McDonough, Thomas M. *The Law and the Gospel in Luther: A Study of Martin Luther's Confessional Writings.* London: Oxford University Press, 1963. By focusing on the large and small catechisms of Luther, this study delineates Luther's views of the force and function of law as well as the relationship of law and gospel.

Oberman, Heiko A. *Luther: Man Between God and the Devil.* Translated by E. Wallison Schwarzbart. New Haven: Yale University Press, 1990. The thesis of this work is that to get at the essence of Luther's own self-understanding, one must see him not only as a healer of the Church but also as one who believed he was engaged in a cosmic struggle against Satanic attacks on the kingdom of God.

Pelikan, Jaroslov. *Luther the Expositor: Introduction to the Reformer's Exegetical Writings.* St. Louis: Concordia, 1959. This comprehensive discussion situates Luther's hermeneutics within the history of Christian attempts to understand Scripture. The work also examines select biblical passages with an eye to the practice and conclusions that emerge from Luther's exegesis.

————. *Spirit vs. Structure: Luther and the Institutions of the Church.* New York: Harper & Row, 1968. A concise summary of the positions Luther took regarding the Catholic priesthood, monasticism, infant baptism, and the sacramental system. This short study examines the difficulties Luther had not only in articulating the conflict between spirit and structure but also his need to present an ecclesiology that saw spirit in and through structure.

von Loewenich, Walther. *Luther's Theology of the Cross.* Translated by H. Bouman. Minneapolis: Augsburg, 1976. The classic 1933 study of Luther's view of faith and the hidden God. The author's claim is that the theology of the cross touches the whole of Luther's theology of salvation.

JOHN CALVIN

Born: 1509, Noyon, France
Died: 1564, Geneva, Switzerland
Major Work: *Institutes of the Christian Religion* (1536, 1539)

Major Ideas

Though God's essential nature is incomprehensible, partial knowledge of God is available through God's self-revelation.

The Bible is the sole source of this adapted revelation.

The Bible reveals God as the triune creator of everything, actively and universally ruling all aspects of the continuing creation.

The Bible reveals humanity as having fallen into sin through Adam, thereby losing all free will and ability to restore itself to right relationship with God and creation.

Nonetheless, by God's mysterious eternal decree, some are predestined to election to salvation through the person and work of Jesus Christ, God's self-revelation as redeemer; others are predestined to condemnation.

Individuals are united to Christ through membership in the true church, which is marked by the Word rightly proclaimed and the sacraments correctly administered.

John Calvin's system of ideas became widely accepted by Protestants as the essential means for understanding the Bible. This ability to direct the acceptable interpretation of the source of Protestant authority had social, political, and religious applications. Through the wide success of these applications, Calvin became one of the makers of the modern mind.

John Calvin (from the latinized form of Jean Cauvin) was born in the episcopal town of Noyon, France, to Jeanne and Gérard Cauvin. (A second-generation reformer, Calvin was eight years old when Martin Luther nailed the Ninety-five Theses to the Wittenberg door.) Calvin's father held several important offices at the cathedral in Noyon and saw to it that his son had the advantages of cultured society, including a benefice to subsidize his studies.

In 1523, Calvin went to study in Paris, where he attended both the Collège de la Marche and the Collège Montaigu. In the first he learned Latin under Mathurin Cordier, a future Protestant educator, and in the second he was exposed to the finest in scholastic dialectic and debate. He received the Master of Arts in 1528. At his father's urging, Calvin switched from theology to law and continued his education at the University of Orleans. He transferred to the University of Bourges in 1529, where law studies were pursued through humanist methods. During this time, he studied Greek under the German scholar Melchior Wolmar. He received his law degree in 1531, the year his father died. Soon after Gérard's death, Calvin left the practice of law and returned to Paris and the pursuit of classical literature, continuing his studies in Greek and Hebrew. His first published work, *Commentary on Seneca's Treatise on Clemency* (1532), was a scholarly piece of Erasmian humanism. It reveals little interest in or commitment to religious matters on the part of Calvin.

By 1534, religion loomed large in Calvin's life; he was on the run from French authorities because of his evangelical views. The time and nature of his conversion is much debated. In October of 1533, the humanist Nicolas Cop, longtime friend of Calvin and rector of the University of Paris, gave an address sympathetic to Lutheran views. Calvin's connection to the address is unclear; some believe he helped write it. However that may be, reaction to it caused him to flee the city. By spring of 1534, Calvin resigned his clerical income, having come over to the Reformation side of the religious question by a "sudden conversion to docility." When the Affair of the Placards made France unsafe, Calvin left for Switzerland.

Taking refuge in Basel, Calvin finished the first edition of the *Institutes of the Christian Religion*, publishing it in 1536. Although diverse works including letters, commentaries, sermons, and other books must be taken into account for a full assessment of John Calvin, the *Institutes* is the best single source for his mature thought. The *Institutes* was constantly revised by Calvin and the final edition was not released until 1559. The first edition was one book with six chapters; the final form was five times larger, with four books containing eighty chapters total.

The context for the constant revising of the *Institutes* was Calvin's struggle to implement the Reformation in the city of Geneva. In 1536, Calvin was convinced by Guillaume Farel to take on the task of transforming Geneva into a Protestant city. His attempts met initial failure and in 1538 Calvin was exiled to Strasbourg. There he was pastor of a French refugee church for about three years. In 1541, he returned to Geneva and started over again. Opposition remained strong; Calvin was not granted citizenship until eighteen years later. His influence was great in the city of Geneva but depended mainly upon the force of his arguments and their application. He delivered these with confidence that they were not his alone but those of the Bible and the God behind the Bible. From 1559 until his death in 1664, John Calvin was the uncontested leader of Geneva, the center of an international Reform movement with profound influence on various cultures from Switzerland to England, Scotland to the Americas.

Institutes of the Christian Religion

The *Institutes* were conceived as a teaching tool and born as a political defense. John Calvin began writing in order to set out in an orderly manner the elementary principles of Christian belief as a catechetical tool for his community of believers. The force of historical circumstance in the form of Francis I's persecution of French Protestants turned the first edition toward an apologetic design. The second edition produced in 1539 was enlarged and revised for the purpose of teaching how to rightly read and understand the Bible. The book was continuously modified with this aim in mind until Calvin pronounced it satisfactory in the 1559 edition.

Calvin understood his life's work as the exposition of the revelation of God that was found solely in the Bible. The *Institutes* is not a systematic theology but an organization of biblical themes to aid the reader of Scripture in understanding the text. Calvin drew heavily on the Christian tradition of Luther and especially Augustine. He also showed skill in Scholastic dialectic and humanist analysis and rhetoric, but his greatness lay in his ability to organize and clarify the Bible's varied writings into a coherent scheme compatible with Protestant insights.

Book 1 of the 1559 *Institutes* treats the knowledge of God as creator and world sovereign. Calvin began with the assumption that neither religious experience nor philosophical reasoning apart from biblical revelation is helpful in obtaining knowledge of God. Though God reveals God's self in nature, universal human sinfulness blinds us from perceiving God as God truly is. Not denying that the deity has left a kind of general revelation in nature, Calvin nonetheless said its only consequence is to remove all excuse before God. Through the Bible alone has God given a source for revelation that is trustworthy. The Scriptures in both Old and New Testaments are inspired for the revealing of God to those to whom the divine chooses to be known. This revelation is accommodated to the comprehension of human beings—God's essence remains unknown—and is unveiled only to that portion of humanity that God elects to receive it.

The God revealed in the Bible is shown to be the triune God who creates all things and is constantly, actively ruling every level of the continuing creation through divine will. This divine will is displayed in the Bible, both Old and New Testaments. Though they differ in presentation, when properly understood they both present a unified witness to the one unchanging will of God. For Calvin, the old covenant of law and the new covenant of grace are equal sources for standards of Christian behavior to be enforced upon everyone in Christian society. Calvin's legalism is tempered by distinguishing between the moral law, which must be kept in all places at all times from the temporary civil or ceremonial types, but the application of God's will through biblical revelation to the affairs of society is firmly established. By a commentary on the doctrine of Providence, Calvin pointed out that these laws are not only established by God but that God is actively carrying their deepest purposes out in the world. The fact that we cannot penetrate or understand these deepest purposes in no way undermines the fact of God's complete and working sovereignty.

The second book deals with God's revelation of God's self as redeemer in Jesus Christ. Redemption is necessary, for the human predicament is revealed in the Bible as one of fallenness. Through Adam all have been infected by Original Sin to the extent that free will and any ability to restore oneself to right relationship with God and God's ongoing creation have been completely lost. Humanity has no power within to help itself. The good news is that God has not abandoned humankind. The Law of the Old Testament has revealed our plight, and the person and atoning work of Jesus Christ provides redemption. Through Christ's ministry as prophet, king, and priest he has provided the sole and essential means for reconciliation with God. In Christ, God was reconciling to God's self those who were elected to be redeemed.

The third book addresses how humanity participates in the grace provided in Jesus Christ, the benefits derived, and the effects that follow. Salvation is gained by believers' communion with Christ, which is established by faith alone. This faith is both a matter of trust in God's action and an "assured knowledge of God's good will." This faith itself is a gift of grace given according to God's sovereign choice without regard for the condition of the recipient. In this way Christ enters the believer, and the benefits of regeneration, justification, and sanctification follow. Regeneration is the beginning of a new life in which the believer and the believer's works are justified by faith alone in the sense that the righteousness of Jesus Christ covers one's former sinfulness before God.

In this context, Calvin presents the doctrine of predestination. Salvation is totally dependent upon God's initiative. Through Christ God chooses some for salvation. This relation to Christ which brings salvation is determined by God, not the sinner. God's will is eternal and unchanging and thus the willing of salvation is eternal and unchanging. Some are predestined, then, to be elected to salvation for the glory of God.

Calvin's doctrine of predestination was not novel. Both Augustine and Luther had already exhibited this line of thought. Calvin went further than they, however, in taking the idea to its logical conclusion. Not all are saved. If the destiny of all is in God's sovereign hands, then those who are damned are damned according to God's decree—and this apart from reference to any aspect of their individual condition, since all deserved damnation. Double predestination is the logical consequence of the principle that sovereign God and sinful humanity are separated by a gap that only God in Christ can cross. Calvin wrote: "We call predestination God's eternal decree, by which he determined with himself what he willed to become of each man. For all are not created in equal condition; rather, eternal life is foreordained for some, eternal damnation for others." (III, xxi, 5)

Calvin saw the difficulties involved in holding this position. He ruled out of bounds questions about why a loving God would hold fallen humanity responsible for sin that they could not be expected to conquer. To ask why of the incomprehensible God behind the accommodating revelation of the Bible is useless and impudent. Humanity can only discover answers as to *whether* God acted in such and such a way, not *why*. Only God from the unknown depths of mystery can answer why; what we know is what God has revealed to be so in Scripture, not why it might or might not be ordained. To the elect, this is the best of news; to the nonelect, this revelation has the "smell of death."

As to the damnation of the non-elect, Calvin was unmoved by arguments of earthly conscience or human reason; he stood his ground on the revelation of Scripture. In his understanding, which he held as obviously correct, the Bible said it, he interpreted it plainly, and that settled it.

Book 4 of the 1559 *Institutes* deals with ecclesiology. Calvin held orthodox Protestant views of the church as the invisible assembly of the elect and the visible community of professed believers. This communion of believers has as its true marks the Word proclaimed and the sacraments rightly administered. The sacraments are two in number, baptism and the Lord's Supper. Calvin advocated infant baptism. Concerning the Supper he was more original, holding a middle ground between the material ubiquity of the Lutherans and the memorial signification of Ulrich Zwingli.

In conformity with his biblical perspective, Calvin's view of the organization of the visible church was specific. He advocated a fourfold hierarchy of offices: pastor, elder, deacon, and teacher. He did not believe that church and state were separate, but he did hold that they had separate responsibilities and jurisdictions. Only the church can rule on matters of a spiritual nature and on what is acceptable in terms of morals for society. The state's connection to the church consists in the state's responsibility to enforce the universal moral laws promulgated by the church. The church should not rule the state; church officials are not above magistrates. Rebellion against immoral magistrates is forbidden, change is up to God. Church and state should exist as two powers with separate jurisdictions within the same society, but the state is obligated to protect both the church and true faith. Through membership in the church, humanity is unified with Christ and society is given a code for Christian behavior.

W. LOYD ALLEN

Further Reading

Bouwsma, William J. *John Calvin: A Sixteenth-Century Portrait*. New York: Oxford University Press, 1987. An interpretation of Calvin as a French intellectual, an evangelical humanist, and a rhetorician.

McNeill, John T. *The History and Character of Calvinism*. New York: Oxford University Press, 1954. A standard account of Calvin's life and teaching along with a survey of his influence to the present.

Parker, T. H. L. *John Calvin: A Biography*. Philadelphia: Westminster Press, 1975. The best single Calvin biography.

Wendel, Francois. *Calvin: Origins and Development of His Religious Thought*. Translated by Philip Mairet. New York: Harper & Row, 1963. First published in French in 1950, this is still the best single volume on the thought and theology of John Calvin.

SAINT TERESA OF ÁVILA

Born: 1515, Ávila, Spain
Died: 1582, Alba de Tormes, Spain
Major Works: *The Life of Teresa of Jesus* (1565), *Way of Perfection* (1565–79), *Book of the Foundations* (1573–82), *Interior Castle* (1577)

Major Ideas

God dwells within the soul.

The soul travels within herself to unite with God.

One image for the soul is an interior castle with many mansions.

By practicing mental prayer, the soul enters the interior castle.

The first three mansions correspond to the purgative way, where the beginner works to cultivate virtues and imitate Jesus Christ.

The first manifestation of supernatural prayer, which is called passive recollection, marks the transition from the purgative way to the illuminative way of the fourth and fifth mansions.

With the increased quieting of the senses and faculties in the fourth mansions, the soul experiences the Prayer of Quiet.

As the soul becomes more passive with respect to God in the fifth mansions, her prayer is called the Sleep of the Faculties.

The sixth mansions, which is the Spiritual Betrothal, is the transition to the unitive way.

The soul experiences the plenitude of unitive love in the Spiritual Marriage of the seventh mansions.

The iconographic depiction of Saint Teresa of Ávila with pen in hand indicates her stature as a woman of learning within the Christian tradition. Although she was canonized a mere forty years after her death in 1582 and proclaimed a doctor of the Roman Catholic church in this century, there is little evidence from Teresa's upbringing and early years in the convent or in the prevailing cultural attitudes toward women in her time to propose her as a candidate for the highest honors that the Church bestows. On the contrary, Teresa's spiritual inclinations were anything but compelling proof of love for God until after the famed conversion that took place around her fortieth year, while the antifeminism of sixteenth-century Spain militated against elevating women to positions of authority within the Church.

In spite of the disadvantages of her sex and meagre education, Teresa emerged as a powerful leader in the reform of the Carmelite order, the author of masterpieces of mystical literature, and spiritual counselor to princes of state and Church as well as to ordinary folk and the nuns under her jurisdiction.

A lively and intelligent young woman, Teresa was sent to the Augustinian convent of Saint Mary of Grace at the age of sixteen by a father who feared that his motherless daughter was falling prey to frivolity and scandal. During her eighteen-month stay with the Augustinians, Teresa was prompted by the example of one particularly devout nun to consider a religious vocation. Not until a life-threatening illness set her thinking about her immortal soul did she settle on the religious life rather than marriage. She entered the Carmelite convent of the Incarnation in 1536 and professed in November of the following year. Thus began a twenty-year ordeal in which Teresa suffered not only grave physical illnesses and the emotional loss of her father but also the spiritual agony of feeling herself hypocritical.

After reading Francisco de Osuna's *Third Spiritual Alphabet* while she was visiting her uncle in 1538, Teresa began to practice and teach the form of mental prayer that she found described by the Franciscan priest. In the eyes of her Carmelite sisters, for whom prayer was a matter of reciting formulaic words in rote fashion, Teresa was almost saintly with her practice of prayer that required the concentration of one's mental and physical energies in order to think about the significance of the words that were being uttered or said silently. She confesses in her autobiography that while others praised her for her piety, she went for long periods of time without praying at all. As the years passed and Teresa realized that there was more to the religious life than adhering to rules of the convent and Church and assisting at devotions and liturgies, she became increasingly dissatisfied with herself and with life in the noisy, crowded convent where over 100 women, most of whom, like Teresa, had chosen the religious life for want of a better option, gave more attention to gossip than to prayer.

An unmistakable Augustinian note of anguish resonates in the pages of her autobiography as Teresa describes the months of spiritual conflict when on the one hand she heard God calling her and on the other, the call of the world. The crisis erupted around 1556, after which she, like Augustine, felt herself irrevocably and joyously committed to God. During the years until her death in 1582, she toiled unceasingly in the vineyard of her Lord, harvesting a reform of the order that resulted in the foundation of seventeen convents and two monasteries for men and a bounty of mystical literature.

The Mystical Way

In her autobiography and in the *Way of Perfection* are chapters and passages that treat the mystical way. In the *Life*, for example, she develops water imagery to express the life of prayer, making the valuable distinction between watering the garden of the soul by one's own effort, which is mental prayer or meditation, and having the garden watered by the Holy Spirit, which is contemplation. Chapters 10 to 21, wherein Teresa describes the stages of prayer in terms of watering the garden of the soul, constitute a mini-mystical treatise. The fullest treatment of the inner life is the *Interior Castle*, (1577), written when Teresa herself had experienced the higher reaches of the mystical life. In the *Interior Castle*, Teresa offers a map of the mystical way as she

herself knew it, one cleared of the Scholastic terminology that cluttered many contemporary treatises by learned men. Although Teresa was uncomfortably aware of her deficiencies as a woman of little education, her writing is all the more appealing because she does not labor under the burden of the erudition that she admired in male theologians but which proved inaccessible to the average person, secular or religious, whose desire to nourish the interior life needed the encouragement and wisdom of a guide whose foremost qualification was experience.

Having suffered from want of adequate spiritual direction, Teresa was sensitive to the needs of men and women in their quest for God. Hence she writes in a language that is understandable and, by dint of her charmingly familiar images, appealing as well. Hers is an endearing style, in large part because she did not employ theological terms; she has proved to be helpful to spiritual aspirants precisely because she remained true to herself, in her experience and in her manner of expressing herself. Although she does not admit in the *Interior Castle* that the experiences she relates are her own, it is evident that such references as the one to "a woman I know" are to herself.

The Interior Castle

The unifying image of the *Interior Castle* is the soul as an inner castle, which, she confides, came to her as an inspiration when she implored God's assistance in complying with her superior's directive to write for the spiritual edification of others. The interior castle of the soul contains seven mansions, each of which in turn is constituted of an indeterminate number of mansions. In the innermost mansions, which is the center of the soul, dwells God. Hence in the mystical journey the soul moves ever more deeply within herself, to see the One who has resided there always but whom she has been unable to see because of the imperfections that cloud her sight.

Just as Teresa's journey in writing the *Interior Castle* begins with the gift of an image, so does the soul embark on her journey when she is made aware of the primordial desire in her life, which is to love God intimately, intensely, and immediately. The gift of desire is a reminder, also, that mystical union is a union of wills wherein the soul is transformed by God's love so that her will is brought into conformity with the will of God. Thus mystical union is called the transforming union, being differentiated from the soul's essential union with God whereby she exists. The latter union makes possible the soul's physical existence, while mystical union is a gift that floods the soul with spiritual life. Mystical union has been termed the union of likeness in recognition of the understanding that by love the soul becomes like God, although she never loses her personality in God in a pantheistic sense.

The journey to mystical union can be long and arduous, requiring, according to Teresa's map, entering into the seven mansions of the soul. First, however, the soul must gain entrance into the castle itself, which is done through prayer and meditation. Instructed by her own practice of mental prayer, Teresa realized that no progress could be made until the soul ceased to rely on vocal prayer, which is the rote recitation of words, and began to think about the words she said to herself or aloud. In advocating mental prayer, Teresa, as a woman, was taking the risk of running afoul of the Inquisition, which had been particularly suspicious of women who practiced and taught mental prayer since the Edict of Toledo had been directed against the *alumbrados* in 1525. Among the *alumbrados*, who were pronounced heretical by the Edict, were several charismatic women. Whereas the Inquisition considered mental prayer dangerous for women because their need for the Church as a mediator between them and God might lessen, thus threatening ecclesiastical authority, in Teresa's eyes the greater danger was that for want of using their minds women would be thwarted in their quest for God. Hence she is adamant in her counsel about mental prayer, asserting without reservation that the soul cannot begin the journey inward unless she prays in this fashion.

The general plan of the *Interior Castle* is that the first three mansions represent the active part of the journey, wherein the soul is primarily aware of what she is doing to become pleasing to God, while mansions four through seven are the passive stage, characterized by the soul's consciousness of God's acting upon her. With respect to the traditional tripart division of the mystical way, mansions one to three correspond to the purgative way, four and five to the illuminative way, and six and seven to the unitive way.

Mental prayer, devotional reading, edifying conversation, and good works are the means by which the soul purges imperfections and cultivates virtues in the first three mansions. The soul discerns progress in the purgative way by the degree to which she is humble and charitable and the senses and faculties are quieted in prayer. The five exterior senses and the interior senses of imagination and fancy reside in the lower part of the soul while the faculties of memory, understanding, and will are in the higher part. Spiritual sweetness, which is the good feelings that come during devotion, prayer, reading, conversation, and doing good works nourish the soul's desire for perfection in the first two mansions, but toward the end of the third mansions, such spiritual sweetness dries up so that the soul does not understand what is happening and fears that she is backsliding. These times of aridity, however, indicate progress, in that God relates to the soul in ways that are too delicate to be discerned by the senses and emotions.

In the third chapter of the fourth mansions, Teresa describes the Prayer of Recollection, which marks the transition from the purgative way to the illuminative way. The Prayer of Recollection is the first form of supernatural prayer that Teresa herself experienced; by supernatural she means that the soul is aware not of what she does but of what is being done to her. Specifically, the soul closes her eyes without willing it and feels a temple of solitude being built up about her. Teresa compares the recollected soul to a hedgehog, for the senses and faculties are gathered together and quieted so as not to disturb the soul. Unlike the hedgehog, the soul cannot recollect herself at will; she is passive, and recollection is a gift, an infused loving.

In the other chapters of the fourth mansions, Teresa describes the Prayer of Quiet, in which recollection of the senses and faculties is deepened. With no effort on her part, the soul is watered abundantly, and she feels peace, quiet, and humility. The faculties are absorbed and amazed at what happens to the soul. Realizing that people may try to force supernatural prayer, Teresa emphasizes toward the end of the fourth mansions that God alone can bestow the Prayer of Quiet and its accompanying consolations. The soul is not to desire consolations but rather to accept God's will in imitation of his Son.

Teresa names the prayer that characterizes the fifth mansions "the Sleep of the Faculties" for the reason that the faculties and senses are so deeply recollected they cannot discern when God enters the soul. Teresa employs the image of the silkworm transformed into a butterfly to express the changes the soul undergoes. Intensely affected by the experience of being quieted in prayer, the soul yearns to suffer and even to die for God. Realizing, however, that her will is not yet conformed to God's, and aware of the dangers of overconfidence, she is reminded to improve in charity. From her own experience and that of others, Teresa recognized the perils of self-delusion, pride, and zealousness. Thus in mansions four and five, as the soul is receiving gifts of infused prayer and love, she warns the traveler of the inner way not to trust in herself but rather to rely on God and to grow in charity.

The Spiritual Betrothal

The Spiritual Betrothal of the sixth mansions is the transition from the illuminative way to the unitive way. This stage is the most dangerous of the journey, for the soul easily can fall victim to her own pride and self-delusion. Clearly referring to her own experiences, Teresa describes the extraordinary phenomena that characterize the sixth mansions. Wounds of love, rapture, flights of the spirit, and jubilation, with their often attendant visions and locutions, not only are not necessary to spiritual perfection but can be obstacles for the soul whose

pride tempts her to boast of her gifts and consider herself superior to others on their account. Like her friend and director, Saint John of the Cross, Teresa cautions her readers not to depend on extraordinary phenomena.

In describing and explaining the understandings that may come to the soul during a rapture, for example, or a jubilation, Teresa refers to the categories of corporeal, imaginary, and intellectual/spiritual to define the kinds of visions and locutions that she knew from experience. In response to the pressing question about how to discern if the understandings have their source in God or the soul, which speaks to their being genuine or not, Teresa offers two criteria. If the vision or locution occurs unexpectedly and if the effects are positive in the sense that the soul is at peace, joyous, and humble, they are from God.

In the middle chapter of the sixth mansions, Teresa sounds a note of caution: She stresses the need to continue to meditate on the Sacred Humanity. Her counsel reflects the debate in theological circles as to whether the contemplative had further need of meditation once she had tasted the gifts of infused love. Clearly Teresa thought that even the most sublimely graced contemplative needed to meditate on the life and work of Jesus Christ and strive to emulate him.

Although the soul has progressed far along the mystic way when she enjoys the sixth mansions, her life is not without suffering. A major theme of these chapters is suffering, reflective perhaps of the fact that Teresa herself suffered when other people derided her or pronounced her saintly, when inept confessors misled her, when illness afflicted her, or when earthly consolations lost their appeal and spiritual ones dried up. So intense can be the suffering in these mansions that Teresa sees the soul as suspended between heaven and earth. Her ultimate advice, as in previous mansions, is to do works of charity and trust in God.

Teresa marks entry into the Spiritual Marriage of the seventh mansions with a spiritual vision of the Trinity. In Spiritual Marriage, the inner restlessness and longing are transformed into the peaceful certainty that she rests habitually in God's presence. The highs of rapture and lows of aridity that made the soul restless in the sixth mansions vanish, giving way to the harmony of the active Martha and contemplative Mary. Her will conformed with the will of God, the soul enjoys the favors of unitive love. Prayer, which Teresa says elsewhere is simply talking with God, has been transformed from an event in time to an uninterrupted conversation with God, whom she now calls her Beloved Companion. Thus the soul enters into the deepest part of herself, drawn there by the transforming love of God.

MARY E. GILES

Further Reading

Dicken, E. W. Trueman. *The Crucible of Love.* New York: Sheed & Ward, 1963. This is reading for the mystical theology of Saint Teresa.

Green, Deirdre. *Gold in the Crucible. Teresa of Avila and the Western Mystical Tradition.* Longmead, Shaftesbury, Dorset: Element Books, 1989. Especially helpful on the issues of feminism and Teresa's connection with Jewish mysticism.

Hatzfeld, Helmut A. *Santa Teresa de Ávila.* New York: Twayne, 1969. Like other volumes in the series, this one is a concise introduction to the saint, her life and work.

Swietlicki, Catherine. *Spanish Christian Cabala: The Works of Luis de León, Santa Teresa de Jesús, and San Juan de la Cruz.* Columbia: University of Missouri Press, 1986. Helpful in seeing Teresa relative to other Spanish mystics in the matter of the influence of Jewish mysticism.

MICHEL DE MONTAIGNE

Born: 1533, at the château de Montaigne near Bordeaux, France
Died: 1592, on the same family estate
Major Work: *Essays*, 1588 (comprising variants from previous editions as well as numerous marginal additions to the 1588 edition). (His *Travel Journal* [1580–81], written as a private diary, was published some two centuries later.)

Major Ideas

An acceptance of the duality of the human condition (man's spiritual aspirations counterbalanced by the physical limitations of the body) enables man to pursue the masterpiece of living well.

A life committed to moderation is superior to one that has allowed excesses and extremes.

The senses through which man knows the world are imperfect and limit his ability to claim knowledge of anything (God alone is omniscient).

Man's inability to say definitively either "I know" or "I do not know" leads to an interrogative formula, "What do I know?" ("Que sais-je?") to reflect the cautious suspension of judgment man must consider.

All living things, including human beings, are in a state of constant flux; being consists of movement and action.

Study of the self is man's primary duty and responsibility.

Montaigne's fame derives not from any rigorous philosophical system but rather from an extremely appealing analysis and commentary on nearly all philosophical currents dating back to antiquity. The thousands of references to classical poets, writers, and philosophers form the backdrop for a comparison with his own experience and reflection. The great texts of the ages have survived because they tell us something of value. The *Essays* of Montaigne, the philosopher, juxtapose insights from the past with contemporary thoughts and ideas to create a timeless metaphor situated at the creative point of tension between the two worlds. His goal is nothing short of writing a primer on how to live life, and the *Essays* proceed in a fashion that encourages the reader to explore the text of his or her own life.

Michel de Montaigne was born on his family's estate near Bordeaux and was the first to carry the recently acquired noble name that came with the property. In the *Essays*, however, he notes a discomfiture with titles that set men apart from each other. Wet-nursed by peasants according to his father's desire that the child feel close to common people, the boy learned Latin at an early age and entered school speaking not a word of French. His fluency in Latin intimidated the faculty at the Collège de Guyenne, where Latin and Greek were studied. The essay "Of the Education of Children" records Montaigne's unenthusiastic appreciation of schooling in the sixteenth century. He continued in philosophy at the University of Bordeaux until political turmoil there led to his transfer to Toulouse and the pursuit of law.

Although much is known about Montaigne's personal life, some mystery remains concerning his influence and political involvement in court intrigues and political maneuverings during the turbulent events of the sixteenth century. It is generally conceded that Montaigne was a far more important player than he himself acknowledged. As mayor of Bordeaux for two terms, his was a steady voice of tolerance during the religious upheaval so characteristic of the period. His own siblings reflected the split between Catholicism and Protestantism, a schism that led to violence in France after 1545 (the Council of Trent) and the decision of François I to punish heretics and unrepentant theologians.

The essayist's public career began in 1554 with a regional appointment in Perigueux; shortly thereafter, in 1557, Montaigne was named to the Parliament of Bordeaux, where he met his great friend, the poet Étienne de la Boétie. Thus began a passionate friendship described by La Boétie as a "marriage of souls" and by Montaigne in these terms: "Our souls mingle[d] and blend[ed] with each other so completely that they efface[d] the seam that joined them." La Boétie died in 1563 at the age of thirty-three, whereupon his friend went into mourning. Two years later, Montaigne married Françoise de la Chassaigne, the daughter of a colleague in the Bordeaux Parliament. This union produced six children, of whom only one daughter survived early childhood. Montaigne speaks relatively little of women in his writings, reserving the most fervent pages on love and friendship for male relationships. Women, it seems, stir the physical passions and tempt man to stray from the desired confines of moderation. For whatever reason, women simply do not occupy a central role in Montaigne's writing.

Before reaching the age of forty, Montaigne chose to retire from public life (1571) and begin writing his *Essays*. This decision scarcely changed his public involvements; indeed, the major political posts and numerous intrigues lay ahead of him. The renunciation of public life coincided with the decision to undertake an investigation of his private universe, now severely shaken by the untimely death of La Boétie. The *Essays* can be viewed as a desire for dialogue and introspection at a time when Montaigne was ill at ease in a world adrift on a sea of religious intolerance. Political leadership had proven ineffective in restoring civil order. With the public sphere approaching chaos, the philosopher turned inward.

As the writing of the first two books of the *Essays* progressed, Montaigne became increasingly involved in political affairs and was named to the court of Henry of Navarre in 1577. His first attack of kidney stones occurred the following year, at which time the pain and suffering led to reflections on man's mortality, the topic most frequently raised in his work. A trip to Italy in search of relief from bouts with gout, the kidney stones, and rheumatism led to the title of Roman citizen being bestowed on Montaigne shortly before his return to Bordeaux as mayor. The first edition of the *Essays* (the A text) appeared in 1580 and was followed in 1582, 1587, and 1588 (the B version) by appreciably augmented

and corrected editions. During the last years before his death in 1592, Montaigne wrote numerous additions in the margins of the fourth (1588) edition. After his death, the 1588 text along with the marginal additions and other variants became the final (C) edition known as the Bordeaux text.

Essays

Much energy has been expended attempting to codify the *Essays* into neatly fitting philosophical clusters beyond the author's obvious tripartite organization. One scheme popular among exegetes divided the work into the Stoical, skeptical, and Epicurean periods, that is to say, material produced at various stages of his life: the early 1570s, the mid-1570s, and from 1578–1592, respectively. Today, we tend to look at the *Essays* from a more holistic point of view, agreeing with Montaigne that the text reveals an organic process from beginning to end and that the author through the writing of the *Essays* becomes consubstantial with the text: "I have no more made my book than my book has made me."

Because of the vast erudition, inexhaustible curiosity, and thirst for knowledge one finds in the *Essays*, Montaigne complements another great sixteenth-century French writer, François Rabelais, who died when Montaigne was twenty. Rabelais's hyperbolic characters with their gargantuan appetites embody a philosophy calling for a *well-filled head* ("une tête bien pleine") in contrast to Montaigne's appeal for a *well-made mind* ("une tête bien faite"). Modern pedagogues would surely term Montaigne an advocate for interactive, student-centered learning.

The very first essay, "By Diverse Means We Arrive at the Same End," reveals a mind free of dogmatism and open to creative methods of approaching ideas and problems. As the title indicates, it may initially appear that subjects discussed earlier have little or no bearing on the matter at hand. Some essays do not follow this pattern, however, as if Montaigne were checking his reader's attentiveness, but many, such as the essay "On Some Verses of Virgil" can truly disconcert the reader who sees little if any connectedness with the announced title. Montaigne's method of achieving the same result, while employing an unorthodox *modus operandi* in the process, reflects a rich and appealing style sometimes described as sensual. Each essay is a kind of palimpsest that invites the reader to come on board first at this level, then at that one. Paradox and ambiguity are cornerstones of the composition, too, since they illustrate man's inability to *know* definitively and thus remind him of his limitations and his human condition.

"Que Sais-je?"

The "Apology for Raymond Sebond," the longest of the essays, is scarcely a defense of Sebond's *Natural Theology*, which posits the notion that God is revealed to man through His creation, the world. Indeed, very little of the lengthy essay deals with Sebond at all. Montaigne's strategy is to examine Sebond's theology in order to present his own view that man can claim to know very little. "What do I know?"—"*Que sais-je?*"—Montaigne's celebrated motto, appears well into the Sebond essay and allows the author to elaborate his view that man's finite condition renders him incapable of saying either "I know" or "I do not know." Rather, the "*Que sais-je?*" goes unanswered; Montaigne suspends judgment and undertakes an investigation and self-portrait of the only subject man can know

something about: himself. The moral becomes: "The true mirror of our discourse is the course of our lives."

The final essay, "Of Experience," contains perhaps the most celebrated maxims, as Montaigne concludes his monumental project with an eloquent plea for mankind to accept the human condition, the duality of body and soul, and the notion that happiness, wisdom, and goodness coexist necessarily with pain and suffering.

The *Essays* are a preparation for Montaigne's death; complete detachment from this world is made bearable once man has fully embraced all that life has to offer, both for good and for ill, since only that which has been fully possessed can be let go without regret: "I unbind myself on all sides; my farewells are already half made to everyone except myself. Never did a man prepare to leave the world more utterly and completely, nor detach himself from it more universally, than I prepare to do." "There is nothing so beautiful and legitimate as to play the man well and properly," he writes in "Of experience."

Montaigne concludes with this humble admonition that certainly influenced the final page of Proust's *Time Recaptured*: "There is no use our mounting on stilts, for on stilts we must still walk on our own legs. And on the loftiest throne in the world we are still only sitting on our own rump."

ROBERT FRYE

Further Reading

Bowen, Barbara. *The Age of Bluff*. Urbana, Chicago, and London: University of Illinois Press, 1972. An analysis of the intellectual milieu in which Montaigne wrote and a valuable reminder that the emphasis placed on creativity is a modern concept.

Cottrell, Robert D. *Sexuality/Textuality: A Study of the Fabric of Montaigne's Essays*. Columbus: Ohio State University Press, 1981. For the advanced student, a perceptive study of two key concepts in Montaigne, *accouplage* (coupling)

and *contexture* (textuality), to suggest a powerful link between sexual impulse and writing.

Frame, Donald M. *Montaigne: A Biography*. New York: Harcourt, Brace & World, 1965. A sound source of information about the man and his work.

Sayce, Richard A. *The Essays of Montaigne: A Critical Exploration*. London: Weidenfeld & Nicolson, 1972. A thoroughly readable and literate overview of the *Essays* by one Montaigne's most distinguished critics.

SAINT JOHN OF THE CROSS

Born: 1542, Fontiveros, near Ávila, Spain
Died: 1591, Úbeda, Spain
Major Works: *Ascent of Mount Carmel (1578–88)*, *Dark Night of the Soul (1582–88)*, *Spiritual Canticle (1578–88)*, *Living Flame of Love (1585)*

Major Ideas

Substantial union with God is that by which the soul exists.

The union of likeness, also called transforming or mystical union, is that by which the soul becomes like God.

God is darkness to the soul in that the divine is essentially other than the human.

Since the means must be proportionate to the end, the soul must travel in darkness to the Divine Darkness. The journey in darkness is named the via negativa.

Night is the image for the dark journey of detachment as the soul actively purges herself of desires for that which is specific, concrete, and particular and as God purges her of desires and dependencies.

Detached in terms of her senses and higher faculties, the soul knows only the dark, confused, and general, which is God.

In the experience of being purged by God, suffering is epistemology.

Love is both the mode and content of knowing.

Although Saint John of the Cross is one of the most celebrated poets in the Spanish language and revered as well for the depths of his love for God, which the Catholic church acknowledged by canonizing him in 1726, he also deserves mention as a thinker of the first order. Trained in theology at the renowned University of Salamanca, he combined the genius of the disciplined mind with the gifts of the poet to produce a corpus of mystical theology without equal. In his prose writings, he accomplished the extraordinary feat of subjecting mystical experience to intellectual analysis without deadening the spirit that informed all the activities of this gentle man.

The seeds of Saint John's vocation as a mystical theologian were sown early in life. His family's poverty might have prevented Juan de Yepes from receiving the education that he deserved were it not for the generosity of a patron who recognized the youth's exceptional intelligence and spiritual sincerity. After attending the College of the Society of Jesus at Medina del Campo, the young man took the Carmelite habit in 1563 and in the following year entered the University of Salamanca to pursue a three-year course in arts, returning in November of 1567 for a year's course in theology.

Saint John's interest in intellectual matters continued throughout his life, as evidenced in the posts he held as rector of the College of the Reform at Alcalá de Henares (1571) and of the Carmelite college in Baeza (1579–82). But the intellectual search for God was not the exclusive concern for Saint John; his greater vocation was to love God intimately and intensely. To further the spiritual vocation of which intellectual understanding was only one aspect, Saint John joined the reform movement that the Carmelite Teresa of Ávila was directing, taking the vow of the Reform in 1568 and giving himself over to the hermetic life for two years before assuming other responsibilities in the Discalced community.

Saint John's profound love for God overflowed into mystical poetry, which in turn occasioned prose commentaries that he wrote at the behest primarily of nuns who sought spiritual guidance through his poetry. His major works thus are explications of the poems "Dark Night of the Soul," "Spiritual Canticle," and "Living Flame of Love."

Saint John's life was not easy even though he was

167

much loved by the nuns he confessed and by other associates, both religious and secular, who appreciated the beauty of his extraordinary soul. Imprisonment at the hands of the Calced brothers, public humiliation by the Discalced, and an agonizing death, the result of an ill-treated infection that spread throughout his body, brought a full measure of suffering to this saintly man. His suffering is not without significance in considering Saint John of the Cross as a thinker. When he goes beyond the limits of Scholasticism, as he must, in his mystical theology, the categories for understanding that he creates are experiential. Among these categories, suffering is a principal experience.

The Mystical Treatises

The mystical treatises form a progression. The *Ascent of Mount Carmel* and *Dark Night of the Soul* make up a treatise in two parts that presents the principles of the *via negativa*, which are crucial to understanding the theology of the *Spiritual Canticle* and *Living Flame of Love*. The emphasis in the first treatise is on the process of detachment, or purgation, up to the experience of union known as the spiritual betrothal and marriage. The *Spiritual Canticle* refers briefly to purgation, concentrating on the increasingly subtle consciousness of union, while the *Living Flame of Love*, repeating in part the understandings about purgation, also moves into the exceedingly difficult task of suggesting, if not analyzing, the higher reaches of union.

Because the point of exposition in the *Ascent of Mount Carmel* and *Dark Night of the Soul* is to elucidate the way of detachment, this treatise is the most speculative of the three and therefore the most accessible to the reader who, not necessarily engaged in the spiritual journey, is in search of intellectual understanding rather than spiritual guidance. The intellectual categories, however, do not preclude the experiential, as evidenced by the *Dark Night of the Soul*.

The first treatise particularly illustrates how Saint John combines Scholastic methodology on the one hand and the experiential–descriptive approach on the other. At a glance, the treatise reveals the Scholastic inclination to break up a text into smaller and yet smaller segments so as to analyze each one in turn and then reconstitute them into a whole. Thus Saint John provides an introductory exposition of the first stanza of the poem he is explicating, after which he proceeds phrase by phrase in analytical fashion. In addition to the Scholastic procedure, Saint John shows his indebtedness to the Salamancan training by employing categories to explicate the psychology of the soul and by detailing increasingly discrete experiences.

There are two major keys to understanding the mystical theology of the *Ascent of Mount Carmel* and *Dark Night of the Soul*. The first is to read the text in this order:

1. Active purgation of the senses: *Ascent*, book 1
2. Passive purgation of the senses: *Dark Night*, book 1
3. Active purgation of the spirit: *Ascent*, books 2 and 3
4. Passive purgation of the spirit: *Dark Night*, book 2

The second is to begin reading with chapter 5 of book 2 of the *Ascent of Mount Carmel*, in which Saint John makes the distinction between substantial union and mystical union, which also is called the "union of likeness" and "transforming union." The reason for the latter terms is that God transforms the soul so that her will is conformed to the will of God and there is effected a likeness of the divine and human in terms of the will. The image of human love—the bride and the bridegroom—elsewhere occurs in Saint John's writings, notably in his poem "Spiritual Canticle," where it expresses the unity of lovers who retain their individuality while in their intimacy they are "oned," that is, they become like one person.

The Journey of Detachment

Although all of Saint John's commentaries explicate to some degree the journey of detachment, the *As-*

cent of *Mount Carmel* and *Dark Night of the Soul* provide its most detailed map. Tracing the way on the map of the two-part treatise thus provides the rationale for detachment that other treatises assume or merely sketch.

In the active night of the senses, the soul labors to know herself so as to purge the imperfections that make her unlike God. The work is to rid herself of the desires that come in a natural way through the five exterior senses and the interior senses of imagination and fancy. Saint John stresses that our desires for things, rather than the things themselves, are the obstacles on the journey. He makes the distinction between privative desires as those that deprive the soul of God and the positive ones that deposit in the soul the effects of wearying, tormenting, darkening, defiling, and weakening her.

Unable to complete the immense task of purging the senses on her own power, the soul may undergo a cleansing by God, thus entering into the passive night of the senses. As the soul is being cleansed of the spiritual imperfections of pride, avarice, luxury, wrath, gluttony, envy, and sloth, the soul experiences a disturbing absence of God in that the good feelings, or spiritual sweetnesses, that have accompanied her prayer and devotion up to this time dry up.

Saint John gives three signs by which to determine if the aridities originate in God or in the soul's own lukewarmness. If the soul derives no consolation in religious or worldly affairs; if she fears she is failing God; if she is unable to meditate or employ the imagination in prayer, devotion, or reading; and if these three signs are present together in the soul, they indicate the transition from the active to the passive, from the natural to the supernatural, from meditation to contemplation, which is infused loving. If the soul discerns these signs, she is to rest quietly, for God, rather than she, is taking the initiative in the relationship.

In the active night of the spirit, the soul labors to cleanse the faculties of memory, understanding, and will. With respect to understanding, she is to detach herself from knowledge that is specific and concrete, thus human, in nature; since memory is the repository of knowledge, it too must be cleansed, as must the affections of joy, hope, grief, and fear in the will.

The explanation of the purgation of understanding reveals Saint John's training in traditional epistemology; he explains the categories of natural and supernatural understanding on the basis of a process whereby we acquire information about exterior reality through the senses, retain the data as images in the imagination, and conceptualize the images. If the elements of exterior reality, senses, images, imagination, understanding, and concepts are present, the mode and content of knowing/understanding are natural, but if one or more of the elements are absent, the mode of understanding is supernatural, though the content is not necessarily supernatural. In natural corporeal understanding, all elements are present, but in supernatural corporeal understanding, exterior reality is absent. In supernatural imaginary understanding, both exterior reality and the senses are absent, while in supernatural spiritual understanding the imagination and images are also inactive. In supernatural corporeal and imaginary understandings, the mode of understanding is supernatural, but the content is natural because the subject understood is specific, particular, and concrete. At the level of supernatural spiritual understanding, which always is supernatural in mode, there is a difference between the content that is specific and particular and that which is dark, confused, and general. Because spiritual understandings that are specific and particular can by their nature be conceptualized, they are not supernatural in content. Only understandings that exceed rational understanding and conceptualization can be classified as supernatural in both mode and content. Because these understandings present themselves to the soul as dark, confused, and general, no word or image can contain them. Dark, confused, and general understanding is understanding of God as God is. By the purgation of the faculty of understanding, the soul comes not to depend on specific, natural knowledge, which would be knowledge about God, but to receive understandings that are God himself.

As Saint John moves into the discussion of the passive night of the spirit, his approach falters in analysis but gains in wisdom. There are no categories into which he can fit the soul's consciousness of being overwhelmed by that which she does not understand. Saint John's method here is to identify, describe, and explain the primary experience of the spiritual night—suffering. Much of the *Dark Night of the Soul* is devoted to the suffering that the soul undergoes as the mediators of God are taken away, until the pain itself is the sole indicator of the divine presence. Saint John the mystic knows the impossibility of understanding the mind of God; Saint John the theologian does not give up on the task of explaining the many reasons for the pain that floods the soul's consciousness.

For Saint John, the mystic and theologian, suffering is epistemological in that the soul knows God by means of her pain. When understandings fail the mind and the soul feels herself suspended over the abyss of unknowing, her comfortable notions of God shattered, stripped of illusions and supports, and her consciousness is flooded with suffering. Although Saint John explains several reasons for the soul's pain, from the perspective of knowing, the principal one is that her desire for God causes pain: In her longing to know and love God, she feels abandoned. But if she did not already desire God, she would not suffer. Hence her pain–desire is her mode of knowing. Furthermore, since the pain–desire is to her dark, confused, and general, it is not only the mode but also the content of knowing.

With the faculty of understanding darkened, the soul moves freely and securely in faith. Her memory similarly purged, she is freed from the specific hopes that were generated by experiences in the past so that she can move in an attitude of hoping. And with the will released from the bonds of particular desires, her desire for God bursts forth in boundless charity. Thus these chapters in the *Dark Night of the Soul* are a model of fidelity on the part of a man who loved God beyond all measure and yet, for the edification of those who sought his counsel, did his best to measure intellectually the source, the way, and the destiny of that love.

Spiritual Love

The darkness that overwhelms the soul as she is caught to God in unitive love cedes to images of erotic love and fire in the *Spiritual Canticle* and *Living Flame of Love*, respectively. Although the suffering of the dark night is not denied in these commentaries, its reality is given different expression, which reveals hidden recesses of meaning. For example, the imagery of the soul as bride and God as bridegroom provides a context in which to explore the deepening of love from the consciousness of spiritual betrothal to that of spiritual marriage. In marriage, the transformation of the soul is further transformed so that she is made divine and becomes God by participation. The experience of human lovers thus opens up a vista of loving wherein the soul feels herself being moved from transformation to transformation, as it were, reminiscent of the Pauline image of love as going from glory to glory.

Transformation as a process rather than a single act is suggested, moreover, in the exquisite imagery of fire and flames, as Saint John shows the soul being wounded and hollowed out by the living flame of the Holy Spirit. So emptied is the soul of particular desires, understandings, and memories that nothing whatsoever stands between her and God. Subject and object no longer are real for the soul who, once having known God through his creatures, now knows creatures through God. To suggest a consciousness without dualities—in which there is no inside or outside—Saint John portrays the higher faculties as being illumined from within rather than lit from without. As all contraries are resolved and dichotomies dismissed, suffering ceases; the soul sees the absolute oneness that was there all along. Thus the soul journeys by love to a loving that bears a unique, wondrous knowing.

MARY E. GILES

Further Reading

Dicken, E. W. Trueman. *The Crucible of Love.* New York: Sheed & Ward, 1963. An excellent introduction to the mystical theology of Saint John of the Cross.

Stein, Edith. *The Science of the Cross.* Chicago: Regnery, 1960. A perceptive and inspired theology of the cross, which was for this martyred nun a lived reality.

Tavard, George H. *Poetry and Contemplation in St. John of the Cross.* Athens: Ohio University Press, 1988. A commendable endeavor to fuse the poetic and theological.

FRANCIS BACON

Born: 1561, at York House in the Strand, London, England
Died: 1626, Highgate, near London, England
Major Works: *The Advancement of Learning* (1605), *Novum Organum* (1620), *De Augmentis Scientiarum* (1623)

Major Ideas

The purpose of scientific knowledge is to make possible great works for the betterment of the human condition.

Experiments are essential to the testing of theories.

The human mind is prey to certain typical intellectual failures.

In the generation and testing of theories, the negative instance is fundamental.

The goal of the science of nature is the discovery of "forms," the unobservable organization or structure of the particles of which all things are composed.

Francis Bacon, the central thinker of the English Renaissance, is often regarded as the father of modern empiricism.

It is no easy matter to recount in brief Bacon's life. He wrote, with extraordinary learning, about law, politics, history, and morality. More than this, Bacon played a very active role in the somewhat cruel political life of the England of his times. It is nonetheless true that Bacon is best known and justly famous for his effort to lay for the sciences a solid foundation, to clear for the study of nature a place amid what he took to be the desperate confusions of Scholasticism.

In 1573, Bacon went to Trinity College, Cambridge. One might speculate as to what he studied as a youth; we do know that he told his biographer, Rawley, that it was at Cambridge that he "fell into a dislike of the philosophy of Aristotle." Though he was born into prominent and politically well-connected family—his father was lord keeper under Elizabeth I and his uncle, Burghley, was lord treasurer—when his father died in 1579, Bacon was left only a small inheritance. He took up the study of law with renewed vigor and in 1582 became a barrister. Two years later he entered the House of Commons, where throughout his life he would represent many different constituencies.

Bacon was to make something of a profession of seeking the favor of those in high places. He became a close friend of the Earl of Essex, a favorite

of Elizabeth's. Bacon had hoped for the post of attorney-general, but this went to his archrival in matters of the heart as well as of politics, Coke. To console his friend, Essex gave Bacon an estate.

In 1600, Essex led the disastrous Irish expedition. He was subsequently tried for insubordination. Having fallen out of favor with the Queen, Essex then led an equally disastrous insurrection. Bacon, who had for some time been playing Essex off the Queen (who seems never to have liked Bacon), played an instrumental role in the prosecution. Essex was convicted as a traitor and executed in 1601. It is, we may speculate, for behavior such as this that Pope calls Bacon "the wisest, brightest, meanest of mankind."

With the ascension of James I in 1603, Bacon's political fortunes improved. Between 1603 and 1621 (a period of impressive intellectual output), Bacon was knighted, appointed attorney-general, made lord keeper, lord chancellor, Baron Verulam, and finally created Viscount Saint Albans.

In 1621, his public life was to end suddenly. Bacon, who had had economic troubles since 1598, was charged with bribery. He was convicted after admitting his guilt, heavily fined, and briefly imprisoned in the Tower of London.

Bacon remained intellectually active and productive until his death. The story of his death, as reported in Aubrey's *Brief Lives*, is well known. Thomas Hobbes (Bacon's friend and sometime secretary) and Bacon were riding near Highgate during winter. It occurred to Bacon that snow might preserve flesh. They had a woman gut a chicken, and they proceeded to fill the fowl with ice. Bacon took a chill and died days later.

The Great Instauration

Bacon writes at the start of his preface to *The Great Instauration* (1620): "That the state of knowledge is not prosperous nor greatly advancing; and that a way must be opened for the human understanding entirely different from any hitherto known, and other helps provided in order that the mind may exercise over the nature of things the authority which properly belongs to it." This at once makes clear Bacon's great pessimism about the present state of the sciences, as well as his great optimism for the intellectual capacities of man once the mind comes to be properly directed.

The *Instauration*, the great plan for the complete reconstruction of the sciences, was to consist of six parts:

1. A Division of the Sciences;
2. The New Organon—Bacon's proposed method for the carrying on of science;
3. The Phenomena of the Universe—the experiential basis, the data of the sciences;
4. The Ladder of the Intellect—examples of the new method in use;
5. Forerunners of the New Philosophy—tentative and provisional conjectures made before the application of the new method;
6. The New Philosophy—the setting out of the science that was to be established according to Bacon's account.

This is a grand plan indeed. Though Bacon himself recognized that the sixth part was beyond his powers, the remainder of the *Instauration* was completed by him only to various degrees. The first is to be found in *The Advancement* and in the expanded and Latinized *De Augmentis*, the second in the *New Organon*. Little progress was made on the other parts. (Though one might look at the *Historia Densi et Rari*; *Historia Sulphuris, Mercurii, et Sallis*; *Historia Vitae et Mortis*; and the *Sylva Sylvarum* for bits and pieces of this work.)

Division of the Sciences

Bacon's classification of the sciences is to be found in book 2 of the *Advancement* and in books 2 to 9 of the *De Augmentis*. He claims to be classifying the various branches of learning rather than the sciences (which we call "philosophy"), and these he singles out as "poesy," "history," and "philosophy." To these correspond the three faculties of the intellect: imagination, memory, and reason.

The third book of the *De Augmentis* begins with a familiar distinction between revealed knowledge of the divine and natural or sensory knowledge. Natural knowledge is itself divided into knowledge of the divine (natural theology) and that concerning nature and man. Common to all these branches of science is "First Philosophy." What Bacon says of this is none too clear, but it does include certain canons of reasoning, for example, the law of non-contradiction (a statement cannot be both true and false) and the law of excluded middle (a statement must be either true or false).

The study of nature is again divided into the speculative and the operative. (We would say the theoretical and the applied.) Here we find a feature much emphasized by Bacon: The purpose of knowledge is to make possible great works. "Human knowledge and human power," he writes, "meet in one; for where the cause is not known the effect cannot be produced."

Speculative natural philosophy is divided into "physic" and "metaphysic." Corresponding to these on the applied side are "mechanic" and "magic" (called so because its deep understanding of nature makes possible great wonders).

Physic and metaphysic are distinguished by Bacon's making use of the Aristotlean doctrine of the four causes. Within the purview of physic are efficient and material causes, while metaphysic studies final and formal causes. This terminology is not particularly helpful. Of more use is the following:

Physic deals with the "common and ordinary course of nature" and metaphysic deals with the "eternal and fundamental laws" of nature. Metaphysic is, then, deeper; its laws serve to explain the manifest variety of nature. Thus Bacon says that physic studies "variable causes." He gives the following example: "Fire is the cause of induration [hardening], but respective to clay. Fire is the cause of colliquation, but respective to wax." Physic deals with certain correlations that are manifest at the phenomenal level (but which may, nonetheless, require careful observation). Fire causes certain effects in clay and certain other effects in wax. These are important regularities, but they are not fundamental laws of nature.

Metaphysic is devoted to the study of final causes (ends) and to the study or discovery of formal causes (forms). The inclusion of final causes in metaphysic is rather strange. While Bacon is famed for his view that the search for final causes is responsible for much stagnation and mischief in the study of nature, he concedes that there are final causes and he indicates that it is proper to regard natural phenomena as the intentional product of a superior will. (In any case, the role of final causes would appear to be entirely discontinuous with the method of the study of nature that Bacon proposes.)

The notion of formal causes or forms is a fundamental and difficult issue in the interpretation of Bacon. It is clear that the discovery of forms is the chief aim of science. While Bacon is no uncritical atomist, he does regard the furniture of the universe as composed of particles arranged in various ways. And it seems likely that by the form of something is meant the structure or organization of these particles. Thus the form of gold or the form of heat is some manner of organization of minute particles.

A number of issues are significant. First, forms will be unobservable. They are the "hidden" and real nature of the furniture of the universe. Second, formal causes are not to be regarded as efficient causes—events determining other events. And the laws—which Bacon sometimes inaptly identifies with the forms—are not to be, except in a most indirect fashion, understood as correlating antecedent events and effects. Like much of what is most

compelling about contemporary science, Bacon's forms, his "fundamental laws," show us what it is for a certain property, for examples, heat and whiteness, to be instantiated in a given particular. This is what Bacon is pointing to when he writes: the "Form of a nature is such that given the form the nature infallibly follows." Whatever the form of gold is, gold is present if and only if something with that form is present. The study of forms is the study of what it is that is responsible for instantiation, for the fact that something has a given property.

In virtue of his acceptance of the distinction between the mind and the body, Bacon distinguishes the sciences of the body from the sciences of the intellectual realm. However puzzling much of Bacon's discussion here is, he is clear about the fact the study of humanity will make use of the same methodology as the study of nature. In this way, Bacon is what later generations would call a "methodological monist."

Criticism of the Sciences

Why is it that Bacon regards so darkly the state of learning of his times? He heaps much ridicule upon the Scholastics (he is a withering—if not very insightful or original—critic of Aristotle), the Renaissance humanists, and the alchemists.

Bacon's chief complaints are economically put in the following: "The axioms now in use having been suggested by scanty and manipular experience and a few particulars of most general occurrence are made for the most part just large enough to fit and take these in and therefore it is no wonder if they do not lead to new particulars. And if some opposite instance not observed or not known before chance to come in the way, the axiom is rescued and preserved by some frivolous distinction, whereas the truer course would be to correct the axiom itself."

Bacon's criticisms here are more subtle than is often noted. He is, of course, pointing to the precipitousness of much ancient and contemporary theorizing. From few data it launches itself into the construction of general principles. The principles then being regarded as true, deductively valid explanations were constructed and then protected against recalcitrant data in an *ad hoc* way. This "method" Bacon calls for obvious reasons the "Anticipation of Nature."

It should be clear, however, that Bacon is also demonstrating that such theories are extremely limited and unfruitful in the sense that they apply to a narrow range of particulars and have no observational consequences outside their original preserve. Such theories will not allow us to make new discoveries or to make predictions in surprising places. But a theory that, for example, explains both the behavior of celestial bodies and the behavior of tides is a better theory than one limited to celestial bodies.

Furthermore, one is unlikely to get theories of such explanatory power and elegance by making uncritical use of the categories of common sense. Bacon notes that "the discoveries that have hitherto been made in the sciences are such as to lie close to vulgar notions"; they barely go beneath the surface. It is for this reason that Bacon is rightly critical of the careless way in which previous thinkers had divided the natural world into species, genera, etc. Rather we must aim to carve nature at her joints, he urged; we must aim to discover the causally and thus explanatorily relevant properties of nature.

The Idols

How can it be that the sciences have reached such a point? Bacon must obviously have thought that the human cognitive apparatus is up to the task of discovering the truth about the natural world. Yet we can well wonder about the source of his optimism given his unflattering picture of past investigation. Bacon's view about human cognitive abilities can be likened to Seneca's in the moral sphere: "At our birth nature made us teachable and gave us reason, not perfect but capable of being perfected." Still, the human mind can be corrupted. And according to Bacon, unless one takes great care, it typically will become corrupted.

Bacon's Idols—introduced in book 1 of the *Novum Organum*—are certain typical ways in which the human mind is prey to systematic and pernicious intellectual failures. Bacon speaks of four classes of Idols.

The "Idols of the Tribe" are so called because they have "their foundation in human nature itself." Among these are the tendency to be struck by and to give priority to data that are salient or easily recalled; the tendency to cleave to what we already believe even in the teeth of the evidence; the tendency to pay great attention to evidence that confirms our view, but to ignore and fail to notice data that disconfirm our opinions. Most important among the Idols of the Tribe are the limitations and failures of the senses.

The "Idols of the Cave" are deficiencies that arise due to an individual's habits, education, and other developmental accidents. Some of us may be very good at logic and some very poor; some good at distinguishing between things that are apparently similar, some very poor.

The "Idols of the Market-Place" are deficiencies that have their basis in language. First, since we can give names to what does not exist (for example, Aristotle's *primum mobile*), words can lead us radically astray. Second, a single word (for example, "humid") can be applied to a variety of different properties in different substances. This kind of abstraction can seduce us into making claims that have no basis in nature.

Last are the "Idols of the Theatre," which are patterns of thought that are the result of allegiance to false schools of thinking. For example, an Aristotelean might be unable to give due consideration to Bacon's own notion of "form."

The doctrine of the Idols anticipates much that is to be found in contemporary theory of methodology and social psychology. What Bacon is urging here is that we have good reason to be suspicious of our own beliefs, given what we know about the way our minds are apt to go astray. In this way the doctrine is part of a tradition that includes Descartes's *Regulae* and Spinoza's project for improving the understanding. In any case, it is clear that Bacon thinks that a theory of knowledge will be of use to us in the matter of giving practical epistemic advice only if it pays close attention to human psychology.

The New Method

Bacon termed his own method the "Interpretation of Nature." In brief, it is a methodical, indeed, meant to be mechanical, process whereby axioms are arrived at slowly and deliberately rather than by "flying from particulars to the most general axioms." Induction, of course, is a way of moving to general conclusions, of the Form all *A*s are *F*, from a finite number of particular observations: This *A* is *F*, that *A* is *F*, and so forth. Bacon condemns induction by simple enumeration largely because it seeks only to confirm hypotheses and because, at least as practiced, it is haphazard.

Bacon's own method begins with the gathering of a "complete and accurate natural and experimental history." This is to provide data for the method. It is here, in particular, that Bacon's often mentioned failure to pay sufficient attention to the role of hypothesis in science becomes apparent. For how, we must ask, are we to know where to look for the relevant data without being guided and directed by some tentative hypothesis?

Once one has the relevant data, one is able to make use of the method of induction Bacon recommends. In some of the most famous pages of the *Novum Organum*, Bacon illustrates his method by means of an example concerning heat.

The goal of the method, as we have already suggested, is to discover the form of heat. Toward this end, one arranges the natural history of heat into Tables of Presence, Absence, and Comparison. (I will ignore the last for brevity's sake.) Thus:

TABLE OF PRESENCE

Rays of the Sun
All Flame
Ignited Solids
Boiling Liquids

TABLE OF ABSENCE

Rays of the Moon and Other Celestial Bodies
Ignus Fatuus, Static Electricity, Sparks
Unignited Solids
Liquids in their Natural State

Bacon provides many such examples. Since the object is to find the form of heat that is the nature under investigation, one wants cases in the Table of Presence in which heat is present but that concern many different kinds of substances. In this way one will not be seduced by merely salient copresent natures. The form of heat must have something to do with what is common to all cases in the Table of Presence. In turning to the Table of Absence, one searches for cases that share many of their natures with the cases in the Table of Presence but in which the nature under investigation is absent. Thus, all of the natures present in both tables can be ignored as the form of the nature under investigation. It is perhaps surprising that given the resources of his method Bacon, after surveying the tables of heat, suggests that its form is "a motion expansive, restrained and acting in its strife upon the smaller parts of bodies." This seems to anticipate the modern view that heat is molecular motion. This conclusion, Bacon emphasizes, is only the first step, a "first vintage." But it must also be emphasized that Bacon is not clear about how investigation is then to proceed.

Two features of the method should be emphasized. In a comparison of the tables, Bacon notes that experiments will be suggested. One will need to ascertain whether or not, in unclear cases, the nature under investigation really is present or absent. To determine this, experimental and controlled environments will be necessary. Second, the method is rightly regarded as anticipating the view that in the sciences one must seek not to confirm a theory by looking for positive evidence; rather one must seek data that would disconfirm one's view. Bacon recognized the importance of the negative instance in scientific methodology. While it is true that Bacon's method can be criticized on many fronts, it should not be forgotten that he properly emphasized the role of experiment and the centrality of seeking disconfirming evidence.

It is not apparent how it is that from the tables one is to arrive at the form of a given nature, since that is something unobservable. Conjecture and hypothesis must be at work if the method is to get off the ground. Bacon was aware of the difficulties here but even so he seemed to think that the method, rightly used, will single out some one form.

Bacon is typically regarded as failing to understand the importance of mathematics in the sciences. He does know that careful quantification will be necessary in making observations, but it must be admitted that, for Bacon, mathematics remains an "appendix" of science.

We have already mentioned the most familiar criticism of Bacon: That he does not comprehend the role that conjecture or hypothesis must play in science. Indeed, the term "Baconian" is, in some circles, a term of derision, pointing to a methodology that would seek the simple facts and then, somehow, purified of all hypothesis, reach the single, correct explanation of the phenomena. This is a naive picture, both of scientific methodology and of Bacon. He is, of course, at pains to criticize an *ad hoc* unresponsiveness to the data of scientific practice. As a result, it is not surprising that he might fail to appreciate the role that hypothesis must play in science. Indeed, his discussion of his own method makes it apparent that conjecture will play a role. Even so, it must be owned that Bacon, largely because of his antipathy to the scientific practice of his times, undervalued the legitimate role of hypothesis in science.

Still, if Bacon is rightly criticized for certain failures, he remains a figure of enduring importance in the history of scientific methodology. The wonder is not that he failed to anticipate all that is currently regarded as sound scientific practice. Rather, the wonder is that he anticipated so much.

DION SCOTT-KAKURES

Further Reading

Hesse, Mary. "Francis Bacon." In *A Critical History of Western Philosophy*, J. O'Connor, ed. London: Collier, 1964. A short and philosophically sophisticated essay that, in many ways, has set the agenda for the contemporary discussion of Bacon.

Quinton, Anthony. *Francis Bacon*. New York: Hill and Wang, 1980. A very useful and historically informed discussion of the significance of Bacon's philosophical works.

Urbach, Peter. *Francis Bacon's Philosophy of Science: An Account and Reappraisal*. La Salle, Ill.: Open Court Press, 1987. A provocative work that seeks to defend Bacon against standard criticisms.

GALILEO GALILEI

Born: 1564, Pisa, Italy
Died: 1642, Florence, Italy
Major Works: *The Sidereal Messenger* (1610), *The Assayer* (1623), *Dialogue on the Two Great World Systems* (1632), *Discourses on Two New Sciences* (1638)

Major Ideas

Observation bears out the truth of the Copernican theory that the earth is not the center of the universe.
Aristotle's claim that heavier bodies fall faster than lighter ones can be disproved by observation.
Controlled experimentation and the use of quantitative methods of reporting observations yield better results than do casual observations and extended discussion of qualities and tendencies.
Authoritarian pronouncements about real phenomena must be tested against the evidence given us in nature.
The universe is written in the language of mathematics.

Galileo Galilei is best known as the central figure in the great scientific revolution that transformed European thought in the seventeenth century. That revolution began hesitantly with the publication of a sun-centered cosmology in 1543 by Nicolaus Copernicus, whose methods of argument were still distinctly medieval. It was completed with the work of Isaac Newton, who was first to achieve a full and clear formulation of the basic laws of motion and gravitation that became the foundation for the modern science of physics.

Galileo's birth into the household of the well-known musician Vincenzo Galilei, following some years after the death of Copernicus, gave him the advantage of the mature flowering of the Renaissance. His death, within a few months of Newton's birth, was in a world beginning to feel the influence of Descartes and soon to see significant support for science as a deliberate enterprise through the formation of groups such as the Royal Society of London and the French Académie des Sciences. Where Copernicus had made a first tentative tug at the helm of natural philosophy, Galileo spun the wheel clear around to take the ship of thought out of the straits of authoritarianism and steer it toward the open seas of free scientific inquiry.

Galileo received a broad education, including some study of medicine at the University of Pisa. But his natural interests led him toward physics, and he left in 1585 without a degree. His talent and accomplishments became well enough known that he obtained a position teaching mathematics at the University of Pisa in 1589. But after conflicts with Aristotelian philosophers there, he moved to the chair of mathematics at the University of Padua in 1592, where he taught until 1610. He provides one of the first models for the modern consultant, having advised the city of Venice, among others, on such things as optics, ballistics, and fortifications.

Galileo might have simply lived another twenty years as a successful academic whose thoughtful experiments helped lay the foundations for the birth of physics had it not been for the advent of the telescope. Though Galileo did not invent this instrument, as soon as he saw one, he understood its working principles and quickly produced the first of a series of telescopes of increasingly better quality.

When he turned his telescope toward the skies in the summer of 1609, he made a stunning series of discoveries that transformed both his own life and the history of ideas in European civilization. He became a celebrity, both for good and for ill, and fell into a conflict with the Roman Catholic church that remains a touchstone for every discussion of the proper relation between science and religious belief.

Galileo's telescopes were good enough that within a matter of months he discovered spots on the sun, mountains on the moon, phases of Venus like those of our moon, four satellites orbiting Jupiter, "ears" on Saturn (later recognized as rings), and the starry makeup of the Milky Way. The image quality was still poor by modern standards, how-

ever, and many who looked through the first telescopes could not easily confirm Galileo's reports. In
March of 1610, he published a small book, *The
Sidereal Messenger*, describing some of these discoveries. He was shortly rewarded with an appointment as philosopher and mathematician to the
Grand Duke of Tuscany, which enabled him to resign his duties in Padua and pursue his studies in
whatever way he chose.

Galileo had already been sympathetic to the Copernican way of thought, but the new discoveries
armed him with the first really compelling arguments in its favor. The paths of Jupiter's moons
made it clear that objects other than the earth could
be centers of motion, and the phases of Venus
proved that it is sometimes beyond the sun, thus
eliminating Ptolemy's earth-centered cosmology.
Discussion of this new information caused quite a
stir, with Galileo being at its center not only in his
role as discoverer but also because he was very
articulate. He took advantage of his celebrity to
present both arguments and demonstrations in favor
of his anti-Aristotelian views on falling bodies as
well. He seems to have relished the attention, but
his self-assurance bordered sometimes on arrogance, and he was not always gracious to his opponents. Of these he had a number, in several cases
owing to other, extraneous disputes.

The opposition of the Catholic church was to
some extent social or political as much as it was
religious, since threats to its authority represented
in church thinking an undermining of the entire
social order. Neither was this opposition by any
means monolithic. Leading Jesuit astronomers were
among Galileo's friends in the early years, as was
Maffeo Cardinal Barberini, who was to become
Pope Urban VIII in 1623. Nevertheless there were
denunciations to the Inquisition that led to Galileo's
being instructed early in 1616 not to advocate the
Copernican theory, though it remains difficult to
determine precisely how strong a prohibition was
imposed.

For some time Galileo turned to other things. He
took what we see as the wrong side in an argument
about several comets that were seen in 1618. A later
stage in that dispute led to *The Assayer*, which

appeared in 1623. It is seen by some as a masterpiece of polemical philosophy, including detailed
exposition of the underlying principles of experimental science and the empiricist position. But for
its physical thought it seems today a minor and
relatively uninteresting little book—unless Pietro
Redondi could be right in his recent (but generally
disputed) proposal that Galileo's discussion of atomism here was in some people's eyes even more
heretical than his Copernicanism.

In 1624, Galileo visited Rome and received what
he took to be encouragement to undertake the project that, after several interruptions, finally appeared
in 1632 as the *Dialogue*. In four "days" of Socratic
conversations among its characters, Simplicio presents the traditional Aristotelian views while Salviati speaks for Galileo in advocating new thinking.
Sagredo acts as a supposedly impartial listener, who
of course is finally more impressed by Salviati's
arguments. In its writing, the *Dialogue* was very
effective; the wit, the style, and the use of vernacular Italian rather than Latin all helped it reach a wide
audience. The quality of its physics is mixed. On
the one hand, Galileo is very telling in his use of
falling bodies to emphasize that proper understanding of inertia does away with the whole family of
anti-Copernican objections that suppose a moving
earth would leave loose objects behind. But on the
other hand, he presents arguments about the movement of sunspots and about the origin of tides that
are quite specious. So the real importance of this
work lies not so much in any of its details as in its
overall thrust of forcing the reader to seriously contemplate the Copernican possibility and to do so in
physical rather than purely philosophical or authoritarian terms.

The book was hardly off the press before it was
denounced, and within a few months the Holy Office ordered its sales stopped. Galileo was summoned to Rome for trial on charges of transgressing
orders not to teach or defend the motion of the
earth, and of falsely attributing the tides to the
earth's movement. At first he attempted the defense
that he had not really advocated the Copernican
view at all, presenting it only as a hypothesis and a
rather weak one at that; but no actual reader of the

book would have gotten such an impression. In the end he was forced in 1633 to "abjure, curse, and detest the above-mentioned errors and heresies." He had always considered himself a loyal Catholic, and as Langford says, it was Galileo the scientist who wrote, but Galileo the believer who recanted.

In the tragedy of that trial, we can see one positive outcome: When Galileo returned to live out his life near Florence under house arrest, he resumed work on some less controversial problems in physics. His work in this area was largely done between about 1590 and 1610, and he had been planning to publish it when interrupted by the astronomical discoveries. Subsequent disputes as well as intermittent illness had kept him distracted. Now he finally took up these ideas again and integrated them into the *Discourses on Two New Sciences*, published at Leyden in 1638 away from the control of Catholic censors. Free from the emotional debate on Copernicanism, this is the work that best shows us Galileo as a worthy builder of the foundations of physics.

Two New Sciences is also in dialogue form, utilizing the same three characters. But it is less consistent in style, less polished and accessible. This is partly due to the more technical subject matter, but also stems from its being completed as time was running out and Galileo's health was very poor. The subjects dealt with include the strength of materials, impacts, friction, floating bodies, motion through resisting media and through vacuum, string vibrations, and parabolic trajectories.

In the first day of *Two New Sciences* is a clever argument against Aristotle's claim that heavier bodies fall faster. We are asked to envision two small bodies falling slowly side by side; if joined together by even a tenuous connection they now constitute a larger body—but do we really believe that now they will fall twice as fast? The second day of the *Dialogue* similarly has ingenious arguments about motion on an inclined plane to clarify what should happen in vertical fall and in unimpeded horizontal motion. Both of these examples illustrate Galileo's great talent for using "thought experiments" to mediate between vague theoretical expectations and the difficulties of real-life experiments,

such as frictional forces and lack of precise timekeeping instruments. Galileo ranks with Einstein as one of the most creative users of this method of developing convincing physical theories.

Galileo deserves credit for advocating extended and well-controlled experiments, in preference to mere collection of assorted casual observations. He also emphasized the importance of quantitative methods over discussions of qualities and tendencies. As Ira Cohen has suggested, while Galileo was hardly the first scientist to do experiments, he was one of the first who made both experiments and mathematical analysis integral parts of his science. This does not mean, however, that he fully anticipated Newtonian physics. In spite of his extensive contributions, as Drake points out, Galileo did not have in mind the grand program we know as "the mechanical philosophy"; that is due more to Descartes. But he did pioneer something we are accustomed to expect in science today, placing a high value on unforeseen discoveries and novel explanations—a goal for which the universities of Galileo's time did not ordinarily strive.

An important part of Galileo's story is his personal style. In comparison with his slightly younger contemporary Kepler, Galileo impresses us less as a mystic and more as the first example of a modern scientific personality. He was no less concerned to achieve scientific results than to convey them effectively, taking great pains to rework his ideas into more and more convincing arguments. He was a skilled debater, not above exploiting opportunities to make his opponents look ridiculous. Unfortunately, as de Santillana has pointed out, Galileo's celebrity in his own time had all too little to do with real understanding: "His was the tragedy of an excess of gifts; . . . his contemporaries could easily recognize a master; but what remained with them of his 'incomparable demonstrations' was as dim as the memory of a symphony to the untrained ear."

Galileo's contributions to science have an important philosophical component. Most obvious is his insistence that authoritarian pronouncements about real phenomena must be tested against the evidence given to us in nature. This was not mere rebellion; he saw it as ultimately aiding true spirituality. When on trial, he said, "It would be to the greatest detriment of souls to be forbidden to believe that which is later made plain before their eyes." Salviati speaks powerfully for him in the first day of the *Dialogue*: "If what we are discussing were a point of law or of the humanities, in which neither true nor false exists, one might trust in subtlety of mind and readiness of tongue and in the greater experience of the writers, and expect him who excelled in those things to make his reasoning most plausible, and one might judge it to be the best. But in the natural sciences, whose conclusions are true and necessary and have nothing to do with human will, one must take care not to place oneself in the defense of error; for here a thousand Demostheneses and a thousand Aristotles would be left in the lurch by every mediocre wit who happened to hit upon the truth for himself."

Galileo also insisted that natural philosophy could not disdain mathematics. One of his best-known statements comes from *The Assayer*: "Philosophy is written in this grand book, the universe, which stands continually open to our gaze. But the book cannot be understood unless one first learns to comprehend the language and read the letters in which it is composed. It is written in the language of mathematics, and its characters are triangles, circles, and other geometric figures without which it is humanly impossible to understand a single word of it." In the words of Langford, this is the divorce of science from philosophy—true science, demonstrative knowledge, must be mathematical; mere concepts of potency and final cause are practically useless.

DONALD E. HALL

Further Reading

Drake, Stillman. *Galileo at Work: His Scientific Biography*. Chicago: University of Chicago Press, 1978. A wealth of detail on how Galileo did his physics, based on preserved papers and correspondence.

Finocchiaro, Maurice A. *The Galileo Affair: A Documentary History*. Berkeley: University of California Press, 1989. New English translations of some correspondence, minutes of the Inquisition, and other important documents. The 43-page introduction provides an excellent summary of Galileo's controversy with the Church; also valuable are a chronology of events, a biographical glossary of all the important characters involved, and a selected bibliography from the extensive literature on Galileo.

Gingerich, Owen. "The Galileo Affair." *Scientific American* (August, 1982): 132–43. Views of a modern astronomer.

Langford, Jerome J. *Galileo, Science and the Church*. Ann Arbor: University of Michigan Press, 1971. A more balanced evaluation than in biographies from the 1950s by Koestler (anti-Galileo) and de Santillana (pro-Galileo).

Redondi, Pietro. *Galileo Heretic*. Translated by Raymond Rosenthal. Princeton: Princeton University Press, 1987. A masterful portrayal of the "theater of shadows" that was the world of arcane theological dispute in 1620s Rome, even if its central conspiratorial theory is doubtful.

Santillana, Giorgio de. *The Crime of Galileo*. Chicago: University of Chicago Press, 1955. A sympathetic portrayal involving the theory that a key document used against Galileo in his trial was forged.

Shapere, Dudley. *Galileo: A Philosophical Study*. Chicago: University of Chicago Press, 1974.

Wallace, William A., ed. *Reinterpreting Galileo*. *Studies in Philosophy and the History of Philosophy*, vol. 15. Washington, DC: Catholic University of America Press, 1986.

JOHANNES KEPLER

Born: 1571, Weil-der-Stadt, Germany
Died: 1630, Regensburg, Germany
Major Works: *Mysterium Cosmographicum* (1596), *Astronomia Nova* (1609), *Harmonice Mundi* (1618), *Epitome Astronomiae Copernicanae* (1617–21), *Tabulae Rudolphinae* (1627)

Major Ideas

God did not create the universe haphazardly: A rational architecture underlies the structure of the solar system.

Three laws govern the motion of the planets:

1. The planets move in elliptical, not circular, orbits.

2. The velocities of the planets are not uniform but vary at different points in their orbits; the areas swept by the radius vectors in equal times are equal.

3. The velocities of the planets relative to each other can be expressed mathematically: The squares of the periods of revolution are proportional to the cubes of the distances from the sun.

A force emanating from the sun governs the motion of the celestial bodies.

Weight arises from the mutual attraction between two bodies.

Aristotelian physics, which postulates four terrestrial elements (earth, air, fire, water) with weight and one celestial element (the ether) without, is false; celestial matter is not fundamentally different from terrestrial matter, and the physics of celestial motion is no different from that of terrestrial motion.

The work of Johannes Kepler marks a fundamental advance over the Aristotelian physics and Ptolemaic astronomy inherited from antiquity. His immediate predecessor Copernicus, who wrote the first systematic exposition of heliocentric astronomy (*De Revolutionibus*, 1543), had maintained the earlier postulates: Celestial bodies move with uniform circular motions; the visible motions can be modeled by supplying a sufficient number of deferents and epicycles; no motive force is needed, because the planets move of their own nature. Kepler's deep-seated belief that the sun emits a force that pervades the cosmos and drives all the celestial bodies on their courses, a belief which meshed well with his Christian faith, led him to investigate the *causes* of celestial motions and to postulate the existence of a force, now called gravity, which links the cosmos into one organism. His willingness to treat the planets as objects having the same nature as terrestrial bodies enabled him to discard the necessity for circular motions and to adopt elliptical orbits. His mathematical curiosity drove him to make correlations between what had been considered unrelated phenomena and from these phenomena to deduce laws.

Johannes Kepler was born to a respectable family of Weil-der-Stadt, in Württemberg, southern Germany. His grandfather was the mayor of Weil, his father a professional soldier who campaigned in the low countries. After preparatory schooling, Kepler entered the university at Tübingen in 1588. There he was influenced by the astronomy professor Michael Maestlin, a thoroughgoing Copernican. In 1594, Kepler, although he had almost completed his graduate program in theology, was assigned to teach mathematics at the Lutheran school in Graz, Austria. This fortuitous appointment, made over Kepler's protests, must count as one of the turning points in scientific history. He had hardly any pupils, and his additional duties, which included preparing almanacs and astrological forecasts for the Province of Styria, left him the leisure to meditate on the structure of the universe. The results of these meditations appeared in his first book, the *Mysterium Cosmographicum*.

This text is characteristic of all Kepler's works.

Its style, a combination of wild fancy and detailed, sober mathematical investigation, strikes the modern reader as bizarre, and its goal, an attempt to explain the principles by which God created the universe in its existing configuration, recalls traditional philosophical teleology.

In the prefatory chapter of the *Mysterium Cosmographicum*, Kepler outlines the Copernican hypothesis and defends it, not on the basis that it simplifies computation—its usual defense—but on the basis that it describes reality and explains phenomena that hitherto had simply been accepted as "natural": Planets at apogee (farthest from the earth) are at the same time in conjunction with the sun because they are on the other side of the sun from the earth; at perigee (closest to the earth) they are in opposition to the sun because the earth is between them and the sun; Mercury and Venus never appear in opposition to the sun because their orbits are between the earth and the sun; and a number of other points.

It must be remembered that in the fifty years after Copernicus's *De Revolutionibus* appeared, his system had not been widely accepted, largely because it represented celestial motions no better than did Ptolemy's system and was based not on recent data but on Ptolemy's observations of 1400 years earlier. Like most of his contemporaries, Copernicus had treated his heliocentric model as a computational convenience, not as an accurate description of reality. Kepler was not satisfied with this: He wanted to discover the structure of reality.

He recounts in detail how this discovery was made "by a gift of divine Providence." Since God did not create haphazardly, perhaps the mathematician could divine the architecture behind the creation. Therefore Kepler tried to correlate planetary orbits with numbers, ratios, and plane figures, but nothing worked. He then tried to nest the five regular solids between the planetary orbits: Between the earth and Mars he circumscribed a dodecahedron (twelve sides); between Mars and Jupiter he placed a tetrahedron; between Jupiter and Saturn he placed a cube. Then the inner planets: Between earth and Venus was an icosahedron (twenty sides), and

between Venus and Mercury an octahedron. The editions of the *Mysterium Cosmographicum* have beautiful engravings of these nested solids. Kepler then calculated the relative distances of the planetary orbits assuming the intervening solids, and the correspondence with the truth was astonishing: After a little adjustment, everything fit within 5 percent. Thus he seemed to have discovered the geometrical structure that governed the solar system.

The final sections of the *Mysterium Cosmographicum* explain the orbital motion of the planets. These bodies do not move with the same velocities: For example, Saturn traverses its orbit at a slower rate than Jupiter traverses its orbit. Why is this? Kepler accepted Aristotle's theory of motion (an object moves only so long as there is a force acting on the object), and he speculated that the sun emits the necessary motive force, and that this force naturally weakens with distance. The sun is the Father, the motive force is the Holy Ghost, as he metaphorically expressed it. He tried to calculate the ratio between the planet's velocity and its distance from the sun, but failed. In his later *Harmonice Mundi*, he succeeded when he formulated his third law.

The concepts outlined in the *Mysterium Cosmographicum* remained at the heart of Kepler's work: the rationality of the created universe, the mathematical relationships between planetary orbits, the ratio between orbital period and distance from the sun, the force emanating from the sun. This work was still dear to him when he published a second edition with notes twenty-five years later (1621).

Most important for later astrophysics was the importance attributed to the sun. In Copernican astronomy, the sun acted simply as an illuminator; all motion was referred to the center of the earth's orbit, near which the sun happens to be located. It was Kepler who made the sun the dynamically active center of the cosmos.

The *Mysterium Cosmographicum* established Kepler as a leading theoretician. Most important for later astronomy, Tycho Brahe received a copy and responded in a letter that was as gracious as the acerbic Danish astronomer could manage. For twenty years at his observatory on Hveen, an island near Copenhagen, Brahe had been regularly observing and recording planetary positions and had a mass of data of unparalleled accuracy at his disposal. Leaving Hveen in 1597, Brahe had moved to Prague as the "Imperial Mathematician" of Rudolph II. Meanwhile, in 1599, Kepler was forced to leave Graz because of anti-Lutheran agitation. After learning of Brahe's move, he set out for Prague to visit with the Dane. Brahe welcomed the younger astronomer and invited him to join his staff. Brahe was in the process of drawing up a new and more accurate set of astronomical tables, and Kepler was assigned the task of working out the theory of the motion of Mars. Despite the personality conflicts between the two astronomers, Kepler later considered this assignment as an act of Providence, for through his studies of this difficult planet he came to the theories described in his most important work, the *Astronomia Nova*.

In this work, Kepler describes his struggles to correlate Brahe's observations of Mars's orbit with various motions, first circular, then oval, finally elliptical. Continuing the speculations of the *Mysterium Cosmographicum*, Kepler rethought his views on the mechanism by which the sun governed the planets. He knew that the planets' velocities varied inversely with their distances from the sun, and under the influence of William Gilbert's *De Magnete* (1600), he decided that a rotating sun drove the planets by means of magnetic vortices whose energy would be less for the more distant planets. (He makes the analogy with light, whose illuminating power decreases with distance.) First assuming that the orbits are eccentric *circles* (as did Ptolemy), he formulated his *second law* (chronologically the first): The radius vector of the orbit sweeps out equal areas in equal times. This law in its original form, applied to *circular* orbits, did not work for Mars, but left an 8′ discrepancy: Mars was 8′ closer to the earth at the orbital points 90° from aphelion (point farthest from the sun) and from perihelion (point closest to the sun). Now,

such a small amount would have been ignored by earlier astronomers, but Kepler knew that Brahe's observations were accurate to 8′. The discrepancy had to be resolved.

Kepler finally concluded that the planetary orbits are elliptical, not circular and eccentric, and that the sun is at one focus of the ellipse. This is his *first law*. With the ellipse, he could reconcile Brahe's observations with theory and supply a satisfactory dynamic for the sun–planet interaction. In adopting elliptical orbits, Kepler finally broke with the Aristotelian physics that had governed all earlier cosmological speculation. Aristotle had stated that the sublunary world consisted of earth, air, fire, and water, while the celestial world consisted of the fifth element, ether, whose primary *inherent* characteristic is its eternal circular motion—hence no further explanation of celestial motion was necessary. Kepler rejected this theory and laid the groundwork for modern astrophysics: the investigation of celestial motion on mechanical principles. The completion of these investigations in modern astrophysics became possible only with Newton's calculus and Einstein's relativity theory.

While finishing the *Astronomia Nova*, Kepler began investigating optics, as had Ptolemy before him. His results were published as *Astronomiae Pars Optica* (1604). Its chapters discuss parallax and refraction, and show for the first time that vision proceeds by images formed on the retina of the eye. In this work no mention is made of lenses or telescopes. Not until 1610 did Kepler even have access to a telescope; in that year he observed Jupiter, duplicating the observations of Galileo's *Sidereus Nuncius*.

The years from 1611 to the end of his life were restless and troubled. His wife and several children died of disease in the troubles of the Counter-Reformation; his aged mother in Württemberg was accused of witchcraft (several months of the period from 1617–21 were devoted to her defense); and his protector, Rudolph II, abdicated in the face of riots in Prague. As a result of this last misfortune, Kepler moved to Linz, Austria, where he resided for fourteen years. During this period he prepared three major works, *Harmonice Mundi*, *Epitome Astronomiae Copernicanae*, and the *Tabulae Rudolphinae*. Among the minor works of this period are the *Stereometria doliorum vinariorum* (*The Measurement of Wine Casks*), in which he developed a precursor of the calculus to measure the volume of irregular solids; the *Somnium*, the first science-fiction adventure, a trip to the moon; and a number of astrological almanacs, which he regularly produced to supplement his irregular income as imperial mathematician.

In the *Harmonice Mundi*, Kepler elaborated concepts first outlined in the *Mysterium Cosmographicum*. The basic principles of the cosmos are based on geometry: Specifically, the regular polygons are archetypal forms in the human soul as well as in the celestial world; when the planets in their orbits form angles corresponding to the angles of these polygons (for example, 90° square, 60° trine), they inspire and excite the soul. Kepler pursued this line of thought in his astrological writings. Musical harmony is also based on these angles: The ratios of the musical scale (octave, fifth, and so forth) can be derived from the polygons by suitable construction. Furthermore, the planets' orbital velocities create a harmony: (1) There is a simple ratio between the planet's velocity at aphelion and its velocity at perihelion; (2) the squares of the periods of revolution of any two planets (the time in which they complete one orbit) are proportional to the cubes of their mean distances from the sun. This latter is Kepler's *third, or harmonic, law*, and his joy at its discovery was unbounded. In the final chapters of *Harmonice Mundi* he assigns musical "notes" to the planets at aphelion and perihelion and demonstrates by the variations in the "tunes" thus played by each planet the eccentricity of the orbit of each: Venus, with an almost circular orbit, plays a monotonous tune; the very eccentric Mercury runs up and down the scale.

Much of *Harmonice Mundi* has been termed mystic fantasy, but this fantasy, as always, was founded on carefully observed fact and aimed at explicating the dynamics and structure of the solar system. Kepler's imaginative mind structured and explained data in terms strange to us, but this exuberant imagination did succeed in discovering his three laws of planetary motion.

In the *Epitome Astronomiae Copernicanae*, Kepler summarized his own—not Copernicus's—work on astronomy: The nested polygons of the *Mysterium*, the elliptical orbits, and the sun's propulsive force all appear. New in this book was his long theoretical justification of his third law. He establishes that a planet's velocity on its orbit depends on four factors: (1) the length of the orbit; (2) the density of the planet; (3) the volume of the planet; and (4) the emanation from the sun, by which the sun sends into space a magnetic whirlwind that both carries the planets along and makes them rotate. The greater (1) and (2) are, the slower the planet; the greater (3) and (4) are, the faster the planet. One consequence is that the large, slower planets farther from the sun (Jupiter, Saturn) must be less dense, while those closer to the sun, particularly Mercury, must be very dense. Not knowing of the existence of Neptune or Pluto, Kepler could defend this law with telescopic observations showing the great size of the known outer planets. For him this third law simply stated a fact about the six known planets. In this work Kepler also developed an accurate theory of lunar motion: He was the first to calculate for the moon an elliptical orbit that is modified by the influence of the earth *and* the sun.

The *Tabulae Rudolphinae* (*Rudolphine Astronomical Tables*), Kepler's last major work, appeared three years before his death. These tables, whose remote ancestors were Ptolemy's *Handy Tables*, enabled astronomers to determine the position of any celestial body at any date, past or future, with unparalleled accuracy, and they quickly superseded all other tables. Their accuracy served as proof of the truth of Kepler's astronomical theories. The use of the tables was explained in a preface, but the reader was referred to the *Epitome* for an explanation of their theoretical basis.

Kepler's work is an example of the deduction of general laws from a mass of observations—the essence of science. But it was primarily his attempt to apply physical principles to astronomical data that marks his break with ancient astronomy. His work was completed by Isaac Newton, who re-worked his ideas about the sun's emanations and his three laws into a theory of universal gravitation and thus made Kepler's speculations into principles of astrodynamics.

MARK T. RILEY

Further Reading

Caspar, Max. *Johannes Kepler*. Stuttgart, 1948. 2d ed., 1950, English translation by C. Doris Hellman. New York, Abelard-Schuman, 1959. The definitive biography. Much of this biography has been reworked in Koestler's *Sleepwalkers*.

Duncan, A. M. *Johannes Kepler: Mysterium Cosmographicum/The Secret of the Universe*. New York: Abaris Books, 1981. This facsimile of the second (1621) edition with a facing English translation is an excellent introduction to the guiding themes of Kepler's thought.

Koestler, Authur. *The Sleepwalkers*. New York: Macmillan, 1959. The best part of this history of man's changing view of the universe is the long section on Kepler, which has been published separately as *The Watershed* (Garden City, N.Y.: Anchor Books, 1960). The author describes Kepler's scientific achievement; he is most successful at analyzing Kepler's psychology.

Koyré, Alexander. *The Astronomical Revolution*. Ithaca, N.Y.: Cornell University Press, 1973. Originally published in French, this detailed description of Kepler's scientific thought includes extensive translations from Kepler's original text. It is practically an anthology of the major works.

Stevenson, Bruce. *Kepler's Physical Astronomy*. New York: Springer-Verlag, 1987. A review of physics and mathematics in the *Mysterium Cosmographicum*, *Astronomia Nova*, and the *Epitome*, the author shows the importance of Kepler's speculations in physics for the development of his astronomical laws.

THOMAS HOBBES

Born: 1588, Westport, Wilshire, England
Died: 1679, Hardwick Hall, Derbyshire, England
Major Works: *De Cive* (1642), *Leviathan* (1651), *De Corpore* (1655), *De Homine* (1658)

Major Ideas

Knowledge is derived from sense experience and from reason: From sense experience we derive historical knowledge and prudence, and from reason we derive scientific and philosophical knowledge and wisdom.

Scientific or philosophical reason is essentially the same as that which is employed in mathematics, moving from definitions, axioms, and postulates to theorems derived logically from them.

Thought, sensation, memory, and imagination are nothing but a motion of some substance inside our heads; they are generally caused by motions of things outside us; consequently, secondary qualities (such as colors) do not exist in things, but are purely mental events caused by minute motions that stimulate our minds to produce certain sensations.

Only matter exists; there is no such thing as a purely spiritual being: This includes God.

Religion arises out of fear, ignorance, and efforts by rulers to maintain their advantage over their subjects.

Good and evil are simply what people desire or dislike; right and wrong are what are permitted or forbidden by law.

Human actions arise out of a desire for self-preservation, and the laws of nature permit any action reasonably intended for that purpose.

Monarchy is the best form of government.

Thomas Hobbes grew up during a time of considerable turmoil in England. His mother said that he was born prematurely because she was terrified at news of the approach of the Spanish Armada and feared an invasion by murderous idolaters. His father, a vicar, was evidently a drunk and had a rather pugnacious disposition. After staying up too late one Saturday night, he fell asleep in the middle of his service the following morning. Upon awakening, he announced to the congregation that clubs were trumps. After becoming involved in a brawl in front of his church with another clergyman, he fled to London and disappeared, leaving his family to fend for themselves. Thomas's education was looked after by a rich uncle, who sent him to Oxford University when Thomas was fourteen years old. He later served as tutor to a wealthy young man, and enjoyed the benefits of a splendid library and foreign travel associated with that position. Hobbes was disenchanted with Aristotelianism even as a student, but became thoroughly convinced of the inadequacies of Aristotle's philosophy during his visits to the Continent. At the same time, he was introduced to the earth-shaking discoveries of the great scientific and philosophical minds of the time: Copernicus, Galileo, Descartes, Gassendi, Harvey, and Bacon.

Hobbes rejected the theories concerning the nature of things that most ancient and medieval philosophers held. Contrary to the traditional view, he held that common nouns do *not* represent things. They are merely *names* that enable people to generalize about individual things that happen to have certain resemblances to one another.

He held that logic is never a source of knowledge as such. Knowledge of the existence of things comes only through sense perception. Logic provides a method for arriving at the relations between things—particularly causal relationships.

Sensations, he believed, are merely the result of the motions of objects pressing upon our sense organs. There is nothing but matter and the motions of material things, both outside our bodies and within them. Thus, even though we may be inclined to think that the images of our imaginations and dreams are immaterial things, that is not the case.

Once an object (for example, a tolling bell or a fluttering moth) has set up a motion within us, creating the sensation of sound or sight, that motion may continue for a considerable time, like the waves of the ocean. With our eyes shut, we may continue to see an image of the thing we have stared at because of the motion it has initiated; and during our sleep, those same motions, more attenuated and "decayed," may give birth to new images. Memory is simply the resonance of an old, fading motion. There is a constant interaction between the brain and other parts of the body, so that certain trains of thought (motions within the brain) can either be initiated by stimuli to other parts of the body or lead to arousal of those parts.

Only Matter Exists

It was an essential part of Hobbes's system that there are no disembodied spirits or souls. Only matter exists. He held that the idea of an "incorporeal substance" is self-contradictory. Hence, God must be a "most pure, simple, invisible, spirit corporeal."

The properties of things are what determine the sorts of things they are. Most properties, however, are variable, and are simply the effects those things have upon our sense organs and brains. Thus, though we customarily say that an apple is red, the "redness" does not exist in the apple itself—it is merely the effect the apple has on the eyes of a normal person. The only qualities that inhere in things themselves are extension (occupancy of a certain amount of space in various directions) and figure (a certain shape). The implication of this is that an object's extension and figure are independent of anyone's perceptions of it but its other qualities are not.

Hobbes attributed man's religious inclinations to fear and ignorance, especially ignorance of the causes of things. When people do not understand what brings about good or evil fortune, they tend to make up imaginary causes or to trust the authority of others whom they believe are wise in such matters. When they lack understanding of the causes of things that frighten them, they assume that there

must be some invisible power that controls their destinies. Clever men, eager to use any device to control others, have exploited these propensities to superstition to persuade others to obedience, peace, and civility. "The first founders and legislators of commonwealths . . . have in all places taken care, first, to imprint in their minds a belief that those precepts which they gave concerning religion might not be thought to proceed from their own device but from the dictates of some god or other spirit, or else that they themselves were of a higher nature than mere mortals, that their laws might the more easily be received. . . . Secondly, they have had a care to make it believed that the same things were displeasing to the gods which were forbidden by the laws." And finally, they prescribed various ceremonies and festivals by which the gods' anger was supposed to be appeased, thus deflecting from themselves onto their insufficiently observant subjects the blame for defeat in war and for other calamities that might have afflicted their people. Thus the people were "less apt to mutiny against their governors" and being entertained by festivals and rituals in honor of the gods would be kept from "discontent, murmuring, and commotion against the state."

Hobbes believed that all human beings are equal—not in their bodily strength or in their mental capacity but in their vulnerability to being killed by others. The weakest, he said, have strength enough to kill the strongest, and the least intelligent enough practical wisdom to kill the most intelligent. Since all persons want more or less the same things, they are in constant competition. Sometimes this competition is for things that are essential for the preservation of their lives, but at other times it may simply be for what will give them pleasure. If one person has more than others, he may expect his neighbors to unite in order to deprive him, "not only of the fruit of his labor, but also of his life or liberty."

People are inclined to fight with one another to gain what they do not yet have or to protect what they do have against others who want to take it from them, and sometimes simply for glory, for "trifles, as a word, a smile, a different opinion, and any other sign of undervalue."

The War of All Against All

Thus, as long as there is no common power to maintain order, all people are in a state of war with one another—a war of all against all. This war exists even when no arms are being employed; it is a kind of cold war, in which everyone is in constant danger from everyone else and constantly apprehensive about that danger. This situation, which Hobbes calls the state of nature, is such that no one can trust anyone else, and everyone is in constant fear of violent death. Consequently, none of the benefits of civilization are possible in that state—no agriculture, no education, no exports or imports, no society, and, worst of all, "the life of man solitary, poor, nasty, brutish, and short."

Put in another way, the state of nature is one in which there is no government, no law, no sense of right and wrong. It is a state of anarchy, in which everyone has a right to anything, even to another's body. Where there is no law, there is no right or wrong, no justice or injustice. Everything is permitted because there is no force, except each individual's own ability, to stop anyone from doing anything he or she pleases.

Hobbes maintains that all persons have a natural liberty or right to do whatever is necessary, in their own judgment, to preserve themselves. Reason leads to certain laws of nature that forbid a person to do anything that may be self-destructive or to omit doing anything that may preserve oneself. From this, Hobbes writes, it follows that everyone ought to seek peace. Because life in the state of nature is so precarious, it is necessary to do whatever one can to get out of that state and into a safer one. To get out of the state of nature, which is a state of war, it is necessary to seek peace.

Law and the Social Contract

Since the state of nature is one in which there is no law, it follows that a state of peace must be one in which there is law. And since a state in which there is law is one in which people do *not* have a right to all things (for law imposes duties on people and places restrictions on them), in order to get out of the state of nature it is necessary for each person to

give up some of the rights he or she has and assume some obligations.

This is not to say that people should give up *all* of their rights, for Hobbes makes it clear that some rights are inalienable—that is, cannot be given to anyone else. The rights of life, liberty, and having "the means of so preserving life as not to be weary of it" are inalienable, for they are the very purpose for which other rights are given up.

Therefore, Hobbes says, people should enter into a social contract, a voluntary agreement in which each person gives up certain rights on the condition that others do so as well. No contract, however, has any meaning unless there is someone to enforce it. Consequently, the contracting parties must agree with one another to appoint or elect some person whose duty it will be to enforce the conditions of their agreement. Once this is done, that person is known as the sovereign, and the others are the subjects. It is important to remember that the contract is between the subjects and that the sovereign is not a party to it. The sovereign remains outside the contract, for his task is to *enforce* the agreement. If the sovereign were a party to the contract, it would be necessary to find *another* person to enforce the agreement between the "sovereign" and the subjects. Since this leads to an infinite regress, Hobbes avoids it by leaving the sovereign in the state of nature. Thus, the sovereign can commit no injustice, for injustice is a violation of the law and the sovereign is not subject to the law.

Sovereigns have a wide range of powers, according to Hobbes, and they cannot forfeit them since they cannot breach a covenant they have never entered into. Hobbes was firmly opposed to any separation of powers. He argued that the best government is one in which the sovereign enjoys the powers of the executive, the legislature, and the judiciary, for it is the most efficient and the most stable, so long as the sovereign remains physically and mentally fit. Hobbes believed that one of the most important of the sovereign's powers is the power of censorship, for actions proceed from opinions, and if peace is to reign, it is essential that subversive opinions be repressed.

Finally, Hobbes believed that the sovereign

should have the power to punish wrongdoers. More-over, Hobbes's conception of punishment was rather specific. He argued that penalties must be carefully designed to fulfill a specific purpose: "that the will of men may thereby the better be disposed to obedience." Thus, a penalty that is too light would be nothing more than a fee for the privilege of committing a wrong, while the imposition of one that is too heavy Hobbes characterized as an act of hostility. In any case, he believed that the aim of punishment is *not* revenge, but deterrence—a far cry from the theory advocated a century later by Immanuel Kant, who believed that the only morally acceptable justification for punishment is retribution.

It is appropriate to conclude by noting that Hobbes anticipated many of the major principles that went into the founding of the American repub-lic, including not only the doctrine of inalienable rights, but also such a specific right as the right not to be compelled to testify against oneself, incorporated into the Fifth Amendment to the Constitution. Nevertheless, Hobbes was no believer in democracy. On the contrary, he was a powerful and consistent advocate of a virtually unlimited monarchy. He did not place a high value on personal liberty. Efficiency, law and order, and above all the preservation of peace are the principal aims of good government. Hobbes did not believe that freedom of the press, freedom of speech, or even freedom of religion are necessary constituents of individual happiness. More important than all of these is the preservation of the state itself and the struggle to avoid slipping back into the state of nature, that dreadful situation in which everyone is at war with everyone else.

Burton M. Leiser

Further Reading

Brown, K. C. *Hobbes Studies*. Cambridge, Mass.: Harvard University Press, 1965. This volume contains some exceptionally fine discussions of various aspects of Hobbes's philosophy by some outstanding Hobbesian scholars, including Leo Strauss, A. E. Taylor, Stuart M. Brown, Jr., John Plamenatz, Howard Warrender, and others. Among the topics considered are Hobbes's analysis of "liberty," his views on God, his political theories, and his theory of punishment. In addition, there are extended discussions of the Taylor thesis, that Hobbes's ethical theory is logically independent of his egoistic psychological theory, and the Warrender thesis (see below).

Durant, Will and Ariel. *The Age of Louis XIV*, *The Story of Civilization*, vol. 8. New York: Simon and Schuster, 1963. Chapter 20 on English philosophy contains a brief but excellent summary of Hobbes's life and thought, written in the Durants' usual lucid style.

Flew, A. G. N. "Hobbes." D. J. O'Connor, *A Critical History of Western Philosophy*. New York: Free Press, 1964. This is in every way the best all-around short introduction to Hobbes that one is likely to find. It is well-organized, well-written, and quite thorough, containing a good summary of Hobbes's major works and of his principal theories on matter, metaphysics, language, liberty, and politics. Flew places each of these theories in its historical context, gives helpful accounts with generous quotations from Hobbes's contemporary critics, and adds an insightful critique of his own.

Peters, Richard. *Hobbes*. Baltimore: Penguin Books, 1956. An excellent introduction to Hobbes's life and thought. Peters is a distinguished philosopher himself. He writes clearly, intelligently, perceptively, and critically.

Warrender, Howard. *The Political Philosophy of Hobbes: His Theory of Obligation*. Oxford: Oxford University Press, 1957. An extremely influential and controversial book, thorough, fascinating, and well written. Warrender's thesis is that according to Hobbes, people are obliged to obey the laws of nature even in the state of nature, for they are God's commands, and that it is only because they are God's commands that people can bind themselves by a valid covenant to obey a human ruler.

PIERRE GASSENDI

Born: 1592, Champtercier, Provence, France
Died: 1655, Paris, France
Major Works: *Exercitationes paradoxicarum adversus Aristoteleos* (1624), *Disquisitio Metaphysica, seu dubitationes et instantiae adversus Renati Cartesii metaphysica et responsa* (1644), *De vita et moribus Epicuri* (1647), *Syntagma philosophicum* (1658)

Major Ideas

Aristotelianism is useless as a philosophy or basis for science.
Skepticism, in a mitigated form, allows for limited knowledge.
Epicurean atomism is the best hypothesis for explaining the natural world.
Epicureanism can be modified so that it is compatible with Christian beliefs.

Pierre Gassendi is best known for his revival of the atomic theory of Epicurus, advanced as a hypothetical system for modern science. He developed this view as a way of dealing with the results of applying skepticism to Scholastic philosophy. He avoided the consequences of complete skepticism by advancing a mitigated skepticism, what he called a *via media* between dogmatism and skepticism. Gassendi, a Catholic priest, also Christianized ancient Epicurean thought by rejecting its views about the nature of the soul and the role of Divine Providence. Instead he accepted the teachings of his church on faith. He was one of the most serious critics of Descartes's philosophy.

Gassendi studied at Digne and Aix in Provence. He was a prodigy and was appointed a professor at the age of twenty-one. In 1614, when he was twenty-two, he received a doctorate in theology at Avignon, and was ordained as a priest two years later. He became professor of philosophy at Aix in 1617, and remained there until 1623, when the university was taken over by the Jesuits. His course there developed into a massive critique of Aristotelian philosophy and a statement of his mitigated skepticism. He published the first part, criticizing the basic features of Aristotle's system, in 1624. The second part, developing his skepticism, was set aside because of the condemnation of anti-Aristotelianism in Paris in 1624, and was published posthumously in his complete works in 1658.

After leaving his university post, Gassendi became part of an avant-garde scientific group patronized by Peiresc in Provence. In 1625, Gassendi visited Paris, and there formed a lifetime friendship with Father Marin Mersenne, a central figure in the scientific revolution and in the development of modern ideas. Gassendi worked with various scientists and mathematicians, and produced important observations in astronomy tending to confirm the Copernican theory. He joined Mersenne in fighting off alchemists and astrologers. He also wrote a sharp critique of Herbert of Cherbury's *De Veritate*.

From his attack on Aristotelianism, and his development of a skepticism about metaphysical knowledge, he became interested in presenting a theory that could avoid skeptical criticism and provide a basis for modern scientific knowledge. He found such a theory in the writings of Epicurus. For the rest of his life, he was editing Epicurus's texts, establishing the most correct information about Epicurus, answering arguments leveled against Epicureanism, and developing a modified Epicureanism.

Gassendi was made provost of the Cathedral of Digne in 1634. In 1645, he was appointed to the chair of mathematics at the Royal College (now the College de France). In 1641 he was asked by Mersenne to write out his opinions of Descartes's new metaphysical system, which had just appeared in Descartes's *Meditations*. Gassendi attacked Descartes's theory from both a skeptical and a materialist point of view. His objections, the fifth set appended to the 1641 edition of the *Meditations*, outraged Descartes, who wrote a very nasty reply. Gassendi expanded his critique into a full-fledged work, the *Disquisitio Metaphysica* of 1644, which was perhaps the most complete answer to Descartes developed at the time.

After this, Gassendi began publishing a series of works on Epicureanism, starting with his thorough humanistic study *De Vita et moribus Epicuri* in eight books in 1647. In the best learned tradition of the time, Gassendi sifted out the facts from fictions about the historical Epicurus. In 1649 he published a most careful analysis of the tenth book of Diogenes Laertius's *Lives of the Philosophers*, the book on Epicurus and Epicureanism, from which most of the criticisms of Epicureanism had come. In the same year he published a systematic exposition of Epicurus's philosophy with an answer to those who claimed this philosophy was anti-Christian.

Gassendi's most complete presentation of his own ideas, and his interpretation and modernization of Epicureanism, appeared only after his death, in a work he had been composing for years, *Syntagma philosophicum*, which takes up the first two folio volumes of the complete works, published in 1658.

Exercitationes paradoxicarum adversus Aristoteleos

In the first part of this work, Gassendi followed in the tradition of the Renaissance humanists Francesco Patrizi and Pierre de la Ramée (Peter Ramus) in seeking to demonstrate the weak, dubious, and erroneous features of Aristotelianism. He criticized the jargon of the Scholastics and their arguments and inquiries. He attacked the Aristotelians for slavishly following their master instead of openly inquiring about the world. He showed the unclarity of some of Aristotle's definitions, the uselessness of his demonstrations, and the contradictions in his philosophy. It is a most detailed, almost stupifying critique.

The second book moves from textual analysis to a skeptical examination of the whole Aristotelian enterprise. Using the skepticism developed in the ancient Greek texts of Sextus Empiricus, together with the modern skeptical efforts of Montaigne,

Charron, and Sanches, Gassendi first sought to show the artificiality of Aristotelian logic and its worthlessness as a means of discovering truths. Proofs, according to Aristotle, begin with universal propositions, such as "All men are mortal." But we can tell if this is true only if we have examined every case, past, present, and future—all men who ever have or will or could exist. Since this cannot be accomplished, we can never arrive at a universal proposition from which to commence our proof. In fact, the conclusion of a syllogism, such as "Socrates is mortal," is not really a conclusion, but is part of the evidence for the universal premise. Hence, Aristotle's method of demonstrating truths turns out to be circular.

From this examination of Aristotle's method, Gassendi concluded that "knowledge such as Aristotle describes it cannot exist." He applied a range of skeptical objects to undermine the possibility of science, or knowledge, in Aristotle's sense. Our faculties can be doubted, our information can be doubted. Hence, as Francisco Sanches a generation earlier had said, *nihil scitur* (nothing is known).

Having developed a complete skepticism against Aristotelianism, Gassendi then introduced his "mitigated skepticism," namely, that we possess a kind of knowledge in spite of all of the difficulties. Although we cannot know the essences of things, what they really are, and why they are what they are, nonetheless we do know how they appear to us. Sciences can be developed on the basis of these limited data. We can find sufficient certainty and evidence in terms of appearances to deal with questions that concern us. Gassendi applied his "mitigated skepticism" even to mathematics, saying "whatever certainty and evidence there is in mathematics is related to appearances, and in no way related to genuine causes or the inner natures of things."

Gassendi began to see Epicurean atomism as the best way of understanding or relating experiences. Epicureanism was for him a hypothetical system rather than a metaphysical one. He felt that Epicurus's views had been misrepresented and misunderstood. Hence, before he could present his hypothetical Epicureanism, he had first to do a great deal of scholarly, humanistic research to establish the correct texts of Epicurus and to interpret them. He was also concerned to obviate the Christian religious objections to Epicurus's philosophy. Hence, in interpreting his view, he sought to show that, if restricted and modified, it could be compatible with orthodox Christianity.

Gassendi's life of Epicurus, his materialist critique of Descartes's views, and his edition of the Epicurean texts were preparations for the presentation of Gassendi's atomistic philosophy.

Syntagma philosophicum

Gassendi's final work, the *Syntagma philosophicum*, begins with a book on logic, evaluating the ways of finding truth. He discusses Aristotelian, Stoic, and Epicurean theories and shows how they were criticized by the skeptics. As long as one is trying to find out the real nature of things, one is bound to fail. But if one will accept a shadow of truth, rather than truth itself, one can gain positive results. Gassendi proposed a *via media* between skepticism and dogmatism that he found in the empirical side of Epicureanism. If one restricts inquiry to what can be known in the world of appearances, then it is possible to establish some standards for judging what is true and what is false, and on this basis one can develop a tentative science.

Gassendi applied his hypothetical view of a science of appearances to working out a theory of the empirical natural world that would encompass the results of such figures as Copernicus, Galileo, Gassendi himself, and other early modern scientists. Instead of offering a metaphysical theory, as Descartes or Hobbes did, Gassendi offered an atomic model as a way of connecting various phenomena. The atomic world was described in terms of visible properties. And relations among atoms were offered as ways of explanation of natural phenomena. Gassendi thought it was possible to describe all that is known about nature in this manner. One can predict future observations on the basis of this hypothetical atomism. As long as one does not turn the hypothetical atoms into metaphysical atoms, one does

not become enmeshed in dogmatic and unverifiable theorizing.

Gassendi's tentative atomism rivaled Cartesianism and Scholasticism as the best way of understanding man's knowledge of nature during the seventeenth century. Some of the Jesuits, who forced the condemnation of Cartesianism in the latter part of the seventeenth century, proposed Gassendi's atomism as the best science to be taught and studied. For better or worse, Gassendi's view was replaced by Newton's physics, in part because there did not seem to be any way of really applying Gassendi's model to nature, since one did not know what atomic configurations best accounted for what observations. It was only with the development of modern chemistry in the nineteenth century that scientific atomism began to develop as a serious way of explaining phenomena.

In ancient times, Epicureanism atomism had been condemned as irreligious. When the views of Epicurus and Lucretius were revived during the Renaissance, similar complaints were made about ancient atomism. Gassendi took it upon himself to explicate what Epicurus in fact said, to answer misguided criticism, and to modify Epicureanism by reference to modern scientific knowledge and to traditional Christian doctrines. In areas where Epicureanism was clearly in opposition to Christian teaching, Gassendi abandoned such parts of the theory and said that he accepted whatever the Church taught. He did not accept Epicurus's view of the physical and mortal nature of the soul and of the non-Providential nature of the course of events. He was willing to some extent to utilize Epicurus's empirical theology, as a way of explaining how people come to their notions about God.

Although it might seem that Epicureanism, as a materialist view, would have to conflict with Christianity, Gassendi provided a reconciliation by dropping parts of Epicureanism. The Church never challenged his orthodoxy or censured his works, but some scholars since have assumed that he must have been a freethinker. His views were disseminated all over Europe. Some of his work was translated into English, and provided the basis for a Neo-Epicureanism that was accepted by many leading English-speaking thinkers. John Locke, among others, was influenced by his views and adopted some of them in his own empirical philosophy.

In the eighteenth century, Gassendi's views were replaced by Newtonianism as the philosophy of modern science. Gassendi's writings, ponderous humanistic philological tomes, were set aside for shorter expositions and arguments. Gassendi has been remembered as an early materialist (albeit a hypothetical one), as the reviver of Epicurean atomism, and as one of the most acute critics of Descartes. He is just beginning to be read and studied again and to be awarded his rightful place as one of the major figures in the making of the modern mind.

RICHARD H. POPKIN

Further Reading

Jones, Howard. *Pierre Gassendi: An Intellectual Biography*. Nieuwkoop: De Graaf, 1982. Concentrates on Gassendi's intellectual development.

Joy, Lynn S. *Gassendi the Atomist, Advocate of History in an Age of Science*. Cambridge: Cambridge University Press, 1987. An excellent recent study showing the philosophy behind Gassendi's way of presenting his ideas.

Popkin, Richard H. *The History of Skepticism from Erasmus to Spinoza*. Berkeley: University of California Press, 1979. Chapters 5 and 7 deal with Gassendi's mitigated skepticism.

Spink, J. S. *French Free-Thought from Gassendi to Voltaire*. London: Athlone, 1960. Portrays Gassendi as being in the line of freethinkers before the Enlightenment.

RENÉ DESCARTES

Born: 1596, Le Haye in Touraine, France
Died: 1650, Stockholm, Sweden
Major Works: *Rules for the Direction of the Mind* (written c. 1630; published 1701), *Treatise on the World* (1633, but published posthumously), *Discourse on Method* (1637), *Meditations on First Philosophy* (1641), *Principles of Philosophy* (1644)

Major Ideas

The method for the discovery of truth is analytic and consists of four rules: (1) Accept nothing as true except what can be clearly perceived to be so and nothing more than can be perceived so clearly and distinctly that one cannot have occasion to doubt it. (2) Divide up each problem into as many parts as possible and resolve each in the best manner possible. (3) Carry on one's reflections in due order, beginning with the most simple and proceed little by little, or by degrees, to knowledge of the most complex. (4) Make enumerations so complete and reviews so general that one can be certain of omitting nothing.

An idea is perceived "clearly" if it is present and apparent to an attentive mind, and "distinctly" if it is perceived as so precise and different from all other objects that it contains nothing that is not perceived clearly.

"I think, therefore I am" ("I think, I am") is perceived as true every time a mind thinks.

The cause must be as perfect or more perfect than the effect.

God is the supremely perfect and consequently eternal and necessarily existent and creative substance.

Mind and matter are two clearly distinct created substances; the essence of matter is to be extended (in space), but the essence of mind is to be unextended and to think.

With the exception of the creative and sustaining power of God, no substance needs another in order to exist.

Descartes is frequently called the father of modern philosophy, and with good reason. He set the framework for the philosophical task for the modern period and gave that period its problems. He attended the Jesuit school La Flèche, and, with the exception of mathematics, was somewhat disappointed in his course of instruction. This is perhaps the reason that his own early interests seem to have been directed toward mathematics and physics. In 1618, Descartes went to Holland to serve in the army of Maurice of Nassau, which gave him the opportunity to travel around Europe.

Released from the army and with an independent income, Descartes returned to Holland in 1628, where he remained, except for short visits, until 1649. Around the time of his return to Holland, he wrote his *Rules for the Direction of the Mind*, which was not published until 1701, and by 1633 he had finished his *Treatise on the World*. The condemnation of Galileo by the Church, however, caused Descartes to suppress publication of the volume, and it was not published until after his death. In 1637, he published his *Geometry*, *Dioptric*, and *Meteors*, which were prefaced with his even more famous *Discourse on the Method of Rightly Conducting the Reason and Seeking for Truth in the Sciences*. The method, which is given in part 2 of the work, is the one summarized above, and it is a condensation and generalization of the *Rules for the Direction of the Mind*.

Although Descartes regarded his method as general enough for application to any subject matter, in the *Discourse* it is applied to philosophy. The steps in the strategy of the application of the method in the *Discourse* are repeated in more detail in the *Meditations on First Philosophy* (1641) and to some extent in the *Principles of Philosophy* (1644), and apparently the same steps were to be repeated again in a dialogue that he began but never completed.

Descartes's Method

The first step in this strategy of applying the method to philosophy is to take the first rule of the method seriously and to attempt to doubt all of one's beliefs. It turns out in Descartes's actual application of the method that it is not truth that Descartes apparently seeks and perhaps not even certainty, as many have suggested, but indubitability. In the method, he speaks of accepting as true only what is presented to his mind so clearly and distinctly that he has "no occasion to doubt it," but in the actual use of the rule in the *Discourse* he puts it a little stronger: He is to reject any belief about which he "could imagine the least ground of doubt." Beliefs about which there is no possibility of doubting are his concern; it is the absolutely indubitable that Descartes, in fact, seeks.

The universality of this possibility of doubt is presented by (1) arguing that since we are sometimes deceived by the senses in their deliverance to us of the external world, it is then quite possible to suppose that nothing is just as our sense cause us to imagine it to be and (2) arguing that since we frequently make errors in matters of deductive reasoning and of calculating in mathematics, we can imagine that all such reasonings and calculations are in error. Likewise, since all the same thoughts and conceptions we have while awake also come to us in sleep, without any of them being true at the time, Descartes concludes with the possibility that everything that ever entered into his mind appears to be no more true than a dream.

This same point of the universal possibility of doubt is made even more strongly and dramatically in the *Meditations*. Here Descartes brings up the belief in an all-powerful creator God and asks the question: How do I know that God has not brought it about that there is no earth, no heaven, no extended body, no magnitude, no place, and that nevertheless they appear to exist as they do? As for the mistakes in the reasonings and calculations in "Arithmetic, Geometry and other sciences of that kind," one cannot argue that the good God who is the fountain and who has created us would not allow such, for we do as a matter of fact make such errors.

Bringing God in at this step and in this way opens the door for Descartes to introduce the possibility of an all-powerful, evil genius, who has employed his whole energies to deceiving Descartes. The pos-

sibility of such a malign demon would apparently bring every belief into doubt.

"I Think, Therefore, I am"

The second step in the application is to find one truth that breaks the back of the universal possibility of doubt. In the *Discourse* it is, "I think, therefore I am." (*Cogito, ergo sum; Je pense, donc je suis.*) In thinking all his beliefs false, it is "absolutely essential" that the thinker exist. Since the "therefore" seems to suggest that there is a premise, "I think," which necessarily yields a conclusion, "I am," many have supposed Descartes's claim to be a logical one.

In the *Meditations*, Descartes phrases the *cogito* quite differently. There he says that the proposition "I am, I exist," is necessarily true each time that he pronounces it or mentally conceives it. Even a malignant demon, bent on deceiving him, could not cause him to be nothing so long as he *thinks* that he is something.

The third step in Descartes's strategy is to use the *cogito* to answer the question of the nature of the "I." In the *Discourse*, he had shown that if he thought, he existed. At the same time, he says, he was given no reason to think that he would continue to exist if he did not think. From this he concludes that he is a substance whose whole existence consists in being a thinking thing, one that requires no place and depends on no material thing. The "I," then, is distinct from the body, and if there were no body, the "I" would remain just as it is.

At this third step in the *Meditations*, Descartes lets us know exactly what is happening here. The concept of the inherited medieval "soul" is being altered and is becoming the modern "mind." The question of the "I" is raised in the context of how Descartes would previously have answered the question, "What am I?" First, he tells us, he would have said that the "I" had a body. And further he would have said that the "I" is nourished, that the "I" moves, that the "I" has sensations and that the "I" thinks, all of these activities he had attributed to his soul. This is the medieval Aristotelian soul, the form of the body, with its vegetative aspect that nourishes (and reproduces), its animal aspect that senses and moves, and its human aspect that thinks. After the *cogito*, the vegetative and animal aspects of the human soul are turned over to the body, which, as we have seen, is not at all essential to the new "I." What we have here is the medieval Aristotelian mind with the lower functions of the soul amputated, and it has now become a substance, something that does not need anything else in order to exist. The mind is quite distinct from the body and, apart from God, it exists in its own right quite independently of the body. The essence of new "I" is to think; and doubting, understanding, asserting, denying, willing, refusing, sensing (not bodily sensing), imagining, and perceiving—all become modes of thinking.

Proofs of God's Existence

The fourth step in the strategy is to prove the existence of the supremely perfect being, God; Descartes offers us three proofs that he proposes as accomplishing this. Although the first two proofs appear to run together in the *Discourse* and *Meditations*, in the "Reply to the Second Objections" he lists them as quite distinct proofs and treats them as such in the *Principles*. The first is based on the presence in his mind of the idea of a supremely perfect being. The second is based on the cause of his own existence as an imperfect being; and the third, on the idea itself of a supremely perfect being that must contain within it the necessity of its own existence.

In the *Meditations*, the first proof is put within the context of the kinds of ideas Descartes finds in his own mind. He finds a group of ideas he calls innate, because they appear to arise from the nature of his own mind. They are ideas such as "thing," "concept," "truth," and "consciousness." There is another set he calls factitious, since they appear to be made by him from other ideas in his mind. These include such ideas as the idea of a unicorn (made from the ideas of a horn and a horse) and that of a mermaid, (from the ideas of a fish and a woman). Then there are ideas he calls adventitious, because they appear to come from without him and through

the senses. These include ideas such as the idea of the sun he sees above him or the idea of the fire burning in the fireplace before him. It is this third group that his process of doubting had called into question: it was possible for him to doubt that there was anything external to his mind that was the source of these ideas.

The first proof for the existence of God focuses on one particular idea that Descartes finds among all these others, the idea of a supremely perfect being, or God. In order to show that in the case of this particular idea there must be a source of this idea without himself, Descartes utilizes a medieval principle that he never puts in his crucible of doubt: The cause must contain as much perfection or reality as the effect. The application here is of this form: There must be as much perfection or reality in the cause of an idea as in the idea itself.

The question that the acceptance of this principle raises is this: Could Descartes's nature be the cause of the idea of a supremely perfect being? In short, is it an innate idea based on his nature in the sense of those innate ideas above? No, he concludes, since he is not perfect, a fact that is obvious from his doubting; for example, he does not have perfect knowledge. His own nature could not be the cause of this idea of a supremely perfect being.

Is it a factitious idea, manufactured by Descartes from, say, his own nature with his own imperfections removed? For example, is the perfect knowledge of the completely perfect being simply an idea of Descartes's own knowledge with the ignorance removed? He gives two reasons for rejecting this. One, God's perfections are not negatively defined as is perfect knowledge in this case, by contrast to Descartes's own imperfect knowledge. In God, perfection is a positive property. Two, the idea of a supremely perfect being is simple, not made up of a number of different perfections, whether negative or not, such as perfect knowledge, perfect power, and so forth, combined together. As a simple idea, the idea of a supremely perfect being cannot be fabricated from a number of other ideas. Thus, he concludes, this idea of a supremely perfect being is not an innate idea with his own nature as the cause, nor is it a factitious idea gotten by negation or by compilation of other ideas. Its only source must be a being other than Descartes's mind and one that contains as much perfection or reality as the idea itself does. Descartes concludes that he is no longer alone in the universe. Instead of a malignant demon, there exists (in addition to himself) a supremely perfect being, namely, God.

The second proof is somewhat analogous to the first and rests on the same medieval principle, that there must be as much perfection or reality in the cause as in the effect, but this time the proof rests on Descartes's existence, which he has already proven. He raises this question: Am I the cause of my own existence? Had he had the power to create himself, he argues, then he would have had the power and will to create himself supremely perfect. In short, if Descartes were the cause of his own existence, he would be God. But, of course, it has already been established that Descartes is far from perfect and, consequently, not his own creator. Descartes cannot avoid this problem by suggesting that he has always existed. Since he is temporal, his existence can be divided up into moments, and it would take as much power to sustain Descartes in each of these moments as it would take initially to create him.

Suppose, however, that the cause of Descartes's existence were something less than the supremely perfect being—for example, his parents. Whatever Descartes's creator might be, it must be capable of creating him with the idea of a supremely perfect being. Thus the cause of Descartes's existence must contain as much perfection or reality as that contained in the idea of a supremely perfect being. The cause of his existence could not, then, be his parents, who are likewise imperfect. Thus the basis of the first proof is called in to support this one.

The possibility that there might be a number of causes of Descartes's existence and of the idea of a supremely perfect being in his mind is considered. Here again, as in the first proof, the perfection of simplicity is pointed to. The idea of God has simplicity as one of its perfections and its cause cannot be a compounded cause. Descartes concludes, then, that he is not alone in the universe and that the cause of his idea of a supremely perfect being is also the cause of his own existence and that the cause has

imprinted the idea of a supremely perfect being on his mind as the mark, or signature, of its creator.

The third proof for the existence of God, which Kant referred to as Descartes's ontological proof, is separated from the previous two in the *Meditations* and placed after a discussion of truth and of the nature of matter, that is, extension. No doubt Descartes did this for heuristic purposes and to make the proof appear stronger coming right after a discussion of extension, whose proofs serve as an analogy for this third proof. The proof is simply this: Just as the idea of a triangle contains the necessity of the degrees of its three angles being equal to the sum of two right triangles, so the idea of a supremely perfect being contains the necessity of its existence, which is one of its perfections. If the idea did not contain the necessity of its existence, then it would not be the idea of a supremely perfect being.

After the replacement of the possibility of the earlier malign demon by the necessity of the existence of the supremely perfect being, the fifth step in Descartes's strategy in the application of his method is to find and support the criterion or mark of truth, clearness, and distinction of perception that has guided him in the proof of his own existence, the discovery of his own nature, and his treatment of God's existence. The supremely perfect being, or God, who has created Descartes and printed his mark upon his mind would not allow him to be deceived by those things that he clearly and distinctly perceives to be so. If God did allow him to be deceived by what he clearly and distinctly perceives to be so, then God would be not the supremely perfect being but the malign demon of the doubting stage. How is Descartes to account for error, then? He is not merely an intellect viewing clear and distinct ideas; he is also a will accepting some ideas as true and rejecting others as false. The will extends beyond clear and distinct ideas, and this is the source of error—accepting ideas as true that are not clearly and distinctly perceived to be so.

The Existence of Material Objects

The sixth step in Descartes's overall strategy is to turn to material objects, whose existence he earlier found he could doubt, to see if there was anything about them that he could clearly and distinctly perceive to be so. He finds this certainty in ideas of the quantified extension of these physical objects in length, breadth, and depth, which also gives rise to ideas of size, shape, position, and local motion. It is this property of quantified extension that Descartes clearly and distinctly perceives to be the nature of matter. And disregarding whether or not there exist material objects of some particular size or shape, he finds that he can clearly and distinctly perceive certain truths about that size and shape. Whether or not there exists a material object with a triangular shape, for example, the sum of the three angles of a triangle must necessarily equal that of two right angles. Descartes thus finds as certain the truths he formerly believed concerning figures and numbers and other matters of arithmetic and geometry, which he formerly found subject to doubt in the presence of the possible malignant demon.

The seventh step in Descartes's strategy is to restore confidence in the existence of material objects. The belief that there are material objects having quantified properties of extension is restored on the basis of the impossibility of God's simultaneously being the supremely perfect being and being a deceiver. The adventitious ideas of the material objects must have a cause. If they had any cause other than material objects that were created by God outside us, then God would be a systematic deceiver; but God, the supremely perfect being, cannot be a deceiver. We, however, are still never certain that any particular physical object, which appears to be given to us in sensation, truly exists, for our senses do not give us clear and distinct perceptions of which we can be certain. But we can be certain that there are material objects outside forming a material world that has the above-quantified properties of extension.

In 1649, Descartes accepted an invitation from Queen Christina of Sweden to join a distinguished circle she was assembling in Stockholm and to instruct her in philosophy. Descartes accepted, but unable to survive the Swedish climate and her rigorous schedule he caught pneumonia and died there in 1650.

Descartes left modern philosophy the legacy of a dualism of two distinct and independent kinds of created substances, minds, which were unextended in space and were thinking, and material bodies, which were extended in space and could not think. As noted above, Descartes concluded that he was a mind with a material body. He received adventitious ideas from the external world through the senses of his material body. His mind thought about these ideas and made decisions to act so as to set his material body in motion and affect that external world. In short, Descartes's mental substance and his material body appear to interact causally. But Descartes never explains how this interaction could take place. Most of modern philosophy and a good deal of contemporary philosophy can be viewed as attempts to handle this problem bequeathed by Descartes.

BOWMAN L. CLARKE

Further Reading

Doney, Willis, ed. *Descartes: A Collection of Critical Essays.* Garden City, N.Y.: Doubleday & Company, 1967. An excellent collection of essays treating different aspects of Descartes's philosophy. The essays on the *Cogito* by A. J. Ayer and J. Hintikka are recommended, along with the essays by A. Kenny, A. Gewirth, and W. P. Alston. Extensive bibliography.

Grene, Marjorie. *Descartes.* Minneapolis: University of Minneapolis Press, 1987. A solid and very readable book on Descartes's thought.

Kenny, Anthony. *Descartes: A Study of His Philosophy.* New York: Random House, 1968. Kenny (also represented in the Doney collection) offers a perceptive and useful examination of Descartes's principal ideas.

Smith, Norman Kemp. *New Studies in the Philosophy of Descartes: Descartes as Pioneer.* London: Macmillan, 1952. A distinguished scholar undertakes a careful analysis of Descartes's ideas, emphasizing Descartes's original contributions to Western thought.

HENRY MORE

Born: 1614, Grantham, Lincolnshire, England
Died: 1687, Cambridge, England
Major Works: *An Antidote against Atheism* (1653) *The Immortality of the Soul* (1659), *A Collection of Several Philosophical Writings of Dr. Henry More* (1662), *Enchiridion Ethicum* (1667), *Enchiridion Metaphysicum* (1671), *Theological Works* (1708)

Major Ideas

All knowledge is conditional on the validity of our faculties.
The world consists of active spirits and inert matter.
God's existence can be proven.
The Platonic theory of the universe best fits with the findings of modern science.

Henry More, a leading member of the Cambridge Platonists, was a prolific writer. He spent his entire adult life, first as a student and then as a fellow, at Christ's College, Cambridge. In his student days at Cambridge, he fell into a complete skepticism, which was overcome only when he read the mystical writing *Theologia Germania*, a work that also played an important role in Martin Luther's development. More then carefully studied the writings of Plato and the Neoplatonists. His earliest publications, some in the form of poems, are based mainly on his readings of Plato and Plotinus.

More then became heavily influenced by his reading of the Jewish cabala and the writings of Descartes. He was briefly a most enthusiastic follower of Descartes and corresponded with him. Initially he saw Descartes's physical system as similar to his own Platonic–cabalistic view of the world, in which matter is inert and is activated and moved by spirit. More saw his own spiritualistic Christian view as not only compatible with the findings of modern science but the very basis of it. However, he soon turned against Cartesianism because he saw that a purely materialistic view of the world might emerge from it, which would be in opposition to Christianity as a picture of the spiritual real world.

More spelled out his own philosophical theory in a group of works published in the 1650s, *An Antidote against Atheism* (1653), *Conjectura Cabbalistica* (1653), *Enthusiasmus Triumphatus* (1656), and *The Immortality of the Soul* (1659). The first and last of these start with the development of a total skepticism, insisting that it is not possible to find any principles that could not possibly be false. Since all our alleged knowledge depends on the veracity of our faculties, it is always possible that whatever our reason and our senses reveal to us as true could actually be false if our faculties are false or deceptive. This "irremedial" skepticism is offered to dispense with Descartes's answer to skepticism, and with Descartes's dogmatic theory.

More then dismissed the actual skeptics as people who are completely unreasonable. In spite of the difficulties, and the skeptical possibilities, any sane person accepts the reliability of his or her senses and reason. Within this postskeptical framework, the reasonable person can be convinced of the existence of God, both from the nature and content of the idea itself and from the inordinate variety of examples of design in the observed universe. And the reasonable person can then understand the nature of the created, inactive physical world and the active spiritual world. More over and over again insisted that the first chapters of Genesis spelled out the essential truths of modern science, including the Copernican theory and the theory of the circulation of the blood. In this sense he said that he and Descartes had come to the same conclusions, but he, More, took the high road, and Descartes the low one: Descartes arrived at his view from strictly materialistic considerations, while More did so from spiritual ones.

More developed a physical theory in which spirits were described as active forces and causes.

He called these "indiscernible" spirits, spirits that expanded and contracted and interpenetrated all physical objects. More came to see Descartes as a "nubbilist," one who denied that spirits could be extended. The spirits, according to More, were part of a Neoplatonic world of entities created by God. To deny them extension was to deny them existence and hence to propound a kind of atheism.

The spirits could be understood metaphysically and theologically. More's physics, which was worked out in detail, influenced Isaac Newton, who had probably been a student of More's and was an associate for years thereafter. The notion of space as the "sensorium of God" was taken by both More and Newton from some Jewish cabalistic tracts. More was one of the translators and editors of the *Kabbala Denudata*, of 1670, a compendium of medieval and modern cabalistic writings, translated from Hebrew and Aramaic into Latin. In the midst of this project More decided that the cabala was nonsense, though he had said "there are jewels in that rubbish." It was, for him, an irrational formulation of his theosophy, as was also the very popular view of the time presented by the German mystic Jacob Boehme. More's rejection of cabalism appears in the middle of the translations.

More's concern about spirits led him to be a leading theoretician of witches and an empirical observer of the effects of witch behavior. More and his follower Joseph Glanvill insisted there could be no proof of the impossibility of the existence of witches, since every matter of fact is possible. People like Hobbes who dismissed witches as impossible beings did not realize that everything that can be conceived is possible. It is a matter of empirical investigation to determine what actually exists in the world. The question then became for More and Glanvill one of determining the best way to account for some of the strange events that were reported: Were active spirits causing these happenings? Or was some other more mundane theory true? More and Glanvill carefully gathered up cases of unusual occurrences, and insisted that only the theory of active witch spirits could really explain these events. Then, they argued, if there is adequate empirical evidence of the existence of witches, there is

nothing odd about the possible existence of other types of spirits, including souls and angels. If witches do not or cannot exist, then the whole spiritual world is cast in doubt.

More and his private student Lady Anne Conway (women could not attend the universities then), his later collaborator, developed a spiritology, a theory of the way the world of spirits, God, and matter operate in cosmic harmony. (The correspondence of More and Anne Conway, published in *The Conway Letters*, is a rich source of understanding their views.) In defending the theory in More's works and in Conway's *The Principles of the Most Ancient and Modern Philosophy*, they developed a strong critique of the metaphysical theories of Descartes, Hobbes, and Spinoza, arguing that none of those theories could explain or account for the events in question; such thinkers had no principle of activity or productive causation, since their conception of matter was of something that is inert—pure extension. In contrast, More and Conway offered a dynamic world, which on the one hand was a way of explaining the world of modern science and on the other was a way of connecting theosophy and science, since the spiritual world was a Platonized Christian one. (Leibniz said he got his concept of the "monad" as a basic source of activity from reading Conway's book, and he then developed his own spiritualized picture of the world, his monadology.)

The Neoplatonic construction, developed out of the ideas of Plato, Philo Judaeus, Plotinus, Proclus, and the Renaissance Florentine Platonists, made for a fairly vague Christian world-view, vague in its relationship to the historical events of Christianity. Conway joined her version with the mysticism of Boehme, and eventually with that of the mystical Quakers, whose movement she joined. More detested the Quakers as one of the worst kinds of enthusiasts, and he offered a very Latitudinarian (broad-minded) version of Christianity, often stated in Platonic terms.

More's writings in the 1660s emphasized both theological questions and ethical ones. More was a moderate millenarian, that is, someone who foresaw the return of Jesus and then his thousand-year reign on Earth. More was trying to defuse or eliminate some of the worst intellectual excesses of the Puritan revolution, which was fired by the expectation of an early fulfillment in England of the millenarian expectation. More's *Enthusiasmus Triumphatus* was an attempt to diagnose the kind of insanity that was involved in the religious believer who was totally sure of his or her beliefs and was willing to perform all sorts of drastic actions on the basis of such a belief. After the Restoration, More tried to present a moderate theology that could be acceptable to nondogmatic Puritans and liberal Anglicans, and still encompassed the millenial reading of Scripture as foretelling the end of days at some indefinite period in the future. More, who had worked with Isaac Newton for years on deciphering the symbols and the prophecies in the books of Daniel and Revelation, broke with Newton around 1680, apparently because of the conflict between More's liberal, vague, and less definite interpretation of the Scriptures and Newton's more fundamentalistic readings.

More also published the *Enchiridion Ethicum* in 1667 (English translation, 1690) giving a rational account of human ethical behavior. This became the most popular of his works at the time. He developed a calculus of ethics to determine what is virtuous action according to right reason. We also need a passionate commitment, a kind of Christian love to lead us to good and right actions, More contended.

Although More was not the most precise or consistent thinker of his time, he was one of the liveliest, wittiest, and satirical polemical writers of his day. He was important in relating some of the central Platonic and Neoplatonic ideas that emerged during the late Renaissance with a new picture of the world that was developing from the mathematical science of Galileo and Descartes. Unlike the Scholastics, who still dominated the universities, More did not oppose the "new science" but, on the contrary, became one of its most ardent supporters because he believed that the basic picture of a mathematically explicable material world was entirely compatible with his dynamic spiritualistic metaphysics and with his Platonic reading of Christianity. For him, religion, metaphysics, and science, when properly understood, walk hand in hand. Those who tried to make the material world self-explanatory, which is what More saw Descartes, Hobbes, and Spinoza as doing, prepared the way for a dangerous atheism. More tried to make people see that not only was modern science compatible with the Bible but that it was actually, when properly understood, part of the ancient wisdom of the Hebrews as revealed by the cabala.

Some of More's views look very anachronistic now, but they help us understand the options that existed in seventeenth-century thought for combining the new scientific ideas and some of the now-forgotten or rejected metaphysical religious views. At the time, there was not simply a warfare of science and religion; there were also those like More, Conway, Newton, and perhaps Leibniz, who advocated a harmonious combination of a religious theodicy and a mathematical physics of nature. Much of this was swept away as the Enlightenment joined Newton's physics to either a complete empiricism or a complete materialism. The Cambridge Platonism of More and Cudworth came to be regarded as a dead end, the unfortunate last gasp of a religious metaphysics that was no longer of significance.

With the present attempt to understand more fully how modern science developed, there has been a reexamination of the many threads that were woven together in the seventeenth century—the magical, hermetic ideas, the cabalistic ones, the Platonic and Neoplatonic ones, as well as the purely mathematical and physical theories. As a result, there is now a revived interest in seeing More as one of the chief thinkers contributing to the making of the modern mind. He may have turned out to be a transitional figure, but in his day he was a significant force in providing interest and concern about new scientific ideas and in seeing them in terms compatible with religion and a spiritualistic metaphysics.

RICHARD H. POPKIN

Further Reading

Cassirer, Ernst. *The Platonic Renaissance in England*. Edinburgh: Nelson, 1953. Basic study of the Renaissance and Cambridge Platonism in England.

Colie, Rosalie. *Light and Enlightenment: A Study of the Cambridge Platonists and Dutch Arminians*. Cambridge: Cambridge University Press, 1957. Important book in presenting the ideas of the Cambridge Platonists, and in connecting them with their allies among the Dutch liberal Protestants.

Hutton, Sarah, ed. *Henry More (1614–1687) Tercentenary Studies*. Dordrecht: Kluwer, 1990. Contains articles by many historians of philosophy and science, such as Alan Gabbey, Allison Coudert, R. H. Popkin, and Sarah Hutton, as well as a bibliography of More's writings and of modern studies dealing with him, compiled by Robert Crocker.

Inge, William. *The Platonic Tradition in English Religious Thought*. London: Longmans, 1920. An appreciation of the Cambridge Platonists by a twentieth-century Neoplatonist.

Koyré, Alexandre. *From the Closed to the Infinite Universe*. Baltimore: Johns Hopkins University Press, 1957. Chapters 5 and 6 present More's theory of the universe in relation to other theories of the "new scientists."

Lichtenstein, Aharon. *Henry More. The Rational Theology of a Cambridge Platonist*. Cambridge, Mass.: Harvard University Press, 1962. A careful account of More's attempt to reconcile reason and theology.

Nicolson, Marjorie, ed. *The Conway Letters*. New Haven: Yale University Press, 1930.

Popkin, Richard H. "The Third Force in Seventeenth-Century Philosophy: Scepticism, Science and Biblical Prophecy." In E. Ullman-Margalit, ed., *The Prism of Science* (Boston: Reidel, 1986), pp. 21–50; and " 'The Incurable Scepticism' of Henry More, Blaise Pascal and Soren Kierkegaard." In R. H. Popkin and C. B. Schmitt, eds., *Scepticism from the Renaissance to the Enlightenment.*, *Wolfenbuttler Forschungen*, 35: 165–184. The first article presents More as a leader of a "third force" in European ideas, which influenced the development of a new metaphysics of a new science.

RALPH CUDWORTH

Born: 1617, Aller, Somerset, England
Died: 1688, Cambridge, England
Major Works: *The True Intellectual System of the Universe* (1678), *A Treatise Concerning Eternal and Immutable Morality* (1731)

Major Ideas

There is an ancient wisdom (prisca theology), *known to all peoples.*
We can have only limited knowledge of God.
All people, even atheists, have an idea of God.
The political explanation of religion is not adequate to explain Christianity.
A survey of religious knowledge, pagan and Judeo-Christian, shows what true religion is.
There is a rational basis for moral behavior.

Ralph Cudworth was the best metaphysician of the Cambridge Platonists. He studied at Emmanuel College, Cambridge, the original seat of the Cambridge Platonism. He was a Puritan sympathizer, and in 1645, when the Puritans prevailed, he was appointed master of Clare College, Cambridge, and regius (royal) professor of Hebrew at Cambridge. In 1654, he became master of Christ's College, where Henry More was a fellow. He remained there for the rest of his life.

The True Intellectual System of the Universe

Cudworth worked for years on his *True Intellectual System*, and published only the first part (which is 899 pages long). The second and third parts have disappeared. He received permission to publish it in 1671, but it did not come out until 1678. Though the work is now difficult to read, it played an important role in European philosophy for almost two centuries. It was translated into Latin by Mosheim (1733) and was discussed by leading philosophers and theologians in Europe and America.

Cudworth starts from a common assumption of Renaissance and Cambridge Platonists, that there is an ancient wisdom, a *prisca theology*, going back to the first wise men, Moses and Hermes Trismegistus, and is knowable by all mankind. The core of this wisdom is knowledge of God. However, this knowledge is beclouded by the variety of different religions developed by human beings, both pagan and monotheistic. The situation is becoming so confused that atheistic views are being raised, denying even that there is a God.

Cudworth set himself the task of refuting atheism both by making clear the limits of what we could know about God, and by undertaking an intensive investigation of all known religions and atheistic views to show that they all point to an original pure religion, which is incorporated in Christianity. When one recognizes this, one can see that the seventeenth-century forms of atheism, which he saw as coming from the ideas of Descartes, Hobbes, and Spinoza (whose *Theological Political Tractatus* had just appeared) can be refuted, or shown to be implausible and unconvincing.

Cudworth started with a type of skepticism, much like that of Henry More, used to brush aside demands for complete knowledge and understanding of fundamental concepts. We have to recognize that our understanding is limited and finite. "Truth is bigger than our Minds." We cannot form a complete and adequate conception of God, or ourselves, or even of any substantial thing. This does not mean that we have any real reason to doubt the existence of God, ourselves, or material beings. Within limits we can understand enough. We can show the plausibility of some views and the implausibility of others.

Cudworth then contended that our inability to comprehend God as an infinite, eternal Being does not stop us from having some conception of the deity. Hobbes and Spinoza may think that if something is incomprehensible, then it is impossible for it to exist. But, Cudworth said, even the atheist must conclude that what now exists must come from something, and that something must be infinite in duration, and eternal without any beginning. Otherwise, one can ask, Why is there now something in existence rather than nothing?

If the atheist contends that the terms "infinite" and "eternal" signify nothing, Cudworth answers that though we have "no full comprehension and adequate understanding" of infinity and eternity, yet we have some notion, comprehension, and apprehension sufficient to make demonstrations about a perfect immutable nature. Both pagan and Christian thinkers have offered such demonstrations.

The basic answer to ancient and modern atheism is that pagan, Jewish, and Christian thinkers have all been aware of the idea of God as an infinite, eternal being. Even ancient atheists, denying the existence of God, knew this idea, but contended that no being corresponded to it. "God" is a concept known in various languages, and people have the same notion or conception in their minds when they talk or write about it.

Most of the *True Intellectual System* is the setting forth of the evidence that pagans, Jews, Christians, and Muslims have all expressed, no matter how obscurely, the idea or belief in one God. Cudworth referred to the research that had been presented a generation earlier in the massive work of the Dutch scholar Gerard Vossius, on the origin and development of gentile theology. Pagan views were classified and shown to be derivative from biblical ones. For instance, both Cudworth and Vossius claimed that Democritus got his theory from one Moschus. (Moschus is another name for Moses.)

The classification and inspection of pagan views showed, according to Cudworth and Vossius, that the pagan authors did not really offer polytheistic theologies but, rather, accepted that there is one supreme self-existent deity, plus other inferior, generated gods. There have been many names for one and the same supreme God. Manicheanism alone might be a form of genuine polytheism. Cudworth claimed that pagan views, when properly classified

and analyzed (with the one exception just mentioned), all set forth a belief in one Supreme Being. This showed both the naturalness of a monotheistic view and the unnaturalness of atheism. The basic defect of paganism is its inclusion of lesser deities that supposedly have some divine power.

Cudworth was unwilling to claim that all the elements of true theology could be found in the ancient pagan views. The fundamental notion of the divine Trinity is not a natural development but was revealed darkly to the ancient Hebrews, who have traces of it in their literature. It was then communicated to the Egyptians and Greeks and was made clearest by the early Christians. The pagan Platonists who lacked the clarity of revealed truth turned Trinitarianism into a belief in three Gods. Nonetheless, Trinitarian Christianity, Cudworth claimed, is the correct expression of the most ancient revelation received by the early Hebrews and somewhat known to the most rational pagans.

Having provided a basis for his religious philosophy, Cudworth turned to rebut a threat that was growing in his time, that of interpreting religious movements as solely social and political developments (as Hobbes and Spinoza were doing). Religion was not based simply on fear or superstition, as Spinoza claimed, nor was it (as Hobbes contended) the result of power-hungry politicians who used religion to make people obey them. If the latter view were taken seriously, then all of the research of Vossius and Cudworth could be accounted for in political terms, without indicating anything about religious truth. So, Cudworth argued against the plausibility of the political and social reading of religious history. He insisted that such a reading could not account for the idea of a supreme deity, which people have had from time immemorial.

Cudworth contended that though politicians often make use of religion for their own benefit, this does not explain the universality of religion. How could all of mankind everywhere and at every time be taken in by a political hoax? If religion is a fraud, is it not strange that in the whole history of the world, people should not have suspected this, or found this out?

Theistic religion is obviously not a fraud since all

mankind acknowledge a supreme deity, an eternal necessary being, as Cudworth had shown in his anthropological excursions. If there were no such God, is it conceivable that people could form the idea, or that politicians could make people believe in such a being? The idea cannot be compounded out of other ideas (which lack the perfections of this idea). Our imperfect beings could not create the idea of an infinitely perfect being out of nothing. "We affirm, therefore, that were there no God, the idea of an absolutely and infinitely perfect being could never have been made or feigned, neither by politicians, nor by poets, nor philosophers."

The universe that this supreme being has created consists of conscious minds, material things, and unconscious "spiritual plastic powers." The latter act and cause events in both mind and matter. God orders the world through these powers, and they provide the spiritual means by which events happen. Cudworth's plastic natures, like Henry More's indiscernible spirits, present an explanation of how and why the material and mental world goes on through the actions of spiritual forces. His theory was taken up by some of the religiously inclined scientists and was challenged by Pierre Bayle, who sought to show that it could lead to a kind of atheism, since the plastic powers could operate without divine intervention. Since the powers were everywhere, Bayle argued, Cudworth's theory bordered on a kind of Spinozistic pantheism.

A Treatise Concerning Eternal and Immutable Morality

Cudworth's *Treatise Concerning Eternal and Immutable Morality* was only published forty years after his death. It and other unpublished works may have been known to John Locke and the Earl of Shaftesbury, since Cudworth's daughter and heir, Lady Masham, was a close friend of Locke's and knew Shaftesbury.

Cudworth contended that any knowledge, including knowledge of good and evil, is about concepts, not sensations. The concepts deal with eternal truths, which are ideas in the Divine Mind. We, as human beings, cannot know the mind of the Supreme Being, and can judge our knowledge only in terms of the clarity and distinctness of our ideas; this is the greatest guarantee of knowledge that we can have. Our knowledge of what is good is what we find in our ideas. Actions do not become good because God wills them, but they are good in themselves, and God wills them because they are good. In this, Cudworth was following Plato's discussion in the *Euthyphro*.

We are not moved to act by reason alone. We act both by instinct and inclination, and also by intellectual considerations. We can try to act so that we choose the best. Whether or not we succeed depends both on our knowledge and the factors that influence our inclinations. If we are motivated by love in the Platonic sense, then we will act better than if we are differently motivated. We have the ability to prefer a spiritual life to a carnal one, and therefore point out the direction of our choices. When we can do this, we are capable of achieving a good life that transcends egoism or self-love and is harmonious.

Cudworth's moral theory greatly influenced that of Richard Price later on in the eighteenth century.

Cudworth's *True and Immutable System* and his treatise on morality were the most substantial metaphysical achievements of the Cambridge Platonic movement. Though neither work is complete or finished, they put together the dominant ideas drawn from Plato, the Neoplatonists, and the Renaissance Platonists in an overall system, which was presented as a significant alternative to those of Descartes, Hobbes, and Spinoza. Like Henry More, Cudworth started with a kind of skepticism, admitting that knowledge was limited by human fallibility. In so doing, Cudworth distanced himself from trying to defend his views dogmatically, as Descartes tried to do.

The other Cambridge Platonists presented their views in fragmentary form, as sermons, brief statements, or polemics (as in the case of More). Cudworth set out to put it all together. His imposing title indicates what he sought to achieve. He offered a rebuttal to materialism and atheism, ancient and modern, both in the form of his vast examination of all sorts of religious and irreligious views and in his analysis of what is involved in having conceptual knowledge. He offered an epistemology and a metaphysics to justify limited knowledge of a spiritual cosmos, compatible with Christian belief.

Cudworth's massive effort can be seen as one of the last attempts to justify a religious picture of the world in the face of the rising irreligion of the time. His effort greatly influenced Sir Isaac Newton. (There is a still-unpublished fragment of Newton's *On the Origins of Gentile Philosophy*, which is a detailed attempt to find the basic true religion behind all the human formulations, using the method of Cudworth and Vossius. There are also some notes by Newton entitled "Out of Cudworth" that have just been published.)

Cudworth's effort was seen as a bulwark against deism and atheism during the next century and a half. The Latin edition made Cudworth a major figure in Continental thought. His ideas and methods influenced many thinkers, even David Hume, whose *Natural History of Religion* is in some ways an ironic comment on Cudworth.

Cudworth, Vossius, and Newton were seen as trying to stem the tide of secular and naturalistic interpretations of Judeo-Christianity (though each of them was accused of giving up crucial aspects of Christianity in order to make their case). By and large they were rejected by the Enlightenment, and when modern philosophy was regarded as a strict development from Descartes to Locke, then to Hume and Kant, Cudworth and the Cambridge Platonists no longer remained part of the story of how modern philosophy grew.

RICHARD H. POPKIN

Further Reading

Colie, Rosalie. *Light and Enlightenment: A Study of the Cambridge Platonists and the Dutch Arminians.* Cambridge: Cambridge University Press, 1957. A study of the relation of the ideas of the Cambridge Platonists to those of their Dutch liberal Protestant friends.

Popkin, Richard H. "The Crisis of Polytheism and the Answers of Vossius, Cudworth and Newton." In J. E. Force and Richard H. Popkin, eds., *Essays on the Context, Nature and Influence of Isaac Newton's Theology.* Dordrecht: Kluwer, 1990. This volume also contains Newton's notes, "Out of Cudworth."

Tulloch, John. *Rational Theology and Christian Philosophy in England in the Seventeenth Century.* 2 vols. Edinburgh: W. Blackwood and Sons, 1872. An overall study of the Cambridge Platonic movement.

BLAISE PASCAL

Born: 1623, Claremont, Auvergne, France
Died: 1662, Port-Royal, France
Major Works: *Conversations with M. de Saci* (1655), *The Provincial Letters* (1656–57), *On the Geometrical Mind and on the Art of Persuasion* (1657–58), *Pensées* (1662)

Major Ideas

The weakness of human reason leads to ultimate, complete skepticism.
The misery of man without God is the ordinary human condition.
Scientific knowledge cannot provide happiness.
There is the need for grace to be moral and happy.
It is the nature of science that it is at best only hypothetical.
Mathematics is true only as an axiom system.
Ultimate knowledge is based on faith.
Man has no choice but to seek God or reject Him.
With faith, one can provide "proofs" of the Christian religion.

Pascal, one of the greatest mathematical and scientific geniuses of the seventeenth century, is most famous for his religious–philosophical views. After achieving great fame for his mathematical discoveries, including the development of probability theory, his invention of the adding machine, and for his experimental and theoretical work on air pressure and the nature of the vacuum, Pascal had an overwhelming religious experience when crossing the Seine River in Paris during a storm. He wrote down what he experienced in a document called "The Memorial," which he kept with him, sewn in his clothing, up to his death. He said he experienced the presence of the God of Abraham, Isaac, and Jacob, not the God of the philosophers. From then on he devoted himself chiefly to philosophical–religious concerns. He joined the rigid, reform-minded Catholic group the Jansenists, and moved to their monastery at Port-Royal outside of Paris. His *Conversation with M. de Saci* reports a discussion he had about the merits of Montaigne's skepticism and Epictetus's Stoicism with one of the chief Jansenist theologians when he arrived at Port-Royal.

The Jansenists were opposed by the Jesuit theologians, who sought to have the former condemned. Pascal became one of the chief polemicists for the Jansenists, and wrote a wonderfully ridiculing, devastating critique of the Jesuit views in his *Provincial Letters*. In spite of his brilliant attacks, the Jansenists were condemned by the pope, and leaders like Antoine Arnauld had to flee to the Netherlands.

Port-Royal was not just a monastery. It was also a school for the education of the best and brightest minds of France of the time. Arnauld and Pierre Nicole wrote logic and grammar books for the students that became important in the history of philosophy and the history of linguistics. Pascal's *Geometrical Method* is believed to be the preface for a mathematical text, a preface in which Pascal evaluated the nature of mathematics.

The most extended statement of Pascal's views appears in his *Pensées* (*Thoughts*). This incomplete work was apparently begun in 1659. It is described in a lecture Pascal gave at Port-Royal as an apology for the Christian religion. At the time of his death, the work consisted of writings on slips of paper, some organized under titles, some not. The writings range from essays of several pages to just a word or two. From the time the *Pensées* were found in his monastic cell to the present, there has been ongoing revision of the order of presentation of the papers. Nonetheless, from their first publication they have constituted one of the most forceful statements of the religious point of view and of the desperate human situation in which human beings find themselves suspended in time and space, between the infinitely large and the infinitely small, without guidance as to what to do, and how to live unless they "hear God" and accept divine guidance.

Pascal was a child prodigy who made important mathematical discoveries before he was twenty. His father, a royal treasurer, introduced him to the scientific circle around Father Mersenne in Paris. The young Pascal did some important experiments on air pressure after learning of the invention of the barometer, including carrying inverted tubes of mercury up a mountain, and up a church tower, to measure the changes in air pressure. He invented the adding machine, one of the major achievements of the early scientific revolution. (His adding machine is the direct ancestor of the modern computer.) He did a series of experiments to challenge the Scholastic claim that nature abhors a vacuum by showing how vacuums could be created. The supposed abhorrence was due to atmospheric pressure.

Pascal contended that in science, in contrast to theology, one should be guided not by authority but by experiments. We can never know the ultimate truths about nature because nature is ever active. Instead we can know only some of the effects of nature's activities. Through experience, experiments, and reasoning, we can frame hypotheses about how nature operates. These hypotheses have to be revised or changed as our historical experience develops.

Pascal was a strong supporter of Copernicus and Galileo, regarding them as scientists offering the best presently available way of understanding the data we possess. Pascal followed them in offering mathematically formulated mechanical theories about how nature operates.

In interpreting his scientific discoveries, and in arguing against the Scholastic professors of physics, Pascal realized the limited nature of scientific discovery. In his preface to the unfinished treatise on the vacuum, and in his answer to Father Noel, he pointed out that one can never fully establish a scientific truth. One can confirm and confirm. One can design experiments and test. But no amount of confirmation suffices, since one negative instance is enough to disprove a scientific view. One can falsify but never really verify proposals in sci-

ence (a view much like that offered in the twentieth century by Karl Popper).

In evaluating what can be established in mathematics, in his *On the Geometrical Spirit*, Pascal examined the nature of an axiomatic system. One can establish truths within the system, but the relevance of these truths to the world depends upon the truth of the axioms. This cannot be determined within the system. All one can say is that the axioms are the clearest and most evident items within the system. Pascal's analysis of the nature of mathematical systems seems to be closer to twentieth-century mathematical logic than that of any of his contemporaries.

Pascal never abandoned his mathematical or scientific interests when his concern turned to religious matters. But the examination of humanity's plight and the possibility of salvation became central for him. Any human attempt to find answers to life's basic problems leads to skepticism. Pascal, in his *Conversations with M. de Saci*, had portrayed total skepticism as the state of "misery of man without God." The human being has a faint idea of real happiness, but is unable with only human resources to achieve it. So, one has to go beyond or outside of the human rational world and seek genuine assurance by nonrational means, by instinct and revelation.

Pensées

Pascal's unfinished masterpiece, the *Pensées*, gives the most extended presentation of his views. The work, as presently organized, begins with a series of statements and vignettes dealing with the ordinary human situation and with how people deal with it. Pascal tried to make readers realize that they are oppressed by their situation, that they do not know what to do about it, and that they realize they have to find an answer that will yield both knowledge and happiness. They also realize that they cannot accomplish this goal by human means, and by rational endeavor. The goals people seek in ordinary life are shown to be of no real worth and will not bring us *real* happiness.

So, what should we do? We realize that our faculties are unable to help us find the kind of knowledge we seek. Our senses are fallacious, and our reasoning is inconclusive or contradictory. We have no rationally guaranteed principles on which to base our quest for knowledge and happiness. We find that the only principles we have are instinctive and not evidential: "The heart has its reasons that the reason knows not of." These heartfelt principles may or may not be true, depending upon the source of our faculties. If they are formed by chance, or by some demonic force, then the principles are false or dubious. If the principles are revealed to us, then they could be true. But how do we tell? Any attempt to examine the situation involves using the very faculties whose veracity is in question.

The more we investigate the matter, the more we are led into total skepticism. But such is the human predicament that nature will not allow us to rest in complete doubt: "Nature confounds the sceptics and reason confounds the dogmatists." When we reach this impasse, we see that we have no choice but to abandon the rational attempt to find a solution, and "learn that man infinitely surpasses man, and hear from your master your real state which you do not know." At this point Pascal writes, one should listen to God.

Thus, knowledge is gained through a religious event. When one has quieted the rational search for knowledge and has submitted to the will of God and received divine revelation, then one can gain certain knowledge and find a way to happiness. Natural science and mathematics cannot yield these results, since they rest on principles known only by instinct or intuition: They cannot be established to be true.

However, human beings try in many different ways to avoid confronting the actual human situation. They engage in all sorts of diversions and adopt foolish philosophies in order to cover up their real ignorance. They invent a god of the philosophers, as Descartes did, who has no genuine relation to their existential problems. In the brief moment when we are on earth, suspended between the infinities of time and space, it is too dangerous to refuse to recognize our situation. Diversions like gambling, dancing, fighting, and philosophizing are akin to fiddling while Rome burns. We have a

brief moment in which to find an answer. When we realize our situation we will also realize that knowing *the* answer can make an inordinate difference—an eternal difference, in understanding why we are here, and what we can achieve. One answer, the religious answer—if we can bring ourselves to accept it, and if it is also true—can bring us eternal happiness.

Pascal's Wager

Since accepting this answer is not a matter of reason and evidence, Pascal presents the choice as a wager. There are two possibilities, either God exists, or God does not exist. We have no means of telling rationally which is the case. But it can make an enormous difference if God does exist. This could transform our present and future existence. If God does not exist, then we are left in our hopeless quagmire. A prudent gambler, seeing the odds, would place his or her bet on the religious possibility. As Pascal insisted, one has everything to gain and nothing to lose. Living an unbeliever's life could be extremely dangerous, if God exists. If God does not exist, it really does not matter what one does. And, Pascal insisted, one has no choice but to bet. Not to bet on God's existence is itself a bet on God's nonexistence, and it stops one from benefiting if there is a God. One is faced, as William James later said, with a forced option, and a monumental one.

Pascal was well aware that betting on the option with the best odds does not make one a religious person. He was also aware that there were many versions of the religious option—Judaism, Christianity, Islam, Hinduism, Buddhism, and animism, among others. Finding religion, and the right religion, requires superhuman effort. One can want to believe, and one can hope that one will be a true believer. One can prepare for this state of affairs. But only God can provide the grace that makes one see the light. Once one has received this grace, then one can judge the evidence for particular beliefs. Pascal claimed that accepting miracles, prophecies, and so on, is not the result of evidence but that it is not unreasonable to believe them. Believing or disbelieving results in whether one has grace or not, "so that it appears in those who follow it [true religion] that it is grace and not reason, which makes them follow it; and in those who shun it, that it is lust, not reason, which makes them shun it."

Pascal was one of the most brilliant figures in the seventeenth century and one of the greatest writers in the French language. He made great contributions in mathematics, physics, philosophy, and theology. He was an unsystematic but very insightful thinker who did not fit in the main lines of seventeenth-century philosophy, as he was neither a rationalist nor an empiricist. He provoked Voltaire, who led Condorcet to produce an edition of his works, showing that Pascal was more than just a religious thinker. He greatly influenced later nonrationalist philosophy and theology and has been much studied by existentialist thinkers in our century.

RICHARD H. POPKIN

Further Reading

Bishop, Morris. *Pascal, The Life of Genius.* Westport: Greenword, 1970. An excellent intellectual biography.

Davidson, Hugh M. *Blaise Pascal.* Boston: Twayne, 1983. A good overview of Pascal's thought.

Goldmann, Lucien. *The Hidden God.* London: Routledge, 1976. An important Marxist interpretation of Pascal and Jansenism.

Krailsheimer, A. *Pascal.* New York: Oxford, 1980. A survey of Pascal's writings and ideas.

Mesnard, Jean. *Pascal. His Life and Works.* New York: Philosophical Library, 1952. Presentation by one of the leading French Pascal scholars.

Popkin, Richard H. "Pascal." In *Encyclopedia of Philosophy*, vol. 6, pp. 51–55. New York: Macmillan, 1967. Also, "Introduction" to *Pascal. Selections*, pp. 1–17. New York: Macmillan, 1989. (This volume also contains an extensive bibliography.)

Rescher, Nicholas. *Pascal's Wager: A Study of Practical Reasoning in Philosophical Theology.* South Bend, Ind.: University of Notre Dame, 1985. A careful examination of the dynamic structure of Pascal's religious wager.

GEORGE FOX

Born: 1624, Drayton-in-the-Clay, Leicestershire, England
Died: 1691, London, England
Major Works: *The Journal of George Fox* (1674–5; published 1694)

Major Ideas

God can be experienced by every person through the presence of the indwelling Christ or Spirit.
Every human being must be respected because there is "that of God" in everyone.
Social inequalities are, therefore, abhorrent and must be eliminated.
Worship takes place wherever the soul discovers God; it requires none of the traditional paraphernalia.
There is no distinction between clergy and laity, for all can and should know God directly.

George Fox, founder of the Friends or Quaker movement, made a powerful impression on persons at all levels of English society, from illiterate farmers to Oliver Cromwell and King Charles II. The secret of this impact doubtless lies deeper than Fox's words and actions, but these played their part. "For in all things he acquitted himself like a man," William Penn, a convert to the Friends movement in 1667, wrote, "yea, a strong man, a new and heavenly-minded man; a divine and a naturalist, and all of God Almighty's making."

Born in July 1624 at Drayton-in-the-Clay or Fenny Drayton in Leicestershire, Fox had a devout upbringing. His father, Christopher, a weaver, was called "Righteous Christer" by neighbors. His mother, Mary Lago, Fox says, was "an upright woman" who was descended from martyrs. His parents taught him as a child "how to walk to be kept pure," and God taught him "to be faithful in all things, and to act faithfully two ways, viz., inwardly to God, and outwardly to man. . . ." A common saying floated around that "if George say Verily, there is no altering him."

A deeply sensitive, perhaps overly serious, person, at age nineteen Fox broke off "all familiarity or fellowship with old or young" as a consequence of an awakening to the vanity of superficial believers ("professors"). He spent the next several years, the period of the English Civil War, wandering around the country as a "Seeker." He himself described the experience as "some years" of "temptation" almost to the point of despair. Everywhere he went, Fox found evidences of superficial Christianity among both clergy and laity.

Early in the year 1646, Fox began to experience a series of "openings" (revelations): that only the regenerate are true believers; that education at Oxford or Cambridge "was not enough to fit and qualify men to be ministers of Christ"; that God, the Creator, "does not dwell in temples made with hands"; that Christ alone could unlock the Scriptures; and, most important of all, "There is one, even Christ Jesus, that can speak to thy condition." After a meditative walk a short time afterwards, he felt himself "taken up in the love of God" and found the truth "opened unto me by the eternal Light and power," and with it "all appeared that is out of the Light." Elsewhere in his *Journal*, he described how he saw "an ocean of darkness and death" swallowed by "an infinite ocean of light and love."

These "openings" prompted Fox to undertake a preaching mission throughout the English Midlands against superficial religion. His initial success at Mansfield filled him with a sense of urgency. In 1652, he won the hearts of Margaret Fell and her children and with it a haven at the Fell home, Swarthmore. The attraction of thousands to Fox, however, aroused suspicion and hostility to his movement. Fox spoke like a prophet, claiming direct inspiration, "not by the help of man, nor by the letter, . . . but . . . in the Light of the Lord Jesus Christ, and by his immediate Spirit and power, as did the holy men of God, by whom the Holy Scriptures were written." Both Anglicans and Puritans thought such claims blasphemous, and they made Fox and his followers pay a high price for them, at first in the form of mob reaction and then by formal court sentence. Fox himself was imprisoned eight times.

After a tragedy involving one of Fox's ardent disciples, James Nayler, who briefly yielded to the urging of his own admirers to claim that he was the Messiah, Fox turned his attention to organization of his movement. Unlike many other Nonconformist leaders, Fox appreciated and possessed gifts for organization. In the first phase, 1656–60, Fox used the general meeting to formulate plans for holding meetings for worship; conducting simple business matters; collecting funds to care for the poor, the imprisoned, and "the publishers of truth"; disciplining the disorderly; caring for the flock pastorally; and performing marriages without normal legal proceedings. In the second phase, beginning in 1666, he established monthly, quarterly, and yearly meetings. Fox himself logged thousands of miles throughout his own country and abroad. He visited Scotland and Wales several times. In 1669 he went to Ireland. In 1671 and 1672 he toured the West Indies, in 1672 and 1673 the American colonies, and in 1677 and 1684 Holland and Germany.

Notwithstanding his cultural deficiencies, Fox possessed a charisma and an insight that attracted the notable. Besides Margaret Fell, whom he married in 1669, and her children, he won William Penn, son of Admiral William Penn; Colonel David Barclay and his son Robert, the most notable of the apologists for Quakerism; Isaac Penington, converted after years as a "Seeker"; and Thomas Ellwood, secretary of John Milton and, subsequently, editor of Fox's *Journal*.

The early Friends had a profound social impact. Fox was more than a thinker; he was also a prophet and reformer who displayed his true genius in the way he worked out an organization to implement his religious ideals. At the time of his death on January 11, 1691, in London he left behind a permanent society that could transmit his contribution to posterity.

The Light Within

George Fox was a highly original thinker. Although he owed much to a melange of ideas current in

England during the mid-seventeenth century, he handled the views of others selectively with a constructive imagination in his own individual manner. His extreme sensitivity equipped him with unusual discrimination, but what mattered above all else was his vivid, firsthand religious experience. He "saw" more than most others, but he shaped his ideas without conscious imitation or conformity.

Students of Fox do not agree regarding major influences on his thought. He knew the Bible well, much of it almost by heart. Born in the heyday of Puritanism, Calvinism obviously had a major impact, but Fox departed from Calvin on the concept of human depravity, believing in the possibility of perfection before death. Rufus Jones ascribed Fox's mystical tendencies to the Familists, originated by the Dutch mystic Henry Nicholas (b. 1501), and Jakob Boehme (1575–1624), the German theosophist whom Fox cited by name. One obvious debt was the way he described sanctification as being lifted up to the paradise of God. Fox spent several years exploring the ideas of different contemporary sects, but he found none of them to his liking.

Fox squared all ideas he swept into his fertile mind with his personal revelations. At the core stood the conviction that the light of Christ is in everyone, based on John 1:9: "That was the true Light that lighteth every man that cometh into the world." Fox did not distinguish sharply between Christ and the Spirit, but, as in the Gospel of John, the Word through which God created the world became flesh in Jesus and is now present to us through the Spirit. Although Fox preferred the term "the Light" or the "Light Within," he employed numerous other phrases to describe the experience: "that which is pure in you," "the pure Seed of God," "the presence of the Great God, and our Lord and Saviour Jesus Christ," "the Truth," "that which is eternal," "the Life" or "the Life of God," "that of God in everyone," "the Power of God," "the Spirit," "your present Guide," "that which makes for peace and love," and "he that inhabits eternity."

The Light Within is the source of knowledge of God, Christian character, and unity. For Fox, knowledge of God, though "experimental" (experiential), is, as in the Old Testament prophets, an ethical knowledge. To know "what is pure in you" is to "guide you to God, out of confusion, [where] all the world is" (Epistle 4, 1652). On the one hand, the Light condemns all behavior "contrary" to God's expectations and will for humankind. The light "shows you the deceit of your hearts, and judges that which is contrary to God" (Epistle 60, 1654). It "shows you sin, and the evil of the world, and the vain fashions of it, that pass away" (Epistle 85, 1655). It draws you "out of the world's honour, and friendship, and words, and ways, and fellowships, and preferments, customs and fashions" (Epistle 102, 1655). On the other hand, the Light may restore those who pay attention to it not merely to the state of innocence before the Fall but to the state of perfection exhibited by Christ. Even if one "falls" after coming to a knowledge of the Light, one can be renewed in the image of God and "be made by him like to God, pure, holy, perfect, and righteous" (Epistle 32, 1653). Himself a "once-born" type, Fox believed in the possibility of perfect obedience to God. The "unchangeable power of God," he insisted, "will keep you in righteousness and truth and love and unity and dominion over all the unclean spirits and rough ways and mountains within and without" (Epistle 181, 1659). Against the Calvinists, who held that, though saved, Christians still sinned, Fox contended that Christ not only redeemed human beings and returned them to a pre-Adamic state "but to a state in Christ that shall never fail" (Epistle 222, 1666).

Although Fox saturated his addresses and letters with Scriptures, he could not accord the latter a final authority, such as Puritans ascribed to them. He wanted all "to have the same Spirit manifested in your understandings which was in them which gave forth the Scriptures" (Epistle 20, 1652). All of them "possessed the Life, which these words proceeded from, and the secrets of the Lord were with them" (Epistle 51, 1653), but they were not the Life itself in which believers must live.

Fox's insistence on the universal availability of the Light laid the foundation for his radical emphasis on human equality. He refused to pay special respect to the privileged by addressing them with the plural "you" or doffing his hat. Among the Friends themselves he refused to distinguish male and female, for "the Son of God is but one in all, male and female" (Epistle 25, 1653). He rebuked Quakers who did not wish women to speak in meetings where men were present nor to hold separate meetings and argued that "the power and spirit of God gives liberty to all" and that "women are the heirs of life as well as the men, and heirs of Grace, and of the Light of Christ Jesus, as well as the men, and so stewards of the manifold grace of God" (Epistle 320, 1676).

The concept of immediate presence accounts also for Fox's powerful salvos directed toward the established Church. True worship is "worship in spirit and truth" and not in temples made with hand, "steeple houses" (Epistle 19, 1652). Scriptures, Fox insisted, do not support such customs as sprinkling of infants, use of the word sacrament, timing sermons with an hourglass (Epistle 58), temples, tithes, oaths (Epistle 165, 1658), the Mass, or the Book of Common Prayer (Epistle 171, 1659). The Spirit teaches inward rather than outward prayers, songs, and fasts (Epistle 167, 1658). What God requires is "to love mercy, to do justice, and to walk humbly with God, who will judge the world in righteousness" (Epistle 353, 1678).

E. GLENN HINSON

Further Reading

Brinton, Howard H. *The Religion of George Fox, 1624–1691, as Revealed by His Epistles.* Wallingford, Pa.: Pendle Hill Publications, 1968. Three basic ideas of Fox drawn from the New Testament.

Jones, Rufus M. *George Fox, Seeker and Friend.* New York and London: Harper and Brothers, 1930. The classic study of the origins and development of Fox's thought.

King, Rachel Hadley. *George Fox and the Light Within, 1650–1660.* Philadelphia: Friends Book Store, 1940. A scholarly interpretation of Fox's philosophy.

Noble, Vernon. *The Man in Leather Breeches.* London and New York: Elek, 1953. A serious scholarly biography.

BENEDICT SPINOZA

Born: 1632, Amsterdam, the Netherlands
Died: 1677, near The Hague, the Netherlands
Major Works: *Principles of the Philosophy of René Descartes* (1663); *Thoughts on Metaphysics* (1663); *Theological-Political Treatise* (1670); *Ethics Demonstrated According to the Geometrical Order* (posthumous, 1677); *Short Treatise on God, Man, and his Well-Being* (posthumous, 1851).

Major Ideas

There can be only one infinite, divine substance, comprising all of reality.

Infinite substance must have an infinity of attributes.

God and nature (understood as substance) are identical inasmuch as God is infinite.

Substance is self-caused and depends on nothing other than itself, whether for its existence or for its differentiation into various modes.

What we perceive to be a world consisting of numerous and different finite creatures is actually the whole of God or Nature in its attribute of extension.

Since thought and extension are attributes of the one substance, the problem of dualism is overcome.

Philosophy and religion are distinct and separate approaches to the divine, the former dealing with rational truths about God, the latter with obedience and worship.

The problem with religion and theology is that they confuse their approach to God with rational truth and turn from piety to dogmatism and superstition.

Freedom of judgment and freedom of inward piety are inalienable rights of human beings.

The just exercise of sovereign power by a contractually or covenantally constituted government is suitable to the preservation of liberty in religious as well as civil matters.

Baruch or Benedict Spinoza, the greatest Western Jewish philosopher after Maimonides and, arguably, the most brilliant metaphysician among the continental rationalists of the seventeenth century, was the child of a Portuguese Jewish family that had migrated to the Netherlands at the end of the sixteenth century. There, in an atmosphere of religious toleration, Spinoza was trained in the religious and philosophical traditions of Judaism. He was, at an early age, tutored in Hebrew and in the Old Testament, the Talmud, and the mystical tradition of the cabala. His earliest encounter with philosophy, apart from the Neoplatonic elements of the cabala, was surely his reading of Maimonides. He was a superb linguist, conversant in Portuguese, Spanish, Dutch, Hebrew, and Latin. He learned the Latin language, in which his major philosophical works were written, from Christian teachers, one of whom, Francis van den Ende, was a Cartesian mathematician who offered the young Spinoza instruction in mathematics and contemporary philosophy as well.

By the age of twenty-four (1656), Spinoza had reached conclusions concerning God and the world and concerning the interpretation of Scripture that were unacceptable to the Jewish community in the Netherlands. After attempts to convince the young philosopher of his errors, the rabbis of Amsterdam solemnly excommunicated and anathematized him.

Following his excommunication, Spinoza fled Amsterdam and entered a life of relative seclusion. He chose to earn his living as a lens grinder and to spend his quiet hours in philosophical meditation and writing. Spinoza's correspondence, beginning in 1660, with Henry Oldenburg, secretary of the Royal Society, indicates not only his profound immersion in the thought of Descartes, Bacon, Boyle, and Huygens but also his progress in writing various works, including his masterpiece, the *Ethics*. Of Spinoza's works, only three were published during his lifetime: the *Principles of the Philosophy of René Descartes*, published in 1663 with a preface by his friend, Ludwig Meyer, and with the *Thoughts on Metaphysics* as an appendix; and the *Theological-Political Treatise*, which appeared anonymously in 1670. The correspondence contains evidence of Spinoza's hopes in 1675 to publish the *Ethics* together with an account of the complaint against his purported atheism, spread by a group of unnamed "theologians" and "Cartesians." Warned by friends that "the theologians were everywhere lying in wait" for him, Spinoza withheld publication.

In 1673, Spinoza was offered the chair of philosophy at the University of Heidelberg by the elector of the palatinate. The letter, written by one of the professors, Ludwig Fabritius, includes assurances of academic freedom in Spinoza's pursuit of his ideas, noting the Elector's confidence that Spinoza would not "disturb" public religion. Spinoza's polite refusal of the position noted both that he feared for his time, granting the burden of teaching, and that he wondered about the "limits within which the freedom of [his] philosophical teaching would be confined," given his assumption that religious disturbances arose not so much from actual beliefs as from "love of contradiction" and desire to distort and debate.

In his own time and for a full century after his death, Spinoza's philosophy was not only largely unappreciated, it was often thoroughly despised and, because of its radically different conception of the divine, branded heretical by Jews and Christians alike, and, indeed, viewed as atheistic. (Spinoza, of course, never denied the existence of God, but he defined God in a manner so unacceptable to most of his contemporaries that they viewed his belief as a form of atheism.) Revival of interest in Spinoza and the total reappraisal and revaluation of his work began toward the end of the eighteenth century with the early German Romantics—Lessing, Goethe, Herder, and Novalis. Far from identifying Spinoza as an atheist, the last of these referred to him as "a man intoxicated with the divine." The philosopher and theologian Schleiermacher called him "holy," and Hegel has been quoted as stating that "to be a philosopher, one must first become a Spinozist."

Theological-Political Treatise

In the *Theological-Political Treatise*, as intimated by the title, Spinoza addresses the great question of the relationship between theology or religion and politics. Specifically, he takes as his point of departure the freedoms of conscience and judgment with regard to religion experienced by citizens of the Dutch republic and the remaining problems that he sees about him in the claims made by competing religions upon the public good. People hold a series of "misconceptions" about religion that "like scars of [their] former bondage" lead to superstition and threaten to return the republic to a condition of spiritual slavery. Spinoza notes that those who use their belief in a Supreme Being as a justification for their own success or as a means of release from ill fortune most easily fall prey to superstition and, most typically, "clog men's minds with dogmatic formulas" and turn religion into an oppressive system.

These abuses, Spinoza argues, arise out of a mistaken view of religion. A right understanding of the Bible not only "leaves reason absolutely free," but also demonstrates that "Revelation and Philosophy stand on totally different footings." In arguing this point, Spinoza became one of the first scholars to apply historical and critical judgment to the text of Scripture and to recognize not only that a careful reading of the text indicated problems of authorship—such as the multiple, non-Mosaic authorship of the Pentateuch, the "five books of Moses"—but that such a reading also made clear that the religious statements and demands made in Scripture were adapted by its authors to the "popular intelligence" of ancient Israel. Thus, the Mosaic law does not attempt to convince Israel by reason of the truth of certain ideas about God, but to bind Israel by oath and covenant to a pattern of life promising reward for obedience and punishment for disobedience. This, argues Spinoza, is not a matter of knowledge but rather a matter of faith leading toward obedience. Similarly, the Gospel enjoins faith and obedience: It does not bestow rational knowledge of God.

Even seemingly rational statements about the divine attributes offered by Scripture are offered not for the sake of rational knowledge of the divine being but in order that people of all sorts, even the most ignorant, will be drawn to acknowledge the superiority of the God who is one, omnipresent, all-powerful, just, and forgiving. The attributes lead to devotion.

This radical distinction between theology and philosophy, obedience and knowledge, and faith and reason allowed Spinoza to free both religion and rational inquiry from their traditional antagonisms, and to cut in a single blow the Gordian knot of scholastic argument on the problem of revelation and reason. It is totally opposed to the nature of both approaches to the divine that one ought to be subordinated to the other—whether reason to faith or faith to reason. Spinoza could criticize the rabbis (and by extension the Christian theologians) for claiming that reason and philosophy ought to be subservient to Scripture and that a rational truth ought to be set aside when it appears to contradict a biblical statement. He also criticized those who held that a doctrine like the incorporeality of God ought to be held on the basis of a text in Scripture rather than on the basis of reason—even though reason clearly attests to the same view. It cannot be proved by reason, Spinoza noted, but known only from biblical religion that human beings are "saved by obedience alone"—while, on the other hand, it must be reason, standing on its own abilities of discernment, that decides for the incorporeality of divine being against the passages in Scripture stating that God has hands and feet.

It would be utterly foolhardy, Spinoza concludes, to assent to anything against the dictates of reason. Reason is the greatest of the divine gifts, a living light, and a far higher manifestation of "God's Word" than any "dead letter." This does not mean, of course, that religion must be rejected, but only that its certainties be understood as belonging to the realm of morality rather than to that of rationality or philosophy. Freedom of thought insures the separation of religion or theology from philosophy and, therefore, insures also the integrity of both.

The separation of religiosity from rationality or theology from philosophy, grounded on a principle of freedom of thought, leads Spinoza back at a somewhat higher level to his original point—the importance of a right understanding of religion and of freedom of thought in relation to the state. Specifically, Spinoza proposes to identify the "right and ordinance of nature" as the foundation of any view of the state and to define the extent and limit of freedom of thought in "the ideal state." Spinoza points out that "nature" as such is not ruled by the laws of reason and that "nature," understood in an abstract and general sense, has the right to do whatever is naturally possible. Even so, human beings, living according to nature and the "laws of desire," can do as they will to please, preserve, and protect themselves. Nature, in short, does not forbid strife, hatred, anger, or deceit. This does not mean, of course, that nature is evil—but only that nature is far greater and wider than the human sphere and that the ultimate good of nature cannot be discerned by beings who know only a part of the whole.

Granting that the laws of nature as a whole do not necessarily serve the specifically human interest of "man's true benefit and preservation," the individual and corporate life of humanity can better be governed by "the laws and assured dictates of reason." Whereas certain individual rights, such as freedom of judgment and feeling or freedom of inward piety are inalienable, the natural rights of individuals to self-preservation must be handed over, in and through a covenant or compact, to the "body politic" in general, to the end that it has a "sovereign right."

Spinoza assumes that irrational commands that could disturb public peace and harmony and precipitate the ruin of a society are virtually impossible in a democracy governed by the rule of the majority—with the result that he advocates the full possession of sovereign right by a democratic government both in temporal and in spiritual matters.

Since God reigns in the world not by the immediate exercise of divine power but through the agency of temporal rulers, religion must be exercised within the bounds set by temporal authorities and must support "public peace and well-being." Inward piety, of course, Spinoza comments, is an inalienable right of the individual, but the outward exercise of one's religion must conform to the rule of justice and charity as understood by the laws of the state. Even so, the authority of the sovereign extends even to judgments in matters of morality, to membership in or excommunication from the church, and to works of charity. Indeed, it is by the reservation of ultimate right in all of these matters to the temporal power that the right of individuals to think and speak freely is best and most fully preserved. "The true aim of government," writes Spinoza, "is liberty." Government, rightly constituted, will therefore enable human beings "to develop their minds and bodies in security, and to employ their reason unshackled; neither showing hatred, anger, or deceit, nor watched with eyes of jealousy and injustice."

Ethics

Spinoza's *Ethics* represents his most concerted attempt to come to terms with the great philosophical questions of the existence and identity of God, the nature and origin of the human mind in relation to God, the origin and nature of the emotions, the power of the emotions as they restrict freedom of choice, the nature of understanding or intellect as the basis of human freedom, and the intellectual love of God as the foundation of eternal blessedness. The *Ethics*, then, contains far more than is typically associated with the subject area of "ethics": It serves Spinoza as the vehicle for the exposition of an entire system of the rational knowledge of God, world, human nature, and human destiny, paralleling but not restrained by the concerns expressed by religion in terms of piety and obedience.

The order and style of the *Ethics*, indicated by its full title, *Ethics, Demonstrated According to the Geometrical Order*, consists in a single, massive, deductive argument from fundamental propositions to final goals, halted in its course only by an occasional excursus or appendix, like Spinoza's "digression on the nature of bodies" (after part 2, prop.

xiii) which follows, in fact, quite naturally from the preceding discussion of the body as "the object of the idea constituting the human mind."

Five terms, defined by Spinoza at the very beginning of the *Ethics*, are crucial to his thought: *substance*, *self-caused*, *attribute*, *mode*, and *God*. His view of substance draws on the Cartesian definition—"an existent thing which requires nothing but itself in order to exist." A substance, according to Spinoza, is "that which is in itself, and is conceived through itself," which is to say, substance must be both ontologically and epistemologically independent. A substance, moreover, must be different in nature and attribute from every other substance and, consequently, cannot be produced by any other substance. This means that substance is and must be self-caused, which is to say, the nature of a substance is such that it involves its own existence.

Attribute and mode are, for Spinoza, the fundamental characteristic and the modification of substance, respectively. The attribute of any substance is what "the intellect perceives as constituting the essence of substance." The mode indicates the way a substance is conceived or disposed, not in itself, but in relation to other things. Spinoza not only assumes that different substances cannot share attributes but also that the greater the substance, the greater will be the number of its attributes—with the result that absolutely infinite substance must have an infinite number of attributes. These definitions lead Spinoza to the conclusion that there can only be one substance and that the one substance is God, who alone is necessarily existent, self-caused, and infinite.

Once Spinoza has postulated the identity of God with substance, he can argue that the two fundamental Cartesian substances, thought and extension, are in fact only primary attributes of the one substance. There remains, therefore, no problem of dualism: The one absolute substance acts in ways that we perceive as thought and extension. The definition of mode now becomes of paramount importance to Spinoza's teaching concerning the world. If God is the one substance or "nature" and there is a fundamental, substantial identity between "nature producing" (*natura naturans*) and "nature having been produced" (*natura naturata*), then the difference between infinite being and finite being must be one of disposition or arrangement rather than one of substance.

God, as the ultimate and sole substance, is not determined in his actions by any other being or substance and is, therefore, free. Nonetheless, God produces the entire order of finite things necessarily as the result of the infinite perfection of the divine attributes: God cannot either refuse to produce the order of finite things or produce another, different order. Spinoza's God is not, after all, transcendent and "other." God is nature itself and necessarily expresses his perfection in the perfect modification, arrangement, and disposition of his attributes in and through the diversity of the finite order. The one infinite nature or God can, thus, be understood in two ways—either as the One God and as *natura naturans* or as the infinite order of finite things and as *natura naturata*.

This view of God as nature and of the order of finite being as an infinite series of modifications in the divine substance does not, on the surface, harmonize easily with the high value set by Spinoza's *Theological-Political Treatise* on human freedom. Spinoza does, in fact, deny what is usually identified as "free will." The entire finite order is conditioned and is predisposed to move and act as it does. Human beings are no exception. Nonetheless, Spinoza readily acknowledges that we experience freedom, particularly in the form of freedom from external coercion. He can also speak of the freedom of the mind and its exercise of reason over the emotions—a freedom that corresponds with his distinction between rational knowledge of the world order and a more or less confused and vague "imagination" arising directly from the senses.

Just as Spinoza can argue the right of nature in general to do whatever is possible, so also can he argue that every individual thing, as determined by its own individual nature, has an inclination (*conatus*) to maintain its being and increase its power. This inclination, which belongs to nature itself, can be guided by reason away from "servitude" to the emotions toward a freedom grounded in understanding and love of God, which is to say, towards a clear, unimpeded understanding and appreciation of the ultimate order of nature. The virtuous life known to reason is, according to Spinoza, the life most conducive to the identification of what is useful to humanity and to the preservation of one's being, and is therefore the life that, given the right development of understanding, proceeds most naturally from our most fundamental inclinations. Within the large-scale determinism of Spinoza's system, therefore, understanding and reason function as the natural means of opening the individual to the higher possibilities inherent in and, in a sense, determined by nature as a whole.

Life in "obedience to reason" brings about agreement "in nature" among individual human beings. Both at an individual level (as expressed in the *Ethics*) and in the context of civil society (as discussed in the *Theological-Political Treatise*), freedom, whether from the internal coercion of the emotions or from the external coercion of political forces, belongs to the ultimate harmony of nature as discerned by reason. Spinoza can, therefore, allow for moral progress, granting the possibility of intellectual or rational clarification, just as he can explain the modification, change, and development of physical things in the natural order—as evidence of the life of nature as a whole in its realization of the possibilities inherent in it and, equally, as evidence of the fundamental inclination of all things to preserve themselves in being. Freedom then, belongs not to a realm of volitional or moral indeterminacy, but to the intellectual grasp of inherent possibilities in the world order. What Spinoza does not answer is whether or not this improvement and the freedom it brings is a possibility for all human beings.

RICHARD A. MULLER

Further Reading

Hallett, H. F. *Benedict de Spinoza. The Elements of His Philosophy.* London: University of London, Athlone Press, 1957.

Parkinson, G. H. R. *Spinoza's Theory of Knowledge.* Oxford, Clarendon Press, 1954.

Roth, L. *Spinoza, Descartes and Maimonides.* Oxford, Clarendon Press, 1924. A significant comparative study that places Spinoza's thought into the context of the philosophies that were most influential in his development.

Wolfson, H. A. *The Philosophy of Spinoza.* 2 vols. Cambridge, Mass.: Harvard University Press, 1934. A valuable study that documents closely Spinoza's relationship to Jewish philosophy and mysticism.

JOHN LOCKE

Born: 1632, Wrington, Somerset, England
Died: 1704, Oates, Essex, England
Major Works: *First Letter on Toleration* (1689), *Second and Third Letters on Toleration* (1690 and 1692), *Essay Concerning Human Understanding* (1690), *Treatises on Government* (1689)

Major Ideas

There are no innate ideas.
Human knowledge is derived either from sense experience or from introspection (reflection).
Ideas are signs that represent physical and mental things.
Things have primary qualities (solidity, extension, figure, motion or rest, and number) and secondary qualities (all others, including color, sounds, smells, flavors, and so forth).
Bodies actually possess the primary qualities, but the secondary qualities are merely the effects observed by those who perceive them.
Good is whatever produces pleasure and evil whatever produces pain.
Liberty is for the sake of pursuing happiness.
The state of nature, prior to the existence of human government, is subject to the rule of natural or divine laws, which are revealed through the exercise of reason.
The chief reason for establishing governments is the preservation of private property.
Civil government comes about as a result of a social contract.

Although a number of philosophers have been called the founders of modern philosophy, in many important respects John Locke deserves that name above all others. His political theories have had a profound effect upon virtually the entire world, Western and non-Western, through their impact upon the British, the French, and the Americans. The founding fathers of the United States drew directly upon his ideas as they formulated the Declaration of Independence and the Constitution—especially the provisions concerning the separation of powers, separation of church and state, religious liberty, and the rest of the Bill of Rights. The British Constitution too was based upon his ideas. Through Voltaire, Rousseau, and Montesquieu, his theories spread through the French intellectual community.

His theories of knowledge and of the nature of matter marked the most radical break with the Aristotelianism that had dominated philosophical thought through the Middle Ages. More importantly, they set the agenda for the empiricism that was to dominate philosophical and scientific thinking from the seventeenth through the twentieth centuries, at least in the English-speaking world. In a very real sense, one may properly say that most philosophy in North America, Great Britain, and the British Commonwealth has been a commentary on Locke and an elaboration of his theories.

Locke studied medicine and helped Robert Boyle, the discoverer of some of the most important laws of physics, in his laboratory experiments. Through these experiences, he acquired firsthand knowledge of scientific method that was to be of the utmost importance later as he developed his theories on the nature of matter and the sources of human knowledge.

Locke was convinced that one of the chief reasons for the failures of past philosophers was their lack of attention to the real sources of human knowledge. Many of their mistakes arise because of the "rubbish" that led to so many of the dogmas in which they believed.

Locke divided human knowledge into three major parts: natural philosophy (logic, mathematics, and the natural sciences); the practical arts, including morals, politics, and what we would now call the social sciences; and "the doctrine of signs," including ideas and the words we use to communicate about them.

Many philosophers before Locke, including such eminent authorities as Plato in ancient times and Descartes more recently, had believed that human beings are endowed with certain innate ideas. These ideas were presumably implanted within the mind at or before birth, and needed only to be called forth to do their job. Plato's entire philosophical system was based upon this theory. He thought that education consisted essentially in helping people to become aware of the ideas that were already in their minds—much as the experienced birdwatcher helps novices become aware of the sounds they have always heard while walking in the woods but never knew they were hearing. Locke devoted considerable energy to proving that there was no reliable evidence that such innate ideas exist. There is no evidence whatever that there is universal assent to any so-called self-evident idea. In the realm of morals, this would appear to be so obvious as to need no argument. Those who argue for innate ideas usually explain away the fact that there is so much controversy over moral principles by saying that people who differ from them are morally blind, but this is simply begging the question.

As for logical and mathematical truths, Locke pointed to the obvious fact that most persons have not the foggiest idea what they might be. It takes long and methodical training to teach the ideas, and children and feeble-minded persons certainly have no grasp of them, as they would if those ideas were "innate."

The Mind as a "Tabula Rasa"

The human mind, according to Locke, is a *tabula rasa*, a blank slate or sheet of paper, ready from the moment of its creation to receive sensations from the outside world and impressions from within. Such are the materials out of which the only knowledge we are capable of having is formed. Once the mind has received the data of sense experience and reflection, it has the power to analyze and organize them. Through this process, it constructs more complex ideas and discovers relationships among

them that the raw data would not necessarily have revealed.

Locke concluded that things *cause* us to have certain ideas. The ideas thus generated, he said, are the *qualities* of those things. Thus, he said, "a snowball having the power to produce in us the ideas of white, cold and round, the powers to produce these ideas in us as they are in the snowball I call qualities; and as they are sensations or perceptions in our understandings, I call them ideas."

Primary and Secondary Qualities

He distinguished three kinds of qualities. Primary qualities, he said, are those that are "utterly inseparable" from a thing. The shape, number, solidity, and state of motion or rest are among such qualities. Locke thought that they were inherent in the objects themselves, and that our perceptions of them were somehow like those objects. Secondary qualities are the "powers" of things to produce certain sensations in us. The submicroscopic particles of things interact with our bodies in such a way as to produce sensations of color, sound, taste, smell, and touch. These "qualities" are not inherent in the objects themselves, but are produced within us by them. Finally, tertiary qualities are the powers of things to produce physical changes in other things. For example, fire's capacity to convert lead from a solid to a liquid is a tertiary quality.

Earlier philosophers had supposed that things were *substances*. The paper on which I am writing is yellow, has a certain size and shape, and has a very faint, musty odor. Once I have described the paper, just what is the *paper* that I have described? They thought that it was a kind of substrate, a *foundation* that *supported* or *had* the various qualities of yellowness, mustiness, and rectangularity. However, Locke's analysis led him to conclude that empirical evidence (sense evidence) for the substrate could never be found, for the only evidence we could ever have would be for the *qualities* of things. He concluded that neither material nor spiritual substances were knowable and that the very idea is so obscure as to be incapable of meaningful analysis. He was not ready to go as far as some of his followers did—namely, to give up the idea of substance altogether. He simply concluded that substance is "a supposed I know not what to support those ideas we call accidents" (the qualities we have just been discussing).

It was even more difficult for Locke to give up the idea of purely spiritual substances, such as the human soul and God, for much of Christian theology rested upon it. His writings are not clear on the point, for he wavered between thinking, like Hobbes, that nothing but matter exists, and supporting traditional religious ideas.

Locke firmly believed that happiness, which he called "the utmost pleasure we are capable of," is the only thing that is capable of moving people to desire anything. We call things good, he said, if they promote pleasure, and evil if they produce pain. Pleasure and pain, incidentally, are not only physical or bodily sensations, but *any* "delight" or "uneasiness" that a person might experience. Locke cites sorrow, anger, envy, and shame as examples of pain that are not always accompanied by physical manifestations or caused by physical intrusions.

Like many others before him, Locke believed that theoretically, at least, it makes sense to think of a state of nature—a state in which human beings might have lived before organized societies with laws and governments were set up. But unlike his predecessor, Thomas Hobbes, who believed that no law but the law of the jungle—self-preservation—exists in the state of nature, Locke concluded that certain laws govern human behavior at all times, whether or not a human government capable of enforcing them exists. In the state of nature, every person has equal rights relative to every other person. Human beings naturally employ reason, and as reasoning beings they simply would not allow themselves to slip into a Hobbesian state of nature in which every person is at war with every other.

Locke's view of the state of nature was of an Edenlike arrangement in which people lived strictly according to reason, with no need to resort to lawyers, police, or courts because they got along so splendidly with one another. In that state, people would enjoy "perfect freedom to order their actions and dispose of their possessions and persons, as they think fit, within the bounds of the law of nature; without asking leave, or depending upon the will of any other man."

In addition to enjoying such complete freedom, people living in the state of nature would be absolutely equal, with none having more than any other. However, the liberty each one would have is not license to harm anyone else. The law of nature commands that no one harm any other in his "life, health, liberty, or possessions." Nor, for that matter, may a person arbitrarily and without some good justification destroy himself or his own possessions. This is based upon the law of nature, according to Locke, and this in turn appears to be based upon certain religious doctrines, among them the belief that ultimately everything, including every human being, is the property of God, who has not granted permission for their destruction.

Theory of Property

Locke believed that labor is the justification for the institution of property. In the state of nature, anyone who converts an article from one state to another acquires a right to possession of it. The person who plants a garden and tends it has a right to the crops it produces. So long as a shell rests on the sands of the beach, it belongs to no one; but once someone picks it up and treats it as a thing of beauty, it becomes his property. Thus, unlike Hobbes, who held that property comes into existence only after laws are devised to define its limits, Locke believed that property is a natural right that exists independent of government. Indeed, the principal purpose of government, in Locke's view, is "the preservation of property."

Locke believed that in theory no one should have more property than one can use. This is particularly so with regard to perishable things, like fruits. A person who gathers an enormous quantity of plums cannot decently claim ownership over them because they cannot all be eaten before they rot, and waste is wrong. However, the invention of money, and especially the discovery that certain metals are virtually indestructible, enabled some persons to accumulate vastly unequal portions of the earth's wealth. Although this is theoretically undesirable, Locke concluded, the sanctity of property is such that its unequal distribution has to be tolerated.

The People as Sovereign

Once reason has persuaded people to set up a government by entering into a social contract, as it inevitably will, it would not be a Hobbesian government, in which the people are subjects and a single individual is sovereign. On the contrary, since people enter into a social contract and consent to the rule of law, sovereignty rests with the people and not with the king. Since that is the case, it follows that the people who have placed the sovereign on the throne also retain the right to remove the ruler from it if the sovereign fails to govern in accordance with their wishes.

Locke's doctrine had enormous influence on the founding fathers of the United States of America and contributed significantly to both the American and the French Revolutions. In this revolutionary democratic theory, the legislature rather than the executive is to exercise the supreme power of governing, since it will be more directly answerable to the sovereign people. Moreover, the executive and the legislature are to be separate and distinct, so as to enable each to serve as a balance against the other, preventing either from overwhelming the other or usurping the rights and prerogatives properly belonging to the people by right of nature.

People enter into society to preserve their property, according to Locke, and they submit to the authority of government and laws as a means of safeguarding what is rightfully theirs. Therefore, Locke says, "whenever the legislators endeavor to take away and destroy the property of the people, or to reduce them to slavery under arbitrary power, they put themselves into a state of war with the people who are thereupon absolved from any further obedience, and are left to the common refuge which God has provided for all men against force and violence." Thus, if the government breaches the trust placed in it by the people, it forfeits the power

the people have entrusted to it, "and it devolves to the people, who have a right to resume their original liberty and, by the establishment of a new legislative, such as they shall think fit, provide for their own safety and security."

In response to the charge that this advocacy of rebellion might lead to constant instability and frequent violent changes of government, Locke responded that "revolutions happen not upon every little mismanagement in public affairs." People are generally quite tolerant of their governors. It takes a long chain of abuses to provoke the people into taking the law into their own hands. Furthermore, Locke argued, knowledge that the people *might* rebel is the best hedge against an abusive government: If the officials know that their positions are in jeopardy, they will be less likely to abuse their prerogatives.

If the purpose of government is the well-being of humankind, Locke asked, then which is better: that people should always be exposed to limitless tyranny, or that rulers should be subject to removal if they use their power for the destruction rather than the preservation of the people's property? In any event, he said, whether a person be the ruler or an ordinary citizen, if he or she forcefully invades the rights of the people and lays the foundation for the destruction of a lawful government, then such a person "is justly to be esteemed the common enemy and pest of mankind, and is to be treated accordingly."

If a major controversy arises between the people and the ruler, who is to judge between them? Locke's answer was straightforward and unequivocal: "The proper umpire in such a case should be the body of the people," for they are the source of the trust that was placed in the ruler in the first place. If the ruler refuses to submit to the judgment of the people, then "the appeal lies nowhere but to heaven," and a state of war exists between the ruler and the people, who have the right to recall the power that they entrusted to the ruler and place it in another whom they believe can be relied upon to serve them more faithfully.

BURTON M. LEISER

Further Reading

Jenkins, John J. *Understanding Locke: An Introduction to Philosophy through John Locke's Essay*. Edinburgh: Edinburgh University Press, 1983. One of the best introductions to Locke's *Essay* available in English. It was derived from lectures that Jenkins had delivered in a first-level class at the University of Edinburgh, and is therefore reasonably readable and not tiresomely pedantic. It is not purely expository, though, for Jenkins uses Locke as a vehicle for discussing philosophical issues as such.

Martin, C. B., and D. M. Armstrong. *Locke and Berkeley: A Collection of Critical Essays*. Notre Dame and London: Notre Dame University Press, 1968. A wide-ranging collection of essays by some outstanding philosophers and specialists in the history of ideas, this volume includes essays on virtually every aspect of Locke's philosophy. The essays generally place Locke in historical perspective as well, particularly with respect to his influence on his successors in the British empiricist tradition.

O'Connor, D. J. *John Locke*. London: 1952. A thorough, well-written introduction to all aspects of Locke's theories, well organized and thoughtful.

Yolton, John W. *Locke and the Compass of Human Understanding: A Selective Commentary on the "Essay."* Cambridge: Cambridge University Press, 1970. More suited to advanced students, this book is devoted to a careful dissection of some of Locke's principal doctrines and an analysis of their place in his works and the consistency with which Locke adheres to them. It is very scholarly and most useful for those who are already familiar with Locke's philosophy.

NICOLAS MALEBRANCHE

Born: 1638, Paris, France
Died: 1715, Paris, France
Major Works: *The Search after Truth* (1674–75); *Dialogues on Metaphysics and Religion* (1688); *Treatise on Nature and Grace* (1680)

Major Ideas

We see all things in God.
The world of intelligible extension exists only in God and is coeternal with God.
To be is to be conceived.
All that we are aware of are ideas and feelings.
We have no direct or indirect knowledge of an external physical world.
God is the sole efficacious cause of all events; there are no secondary causes; so-called causal sequences are just occasions of God's acting.
There is no interaction between mind and matter.
There is no necessary connection between events.

Nicolas Malebranche, a priest, developed his philosophy from carefully studying that of Descartes and then presenting a theory that he believed overcame some of the crucial difficulties in the Cartesian system, difficulties that opponents had been raising for some decades after the publication of Descartes's *Meditations* and his *Principles of Philosophy*.

Malebranche began his own theory by contending that we do not have to justify the application of the ideas in our minds to the understanding of reality, if we recognize that our ideas are illuminations, visions of the Divine Mind, rather than just modifications of our mind. Hence, his famous phrase, "We see all things in God," rather than in ourselves. In this connection he cited Saint Paul's statement that in God we live and move and have our being.

Some of the ideas that we know of are necessary, eternal, and unchanging, such as the truths of mathematics. Since we ourselves are contingent, temporary, and changeable beings, we ourselves cannot be the place where these ideas exist. Rather, these ideas must exist in a necessary, eternal, and immutable being. Such a being is God.

The mathematical ideas we know are truths about intelligible extension, that is, extension conceived mentally rather than observed empirically. These truths have always been true and will always be true. Their truth does not depend on any happenings in the world. Therefore they cannot be, as Descartes claimed, the result of the will of God, but must be coeternal with God. They must constitute a world of Platonic Ideas located in the Divine Mind, but not produced by it. They are uncreated, always existing, as God also is.

When we examine the contents of our minds, we find that we are aware of ideas, which can be defined, rationally conceived, and comprehended. We are also aware of feelings (*sentiments*), which can be described but not really understood. We cannot give clear and distinct conceptions of these feelings. We cannot explain why they have the characteristics that they do.

Neither the ideas we are aware of, which are of intelligible extension, nor the feelings give us any direct or indirect knowledge of an external physical world or any information about such a world. In fact, Malebranche claimed, we would not even know that there actually is such a world except for the fact that it happens to be mentioned at the very beginning of the book of Genesis as something that God has created. So, our knowledge of the physical external world comes to us by revelation rather than by any human rational or scientific process.

We find that there is no necessary connection

between our ideas, between our ideas and our feelings, or between different feelings that we have. We are unable to perceive or conceive how one event causes or produces another. We do not perceive or conceive any power in antecedent events to cause subsequent ones, or any linkage between one state of affairs and another. We are not able to deduce the occurrence of one event from another. The notion of productive power is to be found only in God, not in created beings.

If God is omnipotent, Malebranche argues, then all power must be in God. If any entity other than God had any power whatsoever to produce another event, then God would not be fully omnipotent and would be limited, limited to the extent that there would be something that could occur independent of God's will.

The conclusion of this line of reasoning is that God must be the sole and unique cause of all events that we know or experience. As Malebranche said, all the angels and all the devils in the world could not move a piece of straw unless God so wills. All the angels and all the devils lack the power to do anything in and by themselves. What we see as supposed causal sequences are *occasions* of God's actions. When one billiard ball strikes another, and the second one then moves, it is not because one billiard ball has caused another to move. Rather, on Malebranche's account, on the occasion of the one ball's moving, God causes the second ball to move. (Hence Malebranche's theory is called "occasionalism.")

The world is intelligible because God, fortunately, acts by general rules or laws. Since God causes all events, he would have to decide in each and every case what would happen. However, to obviate this, Malebranche insists that God runs the universe economically, using the fewest general laws to make events happen. Hence we can expect that the sequences we have perceived will be repeated on other occasions, although there is no necessary connection involved in the sequence. A consequence of this theory is that mathematics is about necessary truths (uncaused by God), but natural science is about contingent ones, contingent always on the will of God.

Malebranche applied his view to the relationship of mind to body. Descartes had claimed that mental events and physical events interacted, and that the mind could influence the body and the body could influence the mind. A thought could lead to an action, and a physical event like a pin's entering one's flesh could cause a mental event, pain. Descartes's opponents argued that this was one of the most questionable aspects of the Cartesian theory, because Descartes could not explain how an unextended mental event and an extended physical event could interact or influence each other.

Malebranche offered a solution to this problem. For Malebranche, there is not and cannot be any such mind–body interaction, since neither the mind nor the body has the power to cause anything. The apparent interaction is just a case of God's acting in the mental world, and God's acting separately in the physical world. When, for instance, somebody strikes a key on a piano and a sound is heard, the first event (physical) is not the cause of the second (mental), but rather the first is the occasion of God's causing the second.

Malebranche's theory sounded extremely peculiar to his contemporaries, though they saw that it was amazingly consistent and could account for everything going on in the world. He was criticized by Antoine Arnauld, the Jansenist follower of Descartes, by the skeptics Simon Foucher and Pierre Bayle, by G. W. Leibniz, and by John Locke, among others. Certain elements of his theory influenced George Berkeley, who was called the Irish Malebranche, and David Hume, who adopted Malebranche's views about causality and the idea of necessary connection.

Malebranche originally studied philosophy and theology at the Sorbonne in Paris. He then joined the pious, mystical Augustinian order, the Oratory, and was ordained a priest. He spent the rest of his life as an Oratorian. In 1664 he came across Descartes's work *Treatise on Man*, and he then devoted himself to the careful and serious study of Cartesian philosophy, mathematics, and science. In 1674–75, he presented the results of his studies in the *Search After Truth*. The views developed therein led to a host of controversies, philosophical and theological. He was attacked by skeptics for being too dogmatic, by Cartesians for having given up some of the master's crucial theories and ideas, and by theologians for offering a system that seemed at variance with some basic Christian views. He was accused of making God the cause of all evil events.

Malebranche spent the rest of his life arguing against his philosophical and theological critics. He wrote a series of clarifications to add to the *Search After Truth* to further explain his views. He presented a simplified version of his theory in dialogue form in the *Dialogues on Metaphysics and Religion*, in which he had a theologian–philosopher (himself) explaining his theory to a student and answering the objections that were raised. He tried to explain the supposed irreligious aspect of his theory in the *Treatise on Nature and Grace*. (This led to a very heated exchange with Antoine Arnauld.)

Malebranche insisted that he was not making God the author or cause of evil. The physical events that cause a murder or a rape, like all other physical events, are occasions of God's acting. When God causes a finger to press a trigger, God also causes a bullet to emerge from the gun. Further, God causes the bullet to enter a person's flesh, and further causes the heart of that person to stop beating. The whole sequence consists of occasions of divine action. The moral character of what is involved is not to be found in these occasions, which are just extended events, but in the intent, the thoughts, of the person with the gun. It is the intent that makes the event evil, not the sequence. (But, critics asked, Who is responsible for the intent? Is this not also an occasion of God's action on somebody's mind?)

Malebranche was also accused of Spinozism, of holding a theory that amounted to Spinoza's, in that he argued that God is the only actor in the universe,

and that everything existing is actually just an aspect of God. Malebranche argued in reply that though God was the sole cause of all events, God was not the sole substance, that minds, bodies, and spirits also exist. And, on the basis of his theory of intentions, people and spirits can be moral agents, if not actors. Hence, he claimed he was not advocating either Spinoza's pantheism or his total determinism.

In France, both Cartesianism and Malebranche's theory were attacked and condemned by Church authorities. However, Malebranche was seen as one of the major metaphysicians of the time, rivaling Spinoza, Leibniz, and Locke. He has been classified as one of the major Continental rationalists. His chief works were translated into Latin and and into English at the time, and were studied all over Europe. At Trinity College, Dublin, where Berkeley studied, Malebranche was very influential, and Berkeley's views can be seen as developing from both Locke's and Malebranche's. Berkeley, in fact, claimed to be improving on Malebranche's theory by introducing finite spirits, people, capable of initiating actions. Young Hume studied Malebranche and used sections of his text as part of his famous analysis of causal reasoning. Hume told a friend that if he wanted to understand what Hume had accomplished in his philosophy, he should first study Descartes, Malebranche, Bayle, and Berkeley.

Malebranche remained influential in French thought, and in recent years is again being seen as one of the major figures in modern philosophy. His works are again being translated, and he is being discussed both as an original and controversial thinker and as someone who, opposed by Locke, Leibniz, and others, helped inspire the next stage of the development of philosophy.

RICHARD H. POPKIN

Further Reading

Church, Ralph W. *A Study of the Philosophy of Malebranche.* (Reprint of 1931 edition.) New York: Associated Faculty Press, 1970. A statement of the major features of Malebranche's philosophy, put in terms of twentieth-century issues.

Hobart, Michael E. *Science and Religion in the Thought of Nicolas Malebranche.* Chapel Hill: University of North Carolina Press, 1982. An examination of how science and religion relate in Malebranche's theory.

McCracken, Charles. *Malebranche in British Philosophy.* Oxford: Oxford University Press. Discusses Malebranche's influence on the last of the Cambridge Platonists, and on Berkeley. There is also an appendix on Malebranche's influence on Colonial American thought.

Walton, Craig. *De la recherche du bien: A Study of Malebranche's Science of Ethics.* Dordrecht: Kluwer, 1972. An examination of how Malebranche explained moral thought and action.

ISAAC NEWTON

Born: 1642, Lincolnshire, England
Died: 1727, London, England
Major Works: *Philosophiae naturalis principia mathematica* (1687, 1713, 1726), *Opticks* (1704, 1717, 1721, 1730)

Major Ideas

Invention of differential and integral calculus.
Clarification of concepts of inertia and force.
Formulation of three laws of motion, making possible the science of rational mechanics.
Proof of the composite nature of white light.
Construction of the first reflecting telescope.
Insistence on the experimental basis of true science.

Isaac Newton brought the foundations of physics into the form that remains the starting point today for every student of science. After the inconclusive struggles of Galileo and his other predecessors, it was only with Newton that Aristotle's retrogressive concept of falling bodies "seeking their natural place" finally and decisively died. The mathematical and philosophical aspects of Newton's work deeply affected the science and eventually the whole learned culture of the century that followed. His creative genius was so striking that he became a challenging role model for every physicist since, as well as an icon representing science in the public mind in a way never approached by anyone other than Einstein.

Large portions of Newton's voluminous papers were never available to historians until recent decades. Their study has replaced the traditional overly heroic image with that of a much more complex man, major parts of whose life and activities are surprisingly at odds with the modern idea of dedication to rational science.

Newton's father was a successful but not wealthy farmer in rural Lincolnshire, who died several months before Isaac's birth. His mother Hannah remarried three years later (this time into significant wealth), but left young Isaac to spend most of his childhood in his grandmother's care. He thoroughly disliked his aged stepfather, after whose death Newton's mother returned when he was ten, bringing three younger children with her. These must be major contributing factors to his dour and suspicious personality, which isolated Newton from his peers and led to repeated harsh disputes that poisoned most of his life.

Young Isaac received a few years of schooling in the neighboring village of Grantham, where he exhibited strong curiosity and mechanical aptitude. A brief period during adolescence of attempted grooming to run the family estate was a debacle, and the intervention of some who recognized his true talents enabled him to enter Cambridge University at eighteen. But the academic condition of Cambridge during the turmoil of the Civil War and the Stuart Restoration was an embarrassment; its main advantages for him seem to have been the freedom to devote himself to study and the books to do it with, and he largely taught himself. (The famous retreat from Cambridge to his country home during the Plague Years may not have made much difference in his intellectual activities.) After receiving his bachelor's degree in 1665, he remained in Trinity College, where he became a permanent fellow in 1667. To this was added the M.A. in 1668 and the Lucasian Professorship of Mathematics in 1669.

Cambridge in general and Trinity in particular were in a period of disastrous decline during Newton's tenure, and neither lecturing nor tutoring made significant demands. He applied most of his time to study of natural philosophy, mathematics, alchemy, even history and theology. He always did this with a characteristic thoroughness and intensity that not only conquered every subject but earned him a reputation for staying up all night and forgetting whether he had eaten his meals. His studies were done for his own satisfaction and were usually left in somewhat unfinished states as he jumped on to other interests. He did not merely neglect to publish important work but generally showed considerable aversion to doing so. The jealous, hostile reaction from Robert Hooke to Newton's first paper, submitted to the Royal Society in 1672, probably only reinforced Newton's native tendency to withhold his work from criticism.

After a deep psychological crisis in 1693 (the reasons for which remain subject to debate), Newton's creative work was effectively ended. Having become involved in university politics in the late 1680s and elected to the Convention Parliament of 1689, his interests became more and more centered in London. He gained political appointments in the Mint as warden (1696) and master (1699), remaining in the latter post to the end of his life. These ordinarily would have been sinecures, but he brought his characteristic intensity to the positions and was one of the first prominent exemplars of the radical concept of responsible civil service.

As an undergraduate, Newton was greatly stimulated by both the natural philosophy and the analytic geometry of René Descartes, and his first investigations in mathematics and optics grew directly from that interest. Twenty years later he asserted his independence not only by rejecting the physics and philosophy of Descartes but by denigrating his analysis as well. Most of Newton's original work in mathematics was done in 1664–66, but published only much later or not at all. (John Collins urged him in vain to publish in the early 1670s. Work on a book in the early 1690s was aborted, and some of the material later ended up in the *Opticks*. The *Arithmetica universalis* of 1707 was put out by Whiston, and represented a rather thrown-together collection of Newton's earlier work.)

The Invention of Calculus

Newton made important contributions to the theory of infinite series, including the invention of a "Taylor series" twenty years before Brook Taylor. Aspects of that work and of John Wallis's "method of indivisibles" led him to invent new methods for dealing with the problems of quadratures and tangents of curves, resulting in what we now know as the calculus. (The notation and terminology most used today is that of his rival Leibniz, who developed the calculus a few years later independently of Newton.) He also did important work on the classification of cubic forms.

In those same years, 1664 to 1666, Newton also made many experiments on the refraction of light, especially its dispersion by prisms. In particular, he showed not only that sunlight could be separated into spectral colors but also that recombining those colors produced white light again. Many other ingenious experiments answered various objections and clearly established that different colors were different kinds of light, not merely modifications or differences in strength of a single kind. Newton also observed comets and learned how to grind lenses. It was his invention of the reflecting telescope that brought him recognition and membership in the Royal Society of London in 1672. He then submitted a paper on his theory of colors, in which unfortunately two major issues were not kept separate. Newton's particulate view of light was contrary both to popular notions of vibrations or vortices in a pervading ether and to interference phenomena he and others had observed in thin films, and in hindsight we can see that he was wrong. But his revolutionary demonstration of the composite nature of white light, while equally unpopular in some circles, was exactly on target. Partly due to confusion of these issues, there was a very bitter exchange between Newton and Hooke, which contributed much to Newton's reluctance to publish his other work. Though Newton's own contributions to optics were essentially complete at this time, he did not write most of the *Opticks* until twenty years later, and he delayed its publication another ten years beyond that until after Hooke's death.

Newton's Laws of Motion

Newton was also well started on his study of motion and gravitation in the mid-1660s, though he went on to other things before making it into a coherent whole. But the threat around 1680 that Robert Hooke was going to take credit for some of the ideas Newton had been sitting on drew him back to the subject, and it was the writing of the *Principia* from 1684 to 1687 that forced him to clarify his ideas and produce his laws of motion as we now know them:

1. Any massive object persists in its state of rest or of motion unless an external force acts upon it.
2. An external force produces acceleration proportional to that force and inversely proportional to the mass upon which it acts.
3. For every force acting on a body there is an equal and opposite reaction from the body upon its neighbors.

The help and encouragement of Edmond Halley was very important in finishing the *Principia*, but not in the sense that Halley wrested from Newton's grasp a work that had lain already complete for many years. The key to this step forward came only with persistent effort and lay in emphasizing the property of inertia and clearly differentiating it from external forces, especially in the case of uniform circular motion; in fact, this was not fully achieved until the second edition. Recognition of the laws of motion and of the inverse-square law of universal gravitation were strongly linked with each other, since motions of planets and comets provide the clearest test for any theory of motion. The competing vortex theory of Descartes was quite explicitly debunked.

Newton's predecessors (especially Galileo) and contemporaries (such as Christiaan Huygens and Hooke) had achieved considerable partial understanding of these laws. But it was Newton's crystallization of the physics, coupled with his new mathematical techniques for extracting predictions from these general laws, that clearly was the launching point for physics as a well-founded quantitative science. He demonstrated its power by explaining the ocean tides, the moon's motion under the combined influence of earth and sun, the mutual perturbations of Jupiter and Saturn, the orbits of comets, the nonspherical figure of the earth, and the equinoctial precession.

Major portions of Newton's career were taken up with studies of a very different nature. He gathered voluminous material on alchemy and performed many experiments himself; his personal "Index chemicus," never published, is probably the most thorough survey of alchemical literature ever made. He seems to have hoped that a quantitative approach, together with concepts of universal interparticle attractions somewhat analogous to gravity, would turn this, too, into a unified and rational science. Newton also delved deeply into theology and interpretation of prophecies, and related questions of ancient history. He worked for many years on *The Chronology of Ancient Kingdoms Amended*, which was published the year after his death. In his own eyes this was another major work, but to us it seems that he was not as good a historian as he was a physicist, allowing his work to be too much influenced by religious presuppositions. Part of Newton's isolation from the society around him lay in his holding strong Arian beliefs (a form of Unitarianism) at a time when only Trinitarian doctrine was publicly acceptable; if his true beliefs had become known, even he would have lost position and respect as did his friend and follower William Whiston. (It must have been a bitter private irony for him to be for so many years a fellow of Trinity College.)

Also of interest is Newton's role in the Royal Society of London, which had been founded in 1662 during his undergraduate days and had received him into membership in 1672. His rivalry with Robert Hooke lasted until Hooke's death in 1703, and was one factor in his remaining at arm's length from most Society activities for three decades, even after he lived in London. At the turn of the century the Society might fairly be described as moribund; its first generation had passed on, many of the members were only dilettantes, and it staggered through several years with presidents chosen purely for their political influence and with no interest whatever in science. Newton deserves some credit for the Society's revival after his election to the presidency in late 1703. He did not hesitate to capitalize on his fame to retain that post until his death, and at times was insufferably autocratic. To Newton's great discredit, he used the Royal Society as a tool in the second and third great vendettas of his life. The former was with Astronomer Royal John Flamsteed, over control of the publication of the monumental star catalog that was his lifework. The latter was the dispute with the German philosopher–mathematician Gottfried Wilhelm Leibniz over priority in the invention of calculus. We now know that a report favoring Newton from a supposedly neutral committee set up by the Society was in fact largely ghostwritten by Newton himself. One wonders in vain whether his obsessive and vindictive personality stood in the way of his being an even greater figure than he is in the history of thought, or whether that anguished intensity was what somehow made his creativity possible.

The Necessity for Experimentation

For much of his life, Newton was usually content to let others make public statements about philosophical and theological issues; this reflected both his natural reticence and the need to avoid the doctrine of the Trinity. Newton's most careful statements about the foundations of his work come in the General Scholium to the *Principia* and the "Queries" at the end of the *Opticks*, particularly in the second and later editions. He insisted that natural science must be firmly based on experiment, though he showed very little concern for applied science. "For since the qualities of bodies are only known to us by experiments, we are to hold for universal all such as universally agree with experiments . . . We are certainly not to relinquish the evidence of experiments for the sake of dreams and vain fictions of our own devising."

Newton's work in optics especially shows him putting this into practice; there is both a sustained series of experiments in order to rule out other interpretations, and a care for both quantitative description and accuracy in measurement. He was also suspicious of multiple *ad hoc* explanations, insisting that science should be based on principles with broad explanatory power: "And what certainty can there be in a Philosophy which consists in as many Hypotheses as there are Phaenomena to be explained[?]"

Newton's law of universal gravitation says that two massive bodies affect each other at any distance, even across empty space, and this was philosophically disturbing. He was criticized by Leibniz and others for introducing "occult quantities" into science. His most famous statement, "I frame no hypotheses," should not be given too much weight out of context. It comes from the second edition of the *Principia* and is essentially a defensive position, designed to force the issue that we must accept the empirical evidence that there is an inverse-square interaction quite apart from whether we even attempt any detailed picture of how that action is transmitted: "It is enough that gravitation actually exists and acts according to the laws we have exposed." In a letter to Richard Bentley, he said, "Gravity must be caused by an agent acting constantly according to certain laws, but whether this agent be material or immaterial is a question I have left to the consideration of my readers." Newton had certainly explored some imaginative hypotheses of his own, for instance, about possible relations of gravity to chemical affinity or electrical action, but knew when he did not have proof for them.

Newton saw knowledge both as power over things and as revelation of God; he said he had written the *Principia* "not with a design of bidding defiance to the Creator but to enforce and demonstrate the power & superintendency of a supreme being." His impact upon eighteenth-century philosophy is not entirely what he would have intended. David Hume in particular was responsible for transforming Newton's metaphysics by dealing God out of the picture, leading to the extreme a century later of Laplace's remark about God, "I have no need of that hypothesis." While Newton did develop a mechanistic world picture with atoms, void, and action at a distance, it was by no means a self-sufficient world. He would have disagreed with the deist caricature of a God who sets the world in motion like winding up a clock and leaves it to run itself, just as vehemently as he did with the Cartesian vortex cosmology. Newton's

God was immanent, continually and directly responsible for making things run in such an orderly way. So "Newtonianism" in its later incarnations is not something Newton himself would have subscribed to.

DONALD E. HALL

Further Reading

Andrade, E. N. da C. *Sir Isaac Newton*. London, 1954; reprint: Westport, Conn.: Greenwood, 1979. Best of the many older short popular biographies.

Brewster, Sir David. *Memoirs of the Life, Writings, and Discoveries of Sir Isaac Newton*. 2 vols. Edinburgh: T. Constable, 1855. The classic biography of Newton.

Christianson, Gale E. *In the Presence of the Creator: Isaac Newton & His Times*. New York: Macmillan, 1984. An excellent new general biography.

Cohen, I. B. *The Newtonian Revolution in Science and Its Intellectual Significance*. Norwalk, Conn.: Burndy Library, 1987. Views of a leading Newton scholar.

Herivel, John. *The Background to Newton's Principia*. Oxford: Clarendon Press, 1965. Detailed study of the development of Newton's work from 1664 to 1684.

Manuel, Frank E. *A Portrait of Isaac Newton*. Cambridge: Harvard University Press, 1968. Speculative psychological biography, influential in modern revision of the traditional heroic picture of Newton. For balancing critical comments, see Westfall.

Palter, Robert, ed. *The Annus Mirabilis of Sir Isaac Newton, 1666–1966*. Cambridge, Mass.: MIT Press, 1970. Proceedings of a symposium on the 300th anniversary.

Wallis, Peter, and Ruth Wallis. *Newton and Newtoniana, 1672–1975*. Folkestone, England: Dawson, 1977. An exhaustive bibliography.

Westfall, Richard S. *Never at Rest: A Biography of Isaac Newton*. Cambridge: Cambridge University Press, 1980. A thorough and extensive scientific biography, including a valuable bibliographical essay as an appendix.

GOTTFRIED WILHELM LEIBNIZ

Born: 1646, Leipzig, Germany
Died: 1716, Hanover, Germany
Major Works: *Discourse on Metaphysics* (1686), *On the Ultimate Origination of the Universe* (1697), *Theodicy* (1710), *The Principles of Nature and Grace* (1714), *Monadology* (1714), *New Essays on Human Understanding* (posthumous: 1765)

Major Ideas

There is an infinity of individual substances.

The irreducible, indivisible, indestructible unit of substance is the "monad."

God is the ultimate, necessary being who is the sufficient reason for the existence of all other beings and who is the creator and orderer of all monads.

Each monad is different from and independent of all others, but nonetheless linked together with all other monads in a universal and harmonious system.

Since God is good, God will always act, both in creation and in providence, for the best.

This order of creation is, therefore, "the best of all possible worlds" as evidenced by the order of the system as a whole.

The great transitional thinker between seventeenth- and eighteenth-century rationalism on the continent of Europe was Gottfried Wilhelm Leibniz. He was a man of wide interests—philosophical, mathematical, scientific, and theological—who had learned much from the study of the great philosophers of his time, Descartes, Hobbes, and Spinoza. Nonetheless, he found their systems to be arbitrary and incapable of dealing with the very problems they raised. His own philosophy attempted to retain the ground gained by rationalism but to move toward a philosophical theism capable of resolving the problem of Cartesian dualism without falling into a philosophical monism or pantheism like that of Spinoza and capable of being reconciled with traditional Christian views of God, world, and human responsibility.

Leibniz's father, Friedrich, was professor of moral philosophy at the University of Leipzig and a staunch Lutheran. Leibniz demonstrated considerable precocity and entered the university at an early age to study law. When the university refused to grant him the degree of Doctor of Law on grounds of his age—he was twenty—he left Leipzig for the University of Altdorf, near Nürnberg. There he was received considerably more graciously, and he earned his degree for a dissertation *On Difficult Cases in Law*. It was during this period of Leibniz's life that he came under the influence of the "encyclopedists" of Herborn, Johannes Alsted, Johann Bisterfeld, and their pupil Johannes Comenius, later bishop and theological mentor of the Bohemian Brethren.

Two of Leibniz's early works in particular manifest the influence of the Herborn school—the *Dissertation on the Art of Combinations* (1666) and the *New Method for Learning and Teaching Jurisprudence* (1666). From these thinkers Leibniz gained not only an entry into new currents of metaphysics in the seventeenth century but, more specifically, an interest in the issue of universal order harmony in relation to the existence and life of individuals. This latter issue was to remain a central concern of Leibniz's philosophical enterprise.

During Leibniz's residence at Altdorf, his abilities attracted the attention of the archbishop-elector of Mainz, who took the young Leibniz into his service as librarian and political adviser. The position was so congenial to Leibniz's own philosophical agenda that he refused academic offers, including a professorship at Altdorf. The elector was active in the international politics of the age, and Leibniz found himself sent on missions to the capitals of Europe, where, in addition to fulfilling his political duties, he was able to meet the great philosophers and scientists of the age—Antoine Arnauld, Nicolas Malebranche, Benedict Spinoza, Isaac Newton, Christiaan Huygens, and Henry Oldenburg of the Royal Society. In addition to engaging with these thinkers in philosophical correspondence, Leibniz also entered into an ecumenical dialogue with Lutheran, Catholic, and Calvinist writers, including the famous Bishop Bossuet, in an attempt to foster, on rational grounds, a reunion of Christendom. Three years after the death of the archbishop-elector in 1673, Leibniz left Mainz and entered the service of John Frederick, duke of Brunswick and Hanover. He remained in the service of the Hanoverians until his death in 1716.

Although Leibniz was a systematic thinker in the larger sense, he never produced a major exposition of his thought as a whole. We have from his pen a vast series of short essays, responses to queries, an extensive correspondence, and contributions to the philosophical and literary journals of the day, from which his thought must be abstracted. Crucial essays, like the *Discourse on Metaphysics* and the *Monadology*, serve not as full expositions of his "system" but as outlines or points around which discussion can crystallize.

The Monadology and Discourse on Metaphysics

In 1670 or 1671, Leibniz began to argue that the distinction between mind and matter was a distinction between something like a thought that can continue without moving or changing spatially and, on the other hand, something that must move or change to exist beyond the moment. This perspective enabled him to conceive of all things as essentially motion, albeit two different kinds of motion, and thereby to overcome the Cartesian dualism of thought and extension. In his *Monadology*, Leibniz attempted to identify "simple substances" in the form of monads or atoms as "the elements of things." These simple substances are noncomposite and do not come into existence by "natural means": They are, in short, the building blocks of the universe. God or "the Necessary Being" is "the ultimate unity" of the monads and "the original simple substance" capable of exerting a "force" that creates, regulates, and directs the monads.

Leibniz denied the existence of absolute rest. The force that accounts for all change, although variously distributed, remains constant in Leibniz's universe as the law that supplies the rationale for our changing world. From this view—as opposed to Descartes's deduction concerning his own existence—Leibniz can assert the basic principle of philosophy as "the principle of sufficient reason"— that is, "everything has a reason" or, negatively, nothing exists without there being sufficient reason for its existence. We see here not only a more logical and, indeed, a more self-evident first principle than the Cartesian *cogito*, but also a truly objective foundation for a basic philosophy of the universe and God. As Leibniz commented of the *cogito*, it "is valid . . . but it is not the only one of its kind." There are many "primitive truths"—not necessary propositions of logic, but propositions that rest on "immediate experience": I exist, I am a unity, I know that there is such a thing as "substance," substance is a unity, individualities exist and are substantial, and the like. None of these propositions is purely logical, but all are undergirded by the principle of sufficient reason.

Leibniz's emphasis on the theme of universal harmony led him not only to postulate individualized substances and to refuse to divide the world into two ultimate categories like physical and spiritual, body and soul—or in the Cartesian language, extension and thought—it also led him to postulate an infinite series of gradations in substance, a continuity of things and causes throughout the universe. There are no duplications and no sudden gaps in the order: There may be and are more than a single instance of each substance but there are not two substances that are identical—diversity, in other words, is not a delusion. All is not simply extension, as the Cartesians claim; truly different things exist because of substantial differences. This must be so because of the principle of sufficient reason: Two substances, identical in every respect, would not have "sufficient reason" for their distinction in the divinely appointed order.

Leibniz thus poses a fundamental argument against the Cartesian dualism: The problem is the attribution of reality to both thought or notion and extension. Extension is not truly reality, it is combination or aggregation. It is not the aggregate that is real but its component parts—and, moreover, the material aspect of aggregates can be divided infinitely without coming to any end—so that substance or reality is not to be identified with extension by any account. The absolute individuality, the real substance or Monad, is the locus of the force behind things and therefore of the inner law that determines the conditions of change and motion.

Leibniz identifies the soul with the "monad," the underlying substance of the individual, which cannot be divided and which holds the key to change and development. By the fact of our relation to other existence, we recognize other monads underlying phenomena. Phenomena are real in the sense that they derive from the monads and represent the direction of movement from present to future. What Leibniz has said in this doctrine of monads is, ultimately, that individual things are genuinely individual—that reality is the vast interconnected system of real individualities that cannot be reduced either to a Cartesian dualism or a Spinozistic monism.

This language of the monadic structure of reality, so seemingly foreign to the perspectives of traditional theology and philosophy, was in fact an attempt to overcome problems inherent in the new science and the rationalist world-view for the sake of a traditional emphasis on the value and integrity of the individual. The pantheistic tendencies of rationalism, as clearly manifest in the thought of Spinoza, and the consideration of the world as an ordered system of nature governed by unbreakable laws, as taught in the new science, both tended toward the philosophical and scientific negation of the cosmic or ultimate importance of the individual human being. Scholastic philosophy had argued that man was a microcosm mirroring and, in a sense, summing up the universe; traditional theology had stressed the place of the individual in the divine plan. Leibniz endeavored to have the best of both worlds: the universal order and harmony of the new and, by way of his doctrine of monads, the emphasis on individuality within the order characteristic of the old.

The problem for Leibniz, having thus overcome the problem of Cartesian dualism, was to explain the relationships of these monads, centers or souls, to all things. Each monad is isolated; as Leibniz put it, "The monads have no windows." The connection, of course, is God: It is God who creates the individual monads, who gives them the "sufficient reason" for their own existence, and who alone bears in himself the sufficient reason for His own existence. God provides the power or force that gives life to all things and God guarantees the interrelationship and the movement of things.

In effect, what Leibniz has done is to accept many of the views of modern science but—as he set out to do—merge them with a system of the universe compatible with the older philosophical tradition. He has overcome Descartes's autonomous ego, not by denying it, or refuting it, but by showing it to be logically and physically incomplete: It cannot be the sole starting point of the system, and it is not the only proposition immune to doubt. Leibniz has also placed God in the center of the system rather than at the periphery as the result of a logical deduction; in fact, Leibniz's God who guarantees the ongoing interrelationships of things and the harmony of the universal order is little more than a scientifically more sophisticated version of Aristotle's First Mover.

This is not to imply anything artificial or arbitrary in the construction of Leibniz's system: The position of God in the system as the creator and orderer of all things is central to Leibniz's philosophical and theological program. God is, according to Leibniz, the self-existent and self-actualizing substance upon whom the possibility of all other existences rests. God, then, is the perfect being, perfect in his being and in his knowledge and wisdom in whom the ideas of all other substances subsist eternally:

God . . . is the ground of what is real in the possible. For the Understanding of God is the region of the eternal truths and of the ideas on which they depend; and without Him there would be nothing real in the possibilities of things, and not only would there be nothing in existence, but nothing would even be possible.

Leibniz on the Existence of God

In view of the importance given to God in Leibniz's philosophy, it is not surprising that Leibniz devoted considerable space to the proofs of the existence of God. Elements of these proofs appear in the *Monadology*, the *New Essays*, and the short treatises *On the Ultimate Origination of the Universe* and *On the Cartesian Demonstration of the Existence of God*. Just as the being and will of God are the "principle of things"—the sufficient reason for the existence of things—so is knowledge of God the principle of all the sciences.

According to Leibniz, the ontological argument (based on an account of God's nature) lacks one element: It identifies God as the most perfect being, argues that existence is necessary to perfection, and concludes that God, to be perfect as defined, must exist. Leibniz allows the realist or idealist logic of the argument, including the assumption that existence is a predicate, but claims that the argument, in order to be complete, must demonstrate the *possibility* of the perfect being. This is accomplished teleologically, using the basic premise of Leibniz's philosophy, the principle of sufficient reason. Individual, finite things do not contain in themselves sufficient reason for their own existence: They are the effects of a greater cause. Such contingent things point away from themselves toward a non-contingent or necessary ground of their existence, a self-contained sufficient reason that is also the sufficient reason for its own existence. The argument can also be constructed from the universal harmony of the independent monads: There must be a sufficient reason for the harmony but no single monad, within the order, can explain the order itself. As the orderer of the whole, the self-existent being is also independent; pantheism is avoided. The perfect being, thus, is possible and, as possible, necessary.

Theodicy

Leibniz is perhaps most famous for his work entitled *Theodicy* (a term he invented), indicating a "justification of God" in the face of the existence of evil. The central theme of *Theodicy*, for which Leibniz is famous or, when misunderstood, infamous, is the assertion that this is "the best of all possible worlds." Voltaire, who read Leibniz's theories as proposing a blatant cosmic optimism, accepted the concept of a "best of all possible worlds" until the Lisbon earthquake of 1755 convinced him that to show the goodness of an all-causing God in the face of evil (natural disaster) was not the easy enterprise he had originally thought it to be. *Candide* is Voltaire's satirical rejection of Leibniz.

Arthur Schopenhauer, in the nineteenth century, also rejected Leibniz, and he did so in no uncertain terms: This, said Schopenhauer, is the worst of all possible worlds and is, in and of itself, the great and insuperable objection to the idea of a benevolent creator—God. "This world," comments Schopenhauer, "is the battleground of tormented and agonized beings who continue to exist only by devouring each other."

Correctly understood, however, Leibniz's definition escapes the facile criticisms of virtually all its detractors. Leibniz began with the concept of a good God who, as good, will always act for the best. In an absolute sense—and here we have a reflection of Scotus—God could have created a different world, but in a moral sense, God as good—here a reflection of Aquinas's Aristotelianism—could create nothing but the best world possible.

The root problem addressed by Leibniz's theodicy is the obvious contradiction between the God who wills and therefore creates all things for the good and the obvious existence of evil in the world. Leibniz does not intend either to ignore or to underestimate evil: He only attempts to explain it in the context of his philosophy of a good God and a harmonious world order. There are three kinds of evil, according to Leibniz: "Evil may be taken metaphysically, physically, and morally. Metaphysical evil consists in mere imperfection, physical evil in suffering, moral evil in sin." Like Augustine and the Scholastics (and here we encounter yet another evidence of the deep traditionalism of Leibniz and the reason for the amenability of his philosophy in its Wolffian form with the orthodox system), Leibniz viewed evil as a privation, something without an efficient cause, a deficiency in good things. God, who is the first efficient cause of all things, does not will evil—only permits it.

Here Leibniz adds an original feature to the scholastic argument. Whereas God permits moral evil—that is allows the free activity of moral agents in the world—he is not even said to permit physical evil or suffering. This he wills "hypothetically": There is in God no absolute will that evil events should happen and suffering occur, only a will resting on the "hypothesis" that greater good will come out of the suffering, such as the moral perfecting of the sufferer.

The question still remains, however, as to the existence of the deficiencies in things, the imperfections that lead to physical and moral evil: In other words, we come finally to the question of metaphysical evil. Here Leibniz offers, initially, the standard explanation found in those thinkers from Augustine to the present who would maintain the postulate of a good creator and a good creation: Imperfection belongs, by nature, to all finite things. All created being is finite, all finite things are imperfect (even when they are as good and as relatively "perfect" as any finite thing can be), and the resident imperfection in things is the source of all privations of the good, of all error, misunderstanding, partial truth, and therefore of evil.

The source of evil, for Leibniz, as for virtually all who hold the idealist (or realist) conception of a good absolute, lies in the very nature of finite things. Leibniz asks, "We, who derive all being from God, where shall we find the source of evil?" "The answer," he continues,

is that it must be sought in the ideal nature of the creature, in so far as this nature is contained in the eternal verities which are in the understanding of God independently of his will. For we must consider that there is an

original imperfection in the creature before sin, because the creature is limited in its essence; whence it follows that it cannot know all, and that it can deceive itself and commit other errors.

In other words, Leibniz recognizes and states (far more clearly and bluntly than Augustine or the Scholastics) the limitation of God in his creation of the world: The ideal natures of creatures exist in God's mind, independent of His will. God cannot will that finite things exist without their imperfection—their forms are eternally determined as independent universals. Is God then the cause of evil simply by being creator? Leibniz says no, for the reason that existence itself is a good—it is better to exist than not to exist.

The final explanation of the relationship of God to the created order is made in terms of a Scholastic distinction between God's antecedent and consequent will: Antecedently, God wills the good and only the good, because he is God and he is good—his antecedent good will rests only on his goodness. But the good of existence for things that God wills antecedently is limited by the imperfection of the ideal or universal, the eternal pattern, as it were, of the creature in the mind of God.

God's antecedently good choice to create, therefore, is bound up with the problem of necessarily imperfect created things. What God creates is good not in the antecedent sense of a total and perfect good: God must create imperfect beings. According to his consequent will, unable to create the good in an absolute sense, God wills to create the best possible. Comments Leibniz, "God wills antecedently the good and consequently the best," that is, the best possible. Imperfection there will be, but it will belong to the universal order. The order itself and the lessons it teaches are good. For Leibniz, therefore, "the best of all possible worlds" is not a world without evils but a world in which evil appears as the necessary result of the existence of finite things and is, ultimately, overshadowed by the good, as manifest in the underlying harmony of the world order.

An underlying thread in this system, related both

to the proofs and to the theodicy, is Leibniz's optimistic determinism. God, as the perfect Being, has created according to his perfectly good will the best of all possible worlds: Optimism is the only possible result. But this also implies determinism. God has created the best of all possible worlds and no other. His choice of this world comprehends all possibilities in it—and there can be no defection from the divine order. Even the imperfection that we experience as evil results necessarily from the divine choice. Leibniz's determinism, however, does not imply a denial of free will and the imposition of necessity or constraint upon all choice. The divine determination of all things determines them to be what they are substantially but, in the case of spiritual substances, does not impose necessity; rather, the divine determination assures that voluntary acts will occur on the basis of natural inclination or rational judgment.

We will not fall short of the mark if we characterize Leibniz's thought as the most consistent and noblest attempt of the late seventeenth and early eighteenth century to draw together into one grand totality the most consistent rationalism of the day and the most advanced mathematical and scientific concepts with a philosophical construction of the relationship of God and world that would prove useful and acceptable both to the scientific and to the religious mind of the era. Leibniz had in fact hoped not only to effect a reunion of Protestantism and Roman Catholicism but also to complete the conversion of the world to a rational and scientific system of belief through logical persuasion. At the very least he had hoped to produce a form of rational theism that could function in the context of the new scientific and mathematical view of the universe and that would not encounter the angry response accorded to the philosophies of Descartes and Spinoza.

RICHARD A. MULLER

Further Reading

Broad, C. D. *Leibniz: An Introduction.* Edited by C. Lewy. Cambridge: Cambridge University Press, 1975. A distinguished thinker is prompted by Leibniz's ideas to venture out on his own. The result is a lively account that is both illuminating and critical.

Rescher, Nicholas. *The Philosophy of Leibniz.* Englewood Cliffs, N.J.: Prentice-Hall, 1967. A superb study that stands as perhaps the most convincing recent attempt to reconstruct the Leibnizian "system" out of the vast array of tracts, treatises, and letters.

Russell, Bertrand. *A Critical Exposition of the Philosophy of Leibniz.* 2d ed. London: George Allen & Unwin, 1937. The classic reconstruction of Leibniz's philosophical system.

PIERRE BAYLE

Born: 1647, Carla (now Carla-Bayle), southwestern France
Died: 1706, Rotterdam, the Netherlands
Major Works: *Thoughts on the Comet* (1682), *Philosophical Commentary on the Words of Jesus, "Constrain them to come in"* (1686), *The Historical and Critical Dictionary* (1697 and 1702), *Response to the Questions of a Country Gentleman* (1703)

Major Ideas

All theories—philosophical, theological, and even scientific—can be challenged by arguments that show they are contradictory and/or unbelievable.
Since no beliefs can be proved to be true or false, all should be tolerated.
Morality is completely separate from religious belief; a society of atheists could be more moral than a society of Christians.
Careful unprejudiced erudition and exact reasoning are needed to eliminate the errors of the past and present.
Within a Christian frame of reference there is no way of explaining the existence of evil.

Pierre Bayle is best known for his vast erudition and for his presentation of an inordinate number of paradoxical arguments against all sorts of theories, ancient and modern. He sought to show that the philosophies of the past and the new philosophies of Descartes, Spinoza, Leibniz, Malebranche, and others were fraught with contradiction and absurdity. He also sought to show that any attempt to develop a foundation for rational knowledge in philosophy or theology breaks down when scrutinized in the light of skeptical arguments.

According to Bayle, the various contenders for intellectual power, the various churches and dogmatic philosophical movements, each challenged and persecuted the others without being able to justify their own views. The recognition of the unfounded basis of any philosophical or theological position should lead to complete toleration, since there is no way of telling who is right and who is wrong. All we can do, Bayle asserted, is abandon reason, and accept faith (though he never made clear what faith).

Bayle insisted that there is no rational relationship between religious belief and moral action. By carefully examining the historical record, one can see how immoral so many religious people have been from biblical times up to the present. Hence, a society of atheists might very well be more moral than a Christian one.

All Christian attempts to explain why there is evil in the world, Bayle claimed, either end up making God the cause of evil or justifying the terrible heresy of Manicheanism, the view that there are two gods, one good and one evil. If we cease trying to explain experience in religious terms, we might see that the history of mankind is nothing but the story of the lies, misfortunes, and catastrophes of the human race. The consideration of this skeptical argument against all attempts to understand the world rationally and to justify a religious outlook should lead to a toleration of all views, an acceptance of the human condition as it is, and the living of an undogmatic life.

Pierre Bayle was the son of a Protestant pastor and was raised during the persecution of the Huguenots by the Catholics in France. Because the Protestant colleges had been closed in southern France, he was sent to the Jesuit one in Toulouse. There he was presented with arguments showing there was no rational basis for his Protestant faith. He converted to Catholicism on the basis of intellectual considerations, but he soon convinced himself by arguments that there is no rational basis for Catholicism either, and he reverted to his original faith. Because of his decision he had to flee France, and he then commenced study at the Calvinist University of Geneva. He taught philosophy at Sedan, but he fled to Holland when Louis XIV withdrew the Edict of Nantes, which had tolerated Protestants. He taught in the Huguenot academy in Rotterdam. There he began publishing a series of works criticizing all kinds of beliefs, religious, theological, philosophical, and scientific.

His first book, *Lettre sur la comète,* of 1682 (translated as *Thoughts on the Comet*) was an attack on superstitious beliefs, intolerance, bad philosophizing, and inaccurate history. In this work Bayle advanced his startling thesis that a society of atheists could be more moral than a society of Christians, thereby commenting on how immoral Christians can be. This work was followed by a challenge to a history of Calvinism written by a leading Jesuit, a criticism of the fanciful pipedreams of the Huguenot refugees in Holland, and a critical appraisal of a collection of several writings by Bayle's contemporaries about Cartesianism. This latter publication brought him in contact with Malebranche and other important philosophers of the day.

From 1684 to 1687, Bayle edited and published a very important learned journal, *Nouvelles de la République des Lettres.* He therein discussed the philosophical and scientific work that was appearing by Leibniz, Malebranche, Arnauld, Boyle, and Locke, among others, and established contact with many of these authors. As the result of his acute judgment in his early writings and his journal, Bayle quickly became a central figure in the learned world. Bayle decided in the mid-1680s to devote himself primarily to scholarly writing. He refused a professorship at the University of Franeker, and spent the remainder of his life in Rotterdam carrying on his learned researches and fighting against all sorts of opponents.

In 1686, Bayle published his *Commentaire philosophique sur les paroles de Jesus-Christ, "Contrain-les d'entrer"* (*Philosophical Commentary on the Words of Jesus, "Constrain them to come in"*). The French Catholics had used this text from the New Testament to justify coercive activities to make the Protestants convert. Bayle examined the logic of religious intolerance, and developed the most far-ranging argument for complete toleration of all views. He extended toleration to Muslims, Jews, Unitarians, atheists, and Catholics (who were being persecuted in the Netherlands), a view more advanced than that put forth in 1692 by John Locke in his *Essay on Toleration.*

Bayle presented his view as the outcome of skeptical examination of the claims of various groups to know the truth. All one can claim, he argued, is what appears to be true according to one's conscience. Unfortunately, there is no way of discerning who has a true conscience and who has an "erring" one. Hence, one should grant all persons the right to believe what they will, because the erring conscience cannot be distinguished from a right conscience.

The leader of the French Reformed Church in the Netherlands, Pierre Jurieu, who had been Bayle's original sponsor, was horrified by Bayle's views and saw them leading to irreligion and atheism. As Bayle and Jurieu attacked each other in a pamphlet war, Jurieu denounced Bayle as a secret atheist. For the rest of his life Bayle ridiculed Jurieu's views and tried to show the absurd consequences of Jurieu's claims. Bayle also began developing attacks against the more liberal Protestant theologians in Holland, who were developing a rational version of Christianity compatible with the views of modern science. Up to the very last minute of his life, Bayle was undermining liberal as well as conservative theologies, as well as the philosophies they contained. By the 1690s he was engaged in controversies on many fronts, theological, philosophical, and historical. He had antagonized so many of the French Protestant refugees in the Netherlands that he was forced to give up his teaching post and be an independent, skeptical, polemical scholar.

Bayle's Historical and Critical Dictionary

Bayle's most important work, which grew out of his independent researches, was a biographical dictionary. It became an all important reference work of the time, and Voltaire called it "the arsenal of the

Enlightenment." The work, first published in 1697 in two volumes and enlarged to four volumes in 1702, started out as an attempt to correct all of the errors in earlier dictionaries and encyclopedias, as well as a means of skeptically examining theological, philosophical, and scientific views. The *Dictionary* consists almost entirely of articles about dead persons and movements. The choice of topics was made on the basis of who or what had not been adequately dealt with in the earlier dictionary of Louis Moréri of 1674. Many famous personages, such as Plato, Shakespeare, and Descartes, are omitted, while all sorts of obscure people appear, sometimes at great length. Bayle set forth his articles in the form of biographies running on top of the pages, with lengthy footnotes below, and notes to the notes in the margins. The pages look something like an edition of the *Talmud*, with text immersed in notes, and notes to notes. The heart of the *Dictionary* is in the annotations, where Bayle digressed, discussing and challenging ancient and modern theories on a wide variety of subjects.

Bayle developed skeptical challenges to Scholastism, to Cartesianism, and to the contemporary theories of Leibniz, Malebranche, Cudworth, Locke, Newton, and Spinoza (who got the longest article in the *Dictionary*), as well as many long-since-forgotten thinkers. Bayle criticized various Catholic and Protestant theologies. In two famous articles on Manicheanism, Bayle offered evidence that no Christian theologians of any persuasion were able to set forth a consistent or credible explanation of the problem of evil.

In articles from "Aaron" to "Zueris" Bayle kept up a skeptical attack on theories, ancient and modern, about human nature, history, and religion. He contended that he was just showing the inadequacy of human reason in answering questions about these matters. Especially in the articles on the ancient skeptic "Pyrrho" and the father of paradoxes, "Zeno of Elea," Bayle showed how the skeptical arguments of ancient times could wreak havoc with the new philosophies, especially that of Descartes. In the course of questioning the modern notion of substance and also the distinction between the primary qualities of extension and motion and the secondary qualities of sound, taste, smell and color, Bayle put forth critical arguments that Berkeley and Hume then used in undermining the new metaphysical theories of Descartes and Locke.

Bayle claimed that his skepticism would undermine human rational activity, including philosophical skepticism, and that in destroying reason he made room for faith. He cited Pascal in support of his claim. But Bayle never gave any indication of what a faith that survives skeptical attacks involves. Throughout the *Dictionary* he raised questions about the moral or religious sincerity of the major characters in the Old Testament, of many of the church fathers, and of many of the major figures in the Reformation. Bayle presented news about the immoral sexual conduct, unethical practices, and hypocritical behavior of all sorts of people in the Bible, in the ancient pagan world, and in the political and religious history of Europe. For Bayle, human history was nothing but the story of the lies, misfortunes, and disasters of the human race.

From the moment of its appearance, the *Dictionary* shocked the learned world and the religious establishments. Attacks and bannings made it a bestseller. Bayle promised the French Reformed Church of Rotterdam that he would explain what bothered them most in the next edition. In 1702, he added a great deal more material, including four clarifications in which he strengthened his skeptical criticisms and emphasized the irrationality of religious belief. He also greatly enlarged his criticism of Leibniz's philosophy. Four years later, Bayle answered a host of critics in his *Response to the Questions of a Country Gentleman*. He continued fighting back against his theological and philosophical critics, of all persuasions, up to the very moment of his death. He finished *Conversations of Maxime and Themiste*, an answer to several liberal Protestants, an hour before he passed away. He contended that he was a Protestant in the full sense of the term: He was against everything that had been said and done.

His many opponents accused him of attempting to undermine all philosophy, theology, and science. Bayle said repeatedly that he was a true believer, seeking to destroy reason in order to buttress faith.

He never explained his faith, and many of his opponents from Jurieu on saw him as a secret atheist, or a radical deist, trying to undermine religion while pretending to save it.

Bayle put together all kinds of skeptical arguments into a massive critique of philosophical, scientific, and religious knowledge. He examined and attacked ancient and modern theories and showed the weaknesses in almost any dogmatic view. His criticisms became central for Enlightenment discussions. Leibniz wrote his *Theodicy* as an answer to Bayle on the problem of evil. Berkeley, Shaftesbury, David Hume, Voltaire, Diderot, and many others borrowed heavily from him. Kant developed his antinomies from some of Bayle's arguments.

Thomas Jefferson recommended the purchase of a set of Bayle's *Dictionary* as one of the first acquisitions by the Library of Congress. Bayle was influential throughout the eighteenth century, and he was a seminal thinker in the development of the modern tolerant outlook. But finally his *Dictionary* was replaced by newer encyclopedias, done as team efforts instead of as one man's view of the intellectual universe. Bayle's skepticism was brushed aside by modern positivistic scientific views. However, in the last fifty years, Bayle has been recognized more and more as one of the central figures in the making of the modern mind. To understand Enlightenment thought, one has to go back to one of its richest sources.

RICHARD H. POPKIN

Further Reading

Bracken, Harry M. "Bayle not a Sceptic?" *Journal of the History of Ideas*, XXV, 1964. This rewarding article seeks to show the sense in which Bayle was both a skeptic and a fideist.

Brush, Craig. *Bayle and Montaigne: Variations on the Theme of Skepticism*. The Hague: Nijhoff, 1966. A comparison of these two skeptics, showing their similarities and differences.

Labrousse, Elisabeth. *Bayle*. Oxford: Oxford University Press, 1983. Presents Bayle's place in intellectual history, and offers an important interpretation of what he was for and against.

Popkin, Richard H. *The High Road to Pyrrhonism*. Indianapolis: Hackett, 1989. Several of the articles deal with Bayle's skepticism and the influence it had.

Rex, W. E. *Essays on Pierre Bayle and Religious Controversy*. The Hague: Nijhoff, 1966. Bayle's views put in the context of the religious controversies of the time.

GIAMBATTISTA VICO

Born: 1668, Naples, Italy
Died: 1744, Naples, Italy
Major Works: *On the Ancient Wisdom* (1710), *The Autobiography of Giambattista Vico* (1725, 1728, 1731), *The New Science* (1725, 1730, 1744)

Major Ideas

There is no fixed human nature that remains identical regardless of time, place, and circumstance; human nature develops in accordance with self-knowledge and with insight into the essences of things.

A Divine Providence gives human beings those nonrational creative capacities, operating on associative principles, that will produce false beliefs from which true ones will follow.

The ultimate goal of Providence is the preservation of humanity.

Human history is knowable because human beings have made it, just as nature is known to God because he has made it.

Human beings will act for the sake of their own particular ends, but the socialized nature of those ends will bring about unforeseen changes in society itself.

Historically, society evolves in cycles from one governed by imagination, superstition, and custom to one governed by rational understanding and that, in turn, declines into a society governed by imagination; in a parallel fashion, the political nature of society evolves from anarchy to oligarchy and then to democracy and monarchy, and finally declines to anarchy.

The subject of the new science is the world of nations.

Giambattista Vico was a professor and scholar whose many interests included metaphysics, epistemology, jurisprudence, rhetoric, social and political philosophy, and history. During the early decades of the eighteenth century, when the concept of autobiography was being discussed and reevaluated, Vico proposed a model that was truly a novel one for his time. Autobiography was not to consist of personal confessions. It was to comprise instead a pedagogical evaluation of sources and methods of learning experienced by the author, along with a description of all the arts and sciences.

Vico's own autobiography describes his education and the influences on his thought during the period from his birth to 1731. Like similar personal narratives, however, it relates some dates and details that are inconsistent with other historical records. (For example, the author was born in 1668 and not in 1670 as he claimed.) Despite the errors, this work serves as a good introduction to the man and his ideas. From it we learn that Vico's early education was an unsystematic one, for it progressed by means of tutors and Jesuit schools. The irregularity

in his schooling was due to a severe skull fracture that he suffered from a fall when he was only seven years of age. Although Vico's surgeon predicted that he would either die or remain an idiot for the rest of his life, the young boy recovered fully. After an absence from school for several years, Vico returned to his formal education but, as his teachers soon discovered, he was capable of more advanced work than were others in his age group. Subsequently, at times with a tutor and on other occasions by himself, Vico continued his learning in philosophy, literature, and then law.

In 1686, Vico became the tutor for the Rocca family at the castle at Vatolla (south of Salerno), where he was employed for nine years. This was the only time that Vico lived outside of Naples, and he occupied himself with classical philology, literature, law, and with works by Renaissance writers, such as Giovanni Boccaccio, Dante Alighieri, Francesco Petrarca (Petrarch), and Niccolò Machiavelli. And although according to Vico's *Autobiography*, the years between 1686 and 1695 were spent in relative isolation, he did travel to Naples frequently.

Vico thus remained in contact with its intellectual life, and in 1694 he received his LL.D. from its university. In 1699, the year of his marriage to Teresa Caterina Destito, he won the competition for the chair of rhetoric at the University of Naples. This position provided Vico with a very modest stipend, and for the rest of his life, he was forced to supplement his income through writing ceremonial orations, official histories, biographies, and by means of private tutoring. He retired from his appointment to the university in 1741.

Vico's duties as professor of rhetoric included the delivery of an annual inaugural oration. The six speeches that he presented between 1699 and 1706 proposed the ends or goals of various studies, and philosophically speaking, they expressed a blend of his early Cartesianism with Neoplatonism. The first three orations treated of human nature; the next two of political ends; and the sixth of the Christian goal of learning. Until 1707, Vico's two favorite philosophers were Plato, for his elaboration of the ideal, and Tacitus, for his practical wisdom. He then began to study the work of Francis Bacon, whose writings greatly influenced Vico's thinking; and his seventh oration, "On Method in Contemporary Fields of Study," opens with high praise for the evaluation of the arts and sciences in Bacon's *On the Dignity and Advancement of Learning* (1605).

Vico's "On Method" contains suggestions of what was to become his mature conception of human learning. Here he evaluated the application of a method modeled on the procedure used in geometry to other disciplines. Vico found it inadequate when applied to the physical world and to the realm of practical affairs. For him, the definition of a concept used in mathematics or geometry is determined by convention only. Thus, within the framework of these disciplines, a judgment is true by virtue of its deductive consistency with other judgments, and not by its correspondence with independently existing essences. Vico's conception of the deductive sciences would be consistent with the development of Riemannian geometry in the nineteenth century and with the implications of *Principia Mathematica* (1910–13), by Bertrand Russell and A. N. Whitehead.

In physics, however, or in the natural sciences, the true requires conceptual correspondence with forms existing in God's mind; and since we cannot know such entities, judgments in these sciences must be probable only. In human affairs, moreover, practical and moral problems are too complex to lend themselves to the kind of analysis used in the deductive disciplines. Furthermore: "Knowledge differs from practical wisdom in this respect: those who excel in knowledge seek a single cause to explain many natural effects, but those who excel in practical wisdom seek as many causes as possible for a single deed, in order to reach the truth by induction." Unfortunately, according to Vico, the art of prudence had been widely neglected due to excessive study of the sciences.

In 1710, Vico published *On the Ancient Wisdom of the Italians taken from the Origins of the Latin Language*. Although this book was intended as merely the first volume of a three-part work (the second part on physics and the third on ethics were never completed), it remains one of the most important of his early publications. *On the Ancient Wisdom* proposes that a sophisticated philosophical theory lies embedded in the Latin language. From ancient times, Latin had been made a repository of profound philosophy, especially of Zeno's concepts. Here Vico's error, one that he would severely correct in the works of other thinkers, lay in imposing his own theory onto the writings of the ancients—one that was based on the prejudices of his time. Vico's mature view, however, was that their wisdom was popular (not sophisticated), poetic (not philosophical), and practical (not theoretical).

On the Ancient Wisdom also elaborates one of Vico's most interesting contributions to theory of knowledge, his *verum-factum* conception of truth: The true is what is made or done. For him, it followed that some things are true but not real; for example, figures of geometry, which are "fictions" or human-made abstractions; and some are both true and real, for example, things of the physical world, which God made.

Vico maintained, furthermore, that knowledge is of the "cause" of the true, where cause is the form (that is, the ground or necessary condition) for the true, as generated by the construction of the elements of a system. Indeed, according to the *verum-factum* conception, "to know is to arrange these elements." Revealed theology, having a divine origin, comprises the most certain knowledge of all; and the greatest, most certain human knowledge is of geometry and mathematics, of those systems that we construct by definition and convention. With regard to such deductive disciplines, the true and what is made are convertible in human beings, just as with the natural sciences, knowledge and creation are necessarily connected in God. Human knowledge of mechanics, physics, and morality that requires study of mind is the least certain of all, since the causes of empirical objects are the forms that God creates in his intellect. So although we think about composite entities by associating their images, we cannot fully understand them, which means that we cannot comprehend their forms and interrelations. Thus physics and the natural sciences must use the experimental method of Bacon and Galileo to devise merely probable judgments about nature and the universe.

On the Ancient Wisdom is sometimes considered a transitional work between Vico's early Cartesianism and his later new science. Here he did replace Descartes's concepts of the *a priori*, of clear and distinct ideas as forming the basis for science, with the *verum-factum* conception of truth which, as we have seen, denied any necessary connection between truth and reality in the deductive disciplines—a connection that Descartes and other rationalists had attempted to demonstrate. Moreover, what in Descartes appeared as a sharp disjunction between the theoretical and empirical disciplines, the deductive and natural sciences, became ultimately unified in Vico's epistemology through the application of *verum-factum*. Yet Vico's ordering of knowledge in terms of degrees of certainty, along with his view of the most profound knowledge as consisting of self-knowledge derived from introspection, were also held by Descartes. Nevertheless, Vico was eventually to become the anti-Descartes and the new Bacon of historical studies.

During 1717–32, Vico's studies included the writings of Hugo Grotius, John Selden, Samuel Pufendorf, and Thomas Hobbes. In opposition to his early views, Vico then held that brutes were the ancestral founders of civilization and that intuitional awareness of particulars and feelings are basic forms of apprehension. His conception of intuition as knowledge and of art as involving creative fancy influenced the development of Benedetto Croce's aesthetics and inspired his essay, "Giambattista Vico primo scopritore della scienza estetica" (1901).

In about 1725, while Vico was completing what is referred to as the "negative *New Science*," which consisted mainly of the destructive criticism of existing theories of natural law, Abbe Lorenzo Ciccarelli conveyed Count Gian Artico di Porcía's request for Vico's autobiography, which was to be included in a collection of like essays. After refusing several times, he agreed to submit it, and eventually in 1728, his *Autobiography* along with Porcía's proposal for other such narratives, were published. On July 20, 1725, however, Corsini withdrew his promise to publish the negative *New Science*, and Vico's ambitions suffered a great setback, equal to his defeat in the competition for the chair of civil law. He decided to publish at his own expense, but lacking funds to offer his work in its present form, he decided that if a "positive method were substituted for a negative one," the size of his manuscript would be reduced sufficiently for publication. The revised work, a quarter of its original size, became what Vico would call the first *New Science* (*The Principles of a New Science of the Nature of Nations Leading to the Discovery of the Principles of a New System of the Natural Law of the Gentes*, 1725). Here Vico's problem was how to establish the basic pattern present in the development of the nature of civil society. Its nature could be discovered through a study of the development of the human mind. In the second edition of 1730 (*Five Books by G. B. Vico on the Principles of a New Science of the Common Nature of Nations*), the problem was stated as one of the historical origins of civil society; and in the third of 1744 (*Principles of a New Science Concerning the Common Nature of Nations*), published during the year of Vico's death, it became further reformulated as that of the natural law of the peoples (gentes).

The New Science

In all three editions of *The New Science*, Vico's goal was to create a science of human society, which would be analogous to what Galileo and Newton had elaborated for the realm of nature. In the first edition, Vico attempted to replace the theories of natural law held by, for instance, Grotius, Selden, and Pufendorf, with a correct one. They had erroneously assumed that natural law, which for them really amounted to a principle devised by philosophers, was rational, whereas in fact the natural law of the gentiles consisted of force. Thomas Hobbes, moreover, incorrectly insisted that men came together contractually by virtue of their enlightened reason, whereas according to Vico, gentile society could have arisen only by means of a Divine Providence that used the passions as a means of preserving the human race and its nations. Natural law was coeval with the customs of the nations that were instituted by Providence.

In his *Autobiography*, Vico acknowledged that there is a great difference between the first *New Science* and the second edition, which was for him far superior to the first. In the former, he had considered ideas apart from language, whereas the two naturally go together. This change marks one of Vico's great discoveries—that of the unity between philosophy and philology. In the second edition, moreover, although still interested in the natural law of the gentiles, he was even more concerned with the common nature of nations, as the differences between the two titles would suggest. Comparatively speaking, there is far less difference between the second and third editions. The latter incorporates some corrections and additions, and Vico probably considered it his definitive work. The two later editions present a developmental, his-

toricized conception of nature, society, man, and human institutions. Vico held that there exists an ideal eternal history traversed in time by every nation in its rise, development, maturity, decline, and fall. Every nation develops cyclically from a primitive state that Vico described as poetic in the case of man and his institutions, and as anarchy in that of societal relations, to increasingly more civilized states, only to decline eventually into anarchy. Vico's discovery was thus of the eternal within, not apart from the temporal, of the universal in history rather than of universal history.

The first steps in the building of a world of nations were taken by brute humans. Human institutions occurred in forests, then huts, then villages, next cities, and finally academies. Humanity itself was created by the same processes whereby institutions were created; and thus the former was an effect of the latter when creatures not-yet-human made themselves into humans. The nature of peoples is first crude, then severe, then benign, then delicate, and finally again brutish.

Since the sciences are themselves institutions, we must inquire also about the origins of the new science itself. Its beginnings, for Vico, lay in the coming to self-consciousness of human nature. The mind is naturally inclined by its senses to see itself externally in the body, and only with difficulty does it understand itself by reflection. But because of their self-making, humans are able to know themselves and the process whereby they came to be; and when the one who creates things also narrates them, history is most certain. Just as one comes to know by making the personal history of development from a primitive, brutish state to a civilized one, so the history and new science of the world of nations can be known by being created out of the reality of evolving human institutions. Vico's *New Science* was unique for his time, and no like attempt to trace the progress and decline of the nation would appear until well after his death.

M. E. MOSS

Further Reading

Berlin, Isaiah. *Vico and Herder: Two Studies in the History of Ideas*. London: Hogarth Press; New York: Viking Press, 1976. An introduction to some of Vico's most interesting ideas, such as explanation *per causa*, the difference between "scienza" and "coscienza," "verum" and "certum," and to his concepts of teleological and cultural explanation.

Burke, Peter. *Vico*. Oxford and New York: Oxford University Press, 1985. This work serves as a good, brief introduction to Vico's ideas.

Caponigri, A. Robert. *Time and Idea: Theory of History in Giambattista Vico*. The author considers the central theme of Vico's writings on theory of history as one of the relationship between the historical and the eternal, between the temporal and yet ideal nature of historical development.

Croce, Benedetto. *The Philosophy of Giambattista Vico*. Translated by R. G. Collingwood. New York: Macmillan, 1913. Presupposes some prior acquaintance with Vico's work and presents a thorough evaluation of what is living and what is dead in Vico's philosophy from the vantage point of twentieth-century Italian idealism.

Haddock, Bruce A. *Vico's Political Thought*. Swansea: Mortlake Press, 1986. This work explicates the genesis of Vico's political thought, from his earliest discussions to the *New Science*.

Pompa, Leon. *Vico: A Study of the "New Science."* Cambridge: Cambridge University Press, 1975. A clear and systematic discussion of the *New Science*.

Verene, Donald Phillip. *Vico's Science of Imagination*. Ithaca and London: Cornell University Press, 1981. Verene shows how Vico's concept of *fantasia* develops from his study of myths and demonstrates its importance for his new science, as well as for subsequent philosophy.

GEORGE BERKELEY

Born: 1685, Thomaston, near Kilkenny, Ireland
Died: 1753, Oxford, England
Major Works: *An Essay towards a New Theory of Vision* (1709), *A Treatise Concerning the Principles of Human Knowledge* (1710), *Three Dialogues between Hylas and Philonous* (1713)

Major Ideas

To be is to be perceived. (A physical thing exists only when it is perceived through the use of the senses.)
Physical things are complexes of ideas (sensations).
Since no idea or sensation exists outside the mind, no physical thing exists outside the mind.
The primary qualities (solidity, extension, shape, motion) are as subjective as are the secondary qualities (color, sound, odor, taste, and texture).
The only kind of substance is spiritual substance: namely, that which perceives and thinks.
God accounts for the uniformity of nature and its continued existence when no finite mind perceives it; God causes the perceiving subject to have the ideas that constitute the external world.

George Berkeley is famous as history's ingenious defender of philosophical idealism—the view that nothing exists other than God, finite spirits, and their ideas. The world that we think we encounter, a physical universe that existed long before there were any creatures to perceive it, is only an intellectual construction, according to Berkeley.

The argument for his theory proceeds step by step from the premise that there *is* a world we know, a world of trees, mountains, books, and letters on a page, to the conclusion that since all we know in the experience of these objects is our sensations of them, the objects themselves are nothing but collections of sensations or, as he called them, "sense qualities," such as blueness, hardness, smoothness, and so forth. Such qualities exist only in the mind; hence, "material" objects—what we nowadays call "physical" objects—exist only in the mind. For any physical thing to *be*, to exist, then, it must be *perceived*.

Berkeley developed this intriguing theory, defended at length in both his *Treatise Concerning the Principles of Human Knowledge* and in the *Dialogues between Hylas and Philonous*, after having come to believe, as a result of his studies of vision, that the perception of the spatial features of things—their shape, magnitude, and movements—was derived from and entirely dependent upon fundamental experiences provided by seeing and touching. We do not *immediately* perceive such qualities (solidity, extension, shape, and motion) but only *mediately* or by reference to certain visual and tactual sensations. Analysis of the learning situation shows us, Berkeley concluded, that the "primary" qualities that Locke claimed are objective are just as subjective as are such "secondary" qualities as color and touch, on which we depend for our knowledge of spatial qualities.

Berkeley was educated at Kilkenny School and at Trinity College, Dublin. He became interested in philosophy and, in particular, in the problem of perception and its objects—a problem already presented to him through the work of Locke and Descartes. He became a fellow of Trinity College in 1707 and a short time later became an Anglican priest. His work on the theory of vision was published in 1709, when he was twenty-four. The other two attempts to win assent to his basic theory that material things must be perceived to exist and that they exist only in mind—namely, the *Treatise Concerning the Principles of Human Knowledge* and the *Dialogues between Hylas and Philonous*—were published within the next four years. Thus, his most important work in philosophy was completed by the time he was twenty-eight.

Berkeley was subsequently presented at court by his cousin, Lord Berkeley; he became a senior lecturer at Trinity College and, later, dean of Derry.

Berkeley then conceived the idea of founding a college in Bermuda and after receiving a charter from George I, he married Anne Forster and in 1728 sailed to Rhode Island, where he took up residence in Newport. However, when in 1731 the funds promised by England for the college in Bermuda were not forthcoming, he and his wife returned to England.

He was made bishop of Cloyne in 1734 and for the next twenty years devoted himself to improving the social conditions in his diocese. His last published book was *Siris: A Chain of Philosophical Reflexions and Inquiries Concerning the Virtues of Tar-Water, and Divers Other Subjects* (1744). Tar-water, derived from the pitch of pine trees, was touted by Berkeley as practically a cure-all, and the "divers other subjects" he mentions in his title included such matters as studies of the Trinity, free will, space and time, and God's essential nature.

Despite his eccentricities, Berkeley was a careful thinker and a brilliant writer. The *Principles* is a subtly developed argument for his central theory, and the *Dialogues* is a lively and imaginative presentation of the opposing views of materialism (represented by Hylas) and Berkeley's metaphysical idealism or immaterialism (represented by Philonous).

Although few readers have been persuaded by Berkeley and few philosophers, in his time or later, have been enthusiastic followers, his reputation remains strong because of the degree to which he made credible the claim that empirical knowledge is grounded in sense experience and that there is no knowledgeable way of going beyond such experience. Of course, Berkeley himself attempted to go beyond such experience by arguing for God as the cause of our sense-ideas, but he was no more successful in that enterprise than his materialist opponents were in establishing their own metaphysical position. Ironically, despite Berkeley's philosophical and literary genius, the victors turned out to be the skeptics—culminating in Hume—against whom Berkeley had built his case: in making sense experience fundamental, Berkeley created an empirical philosophy that skepticism was able to exploit.

Treatise Concerning the Principles of Human Knowledge

Berkeley's *Treatise Concerning the Principles of Human Knowledge* is both an argument *against* the proposition that there are "abstract ideas" and an argument *for* the proposition that "*esse* is *percipi*" (to *be* is to *be perceived*). These two ideas are, of course, related: If all knowledge depends on sensations, then no knowledge can be derived from ideas that are presumed to be wholly abstract and without sense content.

In the introduction to the *Principles*, Berkeley argues that a principal cause of difficulties and errors in philosophy has been the notion that there are abstract ideas. It has been supposed that it is possible to draw from the experience of a number of particular things some common feature that is the focus of an abstract idea. Berkeley points out that he does not deny that there are "general" ideas, only that there are "*abstract* general ideas." He maintains that a word becomes general by being made the sign of several particular ideas, not of an abstract idea.

The cause of the mistaken view that there are abstract general ideas is, Berkeley claims, language. Were it not for language with its terms of general signification, there would be no likelihood of anyone's holding the opinion that there are abstract ideas. But reflection on language is sufficient to show to anyone who faces the facts honestly that a general term acts as a sign of a number of particular matters, not of an abstract feature common to them all.

Berkeley begins the main text of the *Principles* with the claim that the "*objects* of human knowledge" are either "ideas actually imprinted on the senses, or else such as are perceived by attending to the passions and operations of the mind, or lastly, ideas formed by help of memory and imagination." From the outset, then, he emphasized his central point—that the mind knows only "ideas" and thus cannot know a world of material objects beyond ideas.

He uses the term "ideas" to include what we would call sensations, as in the sentence "By sight I have the ideas of light and colors . . . ," and again,

"Smelling furnishes me with odors, the palate with tastes, and hearing conveys sounds to the mind. . . ." Finally, he claims forthrightly that groups of such ideas furnished by the senses "come to be marked by one name, and so to be reputed as one thing." And he offers a clear example: "A certain color, taste, smell, figure, and consistence having been observed to go together, are accounted one distinct thing signified by the name 'apple.'. . ." Other examples of collections of sense-ideas that constitute what he calls "sensible things" are a stone, a tree, and a book.

Berkeley then claims that, in addition to sensible things, there is that which perceives them, that which wills, imagines, and remembers: "what I call 'mind,' 'spirit,' 'soul,' or 'myself.' "

Then, having pointed out that no one supposes that thoughts, passions, or products of the imagination exist "without" (outside) the mind, he argues that the same is true of sensations and the objects constituted by them: Sensible things exist only in the mind and cannot exist elsewhere. "Their *esse* is *percipi*," he writes, "nor is it possible they should have existence out of the minds or thinking things which perceive them."

Berkeley concedes that people commonly believe that such objects as houses, mountains, and rivers have an existence distinct from their being perceived—but, he insists, such a belief involves a contradiction. Objects such as houses and mountains are "things we perceive by sense" and since the only objects of sense perception are sensations ("our own ideas") and since sensations could certainly not exist *unperceived*, then it would be contradictory to say, for example, that a house, which is a set of sensations and thus *could not* exist unperceived, *may* exist unperceived.

The author goes on to argue that since the *being* of a sensible thing consists in its being *perceived*, and since only spirits (minds) perceive, "there is not any other substance than *spirit*, or that which perceives."

Nor, Berkeley continues, can the ideas be copies or resemblances of objects presumed to exist independently of perception, for "an idea can be like nothing but an idea."

He rejects Locke's distinction between *primary* qualities (extension, figure, motion, solidity, etc.) and *secondary* qualities (sensible qualities—colors, tastes, and so forth). Since the only ideas we have of such features as extension and solidity are ideas built from sense-ideas, Berkeley argues, these derived features, like the other sense qualities, must be perceived in order to be: Neither the primary nor the so-called secondary qualities can exist outside the mind.

Although Berkeley argues that the idea of material substance (objects existing independently of perception) is contradictory, he takes some time to point out that even if there were any such substance existing without relation to any mind or spirit, then precisely because of that independence, we would never be able to know such a substance. Its existence, then, would make no difference. This, together with the fact that it makes no sense to suppose any such substance, makes the case against the materialist complete. (Berkeley's argument here has a pragmatic cast that foreshadows the philosophical method of William James.)

Berkeley then develops his idea of spirit; more precisely, he argues that no idea of spirit is possible, in that spirit is not like sense-objects, not a set of ideas, but "that which acts"—that which perceives, wills, remembers, and so forth. Spirit cannot itself be perceived, Berkeley argues; it can be known only by "the effects it produces."

Having concluded that we cannot know even ourselves and certainly not other spirits except "by their operations, or the ideas by them excited in us," Berkeley goes on to argue that the works of nature (themselves ideas) would be unaccountable were it not for the presumption that there is some spirit other than a human spirit that causes them. The wonders of nature make evident the wonders of the spirit that realizes them; the order and regularity of nature, together with its harmony and beauty, are evidence of a spirit recognized as being "one, eternal, infinitely wise, good, and perfect. . . ." Berkeley thus contends that "God is known as certainly and immediately as any other mind or spirit whatsoever distinct from ourselves."

By attributing the continuity of nature and its

very existence to God, who enables finite spirits to have the ideas that for them constitute the things of this world, Berkeley builds his case for immaterialism as opposed to materialism.

It is this feature of Berkeley's thought that has been fixed in the popular mind by the famous Ronald Knox limerick:

> There was a young man who said, "God
> Must think it exceedingly odd
> If he finds that this tree
> Continues to be
> When there's no one about in the Quad."

And the reply:

> Dear Sir: Your astonishment's odd:
> *I* am always about in the Quad.
> And that's why the tree
> Will continue to be,
> Since observed by yours faithfully,
> God

Three Dialogues between Hylas and Philonous

When Berkeley found that his *Principles* was not persuading the thinkers of his time—in fact, it was largely ignored and was more laughed at than read—he wrote the *Dialogues*, hoping that the give-and-take of disputational discussion would be more effective than a straightforward essay in making both his negative argument (against abstract ideas and materialism) and his positive argument (that only ideas and the spirits that have them exist and that ideas must be perceived in order to *be*) clear and persuasive.

The basic argument in the *Dialogues* is the same, but it is developed in a very entertaining way in the course of an imaginary dialogue between Hylas (literally, the materialist) and Philonous (literally, the lover of reason, the immaterialist). The latter is, of course, Berkeley's spokesman.

Out of a series of questions and responses comes an argument by Philonous that we here represent as a chain argument:

1. *Sensible things (objects of sense) are such things as apples, wooden things, fires, stones, iron, letters on a page, and so forth.*
2. *We know things of these kinds, sensible things.*
3. *Whatever is knowable by us is perceivable by the senses.*
4. *Anything perceivable by the senses is immediately (that is, not by the use of reason) perceivable.*
5. *Anything immediately perceivable (such as colors, sounds, pains, odors) is a sense quality.*
6. *Sense qualities (such as blueness, hotness, bitterness) are sensations.*
7. *Sensations are ideas ("imprinted on the senses").*
8. *Ideas are only within the mind.*
9. *Whatever is within the mind is perceived.*

Therefore:

Conclusion: Sensible things are perceived.

Note that it follows from this argument that apples, fires, trees, stones, mountains—those objects we apprehend through the use of the senses—are *perceived*, that is, are not simply *perceivable* but are actually grasped by a perceiver in sense experience. That is the radical conclusion common to both the *Principles* and the *Dialogues*.

Hylas, supposing himself to be talking about material (physical) objects that he presumes exist independently of sense experience, finds it possible to assent to propositions 1 through 5. We *do* know apples, trees, and so forth, through becoming aware of their sense qualities (or properties, characteristics) such as redness, sweetness, smoothness, and so forth.

But clever Philonous asks Hylas whether the heat of a fire, which is surely a sense quality, is sometimes a "very great pain," as when one puts one's hand in the fire.

And Hylas agrees that the heat of a fire may be a very great pain.

But, Philonous points out, pressing on with the argument, a *pain* is a sensation only within the mind: For a pain to *be*, it must be *perceived* (felt).

Accordingly, the heat, when it is a very great pain, is also only within the mind; the heat, like any pain, can *be* (exist) only when it is known as a sensation.

What is true of some sensations is true of them all, he then forces Hylas to admit: For them to *be*, they must be *perceived*.

And so the conclusion is forced upon Hylas: The material, physical things of this world, the things we know in the course of experience, are sensations and, hence, such that for them to *be*, they must be *perceived*.

(There are two ways of describing Hylas's mistake, if, indeed, one treats Hylas—Berkeley's invention—as if he were an actual person: Either Hylas failed to realize that throughout the argument Philonous was talking about what might be called "the world of our experience," the "interior world," the world we know as we know the world of our dreams, or Hylas failed to realize that Philonous, after having used the term "sense quality" in such a way that Hylas took him to mean a *causal property*, the capacity of an external physical object to *cause* a sensation, used the very same term in such a way that Hylas took him to mean a *sensation*. Hylas was thus confused and taken in by a switch in the use of the key term "sense quality"—and of corresponding terms, such as "heat.")

Although the *Dialogues* is lengthy, the three dialogues making up an extended work amounting to a book, its central message is that incorporated in the summary above. (It is worth reading as a whole, however, both for the refinements of argument and to make possible a full appreciation of the author's philosophical ingenuity and perceptiveness.)

IAN P. MCGREAL

Further Reading

Dancy, Jonathan. *Berkeley: An Introduction.* Oxford and New York: Blackwell, 1987. An introduction (both demanding and rewarding) to the *Principles* and the *Dialogues*, designed for students and other interested "amateurs." Dancy is careful to point out where his interpretations differ from those of other critics.

Foster, John, and Howard Robinson. *Essays on Berkeley: A Tercentennial Celebration.* Oxford: Clarendon Press, 1985. Twelve philosophical critics from British and American universities, including J. O. Urmson of Oxford, offer fresh discussions of Berkeley's central ideas.

Gaustad, Edwin S. *George Berkeley in America.* New Haven and London: Yale University Press, 1979. Gaustad, professor of history at the University of California, Riverside, here presents a thorough and philosophically literate account of Berkeley's stay in the United States.

McGreal, Ian P. *Analyzing Philosophical Arguments.* San Francisco: Chandler, 1967. Includes an analysis of Berkeley's argument, drawn from the *Principles* and the *Dialogues*, involving a summary and a premise-by-premise critique. The emphasis is on Berkeley's persuasive uses of key terms.

Pitcher, George. *Berkeley.* London, Henley, and Boston: Routledge & Kegan Paul, 1977. One in a series of books in *The Arguments of the Philosophers* series edited by Ted Honderich of University College, London, Pitcher's careful and extensive account of Berkeley's ideas is both analytic and critical.

Urmson, J. O. *Berkeley.* Oxford and New York: Oxford University Press, 1982. A distinguished Oxford scholar's refreshingly brief but perceptive account of Berkeley's philosophy. Urmson finds fault with Berkeley's basic premises but regards him as "one of the most gifted and readable of philosophers. . . ."

VOLTAIRE

Born: 1694, Paris, France
Died: 1778, Paris, France
Major Works: *Letters Concerning the English Nation* (*Lettres philosophiques sur les Anglais*) (1733), *Essay on Manners* (*Essai sur les moeurs et l'esprit des nations*) (1754), *Candide, or the Philosophy of Optimism* (*Candide, ou l'Optimisme*) (1759), *Philosophical Dictionary* (*Dictionnaire philosophique*) (1764)

Major Ideas

All religions of the supernatural are based on ignorance and superstition.
The natural and human evils in the world cannot be reconciled with the view that this is the best of all possible worlds.
The order in the universe indicates that there is a Designer, but not necessarily a moral or immoral one.
People should not be punished for their ideas.
Although we can have no complete explanations of nature, the best accounts of nature are empirical and materialistic.
There is a natural basis for ethics and justice.
The human situation can be improved by eliminating superstition and fanaticism.

Voltaire (born François Marie Arouet) was one of the most prolific and influential thinkers of the eighteenth-century Enlightenment. Born into a prosperous and cultured society (his father was a lawyer with many influential friends), the youth was educated at the Jesuit college Louis-le-Grand. He was already a prolific writer, with an early gift in the composition of satirical verses and plays. His first play, the tragedy *Oedipe* (1718), written during a stay of several months in the Bastille for having offended the Duc de Rohan, was very successful. In 1723 his epic poem *La Henriade*, about King Henri IV, was banned because of its anti-Christian content.

In 1726 he was again imprisoned in the Bastille because of a quarrel with a nobleman and was released on the condition that he stay at least fifty leagues from Paris. He decided to go to England, where he quickly became involved with leading intellectuals there, including Newton's disciple Dr. Samuel Clarke and the philosopher George Berkeley.

When Voltaire returned to France in 1733, he wrote his *Lettres Philosophique sur les Anglais* (*Letters Concerning the English Nation*) showing the advantages of the English liberal democratic developments for human improvement and happi-

ness. The work includes a defense of Locke's empirical theories and of Newton's scientific work, as well as a criticism of Pascal's religious views. The *Letters* was considered too daring and radical in France, partly because of its witty, ironic, biting criticism of the religious and political establishment in France. The publisher was put in the Bastille, and the author, who had become the first of the *philosophes*, an unrestrained critic of accepted ideas and institutions, fled to Lorraine in eastern France, where he lived with his mistress Madame de Châtelet for the next fifteen years. In this period he wrote his *Treatise on Metaphysics* (1734–37), *Elements of Newton's Philosophy* (1738), which popularized Newton's scientific ideas in France, and the philosophical tale *Zadig* (1748). He was named historiographer of France and elected to the French Academy, chiefly for his literary efforts, even though he was still exiled from Paris.

In 1750, after Madame de Châtelet died, Voltaire accepted an invitation from the Prussian king, Frederick the Great, to become the court poet and philosopher in Potsdam. Voltaire and the king had known each other for years, and shared a common critical hostility toward Christianity and all revealed religion. However, Voltaire knew the defects in the king's character—his cruelty and his duplicity—and hesitated about joining him, but finally he joined Frederick at court. Voltaire's official duty was to polish up the king's French writings. Other than that, he joined in great intellectual banquets.

Trouble between the philosopher and the king began over Voltaire's satirizing Frederick's French verses. Soon other matters made the situation intolerable. The king forbade the publication of Voltaire's attack on the Prussian Academy of Science's president, Maupertius, a prohibition that Voltaire ignored. Finally he fled, first to Berlin, and then to the eastern fringe of France (because King Louis XV would still not let him return to Paris). He settled in Geneva in 1755. (His estate there is now the Voltaire Institute and Museum.) Four years later he published his novella *Candide*, his celebrated satirical attack on the optimism expressed in Leibniz's philosophical view that because of God's domination this is the best of all possible worlds.

In 1759, Voltaire moved to Ferney, just inside the French border, and remained there for most of the rest of his life. He became more active in pressing for basic social reforms. In 1762, he led the defense of an unjustly condemned Protestant, Jean Calas. His defense became a clarion call against religious fanaticism and unjust punishment in the *ancien régime* in France. He saw the church and state in France as the main enemies. His forceful writings made him the leading champion of humanistic causes in Europe before the French Revolution. In 1778, he finally returned to Paris, where he was hailed by the populace. He died there a few months later.

Voltaire was not an exact, didactic philosopher, setting forth his ideas in learned treatises. His thought was presented in many different ways and forms during his long life, and was not always consistent. His point of view was developed from the skepticism of Montaigne and Pierre Bayle, the materialism of Gassendi, and the empiricism of Locke and Newton. Early in his career he was an avid student of Bayle's *Dictionary*. In England he learned the value of careful empirical research over the rational theorizing of the Continental metaphysicians. He was most impressed by the way research based on careful examination of experience resulted

in Newton's great all-encompassing physical theory of the universe. Voltaire was also very much impressed by Locke's somewhat skeptical delineation of the limits of human understanding, and by Newton's presentation of a "scientific" proof of the existence of an intelligent Creator. (Voltaire regarded Newton's somewhat heretical Christian views as the result of premature senility.) On the other hand, Voltaire satirized the theories of Aristotle and Descartes, the religious theorizing of Pascal, and the credulous views of French Catholic theologians.

From early in his career, Voltaire was concerned to try to reconcile the Newtonian scientific cosmos with a moral cosmos. He imbibed Bayle's preoccupation with trying to understand whether the existence of evil in the world, especially in human affairs, is compatible with the traditional Christian view of an all-knowing benevolent deity.

The philosophical stories *Zadig* and *Micromegas* emphasized the human inability to comprehend the enormity of the universe and ridiculed the attempt to distort the little that is known about the world into a picture of the whole. Various articles in the *Philosophical Dictionary* mercilessly ridiculed theories being offered by philosophers and theologians to explain the supposedly God-governed universe.

In *Candide*, written a couple of years after the Lisbon earthquake of 1755, one of the greatest natural catastrophes of the eighteenth century as a result of which thousands of people were killed, first by the earthquake, then by an ensuing tidal wave, and finally by the Portuguese Inquisition as a way of placating the deity, Voltaire questioned whether any explanation could be offered to the problem of evil. He had earlier followed Epicurus in saying that either God can remove evil from the world and does not do so or lacks the power to do so; if the former, God is not benevolent; if the latter, God is not omnipotent. In the aftermath of the Lisbon earthquake, all sorts of explanations were offered, including that of Leibniz, as adapted by the English poet Alexander Pope, that this is still the best of all possible worlds, and everything that happens in it is for the best. It is this theory that Voltaire sought to show is bankrupt, totally unacceptable, and unbelievable in the face of the actual evils, physical and moral, that people encounter. Voltaire's answer to the Leibniz–Pope theory is not so much a series of arguments as it is a satirical presentation of a series of caricature situations that show that the theory is ridiculous and cannot be accepted by reasonable persons. (The insufferably naive youth, Candide, having been corrupted by his pedantic teacher, Dr. Pangloss—who uses metaphysical theology to gloss over the natural and moral evils in the world—dismisses all acts of corruption, betrayal, violence, and suffering encountered in his adventures, including the Lisbon earthquake, rapes, murders, and disembowelments, with the protestation that, despite appearances to the contrary, this is the best of all possible worlds. Finally, however, Candide is so buffeted by the realities of this life that he finds even his own rationalizations unconvincing and retires to the countryside to spend his remaining days cultivating his garden.)

What does *Candide* tell us about Voltaire's views about the nature of the universe and its Creator and Designer? Voltaire indicated that we are unable to catch even a glimmering of what is actually going on in the world, nor are we able to judge it. The captain of a ship does not worry about the comfort of the rats on it. We are like the rats in our universe. There is no evidence that the captain of the universe is concerned about us. In his first poem about the Lisbon earthquake, Voltaire said all we can do is suffer, submit, and die. When criticized for such irreligious pessimism, he changed this to read suffer, submit, adore, and die. All we can do, as he said at the end of *Candide*, is just cultivate our gardens.

This passivity toward the universe was coupled with an unyielding attack on the man-made evils that dominated social life in authoritarian Catholic France. From the time of his trip to England to the end of his life, Voltaire exposed the immorality and inhumanity of the way people were mistreated and persecuted in a unfree society. He ascribed much of the evil to the religious tradition and institutions that dominated educational and cultural life in France. He traced the source of the problem to Christianity as a religion, to its institutions, and to its parent, ancient Judaism. Voltaire portrayed biblical religion, both as history and as theology, as the

source of the ills that befall European mankind. He outdid Bayle in construing biblical history, especially in the Old Testament, as an outrageous presentation of an inhumane immorality, a superstitious ignorant comprehension of the world, and a worship of man-made deity. Voltaire mercilessly criticized the religious view in the Bible. He saw the theologians as the ones who have rationalized and institutionalized this odd, malevolent ancient view, and have used it to control and manipulate people. The result is the infamy of eighteenth-century France, which has to be opposed at every turn to bring about a better world.

Voltaire's humanism and humanitarianism was coupled with a most aggressive attack on Judaism and Christianity. Though Christianity was the omnipresent evil force of his time, Voltaire saw Judaism as providing the foul roots on which Christianity breeds, and felt that Europe could only be freed from Christianity by eliminating its source, and substituting the rational paganism of Greece and Rome as the base of European thought and morality. Because of this, Voltaire has been seen, whether intended or not, as one of the authors of modern secular anti-Semitism. During the French Revolution, his views were cited to argue against letting Jews become citizens of republican France.

In spite of his lifelong attack on established religion, Voltaire did not advocate atheism. Rather he offered a kind of deism—that there is a cosmic force that dominates or runs the world, a force that may or may not have moral qualities. He took as the basis for his deism the kind of evidence of design in nature offered by Locke and Newton. But following the critical English deists, he saw no connection between a Designer and the God of Christianity. Like the Scottish philosopher David Hume, whom he admired, he was willing to accept that there probably is an intelligent cause of the order of the universe, but there is no way of inferring any moral attributes from that order. And, as Voltaire is remembered for quipping, "If God did not exist, man would have to invent him."

Voltaire insisted that there is a natural basis for ethics and justice. If people will examine moral and legal questions without prejudice, especially religious prejudice, and will employ reason, they will find natural human laws. These laws will allow for just decisions and just societies. The human condition can be improved to some degree. But Voltaire lacked the great optimism of Condorcet, and saw improvement and the achievement of human happiness severely limited because of so many uncontrollable natural and human factors. But he proposed specific ways in which the educational and judicial systems could be improved to better the human condition.

Voltaire was perhaps the dominant and dominating intellectual of the Age of Reason. He was not as systematic a philosopher as some of the other leaders of the French Enlightenment, but he set the tone for the new way of looking at the world, by rejecting traditional religion and authoritarianism, and by acknowledging limited reason as providing the only way of understanding the cosmos and improving man. Voltaire's irony, ridicule, satire, polemics, and arguments were central in bringing about the great change of outlook in the eighteenth century. For his age Voltaire was the conscience of the civilized European world, a brilliant writer crying out against the many forms of injustice and ignorance.

RICHARD H. POPKIN

Further Reading

Bestermann, Theodore. *Voltaire*. 3d ed. rev. Oxford: Blackwell, 1976. An excellent biography, with bibliographical references.

Edwards, Paul. *Voltaire Selections*. New York: Macmillan, 1989. Contains portions of the philosophical writings of Voltaire. This edition also has an excellent annotated bibliography of works about Voltaire.

Hertzberg, Arthur. *The French Enlightenment and the Jews*. New York: Schoken Books, 1970. A responsible discussion of the subject, including an analysis of Voltaire's anti-Semitism and its influence.

Mason, Hayden. *Pierre Bayle and Voltaire*. Oxford: Oxford University Press, 1963. A scholarly portrait of two notable skeptics.

————. *Voltaire: A Biography*. Baltimore, Md.: Johns Hopkins Press, 1981. Another fine biographical account.

Poliakov, Leon. *The History of Anti-Semitism from Voltaire to Wagner*. New York: Vanguard, 1975. An enlightening historical survey of European anti-Semitism in the eighteenth and nineteenth centuries.

Spink, J. S. *French Free Thought from Gassendi to Voltaire*. London: University of London, Athlone Press, 1960. A helpful account of the development of French thought during the Enlightenment.

Torrey, Norman. *Voltaire and the English Deists*. Hamden, Conn.: Archon Books, 1967. A scholarly discussion of the development of deism in England and its influence on Voltaire.

JONATHAN EDWARDS

Born: 1703, East (now South) Windsor, Connecticut
Died: 1758, Princeton, New Jersey
Major Works: *Religious Affections* (1746), *Freedom of the Will* (1754), *Original Sin* (1758), *The Nature of True Virtue* (1765), *The End for which God Created the World* (1765)

Major Ideas

The world was created out of and is maintained only by the abundance, grace, and love of the sovereign and radically transcendent God, who foreordains all of life according to his providential but hidden will.

Although themselves endowed with will and reason, both of which operate solely within God's providential and determinative designs, human creatures have inhering in them the Original Sin of Adam and thus live a completely contingent existence in God's redemptive scheme without the reception of grace.

In the apprehension of God's will and in the plan of salvation, human reason, nature, and works do not suffice; God's grace alone is effectual, and it is bestowed only in divinely mysterious election of the saints, who are themselves justified in God's sight only by faith.

Such faith, itself a gift of unconditional grace, occurs at an "affective" or experiential level, beyond the capacity of reason, as "a divine and supernatural light" enters the heart and permits human consent to the whole of being.

Until recent decades, Jonathan Edwards was largely remembered in the American cultural tradition as a prototypically grim and severe representative of the most dour forms of Calvinism, an avatar in fact of a frequently caricatured strain of the Puritan legacy. Such a recollection relates only loosely to the man. It *is* accurate to consider Edwards a thinker secured in the theological legacy of John Calvin. It is true also that Edwards stands in familial and marital lineage with the Mathers, the Hookers, the Stoddards, and so on. And it is true as well that some examples of his work like the famous sermon "Sinners in the Hands of an Angry God" (preached at Enfield in 1741) are cast in what seems a "hell-fire and brimstone" mode. In this particular sermon, the key image presents the human state in the metaphor of a spider, dangling over the abyss of death, suspended there on a slender thread in the grasp of a capricious and punitive God.

With the gains made by more recent scholarly work, however, the picture of the authentic Edwards becomes clearer, and the portrait that emerges is of a man indisputably among the most philosophically subtle in the Calvinist intellectual tradition. If his majestic intellect was bent toward keeping alive his bequest from American Puritanism, it was com-

mitted in full to sustaining the most rigorous and thoughtful elements of that inheritance in an age that everywhere conspired against them. And, indeed, when all of Edwards's extant work is taken into account, even "sensationalist" sermons of the Enfield stripe gain altered relief in the context of Edwards's patient and nuanced theological discourse. At least one measure of his sheer magnitude as a thinker is revealed, ironically, in the fact that, virtually singlehandedly, he managed to keep alive for several more generations in America a commanding system of thought that, in his time, was quickly being displaced by several forms of liberal religion.

In 1727, a year or so after completing his education at Yale, Edwards accepted a pastorate—second only perhaps to some in Boston—with the large and very influential congregation at Northampton, there first as an associate and later as successor of his revered maternal grandfather, Solomon Stoddard, who had preached there for over fifty years. Although as a student Edwards had already achieved some reputation as a thinker, the post must have seemed virtually a birthright, for Edwards's own father, Timothy, was a career-long and highly regarded minister in East Windsor, Connecticut, and

young Jonathan was related not only to the Stoddards and the theological dynasty of the Mather
family but, by marriage, both to the old great Puritan Thomas Hooker and to one of the founders of
Yale, John Pierrepont. By upbringing, by education, and by lineage, then, Jonathan Edwards was
aligned with the fundamental creeds of that Calvinist tradition at the heart of the earlier American
Puritan hegemony in New England, and he spent
his own intellectual career in an effort to be true to
this tradition in ways that might sustain it in the face
of new claims on thought in the eighteenth century.

Unfortunately for him, Edwards shared his own
age with powerful liberalizing viewpoints from
without and within New England Congregational-
ism, which made his ministry in Northampton a
rocky affair. The Age of Reason, quickly overtaking American culture, sponsored the modified deism of people like Benjamin Franklin—Edwards's
contemporary—as well as a general species of cultural optimism about the supremacy of reason over
faith and about the potential progress of the human
estate, and this outlook, of course, threatened beliefs in the predestinating and providential designs
of a sovereign God and in the innately sinful character of humankind. Such a cultural movement also
abetted old foes of Puritan thought like Arminian-
ism, with its promises of salvation not by God's
grace alone but by the capacity of free human will
to accept the elected state. Slightly later still, the
enlightened religion of a Charles Chauncy would
insist even further that human moral capacity was
the key to salvation under the shadow of a uniformly
benevolent deity. The problems for any sustained
Puritanism were compounded when, in the 1740s,
waves of revivalism swept through New England.
Often marked by theories of universal redemption,
by emotive preaching, and by "quick" and impassioned conversion, the anti-intellectual character of
this Great Awakening offered for many a powerful
alternative to the stricter requirements of faith
posed in old Congregationalist orthodoxy.

But Edwards also detected concessions in the old
faith from within his community of belief, including liberal tendencies in the thought of his own
widely beloved grandfather Stoddard, which had

increased since the Synod of 1662. These erosions
from within the Puritan tradition, beyond deviations
from Calvinist theological tenets, had mainly to do
with loosened requirements for church membership
and for receiving communion, both now available
even to those who could not claim a decisive spiritual experience that would put them among the
"visible saints." In any event, Edwards attempted to
redress these threats from without and attenuations
from within by renewing the theological system
with full doctrinal consistency and intellectual
rigor, but his efforts, especially his refusal to administer the Lord's Supper, finally led to his being
dismissed from his pastorate in Northampton in
1750.

Most of the remainder of Edwards's career was
spent in a form of exile as he ministered to a few
white families and several hundred Indians at the
settlement in Stockbridge, Massachusetts. Even
with his numerous responsibilities there, he was
afforded a quietude in Stockbridge for his mature
religious and philosophical deliberations, and, at
this remove from the theological controversies left
behind, he returned to those large themes of Calvinism that he sought to reinvigorate within the
crucible of eighteenth-century intellectual conditions. Although some of his most important works
were published posthumously, their power and per-
suasiveness created enough of a following to insure
conservation of major elements of the theological
system for several more decades. His situation in
"defeat," in short, permitted the work that was his
triumph as a thinker, the work that resulted in his
finally victorious admission into the pantheon of
America's greatest thinkers.

The Sovereignty of God

At the center of Calvinist creed is the doctrine of the
radically transcendent and sovereign God, and for
Jonathan Edwards, who faced contemporary theological viewpoints that veered away from any such
idea, the doctrine remained a centripetal force of
belief and faith, even as he worked to restore its
fullest efficacy in and for his own time. Although
this committed belief permeates the whole body of

his writing—treatises, sermons, notebooks, and autobiographical works—it receives its fullest elaboration in his *Dissertation Concerning the End for which God Created the World*. In this work, Edwards makes completely and emphatically clear his notion that all of being depends immediately and ultimately on the character and will of the Creator, however hidden from human view might be the nature of that source or the terms of its sustaining motive.

For a section of the dissertation, Edwards assays what *human reason* can contribute to an understanding of God's purposes in creating and maintaining the world, and he surmises that the partial evidences to be found by looking at the created order, nature and history, posit a God whose end in creation was the completely fulfilled expression of his own glory and perfection. The metaphor Edwards seizes to explain this creative superabundance is the sun, which, fulfilling its defining nature, does not need or require any recipient of its emanating warmth but nonetheless sends out its rays as vital elements of its own character. God, though entirely self-sufficient, sends out emanations of his own glorious nature, and the world was created out of that surplusage of divine being, as if—Edwards thinks—God were not complete without this self-emanation, this overflowing self-expression. As it reflects, or gives, emanations back to its source, then, the world participates dependently in God's purpose of expressing his own goodness and holiness.

Although Edwards finds no initial regard for the world of physical nature or human history in this creating act, he nevertheless sees that the created world is a kind of secondary beneficiary of God's perfected nature as it brims over to provide to humankind "images or shadows of divine things," much as the sun provides light and warmth. Given the finally and inviolably hidden character of the divinity at the source of such images or shadows, however, Edwards recognizes the limits of reason in this matter and turns to the question of what *revelation* discloses respecting the ends of the creation. In measuring what "the scriptures have truly revealed," he argues that the providential acts of God

and the maintenance of moral government among human beings—both decisively figured in the redemptive work of Christ—are subordinate ends in the creation that also, ultimately, work to the purposes of glorifying God. Thus, such ends point to the presence of God in the world and suggest that there is continuing revelation of divine being in the world, boded in "images and shadows" for the possession of humankind. To the extent that the human creature in its dependence can consent faithfully to these emanations in the creation from the Creator, then to that same extent "the glory of God [the sole end of the creation] is both exhibited and acknowledged." Even as Edwards insists that such faithful consent is impossible without one's being elected for God's grace, revelation thus completes reason in its comprehension of the dialectic in the world of the real presence of the hidden God. In answering those theologies that would inflate the capacities of man and truncate the sovereignty of God, Edwards would preach the hidden "God glorified in man's dependence," but, in the redemptive economy, he would also preach that the world continued to receive "a divine and supernatural light."

Original Sin and the Dynamics of Redemption

Despite the view of the participation of the world in effulgences of divine being, which Edwards argued against the most legalistic Calvinism of his age, he remained solidly committed to the doctrine of Original Sin. Stripped by the fall of the spiritual nature that belonged to humankind as created in the image of God, human beings are born into and retain only an animal and physical nature, which, Edwards claims, is completed bereft "of the things of religion." They are by nature innately depraved and alienated from God, so corrupted in will that they cannot by nature choose the course of faith apart from the grace of God. Though men and women are endowed with rational capacity, it is severely constricted in matters of the spirit—clearly and utterly inadequate in the dynamics of salvation.

Consistent with his rendition of the doctrine of God's sovereignty, Edwards asserts throughout his writings the dependent character of human volition in the moral realm and the matter of justification by faith in the soteriological realm, both hinged ineluctably on the principle of *sola gratia*, salvation only by God's free and irresistible gift of grace. Indeed, neither "true virtue" nor "justifying faith" are possible but for those elected to sainthood, those who have been predestined from eternity to receive grace.

The dynamics of salvation, in Edwards's hands, were designed to address two alternative schemes present in the age. First there were those revivalist interlopers who generated "human" means for universal, instantaneous conversion experiences, and then there were those Congregationalist communities that were offering halfway (or more) status to the children of church members and, later, to others, when church membership had formerly been reserved for those "visibly" elected by God, those who had experienced the grace that made both faith in and consent to God possible. Although himself a revivalist, Edwards could not abide the former, the cheap grace they expounded in vulgarly emotive terms being, for him, a slur on God's predestinatory scheme and a scandal to authentic faith. With respect to those closer to home, he feared conquest by the Arminian view of the human capacity to choose grace. For him, in answer to both alternatives, the fundamental requirement was a faith that suddenly or gradually permitted the human heart to know and love God, but this justifying faith, he insists throughout his writings, comes only after God's grace, which itself is not earned or chosen but bestowed by God on those sinners he has elected. For Edwards, the salvific plan could not but occur under the executive principle of God's sovereignty.

Faith and Virtue

Even if he fought against the excesses of revivalist emotionalism, Jonathan Edwards was nonetheless committed to renew the emphasis on "emotion" in the processes of the regeneration of human spiritual existence. For those sinners elected by God to receive grace, a grace they could neither choose nor resist, it was by means of the "affections" that God turned the heart toward the horizon of authentic faith. In works like the majestic *Treatise Concerning the Religious Affections*, like the studied autobiography of the "Personal Narrative," and like the *Narrative of Surprising Conversions*, Edwards took great pains to isolate and emphasize the intuitive, emotive, suasive nature of God's actions upon the hearts of those who would be redeemed, and in this effort to distinguish the true marks of the "religious affections" from those counterfeit emotions stirred up by extremists among the revival preachers, he put his own unique stamp on a theological legacy he thought was turning overly rationalist and legalistic.

In restoring the emotional to religion, Edwards was not interested in the excesses of exuberant expression, except as these revealed the cheapened enthusiasms he sought to resist. Edwards maintains that, within the framework of election and grace, those redeemed would pass through an inward and heartfelt experience that would turn the sinner toward God, prepare the heart for the reception of grace, and ultimately enable that faith eventuating in an intuitive knowledge of God. This experience occurs in the domain of the affections—in the sphere of inward sensibility—as the person undergoes the preparation of his heart for the redemption of his spiritual nature. The creature first suffers the sensations of his own sinful nature (what Thomas Hooker had called "a true sight of sin") and the contingent nature of his life. This is followed with an apprehension by way of natural and biblical revelation of the whelming sense of God's beauty, power, and majesty, an understanding felt now, as never before, by "the reasons of the heart." Such a deepened persuasion teaches, far past mere cognitive assent, the inward convictions of man's dependency and the necessity of grace as the soul is penetrated by a divine light, itself finally illuminating the soul with the fullest "knowledge" of and faith in God the human being can obtain. Thus, beginning with and ending in the sovereign God, the regenerative process in its way replicates God's purposes in creating the world: An emanation stemming from God arrives for the creature who, returning in faith to God, sends a glorifying remanation back to the divine source.

As God's grace makes redeeming faith possible, so too does "the nature of true virtue" operate within the framework of this sovereign system of divine being. The regenerate heart, the redeemed spiritual principle gained in and through the religious affections, also enlivens renewed moral capacity in the human being. But this heightened moral existence must be understood, Edwards thinks, less as right deeds than as an inner disposition of the soul toward the ultimate goodness of divine being, a beautiful harmony of human life with divine life. While authentic faith provides the fullest possible knowledge of God, true virtue consists in the participation of the redeemed heart in the goodness of the God-created world or, as Edwards put it, "in the consent of [human] being to Being itself." As always for Edwards, the whole matter of life is from God, for God, with God, to God—the purpose for which the created order stands.

In addressing the religious issues and alternatives of his day, then, Jonathan Edwards brought to the Protestant tradition in America a theological and philosophical subtlety altogether rare in the history of Christian thought. His powerful and distinct quality of mind, conditioned by a sustaining faith, secures his place in the annals of religious thought, even as his disciples (notably Samuel Hopkins) were finally unable to work at the same capacious level of intellectual control or with the same degree of nuance and refinement. Strong currents of religious and cultural opinion would quickly erode the credibility of Edwards's system in a culture obviously following a different channel. Nonetheless, for those who pursue viable accounts of the experiential character of religious life, of the psychology of faith, or of the ecology of religious perception, Jonathan Edwards remains a rich resource.

ROWLAND A. SHERRILL

Further Reading

Carse, James. *Jonathan Edwards and the Visibility of God*. New York: Charles Scribner's Sons, 1967. In this brief monograph, Carse concentrates on Edwards's interpretations of the forms and means of God's revelation of himself in history and nature.

Cherry, Conrad. *The Theology of Jonathan Edwards: A Reappraisal*. Bloomington and Indianapolis: Indiana University Press, 1990. Published originally in 1966, this critical study, emphasizing the ways Edwards took up large "public" issues of religious thought, remains the most astute, patiently reasoned, and thorough treatment of Edwards's work.

Delattre, Roland A. *Beauty and Sensibility in the Thought of Jonathan Edwards*. New Haven: Yale University Press, 1968. An inquiry into Edwards's moral thought, this study argues that Edwards presents a religious ethics that cannot be understood apart from the aesthetic dimensions of his theology.

Miller, Perry. *Jonathan Edwards*. New York: Meridian Books, 1959. Published originally in 1949, this work, by a leading authority on the New England mind, helped to initiate the contemporary critical study of Edwards as a figure in the canon of American letters.

DAVID HUME

Born: 1711, Edinburgh, Scotland
Died: 1776, Edinburgh, Scotland
Major Works: *A Treatise of Human Nature* (1739, 1740), *An Enquiry Concerning Human Understanding* (1748), *An Enquiry Concerning the Principles of Morals* (1751), *Dialogues Concerning Natural Religion* (published posthumously, 1779)

Major Ideas

All our ideas are derived originally from sense impressions.
Since our beliefs are based not on reason but imagination, they cannot be rationally justified.
We cannot establish the existence of an external, physical world.
Causation must be explained subjectively rather than objectively.
There are no minds distinct from the contents of consciousness.
Ultimately, nothing can be known.
Our moral convictions are based on feeling rather than on reason.
The question of God's existence is an enigma; although the chief arguments that attempt to establish that God exists are subject to telling objections, they still have a residual validity.

David Hume is regarded by many critics as the most important philosopher ever to have written in the English language. His importance results from a number of features of his thought. He discussed in a fundamental and original way issues covering a broad range of central philosophical areas: in epistemology, metaphysics, philosophy of science and mathematics, ethics, and philosophy of religion. He pursued the implications of the empiricist theory of ideas far beyond the level of John Locke, showing that it led inevitably to skepticism. He was one of the most acute critics of orthodox opinions (in whatever field) in the Western tradition. Finally, he formulated the most sophisticated defense of skepticism, or the denial that anything can be known, in the philosophical literature.

Hume's philosophy appears primarily in four works: *A Treatise of Human Nature*, in which most of his main views are developed and defended in detail; *An Enquiry Concerning Human Understanding*, a relatively short work in which some of the main themes of the *Treatise* are repeated in a more popular style; *An Enquiry Concerning the Principles of Morals*, a discussion of some of the more practical aspects of morality; and *Dialogues Concerning Natural Religion*, which is devoted mainly,

but not exclusively, to the teleological or "design" argument for the existence of God.

Hume was born in Edinburgh but spent his childhood in the village of Chirnside, on the border between Scotland and England. He attended the University of Edinburgh for three years but never took a degree. When his family urged him to enter the legal profession, he took a position with a firm of solicitors in Edinburgh, but he soon found the study of law ill-suited to his tastes and began to devote all of his spare time to reading literature and philosophy. In doing so, he overexerted himself and suffered a nervous breakdown at the age of eighteen. On his recovery, he abandoned the intellectual life to join a merchant enterprise in Bristol. But his interest in commerce quickly faded and he departed for France, where, during the next three years, he wrote his most famous book, the *Treatise*.

Hume never held an academic position. He applied for a professorship at the University of Edinburgh but his application was rejected, probably because of opposition from the clergy, who suspected him of being an atheist. After having made his reputation as a philosopher, he shifted his interest to history, publishing a six-volume *History of Great Britain from the Invasion of Julius Caesar to the Revolution of 1688*. A good friend of Benjamin Franklin, he received news of the American Declaration of Independence in 1776 with great satisfaction.

Hume's philosophy was not well received in his native land. His Scottish contemporaries attacked it vigorously, and even viciously, while generally not understanding it. The only eighteenth-century philosopher to appreciate its significance was the German Immanuel Kant, who confessed that it aroused him from his "dogmatic slumbers." Hume received little attention during the nineteenth century but twentieth-century scholars have studied his thought with increasing care and sympathy, fully recognizing its originality and importance.

Epistemology and Metaphysics

Hume begins *A Treatise of Human Nature* with a statement, much like that of Locke, of an empiricist epistemology. "All the perceptions of the human mind," he writes in the first sentence of the book, "resolve themselves into two distinct kinds, which I shall call IMPRESSIONS and IDEAS." "Perceptions" is a general term; it means anything of which we are conscious. "Impressions" are the products of our five senses—colors, sounds, and so forth—as well as feelings of pleasure and pain. "Ideas" are copies of impressions, differing from them only in being less forceful or vivid. It follows from this view that we cannot have any idea that is not traceable back to some impression; thus abstract general ideas of the Platonic kind are impossible. We think by putting simple ideas together, through the employment of memory and imagination, to form complex ones. Since such ideas, however complex they may be, are made up entirely of original materials derived from impressions, the range of our possible knowledge is limited by that of our impressions. Hume draws a number of important philosophical conclusions from these epistemological assumptions.

The physical world, as philosophers and laymen alike have conceived it, has an existence independent of anyone's awareness of it. Locke and others had held that we perceive it through our senses. Hume, however, was unwilling to accept this account. All that we perceive through our senses are impressions and these are not external physical objects but contents of consciousness. They arise in our minds, he writes, "from unknown causes." Since our ideas are copies of our impressions, their ultimate causes must also be unknown. We have no way of leaping the gap between the contents of our consciousness and an external, nonconscious physical world. Although such a world may exist, we can have no knowledge of its existence.

Our inability to have any knowledge of an external world raises a question about the nature of causation. As we ordinarily think of the matter, causation is a connection between two physical objects in which one, the cause, possesses a power that it exerts on the other, the effect. For example, a moving billiard ball, when it strikes another, transfers its causal power to the other, causing it to move. But, if we can have no knowledge of billiard balls as physical objects, obviously we can have none of their causal powers. We can no more perceive this power, Hume contends, than we can perceive the balls themselves. So we need to reinterpret the notion of causation. Rather than being objective, it is subjective. After we have had perceptions that we call billiard balls repeatedly moving in certain ways after colliding with each other, our minds develop the habit of expecting to experience the same kinds of perceptions in the future. Thus when we see what we call a billiard ball moving toward another, we anticipate that the second ball will move in a certain way when it is struck. Causation is just this inward anticipation, based on past experience, that we feel.

Perceptions, Hume has said, are the contents of consciousness. But what is consciousness? Or, more generally, what is a mind that is conscious? If we are to know that minds exist, we must have some idea of them, which requires that we have some sense impression of them. But, Hume says, when he tries to discover his mind, he can find nothing but impressions and ideas, or the contents of consciousness. Since he can have no impression, hence no idea of his mind, he concludes that the mind is unknowable. Carrying his argument one step further, he asserts that minds, as realities different from the contents of consciousness, simply do not exist. As he puts it, "They are the successive perceptions only, that constitute the mind. . . ."

Hume adds one further dimension to his skepticism. After analyzing the process of reasoning, he comes to the conclusion that reason is self-destructive. Through a complex two-step argument he reduces all knowledge to probability and then reduces this probability to nothing. His conclusion, which he entitles "total" skepticism, eliminates the possibility of our knowing anything at all.

In his acceptance of total skepticism, Hume aligns himself with the tradition of skeptical thinkers that had its origins in Hellenistic Greek thought. He sees this tradition epitomized by the Pyrrhonists, to whom he refers in his writings. According to his understanding of them, these philosophers, after reaching the conclusion that nothing could be known, decided that they should believe nothing, therefore adopted a stance of suspension of judgment about everything. Although Hume accepted the first half of this skeptical view, he rejected the second. The fact that we can never give any reasons for what we believe, he argued, does not mean that we believe nothing. On the contrary, we believe many things; for example, that an external physical world exists, that there are objective causal forces at work in nature, and that we have enduring minds. We believe these things, even though our beliefs have no rational basis, because we must do so. As he puts it, "Nature, by an absolute and uncontrollable necessity has determin'd us to judge as well as to breathe and feel. . . ."

Hume's theory of natural belief is his distinctive contribution to skepticism and represents a significant improvement over the positions of most previous skeptics. For him, the destruction of reason does not lead to a debilitating suspension of judgment because he finds in human nature an overwhelming urge to judge and to believe. The fact that we cannot offer any rational support for our beliefs is simply an irrelevancy. We believe anyway, because we are and must be believing animals.

Ethics

Hume's writings on ethics appear mainly in two works, book 3 of his *Treatise* and *An Enquiry Concerning the Principles of Morals*. His views cover three areas of the subject, including *meta-ethics*, with an emphasis on the controversy between ethical objectivism and subjectivism; *normative ethics*, with the defense of a form of utilitarianism; and *applied ethics*, with the application of his normative theory to a variety of practical moral problems.

In his writings on meta-ethics, Hume expresses his most interesting, as well as controversial, ethical views. According to the standard, objectivistic position, ethical properties actually characterize states of affairs. Knowledge is considered to be good for its own sake; it is simply better to know than to be ignorant. Likewise, cruelty is wrong because of its very nature as the infliction of gratuitous pain on another sentient being. Hume rejected this objectivism. No objective state of affairs possesses any moral properties; rather all are in themselves morally neutral. Morality arises only when people react to states of affairs and develop feelings of approval or disapproval about them. Thus, when we say that knowledge is better than ignorance we mean only that we like the one and dislike the other. Or when we say that cruelty is wrong we mean only that we react negatively to it. Hume states this subjectivistic theory in a striking passage in the *Treatise*:

> Take any action allow'd to be vicious: Wilful murder, for instance. Examine it in all lights. . . . The vice entirely escapes you, as long as you consider the object. You never can find it, till you turn your reflexion into your own breast, and find a sentiment of disapprobation, which arises in you, towards this action. . . . So that when you pronounce any action or character to be vicious, you mean nothing, but that from the constitution of your nature you have a feeling or sentiment of blame from the contemplation of it.

His subjectivism in meta-ethics provides Hume with the necessary foundation on which to construct his normative ethics. If the rightness of actions and the goodness of states of affairs are constituted by our feelings about them, to discover what is in fact right or good all we need to do is to find out what people feel approval of. Hume believed he had discovered what those things are. In the first place, we feel approval of whatever is immediately agreeable, or pleasurable, both to ourselves and others. Second, we feel approval of whatever is useful, or whatever produces results that are pleasurable, either to ourselves or others.

Thus Hume's normative ethics is a form of universalistic hedonistic utilitarianism. It is utilitarian because our feelings of approval are directed to the consequences that result from actions; it is hedonistic because the consequences of which we approve are those that are pleasurable; and it is universalistic (rather than egoistic) because everyone's pleasure is taken into account. Nevertheless, it differs from standard hedonistic utilitarianism (like that defended later by John Stuart Mill) in one important respect. Whereas the standard view holds that we ought to maximize pleasure because pleasure is objectively good, Hume denied any goodness to pleasure, or anything else. For him the reason why we ought to maximize pleasure lies simply in the fact that we happen to like it.

Hume's views on practical moral problems are wide-ranging but of less philosophical interest. In various essays and in sections of the *Treatise*, he addresses a number of practical questions, including such topics as private property, justice, government, and international law, as well as many personal attributes, such as pride and humility, love and hate, beauty and deformity, benevolence and anger, malice and envy, and others. His discussions regarding these are guided by his normative theory, derived from his original ethical subjectivism.

Philosophy of Religion

Hume was interested in religious issues all of his life and wrote a number of essays concerned with specific subjects, such as miracles, human immortality, Providence, the problem of evil, and the history of religion. Although he was almost invariably quite critical of religion, the charge made by many of his contemporaries, particularly in Scotland, that he was an atheist seems a gross oversimplification of the quite complex and sophisticated views he held.

By far the most important of Hume's works in this area is his *Dialogues Concerning Natural Religion*, which he apparently wrote over a period of several years but which was not published until 1779, after his death. In the *Dialogues*, three speakers discuss the question of the existence of God. The speakers are, respectively, Demea, who is a conventional believer who defends the orthodoxy of the Christian faith without giving it too much thought; Cleanthes, who is a learned theologian considerably influenced by Newtonian science and by deistic thought; and Philo, who, though a religious skeptic, is far from being scornful of the arguments that theists like Cleanthes can offer in support of their position. The discussion in the *Dialogues* is carried on chiefly by Cleanthes and Philo, with occasional pious interjections from Demea, included mainly for comic relief.

The main theme of the *Dialogues* concerns the question: Is it possible to offer any reasons capable of establishing the conclusion that God exists? Specifically, the discussion centers on the teleological or "design" argument for God's existence, which was the central argument in theological and philosophical disputes in the eighteenth century. This is an argument from analogy. It runs along the following lines: All around us we see manufactured articles, like watches and ships, which we know to have been designed and produced by human beings possessing minds. Likewise, we see the universe in which we live, with all its incalculable size and complexity. By analogy we conclude that it must have been designed and produced by a mind. Furthermore, this mind must possess the qualities, far beyond those of any finite minds, capable of designing and creating such a product. It must, in other words, be an infinite mind, or God.

The main body of the *Dialogues* consists in a series of highly sophisticated arguments in which Cleanthes attempts, with considerable success, to defend the teleological argument against the objections of Philo. Most of his views are reiterations of standard arguments that had been developed by philosophers and theologians of the era and were well known in Hume's time. Philo's counterarguments, on the other hand, were not only ingenious but often original. His attack on the teleological argument was two-edged. He attempted to show that the analogy on which the argument rested was either too strong or too weak and in either case deficient. If the analogy is strong and God's mind is closely related to human minds, his infinite greatness is sacrificed. If, on the other hand, God as infinite is sharply distinguished from humans, the analogy on which the argument rests becomes too attenuated to bear the weight that is placed on it.

Since his time, Hume scholars have perennially argued the question: Which of the characters in the *Dialogues* was speaking for Hume? Demea, of course, is out. Most commentators incline toward Philo, although some favor Cleanthes. Finally, some defend the view that Hume cannot be identified with any one of the three. Whatever the truth, one might say that Hume could well have been speaking for himself when at the end of the *Dialogues* he puts the following words in Philo's mouth: ". . . The cause or causes of order in the universe probably bear some remote analogy to human intelligence. . . ."

OLIVER A. JOHNSON

Further Reading

Anderson, Robert F. *Hume's First Principles*. Lincoln: University of Nebraska Press, 1966. Approaching Hume as a metaphysician, this innovative book by a leading American Hume scholar uses careful and detailed textual analysis to shed important new light on Hume's thought.

Fogelin, Robert. *Hume's Skepticism in the Treatise of Human Nature*. London, Boston, Melbourne, and Henley: Routledge & Kegan Paul, 1985. The book by an eminent American philosopher concentrates on the skeptical elements in Hume's philosophy.

Laird, John. *Hume's Philosophy of Human Nature*. London: Methuen, 1932. A survey and analysis of Hume's writings by a distinguished Scottish philosopher, particularly valuable for its scholarly insight into the influences of earlier writers on Hume's philosophy.

Passmore, John. *Hume's Intentions*. 3d ed. London: Duckworth, 1980. The idea of this book by a distinguished Australian philosopher is to reveal the many facets of Hume's philosophical genius by devoting a separate chapter to each of the major elements in his thought.

Smith, Norman Kemp. *The Philosophy of David Hume*. London: Macmillan & Co., 1941. The classical modern interpretation of Hume in which the author, a notable Scottish historian of philosophy, finds the key to Hume's thought in his ethics of feeling.

Stroud, Barry. *Hume*. London, Boston, Melbourne, and Henley: Routledge & Kegan Paul, 1977. A balanced and judicious general introduction to the major themes in Hume's philosophy written by a major American philosopher from the University of California, Berkeley.

JEAN-JACQUES ROUSSEAU

Born: 1712, Geneva, Switzerland
Died: 1778, Ermenonville, France
Major Works: *Discourse on the Arts and Sciences* (1750), *Discourse on Inequality* (1755), *Émile* (1762), *The Social Contract* (1762), *Letters Written from the Mount* (1764), *Confessions* (1770)

Major Ideas

Man is by nature good; society is the cause of corruption and vice.

In a state of nature, the individual is characterized by healthy self-love; self-love is accompanied by a natural compassion.

In society, natural self-love becomes corrupted into a venal pride, which seeks only the good opinion of others and, in so doing, causes the individual to lose touch with his or her true nature; the loss of one's true nature ends in a loss of freedom.

While society corrupts human nature, it also represents the possibility of its perfection in morality.

Human interaction requires the transformation of natural freedom into moral freedom; this transformation is based on reason and provides the foundation for a theory of political right.

A just society replaces the individual's natural freedom of will with the general will; such a society is based on a social contract by which each individual alienates all of his or her natural rights to create a new corporate person, the sovereign, the repository of the general will.

The individual never loses freedom, but rediscovers it in the general will; the general will acts always for the good of society as a whole.

Jean-Jacques Rousseau was born in 1712 in Geneva, at that time a small city-state. At thirty, he went to Paris, a center of art, philosophy, and science. For Rousseau, the sharp contrast between the happy, bucolic setting of his youth and the sophisticated, artificial Parisian society was definitive; it defined him both as a man and as a thinker. For some time it had been common for philosophers to begin inquiries about morality and politics by asking the question "What is the nature of man?" Rousseau's upbringing, together with his sense of estrangement in Paris, gave him a unique perspective on this question. In his major works, he uses his personal experience to develop a universal understanding of the individual and society.

Rousseau's mother died shortly after his birth and so he was raised by his father and other relatives. As a boy, he read Plutarch's *Lives* and contemporary novels, but did not receive much formal schooling. His youth ended when he was apprenticed as an engraver to a particularly harsh master. In 1728, he ran away from Geneva and eventually found refuge with a wealthy woman, Madame Warens. Madame Warens was the first of a series of wealthy benefactors who lent friendship and sanctuary to Rousseau. He stayed with her intermittently for several years. This friendship gave Rousseau the time and opportunity to educate himself.

In 1742, Rousseau went to Paris. There he met Diderot, d'Alembert, and other French philosophers, some of whom were engaged in producing the *Encyclopedia*. While Rousseau contributed several pieces on music to this project, it was not until 1749 that he found his true subject. In the *Confessions*, Rousseau's personal memoir, he tells of seeing an advertisement for an essay contest administered by the Academy of Dijon. The question for the contest asked whether the restoration of the arts and sciences has had the effect of purifying or corrupting morals. As Rousseau describes it, on seeing the question, he was struck dizzy with inspiration. His *Discourse on the Arts and Sciences* won first place. This essay and a second one, *Discourse on Inequality*, began to develop themes Rousseau eventually treated at length in *Émile* and *The Social Contract*.

Discourse on the Arts and Sciences

The *Discourse on the Arts and Sciences* is a sweeping condemnation of modern society. Perhaps because of the manner of its conception, it is more noteworthy for its soaring rhetoric than for careful argument. Rousseau's central claim is that virtue is found "engraved on the heart" of every person. No special knowledge is necessary, so the advance of knowledge suggested in the question does nothing to improve morals. Rather the reverse is true. One is more likely to find virtue in the simple laborer than in the philosopher or artist. The problem, as Rousseau saw it, is that when a society achieves the leisure to pursue knowledge in art and philosophy, its members become caught up in appearances and illusion. The need to appear correct becomes more important than the truth, and people are led away from the honesty that characterizes more primitive, natural societies.

The *Discourse on the Arts and Sciences* clearly reflects Rousseau's own perception of the difference between Paris and Geneva. In doing so, it also inaugurates his method of analysis: to look within himself for the answers to philosophical questions. In the second *Discourse*, these two features reappear, but this time in the context of traditional "state of nature" arguments.

The terms "state of nature" and "nature of man" are prominent in eighteenth-century discussions of political and moral questions. This was the Age of Reason—many philosophers were critical of society and government, and they sought to give their critiques a rational and empirical basis by appealing to nature. The point was to justify a particular type of government by relating it to human nature, that is, to the defining characteristics of human beings. But to discover such essential characteristics, it also seemed necessary to consider what people were like in a "state of nature," which presumably existed before organized governments arose.

Most thinkers of the period agreed that any legitimate government would have to be based on the consent, real or tacit, of the governed people. However, they differed widely in their understanding of human nature, and their pictures of the state of nature and so, also, in the kind of governments they proposed as necessary and just. Hobbes, for instance, argued that the state of nature is a state of war. Human beings are by nature free and self-interested. Above all, they seek survival. In a state of nature, each person's self-interest threatens and is threatened by the interest of every other person. The result is brutal chaos. But human beings are rational as well as self-interested. Thus, according to Hobbes, to achieve peace and ensure survival, each individual would agree to sacrifice his or her natural rights and freedom and consent to obey the laws of a sovereign whose main responsibility is to maintain order.

Discourse on Inequality

Rousseau's *Discourse on Inequality* is in part a critique of Hobbes's views. Where Hobbes sought to justify existing governments, Rousseau once again offers a condemnation. Like Hobbes, Rousseau argues that people are by nature free and self-interested. But in this case, self-interest is accompanied by a natural compassion that makes people reluctant to hurt each other. The state of nature is not a state of war but one of robust indifference. There are natural inequalities of strength and intelligence, but these are unimportant when taken with natural freedom. They become important only in society. For in society, people start to compare themselves with one another. Vanity, pride, and contempt appear, and so the corruption of people by society described in the first *Discourse* begins. Rousseau argues that people err and mislead each other in their first efforts to construct a government. Their fatal error is to give up their freedom for the illusion of its protection. Instead of achieving protection, they become slaves. The origin of inequality is preoccupation with appearances; inequality then leads to loss of freedom. Both steps lead people away from their true nature.

Several fundamental themes emerge in these first two works. Human beings are by nature good; society corrupts them. The worst corruption is the loss of freedom brought on by social inequality. While many thinkers of the time were concerned with freedom, several scholars have noted that Rousseau's insistence on linking it with equality is unusual. Also unusual is the emphasis on feelings, or, more precisely, on the will, as well as on reason in his arguments.

Émile

If the *Discourses* begin Rousseau's critique of his society, his next major works, *Émile* and *The Social Contract*, furnish his solutions to the problems he saw. Rousseau wrote the two books almost simultaneously. *Émile* describes Rousseau's vision of a youth's education. It is above all an education of will designed with two ends in mind. The first is to avoid the corrupting influence of contemporary society. The second is to create an individual ready to assume the moral and political responsibilities of the new state described in *The Social Contract*. Both books are about the development of freedom, from the natural freedom of the child to the moral and political freedom of the citizen.

Given Rousseau's views on sophisticated society, it is not surprising that the first requirement of the education of the true individual is a rural setting. There the child will be free from the influence of the "arbitrary" will of socialized adults. Rather than learning to conform to the whims of society, the child learns to test himself or herself against the physical necessity of nature. In this way the limits of natural freedom are discovered by direct experience.

Rousseau thought that education should be progressive. The child's education he proposes calls for a prolonged experience of things rather than an introduction to ideas. The only book he allows is *Robinson Crusoe*. Formal religion and in fact all abstractions are postponed until a time when the individual's will and reason have already developed independently.

Although the child's education begins in a state of nature, the aim is not simply to recapture an idyllic, more primitive past, even were that possible, for the adult. Social interaction represents for Rousseau both the potential for human corruption and the possibility of human perfection. The achievement of autonomy—or moral freedom—is, for Rousseau, the perfection of the human will. The transition from natural to moral freedom is based on reason. The individual learns to let reason be the master of passion and thus to free himself from the tyranny of immediate desire.

The Social Contract

The difficulty if one accepts Rousseau's description of the true individual as autonomous and moral is to construct a society that promotes and solicits such citizens. Rousseau thought it necessary that a society's members be willing, active members of their community. *The Social Contract* is Rousseau's attempt to provide a blueprint for such a society. Perhaps the most striking and controversial element of the political theory outlined in the book is his conception of the "general will."

Rousseau's critique of existing governments centered on the loss of freedom. Fundamental to his views on politics is his insistence that people cannot be made to alienate their freedom, as Hobbes, for one, had suggested. On the other hand, Rousseau recognized, the sheer numbers of members of modern society precludes true democracies. The general will is his answer to this conflict of demands. It is the result of the terms of a contract in which each individual transfers all of his or her natural rights and freedom to everyone else in order to create a new corporate person.

The corporate person created by the alienation of individual, natural freedom becomes the sovereign of the new state. It is important for Rousseau that all persons alienate their rights equally (thus avoiding inequalities that lead to loss of freedom) and then rediscover individual autonomy in the shared sovereignty of the general will. As sovereign, the general will decides the founding laws of the society. It always decides for the "good of the whole."

Rousseau's conception of the general will has been both admired and criticized. He himself claimed that the general will is not the same thing as the voice of the majority. A majority may be simply a collection of the shared particular interests of a group of individuals. The general will, however, must always will the good of the whole. Unfortunately, this distinction may be clearer in theory than in fact. How is one in practice to know the general will apart from the voice of the majority? In addition, it may seem that the individual loses too much in a transaction that assigns all rights to the sovereign, even a general will, and leaves no protection for the individual as such.

The Confessions

For much of his later life, Rousseau lived in the French countryside. (He lived for a short time in England with David Hume, with unhappy results.)

Rousseau's later works all focus more directly on his personal life. The most famous of these is the *Confessions*. In the *Confessions* Rousseau tries, with brutal honesty, to tell the story of his life—times of happiness and despair, success and failure. He recounts sexual affairs and his guilt at having given up his children to foundling homes. The book is above all an attempt to explain himself to himself and his public. It has become a classic of self-analysis, but it was not well-received at the time, and Rousseau found himself continuing his efforts at self-analysis for years to come, at times in desperation and with mounting paranoia. He died at the home of a friend in France on July 2, 1778.

CONSTANCE CREEDE

Further Reading

Cassirer, Ernst. *The Question of Jean-Jacques Rousseau.* 2d ed. Edited and translated with an introduction and postscript by Peter Gay. New Haven and London: Yale University Press, 1989. A succinct and penetrating analysis of the unity of Rousseau's work by a philosopher prominent in his own right. Peter Gay's introduction outlines the history of Rousseau scholarship and suggests Gay's own evaluation of Rousseau's contribution to political theory.

Grimsley, Ronald. *Jean-Jacques Rousseau.* Totowa, N.J.: Barnes & Noble Books, 1983. This is a lucid and thorough introduction to Rousseau's work by one of the foremost authorities in the field.

_____. *Jean-Jacques Rousseau, A Study in Self-Awareness.* 2d Ed. Cardiff: University of Wales Press, 1969. This is a study of Rousseau's psychological development based, in particular, on Rousseau's own writings; it is particularly valuable for the details it offers on Rousseau's private life.

ADAM SMITH

Born: 1723, Kirkcaldy, Scotland
Died: 1790, Edinburgh, Scotland
Major Works: *The Theory of Moral Sentiments* (1759), *An Inquiry into the Nature and Causes of the Wealth of Nations* (1776)

Major Ideas

Nature provides a basis in sentiment for virtue.

When we adopt the role of impartial spectators, sympathy is the sentiment that is the basis for moral judgments.

Acting from a sense of duty corrects for any lack of appropriate sentiment in particular instances.

The deity has implanted powerful instincts ("passions"), which lead us to behave in ways that are ultimately beneficial for all.

Self-interest coupled with the predisposition to "trade, barter, and exchange" provides a basis for the division of labor and economic development.

In a market free from monopolies and self-serving public policies, competition among the self-interests of isolated consumers and producers produces a stable and expanding economy.

The self-interested pursuit of wealth may not be individually satisfying but leads to an aggregate increase in wealth that is in the best interests of a nation.

To say that Adam Smith is one of the most influential political economists is to risk understatement; indeed, as Kenneth Boulding has noted, ". . . It is clear that the last two hundred years has been the age of Adam Smith and of his followers and perverters." At the same time, it underestimates Smith to think of him as only being an economist (especially in the twentieth-century meaning of that term); like many (perhaps most) Enlightenment thinkers, Smith sought to understand and demystify the totality of the human condition, and his "economics" is based on extensive studies of human nature and history.

Adam Smith is a biographer's nightmare. Robert Heilbroner writes that he "was a poor correspondent, a jealous husbander of his writings (a number of which he ordered burned from his deathbed), and a man whose quiet and secluded life has not left a rich trail for his biographers."

Smith received his basic education in Kirkcaldy. In 1737, he became a student at the University of Glasgow, where Francis Hutcheson was one of his professors. In 1740, Smith received a scholarship to Baillol College, Oxford, where he remained until 1746, apparently primarily engaged in self-instruction. Unfortunately, little that is definitive is known about Smith's educational experiences at either Glasgow or Oxford—or anywhere else. After spending some time back in Kirkcaldy with his mother, Smith went on to Edinburgh, where he gave a series of public lectures on rhetoric and *belles-lettres*, jurisprudence, the history of civil society, and political economy. On the basis of the reputation he gained from these lectures and enjoying the sponsorship of several notables, Smith was elected to a professorship in logic at Glasgow in 1751. Later in the same year, he assumed the chair in moral philosophy, which he held until 1763. Smith delivered "public class" lectures on "moral philosophy" and "private" (advanced) lectures on rhetoric and *belles-lettres*. The former were divided into four parts covering theology, ethics, jurisprudence, and economics. The second part of the course was the basis for Smith's first full-length book, *The Theory of Moral Sentiments* (1759).

Most of this book is a discussion of moral psychology, which Smith felt was necessary to answer the question as to how moral judgments are formed, and includes among its major arguments: Sympathy is the moral sentiment that is the basis for "moral" judgment of others and ourselves, if we adopt the role of "impartial spectators"; justice, which consists of refraining from harming others, "is the main pillar that upholds the whole edifice" of society; the deity had implanted powerful instincts (passions), which lead us to behave in ways that are ultimately beneficial for all persons; the "voice of conscience" ("the judge within us") facilitates impartiality in our judgments and the achievement of virtue; continued "observations upon the conduct of others, insensibly leads us to form to ourselves certain general rules concerning what is fit and proper either to be done or to be avoided"; acting from a sense of duty "corrects" for the lack of an appropriate sentiment in specific circumstances; and, "Self-command is not only itself a great virtue, but from it all other virtues seem to derive their principal lustre."

It was, by all accounts, a resounding success, occasioning several translations and six editions during Smith's lifetime. Not only did its publication lead to his increased popularity as a lecturer, it so impressed Charles Townshend (to whom David Hume had sent a copy) that he invited Smith to become tutor to his stepson, the duke of Buccleuch, promising him a salary (almost double what he might earn at Glasgow) and a pension for life. This responsibility took Smith to France in 1764, where he remained until late 1766. While Smith spent most of his time at Toulouse, he was able to spend some time in Geneva, where he met Voltaire, and then in Paris where, in addition to his tutorial duties, Smith enjoyed the company of Hume and some of the leading *philosophes* and physiocrats. While the full impacts of these contacts are hard to assess, it is clear that some were important to Smith, especially his associations with the following: François Quesnay, the physiocrat Smith described as "one of the worthiest men in France and one of the best Physicians that is to be met in any country"; Baron d'Holbach, who had translated *The Theory of Moral Sentiments*; and A. R. J. Turgot, who not only addressed many historical issues of interest to Smith but was also working on a major economic treatise while Smith was in France. Smith also took several "expeditions" to various places in France, his obser-

vations on which form part of the "data" for his *An Inquiry into the Nature and Causes of the Wealth of Nations* (1776) (the *Wealth of Nations*).

When his tutorial duties ended late in 1766, Smith spent some time in London editing *The Theory of Moral Sentiments* and advising politicians, especially Lord Shelburne and Charles Townshend. Thereafter he returned to Kirkcaldy in 1767, where, subsidized by a generous pension, he remained working on *Wealth of Nations* for the next six years. This work was still "in progress" when Smith returned to London in 1773, evidently with the prospects for placement in one or another influential post. While he assumed no formal position, he offered advice to several governmental figures on matters like monopolies and the colonial policy, important elements in his research and later in the *Wealth of Nations*, which was ultimately published on March 9, 1776. It too went through several editions and translations before Smith's death in 1790. While the book is discussed more fully below, some of its major arguments include: The leap in productivity resulting from the division of labor requires a market capable of absorbing same; in a market free from monopolies and self-serving public policies, the self-interests of isolated consumers and producers would (through competition) produce an economic condition in the best interests of the whole society; the expansion of the market would lead to surpluses that, when properly reinvested, should guarantee the growth of a nation's economic wealth; the primary role of government is to protect the market from internal and external subversion, the former by preventing monopolies and trade barriers and the latter by providing an adequate national defense; government should also assume responsibility for effective public education. The book had enormous appeal, offering as it does both an explanation of complex phenomena in terms of a simple explanatory framework (comfortable to the thinking of his era) and a set of prescriptions for practical problems.

Smith was appointed commissioner of customs in 1778, which duties he performed at Edinburgh until his death in 1790. The appointment gave rise to a wonderful irony: While Smith was an adamant proponent of free trade, he was to spend years in the Customs House upholding duties and regulations that promoted mercantilism rather than free trade. In addition to faithfully executing his official duties, Smith continued his studies, maintained intellectual discourse through a number of clubs, and worked fairly steadily on revisions for both of his books. Smith's health began to decline in the 1780s, with particular "valleys" in 1784 and 1787. By early 1790, Smith seems to have been anticipating his death: He ordered his literary executors to burn several volumes of manuscripts. Smith died June 17, 1790.

The Theory of Moral Sentiments

The Theory of Moral Sentiments is an attempt to determine the nature of virtue and the power or faculty of mind that leads us to it. Smith argues that virtue cannot be reduced to a single criterion (such as propriety, prudence, or benevolence); ". . . our approbation of all those virtues, our sense of their agreeable effects, of their utility, either to the person who exercises them, or to some other persons, joins with our sense of their propriety, and constitutes always a considerable, frequently the greater part of that approbation." Smith does not believe that self-love, reason, or some special "moral sense" commend virtue to us but, rather, that there is a basis for virtue in sentiment provided by nature.

Smith's primary concern is to explain the method by which we form moral judgments. Toward that end, he begins with a discussion of the principle of "sympathy" (which we might think of as empathy), which he considered the major factor in creating and maintaining a social order. Smith defined sympathy as "whatever is the passion which arises from any object in the person principally concerned, an analogous emotion springs up, at the thought of his situation, in the breast of every attentive spectator" and denotes "our fellow-feeling with any passion whatever." Smith does not argue that there is perfect unison as a result of sympathy but that there is sufficient correspondence for the harmony of society. This concord is produced "as nature teaches the spectators to assume the circumstances of the per-

son principally concerned, so she teaches this last in some measure to assume those of the spectators." By understanding the context of another's behavior, we are able to decide whether or not it is appropriate to the situation, that is, to determine whether it is good or bad. The basis for approving or disapproving of our behaviors is the same as for judging the conduct of others; Smith says that we do this by placing ourselves in the situation of other persons and viewing our behaviors through their "eyes." By judging ourselves as we would judge others in the same situation and having others do the same, we have the basis for a socially approved code of conduct. When we "become the impartial spectators of our own character and conduct," we move beyond the mere desire for praise to the sense that we are worthy of praise.

Smith then examines the respective value of beneficence and justice. While he agrees that friendship, generosity, and charity enhance our lives, it is justice that is essential for the creation and maintenance of a viable society. The want of beneficence may disappoint but "the violation of justice is injury."

At this point Smith considers whether or not the fact that humans are apparently more affected by near rather than distant interests creates a "natural inequality of our sentiments." Smith sets up a hypothetical: Since someone about "to lose his little finger tomorrow, . . . would not sleep tonight," but could "snore with the most profound security"—if he were knew nothing of it—at the loss of a hundred million Chinese, would this person be willing to sacrifice those lives to prevent the misfortune to himself? Smith claimed that "human nature startles with horror at the thought, and the world, in its greatest depravity and corruption, never produced such a villian as could be capable of entertaining it." Smith argues that the deity endows us with conscience that exerts itself on such occasions; "it is he who, whenever we are about to act so as to affect the happiness of others, calls to us, with a voice capable of astonishing the most presumptuous of our passions . . . it is from him that we learn the true littleness of ourselves." The deity makes these imperatives part of human nature to insure collective well-being; in perhaps the original "invisible hand" formulation, Smith tells us that unconsciously obeying this divine plan, "without intending it, without knowing it," we "advance the interest of the society."

Smith argues that we avoid self-deceit by the formulation of general rules of morality. These rules are founded upon experience, based on the sentiments of approval or condemnation responding to particular actions; they are impressed by nature, and are part of the deity's plan, "given us for the direction of our conduct in this life." Regard for these general rules is duty, "the only principle by which the bulk of mankind are capable of directing their actions." Duty overcomes any individual lack of appropriate sentiments in particular instances. Smith does allow that some "deceits" have utility, as when "we naturally confound" wealth with happiness; "it is well that nature imposes upon us in this manner. It is this deception which rouses and keeps in continual motion the industry of mankind."

Smith's account raises some obvious problems. While he argues that virtue is based on natural sentiments, he repeatedly invokes higher standards and divine machinations (at least invisible hands) without effective justification. Smith does not explain how antisocial passions and aberrations come into being, simply assuming that nature's plan will win out in the end. This static psychology, coupled with a utilitarianism that assumes the working out of some "natural" plan, makes for an uncomfortable social philosophy—not because it is inherently conservative but, rather, because of the leaps of faith required to sustain an ostensibly experiential system.

The Wealth of Nations

This is the more famous of Smith's works. As is often the case with "great" works, there is not much in it that was really "new" when it was published in 1776. Its success lay in its timeliness, in what was perceived as a sensible and simple explanation for complex phenomena, and its enthusiastic advocacy of a set of prescriptions for contemporary economic

problems. While there are some discontinuities between *The Theory of Moral Sentiments* and *The Wealth of Nations* (particularly the absence of a discussion of sympathy in the latter), there are some important continuities, most notably Smith's unyielding faith in the positive aggregate effects of an increase in aggregate wealth and in the beneficial operations of an "invisible hand," and his belief that justice (and the enforcement of same) is essential for a viable society.

The Wealth of Nations consists of five "books." Smith begins with a discussion of the division of labor and the market consequences of same. The second book deals with accumulation. Smith then discusses economic development. The fourth book provides a critical analysis of a number of ideas, policies, and systems of political economy. Smith concludes with an extended discussion of the appropriate role of government in a "market" society.

Smith argues that the division of labor is the important development in advancing the wealth of a nation. This "effect" is not the product of human wisdom but, rather, the "slow and gradual consequence of a certain propensity in human nature which has in view no such extensive utility; the propensity to truck, barter, and exchange one thing for another." Humans have constant need for the help of their fellows but cannot expect it on the basis of benevolence. We get others to help us by appealing to their own interests; "nobody but a beggar chooses to depend chiefly on the benevolence of his fellow-citizens." Smith assumes the universality of these characteristics and diminishes the differences between persons in terms of natural talents; in an obvious departure from the ancients (particularly Plato) he asserts that "a philosopher is not in genius and disposition half so different from a street porter, as a mastif is from a grey-hound." Regardless, Smith contends that absent the shared disposition "to truck, barter, and exchange," we would be "of scarce any use to one another."

Using the example of pin-making and arguing by extension, Smith maintains that the division of labor causes a dramatic increase in production, which in turn stimulates the growth of a market capable of absorbing it. The cumulative effect of the self-interested interactions occurring in a "society of natural liberty" is the development of a market economy wherein supply and demand determine prices and profits. Smith argued that as long as nothing interfered with the operations of these interactions between supply and demand, competition would lead labor and capital into production of commodities that had market prices above "natural prices" and away from those that fell below same. As national wealth increases, the "demand for those who live by wages" also increases, as do wages and population. Smith believed that higher wages led to population increases among workers "by enabling them to provide better for their children." Smith contends that "the demand for men, like that for any other commodity, necessarily regulates the production of men." The relationship among the division of labor, growth of population, and increased wealth and income is one of mutual interdependence and support.

Extension of the market creates a need for more capital, which in turn makes frugality and accumulation economic virtues; "capitals are increased by parsimony, and diminished by prodigality and misconduct." While individual industry is important, "parsimony, and not industry, is the immediate cause of the increase in capital." Frugality is the basis for the "perpetual funding" of productive hands; Smith goes so far as to say that prodigals are public enemies. Again, self-interest is the motivating force; we are prompted to save by "the desire of bettering our condition, a desire which, though generally calm and dispassionate, comes with us from the womb, and never leaves us till we go into the grave." When manufacturing capitalists invest these "savings," it leads to increased productivity, economic growth, and increased wealth for the nation. Thus, left to its own devices, the market generates wealth and "occasions, in a well-governed society, that universal opulence which extends itself to the lowest ranks of the people."

Smith believed that we are more likely to promote social benefits unknowingly than knowingly. Each individual consumer and producer is "led by an invisible hand to promote an end which was no part of his intention. Nor is it always the worse for society that it was no part of it." For Smith, the worse thing that can happen is for some force to skew the operations of the market. The two greatest threats come from monopolies and government policies privileging particular interests. Smith generally objected to government policies of control or restraint because they upset the balance of industry and limit the possibility for continued expansion. Nevertheless, Smith was not an economic anarchist. Government was to act to prevent monopolies and other barriers to free trade, to maintain justice generally, to provide for national defense, and to erect and maintain public works necessary for facilitating commerce. Smith recognized that there were some negative consequences of the division of labor that government would have to correct as well. Because a "man whose whole life is spent in performing a few simple operations . . . has no occasion to exert his understanding . . . becomes as stupid and ignorant as it is possible for a human creature to become . . . unless government takes some pains to prevent it," Smith felt that government ought to require and provide for the common people acquiring the "most essential parts of education."

Ultimately, however, it is not government policy but freedom of enterprise and an openly competitive market that should lead to an increase in the aggregate wealth of a nation and all the good that would come from it. Whether or not these assumptions were accurate even in Adam Smith's own day is problematic; John Maynard Keynes would later characterize capitalism as the belief "that the nastiest of men for the nastiest of motives will work for the good of us all." Regardless, through both disciples and critics, Smith's ideas have largely shaped economic discourse for the last two centuries.

DON THOMAS DUGI

Further Reading

Campbell, R. H., and A. S. Skinner. *Adam Smith*. New York: St. Martin's Press, 1982. A brief intellectual biography of Smith by the editors of a commonly used edition of the *Wealth of Nations*.

Heilbroner, Robert L., with Laurence J. Malone.

The Essential Adam Smith. New York: W. W. Norton, 1986. As with most abridgements, this one is somewhat idiosyncratic but does provide a handy compendium of Smith's major arguments. It is based on the Campbell edition, *supra*.

IMMANUEL KANT

Born: 1724, Königsberg, East Prussia (now Kaliningrad)
Died: 1804, Königsberg, East Prussia
Major Works: *Critique of Pure Reason* (1781, 1787), *Prolegomena to Any Future Metaphysics* (1783), *Foundations of the Metaphysics of Morals* (1785, 1786), *Critique of Practical Reason* (1788), *Critique of Judgment* (1790), *Religion within the Limits of Reason Alone* (1793)

Major Ideas

Although all knowledge begins with experience, it does not all arise out of experience.
Knowledge of an orderly world is made possible through the complementary activities of the senses and the mind.
The matter of our experience is due to our senses and its form is contributed by the mind.
The world we know is a phenomenal world; we have no knowledge of things-in-themselves.
The only thing good without qualification is a good will.
One ought to act only according to a principle of action that can be universalized.
One ought to treat all rational beings as ends in themselves and never merely as means.
The categorical imperative must be distinguished from hypothetical imperatives; the commands of the former are unexceptionable, but those of the latter are exceptionable.
The autonomy of the self-legislating will is the basis of human dignity.
Belief in God is a postulate of practical reason.

Immanuel Kant is the most profound of all the modern philosophers. He is also one of the most difficult to understand. Although his difficulty is often attributed (with some justice) to his heavy Germanic style, it is a result mainly of the acuteness, penetration, and complexity of his thought. Nowhere are these characteristics of his philosophy more apparent than in his most important book, *Critique of Pure Reason*. This is not a work to approach lightly, or without a substantial understanding of the history of philosophy from Descartes through Hume, but it can be immensely rewarding to the reader who is able to give it the informed attention it requires.

To understand Kant, it is necessary to begin with David Hume who, Kant wrote, "aroused me from my dogmatic slumbers." Just what were these slumbers? As a student in eighteenth-century East Prussia, Kant was steeped in the tradition of rationalism, particularly as it had been developed by G. W. Leibniz (1646–1716) and his German followers. Two things in Hume's philosophy awakened Kant and set him on the path that would eventuate in his "critical" philosophy. Hume's critique of rational-

ism convinced him that the rationalists based their philosophies on unwarranted assumptions about our knowledge of the nature of reality. However, Hume's empiricist epistemology, derived from a Lockean concept of the mind as a blank tablet on which experience writes, led to a total skepticism in which we can know nothing. Somewhere between these two extremes, Kant believed, the truth must lie.

Kant came from a poor family that was devoutly religious. His parents sent him to a parochial school, at which the seeds were sown for his lifelong antipathy for organized religion. He entered the University of Königsberg at the age of sixteen and graduated six years later. Since there were no formal teaching positions available, he spent the next eight years as a tutor in the homes of various affluent families in East Prussia. He returned to the university in 1755 and received a doctorate with a dissertation on natural science. With his degree he was able to procure a position as a *privatdozent*, or lecturer. For the next fifteen years he lectured widely on philosophy, mathematics, and various areas of natural science. Kant was brilliant in the classroom, with his spontaneity and wit, his enormous erudition, and particularly with his unremitting efforts to encourage his students to think for themselves. At the age of forty-six, he was promoted to professor, a position he held until his death. All of his major philosophical writings date from this relatively late period in his life.

Kant's personal life was uneventful. Engrossed as he was in his teaching and writing, he had little time for other interests. Yet he read widely, particularly in the natural sciences, and he had a number of close friends with whom he socialized on a regular basis. A bachelor, Kant organized his day according to a rigid schedule. He began at five, with breakfast and philosophical reflection; from six to seven he prepared his lectures; from seven to nine or ten he spent in the classroom; he then wrote until noon. Lunch was his main meal, lasting usually until four and spent in conversation with three or four guests. Then came his daily walk, followed by his manservant carrying an umbrella. It is said that the housewives of Königsberg set their clocks by Kant's walk. His evening hours were spent reading until bed at ten.

Kant was the epitome of the Enlightenment. A firm believer in reason, he nevertheless recognized the important role of the feelings in human life. Politically he was very liberal for his time and place, being a strong supporter of both the American and French Revolutions.

Epistemology and Metaphysics

Kant's epistemology and metaphysics are found in his *Critique of Pure Reason*, first published in 1781 with a revised edition in 1787. With the possible exception of Plato's *Republic*, this is the most important philosophical book ever written.

After reading Hume, Kant became convinced that the *a priori*, deductive philosophizing of the rationalists, because it had no basis in experience, led only to empty conclusions. But the empiricist alternative led to an equally unacceptable skepticism. The problem, as Kant saw it, was to combine these two opposed points of view in a synthesis that would draw on the strengths of each but avoid their weaknesses.

Kant began with experience. He accepted the fact that the world that human beings experience is, on the whole, orderly, being made of enduring objects like hills and trees that exist in space and time, and have causal relationships with each other. What assumptions, Kant asked, must we make to explain these facts?

Kant's answer was that our experience of an orderly world of objects results from the cooperation of two faculties—our senses and our minds. The first contribute the matter of our experience, the second contributes its form. Suppose I observe an automobile traveling along a road. Through my senses, I see its color and shape, hear the sound of its engine, and smell its exhaust fumes. But I do more than this. I recognize it to be a physical object, existing in space and time and in causal relationship with the road on which it is traveling. I could not identify the automobile as an objective part of my experience unless I were able to do all of these things. Generalizing, we can say that all represent necessary conditions for us to experience an objective world.

Now, however, we must make a crucial distinction. Our senses provide us only with the content (or matter) of the objective world—with colors, sounds, smells, and so on. But we do not gain our knowledge of the formal structure that experience of an orderly world requires through them. We have no sensory experience of time, for example, or of the causal connections between events. This last point is of great importance because it is one that most of us, including many philosophers, overlook. We take it for granted that we experience time, for example, in the same sense that we experience colors and sounds, and so on. Careful examination of our experience should convince us, however, that we do not. None of our five senses gives us any impression of the all-pervasive but elusive passage of time. What, then, is the source of our knowledge of time, as well as of the other formal elements that give our experience its organized structure? According to Kant, this structure is the result of the creative activity of the mind. When the mind receives the input of the senses—shapes, colors, sounds, and so on—it simultaneously does its work of organizing these raw data into coherent structures or objects in a single unified whole. The result of its activity (of which we are unconscious) and that of the senses working together is the coherent world we experience.

By appealing to the activity of the mind as a necessary agent in the construction of an orderly world, Kant succeeded in overcoming the fatal deficiency in empiricism, which, with its "blank tablet" theory of mind, could never account for the coherence of our experience. In doing so, however, he did not return to a rationalistic conception of the mind as a basic, unchanging substance. Kant's concept of mind is quite different. Rather than describing the mind as a substance, he conceived of it as an activity. Using the technical vocabulary he invented for his philosophy, he referred to it as the *transcendental unity of apperception*. All of these terms, though initially obscure, are illuminating. By "transcendental" Kant means two things. First, the activity in question is not empirically observable; we cannot perceive the mind at work through our senses. Second, the activity is a necessary condition of orderly experience; if it were not occurring, we would not be able to experience the world we in fact do. By "unity," Kant is referring to the mind's organization of our sense data. This activity is, to use another of Kant's terms, one of synthesis. The mind takes the various items brought to it by the senses and unifies, or synthesizes, these to produce the object we experience. The term "apperception" is more difficult to explain. In the illustration given, I do not only observe the object "automobile" but I connect it with the road, the scenery around it and, going further, with its point of origin and destination. In fact I connect it, or could do so, with the totality of my experience. It is, in other words, a feature of a whole world in which I live through time. The ability to integrate my experience of the automobile with the totality of my experiences to form a world is not accomplished through perceptions, which yield only isolated sensations. This necessary ability Kant calls "apperception" to distinguish it from sense perception. It is accomplished by the mind.

We must now consider the other or nonmental side of Kant's metaphysics. The process we have just reviewed gives us knowledge of an organized and unified world. It is easy to conclude that this world is, as we ordinarily believe, an independently existing entity, made up of innumerable physical objects interacting causally with each other over vast stretches of cosmic time. This is not the world Kant is talking about, although a reader may be beguiled into thinking so because of Kant's constant use of the term "objective." This word can be understood in two ways. In ordinary thought, it connotes an independent object that would be just what it is even if never observed by anyone. This is not Kant's meaning. For him, "objective" means a unified construct resulting from the combined activities of the senses and the mind. Kant's "objects," therefore, have no existence in independence of thinking observers.

Generalizing from this account of "objective," we can draw a distinction between what Kant calls the *phenomenal* world and the *noumenal* world, or the world of things-in-themselves. The world that we experience, and can know through the process that has been described, is, for Kant, only the phenomenal world. We can have no knowledge of things as they are in themselves, existing independently in a physical world. The reason why this conclusion must be accepted is that the raw data out of which our world is constructed are provided by our senses and our senses do not present to our mind external, independent realities but only perceptions. Kant often speaks of the external world as being "transcendent," meaning by this that it falls outside our possible experience and knowledge. This is in contrast to the term "transcendental," which, though it refers to something outside of sense perception, is a necessary condition of our experience. To sum up, Kant's "objective" world is, according to our ordinary beliefs about reality, in fact a "subjective" world. This Kant accepted. For that reason he considered his philosophy a form of metaphysical idealism rather than realism. To emphasize this point, the author of a monumental exposition and analysis of the *Critique of Pure Reason*, H. J. Paton, entitles his work *Kant's Metaphysic of Experience*.

The conclusion we have just reached raises an

interesting question. It is clear that Kant believed in an independent world of things-in-themselves. But what reasons could he give for believing this? If our experience yields us knowledge only of a phenomenal world, which is "subjective," we can know nothing of an external, independent reality. Thus it would seem gratuitous to assume that it exists. Rather, it would appear to be dispensable, just as Kant thought the metaphysical substances posited by the Leibnizian rationalists to be. In response to such a criticism, Kant would reply that, unless we assumed the existence of an independent world, whatever its real nature might be, we would have no way in which we could explain the data we perceive through our senses and which are required for us to have any experience at all.

Ethics

In his ethics, Kant's rationalism predominates but, curiously enough, the content of his views can, without great distortion, be described as a rationalized version of Christian ethics. The central concept of his theory is the notion of duty. Kant's conception of the human moral condition is captured by a metaphor he uses in his *Foundations of the Metaphysics of Morals*. The human will, he states, "stands at the crossroads." By this he means that, when we have to make a moral decision, we find that our reason tells us that we ought to act rationally, but our desires or inclinations urge us to act in a way that will satisfy their needs. When we are faced with a conflict between reason and desire, the will must make a decision about which road to take. Because our desires exercise a strong influence on us, the demands of reason seem onerous. So we consider their fulfillment to be an obligation under which we labor, or a duty.

To act morally thus is, for Kant, to act rationally. But to say that we ought to act rationally is not sufficient to tell us what we ought to do. Kant finds the explanation of what constitutes rational action in the "maxims" from which we act. He sometimes speaks of these maxims as "principles of action." What he is referring to are our reasons or motives for acting. A maxim of action, to be rational, must

have a universal validity, because that is what reason requires. Reason, as he puts it, lays down a law for action. Kant calls this rational law the *moral law*. It states: *Act only according to that maxim of action that you can at the same time will to be a universal law.* What Kant is saying is that, if we recognize that human beings as rational beings, have a duty to perform certain actions for certain reasons, this duty applies to everyone, including ourselves. To make an exception of oneself to a law we recognize as binding on everyone else is to act irrationally and therefore immorally.

Developing his theme, Kant points out that we recognize various imperatives to action. Some of these he calls hypothetical; we recognize that we ought to perform some act to gain an end we desire or to further our happiness. Although these are indeed imperatives to act, they are hypothetical because they are avoidable. We do not compromise our rationality if we fail to follow them. The moral law, because it commands us to act rationally, commands categorically. Its command is not rationally avoidable. Therefore Kant calls it a *categorical imperative*.

The will, then, is subject to the categorical imperative, even though it by no means always follows its commands. But in being subject, it is not bowing down to some external power, for the moral law is a law that we, as rational beings, impose on ourselves. Kant speaks of the "self-legislating" will and the "autonomy" of the will. A will that can impose laws of action on itself and then follow those laws Kant believes to have an inestimable worth. Indeed, he asserts, a good will is the only thing in the world that is "good without qualification."

Our possession of a potentially good will gives us a worth that is "above all price." It is the source of human dignity, which separates us as persons from other beings in the world that are things. To treat a human being as a thing—something to be used simply to further our own ends—is to violate his or her humanity. Thus, Kant concludes, we can reformulate the categorical imperative to read: *Act so that you treat humanity, whether in your own person or in that of another, always as an end and never as a means only.*

Kant developed a social philosophy out of this statement of the categorical imperative. He envisions a society in which each person patterns his actions according to the imperative. In this society, which he called *the realm of ends*, many things would be similar to actual societies. People would make use of the talents and skills of others to further their own personal ends, just as we do. But no one would treat others simply as tools or instruments. Rather every person would recognize that everyone else is an end as a self and should always be treated as such.

Religion

According to Kant's epistemology, things-in-themselves are unknowable. If this be true of natural entities, it is even more true of supernatural entities. Kant makes a special point of emphasizing this conclusion as it applies to the concept of God. He devotes considerable space in the *Critique of Pure Reason* to a critical examination of the traditional arguments for the existence of God. All, he concludes, end in failure.

This does not mean that Kant had no religious beliefs. Quite the contrary. His approach to religion was through morality rather than through metaphysics. Although he concluded that the realm of ends is only an ideal, he nevertheless maintained that every moral being has a duty to promote its realization. However much each of us may strive toward this goal, however, we cannot accomplish it by our own endeavors. No more can all of us, striving for the same end, guarantee its realization. Because the full realization of the end would result in the maximum happiness for everyone, the cooperation of nature itself is required. But the cooperation of nature is beyond the control of human beings. Only a superhuman power, or God, can guarantee it. Therefore, since we have an unconditional duty to strive toward such an end, if morality is to have any meaning, we must believe that God exists, is in control of nature, and will bend her to fulfill the goals of humanity.

It is important to recognize that Kant does not consider his moral argument a "proof" of the existence of God. It is, rather, what he calls a "postulate" of practical reason, or an article of moral faith. It is something we can legitimately believe even though we cannot prove it because it supplements the moral law, a law that we all, as rational beings, have a duty to fulfill.

OLIVER A. JOHNSON

Further Reading

Beck, Lewis White. *A Commentary on Kant's Critique of Practical Reason*. Chicago: University of Chicago Press, 1960. This book contains a detailed analysis of Kant's ethics, written by the dean of American Kant scholars.

Körner, S. *Kant*. Harmondsworth: Penguin Books, 1955. In this small book, the author summarizes the main features of the Kantian philosophy and includes a short sketch of the philosopher's life and personality.

Murphy, J. G. *Kant: The Philosophy of Right*. London and Basingstoke: Macmillan and Co., 1970. In this short book, the author, an eminent Kant scholar, surveys Kant's ethics and social philosophy.

Paton, H. J. *Kant's Metaphysic of Experience*. Two vol. London: George Allen & Unwin, 1936. This book, by a renowned English Kant scholar, is written for the serious student of the philosopher. It gives a detailed exposition and analysis of the central argument of the *Critique of Pure Reason*.

Wolff, Robert Paul. *Kant: A Collection of Critical Essays*. Anchor Books. New York: Doubleday & Co., 1967. The book contains a number of essays on various aspects of Kant's philosophy, written by several contemporary Kant scholars.

Wood, Allen W. *Kant's Moral Religion*. Ithaca and London: Cornell University Press, 1970. In this book, the author presents a general interpretation of Kant's views on religion based on an analysis of his main writings on the subject.

THOMAS PAINE

Born: 1737, Thetford, Norfolk, England
Died: 1809, New Rochelle, New York
Major Works: *Common Sense* (1776), *The Crisis* (1776–83), *Public Good* (1780), *The Rights of Man* (1791–92), *The Age of Reason* (1794–96), *Dissertation on First Principles of Government* (1795)

Major Ideas

The rights of humankind originate at birth.

Government should exist only for the security, happiness, and unity of humankind.

Republican government is based on reason and engenders freedom; government by hereditary succession is based on ignorance and reduces people to slavery.

Equality of natural property and the right of suffrage are essential for a free society.

The unrestrained communication of ideas, the right to reform, and freedom of religious belief are all natural rights.

God is the first cause of all things; only by exercising reason can humankind discover God.

A defender of human rights, political independence, and intellectual freedom, Thomas Paine contributed to the revolutionary activities in late eighteenth-century America, France, and England. Representing Enlightenment thought, Paine voiced ideas that have become commonplace. Paine's philosophical contributions are held in esteem less for their innovative nature than for their rhetorical power. At the center of radical political thought, Paine was still able to engage the masses with his simple and succinct style.

Paine's sensitivity to the populace may be due in part to his own humble background. Born in a small village in Norfolk, Paine was apprenticed to his Quaker father's staymaker's shop, where he learned the trade of making women's corsets by inserting steel or whalebones into their fabric. In 1757, Paine was sent to London to serve as a journeyman staymaker, and in 1759, he opened his own staymaking shop in Sandwich. There he met and married Mary Lambert, a maid in service to a woollen-draper's wife. Within a year, however, Mary died.

Paine's first experience with political polemics evolved from his job, first assumed in 1762, as an exciseman. Losing this position in 1765 for stamping goods and collecting duties on goods he had not examined, Paine busied himself with odd jobs: staymaking, teaching, and preaching. Although he was reinstated in the Excise Service with a job in

Lewes in 1768, Paine pursued a rigorous self-education and became interested in politics. He bought a tobacco and grocery shop and married the former shopowner's daughter, Elizabeth Ollive. Both business and marriage failed. In 1774, Paine separated from his wife and was dismissed as an exciseman for inattention to his post. Rallying for excisemen seeking higher salaries, in 1772 Paine wrote *The Case of the Officers of Excise*. He spent an entire winter in London, away from his post, distributing copies of his pamphlet to members of Parliament. The cause failed, but Paine was hooked on politics and reform.

While in London, Paine met Benjamin Franklin, agent for Pennsylvania, whose letters of introduction enabled him to go to Philadelphia in 1775. In the colonies, Paine wrote scientific and political articles for magazines and newspapers, including the bold attack *African Slavery in America*, and he edited the *Pennsylvania Magazine*. His anonymous essay *Common Sense*, which challenged the American colonies to declare their independence from Britain, was a tremendous success in America and France. In 1776, almost 100,000 copies sold in America.

As the war commenced, Paine enlisted in the American army, soon becoming the aide-de-camp to General Nathanael Greene. A series of sixteen essays appearing from 1776 through 1783, *The*

Crisis, promoted morale during the war and presented the colonial cause to Europe. Appointed secretary to the Committee of Foreign Affairs in 1777, Paine obtained from France much-needed supplies, loans, and military assistance. His public attack on Silas Deane, following a controversy over the commission on French supplies, led to his dismissal.

After the war, Paine supported the Pennsylvania Constitution, and in 1780, he was appointed clerk of the Pennsylvania Assembly. He fashioned legislation providing for the gradual emancipation of slaves in Pennsylvania, urged equal rights for women, established the Bank of Pennsylvania, opposed Virginia's claim to unlimited land in the West, and advocated a stronger central government. His services were repaid with 500 dollars from Pennsylvania and a farm in New Rochelle from New York.

An engineer, Paine designed a single-arch bridge he hoped to build across the Schuylkill River in Philadelphia. In April 1787, he returned to France to develop and finance this bridge and found himself at the center of the French Revolution. Back in London in 1791, he joined the pamphlet war, initiated by Edmund Burke's *Reflections on the Revolution in France*, with *The Rights of Man*, a defense of the French Revolution and a challenge to England to revolutionize its aristocratic institutions. Paine became an instant hero to English radical thinkers; the Constitutional Society, of which he was a member, ordered 25,000 copies of his pamphlet. By 1792, when part 2 was published, however, the radical fervor in England had been calmed by strict sedition and treason laws. Paine was charged with sedition, and a mob burned his effigy. Although Paine fled to France before his trial began in 1792, he was found guilty *in absentia* of seditious libel and exiled from Britain.

In France, Paine again rendered his services to the new French republic. He was chosen a delegate to the French National Convention and appointed, despite his inability to speak French, to the Committee of Nine to frame a new French Constitution. His association with the moderate Girondists and his argument for sparing the life of Louis XVI made his position. After England and France went to war

in 1793, foreigners at the French Convention were denounced. Paine was arrested and imprisoned at Luxembourg. Assuming he would be put to death, as many of his inmates were, Paine spent ten months in prison writing *The Age of Reason*, his attack on the superstition and irrationality of institutionalized religion. James Monroe, the American ambassador to France, finally secured Paine's release in 1794 on the grounds that he was an American citizen. Paine bitterly blamed George Washington for the length of his prison term; in a vituperative letter published in 1795, Paine criticized Washington's military and political strategies. Although Paine was reelected to the French Assembly in 1794, his recovery from a fever contracted while in prison prevented him from active participation.

Paine's return to America in 1802 was not a triumphant one. He was known as the notorious author of *The Age of Reason*, with its denouncement of Christianity, and of the *Letter to George Washington*, with its defacement of a founding father. Only Thomas Jefferson really renewed friendship with Paine. Spending his last years quietly in New York City or on his nearby farm in New Rochelle, Paine died in 1809. His request for a grave in a Quaker cemetery was refused, so he was buried unceremoniously on his farm.

Catalyst to the American Revolution

Paine rallied the American colonies to seek independence from Great Britain, and he chastised the wickedness and inhumanity of the institution of slavery. Outspoken about English atrocities in Africa, India, and the Caribbean, Paine, in 1775, joined the first antislavery society in America. In *African Slavery in America* (1775) Paine argues that the slave, the proper owner of his freedom, has a right to reclaim it, however often it is sold. This mental revolution, freeing humankind from the shackles of prejudice, permeates all of Paine's polemics.

Advocating a new method of thinking and a new era of politics, Paine in *Common Sense* outlines the disadvantages and limitations of America's continued attachment to Britain. America constitutes an asylum for persecuted lovers of civil and religious liberty from every part of Europe; thus Europe, not England, is actually the parent country of America. Britain, Paine argues, naturally wants to maintain colonial ties with America for British protection and commercial interests. Separation, not reconciliation, from England represents the only course of action for America to pursue.

Paine encourages immediate action and provides a plan of representative government to employ once independence is achieved. Arguing that a government of our own is our natural right, Paine demands that the crown be demolished and scattered among the people whose right it is, for in America, the law is king. The war debt America contracts, Paine debates, is nothing compared to the work it will accomplish. In almost every article of defense, America abounds: natural resources, knowledge, and character, especially resolution and courage. America has an opportunity to begin government at the right end—to form articles of government and then elect men delegated to execute them afterwards.

Paine's optimism in the American spirit continues through *the Crisis* essays. The first, read by Washington to the troops freezing along the Delaware River just before their battle with the Hessians at Trenton in December 1776, emphasizes that what Britain has done to the colonies constitutes slavery. In "The American Crisis," Paine reminds the colonies that America will never be happy until she gets clear of foreign dominion and that America is justified in waging this "defensive" war against the tyranny of aristocracy. The inspiring rhetoric of "these are the times that try men's souls" reminds weary rebels that "tyranny, like hell, is not easily conquered."

In other *Crisis* essays, Paine establishes or articulates myths shaping the American character. He argues that America's superior mental abilities and talents are reflected in the size of its country. Geography is a powerful justification for American independence. America's eternal youthfulness will undermine the European reverence for the past and tradition. America is morally and ethically right in

maintaining isolationist policies with other European countries engaged in war. Just as children grow into adults independent of their parents, America has weaned itself from child–parent connections with Europe. Citing the success of the American Revolution, Paine concludes in 1783 that "the times that tried men's souls are over," and that the revolution was "an honor to the age that accomplished it."

The value of liberty and the dignity of humankind were the principles on which the American Revolution were based. Characterizing what makes the American Revolution unique, Paine, in the *Letter to the Abbé Raynal* (1782), explains that "our style and manner of thinking have undergone a revolution more extraordinary than the political revolution" and we "enjoy a freedom of mind, we felt not before." Paine maintains that American prejudices as well as oppressions underwent mental examination, and only those consistent with reason and benevolence were retained. This kind of "total reformation," of expanded mind and heart as well as politics, accounts for American success. This kind of revolution is still wanting in England.

Paine's voice continued to be heard during the early days of the American republic. Calling for a Continental Convention to form a Continental Constitution, Paine argues in *Public Good* (1780) that only the United States, not Virginia or any other individual state, can outline new states and incorporate them into the Union. In *Crisis Extraordinary* (1780), Paine proposes raising taxes to meet war expenses, and in *Six Letters to Rhode Island* (1782–83), he convinces Rhode Island to abandon its claims of total state sovereignty and to ratify a revision in the Articles of Confederation allowing Congress to regulate commerce.

When a committee of the Pennsylvania Assembly tried to deprive the Bank of North America of its charter in 1785, Paine supported the bank and opposed the issuing of paper money. Demonstrating how the whole community derived benefit from the bank, Paine alleges in the 1786 tract *Dissertations on Government, the Affairs of the Bank, and Paper Money* that it is the office and duty of government to give protection to the bank. Issuing paper money, warns Paine, reduces the value of currency. Since every generation must be free to act for itself, Paine encourages the making of all future contracts, laws, and treaties with time constraints. "To give limitation is to give duration," Paine concludes.

Contributions to the English Unrest

The Rights of Man (1791) places a system of individual talent, production, and merit in opposition to Burke's adherence to hereditary aristocracy. Part 1, dedicated to George Washington, refutes the infallibility of the Parliament of 1688 to bind posterity forever and Burke's assumption that the British government was regulated by a constitution. Paine advocates radical reform in the British government so the living might exercise their natural rights.

Paine defends the French Revolution as a revolt against despotic principles of government rather than as an overthrow of specific individuals. Individuals entering into a constitution with each other to produce a government is the only mode in which governments have a right to arise and the only principle on which they have a right to exist. This procedure had been followed by the American and French people, but in England the government still presides *over* the people in the metaphors of crown and Parliament.

Paine traces the origin of monarchy to thievery and usurpation. There is no English origin of kings, Paine contends; "kings" are descendants of the Norman line in the right of conquest. The titles assumed by nobility are mere nicknames, and primogeniture is a monster that defies every law of nature. Aristocracy is thus kept up by family tyranny and injustice. The state church of Britain is established by law and is strongly characterized by persecution. Before bad governments can be reformed, Paine expounds, the nefarious principles on which they rest must also be changed.

In part 2 (1792), dedicated to Lafayette, Paine defends freedom of speech. Arguing that publications merely investigate principles of government and invite humankind to reason and reflect, Paine warns that humankind cannot be told not to think or read. The opinion of the world is changed with respect to systems of government, and until humankind thinks for itself, prejudices not opinions result. He foresees government founded on morality, on a system of universal peace, and on the indefeasible hereditary rights of man.

Comparing the old, repressive systems of government with the new, democratic forms, Paine especially praises the American system of representation, offers guidelines for the framing of a constitution, and suggests a plan for improving the condition of Europe. His plan addresses the English national debt, establishes universal education, initiates a progressive tax, provides pensions for the elderly and ill, increases pay for soldiers, abolishes poor-rates, disbands the navy, and stimulates employment. Optimistically, Paine projects future revolutions produced with quiet operation, determined by reason and discussion. Recommending an alliance among England, France, and America, Paine hopes for a confederated Europe in which all the chains of slavery and oppression are broken and all wars cease. "The present age," rallies Paine, "will hereafter be called the Age of Reason, and the present generation will appear to the future as the Adam of a new world."

Paine's response to the English charge of seditious libel, *Letter Addressed to the Addressers on the Late Proclamation* (1792), again points out the dangers of restricting reading and thinking. He reiterates that principles have no connection with time, nor characters with names. Finally, he challenges England to hold a national convention to investigate and to debate the best reforms.

In *Agrarian Justice* (1795), Paine claims that every person has been born to the common property of the earth. The idea of landed property commenced with cultivation and created poverty. Carefully, Paine points out that the fault lies not in the present possessors of land but in the system itself. He proposes a revolution in the system of property and offers a plan reimbursing every person, twenty-one years and older, for the loss of his or her natural inheritance. Based on the principle of justice, not charity, the plan would benefit all without injuring any.

Paine's economic theories also appear in the *De-*

cline and Fall of the English System of Finance
(1796), in which he demonstrates the cause–effect
relationship between war and the national debt.
Paine predicts Britain will go bankrupt if reform in
its financial system does not soon occur.

Reactions to the French Revolution

As a "citizen of France" and a representative to the
French National Convention, Paine wrote *An Essay
for the Use of New Republicans in their Opposition
to Monarchy* (1792). He defines monarchy as absolute power vested in a single person and royalty as a
creation exacting from its victims excessive taxation
and willing submission. Paine's attack again blames
the system of hereditary succession for oppression
rather than particular kings.

Since systems are at fault, Paine strongly pleads
against the execution of Louis XVI. *Reasons for
Preserving the Life of Louis Capet* (1793), a speech
to the National Convention, encourages the French
to avoid new calamity and reminds them of Louis's
assistance to the American Revolution. He recommends that Louis and his family be imprisoned until
the end of the war and then exiled, perhaps to
America, where he may learn that the true system
of government consists of fair, equal, and honorable
representation. As France has been the first of European nations to abolish royalty, Paine further challenges her also to be the first to abolish the
punishment of death and to find a milder and more
effectual substitute. An avidity to punish, Paine
warns, is dangerous to liberty.

By 1795, discouraged that more European revolutions had not occurred, Paine pleads in the *Dissertation on First Principles of Government* for
suffrage based on age, not property. He cautions:
"It is possible to exclude men from the right of
voting, but it is impossible to exclude them from the
right of rebelling against that exclusion." Although
it is impossible for property to be distributed
equally, property is better regulated when rights,
including those of voting, are secure. He strongly
opposed the restrictions on suffrage contained in
the new French Constitution.

Paine also distinguished between the means
needed to overthrow despotism in order to establish
liberty and the means used after that despotism is
overthrown. He believed that if a constitution had
been established in France in 1793, violence would
have been prevented. Lacking a constitution,
France established a revolutionary government
without principle or authority. Paine reminds
France: "The moral principle of revolutions is to
instruct, not to destroy."

The Age of Reason

Paine's attack on institutionalized Christianity in
The Age of Reason (1794–96) comprises his most
controversial work. He disavows any superstitions
or false systems of theology and government that
deny morality and humanity. His attack, stimulated
by the disestablishment of the French Roman Catholic church in 1792, focuses on national institutions
of churches and restrictive systems of dogma. Paine
clearly professes his belief in one God and defines
humankind's religious duties by doing justice, loving mercy, and endeavoring to make its fellow creatures happy. He hoped that a revolution in the
system of government would be followed by a revolution in the system of religion.

Infidelity, explains Paine, is professing to believe
what you do not believe. To be happy, humankind
must be mentally faithful to itself. God communi-
cates through nature to each individual, not through
revelation transmitted by the spoken or written
word. Such "revelation" is not the best evidence on
which to base faith. The Christian tradition, explains Paine, is based on ancient mythology and
Jewish fables. Further, the authority on which the
Bible rests is tenuous. The Old Testament offers a
history of wickedness that corrupts and brutalizes
humankind. The New Testament provides only detached anecdotes of Jesus, and its theory of redemption represents pecuniary justice. Paine challenges
readers to rely on God's gift to them—reason—to
discover God.

God, Paine defines, is the first cause of all things,
and we behold God in creation—the true theology.
Present theology is merely the study of human opinions and fancies concerning God. An imposed sys-

tem of thought, like Christianity, restricts individual discoveries about God and becomes a powerful weapon of control. Systems of religion employ mystery, miracle, and prophecy to obscure the reflection of God human reason is capable of perceiving.

Additionally, Paine substitutes bold educational reforms to replace those connected to restrictive theological systems. Present learning, he alleges, involves knowledge of things to which language gives names. He advocates abolishing the study of dead languages and instituting the study of science and philosophy. The Christian system promotes ig-

norance because it restricts learning to a reinforcement of its rigid dogmas. The Reformation begun by Luther was the first break in the long chain of despotic ignorance. Free thought and liberty go together. Every person of learning is finally his own teacher, and every person has the right to follow the religion he or she prefers. All nations and religions, Paine concludes, believe in a God; the things on which they disagree are the redundancies annexed to that belief. As a deist and a skeptic, Paine disbelieves all institutionalized dogma; he affirms instead, "My own mind is my own church."

MARJEAN D. PURINTON

Further Reading

Aldridge, Alfred Owen. *Man of Reason: The Life of Thomas Paine*. Philadelphia: J. B. Lippincott, 1959. Still a valuable and readable biography.

————. *Thomas Paine's American Ideology*. Newark: University of Delaware Press, 1984. Tracing the intellectual background of Puritans, Locke, Rousseau, and Montesquieu, the study focuses on Paine as an individual thinker from 1775–83 and on *Common Sense*, *The Crisis*, *Letter to Abbe Raynal*. Includes an excellent bibliography.

Ayer, A. J. *Thomas Paine*. New York: Atheneum, 1988. Offers critical analysis of *Common Sense*, *Rights of Man*, *Age of Reason*, but comparisons and tertiary commentary about other political situations are a distraction. Chapters 2 and 4 provide helpful background about political thought of the Enlightenment and Burke.

Butler, Marilyn, ed. *Burke, Paine, Godwin, and the Revolution Controversy*. Cambridge: Cambridge University Press, 1984. Comparative essays about radical attempts to stimulate an English revolution during the 1790s, with emphasis on Paine's contributions to that movement.

Conway, Moncure D. *The Life of Thomas Paine: With a History of His Literary, Political, and Religious Career in America, France, and England*. Edited by Hypatia Bradlaugh Bonner. London: Watts, 1909; Folcroft, Pa.: Folcroft,

1974. Still considered the definitive biography. Despite favoritism toward Paine, it offers the best study of Paine's French period.

Dyck, Ian, ed. *Citizen of the World: Essays on Thomas Paine*. New York: St. Martin's Press, 1988. George Spater's five essays in this volume offer a provocative overview and good introduction to Paine scholarship. J. F. C. Harrison's essay provides a succinct but excellent discussion of religious thought and influence.

Edwards, Samuel. *Rebel! A Biography of Tom Paine*. New York: Praeger Publishers, 1974. Includes critical and analytical commentary on Paine's life, works, and thoughts.

Fennesy, R. R. *Burke, Paine, and the Rights of Man: A Difference of Political Opinion*. The Hague: Martinus Nijhoff, 1963. Comparative study of the ideological debate over human rights and the attempt to generate political reforms in England. Good discussion of Paine's political ideas, 1737–90. Excellent bibliography of primary and secondary sources.

Foner, Eric. *Tom Paine and Revolutionary America*. New York: Oxford University Press, 1976. Readable and well-researched, this study focuses on Paine's American activities prior to 1790.

Hawke, David Freeman. *Paine*. New York: Harper & Row, 1974. Valuable and comprehensive biography.

Powell, David. *Tom Paine: The Great Exile*. New York: St. Martin's Press, 1985. Good introductory biography, but provides limited critical apparatus. Powell gives more attention to the events of Paine's life than to his ideas.

Thompson, E. P. *The Making of the English Working Class*. New York: Random House, 1963. An excellent discussion of the Burke/Paine controversy and Paine's impact on the English reform movement is found on pp. 89–122.

Williamson, Audrey. *Thomas Paine: His Life, Work, and Times*. New York: St. Martin's Press, 1973. A solid discussion of Paine's political and religious ideas, placed in the context of other radical thinking of the day. The biography includes limited bibliographical citations.

Wilson, Jerome D., and William F. Ricketson. *Thomas Paine*. Twayne United States Authors Series, No. 301. Boston: Twayne Publishers, 1989. Excellent survey of Paine's life and major works. Includes annotated bibliography.

MARIE-JEAN ANTOINE NICHOLAS DE CARITAT, MARQUIS DE CONDORCET

Born: 1743, Ribemont, Picardy, France
Died: 1794, Paris, France
Major Works: *Réflexions sur l'esclavage des nègres* (*Reflections on Black Slavery*) (1781), *La Vie de M. Turgot* (1786), *Esquisse d'un Tableau historique des progrès de l'esprit humain* (*Sketch for a Historical Picture of the Progress of the Human Mind*) (1795)

Major Ideas

There is limited certainty in all branches of human knowledge.
Probability theory can be applied to natural and social sciences.
Mankind is infinitely perfectible.
There can be continuous progress and improvement in human affairs.
Mathematics can be applied to the social sciences and to human problems.
Human suffering can be ameliorated through social scientific study.
There are rational and scientific reasons why slavery should be abolished.
There is a reasonable basis for decision making in human affairs.

The Marquis de Condorcet, a protegée of the French finance minister Turgot and of Voltaire, was a great mathematician. Because of his achievements in working out the calculus of probabilities, he became the secretary of the French Academy of Sciences. He was also the first secretary of the Society of the Friends of the Blacks, the group in France advocating the abolition of slavery. He was one of the only *philosophes* of the *ancien régime* to live until the French Revolution, in which he actively participated and ultimately died. Condorcet, who had imbibed the progress theory from his mentor, Turgot, and who saw the application of the achievements of mathematics to social problems as the chief way of bringing about progress, sought to solve scientifically many of the social ills of the time. During the Revolution, he prepared analyses of a wide range of problems concerning taxation, prisons, hospitals, electoral processes, education, and other matters. He proposed a range of liberal, humanistic solutions, some of which are still part of the French scene (such as his scheme for secular public education run by a National Ministry of Education).

Condorcet's most philosophical statement of his views was written at the end of his life, when he was in hiding from the Reign of Terror. He had set forth a liberal plan for a constitution in 1793, which was denounced by the radical Jacobins. Condorcet as a moderate was now regarded as an "enemy of the people." While in hiding, he wrote his classic statement of the progress theory and on the infinite improvability of mankind, *The Sketch for the Historical Picture of the Human Mind*. It was finished shortly before he was captured in 1794. He then either committed suicide or was executed. After the fall of Robespierre, his work was published in 1795 by his widow. It has been recognized as a wonderful statement of the French Enlightenment point of view. Its optimism is all the more amazing when one realizes that the author was being victimized by the very revolution he had helped to create.

Condorcet's Skepticism

Condorcet's philosophy developed from a kind of skepticism that had developed among some of the French followers of John Locke. In the notes to his edition of Pascal's *Pensées*, Condorcet explained that in the moral and the physical sciences we cannot reach the rigorous certainty that we find in mathematical propositions. But this does not mean that we have no sure rule on which to base our opinions in these matters. Following from his studies of probabilities, he declared, "there are sure means of arriving at a very great probability in some cases and of evaluating the degree of this probability in a great number."

Condorcet had read the chapter in Hume's *Treatise of Human Nature* on the probability of chances, and he had seen how probability theory could be applied in both natural and social science. Condorcet accepted the reasons Locke had given to explain why human beings cannot arrive at any necessary science of nature. People can observe what happens in nature but cannot ascertain why it occurs. We cannot even be sure that Newton's laws have to be true, and that nature cannot behave differently at some point. On the other hand, Condorcet insisted, we do find logical certainty in mathematics.

When we examine how it is that we can have certainty in mathematics but not in the natural or social sciences, Condorcet said that the problem is in the human observer, not in nature itself. The world may be completely determined, but we are able to know about it only through empirical observations and intuitively recognized relations between ideas. The generalizations, the laws, that we learn by induction from experience are, as far as we can tell, only probable. We cannot know if future experiences will resemble past ones. Hence, as skeptics like Pascal, Bayle, and Hume had pointed out, our empirical knowledge of the world is slight and uncertain.

Condorcet, as one of the theoreticians of probability theory, saw that one could develop a mathematics of reasonable expectation if one assumed that nature will in fact be uniform. Such a mathematical schema would tell us about relations of ideas, not relations of things in the world.

Condorcet indicated in some of the notes he prepared for his inaugural address when he was elected to the French Academy of Sciences that there is an empirical aspect of mathematical truths as well, which makes even these truths somewhat uncertain. One's basis for asserting that a mathematical proposition is true is the psychological fact that one realizes that it is true. However, this realization may not continue into the future, since our minds may not be constant. Thus all our knowledge, mathematical, natural, and human, is partly empirical, and hence just probable. Instead of stating that all of our knowledge may be dubious, however, Condorcet emphasized the positive aspect—namely, that our knowledge about human affairs can be as precise, exact, and certain as knowledge about natural affairs. One can state the natural and moral sciences in terms of carefully defined terms and reasonings from them. Such statements, as well as statements of mathematical knowledge, are just probable. They all depend upon what is found in experience. All of our knowledge is "fortified by the observation that the fact which was observed yesterday will be observed today if no circumstance has changed." All such knowledge can be stated in terms of probabilities. It may be easier to do this with regard to natural sciences, but it can also be done in the moral sciences. The results may not be as certain, but we can find rules and laws in the social sciences.

Condorcet presented this theory in his inaugural speech at the French Academy in 1782, where it was greeted with dismay and disbelief. It also appears in his work, *Essai sur l'application de l'analyse à la probabilité des décisions rendues à la pluralité des voix* of 1785. (This work has become the basis of the current branch of philosophy called "decision theory.") Condorcet contended that both the moral and political sciences can be stated mathematically. Our knowledge in these areas and our actions can be based on mathematical probabilities.

From the time of his inaugural speech through his activities during the French Revolution, Condorcet insisted that those sciences that deal with human affairs could have the same kind of certainty (probabilities) as the natural sciences, but not necessarily the same degree of certainty. Further, and more important in his theory, was the claim that the scientific results in the study of human affairs could be applied in order to solve human problems and to make human beings happier. The social sciences, rather than either the church or the state, could improve human existence. There could then be endless progress in human affairs. Based on careful observation and reasoning, we should be able "to establish the first principles of ethics, of political, civil or criminal legislation, or of administration." The social sciences thus established would not only describe human existence but would also prescribe how to improve the quality of human existence.

On Human Rights

According to Condorcet, human rights, the natural rights of human beings, can be known empirically. In a note in his edition of Voltaire's writings, Condorcet stated that every reasoning being will be led to the same ideas in morality as in geometry. Such ideas are the necessary result of the properties of sensate beings capable of reasoning: ". . . The reality of moral propositions, their truth relative to the state of real beings, depends entirely upon this truth of fact: that men are sensitive and intelligent beings." Reasonable people should be able to discover the actual state of human affairs and should be able to tell what to do about it in order to make human life better.

Condorcet, who was a good friend of Thomas Jefferson, did not hold that the basic moral truths are self-evident. Rather, he contended that these truths will be discovered by careful scientific examination. We will find it is a fact that all persons are created equal. This will be as obvious to sensate and intelligent beings as the truths of mathematics and physics. With such discoveries based on experience, one could provide a basis for political action; one could discover what ought to be done. But doing it is not part of social science. Political action is an art that tries to bring about rational social choices, based upon scientific knowledge, in given historical situations. Properly directed, it should lead to the endless perfectibility of life on earth.

In Condorcet's final statement of his Enlightenment optimism, in the *Sketch for a Historical Picture of the Progress of the Human Mind*, written in 1793–94 while France was being tormented by the Reign of Terror and Condorcet was in hiding from the Terrorists, he began by insisting that the observation of human societies throughout the various stages of human history would enable people to see how the human race has developed and how it can go on progressing toward greater and greater happiness. The overall picture of the progressive drive of human history "will instruct us about the means we should employ to make certain and rapid further progress that human nature is capable of." The application of rational scientific study to human affairs should lead to an indefinite series of improvements in the human scene. (It is still amazing that Condorcet could write this in hiding as the very ideals he worked for in the French Revolution were being destroyed.)

Condorcet is interesting not only as the theoretician of the progress theory and of mathematical social science as the means for solving human problems but also as a practical philosopher applying his theory to the human problems of the time. Even before the Revolution, Condorcet was actively working on the abolition of slavery. In 1781, he published his *Réflexions sur l'esclavage des nègres*. Shortly before the Revolution, he became the president and chief spokesperson of the Society of the Friends of the Blacks. He tried to show scientifically that all human beings regardless of the color of their skin have the same rights, including that of being a free person. He tried to show scientifically that enslaving people is criminal. As a result of his study of the actual situation in the United States and the European colonies in the Caribbean, Condorcet proposed a systematic way of abolishing slavery over a period of forty years, a way that included preparing the enslaved persons to be viable members of a free society.

During the French Revolution, Condorcet was active in studying the myriad of problems that had to be dealt with. He proposed solutions for reforming the hospital system, the educational system, the tax system, and the prison system. He worked on an unbelievable number of problems, applying his scientific tools to the issues at hand. In 1793, he worked out a liberal constitution for the French republic, which was denounced by the radicals in the National Assembly. Condorcet was forced to flee, and to carry on his scientific studies while in hiding. His final work, the *Sketch*, his greatest philosophical achievement, was published post-humously in 1795. He left many unpublished works, some of which are just now being published for the first time.

Condorcet is gradually being recognized as a basic theoretician of liberal humanism and as a man who saw clearly many of the problems that we are just beginning to try to resolve (such as equal rights for women and for homosexuals). He presented the most complete statement of Enlightenment optimism, which becomes all the more poignant in the light of his own tragedy. Recent studies are showing that there is still much that can be learned from his theory and his insights and his researches.

RICHARD H. POPKIN

Further Reading

Only a few works of Condorcet are available in English. The *Sketch for a Historical Picture of the Progress of the Human Mind* has been translated by June Barraclough (London: Weidenfeld, 1955). Keith Baker has translated the notes for a revised version of Condorcet's inaugural address to the French Academy, *Studies in Voltaire and the Eighteenth Century*, vol. 119 (1977), pp. 7–68. A collection of short works and excerpts from Condorcet has appeared in *Selected Works* (Indianapolis: Bobbs-Merrill, 1976), now unfortunately out of print, but can be found in many college and university libraries.

Baker, Keith M. *Condorcet. From Natural Philosophy to Social Mathematics*. Chicago: University of Chicago Press, 1975. A most important study showing how Condorcet's theory developed.

Manuel, Frank. *The Prophets of Paris*. Cambridge, Mass: Harvard, 1962. Chapter 2, "Marquis de Condorcet: The Taming of the Future," shows Condorcet's role as an interpreter of history.

Popkin, Richard H. "Condorcet's Epistemology and his Politics." In M. Dascal and O. Gruengard, *Knowledge and Politics*, pp. 111–124. Denver: Westview Press, 1989. A study of how Condorcet's theory of knowledge relates to his political views.

Rosenfield, Leonora C., ed. *Condorcet Studies I*. Atlantic Highlands, N.J.: Humanities Press, 1984. A collection of essays by leading Condorcet scholars in America and Europe, dealing with various facets of his views and achievements.

Shapiro, J. Salwyn. *Condorcet and the Rise of Liberalism*. New York: Octagon, 1934. A useful study of Condorcet's role in the development of liberal thought in the nineteenth and twentieth centuries.

Williams, David, ed. *Condorcet Studies II*. New York: Peter Lang, 1987. A second collection of articles by leading American and European Condorcet scholars.

ANTOINE-LAURENT LAVOISIER

Born: 1743, Paris, France
Died: 1794, Paris, France
Major Works: *Opuscules physiques et chimiques* (1774), *Méthode de nomenclature chimique* (1787), *Traité élémentaire de chimie* (1789), *Mémoires de chimie* (posthumous, 1804–5)

Major Ideas

In any chemical reaction, mass is conserved: Matter is neither created nor destroyed; only the form of the matter is altered.

Precise measurements of the weights and volumes of substances involved in experiments must be made if the researcher hopes to explain the nature of the reactions.

Precision and uniformity in nomenclature is necessary for a precise science of chemistry.

Combustion proceeds by the combination of oxygen with a combustible material; animal respiration is a form of combustion.

One of the goals of chemistry is to compile a list of the elements, which are undecomposable materials.

Antoine-Laurent Lavoisier effected a revolution in chemistry analogous to Newton's in physics or Darwin's in biology. His studies of combustion laid the groundwork for the understanding of oxidation and reduction, two bases of chemical change; his emphasis on accurate weights and measures and his formulation of the principle of the *conservation of mass* began the era of quantitative chemistry; his researches in the analysis of plant and animal matter laid the foundation for organic chemistry; and his studies in fermentation and respiration were important contributions to modern biology. In addition to his theoretical work, Lavoisier applied the results of science to industry and agriculture: As a member of the French Academy of Sciences, he wrote dozens of reports on French manufacturing; as a large landowner, he carried out experiments to increase agricultural production and improve the dismal condition of the French peasant. During the early days of the French Revolution, he wrote treatises on the national economy and served on the commission that established the metric system. A victim of the guillotine, he has always been considered the most noteworthy martyr to the excesses of the Reign of Terror.

A lifelong resident of Paris, Lavoisier received his education at the Collège Mazarin, where he received a classical education and the best scientific training available in France. Although his interest in science developed early (he attended a series of popular lectures given by the chemist and geologist Guillaume François Rouelle), he followed family tradition by studying in the Faculty of Law and receiving his degrees in law (1763–64). However, he never practiced, instead devoting himself to scientific investigation.

He first did field work with a family friend, the geologist Jean-Étienne Guettard, who was compiling a geological and mineralogical atlas of France. As part of this work, Lavoisier began a detailed study of the various waters of France. He analyzed potable waters from many sources, for the purpose of determining the influence of the strata through which the water flowed and of increasing the supply of potable water for the urban population. In a paper read before the Academy of Sciences in 1768, Lavoisier described his methods of analysis with a hydrometer, which he had invented to determine the specific gravity of the water, and he presented tables in which were listed analyses of various waters collected in his expeditions with Guettard. Partly as a result of the success of this paper, Lavoisier was elected to the Academy of Sciences, the youngest person ever so chosen.

Much of Lavoisier's chemical work—and that of his contemporaries—derived from the study of gases. In 1648, Van Helmont had created the word "gas" (from "chaos") and had noted that different gases existed, but he had isolated none. In 1659, Robert Boyle developed the first apparatus to isolate a gas and had in fact isolated what we call hydrogen and nitric oxide, although he considered these to be simply minor varieties of common air. Boyle was also the first to rigorously define an *element* as a substance that cannot be decomposed into anything else and to determine that air contained a substance that was required to maintain a flame. Boyle also studied the *calcination* of metals: This is the process in which the metal is heated in air, thus losing its metallic character and producing a *calx* of the metal. (Today the process is called *oxidation* and the calx is called the metal's *oxide*.) Boyle noted that in the process of calcination, the metals gained weight, and he concluded that particles of fire had united with the metals. He also noted that when the calx of the metal was reheated in the presence of charcoal, the metal was reconstituted. (In modern terms, the oxygen from the metallic oxide unites with the carbon to form carbon monoxide or dioxide.)

A decisive advance was made by Joseph Black in 1756. In his studies of alkaline substances like lime, magnesia, and chalk, he was the first to succeed in isolating and identifying a gas, which he called *fixed air* (carbon dioxide). He showed that fixed air was also produced in respiration, fermentation, and the burning of charcoal. Ten years later, Henry Cavendish isolated *inflammable air* (hydrogen) and differentiated it from Black's fixed air. In the 1770s, the brilliant chemist Joseph Priestley isolated several other gases.

While progress was made in the techniques for studying gases, G. E. Stahl (1660–1734) had developed a new theory to explain combustion: All combustible bodies contain an inflammable principle, named *phlogiston*. When a substance burns, it loses its phlogiston; those substances that are consumed by combustion (oil, charcoal) contain primarily phlogiston. For various reasons, phlogiston was considered the lightest of materials.

This was the situation of chemistry when Lavoisier began his researches. The immediate impulse for his researches may have been a visit from Joseph Priestley in October 1774. The English scientist informed Lavoisier of his recent experiment with "the calx of mercury" (mercuric oxide). He had heated this calx in a sealed vessel and had studied the gas that was emitted (now called oxygen). He found that it was insoluble in water and promoted vigorous combustion. He called this gas *dephlogisticated air*, on the theory that since it promoted combustion so well (readily receiving the phlogiston given off by the burning material), it must have very little phlogiston naturally contained in it.

Lavoisier, who called this air "the purest portion of the air" or "eminently respirable air," immediately extended Priestley's experiments: He studied the air left *after* mercury was oxidized and found it to be unlike Black's fixed air. (This was the nitrogen remaining after the oxygen in the air had united with the mercury.) During 1774–77, while experimenting with acids, he came to the conclusion that air, or some fraction of it, entered into the composition of these acids. In 1779, he published his conclusions: The "eminently respirable air" is the principle that makes acids: When combined with charcoal, it makes carbonic acid, with sulfur, sulfuric acid, with nitric oxide, nitric acid, and so on. When combined with metals, it makes calxes (oxides). Because of its acid-forming properties, Lavoisier decided to call this fraction of the air *oxygen* (oxy-, "acid"; -gen, "maker").

In 1782–83, Lavoisier studied Cavendish's inflammable air. Lavoisier and his colleagues exploded a mixture of inflammable air and dephlogisticated air and determined that the resulting liquid was pure water. He gave the name *hydrogen* (hydro-, "water") to the inflammable gas. His conclusions from this experiment were historic: Water is not an element, but the combination of two gases, hydrogen and oxygen, in the ratio by weight of 85 percent oxygen/15 percent hydrogen (modern value 89 percent/11 percent). Hydrogen was soon used to spectacular effect. Following the example of the Montgolfier brothers with their hot-air balloons, experimenters filled several balloons with hydrogen, and intrepid aeronauts flew through the Paris skies. For these balloons Lavoisier developed methods of producing hydrogen on a large scale.

In a treatise on phlogiston (1783), Lavoisier destroyed that theory while setting out his own: (1) Combustion proceeds only in the presence of oxygen, never in a vacuum; (2) in combustion, oxygen is absorbed into the burning substance and increases the weight of that substance; (3) combustion produces light and heat. Phlogiston still had its defenders—Priestley in particular maintained the faith until his death in 1804—but the future of chemistry had been set in another direction.

The development of chemistry has been closely associated with its terminology, which in large part was established by Lavoisier in his *Méthode de nomenclature chimique* (1787). This work marked a complete break with the past—intentionally so, for Lavoisier considered, as did his colleagues in the eighteenth-century Enlightenment, that the art of analysis depends on a finely crafted language. Hence a new departure in chemistry required a new language. In the *Méthode*, Lavoisier listed fifty-five elements, or undecomposable substances, including light and heat, the elementary gases (oxygen, hydrogen, nitrogen), sixteen known metals, and other substances. The principles for forming the names of compounds were listed: Compounds of oxygen are called oxides; salts are given the name of the acid from which they are formed (sulfates, nitrates); and so on.

The *Méthode* was followed in 1789 by Lavoisier's best known work, the *Traité élémentaire de chimie*, which in some ways is a justification of the terminology used in the earlier work. After defining chemistry as the science of determining the composition of the various substances found in nature, Lavoisier lists the elements, which then totaled only thirty-three. Lavoisier had determined that some of the substances previously listed were in fact compounds, and he presumed that others still on his list (potash, soda) would eventually be found to be compounds as well. These lists in the *Méthode* and in the *Traité* are the first tables of the chemical elements.

The *Traité* also describes his experiments in fermentation and his analysis of the products of fermentation. He was aware that the combustion of vegetable products (sugar, alcohol) produces water and carbon dioxide, but he was convinced that these compounds did not exist *in those forms* in the burned substances, but that hydrogen, oxygen, and carbon did—that, in combustion, what we now call a *chemical change* was occurring, not simply a change in physical form. He assumed that the same sort of thing happened in the process of fermentation, and to represent it he wrote the first chemical equation:

Grape juice = carbonic acid + alcohol.

His data, however, could not support an exact determination of the processes. He had established the principle of the *conservation of mass*: "Nothing is created in the operations either of art or of Nature, and it can be taken as an axiom that in every operation an equal quantity of matter exists both before and after the operation."

During his experiments with oxygen, Lavoisier became interested in respiration. He determined that respiration is a slow form of combustion, that in respiration oxygen is exchanged with carbon dioxide, and that the heat liberated by this exchange maintains the organism at a constant temperature. Lavoisier believed that this exchange occurred in the lungs rather than in the muscles. In experiments carried out during the years 1789–91, Lavoisier found that the quantity of oxygen absorbed in respiration—and therefore the heat produced—increases at lower temperatures and is greater during exercise and digestion. Several of these experiments were illustrated by Madame Lavoisier and show Lavoisier's assistant, Seguin, wearing a gas mask through which oxygen was supplied. After Lavoisier's execution, Seguin published the data.

Aside from his chemical work, Lavoisier was continually busy with other projects, particularly those associated with the Academy of Sciences. He usually had himself appointed secretary of the committees on which he served, and in this capacity he produced reports on scores of varying topics, from prison reform to balloon design and hypnotism ("mesmerism"). Benjamin Franklin was a member of the latter committee; indeed the correspondence between Lavoisier and the American continued until the former's death. In 1778, Lavoisier bought a country estate near Blois, and there he conducted experiments on improving crop yields, at the same time addressing the economic difficulties facing French agriculture: the lack of capital, the deleterious effect of the current tax system, and internal trade barriers. This same interest in economics is visible in his work during the Revolution: He was made a director of the Discount Bank and an administrator of the national treasury. In that capacity he published a report on the French economy, the national debt, and the sources of revenue, a serious problem during the Revolution. At the same time he published a statistical study on French agriculture and proposals for the reform of French education, including the establishment of free primary schools and separation of secondary education into training for public service in the existing colleges and for mechanical arts in new vocational institutes. He was part of the commission that developed the metric system; at the time of his death he was working on the gram.

Lavoisier's interest in economics and the national income derived at least in part from his membership in the Ferme Général, the private corporation that collected taxes for the monarchy. In 1768, Lavoisier invested the large fortune he had inherited from his mother in the Ferme, and for twenty years much of his time was spent in travels on behalf of the corporation. In 1771, he married Marie Anne Paulze, the daughter of a fellow tax-farmer. Madame Lavoisier became a valued collaborator in his work. She learned English in order to translate important work in that language for her husband; she studied with the painter David, did a portrait of Benjamin Franklin, and drew the illustrations for the *Traité élémentaire de chimie*. She also acted as the hostess for visiting scientists and for scientific gatherings. The Lavoisiers had no children.

The tax-farmers as a body were unpopular, and after 1790 Lavoisier himself was increasingly the object of attack by extreme revolutionaries, particularly Marat. Institutions with which he was associated, particularly the Academy of Sciences and the Ferme Général, were abolished. In December 1793, all of the tax-farmers were arrested, and on May 8, 1794, they were tried before a revolutionary tribunal, where the testimony was in the hysterical left-wing style that has since become common: "The record of the crimes of these vampires is complete; their crimes clamor for vengeance; the immorality of these creatures is burned into public memory . . ." With reference to Lavoisier, the presiding judge is said to have remarked, "The Republic has no need of scientists." Lavoisier, with his father-in-law, was guillotined that afternoon. Lagrange, the mathematician, said the next day: "It took them only an instant to cut off that head, and a hundred years may not produce another like it."

MARK T. RILEY

Further Reading

Note: Lavoisier's major works were reprinted as *Oeuvres de Lavoisier*, edited by J. B. Dumas and Edouard Grimaux, Paris: 1862–93. Much of his correspondence has appeared in *Oeuvres de Lavoisier—Correspondance*, edited by René Fric, Paris: Académie des Sciences, 1955–64. Almost all of his laboratory notebooks, paper drafts, and reports survive, kept in the archives of the Académie des Sciences in Paris. Consequently, much material is available for a detailed study of the development of his theories and his experiments.

Guerlac, Henry. *Lavoisier—The Crucial Year: The Background and Origin of His First Experiments on Combustion in 1772*. Ithaca: Cornell University Press, 1961. An excellent review of the scientific importance of the combustion experiments.

Holmes, F. L. *Lavoisier and the Chemistry of Life*. Madison: University of Wisconsin Press, 1985. An exhaustive review of Lavoisier's experiments in biochemistry.

McKie, Douglas. *Antoine Lavoisier: Scientist, Economist, Social Reformer*. New York: Henry Schuman, 1952. The best biography in English.

THOMAS JEFFERSON

Born: 1743, Shadwell, Virginia
Died: 1826, Monticello, Virginia
Major Works: *A Summary of the Rights of British America* (1774), *The Declaration of Independence* (1776), *Notes on the State of Virginia* (1782), *A Bill for Establishing Religious Freedom* (1784)

Major Ideas

All human beings are created equal and are endowed with certain inalienable rights.

Governments are established to protect the rights of citizens.

The right to work the land is a fundamental human right; consequently, a state that allows private ownership of land must provide employment to those who do not have such property.

Freedom of religion should be absolute, and citizens should not be taxed for the support of religious institutions.

Universal education is the most effective means of preserving democracy and good government.

The epitaph that Thomas Jefferson wrote for his tombstone is still visible in the burying ground at Monticello:

Here was buried
Thomas Jefferson
Author of the Declaration of American
 Independence
of the Statute of Virginia for religious freedom
& Father of the University of Virginia

These words aptly sum up the chief contributions of an extraordinary man. Born in Virginia to an early settler who was largely self-educated, Jefferson studied at local schools and at the College of William and Mary. He left the college after two years to study for the bar. Two years after his admission to the practice of law, he entered the lower house of the colonial legislature at age twenty-six. In 1775, he was appointed by the Virginia legislature to serve as a delegate to the Second Continental Congress in Philadelphia. He joined a radical group that was advocating separation from Britain. In 1776, fellow members of a committee on which he served, including Benjamin Franklin and John Adams, asked Jefferson to draft a statement of reasons for an irrevocable break with Great Britain— the document that became the Declaration of Independence.

His work in the Virginia legislature included ef-

forts to reform the Constitution and laws of that state, including the creation of a system of free public education. As part of that program, he established the University of Virginia. In addition, he introduced legislation to disestablish the established church, to prohibit all public funding of religion, and to remove all religious disabilities from Virginia's citizens. "I have sworn upon the altar of God," Jefferson said, "eternal hostility against every form of tyranny over the mind of man."

After serving briefly as governor of Virginia, Jefferson retired to his home in Monticello. He subsequently served in the Continental Congress and in the diplomatic service. The Constitution was drafted while he was in France, but upon his return he was instrumental in having the Bill of Rights added to it. He served as secretary of state under George Washington, founded the party that ultimately became today's Democratic party, and was eventually elected president of the United States.

During his presidency, Jefferson acquired the Louisiana Territory, nearly doubling the land area of the United States. He was firmly opposed to the increasing power of the Supreme Court, enunciated in *Marbury v. Madison*, in which Chief Justice John Marshall declared that the Court had the right to decide upon the constitutionality of any legislation. Jefferson held that for unelected judges to have such power was inconsistent with the democratic rights of the people to determine their own destiny. That, he believed, should be left to the democratically elected branches of government.

When it came to foreign affairs, he was anything but indecisive. The United States had no navy worth speaking of when he entered office. Pirates in the Mediterranean were harassing American shipping, both commercial and naval. Following an attack upon an American vessel by Arab pirates, he declared that the United States would give not one more cent of ransom and went to Congress demanding funds for expansion of a naval force capable of dealing with the terrorists of his day.

Jefferson firmly believed in the necessity of every person's maintaining as much personal liberty as possible, and was thoroughly opposed to any kind of behavior that might compromise anyone's range of choices. Thus, for example, he wrote that he was in a state of despair as a result of what he perceived to be the American penchant to buy—on credit—every gadget that was held out to them. Neither governments nor individuals should be permitted to buy on credit, he said, for it is the source of ruin. Love of luxury is a great enemy of liberty. He held that if Americans ran up their debts, they would have to tax such necessities as food and drink, and would end up like the English, laboring sixteen hours a day and giving up fifteen of them to pay for government. In such circumstances, he said, we would "have no time to think, no means of calling the mismanagers to account; but be glad to obtain subsistence by hiring ourselves to rivet their chains on the necks of our fellow-sufferers."

His allegiance to the principles of liberty did not lead him to blind sentimentality or to anything like anarchism. He firmly believed that every society had the right to lay down the principles upon which it would operate, and to exclude from its midst anyone who acted contrary to them. He believed that agriculture was a noble and liberating occupation, and that speculation, banking, and the property laws of England led to the oppression, poverty, and misery that he saw there. He saw little in Europe that he wanted Americans to emulate, except perhaps some aspects of social etiquette. The poorest farmer in America, he said, is two centuries ahead of most Europeans in the things that really

count in life—virtue, freedom, happiness, and scientific knowledge, as opposed to what he called economic "profusion."

Jefferson's Ethics

Jefferson believed, with Locke, that all knowledge comes from experience, and that moral principles are based upon utility. His belief in the pursuit of happiness as the highest goal contributed to his conclusion that agriculture is the best calling a person can pursue. It may produce less economic wealth than manufacturing, but the American farmer enjoys far more freedom, more ease, and less misery than any of the laborers of Europe. In time, however, he came to recognize the vital necessity of creating manufacturing enterprises on this side of the Atlantic.

Jefferson believed that "the earth belongs to the living; the dead have neither powers nor rights over it." He therefore concluded that once a person dies, he should have no further power over his possessions, which should then revert to society. Thus, he would have opposed enabling landowners, through the power of wills statutes, to accumulate vast territories and convey them from generation to generation. Such laws would ultimately vest immense power in a few families and lead to the tyrannical forms of government that had dominated Europe for centuries. A frequent redistribution of property would lead to a better life for all, with greater emphasis on the virtues of friendship, community, and leisure and less on profitability.

This conviction led to his advocacy of the abolition of laws that had led, in Virginia and elsewhere, to the accumulation of vast estates and the development of a landed aristocracy. His success in getting such legislation through the Virginia legislature, he said, "laid the axe to the root of Pseudo-aristocracy." In the old world, Jefferson claimed, people were crowded into small spaces or were overcharged for the land they occupied. But here, he wrote, "every one may have land to labor for himself if he chuses [sic]; or, preferring the exercise of any other industry, may exact for it such compensation as not only to afford a comfortable subsistence, but wherewith to provide for a cessation from labor in old age." He firmly believed that land ownership encouraged people to support law and order and a sense of responsibility that entitled them, if nothing else did, to a control over public affairs and a degree of freedom that was wholly unknown in Europe.

Jefferson believed that every human being possesses an innate moral sense, a conscience, which is as much a part of a person as his arm or his leg. Reason and emotion are both involved in determining a person's actions, and neither should be permitted to dominate exclusively. Right and wrong are determined by conscience and not by reason. Thus, Jefferson contends that there is no difference between the ability of a plowman and that of a professor to make moral decisions. Indeed, he argues that the plowman will often make better decisions than the professor, because "he has not been led astray by artificial rules."

Jefferson disagreed with Hobbes's view that justice was founded on contractual agreements. Like the moral sense with which it is so closely related, our sense of justice is innate, as it must be for a creature destined to live in society.

Jefferson and Slavery

Although Jefferson owned slaves, he was never comfortable with the institution of slavery. In his initial draft of the Declaration of Independence, he included a paragraph condemning the British king for waging "a cruel war against human nature itself" and violating the "most sacred rights of life and liberty" by permitting and encouraging the "execrable commerce" in human beings. In order to keep the southern states in the struggle for independence, he acquiesced in this paragraph's deletion from the official version of the Declaration. He made similar compromises in his drafts of the Constitution of Virginia, realizing that the time was not ripe for determined opposition to slavery. He was, after all, a practical politician as well as a philosopher of politics and law.

Genuine liberty, he believed, could exist only where people could govern themselves. People could be self-governing only if they were able to make intelligent decisions. Therefore, he concluded, free citizens must have an education sufficient to enable them to gather necessary information and use it to make intelligent decisions. If we think the people are not enlightened enough to make wise decisions, he wrote, "the remedy is not to take [control] from them, but to inform their discretion by education." He concluded, therefore, that the state should offer general publicly funded education to all, and considered his contributions toward the founding of a public school system and the University of Virginia among his greatest achievements.

Jefferson was profoundly intolerant of monarchy. After visiting Europe, his abhorrence of kings increased dramatically. He wrote from there: "There is scarcely an evil known in these countries which may not be traced to their king as its source, nor a good which is not derived from the small fibres of republicanism among them. . . . There is not a crowned head in Europe whose talents or merit would entitle him to be elected vestryman by the people of any parish in America."

Like most natural-law theorists, he argued that the laws of nature applied to kings as well as to ordinary people. As early as 1774, he wrote: "The God who gave us life gave us liberty at the same time; the hand of force may destroy, but cannot disjoin them." He declared, "Rebellion to tyrants is obedience to God." And in the Declaration of Independence, he wrote:

> We hold these truths to be self-evident; that all men are created equal; that they are endowed by their Creator with certain unalienable rights; that among these are life, liberty, and the pursuit of happiness; that to secure these rights, governments are instituted among men, deriving their just powers from the consent of the governed.

Separation of Church and State

As a member of the Legislative Assembly in Virginia, Jefferson argued for the complete separation of church and state. He argued for tolerance of unorthodoxy, saying that "it does me no injury for my neighbor to say that there are twenty gods, or no god. It neither picks my pocket nor breaks my leg." He believed that there should be no established church, for that forced people to support ministers of other persuasions. Even forcing people to support ministers of their *own* persuasion was a deprivation of liberty, in his view. He wanted to rid his state of laws inherited from England that made heresy a capital offense and provided for imprisonment of anyone who denied the doctrine of the Trinity or the divine authority of the Scriptures. In his bill for Virginia, he provided:

> [N]o man shall be compelled to frequent or support any religious worship, place, or ministry whatsoever, nor shall be enforced, restrained, molested, or burthened in his body or goods, or shall otherwise suffer, on account of his religious opinions or belief; but that all men shall be free to profess, and by argument to maintain, their opinions in matters of religion, and that the same shall in no wise diminish, enlarge, or affect their civil capacities.

As justification for this radical innovation, he offered the opinion that "our civil rights have no dependance [*sic*] on our religious opinions, any more than our opinions in physics or geometry." To subject people to religious coercion corrupts the very religion it wants to encourage "by bribing, with a monopoly of worldly honours and emoluments, those who will externally profess and conform to it."

He believed that "reason and free enquiry are the only effectual agents against error." Give them free rein, he said, and they would support the true religion, for they were "the natural enemies of error." Truth can stand by itself, he argued, but error needs the support of government if it is to survive. The only justification for subjecting opinion to coercion is to produce uniformity, which succeeds only in making half the world fools and the other half hypocrites. The best way to rid the world of religious sects that would subvert morals is to subject it to reasonable scrutiny and then to "laugh it out of doors."

Freedom of the Press

After being subjected to defamatory accusations in the press, Jefferson defended freedom of the press in his second inaugural address. The offenders would suffer more from public outrage, he said, than from any governmental reprisals. No restraint on the press is needed, he said, as the experiment in allowing unrestrained press freedom has worked and the public has expressed its judgments through the ballot box. "The public judgment will correct false reasonings and opinions, on a full hearing of all parties; and no other definite line can be drawn between the inestimable liberty of the press and its demoralizing licentiousness." He was outraged to learn that a book was brought before the court on the charge that it was inconsistent with accepted principles of religion. "It is an insult to our citizens to question whether they are rational beings or not," he wrote, "and blasphemy against religion to suppose it cannot stand the test of truth and reason."

Jefferson was implacably opposed to unlimited government, both because it was inconsistent with his theory of human rights and because it was utterly inefficient. As he put it, "Were we directed from Washington when to sow, & when to reap, we should soon want bread." Consistently with this opinion, he strongly disapproved of what he considered to be the Supreme Court's usurpation of the power to interpret the Constitution. That power, he believed, belonged equally to each of the three branches of government. Consequently, none of them, including most especially the Supreme Court, had the right to determine for the others what their constitutional powers were.

One of Jefferson's most notable biographers, Dumas Malone, concluded his multivolume study of the sage of Monticello, as Jefferson came to be called, by observing that "he perceived eternal values and supported timeless causes. Thus he became one of the most notable champions of freedom and enlightenment in recorded history."

BURTON M. LEISER

Further Reading

Conant, James Bryant. *Thomas Jefferson and the Development of American Public Education*. Berkeley: University of California Press, 1962. One of America's most outstanding educators assesses Jefferson's contributions to the nation's educational system.

Cunningham, Noble E., Jr. *In Pursuit of Reason: The Life of Thomas Jefferson*. Baton Rouge: Louisiana State University Press, 1987. A well-written biography, emphasizing Jefferson's philosophical contributions.

Malone, Dumas. *Jefferson the Virginian, Jefferson and the Rights of Man, Jefferson and the Ordeal of Liberty, Jefferson the President: First Term, 1801–1805, Jefferson the President: Second Term, 1805–1809, Jefferson and His Time: The Sage of Monticello*. Boston: Little, Brown, 1948–81. This set of volumes comprises a thorough, highly readable study of every aspect of Jefferson's life and thought. The author has sought out all the sources, has organized them into a coherent whole, and provides the reader with a sympathetic but critical view of Jefferson's achievements and foibles. The index to each volume is immensely helpful to anyone interested in pursuing any particular topic related to Jefferson's activities.

Matthews, Richard K. *The Radical Politics of Thomas Jefferson*. Lawrence, Kans.: University Press of Kansas, 1986. A relatively short, lively study of some of Jefferson's most important and controversial ideas. Well worth reading.

JEREMY BENTHAM

Born: 1748, London, England
Died: 1832, London, England
Major Work: *An Introduction to the Principles of Morals and Legislation* (1789)

Major Ideas

Human beings are motivated solely by the desire to gain pleasure and avoid pain.
The morality of our actions is determined by their utility.
Happiness is identical with pleasure, unhappiness with pain.
Pleasure alone is intrinsically good (good in itself) and pain alone is intrinsically bad.
We have a duty to promote the pleasure of every individual equally.
Pleasures differ from one another only in quantity, never in quality.
Human behavior is controlled by the imposition of sanctions.
Justice requires equality but is subordinate to utility.

Although he wrote one of the most influential works on moral and social philosophy published in the eighteenth century, Jeremy Bentham was not interested in theoretical philosophical issues simply for their own sake. Rather, his primary concern was practical. He devoted his life to reform of almost every aspect of society, including government, law, economics, education, and religion. His lifelong interest in reform began with his dissatisfaction with the legal system of England in the mid-eighteenth century.

After graduating from Oxford University in 1763 (at the age of fifteen), Bentham entered a law firm in London to prepare himself for a legal career. He soon became disillusioned by the corruption in current legal practice. Further experience convinced him that the legal system simply reflected a broader corruption that permeated the entire society and infected all of its institutions. Because he had inherited a substantial fortune, Bentham did not have to practice law and so could devote his energies to plans and programs for the reform of the social order.

Bentham carried out his campaign of reform mainly through pamphleteering. He wrote voluminously, exposing a wide variety of social ills of the day. But he went beyond mere criticism to the development of alternative social arrangements. In some, he was successful. Two days after his death in 1832,

Parliament passed the Reform Bill, wresting political power from the landed aristocracy in favor of the general populace, largely as a result of his influence. Sometimes, however, he was unsuccessful. As part of his campaign for penal reform he spent many years and considerable personal resources planning a model prison, which he called a panopticon. His plan, strongly supported by the government, was nevertheless abandoned in its final stages by the political leaders, and the prison was never built. Perhaps because of this disappointment, Bentham took special pains to ensure that his educational reforms would succeed. After his model educational institution—University College, London—was established, he devised a way to enforce its future adherence to his reformist principles. He stipulated in his will that he must attend all meetings of its board of governors. So, on his death, his body (with a replacement wax head) was placed, seated, in a large glass-fronted case, which to this day is a silent presence at all meetings of the board.

Making due allowance for human frailty, Bentham recognized that the pervasive social corruption of his day had its origins in considerable part in unsound philosophical theories. Hence, to eliminate it, he believed it necessary to replace its theoretical foundations. The general social theories of his time that he found inadequate were bound together in a cluster of associated doctrines that included the notions of natural law, natural rights, and the social contract theory of the state. All of these were based on a set of moral presuppositions. But, Bentham asked, how were the moral presuppositions themselves justified? The standard answer was that they were self-evidently true and known to be so by direct intuition. This answer Bentham took to be nothing more than the intellectual sanctification of social beliefs and practices based on our likes and dislikes. Deriding it by the label "ipsedixitism," he maintained that a totally different foundation must be found for social practices and institutions. Rather than relying on a dubious appeal to self-evidence, we must turn to the consequences to which these things lead if we are to justify them. Intuitionism, he argued, must be replaced by the "principle of utility." This is the burden of his one important philosophical work, *An Introduction to the Principles of Morals and Legislation*, published in 1789.

An Introduction to the Principles of Morals and Legislation

Bentham's ethical theory, as well as all of its consequences for social institutions and practices, rests on his principle of utility or, as he often called it, the "greatest happiness" principle. He writes at the beginning of *An Introduction to the Principles of Morals and Legislation*, "The principle of utility is the foundation of the present work . . ."; he then goes on, "By the principle of utility is meant that principle which approves or disapproves of every action whatsoever, according to the tendency which it appears to have to augment or diminish the happiness of the party whose interest is in question. . . ." Elaborating, he identifies happiness with pleasure (and unhappiness with pain). Thus Bentham's ethics is a modern version of Epicureanism, or hedonism. It is usually referred to as hedonistic utilitarianism. According to this theory, the rightness or wrongness of actions is determined by their tendency to have consequences that are pleasurable or painful. Its ultimate foundation, thus, is the thesis that pleasure is the

only thing good in itself or worth having for its own sake, and pain is the opposite.

To apply this ethical theory in practice as a way of justification (or condemnation) of actions, whether these be on an individual or social level, Bentham often made use of the formula "the greatest happiness of the greatest number." As it stands, this phrase contains an ambiguity. Does Bentham mean that an action is right if its performance produces the most pleasure for the largest number of people or for the largest percentage of the total population? It is fairly evident that he means both, but a problem arises when the achievement of one of these goals conflicts with the achievement of the other.

Believing that he had an objective criterion of moral action, Bentham endeavored to make it as concrete as possible. His ultimate aim was to develop a "moral arithmetic," capable of guiding individuals in making decisions and, particularly, governments in the enactment of legislation. If pleasure is the only good and, thus, the only end to be sought, we can determine in any case what we ought to do by summing up the amount of pleasure and pain our contemplated acts will produce and then choosing to perform that act which will result in the greatest balance of pleasure over pain. This act is our duty. Furthermore, we can (within limits) know in any given situation what the right act is because pleasures and pains are quantifiable. The process of quantification, Bentham continued, is carried out through a "hedonistic calculus." Although the calculus is somewhat complex in detail, it contains three main elements. To evaluate a given pleasure (or pain), one must calculate two of its features—its duration and its intensity. A pleasure that lasts ten minutes is twice as good as one that lasts five; an intense pleasure is better than a mild pleasure. Although the calculation of these attributes may be difficult in practice, it is theoretically possible; furthermore, it provides an objective basis for moral actions. Finally, before a decision is made in any situation, one must determine the number of people who will be affected pleasurably or painfully by the actions contemplated and insert this multiplier into the calculations.

An important assumption underlies Bentham's hedonistic calculus and his goal of a practical moral arithmetic. This is that pleasures differ from one another only quantitatively and never qualitatively. To put this in other words, Bentham denies that certain kinds of pleasure are intrinsically superior to other kinds. Rather, if two pleasures are equal in quantity, they must be equal in value. As he put it in his famous aphorism, "Quantity of pleasure being equal, pushpin is as good as poetry." This view is important not only theoretically but historically because John Stuart Mill—Bentham's pupil and successor in the tradition of modern hedonism—disagreed with him on it, arguing that two pleasures equal in quantity could nevertheless be unequal in value because one is a "higher" pleasure and the other a "lower" pleasure.

In his description of human nature, Bentham defended a view of particular importance to his ethical theory. He was a psychological hedonist as well as an ethical hedonist. His *Introduction to the Principles of Morals and Legislation* begins with the words: "Nature has placed mankind under the governance of two sovereign masters, *pain* and *pleasure*. It is for them alone to point out what we ought to do, as well as to determine what we shall do." This passage, because of its "ought," is clearly an expression of ethical hedonism. But, because of its description of human motivation—its claim that we are, by nature, pleasure-seekers—it is an expression of psychological hedonism as well. Such a view of human motivation has implications of a serious nature for Bentham's ethical hedonism, especially for his view that, to act rightly, we must promote the greatest pleasure of the greatest number. Moral action, on this view, requires altruistic action. Indeed, in one of his formulas Bentham states, ". . . Everyone to count for one and no one to count for more than one." In other words, we have a moral obligation to promote the pleasure of all who are affected by our acts equally. But psychological hedonism implies psychological egoism. The pleasure we all seek by nature is our own pleasure. So the question arises: If we are all always egoistically motivated, what meaning can there be in saying that we have an

obligation to act altruistically? This leads to a practical, social question: How can a social order whose individual members are all egoists get those individuals to act altruistically?

Bentham's solution to this practical social problem is his theory of sanctions. Since individuals will perform antisocial acts whenever their doing so will promote their own pleasure, such activity must be discouraged by making its consequences painful to the agent. In other words, sanctions must be imposed on him by punishment for antisocial acts. Society can do this in two ways, either informally, through what Bentham calls the popular sanction, or adverse public opinion, or formally, through what he calls the political sanction, or punishment administered by the judicial and penal systems. But Bentham stresses an important point about sanctions, in particular the infliction of punishment by the state. Since punishment consists in the infliction of pain, it is in itself a bad act, which can be justified only by the fact that, by deterring criminals from antisocial activity, it prevents the production of even greater pain. Therefore, punishment, he concluded, should never be excessive but always limited to a level just sufficient to deter crime.

Bentham's doctrine of "everyone to count for one and no one to count for more than one" struck an egalitarian note in an era notorious for its inequities. In doing so, it laid a theoretical foundation for a new social order based on democratic principles. Yet it is difficult to make it compatible with his hedonistic utilitarianism. If the only criterion to be used in assessing the rightness of actions is the quantity of pleasure they produce, then does it matter whether this pleasure is experienced by the entire populace equally or by a small percentage of it disproportionately? The problem focuses on the concept of justice. To paraphrase a remark made long ago in a famous case, the judge is said to have concluded that it is better that one man should suffer than that a whole nation should perish. The fact that the one man was innocent seems to have been irrelevant in his eyes—as it would apparently have to be in those of Bentham.

To resolve the apparent incompatibility between

his utilitarian theory and the requirements of justice, Bentham distinguished between first-order and second-order goods and evils. The punishment of an innocent person to secure immediate pleasure for society produces a first-order good, but it also produces a second-order evil—the insecurity experienced by all members of the populace when they recognize that they are not safe from being punished for crimes of which they are innocent, whenever doing so will produce social benefits. Because the second-order evil outweighs the first-order good, it is to society's advantage, on utilitarian principles, never to abrogate the requirements of justice.

OLIVER A. JOHNSON

Further Reading

Baumgardt, D. *Bentham and the Ethics of Today*. Princeton: Princeton University Press, 1952. In this book the author, a German-American philosopher, analyzes Bentham's ethical theory and relates it to later developments in ethics, particularly in the twentieth century.

Harrison, Ross. *Bentham*. London, Boston, Melbourne, and Henley: Routledge & Kegan Paul, 1983. This book, in the series "The Arguments of the Philosophers," is an exposition of Bentham's complete philosophy, including its metaphysical foundations. It is written in a style to make it understandable to readers who have no background in technical philosophy.

Mack, Mary P. *Jeremy Bentham*. London, Melbourne, and Toronto: Heinemann, 1962. An intellectual biography of Bentham, covering his life until 1792. It is particularly valuable in tracing the development of his thought.

Parekh, B. *Jeremy Bentham: Ten Critical Essays*. London: Frank Cass, 1974. The book contains ten essays discussing various aspects of Bentham's thought. The authors include both nineteenth- and twentieth-century authorities on Bentham.

Plamenatz, J. *The English Utilitarians*. Oxford: Basil Blackwell, 1949. This relatively short book by an Oxford scholar gives an account of the history of classical utilitarianism as it developed in Britain in the eighteenth and nineteenth centuries. Chapter 4 is devoted to Bentham.

Stephen, Leslie. *The English Utilitarians*. 3 vols. London: Duckworth, 1900. This classic work, by a famous nineteenth-century English intellectual historian, is devoted mainly to the utilitarianism of Bentham and the two Mills. Volume 1, chapters 5 and 6, contain a long account of Bentham's life and thought.

WILLIAM GODWIN

Born: 1756, Knowe's Acre, near Wisbech, England
Died: 1836, London, England
Major Works: *An Enquiry Concerning Political Justice* (1793), *Caleb Williams* (1794), *Memoirs of the Author of a Vindication of the Rights of Women* (1798)

Major Ideas

Humankind is perfectible.

Reason leads to truth; truth leads to justice.

Government usurps private judgment and individual conscience; it is the greatest obstacle to human happiness.

Education and environment determine personality and character.

There are no rights, only duties; the fundamental moral duty is universal benevolence.

Nonviolent reform, not revolution, is the only way to achieve political change.

William Godwin, philosopher, novelist, educator, journalist, and humanitarian, is recognized as the founder of modern anarchism and utilitarianism. His writings, all based on deductive reasoning, probe politics, ethics, epistemology, religion, and psychology. Often misunderstood, his doctrine of perfectibility, "the progressive nature of man," maintains that all humans have the potential to be rational and virtuous. Reason, the faculty of perception and judgment, does not, however, exclude feelings. The moral nature of humankind is determined by regulated affections, seeking benevolence and improvement. All human-created institutions— government, schools, church, and laws—create prejudice, impede independence, and arrest progress. Unequivocally supporting freedom of opinion, Godwin advocated a reformation in human relations and thought.

A precocious child, Godwin was reared in a cold and firm Calvinist environment. From age two, he was distanced from his family by tutors and schoolmasters. By age six, he had determined to become, like his father and grandfather, a Nonconformist preacher. The severity of Master Robert Akers's lessons, including frequent birchings, remained indelible to Godwin, who would later characterize punishments and retribution as barbarous and ineffective. At Norwich, Godwin studied as a private pupil of prominent Dissenting minister Samuel Newton. He entered Hoxton Academy, a radical and

unorthodox Dissenting academy, professing Tory politics. There he studied with Dr. Andrew Kippis, the prominent left-wing intellectual, for five years.

Following his studies at Hoxton and after reading Swift, d'Holbach, Rousseau, Helvétius, and Priestley, Godwin turned republican and rejected the doctrine of eternal damnation. Questioning orthodox Christianity and the Church, he denied the divinity of Christ and renounced Calvinism as a "gloomy doctrine." His ministry at Stowmarket in Suffolk was short-lived, however, following controversies over his administering the sacraments and his ordination. In April 1872, Godwin was expelled from his post; in June 1783, he resigned the ministry. Almost becoming a schoolmaster, Godwin submitted a prospectus for a small school at Epsom, *Account of the Seminary* (1783). He never obtained the necessary twelve students.

Moving to London, Godwin devoted himself to writing. As a journalist, Godwin wrote periodical essays and served as editor of the *Political Herald*. His essays, addressing personal topics, public issues, and literary concerns, were collected and published as *The Enquirer* in 1797 and 1823. During the early 1790s, Godwin responded to the French Revolution and British republican activities. Godwin knew radical thinkers Joseph Johnson, James Mackintosh, John Thelwall, Thomas Cooper, Mary Wollstonecraft, Thomas Holcroft, Horne Tooke, and others. Don Locke claims that *Enquiry Con-*

cerning *Political Justice* (1793) was a reply to Thomas Paine's *Rights of Man* (1791), one of many responses to Edmund Burke's *Reflections of the Revolution in France* (1790), the catalyst for the great Pamphlet War. *Cursory Strictures* (1794), a reply to Justice Eyre's attempt to restrict free thought with his definition of treason, actually saved twelve radicals from execution. The Cabinet deliberated prosecuting Godwin for *Political Justice*. He nonetheless boldly voiced his objections to both radical, revolutionary activities and to repressive, government laws in *Considerations on Lord Grenville's & Mr. Pitt's Bills* (1795).

In March 1797, he secretly married Mary Wollstonecraft, writer and feminist, and adopted her daughter Fanny Imlay. The first great tragedy of Godwin's life was the death of his wife in September 1797. Wollstonecraft died from complications following the birth of their daughter Mary. Godwin candidly recorded Wollstonecraft's life in *Memoirs of the Author of A Vindication of the Rights of Woman* (1798). Although he did not wholly endorse her feminist theories, Godwin acknowledged the improvements her influence brought him. With poignancy, Godwin concludes the biography: "This light was lent to me for a very short period, and is now extinguished for ever!" Godwin cared for his two daughters until 1801, when he married Mary Jane Clairmont, a widow with two children, Charles and Jane. William Jr. joined the large family in 1803.

The financial burdens of this family forced Godwin to open a small shop for a juvenile library, publishing children's books for schools. Godwin's notoriety from *Political Justice* forced them to name their enterprise the M. J. Godwin & Co., and to use pseudonyms for their own works. For the remainder of Godwin's life, he was plagued with financial problems, relying on his friends and disciples for aid. The juvenile library was also to be a constant source of time-consuming commitment and financial concern.

The complications of Godwin's professional life were challenged by those of his personal life. William Jr. ran away in 1814. In 1815, his daughter Mary Godwin and Percy Bysshe Shelley went to Switzerland together and were accompanied by Claire Clairmont, who was having an affair with Lord Byron. A few months later, Fanny (daughter of Mary Wollstonecraft), who was presumably also in love with Shelley, committed suicide. Claire, meanwhile, discovered she was pregnant. Following Harriet Shelley's suicide in 1816, Godwin insisted that Mary and Shelley marry. His relationships with both Mary and Shelley were henceforth strained and painful. Depressed, Godwin often stood silently beside the grave of his friend Richard Sheridan, the symbol of a passing era.

Godwin constantly moved the publishing company to seek less expensive rents, but in 1825, he declared himself bankrupt. Even though the family reunited in 1828, Godwin continued to work under the strain of financial difficulties until 1833, when he received a government pension and the post of office keeper and yeoman usher of the Receipt of the Exchequer. At the age of eighty, Godwin died in 1836, following a week's struggle with a cold and fever. He was buried close to Mary Wollstonecraft at Saint Pancras Church, where they were married.

An Enquiry Concerning Political Justice

Godwin announces in the preface of *Political Justice* that the political events in America and France had exposed the errors in recent political theory and the need for a new study. Godwin's new political theory maintains that all human-created institutions are corrupt and corrupting; they inhibit humankind's ability to develop reason, natural benevolence, and happiness without restraints. Governments, in particular, are established for negative reasons and create enslaving cycles. War and suppression naturally accompany political institutions. In their distress, the oppressed commit violence. The only way to repress this violence is punishment. Political institutions impose class distinctions based on property, and the inequality of conditions is calculated to enhance the imagined excellence of the rich.

Unshackled by these restraints, humankind is perfectible, susceptible of perpetual improvement. The human mind is a faculty of perception. All our knowledge and ideas come from impressions. Thus, education and environment are vitally important to rational thinking and character. Education is the main force for good or ills. The human mind, in itself, is good and pure. Only when private judgment is distorted by government or education do humans fall into error. In essence, we are conditioned by our environment. Our moral improvements keep pace with our intellectual advances, for virtue demands the active use of a rational mind working toward the general good.

Justice involves the application of moral duty and strives to benefit the whole; it prefers that which is most valuable. Judgments are sanctioned by their utility.

Godwin illustrates his utilitarian principle with "the famous fire cause." During a fire, you have the ability to save one of two people from burning to death. One is the philosopher Fénelon. The other is Fénelon's valet—who is also your father. The just and virtuous choice, says Godwin, is for you to save Fénelon because his life benefits the general good.

Godwin argues that individuals and society have no rights, only duties, the treatments you are bound by justice to bestow on others. Rights, treatments you expect others to bestow on you, should be determined by morality. A person unable to exercise his or her understanding falls under a pure state of external slavery. When humankind is reduced to a common standard by laws, it is capable of little more than repeating what others have said, like parrots. The conviction of individual understanding is the only legitimate principle guiding conduct.

All promises and compacts constitute an evil that stands in opposition to the genuine exercise of individual intellect. Sincerity and happiness are not founded in promises (social contracts, marriages, legal agreements). Thus a compact of government should exist only when it is necessary for the welfare of humankind. Such a government is a transaction in the name and for the benefit of the whole, and every member should have some share in the selection of its measures. Conformity to the authority of this government should occur only because humankind sees a greater evil resulting from disobedience. The form of government acquired

should follow a gradual and uninterrupted change until such time as weakness and ignorance shall diminish, and the basis of all government shall also decay. (Godwin's hope was that individuals would become wise enough to govern themselves without the intervention of any compulsory restraint.)

Godwin likewise admonishes violent revolutionary activities as a way to eliminate tyranny or to achieve political change. Force is contrary to intellect. Revolution is instigated by a horror against tyranny, yet it is itself a tyranny. Revolutions interrupt the progress of political truth and social improvements. Godwin disapproves of tyrannicide, which generates new calamities. Gradual reform should seek improvement, not destruction.

Institutions give permanence to systems and opinions; they defy change in us. This renders future advances of the mind tedious and impetuous. Moral improvement results from the repeal of laws, not from multiplying regulations, laws, and authority. Religious conformity is also a system that blinds humankind by promises and penalties; it dupes us into the practice of virtue. Godwin opposes oaths, tests, voting, political parties, and constitutions— any binding agreement with institutions that restricts individual thought.

Governments exert authority by fear of penalty. Punishment, however, by no means accords with any sound principles of reasoning. Godwin advocates abolition of all punishment and criminal law. Punishment, even as a temporary expedient, has no proper tendency to prepare humankind for a state in which punishment shall cease. Reform must consist in removing all extrinsic influences and incitements so individuals may inquire and reason on their own. Punishment cannot achieve reformation.

Coercion and punishment, Godwin alleges, are connected with property. Accumulated property creates class divisions, and the resulting injustices are the foundation of all religious morality. Oppression, servility, fraud, idleness, pride, selfishness, and slavery are the offspring of the present administration of property. The distribution of wealth, Godwin demonstrates, cannot be mandated by laws or government.

Godwin argues that as we deceive others with a

tranquil conscience, we begin deceiving ourselves, and we put shackles on our own minds. We must change the nature of the mind. All government is founded in opinion; destroy this opinion, and the fabric that is built upon it falls to the ground. A revolution of opinions is the only means of attaining political justice, happiness, and benevolence.

Caleb Williams

The original title of *Caleb Williams*, Godwin's popular 1794 novel—*Things as They Are*—indicates that the *status quo* is corrupt. The novel pits the tyrant Ferdinando Falkland, who hides his crime of murder and deception behind a facade of honor and dignity, against Caleb Williams, the naive youth, who is driven by curiosity and justice. Godwin announces in his preface that the novel is "a general review of the modes of domestic and unrecorded despotism, by which man becomes the destroyer of man." Powerful and rich, Falkland can use the corrupt institutions of government as weapons in his relentless pursuit of Caleb, the only person who knows the secret he seeks to hide.

Falkland murders Barnabas Tyrrell. To protect his reputation, he allows Ben Hawkins and his son Leonard to be held guilty and hanged. Creating his own alienation, Falkland becomes a misanthrope. Caleb, while working as Falkland's valet, discovers the cause of his employer's gloomy solitude. Convinced Falkland is guilty but unable to prove it, Caleb forces Falkland's revelation of a crime motivated by the love of fame and reputation. In confessing, Falkland also seals Caleb's fate. The remainder of the novel involves Caleb's many daring attempts at escaping Falkland's machinations to imprison him. Refusing to submit to Falkland's tortures, Caleb vows at least to maintain the independence of his own mind.

Caleb Williams demonstrates the principles of moral and political truth featured in *Political Justice*. A common theme emerges from all Godwinian novels: the tragedy of loneliness and misunderstanding, and the way in which society and its institutions rob humankind of justice and happiness. All of the novels' heroes, victims of socially imposed

conventions and false education, become outcasts of family or society. Their identity struggles are symbolized by the many disguises they adopt. They all discover, although painfully and at great price, "the power which the institutions of society give to one man over others" and the power of the mind to free them from these enslaving institutions.

Political Tracts

Although Godwin is best known for *Political Justice* and *Caleb Williams*, he made other significant contributions to the uneasy political times of his day. In addition to helping to secure the acquittal of twelve radical thinkers of treason charges in 1794, Godwin's *Cursory Strictures* established a precedent in English law. Justice Eyre's construction, interpretation, and manipulation of language and law to secure conviction challenged English liberties and were held in check. Godwin's 1795 tract *Considerations on Lord Grenville's & Mr. Pitt's Bills* argues that constraints against free speech and the right to assemble violate the English Bill of Rights. While Godwin recognizes that the activities of radicals in the London Corresponding Society warrant alarm, these laws, he argues, constitute overreactions. Forcing men into the extremest state of hostility, these bills leave no room for enquiry, compromise, and gradual reform.

In *Reply to Parr* (1801), Godwin responds to attacks on his philosophy and character, affirms his hatred of revolutions, and restates his belief in human perfectibility, utility, and philanthropy. He reproves Thomas Malthus's ratios of population to subsistence and his proposition about sexual appetites. Sexual drive, Godwin argues, can be controlled by moral restraint; vice and misery are not the only sufficient checks upon increasing population. Godwin further expanded his reply to Malthus in the long essay "Of Population" (1820).

In *Letters of Verax* (1815), Godwin warns against reviving the war with France and argues that Napoleon should be recognized as the legitimate French ruler as long as he maintains peace. Godwin declares: "A nation is an artificial individual, the creature of reasoning faculty merely." England has too much to lose in taking arms against such an artifice. (Napoleon was defeated at Waterloo before the *Letters* were published.)

Educational Theory and Juvenile Library

Believing education the great equalizer, Godwin was also aware that education can be used as a powerful weapon of conformity. Education can rob students of individuality and creativity. He felt strongly about the tyranny adults exercise over children, and he opposed any national system of education. Education and enlightenment are the best means of reform, but students should be taught to venerate truth, which must be discovered, not imposed. As Peter Marshall has acknowledged, Godwin was a pioneer of libertarian and progressive education.

In *Letter of Advice to a Young American: On the Course of Studies It Might Be Most Advantageous for Him to Pursue* (1818), Godwin recommends the study of the best models, teaching and learning by example. Histories, especially of Rome and Greece, offer the best examples. He challenges students to read critically and not to be influenced by any one book or author. The better scholar relies on primary sources, letters, public papers, and biographies.

Godwin also placed a high value on the humanities and ancient languages, a classical education. In his *Account of the Seminary* (1783), Godwin advocates a pedagogy governed by the practical not the theoretical; by kindness, not fear; by discovery, not memory; by free writing, not formal composition and grammar; and by self-paced instruction, not standardized competencies. Reading is the key to all knowledge, understanding, and improvement.

Finding most history books too detailed and boring, Godwin wrote *The History of England, for the Use of Schools and Young Persons* (1806) to illustrate ideas and motivations rather than to cite particular battles and dates. He made many classical stories accessible to young readers with *The History of Greece* (1821), *Fables Ancient and Modern* (1805), *The Pantheon* (1806), and *The Looking Glass* (1805). One of the most famous publications of his juvenile library was Charles and Mary Lamb's *Tales from Shakespeare*.

Religious Thoughts

Godwin is often represented as an atheist. Godwin's careful examination of Christian doctrine in *The Genius of Christianity Unveiled*, however, reveals that his disbelief involved institutionalized religion. He was cautious of any belief that infringed on humankind's reasoning powers. Like William Blake, he was critical of anthropomorphism, the view that the Christian God is made "in the image of man." Christianity is a human-created system of fictions and falsehoods, he maintained. God, for example as depicted in the Scriptures, is a tyrant. The doctrine of Original Sin, with its system of rewards and punishments, creates servitude. The human mind cannot be shackled by fear of an omnipotent and omniscient God and an afterlife of retribution. Christian doctrine is essentially intolerant; it leads to controversies and wars. Church hierarchy has made kings and amassed wealth. Its vices are like those of governments. The institutions of religion, like other human-created systems, must dissolve before humankind can fully realize its natural reasoning and religious powers.

MARJEAN D. PURINTON

Further Reading

Boulton, J. B. *The Language of Politics in the Age of Wilkes and Burke*. London: Routledge & Kegan Paul, 1963. Chapter 11, "William Godwin, Philosopher and Novelist," focuses on Godwin's contributions to the 1790–93 political controversy.

Cameron, Kenneth Neill. "William Godwin." In *Romantic Rebels: Essays on Shelley and His Circle*. Edited by Kenneth Neill Cameron. Cambridge, Mass.: Harvard University Press, 1973. A good, brief introduction to Godwin's life and general philosophy.

Clark, John P. *The Philosophical Anarchism of William Godwin*. Princeton: Princeton University Press, 1977. Clark analyzes the ethical and metaphysical bases for Godwin's social and political ideas. He includes an excellent bibliography.

Fleisher, David. *William Godwin: A Study in Liberalism*. New York: Augustus M. Kelley, 1951. An extensive analysis of *Political Justice* and brief explications of Godwin's life and religious views.

Locke, Don. *A Fantasy of Reason: The Life and Thought of William Godwin*. London: Routledge & Kegan Paul, 1980. One of the most scholarly and comprehensive biographies of Godwin. Locke juxtaposes events in Godwin's life with the philosophical content of his writings. His work includes a helpful and detailed chronology.

Marshall, Peter H. *William Godwin*. New Haven: Yale University Press, 1984. This excellent and scholarly biography attempts to place Godwin in a personal, social, and historical context. Chapter 7 offers a superb analysis of *Political Justice*, and the final chapter is an especially concise but thorough review of Godwinian philosophy.

Monro, D. H. *Godwin's Moral Philosophy: An Interpretation of William Godwin*. London: Oxford University Press, 1953; Folcroft, Pa.: Folcroft Press, 1969. Still a standard and quite readable study of Godwin's moral and ethical thought. Monro clarifies misconceptions about Godwin's ideas.

Pollin, Burton R. *Education and Enlightenment in the Works of William Godwin*. New York: Las Americas, 1962. This insightful study traces Mary Wollstonecraft's ideas and influences on Godwinian educational and social theory.

Smith, Elton Edward, and Esther Greenwell Smith. *William Godwin*. Twayne English Authors Series no. 27. New York: Twayne Publishers, 1965. An introductory overview of Godwin's major works.

Tysdahl, B. J. *William Godwin as Novelist*. London: Athlone Press, 1981. Tysdahl's extensive textual analysis of Godwin's novels is especially helpful for those interested in the literary dimensions of Godwin's writings. Tysdahl nonetheless connects themes and motifs with the philosophical thought projected in Godwin's nonfiction.

WILLIAM BLAKE

Born: 1757, London, England
Died: 1827, London, England
Major Works: *The Marriage of Heaven and Hell* (1793), *Visions of the Daughters of Albion* (1793), *America, a Prophecy* (1793), *Europe, a Prophecy* (1794), *Songs of Innocence and of Experience* (1794), *The Book of Urizen* (1794), *The Four Zoas* (1797), *Milton* (1804), *Jerusalem* (1804)

Major Ideas

Imagination is the Divine Being in every person.

All division is contrary to the infinite imagination (the body is not distinct from the soul).

Divisions, which emanate from the Fall (master/servant, rich/poor, male/female) hold some people in bondage; thus, humankind's fallen vision has produced the exploitation, oppression, and tyranny manifested in class stratifications, poverty, slavery, child labor, sexual discrimination, restrictive laws, and wars.

Imagination, unifying and infinite, supersedes reason, divisive and finite.

Rationalism is limited to time, space, sequential operations, natural causality, and measurements.

Science and industry reduce the universe to a vast machine and one unalterable law.

Empiricism limits knowledge to sensory perception; life is revealed to imaginative vision and not to the corporeal eye.

Orthodox religions and deism enslave humankind to a system that promises future rewards or punishments, a dogma that controls human minds.

Eternity is a condition in which no divisions exist; in order for humankind to regain this innocence, it must rediscover Paradise, an act of the poetic genius or imagination.

Blake opposed any system that imposes restrictions, constrictions, conventions, oppressions, or limitations on physical, intellectual, or spiritual activities. Evoking revolutionary content and form in his works, Blake undermines traditional associations, disturbs the expected, rejects the conventions, and destroys comfortable perceptions to force readers to recreate order and meaning, to break the "mind forg'd manacles" that restrict their imaginations. He depicts the destructive conditions resulting from the Doctrine of Contraries, divisions and oppositions in all human endeavors and thought. As an alternative to these fallen visions, he superimposes his Vision of Imagination, the creative energy that seeks harmony and infinity.

Blake's philosophy is submerged in his mythology and entwined in his symbolism. Recurring patterns of thought, nonetheless, appear in his satires and songs, in his political and pictorial prophecies, and in his final prophetic epics. Blake conflates philosophical, religious, scientific, and political fictions that have come to be accepted as truths. He questions established values, discredits the *status quo*, and exposes hypocrisy. Concerned with the issues of the day, Blake inscribes them into the conflicts of his poetic characters, but he also penetrates to the mentally constructed foundations giving rise to oppositions and their ensuing power struggles.

As the second child to a moderately prosperous hosier, Blake, at age ten, was sent to Henry Pars's drawing school in the Strand, the best preparatory school for young artists. At fourteen, Blake was apprenticed to James Basire, engraver to the Society of Antiquaries. These early artistic experiences exposed Blake to antiquity and its mythology, to Gothic art and architecture, and to medieval illuminated books. Blake's voracious reading included the Bible, Dante, Milton, Spenser, Shakespeare, Swedenborg, Gray, Chatterton, early British history, and Percy's *Reliques of Ancient English Poetry*. Blake, a naturally gifted linguist, read French, Latin, Greek, and a little Hebrew.

As a student at the Royal Academy, Blake preferred Michelangelo and Raphael, artists who captured the "human form divine," over the models dictated to him by Sir Joshua Reynolds and G. M. Moser, keeper of the Academy. Unable to "correct" his drawings, Blake became an engraver to the bookseller Joseph Johnson in 1779. Johnson was a Dissenter and radical political thinker. Blake quickly became a part of the radical circle of thinkers who met weekly at Johnson's home.

Against his father's wishes, Blake married Catherine Boucher, the illiterate daughter of a Battersea market gardener in 1782. They remained childless. Catherine learned from Blake how to assist in the printing of his illuminated manuscripts. She also helped Blake with a print shop, which he opened with his brother James in 1784 with inherited money following his father's death. Blake's younger brother Robert became his pupil. The venture ended in 1787, however, when Robert died.

Blake never had any real interest in making money, nor was he ever a comfortable man socially. His politics were radical. While living in Felpham in Sussex in 1803, Blake assaulted a soldier who refused to leave his garden, and allegedly made treasonous remarks about the King and a potential French invasion. Although Blake was charged with sedition and brought to trial, he was acquitted.

Eschewing the empirical and rational philosophy of the Enlightenment (Bacon, Newton, Locke, Berkeley), Blake believed that life could not be contained within quantitative measurements or laws of nature. His art and poetry deprecate reason, sensory perception, absolute dogmas, and scientific analysis; all forge the mental chains that enslave imagination. His works admonish all form of tyranny: kings, priests, parents, nurses, schoolmasters, lawmakers, merchants.

Living during revolutionary times, Blake himself was seen as a revolutionary. He was nevertheless skeptical of any system, republican or monarchial, that limited human imagination. Humankind must change its mind before it could expect to change social or political order. For Blake, religion could not be codified. Man had made his god in the image of himself: This constituted a fallen vision. The "God within" and not the God above is the creative

energy that can redeem humankind from its erroneous dichotomies. Any tyrannical deity that promotes the law of "thou shalt not" and compels humankind to serve him in "moral gratitude and submission" is a satanic being, or in Blake's mythology, an Urizenic figure. Satan is always identified with reason and moral law, and Blake conflates revolutionary themes with apocalyptic imagery.

Poetical Sketches, Satires, and Prophecies

Revolutionary thinking clearly appears in Blake's early poetry. In the dramatic fragment *King Edward III* (1783), Blake subverts the meaning usually associated with "liberty" and illustrates how the English nobles, who define liberty as property, feudalism, and power, use it to instill courage and loyalty among the army. Similarly, in *An Island in the Moon* (1784), Blake's satire demonstrates how slavery, poverty, and gender inequality are preserved by rhetoric that renders these conditions necessary for eternal happiness.

The poetic tracts *There Is No Natural Religion* and *All Religions Are One* (1788) suggest that empiricism and religious doctrines constitute limited mental systems. *The Book of Thel* (1789) admonishes a system of thought that codifies sexuality as evil and champions liberation from culturally induced roles and behaviors. The "Bald tyrant" Tiriel of the 1789 poem entitled *Tiriel* uses lies and curses to force his children into submission, obligation, and duty.

Prophecies and Revolution

In the prophetic book *The Marriage of Heaven and Hell*, Blake maintains "every thing that lives is Holy." The Five Memorable Fancies illustrate the mind's ability to liberate itself from the entrapment of imposed systems of thought. A satire on the biblical Proverbs, the seventy Proverbs of Hell challenge assumptions based on reason. "For man has closed himself up, till he sees all things thro' narrow chinks of his covern," demonstrates the effects of knowledge derived from sensory perceptions. Showing an archetypal rebel who depended on imagination, not reason, a proverb says: "Jesus was all virtue, and acted from impulse, not from rules." A Song of Liberty, the conclusion of *The Marriage*, proposes a spirit of revolt in France and a prophecy of the end of all oppression.

The French Revolution (1791) depicts the political liberation to which Blake alludes in *The Marriage*. It also represents the last book Blake committed to publishing. He etched the remainder of his poetic books and sold them to subscribers, a revolution in his own publishing process.

Visions of the Daughters of Albion continues to attack simultaneously several levels of oppression: economic, sexual, moral, linguistic, and spiritual. Bromion, a slave owner, rapes his slave Oothoon, who is betrothed to Theotormon. Oothoon, who sees no sin in her participation in the crime, refuses to consider herself a "whore" simply because she is so labeled. Bromion, motivated to increase the value of his property, views the act as economic necessity. Theotormon, his mind chained to the fixed referents dictated by language, believes Oothoon tainted and valueless. Blake's vision shows us that what destroys Oothoon's virginity is not Bromion's act, but Theotormon's perception of Bromion's act, an act he knows only through language, which is encoded and limited by the values of a semantic system.

America, a Prophecy and *Europe, a Prophecy* also illustrate the oppression–liberation dialectic at an intimate, sexual level. This level then serves as the mediation for the same conflicts within political and philosophical contexts. America, the shadowy and nameless female liberator, will assist Orc as he frees her from slavery to England (servitude to her father). Europe, however, embodies the female oppressor that dominates through sexual possession. The tyrant Enitharmon, a powerful, external force, ensnares humankind with her dominion—her myth "Woman's love is sin," and her edict "Thou shalt Not." She "groans and cries in anguish and dismay" as Orc hastens to France to rouse rebellion.

The Book of Urizen is a recapitulation of the creation story and humankind's Fall into divisions and imprisonment in its five senses. Separations occur, darkness pervades, Urizen imposes mea-

surements on time and space, Orc is chained, words are measured into laws and codified into the eternal brass book. Urizen forges the world and spreads his "Net of Religion." The Eternals weave curtains of darkness. Its vision reduced, humankind forms laws and deems them from God. Humanity is reduced to unthinking and unimaginative cogs in the mechanism. The story projects analogues to the social, political, and religious measurements of primogeniture, tithes, and titles that segment society into enslaved fragments of existence.

Songs of Innocence and of Experience, Lambeth Books, and Visions

Similarly, the conflicts involving children in *Songs of Innocence and of Experience* represent a mediation of other power struggles that result in dominance, repression, and enslavement. Figures of authority (father, mother, king, priest, nurse, God, law, schoolmaster) are oppositional to children of submission and exploitation. Children are inculcated with the social, religious, and political lies that hold them in check and perpetuate a *status quo* that exploits them. The *Songs of Innocence* demonstrates how dehumanization is veiled by the myth of piety, which creates destructive divisions, and by promises of eternal life. Chimney sweepers are consoled with a platitude that is actually a powerful mental weapon: "So if all do their duty, they need not fear harm." The persona of "the Human Abstract" reminds readers: "Pity would be no more, / If we did not make somebody Poor." The Little Vagabond tells his mother that "the Church is cold. / But the Ale-house is healthy & pleasant & warm." The gates are shut to the chapel built in the midst of the Garden of Love, "And Thou shalt not, writ over the door." These seemingly simple verses satirize eighteenth-century moral instruction books and criticize serious social ills.

Chaos, disease, and pestilence follow Urizen's usurption of power from Fuzon in *The Book of Ahania* (1795). Urizen nails Fuzon's corpse to the top of the Tree of Mystery. Writing silently in his book of iron, he forms iron nets around him. In this revision of the Genesis myth, Urizen seizes Ahania, calls her sin, and then casts her out of his bosom (Garden of Eden) into the World of Loneness. Blake recapitulates the Fall and the designation of sin, around which moral law and judgment are based.

Two of Blake's Notebook Poems, "Auguries of Innocence" and "The Mental Traveller," along with his poem *The Everlasting Gospel*, oppose cultural manifestations that limit vision to one law, one king, one god, one social ordering. Among Blake's targets is sensory perception. The simplistic lines obscure the radical challenges each poses. "The Mental Traveller" indicates how deceptive human senses are when left unchecked:

> *For the Eye altering alters all*
> *The senses roll themselves in fear*
> *And the flat Earth becomes a Ball.*

From "Auguries of Innocence," readers learn that "We are led to Believe a Lie/When we see *not* Thro the Eye." This warning is repeated in *The Everlasting Gospel*:

> *This Life dim Windows of the Soul*
> *Distorts the Heavens from Pole to Pole*
> *And leads you to believe a Lie*
> *When you see with not thro the Eye.*

Blake asks his readers to "see" and to "read" differently than they have. The interpretative frameworks of his poetry ask readers to consider multiple meanings rather than one fixed meaning.

In his prose description *A Vision of the Last Judgment* (1810), Blake portrays a painting (no longer extant) that multiplies its meanings rather than limiting them. The painting, like the Hebrew Bible and the Gospel of Jesus, presents visions or imaginations, representations of what eternally exists. The characters of these visions are representatives of states signified, not actual people or even limited symbolic figures. Most, Blake alleges, interpret the Bible as moral virtue. Liberty cannot exist in this world, many argue, without moral virtue. However, contends Blake, you cannot have moral virtue without the slavery of that half of the human race who hate what you call moral virtue. Moral virtue, like pity, leads to division and slavery.

Blake maintains that mental things alone are truly real. He says: "I question not my corporeal or vegetative eye any more than I would question a window concerning a sight. . . . I look through it and not with it." In a 1799 letter to Dr. Trusler, a short-term patron who did not approve of Blake's watercolors, Blake argues, "As a man is so he sees." He opposed any system or philosophy that blinded the eye of imagination.

The Prophetic Epics

Blake's epics are considered difficult because they defy linear sequence and plot construction. The same philosophic tenets that pervade the shorter verses also pervade these poems. In *The Four Zoas*, for example, the political dialectic lies latent behind the domestic, philosophical, scientific, and epistemological struggles depicted throughout the epic. Under Urizenic tyranny, children are abused, women become slaves, and humankind is trapped by a false form and a net of delusion. Nine nights, which constitute the epic's structure, unfold as recapitulations of the same story: the tyranny, oppression, persecution, revolution cycle.

Los's "dire revenge" and "thoughts of cruelty" victimize humanity as he plots to kill his son. Tharmas struggles to make his will Law. "Infacted madness" reigns. Luvah and Urizen struggle for power. Tharmas rapes Enitharmon. Children are nourished for the slaughter. "When Thought is closed in Caves, Then love shall shew its root in deepest Hell," and mental enslavement occurs. "Terrified at the Shapes/Enslaved humanity put on, he became what he beheld." Urizen confines his daughters in ignorance. Urizen vows to make a new world and to make himself King, and then God.

The conclusion of this epic suggests that this circle of entrapment and conflict continues endlessly because humankind has not yet broken the chains of mental bondage that make freedom impossible.

Milton offers a corrective for binary systems and bifurcations that revolve around gender. Blake argues that the destructive and external Feminine Will results from gender dichotomy, and *Milton* shatters the basis on which any gender divisions (which dictate a subservient role to women) exist. In Eternal Imagination, there are no sexes.

As the title of the epic implies, the poem redeems Milton's fallen vision, his Puritan view of dogma and gender relations. To regain Paradise, Milton must annihilate selfhood, the division of the person and ego. The epic suggests an alternative version of what it is to be human: person and ego, male and female, are unified, not separate distinctions. As Milton sheds his selfhood, Ololon, womanhood as an externalization, must shed her feminine identity, and unite with Milton. As a liberating process, Ololon puts off self and descends into Milton's shadow. The liberated Milton then enters Blake at the end of the epic.

Milton offers a corrective for several visions, all based on bifurcations, including Greek and Roman models of war and love, poetic conventions, philosophies of Rousseau and Voltaire, biblical interpretations, and sociology and psychology. The recovery of Paradise begun in *Milton* continues in Blake's final epic, *Jerusalem*. Its four chapters parallel each other, with each chapter presenting an alternative to the authority that it challenges.

Chapter 1, dedicated to the "Public," revolves around the building of systems that create oppositions and then result in domestic strife, power struggles, and war. Los builds Golgonooza and vows to "create a system, or be enslaved by another man's."

Chapter 2, directed to the Jews, exposes Albion as the Old Testament judge and punisher who exacts vengeance as righteousness. The dichotomies of pity/mercy and masculine/feminine emerge, and war leads to destruction.

Chapter 3, addressed to the deists, shows how they (like the Pharisees) deny forgiveness but plot revenge by way of reason and demonstration. The Daughters of Albion create the myth of genders and exploit the bondage these bifurcations engender. Doubt and despair flourish.

Chapter 4 speaks to the Christians. Weaving dichotomies at their looms, Gwendolen hides falsehood and utters deceit while Cambel disguises jealousy and envy. Male/female separations continue to create strife. England awakens and enters Albion, but Jesus must die for Albion to live.

Jerusalem, like Ololon, is a liberating process, a hermaphrodite beyond corporeal and sexual encasement. At the end of the epic, she enters Albion and gender divisions cease. The recovery of Jerusalem poetically depicts Blake's philosophical belief in infinite imagination, the recovery of a Paradise in which no destructive divisions exist.

MARJEAN D. PURINTON

Further Reading

Bindman, David. *Blake as an Artist*. Oxford: Phaidon Press, 1977. An excellent analysis of the philosophical dimensions of Blake's art and illuminated manuscripts.

Butlin, Martin. *William Blake*. London: Tate Gallery Little Book Series, 1966. A good introduction to Blake's art.

Crehan, Stewart. *Blake in Context*. Atlantic Highlands, N.J.: Gill and Macmillan Humanities Press, 1984. A Marxist analysis of the class struggle depicted in Blake's poetry.

Erdman, David V. *Blake: Prophet Against Empire: A Poet's Interpretation of the History of His Own Times*. Princeton, 1954. Rev. ed. Garden City,

N.Y.: Doubleday and Company, 1969. A detailed political, social, and historical interpretation of Blake's poetry.

Lindsay, Jack. *William Blake: His Life and Work*. London: Constable and Company, 1978. An excellent biography, including textual explications of the poetry and discussions of the art.

Lister, Raymond. *William Blake: An Introduction to the Man and His Work*. New York: Frederick Ungar, 1968. Designed for students unfamiliar with Blake's work, this survey of Blake's art and poetry includes pictorial reproductions, poetic quotations, and excerpts from Blake's letters.

Nesfield-Cookson, Bernard. *William Blake: Pro-

phet of Universal Brotherhood. London: Crucible, 1987. This philosophical analysis of Blake's poetry is arranged thematically to trace Blake's transformation of reason into divine imagination.

Nurmi, Martin K. *William Blake*. London: Hutchinson University Library, 1975. A philosophically oriented introduction for students and general readers. Beginning with a biographical overview, the study emphasizes the philosophical criticisms inscribed in Blake's poetry.

Paley, Morton D. *William Blake*. Oxford: Phaidon Press, 1978. This discussion of Blake's relationship, as poet and artist, to other texts (i.e., Bible, Milton, Dante, Bunyan) includes extensive illustrations (some colored).

Raine, Kathleen. *William Blake*. World of Art Series. New York: Thames and Hudson, 1970, reprint 1988. A chronological and biographical introduction to Blake's art, engraving, and poetry. This readable study includes excellent illustrations and perceptive commentary.

MARY WOLLSTONECRAFT

Born: 1759, London, England
Died: 1797, London, England
Major Works: *Thoughts on the Education of Daughters* (1787), *Mary, A Fiction* (1788), *Original Stories from Real Life*, (1788), *A Vindication of the Rights of Men* (1790), *A Vindication of the Rights of Woman* (1792), *An Historical and Moral View of the Origin and Progress of the French Revolution* (1794), *Letters Written during a Short Residence in Sweden, Norway, and Denmark* (1796), *Maria, or The Wrongs of Woman* (1798)

Major Ideas

Unwilling submission to any person, institution, or custom is limiting, degrading, and destructive.
Reason, infallible and God-given, should control all human thought and action.
Women must have the freedom to cultivate reason, the key to self-improvement and social change.
Environment and education shape character and morality.
Education is the right of all humankind and the vehicle through which women can gain independence and equality.
Humankind is evolving socially toward perfectibility.

Mary Wollstonecraft's ideas and writings have provided the foundation for the feminist movements of the nineteenth and twentieth centuries. Her best-known work is *A Vindication of the Rights of Woman*. She was the first woman to articulate publicly a request for women's suffrage and coequal education. She denied all double standards emanating from the sexual character theory, which ascribed reason to man alone.

Her arguments for increased opportunities and independence for women, however, did not include total equality of the sexes. She maintained a separate sphere ideology, and her hope for women was that they could become better wives and mothers. Although Wollstonecraft is best known as a feminist thinker, her philosophies are not limited to women's issues. She championed radical theories in education and politics, often linking social and political polemics with gender issues. The two false systems of values she attacked were class and gender.

The second of seven children, Wollstonecraft received a typical "female" education at the Yorkshire country school. Resenting the favoritism extended to her older brother by her parents, Wollstonecraft found companionship in Jane Arden, a friend from school, and later from Fanny Blood, her adopted mentor. During the summer of 1777, the family moved to Walworth in South London, and a year later, Wollstonecraft defied her parents by accepting employment as a companion to a wealthy, demanding widow, Mrs. Dawson, in Bath. Wollstonecraft would term this experience "a nightmare of tyranny and humiliation." In 1781, Wollstonecraft returned home to nurse her dying mother and to care for her younger siblings.

In 1782, Wollstonecraft moved in with the poverty-stricken Blood family at Walham Green, South London. Experiencing actual poverty for the first time, she earned a meagre income by sewing. When her sister Eliza suffered a severe depression following childbirth, Wollstonecraft abducted Eliza and the child from her husband's house. This represented Wollstonecraft's first public scandal.

With her sisters Everina and Eliza, together with her friend Fanny Blood, Wollstonecraft opened a school in Newington Green in 1784. Here Wollstonecraft met a circle of rational Dissenters who exerted considerable influence on her thinking. These thinkers included the moral philosopher and minister Richard Price, scientist Joseph Priestley, the Reverend John Hewlett, and Sarah Burgh, widow of the educator James Burgh.

In 1785, Wollstonecraft rushed to Portugal to visit her recently married friend Fanny, who died in childbirth. Although the Newington Green School failed, Wollstonecraft wrote her first educational tract, *Thoughts on the Education of Daughters*, and she sent Fanny's family to Ireland with the ten guineas she received from the book. In Ireland, Wollstonecraft was a governess to Lady Kingsborough, an experience she describes as "disagreeable." She was dismissed in 1787. Wollstonecraft's first attempt at fiction, *Mary*, describes her friendship with Fanny and voices her resentment of trivial aristocratic women.

Wollstonecraft returned to London as a reviewer and editorial assistant for Joseph Johnson's liberal journal, the *Analytical Review*. She reviewed controversial contemporary works and translated works from French, Dutch, and German, which she taught herself to read. Here Wollstonecraft met a second group of influencial radical thinkers: philosopher William Godwin, political writer Thomas Holcroft, Swiss painter and writer Henry Fuseli, painter and poet William Blake, educator and author Anna Barbauld, publisher Thomas Christie, radical activist Thomas Paine, and authors Mary Hays and Eliza Fenwick.

In 1790, Wollstonecraft contributed to the political polemics of this revolutionary period with *A Vindication of the Rights of Men*, one of thirty replies to Edmund Burke's conservative tract *Reflections on the Revolution in France*. After an unsuccessful and unhappy affair with Henry Fuseli, Wollstonecraft traveled to Paris in 1792. Her observations of postrevolutionary Paris are recorded in *An Historical and Moral View of the Origin and Progress of the French Revolution*. In Paris, Wollstonecraft fell in love with the American writer and speculator Gilbert Imlay. She named their child, born in 1794, Fanny, for her friend. Claiming to be Imlay's wife and therefore an American citizen, Wollstonecraft escaped arrest and imprisonment in Paris.

Following Imlay to London in 1795, Wollstonecraft discovered his infidelity and she attempted suicide. Recovering and hoping to keep Imlay's love, Wollstonecraft agreed to take her one-year-old child and to go to Scandinavia as Imlay's business emissary. There she composed *Letters Written during a Short Residence in Sweden, Norway, and Denmark*. Returning to London, Wollstonecraft learned Imlay had again forsaken her. She tried suicide a second time by plunging into the Thames from Putney Bridge. Thames boatmen dragged her unconscious from the water.

Shortly following Wollstonecraft's recovery from this suicide attempt, Mary Hays reintroduced her to William Godwin. Their friendship "melted into love," as her letters reveal. Neither believed in the institution of marriage, but in 1797, when Wollstonecraft became pregnant, they agreed to marry. She was working on another novel, *Maria, or The Wrongs of Woman*, when her second daughter Mary was born. Eleven days after Mary's birth, Wollstonecraft died from birthing complications and inadequate medical attention.

Educational Theories

Wollstonecraft encourages self-respect, independence, and intellectual inquiry in her educational writings. Education represented the solutions to women's lack of physical and mental development and a process through which they could achieve reason, equality, and virtue. In *Thoughts on the Education of Daughters*, Wollstonecraft reiterates Locke's emphasis of environment and experience on education. From the nursery, girls should cultivate reason and learn to govern their instincts to dominate over passions. Affection, not rigid requirements of behavior and needless restraint, generates better conduct and manners.

Wollstonecraft encourages examples over precepts as teaching strategies. Mrs. Mason, Mary and Caroline's governess in *Original Stories from Real Life*, demonstrates this with her anecdotes that provide moral instruction. Stories, claims Wollstonecraft, should amuse and instruct, and children should be permitted to enter into conversation and to pose questions. Deploring rote learning, Wollstonecraft encourages understanding, analytical thinking, and associations of ideas. She argues that the principles of truth are innate, but children, unless they reason, cannot discern such principles from fictions.

Wollstonecraft demands that parents take more responsibility for the education of their children.

She encourages mothers to nurse their own children and not leave young ones to the care of servants, who teach only cunning. Boarding schools, likewise, provide inadequate education for women. It is the duty of parents, she argues, to preserve the child from receiving wrong impressions and prejudices.

Wollstonecraft's most radical educational tenet asserts that boys and girls should receive the same instruction. Attacking the theories of Rousseau, Fordyce, and Gregory, whose double-standard approach to education limited female intellectual life, Wollstonecraft argues that women should cultivate the same mental and physical activities that men enjoy. In these early educational tracts, as well as in *A Vindication of the Rights of Woman*, Wollstonecraft maintains that female education should be useful; it should prepare women to be rational wives and mothers. The present system merely cultivates female vanity and teaches women to function as submissive, unthinking servants to men. Daughters who imitate their mothers receive an indirect, unconscious form of learning. She seeks to end this imitation cycle that inculcates and perpetuates humiliated social and domestic females.

Women, Wollstonecraft advocates, should spend less time on the exterior accomplishments, affectations derived from dress, cosmetics, cards, and dance, and more time on mental employments like reading, writing, and conversation. Reading is the most rational employment and food for understanding. Furthermore, she encourages women to read weighty materials to exercise and to improve their minds, not sentimental novels for escape. Novels, she asserts, give a wrong account of human passions and perpetuate fictional perspectives. Reason must fill up the vacuums of life, but too many women suffer theirs to lie dormant. Idleness, in men and women, is intolerable.

Political Theories

Wollstonecraft advocates liberty and equality for all humanity. Advancing arguments for political rights, she argues for the removal of traditional injustices of rank, property, class, and gender. At birth, all

human beings as rational creatures inherit rights from God. Conserving old principles and institutions (such as monarchy, church, commerce, and inheritance) hinders progress—humankind's evolutionary process toward perfectibility. The key to freedom lies in the reasoning individual conscience, not in laws or dogma.

A Vindication of the Rights of Men defends Price's sermon on the anniversary of the 1688 English Revolution and specifically his assertion that political authority is derived from the people; she refutes Burke's defense of the established church, civil authority emanating from propertied men, and the hereditary principle of succession. Wollstonecraft raises the question of obedience to a tyrannical parent (and by analogy, to king, to ecclesiastical authority, or to commerce). She cites the 1215 rebellion and the English Magna Carta as the foundation of liberty.

She attacks marriage as an institution that provides men with another article of property—a wife. Girls are sacrificed to family convenience or marry to settle themselves in a superior rank. Property and primogeniture, she argues, are a consequence of a barbarous feudal institution. "The only security of property that nature authorizes and reason sanctions," she writes, "is the right a man has to enjoy the acquisitions which his talents and industry have acquired. . . ." Eliminating rank would make all people more genuine and productive. No friendships or society can generate among unequals. Defending the French National Assembly, Wollstonecraft predicts that liberty will produce glorious change that levels all rank.

Acutely aware of the chaos and the atrocities occurring in France in 1792, Wollstonecraft defends the French Revolution as a positive step toward human perfectibility. She sees the political and physical revolution as an analogue to mental revolution that would attack the foundation responsible for all injustices and inequalities. The Revolution represents a "natural consequence of intellectual improvement." The Revolution has overthrown superstitions, broken the artful chain of despotism, destroyed false notions of duty, and provided room for reason to flourish. The revolution of opinion will continue to overturn the empire of tyranny and to emancipate the mental powers of humankind.

In *An Historical and Moral View of the Origin and Progress of the French Revolution*, Wollstonecraft optimistically asserts: "Out of this chaotic mass a fairer government is rising than has ever shed the sweets of social life on the world." The aristocracy of France destroyed itself, she explains, through the ignorant arrogance of its members, who, "bewildered in a thick fog of prejudices, could discern neither the true dignity of man, or the spirit of the times." She believes that a civilization founded on reason and morality is taking place in the world, but that stability would require time.

Wollstonecraft ascribes the failures of the Revolution to the character of the French people, who were so long held in tyranny that they became incapable of handling their newly achieved freedom. She explains that the minds of the people were not completely ripe for a total change in government from despotism to republicanism; thus, it was politically necessary to maintain the shadow of monarchy. She finds fault with the way the dissolution of the monarchy was handled, but qualifies the mistakes by showing how the French, depraved and volatile, were not ready for the new government. The Revolution was in many ways, she argues, an improper political plan for the degenerate French society. Republicanism is possible only for a people in the highest stage of civilization. Furthermore, the revolutions of states ought to be gradual so wisdom may prevail. France failed because its revolution was not gradual. Still an infant civilization, France was not yet ready for an idealistic government.

Still, Wollstonecraft finds much goodness coming out of bloody Paris. Revolution, even with its mistakes, is a rational and natural part of the growth of civilization. "People thinking for themselves," she writes, "have more energy in their voice, than any government, which it is possible for human wisdom to invent." It is this mental revolution and freedom that Wollstonecraft embraces, and we see evidence of this philosophy in all her writings. She later recanted her harsh assessment of the French people (in letters she composed in Scandinavia).

Political equality and educational reform are the vehicles for social change. In *Letters Written during a Short Residence in Sweden, Norway, and Denmark*, Wollstonecraft argues for prison reform and more tolerance toward servants, while she attacks capital punishment, lawyers, commerce, and meaningless ceremony. Public executions, she alleges, are scenes of amusement, and far from being useful examples, they harden "the heart they ought to terrify." Men of business, she asserts, are domestic tyrants. She cautions the merchants gaining power in Norway: "England and America owe their liberty to commerce, which created a new species of power to undermine the feudal system. But let them beware of the consequence: the tyranny of wealth is still more galling and debasing than that of rank." She admonishes Tonesberg lawyers who undermine morality by confounding right and wrong.

These letters reveal Wollstonecraft's skepticism of any organized religion, the Anglican church, Lutheran piety, or Methodist fanaticism. Piety, either heathen or Christian, constitutes a blind faith in things contrary to reason. She expresses concern for the environment and overpopulation, and she is convinced that knowledge will destroy the factitious national characters that ignorance has supposed permanent. All vices are a result of ignorance.

Because Norwegian farmers maintain communal-like small landholdings, Wollstonecraft professes them the happiest and least oppressed people of Europe. Humankind is debased by any kind of servitude, and she thus deplores the double sexual standards of Denmark. Men, whether fathers, brothers, or husbands, are domestic tyrants; "there is a kind of interregnum between the reign of the father and husband," she writes, "which is the only period of freedom and pleasure that the women enjoy."

Wollstonecraft is as appalled by the poverty of Scandinavia as she was with the poverty of Ireland. She admonishes excessive drinking. Calling intoxication the pleasure of savages, Wollstonecraft says drinking serves as Europe's greatest impediment to general improvement. Wollstonecraft questions the assistance provided by any institutionalized charity, whether hospitals or workhouses. "I have always been an enemy to what is termed charity," Wollstonecraft writes, "because timid bigots endeavouring thus to cover their *sins*, do violence to justice, till, acting the demi-god, they forget that they are men." Benevolence becomes merely tyranny in disguise.

Feminist Theories

Masculine tyranny over women, the double standard at the heart of gender relations, is the focus of Wollstonecraft's attacks in *A Vindication of the Rights of Woman*. Educational restrictions and social customs keep women in a state of ignorance and slavish dependence. Men, she points out, are prepared for a vocation that ensures them a future. Women are prepared only for the present, to be the playthings of men. They are taught to adorn themselves with artificial graces that enslave them to masculine tyranny. Marriage—a contract of obedience and servitude to men—is the only way for women to advance socially.

Why, asks Wollstonecraft, should virtue have different meanings for men and women? She challenges men to become more chaste and modest as she erodes the double standard of socially acceptable behavior. The word "masculine," she asserts, is only a bugbear. We have imposed gender distinctions and limitations on the mind and soul. The sexual distinction that men have so long insisted upon is arbitrary. Women must reform and liberate themselves from the servitude imposed on them by this double standard. Wollstonecraft calls for a revolution of female manners. Women must cultivate reason, think independently, and learn to respect themselves. This female improvement and emancipation will, in turn, liberate and improve all humankind.

Wollstonecraft tried to depict these feminist theories in her two attempts at fiction. In both *Mary, A Fiction* and *Maria, or The Wrongs of Woman*, she portrays women who are victimized by limited feminine education, who submit to unquestionable obedience and duty, who become imprisoned by a society that glorifies the tyranny of men, and who are deprived of economic independence.

The preface of *Maria* reveals Wollstonecraft's desire to exhibit "the misery and oppression, peculiar to women, that arise out of the partial laws and customs of society." In her depiction of Jemima, Wollstonecraft presents the plight of poor, outcast women. Maria, a representative of upper-class women, is manacled in the cell of an insane asylum where her husband George Venables has legally placed her. The literal fetters of the cell provide a concrete image of the metaphoric chains of marriage. All women, regardless of class, are victimized by the myths, customs, and prejudices that endorse a double standard.

In all her writings, Wollstonecraft adamantly asserts that education inculcating reason will eventually emancipate all humankind from all forms of servitude (political, sexual, religious, or economic) and allow all humankind to enjoy their God-given rights.

MARJEAN D. PURINTON

Further Reading

Bouten, Jacob. *Mary Wollstonecraft and the Beginnings of Female Emancipation in France and England*. Amsterdam: H. J. Paris, 1922; Reprint: Philadelphia: Porcupine Press, 1973. An analysis of Wollstonecraft's works in the context of eighteenth-century English and French philosophy.

Ferguson, Moira, and Janet Todd. *Mary Wollstonecraft*. Twayne's English Author Series. General editor, Sarah Smith. Boston: Twayne Publishers, 1984. A superb introduction to Wollstonecraft's life, including analyses of major works and an excellent annotated bibliography.

Flexner, Eleanor. *Mary Wollstonecraft: A Biography*. New York: Coward McCann and Geoghegan, 1972. Flexner emphasizes Wollstonecraft's life experiences as the basis for her writings, rather than the intellectual trends of the period.

George, Margaret. *One Woman's "Situation": A Study of Mary Wollstonecraft*. Urbana: University of Illinois, 1970. Considers Wollstonecraft as a feminist and rebellious writer who refused the female role prescribed by eighteenth-century society and who helped create a history for women.

Nicholes, Eleanor L. "Mary Wollstonecraft." In *Romantic Rebels, Essays on Shelley and His Circle*. Kenneth Neill Cameron, ed. Cambridge: Harvard University Press, 1973. Good short introduction to her life, ideas, and major works. Nicholes stresses the personal nature of Wollstonecraft's literary works.

Nixon, Edna. *Mary Wollstonecraft: Her Life and Times*. London: J. M. Dent and Sons, 1971. The narrative focuses on the events surrounding Wollstonecraft's life and her relationships with Fuseli, Imlay, and Godwin.

Sustein, Emily. *A Different Face: The Life of Mary Wollstonecraft*. New York: Harper & Row, 1975. The best biography of Wollstonecraft, with excellent analyses of her works and the eighteenth-century philosophies influencing her thought.

Tomalin, Claire. *The Life and Death of Mary Wollstonecraft*. New York: Harcourt Brace Jovanovich, 1974. Chapters 4, 6, and 11 are helpful examinations of the radical thinkers that helped to shape Wollstonecraft's own ideas.

Wardle, Ralph. *Mary Wollstonecraft: A Critical Biography*. 1951. Lincoln: University of Nebraska Press, 1967. This readable biography is still a standard. Especially good discussion of Wollstonecraft's French Revolution experiences (chapters 6 and 7). Wardle details reactions to *A Vindication of the Rights of Woman* and Wollstonecraft's influence on feminist thinking.

THOMAS ROBERT MALTHUS

Born: 1766, Guildford, Surrey, England
Died: 1834, Bath, England
Major Works: *Essay on the Principle of Population* (1798), *Principles of Political Economy* (1820)

Major Ideas

Population, when unchecked, increases in a geometric ratio, while subsistence increases only in arithmetic ratio.

Accordingly, there is a strong and constantly operating check on population because of the difficulty of subsistence.

The price of food will tend to increase, owing to the necessity of employing additional land of inferior quality to increase production: This is the law of diminishing returns.

Thomas Robert Malthus, whose life overlapped the Napoleonic Wars and the beginnings of the Industrial Revolution in England, best described the forces underlying the economics and the population dynamics of the traditional society that was coming to an end in his day. His theories, controversial in his lifetime and even more so today, form the basis of arguments over government social welfare policies. A kindly clergyman, he was reviled by Marx as "a shameless sycophant of the ruling classes." On the other hand, he was praised by John Stuart Mill on the grounds that only since Malthus's time "has the economical condition of the labouring classes been regarded by thoughtful men as susceptible of permanent improvement." (Before him, the laborer's condition had been considered hopeless.) Malthus showed that population growth can be analyzed empirically and can form the basis of public policy decisions. He is one of the few political thinkers whose arguments can be—and are—treated as if they had been written by a contemporary.

Born of a well-to-do family, Malthus was educated in mathematics at Cambridge, where he formed a wide circle of lifetime friends. In 1788, he was ordained into the Church of England (a common fate for the younger sons of the gentry) and served as a pastor in Surrey for a few years. From 1803, however, he held a sinecure that allowed him time for traveling and for developing his economic theories. In 1819, he was elected to the Royal Society. In his later years he testified before Parliament

and wrote treatises that led to the Poor Law Amendment Act of 1834.

Much of Malthus's work arose from his opposition to the utopianism of two earlier political thinkers, the Marquis de Condorcet and William Godwin. Both believed that social evils arise from imperfect political arrangements and that scientific reason, benevolence, and equality will be more common in future societies. Godwin developed these ideas further: The coercive state will gradually yield to a regime of peace, sincerity, and respect for individuality; eventually a brief period of daily work—perhaps two hours—will suffice for all, once artificial wants and superfluous needs are eradicated; property, including marriage, will disappear. Most of his contemporaries believed that population growth was desirable for supplying the workers, farmers, and soldiers necessary for a strong nation.

Malthus, influenced by his tenure as a curate among the poor of Surrey, countered these visions with arguments derived from his observations and from his reading in history and economics. He stated that "the power of population [growth] is infinitely greater than the power in the earth to produce subsistence," that population increases geometrically in the ratio 2, 4, 8, 16, 32 . . .) while food production increases only arithmetically (2, 4, 6, 8, 10 . . . ; twice as much land may produce twice as much food). He cited the rapid population growth of British North America (which had doubled in numbers every twenty-five years since the first settlement) as evidence for the exponential growth of population, given virtually unlimited resources and room to expand. Therefore population will always outrun the food supply, being checked only by (1) malnutrition and disease, or (2) by voluntary measures such as late marriage. (He doubted that war was a limitation on population; rather the reverse.) This was the central argument of the first edition of the *Essay on the Principle of Population*, and its six subsequent editions grew successively larger with supporting data gathered in travels to Scandinavia, Russia, Germany, France, and Switzerland.

Malthus's argument was based on observation and common sense, not on statistics. The first comprehensive British census was published in 1801, *after* the first edition of the *Essay*. To be sure, Malthus used the data from this census in the later editions, but at no time did he have the information necessary for rigorous proof. Modern studies have shown that in fact Malthus's assumptions were correct for the old regime: As the rate of population growth increased, wages declined and prices rose (these are, of course, two sides of the same coin); as real wages declined, the average age of marriage rose and the reproduction rate declined. Thus voluntary restraint did affect population growth.

It was unfortunate for Malthus's reputation that he—like everyone else—failed to foresee the changes already in process in his day. The Industrial Revolution in agriculture and the settling of North America and Australia were about to increase greatly the world's food production, lowering the price of food and increasing the purchasing power of consumers manyfold. In addition, the birth rate in industrialized nations began to decline rapidly, a trend that has continued, to negative rates in some countries. (Twentieth-century neo-Malthusians ask, "Can the increases in agricultural productivity continue to keep up with the birth rate in the nonindustrialized nations?" This was, of course, Malthus's very question.)

Also unfortunate for Malthus's reputation was his position on the Poor Laws, a position that was consistent with his theories of population dynamics, but seemed cruel. The Poor Laws established in each parish a property tax whose proceeds were used to support the infirm and the unemployed. Malthus, in common with others who advocated the principle of natural law in political matters, supported the abolition of the Poor Laws on the grounds that, although they had been instituted for benevolent purposes and were valuable for short-term relief, in the long run they produced incurable evils: They increased population without increasing the food supply, and therefore increased the price of food and lowered real wages. Welfare payments had become a subsidy that supplemented the laborer's wages, thus raising the effective wage rate, which would then require an increased subsidy. This leads to a spiral of ever increasing pauperism. In short, the Poor Laws, rather than helping the poor, simply increase their poverty. Understandably, this view seemed heartless. In the novel *Melincourt*, Thomas Love Peacock has a Malthus figure denounce the fact that paupers marry *even in the workhouse*, thus making it a "manufactory of beggars and vagabonds." In *Surplus Population*, an anti-Malthus melodrama, William Cobbett has his Malthusian rail against "that great national scourge, the procreation of the human species!"

The problems addressed by Malthus are still discussed: How seriously do welfare benefits modify an individual's will to work? Have large-scale welfare schemes (such as the "Great Society") increased dependency? Do such schemes institutionalize poverty in the midst of prosperity? American neo-Malthusians have stressed the dangers of the increase of the world's population. Paul Erlich, the author of recent books on this topic, might echo the sentiments of Cobbett's Malthusian.

Malthus's other contribution to economic thought was his opposition to Say's Law, which states: If capital and the resulting supply of goods increase, the level of demand will also increase, that is, goods will always find consumers. Malthus disagreed. He considered that population, capital accumulation, a prosperous agriculture, and labor-saving machinery by themselves could not generate sustained growth. He postulated the need for *effective demand* for noncapitalist consumption by those in possession of the surplus wealth that is created when high prices cover all production costs and yield a good return on capital. This theory implies that high prices are necessary for prosperity. It is, indeed, observable that prices in prosperous, developed countries are higher than in underdeveloped countries. Malthus's theory was developed during the depression following the end of the Napoleonic Wars in 1815, when unemployment was high despite England's industrial capacity, and prices fell. The economist John Maynard Keynes, facing the problems of the postwar depression of the 1920s and 1930s, joined Malthus in rejecting Say's Law, and he revived Malthusian economics in opposition to classical economics.

As a consequence of his theory of effective demand, Malthus advocated *protectionism* in the form of the Corn Laws, which supported the price of grain at a fixed level and limited grain imports. He considered that free importation of grain into England would lower prices for domestic grain, reduce landowners' income, and thus decrease effective demand and prosperity in the economy overall. (In addition, he thought that Britain should be self-sufficient in food production on grounds of national security.)

Malthus's influence has been great. Two years after Darwin returned from his voyage on the *Beagle*, he happened to read the *Essay* and was struck by the idea that under the circumstances described in that work, "favorable variations would tend to be preserved and unfavorable ones to be destroyed. The result would be the formation of a new species." The entire struggle for existence "is the doctrine of Malthus applied . . . to the whole animal and vegetable kingdoms." It is recognized today that Malthus confronted many problems that still arise in studying the economies of the underdeveloped countries, even if he lacked the data and the statistical methods to resolve these problems.

MARK T. RILEY

Further Reading

James, Patricia. *Population Malthus; His Life and Times*. London, Boston: Routledge & Kegan Paul, 1979. This standard biography includes many unpublished letters.

Keynes, John Maynard. "Malthus" in *Essays in Biography*. Edited by Geoffrey Keynes. New York: W. W. Norton, 1963. This is published as vol. 10 of *The Collected Writings of John Maynard Keynes*. Royal Economic Society. London: Macmillan, 1972. Keynes did much to rehabilitate Malthus's reputation.

Winch, Donald. *Malthus*. Oxford and New York: Oxford University Press, 1987. Not a biography, this is the best short introduction to the development of Malthus's theories and the contemporary events and situations that prompted them.

GEORG WILHELM FRIEDRICH HEGEL

Born: 1770, Stuttgart, Germany
Died: 1831, Berlin, Germany
Major Works: *Phenomenology of Spirit (Phänomenologie des Geistes, 1806); Science of Logic (Wissenschaft der Logik, 1812–16); Encyclopedia of the Philosophical Sciences in Outline (Enzyklopädie der Philosophischen Wissenschaften im Grundrisse, (1817, 1827); Philosophy of Right (Grundlinien der Philosophie des Rechts, 1821)*

Major Ideas

To identify the categories inherent in our own subjective thinking is at the same time to identify objective reality's fundamental character or meaning.

"The Idea," "reason," or "God"—the full actualization of which is spirit—is reality's fundamental character.

The stages both of nature and of human activity are stages through which the Idea passes in becoming actual as spirit.

As beings with the power of thinking and so of willing and acting freely, we human beings are the bearers or vehicles of reality's actualization as spirit.

Although he is often thought of as the philosopher from whose idealistic "mystification" Karl Marx distinguished his own philosophical materialism, Hegel was not an idealist in the usual sense of the term, nor can his kind of idealism be contrasted in any simple way to materialism. Hegel did not agree with such a "subjective" idealist as George Berkeley in saying that things exist, or have reality, only if they are perceived by a human or divine "mind." Nor did he agree even with Immanuel Kant, his immediate predecessor with whom he otherwise had much in common, in maintaining that things as we know them—as contrasted with *un*knowable things as they are in themselves—are constituted as objects by the functioning of our minds. Things do exist independently of anyone's having knowledge or experience of them, Hegel made clear as against Berkeley and, in contrast to Kant's distinction between the "phenomenal" world of knowable objects and the "noumenal" world of unknowable things in themselves, Hegel maintained that the world of knowable objects is *the* world: As we know or experience it, so "what is"— whether it be a stone, a tree, a dog, a person, or God in the sense of the Absolute that all finite beings manifest—really is.

Hegel nevertheless *was* an idealist, however. For if the world is knowable by us, he reasoned, then— since knowing is an activity of thinking, and since thinking has its own inner principles and concepts—this world's fundamental character must be as we necessarily, that is, logically and validly, think or conceive it to be. As our thinking necessarily thinks or conceives it to be, so "what is" must be, such that by "deducing" in the science of logic the "necessary forms and self-determinations of thought," we thereby at the same time come to know the fundamental character or meaning of everything that is. "What is, is reason," then, according to Hegel, not in the sense that our subjective reasoning creates or invents the world of beings but, instead, in the sense that our subjective reason ("self-conscious reason") comprehends or grasps the "reason which *is* in the world." "Nothing is actual except the Idea," to be sure, Hegel said, and in saying this he surely was an "idealist." But "the Idea," "the Absolute," "God," is not a "chimera" or "phantasm"; it is the fundamental character of "what is," and to call it "the Idea" or "reason" is only to indicate that our knowledge of it is by way of knowing the principles and concepts of logic, "the logical Idea."

As is suggested by his identification of the deductions in the science of logic, "the logical Idea,"

331

with "the exposition of God as he is in his eternal essence," Hegel had a strong interest in religion and, specifically, Lutheran Christianity. Indeed, his original plan was to enter the Lutheran ministry, and, upon completing Gymnasium in 1788, he began a program of theological study at Tübingen Seminary (where he shared quarters with Friedrich Hölderlin, the poet, and Friedrich Schelling, the philosopher who was to become his most prominent philosophical friend and rival and, later, his successor as professor of philosophy and rector of Berlin University).

Having shifted his interest from theology to philosophy, but unable to secure a university post after his graduation from the seminary in 1793, he then worked as a tutor in Bern and Frankfurt. At Schelling's invitation, he moved to Jena in 1801, where, after submitting a dissertation on the orbiting of the planets, a critique of Kepler and Newton, he received his postdoctoral *habilitation*, the right to teach in a state university. Only in 1805, however, did he finally become an associate professor (with a very small salary) at the University of Jena. His tenure in this position turned out to be short. For in 1806 Napoleon defeated the Prussian Army at the Battle of Jena, the university was closed, and Hegel was forced to leave the city with his one copy of his just-completed first major work, *Phenomenology of Spirit*, in his hands and ready for the publisher.

After working as editor of a newspaper in Bamberg in 1807, Hegel then became headmaster of a Gymnasium in Nuremburg in 1808, where he served until 1816. During this period, in 1811 at age forty-one, he married Marie von Tucher, age twenty, and, in 1812, his *Science of Logic* was published in three volumes. Then in 1816, at age forty-six, Hegel secured his first genuine university appointment. He became a full professor of philosophy at the University of Heidelberg, where, in 1817, his *Encyclopedia of the Philosophical Sciences in Outline* was published.

In 1818 Hegel was appointed to the position as professor of philosophy at Berlin University, for which he is best known and in which he remained until his death in 1831. His *Philosophy of Right* was published in 1821, a revision of his *Encyclopedia* was published in 1827, and, after his death, his lectures on the history of philosophy, on the philosophy of history, on aesthetics, and on the philosophy of religion were edited and published by his students. He had become rector (president) of Berlin University in 1829.

Hegel was then and continues today to be one of the major enduring influences on philosophical thinking. Karl Marx, for example, in the generation directly after Hegel's, "openly avowed [him] self the pupil of that mighty thinker." And even though Hegel's influence diminished somewhat during the last half of the nineteenth and the first half of the twentieth centuries, it increased again around the middle of the twentieth century. Martin Heidegger's and Jean Paul Sartre's existentialist philosophies owe much to Hegel and even adopt much of Hegel's vocabulary, and in philosophical theology both the Catholic theologian Hans Küng and the Protestant theologian Paul Tillich acknowledge their indebtedness to Hegel. (When Tillich first came to this country, he was asked by students at Union Theological Seminary and Columbia University where he stood philosophically. His answer: Somewhere between Hegel and Schelling.) Even today the Hegel Society of America is an active and thriving professional association whose journal, *The Owl of Minerva*, serves as a focal point for Hegel scholarship, and, as the brief bibliography attached here indicates, important books about and building upon Hegel's thought continue to be published and discussed.

Encyclopedia of the Philosophical Sciences in Outline

"God does not remain petrified and dead," Hegel says in the introduction to part 3 of his *Encyclopedia*; "the very stones cry out and raise themselves to spirit." This formula points to the three main parts both of his *Encyclopedia* and of his philosophical system as a whole. "God"—the Idea, the Absolute, reason, "*the* Being," being-itself, of which all other beings both natural and spiritual, are finite actualizations or "differentiations"—comprises the subject matter of part 1, *Logic*; "stones," along with all other natural, prespiritual finite beings, comprise the subject matter of part 2, *Philosophy of Nature*; and "spirit," namely, the world of thinking (and therefore free) beings, comprises the subject matter of part 3, *Philosophy of Spirit*.

Knowing is an activity of thinking, we need to note in order to make at least some sense, first, of Hegel's *Logic* and then of his *Philosophy of Nature* and *Philosophy of Spirit*. To know any object, a piece of sugar, say, to use Hegel's own example, is—by thinking—to assimilate it within oneself in the form of thought, conception. "In thinking an object," as he puts it, "I make it into thought and deprive it of its sensuous aspect; I make it into something which is directly and essentially mine." As comprehended in thought, the piece of sugar is no longer alien or strange to us. Even though the piece of sugar is still there before us, in the bowl, it is no longer something that is simply given to our senses of sight and taste; instead, insofar as by thinking we comprehend it conceptually, "it then ceases to stand over against me and I have taken from it the character of its own which it had in opposition to me."

But how is this possible? Not merely by seeing and tasting the piece of sugar, Hegel argues. For, as Immanuel Kant demonstrated in his *Critique of Pure Reason* (1781), by seeing and tasting we can sense only such qualities as hardness and sweetness; we cannot know the piece of sugar as a piece of sugar, that is, as an object that unites or *has* these qualities. The piece of sugar's unity cannot be sensed. Yet we surely do experience the piece of sugar as a piece of sugar, as a whole, a unity, rather than merely as a collection of sense-qualities; we know it as a unity-in-difference. How? the unity of which we are aware must be contributed by our own thinking. "When . . . we look at a piece of sugar, we find it is hard, sweet, etc. All these properties we say are united in one object. Now it is this unity that is not found in the sensation." Instead, Hegel maintains, "it is evident only to thought."

Hence in addition to the principles of the "common logic," the laws of identity, contradiction, and excluded middle, there are concepts—thought-determinations (*Denkbestimmungen*) or categories—that are internal to our thinking that we bring *to* experience, so to speak, that make our knowledge of objects as objects possible, and it is the task of *Logic*, according to Hegel, to identify these concepts by analyzing our conscious, subjective thinking. There is a crucial disagreement between Hegel and Kant at this point, however. For whereas Kant draws the conclusion that, since objects are constituted as objects by the functioning of our subjective thinking, the objects of which we have knowledge ("phenomena") differ from things as they are in themselves ("noumena"), Hegel points out that, "though the categories, such as unity, or cause and effect, are strictly the property of thought, it by no means follows that they must be ours only and not also characteristics of the objects." He then concludes, instead (for reasons that cannot be explained here), that the categories of logic comprise "thoughts accredited able to express the essential reality of things." For Hegel, then, in disagreement with Kant, "logic therefore coincides with metaphysics, the science of things set and held in thoughts"; as we think or conceive "what is" by means of the categories inherent in our subjective thinking, so, according to Hegel, "what is" really is. "What is, is reason," not in the sense that it exists only in our subjective reason but, instead, in the sense that, as we conceive it in our rational thinking, so "what is" really is.

Thus the question at issue is, If an object is known by us, then by what thoughts or concepts do we necessarily think it? Or, in another way of posing the same question, If it is to be thinkable by us, what must any being's fundamental character be? And the answer, Hegel maintains, is "the logical Idea," the highest and most adequate category of which is "the Notion," or, what is somewhat easier to explain, the concept of "concrete universality." No matter what the "what is" may be, Hegel contends, be it a piece of sugar, a stone, a tree, a dog, an "I," or being-itself—God—we think or conceive it as containing three "dialectical" aspects or "moments": universality, particularity, and individuality. Since thinking necessarily thinks it so, everything that *is* is rational, in that (although in varying degrees) it is "syllogistic"—"dialectical"—in form. "The syllogistic form is a universal form of all things," as Hegel puts it; "everything that exists is an individual [*Besondere*], which couples together the universal [*Allgemein*] and the particular [*Einzeln*]." (This is at bottom what Hegel means by his now-famous and often-misunderstood statement, "What is rational is actual and what is actual is rational.")

Now if (according to Hegel's *Logic*) we "deduce" this syllogistic form to be the fundamental character of everything that is, including God, then (as he claims in the *Philosophy of Nature* and the *Philosophy of Spirit*) we "apply" logic to the worlds of nature and spirit by "recogniz[ing] the logical forms under the shapes they assume in nature and spirit," that is, by comprehending natural and spiritual beings as expressions of this syllogistic form. Moreover, since the degree to which a being expresses the syllogistic form is also the degree to which the being is "true" or "actual," we can trace out, in nature and spirit, the stages through which the Idea, reason, God, passes on its way to becoming fully actual.

Since "nature is weak and fails to exhibit the logical forms in their purity," we can most easily clarify what it means to say that to be something, not no-thing, is to be syllogistic, rational, by first considering spirit. Then, albeit only briefly, we can consider nature and show how stones, trees, dogs, and even humans (considered as biological/psychological organisms rather than as bearers of spirit, thinking beings), progressively actualize the Idea's syllogistic form.

Spirit is "*thinking* being," and a thinking being is an "I," a person; it is "thought as a *thinker*." Consequently we can understand what Hegel means by saying that "what is, is reason" by analyzing the "moments" comprising us as "I"s, thinking beings, persons.

First of all, I can distinguish within myself the "I" that is actively thinking from any and all of its possible contents, that is, from all particular thoughts that it might think. "When I say 'I'," as Hegel explains in his *Philosophy of Right*, "I *eo ipso* abandon all my particular characteristics, my disposition, natural endowment, knowledge, and age. The ego is quite empty, a mere point, simple, yet active in this simplicity."

This active but so far empty "I" is the "I" *qua* universal. But as a thinking "mere point," I also will and act. That is, I make myself particular or determinate; the "I" does not remain empty but in its activity it wills a content and so differentiates itself. If, for example, I will to affirm or believe a proposition, then in doing so I make myself determinate, particular, restricted; I hold *this* belief rather than other beliefs, and to this extent I am particularized, differentiated. My beliefs, opinions, and practical purposes are particulars that are now contents of myself *qua* "I." *Qua* "I" I am universal in my activity of *willing* these contents, but I am particularized, differentiated, in having *willed* these contents. I am both universal and particular; specifically, in Hegel's language, I am a self-differentiated universal.

As Hegel puts it, "Every self-consciousness knows itself (i) as universal, as the potentiality of abstracting from everything determinate, and (ii) as particular, with a determinate object, content, and aim." I am also in unity with myself in my differences or particulars, at least in some degree—since otherwise my beliefs and actions would not be *mine* at all—and to this degree I am an individual; that is, I actualize the syllogistic form and so am in this sense rational, "true." For "these moments [of universality and particularity] are only abstractions; what is concrete and true (and everything true is concrete) is the universality which has the particular as its opposite, but the particular which by its reflection into itself has been equalized with the universal. This unity is individuality . . . in accordance with its concept [that is, its Notion or syllogistic form]."

A being—and of course being-itself, the Idea, as well—is "true" or "actual," then, to the degree to which it exhibits the syllogistic form, concrete universality, that is, to the degree to which it is a universal that is both differentiated and in unity with itself in its differences. Hence it follows, according to Hegel, that we can distinguish degrees of "truth" or "actuality" within the spheres both of nature and of spirit.

A stone, for example, exhibits the syllogistic form only minimally. A stone is differentiated, to be sure, in that it is made up of grains of sand, and it is in unity with itself in its differences at least to the extent that the grains of sand are bound together in a whole. But its unity is only accidental. A stone does not have a center, a self, in which the differences, the grains of sand, are united; instead, the grains of sand remain "mutually external" to one another. Rather than concrete universality, a stone exhibits "asunderness."

A living plant, however, exhibits the syllogistic form to a greater degree and so is more "true" or "actual." For "in the plant," as Hegel explains, "we see a center which has overflowed into the periphery, a concentration of the differences, a self-development from within outwards, a unity which differentiates itself and from its differentiation produces itself in the bud." But a plant nevertheless does not exhibit the syllogistic form (the Idea) adequately, and so lacks "truth" or "actuality," for the reason that it lacks a definite center. It is not conscious, "and consequently the organs are not held in complete subjection to the unity of the subject."

The syllogistic form, the Idea, is exhibited in a greater degree, then, in an animal, since in an animal there is a conscious, "feeling" center in which the animal's differences are united. Here "the whole is so pervaded by its unity that nothing in it appears as independent, every determinateness is at once ideal, the animal remaining in every determinateness the same one universal." For "the animal is self-existent subjectivity and has feeling" so that "the animal is self-determined, from within outwards, not merely from outside." But while the animal's center is conscious, it is not yet *self*-conscious—the animal's self feels, but it cannot *think*—and so it is not fully in unity with itself in its differences, not *free*; "in the animal, the soul is not

yet *for* the soul," as Hegel puts it, "the universal as such is not yet *for* the universal." And to this extent it falls short of "truth" or "actuality"; it is not yet an adequate expression of the syllogistic form, the Idea.

It is only in spirit, then, that is, as thinking being, an "I," that the syllogistic form, concrete universality, can be (even if in fact it is not) fully expressed. This is so because thinking being's center, the universal "I," freely wills its differences—specifically, its theoretical beliefs and practical actions—whereas the animal's center, the "animal soul," "has no will and must obey its impulse if nothing external deters it." *Qua* "I"s, bearers of spirit, we human beings are free from determination by everything external to us, whereas the animal's center is "tied to one determinateness," namely, whatever happens to be its strongest impulse.

As thinking beings, "I"s, bearers of spirit, we human beings therefore have it as our specific potentiality, our "specific Notion," as Hegel puts it, to exhibit the syllogistic form, concrete universality, in full and so to be fully "true" or "actual." But for us this is not something that is immediately given. We have to actualize this potentiality and, according to Hegel, it is our *duty* to do so. "To such an extent as man is and acts like a creature of nature," as he puts it in his *Logic*, "his whole behavior is what it ought not to be. For the spirit it is a duty to be free, and to realize itself by its own act." We are not born as concrete universals. We are born as animals, beings in nature, who by virtue of our power of thinking have the potentiality for spirit, and we thus have the duty to develop and express this potentiality.

By willing—deciding what propositions to believe and what actions to do—in obedience to the Idea, reason, God, we develop our potentiality for spirit. We are free—that is, we fully express the syllogistic form within ourselves, or, again, the Idea is actual within us as spirit—if and when we "will what is rational." We do this in our practical activity, Hegel maintains, by forming and obeying the laws and customs of a "genuinely organized" state, namely, a "community of existence" wherein everyone treats everyone always as a free "I" and never as an unfree "it" (which is the reason why, in a frequently misinterpreted passage in *Philosophy of Right*, Hegel refers to the state as "the march of God in the world"); and, in our theoretical activity, our knowing, we do it finally in philosophy, namely, by knowing, comprehending that "what is, is reason," or, in other words, that "what is rational is actual and what is actual is rational."

CLARK A. KUCHEMAN

Further Reading

Fackenheim, Emil. *The Religious Dimension in Hegel's Thought*. Boston: Beacon Press, 1970 (by arrangement with Indiana University Press). A useful resource for anyone interested in the religious implications of Hegel's thought.

Findlay, J. N. *Hegel: A Re-examination*. Oxford: Oxford University Press, 1958. A perceptive analysis by an eminent scholar.

Kucheman, Clark A. "Abstract and Concrete Freedom: Hegelian Perspectives on Economic Justice." *The Owl of Minerva*, 15 (1), Fall, 1983. A discussion of the economic dimension of Hegel's work.

Lauer, Quentin. *A Reading of Hegel's Phenomenology of Spirit*. New York: Fordham University Press, 1976. A helpful guide.

Reyburn, Hugh A. *The Ethical Theory of Hegel: A Study of the Philosophy of Right*. Oxford: Clarendon Press, 1921. In spite of its age, this remains one of the most thorough, accurate, and clearly written accounts of Hegel's moral and political philosophy.

Taylor, Charles. *Hegel*. Cambridge: Cambridge University Press, 1975. The best of the contemporary interpretations of Hegel's thought. It also relates Hegel to the historical period in which he was writing and describes the influence of Hegel upon Karl Marx and upon contemporary philosophy and social theory.

Wiedmann, Franz. *Hegel: An Illustrated Biography*. Translated by Joachim Neugroschel. New York: Pegasus, 1968. For a look at Hegel's personal background.

CARL FRIEDRICH GAUSS

Born: 1777, Brunswick, Germany
Died: 1855, Göttingen, Germany
Major Works: *Disquisitiones Arithmeticae (Arithmetical Investigations)* (1801), *Theoria Motus Corporum Coelestium in Sectionibus Conicis Solem Ambientium (Theory of the Motion of the Heavenly Bodies Moving about the Sun in Conic Sections)* (1809), *Disquisitiones Generales Circa Superficies Curvas (General Investigations of Curved Surfaces)* (1827)

Major Ideas

Mathematics requires a new rigor in which Greek standards of precision are applied to the subject matter of contemporary mathematics.

The goal of science is the pursuit of truth "for its own sake."

Due to its intrinsic independence from the material and the practical, "mathematics is the queen of the sciences."

Arithmetic, on the other hand, is the "queen of mathematics," since it is the most disinterested and pure.

The logic that holds together mathematics also pervades the universe; we understand the universe by discovering its underlying mathematical theories.

Carl Friedrich Gauss is regarded as the greatest mathematician since Newton. Many consider Gauss to be the greatest mathematician of all time. Like Newton, Gauss was a scientist in a time when there was no clear distinction between the activity of a mathematician and that of a physicist. But, whereas Newton's main interest in mathematics lay in its application to science, Gauss found mathematics to be of intrinsic value. Gauss worked with equal success in pure and applied mathematics, but placed a higher value on the former. The development of a logical and complete theory was the goal of both his mathematical and his scientific work. His experimental activity in science inevitably led to the development of theoretical work.

To Gauss's creativity and depth of insight was added a new sense of rigor that enabled him to reorganize or develop major areas of mathematical and scientific research and that changed the way that mathematics was to be done by his successors.

Mathematics and science were placed in a new relationship in Gauss's scheme. According to eighteenth-century views, mathematics served essentially as a tool for scientific use, and science tended to be valued for its practical advantages. In Gauss's new vision, theoretical considerations held an inherent primacy, resulting in the supreme position of mathematics among the sciences.

Gauss entered elementary school in 1784. His teachers observed and nourished his unusual ability in arithmetic and helped to arrange for his admission to secondary school in 1788, where his studies included Latin and High German.

Gauss entered the Collegium Carolinum in 1792, where he was a student of Latin and Greek and benefited from its excellent library. There he acquired a broad foundation of mathematical knowledge. His early interest in arithmetic led to his investigation of the distribution of prime numbers.

In 1795, Gauss entered Göttingen University, chosen for its extensive mathematical library. There he completed most of his first major work, *Disquisitiones Arithmeticae*, including its two proofs of the law of quadratic reciprocity (his "golden theorem") in 1796. In that same year he used number theory to prove the constructibility of the regular polygon of seventeen sides, and thereby solved a geometric problem dating back to antiquity.

Gauss returned to Brunswick in 1798. He completed his dissertation, in which he proved the fundamental theorem of algebra, and received the doctoral degree from the University of Helmstedt in 1799. *Disquisitiones Arithmeticae* was published in 1801.

The discovery of the planet Ceres by an Italian astronomer in 1801 led to a shift in Gauss's major interest from pure mathematics to astronomy. Gauss computed the orbit of Ceres and successfully predicted its rediscovery a year later, resulting in his becoming a celebrity in the field of astronomy.

In 1807, Gauss moved to Göttingen to become director of its astronomical observatory.

His second major work, *Theoria Motus*, was published in 1809. *Theoria Motus* is a treatise in theoretical astronomy on the determination of the orbits of planets and comets. In the period from 1807 to 1818, Gauss continued his astronomical work, produced a paper on Gauss sums, second and third proofs of the fundamental theorem of algebra, and a paper on the hypergeometric series. The remaining four of his six different proofs of the law of quadratic reciprocity are believed to have been found by him by 1808. In a review written in 1816, Gauss indicated his success in grasping non-Euclidean geometry and he is credited with being the first to do so.

From 1818 to 1832, Gauss participated in a project undertaken to survey the kingdom of Hanover. This work led to two major theoretical works in geodesy and also to an important paper in pure mathematics, *Disquisitiones Generales Circa Superficies Curvas*, in which he introduced "intrinsic" geometry—concerned with the local properties of a surface, such as its curvature—and thus set the foundation for the development of modern differential geometry.

In 1831, Gauss's major interest shifted to physics. In an 1832 paper he defined an absolute measure of magnetic force, and in 1838 he published a general theory of terrestrial magnetism from which he successfully predicted the location of the magnetic South Pole. He made contributions to potential theory and to the theory of electro-magnetism.

Gauss published a paper on biquadratic residues in 1831 in which he introduced the Gaussian integers and thus began the field of algebraic number theory.

During the final years of his life, from 1838 to 1855, Gauss worked in his astronomical and magnetic observatories in Göttingen, and he continued to pursue his interests in both mathematics and physics. He learned Russian in order to read the work of the Russian geometer Lobachevsky. A fourth, final, and improved version of his doctoral dissertation was presented in 1849 at the time of his golden jubilee.

Gauss made major contributions to every field of mathematics. He reorganized number theory and established its future direction. He founded the subject of modern differential geometry and thus provided the mathematical basis for the later development of the theory of general relativity by Einstein. He set new directions for research in astronomy and geodesy.

Gauss died on February 23, 1855. In the words of mathematician Eric T. Bell, "He lives everywhere in mathematics."

The New "Inner" Rigor

Gauss brought to mathematics a new rigor that was to redefine the standards for the work of his successors. The work of Gauss is characterized not only by the completeness of its overall form but also by a completeness of the details of its inner structure, the latter of which defines him as the first of the modern rigorists.

Gauss had studied the works of Archimedes and Newton, well-known masters of the completed presentation. He held them in high esteem, referring to Newton as "summus." Following their example, Gauss sought to produce work complete in form—logical, unified, and concise. *Disquisitiones Arithmeticae, Theoria Motus*, and *Disquisitiones Generales* stand as superb examples of Gauss's ability to produce complete and unified theories.

But Gauss's unique contribution to the standards of modern rigor lay not in his ability to achieve classical completeness of external form but rather in his ability to further refine the inner workings of his theories. Indeed, he saw the latter as his major occupation. As he simply stated, "One must pursue the tree to all its root fibers. . . ." He referred to this as "rigor antiquus," reflecting the fact that the Archimedean standard of precision had been abandoned in the eighteenth century.

Gauss rendered the rigor of the Greeks applicable to the mathematics of his day.

First of all, he insisted that mathematical results, then generally accepted on the basis of intuition or induction, must submit to logical demonstration in order to establish their mathematical validity. In fulfillment of this standard, he provided the first correct proofs of such landmark results as the fundamental theorem of algebra (a theorem in complex analysis that states essentially that every polynomial equation has a complex root), and the law of quadratic reciprocity, which is concerned with the solvability of certain pairs of quadratic congruences and is crucial to the development of number theory.

Second, he tightened the way in which logic is used within a mathematical proof. Rigor is always a matter of degree, and Gauss set a new standard for what may be regarded as evident. His criticism of the work of other mathematicians in his doctoral dissertation and in *Disquisitiones Arithmeticae* shows his dissatisfaction with the way in which much of recent mathematics was done. In his analysis of Legendre's incorrect proof of the law of quadratic reciprocity, he asserts the unacceptability of using that which is merely plausible or even probable, and he warns of the danger of circular logic.

A third element of Gauss's inner rigor is the setting of new standards of precision in the use of mathematical techniques.

Gauss noted the importance of the use of computational devices in the mathematics of his time, as against that of antiquity. Such devices serve to shorten, simplify, consolidate, and sometimes even to make possible methods of calculation and proof.

But the benefits to mathematics brought by the increased use of such methods were accompanied by serious dangers to logic and beauty. In reaction to the work of his contemporaries and recent predecessors, Gauss warned against the merely mechanical use of techniques that leads to their application in contexts where they have no validity.

Gauss's own work on topics related to the convergence of infinite series provides an illustration of this aspect of his rigor. He saw that methods for computing sums of infinite series must be restricted to those series that actually do converge, so that a precise definition of convergence and convergence tests are required for the development of a sound theory. His paper on the hypergeometric series published in 1813 was the first systematic approach to infinite series. His work set a new standard for the treatment of infinite processes and established for all of mathematics the importance of knowing the exact conditions under which a given method is applicable.

Mathematics as the Queen of the Sciences

For Gauss, "mathematics is the queen of the sciences, and arithmetic is the queen of mathematics."

The eighteenth-century belief in the mathematical nature of the universe was raised to a new level in the work of Gauss. Mathematics was indeed a tool for scientific use. But for Gauss, the relationship of mathematics to science was not that of mere servant. In his view, mathematics *governed* the behavior of the universe; to understand the universe, therefore, we must discover and develop its underlying mathematical theories.

Mathematics, moreover, provided a model for the way in which scientific theories were to be developed. Gauss's first major work, *Disquisitiones Arithmeticae*, provided such a model for his later work in both mathematics and science. His classic treatise in astronomy, *Theoria Motus*, like its mathematical predecessor, is described as rigorous, concise, and complete. *Theoria Motus* contains Gauss's first publication of the method of least squares, a mathematical method whose essential role in his analysis of data in both astronomy and geodesy gave further evidence of the fundamental congruity of mathematical thought and the behavior of the universe.

Gauss's elevation of mathematics from servant to queen of the sciences arose also from his belief, expressed in the *Inaugural Lecture on Astronomy* (undated), that the primary goal of science is the pursuit of truth "for its own sake." In this work, he praises Archimedes for ranking pure mathematics as first among the sciences, a position that it warrants by virtue of its intrinsic independence from the material and the practical.

As a consequence of Gauss's vision, the very nature of mathematics was redefined for his successors. Mathematics regained its identity as a distinct science and the near identification of mathematics and physics that had prevailed since the time of Newton ended. *Disquisitiones Arithmeticae* stands as a monument to Gauss's new vision.

Gauss not only redefined mathematics, he also redefined arithmetic as a subject within it. In his preface to *Disquisitiones Arithmeticae*, Gauss distinguishes higher arithmetic, which is concerned with general properties of numbers, from elementary arithmetic, which is concerned with counting and calculation. Higher arithmetic, now called number theory, forms the subject matter of *Disquisitiones*

Arithmeticae, in which he refers to it as "this divine science." Gauss values higher arithmetic as the most disinterested and pure of all of mathematics. He values its supreme elegance of theory and notes the special joy and passion that accompany its study. Qualities such as rigor and conciseness which are perhaps only *useful* to the other sciences are absolutely *necessary* for arithmetic.

Gauss's own work was a major contribution to the new position of arithmetic within the mathematical sciences. For, in *Disquisitiones Arithmeticae*, he placed the rather isolated results of his predecessors on a sound basis within a newly organized theory, and by adding his own work defined the subject of modern number theory.

SUSAN WILLIAMSON

Further Reading

Buhler, Walter K. *Gauss: A Biographical Study.* Berlin, Heidelberg, and New York: Springer-Verlag, 1981. Designed for the contemporary mathematician and scientist. Provides a summary of the contents of Gauss's work and includes many passages from his writings.

Dunnington, G. Waldo. *Carl Friedrich Gauss: Titan of Science.* New York: Exposition Press, 1955. A comprehensive and authoritative biography that describes Gauss's life against its historical setting. Contains a chronological listing of Gauss's 155 published works and a bibliography of secondary literature.

Gauss, Carl F. *Disquisitiones Arithmeticae.* Translated by Arthur A. Clarke. New Haven: Yale University Press, 1966.

————. *General Investigations of Curved Surfaces.* Translated by Adam Hiltebeitel and James Morehead. New York: Raven Press, 1965.

————. *Theory of the Motion of Heavenly Bodies.* New York: Dover, 1963.

————. *Inaugural Lecture on Astronomy and Papers on the Foundations of Mathematics.* Translated by G. Waldo Dunnington. Baton Rouge: Louisiana State University, 1937.

Hall, Tord. *Carl Friedrich Gauss: A Biography.* Cambridge and London: MIT Press, 1970. A readable explanation of the problems Gauss sought to solve, together with his methods of solution. Designed for the general reader.

ARTHUR SCHOPENHAUER

Born: 1788, Danzig, Poland
Died: 1860, Frankfort-am-Main, Germany
Major Works: *On the Fourfold Root of the Principle of Sufficient Reason* (1814), *The World as Will and Idea* *(Representation)* (1818), *On the Will in Nature* (1836), *The Two Fundamental Problems of Ethics* (1841), *Parerga and Paralipomena* (1851)

Major Ideas

The world is nothing but the product of our perception and reason and exists only through and for the perceiving subject.
Reality is in itself nothing but will (an aimless energy), and will is known only as idea (representation), the objectivity of the will.
The body is the will objectified.
The arts objectify the will by representing individual things and therefore the Platonic Ideas.
The will we know is the will-to-live, and to live is to desire, and to desire is to suffer.
The way to salvation, to escape from suffering, is through knowledge of the nature of will, a knowledge that prompts denial of the will.

Arthur Schopenhauer comes immediately into focus when one sees him as possessed by an idea: All reality is fundamentally *will*—a blind striving that is never-ending, that manifests itself as life, that realizes itself in suffering, and that triumphs only in its own denial.

Schopenhauer was born into a rich merchant family in Danzig, but at the age of five, after Prussia annexed Danzig, he was taken by his parents to Hamburg. At the age of nine, he was sent to Le Havre to learn French, and at fifteen he was sent to stay with a clergyman named Wimbledon to learn English. While still in his teens he spent some time in Paris, then in Switzerland and Vienna.

His father, Heinrich Schopenhauer, who had always been sympathetic and encouraging to his son, committed suicide in 1805, and the young Schopenhauer was then free, through his inheritance, to abandon his job in a mercantile house and to develop his interest in philosophy.

For some time he lived with his mother in Weimar, but although she was the center of an active literary circle and had Goethe as a constant visitor to her salon, Arthur was dissatisfied. He disliked, if not hated, his mother, and his aversion to women, which he later expressed in his "Essay on Women," together with his aversion to the ro-

manticism of the Weimar circle and his love for philosophy, led him to depart from Weimar and to enter the University of Göttingen.

At Göttingen, Schopenhauer was profoundly drawn to the ideas of Plato and Kant, and these perspectives—the one involving an emphasis on the pure Ideas, the Form of things, and the other emphasizing the role of the knowing subject in the forming and conceiving of the world—were to influence, if not determine, the whole course of his thinking and his life. The third significant influence on his work and life were the scriptures of Hinduism and Buddhism, with their emphasis on life as suffering and on the denial of desire as the way to freedom and detachment.

After studying in Berlin, where he attended Fichte's lectures (which he did not admire), he returned to Weimar to write his thesis for the doctorate at Jena, *On the Fourfold Root of the Principle of Sufficient Reason* (1814). Two years later his essay "On Vision and Color," influenced in part by correspondence with Goethe, who found fault with Newton's theory of light, was published.

He moved to Dresden and wrote the work that was to become his masterpiece, *Die Welt als Wille und Vorstellung* (*The World as Will and Idea*—or *The World as Will and Representation*), published in

1818. The book received very little attention and did nothing at the time to contribute to Schopenhauer's reputation; a second edition in 1844 was also a failure; finally, with the third edition in 1859, he achieved the respect and attention he was sure he deserved.

When in 1819 he was appointed to the faculty at the University of Berlin, he scheduled his lectures at the same time as those given by Hegel, then regarded as the greatest philosopher in Germany. Unfortunately, again, he failed to draw any auditors from his famous colleague, and Schopenhauer gave up the profession of teaching altogether.

Fame finally came to Schopenhauer in the 1850s, mostly because materialists and anticlerics in England and Germany, as well as mystics and devotees of the Eastern religions, began to use his works in support of their various causes. New editions of his books appeared in rapid succession. He continued to write, to take long walks with his poodles, to dine out, and to retire early. After a decade of success, in 1860 he had a heart attack followed by pneumonia, and on the morning of September 21, he quietly died on the sofa after breakfast.

The World as Will and Idea

Schopenhauer's masterpiece begins with a grand flourish:

> "The world is my idea": this is a truth which holds good for everything that lives and knows, though man alone can bring it into reflective and abstract consciousness. If he really does this, he has attained to philosophical wisdom. It then becomes clear and certain to him that what he knows is not a sun and an earth, but only an eye that sees a sun, a hand that feels an earth; that the world which surrounds him is there only as an idea, *i.e.*, only in relation to something else, the consciousness, which is himself.

As if suspecting that his claim would be too radical to be taken seriously, Schopenhauer insists that what he is proposing is an *a priori* truth, a truth that reveals the general character of all actual and possible experience. He underscores his certainty by writing that "no truth . . . is more certain, more independent of all others, and less in need of proof than this, that all that exists for knowledge, and therefore this whole world, is only object in relation to subject, perception of a perceiver, in a word, idea [representation]."

As one reads on, it becomes apparent that Schopenhauer intends his claim to be taken literally and in all seriousness. *The* world is *my* idea, he declares at the outset, but this truth is not to be taken as an expression of solipsism (the belief that nothing exists except as the content of the subject's thinking). Nor is the claim to be taken to mean that since *my* world is *my* idea, and *your* world is *your* idea, and so forth, reality is only in minds. For, as it turns out, Schopenhauer regards the "idea," the experience (image, perception, conception, feeling) in mind, as the phenomenal or subjective aspect of the fundamental and universal *will*, a pervasive, striving power that is the very center of being.

Schopenhauer asks whether the world we know as our idea is *only* an idea—that is, whether reality consists of ideas (our experiences) and nothing more. He argues that we realize that our bodies are the objectifications of our wills: What we do with our bodies is what we will. In knowing the activities of our bodies, we directly know our wills. This knowledge is not based on one of the four kinds of truth specified in the earlier work *On the Principle of Sufficient Reason*, namely, what Schopenhauer calls "logical, empirical, transcendental and metalogical" truths. He calls the truth—that "the body is the objectivity of will"—a "philosophical" truth. The proposition that reality is will and its representation, its objectification, is an extension of the directly known philosophical truth that our bodies are the objectification of will.

The ideas or representations in our experience are products of a forming intellect, Schopenhauer argues. Profoundly and almost without qualification influenced by Kant (although he also acknowledges a debt to Descartes and Berkeley), Schopenhauer not only stressed the formative influence of the intuition and the intellectual powers but also related the phenomena and the exercise of those powers to *will*, the power to determine action.

Schopenhauer insists that there is more to existence than the worlds we form in the intimacy of consciousness. There is that which is objectified in and through us. Schopenhauer calls it "will," and he insists that will is what Kant called the "thing-in-itself," what we cannot know except as the unknowable reality that manifests itself, in part, as the directly knowable will of the individual person.

Schopenhauer denies that the relation of cause and effect exists between the object and the subject. The knowing subject does not know itself as object; it knows itself only in knowing. But the object of experience is not what affects the subject, for the object is a *representation* (or reorganization) of the phenomenal data formed by the subject. In other words, Schopenhauer argues, realism is mistaken in presuming that objects causally affect subjects (persons). The world is not something outside us that determines us; the world *is* our representation. Nor is the philosophical idealist correct in maintaining that the subject causes the object. The object *is* the representation of the subject; neither one is a cause or is an effect of the other.

Early in the first book of *The World as Will and Idea*, Schopenhauer asks, "What is this world of perception besides being my representation?" and he follows immediately with the question, "Is that of which I am conscious only as representation just the same as my own body, of which I am doubly conscious, on the one hand as *representation*, on the other as *will*?" He then indicates that the answer to the second question is affirmative and will be the subject matter of the second book.

The body, then, is an idea, a representation. Space, time, and causality are forms of objects that are functions of modes of perception of the knowing subject. But the knowing subject knows itself also as *will*, as the drive toward the formation of objects and toward life itself.

We are eager to understand what Schopenhauer means by "will," for if there are two aspects of reality, the will as thing-in-itself and the world as the knowing subject's representation, it would be illuminating to know what the world *beyond* experi-

ence is and, hence, if Schopenhauer is right, what the *will* in itself is.

Unfortunately, Schopenhauer, like Kant (from whom he derived the idea), maintains that the "world" is inconceivable except as a representation: Without consciousness and the knowing subject, there would be no world. But the will is not part of the world we know; the will is not an object of and for the subject. The will is a "thing-in-itself" and so, by definition, not knowable as object.

Still, Schopenhauer presumes himself to be saying something significant when he writes of the will as the unknowable and fundamental aspect of reality. And he concedes that we can be conscious of ourselves as *wills*. Can we find in Schopenhauer, then, a connection between the personal will of which each of us is conscious and the cosmic Will, the fundamental force of reality?

First of all, how do we become conscious of ourselves as "willing"? Schopenhauer answers—as would most modern philosophers—that we become conscious of our wills *insofar as we act*. I know that I have willed to turn on the light in that I find that I have turned on the light. To "will," then is to act in one way rather than another when not to act in that way is possible. The point is not that by reference to action we find clues as to how the will operates; the point is that talk about the "will" is nothing more than talk about how we give way to tendencies to act in one way rather than another that is possible.

But what of the cosmic will, the will as thing-in-itself? If we identify will with the incentives to action that we find in ourselves, we tend to move from the specific to the general; we tend to attribute to the cosmic will, whatever it may be, the origin in appetite and interest that we find in ourselves. At that point, Schopenhauer's claim (or proposal) that the world-in-itself is will takes on an anthropomorphic cast: We see the underlying reality as a kind of irresistible impulse, a drive to be one way rather than another, a cosmic interest.

However, there is nothing in Schopenhauer to confirm such an interpretation. On the contrary, there is the constant warning from the author himself that says, in effect, there is that—we know not what—that manifests itself as individual wills and worlds. Schopenhauer chooses to call the unknowable force or power in reality by a term related to (but not identifiable in meaning with) the will of which we are conscious in the action of our bodies, namely, "will."

Given this broad interpretation, Schopenhauer's "metaphysics" becomes a kind of poetry—that is, an original and illuminating piece of description, involving a departure from conventional uses of terms. One comes to suspect that Schopenhauer's "will" is something like the contemporary physicist's "energy." Bryan Magee, in his extraordinary book *The Philosophy of Schopenhauer*, writes that "Schopenhauer is saying that . . . energy is itself what is ultimate in the world of phenomena." And he calls attention to Werner Heisenberg's remarks in *Physics and Philosophy*: "Energy is in fact the substance from which all elementary particles, all atoms and therefore all things are made, and energy is that which moves." And, again, "Since mass and energy are, according to the theory of relativity, essentially the same concepts, we may say that all elementary particles consist of energy. This could be interpreted as defining energy as the primary substance of the world."

If we interpret "will" as meaning "energy," much of the drama and mystery of Schopenhauer is lost, but much in the way of credibility is gained. If we think of the world as an incomprehensibly complex churning and plunging forward of energy—the primal force, the power to make a difference (we must use the concept of time to visualize the process)—then it makes sense that something of that force is known to us as "will" and that when we are driven to act, we are realizing in action a turn that the primal force can take.

Magee discusses Schopenhauer's problem of finding a term for the noumenon, the unknowable reality beyond experience. He tells us that Schopenhauer rejected the word "force" precisely because of its scientific connotations and chose instead a term that calls attention to a reality known to us both as subject and as object, the term "will." In chapter 18 in the supplements to the second book of *The World as Will and Representation*, Scho-

penhauer writes that "the act of will is indeed only the nearest and clearest *phenomenon* of the thing-in-itself. . . . Therefore in this sense I teach that the inner nature of everything is *will*, and I call the will the thing-in-itself." If one then asks, writes Schopenhauer, what the will is apart from its manifestation "in the world and as the world," one asks for an account of the unknowable; in other words, one asks for the impossible.

It becomes clear that it would be a mistake to think of Schopenhauer's reality, the world-in-itself, what he calls the "will," as a conscious and deliberate striving toward objectives. Schopenhauer repeatedly describes the will as "blind impulse," as without consciousness. But when the will manifests itself as the individual wills of persons, it can be characterized as the "will-to-live." The will-to-live does involve cravings and the setting of goals, and it is exercised in competition, conflict, and the futile effort to satisfy desires that are continually frustrated. Accordingly, Schopenhauer concludes, the world is fundamentally an evil place, a manifestation of a purposeless striving that is at best boring, at worst painful without remedy. And the only way to free oneself from such a world is to deny the will that that world objectifies. An "empty nothingness," writes Schopenhauer, is preferable to the "incurable suffering and endless misery" that are "essential to the phenomenon of the will, to the world. . . ."

How is a denial of the fundamental reality, will, possible? Schopenhauer suggests that this denial can be achieved through a concentration of the knowledge that all is will and that the manifestation of will in phenomena to which suffering is intrinsic is nothing that a rational person can accept. Schopenhauer calls attention to the sages and saints who have accomplished a denial of the will. He does not urge an escape to the Buddhist state of Nirvana, somehow a positive outcome of the denial of the will. He insists that to have nothing, to become nothing, through the denial of the will, is to achieve an "ocean-like calmness of the spirit, . . . deep tranquillity, . . . unshakeable confidence and serenity. . . ." He agrees that the denial of the will leaves us with nothing, but he argues that to one who has accomplished such a denial, the world, which is the objectification of will, is itself nothing. Accordingly, he suggests, nothing is lost, and nothing (which is better than anything) is gained.

Art as the Objectification of Ideas

If there is any way of escaping the bondage of the will that underlies all phenomena, it is by way of art, Schopenhauer argues. The artist is a genius at the isolation of the Idea, the Platonic universal. Where the gardener sees a particular tree, the artist sees and expresses treeness, the essence of the tree. And since Ideas (universals) are abstracted from individual things and exist apart from interests, art takes us beyond the clutches of the will (if anything can) and gives us peace in contemplation.

Schopenhauer denies that Kant's thing-in-itself can be identified with Plato's Idea. The Idea is a representation and hence *not* a thing-in-itself, but the Idea is an aesthetic object of the highest degree of generality and can be enjoyed by the beholder in a fairly will-less condition.

An object is beautiful, Schopenhauer contends, if it is an object of aesthetic contemplation, that is, if it "makes us *objective*" in that "in contemplating it we are no longer conscious of ourselves as individuals, but as pure, will-less subjects of knowing."

The source of aesthetic enjoyment is sometimes simply in the apprehension of the Idea and at other times consists of the "bliss and peace of mind of pure knowledge free from all willing. . . ."

Although the will objectifies itself in Idea in all the arts, which Schopenhauer arranges from architecture (the lowest grade of the objectivity of the will in art) through tragedy (the highest grade of objectivity, presenting the "conflict of the will with itself"), Schopenhauer gives a special place to music. The arts other than music objectify will by means of the Ideas, but music is "a copy of the will itself. . . ." The other arts depict individual things in order to present the Ideas of those things, but music directly copies the will. The other arts, Schopenhauer writes, "speak only of the shadow, but music of the essence."

An Ethics of Compassion or Sympathy

In the statement of his ethical position in *The World as Will and Representation*, Schopenhauer makes it clear from the outset that he does not intend to lay down moral principles or to issue "ought" injunctions. The will is free, and it cannot be brought to its knees by commands.

Other philosophers, such as Kant, have attempted to base ethics on *a priori* principles, but Schopenhauer takes as the starting point each person's knowledge of suffering. By recognizing that suffering is inevitable in life (in that to live is to desire, and to desire is to will the satisfaction of a need or want, itself painful), we can come to the point of identifying the lot of others with our own and thereby overcome the egoism that stems from an absorption in one's own suffering as an individual. Pure affection, then, is sympathy or compassion, a recognition of the universality of suffering and a willingness to act for the elimination of suffering.

Schopenhauer argues that weeping, like laughter, distinguishes the human being from the animals. Weeping occurs only when suffering is reflected on. Whatever the cause, weeping is immediately occasioned by sympathy with ourselves. A progression to sympathy for others then occurs once the weeper recognizes in the pain of another what is common to all humanity. And since sympathy with oneself strengthens the resolve to do what is possible to eliminate or reduce one's own suffering in the future, sympathy for others motivates a resolve to remember the finiteness of others and to act in pure love—which, for Schopenhauer, is sympathy—and to seek to reduce the suffering of others.

The concern to eliminate suffering once suffering is recognized as a universal feature of the human condition finally leads to the denial of the will-to-live, Schopenhauer maintains.

Although Schopenhauer regarded reality as fundamentally evil in that the will manifests itself as desire, thereby making suffering inevitable, he provides a kind of escape through the use of reason and the self-knowledge that reason makes possible. To understand the human condition, he says in effect, is to make oneself strong enough to overcome it. In the eternal calm of knowledge, contemplation of the Ideas, and immersion in the Forms that art embodies, one finds asceticism possible: a pervasive constraint that shows itself in chastity, fasting, and other self-disciplines by which will attains a kind of *stasis*, an equilibrium in the midst of turmoil, that is the only salvation worth having.

An Unphilosophical Postscript: Schopenhauer on Women

Schopenhauer's notorious essay "Of Women," which appeared in the collection *Parerga and Paralipomena*, is perhaps better viewed as symptomatic of his neurotic repugnance toward his mother than as the well-considered position of a brilliant philosopher. His ideas and feelings about women do not stem from his philosophy of the will as thing-in-itself; on the contrary, his philosophy may very well stem from the frustrations of his will that were occasioned by his efforts to tolerate and live with his mother as in his peculiar and tortured way he saw her. In any case, his essay "On Women" is not a sign of his genius as a philosopher; it is a curiosity that, like Nietzsche's rantings about women, understandably continues to provoke some interest and resentment.

A smattering of remarks suggests the tone and range of the essay:

"You need only look at the way in which she is formed, to see that woman is not meant to undergo great labor, whether of the mind or the body." "Women are directly fitted for acting as the nurses and teachers of our early childhood by the fact that they are themselves childish, frivolous and short-sighted." "A man reaches the maturity of his reasoning powers and mental faculties hardly before the age of twenty-eight; a woman at eighteen. And then, too, in the case of woman, it is only reason of a sort—very niggard in its dimensions." ". . . It will be found that the fundamental fault of the female character is that it has no *sense of justice*. . . . They are dependent, not upon strength, but upon craft; and hence their instinctive capacity for cunning, and their ineradicable tendency to say what is not true." "And since women exist in the main solely for the propagation of the species, and are not destined for anything else, they live, as a rule, more for the species than for the individual. . . ." "It is only the man whose intellect is clouded by his sexual impulses that could give the name of *the fair sex* to that undersized, narrow-shouldered, broad-hipped, and short-legged race. . . ." "That woman is by nature meant to obey may be seen by the fact that every woman who is placed in the unnatural position of complete independence, immediately attaches herself to some man. . . . If she is young it will be a lover; if she is old, a priest."

Schopenhauer's Moral

What, if anything, does Schopenhauer say that is worth thinking about? It is not that there is a cosmic evil will that aims at our misery. He does not argue that, and if he did, there would be no reason to believe him. He was pessimistic, and he thought that life is more trouble than it is worth. That was his problem; it need not be ours. His views on women are obviously symptomatic of a neurotic condition beyond the scope of this essay.

But what Schopenhauer accomplished is something that philosophers through the ages have attempted, without much success. The world as we know it is largely our own creation: The color, the sound, the odor, and the worth of it are functions of our interests and consequent interpretations and conceptions. But there is an underlying, restless energy that cannot be turned aside, that determines the limits of our creativity, and that finally overwhelms us. And there is little that we can do about it, argues Schopenhauer—except acknowledge it, train ourselves to live in spite of it, and find our peace in art and in enduring ideas.

IAN P. MCGREAL

Further Reading

Hamlyn, D. W. *Schopenhauer. The Arguments of the Philosophers.* Edited by Ted Honderich. London, Boston, and Henley: Routledge & Kegan Paul, 1980. An intelligent, informed, and philosophically acute account of Schopenhauer's central argument, with critical remarks that do justice both to Schopenhauer and to Hamlyn.

Magee, Bryan. *The Philosophy of Schopenhauer.* Oxford: Clarendon Press; New York: Oxford University Press, 1983. A brilliant, searching series of essays on Schopenhauer's thought, including a section of appendices that touches perceptively on Schopenhauer's influence on Wittgenstein, Wagner, and a number of extraordinary creative writers.

Taylor, Richard. *The Will to Live: Selected Writings of Arthur Schopenhauer.* Garden City, N.Y.: Anchor Books, Doubleday 1962. A well-ordered and dramatic presentation of passages from Schopenhauer, drawing from his major works, and clarified by an introduction that illuminates Schopenhauer's intention and the direction of his creative imagination.

AUGUSTE COMTE

Born: 1798, Montpellier, France
Died: 1857, Paris, France
Major Works: *The Positive Philosophy* (*Cours de philosophie positive*, 6 vols.) (1830–42), *The System of Positive Polity* (*Système de politique positive*, 4 vols.) (1851–54), *The Catechism of Positive Religion* (*Catéchisme positiviste*) (1852)

Major Ideas

All human thinking, both for individual persons and for historical cultures, follows the law of the three stages: first seeking explanation in animistic purposes (the theological stage), then in abstract entities (the metaphysical stage), and finally in lawful observable correlations among variables (the positive stage).

There is a definite order among the positive sciences, in which the lower, simpler, and more general are presupposed by the higher, more complex, and more particular; this ordering provides both for the unity of the sciences, as successive branches from a common stem, and also for the recognition of historically emergent distinctive methods within different empirical subject matters.

The crowning science, the most complex and consequently the last to emerge as an empirical domain of invariant lawfulness, is sociology.

Sociology and positive philosophy finally will ground an urgently needed reorganization of politics, ethics, and religion.

Religious ritual, when brought into harmony with scientific intellect, is vital for the cultivation of feeling, thus providing motivation for the transformation and nurture of healthy society.

Auguste Comte has the distinction of founding both a new school of philosophy, positivism, and a new science, sociology. The two are intimately entwined, since Comte's positivist understanding of the sciences led him to anticipate a science of society, and, reciprocally, since Comte's sociology was to be thoroughly positivist in method and content. In addition, Comte believed from his youth that the progressive dynamic of history required deep reform in ethics, politics, and religion to restore lost unities of thought and feeling. This led him beyond philosophy and science, to the founding of a new positivist religion, the religion of humanity.

Comte, ungainly and physically unattractive from childhood, showed immense intellectual powers at an early age. At only fourteen, he had rethought his religion and politics and had dismayed his ardently Catholic and royalist family by announcing his atheist and republican conclusions. At fifteen, he had achieved the highest score for all applicants on the entrance examinations for L'École Polytechnique, the famed school of advanced science in Paris, but because of his youth he was denied admission until a year later. Eventually departing his native Montpellier for Paris in 1814, he happily divided his time between intense study (of such great scientists as Carnot, Lagrange, and Laplace) and rebelliousness. After only two years, Comte was sent home when a student demonstration, in which he took a leading role, resulted in the closing of the school for radicalism and later in its royalist reorganization.

Against his family's wishes, Comte soon returned to Paris to study privately and to support himself (meagerly) by tutoring in mathematics. During this time he read widely, taking a great interest in Condorcet's writings on human progress, Hume's skeptical epistemology, and Adam Smith's political economics, among many other authors. After a year of this, Comte accepted the position of secretary to the visionary social thinker, Henri, Comte de Saint-Simon. Saint-Simon, forty years his elder, had already stated the law of the three stages (see below) and was full of ideas on the restructuring and reform of society. After seven years, Comte, at first an admiring disciple, broke away with much acrimony.

In the next year, 1825, Comte married, despite extremely limited financial resources gained from tutoring. The marriage was stormy and ended in 1842, but during this period Comte gave the great course of private lectures, begun in 1826, that resulted in his six-volume *Cours de philosophie positive*. The complex course of seventy-two "*séances,*" fully outlined from the start, was interrupted after only the third lecture, when Comte suffered a nervous breakdown requiring institutionalization and slow, painful recovery (during which he attempted suicide by throwing himself in the Seine), but in 1828 the thread was taken up, and in the years 1830–42 the volumes appeared exactly as initially outlined.

The final period of Comte's life, following his divorce and the appearance of the *Cours*, was devoted to fulfilling his early commitment to the reform of society and religion, based on the intellectual foundations he believed his *Cours* provided. Despite growing fame, Comte never found a regular academic position and depended in large part on charitable subscriptions raised by admirers (importantly including John Stuart Mill) in England as well as France. In 1845, he met the beautiful, gentle, and educated Madame Clothilde de Vaux and fell in love—so deeply that, after her untimely death in the next year, he gave homage to her with a ritualized trip each Wednesday to her grave, invoked her virtues aloud three times a day, and incorporated elements of feminine mysticism in his religion of humanity. The major books of this period were his *Système de politique positive* and his *Catéchisme positiviste*. He died of cancer in 1857, still at work on another attempt at reconciling religion and science, *La synthèse subjective*, of which only the first volume (1856) was completed.

Comte's Theoretical Analysis

The key to understanding Comte's ideas is the law of the three stages, first enunciated by Saint-Simon but developed by Comte into a theory of historical progress and a framework for interpreting all human thought.

At the start, we think anthropomorphically, giving explanations in terms of qualities like our own. Just as the child kicks the toy that has tripped him and calls it naughty, so in early human history the seers and prophets invoked nymphs, demons, and divinities to explain their world. With the logical tendency for unification at work in all theory, the trend even in primitive theological thinking was toward monotheism; but the whole enterprise of thinking in such categories shows immaturity.

In youth, we put away the animist trappings of childhood, thinking instead in terms of "forces" and other impersonal, behind-the-scenes entities of abstract metaphysics. So, likewise, the best of ancient thinkers rose from the first (theological) to the second (metaphysical) stage of understanding. This was an advance, especially as abstract concepts became unified into ever more powerful systems. But it still allowed the obscurity and ultimate futility of unperceivable entities to enter thinking.

The fully mature stage of thought finally rose only when scientists, led by the example of Newton's rejection of "hypotheses" to account for the mathematical regularities of gravitation, resolved to think solely in terms of the lawful relations between observables. This rejection of any appeal to what cannot be positively perceived marks the attainment of the positive—and highest—stage of human thought, whether in an individual, in a society, or in a subportion of society such as the elite community of scientists, philosophers, and other thinkers who take the sciences with sufficient seriousness.

Comte goes into much detail, in his six-volume work, to examine the sciences in their logical relations to one another. Shorn of this detail, his position is that the most general and inclusive sciences were required first, as the logically necessary preparation for the more particular ones. Mathematics, as the abstract or fundamental study of the forms of existence common to all things, is presupposed for the successful study of physics, which can be divided into celestial physics (astronomy) or terrestrial physics, either general (physics proper) or special according to the empirical elements (chemistry). Astronomy made important strides before terrestrial physics; but chemistry had to wait for its germination until general terrestrial physics had first come into flower. Biology, in like manner, depended upon chemistry for its emergence as a lawful science. Biology is less comprehensive than chemistry, since the domain of living forms is less extensive than the domain of all forms exhibiting chemical laws. Correspondingly, biology, though logically depending upon chemistry, has positive laws of its own that are not merely the laws of chemistry; and this is just as should be expected, since living matter is observed to behave very differently from nonliving chemical entities. Thus Comte rejected methodological reductionism of higher sciences to the lower, despite the fact that the former presuppose the latter.

In the same way, human society is far less general than the biological realm as a whole, though society clearly presupposes and depends on the laws of life. This means that the laws of human society, as they are uncovered, will inevitably have their own quasi-autonomy despite the complete grounding of sociology in biology, biology in chemistry, chemistry in physics, and physics in mathematics. This methodological uniqueness, for Comte, does not in the slightest soften the invariant character of social laws. Early in his *Cours*, indeed, "social physics" is what he terms the positive scientific study of society; only after several volumes does he introduce his newly invented word, "sociology," for what he believed would be the "final science."

On Comte's classification of the sciences, it stands to reason that the rise of sociology had to await the establishment of all the prior disciplines. This centuries-long delay left the field of human society vulnerable to domination by the immature prescientific modes of thinking, theology and metaphysics, as long as the benefits of the positive mode in this area were unavailable. Thus, on Comte's analysis, adding the Law of the Three Stages to the classification of the sciences reveals that the moment is ripe—and inevitable—for radical social reform.

Comte's Social Synthesis

Comte had announced, at least as early as 1822, during his association with the social reformer

Saint-Simon, that he wanted to point the way to a better political, ethical, and religious order. In Comte's mind, the great effort of developing the positive philosophy was largely a means for the sake of providing a responsible scientific foundation—something far beyond even Saint-Simon's aspiration—for a positive polity and a positive religion. Doubtless Comte would have been disappointed in posterity for tending to take his efforts at social synthesis as less memorable than the preceding philosophic analysis.

The positive polity developed in his *Système de politique positive* was an elitist vision of a rational, harmonious society, with all members living generously for one another, the whole inspired and led by altruistic scientist-priests. Some have speculated that Comte's unconscious model was an idealized L'École Polytechnique, his days of youth fondly remembered through rose-tinted glasses. On the other hand, if one grants Comte the inevitability of the law of the three stages, then there is nothing fantastic about anticipating a much more rational society than anything hitherto encountered among humans. And if one is convinced, with Comte, that a fully determinate science of society is immanent, then all aspects of society, including ethics and religion, can in principle be engineered.

Comte took the domain of ethics and religion with utmost seriousness. Some commentators have criticized the absence of any science of psychology in his classification, leaving sociology as the "final" science; but it is not fair to charge that Comte ignored the individual person. Sociology was to be the overall name for what Comte called the "study of man," and this study was to include careful attention to the individual person as well as to people in relations. In his *Catéchisme positiviste*, Comte characterized the "individual" aspect of sociology as the study of *moral laws*. This emphasis on morality again illustrates what was on Comte's mind as he laid out the logical structure of the sciences: The whole edifice of science, rising from generality to particularity, finally focuses on human society—and within society, because of its still greater particularity, on morality.

Morality, however, needs to be motivated. The

fundamental motivator in human life is religion. In reformed positivist society, religion, though essential, will not remain at the merely theological level of thinking; that is, it will dispense with the gods or with God. Instead, it will find inspiration in humanity, as the Great Being. Comte developed a positivist calendar (with thirteen months of twenty-eight days, each dedicated to a hero of humanity, for example, Archimedes, Gutenberg, Shakespeare, or Descartes) for use in veneration of human achievements of many sorts. A positivist priesthood would preach rational truth and nurture social feeling and cooperation within society. The split between faith and reason, authority and autonomy, ritual and science, would at long last be fully overcome.

Comte believed that this religion of humanity, an intrinsically universal religion, would be especially attractive to those who, within the prepositivist stages of history, have been systematically excluded. These are the various downtrodden proletariats of the world, and, of course, women everywhere. Comte concludes his *Catéchisme positiviste* with the following reflection on his hopes for universal positivist religion: "Though it be yet very greatly hampered, especially at its centre, by the prejudices and passions which, under different forms, reject all wholesome discipline, its efficacy will soon be felt by women and proletaries. . . . But its best recommendation must come from the exclusive competence of the Positive priesthood to rally everywhere the honest and the thoughtful, nobly accepting the whole inheritance of mankind."

There is irony in the fact that the principal actual inheritors of Comte's mantle, the logical positivists, adopted instead a disdainful attitude toward the cognitive value of ethics and religion, focusing rather on Comte's rejection of nonempirical modes of thought and on his fascination with the sciences. We do well, however, to recall that Comte himself saw no necessary conflict between the sciences and religion rightly understood.

FREDERICK FERRÉ

Further Reading

Lévy-Bruhl, Lucien. *The Philosophy of Auguste Comte*. Translated by Kathleen de Beaumont-Klein. New York, G.P. Putnam's Sons, 1903. [English translation of *La Philosophie d'Auguste Comte*, Paris, 1900.] Lévy-Bruhl provides a thoughtful and authoritative analysis of Comte's philosophical ideas.

Mill, John Stuart. *Auguste Comte and Positivism*. London, Kegan Paul, 1865. Mill, as one of Comte's supporters through thick and thin, and as one of the leading British philosophers of the nineteenth century, provides an interesting and well-written treatment of Comte's ideas despite various disappointments with Comte's personality.

Simon, W. M. *European Positivism in the Nineteenth Century: An Essay in Intellectual History*. Ithaca, N.Y.: Cornell University Press, 1963. Simon traces influences of Comte's thought. No attempt is made to follow parallel influences in South America.

Whittaker, Thomas. *Comte and Mill*. London, A. Constable & Co., 1908. Whittaker offers perspective on the mutual relations of positivism and utilitarianism, stressing the utilitarian aspects of Comte.

JOHN HENRY CARDINAL NEWMAN

Born: 1801, London, England
Died: 1890, Edgbaston, England
Major Works: *Essay on the Development of Christian Doctrine* (1845), *Idea of a University* (1858), *Apologia pro vita sua* (1864), *Essay in Aid of a Grammar of Assent* (1870)

Major Ideas

All things human develop and change in time, including the Church institution and doctrine.
It is a collective responsibility to see that ideas develop rightly and in a continuous fashion.
A university is a place of teaching universal knowledge to produce intelligent members of society by fostering cultivation of the mind and formation of the intellect.
Religion and knowledge are not opposed to each other, not because they are irrelevant to one another but because they are indivisibly connected—religion forms part of the subject matter of knowledge.
Certitude is "an assent, deliberate, unconditional and conscious, to a proposition as true"—which does not mean we cannot "allow in the abstract that it is possible that we are wrong" but there can be no "degree" of certitude.

It is difficult for us in more irreligious times to fully comprehend the impact that the thought and consistent action of a man like John Henry Newman, a bookish, saintly pastor, had on the England of his times, government and university as well as church and society as a whole. The establishment of the Church of England was more a political if not to say a personal move of the ruler than a religious movement, yet once it was undertaken it was bolstered by the thought of the Protestant reformers who were being used so effectively to establish new state religions on the Continent. In time, segments of the new church were deeply influenced by them. The Anglican communion as a whole, though, sought to keep much of the traditional Catholic thought and practice, seeking a *via media* between the reformers and the erring Roman Catholic church.

John Henry Newman, who was born in London in 1801, was brought up in a strongly religious family and was himself a devout man. His keen questing mind therefore did not leave religion out of its investigations. In fact, religion always remained central even while he gave his powerful intellect freedom to question deeply and freely. He was in the truest sense a theologian; his faith was seeking understanding: *fides quaerens intellectum*.

At fifteen this brilliant young man went up to Trinity College, Oxford, and six years later, in 1822, he was elected a fellow at Oriel. Religiously he gradually moved from a fundamentalistic evangelical outlook to a more traditional Catholic one. It was through no ambition on his part but rather due to his keen intellect, deep devotion, and exceptionally well-developed gift for expression that he emerged as the leader of the Oxford Movement, which sought to reaffirm the catholicity of the Church of England. His intellectual sincerity pushed him on relentlessly until, almost against his will, he left the movement and entered the Roman Catholic church.

Essay on the Development of Christian Doctrine

Newman's *Sermons and Essays* as well as the tracts he wrote are important in tracing the development of his thought—a development that led to the publication in 1845, a month after his reception into the Catholic Church, of his *Essay on the Development of Christian Doctrine*. He examined deeply the pretensions of the Anglican church and found them wanting. It became clear to him that there had to be a development of doctrine just as there is development in every other sphere of human life. Newman kept the full Christian tradition but he viewed it historically, as a movement whose ideas and practices were in continual development. Within the Roman Catholic church, that development had been constant and not discontinuous so that, with due development the Church of Rome still taught what it had taught in apostolic times.

The Development of Christian Doctrine was written nearly fifteen years before Darwin published *The Origin of Species* in 1859. Darwin's theory of development was the foundation from which Newman was able to build a defense of Christian truth to confront the scientific skepticism that was spreading widely among the educated in the late nineteenth century. In writing *The Development of Christian Doctrine*, Newman concluded that although there had been some corruptions in practice and exaggerations of devotion, the changes in doctrine in the Roman Catholic church had been the result of collective meditation on the original revelation of God in Christ and that the Catholic church in all ages had been guided into all truth by the Spirit as Christ had promised.

As a man of scrupulous intellectual integrity, Newman followed his reason and at very great cost joined the Roman Church. In doing this he deeply pained loved ones, turned some dear friends into enemies, and lost his livelihood and home. Yet such was the stature of the man and the power of his clear rational argument that many in high position and low, in government and university and church, followed him out of the establishment and into the "foreign" church, even while their counterparts strongly condemned him, calumniated and derided him, questioning his motives and integrity.

Apologia pro vita sua

Newman's *Apologia pro vita sua*, which he published a month after his conversion to the Roman Church, must be seen in the light of his earlier work on the development of doctrine if it is to be rightly assessed. It is not an autobiography. Rather, in it he sought "to give the true key to my whole life"; he sought to "draw out the history" of his mind. It was the theory of development applied to one person's ideas as he had already applied it to the collective mind of the Church. In the process, he was able to defend the Church as well as himself.

In a country where the monarch had declared himself the head of the Church, there was no room in the universities that were so completely under the control of the state for a thinker who so effectively challenged the establishment. Newman had to resign the university position that he had held for twenty-three years and depart from the scene that had been his home for even longer. Nine years after his conversion and exile, the religious tests were removed at Oxford and Catholics could begin to attend the university.

In the hope of providing a milieu in which true academic freedom could find its home, Newman accepted in 1851 an invitation to establish a new university in Dublin. He set forth his guiding principles in his very significant *Idea of a University*, actually a series of lectures (with some addenda) that he had given at Dublin in preparation for the opening of the university. Only a man who had a profound grasp of the fact that ultimately all truth is one and that authentic scientific truth can never contradict the truths of faith could have been so boldly committed to academic freedom and the search for truth at every level of the mind in every level of being. At the same time, he stoutly maintained that no university education could claim to be universal if it did not include the study of theology, a true science and wisdom of what is ultimate in the life of the human person. But Ireland in the middle of the nineteenth century was too poor and too completely subject to its English overlords to be able to support the courageous venture of this zealous priest. After eight years of valiant struggle, Newman had to admit defeat. He resigned his post as rector of the university and returned to England to give his full attention to being superior of the Oratory of Saint Philip, which he had established near Birmingham in 1848.

The Grammar of Assent

The aging man might have been defeated in this undertaking, but he was not dispirited and continued to wield his powerful pen. John Henry Newman was not a theologian in the usual academic sense. Rather, he dealt with modern problems of faith in a way that was based in historical study and human experience. He wrote not just for the academic or professional thinker but for "the man of ordinary intelligence." He respected the intelligence of the common person, one who might not have had much opportunity for university learning but knew how to think for himself. More extraordinary for his time, he respected the intelligence of women. He told a friend that he had written the last hundred pages of his *Essay in Aid of a Grammar of Assent*, which is a powerful, clear, and fundamental epistemology, published in 1870, "especially for such ladies as are bullied by infidels and do not know how to answer them—a misfortune which I fear is not rare in this day." This section of the *Grammar* draws out from history and from the universal experience of moral obligation the accumulating probabilities that Christianity is a true revelation from the Divine Creator of all things, that final acceptance of it is an act of will and a duty, and that faith in it, since it comes from God, is certain—but it cannot be freely accepted until it is seen to be reasonable and worthy of credence. He added that this is the way both factory girls and philosophers are converted. The seventy-year-old man had lost none of his clarity and precision of thought. His writings and espe-

cially his sermons were less theory than a diagnosis of experience. This is why Newman is still sought as a guide for seekers after truth.

Newman was the victim of a great deal of jealousy and suspicion as his humble, tireless service brought him into ever greater prominence in his adopted Church. Nonetheless, he retained his independence of thought and held some positions not popular among the more powerful in the Church at that time but which in the end would indeed prevail. His article "On Consulting the Faithful in Matters of Doctrine" (*Rambler,* 1859) was received with indignation by most of the hierarchy, yet a hundred years later the greater part of its teaching was incorporated into the decrees of the Second Vatican Council. At the time the pope was in the process of losing his temporal power, Newman held that it was not essential for the pope's spiritual authority for him to exercise temporal authority; rather Newman thought the papacy would be better off without the latter. In spite of all this, Newman's true greatness was finally acknowledged in 1879 when the venerable father was elevated to the cardinalate by Pope Leo XIII. John Henry Cardinal Newman died eleven years later at the age of eighty-nine, a much-loved and revered father, still guiding the destinies of the oratory he so loved.

M. Basil Pennington, O.C.S.O.

Further Reading

Martin, Brian. *John Henry Newman. His Life and Work*. New York: Oxford University Press, 1982. A concise, up-to-date biography that places all the works of Newman in their full context and traces the evolution of his thought. This critical assessment of the gentle but controversial saint by a fellow Oxford don draws much human color from Newman's *Letters and Diaries*.

O'Connell, Marvin R. *The Oxford Conspirators. A History of the Oxford Movement. 1833–1845*. New York: Macmillan, 1969. A comprehensive study written from a Roman Catholic perspective, of the movement that so profoundly influenced Newman's life and thinking even while it was profoundly influenced by him.

RALPH WALDO EMERSON

Born: 1803, Boston, Massachusetts
Died: 1882, Concord, Massachusetts
Major Works: "Nature" (1836), "The American Scholar" (1837), "The Divinity School Address" (1838), *Essays: First Series* (1841), *Essays: Second Series* (1844), *Representative Men* (1850), *The Conduct of Life* (1860)

Major Ideas

The natural world is coursed through with the immanent flow of a deity—a "world-soul"—both in and above the world.

The divine spirit can be approached in the immediacies of experiential existence.

The principle of immanence reveals that there is a democracy of spiritual possibility, that personal experience and vision have precedence over abstract intellect and tradition, and that each generation needs to find revelation anew.

What prevents the full realization of the human soul is only the clouded and habitual "sight" blocking imagination and insight of the gifts of spiritual fullness presented by the circumambient world.

The tactic and horizon of human knowledge and possibility therefore reside in a complex form of self-reliance that can lead to a union of the human soul with the "Over-Soul."

Ralph Waldo Emerson's family lineage in many respects followed out the broad history of New England. His Puritan and Congregationalist forebears, over the course of several generations, had gradually departed the full rigors of earlier Puritan piety, embraced the age of enlightenment, and entered the realm of liberal and rational religion espoused by William Ellery Channing. By the time of young Waldo's coming of age, the Harvard that had trained the old, great Calvinist Jonathan Edwards would now instruct this Emerson in the outlook of Channing's "Unitarian Christianity," a spiritual curriculum he resisted virtually from the outset. In later years, he would refer to the "pale negations" of Unitarianism he believed should be displaced by a new vision of existence.

To the extent that he was tutored at others' hands, Emerson was held in thrall by the romantic imagination that flourished in the Anglo-European world in the first three decades of the nineteenth century—the liberating forms of experience and expression he found in Samuel Taylor Coleridge, Thomas Carlyle, the Schlegels, Schelling, and Goethe, among others. Their works, for him, gave rise to radically new understandings of God, nature,

culture, and history, plunged deeper into the mysterious forces of life, emphasized the affective and intuitive course and conduct of life, and discerned bold, altered horizons of human possibility. Perhaps because sharing similarly Calvinist backgrounds, Carlyle particularly engaged Emerson's attention, and they became lifelong correspondents. For his own part, Ralph Waldo Emerson not only came to the fore as the most prominent champion of romanticism in America but also increased its power and moment in the burgeoning new nation by lending the movement a quite distinctively New World energy and implication.

Emerson's intellectual career was played out in his role as a "public philosopher." His thought was dedicated to exploring what he took to be the central issues of meaning facing the cultural imagination of his day and to proselytizing for a surer, better understanding of life for his contemporaries. Although his works were studied and artful, they were not prepared within or for—and indeed were aimed quite beyond—any narrowly academic or "intellectual" framework: He was always vigilant with respect to the broadly open forums in which he would have his hearing. If some of his auditors felt he rotated in the vapors and whirled in mystifications, Emerson nonetheless attempted to deliver his ideas to them in ways consonant with their lives and with maximum rhetorical effect. His most consistent *metier* was the essay-length work which, in his hands, bore resemblance to the structure and order of the classical oration. Whether utilized in sermons as he entered pulpits in his early career, then in lectures as he toured from one podium to the next, or finally in more formal essays as he gradually retired to his study, his works, designed to be heard or read in one sitting, practiced a psychology of exhortation. And, as with the classical oration, when rhetoric was still a fully substantive and not simply a technical art, Emerson's "addresses" had as the crucial subject the well-being of the community, although this was a matter of spiritual vision for him more than it was an affair of statesmanship as for, say, old Cicero in *his* forum.

In the early 1830s, after resigning his ministry because he could not assent to the administration of the sacraments as "a divinely appointed, sacred ordinance of religion" and after some travel in England where he met a series of romantic notables, he took up the lecture tour in America. With the publication of "Nature" in 1836, he fairly burst upon the scene, and the controversy about him continued in ensuing years as he flew in the face of the reigning orthodoxies. Dismissed as a mystic, labeled a "transcendentalist" (a term Emerson resisted), his views seemed too fluid for most of his contemporaries to categorize precisely. Whatever he was, some found him clearly unnerving, espousing, as it seemed to them, what religious worthy Andrews Norton called "the latest form of infidelity." Many others, however, found in his thought a vital new endowment of spiritual truth, a vision boldly commensurate with the character and aspirations of young America, a sense and conduct of life appropriate and abundant for democratic society. He achieved his ultimate place in the American pantheon with a set of ideas remarkable for their lifelong consistency and with the public forms of delivery that carried them far and wide.

The World of Spirit and the Spirit of the World

When Emerson published his "Nature" essay in 1836, it was quickly dismissed by many as so much pantheistic ranting, but in it he had established, at least in broadest outline, the intellectual agenda and the coordinates of ideas and themes that would characterize virtually all of his subsequent work, including the poetry he wrote sporadically over the years. As a religious and cultural manifesto for the age, the essay calls immediately for the generation to discard the sterilities of tradition, the "dry bones" of the past, and to discern its "own original relation to the universe." A new, intuitive response to experience is required, he insists, to give to the age a "religion of revelation to us," a vision of spiritual possibility precluded if his contemporaries were content only to live out the beliefs inherited from their forebears. "Nature" does more than simply throw down Emerson's revisionary gauntlet, however; it traces out the nature and connection of the world and the self, both radically redefined, and adumbrates the prospects for the human spirit on the bases of these altered philosophical foundations.

In broadest assumptions and proposals, this essay, along with many others that followed, depicts the universe in terms that, in several senses, belong to a species of idealism: The universe is made up of both a realm of pure and unified spirit and another, apparently fragmented realm of natural and material forms and forces. But neither of these spheres, for Emerson, is static: Both are fluid, mutable, and mysterious, and each exists in "corresponding motion" with the other. This essential reciprocity of life, a kind of spiritual organicism, occurs because the realm of pure spirit—the "Over-Soul," "the universal Soul," the "Supreme Mind," depending on which momentary designation Emerson's style prefers—not only exists above but flows continuously through the world of nature, thus making its discrete essences ("space, the air, the river, the leaf" and even those mortal arts that appropriately mix nature with human will) resonate with a spirit unifying the phenomenal world beyond the level of its material appearances. Vistas, visages, and scenes of astonishing beauty and sublimity, under a romantic aesthetic, clearly portend the allusive harmonies of such a Supreme Mind or Soul, but even all of the blemished, sordid, and disagreeable aspects of nature—"swine, spiders, snakes, pests, mad-houses, prisons, enemies"—will eventually vanish with the full "influx of spirit" that creates a "correspondent revolution" even in such brute examples of material life. In this way, Emerson declares, "is the phenomenon perfect."

Thus broadly understood, then, the environing world, indwelt with universal soul, brims over with spiritual possibilities, there to be seized. Maintaining the transcendence of the Over-Soul, Emerson evades the charges of pantheism against him. But envisioning the overflow of the transcendent realm into and throughout the natural world, he proposes a form of immanence that lends credibility to his call for "a religion of revelation." In the degree that people conform their beliefs to and understand their experiences only within the history and tradition of earlier revelation as codified in Scripture and doctrine, then in that same measure will they fail to realize the spiritual and religious qualities of their own immediate experience. They will simply succumb in fragmented lives to the forces and factors of material history. To the extent that they live and move and have their being in correspondence with a world replete with currents of divinity, then to that same extent will they recognize their own participation in and with a community of life unified by the Supreme Mind and moving toward a horizon of spiritual perfection. Emerson knew that such a recognition by his contemporaries, steeped in the stale habits of tradition and social conformity, could stem only from a new imagination of the world of their experience, a fresh and "original relation to the universe."

The Human Condition and Prospect

Emerson's views of the nature of the human being and its situation is also proposed in "Nature," though again it is continuously elaborated in other theoretical and exhortative essays like "Self-Reliance" and "The American Scholar" and in the portraits he presents in *Representative Men* (1850). In its rudiments, the "self" for Emerson is bifurcated in a fashion similar to his conceptions of the universe in which the human self must be understood. One element of the self, which Emerson calls "the Not-Me," is part and parcel of nature—that is, it belongs to and participates in the material or phenomenal world in all its brute and intractable character. This aspect of the self refers to embodiment, to sensate and temporal existence, to all the stuff that flesh is heir to. The other element of the self, "the Me" in Emerson's scheme, is the soul, which belongs to the sphere of spirit, for it is nothing other than the stuff of divine immanence inhering in the world, in this case the human body. The human soul exists in full continuity with the universal "Over-Soul," possesses its purity, borrows of its unity and harmony. Therefore, the soul is the *essential* "self," in Emerson's theory, because it belongs to and in its way partakes of the eternal, the ethereal, the ideal realm of spirit, the universal soul, the Over-Soul, the Supreme Mind—associations that must be kept steadily in view in order to avert some typical and long-standing misconstruals of Emerson's thought and intention.

If the essentially human self belongs to the eternal, it does not automatically enjoy full union with the Over-Soul: The spiritual self is fragmented away from its spiritual home by virtue of its encasement in the world of material forms and forces. However much the natural world is suffused with currents of deity that hold out promises of a reunion of the essential self with its sources in spirit, the embodied self inherits perceptions of the world that blunt its ability to see and seize nature's spiritual resonances. What is required, in short, is an altered relationship between the "Me," the essential self, and the "Not-Me," the environing world. For Emerson, then, the struggle for the self in seeking its ideal measure is a struggle to see the world anew, to recast the imagination, to intuit the spiritual dimensions in natural forms that sheer, strict rationality cannot perceive. Nothing else, or less, can restore to human sight the revelatory character of the world, and, without such new vision, the effort of the human soul to reunite with the Over-Soul cannot be accomplished.

As Emerson presents the matter in "Nature," the human soul can spiral upward toward the fully spiritual realm through the natural forms and uses presented to it in its immediate experience. The images and metaphors of "sight" and "vision" in this process are not merely tropes but, in fact, reflect Emerson's sense of the means for being authentically in the world. Seen only at the brute level, the forms of nature are dealt with as "Commodity"—the exigent uses to which the world is put as it supplies raw material—and all people are *naturally* involved. But, for those who have eyes to see, nature also presents to humankind the higher forms and uses of "Beauty": Envisioned at this level, nature gives grounds for no merely formal aesthetic but proposes to the emotions the rightnesses of sublime moral perfection that unify and dignify all aspects of a world so created. At a higher level still, again for those tutored in the new vision, nature presents to the beholder its portion of "Spirit," the world perceived as permeated by divinity, made perfect by the presence in it of the Supreme Mind. By mounting upward through "the spires of form"—Commodity, Beauty, Spirit—thus bodied forth, thus revealed in nature, the self, having now "come to look at the world with new eyes," realizes itself as spirit, gains the intuition of its own divinity, participates again in the universal current of spirit. Only in this way, Emerson claims, can a human self achieve its fullest spiritual prospect, "a dominion such as now is beyond his dream of God—he shall enter without more wonder than the blind man feels who is gradually restored to sight."

Democracy and Self-Reliance

In constructing the condition of the essential self in relation to the spiritual immensities, Emerson might at first blush seem to repudiate the hard facticity of the world and to recommend a kind of elitist spiritual possibility, but he knew full well that the realization of the ideal prospects of the human soul depended on the self's saturation in the experience of life around it and that such a realization was as open to the common man as to any erudite philosopher or imperial emperor. In "Nature," he suggests such a "spiritual democracy" as he calls his fellows toward their own greatness of soul: "All that Adam had, all that Caesar could, you have and can do. Adam called his house, heaven and earth; Caesar called his house, Rome; you perhaps call yours, a cobbler's trade; a hundred acres of ploughed land; or a scholar's garret. Yet line for line and point for point your dominion is as great as theirs, though without fine names. Build [see] therefore your own world." Of course, this egalitarian outlook with respect to *who* could achieve a corresponding spirit is coterminous in Emerson's thought with his idea of *what* in the phenomenal world might be a reservoir of spirit. With this notion, Emerson posits what might be termed a "democracy of experience"—that is, a sense that the meanest or most mundane aspects of life could be equal in spiritual potential with the grandest vista and the most exotic life. It is one thing to recognize the stirrings of spirit in Greek art, he declares in "The American Scholar," but "I embrace the common, I explore and sit at the feet of the familiar, the low. Give me insight into today, . . . the meal in the firkin; the milk in the pan; the ballad in the street; the news of the boat; the glance of the eye; the form and the gait of the body; show me the ultimate reason of these matters; show me the sublime presence of the highest spiritual cause lurking, as always it does lurk, in these suburbs and extremeties of nature." If everyone has access to spirit, everything could be seen as equally plenteous: The world of "Commodity" and the world of "Spirit" are, in a word, interpenetrating, as "one design unites and animates the farthest pinnacle and the lowest trench."

To be gathered in and to live by the "doctrine of soul," as Emerson refers to it in "The Divinity School Address," required an extraordinary effort of individual will, for it means seeking one's own way, plumbing one's own experience, and refusing the comforts of repose in conformist attitudes. If the only one who ever fully followed out the ultimate reaches of the soul was Jesus, according to Emerson, each and every person who could be "Man Thinking"—the radical image of the one who would learn resolutely from nature and experience as well as from books, who set his or her own inveterate conduct of life—could also meet the spiritual horizon. For many over the generations, this has seemed an endorsement on Emerson's part of a kind of triumphant individualism, an enthusiasm for unfettered personal freedom that might be heedless of the common life. Nothing could be farther from the truth. When Emerson argues the case for the self's personal course, it is clear that he sees this as a matter of philosophical vision as well as social action. Indeed, it must be remembered that in Emerson's version of "Self-Reliance" the *essential* self is the soul, the spirit, the mind, which is part of the Over-Soul, the Universal Spirit, the Supreme Mind. To be reliant on the "self," then, is to rely on the "soul," to intuit the dependency of the self on the divine source and springs of the self, to consent to that spirit which flows through all of creation, to follow a conduct of life that makes one part and parcel of the whole of spiritual life.

As a philosopher for his time and for his place, Emerson met young America in full stride. Forging its own identity, the emerging nation received him as its apostle to a culture ambitious to break with tradition, to take the measure of its own breath and abundance, to seize its full possibilities, and to locate the terms of its own authenticity. For the expectant country, he himself in many respects became the "New Teacher" he had called for in "The Divinity School Address," crafting a new metaphysics from the near-at-hand, creating a philosophy grounded in and appropriate for democratic vistas, standing as the exemplar of "Man Thinking" in an American mode. In the twentieth century, he retains a central place in the American cultural canon even if now, as it must frequently have seemed then, his estimate of humanity appears too high, his treatment of evil stunted, any sense of complexity washed over and out by his tidal conceptions. He was like no other, this shy man with his bold vision, an American original.

ROWLAND A. SHERRILL

Further Reading

Allen, Gay Wilson. *Waldo Emerson: A Biography.* New York: Viking Press, 1981. Allen's magisterial critical biography treats Emerson's thought in the contexts both of the age and of the personal history with which Emerson's ideas were so fully intertwined.

Cady, Edwin H., and Louis J. Budd, eds. *On Emerson.* Durham: Duke University Press, 1988. The essays in this collection, gleaned from the pages of the scholarly journal *American Literature*, inquire into a number of important facets of Emerson's life and thought.

Howe, Irving. *The American Newness: Culture and Politics in the Age of Emerson.* Cambridge: Harvard University Press, 1986. Following from Howe's Massey lectures, this volume explores the way Emerson's thought in part shaped the tenor of

his time in America and is especially astute about the political dimensions of his work.

Robinson, David. *Apostle of Culture: Emerson as Preacher and Lecturer.* Philadelphia: University of Pennsylvania Press, 1982. Tracing out the evolution of Emerson's thought over the entire course of his intellectual career, Robinson studies the shifting modes and emphases involved in Emerson's movement from pulpit, to podium, to study.

Whicher, Stephen. *Freedom and Fate: An Inner Life of Ralph Waldo Emerson.* Philadelphia: University of Pennsylvania Press, 1953. This book remains the best account of those elements of Emerson's sense of life that constricted the soaring optimism many have thought definitive for him.

JOHN STUART MILL

Born: 1806, London, England
Died: 1873, Avignon, France
Major Works: *A System of Logic* (1843), *Principles of Political Economy* (1848), "On Liberty" (1859), "Utilitarianism" (1863), *An Examination of Sir William Hamilton's Philosophy* (1865), *Three Essays on Religion* (1874)

Major Ideas

All knowledge is derived originally from sense perception.

Matter, or the external world, can be defined as the permanent possibility of sensation.

Mind is reducible to successive conscious states.

True inference is always accomplished through induction rather than deduction.

Pleasure alone is intrinsically good and pain alone is intrinsically bad.

Pleasures differ from each other qualitatively as well as quantitatively, a "higher" pleasure being intrinsically better than a "lower" pleasure.

The only justification society has in interfering with the liberty of action of any individual is self-protection.

Given the existence of evil, God cannot be both omnipotent and morally good; if he exists, he must be limited in power.

Although John Stuart Mill published substantial works in almost every area of philosophy, his main interests were in ethics and social thought. The reason for this is understandable. His father was James Mill, who was, along with Jeremy Bentham, a leading member of the Philosophical Radicals. This group of reformers was dedicated to the task of ridding society of its injustices and modeling it according to the utilitarian tenets advanced by Bentham in his influential work, *An Introduction to the Principles of Morals and Legislation* (1789). Brought up in surroundings of constant discussion and ferment concerning social issues, Mill soon found himself following in the footsteps of his father and Bentham.

Mill was educated at home. He began to study Greek at the age of three and Latin at eight. By fourteen, he had read widely in the ancient classics, history, economics, mathematics, and logic. He began publishing scholarly writing at sixteen.

Mill's remarkable education had a special purpose—to groom him for leadership in the reform movement of the Philosophical Radicals. In this goal it was eminently successful: Mill became the chief spokesman for liberal causes in nineteenth-century England. But it had an unfortu-

nate side effect: Intellectual force-feeding led him to a nervous breakdown at the age of twenty.

Mill never held an academic post. Instead he worked for thirty-five years in the offices of the East India Company. His position gave him considerable free time, and he wrote on a wide variety of topics, ranging from technical philosophy to current social problems. Much of his writing consisted of short pieces, but he also published several substantial books and influential essays. After his retirement, he spent much of his time in Avignon, in southern France, although he served from 1865 to 1868 as a member of Parliament.

Although Mill was educated to carry on the utilitarian tradition and although he clearly attempted to do so, a study of his writings reveals a gradual but widening gap between his thought and that of his teachers. In particular, Mill found himself unable to confine himself to the narrow and rigid tenets of Bentham's philosophy. Its stark intellectualism, he concluded, unduly ignored the emotional side of human nature, and its egoism offered no satisfactory account of our social feelings. In his development of the Benthamite position, Mill added a strong, and needed, humane dimension. But, in doing so, he often reached conclusions that seem inconsistent with his utilitarian assumptions.

A System of Logic

Although *A System of Logic* is concerned in part with logic, its scope is much broader, most of its voluminous contents being devoted to what Mill called "induction," or scientific method. The reason for this emphasis lay in Mill's empiricist theory of knowledge. If all of our knowledge has its origin in sense perception, we cannot expand on what we know through the method of deduction, which only makes explicit the knowledge we already possess. We need, therefore, a logic of discovery: This is induction.

An apparent exception to Mill's view is mathematics, which seems to be deductive yet expands our knowledge. Mill argues, however, that mathematics is an inductive science, its foundations lying in experience. When, for example, a geometer concludes that two straight lines *cannot* enclose a space, he means that he has never observed such a phenomenon and is unable to conceive of its occurrence. The necessity expressed in the word "cannot" is psychological rather than logical.

Induction rests on the principle of the uniformity of nature, or the view that causes operating in the past will continue to operate in the future. Since the ultimate aim of science is prediction, the notion of the uniformity of nature is fundamental to it. But this raises a question: How can we justify this axiom? It is certainly not self-evident; rather, Mill holds, we must found it on past experience. The axiom is, itself, an inductive generalization, based on our past experiences of uniformities in nature. But, according to some critics, this justification begs the question. All that our repeated experiences tell us is that nature has been uniform in the past, but what we need is to justify our belief that it will continue to be so in the future and, of this, past experience offers us no guarantee. Nevertheless, Mill made an important contribution to scientific method through his analysis of four methods of inductive reasoning. Now known as "Mill's methods," these are the methods of "agreement,

difference, residues, and concomitant variations." No full account of these methods can be given in a limited space. Suffice it to say that they are designed to aid the scientific investigator in his or her work by helping to locate, among the complex array of data, the precise cause producing the particular phenomenon he or she is attempting to explain.

An Examination of Sir William Hamilton's Philosophy

Written as a critique of the philosophy of the Scottish philosopher William Hamilton (1788–1856), the *Examination of Sir William Hamilton's Philosophy* would appear to be of little importance, as was its target. Nevertheless it is important, not because of its criticisms of Hamilton but because of its inclusion of Mill's own views on epistemology and metaphysics. The basis from which Mill argues is the epistemological thesis that everything we can know must be known through sense perception. Hence our knowledge must be limited to what our senses reveal—conscious experiences of sounds, colors, and so forth. Nevertheless, we believe in the existence of an external material world independent of our conscious states.

The belief in an external world is to be explained, Mill maintains, by the psychological association of ideas. Some of our perceptions repeatedly go together, forming a group—say, our ideas of color, brightness, warmth, and roundness. We associate this group of ideas together, calling it the sun. But that does not mean we are aware of an external, physical object; rather, all we know are the conscious experiences we group together and give a name. Mill uses this epistemological theory to draw an ontological conclusion. By the concept "matter" we mean the "permanent possibility of sensation." By defining matter in this way, Mill was able to avoid postulating the existence of an external world, which, if it actually existed, would in any case be unknowable.

We also believe that we have minds, Mill writes. But it is apparent that we cannot be directly aware of our minds as real entities. All that we can introspectively observe are our conscious states. As in the case of matter, mind must be defined as the permanent possibility of introspection. As Mill concludes: "We have no conception of Mind itself, as distinguished from its conscious manifestations. We neither know it nor can imagine it. . . ."

Such a theory of the mind has problems, which Mill recognizes. If the mind is only a series of conscious states, how to explain memory? Can a series of conscious states remember previous states or, if memory is to occur, must there not be a permanent entity different from the states themselves to perform this task? Mill confesses himself unable to account for memory: "I think, by far the wisest thing we can do, is to accept the inexplicable fact [of memory], without any theory of how it takes place. . . ."

"Utilitarianism"

Mill's "Utilitarianism" is the centerpiece of his philosophy. After beginning by reaffirming the hedonistic theory of his mentor, Jeremy Bentham, Mill soon wanders from the strict hedonist path. His first diversion turns on the evaluation of different kinds of pleasure. Bentham had maintained that qualitatively pleasures are all on a par and, therefore, in evaluating them we must rely on quantitative measures alone. Mill could not accept this narrow doctrine. He believed that some *kinds* of pleasure, whatever their quantity, are intrinsically superior to others: "It is better to be a human being dissatisfied than a pig satisfied; better to be Socrates dissatisfied than a fool satisfied." Whether the distinction is consistent with hedonism or not, most people would surely agree with Mill on this point.

Mill's second major divergence is his rejection of Bentham's egoism. Although he was a psychological hedonist (in that he believed each person seeks his or her own pleasure), Mill denied that this theory of human motivation implies egoism. Even though we are by nature pleasure-seekers, we can be trained through proper development of our feelings to find pleasure in the pleasure of others.

"On Liberty"

Mill's essay "On Liberty" is one of the great defenses of individual human liberty in Western literature. Mill states his theme near the outset, writing: "The only part of the conduct of anyone, for which he is amenable to society, is that which concerns others. In the part which merely concerns himself, his independence is, of right, absolute." The denial that society has any right to impose on the private activities of citizens was extraordinarily influential, particularly in the development of liberal ideals and practices in nineteenth-century Britain and elsewhere. It remains a living defense of freedom today. Nevertheless, as a theory, Mill's concept of individual liberty raises problems. In particular, we can ask: How do we distinguish between those activities that affect ourselves only and those that affect others as well? In fact, do we ever do anything of importance that affects us alone, and has no effects on anyone else?

Mill's essay "On Liberty" is a defense of a liberal social order and Mill himself was a believer in democracy. Nevertheless, he saw dangers in democracy because it could result in a tyranny of the majority. Warning against this danger, he wrote: "If all mankind minus one were of one opinion, and only one person were of the contrary opinion, mankind would be no more justified in silencing that one person, than he, if he had the power, would be justified in silencing mankind."

Principles of Political Economy

The *Principles of Political Economy* is devoted to economic theory. Although its details are of importance mainly to the economic historian, the book has interest for a wider audience, for Mill's analyses of economic arrangements and conditions are carried out against the background of a system of values. This system, grounded in his utilitarian ethics, is enriched by his constant concern for individual liberty, self-development, and social justice.

For the student of Mill's thought, the most important features of the *Principles* are the changes Mill made in it. The book went through seven editions, from 1848 until 1871. The first edition was dominated by the *laissez-faire* theory of the classical economists, but succeeding editions revealed a steady movement in Mill's mind in the direction of socialism. Although Mill did not embrace socialism, fearing that too much governmental power would pose dangers to individual liberty, he came increasingly to be convinced that social justice can hardly be realized through the economics of unbridled capitalism.

Three Essays on Religion

The *Three Essays on Religion*, though written earlier, were published together in one volume only after Mill's death, in 1874. They reveal an ambivalence in his views on the fundamental questions of religion. Two points in the essays are of particular philosophical importance—the existence of God and the problem of evil. Mill rejected any *a priori*

"proof" of the existence of God but was willing to concede that the argument from design, because it was based on empirical evidence, had at least some plausibility. On the problem of evil, he was vehement. Given the obvious existence of evil, God could not be both omnipotent and all-good. Rather, an omnipotent being who would allow such evil is not worthy of our worship. Mill's most forceful statement of this judgment, though it appears in his *Examination of Sir William Hamilton's Philosophy*, sums up his argument in the *Essays*: "I will call no being good, who is not what I mean when I apply that epithet to my fellow-creatures; and if such a being can sentence me to hell for not so calling him, to hell I will go." To summarize Mill's religious views, although he found some basis for belief in a deity if that deity is limited in power, and he conceded the utility of religious belief, he was more inclined toward what he called a "religion of humanity" than to one that trusted in the supernatural.

OLIVER A. JOHNSON

Further Reading

August, Eugene. *John Stuart Mill*. New York: Charles Scribner's Sons, 1975. A survey of Mill's philosophy designed for the general reader rather than the specialist.

Bain, Alexander. *John Stuart Mill*. London: Longmans, Green, and Co., 1882. This intellectual biography is important because written by a distinguished philosopher who was both a follower and friend of Mill.

Berger, Fred R. *Happiness, Justice, and Freedom*. Berkeley, Los Angeles, and London: University of California Press, 1984. A detailed exposition and analysis of Mill's moral and political philosophy.

Mill, John Stuart. *Autobiography. The World's Classics*. London: Oxford University Press, 1924. In this famous autobiography, Mill tells the story of his life to 1870. Of special interest is his account of his remarkable education.

Schneewind, J. B., ed. *Mill: A Collection of Critical Essays*. Modern Studies in Philosophy. Garden City, N.Y.: Doubleday & Company, 1968. In this collection of essays, a number of distinguished philosophers discuss various aspects of Mill's thought.

Stephen, Leslie. *The English Utilitarians*. 3 vols. London: Duckworth, 1900. This classic work, by an eminent nineteenth-century English intellectual historian, is devoted mainly to the utilitarianism of Bentham and the two Mills. Volume 3 contains an account of John Stuart Mill's life and thought.

CHARLES DARWIN

Born: 1809, Shrewesbury, England
Died: 1882, Downe, Kent, England
Major Works: *Journal of Researches into the Geology and Natural History of the Various Countries Visited by the H.M.S. Beagle* (1839), *On the Origin of Species by Means of Natural Selection* (1859), *The Descent of Man, and Selection in Relation to Sex* (1871)

Major Ideas

Species are related to each other by descent, with the changes from their common ancestors being caused by the survival and reproduction of advantageous genetic variants.

Overpopulation and the resulting shortage of food create the pressure that causes organisms that have advantageous genetic variants to produce a greater number of surviving offspring than those that do not have these variants.

Man and apes are descended from a common primate ancestor.

Secondary sexual characteristics have evolved as part of a complex set of reproductive behaviors.

Charles Darwin, English geologist and naturalist, was the first to unite several ideas prevalent in his time so as to describe convincingly the process of organic evolution. In doing so, he revolutionized biology and anthropology. Indeed, no area of human thought, scientific or popular, has remained unaffected by his theory of evolution. Darwin also made important contributions to geology, botany, and ecology.

Darwin came from a prosperous and able family: One grandfather was Erasmus Darwin, a physician and poet known for his evolutionary speculations; another was Josiah Wedgwood, the famous industrial potter. Darwin showed little academic prowess as a youth. In 1825, he was sent to Edinburgh to study medicine, the chemical and pharmaceutical parts of which he found dull, the practical parts (especially surgery), horrifying. Abandoning this endeavor in 1827, Darwin's father sent him to Cambridge to prepare for the ministry, a common resort of younger sons in that era. Darwin found these studies useless, and he received his degree without distinction in 1831. However, at both Edinburgh and Cambridge, Darwin indulged his passion for geology and natural history, in company with the zoologist Robert Grant, who accepted Lamarck's teachings on evolution, and with the geologist Adam Sedgwick and, most importantly, with J. S. Henslow, professor of mineralogy and botany at

Cambridge. The latter interested himself in Darwin's career and secured an invitation for Darwin to join, as a naturalist, the ship H.M.S. *Beagle* on a voyage to survey the coast of South America. Because of the theories it inspired, this voyage (1831–36) was the single most important event, not only in Darwin's life, but in the history of biology.

Three developments were converging in the 1830's: (1) new information about the earth's geological development, (2) new applications of evolutionary thought, and (3) new studies of population dynamics.

Geological Development

Informed speculation about the earth's structure and history had begun in the 1700s with information derived from the widespread construction of canals throughout southern England. Geologists recognized, after seeing the excavations, that layers of rock (*strata*) were uniform over wide areas and that fossils embedded in these strata were remains of earlier life. At first *catastrophism* prevailed, the theory that the earth has been periodically subject to sudden, catastrophic upheavals that left, for example, marine strata and seashells elevated thousands of feet high in the mountains. According to this theory, fossils were the relics of previous creations of plant and animal life different from today's. These earlier (*antediluvian* = "before the Flood") forms of life had been destroyed in these periodic disturbances. The foremost researcher of fossils, the Frenchman Georges Cuvier (1769–1832) adopted this theory. Catastrophists believed that, since the most recent catastrophe, Noah's Flood, the earth's surface had been stable.

This view was challenged, first by James Hutton, who in 1785 suggested that the stratification of rocks and the embedding of fossils was still going on and that the geological results visible on the earth are the results of ongoing processes. This *uniformitarian* theory was put in definitive form in Charles Lyell's *Principles of Geology* (1830–33). According to Lyell, the ordinary action of rain and waves was sufficient to deposit the observed strata, which had then been gradually elevated by earthquakes and volcanism over long periods of time, rather than in one upheaval. (Lyell had studied these processes in the volcanic areas of Sicily.) A corollary of this theory was that the earth must be far older than previously imagined, to allow time for the extensive changes in surface features to occur. Darwin had the first two volumes of Lyell's text with him on the *Beagle*.

Evolutionary Thought

Generally prevailing since antiquity was the belief that a *species* is a fixed, absolute form; that each individual is the manifestation of an immutable type. (Each lion is the embodiment of the unchanging concept of lionness.) The entire thrust of Aristotelian biology led to this conclusion. On the other hand, the concept of evolution was familiar to the Greek philosophers as a speculative idea. Democritus and the atomists believed that, while species arose independently, only the fittest survived—this did not necessarily contradict Aristotle. Others suggested that more perfect forms of life arose from the less perfect. In modern times, the first complete theory of biological evolution was that of Jean-Baptiste de Monet, Chevalier de Lamarck (1744–1829). Lamarck, an outstanding researcher of invertebrate zoology, suggested that in any living creature organs increase in effectiveness

if used and deteriorate if not used, and that this increase or deterioration will be passed on to its offspring. This is called *the inheritance of acquired characteristics*, and this concept, though rejected by biologists, was influential among nineteenth-century social thinkers.

Population Dynamics

Finally, the basis underlying the growth and decline of populations was outlined by Thomas Malthus in his *Essay on the Principle of Population* (1798). Malthus argued that the unchecked rate of increase of any population was geometrical, doubling while the rate of increase in food production was much less. Under these circumstances, population will grow until it reaches the limits of the food supply, and thereafter poverty, starvation, and death will be inevitable. These are the sanctions that Darwin later saw to be the driving forces behind natural selection.

During the *Beagle*'s five-year voyage, Darwin was able to make many contributions to geology. He showed that granite is an igneous rock, like lava, thus proving that volcanism was widespread; he saw the elevation of the earth's surface after a severe earthquake in Chile; he observed a fossil forest in Peru at an elevation of 7,000 feet, the fossil trees being buried under thousands of feet of sedimentary deposits. From these and other observations he concluded that the age of the earth must be far greater than had been imagined. He observed coral reefs throughout the Pacific and deduced their origin and manner of formation. His book *The Structure and Distribution of Coral Reefs* (1842) laid the foundation for all further study. Most of his geological observations were published on his return in *Journal of Researches into the Geology and Natural History of the Various Countries Visited by the H.M.S. Beagle* (1839).

Natural Selection

During the course of his geological work, Darwin began to notice evidence that made him question the prevailing view that species are unchanging. He knew from his fossil discoveries in Argentina that some species had become extinct, while close relatives survived. He found one similar species of living animal replacing another as he traveled south along the coast. Most important, however, were his observations on the Galapagos Islands, 650 miles off the coast of Ecuador. There he found some fourteen species of finches, today called Darwin's finches, which varied among themselves in food habits, size, and shape of bill. Darwin hypothesized that the ancestor of all these species had come from the mainland; the line had then differentiated itself into the present variety. One species had changed into fourteen.

When he returned to England, he continued thinking about this variability. He found that—if species do change—an easy explanation is available for (1) certain similarities between existing species: The bones in the arm of a man, the foreleg of a dog, and the flipper of a seal all correspond, despite the differences in the organisms. (2) He could see why organisms are not randomly distributed, but fall into genera, families, and phyla, and (3) why the same behavior occurs in different animals—horses, cats, and men all yawn. (4) He could understand why certain unusual species occur only on one continent, while closely related species may occur on others: All kangaroos are in Australia; all llamas and jaguars are in South America, while camels and leopards are in Asia. (Older theories had held that there were "centers of creation," which resulted in the distinctive populations of the different continents.) These phenomena were understandable if species were related by descent from common ancestors. Darwin did not, however, understand what could cause these changes until, in 1838, he read Malthus's *Essay*. He immediately saw that a population that outruns its food supply creates the conditions for an ever-increasing variability in that population. He argued as follows:

1. The number of individuals in a given species remains more or less constant;
2. more offspring are produced than can survive; mortality is high;
3. the individuals of any species are not identi-

cal; therefore some will be better adapted to their ecological niche and will survive and leave more offspring;
4. these offspring will resemble their parents in their greater adaptation to the environment;
5. since conditions vary in different places, successive generations will come to differ from their common ancestor and from each other.

Thus *natural selection*, the process by which a population becomes better adapted to its environment, leads to the creation of a new species.

Darwin never knew the mechanism by which variations occur and are transmitted to offspring. Like most biologists of his time, he rejected Lamarck's theory of the inheritance of acquired characteristics, but he had nothing to put in its place. In 1865, Gregor Mendel proved that traits were inherited in the form of particles (now called *chromosomes*) that obey simple laws; Darwin was not familiar with Mendel's work. In 1900, Hugo de Vries studied—and named—the phenomenon of *mutation*, which supplies the source of variation. In 1953, Francis Crick and James Watson deciphered the structure of DNA and showed how genetic information is coded in the chemical structure of *genes*, which make up the chromosomes.

Darwin had developed his theory of natural selection by 1838, but he did not publish it. After sending his report on the *Beagle* voyage to the press, he began eight years of research into the classification of barnacles, during which he discovered how much variation is possible in nature. Publication of this work (*Monographs on the Cirripedia*—1851–54) established him as a respected scientist. In 1856, Darwin had begun to write an essay on natural selection and had discussed the topic with a friend, the geologist Charles Lyell, who urged him to publish his views. At that very moment Darwin received an essay on natural selection from Alfred Wallace, who, like Darwin, had traveled in the Pacific and had developed similar views on the causes of natural selection. Darwin was astounded at the correspondence between his views and Wallace's. Both Darwin's and Wallace's papers were read to the Linnean Society in London in 1858. Darwin's book, *The Origin of Species*, was published the next year and was an immediate success. It is still in print today.

Theological Reaction

Theological reaction was vigorously hostile. The traditional world view had been static: God had created the earth and its species as we see them today. No educated person in Darwin's time doubted that the earth was several million years old; no one doubted that there had been periodic catastrophes, as represented by Noah's Flood; nevertheless the basic form of the earth and the types of its inhabitants had not changed. Also popular was the *argument from design*, which states that the complexity of each specific form (for example, the human hand, the bird's wing) and its careful adaptation to the organism's way of life cannot be the result of chance; it must be the result of someone's plan. Darwin had tried to show that natural selection alone adapts an organism to its environment, supplying these admirable forms by the force of population pressure. The genius of a supreme designer was replaced by the blind necessity of survival. Not surprisingly, Darwin's theory aroused the hostility that still limits the teaching of evolution in the American schools. Darwin was indeed troubled by this reaction and by the hostility, which he had foreseen, but in time his theory triumphed in the intellectual world.

Darwin wrote other books elaborating different aspects of his work. Among these was *The Descent of Man, and Selection in Relation to Sex* (1871), in which he applied the theories of *The Origin of Species* to humankind specifically. He showed that vestigial organs (the appendix, the muscles that move the ear) are signs of evolutionary change; that man and apes descend from a common ancestor, a primate; that most aspects of man's physical and mental activity show their kinship with the ape; and that, since the moral sense has arisen through evolution, any social animal would develop similar moral instincts given a suitable stage of intellectual development. To this book Darwin added an essay on the mechanisms of *sexual selection*—antlers,

colorful feathers, skin coloration—and their role in reproduction and the evolution of species. During these decades the first Paleolithic human remains were discovered—in 1856 the first Neanderthal skull was uncovered—and these relics of early man promoted the acceptance of evolutionary thought.

Evolutionary theory was occasionally applied in inappropriate areas. The philosopher Herbert Spencer (1820–1903) had speculated on evolution even before Darwin's theories became known, and he pounced eagerly on Darwin. (Not the first or last time that philosophers have misappropriated science for their own purposes.) Spencer applied natural selection to human societies, believing that such societies had developed from originally simple forms to the complex forms visible today. He viewed human individuals and societies as in constant competition with each other, with the weakest going down to defeat. Spencer's phrase for this process was "the survival of the fittest." Spencer's application of Darwin's natural selection to societies was inappropriate because, in order to see examples of evolution in human history, Spencer had to adopt the Lamarckian view that acquired characteristics (thrift, energetic activity, aggressiveness) can be inherited. Nevertheless, Spencer's ideas, now called *social Darwinism*, had a vogue in the final decades of the nineteenth century. They were used to justify warfare, seen as a form of competition that would produce a stronger race. World War I sent Spencer back to the shadows.

In the last years of his life, Darwin devoted himself to studies in botany, with books on orchids (1862), cross- and self-fertilization (1876), climbing plants (1875), insectivorous plants (1875), and the effects of earthworm activity on plants (1881), his last book. Among the souvenirs of his *Beagle* voyage may have been a parasitic infection that enfeebled his health for many years. He died in 1882 from a heart attack, perhaps brought on by the parasite.

Darwin's mild and kindly disposition had kept him personally aloof from the turmoil caused by his theories, and at his death he was hailed as England's greatest scientist. He was buried in Westminster Abbey as a token of his nation's respect for his achievements. He had married Emma Wedgwood in 1839, and seven children survived to adulthood; several of his children and grandchildren have been prominent in mathematics, astronomy, botany, engineering, and the arts. His family is a good example of the inheritability of genius.

Debates about the details of Darwinism continue in modern biology. Darwin believed that evolution proceeds gradually, with small changes accumulating over long periods of time. Some biologists, arguing from the fossil record, suggest that on the contrary, evolution proceeds by *punctuated equilibrium*, periods of rapid change interspersed with long periods of stability. These periods of rapid change are produced by the joining and separation of continents in their drift (the most widely accepted suggestion), by eras of heavy volcanic erup-

tions, leading to atmospheric changes, or by large meteors colliding with the earth. The latter suggestion has received much publicity in the popular media, but is not universally accepted among scientists. Another debate concerns the purposefulness of evolution. Darwin considered that the process was essentially blind, with no preestablished goal. Some biologists have revived Lamarck by suggesting that certain acquired traits can be inherited or that an organism's current genetic coding may affect the future evolution of that organism. These suggestions can be tested only by study of the patchy fossil record, not in a laboratory or other controlled setting, so the debates about details continue. However, Darwin's broad outline of evolution continues to be the prevailing view of the history of organic life on earth.

MARK T. RILEY

Further Reading

Bowler, Peter. *Evolution: The History of an Idea.* Rev. ed. Berkeley and Los Angeles: University of California Press, 1989. A complete study of the concept of evolution from antiquity, with special attention to Darwin's importance in popularizing it. Bowler also discusses the debate about scientific creationism.

Brent, Peter. *Charles Darwin, A Man of Enlarged Curiosity.* New York: Harper & Row, 1981. There is no definitive biography of Darwin. This popular, but thorough, treatment is sympathetic to its subject.

Gould, Stephen Jay. *Ever Since Darwin: Reflections in Natural History.* New York: W. W. Norton,

1977, and *The Panda's Thumb.* New York: W. W. Norton, 1980. Essays on current evolutionary theory by a lively debater. Gould presents the arguments for the punctuated equilibrium theory of evolutionary progress.

Hofstadter, Richard. *Social Darwinism in American Thought.* Rev. ed. New York: George Braziller, 1959. The best-known treatment of social Darwinism. The reader must be cautious: Hofstadter greatly exaggerates the influence of social Darwinist thought, attributing virtually all the problems of industrial society to Herbert Spencer and his followers.

SØREN KIERKEGAARD

Born: 1813, Copenhagen, Denmark
Died: 1855, Copenhagen, Denmark
Major Works: *Either/Or* (1843), *Fear and Trembling* (1843), *Philosophical Fragments* (1844), *Concluding Unscientific Postscript* (1846), *Sickness unto Death* (1848)

Major Ideas

As human beings, we are often in situations in which we must choose between incompatible alternatives. God may place us religiously in paradoxical situations of anguished choice as a test of faith.

There are objective problems, but they cannot be answered objectively for the person, who must decide about his or her subjective relation.

We live aesthetically without commitment, but ethical situations demand decisions from us that are decisive.

The individual is more important than the universal.

Uncertainty permeates human life and is only overcome by human decisiveness.

Paradox stands at the center of all human existence.

The essential self lives inwardly in ways that cannot be given full outward expression.

Sometimes known as the "melancholy Dane," Søren Kierkegaard was a local celebrity in what he liked to call a provincial town. He seldom traveled outside Denmark and did not like Berlin, the great philosophical center, when he did go. His fame comes partly from opposing Hegel, the dominant philosopher of the time, for his rebellion against the established church as lifeless, and for his championing of the individual against "mass man." He is acknowledged as the father of "existentialism," which became well known only a century later when popularized and developed by French writers (such as Jean-Paul Sartre and Albert Camus) in novels and plays. He broke off a love affair with a young girl and never married, saying his disposition was too melancholy. Although he wrote profusely, he never worked but lived comfortably on his inheritance.

As much as with any philosopher, Kierkegaard's own life figures prominently in his writing. He comments on his broken engagement, his unhappy childhood, and his loneliness as an isolated figure. He claimed to be inwardly unhappy, although he was a known and somewhat celebrated local figure. He opposed the notion of "progress" and maintained that all human beings stand where everyone before them has stood. The advances of science, and even of civilization, do not take the burden of decision off the individual.

Kierkegaard struggled all his life with the idea of becoming a country parson, but never did. He died in conflict with the church, denouncing it for making faith and the religious life too easy and too respectable (see *The Attack on Christendom*). He felt that, ultimately, each individual stands alone.

Subjectivity

"Subjectivity" is the concept most often associated with Kierkegaard. He develops this in relation to the interpretation of Scripture (primarily in his *Concluding Unscientific Postscript*). There is a "scholarly, historical" approach that attempts to determine the facts and make judgments based on the evidence. Such objectivity is necessary, Kierkegaard claimed, but most important are a person's relationships to these factors. Each individual must decide how he or she stands in relationship to the evidence and what resolving these questions means. These are objective questions, but the individual also has subjective concerns. These two approaches cannot be reconciled, and we must all learn to live in that tension. Kierkegaard's approach opposes the Hegelian notion of the dialectic, a synthesis between thesis and antithesis. Kierkegaard sees no synthesis, no reconciliation between life's oppositions. A person can allow decisions to be made for him or her, but that means a loss of individuality.

God places the religious individual in a similar situation, demanding faith in a situation of unrelieved anxiety. Faith for Kierkegaard is not a safe, contented matter but one of constant anxiety. In *Fear and Trembling*, he stresses the concept of "dread," which is different from physical fear. Dread has no specific object and reflects essentially the emptiness of the self. The self is not born; it is made, constituted by the many decisions that must be made. But the task fills a person with dread upon realizing how difficult it is. Such freedom is thrust upon one and is not necessarily what one chooses. Consequently, we may seek escape from responsibility and let someone else choose for us.

Either/Or

In *Either/Or*, Kierkegaard celebrates the aesthetic life as one in which one lives and enjoys the present moment. All decisions and seriousness are set aside. One avoids commitments as restrictive. However, just as there is a subjective as well as an objective problem, so there are times of ethical demands when a choice cannot be avoided; one is then forced to decide between incompatible alternatives. We seek to avoid such decisions when we can, Kierkegaard acknowledges, but they add seriousness and stability to life. The personality grows in choice and declines in indecision. We seek support, but that means giving up our autonomy to the group. Yet it is wrong to say that Kierkegaard despises the aesthetic. There really is a lot we should enjoy. The issue is just not to avoid decision by continued enjoyment.

In his *Concluding Unscientific Postscript*, Kierkegaard wants to oppose historical understanding by saying that the future is more important than the past and is not controlled by the past. We make the mistake of seeing the past as finished and then treating the future as if it were just as fixed, whereas human futures are open and contingent and subject to decision. Necessity appears as we look at the fixity of the historical record, but we really need to take the openness of the future and use that as our model for understanding how the past came to be. We need to discover our freedom by discovering how the past need not determine the future. And if outer circumstances seem fixed, that is because we have not understood how different our inner life is.

Kierkegaard's writing style is often unusual, with a dramatic or literary flair. This is partly because he worries a great deal about communication; he thinks it very difficult to make one aware of the truth. Like Socrates, whom he admires, he believes in indirect techniques that allow the other person a freedom of determination. The writer's job is not to convey truth, which on the subjective level Kierkegaard thinks is impossible, but to awaken the reader to an awareness of the problems involved. Thus, awareness is the goal, not conversion to a point of view. The author needs to keep a distance from the reader so that the reader develops a sense of how she or he relates to that question; the author's aim is to shift the burden of decision onto the reader.

"Chance" and the "moment" are important concepts for Kierkegaard, because everyone wants to escape necessity and stay free. Recognizing the role of chance in life helps one to see how much is contingent and how little overall control there is. If we can cut ourselves free and stand in the moment only, we can be happy, unburdened by the past. But we can also get free of past lines of determination and exercise our options, if we do not let the right moment for decision go by. In action we may not be so aware of the importance of chance, but if we see the unstructuredness of our inner lives, then we see better how little is determined for us. Uncertainty is a state we live in constantly, if we are not fooled by an outward appearance of fixed states. (This is the fundamental theme of Kierkegaard's *Sickness unto Death*.)

Kierkegaard borrows the midwife image from Socrates. The author/philosopher's job is not to convince or to put ideas into people's heads but simply to assist them in bringing to birth thoughts of their own. This requires passion; no originality is easy and no decision obvious. Thus, one reason to write is to try to stir up passion in order to facilitate decisiveness. Kierkegaard is not "antirational," as is sometimes said, but he does believe that unaided reason cannot often bring the individual to decide about matters of life importance, particularly ethical problems and religious matters. The birth of a decision is not an easy process. It requires a teacher in the sense not of one who lectures, but in the sense of one who raises the level of awareness and intensity. An age that lacks passion, as Kierkegaard thought was true of his time, cannot act decisively in the midst of uncertainty.

God figures prominently on all of the pages of Kierkegaard's writings. It is struggling with religious problems that brings Kierkegaard to his novel philosophical ideas. He says that the self becomes a self only in relationship to God. This is partly because we begin as blank entities and need the challenge of a strong personality to draw us along. But God is always a paradox for Kierkegaard, always a challenge, and always the one who disturbs the individual most. To deal with God is difficult but necessary, so that Kierkegaard does not really see the possibility of religion's unimportance. He takes its centrality in life for granted. His was a religious age but he thought it lacked inner commitment.

Kierkegaard often speaks of the poet and surely sees himself in that role. A poet has an inner suffering, he feels, that can be expressed in beautiful words, but only symbolically and indirectly. Philosophical truth is like poetry in its form, for both the poet and the philosopher are in conflict with existence. But struggle is necessary and nothing is learned by smooth passage. Truth cannot be directly stated, or at least the truths important to living individuals cannot be. No one can be an authority for another or guide that person to truth. One can be a witness but cannot say what is true for another. Thus the beauty of poetry and its impact is a good image for Kierkegaard of how philosophy should go about influencing people.

In writing a little review of his life as an author (in *The Point of View*), Kierkegaard sees himself as a religious writer who wants to make people aware of life's dilemmas. He argues that there was a single plan to his whole written production, but this statement was no doubt made partly tongue in cheek, since the writings are so vastly different and so heterodox in nature. Kierkegaard stresses that life is understood backwards, although it must be moved forward. Understanding is retrospective but in many ways deceptive, since actions do not develop logically from their origin. However, Kierkegaard's is primarily an "inner rebellion," since he thinks the inner life is where the crucial battles must be fought. Hegel makes life progress from inward to outward manifestation. Kierkegaard thinks the inner and the outer will always be a conflict of irreconcilables. But these tensions are what give life its meaning—but also its dread.

FREDERICK SONTAG

Further Reading

Arbaugh, George. *Kierkegaard's Authorship: A Guide to the Writings.* Rock Island, Ill.: Augustana College Library, 1967. An essay systematizing Kierkegaard's prolific writings.

Lowrie, Walter. *Kierkegaard.* New York: Oxford University Press, 1938. This work by the translator of Kierkegaard remains the most solid and reliable introduction to the genius of Kierkegaard.

Malantsckuk, Gregor. *Kierkegaard's Thought.* Translated by Howard V. Hong and Edna H. Hong. Princeton: Princeton University Press, 1971. A scholar's impressive and successful attempt to add structure to Kierkegaard's often paradoxical, dialectical, and poetic writings.

Sontag, Frederick. *A Kierkegaard Handbook.* Atlanta: John Knox Press, 1979. An introduction to the key concepts in Kierkegaard's writings.

Thomte, Reidar. *Kierkegaard's Philosophy of Religion.* Princeton: Princeton University Press, 1948. Philosophy of religion is the key to much of Kierkegaard's wider philosophical writings.

Thulstrup, Niels. *Kierkegaard's Relationship to Hegel.* Translated by George Stengren. Princeton: Princeton University Press, 1980. Kierkegaard's rebellion against Hegel's systematic thought is helpful in the attempt to understand what Kierkegaard is trying to say and in what way it is novel and illuminating.

HENRY DAVID THOREAU

Born: 1817, Concord, Massachusetts
Died: 1862, Concord, Massachusetts
Major Works: *A Week on the Concord and Merrimack Rivers* (1849), "Civil Disobedience" (1849), *Walden, or Life in the Woods* (1854)

Major Ideas

The search for ultimate reality begins with simplification and the dispelling of the superfluities of life, and with the desire for clarity of vision and spiritual alertness.

There exists within each human being a moral sense and an intuitive capacity for the apprehension of spiritual truths.

Transcendental spiritual truths are revealed through nature.

The divine source of all things exists in nature, yet divine reality is not exhausted by nature.

Reformation, even the reformation of society, begins with the reforming of the individual.

Action from principle brings about change in institutions and governments.

Thoreau had not yet graduated from Harvard when he read Emerson's "Nature," and it would be three more years before he became an intimate of that essay's author and a member of Emerson's circle. Yet the young Thoreau seemed destined for that loosely knit group of New England intellectuals, poets, and reformers over whom Emerson presided and who went by the name transcendentalists. With this group, whose number included Bronson Alcott, Margaret Fuller, Orestes Brownson, and Ellery Channing, among others, he was influenced by the sentiments of European romanticism and the epistemology of German idealism. From philosophers like Kant and Hegel, the transcendentalists took the view that knowledge comes not from experience but rather through the intuition of the mind itself. Emerson said it summarily when he observed that whatever belongs to intuitive thought is transcendental. From poets like Goethe, Coleridge, Wordsworth, and Carlyle, these representatives of America's romanticism inherited an exalted conception of the human spirit and imagination, a confidence in the authority of experience and the individual conscience, and an appreciation of nature as a medium of spiritual truths.

Yet long before Thoreau himself became a transcendentalist, he was already inclined by a natural disposition to accept the opinions that Emerson's "Nature" more clarified for him than introduced.

He wrote in his *Journal*, for example, of the early attraction that nature held for him and of a trip to Walden Pond when he was four years of age. As he remembered that visit to the pond, it was for him a spiritual awakening, in many ways akin to the awakening that is the subject of the first book of Wordsworth's *The Prelude*. In a related vein, his mother, Cynthia Dunbar Thoreau, related that Henry would sometimes be found awake at night gazing at the stars. He told her that he had been looking through them to see if God could be seen behind them.

For the most part, however, Thoreau's public life was not remarkable from the perspective of his contemporaries or ours. He showed promise as a student at Concord Academy and at some financial sacrifice to the family was sent to Harvard College. There he would have encountered Scottish "common sense" philosophy with its un-Lockean emphasis on innate ideas. As we have already remarked, he read Emerson's "Nature" during his senior year; it is possible, though not probable, that he heard Emerson give the Phi Beta Kappa address, "The American Scholar." Following his commencement in 1837, he experienced the usual crisis of new baccalaureates: He needed to decide on a career and employment. His stint as schoolmaster of the Concord Center School concluded after only two weeks and a disagreement with the school board. More promising was his decision to reopen the Concord Academy with his elder brother John in 1839, and the two proved to be innovative educators supplementing the traditional curriculum with practical application and field trips.

During this same period, he commenced his real life's work with the first entry in the *Journal* in 1837, and before he died, this record of his interior life would swell to fourteen printed volumes. Here he prepared the material that later appeared in his lectures, essays, and books. Emerson too was certain that his young protégé would be a writer of distinction and encouraged his talent. He arranged for Thoreau's invitation to speak at the Concord Lyceum in 1838; he used his influence in getting Thoreau's poetry and essays published in the transcendentalist periodical, *The Dial*; he sent Thoreau off to Staten Island to his brother's house in the hope that Henry would make valuable contacts in the publishing world. In the end, however, Emerson was disappointed with Thoreau's prospects as a writer and concluded that Henry was content to remain "the captain of the huckleberry party."

Perhaps because of his discouragement with the public life that Emerson hoped for him, in part certainly because of the tragic death of his beloved brother John in 1842, but principally because he wished to write and to put into practice his theories, Thoreau decided to withdraw to Walden Pond a mile and a half south of Concord for a period that would be the most productive of his short life. He moved into his cabin by the pond on Independence Day 1845 and stayed there in the woods for two years. He passed his famous night in the Concord jail for not paying poll taxes in July of 1846 and so laid the foundation for his most famous essay, "Civil Disobedience." In that same year, he took his first trip to the Maine woods, which adventure provided material for the essay "Ktaadn and the Maine Woods" and later for his best travel book, published posthumously as *The Maine Woods*. He continued such travels until within a year of his death from tuberculosis in May—making two more trips to Maine, an excursion to Canada, four visits to Cape Cod, and a last visit with Horace Mann, Jr. to Minnesota in 1861. His most famous trip, however,

was the outing that he had with his brother John during the summer following their first year as teachers at the Concord Academy. It was a two-week boating and hiking expedition on the Concord and Merrimack Rivers to New Hampshire's Mount Washington, and the memorializing of that adventure just three years before his brother's death was the work Thoreau set himself to during his first year at Walden. The second year by the pond produced a draft of one of the greatest books in world literature, his *Walden* (1854).

Perhaps because it was culled from the journals of the period most dominated by Emerson's influence, *A Week on the Concord and Merrimack Rivers* (1849) was more derivative in its transcendentalism than any of Thoreau's later writing. Familiar transcendental sentiments about nature are voiced; transcendental themes are the topics of the lengthy digressions that interrupt the narrative; a transcendental *persona* of the hero-poet is developed. Typically, nature, like the river on which the two brothers sail, is seen as constant, harmonious, and permanent; and the river, itself a symbol of nature's laws and time, offers the hero-poet of this adventure a unique vantage for seeing both nature and society on the shore. And, while others slumber on the bank, the poet in a kind of waking dream floats serenely on the bosom of the water, content to drift "to whither it will bear me." Or again, the boat on which the brothers sail is said to be painted green below with a blue ribbon around the top—a kind of amphibious animal of two elements, presumably akin to the poet and to the narrator himself, who seeks an equipoise between the substantial material world below and the world of spirit and thought. The tendency to view the world as an extension of the human mind, so characteristic of Emerson, threads its way through the *Week*. The reader is reminded at frequent junctures that the river on which the narrator travels is the river of his own thoughts. Even the digression on the river's fish in the opening chapter, "Saturday," becomes in the words of one Thoreau interpreter a mere "catalog of thoughts," which it would seem the author was out to make his catch. The shiners—to take but one of the kinds of fish in this digressive meditation—are suspended between elements, like the boat itself and the voyagers in the boat, "half in the water, half in the air."

Such Emersonian emphasis on symbol, thought, and spirit, however, is never allowed to subvert Thoreau's commitment to the facts of nature and to what might be called his pantheism. For Thoreau, nature's reality and substantiality are never in doubt as they are in Emerson; nature is never simply the medium of spiritual truths. Even in this most transcendental of Thoreau's writing, the conviction central especially to *Walden*—that the divine penetrates the whole of the natural world (though it is not exhausted by nature, as in pantheism)—is apparent and is perhaps the cause for much of the *Week*'s tentativeness. Even as he reaches for the symbolic and universal in nature, he remarks on nature's particularity, wildness, and impenetrability. Early in "Friday," for example, he observes that the landscape is something solid and real and then remarks with a characteristic matter-of-factness—"and I have not put my foot through it yet."

In the *Week*, the voyager's resolve to submit himself to wherever the currents may carry meets with resistance from nature; it is also tested by the society of farmers and merchants and prudent citizens who busy themselves with commerce and government and place obstacles in the poet's and in nature's path. The shad, so the narrator discovers, are not free to follow their destinies because Billerica's dam blocks their passage up the Concord. But the narrator is conscious too that the voyager in following his destiny encounters difficulty as well when society crowds around nature's boundaries. It would be of interest to the people of Wayland, Sudbury, and Concord, the narrator remarks, to demand the leveling of the dam.

Thoreau may have had in mind at this period the leveling of other dams as well, for in the summer of 1846 he went to jail for refusing to pay the poll tax. He had for several years withheld payment of the tax on the ground that it was used exclusively for the benefit of a government of which he disapproved, but the precipitating cause of his arrest may have been the commencement of the Mexican War. In 1848, he presented before the Concord Lyceum the lecture "The Rights and Duties of the Individual in Relation to Government," which would be published the next year as "Civil Disobedience."

Thoreau's journals also reveal that the horror of slavery was very much on his mind, and he may have acted as a "conductor" on the underground railroad even during his Walden stay. The passage of the Fugitive Slave Law and the capture of Anthony Burns in Boston and his return to slavery, however, galvanized Thoreau's social protest and nudged him toward the sanctioning of the more violent means of social resistance practiced by Captain John Brown. Before an abolitionist meeting in Framingham, he delivered an angry denunciation of slavery in a lecture published the same year in *The Liberator* as "Slavery in Massachusetts" (1854). As the circumstances in the country changed and more drastic measures were called for, Thoreau moved beyond his call for noncompliance with social injustice. At the end of the decade, he wrote his "Plea for Captain John Brown" immediately on the heels of Brown's raid at Harper's Ferry, and the following year his "Last Days of John Brown" was read at the memorial service for the burial of Brown's body in North Elba, New York. The seer of Walden and the exemplar of nonviolent resistance ended an angry prophet at last, yet he never relinquished his conviction that "action from principle" changes persons and society.

Walden

There is a variety of opinion about the kind of book *Walden* is and what models may have been used in its writing. It has been described as autobiography, pastoral, extended familiar essay, and literary excursion. The influence of Asian and especially Indian religious scripture on Thoreau's thinking, together with its original title, *Walden, or Life in the Woods*, prompted one critic to speculate that it might be "a forest treatise" or a soul's journey popular in Hindu literature. Critics have cast about as well for a possible exemplar for Thoreau's masterpiece. Among the proposed candidates have been *Pilgrim's Progress, Robinson Crusoe, Gulliver's Travels, The Prelude* and, farther afield, the *Bhagavad-Gita*. In fundamental respects, however, this book is like its author, singular and a kind unto itself. In a sense, of course, it is a pilgrim's progress, a story about solitude and the fronting of the unembellished facts of life, a social satire, a saga of the poet's formation, a religious epic. Yet its themes are more basic still, its scope more embracing. Though its immediate subject was ordinary enough, *Walden* locates the commonplace in relation to the exceptional, the universal, and the cosmic.

Within the cyclic rhythm of ordinary time, of the day and of the year, it evokes a time-out-of-time, the time of the beginning; it alerts the reader to a mythic time that can also be experienced as present tense. It was, the narrator reports, on long winter evenings that he received visits "from an old and original proprietor" (God) and from "an elderly dame" (Nature) who resides in the neighborhood, though "invisible to most persons." The water of Walden, we are told elsewhere, is unchanged and perennially young, and Walden Pond was in existence perhaps on that spring morning when Adam and Eve were driven from Eden. The change, says the narrator, is in "me," and so the theme of the Fall is added to that of creation and paradise.

The narrator thus understands himself to be poised not so much between a material and a spiritual world as between a sacred one and one that humans defile. The higher laws, which in the *Week* indicated a truth beyond the phenomenal world, are in *Walden* associated with the undefiled purity of Walden's springtime and the world's. The question is here no longer one of getting beyond nature and materiality. Thoreau's experiment, which is more like the Bay Colony Puritan's holy experiment than the utopian adventures at Fruitland and Brooks Farm, concentrates on strategies for crossing over "an invisible boundary" to a world where "new, universal, and more liberal laws" establish themselves not only "within" but significantly also *around* the self.

Walden then is about the crossing of a threshold, an invisible boundary, into an aboriginal world of purity and sanctity, a world Thoreau thought contemporary American society with its devotion to commerce was incapable of seeing or even imagining. The book is also about the spiritual discipline necessary for coming into the presence and possession of the sacred world that had been "bleared, smeared with trade." What Thoreau proposes is an ascetic life of deliberateness, voluntary poverty, and simplicity. What he seeks is the dispelling of delusion and all that is false, a deliberate wakefulness, and, above all, a fronting of the essential facts of life. To use his language and the language of mysticism, his purpose was the attainment of an inner clarity of vision. It was also to achieve an appreciation of and participation in the pure and purifying world of nature that can fairly be described as sacramental. He thus begins the morning—that auroral hour of reawakening—with a sacramental rite of purification, a bathing in Walden, whose waters, he says, are as pure and sacred as those of the Ganges. He regrets that the only use his neighbors make of Walden's water is to pipe it to the village for the washing of dishes. Bathing in the pond is often followed by a morning of uninterrupted meditation and periods of "rapt revelry." Yet, even the journey inward that meditation initiates carries the mediator once more back into the world and delivers him into the fullness of the present moment and the world around of sight and sound.

Thoreau's holy experiment was for him an act of moral reform, and it began, as he believed it should, with himself. *Walden*, however, enlarges the circle of reform to include the neighbor as well—an intention that the narrator makes clear in its first chapter. It is thus in the part of chanticleer, the rooster of Chaucer's *Canterbury Tales*, that the narrator announces his intention to "brag lustily" and so to wake others at the first dawn. It is as the practical Yankee that the narrator calls into doubt the common sense of the economic principles on which the lives of his fellow New Englanders are built.

Though Thoreau believed that Christianity had long since hung its harp on a willow branch and ceased to herald the dawn of a new day, he evoked the language and frequently the phrasing of the New Testament to question the soundness of life built on the nineteenth century's reigning social and economic philosophies. Even more arresting, however, is Thoreau's fresh appropriation of the New Testament's language in the last two chapters, "Spring" and "Conclusion." Having passed from autumn through winter into spring, the cycle of the seasons rounds on itself and is complete, and the pattern of death and rebirth that nature represents and the story of the "beautiful bug" confirm a resurrection (if not Christian) faith that there is "more day to dawn."

"Civil Disobedience"

The Jewish theologian Martin Buber wrote from Jerusalem that there was something about "Civil Disobedience" that spoke directly and persuasively to him. He said that it was the essay's personal element and its rootedness in concrete historical circumstance, in the "here and now," that won him over and gave to Thoreau's words a validity for all history. Others like Mohandas K. Gandhi and Martin Luther King, Jr. discovered the genuinely revolutionary character of the principles Thoreau sets forth in his little essay. Ironically, however, the genesis of the essay was not in an event so momentous as those of Gandhi's South Africa or King's Alabama. As circumstances would have it, one July evening in 1846, Thoreau walked to Concord from Walden Pond intent on retrieving a pair of shoes at the cobbler's shop when he was arrested by the local constable Sam Staples and asked to pay his poll tax. Staples even offered to pay it for him, but Thoreau refused in what was largely a symbolic protest against slavery. Yet, like so much that Thoreau wrote, his night's experience in the Concord jail became the touchstone for ideas elaborated later on, first as a lecture in 1848 before the Concord Lyceum and then as a published essay the following year.

It is noteworthy, however, that Thoreau thought

of this direct personal act of disobedience as essentially revolutionary, as an act cut from the same pattern and in the same spirit as the American Revolution. As he thought of it, the principle of civil disobedience was to serve neither the cause of anarchy or reform. Resting it on the right of individuals to refuse allegiance to and to resist governments, Thoreau believed the principle of civil disobedience was essentially revolutionary and in the revolutionary tradition of 1775. To be sure, Thoreau begins the essay with the famous statement that the best government "governs not at all." He reinforced the impression of his anarchism when he declared that governments did not concern him much. The individual has no duty to make governments better or even to eradicate the worst injustice, though he confesses that no one should follow private pursuits at the expense of others or on another's shoulders. On the surface, that seems as far as Thoreau is willing to go. Yet he did go farther in the *Week* in criticizing the textile industry in New Hampshire, and in *Walden* he excoriated America's consumerism and materialism. In "Slavery in Massachusetts" and in "A Plea for Captain John Brown," he approved the use of violence in the cause of abolition. So also in "Civil Disobedience," for all his disclaimers, he proposed a principle for dealing with social evil and effecting social change.

Without becoming what he called "a no-government man," Thoreau expressed in this essay the conviction that conscience and the moral sense resides not in institutions but in individuals and that change in governments comes about when the individual person acts on the basis of conscience. Social change is brought about when the individual directly confronts the state and performs the right. Nor is it important that this action from principle be a part of a reform program or that it be a grand gesture. Taking his own case, he said that he met the American government "face to face" each year in the person of Sam Staples, his neighbor and the tax collector, and that the simplest way of dealing with his grievance with the state was not to pay his poll tax. He did pay the highway tax and supported schooling "after his own fashion." In spite of his quiet declaration of war on the state, he acknowledged the "use" and "advantage" the state might bring, though he makes plain that the state is never an end in itself. Yet the pilgrim's journey, as Thoreau writes near the conclusion of the essay, indicates a higher destiny where truth is undefiled and where there exists "a more perfect and glorious State," and from his journeying there Thoreau refused to be deflected.

THOMAS E. HELM

Further Reading

Harding, Walter. *The Days of Henry Thoreau.* New York: Alfred A. Knopf, 1965. A standard biography giving a detailed account of Thoreau's life.

Hick, John, editor. *Thoreau in Our Season.* Amherst, Mass.: University of Massachusetts Press, 1966. An valuable collection of essays emphasizing the political character of Thoreau's thought.

Krutch, Joseph Wood. *Henry David Thoreau.* New York: William Sloane Associates, 1948. An admiring biography and a good introduction to Thoreau's thought, with frequent quotation from Thoreau's writing.

Paul, Sherman. *The Shores of America: Thoreau's Inward Exploration.* Urbana, Ill.: University of Illinois Press, 1958. An examination of Thoreau's intellectual development with an emphasis on the relation of Thoreau's life and writing.

————, ed. *Thoreau: A Collection of Critical Essays.* Englewood Cliffs, N.J.: Prentice-Hall, 1962. Previously published essays giving a wide sampling of views on Thoreau and his writing.

Wagenknecht, Edward. *Henry David Thoreau: What Manner of Man?.* Amherst, Mass.: University of Massachusetts Press, 1981. Valuable among other things for its exploration of the religious themes in Thoreau's writing.

Wolf, William J. *Thoreau: Mystic, Prophet, Ecologist.* Philadelphia: Pilgrim Press, 1974. A look at Thoreau's religious attitudes and their relation to his ecological concerns.

KARL MARX

Born: 1818, Trier, a small German town in the Western Rhenish province of Prussia
Died: 1883, London, England
Major Works: *The Communist Manifesto* (with Engels: *Manifest der Kommunisten*, 1848), *A Contribution to the Critique of Political Economy* (1859), *Capital* (*Das Kapital*, 3 vols.: 1867, 1885, 1894)

Major Ideas

The whole of what is called world history is the creation of human labor.

Capitalist development prevents human beings from reaching their full potential as self-determining beings.

Only when capitalists are overthrown, private property is abolished, and communal ownership of the means of production is established by an initial dictatorship of the proletariat can economic justice be achieved.

The impact of Karl Marx's philosophy and theories of social development cannot be overestimated. His ideas of human relationships and capitalist development have brought about changes in the world during the past hundred years that will be felt for years and perhaps centuries to come. Revolutions have been started with the goal of developing a state utilizing Marx's ideas as the foundation. We have seen such revolutions in Europe, Asia, Africa, and South America. Even where his ideas of social organization have ultimately been rejected, the effects of his influence tend to be profound (as in the recent rebellions against Soviet domination).

Karl Marx was born into a family that had recently converted from Judaism to Protestantism. His father was a lawyer. At the age of seventeen, Karl attended the University of Bonn to study law, but his behavior at the university (drinking, dueling, and so forth) led his father to withdraw him from Bonn and send him to the University of Berlin.

At the University of Berlin, Marx decided to major in philosophy, and he joined a group of radical students and lecturers known as the "Young Hegelians," who maintained that religion is nothing more than a human invention designed to explain the unexplainable. Marx's time with the Young Hegelians was significant in his intellectual development.

Marx began to raise critical questions about the role of ideas in the shaping of social organizations and in social relationships. He became interested in using knowledge as a means for emancipating the victims of society, and he argued for the unity of theory and practice. As a result of his association with the Young Hegelians, he became editor of the *Rheinische Zeitung* in 1842—a radical newspaper critical of the treatment of the disadvantaged by both Prussia and Russia. In January 1843, the newspaper was shut down by the government.

In April of 1843 Marx married Jenny von Westphalen, his childhood sweetheart. After months of trying to obtain an academic position but being unable to do so, he and his wife left for Paris, where they lived until 1845.

Paris was a gathering place for radicals and revolutionaries and was a center of political activity. Marx met many radical socialists during this period, but of all the relationships he developed during those years the most significant was his friendship with Friedrich Engels, with whom he later wrote the *Communist Manifesto*. In 1844, Marx helped found an influential radical journal (the *German-French Annals*) and began the writing of his economic and political essays.

In response to his attacks on the Prussian aristocracy, the Prussian government on April 16, 1844, issued an order for Marx's arrest on the charge of high treason. The French government then expelled him from Paris, and he moved to Brussels, where he lived in exile for three years.

In 1847, the Communist League commissioned Marx and Engels to write a document about its aims and beliefs; the resultant document was the *Communist Manifesto*, published in 1848.

While in Brussels, Marx had helped to buy arms for an abortive workers' revolution and, as a result, he was no longer welcome in Brussels. In 1849, he moved to London, where he remained for the rest of his life.

In 1851, Marx became the London correspondent for the *New York Daily Tribune* (although most of the articles were actually written by Engels). He remained with the paper for approximately ten years. From 1864–72, he was involved in the International Working Men's Association (the First Internationale). This group was not as radical as the Communist League; although they supported workers' rights and attempted to organize workers in England, France, Germany, and Poland, they did not advocate communism or violent revolution.

The first volume of *Das Kapital* (*Capital*) was published in Germany on September 14, 1867. The first translation appeared in Russia in 1872, and the English translation followed in 1887. Marx was working on *Das Kapital* for nearly twenty years but was unable to finish it before his death. Engels brought out the second volume in 1885 and the third volume in 1895.

The basic premise of Marxism is that our perception of the material world is conditioned by the society we live in. History is a process of the continuous creation, satisfaction, and recreation of human needs. Fundamentally, the history of the world's societies has been a history of the struggle for wealth and private property, and labor is the force of that struggle. As human beings struggle with their environment in an attempt to satisfy their needs, they are limited by the conditions of the societies in which they work: technology, ideology, divisions of labor, and so forth. Therefore, human history is determined by the relationships of labor to ownership.

In *The German Ideology* (written with Engels and published 1845–46), Marx discussed for the first time in detail his understanding of human history and the development of capitalism. According to Marx, the various stages of the division of labor can be categorized as preclass systems, Asiatic societies, the ancient world, feudalism, and the origins of capitalist development.

Preclass societies are characterized by communal ownership of property and a simple division of labor (gender related). Nomadic groups tended to develop these types of societies. The *Asiatic societies* were the earliest kind of class societies with powerful tyrants as rulers. In what Marx calls the *ancient societies*, land became private property, large cities were created, and a slave population came into being; there was a large gap between the rich and the poor. The *feudal societies* developed in Europe with the downfall of the Roman Empire: A large class of serfs worked the land for a small class of aristocrats. With the rise of commercial trading cities such as Venice and Genoa, feudalism came to an end and capitalism took its place. *Capitalist societies* are characterized by two major classes: the *bourgeoisie*—those who control capital (wealth and the means of production)—and the *proletariat* (the laborers who produce wealth and are used as means toward that end).

According to Marx, all of these societies except for the Asiatic follow each other in sequence. The Asiatic societies can exist in the same time-frame as preclass and ancient societies. All types of societies, however, are determined by the social regulation of labor. In other words, the economic structure of society determines the legal and political superstructure as well as the dominant social consciousness of the society, the laws, and the dominant class. The prevailing ideology is the ideology of the ruling class, the owners of the means of production. For Marx, the means of production include tools, machines, land, and the technology needed to utilize them for productive purposes.

In a capitalistic system, the bourgeoisie, those who own the means of production, control the economic and political structures of "their" society; the power to shape society lies in the hands of the owners, and they maintain their position through a dominating ideology. The interests of the capitalist are preeminent and tend to be in conflict with the interests of those who comprise the remainder of society. The institution of private property is indispensable to any capitalist ideology.

The proletariat (and the nonworkers) make up the remainder of society, and they suffer from the domination of the capitalist owners. But until they become a self-conscious group and overcome the factors of alienation and false consciousness brought about by the manipulative techniques of the bourgeoisie, they cannot challenge and overcome the power and ideology of the capitalists.

Alienation is the workers' state of being "other," resulting from domination by those whose power comes from the workers; the workers, hence, are opposed by forces of their own creation that confront them as alien forces. In capitalist societies, work is a means to an end (the end being the wealth of the owners). According to Marx, work should be the end, related to the interests of the workers. Alienation in work is fourfold: The workers are alienated from (1) the products of their labors, (2) the forces of production, (3) themselves, and (4) the community.

The workers work for others and produce objects over which they have no control, objects that they may or may not need. For them, work becomes a mere job, undertaken in order to acquire the wages by which material goods can be purchased. The goods that are bought by the workers may be goods that they themselves have produced; hence, the workers are, in effect, paying for their own labor with the money received for producing the goods they purchase. Since workers do not own the means of production, they lose control over their own ability to create through labor: They lose their freedom. Consequently, the workers, through losing their freedom by being used as mere instruments, are dehumanized in the process of being perpetually dominated by the owners of capital.

False consciousness is another factor acting as a barrier to the proletariat's move into a class for itself. "False" consciousness is the contradiction between understanding and practice. Workers in a capitalist society may believe themselves to be free, but in practice they are the slaves of the dominating class, the owners. Workers who believe that social mobility is open—that by their labor they can change their class status—can accept class inequalities, but if in practice they find that they cannot move from the working class to the class of owners, they begin to question their understanding.

In the questioning of their understanding, the workers who have suffered from false conscious-

ness will begin to see how their interests as workers are similar and will move toward organizing on the basis of those common interests. In the process of organizing, the workers become a class for themselves, the "proletariat."

When the laboring class, the proletariat, emerges as a class conscious of its status and of the causes of its oppression, it undertakes a struggle for control with the bourgeoisie. When the bourgeoisie is overcome, through violent revolution if necessary, a new society emerges, one that is classless and in which private property is abolished.

To understand Marx's conception of social change, one has to understand the concept—derived by Marx from Hegel—of dialectical materialism. Hegel wrote of dialectical processes—opposing forces producing through conflict a resolution or synthesis: Through the conflict of opposites, thesis and antithesis, a new order or synthesis emerges. In the case of opposing social forces, Marx pointed out, a new social order emerges rooted in material conditions.

Before the classless society resulting from the abolition of private property and involving the common ownership of the means of production can be attained, Marx argued, the proletariat has to destroy all remnants of bourgeois society. A dictatorship of the proletariat is necessary to ensure the orderly removal of the vestiges of bourgeois power. The duration of that dictatorship varies according to the conditions in the society being transformed. Once the state has succeeded in achieving a classless society, it withers away, since it is no longer needed.

A major criticism of Marxism is directed to the notion of inevitability, the theory that class differences must lead to conflict resulting in a new social order: Capitalism, because of its inherent contradictions, must give way to socialism and communism. If the theory were true, one would expect that revolutions culminating in communism would have occurred in the United States and Great Britain rather than in Russia and China. Critics of Marxism suggest that societal change is not evolutionary but situational: Change of the kind Marx envisaged is not inevitable but may occur when circumstances both permit and encourage movements leading to shifts in power.

Another major criticism of Marxism is directed toward Marx's theory of economic determinism, the view that the dynamic relationships in a society are determined solely or primarily by economic factors: Wealth, power, and prestige are affected primarily by relationships to the means of production. This unidimensional approach, according to the critics, does not adequately address such factors as race and gender. Accordingly, Marx minimized the effects of racism and sexism by reducing them to economically determined class relations.

Finally, critics of Marx contend that Marx's ideal of the classless society is unrealistic and utopian.

For one thing, the Communist states have so far not achieved their objective of becoming classless societies and, consequently, they have not withered away as dictatorships; on the contrary, either the dictatorial ruling classes have persisted, using violence and intimidation to maintain power over the people, or they have themselves been displaced by groups desiring a new social order. After all, it is pointed out by critics, all human societies involve inequalities that persist; when one kind of imbalance is corrected, another takes its place. In fact, to conceive a "society"—which necessarily involves the attempt to organize classes of persons into an effective whole—as "classless" is itself a contradiction in terms.

TERRY KERSHAW

Further Reading

Avineri, Shlomo. *The Social and Political Thought of Karl Marx*. Cambridge and New York: Cambridge University Press, 1976. Avineri stresses the significance of Hegel's influence on Marx.

Jordan, Z. A. *The Evolution of Dialectical Materialism: A Philosophical and Sociological Analysis*. New York: St. Martin's Press, 1977. A comprehensive study of the philosophy of dialectical materialism. Jordan argues that dialectical materialism has never been a single, continuous, or uniform doctrine. He suggests that Marxism is not a coherent body of thought but a "wide and vaguely circumscribed collection of views, often incompatible with each other."

Moore, Stanley. *Marx on the Choice Between Socialism and Communism*. Cambridge, Mass.: Harvard University Press, 1980. Moore carefully distinguishes between socialism and communism, and discusses Marx's changing views on the transition to a Communist society.

Tucker, Robert. *Philosophy and Myth in Karl Marx*. 2d ed. Cambridge: Cambridge University Press, 1972. One of the first books in English to reevaluate Marx in light of Marx's own writings.

Weeks, John. *Capital and Exploitation*. Princeton: Princeton University Press, 1981. An excellent discussion and analysis of Marxian economics.

HERBERT SPENCER

Born: 1820, Derby, England
Died: 1903, Brighton, England
Major Works: *Social Statics* (1850), *The Principles of Psychology* (1855), *Education: Intellectual, Moral, and Physical* (1861), *First Principles* (1862), *The Principles of Biology* (Vol. 1, 1864, Vol. 2, 1867), *The Study of Sociology* (1873), *Descriptive Sociology* (1874), *The Principles of Sociology* (1879–97), *The Principles of Ethics* (1879–93), *The Man Versus the State* (1884), *An Autobiography* (posthumous, 1904)

Major Ideas

"Life under all its forms has arisen by a progressive, unbroken evolution."

The law of evolution provides a philosophical generalization capable of scientifically explaining all phenomena.

Evolution is change from an incoherent homogeneity to a coherent heterogeneity.

As organisms increase in size, they increase in structure, and the progressive differentiation of structure is accompanied by the progressive differentiation of function.

Evolution establishes definitely connected differences; specialization produces interdependence.

Culture change is better explained in terms of sociocultural forces than as a result of the actions of great men.

Artificially protecting the weak prevents adaptations that would result in the "organic" improvement of the human race.

Herbert Spencer has had an enormous intellectual impact in many areas, both scholarly and popular. For most of his productive life, Spencer enjoyed great acclaim from people of all classes and many nations, but especially from the United States. Although his reputation may have waned, his influence continues.

Perhaps Spencer's most pervasive effect has been on our language for analytic discourse; he either coined or popularized such important ideas as evolution (first used in 1854 as a less value-laden term than progress), superorganic, "survival of the fittest" (in 1852, seven years before Darwin's *Origin of Species*), system, equilibrium, institution, structure, function, differentiation, adaptation, and social development. These concepts and the theories associated with them have had great impact, even if often unacknowledged, on the development of modern sociology and anthropology; further, the publication of *Descriptive Sociology* (beginning in 1874) marked the beginning of systematic, fact-based, comparative sociology. Spencer also influenced academic disciplines in a confrontational way, as in his "dispute" with the academic histo-

rians of his day wherein he attacked them for failing to present essential facts because of focusing too much on the lives of "great men" and not enough on the "natural history of society." In the United States, Spencer had a profound effect not only on academics, most notably William Graham Sumner at Yale, and the business elite (Andrew Carnegie was a devoted "student") but on political thought and public policy generally; indeed, if we can trust Oliver Wendell Holmes's dissent in *Lochner v. New York* (1905) wherein he said, "The 14th Amendment does not enact Mr. Herbert Spencer's *Social Statics*," he even affected constitutional law. Spencer's writings were most enthusiastically embraced by U.S. social Darwinists (ultimately, ironically, often by preachers)—although, in truth, not without some violence to his ideas. Although perhaps best known for his sociology and evolutionary theory, his *Education: Intellectual, Moral, and Physical* (1861) had the greatest distribution, both in sales and translations, with its popularity based in his "modern" and utilitarian prescriptions. Spencer clearly had a wide range of influence.

Recounting Spencer's life and intellectual development is no small feat; Spencer's own *Autobiography* runs to 1,200 pages and his collected works take up a great deal of shelf space. Spencer was born April 27, 1820, in Derby. His early education was largely free from restraint, despite the fact that his father had run a school and given private lessons to the local elite; Spencer notes, "I doubt not that had he retained good health, my early education would have been much better than it was" but, as it was, his father "allowed [him] to pass the greater part of this period without the ordinary lesson-learning." Thus, his early education consisted mostly of roaming the countryside engaged in elementary scientific exploration (particularly in entomology) and in informal discourse and reading in science. He was sent to his uncle Thomas Spencer at thirteen for his formal education. Nevertheless, his education was not as thorough and orthodox as most, being relatively strong in science and mathematics, modest in logic and political economy, and weak in language, classics, history, and literature. Despite his uncle's urging, Spencer declined university attendance.

At seventeen (1837), Spencer took a position with the London and Birmingham Railway, working on several lines throughout the Midlands until the 1840s. He continued his scientific "experimentation," presenting papers and publishing articles in engineering and other magazines. His most important intellectual discovery came when his examination of fossils from railroad cuts led him to read Charles Lyell's *Principles of Geology,* important because his "reading of Lyell, one of whose chapters was devoted to a refutation of Lamarck's views concerning the origin of species, had the effect of giving [him] a decided leaning to them." Spencer's evolutionary theory would always retain some Lamarckian elements, particularly a belief in the inheritance of acquired characteristics.

In the 1840s, Spencer was involved in several projects. After he was "laid off" from the railroad, Spencer wrote a number of letters to *The Nonconformist* on the proper sphere of government. With Joseph Sturge he established the Complete Suffrage Union, which ultimately came to little. Later (1844) Sturge invited Spencer to come to Birmingham as

subeditor of *The Pilot,* a radical paper. Shortly thereafter he went back to engineering for a couple of years (until 1846).

In 1848, Spencer moved to London as subeditor of *The Economist,* a position that gained him access to London's intelligentsia. In 1850, he published *Social Statics,* which was largely a critique (intended as an improvement) of Bentham's utilitarianism and an argument that there is a perfect morality toward which humans are tending (as a matter of necessity). In it, Spencer articulated a radically liberal system of rights, for example, arguing that voluntary citizenship confers equal privileges, including the "law of equal freedom." There followed for the next forty years a prodigious production of articles and books.

Spencer's essays and books in the 1850s show him grappling with and finally coming to grips with evolutionary theory. There was some foreshadowing of the importance of evolution in *Social Statics,* with its themes of necessary progress and adaptation toward perfection. In 1852, Spencer published "The Development Thesis" and "A Theory of Population," the former denying special creation (and advocating evolution) and the latter principally famous for his use of the expression "survival of the fittest." In "On Manners and Fashion" (1854), he first used the term "evolution" as a means of transcending the biological denotation of words like "epigenesis" and the "anthropocentric meaning" of words like "progress." The first edition of *Principles of Psychology* (1855) asserted that "life under all its forms has arisen by a progressive, unbroken evolution; and through the immediate instrumentality of what we call natural causes." While Spencer continued to work out evolutionary ideas that he began to formulate in the 1840s, he still lacked a synthesis.

Edward Preble has written that Spencer was one of the tidiest men that ever lived and could no more abide a disorderly universe than an untidy saltcellar. Preble further suggested that Spencer was obsessed with the need to fit all of nature into a neat, perfectly axiomatized system. Regardless of the merits of psychobiography, it is true that by 1857 Spencer saw the need for a general law of evolution in

"Progress: Its Law and Cause." In 1858, he developed the idea of synthesizing the scientific data of fields from biology to ethics in terms of evolution, and in 1860 he issued a prospectus for his "synthetic philosophy" wherein he proposed to treat "general facts, structural and functional, as gathered from a survey of societies and their changes; in other words, the empirical generalizations that are arrived at by comparing different societies, and successive phases in the same society." Clearly, sociology was a focal point for his research. Spencer believed that while science seeks general laws, it is done in a "discipline-based" way; he conceived of his task as one in philosophy, which he thought was "knowledge of the highest degree of generality." His formula was to rise by induction from established sciences to general laws that could then be used (by deduction) to flesh out more poorly developed sciences (interestingly, Spencer saw an inverse relationship between complexity of subject matter and the degree of development in science, with the most developed sciences having the most "backward" subjects). Spencer believed that evolution was the basis for a genuine philosophy, an overarching generalization that would hold for everything.

Spencer wrote *First Principles* (1862) as a blueprint for the rest of the "synthetic philosophy." In it he stated, "Evolution is an integration of matter and concomitant dissipation of motion; during which the matter passes from a relatively indefinite, incoherent heterogeneity; and during which the retained motion undergoes a parallel transformation." He maintained that while ". . . it may seem to some extent a coincidence that the same law of metamorphosis holds throughout all its divisions," when we remember that "these are mere conventional groupings, made to facilitate the arrangement and acquisition of knowledge" and "regard the different existences with which they severally deal as component parts of one Cosmos, we see at once that there are not several kinds of Evolution having traits in common, but one Evolution going on everywhere after the same manner." He argued that so understood, evolution is "not one in principle only, but in fact" and that "there is a single metamorphosis universally progressing."

Spencer then went on to *The Principles of Biology* (1864 and 1867) and a recast edition of *The Principles of Psychology* (1870 and 1872). Realizing that completion of the sociology would require "an immense accumulation of facts so classified and arranged as to facilitate generalization," Spencer hired David Duncan to search histories and ethnographies for this data several years before he actually planned to begin work on *The Principles of Sociology*. The collected data resulted in several volumes of *Descriptive Sociology*. At the urging of E. L. Youmans and others, Spencer diverted from his quest to write a series of articles that became *The Study of Sociology* (1873), which was a methodological "primer" for social science, famous for Spencer's criticisms of historiography (asserting that "the only history that is of practical value, is what may be called Descriptive Sociology"). *The Principles of Sociology* and *The Principles of Ethics* were published irregularly from the mid-1870s until 1896, when the "synthetic philosophy" was completed. The major diversion during this period was his publication in 1884 of *The Man Versus the State*, a collection of essays more polemical than scholarly. Indeed, it should be noted that Spencer was never reluctant to "go off" on one or another current issue, a trait that contributed to some succeeding scholars dismissing him out of hand.

Evolutionary Theory

Despite Spencer's criticisms (and often ignorance) of history, his evolutionary theory is really an evolutionary theory of history. Spencer believed (mostly) in a unilinear evolution of organisms, humans, and society, that is, in a unidirectional progressive movement from the simple to the complex. He maintained that nature moves forward in a line (sometimes looking like a tree) from energy to life, to mind, to society, to civilization, and then on to more highly differentiated and integrated civilizations. Since this evolutionary process is pervasive in nature, progress is "not an accident, but a necessity." He argued that the movement of society was from a largely amorphous, unintegrated mass to a civilization where there is a high degree of differentiation among the individuals composing it, with integration corresponding to the level of differentiation. To his conception of inevitable progress Spencer added the notion of the "survival of the fittest"; he believed that the natural process of eliminating the unfit (those unable to adapt to environmental challenges) during each stage of evolution insured a constant improvement in the quality of the human race. Thus, Spencer maintained that the progress of society was toward a stage in which it will be made up of individuals in equilibrium with their environment.

Spencer argued that the development of society was originally influenced by two types of factors: (1) external, including climate, surface, flora, fauna, and (2) internal, including the physical, emotional, and intellectual traits of the units. (It is important to remember that Spencer does not limit society to human beings.) As society advances, it is affected by the derived factors of environmental transformation, increasing size and density, and the reciprocal influence of society and its units, superorganic environment, and products. Like an organism, social bodies increase in structure as they increase in size ("scale complicates," we say today), and the progressive differentiation of structure is accompanied by progressive differentiation of functions. Evolution establishes not just differences but definitely connected differences, mutuality, such that a vast aggregate is formed by the union of minute individuals. The discreteness of the social organism does not prevent subdivision of functions and mutual dependence of the parts, so that the aggregate is rendered a living whole. This does not mean that the aggregate has any being or will apart from the units composing it; it is a whole only insofar as the parts are functionally interrelated with one another.

Spencer maintained that the original social clusters were not only small but lacked density. Integration came with the formation of a larger mass and its progress toward the coherence resulting from closeness of parts. Size augmented social growth, which proceeded by compounding and recompounding. Where large simple groups existed, some kind of head was found; this was the first social differentiation, and it was followed by further differentiation within the coordinating agencies—conforming to the law of proceeding from the general to the specific. In developed aggregates, the combination of actions that constitute the life of the whole makes possible component actions that constitute the lives of the parts. When highly differentiated, the parts cannot perform one another's functions very well, if at all, yet vitality increases as fast as the functions become specialized.

Spencer held that the "hypothesis of evolution" implies that all societies began their development in like ways. The first stage was for outer and inner systems to be marked off from one another, followed by the rise of a third system lying between the first two that facilitates their cooperation. These are the sustentative, regulative, and distributive systems. The general law affecting differentiation of the sustaining system is that it progresses as the divisions become more localized. As the differentiation continues (ultimately down to the individual), the need for channels of communication (or a distributive system) arises. The regulating system, the structure for carrying on outer actions, is determined by the character of things around it; it develops what is appropriate for dealing with surrounding organisms. The first step is development of simple headship in a tribe in conflict with other tribes. The union of smaller social aggregates tends to initiate a central coordinating agency. The development of the regulating system always begins with the rise of a superior coordinating center exercising control over inferior centers, accompanied by the cooperation of the components in conflicts with other aggregates (Spencer believed that action toward external enemies stabilized political centralizations—a lesson not lost on contemporary political leaders). The dominant center increases in size and complexity during the evolution of supreme regulating centers. Thus, in the metamorphoses of society, the effects of surrounding influences affected inherited tendencies and structure became adapted to activity.

According to Spencer, the two main forms of society and the state are the predominantly military and the predominantly industrial. The former is a more primitive and barbaric form of organization, which is rigidly organized with the individual's role defined by the exigencies of military preparedness and authoritarian government. The chief organizing principle is status and there is little mobility. The purpose of its economy is not to increase individual happiness through material welfare but to enhance collective power for conquest; cooperation is enforced and not voluntary.

Spencer maintained that while it may well have been the case that the first need of primitive human beings was for discipline and that this need was well fulfilled by military society, the arrangement necessarily leads to a deficiency of intellect and inventiveness. He saw regimentation suppressing as dangerous the very differences marking the gifted individuals by which the species would be improved. Thus, as the military society expanded and achieved peace and stability, it evolved into a predominantly industrial state. In the industrial state, there is an increased division of labor and greater attention to commerce, which, unlike militancy, promotes and needs individuality and inventiveness; commerce requires freedom and is destroyed by restrictions on same. Hence, status is replaced by contract as the basis for the individual's position; cooperation is voluntary and there is the gradual elimination of all coercion. The purpose of society is redefined to be that of assuring maximum liberty and happiness for individual members instead of increasing power through regimentation. Thus, as industrial society develops, there is a progressive diminution of government. (Spencer saw government as "proof of still-existing barbarism.")

Spencer believed that state interference with the "natural laws" of society (and the economy) would slow the natural progress of society toward an "equilibrium of static repose." Artificial political measures and conscious institutional changes cannot change defective natures; "There is no political alchemy by which you can get golden conduct out of

leaden instincts." (Again, this is the Lamarckian influence in Spencer; artificially protecting the weak prevents adaptation and the improvement of the race—people adapting themselves results in the improvements becoming "organic" in the race.) Also, if people get accustomed to the idea of the state providing for them, they lose the spirit of initiative and enterprise essential for the realization of the goals of happiness through material welfare (an idea with more than a little contemporary currency in one form or another on both the left and the right).

Education, voluntary and based primarily on physical science, is desirable because it leads individuals to confront and deal with problems on their own. (Spencer's views on a proper education closely parallel his own experience and emphasis on science; after science—a subject that helps in our struggle to adapt to our environment—he would have people study the social sciences [for similar reasons] and art, which is good in itself.) Spencer would limit the proper spheres of governmental activity to maintenance of order (evidently not all barbarism is gone) and the administration of justice. He believed the proper place for sentiment to be the private sector (especially the family) and not the public; the family's habit of artificially supporting some of its members should not be a guide for society. It needs to be realized that "public interests and private ones are essentially in unison" and, further, that the state cannot and ought not create rights nor have any "divine rights" of its own. Spencer viewed government as only a committee of management with no intrinsic authority of its own; it enjoys only the ethical sanctions freely granted to it by the citizens. It is only to sanction and better define "those assertions of claims and recognitions of claims which naturally originate from the individual desires of men who have to live in the presence of one another."

Spencer had a utilitarian ethics in that he believed that the good is pleasure, although he suggested that it is not necessarily or even primarily *immediate* satisfaction: Human beings have intelligence, which when used in considering pleasures can give them a sense of what is for their long-term good. Spencer said that his "ultimate purpose, lying behind all proximate purposes, has been that of finding for the principles of right and wrong in conduct at large, a scientific basis," that is, to establish a science of conduct, a systematic method for adjusting behaviors in terms of ends. Moral consciousness and duty are rules of mind that stress the need to think in terms of the long run. On the basis of the latter, Spencer felt that he had overcome the apparent contradiction between altruism and egoism. Recognition of our "definitely connected differences" and of our inability to perform another's function—which comes with a high level of differentiation in the industrial society—causes egoism to be altered by the simultaneous awareness that we have to help others to insure that they will help us gain satisfaction.

DON THOMAS DUGI

Further Reading

Hofstader, Richard. *Social Darwinism in American Thought*. Rev. ed. New York: Braziller, 1959. Shows how some of Spencer's ideas were adopted and adapted by the Social Darwinists.

Peel, J. D. Y. *Herbert Spencer: The Evolution of a Sociologist*, New York: Basic Books, 1971. An interesting attempt to place Spencer in the history of sociological thought.

GREGOR JOHANN MENDEL

Born: 1822, Heinzendorf (now Hynčice), Czechoslovakia
Died: 1884, Brno, Czechoslovakia
Major Work: *Versuche über Pflanzenhybriden* (*Experiments in Plant Hybridization*) (1866)

Major Ideas

The inheritance of characteristics is governed by pairs of discrete elements derived from each parent.

These parental elements pass into the germ cells of the offspring without influencing each other; this is the law of segregation.

The inheritance of one element does not govern the inheritance of any other element; this is the law of independent assortment.

The painstaking work of Johann Mendel (he adopted the name Gregor only on entering the Augustinian monastery in Brno), carried out over many years and presented straightforwardly in his major scientific paper, explicated the mechanism of heredity and the process of evolution, and thus laid the basis for all further work in genetics. His work removed the inheritance of traits from the realm of speculation and made it the subject of statistical analysis. Unknown to the scientific world during his lifetime, his contributions were not recognized until twenty years after his death, when several experimenters had begun to duplicate his work.

Born of a peasant family, Mendel showed exceptional intellectual abilities and was sent to a secondary school and then to a Gymnasium in Troppau (now Opava), Moravia, where he completed the course in 1840. After a period of illness and with financial help from his sister, he attended the University at Olmütz (now Olomouc), completing the course in philosophy, which also included physics, mathematics, and statistics. In 1843, although he felt no vocation for holy orders, he entered the Augustinian monastery in Brno, largely because he saw no other way of supporting himself. His entry, however, was propitious, for it was there, freed from money worries, that he was able to pursue the studies for which he is known.

The monastery was a center of scientific activity, particularly research in agriculture. One of the teachers there, Matthew Klácel, directed an experimental garden and was investigating the causes of genetic variation in plants. Mendel's abilities were

appreciated at the monastery, and he was sent to the University of Vienna to study physics, chemistry, and biology. Among his teachers was Franz Unger, who had studied fossil plants and the variability of cultivated plants, and who surmised that new plants evolved by combining simple elements within their cells, although he had no concrete evidence of the existence of these elements.

In 1856, after his return from Vienna, Mendel began his famous series of experiments with peas. From family experience (his father had been a professional gardener) and from his reading in Vienna, Mendel was familiar with hybridization, the chief method for improving cultivated plants. Following Unger's surmise, Mendel devised an experimental method for finding the simple elements of inheritance: Over a ten-year period, he cultivated about 30,000 pea plants, analyzing seven *pairs* of seed or plant characteristics. These pairs included smooth vs. wrinkled seed, green vs. yellow seed, tall vs. dwarf plants, and various pod and/or flower placements. His hypothesis was that in a hybrid, these characteristics are due to elements derived from each parent plant. The hybrid inherits one element from each parent, for example, from one, the element for smooth seeds; from the other, the element for wrinkled seeds; and neither element modifies the other. This is Mendel's *law of segregation*. However, the first generation of hybrids all display only one of the characteristics, the *dominant* one. (The other is *recessive*.) In the second generation, both ancestral traits appear again: Some plants will have smooth seeds, some will have wrinkled.

Mendel reduced the variables in his experiments to a minimum in order to get meaningful statistics. He cultivated 14,000 pea plants that differed in only one characteristic and found that in the second generation, the ancestral traits appear in the ratio 3 dominant to 1 recessive. His results are shown in the following chart, where *S* is smooth (dominant) and *W* is wrinkled (recessive):

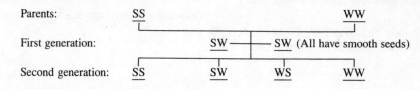

Parents:	SS				WW
First generation:			SW —— SW (All have smooth seeds)		
Second generation:	SS	SW		WS	WW

The second generation types appear in equal numbers, but since *S* is dominant, ³/₄ of the plants have smooth seeds.

Mendel cultivated plants which differed in two, three, or more traits and found that the inheritance of one trait implied nothing about the inheritance of another. He found that all seven characteristics occurred independently, yielding 128 (2^7) different types in the second generation. This is his *law of independent assortment*. He was able to prove his two laws because he (1) carefully selected his experimental subjects for a limited number of traits and (2) had a large population, which allowed him to treat the result statistically. Such a method of handling raw data was new.

(Mendel's elements were, of course, *genes*, a name coined by Johannsen in 1909. Mendel was unaware of *chromosomes*, which were first observed in 1873. The connection between genes and chromosomes was made by the American biologist T. H. Morgan, who, beginning in 1910, made extensive studies of the genetics of *Drosophila*, the fruit fly. Morgan discovered that Mendel's law of independent assortment is true only for genes that occur on different chromosomes—which happened to be the case for the seven pea elements. Genes that occur on the same chromosome are usually inherited together.)

Mendel presented his results in 1865 in lectures presented to the Brno Natural Sciences Society and in his paper "Versuche über Pflanzenhybriden," published in 1866. Disappointingly, there was no response. Mendel attempted to verify his results with peas by doing similar experiments with *Hieracium* (a genus of common European weed), but without great success. Moreover, in 1868 he was elected abbot of the monastery, and the rest of his life was devoted primarily to official business and to a lengthy conflict with the Austrian authorities over taxes on religious property. He did publish a paper on *Hieracium* and several papers on meteorology. Beginning in 1877, with his support, weather forecasts for Moravia were issued, the first in central Europe.

Mendel read Darwin's works, but the reverse was not true; so Darwin, who searched for an explanation of the causes of variations, never knew that Mendel's results could supply an answer. Only in 1900, when three scholars (de Vries, Correns, and von Tschermak) each working independently duplicated Mendel's results, was he rediscovered. Each found, just before his work was completed, that he had been anticipated thirty-five years before by an Augustinian monk. Mendel was given posthumous credit as the founder of modern genetics.

MARK T. RILEY

Further Reading

[Mendel's original documents are preserved in the Mendelianum, a museum located in the former Augustinian monastery in Brno.]

Bowler, Peter. *The Mendelian Revolution*. London: Athlone Press, 1989. A description of the influence of Mendel's work on later scientific and cultural thought.

Iltis, H. *Life of Mendel*. Translated by E. and C. Paul. 2d ed. New York: Hafner Publishers, 1966.

A translation of *Gregor Johann Mendel. Leben, Werk, und Wirkung*. Berlin: J. Springer, 1924. The standard biography of Mendel.

Stern, C., and E. R. Sherwood. *The Origins of Genetics. A Mendel Source Book*. San Francisco: W. H. Freeman, 1966. This text includes Mendel's chief papers and his letters to other scientists.

JAMES CLERK MAXWELL

Born: 1831, Edinburgh, Scotland
Died: 1879, Cambridge, England
Major Works: *On Faraday's Lines of Force* (1856), *On the Stability of the Motion of Saturn's Rings* (1859), *A Dynamical Theory of the Electromagnetic Field* (1865), *On the Dynamical Theory of Gases* (1867), *Theory of Heat* (1870), *A Treatise on Electricity and Magnetism* (1873)

Major Ideas

Electricity and magnetism are two aspects of a single unified force of nature, best described as dynamical fields.

Light consists of transverse electromagnetic waves, and is but one portion of a broad spectrum of such waves.

Thermodynamic laws and properties of gases may be derived from a statistical description of molecular motion.

Analogies are a valid and important tool in physical theory.

James Clerk Maxwell is best known for his formulation of "Maxwell's equations," which govern all electromagnetic phenomena. But he worked in many other areas as well and may best be described as "a physicist's physicist." He was somewhat shy and eccentric; neither his personality nor his scientific work was such as to make him famous in the colorful fashion of Galileo, Newton, or Einstein. His contributions, however, have been just as central as theirs in making physics what it is today; he is revered as much as they by modern scientists for his great skill and insight in developing fundamental theory.

The Clerk Maxwells were landed gentry from Galloway in southwestern Scotland. James was the only surviving child of middle-aged parents, and his life was strongly affected by his mother's death when he was eight. His father was nominally a lawyer in Edinburgh but had plenty of time to devote to the encouragement of this very bright and curious son—for example, by taking him to meetings of the Royal Society of Edinburgh.

James Maxwell was educated at the University of Edinburgh and then from 1850 at Cambridge, where he became a fellow of Trinity College. He held professorships at Marischal College in Aberdeen (1856–60) and Kings College in London (1860–65), but he was not really successful as a teacher. He spent 1865–71 in semiretirement on his estate, where he could devote himself fully to his research. He was lured back to Cambridge to be its first professor of experimental physics and founder of the famous Cavendish Laboratory.

Maxwell's work in physics was very wide-ranging, and he had a good sense of which problems were ripe for fruitful work to be done. His mix of caution and boldness was such that even while his work was path-breaking, very little of it has ever been superseded, only added onto. Maxwell made important contributions to the understanding of color vision and produced the first color photograph; he was the first to use polarized light to study distributions of stress in solid materials; he showed what the nature of Saturn's rings must be; and he wrote the first major paper on servomechanisms, from which the whole field of cybernetics later grew. But it is especially for his work on the kinetic theory of gases and on electromagnetism that he is famous. In both cases he laid the foundations on which the entire subject still stands today.

Electromagnetic Theory

Maxwell developed his formulation of electromagnetic theory in a series of major papers from 1855 to 1865. These began with careful analysis and quantification of Faraday's idea of space-filling lines of force. They culminated in his introduction of the concept of displacement current and consequent deduction that transverse electromagnetic waves should exist and travel at the speed of light, thus finally settling the ancient question of what light really is. These papers were followed by the *Treatise* of 1873, in which he does not merely recount his previous work in tidier form, but reformulates and extends it still further. Here, for instance, the theory of radiation pressure is first developed.

One encounters in these works a series of approaches to the subject not entirely consistent with one another. Maxwell used several mechanical analogies to develop his understanding of electric and magnetic fields; these have sometimes been taken too seriously as literal models for the properties of an all-pervading "ether." In the 1865 paper, Maxwell has largely laid these models aside and become willing to accept electric and magnetic energy as fundamental in their own right; he advocates that it is only the presence and flow of energy that is to be understood literally from the theory. Everitt points out the danger of selective quotation; though the *Treatise* says "there must be a medium or substance in which . . . energy exists after it leaves one body and before it reaches [an]other," Maxwell also says later that ether is a "most conjectural scientific hypothesis."

It took about twenty years before Maxwell's theory was widely accepted. Among the reasons for this were the difficulty of following his mathematics without the aid of modern vector notation, philosophical preference for Weber's action-at-a-distance theory among German scientists, and the lack of strong experimental confirmation until Hertz's work on radio waves in 1887. But there are two direct lines from Maxwell's work to Einstein's. First, Maxwell's comments on propagation of light through moving ether directly stimulated Albert Michelson to his famous interferometer experiment, which provided one of the most important reasons for invention of the theory of relativity. Second, it was in attempting to reconcile Maxwell's field equations with Newton's laws of motion that Einstein recognized it was Newton who must yield.

Kinetic Theory of Gases

In 1859, Maxwell took up some estimates by Rudolf Clausius of the properties of gases in terms of a model in which all molecules move at the same speed. Maxwell realized the importance of extending this model to include a statistical description of particles moving with all possible speeds. He showed that the probability for each possible state of motion is an exponential function of the energy required, giving what is now known as the Maxwell-Boltzmann distribution. Maxwell showed how the phenomena of diffusion, viscosity, and thermal conductivity could be related to molecular transport of mass, momentum, and energy. With assistance from his wife, he carried out experiments on viscosity that verified predictions of the new theory. In the course of further work in this area, Maxwell introduced such important concepts as relaxation time and viscoelasticity. Many years later, some of his last work created the science of rarefied gas dynamics.

But one of the most important aspects of the new kinetic theory of gases was the way it established statistical description as a valid and useful way of understanding complex physical systems and predicting their behavior. In his *Theory of Heat* (1870), he introduced the imaginary molecule-sorting creature we now know as "Maxwell's demon" in order to show that the second law of thermodynamics must have only a statistical certainty. Experience with the kinetic theory was invaluable in easing the way for probabilistic interpretation of quantum mechanics many years later.

As already illustrated by his work on gases, Maxwell was not one to neglect experiment, even though it is certainly his theoretical work for which he is best known. He was not only concerned to base his theory on strong observational foundations but was more than willing to experiment himself. He had been an inveterate tinkerer in his youth, and he always remained creative in devising new measuring techniques. He did important experimental work on color vision and on basic electrical units and standards, and he finally devoted the last major block of his career to the creation of the Cavendish Laboratory. His belief in the importance of experimental work for students had a lasting influence on science curricula.

Maxwell's theoretical work is characterized by very thorough exposition, and extensive use of mathematics that is free and creative yet closely tied to physical meaning:

> . . . We shall endeavour to put our calculations into such a form that every step may be capable of some physical interpretation, and thus we shall exercise powers far more useful than those of mere calculation—the application of principles, and the interpretation of results. [Inaugural lecture, King's College, 1860]

Maxwell, like Galileo and Einstein, emphasized visual thinking. He made extensive use of analogies, and invented many of the central techniques of vector calculus that were later developed by Gibbs and Heaviside. His style of work has had an enormous influence in textbooks on theoretical physics ever since.

Scientific Analogy

Maxwell was more overtly interested in philosophy than most physicists, and was concerned with the philosophical underpinnings of his theories. In particular, he wrote thoughtfully about the use of analogy in general, as well as stating carefully what he meant in his own use of specific analogies in his theories:

> . . . It is a good thing to have two ways of looking at a subject, and to admit that there *are* two ways of looking at it. Besides, I do not think that we have any right at present to understand the action of electricity, and I hold that the chief merit of a temporary theory is, that it shall guide experiment, without impeding the progress of the true theory when it appears. ["Faraday's Lines of Force," 1856]

Maxwell was influenced by the Scottish commonsense tradition and by the dynamical theories of William Hamilton (who taught him at Edinburgh) and William Whewell (whom he knew at Cambridge). He had learned from Hamilton of the relativity of knowledge; one can see care in his work to maintain the distinction that our knowledge is of relations between objects rather than of the objects in themselves.

In retrospect, we can see the deepest significance of Maxwell's work in his careful development of the whole notion of physical "fields." Beyond any of the particulars of the electromagnetic case with which he was dealing, he gave us much of the philosophy and techniques for describing natural phenomena in terms of fundamental forces that have a reality of their own spreading through all space. In this he succeeded where Descartes failed in creating a worthy alternative to the mysterious interaction between distant particles that always seemed such a weakness in Newtonian mechanistic theory, yet without falling into the opposite trap of giving too much reality to ghostly imponderable fluids. All the elaborate development of quantum field theories in this century owes much to Maxwell's general model of the meaning of physical fields. In particular, the theme of unification in modern physics is an ongoing attempt to echo his magnificent achievement in the theory of electromagnetism.

DONALD E. HALL

Further Reading

Everitt, C. W. Francis. *James Clerk Maxwell: Physicist and Natural Philosopher*. New York: Charles Scribner's Sons, 1975. The best modern scientific biography of Maxwell, by a practicing physicist. Includes a good bibliography of earlier sources.

————. "Maxwell's Scientific Creativity." In *Springs of Scientific Creativity*, edited by R. Aris, H. T. Davis, and R. H. Stuewer. Minneapolis: University of Minnesota Press, 1983. Interesting analysis of psychological factors contributing to Maxwell's style and accomplishments.

Goldman, Martin. *The Demon in the Aether: The Story of James Clerk Maxwell*. Edinburgh: Paul Harris Publishing, 1983. A mixed personal/scientific biography useful for its picture of Maxwell's relation to such associates as Michael Faraday, William Thomson, and Peter Tait.

Hendry, John. *James Clerk Maxwell and the Theory of the Electromagnetic Field*. Bristol: Adam Hilger, 1986. A detailed study with emphasis on the philosophical views underlying Maxwell's work.

Tolstoy, Ivan. *James Clerk Maxwell: A Biography*. Chicago: University of Chicago Press, 1981. A short nontechnical biography with emphasis on Maxwell as a person.

Tricker, R. A. R. *The Contributions of Faraday and Maxwell to Electrical Science*. Oxford: Pergamon Press, 1966. A helpful summary account.

DIMITRI IVANOVICH MENDELEEV

Born: 1834, Tobolsk, Siberia, Russia
Died: 1907, Leningrad, Russia
Major Works: *Osnovy khimii* (*Principles of Chemistry*) (1868), "On the Place of Cerium in the System of Elements" (1870, in Russian), "The Periodic Law of the Chemical Elements" (1889, in English)

Major Idea

Elements placed according to the value of their atomic weights present a clear periodicity of properties.

Dimitri Ivanovich Mendeleev (or Mendeleyev), a researcher in many areas of physical chemistry, including the liquification and compressibility of gases, and active in developing procedures for modernizing the Russian iron, coal, and petroleum industry, is best known today for his discovery of the periodic table of elements. Proceeding by analysis of the nature of the elements known in the mid-1800s and using the recently standardized atomic weights, he arranged the elements in a table that graphically showed the relationship between them. In Mendeleev's later years, he was active in government service, becoming one of the czar's privy councillors and producing a series of reference books of industrial knowledge. He was honored for his work throughout Europe.

Born to an old merchant family in Tobolsk, Siberia, Mendeleev showed an early liking for science and industry. His mother owned a glass factory, and throughout his life he endeavored to apply the results of science to industry and commerce. After graduating from the gymnasium in Tobolsk, he studied at the Main Pedagogical Institute in Saint Petersburg, graduating in 1855. His work there prefigured his later career: He began to investigate the relationship between the crystal structure and the chemical composition of substances, and whether these properties have anything to do with molecular configuration. This was to develop into his success in correlating chemical properties and atomic weights in the periodic table. After 1857, he taught and experimented at the University of Saint Petersburg. Appointed to the chair of chemistry in 1867, he found it necessary to write a chemistry textbook for his classes. This book, *Osnovy khimii* (*Principles of Chemistry*) went through eight editions during his lifetime (1st ed., 1868–71; 8th ed., 1906) and was his chief work. While working on the first edition, he had the insight that produced the modern periodic table.

By the mid-1850s, it had been shown that the elements could be placed into categories according to similarity of chemical activity: Fluorine, chlorine, bromine, and iodine formed the halogen group; oxygen, sulfur, selenium, and tellurium were another group; nitrogen, phosphorus, arsenic, antimony, and bismuth a third. It had also become clear that an atom of any given element can combine only in certain ways with an atom or atoms of another element. A fluorine atom combines with one hydrogen atom, an oxygen atom with two, a nitrogen atom with three, a carbon atom with four, to form HF, H_2O, H_3N, and H_4C, respectively (using modern notation). These ways of combining are called the *valence* of the element: Fluorine is said to have valence of one, oxygen two, nitrogen three, and so on. (The valence of an element may vary, and in modern physics the general concept of valence has been subdivided into more precise categories. Today valence is explained by the number of electrons in the outer shell of the atom, but this explanation was not available to Mendeleev, who in fact rejected the existence of the electron and the concept of the ion as an electrically charged particle.)

Several chemists had already drawn up charts that arrayed the elements in horizontal and vertical rows according to atomic weights. Indeed, the chemist Lothar Meyer had constructed a table much like Mendeleev's, but unfortunately had not published it. In writing *Osnovy khimii*, Mendeleev had the inspiration of arranging the elements according to their valence and their atomic weights, which had recently been standardized on an *empirical basis*—that is, solely according to their chemical properties—at the first International Chemical Congress at Karlsruhe in 1860, which he had attended. He noted that there were regular progressions in the differences between the atomic weights of the elements in each group (the elements in the vertical columns of the final periodic table). He cited the following examples:

Element	Atomic Wt.	Element	Atomic Wt.	Element	Atomic Wt.
Chlorine	35.5	Bromine	80	Tellerium	127
Potassium	39	Rubidium	85.4	Cesium	133
Calcium	40	Strontium	87.6	Barium	137

To complete the table, Mendeleev wrote the names of the elements, their atomic weights, and their chemical properties on cards and played "chemical solitaire" with them until he had the correct arrangement. (He was, in fact, fond of solitaire.) He made a table whose eight vertical columns contained elements of the same valence and whose horizontal rows arrayed the elements in order of ascending atomic weight.

Mendeleev arranged his table by *logical deduction* from chemical facts. Only in the twentieth century, after the researches of Rutherford, Bohr, and others had explicated the structure of the atom, could a physical explanation be given for the nature of each group. Mendeleev announced his discovery in several papers delivered in 1869 and in a later edition of *Osnovy khimii* he summarized the studies that had led to the discovery.

His periodic table was not readily accepted at first: The industrial, empirical chemists were not interested; others objected on the grounds that the atomic weights given for certain elements were incorrect, while still others claimed prior discovery. His atomic weights and the table gained general acceptance only when Mendeleev was able (1) by using his table, to correct the previously announced atomic weight of cerium (its place in the table implied an atomic weight of 138, instead of the accepted 92), and (2) from gaps in the table, to predict the discovery of new elements and forecast some of

their properties. Specifically, he predicted new elements in the groups containing aluminum and silicon. When these elements were discovered (gallium, germanium, and scandium), Mendeleev's work was universally accepted as proven. He also predicted new elements falling between hydrogen and lithium, between fluorine and sodium, and between chlorine and potassium—these were helium, neon, and argon, discovered in the 1890s—and he suspected the existence of a series of elements that were later found to be the rare earths.

While working on the periodic table, Mendeleev was also studying gases. In 1860, he had discovered that each gas has a *critical temperature*, the temperature at which the gas may be liquified by pressure alone. In 1870–71, he turned to research on the cooling and compressibility of gases. While investigating gases, he hoped to find the *ether*, the universal fluid permeating the universe, which in his system must occupy the place just above hydrogen. Although this pursuit was chimerical, he did derive precise equations for the behavior of gases in a real—as contrasted with an ideal—environment. He then turned to atmospheric research, investigating the temperature of the upper atmosphere. He made a balloon ascent in 1887 to further these investigations.

In 1890, because of political upheavals at the University of Saint Petersburg, Mendeleev felt obliged to resign his professorship. His retirement was busy and full of honors: He was commissioned to do research on smokeless powder, he studied the tariff, he was director of the Central Board of Weights and Measures, and he helped design an icebreaker for Arctic research. He presented a summary of his work in English in his Faraday lecture, "The Periodic Law of the Chemical Elements," delivered in London on the twentieth anniversary of his discovery. In 1902, he visited the Curies in Paris to study radioactivity. At his funeral in 1907, students of the University of Saint Petersburg lifted the periodic table of the element high above the procession as their tribute to the great scientist's career. In the modern periodic table, the transuranic element of atomic number 101, atomic weight 258, has been named mendelevium; thus contemporary physics commemorates the discoverer in his discovery.

MARK T. RILEY

Further Reading

Petrianov-Sokolov, I. V. *Elementary Order: Mendeleev's Periodic System*. Translated by N. Weinstein. Moscow: Mir Publishers, 1984. A discussion of the background and scientific basis for Mendeleev's primary work.

Pisarzhevskii, Oleg. *Dimitry Ivanovich Mendeleyev, His Life and Work*. Moscow: Foreign Languages Publishing House, 1954. One of the few biographies available in English. The biography by Daniel Posin, *Mendeleyev: The Story of a Great Scientist*, is a fictionalized narrative, difficult to take seriously.

CHARLES SANDERS PEIRCE

Born: 1839, Cambridge, Massachusetts
Died: 1914, Milford, Pennsylvania
Major Works: "The Fixation of Belief" (1877), "How to Make Our Ideas Clear" (1878), *The Collected Papers of Charles Sanders Peirce* (8 vols., 1931–35, 1958)

Major Ideas

What we expect from our forms of inference is that they give us true conclusions from true premises—if not all the time, then at least most of the time.

Beliefs are established habits of action.

Consider all the possible effects that might conceivably have practical bearings, we conceive the object of our conception to have: Our conception of these effects is the whole of our conception of the object.

The opinion that is fated to be agreed to by the community of those who follow the scientific method indefinitely is what we mean by truth.

The phaneron *is all of that which is before the mind and its aspects: Firsts, feelings or qualitative possibilities; Seconds, actualities; Thirds, laws, habits, or customs.*

A sign is something in the phaneron that stands for something else in the phaneron and gives rise to an interpretant in the phaneron by virtue of some habit, law, or custom.

All mental activity is of the nature of sign activity and every thought is a sign, which by virtue of some habit gives rise to another sign of the same object.

Charles Sanders Peirce is accredited by William James as being the founder of pragmatism. Many today would consider Peirce to be the greatest of the American pragmatists, if not the greatest philosopher the United States has produced. He was the son of a Harvard professor, Benjamin Peirce, who was probably the greatest American mathematician of his day. Under the influence of his father, Charles Peirce developed a strong and early interest in mathematics and the natural sciences. He graduated from Harvard in 1859 and later enrolled in the Lawrence Scientific School and received his degree in chemistry in 1863. Except for a five-year period (1879–84) teaching at the new Johns Hopkins University, he held no teaching position. For most of his career, Peirce was a physicist for the United States Coast and Geodetic Survey, from which he retired in 1891. He retired to Milford, Pennsylvania, where he lived in relative isolation with his second wife until he died.

A person seriously interested in Peirce's ideas faces a severe difficulty. First, Peirce published very little in a finished form. Secondly, Peirce appears to have changed his mind over the years of his philo-sophically productive career (1866–1914), and a large part of this material is in the form of working scraps, some of which are undated. Murray G. Murphey has been able to detect the development of what he calls the four philosophical systems. This is probably the most elaborate hypothesis of the chronological development of Peirce's philosophic ideas, but the unfinished nature of his papers and their dubious chronology makes any such hypothesis highly speculative.

Two published essays are generally thought to be the beginnings of Peirce's pragmatism, which he later referred to as pragmatism to distinguish his position from James's. The first essay is "The Fixation of Belief." Here we find Peirce developing his theory of the function of logic, of the scientific method, and of the nature of belief. The object of reasoning is to acquire new beliefs (conclusions) on the basis of beliefs that we already accept (premises). That which determines us to draw one conclusion rather than another from given premises is some habit of the mind, which Peirce calls a guiding (or leading) principle of inference. For example, if from the premise that Socrates is human we draw the conclusion that Socrates is mortal, then the habit of the mind, or the guiding principle of the inference, is: If any given thing is human, then it is mortal. A guiding principle, or habit of the mind, is logically good provided it would never (or in the case of probable inference, seldom) lead us to draw a false conclusion from true premises. Good reasoning, then, has survival value.

Peirce saw three consequences of the above analysis of inference. First, it gave him a way of distinguishing logical guiding principles from probable ones. Those guiding principles that will always give true conclusions from true premises are logical guiding principles. Peirce proposed that the logical guiding principles could be determined diagrammatically, either by the use of truth tables (which led him independently to invent the procedure) or by Venn diagrams (involving overlapping circles) or other diagrams that he invented.

Peirce went on to distinguish three forms of inference: first, the *deductive* forms of inference, which he took to be logical guiding principles; second, the *inductive* form of inference, which renders probable conclusions (from which he developed a rather elaborate and contemporary theory of probability); and, third, a form of inference he called *abduction*, which yields as a conclusion a hypothesis—something that if true would explain the truth of the facts in the premises. Peirce insisted that the formulation of a hypothesis is a form of inference rather than a wild guess, because the hypothesis has the function of explaining the given premises.

The second important consequence of the above analysis of inference has to do with the nature of belief. Take, for example, the above nonlogical leading principle: "If any given thing is human, then it is mortal." What is the difference here between the belief that all human beings are mortal and this habit of the mind that is a guiding principle in the above inference concerning Socrates? None. Beliefs, too, are habits of the mind. When we believe a given proposition, we have an established, or to used Peirce's term, a fixed habit of acting in a certain way under certain conditions. (How beliefs such as "So-and-so is mortal" are habits is treated in more detail in the discussion of

the second above-mentioned essay, "How to Make Our Ideas Clear.")

The third consequence from the above analysis of the reasoning process is that doubt, the opposite of belief, consists in *not* having such a fixed habit of acting under certain possible conditions. Doubt is an uneasy state of the mind from which we try to free ourselves. One is in a most uneasy state if one does not know whether a certain person being considered is friend or foe. It is this type of uneasy state of the mind, or possible uneasy state of the mind, that gives rise to inquiry, whose sole object is to fix belief.

Methods for Fixing Beliefs

There are a number of ways to fix belief-habits. Peirce mentions four: the method of *tenacity*, the method of *authority*, the *a priori* method, and the *scientific* method. One is following the method of *tenacity* if one refuses to change one's beliefs; that is, one always acts the same way, given the same conditions, that one has in the past. One is following the method of *authority* if a person acts a certain way under certain conditions because some given authority tells him or her to act that way under those conditions. One is following the *a priori* method when a person acts a certain way under certain conditions because he or she is inclined so to act under those conditions, or feels it is reasonable so to act. One is following the *scientific* method when a person takes all beliefs as hypotheses to be spelled out pragmatically in terms of future expectations and to be tested by future experiences of the community of scientific inquirers.

We all use all four of these methods for fixing our beliefs, Peirce tells us, and all four have positive value and should not be ruled out indiscriminately. If one wants consistency and decisiveness of action, then one should use the method of tenacity. If one wants a social group to have internal stability, then, as every totalitarian leader knows, the method of authority should be used. If one wishes to feel good about one's beliefs or to be in style, then the *a priori* method should be used. If one wishes the truth, then that person should be a member of a community that uses the scientific method.

The point Peirce wished to make here is that a person's goals determine the choice of method. How it is that the scientific method is the only one that guarantees *truth* will be explained after a discussion of the pragmatic criterion of meaning.

The Pragmatic Criterion

In the essay "How to Make Our Ideas Clear," Peirce proposes what is sometimes called the "pragmatic" criterion of meaning. In fact, according to James, Peirce read this paper to the Metaphysical Club in Cambridge and it was in his paper that the term "pragmatism" was first used. It must be noted, too, as Peirce later said a number of times, that the pragmatic criterion is the criterion for the meaning of general, scientific terms. If we take seriously the former discussion, then if we wish to clarify the meaning of a general term in the expression of a belief-habit, we need to determine what actions believing a proposition applying that term to a particular object produces with reference to that object.

Peirce's first formulation of the pragmatic criterion is: "Consider what effects, that might conceivably have practical bearings, we conceive the object of our conception to have. Then, our conception of these effects is the whole of our conception of the object."

The expression "effects that might conceivably have practical bearings" has a lot packed into it. First, "effects of the object" later becomes "possible effects of the object," so that we are then concerned with the disposition of the object to affect us in certain ways. "Conceivable practical bearings" means all the possible ways we would act, under specified conditions, toward the object because it has these effects. The meaning of a general term involves the conceivable ways in which we expect the object of the term to act if we were to behave in such-and-such a way under certain conditions.

What is involved in belief and meaning, according to Peirce, are the possible interactions between believer and the object of belief. To believe that something is of a certain kind, then, is habitually to expect certain effects when we act toward *x* in certain ways under certain conditions; if our belief is true, then *x* in turn affects us, or habitually reacts to us, in the anticipated ways.

Theory of Truth

If we had a community of investigators using the scientific method to fix their beliefs, that is, taking beliefs as hypotheses, spelling out their meanings by reference to the pragmatic criterion of meaning, and performing the specified actions under the specified conditions (testing the hypothesis), revising the hypotheses when they do not get the anticipated effects, and repeating the testing procedure again, then what that community would come to believe in the long run, Peirce maintained, would be the truth. He pragmatically characterized truth in this way: "The opinion which is fated to be ultimately agreed to by all who investigate [use the scientific method to fix their beliefs] is what we mean by the truth, and the object represented in this opinion is the real."

Another question that preoccupied Peirce was, What is there to be investigated? or, What is before the mind? In answer to this, he developed what he called phaneroscopy, or phenomenology, that is, a theory of the *phaneron*, "the collective total of all that is in any way or in any sense present to the mind." His answer is that what is before the mind exemplifies elements of three categories: Firstness, Secondness, or Thirdness. Firstness is qualitative possibility. It is monadic in that it has no essential relationship to anything else. The quality of being white would be a First. As Hume suggests, white in itself tells no tales about anything else: It is just what it is. Secondness is actual fact and it is diadic; to be that particular actuality, it has to have certain relations to some other thing—spatial and temporal relations, for example, or causal relations. Thirdness is law, habit, or custom and, according to Peirce, it is triadic. (However, it is most difficult, if not impossible, to see how all laws, habits, conventions and customs essentially involve three things just as actuality involves two and is diadic, and quality involves only itself and is monadic. This neat thesis is probably due to Peirce's eagerness to argue that the three categories are both needed and sufficient and to do so by the use of his newly developed logic of relations.)

One thing that makes Peirce's phaneroscopy exciting is the way in which he characterizes mental activity. All mental activity is sign activity and all thoughts are signs. Now, a sign is something that stands for some object for some interpreter; that is, the sign by virtue of some habit, law, or custom gives rise to some interpretant. Thus all sign activity is triadic, involving a sign, an object of the sign, and an interpretant of the sign; that is, the way in which the interpreter interprets the sign as standing from that object. The interpretant is itself another sign of that same object. This is the way in which we took the general term "is human" to be applicable to (a sign of) Socrates earlier, and it gave rise to the term "is mortal" as a sign of Socrates by virtue of a habit of mind.

Since what is before the mind can be a First, Second, or Third, then instances of each can function as signs, but also they can be taken as signs of a First, Second, or Third, and call up a First, Second, or Third as an interpretant. If, for example, taking a certain thing as the sign of an object gives rise to a First, some quality of feeling, as an interpretant, then it is an emotional interpretant. An example would be one's taking certain sensible qualities as a sign of a lion and its giving rise to a feeling of fear. If the sign gives rise to a Second as an interpretant, an action or an exertion of effort, it is an energetic interpretant. An example would be one's taking certain sensible qualities as a sign of an oncoming car and then jumping out of the way. If taking a sign as the sign of an object establishes a habit of the mind, then it is a logical or conceptual interpretant, and it fixes a belief about the object of the sign. Also, a sign may stand for some object by virtue of some qualitative similarity (an icon; for example, a picture), or by virtue of some fact of dynamic relatedness (an index; for example, a weather vane) or by virtue of some law, habit, or custom (a symbol; for example, the English predicate "is human"). These facts led Peirce to spend hours working on classifications and reclassifications for all of the kinds of possible signs.

BOWMAN L. CLARKE

Further Reading

Esposito, Joseph L. *Evolutionary Metaphysics.* Athens, Ohio: Ohio University Press, 1980. This is a recent work that deals with Peirce as a metaphysician and concentrates on his work prior to and around 1865, particularly the early development of the categories.

Murphey, Murray G. *The Development of Peirce's Philosophy.* Cambridge, Mass.: Harvard University Press, 1961. A major work by Murphey on the development of Peirce's "four systems" mentioned above. It is the elaborate detailed hypothesis of the historical development of Peirce's ideas and is still a hypothesis well worth considering.

Thompson, Manley. *The Pragmatic Philosophy of C. S. Peirce.* Chicago: University of Chicago Press, 1953. This is a rather careful and systematic study of Peirce's ideas that have to do with what has become known as pragmatism.

WILLIAM JAMES

Born: 1842, New York, New York
Died: 1910, Chocorua, New Hampshire
Major Works: *The Principles of Psychology* (1890), "The Will to Believe" (1897), *The Varieties of Religious Experience* (1902), *Pragmatism* (1907)

Major Ideas

Human consciousness is selective; it concentrates on some things and ignores others.

Ideas and beliefs are essentially plans for organizing and structuring our experience and world.

One cannot prove finally whether human action is free or determined, but there are good reasons, especially moral ones, for believing that human action involves freedom.

A person's psychological makeup affects his or her religious experience, and that experience is best evaluated in terms of its moral quality.

Pragmatism consists of two parts: It is a method for the determination of meaning, and it is a theory about the nature of truth.

The truth or falsity of a judgment, its agreement or disagreement with reality, depends on obtaining or failing to obtain corroboration of the expectations that follow from the judgment in question.

The best-known American philosopher of his day, William James is most famous for his contributions to the development and popularization of pragmatism. A theory about the nature of meaning and truth, James's pragmatism leads to *meliorism*, as he liked to call it. His view holds that fulfillment and salvation for humankind and nature are neither necessary nor impossible and that our actions make a vital difference in whatever happens. It implies that process, change, and open-endedness characterize all existence, that human existence is permeated by freedom, and that hope, which is at the heart of human life, finds its natural expression in religious faith. These concerns and convictions emerged from a life and career that were an intellectual and spiritual odyssey. James's journey took him from medicine and physiology to philosophy, with pioneering contributions to psychology in between.

James's father, Henry James, Sr., was an independently wealthy man whose major interests included theology and the education of his children. Even before William James was out of his teens, the family, including William's younger brother, Henry James, Jr., who became a brilliant novelist, had been to Europe many times. Art and science were William's early interests, but the latter won out, and

in 1869 he received the M.D. degree from Harvard Medical School.

Poor health restricted James's activities after graduation, but in 1872 he became an instructor in physiology at Harvard. While traveling in Europe, he became acquainted with novel developments in psychology. Thus, not only did he begin to teach psychology in 1875, but also he organized one of the United States's first laboratories for psychological studies. In addition, James found that psychology raised basic philosophical issues, and these questions ultimately captured and held his attention in ways that problems peculiar to physiology and psychology could not.

By 1879, James was also teaching philosophy at Harvard, and in the late 1870s and the 1880s he wrote and published papers that concentrated on the nature of rationality and the freedom–determinism controversy. In 1890, after twelve years of work, James published his two-volume *Principles of Psychology*. In this book, which is still of great importance, James tried to delineate the foundations, boundaries, and findings of the relatively new science of empirical psychology. He found, however, that the task of securing the foundations of the new science was especially difficult, for philosophical assumptions were involved at every turn. James saw that a sound psychology requires a firm philosophical base, and he worked to clarify issues in both areas.

Spent mostly at Harvard, the last twenty years of James's life were occupied primarily with the teaching and writing of philosophy, culminating in his development of pragmatism. A gifted writer and an eloquent speaker, James was much in demand at home and abroad. His Gifford Lectures at the University of Edinburgh, Scotland, in 1901–02 became his famous book *The Varieties of Religious Experience*. An invitation to lecture at the Lowell Institute in Boston during the winter of 1906–07 led to another crucial work, *Pragmatism*, which James subtitled *A New Name for Some Old Ways of Thinking*. By the time of his death in 1910, James was well known both for his contributions to psychology and for his often-controversial philosophical views.

The Principles of Psychology

James believed that psychology and philosophy are closely related in the following way: Both need to emphasize the description of human experiences as well as the goal of finding causal explanations. Putting that principle into practice, he found five basic characteristics about human consciousness and thought:

1. Thought is personal; experiences are owned—they belong to someone.
2. Thoughts and experiences are constantly changing. No two experiences are ever identical. James did not deny that we experience the same objects over again, but only that our experience of an object has different qualities on different occasions. Moreover, even though change is always taking place, he stressed that nothing is ever totally wiped out in experience. Every experience leaves its mark, although not in a way that eliminates autonomy and freedom in the present moments of conscious awareness.
3. There is continuity as well as change in thought and experience. Conscious awareness is not chopped up into bits. Rather, consciousness flows like a stream—the concept of the "stream of consciousness," which plays important parts in literary creation and theory, has its origins in James. In addition, within this flow one basic structural feature stands out. Some object, person, or concept is focused on, but always against a broader, richer background or horizon. The focal point is "fringed" by a field of perceptions, feelings, time, and space, all of which play their parts in constituting the meaning of the central object and our experience. As our attention moves, different objects come to be at the center, but the figure–ground structure remains essential.
4. Thought is cognitive. It deals with something other than itself. This is James's way of asserting that we inhabit and know a world that is not entirely of our own making, however much our words and deeds may affect what goes on within it.
5. Consciousness is selective. It concentrates on some things and ignores others. James placed particular emphasis on this fifth characteristic. Consciousness is not passive. It is an organizing force that creates and brings specific patterns of meaning to light. Consciousness inhabits a rich and ambiguous field from the outset, but the particular world we inhabit is largely due to the interests that we bring with us, some of which are instinctual, and to the choices that we make.

This emphasis on the selectivity of consciousness suggests that freedom plays an important part in James's understanding of human existence. He believed that we inhabit a world of freedom. Meaning and value are largely determined by our choices, and the significance and quality of human life are primarily our responsibility. The roots of freedom are in the selective powers of consciousness. For James, the assertion that we are free means that in present moments of conscious awareness we always have some power to control our concentration of attention on persons, feelings, ideas, or objects in the world. James denied that what we attend to in the present and in the future is exhaustively deter-mined by what has already taken place. In addition, he held that our acts of attending and thinking are choices that naturally result in action. Our efforts may be insufficient to accomplish what we want, but through an original capacity to concentrate at-tention, which can grow and develop, human life and the world as a whole become permeated with novel purposes, values, and actions, which are the results of our freedom.

Determinism, Freedom, and the Will to Believe

Many of James's views conflicted with the deter-ministic theories held by some of his contempo-raries. These theories dealt with human conduct in terms of cause and effect relationships in which the past exhaustively fixes the present and the future. James defended freedom against this determinism in an interesting way. First, he argued that it is impossible to demonstrate conclusively either that human action involves freedom or that it is totally determined, because once an act has occurred, there is no possibility of exactly duplicating the circumstances to see whether the act could be al-tered. But if final demonstrations are ruled out, it still possible to have a well-grounded belief in the reality of freedom.

Our existence is characterized by feelings that the future is genuinely open-ended, that we do shape its course in the present moment, and that our actions are not adequately explained as fixed results of causes in the past. Furthermore, these undeniable feelings of freedom are fundamental to our experi-ences of moral striving and our convictions that life's quality can be improved. James believed, therefore, that the meaning and intelligibility of our lives depend largely on the existence of freedom, and he held that this fact gives us sufficient practical grounds for believing in freedom and rejecting de-terministic theories.

James's position on these and related issues is especially well illustrated in essays such as "The Dilemma of Determinism" and "The Will to Be-lieve." The latter argues that there are times when

we are confronted by situations in which we must make a decision without having all of the evidence we might like to possess. Life does not always allow us the luxury of waiting until we have conclusive data confirming the correct course of action. James's goal was to delineate some of the basic characteristics of such situations and to defend the view that the rational course of action in these cir-cumstances is not to flee from reality by claiming the necessity of having to wait for more objective evidence before deciding what to do. Rather, James urges us to face such circumstances squarely, to meet them with full awareness of the risk and uncer-tainties that they involve, and then to choose the course of action that is most likely to add signifi-cance and fulfillment to our lives.

What James called the "religious hypothesis" provides an example. If religion is taken generically, James found that it makes the following claims. First, it asserts that "the best things are the more eternal things, the overlapping things, the things in the universe that throw the last stone, so to speak, and say the final word." Second, religion affirms that "we are better off even now if we believe her first affirmation to be true." These claims, James believed, constitute an option that is living, forced, and momentous. The point that James stressed is that when one is confronted by genuine options such as those that occur in religion, one is entitled to commit oneself positively toward the claims of reli-gion without being branded irrational—provided, of course, that one acts with a clear awareness of what he or she is doing.

The Varieties of Religious Experience

Hope is at the heart of human life, and one of its natural expressions is in religious faith. James was no starry-eyed optimist. He had a profound sense of the negativity and evil that haunt existence. He knew that life smells of death. Yet pessimism was not his choice. In a world of freedom, hope can spring eternal. Hope is a quality peculiar to human life. It entails the feeling that the past and the pres-ent are not good enough and that the future can be better. As James understood it, hope is best embodied in what he called the "strenuous mood." This lifestyle involves a deep desire to find lasting meaning, a passionate concern to relieve suffering and to humanize existence, and a sense of urgency about developing and using one's talents to the utmost. Only hopeful persons can live this way.

The Varieties of Religious Experience does not give high marks to every form of religious life, but it makes clear James's conviction that religious faith is instrumental in releasing human energy toward the moral ends of the strenuous mood. In turn, the strenuous mood points toward a need for religious faith. Any sensitive person knows that human powers are limited. Try as we may, human efforts alone seem insufficient to eliminate destruction and death. The hope that the strenuous mood entails, then, may not be sustained unless that mood points beyond itself, trusting that life is supported by divine power that can aid us in achieving our best ideals and that can save us from the clutches of negativity and absurdity.

Caught in the ambiguity and frustration of human finitude—somewhere between ultimate success and total failure—the strenuous mood points toward religious faith as a source of courage. James contended, however, that some religious perspectives are more adequate than others. He opposed theologies that imply that the world and human existence are essentially complete and finished by virtue of their relation to a God, or an Absolute, who comprehends all being from a perspective of eternity. Instead, James inclined toward a finite God—one limited either in power or knowledge or both. Better than other concepts, he thought, such a view of God fitted a world that is characterized by freedom, open-endedness, and change, and in which a real struggle with evil is taking place.

Pragmatism

James's pragmatism is in many ways a natural extension of his earlier ideas, especially those involving freedom and religion. It involves both an empirical method for clarifying the meaning of concepts and theories and a theory about the nature of truth. With respect to the clarification of meaning, pragmatism rests on the following principle: Meaning is revealed by examining a concept or theory with respect to the practical consequences in future experience that the object of the concept or theory leads us to anticipate. A complete account of such consequences would constitute a full analysis of the meaning of the concept or theory in question.

This approach to meaning provides a good starting point for handling disputes. For example, if we are faced by two claims that seem to be in conflict, but no practical differences can be delineated concerning the results that will hold if they are true, then the dispute can be dismissed as purely verbal. However, if substantive differences are present, the pragmatic approach will reveal them. In addition, it will help us to find out the truth or falsity of the claims by urging us to see whether the consequences we are led to expect really do occur.

In *Pragmatism*, James illustrated his approach to meaning in clarifying the major differences between a scientific materialism and a view—James calls it "theism"—that asserts the existence of a purposeful, creating God. If we look from the present back toward the past, James believed, no difference between the two views can be specified. Either perspective is capable of accounting for what has happened thus far. But when materialism and theism are contrasted with respect to what they promise and the expectations they produce in us, crucial differences in the two views begin to appear. The materialism that James has in mind leads us to expect the ultimate negation of human ideals and achievements. Such a world is finally devoid of hope, and life in this world will have a hollowness because the future is basically closed. On the other hand, a theistic perspective allows room for hope. It suggests that finitude, death, and evil are not the final words. Theism posits the hope that "an ideal order . . . shall be permanently preserved." It asserts that because of God's presence "tragedy is only provisional and partial, and shipwreck and dissolution [are] not the absolutely final things."

It is not enough for us, however, simply to specify differences in meaning or to discover that some disputes are merely verbal. We also need to know the truth or falsity of our claims. James held that an examination of the concept of truth itself can help us in this quest. After a pragmatic analysis of the meaning of the concept of truth, James concludes that truth is a property of those ideas or beliefs that produce expectations concerning our future experience that do, in fact, get fulfilled. Thus, truth is synonymous with verification: An idea is true to the degree and only to the degree that it is empirically corroborated. This definition, in turn, suggests that truth has a temporal quality. James believed that ideas or beliefs *become* true as the expectations they produce are fulfilled. Truth itself is in the making.

James's views clashed with the claim that truth is absolute, eternal, and forever unchanging. He argued that thinking in terms of absolutes takes us beyond actual experience, which does not demonstrate that truth is complete, fixed, and unchanging, although experience does show that some ideas have been validated for a very long time. At best, James contended, the notion of absolute truth serves as a helpful limiting concept. It refers to what would be the case if all possible inquiry and experience were completed. But as a limiting concept, absolute truth remains unattainable; it reminds us instead of our finitude and fallibility.

James's denial of the completely static nature of truth led him to equate it with concepts such as usefulness, expediency, and workability. The true is what works, or what is expedient or useful. Some critics found such moves dangerously ambiguous, for it seemed that James ignored the possibility that some ideas or beliefs could be useful or expedient without being true. In James's account, the critics argued, truth seemed to be reduced to subjective opinion.

Aware that such objections might arise, James tried hard to answer his critics. The truth of beliefs or theories, argued James, involves their being expedient or useful over "the long run" and "on the whole." This was James's way of stressing the need for repeated testing and for obtaining consistency and coherence among all the beliefs and theories that we think are true. These qualifications are communal. They invalidate a narrowly subjective interpretation of expediency and usefulness.

In stating his theory of truth, James no doubt used words that left him open to charges of unwarranted subjectivism. Nor it is clear that he put all those indictments to rest. But he did challenge a tradition about truth that was not as clear as it appeared to be. While showing that possession of truth depends on an ongoing, critical sifting of experience, his pragmatism complements the other parts of his philosophy by helping us to discern and evaluate the varieties of life's meanings.

JOHN K. ROTH

Further Reading

Allen, Gay Wilson. *William James: A Biography.* New York: Viking Press, 1967. This study of James's life emphasizes his views about pluralism, empiricism, and theism and underscores how James's *Pragmatism* interprets the universe as one of flux and change.

Barzun, Jacques. *A Stroll with William James.* New York: Harper & Row, 1983. An arresting interpretation of James's thought by a creative and influential scholar.

Flower, Elizabeth, and Murray G. Murphy. *A History of Philosophy in America.* 2 vols. New York: G. P. Putnam's Sons, 1977. Flower and Murphy suggest that James's *Pragmatism* can still alert us to the subtlety and richness of experience, the purposeful quality of thought, and the active character of knowing.

Ford, Marcus Peter. *William James's Philosophy.* Amherst: University of Massachusetts Press, 1982. Ford offers a succinct overview that compares James's thought to the process philosophy of Alfred North Whitehead.

Myers, Gerald E. *William James: His Life and Thought.* New Haven: Yale University Press, 1986. Myers provides an extensive study of James's thought and the milieu in which it appeared.

Roth, John K. *Freedom and the Moral Life: The*

Ethics of William James. Philadelphia: Westminster Press, 1969. Surveying the entire range of James's writings, Roth offers an interpretation of the moral philosophy of William James.

Smith, John E. *The Spirit of American Philosophy.* New York: Oxford University Press, 1963. Smith contends that James's philosophy is distinctively American because it underscores the vitality and variety of experience and accepts the challenge of adventure in an open-ended existence.

Wild, John. *The Radical Empiricism of William James.* Garden City, N.Y.: Doubleday & Company, 1969. Interpreting James's psychology and its similarities to European phenomenology and existentialism, Wild emphasizes James's convictions about the freedom of the mind and the strenuous life.

FRIEDRICH NIETZSCHE

Born: 1844, Röcken, Germany
Died: 1900, Weimar, Germany
Major Works: *The Gay Science* (1882), *Thus Spoke Zarathustra* (1883–85), *Beyond Good and Evil* (1886), *On the Genealogy of Morals* (1887)

Major Ideas

Self-deception is a particularly destructive characteristic of Western culture.

Life is the will to power; our natural desire is to dominate and to reshape the world to fit our own preferences and to assert our personal strength to the fullest degree possible.

Struggle, through which individuals achieve a degree of power commensurate with their abilities, is the basic fact of human existence.

Ideals of human equality perpetuate mediocrity—a truth that has been distorted and concealed by modern value systems.

Christian morality, which identifies goodness with meekness and servility, is the prime culprit in creating a cultural climate that thwarts the drive for excellence and self-realization.

God is dead; a new era of human creativity and achievement is at hand.

Friedrich Nietzsche's rebellious spirit found expression in the style of his writing. He had little patience for attempts at the rigorous definition of terms, sustained logical analysis, and proofs about the ultimate nature of things, all of which in his view typified previous philosophy. Flashes of insight, aphoristic expressions, and proclamations are characteristic of his work. His ideas often appear to be nonsystematic and disconnected, characterized by conflict and even contradiction. Nietzsche did not try to explain away these tensions to make things easy for his readers.

Connections do exist between Nietzsche's disparate assertions, but he challenges us to figure out the appropriate links for ourselves, if we can. And even then Nietzsche did not want his readers to be overly confident that they had arrived at a final truth beyond criticism. "Every philosophy," he once wrote, "is a foreground philosophy. . . . Every philosophy also *conceals* a philosophy." Nietzsche, we might say, undermines or deconstructs even his own thought—not to detract from its value but to insist that we always need to dig deeper and should be suspicious about stopping inquiry too soon.

Nietzsche's philosophical style is a miniature of the world he experienced. This world has some pattern and structure, but it does not form a completed rational system. "There are no moral phenomena at all," Nietzsche observed, "but only a moral interpretation of phenomena." Life moves, and Nietzsche tried to describe the features of human existence as he saw them. His bold interpretations and inquisitive probes evaluated broad trends in the development of morality and religion. They did so partly by exploring the "death" of God.

Nietzsche was born in 1844 in the little Prussian town of Röcken. His father, a Lutheran pastor, died when Nietzsche was only five, but the family saw that he received good schooling. Greek and German literature were his early interests, and he also worked to develop skill as a poet and musician. By 1865, Nietzsche was studying at the University of Leipzig. Not only had he given up an earlier idea to enter the Lutheran ministry, but also he was essentially alienated from the Christian faith. In 1869, he accepted an offer to teach classical philology at the University of Basel, Switzerland. His teaching career was interrupted by service in the ambulance corps of the German army during the Franco-Prussian War. Illnesses contracted during his military duty left him in a weakened condition, and in 1879 poor health forced him to end his teaching career.

The next decade of Nietzsche's life was marked

by a search for medical help to restore his health and by the development of philosophical themes that had already started to emerge in his years at Basel. While there, Nietzsche had analyzed Greek civilization and contrasted it with his contemporary German society. He believed that the height of Greek culture had been realized in instances where two main tendencies had been carefully blended. One of these seemed to Nietzsche to be symbolized by Dionysius, the god of wine and revelry. It incorporated an emphasis on instinct, passion, and the primordial forces of nature. Where this tendency dominated, people were characterized by unrestrained desires for conquest, passionate love, and mystical ecstasy. The other tendency was symbolized by Apollo, the god of art and science. Self-control, measured behavior, and serenity were traits that came to the fore when the Apollonian spirit was in command.

In Nietzsche's analysis, ancient Greek life had been characterized primarily by Dionysian traits, but, after a period of successful blending, the Apollonian qualities became dominant. The fruitful merger between the two tendencies, which had been the greatness of Greece, did not last, and the result—the suppression of Dionysian qualities and dominance of the doctrine "nothing in excess"— was a prelude to the tame mediocrity that would later become the central motif of Western civilization through the rise and spread of Christianity. Thus, Nietzsche's analysis entailed that, in contrast to the highest culture of Greece, nineteenth-century Europe and Germany in particular were sick and in need of an infusion of passion and a desire to excel. Such changes might outstrip the conventional dictates of prudence and Christian morality that had taken over Western civilization.

Nietzsche viewed existence as a struggle. His understanding of life, moreover, was influenced by the Darwinian conception that nature encourages the survival of the strong and fit and the elimination of the weak. The sickness of his own society was evidenced, Nietzsche thought, by the fact that the powers in control were those that advocated leveling everything down to mediocrity so that the strong were held in check and the weak could survive.

Nevertheless, there was a chance for at least a few individuals to become something more than the stifling structures of society tended to permit. If society's sickness could be exposed, and if a sketch of genuine excellence in life could be set forth, there was hope that some unique individuals ("supermen" or "overmen") might transcend the low state into which life had lapsed and help to transform life's quality.

Nietzsche's most significant attempts to perform these tasks are found in the writings he published in the 1880s. These works include *The Gay Science*, *Thus Spoke Zarathustra*, *Beyond Good and Evil*, and *On the Genealogy of Morals*. By the end of the decade, however, Nietzsche's literary output had ceased. In January 1889, while in Turin, Italy, he suffered a serious mental breakdown and never recovered. Nietzsche died on August 25, 1900.

Self-deception and the Will to Power

"We are unknown to ourselves, we men of knowledge—and with good reason." Thus begins *On the Genealogy of Morals.* Nietzsche's theme was that even though people may regard themselves as well informed, sophisticated, and knowledgeable, their lack of courage keeps them from uncovering what lies at the foundation of human existence and morality. Previous attempts to speak to such issues reveal more about the decadence of Western civilization than they do about how things really are. Nietzsche sought to check this plague of self-delusion. He worked to lay bare facts that people had suppressed and hidden, envisioning himself as a therapist who could free his readers from the cultural restrictions that stifle excellence. But the freedom that emerges might be overwhelming. "Independence is for the very few," said Nietzsche. "It is a privilege of the strong." For the few who resist retreating into the security illusions provide, this twilight of the idols of conventional morality and religion is the dawn of a new hope.

Nietzsche felt that it is self-deception not to admit honestly that "life simply *is* will to power." He was no advocate of the democratic ideal of human equality. Such a doctrine, he thought, only levels the quality of life toward mediocrity. Individuals vary greatly in their talents and abilities, and there are basic qualitative differences that leave them unequal as persons. Nevertheless, according to Nietzsche, individuals will do what they can to assert power. Each will strive to achieve and hold a position of dominance. This tendency means that struggle is a basic fact of life. There is fierce competition for the top positions of power. If anyone falters at the top, someone else takes over.

Beyond Good and Evil

As Nietzsche interpreted the course of human history, Western culture has been dominated by an unfortunate distinction between "good" and "evil," a distinction that the Christian religion in particular has done much to encourage. Spurred by a deep hatred of aristocratic ways they could not emulate, the masses of humanity, often supported by religious leaders, have indulged in a revenge-motivated negation of the qualities of an aristocratic life. As Nietzsche saw things, the "good" of the good–evil distinction has emphasized equality, self-lessness, meekness, humility, sympathy, pity, and other qualities of weakness. It has castigated the noble, aristocratic qualities—self-assertion, daring creativity, passion, and desire for conquest—by calling them evil. The prevalence of this concept of evil, Nietzsche contended, is responsible for weakness and mediocrity among those in dominant positions. It has annihilated the qualities that are essential for excellence in life. For Nietzsche, the low state of contemporary society indicated that not much had been done to fulfill these needs for excellence.

Human existence, however, need not end on this dismal note. If Nietzsche sometimes regarded himself as a voice crying in the wilderness, he also thought human life could redeem itself by going beyond good and evil. "Must not the ancient fire some day flare up much more terribly, after much longer preparation?" he wrote; "More: must one not desire it with all one's might? even will it? even promote it?" The spirit of nobility—affirmation of life, struggle, and conquest, and a passionate desire

to excel—these characteristics need to be uplifted. Nietzsche's aim, however, was not to duplicate the past but to put these essential qualities back into contemporary life.

Thus Spoke Zarathustra

The most dramatic and emotional expression of Nietzsche's call to all humankind to throw off the restraints of conventional morality, which he called a "slave morality," and to liberate themselves through the exercise of creative power, thereby creating a new morality of individual power, is his masterpiece *Thus Spoke Zarathustra*. This long impassioned work is in the form of an account of the travels of Zarathustra, a figure based on the 6th century B.C. Iranian prophet Zoroaster (Zarathustra is the Latin form of the name) but adapted to Nietzsche's poetic and philosophical ends. Zarathustra is a vital and sometimes explosive advocate of Nietzsche's radical view of life.

Zarathustra travels from town to town, preaching the word of a new "religion," earth-centered, humanistic, and rebellious: "*I teach you the overman.* Man is something that shall be overcome. What have you done to overcome him? . . . The overman is the meaning of the earth. Let your will say: the overman *shall be* the meaning of the earth, and do not believe those who speak to you of otherwordly hopes! . . . Behold the good and the just! Whom do they hate most? The man who breaks their tables of values, the breaker, the lawbreaker; yet he is the creator."

When Zarathustra meets a hermit saint in a forest, the saint speaks of praising God. Zarathustra reflects on what he has heard: "Could it be possible? The old saint in the forest has not yet heard anything of this, that God is *dead!*"

The proclamation of the death of God was a fundamental ingredient in the revaluation of values Nietzsche advocated. This proclamation emerges from his conviction that the morality of mediocrity and affirmations of God's existence, especially as the latter are understood in Christianity, stand inextricably tied together. Nothing, argued Nietzsche, has done more than Christianity to entrench the morality of mediocrity in human consciousness. In Nietzsche's view, the Christian emphasis on love extols qualities of weakness. Christianity urges that it is our responsibility to cultivate those attributes, not because of an abstract concept of duty, but because it is God's will that we do so. As this conception develops, Nietzsche argued, it binds people in debilitating guilt. It also leads them to an escapist tendency to seek fulfillment beyond this world.

Arguably one-sided, Nietzsche's critique was loud and clear: Christianity, with its conception of a transcendent, omnipotent, omniscient, just, and loving God, denies and negates too much that is valuable in this world. Institutionalized by church and state, Christian theology and morality have made prisoners of Western humanity. Christianity claims that true freedom exists in serving God, but it denies a genuinely creative freedom by asserting that the world and its value structure are fixed by the will of God. It claims to offer people release from sin and guilt, but it does so at the expense of reducing them to mediocrity. Christianity advances a doctrine of love and charity, but this teaching actually rests on a feeling of hatred and revenge directed toward the qualities of nobility.

Nietzsche did not deny that the long dominance of the Christian faith is a real manifestation of the will to power and that certain individuals have revealed unusual qualities of strength in establishing Christianity's authority. But he was convinced that the result has been to place an inferior breed in control of life. By proclaiming that God is dead, Nietzsche believed the underpinning of Christian morality might be eliminated, thus making it less difficult to move beyond our conventional understanding of good and evil.

The issue of God's existence, believed Nietzsche, is more psychological than metaphysical. Belief in God is a tool used to distort the facts of life and to attack and to bring to submission individuals of noble character. Nietzsche's aim was not so much to prove or disprove the existence of God but to show that belief in God can create a sickness. He wanted to convince people that the highest achievements in human life depend on the elimination of this belief.

Nietzsche, then, assumed that God does not exist and concentrated on what he took to be the psychotherapeutic task of freeing people from the idea that they are dependent on God.

The Madman

If one argues that Nietzsche's philosophy begs the question of God's existence, Nietzsche is not without a powerful rebuttal. His is not a logical disproof of God's reality but an appraisal of human experience, which notes that, from a functional point of view, the credibility of God's existence is crumbling. Nietzsche advanced this argument in his 1882 book, *The Gay Science.* There he spoke of "a madman" who runs into a marketplace crying incessantly, "I seek God! I seek God!" This action provokes laughter from the men in the marketplace, who, Nietzsche reports, do not believe in God. In jest, they ask the madman whether God is lost, hiding, or traveling on a voyage. But with piercing vision, the madman confronts his tormentors with this announcement: "God is dead. God remains dead. And we have killed him."

Significantly, Nietzsche's story involves both people who do not believe in God and the claim that people have killed God. Although nineteenth-century Europe was still dominated by Christian concepts, Nietzsche believed that the strength of Christianity was far less than it had been. People professed to be Christians and to have faith in God, but their confessions were habitual responses that lacked depth and authenticity. Nietzsche argued that developments in science and technology had eroded the idea of human dependence on God. Although those developments had not succeeded in eliminating the mediocrity that Nietzsche so much deplored, they were creating signs of a new trust in human power, and the possibility of progress through human efforts could be discerned. Philosophical critiques of theological arguments and the ever-present conflict between the presence of unmerited suffering and the assertion of God's omnipotence and goodness were also taking their toll on religious belief. Thus, a combination of factors were turning attention away from God and toward humanity and its world. Functionally speaking, this change of outlook constituted what Nietzsche so dramatically called the "death of God" in Western civilization.

If people in the nineteenth century already lived in a world largely devoid of God, Nietzsche doubted that they realized it completely. Those who hear the madman's announcement stare at him in astonishment. These men, who are really Nietzsche's contemporaries, do not give God a place of importance. They have put God to death, but they lack a full awareness of the meaning of this fact and its significance. The madman, who sees the awesome possibilities of God's death far better than do the men in the marketplace—and thus grasps with an uncommon intensity what it might mean to seek God in a godless world—puts his point this way: "Lightning and thunder require time, the light of the stars requires time, deeds require time even after they are done, before they can be seen and heard. This deed is still more distant from them than the most distant stars—*and yet they have done it themselves.*" The madman believes that he has come before his time. People have killed God, but they are not yet ready to confront this fact and its importance.

The death of God is an awesome matter, as Nietzsche's madman understands and underscores when he asks, "What did we do when we unchained this earth from its sun?" In a series of rhetorical questions, he suggests that the death of God leaves us disoriented and in darkness. "Is there any up or down left? Are we not straying as through an infinite nothing? Do we not feel the breath of empty space? Has it not become colder? Is not night and more night coming on all the while? Must not lanterns be lit in the morning?"

Nietzsche's appraisal, though, was not that this dizzying instability should be the occasion for despair and sorrow. On the contrary, the death of God, however disorienting it may be, is an occasion to affirm life. It signifies a release, a new awareness of freedom and responsibility, and an opportunity for creative action. This situation, Nietzsche acknowledged, is full of uncertainties. It is not clear how people will react when made to understand that God is dead. There is no guarantee that they will take excellent advantage of the new freedom and opportunity for creativity available in a world where God's control is absent. Nevertheless, Nietzsche retained a guarded optimism: "At long last the horizon appears free again to us, even granted that it is not bright; at last our ships may venture out again, venture out to face any danger; all the daring of the lover of knowledge is permitted again; the sea, *our* sea, lies open again; perhaps there has never yet been such an 'open sea.' "

Nietzsche's philosophy places strong demands on those who would live by it. He urged such people to consider that life is an eternal recurrence. Therefore, one ought to choose so there would be no need for regret. The goal would be to act so that, if we were confronted by an identical situation an infinite number of times, we could honestly say that we would do nothing differently. Nietzsche found that life is not without rhyme or reason. But, he contended, "we invented the concept 'purpose.' In reality purpose is *lacking.*" Human consciousness seems to exist for no purpose that transcends itself, and there is no rationality that adequately answers every question "Why?" Yet, affirms Nietzsche, if we live as far as possible with an honesty that moves beyond self-deception, life can have the meaning we give it.

JOHN K. ROTH

Further Reading

Hayman, Ronald. *Nietzsche: A Critical Life.* New York: Oxford University Press, 1980. Hayman's biographical approach stresses the critical theory that Nietzsche helped to develop.

Heller, Erich. *The Importance of Nietzsche: Ten Es-* says. Chicago: University of Chicago Press, 1988. An eminent Nietzsche scholar appraises Nietzsche's work.

Kaufmann, Walter. *Nietzsche: Philosopher, Psychologist, Antichrist.* Princeton, N.J.: Princeton

University Press, 1950, 1974. Authored by an eminent scholar who did much to make Nietzsche's thought accessible to English-speaking audiences, this book remains one of the standard interpretations of the German thinker's entire body of work.

Koelb, Clayton, ed. *Nietzsche as Postmodernist: Essays Pro and Contra.* Albany: State University of New York Press, 1990. Distinguished contemporary scholars appraise how Nietzsche's thought clarifies or complicates the debate about what philosophy is and how it works.

Krell, David Farrell, and David C. Wood, eds. *Exceedingly Nietzsche: Aspects of Contemporary Nietzsche Interpretation.* New York: Routledge, 1988. Contemporary scholars discuss and appraise Nietzsche's work and its significance for late twentieth-century life and thought.

Magnus, Bernd. *Nietzsche's Existential Imperative.* Bloomington: Indiana University Press, 1978. This helpful account of Nietzsche's philosophy focuses on *Thus Spoke Zarathustra* and emphasizes Nietzsche's theory of eternal recurrence.

Nehamas, Alexander. *Nietzsche: Life as Literature.* Cambridge, Mass.: Harvard University Press, 1985. Nehamas's interpretation is one of the most influential in recent Nietzsche scholarship.

Schacht, Richard. *Nietzsche.* London: Routledge, 1983. A detailed and penetrating critical study of Nietzsche's philosophy.

Solomon, Robert C., ed. *Nietzsche: A Collection of Critical Essays.* Garden City, N.Y.: Anchor Press/Doubleday, 1973. This volume contains more than twenty essays—each one by a distinguished author—on various aspects of Nietzsche's thought.

SIGMUND FREUD

Born: 1856, Freiberg in Moravia (formerly Austria, now Czechoslovakia)
Died: 1939, London, England
Major Works: *Studies in Hysteria* (first German edition, 1895), *The Interpretation of Dreams* (first German edition published 1899, dated 1900), *Five Lectures on Psychoanalysis* (first English edition, 1910), *Beyond the Pleasure Principle* (first German edition, 1920), *Group Psychology and the Analysis of the Ego* (first German edition, 1921), *The Ego and the Id* (first German edition, 1923), *The Future of an Illusion* (first German edition, 1927), *Civilization and its Discontents* (first German edition, 1929–30)

Major Ideas

Human behavior is the result of both heredity and environment.

By means of the techniques of free association and analysis of symbols, we may learn about the structure and functioning of self.

The model of self should be constructed in terms of the "id" (which represents drives), the "ego" (which represents reason), and the "superego" (which represents conscience-restraints or self-judgment).

The two principles of mental functioning are survival and pleasure.

Fundamental human drives—eros and thanatos—that arise in the unconscious are expressions of the id; the successful repression of id impulses is called "sublimation," which is a prerequisite of civilization.

Infant behavior exhibits primitive sexuality; the roots of neurosis or intrapsychic conflict lie in infant experience.

Children may feel both jealousy and hostility toward one parent and love for the other (Oedipal complex).

Motivations originate from unconscious wishes; conflict between these wishes is expressed in both normal and pathological behavior.

Dreams are disguised representations of repressed wishes; the manifest appearances of dream-images can disguise latent wishes.

In recent times, Sigmund Freud has been narrowly associated with the concept of human sexuality. Nevertheless, he remains one of the most influential twentieth-century thinkers of the Western world. His concepts of drive, libido, psychosis, and "psychoanalysis" (a term he first used in a paper published on March 30, 1896) have so pervaded our ways of thinking that it is difficult to imagine interpreting a world that is not structured by these concepts. Yet Freud began to develop his "new science of psychoanalysis" only after the age of thirty.

The Early Years: The Development of Psychoanalysis

During most of Freud's college years, while under the strong influence of a school friend, he intended to study law and to engage in solving societal prob-

lems. At the same time, he was attracted to Darwin's theories of nature and evolution, because he believed that they would greatly increase an understanding of the world. It was not until late in his senior year, after he had heard Professor Carl Brühl read an essay on nature, that Freud decided to enter medical school. Thus in the autumn of 1873, at the age of seventeen, he enrolled in Vienna's university, where, letting his strong curiosity lead his choices whenever possible, he pursued a wide range of courses. Although Freud himself said that he curbed a youthful tendency to speculate, he did attend Franz Brentano's seminar in philosophy and another on Aristotle's logic.

In 1877, Freud joined the Physiological Institute of Ernst Brücke, his professor in a course entitled "The Physiology of Voice and Speech," at the University of Vienna. (Brücke, Freud later said, had been his most important teacher.) While working in the physiology laboratory, Freud engaged in research projects that yielded what were then major discoveries, for example, the demonstration that the cells of the nervous system of lower animals are continuous in nature with those of higher animals. This finding contradicted the accepted view that there exists a fundamental difference in kind and nature between the systems of lower and higher animals. Freud continued his investigations in Brücke's Institute even after graduation from the university.

During the summer of 1879, Freud was called upon to complete a year of obligatory military service. He was able to endure it by translating four essays by John Stuart Mill from his collected works. These writings formed one of the five books by the same author that Freud eventually would render into German. His former professor, Franz Brentano, had recommended Freud to Theodor Gomperz, editor of the German collection of Mill's works.

Two years later, in 1881, Freud graduated from medical school and held the position of demonstrator from May 1881 to July 1882. Because of his poor financial resources and at Professor Brücke's urging Freud then began his training at the Vienna General Hospital. If finances had permitted, however, he would have preferred a career in pure research. Freud's medical internship was in surgery, internal medicine, dermatology, and psychiatry under Theodor Meynert. It was from his study of "Meynert's Amentia" (acute hallucinatory psychosis) that Freud gained the concept of "wish-fulfillment," which he was to apply to dream analysis and to the functioning of the unconscious mind. While at Vienna's General Hospital, Freud continued to study the anatomy of the brain and also wrote papers on diseases of the nervous system.

In 1884, he began his research on cocaine. After a few years of experimentation, Freud became very enthusiastic about its capacity to alleviate depression, fatigue, and even to cure morphine addiction. For a brief period Freud himself ingested cocaine regularly, but apparently never felt its habit-forming powers. Nevertheless, by 1886, widespread cases of such addiction were reported; and the following year Freud felt compelled to respond to criticisms of his earlier recommendation that it be used to treat morphine addiction: First, when he had initiated his experiments there were no known cases of cocaine addiction, and habit formation was assumed due to the patient's character rather than to substances ingested; and second, the variable that determined addiction consisted of the lability of cerebral blood vessels.

One year after he had begun his research on cocaine, Freud was appointed *privatdozent*. Aided by a small grant, he went to Paris to study under the neurologist Jean-Martin Charcot. Freud worked in the Salpêtrière hospital, where Charcot was applying hypnotism to the treatment of hysteria as well as other functional diseases. By means of a thorough and systematic study, Charcot showed that hysteria manifests itself in a variety of forms in both the male and female sex. At this time, the proposal that males also exhibit hysterical symptoms was a highly controversial one. Moreover, Charcot held that such physical disorders derive from a psychological origin. Freud remained in Paris for about a year as a pupil and translator of Charcot's works, and this experience strengthened his determination to investigate hysteria from a psychological point of view.

Freud returned to Vienna by way of Berlin and Adolf Baginsky's clinic, where for some weeks he studied children's diseases. Upon resigning from his position at Vienna's General Hospital, he opened a private practice and married Martha Bernays. Subsequently, Josef Breuer, a Viennese physician and internist whom Freud had met while he was working at the Institute of Physiology, told him of his success in curing symptoms of hysteria through recollection and subsequent catharsis. Later Freud would write that from the beginning he employed hypnosis not only to give therapeutic suggestions but also to trace the history of such symptoms. Appropriately, Freud's first book on the aphasias, published in 1891, was dedicated to Breuer. It includes the most valuable of Freud's neurological writings; its excellent organization and clarity resemble his later work. By this time Freud was already thirty-five years old.

The Case of Anna O

In mid-November of 1882, Breuer told Freud about a patient, Anna O (Bertha Pappenheim), whose complaints included paralysis of limbs, disturbances of sound and sight, an inability to ingest food, and a nervous cough. Treatment of her case began in December 1880, and concluded under somewhat unusual circumstances in June of 1882. Freud was disappointed that hypnotic suggestion had not been fully successful for this patient. On one occasion after she had related in great detail the circumstance under which a symptom first appeared, it suddenly disappeared. The patient then tried what she described as the "talking cure" or "chimney sweeping" with each of her disorders until they all had vanished. Unfortunately, however, Breuer's interest in his patient eventually provoked problems with his wife; perhaps because of guilt and caring for the latter, he ended the treatment. On the very evening after he had terminated his case, Anna O suffered a hysterical childbirth (pseudocyesis). Dr. Breuer temporarily calmed her through hypnosis, but the following day he left for Venice on a vacation with his wife. During the next year she again experienced regressions, but slowly the intelligent and pretty woman began to improve. By the age of thirty, she had become the first social worker in Germany and one of the first in the world. She founded a periodical and devoted her life to humanitarian causes, which included the welfare of women and children.

The case of Anna O constituted the very beginnings of psychoanalysis, and its importance led Freud to describe Breuer as its true founder. The latter, however, did not agree with Freud that sexual disturbances were essential factors in both neurosis and psychoneurosis and thus he did not accept the generalizations about their essential components that Freud had drawn from his diagnosis of the cause of Anna O's symptoms. Nevertheless, Freud was convinced that Breuer's work with this patient, which resulted in the discovery of the "cathartic method," should be published. Finally Breuer consented to such publication with the proviso that the ingredient of sexuality as a determinate of hysteria

be downplayed. The book *Studies in Hysteria* (*Studien über Hysteria*, 1895), a joint work, represents the conclusions that Freud and Breuer reached about Anna O, along with four other cases written up by Freud.

The arguments about Anna O hastened a dissolution of Freud's friendship with Breuer, and by 1896 Freud was avoiding contact with his former colleague. As Freud's friendship with Breuer waned, his affection for Dr. William Fliess, an ear, nose, and throat specialist from Berlin, grew. Fliess better understood Freud's theories and supported him both emotionally and intellectually, encouraging attention to the role of jokes as providing hidden psychological material. Indeed, Fliess published his own ideas regarding infant sexuality in the mid-1890s, before Freud had completely absorbed such concepts. Fliess also advocated the notion of human bisexuality, which Freud later was to develop within the framework of psychoanalytic theory.

Free Association

Freud soon replaced hypnotism with the method of free association, which allowed him to isolate the phenomena of the patient's resistance to uncovering repressed emotional traumas and the transference of emotions associated with one person to another, for instance from the analysand to the analyst. He dated the beginning of psychoanalysis from the use of free association as a powerful tool of psychological technique. This method evolved gradually between 1892 and 1895, out of the use of hypnotic suggestion and questioning. Nevertheless, Freud's chapter on psychotherapy in his *Studies in Hysteria* is usually regarded as the inception of the method, although he still described it as Breuer's cathartic method. Freud then turned the new method on himself, perhaps in July 1895 when he analyzed one of his own dreams. By 1897, self-analysis became part of Freud's regular procedure. Its use yielded further insight into the internal causes of human behavior and led to Freud's suggestion that as part of their training, analysts undergo self-analysis. Through the use of this procedure, Freud hoped to infer the structure of mind and the forces that interact in it.

During the spring of 1895, he planned first "to investigate what form the theory of mental functioning assumes if one introduces the quantitative point of view," that is, to develop a sort of economics of nerve forces; and second to extract from psychopathology information useful for normal psychology. He never finished the project, yet his ideas on human drives, repression and defense, mental economy with its contending forces of energies, and on the person as driven by wish-fulfillment are outlined in his notes. Although Freud was attempting to establish psychology as a natural science based on neurology, he was in fact on the verge of discovering not a psychology for neurologists but a psychology for nonmedical psychologists. The physiological and biological causal ground for behavior was never neglected by Freud, but he increasingly concentrated on exploring the effects of the unconscious mind upon dreams, slips of the tongue, jokes, psychosomatic symptoms, and defense mechanisms. Many years later, Franz Alexander would investigate the physiological origins of psychosomatic illnesses and develop the new concept of mind–body relationship that Freud's theories suggested.

The Interpretation of Dreams

Freud's interest in dream interpretation began with noticing that, while freely associating, patients described their dreams. He also observed that the hallucinatory experience of psychotics lends itself to an interpretation in terms of the concept of wish-fulfillment. On the night of July 23 and 24, 1895, Freud dreamt the "Irma dream," which was used as a paradigm for his early conception of dreams as representations of wish-fulfillments.

It is frequently remarked that Freud's *The Interpretation of Dreams* is his major work. Indeed, in the preface to its third English edition, Freud himself wrote: "Insight such as this falls to one's lot but once in a lifetime." The writing of this work dovetailed with the development of Freud's own self-analysis, which was greatly stimulated by the death

in 1896 of his father, Jacob Freud. Thus, in the preface to the second edition, Freud mentioned that he had come to see his book as "a piece of my self-analysis, my reaction to my father's death, that is, the most significant event, the most decisive loss, of a man's life." This expanded edition also elaborated on the description of a dream by adding that it is the *disguised* fulfillment of a *repressed* wish.

Although somewhat shorter than subsequent editions, the first printed version of *The Interpretation of Dreams* does distinguish between manifest and latent dream content, a distinction that serves to explain distortions and conflicts that our dreams embody and disguise. It also describes the "oedipal complex," emphasizes the importance of infantile life for the adult; and provides an epistemological basis for belief in the existence of the unconscious, along with an approach to it by way of dreams. As Freud himself put it, the interpretation of dreams is the *via regia*, or royal road, to understanding the unconscious mind. All of these notions were to be further illustrated and developed in his subsequent writings. *The Interpretation of Dreams* offers, moreover, a picture of Freud's own milieu, of the Viennese medical world, and of the position of his fellow Jews in Viennese society.

In the first six chapters, Freud provided a general theory of dreams, suggestions on how to treat varieties of dreams, as well as investigations by other authors. He thus surveyed the existing literature on dreams, including philosophical treatises and psychological monographs. Although he found such work tedious, Freud forced himself to perform this research in order to avoid criticism that the book was unscientific or that it neglected important material. The seventh chapter, highly technical and philosophical, presents a theory of mind. In 1909, when Freud's other theories and concepts had begun to be recognized, a second edition was printed. In all, there were eight editions published during his lifetime, the last in 1919.

In December of 1908, G. Stanley Hall, the founder of experimental psychology in the United States and president of Clark University in Worcester, Massachusetts, invited Freud to deliver a series of lectures on the occasion of that university's celebration of the twentieth year of its foundation. Freud presented the five lectures in German the next year. His honorary doctorate was the first academic recognition of his work. Soon thereafter, the English version of his talks, entitled *Five Lectures on Psychoanalysis*, along with his psychobiographical essay, "Leonardo da Vinci and a Memory of his Childhood," were published. In 1909 two other important papers by Freud also appeared in print. One was entitled " 'Little Hans'—Analysis of a Phobia in a Five-Year-Old Boy." This essay treated the first psychoanalysis of a child; the other presented the famous case of the Rat Man, or "Notes Upon a Case of Obsessional Neurosis." The following year, the so-called Wolf-Man, a Russian aristocrat, entered analysis with Freud. This case was completed in 1914, and Freud published its results four years later under the title "From the History of an Infantile Neurosis." After 1919, attacks on psychoanalysis waned somewhat, as the fame of Freud's methods grew.

In 1920, 1921, and 1923, three relatively short works that express Freud's mature views were also published. *Beyond the Pleasure Principle* states the first revision in print of his drive theory. From the 1880s on, Freud had quoted Schiller's line that hunger and love move the world. For Freud these terms meant self-preservation and sexual satisfaction. In short, drives are self-protecting or sexual. As early as 1915 Freud had admitted that he needed to redefine his conception of these forces. Nevertheless, he then simply restated the definition that he had published ten years earlier in his *Three Essays on the Theory of Sexuality:* A drive is the "psychical representative" of "stimuli originating within the body," that is, "the demand for work imposed on the mind by its connection with the body." Two basic principles of mental functioning had already been described in 1911 as reality and pleasure. It was not, however, until *Beyond the Pleasure Principle* that Freud reclassified the drives into those of life (eros) and those of death (thanatos). The compulsive repetition of a trauma, Freud believed, "went beyond the pleasure principle" and could be an expression of the death drive.

Two other major works by Freud were *Group Psychology and the Analysis of the Ego*, his most significant venture into social psychology, and *The Ego and the Id*, which further elaborated the concept of mind outlined in *Beyond the Pleasure Principle*. Earlier, in *The Interpretation of Dreams*, Freud had equated the unconscious with repressed material, and the conscious with the function of mind that represses, that is, with the ego. Later, however, in *Beyond the Pleasure Principle*, Freud wrote that part of the ego itself is unconscious. In *The Ego and the Id* Freud asserted, moreover, that the superego results from the child's earliest object-relations. In 1924 he published "The Dissolution of the Oedipus Complex," the first paper that investigates the differences between the sexual evolution of boys and girls. This work would be continued later by Erik Erikson, an analysand of Freud's daughter, Anna, and published in his *Childhood and Society* as well as in other works.

At the age of seventy, Freud published a revised theory of neurosis and his response to Otto Rank's conception of the birth trauma in *Inhibitions, Symptoms and Anxiety* (1926). During the year that followed, Freud's psychoanalytic critique of religion appeared under the title of *The Future of an Illusion*. This work was followed by *Civilization and its Discontents* (1929), which gives a very pessimistic view of the human ability to sublimate aggressive drives. *Civilization* also includes a detailed treatment of the use of "superego," "conscience," "sense of guilt," "need for punishment," and "remorse" in understanding human behavior. In 1938, the year that *Moses and Monotheism* was published, Freud moved to England to escape Nazi persecution of Jews. The next year he closed his practice and died of the cancer that had plagued him for many years.

M. E. MOSS

Further Reading

Gay, Peter. *Freud: A Life for Our Time.* New York and London: W. W. Norton, 1988. This is the best biography of Freud from the perspective of a humanist. Gay has had the advantage of Jones's work, along with recent scholarship. *Freud* includes an excellent up-to-date bibliography.

Jones, Ernest. *The Life and Work of Sigmund Freud.* 3 vols. New York: Basic Books; London: Hogarth Press, 1953–57. Jones's work is still one of the best biographies of Freud, especially from the perspective of his scientific and medical achievements. Jones, a physician, was friend and confidant of Freud. *Life and Work* has been edited and abridged in one volume by Lionel Trilling and Steven Marcus (New York: Basic Books, 1961).

Masson, Jeffrey. *The Assault on Truth: Freud's Suppression of the Seduction Theory.* New York: Penguin, 1985. Masson's view that Freud suppressed that theory because of the criticism of the Vienna medical community has been the subject of much controversy. Gay, for example, dismisses it and refers the reader to the Ernest Jones's account of what happened.

Ricoeur, Paul. *Freud and Philosophy: An Essay on Interpretation.* Translated by Denis Savage. New Haven and London: Yale University Press, 1970. This is a philosophical analysis of Freud's concepts from the perspective of philosophical hermeneutics. A difficult but worthwhile book.

MAX PLANCK

Born: 1858, Kiel, Germany
Died: 1947, Göttingen, Germany
Major Works: (Quantum theory, Planck's constant) Collections of essays and lectures: *A Survey of Physical Theory* (1920), *The Philosophy of Physics* (1936), *Scientific Autobiography and Other Papers* (1949)

Major Ideas

The energy of electromagnetic radiation (such as light, X-rays, and radio waves) is found only in discrete packets of fine size: quanta.

The amount of such energy must be a whole-number multiple of h *(Planck's constant: 6.55×10^{-27} erg-seconds).*

On December 14, 1900, forty-two-year-old conservative academic Max Karl Ernst Ludwig Planck fired physical science's version of the shot heard round the world. It was during a lecture to the German Physical Society on this date that Planck introduced a new fundamental constant of nature. He remarked some time later that he envisioned far-reaching consequences for his discovery, rivaled in importance only by the ideas of Newton. This was an accurate assessment. Planck brilliantly pointed out the way in which the received (Newtonian) view of a continuously changing nature must be abandoned. Planck's description of nature suggested that instead of continuity, nature exhibits fits and starts. Smooth mathematical descriptions of nature must give way to statistical analysis of countless corpuscular entities, which behave for all intents and purposes in a random fashion. Thus Planck spawned a revolution in science whose effects are still being felt and pondered.

Revolution, however, was not part of Planck's demeanor. Grandson of a pastor and son of a law professor, Planck's mindset was thoroughly conservative. He gave up old ideas only very reluctantly and resisted even the widely accepted interpretation of his own ideas in science.

Planck studied in Munich and Berlin, in the latter place benefiting from the luminaries Kirchhoff and Helmholtz (although he was unimpressed by their teaching abilities). For several years after obtaining his doctorate (1879), he was *privatdozent* at Munich. In 1885, probably through paternal connections, he was appointed to a permanent position

at Kiel, where he stayed until 1889, when he was offered a position at the prestigious University of Berlin. In addition to his professorial duties, Planck was heavily involved in various scientific institutes and societies. These positions gave Planck a very high profile and the political power to convince the government of the need for fiscal support of physical science. The money that made possible many of the advances in German science was made available through the untiring efforts of this able administrator. Planck's scientific genius was recognized worldwide, and the Swedish Academy of Sciences rewarded him with the Nobel Prize in physics for 1918, even though his discovery had not yet resulted in a coherent theory.

Planck often cast himself as a peacemaker between warring factions, whether the battle was political or scientific. His spirit of compromise brought him serious distress during the reign of the uncompromising Nazi regime. He was an opponent of Hitler, but for the sake of the survival of his institute, he did not resist openly, hoping that the more radical policies of the government would ameliorate. The weight of this misapprehension became all too evident to Planck as his only surviving son of his first marriage, Erwin, was executed for allegedly conspiring to assassinate Hitler. In addition to this calamity, Planck's first wife died in 1909, another son was killed in the First World War, and both of his daughters died from complications relating to childbirth. His triumphant pilgrimage in the face of devastating tragedy has been likened to that of Job.

The Discovery of the Quantum

The young Planck's chosen field of physics was thermodynamics (the study of the properties and effects of heat), an area seemingly far removed from the theoretical atomic physics with which his name would become associated. In particular, Planck wanted to establish connections between classical thermodynamics and electrodynamics (study of electromagnetic radiation). It had been shown that many physical systems are irreversible, that is, they inexorably proceed to an equilibrium state corresponding to maximum entropy (a measure of the inherent disorder in a system). Boltzmann had shown that in systems of numerous particles the equilibrium state was the most probable state of a system and that this state could be calculated by statistical methods, assuming the motion of each individual particle to be random. One could not predict the precise motion of each individual particle, but the mean value of the system could be calculated, and this mean value always moved toward the most probable (random) distribution of the individual pieces. Further, since the temperature of any body is but a measure of the motion of its individual molecules, the advance of entropy corresponds to a decrease in temperature in that body as its molecules slow down.

When Planck began his professional career, these principles of thermodynamics were accepted laws, but no one had yet rigorously developed a theory of entropy for bodies emitting electromagnetic radiation. Michelson had applied statistical techniques to radiation in 1887, but his methods were not aimed at the specific problems that occupied Planck. Planck investigated the relationship between heat (which required statistical rules for its analysis) and electromagnetic radiation (which obeyed precise *continuous* mathematical laws). Planck thought that he could discover laws for radiant energy's march toward equilibrium that did not require the distasteful (to Planck) statistical methods of calculation. That there was a relationship between heat and electromagnetic radiation was and is obvious, as evidenced by the fact that a hot body (such as a branding iron) glows. It emits heat and light. The

quantifying of this relationship proved to be one of physical science's most difficult challenges in the late nineteenth century. In order to study this relationship, physicists often focused on an object called a blackbody, which is a perfect emitter and absorber of radiation, and which, when in thermal equilibrium with its surroundings, emits radiation of all frequencies. These qualities, plus the fact that laboratories could create a reasonable approximation of a perfect blackbody (a cavity was used), made the blackbody the perfect object for this inquiry.

However, the study of blackbody radiation at thermal equilibrium led to experimental results that could not be explained by classical electromagnetic theory. It was known that the energy of an emission from the blackbody at any wavelength is proportional to that wavelength. Classical theory predicted that as the wavelength increased, the energy emission tended toward zero. This much was confirmed by observation. On the other hand, classical theory predicted that as the wavelength became shorter (and hence the frequency greater), the energy increased toward infinity. Such a scenario is, of course, impossible, and actual experiments showed that as the wavelength decreased beneath a certain level, the energy output dropped to zero. This breakdown of theory was known as the "ultraviolet catastrophe" and led to novel ways of approaching the problem.

The process that led Planck to the formulation of the quantum of action was a combination of genius, inspired guesswork, inconsistency, and tinkering. Planck later deemed his proposal of the elementary quantum "an act of desperation" driven by his unrelenting compulsion to solve this problem. To explain the energy distribution (and hence the entropy) in the blackbody radiation spectrum, Planck was forced to employ Boltzmann's statistical methods. This maneuver necessitated the combination of ideas from corpuscular theory and field theory, a combination that Einstein later called inconsistent. Maxwell's radiation equations and Boltzmann's particle equations dealt with two vastly different types of entities. Planck's mathematical tinkering brought the two together, and he did not fully realize what he had done. Planck's inconsistent reasoning proved portentous.

The only way to explain the experimental results concerning the blackbody spectrum was to assume that the energy emissions in question could not just assume any arbitrary value from zero to infinity, but that the energy could only be emitted in whole-number multiples of a constant. The presumed continuous fieldlike nature of radiation led to the ultraviolet catastrophe; however, if the energy were assumed to be particlelike as emitted, then the catastrophe could be averted. In this way Planck's constant was born. Planck named his constant h and calculated it to be 6.55×10^{-27} erg-seconds. The smallness of this number explains why it had not been discovered sooner. Only at very small wavelengths and correspondingly high frequencies do the problems arise. For normal macroscopic bodies, the number of quanta (the name for the small packets of radiation) is so large that their *individual* behavior can be ignored. Their average value approaches classical norms.

Planck explains in his 1906 book *The Theory of Heat Radiation* that "we shall assume that the emission does not take place continuously . . . but that it occurs only at certain definite times, suddenly, in pulses." The behavior of these quanta for the purposes of quantifying the entropy (progress toward the most probable state) of the radiating system is in many respects like that of the particles that were the subject of Boltzmann's statistical analysis. Like individual gas molecules, the individual quanta were too small to be measured directly. But the behavior of the body of which they were a part could be described very accurately by probability calculus, treating the behavior of the individual quantum as random. Foreshadowing his later interpretation of the quantum, Planck wrote in 1906:

This will not be regarded as implying that there is no causality for emission; but the processes which cause the emission will be assumed to be of such a concealed nature that for the present their laws cannot be attained by any but statistical methods.

Interpretations of the Quantum

For several years after its discovery, Planck and others were not convinced that the quantum was anything but a convenient mathematical trick for solving a sticky problem. It was postulated originally as a conjecture, and an *ad hoc* conjecture at that. It took some time for the profound physical significance of Planck's discovery to come to light. One of the earliest scientists to make use of Planck's quantum was Albert Einstein. Einstein used Planck's ideas in part to explain the anomalous photoelectric effect (radiation-induced scattering of electrons from the surface of a metal). This effect could be explained adequately only on the assumption that light comes in packets of a size proportional to Planck's constant. Einstein was highly significant in the advance of quantum theory because he went farther than Planck in quantizing radiation. Planck had originally stated that radiation was *emitted* in discrete packets; Einstein said that it *existed* only in discrete packets, subsequently named "photons." Planck, who early in his career disdained the atomic theory even of matter, grudgingly came to accept, after years of trying to salvage continuity, the radically nonclassical atomistic interpretation of energy that he himself had initiated.

Niels Bohr made important use of Planck's quantum in his model of the atom. Until Bohr encountered Planck's ideas, no one could explain why the electrons circling the nucleus of an atom do not crash into the nucleus. Bohr postulated, again *ad hoc* but roughly accurately, that electrons could occupy only specific energy levels whose values are delimited by Planck's constant. In addition, Werner Heisenberg (a collaborator of Bohr) proposed his now-famous uncertainty principle, which stated that Planck's constant is used to define the ultimate limit of the accuracy of measurements of subatomic particles. Bohr and Heisenberg were largely responsible for developing the most far-reaching interpretation of quantum reality through their espousal of the "Copenhagen interpretation" of quantum mechanics. This interpretation denied the sense of any statement that claimed causality at the level of the quantum and of any statement purporting to establish the real existence of subatomic particles such as electrons.

Planck was exceedingly uncomfortable with this positivist reading of contemporary physics. He clung steadfastly until his death to the belief in the simple reality of the subatomic particle and to the absolute reign of the law of causality. The majority of physicists then and now side with Bohr and Heisenberg against Planck and Einstein, but Planck could not be swayed. His commitment to make sense out of a sensible universe disallowed any belief that there was not a causal explanation for every physical phenomenon. Planck insisted that while the law of causality and the real existence of elementary particles can never be proven, they must be assumed as the basis for further rational inquiry. Science must always recognize the presence of a decidedly irrational element, Planck contended. This element, the metaphysical assumption of realism and causality, is the only possible impetus that can drive scientific investigation.

D. BRIAN AUSTIN

Further Reading

Planck's own works exist in English almost exclusively as collections of essays and lectures. Among the more useful of these for the layperson are: *A Survey of Physical Theory*. Translated by R. Jones and D. H. Williams. New York: Dover, 1960 (orig. pub. 1920); *The Philosophy of Physics*. Translated by W. H. Johnston. London: George Allen & Unwin, 1936; and *Scientific Autobiography and Other Papers*. Translated by Frank Gaynor. New York: Philosophical Library, 1949.

Heilbron, J. L. *The Dilemmas of an Upright Man: Max Planck as Spokesman for German Science*. Berkeley, Calif.: University of California Press, 1986. The author provides a very lucid account of the life and work of Planck. Scientific explanations are clear and entirely nontechnical, making this book a valuable resource for the interested layperson.

Jammer, Max. *The Conceptual Development of Quantum Mechanics*. New York: McGraw-Hill, 1966. An unparalleled historical source that recounts the theoretical development of quantum theory from its inception through the various debates about its proper interpretation. Jammer includes a semitechnical discussion of the blackbody problem, Planck's starting point.

Mehra, Jagdish, and Helmut Rechenberg. *The Historical Development of Quantum Theory*. 5 vols. New York: Springer-Verlag, 1982. An exhaustive narration of the events leading to the development of quantum theory. The authors begin with an analysis of nineteenth-century physics and the difficulties that caused the twentieth century to begin on such a radical note. Volume 1 is especially informative about Max Planck.

EDMUND HUSSERL

Born: 1859, Moravia, Austria
Died: 1938, Freiburg, Germany
Major Works: *Logical Investigations* (2 vols., 1900–1; 2d ed., 1913); "Philosophy as Rigorous Science" (1910); *Ideas: General Introduction to Pure Phenomenology* (vol. 1, 1913); *Cartesian Meditations: An Introduction to Phenomenology* (1913); *The Crisis of European Sciences and Transcendental Phenomenology: An Introduction to Phenomenological Philosophy* (1954)

Major Ideas

The edifice of scientific knowledge must be built up by rigorously securing each step through direct intuitive insight, without presuppositions.

Phenomenology provides a founding "first philosophy" for all knowledge by its method of describing the essence of "the things themselves" as they are constituted in consciousness.

The ultimate foundation for the constitution of everything that appears in consciousness is the transcendental ego, making phenomenology idealistic and transcendental.

Conscious experience is intentional in nature, always having both a subject and object pole.

The lifeworld is the practical, everyday world that provides the foundation for all specialized activities and that must be phenomenologically described.

Edmund Husserl is recognized as the founder of phenomenology and as one of the foremost philosophers of the twentieth century. Quite apart from phenomenology's own status as a distinctive approach to philosophy, it particularly influenced existentialism and inspired movements in psychology, sociology, aesthetics, and philosophy of religion. Standing in the great tradition of attempts at "first philosophy," the attempt to lay foundations for all areas of knowledge, Husserl understood himself as offering a new and much-needed orientation for philosophy. The theme of "beginning" pervades his thought. He desired to find the roots, the proper starting point, with such intensity that he continually revised his own work. His last four major published works are all intended to be new "introductions," that is, beginnings, to phenomenology. Toward the end of his life, he claimed only to have reached the status of a beginner. This "philosopher of infinite tasks," as one commentator described him, drew people as much by his single-minded devotion to truth as by the concrete results of his method.

Husserl was born a Jew in Moravia, part of the Austrian empire. After being educated in Vienna, he went to the University of Leipzig to do work in mathematics and physics, followed by further work in mathematics at the University of Berlin. His focus on mathematics and logic issued in his first work on the philosophy of arithmetic, a psychologistic treatment in the tradition of John Stuart Mill. This approach attempted to place logical truths on an inductive and psychological basis. After criticism by Gottlob Frege, Husserl himself sharply repudiated psychologism and moved toward what came to be called phenomenology in his massive *Logical Investigations*.

Even after the success of that work, he suffered academic and personal frustration in the early years of the century, doubting his ability as a philosopher. He emerged with a more mature conception of phenomenology, taking it in an idealistic direction that surprised some supporters of the realism of the earlier work. These ideas were expressed in a popular essay, "Philosophy as Rigorous Science," and in perhaps his major book, *Ideas*. After another decade of reassessment, he published *Cartesian Meditations* and *Formal and Transcendental Logic*, which represented the height of his idealism.

In the waning years of his life, the perpetual beginner began once again and turned in a more realist and historicist direction in two final works,

The Crisis of European Sciences and *Experience and Judgment*. The former of these books was unfinished and the latter was heavily edited by a student, making their interpretation notoriously difficult.

Husserl first taught at the University of Halle (1887–1901), then at the University of Göttingen (1901–16), and retired at the University of Freiburg in 1928. He had named Martin Heidegger to be the successor to his chair at Freiburg and as the one to carry on the phenomenological program. At the time of Heidegger's accession to the chair, however, the two clashed on the nature of phenomenology.

Under the burgeoning National Socialist regime, Husserl's Jewish status resulted in increasingly repressive measures. After his death in 1938, his works had to be smuggled out of the country to avert their destruction. This was no small task since his unpublished manuscripts amounted to nearly 45,000 pages in shorthand.

His thought can be approached in terms of the transcendental phenomenology of the second edition of the *Logical Investigations* and the *Ideas*, supplemented by later changes represented in the *Cartesian Meditations* and *The Crisis of European Sciences*.

Transcendental Phenomenology

Husserl's passion for rigor led to his desire for a certain foundation of all the sciences. The phenomenological method was elaborated in order to provide the requisite certainty. Like Descartes, whom Husserl resembles in so many ways, the measure of true knowledge and of adequate foundations was "apodictic" knowledge, knowledge that is indubitable.

The way to such certainty was to turn away from untested common sense, which Husserl termed the "natural attitude," from tradition, and from theoretical speculation. The famous slogan of the phenomenological movement was therefore "to the things themselves." Consequently, phenomenology in Husserl's eyes was understood throughout his philosophical journey as a descriptive science of direct experience. Although sometimes understood

in the early years in realist fashion as being concerned with objects of the external world, phenomenology for Husserl was closer to the idealist tradition. First of all, he was not interested in what actually occurs, with empirical facts, but with the nature of what can possibly occur, namely, with the essential structures of experience. Thus he described phenomenology as a science of essences. Second, he was concerned with the way experience is constituted by the mind, or the transcendental ego. Third, he was concerned with the way objects subjectively appear to human consciousness, not with an impersonal or behaviorist characterization. For example, Husserl's influential phenomenology of internal time-consciousness, rather than breaking up time into an objective and sharply demarcated past, present, and future, describes the way people synthetically experience the present as including the "just-past" (retention) and the anticipated near-future (protention). Like Gestalt psychology, which was a parallel development, experiences were not atomistically broken up into their parts but were described in the holistic way in which they appear. Also in the context of psychology, Husserl's emphasis on conscious experience set his thought against a preoccupation with the unconscious.

His philosophy was based on intuition, direct "seeing" of the contents of consciousness. No higher court of appeal was possible than the direct givenness to intuition of what is experienced. At the heart of his philosophy is the appeal to move from inadequate conceptions to their "fulfillment" in adequate intuition. The validity of Husserl's thought stands or falls with the confidence he placed in this capacity to encounter the things themselves in consciousness and to be able to bracket extraneous influences such as the "sediments" of tradition and of language. It was "evidence" in this sense that was his constant point of reference. Husserl never retreated from this belief, although in the period of the *Crisis* he himself strained it to the utmost.

It was this direct insight into the essence of what he termed transcendental subjectivity that caused Husserl adamantly to oppose explanation of experience in terms of historical causes (historicism) or psychological causes (psychologism). He was not opposed to history, psychology, or any of the sciences, but he believed that their methodology presupposed—and left unclarified—what phenomenology had finally uncovered. Indeed, he was convinced that philosophy itself had not even yet begun. Despite such bold claims, Husserl saw his work as only the beginning of what he hoped would be a long line of patient researchers who would step by step build up the edifice of scientific knowledge.

One of the first results of his phenomenology was the insight that conscious, active experience is "intentional." This idea, with roots in medieval Scholastic theology and particularly in the thought of his teacher Franz Brentano, became the centerpiece of the phenomenological movement. Consciousness is dynamic with a vectorial or from–to orientation. Consciousness is consciousness-of.

Several ideas central to Husserl's advanced phenomenological perspective are laid out in *Ideas*. First of all, with respect to intentionality, he distinguished between the object that is intended and the act of intending. The first he termed the *noema* and the second he termed the *noesis*. In perceiving a box, for example, one intends an actual box; the noema, however, is not the actual box. One may intend a box and be mistaken. Furthermore, the noema includes more than what directly appears; it also includes what is "cointended," that is, the sides that one does not see and perhaps the inside of the box. These "inner horizons" form part of the meaning-construct of a box. The "outer horizons," the room, perhaps other boxes, are also cointended. Later, Husserl would speak of the sediments of tradition that go into the background or outer horizon of such a perception. Perceptions also usually involve fringes or shadings, where what is in the foreground becomes blurred. Like Aristotle, Husserl did not want to supply any more precision than the subject matter allowed.

The noesis is the subject pole that refers to the act by which one intends a noema. One may perceive a box, or imagine a box, or remember a box—different noetic acts but the same noema. Conversely, one could have one type of noesis, imagining, and many different noemata. Much of the focus of phenomenologists was on noeses rather than on noemata, although one cannot actually separate the two.

Another major issue in *Ideas* for Husserl was that of the phenomenological reduction, a concept that he struggled continuously to make clear. One interpreter suggested at least six different meanings of reduction in Husserl. Basically, however, one can indicate two primary types of reduction, which Husserl also called "brackets" or the *epoche*. The "phenomenological" reduction *per se* brackets prejudices that arise from the tradition or common assumptions from the natural attitude, as well as any evaluation of the way the thing is "in itself." Husserl was convinced that such suitably "reduced" phenomena opened up a new frontier of philosophical exploration. It is important to note that, unlike Descartes, he did not doubt the existence of the external world, as some have thought. Rather, he set to one side the question of the actual existence of the things in consciousness, neither deciding for nor against. This neutrality is one of the most misunderstood notions of Husserl. On the one hand, his point was that one could not properly address the metaphysical question of the existence of some "thing in itself" until one understands how to go about doing so through phenomenological analysis of the relevant acts. On the other hand, it is also true that Husserl virtually collapsed the issue of being or ontology into the arena of reduced phenomena, thus giving rise to the charges of extreme idealism.

The second type of reduction, the "eidetic" reduction, reflected Husserl's concern to describe the essential structures of experience. He insisted that phenomenology was not interested in actual experiences, in empirical facts, but in the nature of possible experiences. The eidetic reduction brackets what is accidental to an experience and focuses on what is invariant or what remains common to many such experiences. An important technique in discerning such essences was "free variation" of an experience in imagination in order to "see" it from all possible angles. Husserl's firm belief that one could intuit essences is one of the most controversial of his convictions.

Cartesian Meditations and *The Crisis of European Sciences*

In the *Cartesian Meditations*, Husserl went even further in an idealistic direction, elaborating a transcendental study of self. He still spoke of the givenness of the noema, but he emphasized the constructive or "genetic" role of the ego. One could imagine the external world not to exist, but one could not doubt the existence of this transcendental ego, which is the foundation of reality. This Cartesian emphasis on the ego and emphasis on doubt or suspension of presuppositions was rejected by Husserl's most famous disciple, Martin Heidegger, and by many later thinkers who were otherwise influenced by Husserl.

One of the great challenges to such an idealist position based on the transcendental ego is the problem of intersubjectivity. Husserl gave an ingenious, if not satisfactory, response to this problem in the *Cartesian Meditations*. He argued that each self is a monad that constitutes reality, including the reality of other selves. However, each other self is intended as a self that in turn constitutes experience. The other is perceived through empathetic pairing of an inner horizon to the bodily outer horizon.

Although continuing to reflect deeply on the issue of intersubjectivity, Husserl rather quickly moved in a different direction in his enigmatic last writings. Experiencing personally the crisis of Europe, suffering the death of a brilliant son in World War I and restrictions on his own movement with the later rise of National Socialism, he called as he always had for a return to rational foundations. In his last book, he took up the issue of history, tradition, and the everyday world in a new way. The very influential *Crisis* was an unfinished book whose order and meaning is uncertain, making its interpretation perilous. Nevertheless, Husserl's new notion of the lifeworld has been one of his most fecund notions. Perhaps under some influence from Heidegger and other existentialists, he came to see the importance of the lifeworld, the everyday world that forms the foundation for everything people do. As he pointed out, before and after scientists become scientists, they are persons who dwell in an environing practical world deeply shaped by tradition. It is possible that at the end of his life Husserl had come to believe that this is the proper starting point for phenomenology, which would provide the necessary first philosophy.

As part of his studies in this work, he came to see that bracketing history was not as easy as he had earlier envisaged. He saw how the objectification of the sciences had penetrated back into the lifeworld itself and colored its interpretation. So for the first time he suggested the need for an essential historical analysis, which David Carr calls a "historical reduction" in line with the other reductions, that enables one to have the necessary unbiased intuition. Some see this new step as a rejection of all that he had done before. On the other hand, it can be seen as a propaedeutic enabling one to do that which he had always demanded, to turn to the things themselves without bias.

Husserl himself said in his last years (in *Crisis*), "Phenomenology as science, as serious, rigorous, science—*the dream is over.*" This remark has been interpreted as indicating an awareness of the failure of his original program. Most likely, it is not a personal rejection of phenomenology but a sober recognition that what had been a burgeoning program attracting many disciples had fallen to the wayside with its founder, having been overtaken by other philosophical movements.

It is also true, however, that Husserl was often his own best critic and that he was never satisfied with what he had done, despite his hope that he could lay a foundation on which generations of scholars could build. Key elements that he stressed—foundations, certainty, subjectivity—have come under increasing attack. Nevertheless, his repeated attempts to be a proper beginner have been the fertile source of much of the philosophy of the twentieth century.

DAN R. STIVER

Further Reading

Carr, David. *Phenomenology and the Problem of History*. Northwestern University Studies in Phenomenology and Existential Philosophy. Evanston: Northwestern University Press, 1974. A detailed analysis of the whole of Husserl's thought by the translator of *Crisis*, with special emphasis on the issue of historicity.

Lauer, Quentin. *The Triumph of Subjectivity: An Introduction to Transcendental Phenomenology*. 2d ed. New York: Fordham University Press, 1978. A clear, critical introduction that stresses Husserl's assimilation of the problem of being to that of meaning and subjectivity.

Natanson, Maurice. *Edmund Husserl: Philosopher of Infinite Tasks*. Northwestern University Studies in Phenomenology and Existential Philosophy. Evanston: Northwestern University Press, 1973. An introduction to Husserl that is both sympathetic to Husserl and yet interprets him in light of the existential turn in phenomenology.

Ricoeur, Paul. *Husserl: An Analysis of his Phenomenology*. Translated by Edward G. Ballard and Lester E. Embree. Northwestern University Studies in Phenomenology and Existential Philosophy. Evanston: Northwestern University Press, 1967. A series of detailed essays on Husserl's thought by one of the most respected French interpreters. Ricoeur stresses the difference between Husserl's phenomenology as a method and as an ontology.

Spiegelberg, Herbert. *The Phenomenological Movement: A Historical Introduction*. 2 vols. Phaenomenologica, no. 5. 2d ed. The Hague: Martinus Nijhoff, 1971. The standard history of the phenomenological movement with special stress on the thought of Husserl.

HENRI BERGSON

Born: 1859, Paris, France
Died: 1941, Paris, France
Major Works: *Time and Free Will* (1889), *Matter and Memory* (1896), *Laughter* (1900), *An Introduction to Metaphysics* (1903), *Creative Evolution* (1907), *The Two Sources of Morality and Religion* (1932)

Major Ideas

There are two methods of intellectual inquiry: intuition and analysis.

Analysis understands reality in terms of stability, predictability, and spatial location; intuition, on the other hand, experiences growth, novelty, and temporal duration.

True duration is experienced only in the human person, and that duration is preserved in memory.

Memory, while being informed by sense impressions, is not absolutely dependent upon the matter of the brain.

Freedom is the personal event of self-creation.

An inexhaustible, vital impulse orients all of creation to greater perfection and as such lies at the core of evolution.

Mysticism, as ultimate transcendence, experiences the unity of all things and expresses itself in a call to universal love; this is the insight of dynamic religion and morality.

Closed societies with their concern for social order and cohesion produce religions of authority, ritual, and hierarchy, as well as a morality focused on law.

Henri Bergson taught for twenty-one years at the Collège de France. He was a member of the French Academy and a recipient of the Nobel Prize for literature. In his own lifetime he enjoyed an international reputation as the most important French philosopher of the day. His writings influenced discussions in the fields of psychology, biology, literature, ethics, and religion. His thoughts on intuition, memory, evolution, and society were widely discussed. He was known in the early years of the twentieth century as the great champion of the inner spiritual life of the individual and the spokesperson for the dynamic creative force at the heart of the evolving universe.

The Intuition of Duration

In his *Introduction to Metaphysics*, Bergson sets in contrast two methods of intellectual inquiry: intuition and analysis. They are two complementary yet fundamentally different ways of reflecting on reality. Although they both reveal something of the character of being, Bergson argues for the superi-

ority of intuition as that method of knowledge that grasps the essential nature of time.

When Bergson was young, he studied the work of Herbert Spencer (1820–1903). Spencer sought to describe the whole of reality from the perspective of the mechanical forces of natural selection made famous by Charles Darwin (1809–82). Initially Bergson was pleased with Spencer's nineteenth-century scientific analysis until he realized that it lacked a real awareness of our own awareness of the flowing continuity of all things. For Bergson, life was not only a vast series of interplays of natural causes and effects but, also, a dynamic active unfolding. Life, he argued, is immensely richer than our intellectual cognition of it.

The analytic method as used in the sciences attempts to grasp in precise terms the whole of reality and thus offer certainty and predictability. This is why in the West there has been a great respect for theory, explanation, and demonstrability. Since the time of the Greeks, mathematics has shown itself to be a powerful vehicle through which humanity can discover order. Language itself is a tool seeking to impose clarity and simplicity on the flow of experience. The mathematical and theoretical constructs are thus symbols that seek to understand the nature of a particular being in terms of common and familiar points of reference. Scientific analysis, which tends to understand reality in terms of stability, predictability, and spatial location, offers to alleviate the anxiety experienced when we find our world too complex or dangerous.

This approach, while valuable, has the problem that it offers only a photograph, a snapshot so to speak, of what is essentially a dynamic, active world. It is never able to penetrate into the essence of things but remains only on the surface. This critical method selects the perspective of a scientific discipline and is thus limited to that perspective. Further, it focuses on the elements that a particular object shares with other objects rather than on what is unique and unpredictable. Indeed, Bergson would argue that the symbol system itself acts as a veil preventing one from getting at the fullness of being. That is why he writes that true metaphysics is the science that claims to dispense with symbols in order to get at reality itself.

If symbols distance the object known from the knower, then what is needed to overcome this conceptual distance is an intellectual sympathy that experiences being as a whole, as a dynamic continuum. This sympathy is called intuition by Bergson. Intuition enters into the interiority of an object to get at what is unique. It is an immediate nonconceptual knowledge, a direct participation and identification with the object of thought. Bergson does not dismiss the value of science, mathematics, or logic, but he does emphasize their inability to understand the whole of reality. For him, the empathic identification with being offers a deeper and more complete avenue of knowledge. Intuition may be a spontaneous insight or the result of a sustained effort to turn attention to one's consciousness. In either event, it offers a richness of knowledge beyond that given only to the senses. Contrary to materialistic empiricism, which claimed that what was known by the senses in contact with material reality was all that could be known, Bergson focused on the intellect's ability to have an intuitive awareness of time.

By turning to the data of human consciousness, our presence to ourselves is a presence to our own time. This time he calls "duration" (*durée*), or real time, in contradistinction to the time of clocks and celestial movements. This inner time is our own awareness of our past, present, and future, known in one introspective glance. Unlike analysis, where the mind is outer-directed, in intuition the mind redirects its attention to itself in an attitude of disinterested contemplation. In this way, the person achieves meaning and sees at once the complete pattern of relationships, just as one sees, so to speak, the intention of the poet in the words of the poem.

The words of the poem, the natural world, appear stable and static; yet the intention of the poet, the inner life of persons, is ever-creating, novel, and unpredictable. Duration, grasped by intuition, is the organizing principle of the personality, the point of unity that underlies the multiplicity of self-expressions. Here is the core of the individual where past, present, and future interpenetrate to form the inexhaustible richness and depth of the human. This core expresses itself not in a utilitarian manipulation of the world (one aim of science and the goal of all animal instinct) but in art, philosophy, and religion. So music captures the motion that underlies reality, while art offers a contact with human consciousness. Philosophical introspection and religious mysticism are not irrational or purely emotive acts but intellectual activities that seek to make the implicit core of being explicit.

There is no time in matter, only location in space. It is the human person who alone communes with time and is able by the creation of symbolic representations of duration to project into matter temporality. Science, with its analytic methods, sees things like successive beads on a string, as separate states. A philosophy of the intuition of duration sees lived time as a fluid, indivisible continuum. As Bergson put it in his *Creative Evolution*, "To exist is to change, to change is to mature, to mature is to go on creating oneself endlessly." For Bergson, Spencer's philosophy was that of inert matter, not that of dynamic growth. Mechanistic thinking leveled off the uniqueness and inexhaustible creative depth of the human personality. That is why in his work on laughter (*Le Rire*) he argues that we respond with the social corrective of laughter when we see the self or the other acting like a mechanical, repetitive thing rather than adjusting to reality. Thus Don Quixote is the object of laughter when he molds his perceptions to his preconceived ideas and sees giants rather than windmills.

Memory

At the depth of the human personality is memory. Bergson in his most difficult work, *Matter and Memory*, seeks to describe the nature of memory and thus critique such authors as Hippolyte Taine (1828–93) and Alexander Bain (1818–1903), who claimed that all mental images are only the result of the association of sensations. The idea that Bergson rejects is that ideas are recorded on specific brain tissues just as sound is recorded in the grooves of a gramophone record. He argues that memory is our ability to unify duration so that our many isolated sensations throughout time form a focused image of a particular person, event, or thing. Memory binds perceptions into a continuum. Memory brings the past into the present so that the world becomes "for me." Memory makes the world personal, with patterns of significant perception and meaningful acts. Thus memory transcends the separateness of sense impressions taken one by one by bringing experience into an organic ever-expanding whole. Memory, as Bergson understands it, becomes the doorway to the core of the person—a theme that stands at the center of the important novel *À la recherche du temps perdu* by Marcel Proust (1871–1922).

This dynamic activity of memory that retains all experiences is limited by matter. The function of the brain is to focus consciousness on survival needs. This move away from the total picture captured by memory to the particular is required, for we must deal selectively with our environment by adapting to the necessities of the moment. In dreams, however, when the memory is freed from this connectedness, the unconscious expresses itself.

In these ideas, Bergson would be in harmony with the emerging tradition of psychoanalysis. He would also anticipate a later author, Maurice Merleau-Ponty (1908–61), for whom the dynamic personal aspect of the human is mediated through yet limited by the materiality of the body. Indeed, in a broad sense, here is a foreshadowing of the phenomenological/existential tradition of the twentieth century, which sees the person as able to create a meaningful world in the world of things. As Bergson puts it in *Matter and Memory*: ". . . spirit borrows from matter the perceptions on which it feeds and restores them to matter in the form of movements which it has stamped with its own freedom."

Freedom

Memory operates in two spheres: in a mechanical way by rote recall of those ideas necessary to deal with the demands of the present, and as a vehicle of independent recollection of the past. Bergson believes that this latter sphere carries with it the continuum of personal identity, which, because of its noncongruence with matter, offers the real possibility of personal immortality. In other words, interiority is different from, yet complementary to, exteriority; the "deep self" is other than the "outer self." This dualism, like that of time and space, quality and quantity, is the framework from which Bergson discusses freedom and determinism.

Many in the history of philosophy have made the error of discussing freedom in terms of what was chosen. In essence, this was to look upon freedom in terms of the determinism or indeterminism of objects "out there." Freedom, Bergson argues, needs to be examined in terms of duration, not space. We not only choose from among possible objects but create possibilities in acts in which we create ourselves. In freedom, we turn from our superficial and spatialized self to the unity of the self experienced through intuition and memory. Freedom sums up the past and sets a direction for the future. As he puts it in *Time and Free Will*, we are free when our acts spring from our whole personality and express it, as in the relationship between an artist and his work.

Freedom is not a constant quality, for the moments in which we fully grasp the self are rare. There are, however, acts that so project the whole self into the future that they offer real orientation and meaning to the person. Determinism is the result of preset patterns; freedom is an event that creates the future. Thus, freedom is not reasoned about but lived and intuitively experienced. These themes would be the object of much discussion by the later existentialists.

Élan Vital

Bergson's idea of "élan vital," a vital impulse or life force, is presented in his most celebrated book, *Creative Evolution*. This French philosopher, born the same year as the publication of Charles Darwin's *Origin of Species* (1859), would use the idea of a life force to accept Darwin's theory of evolution as well as to repudiate its materialistic and mechanistic connotations. For Bergson, the core problem with nineteenth-century Darwinian theory was that it was an extension of the Newtonian mechanical worldview whereby biological changes were understood to be governed by the rigid laws of cause and effect. What is missed in this view is that the universe has within it a vital impulse driving it to greater and greater complexity, creativity, and adaptability, as spirit struggles with the resistance of matter.

Here is the metaphysical vision, an intuition of real duration at the core of the cosmos. If the essence of the person is self-forming growth of which we are conscious over the continuum of time, then there exists a similar power with the evolutionary advance of all species. These themes, with their emphasis on activity, would be developed in different ways throughout the twentieth century by writers as diverse as Samuel Alexander (1859–1938), Alfred North Whitehead (1861–1947), and Pierre Teilhard de Chardin (1881–1955).

Religion and Morality

Our deepest solidarity with the universe stems from the fact that we participate in its source. Just as the dynamic thrust of the vital force of the cosmos calls the whole of the creation to greater complexity, self-mastery, intelligence, and intuition, so also the great goal of religion and morality is to aid in the achievement of spiritual and moral perfection. With this in mind, Bergson claims in his last book, *The Two Sources of Morality and Religion*, that the universe is a "machine for the making of gods."

God in *Creative Evolution* is uninterrupted life, action, and freedom. Bergson, a Jew who in later life expressed his attraction to Roman Catholicism, rejected the charge made by some Thomists of his day (especially Jacques Maritain, 1882–1973) that his philosophy amounted to pantheism. He thought in theistic terms of God as a free creator generating both matter and life. "Élan vital" was the vehicle of divine creativity and activity. This dynamic spirit, this inexhaustible mystery at the core of being, defies clear-cut definitive rational or empirical distinctions. It is only the mystics and the saints who in acts of intuition and love are able to grasp the meaning and unity of all experiences. They alone fully apprehend, as he puts it in his *Two Sources*, "the point of intersection of the timeless with time."

Genuine mysticism is the guiding force that creates what Bergson calls open religion and morality. In the insight that in essence all persons are one, there emerges in open religion and morality a world-view of universal brotherhood and love. This was the wisdom of the founders of world religions and as such they served as ideal models for their followers. Open dynamic religion and morality are clear and profound manifestations of the life force, calling humanity to leap beyond the limits of all that encloses society in the experience of limitless aspiration. This transcendence gives human life purpose and ultimate significance.

In contrast to an open society based on aspirations and idealism in touch with the ever-creating divine impulse, Bergson offers an analysis of closed societies influenced by his reading of two French sociologists of primitive religious phenomenon: Émile Durkheim (1858–1917) and Lucien Lévy-Bruhl (1857–1939). A closed society creates structures to defend itself against the awareness of intelligence, which experiences in its attempts to impose order on the natural world an unfriendly cosmos of tragedies and death. Hence, static religion responds by creating deities whose function it is to offer a sense of comfort to threatened humanity. A powerful helping deity is understood to be protecting the faithful in this life and in the next. The myths of static religion in this way offer confidence and reassurance while the rituals of religion provide strength, discipline, and social cohesion.

In open societies, morality is centered on trustful love and risk-filled self-donation. In closed societies, morality is centered on laws interpreted as the fixed order of nature designed to restrain an egotism that would, if given free rein, destroy social order. In closed societies, which emphasize hierarchy, authority, and group solidarity, intense social pressures create for the individual a strong sense of obligation to conform. In such a tightly structured situation, defensiveness forms an ethic of loving the fellow citizen while hating the enemy. In a morality of aspiration informed by the vital forces within all things, the goal is to unite humanity by transcending the artificial boundaries between persons.

LAWRENCE F. HUNDERSMARCK

Further Reading

Alexander, Ian W. *Bergson: Philosopher of Reflection*. London: Bowes and Bowes, 1957. A positive appraisal of Bergson with special attention to repudiating the charge that his was a philosophy of the irrational.

Gallagher, Idella J. *Morality in Evolution: The Moral Philosophy of Henri Bergson*. The Hague: Martinus Nijhoff, 1970. This work sets the major claims of Bergson's *Two Sources of Morality and Religion* within the context of his total philosophical effort.

Gunter, Pete A. Y. *Henri Bergson: A Bibliography*. 2d ed. Bowling Green, Ohio: Philosophy Documentation Center, 1989. This is an indispensable bibliographic guide to the entire corpus of Bergsonian literature up to 1985. Gunter, aside from listing all the works of Bergson and all available translations, cites close to six thousand studies on Bergson's philosophy and its influence.

Kolakowski, Leszek. *Bergson*. Oxford: Oxford University Press, 1985. A short, easy-to-read overview with special attention to Bergson's critics and followers.

Levi, Albert William. *Philosophy and the Modern World*. Bloomington: Indiana University Press, 1959. Bergson is one chapter in this sweeping, competent overview of twentieth century thought. Helpful in situating the French philosopher is Levi's introductory chapters, which deal with the problems of fragmentation, rationality, irrationality, and the distinction between clock time and real time.

Maritain, Jacques. *Bergsonian Philosophy and Thomism*. New York: Greenwood Press, 1968. This is the famous, or as some would say, infamous, critique of Bergson from the perspective of Thomism by a former student.

JOHN DEWEY

Born: 1859, Burlington, Vermont
Died: 1952, New York, New York
Major Works: *Ethics* (1908, revised 1932), *Democracy and Education* (1916), *Reconstruction in Philosophy* (1920), *Human Nature and Conduct* (1922), *The Quest for Certainty* (1929), *Experience and Nature* (1929), *Art as Experience* (1934), *Logic: The Theory of Inquiry* (1938)

Major Ideas

Pragmatism emphasizes the pervasive but often-overlooked role of practical activity in inquiry and experience.
The history of philosophy is a misguided quest for certain knowledge of an unchanging reality.
Scientific method, as a method linking the acquisition of knowledge to practical activity, is to be generalized and adopted as the method of all inquiry, including all aspects of philosophical inquiry.
Knowledge is properly understood as warrantedly assertible belief.
Art is experience aiming at the production of objects that, as experienced, yield continuously renewed delights.
Ethics involves relating the desirable to the desired.
Education is best practiced as the art of inquiry rather than as the mere transference of factual knowledge.

John Dewey is the most systematic exponent of the distinctively American school of philosophical thought known as pragmatism. Though Dewey is perhaps better known as an educator, social reformer, and political theorist, his writings in these areas are best understood as specific implementations of his own articulation (some would say transformation) of the pragmatic tradition he inherited from William James and Charles Sanders Peirce.

Much like James, Dewey takes as the primary challenge to philosophy the task of reconciling the intransigent conflict between science and values, broadly construing the latter to include aesthetics, politics, and ethics. The pragmatists argued that this conflict, which had dominated philosophy since the seventeenth century, was the inevitable result of a radical and unwarranted disconnection of philosophical inquiry from practical activity. This unwarranted separation, Dewey argues, has characterized Western philosophy since the pre-Socratics: The history of philosophy is the history of the progressive reification of this artificial separation. To remedy this separation, Dewey presents a theory of inquiry and a corresponding epistemology and metaphysics that are essentially grounded in practical activity. According to Dewey, it is the discon-

nection of philosophical inquiry from practical activity that has systematically warped our theories of education and politics and impeded our understanding of aesthetic and ethical values.

It is curiously fitting that the author of this revisionary architectonic was born and raised in the heart of rural New England, in the town of Burlington, Vermont. Dewey attended the University of Vermont, receiving his undergraduate degree in 1879. It was only in his last year at the university that he developed an interest in philosophy. Over the next several years, Dewey continued his studies in philosophy privately while earning a living as a high school teacher. In 1882, Dewey enrolled in the recently formed graduate philosophy program at Johns Hopkins University. There Dewey was taught by the founder of pragmatism, Charles Sanders Peirce, and he was introduced to the writings of the other great pragmatist, William James. It was at Hopkins as well that Dewey came under the sway of the writings of Hegel, the philosopher who, along with Peirce and James, had the most profound effect upon Dewey's own philosophical development.

Upon completion of his graduate studies in 1884, Dewey accepted a teaching position at the University of Michigan. Already he had begun to produce in earnest a body of published work that would span six decades and be rivaled in quantity only by that of his arch philosophical rival, Bertrand Russell. Dewey moved on to become chair of the department of philosophy, psychology, and education at the University of Chicago in 1894. During the Chicago years he founded what came to be known as the Dewey School, a laboratory school in which his educational theories could be implemented and tested. He became an outspoken advocate for social reform and for his liberal political agenda. Friction over the Dewey School led to Dewey's move from Chicago in 1904 to Columbia University, where he remained on the faculty until his retirement in 1930. In 1937, Dewey chaired the famous commission that vindicated Leon Trotsky of the charges made against him at the Moscow trials: In 1941, he led the highly publicized fight for academic freedom against the decision by the City College of New York to refuse Bertrand Russell permission to teach there. He continued to work actively in philosophy until shortly before his death in 1952.

The Quest for Certainty

The target of much of Dewey's philosophical writing is traditional philosophy itself. Dewey argues that the philosophical quest throughout history, in all of its various guises, has been characterized by an interrelated set of epistemological, metaphysical, and methodological commitments, commitments that are systematically misguided. The *epistemological* commitment has been to the quest for and attainment of *certain* knowledge; the *metaphysical* commitment has been to the location of the appropriate object[s] of this knowledge in a higher reality, an unchanging realm of "pure being"; the *methodological* commitment has been to a method of inquiry that completely rejects any role for practical activity.

The interconnection of these three traditional philosophical commitments can be made readily apparent. Practical activity is by its nature uncertain; it deals with individualized situations that are never exactly duplicable. All such activity, moreover, essentially involves change. Practical activity involves change and uncertainty; the quest of traditional philosophy has been for certain knowledge of an unchanging reality. The method of philosophical inquiry appropriate to this quest thus has not concerned itself with the inherently uncertain realm of practical action but has focused instead on the certain knowledge of an unchanging realm presumed to be accessible only through reason and pure intellection.

Dewey argues that it is precisely the radical uncertainty surrounding action, the constant peril of acting in an almost completely uncontrolled and unpredictable environment, that first led primitive men to the postulation of a supernatural realm, the secrets of which were accessible only through oracle and omen. It was only later, with the Greek philosophers, that this supernatural realm began a process of transformation to a realm of pure, unchanging being, a realm of which certain knowledge was attainable through the exercise of pure intellection and reason. Metaphysically, the realm of action was demoted to a realm of mere "appearance" and "becoming," as opposed to the realm of reality and being. Epistemologically, this realm of action was demoted to a realm of which only belief or opinion, as opposed to knowledge, was possible. Methodologically, the method of inquiry appropriate to the formation of mere opinions governing actions in the realm of appearance was ignored in favor of the method of inquiry appropriate to the rational attainment of knowledge of reality.

Dewey argues that despite the wholesale rejection of Greek philosophy by the seventeenth-century modern philosophers, the fundamental metaphysical, epistemological, and methodological commitments of the Greeks and medievals were actually reified by the moderns into unquestioned assumptions, assumptions that systematically excluded a role for practical activity in philosophical inquiry. The significant change ushered in by the seventeenth-century thinkers was thus certainly not the abandonment of the fundamentally skewed commitments of Greek philosophy. Dewey saw the significant change to be the abandonment of the teleological science of the Greeks—a science governed by a method of inquiry divorced from practical activity—in favor of modern science governed by a practical method, the experimental method.

It is the scientific *method*, Dewey argues, that holds the key to unlocking the systematic errors of traditional philosophy and to banishing the intractable conflicts between science and values that have characterized philosophy since the seventeenth century. It is method that provides the key, because although the scientific method is one that essentially connects the quest for scientific knowledge to experimental activity, the knowledge obtained through use of this method is nonetheless taken to be certain knowledge of an antecedently existing scientific reality. The method used links knowing to practical activity, but the account of knowledge and reality continues to be one built upon a denial of any such linkage.

It is this fundamental inconsistency, in Dewey's view, that leads to the intractable conflicts between science and values. Philosophers insist that there are values of which we can have certain knowledge and contend that scientific inquiry reveals ultimate reality. But scientific reality, the deterministic reality of matter in motion, allows no place for values. The commitment to science thus leads philosophers to a denial of values, while the commitment to values leads philosophers to a reality fundamentally incompatible with that dictated by science.

It is through articulating the problem of philosophy through its history that Dewey motivates his positive resolution of this problem. Clearly, Dewey maintains, it is the quest for certain knowledge of ultimate reality, and the radical separation between knowledge and practical activity that this quest involves, that has led philosophy into its current morass. Just as clearly, it is the abandonment of this quest that will lead philosophy out of the morass. Science points the way for Dewey, not because it discloses certain knowledge of a true reality, but because it employs a method of inquiry that intrinsically links knowledge and practical activity and hence implicitly rejects the quest for certainty attainable only through a methodological rejection of a role for practical activity. Dewey's championing of the scientific method is the championing of the

adoption in a particular area of inquiry of a method that in Dewey's view, ought properly to be extended to all areas of inquiry—a method of inquiry that forges an intrinsic connection between knowledge and practical activity.

The Pragmatic Theory of Inquiry

The key concept in Dewey's general theory of inquiry is that of a situation. Situations are transactions between an organism and its environment, where this environment is understood as that part of the world with which the organism interacts. Such situations are contextual wholes, and immediate experience is always of such contextual wholes. Inquiry is "the controlled or directed transformation of an indeterminate situation into one that is . . . determinate in its constituent distinctions and relations. . . ." Sentient organisms have the ability to respond dispositionally so as to resolve problematic (indeterminate) situations through such activities as foraging for food and taking flight. Human beings are distinguished from other such organisms through being sophisticated *linguistic* beings, trained by their communities into very complex sets of language-infused habits, including habits of inference. These habits are governed by norms of reasonableness, or appropriateness. These sophisticated, norm-governed habits of inference constitute a powerful set of tools through which human beings are able to render progressively more determinate the indeterminate situations they experience. Lower animals are comparatively hard-wired; they either have a disposition to respond to a potentially hostile situation or they do not. Human beings, on the other hand, have internalized through training certain linguistic habits that allow them to distinguish, for instance, safe situations from dangerous ones. To recognize a situation as dangerous *is* to have internalized the habit of inferring that one ought to flee, or at least to proceed cautiously, and to be so disposed as to act accordingly. Moreover, further experience will refine the agent's ability to discriminate safe from dangerous situations and the responses appropriate in each. It is in this way that particular areas of inquiry advance, and it is such advances that bring about general advances in the method of inquiry itself. Far from shunning practical activity, inquiry, including philosophical inquiry, *is* a socially inculcated activity. The mastery of this activity allows humans to act intelligently so as to transform indeterminate, uncertain, perilous situations into determinate, satisfying ones.

Knowledge as Warranted Assertibility

Knowledge, for Dewey, is the outcome of successful inquiry. The outcome of successful inquiry is the determination of an indeterminate situation. Such determination is accomplished through application of the culture's internalized habits of inference in appropriate ways. A belief that results from such successful inquiry is knowledge in virtue of being warranted by such culturally internalized, experientially vindicated norms of inference. The mistake of traditional philosophy was to demand of knowledge that it be *certain*, where this is taken to require that it be placed upon a more solid ground than the method of inquiry sketched above is able to supply. But Dewey argues that successful inquiry provides all the evidence there can be for knowledge; moreover, the outcome of successful inquiry is all that knowledge has to be. Dewey's theory of knowledge is thus not just another account of what we know for certain; it constitutes the abandonment of the claim that the task of epistemology is to determine what we know for certain. Of course, the result disturbing to traditional philosophy is that what is successfully settled through inquiry stimulated by one indeterminate situation may become unsettled in the face of new situations, or in the face of new and superior methods of inquiry. No knowledge is certain, hence no knowledge is immune in principle from revision on Dewey's account. Far from viewing this in-principle revisability as a shortcoming of his theory of knowledge, however, Dewey sees this as a necessary feature of any account of knowledge that pretends to include the continually evolving outcomes of scientific inquiry among the things that human beings "know."

Education as Training

Dewey's influential writings on education are straightforward proposals for the practical application in the classroom of his revolutionary theory of inquiry. Traditional educational approaches were based upon the mistaken traditional views of knowledge and the proper method for its acquisition. The child was thought of as a passive, empty mind, the classroom, as the venue in which knowledge was to be poured into this mind. The educator's task was to fill the mind in the most efficient fashion. For Dewey, the child is an interactive creature. Inquiry is the art of problem solving and knowledge acquisition, an art the child must master in order to flourish as an independent individual capable of successfully undertaking its own inquiries and successfully carrying out its own projects. The difference is subtle but profound: For traditional education, the child is a mental receptacle in need of filling; for Dewey, the child is a primitive interactor in need of developing the sophisticated skills of interaction, the art of inquiry, necessary to lead an independent and satisfying life.

Inquiry is a skill, Dewey maintains, a skill in which the child must be trained through practice—thus the motto, "Learn by doing." The educator's task is to inculcate the child with norm-governed habits of inference that allow the child not only to understand the products of past inquiry but, equally importantly, to be able to carry on the self-corrective enterprise of inquiry on its own. Only such a properly trained mind is an independent mind, and a democracy can function effectively only if it is comprised of such independent minds.

Science and the Metaphysics of Experience

Just as Dewey's theory of knowledge is a pragmatic attack upon the quest for certain knowledge, and his theory of inquiry is a pragmatic attack upon the traditional method of inquiry employed in the pursuit of that knowledge, so too his metaphysics is a pragmatic attack upon the traditional philosophical quest to discern the true, unchanging reality that is held to be the proper object of certain knowledge.

There is no unchanging realm of being, no antecedent reality that it is the unique office of philosophy to uncover, Dewey claims. It is this commitment to a reality transcending the realm of practical activity that has systematically skewed most, if not all, of the defining dualisms of traditional metaphysics, including those between subject and object, mind and body, form and matter, and appearance and reality. Dewey's metaphysical writings are thus largely taken up by efforts to demonstrate that these dualisms, properly understood, are dualisms both components of which are comprehended *within* the natural realm of practical activity, not dualisms between one component within the natural realm (for example, body) and another existing in some higher realm (mind).

Dewey's account of experience plays a crucial role in his efforts to carry out this metaphysical agenda. Experiences of situations are emergent in nature as the product of complex interactions of organisms and their environments. Mental awareness of such experiences is emergent in nature as the product of the even more complex norm-governed interactions constituted by language and communication. Experiences are the psychophysical events that result when merely physical events attain the level of organization and complexity of interaction we term "living." The experiences of complex organisms are suffused by immediate felt qualities such as pleasure and pain, red and green, and fear and anger. These qualities of feeling are real, yet they are not physical properties either of the organism or its environment. Rather, they are psychophysical properties that are the result of the interaction of the organism with its environment.

Such psychophysical experiences suffused with qualities of feeling manifest a level of complexity of interaction of natural events that transcends the merely physical. Yet this level of complexity falls far short of that necessary to constitute mental activity. Animals with minds not only have experiences suffused with qualities, they *know* that they have them. To have such knowledge is to be aware of meanings, and to be aware of meanings is to

have achieved the higher level of norm-governed interaction marked off by language and communication—a level achieved through the internalization of habits of inference governed by norms of appropriateness. Thus, for Dewey, thought is essentially linguistic, for only through language can an organism develop to the level of complex norm-governed interaction at which distinctively mental properties manifest themselves. The level of the mental is the level at which organisms develop the linguistic capacity to discriminate particular qualities and objects of experience such that these qualities take on significance. This third level of complexity of interaction among natural events is not distinguished from the levels of the physical or the psychophysical in virtue of somehow transcending nature. Rather, it is distinguished as a higher level of complexity of interaction *among* natural events.

With the development of mental abilities, qualities of experience come to signify qualitative differences in objects and events, differences that have import for yet other objects and events that have occurred or have yet to occur. In short, qualities come to mean something for humans: A red traffic light means stop or suffer the consequences. As qualitative experience becomes more meaningful, more funded with significance, it becomes, as a result, subject to a greater degree of control by the individual whose experience it is. Knowing whether an experienced situation is dangerous rather than joyful, whether it is populated with objects that are explosive rather than edible, is what allows us to render indeterminate situations determinate through inquiry and intelligent action.

Situations as immediately experienced are qualitatively unique and incapable of duplication; moreover, these immediate qualities undoubtably exist. Yet the effective control of such qualitatively rich experienced situations depends precisely upon the determination of those qualities of experienced situations that *are* duplicable and repeatable. It is the identification of these features that facilitates comparison, the discovery of hidden relationships, and the identification of regularities: features that allow for greater predictive control of situations. The systematic search for such hidden relationships and regularities is the office of scientific inquiry.

Science, Dewey argues, systematically ignores much of the immediate *qualitative* nature of experience to allow for the discovery of patterns and relationships among objects that are more susceptible to *quantitative* relation and comparison. Science, in short, looks for general quantitative interrelationships where immediate experience emphasizes specific qualitative difference. Thus, to the physicist, two radically different qualitative experiences of the colors red and green are merely quantitatively comparable frequencies of light waves.

Science abstracts away from the qualitative fullness of immediate experience so as to disclose hidden quantitative relationships, relationships that in turn allow for the more effective control of immediately experienced situations in the pursuit of value. For Dewey, the qualities of immediate experience that are appropriately ignored by science are nonetheless undeniably real. Thus, science, far from disclosing a reality to which the world of immediate experience stands as mere appearance, shows itself in fact to be an instrument allowing individuals vastly greater control over the qualitatively rich situations confronted in immediate experience.

Art as Experience

If science, properly understood, pares away from the richly qualitative nature of immediate experience, then art, Dewey argues, performs virtually the opposite function. The artist is possessed of the greatest sensitivity to the qualitative richness of immediate experience. The process of artistic creation is an experience through which the artist adds to his materials properties and efficacies that they did not possess in their earlier state. Art, for Dewey, is a mode of practice (both a "doing" and an "undergoing"). More specifically, art is the term for modes of practice that are productive of objects and ends affording continuously renewed delights. The object or goal of artistic activity, whether it be a painting, a musical score, a house, or even a scientific discovery, is an end-in-view, the aesthetic perception of which provides a plan to be undertaken by the artist in action. The end-in-view is present at each stage of the process as the meaning of the process. Only with such an end-in-view, however obscure, informing the creative activity does the realized object (except through sheer coincidence) constitute an object of aesthetic value, a source of heretofore undisclosed meanings and possibilities.

Ethics: The Desired and the Desirable

Traditional philosophy provides a particularly unsatisfactory account of ethical value. The fundamental question of ethics is "How can I decide what I should do?" On traditional accounts, the task of answering this question, of determining what it is desirable to do, is relegated to the realm of certain knowledge accessible only through reason. Determinations of desirability are thereby disconnected, perversely, from the desires that lead to practical action. This disconnection renders such accounts incapable either of providing a satisfactory account of the metaphysical status of values, or of responding to the question "Why should I be moral?" Dewey's theory of inquiry, through connecting knowledge to practical action, simultaneously reconnects desire to determinations of desirability. For Dewey, to have a desire is both to experience, through application of the appropriate inferential norms, a situation as lacking in some determinate respect, and to tentatively project and endorse as warranted by such norms an end-in-view of which the enacting will redress the lack. Clearly, one's desires are for what is desirable only if one is warranted in claiming that there is a lack in the particular situation and if the projected end-in-view is the best way, all other things considered, to redress that lack. Such a determination clearly involves a determination of whether the particular end-in-view conflicts with the agent's other warranted ends-in-view. A person can desire what is not desirable if his projected end-in-view is not appropriate for redressing what is lacking in his situation, just as a person can believe what is not believable if his belief is not in fact warranted in the given situation. Just as the believable, what it is warranted to believe, is the outcome of successful inquiry into what to believe, so too the desirable is the result of successful inquiry into what to do. In place of the radical disconnection between the desired and the desirable, Dewey offers an intrinsic connection, a connection he believes simply explains away many of the intransigent problems that have plagued ethical theory. Moreover, the fundamental conflict between science and values, the conflict that Dewey believes has dominated philosophy since the seventeenth century, is largely resolved. The conflict arose because science was thought to mandate one account of ultimate reality, while values were thought to mandate an incompatible account of ultimate reality accessible only through a different method of inquiry. Dewey has demonstrated, however, that the method of inquiry appropriate for ethical values is simply an extension of that appropriate for science. Moreover, since neither science nor values, properly understood, involves any claim concerning a transcendent reality, the question of incompatible realities simply does not arise.

Philosophy, Dewey argues, is less than has been thought: It is not, properly understood, a quest for *certain* knowledge of an *ultimate* reality. But because philosophy is less, it is more—more relevant to understanding both the world in which humans live, and how to make that world better. Dewey demonstrates this relevance in his writings through tracing the impact of this philosophical reorientation on education, ethics, and politics. But Dewey does something much more. Perhaps not since Socrates himself has a philosopher demonstrated the relevance of his philosophy through his actions. Dewey's was a life not of mere reflection but of intelligent, reflective action in the pursuit of value. As such, it stands as a paradigm not only for what a philosopher's life should be but for what a human life should be.

PAUL E. HURLEY

Further Reading

Hook, Sidney. *John Dewey: An Intellectual Portrait.* Westport, Conn.: Greenwood Press, 1951. An engaging portrait (originally published in 1939) of both the man and his thought by one of his most distinguished students, himself an eminent philosopher.

————. *John Dewey: Philosopher of Science and Freedom.* New York: Dial Press, 1950. An anthology of essays presented at a symposium in honor of Dewey's ninetieth birthday. These essays cover the entire range of Dewey's writings, and many of them, in particular, essays by Ernest Nagel, Wilfrid Sellars, and Hook himself, merit particular attention.

Schilpp, Paul Arthur. *The Philosophy of John Dewey.* New York: Tudor, 1951. A volume in the *Library of Living Philosophers* series, containing insightful criticism of all phases of Dewey's thought by many different scholars, as well as an extensive reply by Dewey to each of the criticisms. Contains an extensive bibliography of Dewey's writings.

Sleeper, R. W. *The Necessity of Pragmatism.* New Haven: Yale University Press, 1986. A highly engaging attempt to come to grips with the central tenets of Dewey's pragmatism.

Thayer, H. S. *The Logic of Pragmatism: An Examination of John Dewey's Logic.* New York: Humanities Press, 1952. A detailed and critical analysis of Dewey's theory of inquiry.

ALFRED NORTH WHITEHEAD

Born: 1861, Ramsgate on the Isle of Thanet, England
Died: 1947, Cambridge, Massachusetts
Major Works: *The Concept of Nature* (1920), *Science and the Modern World* (1925), *Process and Reality* (1929), *Adventures of Ideas* (1933)

Major Ideas

The basic concrete entities are not enduring substances, but events (later: "actual entities" or "actual occasions") related by their space-time relations and exemplifying their qualitative and mathematical patterns (later: "eternal objects").

Time is differentiated from space by the acts of inheriting patterns from the past (later: "causal prehensions").

Enduring perceptual and physical objects, as well as scientific objects and minds, or souls, are repetitions of patterns inherited through a series of events, or occasions.

Physical causality is the inheritance of patterned energy from the past along the lines of the Minkowski cones constructed for special relativity theory.

The paradigm for an actual occasion is a complete, momentary human experience, exemplifying causal prehensions in its acts of remembering and sensing, and conceptual prehensions in its acts of exemplifying these above patterns (eternal objects).

The completeness of an actual entity, like a human experience, lies in the integration ("concrescence") of all the various acts of prehending into one act according to some one aim ("the subjective aim").

This concrescence of an actual entity toward some one aim ("final causality") is its process of becoming, distinguishable from its acts of inheritance from the past ("efficient causality"), and which gives rise to the process of temporal transition.

God, too, is an actual entity, the concrescence of all acts of experiencing (prehending) into one everlasting act of experiencing ("God's Consequent Nature"), and it is God's conceptual prehensions of eternal objects that serve as lures (providing "subjective aims" for finite actual occasions) and form the basis of order ("God's Primordial Nature") in the cosmos.

Alfred North Whitehead has frequently been called the last great systematic philosopher, and with some justification. His career can be divided into three periods, each of which is dominated by interests that can roughly be characterized by his various titles at the educational institutions where he taught and the themes that at the time dominated his published work. From 1884 to 1910, he was a fellow in mathematics at Trinity College. This period, which could be referred to as his mathematical period, begins with the publication of his *Universal Algebra*, which consists of a systematization of Boolean Algebra and several applications to logic and to space, and it culminates with the writing of the three volumes of *Principia Mathematica* (1910–13) with Bertrand Russell. In this work, Whitehead and

Russell set out to demonstrate Frege's logistic thesis that mathematics could be reduced to logic. Utilizing the new symbolic logic systematically synthesized by Frege and his definition of the natural numbers in terms of classes of classes, the first three volumes set out to axiomatize logic and to show how arithmetic could be deduced from the proposed system. According to Russell, there was to be an analogous fourth volume on the foundations of geometry, which was to be written by Whitehead. This volume was never published, as such, but the program of such a volume lies behind much of Whitehead's subsequent thought and eventually finds its final formulation in part 4 of *Process and Reality*.

There is also a memoir, entitled *On Mathematical*

Concepts of the Material World and published by the Royal Society in 1906, in this first period that is an important precursor of Whitehead's next period. In this work, Whitehead utilizes the new logic to axiomatize several alternative conceptual frameworks for Newtonian physics, and then compares them in terms of their logical simplicity. This is perhaps the first utilization of the new symbolic logic to axiomatize a subject matter beyond mathematics, but more importantly than that, it is a good clue as to the way in which Whitehead conceives of a conceptual framework, whether for natural science, as in his second period, or for speculative philosophy, as in his third period. The first conceptual framework is the standard one, which takes, as primitive, spatial points in a three-dimensional space, instants of time, and particles of matter, in with mass, velocity and direction. The latter framework, which he calls Leibnizian, takes particles as paths through space-time and defines the other required concepts in terms of them. This is a precursor of his latter treatment of enduring objects as sequences of events, life histories, so to speak, exemplifying the same pattern throughout the sequence.

Both of these concerns from this first period, a search for the foundations of geometry and the development of the simplest and most general conceptual framework for natural science, become the concern of Whitehead's second period, which might be called his philosophy of natural science period. It begins roughly with his going to University College, London as a lecturer in applied mathematics in 1910 and continues through his position as professor of applied mathematics at Imperial College of Science and Technology, London (1914–24). This period embraces three of his major works of the period, *The Principles of Natural Knowledge* in 1919, *The Concept of Nature* in 1920, and *The Principle of Relativity* in 1922. In *The Concept of Nature*, Whitehead conceives of the philosophy of natural science as an attempt to exhibit all natural sciences as one science. This is done through constructing a conceptual framework in which they all find their niche. Since this inevitably involves some concept of space and time, the concerns of the fourth volume of *Principia Mathematica* are found

here, but something important had happened in natural science that had to be taken account of: the publication of the general theory of relativity by Einstein in 1906.

The basic conceptual framework advocated by Whitehead in this period is best summarized in his "Summary" in *The Concept of Nature*. There he tells us that "the concrete facts of nature are events exhibiting a certain structure in their mutual relations and certain characters of their own." The term *event* is taken in the sense of a space-time "chunk of nature." In these three works, he distinguishes between a number of events. There is first the *percipient event*, that chunk of space-time which is the standpoint of some observation of nature. We always observe nature from within nature. Second, there is what he calls a *duration*, the complete slab of nature that is there for observation by a percipient event. Third, there are the *active conditioning events*, those events that enter causally into the makeup of the percipient event. Fourth, there are all the *passive events*, the other events that make up the entire space-time continuum of events and contribute space-time location to the percipient event. And fifth, there are all the events that are smaller space-time parts, or *subevents*, of any of these events. All events have smaller events as parts.

In addition to events, there are the relations between events. The most important such relation was mentioned above, the part–whole relation, or its converse, the relation of an event extending over another. It is this relation of part to whole among events that Whitehead uses in this period to suggest a construction for geometry, the missing fourth volume of *Principia Mathematica*. He utilizes a technique he calls "extensive abstraction" to construct geometric entities. This technique is to take a sequence of events, each of which is a smaller part of the previous one and with no smallest, then to define geometric elements as the element toward which the sequence converges. In this way the geometric elements are abstracted from the more concrete elements, the events. The other important relation between events is the temporal ordering relation, "earlier than." And since Whitehead in this period was under the influence of the special theory of relativity, even though he contributed an alternative to Einstein's general theory of relativity in *The Principles of Relativity*, he countenances multiple time systems in the temporal ordering of durations and accepts the Minkowski cones for the special theory of relativity in his construction.

In the "Summary" to *The Concept of Nature*, Whitehead mentions, in addition to events and their relations, the characteristics of events. The characteristics of events are due to the objects that ingress into the events. Whitehead distinguishes between events and objects in the following way: Events never reoccur; once an event occurs and passes, it never reoccurs again. On the other hand, objects are recognized by us because they can reoccur, or to use his technical term, can ingress into events over and over. It does not make sense to say, "The same event occurred today that occurred yesterday," unless we mean by "same event" a similar event, similar by virtue of its characteristics, which are due to objects. It does, however, make sense to say, "That is the same color as was the dress you wore yesterday." A color is an object; it can and does reappear.

In the three works that exemplify this period in Whitehead's career, he does not give consistent listings of the kinds of objects. Among those listed are sense objects—such things as colors, tastes, smells, and so forth, the qualitative entities frequently referred to as sense data. He does not use the term, however, since he is not concerned with their givenness but with their qualitative nature, their possibility of reoccurrence and their being spatiotemporally related by virtue of their ingression into events in nature. In fact, he sees his own position as putting the secondary sense qualities back into nature. I observe red there-now, where the dress is, from here-now, where I am. There are also what Whitehead refers to as "perceptual objects," such as a lady with a red dress, but such objects are both of a delusive and nondelusive nature. A pink elephant dancing on the table would be an illustration of a delusive perceptual object. Nondelusive perceptual objects are physical objects. Scientific objects, along with the space-time points required by science, are gotten by the method of extensive abstraction from events (the space-time points, for

example) and from physical objects (the material particles, for example).

The last phase of Whitehead's thought coincides with his move to Harvard and his turn to metaphysics. The introduction for this period is *Science and the Modern World* (1925) and it also includes *Religion in the Making* (1926) and *Symbolism: Its Meaning and Effect* (1927). It is in these works that we find his interest broadening into what he later calls speculative philosophy, or metaphysics, which concerns a conceptual framework that integrates natural science with moral and aesthetic value, religious feeling and theology. In *Science and the Modern World*, for example, we not only have events, their relations and characters, but the concept of "the value realized in an event." The old theory of objects that ingress in events is turning into an elaborate theory of a hierarchy of relational "eternal objects" and their potential for ingression into events, giving rise to the need for a principle of concretion, God. Enduring objects, such as a table, are explicitly treated in terms of long events, each temporal segment of which exemplifies the same pattern or eternal object. In *Symbolism: Its Meaning and Effect*, Whitehead develops and refines the account of the perception of the old percipient event. Here there are two modes of perception, perception in the mode of causal efficacy, the old conditioning events for the percipient event; and the mode of presentational immediacy, a new role for the old durations.

The magnum opus of this period is, of course, *Process and Reality*, without question one of the most difficult books to read in the history of philosophy. For this reason, an understanding of Whitehead's earlier work is essential. This broadening of the earlier conceptual framework of the philosophy of science period to include the concept of the value realized in an event leads Whitehead to adjust the notion of an "event"; in fact, the term is virtually unused in *Process and Reality*. The old concept of an event has been replaced by three new ones, actual entities (or occasions), nexus, and prehensions, each of which in the old terminology is a "chunk of space-time." The actual entity is the refined generalization of the old percipient event. It is distinguished from other events in that it has an aim ("subjective aim") and is the locus of realized value in nature. Nexus are simple events made of actual entities as their parts and have no overall subjective aim. Prehensions, acts of prehending, are subevents within an actual entity, and they concresce together, teleologically guided by the overall aim of the actual entity of which they are parts. Thus a kind of atomism is introduced into the continuum of events by the notion of "the realized value in an event," and the old concept of an event becomes a far more complex one.

The concrescence of the many acts of prehending into the one actual entity, which is an experience of the entire universe as actual and possible from that unique place in space-time, gives rise in Whitehead to two types for process. One is the temporal transition from actual occasion to actual occasion, and within an actual occasion, the other is the process of concrescence, the becoming of the actual entity, and this process is not a temporal process. The first is the area of efficient causality, where occasion inherits from occasion; the second is the area of final causality, where the various prehensions concresce into one actual entity, guided by that entity's subjective aim.

God's envisagement of all the eternal objects acts as a lure to the finite actual occasions in their coming to be. This is the old principle of concretion of *Science and the Modern World* and referred to by Whitehead as God's primordial nature. The consequent nature of God is all the finite occasions, serving as God's prehensions, concrescing together into one primordial, nontemporal, everlasting actual entity according to God's own subjective aim.

Whitehead seemed to be aware himself that his magnum opus was unreadable, and in his later works, *The Function of Reason* (1929), *Adventures of Ideas* (1933), *Modes of Thought* (1938), and *Nature and Life* (1934), he presents the themes of his system in a more popular form.

BOWMAN L. CLARKE

Further Reading

Leclerc, Ivor. *Whitehead's Metaphysics*. London: Macmillan, 1958. This book remains perhaps the best introduction to Whitehead's developed metaphysical system. Unfortunately Leclerc relies heavily on Aristotle to elucidate Whitehead, but by and large Whitehead himself prefers Plato.

Lowe, Victor. *Understanding Whitehead*. Baltimore: Johns Hopkins Press, 1962. The first essay in this collection on Whitehead's development is the best work anywhere on the subject.

Palter, R. M. *Whitehead's Philosophy of Science*. Chicago: University of Chicago Press, 1960. The work here on this subject is unparalleled, but it is highly technical in some parts.

Whitehead, Alfred North. *Process and Reality*. Corr. ed. David Ray Griffin and Donald W. Sherburne, ed. New York: Macmillan, 1978. There are many editions of *Process and Reality*, and unfortunately they differ. Also, all of the editions are filled with misprints. This edition needs mentioning because in the "Editor's Notes" they give the readings of the different editions and in the texts the editors have corrected a number of obvious misprints.

GEORGE SANTAYANA

Born: 1863, Madrid, Spain
Died: 1952, Rome, Italy
Major Works: *The Sense of Beauty* (1896), *The Life of Reason; or the Phases of Human Progress* (1905–6), *Scepticism and Animal Faith* (1923), *Realms of Being: The Realm of Essence* (1927), *The Realm of Matter* (1930), *The Realm of Truth* (1938), *The Realm of Spirit* (1940), *The Last Puritan; a Memoir in the Form of a Novel* (1936), *Persons and Places: The Background of My Life* (1944), *Persons and Places, Vol. 2: The Middle Span* (1945)

Major Ideas

Beauty is pleasure objectified—pleasure regarded as the quality of an object.
Belief in the existence of anything is incapable of proof.
By animal faith we believe in ourselves and a world of which we are a part.
Knowledge is faith mediated by symbols.
Spirit is a form of life in which values are consciously universalized.

George Santayana was a philosopher with the spirit of a poet; he was at the same time a poet preoccupied with a philosophical view of life; and, finally, he was both at once, something different from being a poetical philosopher or a philosophical poet. He has described himself as a materialist—as one who contends that ours is a universe of matter; his philosophy, then, is a naturalism (as opposed to a supernaturalism). At the same time, he argued that sense experience provides data for judgments about the material world, although the resultant knowledge is possible only through animal faith— the natural impulse to take what is given to us in the course of experience as signs of objects not otherwise knowable. Without faith, only skepticism is rational; with faith (in the existence and character of the material world), belief becomes knowledge. In fact, Santayana has defined knowledge as "faith mediated by symbols" (in *Scepticism and Animal Faith*).

Most critics attempting to describe Santayana's distinctive style and method as a philosopher make that identification between the philosopher and the poet—that is, they see that identification in Santayana. But Santayana, who also recognized it, thought it to be inevitable: One cannot philosophically present one's view of life without embodying one's ideals in that view and doing so poetically— that is, by way of literature rooted in the world we

know and formed by the spirit by which we know it. For Santayana, then, it was not surprising that he was both philosopher and poet at once; what was incomprehensible to him was that it could have been otherwise. (In fact, he argued vigorously against the growing emphasis on logical analysis in philosophy, contending that form abstracted from the total activity of life has no significance.)

The philosopher Irving Singer, a critic of Santayana's aesthetics as expressed in *The Sense of Beauty*, argues in his book *Santayana's Aesthetics* that Santayana was not so much preoccupied with the task of defining beauty as he was with expressing the "sense" of beauty, how beauty is realized in the experience of it. And when one appraises Santayana's claim that beauty is "pleasure objectified," Singer's contention becomes credible. (Santayana maintains that human beings have the tendency to suppose that the pleasure they have while looking at something is a "quality of the object." In *The Sense of Beauty*, he writes that "the passage from sensation to perception is gradual, and the path may sometimes be retraced: so it is with beauty and the pleasures of sensation. There is no sharp line between them, but it depends on the degree of objectivity my feeling has attained at the moment whether I say 'It pleases me,' or 'It is beautiful.' ")

One may find it somewhat illuminating to extend Singer's perceptive comment to the whole of Santayana's philosophy. In composing his philosophy of life (or of the world, or of reality) Santayana, the poet-philosopher, both describes and expresses the "sense" of life; he eloquently and vividly objectifies in his writings the experience of life, the sense of being an inquisitive and appreciative spirit in a world one grasps only by the irresistible promptings of animal faith.

If there is a philosophy that is distinctively American, it is that of pragmatism and, in particular, of pragmatism as formed in the writings of Charles Sanders Peirce, William James, and John Dewey. Santayana knew all three (although James, his teacher and then colleague at Harvard, was the only one he knew well); he was enthusiastic about none of them as philosophers (although he respected James and appreciated James's work in psychology), nor were they about him. The opposition was not so much a matter of philosophical conflict as it was of temperamental differences: The pragmatists focused on the practical—the planning and execution of acts, and they related these matters to the problems of philosophy. Santayana, on the other hand, having abandoned Roman Catholicism (except as an imaginative symbol) and having developed a naturalistic, materialist philosophy in which the existence of blind, unthinking matter is not only admitted but insisted upon, created his morality, his aesthetics, and even, in a sense, his religion from his spirited response to matter. He must have appeared to the pragmatists as antagonistic not only to the pragmatic movement but to the philosophical calling itself.

Santayana was born in Madrid on December 16, 1863, the son of Agustin Ruiz de Santayana, who practiced law and was a Spanish civil servant who had served in the Philippines, and Josefina Borras Sturgis Santayana. (Agustin had met Josefina soon after her marriage to George Sturgis of Boston; he met her again in Madrid after she had become a widow, and they were married.)

Because of difficulties in the marriage and Agustin's interest in securing a proper education for George, it was decided that Agustin would take his son to Boston, and they departed from Avila in 1872; the following year Agustin returned to Spain

and George was left with his mother in Boston, to which she had earlier moved with her other children to satisfy her late husband's wish that the three children of their marriage be educated there.

George Santayana attended Boston Latin School and then entered Harvard College in the fall of 1882. He visited his father in Spain at the end of the first year and expressed some doubts about continuing at Harvard, but together they decided it would be best for him to return; he graduated in the class of 1886. He studied for two years at the University of Berlin and then returned to Harvard for graduate work in philosophy, receiving the Ph.D. in 1889. He was invited to join the faculty there, becoming a colleague of his former teachers, William James, George H. Palmer, and Josiah Royce. His first book, *The Sense of Beauty*, was published in 1896 and his next, *The Life of Reason*, appeared in 1905–6. He enjoyed association with his students but was not fond of teaching; in fact, he thought that philosophy is more to be practiced than taught. He retired in 1912, having inherited money from his mother, and the remaining years of his life were spent for the most part in Europe—in Spain, France, England, and Italy. His most important works appeared during these latter years. His final years were spent mostly in Rome, and he died at the Convent of the Little Company of Mary (where he was free to study and write) on September 26, 1952.

The Sense of Beauty

In the preface to *The Sense of Beauty*, Santayana informs us that his book originated in a series of lectures on aesthetics given at Harvard from 1892–95. His principal concern, he notes, is to organize material from various sources (although without acknowledgment) so as to present a clear and sincere account of "those fundamental aesthetic feelings the orderly extension of which yields sanity of judgment and distinction of taste."

Perhaps the most important of the four parts of which the book is composed is the first, "The Nature of Beauty." Here Santayana develops an idea of beauty that is distinctively his own, if not in its fundamental features, at least in its emphasis and its phrasing.

Beauty, he writes, is "value positive, intrinsic, and objectified," and this technical definition is followed by a simpler but substantially equivalent statement: "Beauty is pleasure regarded as the quality of a thing."

Since pleasure is a feeling that is good on its own account, if beauty is pleasure, then beauty is a good and, as good on its own account, an "intrinsic good." Pleasure is objectified in the sense that it is, in effect, projected to its source: The object that pleases is seen as alive with pleasure; pleasure seems to be an intimate aspect of the object, its very "quality."

Santayana prepares for this somewhat surprising claim—not that beauty is *pleasant* but that beauty is *pleasure*—by calling attention to the human tendency to attribute to the objects of perception the qualities of the feelings aroused by such objects. Uncritical minds attribute to nature the feelings that nature provokes; the qualities—distinctive natures—of sense impressions are presumed to belong to the objects that provoke those impressions. Although we would not ordinarily regard pain as the quality of an object that causes pain, we may in the overwhelming delight of a complex aesthetic experience take the pleasure involved in that experience to be, along with the colors or sounds we perceive, a feature of the thing perceived. Thus, Santayana concludes, when the uncritical person says that something is beautiful, what is being attributed to the object is the pleasure that perceiving it occasions. To say that pleasure is "objectified" is to say that pleasure is regarded as somehow belonging to the object said to be "beautiful."

In part 2 of the *Sense of Beauty*, Santayana argues that "all human functions may contribute to the sense of beauty." The functioning of the sense organs, for example, contributes to the beauty of colors, sounds, and movements. But there are more complex vital and social functions, and of them none is more powerful than that of love, especially as prompted by sexual instinct. Spontaneous taste begins with the senses, but as experience broadens the interests of perceivers and education enlarges

the range of aesthetic objects, taste develops and more satisfying experiences of beauty emerge in response to a variety of aesthetic material.

Santayana then explores the role of form in aesthetic experience, that is, in experience undertaken for the sake of the appreciation afforded by the contemplation of objects. Here the values of symmetry, multiplicity in uniformity, and utility are examined, among others. It is apparent that we are now far from the simple pleasures afforded by immediate sense experience; in attending to form we take delight in order, meaningful relationships, and dramatic structure.

Finally, Santayana deals with expression. Just as one may find objects in the world that are pleasant to perceive, so one may take pleasure in expressions—whether in language, music, or other media—that enable us to grasp and appreciate what is not directly present to us and would perhaps, were it not for expression, not be present at all.

Scepticism and Animal Faith

In *The Life of Reason; or the Phases of Human Progress* (1905–6), Santayana began the intensive exploration of experience that was to occupy him during the remainder of his philosophical and natural life. His book of five volumes was designed to argue that the human mind not only makes sense out of experience but appraises the past by referring to an ideal rooted in natural impulses. Mind and body are one: The life of reason does not operate in a vacuum nor does it proceed by a logic divorced from life; thinking is not so much instrumental as it is the expression of the vital relationships arising out of the human animal's encounter with nature. The ideas developed in *The Life of Reason* were to receive more precise and illuminating treatment in subsequent books written by Santayana, particularly in *Scepticism and Animal Faith* and in his survey of the significant aspects of human experience. *The Realms of Being*.

In *Scepticism and Animal Faith*, Santayana begins his account of the conditions of knowing by arguing that an ultimate skepticism is defensible. There is nothing given (no datum of experience) that carries with it proof of its own existence or of anything else. Accordingly, the belief that there is an external world that affects us cannot be justified by any appeal to data.

"Nothing given exists," argues Santayana in a chapter bearing that title. A "datum" is what is simply given, presumably in experience: what we might describe as a color, a flash of light, an odor— although to assume the truth of any such description is to go beyond the data. "Existence . . . , not being included in any immediate datum, is a fact always open to doubt," he writes. He concludes: "For all an ultimate scepticism can see, therefore, there may be no facts at all, and perhaps nothing has ever existed." (The argument supporting this conclusion and the development of the skeptical position is brilliantly conceived and persuasively argued.)

Santayana introduces the term "essence" to designate *what* is given. A datum is an essence, a distinctive character, simply *what*, as such, is given: "Each essence that appears appears just as it is, because its appearance defines it, and determines the whole being that it is or has." If, for example, while attending to a datum, we were to call it "nausea," we would be going beyond the datum were we at the same time to posit a world, a sea, a ship, ourselves, and all the rest. The datum itself is simply, as an essence, a character, what it is: It carries nothing with it that can serve as evidence for anything, even its own existence (which, as datum, it cannot have).

The word "essence," as Santayana acknowledges, has Platonic overtones. But Santayana's essences have no metaphysical status; they do not dwell in a supernatural realm as the common properties of members of a class; they are nothing but the characters (*this* color, *this* sound) presented by data. The "realm of essence," he writes, "is simply the unwritten catalogue, prosaic and infinite, of all the characters possessed by such things as happen to exist, together with the characters which all different things would possess if they existed." The problem of empirical knowledge, then, is the problem of determining whether the essences can serve as the signs of anything existing beyond them.

Santayana's conclusion is that we are driven by our animal instincts to posit ourselves and a world that affects us. "The images in sense are parts of discourse, not parts of nature," he writes; "they are the babble of our innocent organs under the stimulus of things; but these spontaneous images . . . may acquire the function of names; they may become signs . . . for the things sought or encountered in the world." Driven by our animal instincts to believe in a world of objects, we act accordingly: we reach out, we draw back, we remember, we anticipate. "Knowledge," then, "is true belief grounded in experience . . . controlled by outer facts"; knowledge is "faith mediated by symbols." The belief in substance and nature is a natural extension of the animal inclination to believe in the object at hand. And the belief in "spirit" also springs from the positing of a world, for the spirit is "the light of discrimination that marks in . . . pure Being differences of essence, of time, of place, of value. . . ."

The Realms of Being

In the preface to *Scepticism and Animal Faith*, Santayana begins by saying, "Here is one more system of philosophy." But he is quick to point out his is not another fanciful exercise in metaphysics. He intends to appeal to the principles to which every person appeals; he means only to give to "everyday beliefs" and the convictions of "common sense" a "more accurate and circumspect form." He is to write of "Realms of Being," but he means by that term not parts of the universe but, simply, the "kinds or categories of things which I find conspicuously different and worth distinguishing."

The four volumes of *The Realms of Being*, then, develop with acumen and grace the fundamental ideas already made eloquent in his account of the phoenixlike renewal of animal faith that springs from his brilliantly defended skepticism. There are four "realms" of which he treats: *essence*, *matter*, *truth*, and *spirit*.

In remarking on his own philosophy, in the preface to *The Realms of Being*, Santayana indicates his objective of "taking each thing simply for what it is," and he then proceeds to set forth in the simplest possible way certain ideas that are central in his thinking: ". . . All moralities equally are but expressions of animal life . . . ; . . . there can be no knowledge save animal faith positing external facts, and . . . natural science is but a human symbol for those facts. . . ."

Since Santayana devotes four volumes to his exploration into the realms of essence, matter, truth, and spirit, no summary that does justice to the details of his account is possible. However, one may at least suggest the meanings of the key terms.

The term "essence" has been discussed above, and it must be acknowledged that Santayana's genius proves itself in the discovery and elucidation of the realm of essence: To have abstracted and conceived characters, whether exemplified or not, and then to have attended to them without any assumptions or presuppositions took a kind of intellectual, moral, and aesthetic restraint of which few philosophic professionals are capable.

By "matter," Santayana means substance that is posited to give significance to experience; substance is external to thought, passes through various phases, and is regarded as "the source of phenomena unsubstantial in themselves. . . ." Matter is what is posited by animal faith; for the animal, sense experience is a sign of something external that in action gives rise to such experience; the world of nature is a material world. Accordingly, "the field of action . . . is the realm of matter."

Santayana asserts at the outset of *The Realm of Truth* that he means by "truth" what the term means in ordinary conversation; his use of the term follows that of common sense. He then generalizes: "The truth means the sum of all true propositions, what omniscience would assert, the whole ideal system of qualities and relations which the world has exemplified or will exemplify." And he brings out the meaning that common sense affirms: "An opinion is true if what it is talking about is constituted as the opinion asserts it to be constituted. . . . It is a question of identity between a fact asserted and a fact existing." But here, as in the other volumes of *The Realms of Being*, what is illuminating is the searching account that follows, a sensitive review of the kinds and uses of truth, and concluding passages in which Santayana explains how the spirit goes beyond—but preferably not counter to—truth in the building of moralities and value objectives in general.

In *The Realm of Spirit*, Santayana distinguishes between the "self" that is the center of experience, in active response to the world of matter, and the "spirit," by which the author means nothing religious or metaphysical but "only that inner light of actuality or attention which floods all life as men actually live it on earth. . . . It is roughly the same thing as feeling or thought; it might be called consciousness. . . ." However, the spirit, although not substance, is active: It deals with what is given in the way of experience.

The account of spirit is consistent with and, in fact, an outgrowth of Santayana's naturalism and materialism, and yet it does justice to the active dimensions of the human adventure. This final volume in *The Realms of Being* is a drawing together of Santayana's survey of the human condition and, accordingly, of nature; yet it is not ponderous and static analysis. It is a creative account, literary in form and didactic in intent in that it calls attention to the liberating directions in which the spirit can move. The adventure of living and of thinking about living was a single adventure for Santayana.

IAN P. McGREAL

Further Reading

McCormick, John. *George Santayana: A Biography*. New York: Alfred A. Knopf, 1987. A thorough, sympathetic, fair, and illuminating biography, intended in part to encourage an honest appraisal of Santayana in the expectation that his greatness as a thinker and writer will come to be recognized, especially by those who will be prompted to read some of Santayana's works.

Munitz, Milton K. *The Moral Philosophy of San-*

tayana. New York: Humanities Press, 1958. Munitz distinguishes between Santayana's naturalistic ethics, with its endorsement of humanism, and his creative effort to laud the life of the spirit in its encounter with essences. Munitz argues for Santayana's naturalism with its call for a life in which ideals are so related to desires that are rewarding as to eventuate in happiness.

Schilpp, Paul Arthur, ed. *The Philosophy of George Santayana.* New York: Tudor, 1940, 1951. One of the distinguished *Library of Living Philosophers* volumes edited by Schilpp, this volume has the following features: an opening statement by Santayana, partly autobiographical and partly a commentary on his philosophical temper, critical essays by nineteen professional philosophers, both supporters and opponents of Santayana (including Daniel M. Cory, Charles Hartshorne, Stephen C. Pepper, George Boas, Schilpp, and Bertrand Russell, among others), and a fascinating section, "The Philosopher Replies," in this case, an essay over a hundred pages long, entitled "Apologia Pro Menta Sua," in which Santayana comments in turn on the critical essays mentioned above. Includes a bibliography of Santayana's writings from 1880–1951.

Singer, Irving. *Santayana's Aesthetics: A Critical Introduction.* Cambridge, Mass.: Harvard University Press, 1957. A competent critic argues that Santayana's "definition" of beauty as objectified pleasure has more to do with the *sense of beauty* than with beauty itself. He acknowledges Santayana's strengths in aesthetics while regarding Santayana's adherence to a theory of essences as obscuring a number of very important aspects of fine art and beauty.

MAX WEBER

Born: 1864, Erfurt, Germany
Died: 1920, Munich, Germany
Major Works: *The Protestant Ethic and the Spirit of Capitalism* (1904–5), *Economy and Society* (1922), *On the Methodology of the Social Sciences* (1947, posthumous)

Major Ideas

Society must be understood objectively, a procedure that entails refusing to jump to evaluative conclusions.

An important contribution of the social scientist is to alert us to inconvenient facts and the unintended consequences of human action.

Humankind may be constructing its own iron cage: Ironically and tragically, our own presumed success or progress can trap us.

Conflict fills human existence because the attitudes toward life that are ultimately possible are irreconcilable.

In our disenchanted world, violence is the decisive means for politics.

Max Weber established the foundations for modern sociology. As he understood that social science, it would not simply quantify data about human societies but interpret and explain, as far as possible, how and why they function as they do. Weber did not seek explanations that went beyond human experience and history. He believed, however, that sociology must have a theoretical core that critically links it to philosophy. The result was a series of writings—often published first as journal articles—on methodology, politics, economics, and human power. They left lasting marks on social scientific research.

Raised in Berlin, Weber took his academic training in law and economics. In the 1890s, he was a professor at Freiburg and Heidelberg, but poor health prevented him from sustaining his university career. He did find energy to write, however, and in 1904–5 he published what would become one of his most famous and controversial works, *The Protestant Ethic and the Spirit of Capitalism*. It appeared first in article form in a German journal called the *Archiv für Sozialwissenschaft und Sozialpolitik*. Weber helped to edit this influential journal, and, in working to establish both its editorial policy and sound procedures for social scientific research generally, he contributed some of his most important essays on methodology in the social sciences. About the same time, having been invited

to deliver a paper at an academic meeting held in conjunction with the 1904 World's Fair in Saint Louis, Missouri, Weber traveled extensively in the United States. That experience drove home to him the importance of bureaucracy in modern politics and in modern democratic states in particular. Bureaucracy, in fact, became one of his central topics.

Already fifty when the First World War began, Weber served as a hospital administrator during that period. He also managed to complete substantial sections of his multivolume *Economy and Society*, which was published posthumously in 1922. The war experience reinforced his belief that political and economic rivalries make human existence a dangerous, conflict-driven power struggle. By 1919, he was teaching again, this time at the University of Munich. There he gave two especially notable lectures, "Politics as a Vocation" and "Science as a Vocation." Unfortunately, his time in Munich was cut short by an influenza epidemic that swept through Europe. It took Weber's life in 1920.

Weber died unsure that human beings were capable of implementing good answers for the many problems that plagued life. Nevertheless, he firmly believed that the odds could be improved in our favor if we understood better the social structures of our lives and the ways in which those structures not only created problems but might be used to check them as well.

The Iron Cage and Sociology's Methods of Inquiry

In *The Protestant Ethic and the Spirit of Capitalism*, Weber traced how he thought the "work ethic" of Protestant Christianity and the rise of a capitalistic, market economy had nurtured each other. He sought to show that Christian ethics encouraged capitalism as a natural expression. As he reached the end of that study, he used a now-famous image to describe the future that might be unfolding. It was that of an "iron cage." This cage, suggested Weber, traps us within its confines, which are cunning because they are constructed, however inadvertently, by human beings themselves. We are imprisoning ourselves, Weber imagined, with no exit. We are doing so, ironically, through our own ingenuity, intelligence, and rationality—indeed through our own "success" and "progress." Weber summed up his forecast as follows: "No one knows who will live in this cage in the future, or whether at the end of this tremendous development entirely new prophets will arise, or there will be a great rebirth of old ideas and ideals, of, if neither, mechanized petrifaction, embellished with a sort of convulsive self-importance. For of the last stage of this cultural development, it might well be truly said: 'Specialists without spirit, sensualists without heart; this nullity imagines that it has attained a level of civilization never before achieved.' "

Weber's iron-cage imagery did not materialize out of thin air. His social scientific methodology convinced him that the symbol was right. As a thinker trying to understand society scientifically, Weber placed a premium on objective description. He stressed how crucial it is to understand society as it actually exists, which entails refusing to jump to evaluative conclusions. He would try to see how social arrangements—bureaucracy, for example— really worked. His emphasis would be on questions such as: How does bureaucracy function? How it is structured? What roles are played within it? Such analysis, he believed, could be done without deciding whether bureaucracy was good or bad. Indeed, before sensible value judgments could be made, objective description needed to have its say.

When we study human activity in these ways, Weber also affirmed, one of the most important things to emphasize is how meaning and purpose are evident in human situations. Specifically, Weber was intrigued by the "rationality" that operates in social transactions. Continuing to use bureaucracy as an example, Weber's questions would now include: What human purposes generate bureaucratic structures? What kinds of thinking characterize bureaucratic institutions? Once more Weber stressed that these are primarily objective, not evaluative, matters for the person who desires the descriptive, social scientific understanding that is needed for coping with the future.

Weber's approach had a cutting edge. The kind of inquiry he advocated can be directed at any human activity. Such inquiry, moreover, will relativize that activity by analyzing it not only on its own terms but also in a context that brings out the variety of human practices and perspectives. That variety includes different judgments about what is good and evil, right and wrong. One consequence is that, within Weber's methodological framework, no perspective can achieve absolute moral truth. We do make moral judgments, and Weber knew that life is structured so that we must. These judgments often involve claims about their absoluteness, but Weber believed that there is likely to be "eternal conflict" between the different views of good and evil that societies hold. "There is," he argued, "no [rational or empirical] scientific procedure of any kind whatsoever which can provide us with a decision here." Weber found that this outcome gives our existence a tragic character.

Some critics have denounced Weber. Not only did his methodology seem to undercut their own absolutes, but also it appeared that Weber inconsistently put his supposedly "value-free" approach in a privileged position. Weber was clear, however, that his methodology does involve value commitments. Specifically, it involves commitment to the value of objectivity, which he thought we would be hardpressed to do without, even if it cannot be philosophically demonstrated as *the* most important factor in human life. Weber, for one, was willing to follow his chosen method unrelentingly to its various conclusions. Doing so would destabilize some fond assumptions and hopes, but Weber affirmed that illusion's elimination was much better than blindness.

Another emphasis in Weber's thought was on the utility of the "ideal type." Weber regarded himself as an empiricist, but he found it useful to filter data so that clarity about basic structures in human experience stands out. To use the illustration of bureaucracy once more, Weber did not stop with descriptions of actual cases. He also drew from them pure forms or patterns of bureaucracy that would let us see as sharply as possible the characteristics and tendencies that form bureaucracy's logical core. As an ideal type, Weber stressed, bureaucracy may not actually exist. But possessing a grasp of an ideal, we may be better able to identify and discern what we are encountering in our experience.

Facts and Consequences, Ethics and Politics

A crucial responsibility for a social scientist—especially, Weber thought, if he or she is also a professor—is to confront people with "inconvenient facts." Such facts explode conventional wisdom. Among the most inconvenient ones Weber wanted to impress upon us is that human experience and rationality often produce *unintended* consequences. We intend to do one thing, only to discover—frequently too late and to our sorrow—that something quite different has emerged. Hence, as Weber's image of the iron cage makes clear, human existence is often ironic as well as tragic.

Much of the inconvenience of unintended consequences consists in their making life far more complicated that we first assume. The iron cage, for example, certainly has its undesirable qualities, but simultaneously it has comforts and attractions. What we desire and what we loathe are not always clearly separated or even separable. In southern California, for example, people would like to have smog-free air, but how many of its residents will, or even could, get along without their cars? Other solutions to the problem do exist, and no one alone will solve it, but they will also cramp someone's

style. The conspiracy of pressures that result may leave southern Californians caged in poisonous air. Weber uses a different example, but his point is much the same: "This order is now bound to the technical and economic conditions of machine production which today determine the lives of all the individuals who are born into this mechanism, not only those directly concerned with economic acquisition, with irresistible force. Perhaps it will so determine them until the last ton of fossilized coal is burnt."

One of Weber's final efforts as a teacher was to lecture on "Politics as a Vocation." Delivering his views at the University of Munich in a world scarred by a devastating war, in a nation burdened by defeat, and in a city that was the scene of revolution and counterrevolution, Weber remained true to his calling by setting forth a variety of inconvenient facts. One of those was simply his own appraisal that "not summer's bloom lies ahead of us, but rather a polar night of icy darkness and hardness, no matter which group may triumph externally now." Mixing his metaphors, he concluded that "politics is a strong and slow boring of hard boards."

Weber used the term "politics" to refer to "the leadership, or the influencing of the leadership, of a *political* association, hence today, of a *state*." Using that approach, he suggested that a key problem was to define a state. Pointing out the first of several inconvenient facts, Weber asserted that "sociologically, the state cannot be defined in terms of its ends." Sociologically speaking, political regimes have multiple aims. It is impossible to define what a state is by focusing on its objectives. That inconvenience, however, does not mean that the state is beyond definition, although the possible definition turned out to present yet another inconvenient fact. One could define "the modern state sociologically," said Weber, "only in terms of the specific *means* peculiar to it, as to every political association, namely, the use of physical force."

The state, and therefore the realm of politics, involves much more than "a human community . . . within a given territory." It is also, Weber insisted, "a relation of men dominating men, a relation supported by means of legitimate (i.e., considered to be legitimate) violence." However much we might wish it to be otherwise, he concluded, "the decisive means for politics is violence." Weber's point was not that politics is just another name for violence. Nor did he want to nurture a breed of belligerent political leaders. He did believe, however, that whatever its ends may be and however noble they are, the existence of a state depends on its ability to use and to control force. Political leaders and citizens alike, cautioned Weber, lose sight of that inconvenient fact at their peril.

States do not exist without leaders, and likewise the function of a political leader is at once to direct and to serve the state with passion and sound judgment alike. To make his or her state survive and flourish is the political leader's calling. To do anything that compromises those aims is to betray politics as a vocation. Weber contrasted this "ethic of responsibility," as he called it, with an "ethic of ultimate ends." One ingredient of the latter, he suggested, could be an attitude that says one must do what is right and leave the results to God. Such a view has consistency and coherence that give it integrity, but Weber also believed that political responsibility and an ethic of ultimate ends are not easily matched. A political leader can hardly afford to leave the results to God, because violence is so much at the heart of politics.

Certainly a political leader can adamantly stick to a commitment to try to do what is right. That stance may be the highest fulfillment if politics becomes one's calling. Yet such decisiveness and judgment are bound to be influenced by an awareness of political responsibility that pretty well rules out "In God We Trust"—even if that slogan does appear on the state's currency. The vocation of politics, Weber admits, may bestow "a feeling of power," but no one who "seeks the salvation of the soul, of his own and of others," warns Weber, "should . . . seek it along the avenue of politics." Part of the reason, he believed, is as follows: "No ethics in the world can dodge the fact that in numerous instances the attainment of 'good' ends is bound to the fact that one must be willing to pay the price of using morally dubious means or at least dangerous ones—and facing the possibility or even the probability of evil ramifications. From no ethics in the world can it be concluded when and to what extent the ethically good purpose 'justifies' the ethically dangerous means and ramifications." Weber wanted to encourage young political leaders, but he did so through a realism that advised his audience not to undertake politics as a vocation unless they honestly believed that they could endure and even prevail in spite of such ambiguity.

Max Weber saw human affairs dominated by what he called "the disenchantment of the world." He used that term to refer to the belief that "there are no mysterious incalculable forces that come into play, but rather that one can, in principle, master all things by calculation." If Weber concurred with that belief to some extent, his sociology also emphasized that we have good reason to be disenchanted with our own human power because it tends to cage us.

Weber's thinking was oriented more toward diagnosis than toward prescription. He did not think it was the scientific scholar's role to make pronouncements about good and evil, though as an individual citizen that responsibility would be of vast importance. His sociological theories also made him doubt that philosophers could do much more than offer subjective opinions about such matters. "The ultimately possible attitudes toward life are irreconcilable," he thought, "and hence their struggle can never be brought to a final conclusion."

But in those circumstances, Weber went on to underscore, "it is necessary to make a decisive choice." A role that philosophical reflection could admirably fill in that situation, he thought, was to insist that people be prepared to give an account of "the ultimate meaning" of their own conduct. Getting people to think clearly about what they are planning to do and why is not a cure-all—far from it. But neither is that clarification a "trifling thing to do." Such effort, concluded Weber, "stands in the service of 'moral' forces" by encouraging "a sense of responsibility."

JOHN K. ROTH

Further Reading

Aron, Raymond. *Main Currents in Sociological Thought*. 2 vols. Garden City, N.Y.: Doubleday/Anchor Books, 1968, 1970. Aron's discussion of Weber is a good short introduction.

Bendix, Reinhard. *Max Weber: An Intellectual Portrait*. Garden City, N.Y.: Doubleday & Company, 1960. Bendix provides useful synopses of Weber's major works.

Giddens, Anthony. *Capitalism and Modern Social Theory: An Analysis of the Writings of Marx, Durkheim, and Max Weber*. Cambridge: Cambridge University Press, 1971. A leading social theorist compares and contrasts Weber with two other giants of social thought, Marx and Durkheim.

Kasler, Dirk. *Max Weber: An Introduction to His Life and Work*. Translated by Philippa Hurd. Chicago: University of Chicago Press, 1988. Kas-ler's book provides a significant overview of Weber's accomplishments.

Mommsen, Wolfgang J. *The Age of Bureaucracy: Perspectives on the Political Sociology of Max Weber*. New York: Harper & Row, 1974. Mommsen's book explores the depth of Weber's prophetic insight about modern politics and bureaucracy in particular.

Parsons, Talcott. *The Structure of Social Action*. 2 vols. New York: Free Press, 1968. This work contains a detailed and important study of Weber's thought by an influential interpreter.

Scaff, Lawrence. *Fleeing the Iron Cage: Culture, Politics, and Modernity in the Thought of Max Weber*. Berkeley: University of California Press, 1989. Scaff takes earlier interpretations into account in his contemporary reading of Weber.

MIGUEL DE UNAMUNO Y JUGO

Born: 1864, Bilbao, Spain
Died: 1936, Salamanca, Spain
Major Works: *En torno al casticismo (Concerning Purism)* (1895), *The Life of Don Quixote and Sancho* (1905), *The Tragic Sense of Life* (1913)

Major Ideas

History is the immediate historic moment that is happening, while intrahistory is an eternal, historical present.

The intrahistory of Spain is its soul, that which is genuinely pure and vital.

The landscape, language, and art of Castile express the soul of Spain.

To find the soul of Spain is to modernize the nation.

The inspiration for modernizing Spain is Don Quixote, who struggled to create his ideals against the conventions of society.

Don Quixote inspires individuals to find their humanity in the tensions of life, that is, in reason and faith, and in life and death.

To live these tensions is to live tragically and to live in this tragic sense is to live authentically.

The real problem of human life is death.

To agonize, which means to fight against death, is immortality.

Considered by many scholars to be Spain's most influential thinker of the twentieth century, Miguel de Unamuno was himself a paradox who cultivated in his writings paradoxical language in order to express the sense of paradox that for him was the sap of life. He lived, too, in paradoxical times, when Spain, stung by defeat at the hands of the United States in the War of 1898, indulged in self-flagellation while at the same time defending zealously the very defects of national character that had ensured the disaster. The writers and thinkers who gave themselves to the task of criticizing Spain in an attempt to revitalize her are known as the Generation of '98; Unamuno was their spiritual leader, the man who expended his seventy years in unremitting defiance of social and political structures that make difficult if not impossible the struggle to create oneself as an individual and as a consequence to create a unique, dynamic society.

Born in the Basque region, Unamuno was thus bestowed with the singular identity that comes with speaking a language that is utterly apart from all known tongues and belonging to a group that considers itself to be culturally autonomous. His Basque individualism never deserted him, provid-

ing a psychic foundation on which he built his own person.

He lived through the crisis of war—the Carlist wars that brought the bombing of Bilbao in 1873 and 1874, the disaster of 1898, the First World War, and the outbreak of the tragic Civil War in 1936, the year of his death; the crisis of political exile from 1924 to 1930, when his sharp criticism of the dictator Primo de Rivera landed him first on Fuerteventura in the Canary Islands, then Paris, and finally the border town of Hendaye; and the crisis of public humiliation when he was discharged as rector of the University of Salamanca in 1914 for political reasons, and again, in 1936, when for his challenge to the political regime he was expelled from the lifetime rectorship that two years before had been awarded him after his triumphant return from exile.

Not only did Unamuno live through crisis but it was by crisis that he lived. Within his soul raged the never-to-be-resolved battle between reason and faith by which he was made conscious of himself as a human being struggling to create moment by moment the meaning of his existence. There were, however, calm waters to the sea of turbulence. The love he found with his wife and children and the joy of teaching never abandoned him.

Having studied first at Bilbao and then at the University of Madrid, where he received the doctorate in 1883, Unamuno committed himself to teaching as a profession. He taught in Bilbao for seven years, then moved to Salamanca to occupy the chair of Greek Language and Literature before assuming the duties of rector. Unamuno was a brilliant scholar, adept in Greek, Latin, Hebrew, and Arabic, as well as several modern languages. His interests were philological, linguistic, literary, philosophical, and aesthetic, and his ideas are to be sought not only in the essays for which he is justifiably celebrated but also in the novels, drama, and poetry that brought him fame. In whatever form he created for the expression of ideas, Unamuno was always concerned for language, its vitality and creativity. He was passionate about the creative force of metaphor, and he wrote some of Spain's most compelling poetry.

Although Unamuno was an anguished soul bent on creating himself through crisis, he was not without the comfort of love. A chaste, faithful lover, Unamuno had married his childhood sweetheart, who was to him wife, mother of their nine children, and, through the darkness of spiritual crisis, mother. Thus, the constancy of his devotion to teaching was enhanced by the love he enjoyed with his family.

To speak about the ideas of Unamuno is to consider his life in all its aspects, including the familial; life was no abstraction for Unamuno, and philosophy had nothing to do with concepts as if they were bones from which the flesh of living had been stripped. He once said that all his writings, whether essays or poems, were pieces of his heart. He himself *was* his philosophy; to the extent that we meet him as a man of flesh and blood we understand his thinking.

Concerning Purism

The five essays that constitute his first major work, *En torno al casticismo* (*Concerning Purism*), written in 1895 and published in 1902, demonstrate Unamuno's sense of crisis with respect to Spain. In quest of the soul of Spain, Unamuno turns, as did other writers of the Generation of '98, to Castile, penetrating the overlays of false nationalism and dead traditions to find the eternal and genuinely pure Spain. The paradox for Unamuno is that while on the one hand he rejects traditional Spain in order to modernize her, on the other he seeks the traditional as a way to bring Spain into the modern world. The paradox is resolved in understanding that for Unamuno modernization lies in discerning that which is authentically pure.

In search of Spain's soul, Unamuno makes the distinction between history and intrahistory, the former being the immediate historic moment as that which is going, the latter, an eternal, historical present that is the bearer of Spain's collective unconscious or her soul. In order to touch Spain's intrahistory as the seat of her authentic values and traditions, Unamuno celebrates the Castilian landscape in its granite mountains, poplar trees, and wheat fields, the vitality of the language, and, as its purest creations, epic poetry, drama, and mysticism. The tone of the volume is reformist as Unamuno labors to awaken Spain from the torpor of illusions of imperial grandeur to an authentic life in its collective soul, casting off such burdens as extremism, honor, and individualism.

The Life of Don Quixote and Sancho

The Life of Don Quixote and Sancho (1905) carries forward the theme of revitalization, as Unamuno, reflecting on Cervantes's masterpiece, interprets the Castilian knight and his squire as symbols of hope for Spain collectively and for individuals. It has been said that Unamuno made a religion of Quixotism, for he saw in the creative energy of Don Quixote as well as Sancho, who under his master's tutelage is awakened to assert himself as a unique person, redemptive hope for humanity. Rescuing Don Quixote from commentators who saw the knight only within the limits of the novel, Unamuno clarified the significance of Don Quixote in terms of what the knight yearned to be rather than for what he did. That is, Don Quixote symbolizes the quest for personality as opposed to a reductive emphasis on facts and ideas. Lauding Don Quixote's values of glory, action, and doing good, Unamuno claims for the knight the ultimate value in life, which is to strive not to die, to strive for immortality. Thus there is a historical Don Quixote, who is the character created by Cervantes at a particular time, and there is the immortal Don Quixote, who exists outside of the novel to inspire in the hearts of men and women, individually and collectively, the desire to create themselves moment by moment. Unamuno thus regarded Don Quixote and Sancho not as abstractions or allegories but rather as human beings of flesh and blood who, in existential terms, created meaning out of chaos.

The Tragic Sense of Life

The existential thematic of *The Life of Don Quixote and Sancho* is forcefully visible in Unamuno's most profound work, *The Tragic Sense of Life*. The theme that informs the book is Unamuno's own crisis of faith, which had erupted in 1897, leaving him bereft of his childhood religion. Doomed to the darkness of doubt, Unamuno was never to know the comforts of religious belief that had surrounded him as a Catholic until that time. From 1897 on, Unamuno lived the tension of opposites—the secular and the spiritual, knowledge and faith, hope and despair. Until his death in 1936, Unamuno appears to have suffered an ongoing "dark night of the soul," a dying to the old self of religious belief and in that dying a being reborn in faith. Rebirth, however, did not usher in a new life of clarity and confidence; on the contrary, doubt and despair were the hallmarks of faith as Unamuno struggled against the forces of reason to assert the existence of God and the immortality of his soul. The God of reason and the assurances of the Catholic religion had collapsed, and in their place Unamuno could post nothing more certain than his own uncertainties.

Out of his own experience, Unamuno realized that not only he but all persons of flesh and blood are a living conflict of opposites, especially those of faith and reason and of life and death. No solution to the conflict is possible, and the only authentic response to it is struggle. Hence a human being is human insofar as he is conscious of himself as being doomed to physical death and yet, in the anxiety of this awareness, struggling not to die. Her vision of immortality is a continuance of suffering and anxiety mixed with bliss and hope, which characterize life on earth. Thus immortality means simply not to die, to struggle to escape death. In this respect, Don Quixote served Unamuno well as inspiration, for in the knight's unremitting struggle to assert the commendable values of knight errantry in a Spain where the profession was no longer a historical or fictitious truth, the Castilian knight, by his refusal not to struggle, achieved immortality.

Unamuno's relationship to Kierkegaard is evident in the existential obligation to create oneself and in the irrational faith by which a human being asserts the existence of God and the immortality of the soul in the teeth of reason. Unamuno could not have endured the anguish of faith had there not sprung from the aridity of his darkened soul first compassion for himself and then compassion for the world, which in turn bore a human God who is knowable only through love.

The mystery of human existence, which is the mystery of Unamuno's existence as a man of flesh and blood, is the connective theme among all his writings. In his "nivolas," which is the term he fashioned for his narrative fiction, Unamuno recreates over and over his interior struggle. In *San Manuel Bueno, martyr* (1930), for example, the protagonist is a priest who has lost his religious conviction but, out of love for his parishioners whose illusions he does not want to destroy, remains a priest, leading others to believe that he enjoys the faith he ministers to them. The crisis of faith is also essential in two of Unamuno's most famous poems, "The Recumbent Christ of Santa Clara," which is the cry of a desperate soul confronting the terror of nothingness, and "The Christ of Velasquez," an expression of faith inspired by the famous painting.

Ever suspect of institutions, whether political or

religious, Unamuno went to his grave acclaimed on the one hand as the greatest Christian of the twentieth century and, on the other, as Spain's worst heretic. Neither classification would have pleased this unique man who loathed labels and definitions. His struggle was not to accommodate existent models but in authentic existential fashion to create himself on his own terms and by those terms to struggle not to die, to struggle for immortality.

MARY E. GILES

Further Reading

Ferrater Mora, José. *Unamuno. A Philosophy of Tragedy*. Berkeley and Los Angeles: University of California Press, 1962. Essential reading, it is a clear, concise introduction to Unamuno's thinking.

Ilie, Paul. *Unamuno. An Existential View of Self and Society*. Madison, Milwaukee, and London: University of Wisconsin Press, 1967. The emphasis is on Unamuno as a psychologist, moralist, and cultural analyst, studied in light of existentialism.

Ouimette, Victor. *Reason Aflame. Unamuno and the Heroic Will*. New Haven and London: Yale University Press, 1974. A solid analysis of the concept of hero in European culture and in Unamuno.

Rudd, Margaret T. *The Lone Heretic. Miguel de Unamuno y Jugo*. Austin, Tex.: University of Texas Press, 1963. Because Unamuno himself is his philosophy, this biography is required reading.

BENEDETTO CROCE

Born: 1866, Pescasseroli, Italy
Died: 1952, Naples, Italy
Major Works: *Aesthetic as Science of Expression and General Linguistic* (2nd ed. rev., 1922; first Italian edition, 1902), *Logic as Science of the Pure Concept* (1917; first Italian edition, 1905), *Philosophy of the Practical: Economic and Ethic* (1913; first Italian edition, 1909), *Guide to Aesthetics* (1965; first Italian edition, 1913), *History: Its Theory and Practice* (1921; first Italian edition, 1917), *Benedetto Croce's Poetry and Literature: An Introduction to its Criticism and History* (1981; first Italian edition, 1936), *History as the Story of Liberty* (1941; first Italian edition, 1937)

Major Ideas

A work of art is an intuition, an image expressive of and unified by feelings.
Art is lyrical in that it is expressive of life and feeling; it has aesthetic universality that stems from its origin in intuition.
Art is independent of all other expressions of human reason.
Philosophy and history are unified and yet distinguishable; neither discipline can occur without the other.
The task of philosophy is to make explicit the guiding principles and concepts in historical narrative.
History consists of the recreation of the past in the mind of the historian; it is thus contemporary and autobiographical.
History is the story of morality and liberty.

Benedetto Croce was one of the most important European philosophers of the twentieth century, not only for the controversies he stirred and for the polemics he waged against such fashionable views of his time as positivism, materialism, and metaphysical systems of every kind but also for the positive contributions he made to intellectual thought—especially to aesthetics and theory of history.

In 1883, an earthquake at Casamicciola left Croce's parents and his only sister dead and Croce himself physically afflicted for the rest of his life. Subsequently, he devoted his time to learning and writing (his published works include well over seventy volumes), and at least during his early years, the intensity of his research was increased by a desire to forget his painful memories.

Croce's grammar school education began when he was nine years old and took place at a Catholic boarding shcool in Naples, the *Collegio della Carità*, which offered moral and religious instruction. At the end of 1879, he experienced a religious crisis that represented the culmination of a period of questioning, which was stimulated by lectures on the philosophy of religion given by the director of Croce's *Collegio*, Father Attanasio. As a result of this crisis, he discarded the religious beliefs that he had held from childhood. Subsequently in 1880 he attended the *Liceo Genovese* in Naples, and by 1882, he had studied the writings of Francesco De Sanctis and Giosuè Carducci. From De Sanctis he gained guiding principles that he would later use in literary criticism and from Carducci he developed a "contempt for the frivolous and self-indulgent manners of the fashionable world."

After the disaster at Casamicciola in 1882, Benedetto and his brother Alfonso lived with Silvio Spaventa, a distant relative, in Rome. Spaventa provided a passionate but severe political and moral role model for the youths. Croce attended some lectures by Antonio Labriola, who was a Marxist and frequent visitor to the Spaventa household. He fulfilled Croce's "need to reformulate a faith in life, its goals, and its duties." It was then, through Labriola's lectures, that Croce became introduced to the discipline of economics. To Labriola's lectures and to De Sanctis's writings Croce attributed the fact that he never adopted the then-fashionable views of positivism and empiricism.

In 1885, before completing his formal education, Croce returned to Naples and began to administer the estates that belonged to his family. At the same time, he became absorbed in municipal and political history, and he wrote a number of essays that were published in a book on the Neapolitan Revolution of 1799. His next task, which was to give an account of the national and spiritual life of Italy from the Renaissance, prompted Croce to investigate the very nature of history and knowledge; and for the first time he read Giambattista Vico's *Scienza nuova* (*The New Science*). These studies culminated in a 1893 essay, "La storia ridotta sotto il concetto generale dell'arte" ("History Subsumed under the General Concept of Art"), which, by explicating the relations between art and history, demonstrated that intuitional cognition of a particular object was requisite to both aesthetic expression and to historical knowledge.

In 1895, Labriola sought Croce's help on the publication of some essays on Karl Marx. Croce's studies led him to debate with Vilfredo Pareto, the economist and sociologist. As a result of these exchanges, Croce proposed that economic activity consisted of an exercise of will that acted independently of moral choice, a position that he was to maintain throughout his lifetime. For him, the economic act was moreover a universal one in the sense that it was coequal with the other three fundamental expressions of human consciousness: the aesthetic, the logical, and the ethical. In 1900 he published what he later considered to be his definitive work on Marx, translated under the title of *Historical Materialism and the Economics of Karl Marx*.

In 1902, Croce and Giovanni Gentile announced the publication of *La Critica: Rivista di letteratura, storia e filosofia*, a journal that advocated an antimetaphysical and methodological approach to literary criticism, history, and philosophy. Its aim was to further develop a humanistic tradition that consisted of a science of the human spirit. The same year in which Croce started *La Critica* saw the publication of his first major work on aesthetics, later translated as *Aesthetic as Science of Expression and General Linguistic*. Here he argued for the autonomy of art, as distinguished from, for exam-

ple, history, philosophy, and the empirical sciences. Three additional volumes—on logic, economics and ethics, and historiography—followed. These four books purported to give a complete inventory of the activities of the human spirit. Works on Vico and Hegel also were published, and Croce's eminence as a philosopher became recognized by the conferment of a life senatorship in 1910.

In 1920, Giovanni Giolitti, prime minister of Italy, asked Croce to accept the post of minister of education. Croce's tenure lasted for only a year, when Mussolini replaced him with Gentile. During the subsequent twenty years of Fascism, Croce's books were removed from scholastic curricula and Gentile's works took their place. Although Croce was never imprisoned, he was harassed by Fascist thugs. His major works on history completed during this period illustrated the importance he gave to "liberty" as a directive concept for historical narrative and for humankind. At Salerno during 1944, Croce became a minister without portfolio of the new democratic government of Italy, and from 1944 to 1947 he remained president of the Liberal party.

In 1943, *La Critica* was succeeded by the *Quaderni della "Critica."* Unlike *La Critica*, wherein Croce's voice dominated Italian culture to an extraordinary extent, the *Quaderni* had to contend with a variety of views, all struggling for power, which derived from the Resistance cultural legacy. Young critical intellectuals felt that Croce's humanistic liberalism was too elitist, traditional, and conservative to lead the emergence of Italy's "New Culture." The political left began to attack Croce's views. Ironically, the Marxist philosophy that Croce thought he had laid to rest long ago not only would replace his philosophical idealism and political liberalism, but also would claim the former as its legitimate predecessor.

Crocean Aesthetics

Critics have distinguished distinct phases of the development of Crocean aesthetics. Croce's early view described art as cognitive intuitional expression of particular feelings. In the 1902 *Estetica*, Croce also distinguished intuition as form from the content of expression, a distinction he soon discarded and described as a residue of Kantianism in his aesthetic theory. Subsequently, as a result of his own extensive work as literary critic and the suggestions of others, Croce added another defining characteristic to his concept of art—lyricality. Lyrical quality consisted in "the life, the movement, the emotion, the fire, the feeling of the artist. . . . When emotion and feeling are present, much is forgiven; when these are lacking, nothing can compensate for them."

In 1918, Croce published an essay, later translated as "The Totality of Artistic Expression," that further determined Croce's concept of art by describing another of its important characteristics—aesthetic universality. Although Croce did not elaborate on this quality before 1918, his 1913 *Breviario di estetica* (*Guide to Aesthetics*) described a kind of aesthetic universality as intrinsic to the intuitional process, inasmuch as art consisted of an aesthetic synthesis between feeling and image within intuition. This development in Croce's concept of art was due as much to his work as literary critic of writers whom he described as cosmic, such as Dante, Ariosto, Shakespeare, Corneille, and Goethe, as to comments by critics such as the American Joel Spingarn deploring the absence of universality in Croce's list of the defining characteristics of art. The recognition of aesthetic totality required empathy and the acknowledgment that a particular expression resonated in the heart of every person. Some critics have proposed that the addition of universality rendered Croce's concept of aesthetic expression more like that of other expressions of the human spirit, such as the logical and ethical ones. And although a reading of his published works reveals that he consistently maintained the autonomy and uniqueness of art, nevertheless, in his later writings one can discern an increasing emphasis on the circularity of the four fundamental expressions of consciousness, along with an acknowledgment that the rational-ethical will provides the material to be transformed into aesthetic intuition by the creative imagination.

Another important work, published in 1936 and later translated as *Benedetto Croce's Poetry and*

Literature: An Introduction to its Criticism and History, summarized and further clarified Croce's use of the genres in literary criticism. Here the genre of literature became characterized further as resembling art, yet as falling short of genuine lyrical and cosmic expression. With great detail and well illustrated from his earlier critiques, *Poetry and Literature* described the differences between authentic poetic expression and the various forms of nonart, along with their interrelationships. Croce's position was clear: There is "good literature" and occasionally nonpoetic verse may be necessary in genuine poetry.

Theory of History

Croce's conception of history, like his philosophy of art, evolved out of reciprocal relations between *theoria* and *praxis*. During the years between 1886 and 1892, when Croce was absorbed with studies on the kingdom of Naples and the diplomatic relations between Italy and Spain, he became aware of a need for categories of interpretation in historical narrative. While attempting to solve specific difficulties of hermeneutical research, Croce turned to the general topics of history and knowledge. Out of the perplexities that he encountered while pursuing these inquiries emerged his first philosophical essay, entitled "La storia ridotta sotto il concetto generale dell'arte" ("History Subsumed under the General Concept of Art"), which temporarily organized his ideas in terms of categories of art and philosophy. Each of these categories of historical interpretation represented an activity of human consciousness: the *intuitional*, the fundamental cognitive expression of particular objects, on which all knowledge depends; and the *conceptual*, which includes the intuitive but transcends it in the concrete universality of its representation.

Croce's subsequent work with Marx's philosophy resulted in the adoption of a third category of historical interpretation besides the aesthetic and philosophic ones, the *economic*. It represented human practical activity and thus the strivings of human will to achieve immediate goals. Its creations included what Croce named "pseudoconcepts," which consisted of empirical and abstract class names, whose denotation and connotation were limited by need and interest. Among such classifications, for example, were divisions of history into ancient, feudal, Renaissance, or into classical and romantic. Much of historical narrative consisted of such concepts and the pseudojudgments that expressed them. Unlike, however, what Croce termed individual or historical judgments that included categories, pseudojudgments were neither true nor false. Considered as arbitrary and not fixed, they were to be evaluated in terms of utility and need.

The final major category of historical interpretation that was to follow upon "the economic" was one of *moral goodness*. It represented the fourth activity of the human spirit—the ethical will having a relatively universal goal that extended beyond short-term economic needs—and expressed itself, moreover, as the quest for greater degrees of political liberty than those already existing within a particular historical context. Croce's writings on history, as for instance, *La storia come pensiero e come azione* (1937), later translated as *History as the Story of Liberty* (1941), clearly illustrated the importance that he gave to this concept, one doubtless reinforced by restrictions on personal and political freedom that had occurred during the Fascist period.

How did Croce's conception of the functions of mind and their categorical representations lead to his conception of history as autobiography? Early in his career, Croce described his philosophical position as post-Berkelian "absolute" historicism, his epistemology did not fundamentally change. By "idealism" and "absolute historicism," Croce meant that the existence of an object depends on its expression by consciousness. He denied the existence of anything that bears no relation to mind. Mind is foundational to reality in the sense that the synthetic *a priori* aesthetic activity of imagination, that is, intuition, provided the subjects of historical judgment, and the synthetic *a priori* logical act was the source of the categories of historical interpretation. In the Crocean philosophy, the tenet that every objective true judgment expresses an immediate, logical state of mind follows from his epistemic idealism and led Croce to propose that history itself is contemporary. By this assertion he meant that the subject matter of judgment is created by the historian's present interests and needs. Crocean history amounted, moreover, to autobiography, inasmuch as it issued entirely from the unique perspective of the historian's consciousness.

M. E. Moss

Further Reading

Caponigri, A. R. *History and Liberty: The Historical Writings of Benedetto Croce*. London: Routledge & Kegan Paul, 1955. This book presents a useful and thorough treatment of Croce's writings on history from his studies on the Neapolitan revolution of 1799 through the Fascism of Mussolini.

Caserta, Ernesto C. *Croce and Marxism*. Naples: Morano, 1987. The author gives a scholarly treatment of the relations between Croce's philosophy and Marxist doctrine from the years of revisionism to the last postwar period.

Jacobitti, Edmund E. *Revolutionary Humanism and Historicism in Modern Italy*. New Haven: Yale University Press, 1981. Despite its title, this book critically evaluates the development of Croce's philosophy from his early writings through 1914. The author concludes with a chapter entitled "The Prophet Who Failed."

Moss, M. E. *Benedetto Croce Reconsidered: Truth and Error in Theories of Art, Literature, and History*. With a foreword by Maurice Mandelbaum. Hanover and London: University Press of New England, 1987. Moss provides an introduction to Croce's entire philosophy, with special emphasis placed on his aesthetics and theory of history. The discussion includes recent Crocean criticism and scholarship.

Roberts, David D. *Benedetto Croce and the Uses of Historicism*. Berkeley: University of California Press, 1987. Roberts discusses the development of Croce's absolute historicism in relation to Italian and European intellectual thought. His conclusion evaluates Croce's place in the twentieth-century search for modern humanism.

BERTRAND RUSSELL

Born: 1872, Trelleck, Monmouthshire, England
Died: 1970, near Penrhyndeudraeth, Merioneth, Wales
Major Works: *Principia Mathematica* (with A. N. Whitehead) *(1910, 1912, and 1913), The Problems of Philosophy* (1912), *Our Knowledge of the External World* (1914), *Mysticism and Logic* (1917), *A History of Western Philosophy* (1945), *Human Knowledge: Its Scope and Limits* (1948), *Why I Am Not a Christian* (1927).

Major Ideas

The Theory of Types: Sentences may be not only true or false but meaningless because of inconsistent uses of language.
The Theory of Descriptions: Existence is a property of propositional functions; it is not a property of things.
All knowledge of the world is derived from sense data.
We do not know objects directly, but only indirectly, through sensations.
The right action is always that which will, from a purely objective point of view, have the best consequences, that is, the one that will produce the greatest good and the least evil.
Good is whatever produces the greatest satisfaction for the greatest number; one form of satisfaction is as good as any other.
Determinism is probably true, but it does not follow from this that human beings are not responsible for what they do.
Morality is not dependent upon God's approval or disapproval.
All of the proofs for the existence of God are fallacious.
Christ is not divine, and Christianity is a particularly cruel and inhuman religion.
There is very little likelihood that there is an afterlife.

Bertrand Arthur William Russell, 3d Earl Russell, knew virtually nothing of his parents (who died when he was very young) until after he reached the age of twenty-one. His father had appointed two freethinkers as Russell's guardians, but his grandparents had the will set aside and gained custody of the three-year-old future philosopher. Russell described his grandmother as "a Puritan, with the moral rigidity of the Covenanters, despising comfort, indifferent to food, hating wine, and regarding tobacco as sinful." Although he came to detest her religious zealotry, he was profoundly influenced by two texts that she had inscribed in a Bible she gave him on his twelfth birthday: "Thou shalt not follow a multitude to do evil" and "Be strong, and of a good courage; be not afraid, neither be Thou dismayed."

His discovery of Euclid at age eleven marked an important transition point in his life. From that time on, he was intensely interested in mathematics,

partly because of the sheer delight he experienced in deductive reasoning, and partly because of an early belief that all of nature, including human behavior, must operate according to mathematical laws and was therefore completely predictable, if only we had enough information.

After reading John Stuart Mill at age eighteen, he concluded that the traditional proofs for God's existence were fallacious. In the meantime, he had been examining and rejecting many of the doctrines that he had previously been taught, including the theory of free will and the doctrine of immortality.

During his years at Cambridge, he met a number of people who were to become his friends and intellectual colleagues, including, particularly, J. McTaggart, Alfred N. Whitehead, and G. E. Moore.

Russell lived a very long, productive life. He made important contributions to virtually every area of philosophy. And he never stopped inquiring,

searching, and reexamining his earlier views. He
was intellectually fearless and scrupulously honest.
Consequently, he often changed his mind about important questions. He once said that if someone
showed him that the views he had expressed in one
book were wrong, he would not hesitate to publish
another book repudiating the first. Because he often
acted upon that principle, it is difficult to say just
what his views on some subjects were, for the answer depends upon the period of his life to which
one is referring.

He firmly believed in the usefulness of Ockham's
razor, the principle that one should not unneces-
sarily multiply entities in attempting to explain the
universe. It was this principle that ultimately led to
the general adoption of Copernicus's theory that the
sun is at the center of the solar system—for it
offered a simple explanation of planetary motions,
while the competing Ptolemaic theory had to postulate the existence of hundreds of "epicycles."
Russell applied Ockham's razor to mathematics. He
thus rejected Plato's idea that cardinal integers are
timeless entities or "forms." Instead, he argued for
a "minimum vocabulary," that is, an irreducible set
of terms or symbols from which the remainder of a
science can be inferred.

The Theory of Types

Like many philosophers before him, Russell was
puzzled by certain paradoxes that were particularly
resistant to resolution. Epimenides the Cretan, for
example, claimed that all Cretans are liars. If Epimenides is telling the truth, then he must be lying;
but if he is lying, he must be telling the truth.
Similarly, it is reasonable to suppose that every
propositional function (or, in ordinary language,
every term that one might use in a sentence, such as
the word *man*) determines a class (in our example,
all of the male members of the species *homo sa-
piens*). Some classes are members of themselves
(for example, the class of things that can be counted
is itself a thing that can be counted) and others are
not (the class of men that is itself not a man). But if
the class of classes that are *not* members of them-

selves *is* a member of itself, then it is *not*; and if it is
not, then it *is*.

Though many people might be inclined to dismiss such paradoxes as trivial but amusing puzzles,
Russell took them as serious challenges to logical
theory. He developed the theory of types in an
attempt to solve these paradoxes and others. The
theory is too complex to explain here. Suffice it to
say that it is based upon the assumption that the
paradoxes are attributable to faults in language and
not to any contradictions inherent in reality. The
theory proposes to resolve the paradoxes by explaining that words that appear to be the same are
often not really the same, because they refer to
different things or refer differently and are therefore
on different levels. Russell revised the theory a
number of times during his life to meet various
objections that were raised against it, but none of
the revisions was completely satisfactory, even to
him.

The Theory of Descriptions

In rejecting Platonism, Russell concluded that
nouns do not refer to eternally existing things like
those that Plato called "Ideas" or "Forms." Plato's
theory populated the universe with altogether too
many things to satisfy the principle of Ockham's
razor. Although one may talk about unicorns,
golden mountains, and the present king of France, it
is absurd to suppose that any of these "things"
exists in any meaningful sense at all. The problem is
to explain how a nonentity can be the subject of a
proposition: How is it possible to talk sensibly about
things that don't exist? Russell responded by analyzing statements in such a way that existence is
made explicit. Thus, a statement like "A unicorn
has one horn" would be translated into something
like, "If there is anything that is a unicorn, then that
thing has one horn." Some propositions, such as
"The present king of France is bald," implicitly
state that their subjects exist. A full analysis of this
statement would be: "At least one person is a king of
France, at most one person is a king of France, and
there is nobody who is a king of France and not

bald." Since the statement implicitly asserts that a king of France exists, and since there is no king of France, the sentence is simply false. The phrase "the present king of France" refers to nothing at all.

Perception Theory

George Berkeley had concluded that what we sense is in our minds and that we therefore have no evidence of things existing outside our minds. Russell insisted that although we learn whatever we know about a table from sense data (our sense perceptions), what we know *about* is a table and *not* our perceptions. Nevertheless, some puzzles remain: Different people under different conditions may have very different sense data relative to the same table. Different people viewing a table from different angles will see the color differently. *The* color of the table is just the sort of color it will seem to have to a normal viewer from an ordinary point of view under normal light conditions. "But the other colours which appear under other conditions have just as good a right to be considered real," he says, so to avoid "favouritism," we must deny that the table has any one color. All of the table's other properties (shape, size, texture, and the like) are equally variable as perceived under various conditions by different people. Consequently, Russell concludes that we have no direct knowledge of the table's properties, although we may infer what its properties are from the "signs" that our sensations, which are *caused* by the table's properties, reveal to us.

Ethical Theory

Russell abandoned his early belief that goodness and badness are intrinsic qualities of things and adopted the view that we generally call things "good" if we desire them and "bad" if we have an aversion to them. However, he acknowledged that there are some clear exceptions to this rule, for people often condition their desires on what some authority tells them they *ought* to desire. Moreover, they frequently come to believe that their own desires are bad. In the last analysis, ethical judgments

are not based upon anything scientific or philosophical, but upon emotion. There is no objective truth as to good and evil. It all boils down to a matter of taste.

When a person makes an ethical judgment, however, he is not merely expressing his personal feelings. Such judgments are also expressions of how the speaker wishes the world would be and how others would act.

Russell believed that human actions derive from three sources: instinct, mind, and spirit. Instinct is presumably whatever more or less automatically occurs as a result of our animal natures: seeking food and water when one is hungry and thirsty, seeking a sex partner when one is physically mature, fleeing from danger, and so on. Mind as a source of conduct leads to the pursuit of knowledge, and spirit to religious consciousness.

Russell did not believe that it was necessary for human beings to acquiesce in the dictates of nature, though we are all of course limited in what we can do by the laws of nature. In the realm of values, he wrote, "we are kings, and we debase our kingship if we bow down to Nature. It is for us to determine the good life, not for Nature."

In this connection, he held that it was likely that determinism was true. That is, if one could know all the laws of nature, and all there was to know about the condition of the universe at any particular moment, one should in principle be able to deduce what would occur at any future time, and predict accurately what any given individual would do in any future situation. This theory has led some philosophers to deny that individuals have any freedom to decide for themselves what they will do. Their actions are caused, or determined, by previous states of affairs and natural laws over which they have no control. This in turn would lead to the conclusion that people are not morally responsible for their behavior. Russell's view, however, is quite the opposite. He says that if a person's actions had *no* cause, then it would be particularly inappropriate to hold him responsible for what he did, for his actions would have been chance happenings over which he had no control whatever. We hold people responsible because we believe that their acts are conditioned by the influences—educational, moral, and religious—to which they have been subjected. If they were not, it would make no sense to express praise or blame. He concludes that determinism and free will (and thus moral responsibility) are not only fully compatible with each other but require each other.

He thoroughly disagreed with those who accused him of inconsistency for having said that morality was ultimately a personal, subjective matter, while he vehemently expressed his opinions on a wide range of moral issues. He insisted that ethical statements are neither true nor false, but are expressions of the speaker's feelings. The purpose of persuasion in ethics is quite different from what it is in science. It is to rouse people to desire what the speaker desires and is thus akin to preaching. Logical demonstration and moral persuasion are completely different activities, but there is no inconsistency in doing both. He insisted that no amount of logic would persuade him to forgo his right to feel and express ethical passions. "There are some men whom I admire, and others whom I think vile; some political systems seem to me tolerable, others an abomination. Pleasure in the spectacle of cruelty horrifies me, and I am not ashamed of the fact that it does. I am no more prepared to give up all this than I am to give up the multiplication table."

Criticism of Christianity

Russell concluded very early that the traditional arguments for the existence of God are fallacious, and he never saw any reason to revise that judgment. He saw no evidence whatever for the existence of a benevolent deity. Indeed, if the usual inferences are drawn from the world to the existence of some supreme power, it would be more reasonable to conclude that the universe is created by a malevolent demon.

He felt that the Christian religion is particularly infected with absurd beliefs and superstitions. He took pleasure in ridiculing the Roman Catholic church, which "holds that a priest can turn a piece of bread into the Body and Blood of Christ by talking Latin to it." He particularly fulminated against the Church's obscurantism, its repression of intellectually creative people, and its deification of some rather detestable people. He concluded that Christian apologists tended, dishonestly, to overlook the less-desirable traits and doctrines of Jesus of Nazareth, who was, in Russell's opinion, intolerant, vindictive, cruel, and bloodthirsty. He believed that it was impossible to believe that Christianity has had an elevating moral influence, unless one ignored or falsified the historical evidence.

BURTON M. LEISER

Further Reading

Ayer, A. J. *Bertrand Russell.* New York: Viking Press, 1972. An excellent introduction to Russell's life and major theories, clearly written, thorough, and interesting. Ayer is an extremely influential philosopher in his own right, and points out where his views differ from Russell's.

Schilpp, Paul Arthur, ed. *The Philosophy of Bertrand Russell.* New York: Tudor, 1951. This volume in the "Library of Living Philosophers," first published in 1944, contains an intellectual autobiography, more than twenty articles by distinguished philosophers on various aspects of Russell's work, and Russell's responses to his critics.

Wood, Alan. *Bertrand Russell, the Passionate Skeptic.* London: Allen & Unwin, 1957. A well-written, often entertaining biography.

CARL GUSTAV JUNG

Born: 1875, Kesswil, Switzerland
Died: 1961, Zürich (Küsnacht), Switzerland
Major Works: *Symbols of Transformation* (1911), *Psychology and Alchemy* (1944), *Answer to Job* (1952), *Memories, Dreams, Reflections* (1961)

Major Ideas

There are particular personality types characterized by extraversion or introversion, and four personality functions: sensation, thinking, feeling, and intuition.

Within each individual is found a personal unconscious, which is composed of one's personal history, and a collective unconscious, which is composed of images or archetypes common to all people; these images appear frequently in dreams, fairy tales, and myths.

Each individual is so constituted that he or she has an innate drive to fulfillment, or to his or her own destiny. Individuation, or the attainment of personal integrity, occurs in the second half of life.

Dreams arise from the "all-uniting depths" and tend to compensate for deficits in the individual's waking life, facilitating the person's awareness of deficiencies in the personality and thus enabling their development.

The son of a Swiss Reformed pastor, Carl Gustav Jung brought the study of mythology and religion to the discipline of psychology. Prompted by his interpretation of two dreams, he studied medicine at the University of Basel, while reading intensely in the areas of philosophy and religion. He was "irretrievably drawn under [psychiatry's] spell" by Krafft-Ebing's *Lehrbuch der Psychiatrie*, and went on to study psychiatry under Eugen Bleuler at the University of Zürich.

At first a supporter and friend of Sigmund Freud, Jung broke with him around 1913 to found "analytical psychology." Jung's initial dissatisfaction arose from Freud's sexual theory, not only because it seemed to Jung to be reductionistic, but because it left no room for the human spirit. He also became increasingly distressed by Freud's insistence that his ideas, particularly his sexual theory, be treated as "dogma" and "bulwark" (against "occultism"). He valued the work of both Freud and Alfred Adler but viewed their theories as primarily applicable to the earlier stages of life. Jung never abandoned his investigations of religion, myths, legends, folk tales, and the like, and immersed himself particularly in the study of Gnostic thought and alchemy. As he went his own way, he developed a following of his own, and there are currently Jung Institutes in many major cities.

Jung's analytical psychology has also been called "complex psychology." Jung was a pioneer in the use of *word-association* tests as diagnostic tools. That is, upon observing that certain words evoke especially unusual behavioral or verbal responses (delay, repetition, and so forth) in patients, he concluded that there were hidden constellations of feelings and ideas, or "complexes," reflecting "traumatic influences or certain incompatible tendencies." Because these complexes interfere with a person's life, they must be brought to light.

Jung adapted word-association tests to his research into mythology and the history of religions. With the Pueblo tribe in North America, for example, Jung gained insight into the tribe's religious beliefs (about which they would reveal nothing directly) by making "tentative remarks" and watching for "those affective movements which are so very familiar to me." Thus an unusual reaction led Jung to believe he had hit upon a weighty matter. Jung's experiences with groups around the world, especially in North America, Africa, and India, reinforced his assumptions about the existence of universal archetypes and the collective unconscious.

One of Jung's major contributions was the identification of psychological or *personality types*. The two primary types, or attitudes, are *extraversion*

and *introversion*. The extravert typically spontaneously invests his or her energy in the external
world and comes across as outgoing; the introvert is
inward-directed and may seem aloof. An individual
is an extravert or an introvert to a greater or lesser
degree. One or the other personality type typically
is dominant, but neither is found exclusively in an
individual.

As well as a tendency toward one of these types
of personality, each person exhibits dominant *functions of personality*. Jung identified four: sensation,
intuition, thinking, and feeling. By *sensation* Jung
meant what one ordinarily receives through the
sense organs. *Intuition* denotes something rather
like a hunch; it is a perception that apparently spontaneously wells up from within. Both sensation and
intuition are, as it were, "given," in that they are
involuntary responses to some sort of stimulus or
stimuli. They represent not merely different but
opposite ways of perceiving.

By *thinking*, Jung meant the mental process of
understanding or making sense of things as we generally construe the term. It is, we might say, the
"logical" or "objective" approach to things. The
feeling function weighs things, and pronounces
them valuable or not, pleasant or unpleasant.
Again, these functions are opposites, with one being dominant, the other being undeveloped.

The psychological types and functions are the
person's conscious response to life. Jung did not
place individuals into rigid categories, but identified general tendencies or ways of being in the
world. There are certain evidences for the types:
preference for reading a book over attending a party
(introversion), a preoccupation with beauty over
what can be demonstrated (feeling). While Jung
believed that it is important to be aware of one's
tendencies in these areas, the exploration of the
unconscious was Jung's central concern.

The Unconscious

Within each person are found the personal unconscious and the collective unconscious. One element
of the *personal unconscious* would be the above-
mentioned complexes, repressed due to their painful character. Perceptions, not necessarily painful,
of which the individual never became conscious
also reside in the personal unconscious. In this
sense, the personal unconscious is unique to each
individual and reflects his or her personal history.
The *collective unconscious* makes up the prepon-
derance of the psyche and its contents are common
to all people. "The instincts and archetypes together form the 'collective unconscious.' I call it
'collective' because, unlike the personal unconscious, it is not made up of individual and more or
less unique contents but of those which are universal and of regular occurrence." These contents are
the products of countless generations of human experience (for example, fear of the dark).

Archetypes

At the same time, however, there are elements common to everyone, or *archetypes*. Two very important ones that seem to be at the border, as it were, of
the personal and the collective unconscious because
they are found in every person but are shaped by the
particular person, are the persona and the shadow.
The *persona* is the socially and personally acceptable mask (the meaning of the Latin word *persona*)
that the individual presents to others and, to some
degree, to him- or herself. While the persona is not
the "real" person, it is necessary for life in human
society and does, in fact, constitute an element of
the real self. The danger exists that a person will so
identify with his or her persona that the real self
never emerges, or else will not sufficiently develop a
persona and thus remain deficient in that area.

The *shadow* is that part of the personality that
contains all those elements contrary to what the
persona presents to the world. Thus it is kept hidden
from the world and from consciousness. In popular
thought, the shadow is inevitably "the dark side" or
the evil within the individual, which appears in
dreams as murderers, monsters, and the like. While
this is generally true, Jung pointed out that this is
not necessarily the case. The shadow can manifest
in a "bad" person qualities such as order, kindness,

and normal reactions. The individual must acknowledge and come to grips with his or her shadow or else the shadow will, as it were, develop a life of its own in the person. In dreams, the shadow always appears as a person of the same sex as the dreamer (although not every dream figure of the same sex represents the person's shadow).

Alongside the persona and shadow are the *animus* and *anima*, or the masculine side of the female psyche and the feminine side of the male psyche, respectively, thus making, to the degree that they are appropriately expressed, a person "whole." The existence of these elements in the individual enables meaningful interaction between the sexes as well as determines to some degree a person's attraction or aversion to particular members of the opposite sex. Thus, a man, for example, is influenced in his relationships with women not only by his perceptions of his mother (which themselves are determined in part by the innate anima) but by the anima as the "eternal image of woman," not of *a* woman but of the eternal feminine that is part of the collective unconscious. Jung has come under fire for his "sexist" assumptions that the animus is connected primarily with the thinking function, while the anima is connected with the feeling function. The anima and animus are absolutely crucial as messagebearers of the collective unconscious. Jung wrote, "The animus and the anima should function as a bridge, or a door, leading to the images of the collective unconscious, as the persona should be a sort of bridge into the world."

Other *archetypes* in the collective unconscious are found in myths, religions, folk tales, and the like, and are depicted by anthropomorphic figures such as the trickster, the wise old man, and the earth mother. Yet others are represented by the moon, lakes, death, magic, weapons, and so forth. An archetype is not the depiction *per se* but is the "possibility of a certain type of perception and action." This possibility, then, takes on or receives a representation common to the person's culture. One must acknowledge the presence of these archetypes, lest they take on a life of their own, become a complex, and begin to influence one's conscious

life. A wise old man complex, for example, may come to dominate a person's identity and behavior, turning him or her into an unbearable know-it-all. Had, however, the archetype been acknowledged and incorporated into the personality, he or she may have become, for example, a good teacher or helpful counselor.

The culmination of Jung's investigation of archetypes was his discovery of the *self archetype*. The self is the center of the unconscious and the organizing principle of the personality. It is, as it were, both the undifferentiated unity of the beginning of the personality and the integrated unity, which is the goal of the individual's life. Religious images, particularly the mandala, are frequently images of the unity toward which the psyche strives and which the self archetype represents. The *ego*, as the center of consciousness, must recognize, acknowledge, and give expression to the messages of the unconscious. Anything kept out of consciousness cannot play its necessary role in the process of individuation.

Individuation

Fundamental to Jung's thought is the idea that within every person there is a drive toward wholeness, or *individuation*. Just as creation itself has purpose and direction, so each person moves as best as he or she can toward his or her particular destiny, or personal integration, this wholeness being attained to varying degrees and in varying ways or manifestations from person to person. This drive is manifested in the process of individuation, a process that typically occurs at midlife, after other, more materialistic, developmental stages have been negotiated. Just as external, or social and environmental, factors can have a salutary or harmful impact on the growth of the body, so external factors influence for good or ill the course of this innate drive and the process of individuation. Genetic predispositions can also create obstacles to individuation. For the personality to develop fully, each facet of the personality must itself develop fully, or individuate, through the individual bringing it into consciousness. Total self-realization rarely, if ever, is attained.

In the individuated person, the various elements of the personality are not only fully developed but are brought together in harmony. As the individual becomes aware of and expresses these unconscious facets, they themselves become fully developed. In the process, what Jung called the "transcendent function"—also inherent in the person—comes into play, bringing opposite elements into harmony so that the person acts not out of this element, then out of that, but out of both simultaneously and spontaneously, that is, out of the integrated self. While Jung saw individuation primarily as a mid- and post-midlife process, modern Jungians tend to believe that it begins early in life. The impulse toward individuation is then heightened at midlife, and the process is affected by the various helpful or harmful influences encountered throughout life.

The Interpretation of Dreams

Since the key point of Jungian psychotherapy is individuation, the *interpretation of dreams* is of great significance in the process, since dreams are perceived as manifestations of—we might even say, messages from—the unconscious that compensate for deficiencies in the ego or in the waking life. As dreams are remembered, they can contribute more directly to the individual's drive to wholeness. Through the examination of and meditation upon the symbols and structure of dreams, a person can recognize and respond to his or her need to develop the deficient or undeveloped parts of his or her psychic life expressed in dreams. The analyst assists in the *amplification* of the dream through "directed association" and references to similar situations or figures in folk tales, myths, religions, and so forth. Directed association refers to spontaneous connections made on the basis of dream material and related back to the dream. Jung felt Freud's "free association" could too easily lead away from the dream's crucial message.

The individual can also use *active imagination* to enhance interaction with various elements of the dream. A person may, for example, recall a person from a dream and enter into a conversation with that person, or pick up a dream at its end and continue it in his or her imagination, thus making the dream figures present to the waking person, and facilitating (harmonizing) encounters between the conscious and the unconscious. This technique normally is used later on in psychotherapy, and with more mature individuals.

A person may also engage in physical activities representative of his or her un- or underdeveloped aspects. Jung, for example, painted and carved as ways of expressing unconscious drives. An individual with a dominant thinking function may be encouraged to dance or sing. These practices not only bring elements of the unconscious to the individual's awareness, but exercise, as it were, the undeveloped function.

In all this the emphasis is not on individuation *per se*, but on self-knowledge and self-expression. Self-realization, then, is a sort of by-product of the process.

In his concentration on the reconciliation of opposites, and the synthesis of all of the personality's components into one harmonious whole, Jung much resembled the alchemists with whom he was so fascinated. Indeed, we might say that he was in many ways himself a Gnostic alchemist; Jung himself made a direct connection between his work and alchemy in *Memories, Dreams, Reflections:* "I had very soon [after intense study of Gnosticism and alchemy] seen that analytical psychology coincided in a most curious way with alchemy. The experiences of the alchemists were, in a sense, my experiences, and their world was my world. This was, of course, a momentous discovery: I had stumbled upon the historical counterpart of my psychology of the unconscious. The possibility of a comparison with alchemy, and the uninterrupted chain back to Gnosticism, gave substance to my psychology. When I pored over these old texts everything fell into place. . . ."

Because of his openness to, and great interest in, religious and spiritual matters, Jung has found a following not only among psychologists and psychiatrists but among clergy of many faiths as well. While Jung made clear distinctions between analysis and pastoral care in a paper titled "Psychoanalysis and the Cure of Souls," growing numbers of clergy find him helpful precisely because of his deep concern for the human soul and his apparent acceptance of things normally considered "spiritual," transcendent, or numinous. One must be careful to differentiate as best one can, however, between his personal views or faith and his psychological observations and theories.

GARY R. SATTLER

Further Reading

Hall, Calvin S., and Vernon J. Nordby. *A Primer of Jungian Psychology.* New York: New American Library, A Mentor Book. 1973. A brief, but thorough, introduction to the basic elements of Jung's thought with a short, helpful biography.

Jung, Carl G. *Man and His Symbols.* New York: Dell, 1964. Jung edited this collection of articles by some members of his closest circle. His article "Approaching the Unconscious" reflects his final thoughts.

Serrano, M. C. *Jung and Hermann Hesse: A Record of Two Friendships.* London: Routledge & Kegan Paul, 1966. A short book, but entertaining in its personal recollections of the visits of a South American writer with Jung and Hesse. The conversational, anecdotal tone of the book makes the reading of Jung's works an even more pleasant experience.

MARTIN BUBER

Born: 1878, Vienna, Austria
Died: 1965, Jerusalem, Israel
Major Works: *I and Thou* (1923)

Major Ideas

The I-Thou approach to relationships is the only way people can be fully authentic; only a part of our being is expressed in the I-It relationship.
Scripture and biblical commentary are of great importance but are not infallible.
Religious law is not immutable but applicable to the times of its formulation.
Zionism must incorporate Arabs as well as Jews.
Cooperative efforts, such as in the ideal kibbutzim, are to be encouraged, but collectivism is dangerous.

A German-Jewish religious philosopher, Martin Buber, born in Vienna, was a master prose stylist (in his native German) whose achievements included biblical translation and commentary, social reforms, and educational innovations. He studied at a number of top European universities, became a Zionist (though of a rather independent cast), edited several important journals, and embraced Hasidism. Active in adult Jewish education and in opposing Nazi nationalism, he migrated to Palestine in 1938, where he taught at Hebrew University. He was engaged in promoting the idea of the Israeli kibbutz and centered his philosophic teachings around the concept of dialogue—between persons and God, and among persons themselves. There are many facets to the development of his influential thought but none is better regarded than what is popularly known as his "teachings" on the I-Thou dialogue between persons and between the individual and God.

I and Thou

This fundamental teaching, which is found in all of his work, stems from the insight that in relating to things or objects, I do so quite differently from the way that I respond to a person (a "Thou") who addresses me and to whom I wish to relate. Inanimate objects are observed, Buber writes, while persons are spoken to, sincerely communicated with. He cautions that an inadequate relationship results not in the realization of an I-Thou ideal but rather in the more objective—and therefore less desirable—I-It relationship. If we take a less than fully "personal" interest in another, the result will be in an I-It class. If, for instance, I deal with my superior at work on the basis of that man or woman's likelihood of giving me a promotion rather than from a genuine concern for our human relationship, then the result is I-It. The same will be true if a repairman is treated by me solely in his job capacity or a doctor is considered only as a healer, excluding the possibility of my encountering that person's humanity on an obviously deeper level.

The preferred relational level is that of the I-Thou, which signifies a kind of cosmic comprehension of the entire universe. The Thou that I thus encounter is not an object, not a single thing noticed out of the many other possible things I might notice. Rather, the entire universe is grasped in the acceptance of the Thou—not vice versa. Not only, says Buber, is my relationship to the universe changed in each of my I-Thou encounters, but the "I" changes as well. The I of the I-Thou partnership can itself never be an object. Buber's I is understood only in the context of a relationship. If it is in an I-It relationship, the I here exists with only a portion of myself in it. By definition, then, there is a part of me that must be observer in the I-It context, a part of me that must stand outside the relationship to pass a judgment on it.

Contrariwise, the I of the I-Thou situation is a totally involved, totally committed I. Buber argues that God is the archetypical Thou, the basis on which the human I-Thou is modeled. Nor does Buber limit this idea to human encounters. While recognizing that the I-Thou is almost nonexistent below the animal level, Buber holds for the possibility of a measure of ideal interaction with an animal, but such interaction is quite possible (although rare enough) on the person-to-person level. On the highest plane, the human-with-God meeting must be on the I-Thou level from the human perspective. Buber insists that God must be encountered and experienced in dialogue, not merely as thought of and spoken to.

Most relationships are entered into without the fullness of being of both parties. Great loves, great friendships are very rare. Usually we hold back from total involvement for one reason or another and enter into a relationship only with some deep reservations. There is a fear of risk on the part of the person since, again by definition, there is no holding part of the self back in the I-Thou encounter; one commits one's total being. No defense mechanisms are held in reserve—the risk involved is that of the complete I.

There are a number of implications in accepting Buber's position here. One important feature is that the I-It relationship is necessarily one of the past. All knowledge that is objective (and that is what the I-It has to be) is knowledge about one's past, whereas the I-Thou relationship is experienced exclusively in the present. One explanation of this is that in the I-Thou relationship each participant must be willing to accept whatever response is made by the person with whom one is relating. This means that each must be a true listener, a woman or man who will not attempt to predict the response of another but listen clearly without any previous judgment interfering with the hearing.

Buber and Hasidism

Born in 1878, Buber was the child of Jewish parents who were assimilated. His mother left the family when Martin was three years old and the boy was raised then by his grandparents in an area now known as the Ukraine. Critics have noted that one of the important influences on the development of Buber's theory of dialoguing resulted from his search for his absent mother. Buber's grandparents provided him with a background that prepared him for his study of philosophy and art, which he pursued in Austria, Germany, and Switzerland. The grandfather was a wealthy man very much interested in rabbinical Hebrew tradition and linguistics. His grandmother believed in the need to modernize nineteenth-century Jewish culture.

While Buber's doctoral dissertation centered on the thought of two important Christian mystics, Nicholas of Cusa and Jakob Boehme, it was the nihilism and skepticism of modern culture of Friedrich Nietzsche that most gained his attention. It was at this time, at the exact turn of the century, that Buber became a Zionist and editor of the Zionist weekly magazine, *The World* (*Die Welt*). This was at the invitation of the Zionist movement's founder Theodore Herzl in 1901.

But Buber did not remain editor a full year because Herzl's approach to establishing a homeland for the world's scattered Jews was significantly different from Buber's. Herzl emphasized the need for diplomacy to establish a Jewish homeland, while Buber insisted on the need for spiritual renewal and the immediate establishment of agricultural settlements in Palestine. Later, in 1916, Buber was to found his own, very influential journal, *The Jew* (*Der Jude*), which was widely read by Jewish intellectuals throughout the world. It was in these pages that Buber promulgated his idea that was to prove so controversial to many Jews and others—that a binational state be formed in Palestine based on the cooperation of Arabs and Jews.

It was also at the turn of the century that Martin Buber began to seriously study Hasidism. Based on the tradition founded by Israel Ben Eliezer (Baal Shem Tov) in Russia in the eighteenth century—of whose life little is known—Hasidism may be regarded as an eastern European religious-mystical-revival movement. The word *Hasid* is Hebrew for "pious one" and emphasizes the joy of religion as expressed in singing and in dancing, stressing religious commitment, the spiritual life, devotion to good deeds, and adherence to customs, laws, and traditions.

Buber saw in Hasidism a revitalization of Judaism that would—again paralleling his dialogic approach as manifested in the ideal I-Thou relationship—restore a proper balance to human beings in their encounters with God, with each other, and with nature. He wanted Zionism to reflect this "healing" just as Hasidism attempted to do in the eighteenth century. In his volume *Paths in Utopia* (1947), Buber claimed that in the Israeli kibbutz—an agricultural community of cooperating volunteers working in a natural environment—a kind of utopian socialism could be realized but was falling short of the ideal. While he did not label such experiments as failures, he did express disappointment over the fact that the majority of kibbutz dwellers neglected the person–God relationship, partly because they were alienated by inadequate representations of God rather than by the living God himself, who is beyond any representation.

By the middle 1930s, Buber became a major Jewish educational force in Germany. Under the Nazis, he was the director of the entire Jewish adult education program in Germany, where he courageously spoke out against Adolf Hitler's brand of nationalism. The Nazis so restricted his freedom that Buber chose to emigrate to Palestine in his sixtieth year. There he proved again to be an active and influential teacher. He held the post of professor of social philosophy at Hebrew University in Jerusalem until his retirement in 1951.

He was chosen the first president of the Israeli Academy of Sciences and Arts and helped to found the Teachers Training College for Adult Education, which concentrated on developing teachers for the great number of immigrants entering the newly established state of Israel. Part of Buber's success in this area was due to his ability to gain the respect and cooperation of those whose religious and political views differed from his own. This was a monumental achievement, particularly considering Buber's attitude toward a legalism in Judaism which he found objectionable. He taught that revelation can never be regarded in terms of law. Biblical laws are only a human response to revelation and thus have application to the periods in which they are formulated but are not obligations placed on future generations, which will need to make their own responses. Politically, he was also able to work with Zionists who rejected his cooperative efforts aimed at harmonizing Arab-Jewish relations. (At his funeral in 1965, Arab students publicly honored Buber in a very unusual display of respect.)

Toward the end of his life, Buber became interested in psychotherapy. Not surprisingly, Buber wrote of the dialogue aspects of that discipline, emphasizing the need for the patient and therapist to speak and hear each other, and warning the therapist not to remain cloaked in the mantle of a "school" and thus inhibit the dialogue possibilities.

Buber has had a large impact on such Christian thinkers as Paul Tillich, Gabriel Marcel, Ernst Michel, J. H. Oldham, and others, in spite of his insistence that Judaism has most emphasized the spiritual force of the God–man concept. He was critical of certain aspects of Protestantism that teach passivity of human beings in their relationship to God, and he rejected the ideas of some Catholic theologians who held that Judaism somehow was ignoring the concept of the grace of God.

HARRY JAMES CARGAS

Further Reading

Friedman, Maurice. *Martin Buber: The Life of Dialogue.* Chicago: University of Chicago Press, 1976. Considered the best work on Buber in English, this volume includes an excellent bibliography.

―――――. *Martin Buber's Life and Works*, New York: E. P. Dutton. Vol. 1, *The Early Years, 1878–1923* (1981); vol. 2, *The Middle Years, 1923–1945* (1983); vol. 3, *The Later Years, 1945–1965* (1984). This is the definitive biography of Buber in English.

Vermes, Pamela. *Buber.* New York: Grove Press, 1988. A nonscholarly introduction to the life and thought of Buber's central ideas as well as his impact on Christian thinkers.

Urs von Balthasar, Hans. *Martin Buber and Christianity.* London: Harvill, 1961. A critical but appreciative study of Buber's teachings by one of Europe's most widely respected Catholic theologians.

ALBERT EINSTEIN

Born: 1879, Ulm, Germany
Died: 1955, Princeton, New Jersey
Major Works: Scientific papers, originally published in German: "On a Heuristic Viewpoint Concerning the Production and Transformation of Light" (1905), "On the Motion of Particles Suspended in a Liquid" (1905), "On the Electrodynamics of Moving Bodies" (1905), "Planck's Theory of Radiation and the Theory of Specific Heats" (1907), "On the Relativity Principle and its Consequences" (1908), "On the Present State of the Radiation Problem" (1909), "The Foundation of the General Theory of Relativity" (1916), "Cosmological Considerations on the General Theory of Relativity" (1917), "On the Quantum Theory of Radiation" (1917), "Relativity: The Special and General Theory" (1920), "Quantum Theory of Monatomic Ideal Gases" (1925), *Can Quantum Mechanical Description of Physical Reality Be Considered Complete?* (1935)

Major Ideas

Coordinate space and time are not absolute, and the simultaneity of events is observer-dependent, but the speed of light is invariant (the special theory of relativity).

Mass is a form of energy, interchangeable with other forms according to the relation $E = mc^2$.

Gravitational force is locally indistinguishable from acceleration of the frame of reference (the equivalence principle).

Gravitational fields are manifestations of curvature of spacetime, which originates in the stress-energy of the material contained therein (the general theory of relativity).

Motion of massive bodies will create gravitational waves.

Light exhibits quantum properties in the photoelectric effect, with photon energy related to frequency by $E = hf$.

Atoms can be stimulated by the passage of light to emit more photons of the same energy.

Observations of diffusion can be used to determine the dimensions of molecules.

A monatomic gas such as helium should condense at low temperature into a superfluid state.

Understanding of gravitation, electromagnetism, and other interactions should be sought in unified-field theories.

Albert Einstein's mastery of physics and his influence on the form it takes today cannot be matched by any other figure in history except Isaac Newton. The transformation of classical into modern physics is due in large part to Einstein's work. He is also probably the most famous physicist of all time, and his story is deeply embedded in the popular image of that profession. He is an appealing figure because of his gentle, affable character and interest in humanitarian causes, coupled with strikingly creative work and technical brilliance that keep him at the same time forever remote from true popular understanding.

Soon after Albert's birth, his parents moved to Munich, and there he spent his formative years. His father and uncle were proprietors of a small busi-

ness, designing and manufacturing electrical equipment. Here young Albert imbibed early both an interest in the nature of light and electricity and an appreciation for the importance of measurements. Though he is most famous as a theorist, in fact he retained a keen interest in experimental physics in his career. When the family business failed in 1894, the family moved to Italy for a new start. The fifteen-year-old son stayed briefly in Munich, but soon dropped out of school; at least one teacher who considered him a disruptive influence was glad to see him go. Albert spent a few months in Italy before heading to Zurich for further education.

Contrary to a common misunderstanding, there was little doubt at any point about Einstein's mental abilities. He did relate poorly to some retrogressive features of the German schools of the time, and he had the confidence to follow his own priorities about what he learned and how he went about it. He cared for mathematics only as a tool, for instance, being more interested in visual conceptualization and experiments in science. His failure to gain entrance to the Federal Institute of Technology (ETH) in Zurich on his first try has much to do with his taking the exams a year earlier than normal, on top of being a dropout. The year he spent in the progressive cantonal school in Aarau (1895–96) not only gave him automatic admission to the ETH but also provided experiences (especially in its unusually well-equipped new laboratory) much more suited to his mental development.

As a university student, Einstein again followed his own unorthodox path, and his talents were not sufficiently recognized for him to receive encouragement toward an academic career; he failed to win an assistantship to continue graduate studies. After brief experiences with high school teaching and private tutoring, he took a position in the Swiss patent office in Bern in 1902, where he worked for the next seven years. He continued to discuss physics with several close friends from student days, and tried writing some papers, which at first gave no promise of distinction. It was as an outsider that he stunned the scientific community with the three great papers of 1905, which in a single volume of *Annalen der Physik* remade the foundations of three distinct areas in physics.

Over the next two or three years, the importance of these papers was gradually assimilated. Einstein was finally encouraged to submit a dissertation to receive the doctorate (having had an earlier attempt rejected), and to apply for academic positions. After brief appointments at the University of Zurich and the German University of Prague, he returned to ETH; his recommendation for this position from Poincaré commends "the facility with which he adapts himself to new concepts and knows how to draw from them every conclusion . . . when presented with a problem in physics he is prompt to envisage all its possibilities." Einstein finally took a special research professorship at the University of Berlin in 1913. He resigned that position in 1933 as

a direct result of abuses when Hitler came into power, and spent the rest of his life at the Institute for Advanced Study in Princeton, New Jersey. Einstein traveled widely; he missed the award ceremony for his own Nobel Prize in 1922, for instance, because he was lecturing in Japan at the time.

Einstein is most famous, of course, for his theories of relativity. The term is somewhat inappropriate, for the real heart of the theory lies in the study of *invariants*, those physical quantities that do *not* depend on the observer's frame of reference. Einstein actually created two quite distinct theories, the first of which (1905) is called special relativity (SR). SR is a theory of the nature of space, time, and motion, following primarily from careful examination of the meaning of simultaneity. Einstein realized that Newton's assumption of a fixed and absolute universal time was not the only reasonable possibility; if the speed of light provides a natural limit on how fast signals can travel, one should insist on an operational definition of how the readings on two spatially separated clocks can be related to one another. The consequences of this theory include the apparent mass increase and spatial contraction of moving bodies and apparent slowing of the rate of moving clocks ("time dilation"). The word "apparent" is crucial here, because the theory says these represent changes in the way events are described by particular observers, not actual alterations of the moving bodies. SR also led to recognition of the possible interconversion of mass and energy.

Many of the individual elements of SR had already been developed by Lorentz, Abraham, and Poincaré, including in particular the mathematics of the Lorentz transformation of coordinates. But this work was burdened with being an elaborate extension of classical ideas whose meaning seemed to become more obscure as it proceeded. Einstein's revolutionary contribution was in starting afresh and giving an entirely new physical interpretation to the symbols involved; Peter Bergmann says its revolutionary importance is because it is "formally simple, yet conceptually deep." At first, the limited data available on fast electrons contradicted SR, but Einstein was so sure of the theory that he was unperturbed, and after several years new and better data proved him right. By now, a vast array of results from many areas of physics confirms SR.

In attempting to overcome SR's limitation to inertial frames of reference, Einstein was led to general relativity (GR). This is a theory of gravitation, which differs from Newton's in saying that gravity is not merely a field that is created *in* space, but a modification of space-time itself. The first step (1907) was to recognize the principle of equivalence: Being in an accelerated frame of reference would be indistinguishable from experiencing a gravitational field. Gradually Einstein came to realize that this idea was best developed by supposing that gravity represents curvature of space-time, and that he would need much more powerful mathematical tools to describe this. With the crucial help of his friend Marcel Grossmann, he learned tensor calculus and then did much to extend it in developing GR. This work took several years, finally succeeding in late 1915. Einstein showed that GR should have three measurable effects that would differ from the predictions of classical physics: precession of the perihelion of the planet Mercury's orbit, deflection of starlight passing close to the sun, and red shift of the spectral lines of light radiated by a massive body. The first of these immediately resolved an existing puzzle, but it was several years before the second and third could be verified. The drama surrounding an expedition to observe a solar eclipse in 1919, and the subsequent announcement that Einstein's prediction of light bending had been verified, made him a worldwide celebrity. While the number of experiments in which GR can be critically tested remains small, some of them today can be done with high accuracy, and their support for GR appears to be strong.

Three further consequences of GR are of particular interest, two of them having first been pointed out by Einstein himself. In 1916 and 1918, he wrote two papers about gravitational waves, setting out important information about their nature and the circumstances of their production. In 1917, he wrote his first paper on cosmology, beginning the application of GR to the overall structure of the universe. And Karl Schwarzschild showed a solution of the GR

equations that was the first example of what are now known as black holes. All three of these are presently areas of very active research.

Aside from relativity, Einstein's most important work was on early quantum theory. One of the 1905 papers gave a radical explanation of the photoelectric effect. Max Planck, in his explanation of blackbody radiation five years earlier, had with considerable reluctance used a formula suggesting that material substances can interact with radiation only by transfer of energy in finite amounts, not continuously. Einstein was willing to go much further in supposing that light itself comes in discrete packages of energy that we now call photons (light quanta). It was nearly ten years before careful experiments by R. A. Millikan provided strong evidence that Einstein's explanation was correct, and many physicists remained unconvinced of the literal reality of photons until discovery of the Compton effect in 1923. Einstein's 1905 work foreshadows the whole discussion of wave-particle duality that flowered after Louis de Broglie's association of wavelength with momentum in 1923. It was for the photoeffect that Einstein was cited in his Nobel award—relativity was still too controversial. In 1916–17, he did further important work in this area, dealing with the relative probabilities of absorption, spontaneous emission, and stimulated emission of light by atoms. The third of these provides the foundation for light amplification and thus for all the practical applications of laser technology.

It is ironic that in this work Einstein was one of the first to develop the description of atomic processes in probabilistic terms, ten years before statistical interpretation of the wave function came forward as central to the new quantum mechanics. Already in 1916 Einstein expressed discomfort at this element of randomness, and he never fully accepted that aspect of quantum mechanics; he was fond of saying "Der Herrgott wurfelt nicht"— "God doesn't throw dice." His further contributions to this part of physics were in the form of valuable criticism rather than direct development: In an ongoing exchange of thought experiments with Niels Bohr, he forced the Copenhagen school to sharpen their arguments; and in 1935 he wrote a paper (with Podolsky and Rosen) proposing a paradox that remains central to ongoing discussion about the issues of completeness and reality in quantum theory. As Max Jammer has said, "No physicist had more to do with the creation of quantum mechanics than Einstein"—but having decisively influenced the rise and development of this theory, he then no less decisively denied its adequacy once it had gained general acceptance. This rejection represents his feeling not that quantum mechanics is incorrect but that it is incomplete; he always held out hope that some different kind of theory would give a more satisfying account of atomic behavior. This theory should not be a mere appending of "hidden variables" to quantum theory, but should establish new concepts from which the quantum theory would emerge as only a statistical approximation to the truth.

Einstein's scientific work was wide-ranging; other significant items include analysis of the "Brownian motion" of microscopic particles showing how it could be used to determine fundamental constants of nature, an early explanation of the specific heat of solids, improvements on the explanation of blackbody radiation, and development of the quantum statistics of identical particles. Only for Einstein would such accomplishments be of little enough relative importance to barely rate mention. There is one other major theme in his work, that of the unified field, which dominated most of his career after about 1925. He had the misfortune to attempt a very worthy program of theory-building at a time when available data were not yet sufficient (as they were in the 1960s) to suggest that the nuclear forces (rather than gravitation) were the best candidates to be combined with electromagnetic fields in a unified picture. If nothing else, his willingness to explore so many blind alleys in quest of the unified field theory demonstrates that his distaste for quantum mechanics was anything but scientific "hardening of the arteries."

Dealing with such fundamental issues in physics as he did, Einstein was quite aware of the philosophical implications of his work and interested in expressing his views. Those views developed with time, so that one can be misled by conflicting quotes from different stages in his thinking. He was an admirer of Spinoza, and as a student was also quite taken with the ideas of Ernst Mach. He credits Mach's views for much of his inspiration in solving the tangled affairs of electromagnetism and mechanics by the creation of special relativity. But by the time he completed general relativity, he and Mach had grown rather sour on each other. This is one aspect of Einstein's development from an early empiricism and positivism toward more of a realist picture later on, though as Fine says, "Einstein's realism is not the robust metaphysical doctrine that one often associates with that label." He would call it instead a "motivational realism"; that is, Einstein's realism is not any one particular theory but a *program* of trying to construct realist theories in hopes of matching empirical data, even reaping the dividends of successful prediction. In a foreword contributed by Einstein to a translation of Galileo's *Dialogue*, he said, "There is no empirical method without speculative concepts and systems; and there is no speculative thinking whose concepts do not reveal, on closer investigation, the empirical material from which they stem. To put into contrast the empirical and the deductive attitude is misleading."

While Einstein certainly led one of the great intellectual revolutions of all time, he often denied the revolutionary character of his own work. This was partly a reaction against journalistic extravagance in describing that work. But it was also because he felt himself in the deepest sense to be truly carrying on the work begun by Galileo, Newton, and Maxwell. Holton suggests that some of the key elements in his success were an ability to adopt an unconventional point of view when needed to expose a fault in some nagging problem, a willingness to concentrate for years on a single problem without regard to contemporary fashion, and an ability to make great but sure-footed intuitive leaps to new basic principles or viewpoints. No less important was a flair for asking himself childlike questions about such simple things as space and time, and then taking those questions seriously; the most famous example is wondering how a light wave would appear if one traveled alongside it.

Once Einstein was thrust upon the public stage, he endured with good humor most of the inevitable misunderstanding and nonsense generated by the media. He protested, often in vain, that his theory of relativity had no application whatsoever to the social sciences, arts, or ethics. Without taking himself too seriously, he used many opportunities to make very personal statements about education, re-

ligion, pacifism, Zionism, and other issues of the day. In retrospect one can criticize some of these as naive, but on the whole we value them today for their reassurance that one of the most brilliant creators of abstract science could still be a reasonable, gentle, caring, and whole human being. His influence upon the world around him is to be admired along with his monumental physical theories.

DONALD E. HALL

Further Reading

Clark, Ronald W. *Einstein: The Life and Times.* New York: H. N. Abrams, 1971. Widely read popular biography, which is somewhat weak on insight into the scientific work.

Einstein, Albert. *Relativity: The Special and the General Theory.* 1st ed., 1916. 15th ed. New York: Crown Publishers, 1952. An account written by Einstein himself for the general reader who is not conversant with the mathematics of theoretical physics. Although the reader may get lost from time to time and the going is difficult, the reward may be a fundamental grasp of the basic ideas that revolutionized physics.

Fine, Arthur. *The Shaky Game: Einstein, Realism and the Quantum Theory.* Chicago: University of Chicago Press, 1986. Chapters 1–6 examine at length the nature of Einstein's objections to quantum theory.

Friedman, Alan, and Carol Donley. *Einstein as Myth and Muse.* Cambridge: Cambridge University Press, 1985.

Hoffmann, Banesh. *Albert Einstein, Creator and Rebel.* New York: Viking, 1972. Recollections of a former assistant to Einstein, in collaboration with his long-time secretary Helena Dukas.

Holton, Gerald, and Y. Elkana, eds. *Albert Einstein: Historical and Cultural Perspectives.* Princeton, N.J.: Princeton University Press, 1982. Proceedings of a symposium on the centennial of Einstein's birth.

Pais, Abraham. *'Subtle is the Lord . . .': The Science and the Life of Albert Einstein.* New York: Oxford University Press, 1982. A thorough and authoritative scientific biography by a physicist who worked alongside Einstein at the Institute for Advanced Study.

Pyenson, Lewis. *The Young Einstein: The Advent of Relativity.* Bristol: Adam Hilger, 1985. Chapters 1–3 are informative about Einstein's social and educational background, and chapter 9 about his early career.

Sugimoto, Kenji. *Albert Einstein: A Photographic Biography.* New York: Random House, 1989.

PIERRE TEILHARD DE CHARDIN

Born: 1881, Sarcenat, France
Died: 1955, New York, New York
Major Works: *The Divine Milieu* (1957), *The Phenomenon of Man* (1955)

Major Ideas

Evolution, or cosmogenesis, has a direction.

Evolution ascends toward a final point, or Omega, which exerts an attraction on the process although it stands outside of it.

Evolution has a within as well as a without, taking place on both the physical and psychic levels.

Tangential energy moves evolution on the without while radial energy operates on the within.

Ultimately all energy is one, namely, psychic energy, or Love.

Omega is the Cosmic Christ who attracts an increasingly personalizing universe to a kind of cosmic mystical consciousness.

God and the evolving universe are united one with another.

The moral and spiritual responsibility of human beings is to advance the work of evolution and thus to create the future.

If human beings are like poems in the sense of being worlds unto themselves, living unities that defy fragmentation and analysis, then Pierre Teilhard de Chardin is a metaphor for this truth. A complex man in the variety and enormity of his interests, yet simple in the elegant unity of his vision, Teilhard proves the fallibility of attempts to classify human experience. The complexity of this man is apparent in the obvious fact that he was both a scientist and a priest, his simplicity in his insistence on the unity of the truth that he found and created through the two vocations.

Born in Sarcenat, France, in 1881, Teilhard inherited from his father the desire to understand natural history and from his mother a disposition to appreciate the beauty of nature. The poet and scientist in him were manifest at an early age.

Attending the Jesuit school at Villefranche, he passed the baccalaureate at the age of eighteen and entered the Jesuit novitiate at Aix-en-Provence, continuing his studies in French, Latin, and Greek two years later at Laval. With the expulsion of the religious orders from France in 1902, he went to Jersey to continue with the Jesuit community and study Scholastic philosophy.

September of 1905 saw Teilhard on the first of his many exotic excursions, this time to Cairo, Egypt to teach physics and chemistry at the Holy Family College, and also to expand his knowledge of geology and paleontology. In Egypt he encountered the East, which would fascinate him all his life. He also began his publishing career there, writing on scientific subjects.

His scientific studies receded in importance when he traveled to England for final training for the priesthood and ordination and when, in 1914, he joined the army to serve as a stretcher-bearer. In 1919 he resumed his scientific career, studying at the Natural History Museum in Paris and completing a doctoral thesis in 1922. Until April 1923, when he left for China to join the French paleontologist Père Émile Licent, Teilhard taught geology at the Institut Catholique in Paris, garnering a reputation as a brilliant, innovative thinker.

The experience in China was essential to the vision that was growing in Teilhard's mind and heart. In the vast solitude of the Ordos desert, Teilhard not only participated in the discoveries that made famous the French paleontological mission but also nurtured a unique spirituality that bore fruit in the beautiful "Mass on the World," published in Teilhard's *The Hymn of the Universe* (1955).

His return to France in the fall of 1924 occasioned the first of many difficulties he would encounter with his religious superiors about his theological interpretations. The tragedy underlying the years until his death was the recognition on his part that his powerful and confident Christian vision, which was being born out of his intense love for God and the world, would remain suspect in the eyes of the Church and would render him suspect as a Catholic priest as well. Although there is considerable evidence that Teilhard suffered deeply because his work was not accepted by the Church and the writings that were not strictly scientific did not receive the imprimatur necessary for their publication by a member of a religious order, he never abandoned his work or betrayed the vision.

In the next years, he traveled extensively, to India, America, and China, where he lived during the Japanese occupation, leaving at last in 1946. In 1951, Teilhard accepted as a kind of self-exile from France and from recrimination by his order an appointment at the Wenner-Gren Foundation in New York, where he devoted himself to anthropological studies. A man of unfailing charm and intellectual vigor, he attracted many friends and colleagues, their esteem somewhat easing the pain of realizing that in his lifetime the Church would not accept his work or agree to its publication. On April 10, 1955, which was Easter Day, Teilhard collapsed late in the afternoon in New York. His funeral was humble, a quiet ending to a life that was destined to change the thinking and stir the hearts of countless men and women.

The Phenomenon of Man

Among the many writings of Teilhard, two stand out as essential to understanding his vision. The first, *The Phenomenon of Man*, appears to be the more scientific of the two, while *The Divine Milieu* has the look of a spiritual essay. In fact, they express the same vision, with differing points of emphasis.

The Phenomenon of Man was a complete manuscript by 1938, although like his nontechnical works, its appearance in book form would have to await publication until after his death. As Teilhard explains in the preface written in 1947, the book bears the title it does because man is preeminently significant in nature and mankind is organic in nature. The story of evolution that he traces in *The Phenomenon of Man* is unique in his insistence that the human being is the key to understanding evolution. Since consciousness is the aspect that sets human beings apart from other manifestations of evolution, Teilhard seizes upon the phenomenon of reflection as if it were the thread of Ariadne by which to find one's way through the labyrinth of evolution.

Two terms that are essential in Teilhard's vocabulary are "cosmogenesis" and "orthogenesis." The first term indicates the scope of evolution, that he is treating not just an aspect of evolution but the whole of it as a cosmic event. Orthogenesis is a term first used by the biologist Wilhelm Haacke in 1893 and later defined by Gustav Eimer as a general law by which evolution takes place in a noticeable direction. Thus evolution has a drift, even though chance is still operative. Evolution begins with the fact of primordial matter, perhaps the result of an event like, if not the same as, that postulated by scientists as the big bang. In this matter, all of creation is potentially existent. Given primordial matter, evolution ascends through four major stages in four spheres.

Geogenesis is the evolution of the cosmos in the form of prelife in the geosphere. In this stage, matter presses from an undifferentiated state to one of organized forms, moving, for example, from the less complex form of the nucleon to the more complex one of the atom and thence to the molecule. Each manifestation, whether electron, proton, atom, or molecule, is a closed whole with properties unique to itself.

The cosmos continues to be born in biogenesis, which is evolution of life in the biosphere. Here the process is manifest in the evolution of the simple cell to complex cells, to algae, to fish, to amphibia, to reptiles, and to mammals.

"Noosphere" and "noogenesis" are terms that Teilhard coins to suggest the stage of evolution marked by the emergence of human beings and the birth of thought. The phenomenon of man with the power to think is a new and critical point in evolution, for at this time the earth finds its soul, Teilhard says, and with his reason man is able to seize the rudder of evolution and reduce the force of chance.

Through these three stages of cosmogenesis, Teilhard is walking on the fairly firm ground of scientific inquiry, especially in those sections where his paleontological expertise undergirds the discussion. But as Teilhard projects evolution into the fourth stage, that of Christogenesis, what has seemed a real story collapses for his critics into fiction in the camp of science and scandal for those bastioned in theology. In this stage, Teilhard clarifies the spiritual nature of evolution, explaining that the process is not pushed from below but attracted from above; that which attracts is Omega, the final point to which the cosmos has been struggling and continues to struggle to give birth. The Omega is that to which all creation is ascending and that which stands outside of the process but nonetheless energizes it with its attracting power.

Christ, the Omega

Omega, Teilhard asserts, is Christ, whom he also calls the Cosmic Christ, Christ-Omega and Christ-the-Evolver. Before Omega or Christ-Omega is realized, however, cosmogenesis is to move through the stage of survival, which in turn is subdivided into the collective and the hyperpersonal. In the collective, human beings under the pressure of increasing proximity one to another recognize the need to cooperate and coexist; evidence of the collective abounds in such forms as the alliance of science and religion and global enterprises in politics, economics, and governance.

Beyond the collective is the era of the hyperpersonal, when individuals become ever more aware of their uniqueness, not as a factor to alienate them from one another but as a psychic reality that draws them together. In the vision of the hyperpersonal cosmos, Teilhard sounds a familiar mystical note, affirming on a cosmic scale that men and women will realize their uniqueness as intensely as do lovers who in rapturous embrace at last see themselves in the full beauty of their personhood. Individuality is not lost but realized in the consciousness of the hyperpersonal.

The language of the mystic points as well to the reality of Christogenesis, or the realization of Omega, when the cosmos in its particularities is united in an ineffable embrace, each particularity a center of consciousness, centered in itself, and every center touching every other center by dint of being centered in the ultimate Center of Christ-Omega. Omega is visible already in the historical fact of Christ's birth, but the transformation of cosmogenesis into Christogenesis may take 1 or 2 million years.

Two laws control evolution. The first is the law of complexification, whereby evolution builds up units that are ever more elaborate as organizations or systems. Just as there is an increase of physical complexity, so there is increasing complexity of consciousness, of which the nervous system is the judge. The emphasis on psychic complexity reveals the uniqueness of Teilhard's vision, for, arguing by analogy, he posits the existence of consciousness and its evolution along the same lines as physical evolution. That is, just as the emergence of a physical phenomenon on the horizon of evolution is not without precedent, so the advent of thought in human beings has its precursors, whose existence, although not yet detected scientifically, is reasonable to assume given the demonstrable nature of cosmogenesis.

The second law that governs evolution is entropy, the cosmic force that constantly fights against the rise of complexity-consciousness. This law dictates that with each conversion of energy from one form to another, some of the energy is lost as useless heat that diffuses throughout the universe. By the second law of thermodynamics, the whole universe is moving inexorably toward its death.

Teilhard did not accept the inevitability of cosmic death, for he saw evolution moving on a within as well as a without, and the energy that in the final analysis makes possible the entire process defies death. Appropriate to the two forms of evolution—the physical and the psychic—are two manifestations of energy. Tangential energy links units of the same complexity, while radial energy builds up complexity and causes evolution to move forward, or, stated more aptly, to ascend. Ultimately, however, all energy is psychic, and this internal energy Teilhard identifies as love, the transcendent force that in the face of physical death creates life.

If the scientific community repudiated the larger vision of Teilhard and sought his company only on the safe terrain of scientific inquiry, his religious peers and superiors were no less reluctant to follow his star. His vision of Christ-the-Evolver was enough to shatter their confidence in him as a theologian, a role that he shunned for himself in the belief that his theological training was insufficient. His writings took him into the theological arena, however, for he could not posit belief in Christ-Omega without calling into question the belief in a static world and the theology of fall and redemption to which the Church still clung in this century. Teilhard rejected the view of a world created perfect, that is, complete, in which human beings fell from perfection and were redeemed by a Savior. According to that view, redemption means return to a prior perfection. In a world that is evolving, such a static view is not acceptable. Hence Teilhard envisions cosmogenesis as ascending from multiplicity and chaos to a final point of unity and harmony. The geometric model for the ascent is a cone with the rising lines of evolution converging toward Omega. In the process, Christ is both in the process and outside of it; Christ is *within* as the historical Christ who prefigures the consciousness of Christogenesis and as the one who is being created (cosmogenesis-Christogenesis), and Christ is *without* as the Christ-Omega who in his plenitude attracts the process. Thus Christ *is*—Christ-Omega—and Christ is *becoming*—Christogenesis.

In this vision, there is no fall from perfection nor redemption in terms of a return to perfection. Rather, Christ redeems human beings insofar as he and they are cocreators in Christogenesis. As a consequence of this Christology, sin must be rethought; for Teilhard, human beings sin when they are aware of cosmogenesis and refuse to participate in the process. To say no to evolution is to say no to God—which is a theology of sin that sounds familiar even though it looks strange in the new clothes of its language.

The Divine Milieu

Thus Teilhard envisions an evolving cosmos that he understands on the basis of scientific inquiry and whose continuance he affirms from the depths of faith. What the contours of life at Omega would be he could not detail, but he does offer in *The Divine Milieu* insights into its nature as well as the character of those who occupy it. This book is one of the more mystical of his writings; indeed, Teilhard shows himself to be in the tradition of the Christian mystics, especially Saint John of the Cross.

Like Saint John of the Cross, Teilhard discerns the two faces of human experience in activities and passivities. Although we would like to think of ourselves as being in control of our lives, acting upon the world to shape events, the reality is that we experience ourselves as passive far more than we do as active. Yet our activities are essential to the divine milieu, for through them we create the cosmos and give birth to Christ. Teilhard rejects any notion that our daily work is merely something to offer up to God or to occupy our time until we can occupy the kingdom of heaven. Human endeavor is worthwhile in and of itself precisely because we participate in a cosmic enterprise by dint of our work, however humble or distinguished it may be. In these pages Teilhard celebrates the nobility of human endeavor with unmuted joy.

Just as passivities play the larger part in the mystical vision of Saint John of the Cross, so also do they in Teilhard's. Unlike Saint John, however, Teilhard speaks of two kinds of passivities, those of growth and those of diminishment. When we experience ourselves as being acted upon, recipients of life's experiences, as it were, and the gift infuses us with joy, as in the event of giving birth or in some way attending to birth, then the passivity is one of growth. Through the passivity, we touch the wellspring of our existence and are opened to God in joy and love.

Passivities of diminishment do not taste of joy as do those of growth, though eventually their bitterness is transformed into delight. We are diminished externally by the turnings of chance, as with natural disasters, and internally by deficiencies of mind, personality, and body. The ultimate diminishment is death, which presents itself to us as the final absurdity for the reason that we experience ourselves falling into the multiplicity of physical decay and decomposition. All experiences of diminishment are related to death in that they are foretastes of the ultimate bitter dregs we must swallow.

Teilhard does not advocate resignation in the face of diminishment but rather heroic resistance by which we muster every ounce of energy to combat the forces of decomposition. We are to exhaust ourselves in combat until, drained of energy, we accept the inevitable. Teilhard would have not only individuals but also society fight heroically against the forces of diminishment, through such work as medical research. Ultimately, death is defeated, for just as suffering can be transformed into spiritual energy, so can faith in Christ transform death into life.

Like Saint John of the Cross, Teilhard does not court suffering, but he does view passivities of diminishment in the light that illumines the "dark night" for Saint John, that is, as the context for spiritual transformation whereby a person dies to selfishness and is reborn in compassion for the world and love for God. Teilhard the scientist-mystic of the twentieth century speaks a language that differs from his sixteenth-century predecessor, in that the "dark night" for Teilhard has global as well as individual application for a cosmos that is laboring to give birth to the seed it carries within, the seed of Christ-Omega.

MARY E. GILES

Further Reading

Corbishley, Thomas. *The Spirituality of Teilhard de Chardin.* Paramus, N.J. and New York: Paulist Press, 1971. The author's concern is to explore Teilhard's spirituality, with particular attention to the Ignatian roots.

Demoulin, Jean-Pierre. *Let Me Explain Pierre Teilhard de Chardin.* New York: Harper & Row, 1970. Although essentially a compilation of passages from Teilhard's writings, the introduction, bibliography, and glossary of terms make this a helpful companion volume.

Jones, D. Gareth. *Teilhard de Chardin: An Analysis and Assessment.* Downers Grove, Ill.: Inter-Varsity Press, 1969. It is interesting to follow the appraisal of a scholar who, after providing a lucid introduction to Teilhard's concepts and vision, finds his evolutionary humanism inadequate.

Hefner, Philip. *The Promise of Teilhard.* Philadelphia and New York: J. B. Lippincott, 1970. A volume in the series *The Promise of Theology*, it offers a clear, succinct introduction to Teilhard's ideas.

Kraft, R. Wayne. *The Relevance of Teilhard.* Notre Dame, Ind.: Fides Publishers, 1968. Written by a professor of metallurgy, the book is splendid help in understanding the scientific concepts of Teilhard.

Lubac, Henri de, S.J. *The Religion of Teilhard de Chardin.* Garden City, N.Y.: Image Books, 1968. This is essential reading for understanding Teilhard.

JOSÉ ORTEGA Y GASSET

Born: 1883, Madrid, Spain
Died: 1955, Madrid, Spain
Major Works: *Meditations on Quixote* (1914), *Invertebrate Spain* (1922), *The Dehumanization of Art* (1925), *The Revolt of the Masses* (1930)

Major Ideas

Human beings and their circumstances exist in a dynamic interplay.

"I am I and my circumstance" is the phrase that conveys this dynamic interplay.

The individual can influence his circumstance but he cannot disregard it.

How the individual influences his circumstance is his "quehacer vital," or his creative action.

Vital reason as opposed to pure reason is derived from history, which provides a story that leads to the reality of human life.

Human beings create their lives by exercising vital reason and exerting their will.

The hero, or the excellent man, creates the noble life by exerting his will to go beyond the ordinary and the given.

The opposite of the hero, the mass man, is content with his own mediocrity and relies on opinion rather than reason.

Perspectivism means that although each individual sees truth from a unique perspective, truth itself is absolute.

José Ortega y Gasset's position as a philosopher is as problematical as Spain's has been relative to the modern European community. He did not devise a philosophical system as such, yet his writings yield an abundance of ideas such that he gained a reputation as Spain's foremost thinker of the twentieth century. One reason for not considering Ortega a philosopher in the strict sense is that his preferred form was the essay, in which he savored ideas without having to present rigorous proof. His penchant for the essay probably was nourished by the journalist milieu in which he was reared. His father was an influential journalist on the liberal side of the press as well as a popular novelist, while in his mother's family there were numerous politicians, including government ministers. Consequently, when Ortega began to circulate his ideas, he chose to do so in the double arena of journalism and politics.

Before his first articles would appear around 1904, he studied with the Jesuits in Málaga, attended the University of Salamanca in 1898, where he became acquainted with Miguel de Unamuno, and in 1904 received a degree from the Central University of Madrid. That same year saw his first trip to Germany, followed from 1905 to 1907 by visits to Leipzig, Berlin, and Marburg, where he studied with the neo-Kantian philosopher Hermann Cohen, returning in 1911 for further work with the famed scholar. The first visit sparked a lifelong enthusiasm for German culture, which would compel Ortega to urge for his countrymen the same devotion to scientific and objective methodologies that he encountered in Germany. Although Ortega did not want Spain to renounce the qualities that were beneficially Spanish, he did advocate a compromise with German culture so that Spain would be a modern, Europeanized nation. The love affair was not one-sided; until his death, Ortega enjoyed an esteem in Germany that at times, especially after the Civil War, was greater than in his native land.

Ortega's appointment to the faculty of the Escuela Superior de Magisterio in 1908 initiated his career as a sociopolitical teacher and critic. The university provided a context in which to pronounce the ideas that made of bright, restless students his devoted disciples. Teaching in Madrid, he was aptly located to observe the workings of government and, as early as 1909, to launch his attacks. From 1910 to 1936, when he left Spain for the duration of the war, spending his exile in France, the Netherlands, South America, and Portugal, Ortega held the position of professor of metaphysics at the Central University of Madrid. During these years, his concern that Spain modernize and join the European community prompted writings on political and social themes and resulted in his election as a delegate to the legislature when the Spanish republic was declared in 1931.

The preferred medium in which Ortega observed contemporary Spain was the newspaper and journal. He published a series of articles in *El Sol* in 1920, founded two magazines, *España* (1915–16) and the *Revista de Occidente* (1923–36), and published a one-man review, *El Espectador*, for almost twenty years (1916–35).

If teaching and writing for newspapers and journals were realistic modes by which to communicate his ideas, so also were lecture tours and foreign travel. His lecture tour to Argentina in 1928 and the frequent visits to Germany before the Civil War and after it, as well as to the United States in 1949, are evidence of his eagerness to observe the world and to analyze the Spanish condition from a larger perspective.

Meditations on Quixote

The fruits of his observations are not only lectures and journalistic essays but also book-length studies. In 1914, Ortega published *Meditations on Quixote*, a book that in its form suggests what philosophy is for Ortega y Gasset. His method is to meditate *on* the *Quixote* and *with* it—that is, to circle the text with attentive gaze so as to see the circumstances of his life and through them to exit toward the universe in search of connectives and coherence. In the important foreword to the reader, Ortega explains that the essays, which constitute the *Meditations on Quixote*, are motivated by philosophical ideas, although they are not philosophy, which he considers a science. His meditations are simply essays; that is, they are science without explicit proof.

Ortega's technique of meditating on a specific

phenomenon, in this case the novel by Cervantes, indicates his belief that philosophy cannot exist apart from the concrete conditions of human life. Thus he shunned abstractions in favor of the observable fact, no matter how tiny or grand. In his personal case, he had to consider the condition of Spain in its historical and cultural reality as the circumstance through which he communicated with the universe. He rejected nineteenth-century idealism that posited the "I" as a cerebral, contemplative subject for whom, as the center of the universe, things are mere objects. This exaggerated subjectivity he denied in search of a harmony between subject and object such that one would not be the inferior term in the relationship. He saw the "I" not as a substantial being but as one who exists in active correlation with the world, the one not existing without the other. "I am I and my circumstance" rose the soon-to-be famous cry from the *Meditations*; by circumstance Ortega meant *circum stantia*, the mute things that surround us. Later, in *What Is Philosophy?* (1929) Ortega spoke of the world as confronting, surrounding, affecting, pressing at him, and of himself as consisting in occupying himself with this world, transforming it and suffering from it.

Just as Ortega could not regard himself apart from his circumstance, but rather lived vitally related to that which surrounded him, so he could not value understandings as philosophical unless they issued from the dynamic of the "I" and the circumstance relating one to the other.

The *Meditations on Quixote* disclose the kinds of understanding that attention to vital relations generates. With respect to literature, for example, he saw concepts of genre that were not based on formal distinctions but rather on the stance of the writer before his world; under his personal gaze, terms like "lyric," "epic," "comedy," and "tragedy" reveal new faces. Attentive always to the figure of Don Quixote, Ortega suggests that the essence of heroism is the act of will: The hero intends to be himself, to exert himself as being unique. The will to be oneself is heroism. Tragedy is the destiny of the person who exerts his will, refusing to give up the role that he has chosen to play. Don Quixote is the phenomenon that Ortega encounters and on which he formulates not only a theory of the literary hero but one that applies to individuals and societies in their concrete circumstances as well.

That the failure to exert the will in a heroic manner can affect society adversely is seen in one of Ortega's most controversial books, *Invertebrate Spain* (1921), a scathing criticism of Spain that in its concern for the position of the nation in the contemporary world reveals the author's link with the Generation of '98, the writers and thinkers who as a result of Spain's defeat in 1898 were forced to examine the traditional values that had isolated Spain from Europe for centuries. Ortega especially criticized the excessive regionalism of Spain that rendered her spineless, doomed to chaos and fragmentation. Ever alert to the circumstance of history, Ortega sought the cause of fragmentation in the Middle Ages, specifically in the weakened character of the Visigoths who, unlike the Franks, were not pure Germans. Unable to exert creative leadership, the Visigoths failed to establish a cohesive nation; they did not qualify as a select minority, which is possessed of foresight, vitality, and willpower—qualities that the masses by definition lack. Horizontally invertebrate because of excessive regionalism and vertically invertebrate in the absence of a select minority, Spain needed the discipline and order that, Ortega believed, undergirded German society.

The Revolt of the Masses

Prescinding from the idea that Spain suffered from the absence of a creative minority, Ortega extended his critique of modern society to include Western society in general in *The Revolt of the Masses* (1930). In this celebrated book, Ortega elaborates the theory of two classes, the masses and creative minorities, observing that societies advance dynamically when the masses accept themselves as such, allowing the creative minority to govern. Unfortunately, in modern societies, the masses have revolted by their refusal to accept their proper roles. In a penetrating examination of the mass man, Ortega sees that mass man is without direction, self-

satisfied, and preoccupied with his own well-being. Moreover, he relies on personal opinion rather than reason, considers himself perfect, and is without will. The prototype of the mass man is the technocrat, or the specialist, the person who knows very well a small corner of the universe but who is ignorant of the rest. Ortega calls the specialist a "learned ignoramus" who is self-satisfied within his limitations.

The mass man, then, is identifiable by an attitude that is the opposite of the dynamic man of excellence, who represents the creative minority. The man of excellence is a hero in that he exerts his will in service to values and goals that are larger than himself; he lives the noble rather than the common life in that he lives it as a discipline for which constant training, or asceticism, is required. The noble man expends himself, as does Don Quixote, in creative endeavors. The noble man is he who creates a "quehacer vital," that is, a vital task by which he informs his life with meaning.

Ortega shows himself to be existential in his insistence that human beings create the meaning of existence through life-affirming action. Unfortunately, so Ortega observed, society today lacks more than anything else a "quehacer vital," a project of life to inspire and direct all human activity. Western man does not know what to do or be, either individually or collectively.

The Dehumanization of Art

Ortega's interests were not exclusively social and political. He wrote and lectured on a range of topics, including art, education, bullfighting, and literature. His most influential essays on art and literature are *The Dehumanization of Art* (1925) and *Notes on the Novel* (1929). His interest in literature ought not to be surprising in light of his widely praised talent as a writer. He was optimistic about the future of the novel, seeing in the shift away from emphasis on plot to the invention of interesting characters the best hope of the novel. *The Dehumanization of Art* is a brilliant critique of contemporary art in which Ortega praises the artist for deforming reality and making of art something that exists wholly unto itself. Because modern art recognizes no authority other than itself nor claims a redeeming quality outside of its own existence, it can continue to be art.

The years after the Civil War until his death in 1955 were problematical for Ortega. While his fame was on the ascendancy outside of Spain, especially in Germany and the United States, in postwar Spain he enjoyed less favor. The years spent in exile set him apart from the men and women who had endured the war at home, and the younger generation particularly viewed him with distrust for ideas that appeared to be elitist and aristocratic. Nonetheless, Ortega exercised enormous influence over a generation of thinkers and writers and his stature as an essayist of remarkable lucidity and stylistic genius brought fame to Spain as well.

MARY E. GILES

Further Reading

Ferrater Mora, José. *Ortega y Gasset: An Outline of His Philosophy*. New Haven, Conn.: Yale University Press, 1963. A dependable introduction to the thought of Ortega.

Marías, Julián. *José Ortega y Gasset. Circumstance and Vocation*. Norman, Okla.: University of Oklahoma Press, 1970. A student of Ortega's, Marías has been considered the foremost authority on Orteguian philosophy.

Niedermayer, Franz. *José Ortega y Gasset*. New York: Frederick Ungar, 1973. A concise overview of Ortega's life and works, with emphasis on the importance of German culture.

Raley, Harold C. *José Ortega y Gasset. Philosopher of European Unity*. University, Ala.: University of Alabama Press, 1971. The author demonstrates a developed philosophy of Europe in all of Ortega's works.

NIELS BOHR

Born: 1885, Copenhagen, Denmark
Died: 1962, Copenhagen, Denmark
Major Works: *Atomic Theory and the Description of Nature* (1934), *Atomic Physics and Human Knowledge* (1958)

Major Ideas

The electrons that surround the nucleus of an atom can only occupy certain discrete states—those states being defined by Planck's constant, h. "In-between" states are not permissible.

The configuration of electrons in an atom is the primary factor that determines the chemical properties of an element.

Quantum mechanical descriptions of the states of atoms should be considered the most complete possible descriptions.

The classical ideal of complete causal explanation of any phenomenon is impossible to reach and should be abandoned in favor of statistical explanation.

Niels Henrik David Bohr was the child of an auspicious Danish family. His father, Christian Bohr, was an internationally known physiologist who raised two famous children, Harald, the mathematician, and Niels, the physicist. Niels shared his father's love for natural science and passed this love along to his own children, as he continually referred them to everyday experiences as examples of intriguing physical phenomena. Illustrations abound of the warm and familial atmosphere of the Bohr household, an atmosphere that encouraged personal growth and intellectual achievement.

Bohr was awarded his Ph.D. in 1911 by the University of Copenhagen. His thesis dealt quite ably with the electron theory of metals but never gained wide recognition, partly because there were few speakers of Danish who knew enough of the topic to promote its broader publication.

The years immediately following the completion of his degree were very important in Bohr's life. In 1911, he studied with J. J. Thomson; in 1912, he began his fruitful and lengthy relationship with Ernest Rutherford, and in that same year he married Margrethe Norlund, who was to be his faithful companion for more than fifty years. These events set the stage for the most significant single year of Bohr's professional life, 1913. In this year Bohr solved some of physical science's most nagging problems in a trilogy of papers. His initial break-

through came as an insight that Planck's quantum of action should be incorporated into the explanation of the mysterious stability of Rutherford's atom. This insight served to entrench Planck's constant in physical reality to a degree unapproached up to that time. Such a move also guaranteed the further erosion, if not collapse, of many strongly held beliefs from classical Newtonian physics. Bohr's fame increased due to his unrelenting quest for a thoroughgoing and consistent interpretation of these new ideas.

Bohr quickly gained an international reputation, which brought him as much stress as it did comfort. He was in demand from many corners and spent many of his mature years writing and delivering lectures on new themes and old. Bohr worked tirelessly from 1921 until the end of his life administrating what would eventually be named the Niels Bohr Institute for Theoretical Physics in Copenhagen. He played a role in the early stages of the development of atomic weapons, whose use he abhorred and whose strict control he tenaciously sought. All his life, Bohr was exceptionally meticulous about his publications (even personal letters often went through several drafts), and hence did not publish a single book-length work. Three nontechnical, philosophically oriented collections of his essays, however, have been published. In the 1934 publication of *Atomic Theory and the Descrip-*

tion of Nature, Bohr first develops his ideas about complementarity as the core of his philosophy of atomic physics. The two other collections, *Atomic Physics and Human Knowledge* (1958) and *Essays 1958–1962 on Atomic Physics and Human Knowledge* (1963), represent refinements of the basic philosophical positions of the earlier volume and a further branching out into other disciplines as they related to physics. Bohr died at his home on November 18, 1962, shortly after apparently having recovered from an illness.

The Structure of the Atom

The young Niels Bohr, newly graduated with his doctorate, had the privilege of studying with two luminaries in atomic physics, J. J. Thomson and Ernest Rutherford. Thomson is generally regarded as the discoverer of the electron, and Rutherford first proposed the nuclear model of the atom that would provide the foundation for Bohr's own model. Bohr benefited greatly from his contact with these two men, though he clearly sees his collaboration with Rutherford as the most valuable of his scientific life. In 1911, Bohr spent several months with Thomson in Cambridge, where he quickly became aware that Rutherford would be the better mentor in his particular field of interest. So in March of 1912 Bohr moved to Manchester to work with Rutherford, beginning a lengthy friendship and collaboration.

When Bohr encountered Rutherford, the latter had recently proposed that the nucleus of the atom was extremely dense and widely separated from the electrons. Rutherford suggested that the electrons were in orbit around the nucleus, modeled on the shape of the solar system. Compared to the size of the nucleus, the distance between the nucleus and the electrons was great. Also, the electrons had been shown to be exceptionally light in comparison to the weighty nucleus. This model explained many things, and Bohr was highly attracted to it. The simplicity of the model persuaded many other physicists of its value as well.

However, most physicists, including Rutherford himself, were reluctant to believe that the model provided a literal picture of the atom, because of problems in explaining how it could hold together. According to classical electrodynamic theory, a system such as Rutherford's atom, in which orbiting particles were held in position by electromagnetic attraction to the oppositely charged central nucleus, could not hold itself together. The negatively charged electrons should, according to the accepted physics of the day, collapse into the positively charged nucleus, and with all dispatch. This turn of events would make the existence of stable matter impossible. But stable matter *did* exist; hence it was thought that Rutherford's model had some serious shortcomings. This state of affairs did not deter the young Bohr, who, as a matter of character, could not rest as long as such quandaries persisted.

Another such quandary befuddled the world of the natural sciences at the same time. It was well known that the absorption lines in the spectrum of the element hydrogen displayed numerical regularities, but physicists and spectroscopists were at a loss to explain the physical origin of these regularities. Bohr, through his own work on the electron theory of metals and through his close contact with important chemists of the day, was well aware of this puzzling situation.

Bohr's great insight began with the notion that these two apparently unrelated problems might share a common solution. He thought that by taking Planck's quantum of action more seriously than did its discoverer, one might find the key to unlock the dual mysteries of atomic stability and spectroscopic regularity. As Bohr himself explained in a 1955 essay, "In the hitherto entirely incomprehensible empirical laws for the line spectra of the elements was found a hint as to the decisive importance of the quantum of action for the stability and radiative reactions of the atom." This "hint" led Bohr to propose that the electrons did not collide with the nucleus, because the very nature of energy prohibited it. Bohr suggested that the orbits of electrons were quantized in much the same way as were Planck's resonators in the original quantum postulate of 1900. Electrons could not, as the planets could, assume just any position relative to the focus of the orbit. They could only occupy states, called "shells" by Bohr, that were proportional to the angular corollary of Planck's constant. The allowed orbits were calculated by Bohr from the mountain of data accumulated from years of spectroscopic investigations.

Not only were electrons prohibited from assuming orbits in between the discrete ones allowed by Planck's constant, they could not even momentarily be in these states. This meant that an electron could not move continuously from one state to the other, because to do so it would have to traverse the forbidden territory. But experiment showed that atoms did in fact go from one state to another under certain conditions. According to Bohr's theory, which has been thoroughly corroborated, these movements were *dis*continuous, just as radiation was discontinuous (as had been shown by Planck and Einstein). Electrons were said to jump from one stationary state to another (hence the origin of the phrase "quantum leap"). This transition resulted in the emission or absorption of radiation in discrete quantities, a process that explained the hitherto anomalous distribution of spectral lines.

Bohr's well-founded conjectures met with a mixture of praise and skepticism when they were published in the 1913 series of papers. The agreement of his ideas with the experimental data was undisputed, but the radical departure from classical physics was cause for grave concern on the part of many of Bohr's contemporaries. The debate about the proper physical interpretation of Bohr's notions continues, but the practical fruitfulness of the same theories is undebated.

The influence of Bohr's ideas on subsequent physics and chemistry is difficult to overestimate. The quantum revolution that has changed the civilized world of the twentieth century relies heavily on Bohr's atomic model. The shape of the periodic table of the elements depends largely on the conclusions of Bohr concerning the nature of the periodicity of the elements. He was able to predict successfully the properties of hitherto undiscovered elements and the nature of spectral data from hitherto unobserved regions of X-radiation. His observations explained why certain chemicals acted as they did and gave the first comprehensive tool that

accounted for the mechanism of chemical bonding. Though Bohr's model was quickly shown to be inaccurate as a literal picture of the shape of the atom, the practical value of the model continues. Bohr's ideas were exceptionally useful in the description of simple systems, such as the hydrogen atom, but the world had to wait for those who would elaborate on Bohr's foundations before adequate explanations of more complicated systems were offered.

The philosophical repercussions have been no less profound, even though the conclusions reached have been fewer and more tentative. Much of Bohr's contribution to the changing of the thought patterns of contemporary scientists and philosophers can be traced to his uncompromising pursuit of the full implications of Planck's quantum of action. Planck was the first to suggest that radiation was available only in particular size units; Einstein suggested that radiation, including light, existed only in such units (through his work on the photoelectric effect); Bohr showed how this feature of energy had universal consequences for nature and our understanding of it. In a strong sense, Bohr tried to bring to completion the break with classical physics inaugurated by Planck's 1900 discovery. This effort was met with notable success.

Classical physics, epitomized by Newton and carried on with tremendous success by countless others, had no room for energy that had to be quantized, or for noncontinuous entities, or for spontaneous jumps of particles. These new ideas, along with the increasing experimental evidence in their favor, compelled an extensive rethinking of accepted doctrine in the physical sciences. Cherished notions such as objectivity, causality, and determinism simply could not be salvaged in the new system, at least not in the form in which they had been held previously.

The "Copenhagen Interpretation" of Quantum Physics

Nowhere is there written an official doctrine named "the Copenhagen interpretation" of quantum physics, but the writings of Niels Bohr hinge around a few important concepts that are at the heart of the understanding of physical reality that goes by that name. Much of Bohr's perception of the broader meaning of the fundamental physical discontinuity that characterizes quantum physics can be gleaned from his treatment of the notions of complementarity and correspondence.

Ideas that would later coalesce into the principle of correspondence were present as early as 1913 in Bohr's writings. Bohr's electron shells were radically different from anything encountered in physics before the quantum era, yet the world at the macroscopic, everyday level behaved just as the classical world-view predicted that it would. Thus Bohr knew that any very new theory must include within it the expected behavior at the visible level. The new theory met this requirement by proposing, and then demonstrating, that when very large numbers of atoms are involved in a system, the random jumps of the electrons "average out," resulting in the large-scale predictability of classical systems. The discontinuous behavior of matter does not become evident until one examines systems small enough that Planck's quantum of action cannot be ignored. The visible world is much too large for anything as small as Planck's quantum to make a noticeable difference, under most circumstances. But when experimental techniques are sophisticated enough to allow the observation of effects of subatomic events, then Planck's constant can no longer be ignored. Hence, when large numbers of atoms are being investigated, even according to quantum rules, the results *correspond* to classical results. Classical mechanics is then seen as a special case of quantum mechanics.

With the notion of complementarity, Bohr describes the way in which everyday concepts are inadequate to the task of depicting microscopic reality. He has been quoted as saying, "Anyone who is not shocked by quantum theory has not understood it." Complementarity allows the shocking aspects to be brought to light. Early in his career, when he realized the fundamental significance of Planck's quantum of action, Bohr could see, perhaps only hazily at first, that a wholesale revision of classical concepts was going to be needed.

The very notion of cause and effect, the cornerstone not only of classical physics but also of classical thought, assumed that systems varied continuously, moving regularly and predictably from one state to another. The quantum postulate suggested that matter and energy are not continuous but corpuscular, behaving not smoothly but in fits and starts. In such a scenario, our accustomed language and conceptual framework have only limited applicability. The pictures used to explain physical events, pictures drawn from our apparently continuous experience of our everyday world, could not explain atomic reality except in a very limited way. For example, electrons and light cannot accurately be said to be waves *or* particles, but something very different—we do not possess any picture at all to describe it. Hence our various pictures, the only means we have of linguistic description, should be expected to bump into contradictions, such as the wave/particle dilemma.

The debate over whether electrons, light, and other subatomic particles are ultimately wavelike or particlelike is a premier example of a complementary relationship between mutually exclusive descriptions. Both electrons and electromagnetic radiation (including light) stubbornly refuse to be classified as either wave or particle. Numerous experiments apparently confirm both models. To our minds, full of concepts based on the everyday world of classical physics, this makes no sense. Bohr realized this and concluded that our everyday concepts simply do not apply to the subatomic realm. Bohr proposed instead that these mutually exclusive yet jointly necessary pictures provide complementary interpretations of the phenomena. Neither is complete, yet neither is wholly mistaken. This rather vague and apparently inadequate means of description is simply the best we can do. The nature of physical reality precludes our being able, ever, to gain a more precise physical description of these subatomic entities.

In order to describe subatomic phenomena, then, we must resort to descriptions less precise than classical mechanics would tolerate. In quantum mechanics, this means that the most complete description possible is a statistical one. We cannot tell what a given subatomic system will do in the future, but since we know that on the average many atoms together approach classical limits, we can assign a probability to one outcome as opposed to another. Heisenberg's uncertainty principle (which postdated Bohr's early thoughts on complementarity) sets an unsurpassable limit to the accuracy with which any given subatomic particle can be measured. This limit, which gives mathematical rigor to Bohr's notion of complementarity, requires that statistical approximations be the most accurate possible descriptions of individual atomic states. We will never be able to penetrate the atom with an application of our classical pictures to the behavior of what is found there.

Attempts to describe the microscopic run into further trouble when one considers the act of observation. There are dual difficulties here. First, the experimental apparatus is necessarily an object in the classical world, so the information it yields must be interpreted in light of complementarity. Second, observation connects a classical, macroscopic observer to a nonclassical, quantum reality. The classical observer, armed with classical concepts, assumes the existence of a continuous causal chain from the event to the observation of the event. For quantum-level systems, this assumption is grossly inaccurate. In fact, the very act of observation produces unpredictable behavior on the part of the observed system, making an objective description of the event impossible. The most that can be done is to describe the overall observation-event, which involves the inseparable observer-observed system. Again, this causes classical pictures of events to lose their relevance.

Considerations such as these persuaded Bohr to promote the abandonment of the traditional notions of objectivity and causation. Since we would never be able to observe any alleged causal connection between discontinuous atomic states, and since we would never be able to conduct experiments without

a crucial influence by the observer, there was no reason to hang on to these concepts at all.

Bohr's endeavor to eliminate the traditional concepts of causality met with stiff opposition from some of the most celebrated physicists of his day. Planck, Einstein, and Schrödinger all continued to believe that there is an underlying continuity in subatomic events and that causation is universal, despite the apparent obstacles to demonstrating this belief experimentally.

One of the most famous debates in the history of science is the one between Bohr and Einstein. These two brilliant men engaged in sometimes heated exchanges over the proper interpretation of quantum theory. Bohr insisted that random jumps and statistical approximations were permanent parts of physical theory, while Einstein maintained that quantum physics was inherently incomplete and that "God does not play dice." Einstein and others created numerous thought experiments designed to envision situations in which quantum mechanics, and the limits represented by Heisenberg's principle and complementarity, could be shown to be incomplete. Einstein seemed to think that eventually experimental technique would surmount the problems that prohibited a classical space-time description of all phenomena. In each case, Bohr illustrated how the situations envisioned by Einstein would not in fact supersede the limits imposed by uncertainty and complementarity.

Einstein and Bohr never reached agreement on these issues, and both types of interpretations persist. Experiment and consensus since the early days of the theory, however, clearly favor Bohr's interpretation over Einstein's. More and more sophisticated experiments have served to strengthen the idea that the statistical and counterintuitive reading of quantum mechanics defended by Bohr (and refined by many others) is the most adequate.

D. Brian Austin

Further Reading

Folse, Henry J. *The Philosophy of Niels Bohr: The Framework of Complementarity.* Amsterdam: North-Holland, 1985. A thorough discussion of the notion of complementarity, with useful reference to popular misunderstandings of the notion.

Honner, John. *The Description of Nature: Niels Bohr and the Philosophy of Quantum Physics.* Oxford: Clarendon Press, 1987. An interesting analysis of Bohr's philosophy in comparison with other world-views, including mysticism.

Jammer, Max. *The Conceptual Development of Quantum Mechanics.* New York: McGraw-Hill, 1966. An unparalleled historical source that recounts the theoretical development of quantum theory from its inception through the various debates about its proper interpretation.

Mehra, Jagdish, and Helmut Rechenberg. *The Historical Development of Quantum Theory.* 5 vols. New York: Springer-Verlag, 1982, 1987. An exhaustive narration of the events leading the development of quantum theory. The authors begin with an analysis of nineteenth-century physics and the difficulties that caused the twentieth century to begin on such a radical note.

Murdoch, Dugald. *Niels Bohr's Philosophy of Physics.* Cambridge: Cambridge University Press, 1987. An exhaustive account of Bohr's interpretation of physical reality. The book is strong on providing philosophical and cultural context for the various ideas promoted by Bohr. It also includes an engaging account of the debate between Bohr and Einstein.

Rozental, Stefan, ed. *Niels Bohr: His Life and Work as Seen by His Friends and Colleagues.* Amsterdam: North-Holland, 1967. A series of essays by the family and friends of Bohr, including many revealing anecdotes and detailed biographical information.

PAUL TILLICH

Born: 1886, Starzeddel, Germany (present-day Starosiedle, Poland)
Died: 1965, Chicago, Illinois
Major Works: *The Interpretation of History* (1936), *The Protestant Era* (1948), *The Courage to Be* (1952), *The New Being* (1955), *Dynamics of Faith* (1957), *Theology of Culture* (1959), *Systematic Theology* (3 vols., 1951–63), *Perspectives on Nineteenth and Twentieth Century Protestant Theology* (1968)

Major Ideas

Human beings are ultimately concerned with the fundamentals of being and meaning.

The nominalist dichotomy of subject and object leads both to naturalism and supernaturalism; naturalism fails to appreciate the dynamic power and purpose of all being, while supernaturalism fails to appreciate the interpenetration of the sacred and the secular.

God, as Being Itself, is the essential ground and source of all natural and intelligible structures of reality.

Beings from their essence manifest what they are and what they ought to be in their dynamic acts of transcendence.

True symbols and myths participate in what they present and as such serve as avenues to the depth of being.

All reality can be potentially sacramental, for all reality is the interplay of the finite with the infinite.

When the essence of being is manifested in existence, it is in a state of alienation; in human beings, this is experienced as the encounter with nonbeing and in all the acts by which the finite seeks to make itself absolute.

In the movement from essence through existence to essentialization, human beings seek to overcome, by God's grace, the gap between essence and existence.

The Christian understanding of the Incarnation is that the deficiencies of the human existential situation have become absolutely united with the ground of all being, such that Christ conquers all the negativity of existence.

The German-American philosopher and theologian Paul Johannes Tillich, the son of a Lutheran pastor, studied at the Universities of Berlin and Tübingen. He received a doctorate in philosophy at Breslau (1910) and a licentiate in theology at Halle (1912). Ordained in the Evangelical Lutheran Church the same year as the granting of his licentiate, he later served as an army chaplain during the First World War. He held academic teaching positions at various German universities from 1919 until his dismissal by the Nazis in 1933. Accepting a post as professor of systematic theology and the philosophy of religion at Union Theological Seminary, he emigrated to New York. It was in these years (1933–55) that his international fame was established. In the last decade of his life, he was honored with distinguished professorships at Harvard (1955–62) and the University of Chicago (1962–65). His description of the human person as the one who is ultimately concerned about being and meaning could

serve as a description of Tillich's own life efforts. It was this preoccupation with humanity's ultimate concerns that led him to set forth a Christian worldview that saw at the core of being the manifestation of the divine.

Nominalism and the Modern World

Nominalism, a philosophy associated in the late Middle Ages with William of Ockham (d. 1347), was seen by Tillich to be the pervasive yet greatly deficient mentality of the modern mind. Nominalism rejected the reality of universals (as, for example, humanness or goodness) as fundamental qualities of reality in favor of an analysis of particular human beings or particular good acts; universals are abstractions from similar qualities of particular things, names (*nomen*) only, not a grasp of what is constitutive of a reality that underlies and grounds similarities. From a nominalist perspective reason does not participate in being as it seeks to grasp the essence of being but, rather, becomes an instrument for logical analysis of abstract concepts and a tool of manipulation put at the service of human appetites. Science thus emerges as an expression of the human will to have power over the world of nature.

In Descartes (d. 1650), the shift from a focus on the essential characteristics of being to the knowing subject would have a powerful impact on modern epistemology. Later, Immanuel Kant (d. 1804) would offer his famous transcendental method as a way to bridge the gap between the knowing subject and the object that is known. Both Descartes and Kant err, according to Tillich, for they do not argue from a preexisting harmony between humanity and the cosmos but, rather, elevate human reason to the supreme position of critical autonomy. In such a move, the intellect is made the final judge of the ground and meaning of religion and culture.

One of the fruits of the nominalist dichotomy of subject and object (the thinking person and what is thought) was naturalism. This world-view, as Tillich presents it, rejects the interpenetration of the finite forms of being with the Infinite source of meaning at the core of all being. Naturalism as a world-view sees all things in a state of interplay and tension in a self-sufficient secular finitude. By denying the presence of a universal power of being expressing itself in beings, this nominalistic philosophy undercuts the classical Greek claim, as for example in Aristotle (d. 322 B.C.), that individual beings strive toward an end (*telos*). This lack of teleology severs the inherent connection between being and value, for all things are called to be adjusted to a given set of natural conditions (as in Darwinism) rather than to fulfill the essential characteristics of their nature.

Tillich lamented the loss of the ancient idea of love as a dynamic power of being that moves all things toward unity. If there is no universal dynamic orientation of beings, then there are no universal moral demands and morality is reduced to maximizing subjectively experienced happiness (as in John Stuart Mill's ethics of utilitarianism). In its rejection of the claim that the finite can be a vehicle for the infinite, naturalism repudiates the idea that

cultural creations manifest ultimate significance as disclosures of the ground of being. Hence, in the modern world, music, art, and drama are often seen as only the expressions of subjective feelings, while love is increasingly thought to be a private psychological emotion.

The nominalist rejection of universals and the assumption of a radical distinction between the knower and what is known is, according to Tillich, also at the core of supernaturalism with its radical distinction between the natural and the supernatural. Tillich's early controversy with Karl Barth (1886–1968) finds its basis in Barth's claim, often made in Christianity, that humanity is subject to a divine realm situated over and against it. In supernaturalism, the great chasm between the infinite and the finite can be bridged only by divine revelation and human faith. Therefore, knowledge of God is dependent on the infallibility of religious documents and traditions. Theology becomes a rational justification of revelation to show that nothing contradicts reason, yet reason remains incapable by itself of transcending the natural realm.

In the absence of a true interrelationship between religion and culture, Tillich thought, one can find the reason for the quietism of the German churches and an important reason for their destruction by the Nazis. The Ockhamist's exaggeration of the will over the intellect in God leads the supernaturalist to emphasize the divine as an absolute being who wills all things (so the Protestant reformers), as well as to the Kantian claim that God is a guarantor that moral acts will lead to happiness. For Tillich this is a fundamental error, for such a conceptualization disassociates the divine from the core of being while serving to justify ecclesiastical and biblical authority. This view, which sets the divine as radically other than the nondivine, also depreciates all human culture as only various manifestations of the secular.

The Essence of Being

To rectify these manifestations of nominalism (naturalism and supernaturalism), Tillich's life work sought to offer a view of being that saw God as *being* itself (*esse ipsum*). God, as absolute transcendence, remains beyond all human attempts to finally capture and exhaust, while the same God, as absolute immanence, remains the essential ground and source of all natural and intelligible structures of reality.

For Tillich, the unconditioned depth of being can be encountered in the conditional experiences of life. When Tillich speaks of being and the God who makes reality be what it is, he stands in the tradition of Plato (d. 347 B.C.), who saw the Form (or essence) of the Good as that which gave to being its source, end, and value, yet the perfect Good is never fully realized in the imperfect realm of sensible existence. It was Tillich's closeness to the idealist and realist traditions that called him to a never-ceasing struggle with nominalism. Like Augustine (d. A.D. 430), Tillich saw a correlation of the finite and the infinite so that any knowledge of a particular truth or any love of a particular good was simultaneously knowing and loving God. Thus he writes in the first volume of his *Systematic Theology* that one is a theologian ". . . in the degree to which his intuition of the universal logos of the structure of reality as a whole is formed by a particular logos which appears to him in his particular place and reveals to him the meaning of the whole." By a method of correlation, Tillich sought to interrelate the meaning of, and the encounter with, the whole as an answer to the questions and dynamics that emerged from any particular cultural situation.

Tillich sought to reaffirm the ontological foundation of thought, in that he claimed all knowledge to be dependent on a correspondence of being to being itself. Truth is ". . . the essence of things as well as the cognitive act in which their essence is grasped" (*Systematic Theology I*). The essence of anything is what the thing is and what it ought to be. Put in other words, the essence of being is its intelligible manifestation (*logos*) and its dynamic orientation to completion (teleology). Both order and purpose stem from the perfect source and end of all being, God. Infinity is not a realm beyond the finite but rather includes finitude within itself, as it calls the finite to infinite completion. In this dynamic view of being, Tillich stands in the tradi-

tion of Bergson (d. 1941) and Teilhard de Chardin (d. 1955), in that these three men, each in his own way, claimed that at the core of reality is the dynamic of transcendence. Tillich puts it the following way in his work, *The Interpretation of History:*

> . . . There dwells in everything the inner inexhaustibility of being, the will to realize in itself as an individual of active infinity of being, the impulse toward breaking through its own, limited form, the longing to realize the abyss in itself.

Being is in essence good for in its order and in its dynamic orientation it expresses its primal unity with the absolute goodness, which is God. It is only when there is openness to the fundamental essence of existence in a state of ultimate concern that an individual or a culture truly encounters the divine. For Tillich, God is the answer to the question implied in being.

Tillich lamented the triumph of Aristotelianism in the Middle Ages over the Franciscan Augustinian understanding of the immediacy of the divine presence to the creation. This presence is manifested in the power of being in its resistance to nonbeing, as well as in the impulse within being to achieve union. Divine presence also makes itself visible in symbol and myth. The symbolic and mythic aspects of culture do not just point to something other than themselves but, rather, participate in what they present. So the national flag as a symbol participates in the power and meaning of the nation. Symbols and myths have an integrative and/or disintegrative power over individuals and groups, for they serve as avenues to the deeper dimensions of the human psyche and to the depth of external reality. All reality can be potentially sacramental, for all reality is the interplay of the finite with the infinite. All discourse about God is symbolic except the claim that God is being itself. God as the absolute ground of the structure of being is not captured in any structure; therefore, conceptual and experiential order participate in and simultaneously point to this absolute.

Existence

Since full power of being is never poured completely into any particular state of existence, Tillich argues, all beings that do exist have within themselves nonbeing. Existence implies, as Tillich reads the Latin etymology, a standing out (*ex-sisto*) from essence. Existence is a distortion and an estrangement from essence. Hence creation and the Fall from the absolute are identical. As Tillich puts it, "Actualized creation and estranged existence are identical" (*Systematic Theology II*).

This is at the basis of the religious awareness that in this life one is simultaneously present to and alienated from God.

The effects of existential alienation are self-elevation (*hubris*), unbelief, sin, irrationality, and concupiscence. With a focus on the self to the exclusion of God in the state of existence, a person loses his or her unity and essential center. In human estrangement, the meaning and ground of the whole is abandoned in favor of the absolutizing of the self. The awareness of death (the triumph of nonbeing) brings about horror, meaninglessness, and despair as tragedy obscures the essential goodness of being. Losing the primordial unity with the ground of being results in anxiety. In the context of anxiety, an individual must struggle to achieve self-realization. As the title of one of Tillich's most famous works puts it, one must have "the courage to be."

In the existential state, free persons misuse their freedom to create false absolutes. This is why throughout his writings Tillich reminds his readers of the "Protestant principle," which repudiates all the many idols and idolatries created by finite humanity as substitutes for the true infinite. He devotes numerous essays to critiquing various religious, national, economic, and personal "absolutes." The influence of Tillich's Protestant roots is also seen in his often-repeated claim that the existential state is a state of the "bondage of the will," a bondage that humanity is unable to break on its own. This inability and the awareness of the gap between essence and existence leads to a quest for new being.

New Being

Salvation is achieved only by overcoming the gap between essence and existence. In the third volume of his *Systematic Theology*, Tillich describes his whole system as a process moving "from essence through existence to essentialization." Essentialization is more than only a return to one's essential nature; having struggled in the situation of existence, the human being achieves new being by acts of self-transcendence and integration through the power of God's grace. This process of degrees for perfect healing (or essentialization) is reserved for the final and eternal realm known as the eschatological state.

This eschatological reality is made present before the end time in the person of Jesus, whom Tillich believes to be the Christ. Using the fundamentals of his philosophical system, Tillich understands the Incarnation to be the actualization of humanity in a way that did not involve the estrangement of existence from the absolute ground of all existence. This Godmanhood is unique in that only once in human history does existence exist without falling away from essence. He writes, "No philosophy which is obedient to the universal logos can contradict the concrete logos, the Logos 'who became flesh' " (*Systematic Theology I*).

Christianity offers itself as a world-view both of reason, in its claim to have grasped the essential structure of being, and of love, in that it proclaims a union of the divine and the human. The Christ event does not remove anxiety, ambiguity, finitude, nor death in the temporal realm but, as faith claims, takes these dimensions of existence into a unity with God. The essential paradox of Christianity is that one life conquered the conditions of existence. The Incarnation becomes the finite medium by which the infinite ground of being becomes transparent to all being and as such is the eternal conquest of the negativity of existence. Salvation is the overcoming of existential distortions of the divine life that are present, yet obscured, in existence. Salvation, as God's act (as opposed to all forms of self-salvation), expresses itself most fully in the symbols of the cross and the resurrection. The cross symbolizes total subjection to existential estrangement, while the resurrection symbolizes its complete conquest. For Paul Tillich, here is the essence of the gospel, the heart of the good news.

Influence

There is today no Tillichan school, yet Tillich's writings have received a careful reading and have left a significant impact on twentieth-century thought. The attempt to represent the fundamentals of Christianity through a realist ontology speak to many in this century who see in various contemporary philosophies influenced by nominalism a harvest of spiritual and cultural emptiness. Tillich's vocabulary of terms such as "dread," "choice," "commitment," "meaning," and "value" emerges, as it does in modern existentialism, from the human struggle against the destructive forces of alienation and nonbeing. His views on the struggles of existence to achieve essentialization find a receptive hearing among those who see the twentieth century as that age which experiences the complete breakdown of the cosmic securities so important to earlier times. Tillich's idea that anxiety has an ontological basis in the failure to achieve the fullness of being reemerges in the writings of some contemporary psychologists such as Erich Fromm and Rollo May. Also, in modern discussions in the philosophy of religion and in the study of religion, the claim that faith is, in essence, of ultimate concern and that it is a universal dimension of humanity is cited as revealing one important reason for the omnipresent phenomenon of religion despite pervasive secularism.

Tillich sought to find the point or boundary where the polarities of existence interrelate. He sought to delineate how the tensions of life (individual vs. community, divine vs. humanity, religion vs. culture, the holy vs. the secular) were in reality the coincidence of opposites. His conceptualization of the interpenetration of the one and the many was elastic enough for both of these dimensions of being. His discussion of symbol left room for a genuine diversity of approaches toward the divine. His writings reflect the modern suspicion of absolutist claims made by finite individuals and by their institutions. He sought a respectful pluralism without falling into a destructive relativism. As such, the writings of Paul Tillich encourage each reader to struggle with the call of the holy to achieve meaning in a life journey of authenticity.

Lawrence F. Hundersmarck

Further Reading

Dourley, John P. *Paul Tillich and Bonaventure.* Leiden: E. J. Brill, 1975. By comparing Tillich to the thirteenth-century theologian Saint Bonaventure, this text brings out Tillich's indebtedness to the Augustinian Franciscan tradition as well as the Bonaventuran Trinitarian tradition of the coincidence of opposites.

Grigg, Richard. *Symbol and Empowerment: Paul Tillich's Post-Theistic System.* Macon: Mercer University Press, 1985. This is an introduction to the nature and implication of Tillich's symbols.

Keefe, Donald J. *Thomism and the Ontological Theology of Paul Tillich.* Leiden: E. J. Brill, 1971. This is a comparison of Tillich and Saint Thomas Aquinas, with a focus on their respective claims regarding the nature of faith and theology.

Kegley, Charles W. *The Theology of Paul Tillich.* 2d ed. New York: Pilgrim Press, 1982. This revised edition is a reissue and update of the 1952 work, which offered fourteen interpretive essays on a wide range of issues emerging from Tillich's thought. This collection includes autobiographical reflections as well as a reply to the various contributors. The work ends with a comprehensive chronological bibliography of Tillich's publications.

Osborne, Kenan B. *New Being: A Study on the Relationship Between Conditioned and Unconditioned Being According to Paul Tillich.* The Hague: Martinus Nijhoff, 1969. A comprehensive and critical presentation of the idea of essence and existence. Since the author cites Tillich's works in their original languages, this study will be demanding for those who are not conversant with German. However, there is enough English in Tillich's other works so that, together with Osborne's clear summaries, the reader is left with an understanding of the major points.

Thatcher, Adrian. *The Ontology of Paul Tillich*. Oxford: Oxford University Press, 1978. A survey of all the major ontological claims of Tillich regarding being, nonbeing, God, essence, existence, and new being. This is the work to begin with for a sweeping introduction to the fundamentals of Tillich's system.

Thompson, Ian E. *Being and Meaning: Paul Tillich's Theory of Meaning, Truth and Logic*. Edinburgh: Edinburgh University Press, 1981. This work sets forth the problematic of truth, verification, meaning, and logic within the context of Tillich's struggle with nominalism.

ERWIN SCHRÖDINGER

Born: 1887, Vienna, Austria
Died: 1961, Alpbach, Austria
Major Works: *Collected Papers on Wave Mechanics* (1928), *Science and Humanism: Physics in our Times* (1951), *Nature and the Greeks* (1954)

Major Ideas

Partial differential equations representing wave phenomena best describe action on the atomic level.
Quantum physics can explain the persistence and the spontaneous mutation of genetic material.
The Hindu philosophy of Vedanta best matches the insights of modern physics.

Erwin Schrödinger worked not only on theoretical physics, including thermodynamics, quantum mechanics, and general relativity, but also on the philosophy and history of science. Fluent in four languages and an avid writer of poetry, he was a tireless popularizer of modern physics and its application to epistemology and to the discovery of the relationship between mind and matter. He deplored narrow specialization and valued science as a way of synthesizing all knowledge and answering the question, "Who are we?"

Schrödinger's father, a well-to-do manufacturer with scientific interests (he had published articles on plant genetics) was the primary influence on his young son. Schrödinger did not attend public elementary school, but was educated at home, entering the Gymnasium at age twelve. After the usual classical education, he attended the University of Vienna, where he began his studies in theoretical physics under Friedrich Hasenörl and Franz Exner. He served in World War I as an artillery officer on the Italian Front. In 1921, he accepted the chair of physics at Zurich, which had been held by Einstein. During the Zurich period, he wrote papers on a wide range of topics in physics: statistical thermodynamics (the branch of physics that links the micro-world of atoms and molecules and the macroworld of solids, liquids, and gases), the kinetics of gases, vibrations in crystal lattices, the theory of specific heats, and general relativity. In 1926–27, just before leaving Zurich, he completed a famous series of papers on wave mechanics, his chief contribution to physics.

Wave mechanics is one formulation of the laws of quantum mechanics. Quantum theory began in the early 1900s with the investigations by Max Planck, who determined that energy (light, radiation, heat) on the atomic level is emitted not in an infinitely divisible range of values but in discrete packets, called *quanta* (singular *quantum*), the value of which is called *h* or *Planck's constant*. Energy comes in "bits"; it is not a continuum. Planck did not explain the physical reality underlying his constant. This was done by Niels Bohr, who showed that atoms are composed of heavy, positively charged nuclei with light, negatively charged electrons revolving around them like a miniature solar system. In 1913, Bohr published his theory of the spectrum of hydrogen: An electron of any atom can be in any one of a series of energetic states; when it passes from one state to another, it absorbs or emits a quantum of energy equal to a multiple of *h*. By the 1920s, difficulties were arising with Bohr's theory: Noninteger values for the energy emitted were found and the values for helium did not match the theory developed using hydrogen. In 1926, several new approaches attacked these difficulties and established modern quantum mechanics. Among these were Schrödinger's wave mechanics and Heisenberg's matrix theory.

Schrödinger was inspired by the French physicist Louis De Broglie, who suggested that elementary particles have associated with them *waves* whose frequency is a multiple of *h*. De Broglie attempted to unite the wave and particle theory of light and matter but was not able to derive the equations describing his matter waves. This was left for Schrödinger.

Schrödinger postulated that a physical system (matter and/or energy) is a continuum that has wave properties. Each system has its own proper vibration, the frequency of which is the basic physical entity. Matter is analogous to light, both exhibiting at the same time *wave phenomena* (interference patterns, refraction) and *particle phenomena* (most obvious in the tracks seen in cloud chambers). In the atom, some wavelengths are possible; others are not. This explains Bohr's quantum values for the electron: Depending on the atom, only specific values are possible. It was quickly recognized that Schrödinger's wave equations were logically equivalent to Heisenberg's matrix mechanics—and were much easier to use—and with this recognition, wave equations became part of modern quantum mechanics.

Schrödinger immediately became famous in the world of physics, and when Max Planck retired from the chair of theoretical physics in Berlin, the scientific center of the world, Schrödinger was invited to replace him.

Schrödinger stayed in Berlin, writing on quantum mechanics, relativity, and Heisenberg's uncertainty principle until Hitler became chancellor in 1933, when Schrödinger moved to Oxford. He was virtually the only non-Jewish scientist to flee the Nazis. Immediately on his arrival, he learned that he had won the Nobel Prize in physics for 1933. Homesick, he returned to Austria in 1936, but with the *Anschluss* (German annexation of Austria) in 1938, he fled to Rome, then Dublin, where, in 1940, he became director of the School of Theoretical Physics of the Dublin Institute for Advanced Studies. He remained at the Institute for seventeen years, a most productive period for his philosophical thought.

During his stay in Dublin, he did further work on wave mechanics and cosmology, and (like Einstein) unsuccessfully attempted to develop a unified field theory that would link electromagnetism and gravity. However, his best-known works from this period are his studies on the foundations of physics and their implications for philosophy. He was hostile to the positivism illustrated by Ernst Mach's definition of science: "A description of the facts,

with the maximum of completeness and the maximum economy of thought." Schrödinger considered such a goal to be banal, incapable of keeping the work of research going. From his early years, he had felt the need of a metaphysics of science, a term he used in several senses, but chiefly as his name for experiences that give clues about the nature of reality: value judgments, philosophical wonder, puzzle-solving, an awareness of "relationships which have never . . . been grasped either by formal logic or by exact science . . . relationships which keep forcing us back toward metaphysics, that is, toward something that transcends what is directly accessible to experience." Metaphysics was for him the indispensable basis of knowledge.

Like many German and Austrian scientists, Schrödinger considered himself a philosopher—indeed, he may have viewed his philosophy as more significant than his physics. He was particularly interested in two problems that address the bases of scientific thought: *comprehensibility*, the hypothesis that physical reality can be understood by men acting in common, that things happen in processes governed by natural law; and *objectivation*, the removal of the observing self from the world that is studied. The former, of course, has been part of science since the Greeks, but Schrödinger was specifically reacting to the belief that matter on the atomic level is basically incomprehensible.

Schrödinger recognized that events/particles *on the atomic level* have a probabilistic and indeterminate nature: They cannot be observed directly nor can the positions of individual particles be determined; cause and effect do not apply to them. But unlike Heisenberg, Schrödinger believed that this indeterminate nature has nothing to do with any basic uncertainty in the subject–object relationships familiar in our everyday experience. He burlesqued the uncertainty principle in his well-known paradox of the cat. Imagine a cat shut in a steel box along with a Geiger counter, a small radioactive mass, a hammer, and a bottle of cyanide. The radioactive mass is so little that in the course of an hour, there will be a 50–50 chance of *one* atom disintegrating, at which time the Geiger counter will respond, trip the hammer, which will then break the bottle and kill the cat. The uncertainty principle correctly states that the disintegration of one atom cannot be predicted, calculated, or even known. However, at the end of this experiment one can see with no uncertainty if the cat is alive or dead: An atomic uncertainty is transformed into a macroscopic uncertainty, which can then be resolved by looking in the box. This experiment warns us against considering the uncertainty principle as an image of everyday reality. In short, our difficulties in observing on the atomic level do not preclude an accurate model from which predictions and calculations can be made—indeed, Schrödinger considered his wave mechanics to be such a model.

Objectivation, the belief that nature must be put "out there" in order to be examined, is another basis of conventional science. In fact, comprehensibility makes no sense if objectivation is not done. If the subject/observer becomes part of the objects observed, then each observer must see something different and comprehensibility will fail. This principle makes comprehension of the self a contradictory notion: The observer would be observing himself. Therefore, for the study of the self, of "who we are," of the point of contact of mind and matter, comprehensibility and objectivation must be modified.

In *Nature and the Greeks*, Schrödinger studied early Greek thinkers to determine the origin of comprehensibility and objectivation in order to determine where the difficulties with these concepts arose. He continued these investigations in *Mind and Matter* and *My View of the World*, concentrating particularly on the relationship between mind and matter: "Is there a world apart from my perception of it?" As a philosopher with a mystic bent, Schrödinger opted for an answer found in Vedanta (Hindu philosophy had attracted him from his youth): The world *is* the perceiving mind; the Self is universal and identical with the world; the plurality of individuals is an illusion. He traced this thought not only in the *Upanishads*, but also in Plato's universal Forms and Einstein's theory that time is relative to our frame of reference.

Among Schrödinger's contributions to science during his Dublin period was *What Is Life?* (1944), in which he applied physics to the problems of biology and made the suggestion that the chromosome is nothing but a message written in code. A few years later, this book inspired the DNA researches of James Watson and Francis Crick.

Schrödinger returned to Austria in 1956, when he was given his own chair at the University of Vienna. After a period of ill health, he died in 1961.

MARK T. RILEY

Further Reading

Moore, Walter. *Schrödinger: Life and Thought.* New York: Cambridge University Press, 1989. The standard treatment of Schrödinger's life. The author is a physical chemist, and thus competent to treat the science part of this biography. He had access to sources that were not available to—or not used by—Scott (below).

Scott, William T. *Erwin Schrödinger: An Introduction to his Writings.* Amherst: University of Massachusetts Press, 1967. Though superseded by Moore, Scott is valuable for his description of Schrödinger's philosophy.

ROBIN GEORGE COLLINGWOOD

Born: 1889, Coniston, Lancashire, England
Died: 1943, Coniston, Lancashire, England
Major Works: *Roman Britain* (1923, rev. ed. 1932), *Speculum Mentis* (1924), *The Archaeology of Roman Britain* (1930), *An Essay on Philosophical Method* (1933), *The Principles of Art* (1938), *The New Leviathan* (1942), *The Idea of History* (1946, posthumous)

Major Ideas

"Mind" and "body" do not represent two ontologically different substances; these terms denote diverse ways of considering, historically and physiologically, a human being.

The psychological theory of faculties understood as the capacity of parts of mind to work independently and in separation from one another is incorrect; the human spirit is a unity that includes necessary and permanent distinctions, perennially reaffirmed.

Philosophy consists of a method that elucidates and deducts categories and concepts.

The method whereby philosophy examines its history is a historical one; and it is by its epistemic function that philosophy becomes distinguishable from history.

The task of metaphysics is not to contemplate eternal verities; its aim is to make explicit the fundamental beliefs of civilization, natural science, or history at various times.

Historical knowledge is the reenactment in the historian's mind of the thought whose history he is studying.

Art is the expression of feelings that represent the working out of concrete problems present in the artist's own situation; principles of art criticism are to be adjusted in accordance with changes in the arts.

R. G. Collingwood is as well known for his archaeological and historical studies that found their expression, for example, in *Roman Britain* (1923, rev. ed. 1932) and in *The Archaeology of Roman Britain* (1930) as he is for his theory of history as expounded in his address to the Historical Association, *The Philosophy of History* (1930), in *The Historical Imagination*, an inaugural lecture (1935), and in *The Idea of History* (1946). His lifelong task, moreover, was to determine the relations between history and philosophy. In this endeavor he acknowledged the influence of his contemporary, Benedetto Croce, whose theory of history, like Collingwood's, evolved out of his work as a practicing historian. Both philosophers came to regard history and philosophy as interconnected and to maintain that the function of philosophy *vis à vis* history is an epistemic one.

Collingwood also recognized Croce's influence on the development of his philosophy of art, but whereas Croce's aesthetic developed mainly out of his work as literary critic, Collingwood's principles of criticism derived from his activity as painter and composer. Both philosophers agreed that art consists of the expressive and imaginative language of one's emotions. Genuine artistic activity is original, creative, and thus never exactly replicated. Croce, however, also recognized that it is the universal quality of great art which permits it to communicate its complex sentiment from generation to generation.

Collingwood's early education occurred at home and included instruction in Latin and ancient Greek. He was influenced by the aesthetic tastes of his parents and the scholarly pursuits of his father, who was friend and biographer of John Ruskin. Collingwood's formal education took place at Rugby and at Oxford, where he was stimulated by F. J. Haverfield to immerse himself in archaeological and historical studies.

In 1912, Collingwood became a fellow of Pembroke College, Oxford, where he taught philosophy—the discipline that, despite his publications on archaeology and the history of Roman Britain, remained his avocation until his death. By this time he could read not only Latin and ancient

Greek but also modern German and French, and he was sufficiently well versed in Italian to translate Benedetto Croce's *La filosofia di Giambattista Vico* (1911) (*The Philosophy of Giambattista Vico*, 1913). Collingwood would later acknowledge that the influence of Vico's philosophy, especially Vico's concept of mind's creative activity, on his own intellectual development had been a major one. Subsequently, with A. H. Hannay, Collingwood translated G. de Ruggiero's *Storia della filosofia moderna* (1912) (*Modern Philosophy*, 1921) and his *Storia del liberalismo europeo* (1925) (*History of European Liberalism*, 1927), as well as Croce's *Contributo alla critica di me stesso* (1918) (*Benedetto Croce: An Autobiography*, 1927). Collingwood also helped to revise Douglas Ainslie's translation of Croce's *Estetica come scienza dell' espressione e linguistica generale* (3d ed. rev. 1908) (*Aesthetic as Science of Expression and General Linguistic*, 2d ed. rev., 1922), and he translated Croce's article on aesthetics for the fourteenth edition of *The Encyclopaedia Britannica* (1929).

Religion and Philosophy (1916), which was Collingwood's first book, discusses, among other topics, the relations between history and philosophy: "History and philosophy are . . . the same thing." By this cryptic assertion, he meant that neither discipline could occur in abstraction from the other. Every genuine history includes philosophical presuppositions, and every philosophy develops out of concrete, historical conditions.

The publication of *Speculum Mentis* (1924) marks the conclusion of Collingwood's early period. Its aim was to investigate human nature in a new way; and since theory or thought, as Collingwood put it, exists for the sake of action, the goal of *Speculum Mentis* is to provide its reader with a response to the perennial question: How can one achieve happiness? The answer lies, for Collingwood, in the development of a unified human spirit, which is possible only through a comprehensive knowledge that reflects all aspects of human experience as they occur in their interrelationships with one another. He concluded that an understanding of art, religion, science, history, and philosophy is "necessary to a complete and full mental life." This

list of intellectual disciplines, moreover, is not an exhaustive one; it indicates merely a starting point for an inventory of human experience.

The *Outlines of a Philosophy of Art* (1925), subsequently replaced by *The Principles of Art* (1938), was followed by the publication of *An Essay on Philosophical Method* (1933). This work, which represents the beginning of Collingwood's mature period, attempts to answer the question "What is philosophy?" and to distinguish its inquiry from the investigations of the exact and empirical sciences, as well as from history and poetry. Collingwood concluded that philosophy is a branch of literature. But unlike scientific literature, philosophical writing is not technical; unlike historical writing, philosophic discussion is addressed primarily by the author to himself; and unlike poetic expression, philosophy is written in prose. To understand philosophy is to criticize it; and such criticism is guided by its search for what is true. The test of truth is consonance with the experience of those persons who, over the centuries, have worked at philosophy.

By 1932, Collingwood had begun to suffer from the ill health that increasingly plagued him, especially from 1938 onward, when he suffered his first stroke, until his death in 1943 at the age of fifty-three. According to his editor T. M. Knox, Collingwood's affliction consisted of the breaking of tiny blood vessels in his brain, with the result that small parts of it were destroyed. Despite his physical condition, however, from 1935 to 1941 Collingwood served as Waynflete Professor of Metaphysical Philosophy in Magdalen College. During this period he published *An Essay on Metaphysics* (1940), and *The New Leviathan*, Collingwood's last book, appeared in 1942, the year after his illness forced him to resign from teaching. *The Idea of Nature* (1945) and *The Idea of History* were published posthumously and consisted of Collingwood's lectures and papers as edited by T. M. Knox.

The Principles of Art

The Principles of Art, according to its author, represents a replacement rather than a mere revision of his *Outlines of the Principles of Art*, because aesthetic theory and the arts, as well as his own theory, had changed during the years since 1924. A new poetry and a new way of poeticizing, along with some new concepts proposed by artists themselves, had emerged. Thus, in a manner consistent with Collingwood's view that principles of criticism or *teoria* must be adjusted in accordance with changes in *praxis*, he wrote a new work, which took cognizance of what had transpired in the arts during the preceding thirteen years.

The "business," as Collingwood put it, of *The Principles*, is to answer the question "What is art?" For him, an answer required the ability to recognize what is and what is not art, which in turn necessitated a knowledge of how to use the term "art" appropriately. When the proper meaning of "art" is fixed, personal usage corresponds with common convention. A reply to the above question demanded, moreover, a definition of "art."

Collingwood determined that art does not consist of the representation of an object; nor does it have anything to do with a search for eternal Forms or Ideas. Art, instead, is formed of the expressive and imaginative language of one's emotions. As such, it must be generated out of the sensuous emotional experiences of the artist and expressed by an activity of consciousness. As the expression of feelings, the work of art proper is something imagined. Thus art is not to be identified with the physical artifact that stimulates an aesthetic creation in one's imagination. Such an object is constructed to record emotional expressions in a physical medium.

Moreover, there is no distinction of kind between artist and critic, since upon the stimulation of the artifact, at the sound of musical notes or at the sight of a painting, for example, the audience must try to recreate the internal imagery of the composer or artist as it was expressed during an earlier creative act. But how can we be certain that our own imaginative expressions correspond to those of the artist? With study of the artist's work, according to Collingwood, we can have good reasons for supposing that aesthetic images do so correspond.

Bad art amounts to a failure of expression. Great art is prophetic—not in the sense that it foretells the future, but in that the artist tells the audience, at risk of their displeasure, "the secrets of their own hearts."

Collingwood's conception of art as language and his practical suggestions for handling the problems of communication between artist and audience are suggestive and fruitful. In the light of his historicist interpretation of the principles of criticism, however, his distinction between what is and what is not art and his conception of "great art" must remain essentially arbitrary and open to change.

The Idea of History

Collingwood's major writings about history were published posthumously under the title *The Idea of History*. This book was compiled from Collingwood's thirty-two lectures on the philosophy of history (1936) and from a fragment of a major work entitled *The Principles of History*, which was never completed. It also includes two essays on history that were published in 1935 and 1936.

Despite the composite nature of *The Idea of History*, its contents, including the essays in the Epilegomena, are united by a central aim: to conduct a philosophical inquiry into the nature of history, regarded as a special type or form of knowledge with a special type of object. The business of history, for Collingwood, is to apprehend the past, to learn what really happened, whereas the business of philosophy is to make explicit the character of knowledge about the past. Philosophic inquiry, moreover, cannot separate its study of the way the past is known from the study of what is known.

The essay "Human Nature and Human History" (*The Idea of History*, part 5, section 1) distinguishes between the "outside" and the "inside" of an event. The former consists of bodies and their movements, whereas the latter comprises thought. According to Collingwood, the cause of an event, for a historian, does not occur in the relations between external bodies but lies instead in the thought of its agent. One discovers such mental objects by reenacting them in one's mind. It follows that all history amounts to the reenactment of past thoughts in the historian's mind. All such imaginative construction is also critical, because the thought that reenacts the past evaluates it during the act of construction. What is the subject matter of special interest to the historian? The historian investigates the social customs that humans create by thought. These mores are to be considered as a framework within which appetites find satisfaction in ways sanctioned by convention and morality.

In "The Historical Imagination" (*Idea of History*, part 5, section 2), Collingwood described the constructive activity of imagination as *a priori*, because it is the *sine qua non* for historical knowledge. The historian further asks whether his picture of the past is a coherent and continuous one, which amounts, for Collingwood, to asking whether history be true.

With these assertions, Collingwood argued against attempts by some late nineteenth- and twentieth-century philosophers to show that history is a science, that is, to demonstrate that its subject matter consists of what Collingwood called the "outside" of events along with their causal relations. In short, such philosophers treated history as

"closed to mind." Relatively recent illustrations would include Carl Hempel's discussions of the covering law model and also what today is called "quantitative history."

The problems involved in implementing a scientific approach to historical narrative (as, for instance, those of generalization, retrodiction, and verification) have been widely discussed. Yet, if we agree that what Collingwood described as the "inside" of an event, that is, the imaginative reenaction of past purposive thought, forms the subject matter of investigation, then important difficulties still remain. The methodological problems in establishing motive for action in the present are well known and must be greatly increased when we try to determine it as expressed within a culture very different from our own milieu, even if, as Collingwood urged, we rely on evidence for our determination. Nevertheless, Collingwood's conception of history, along with its method and subject matter, as *sui generis* is appealing. Unfortunately his ill health and death prevented him from fully developing his ideas.

M. E. MOSS

Further Reading

Boucher, David. *The Social and Political Thought of R. G. Collingwood*. Cambridge: Cambridge University Press, 1989. Through a synthesis of unpublished and published works, Boucher attempts to give a faithful representation of Collingwood's thought. His aim is not to criticize but to understand.

Donagan, Alan. *The Later Philosophy of R. G. Collingwood*, with a new preface. Chicago and London: University of Chicago Press, 1985. Still the best introduction to Collingwood's later philosophy (writings after 1930), this edition includes a new preface that takes into account the most recent scholarship since Collingwood's unpublished papers have been made available.

Krausz, Michael, ed. *Critical Essays on the Philosophy of R. G. Collingwood*. Oxford: Clarendon Press, 1972. A selection of evaluative essays by some outstanding scholars. These writings cover the entire range of Collingwood's philosophy.

Mink, Louis O. *Mind, History and Dialectic: The Philosophy of R. G. Collingwood*. Bloomington and London: Indiana University Press, 1969. Mink gives a dialectical interpretation of the evolution of Collingwood's work, in terms of a system continually transcending itself.

Rubinoff, Lionel. *Collingwood and the Reform of Metaphysics: A Study in the Philosophy of Mind*. Toronto and Buffalo: University of Toronto Press, 1970. According to Rubinoff, *Speculum Mentis* includes Croce's expression of a master plan. Subsequent works can be seen in terms of the program outlined there.

Van der Dussen, W. J. *History as a Science: The Philosophy of R. G. Collingwood*. The Hague, Boston, London: Martinus Nijhoff, 1981. This work focuses on Collingwood's conception of history, from its inception through its development into the mature works. It refers to unpublished manuscripts available only since 1978.

LUDWIG WITTGENSTEIN

Born: 1889, Vienna, Austria
Died: 1951, Cambridge, England
Major Works: *Tractatus Logico-Philosophicus* (1921), *Philosophical Investigations* (1953)

Major Ideas

Language and the world share a common logical form.

Sentences are logical pictures of the world: The logical relations between the elements of a sentence reflect the relations between the elements in the world.

Sentences can show their form but they cannot say it; Sentences that attempt to say what can only be shown are pseudo-sentences or nonsense.

Language consists of "language games" that reflect forms of life.

For many expressions, the meaning is the use: To grasp the "meaning" of such an expression is to know how to use it.

Ludwig Wittgenstein is distinguished among philosophers for developing two very different philosophical theories, a feat that attests to his reputation as a man both brilliant and eccentric. He was born in Vienna, Austria in 1889. By 1912, an initial interest in engineering had brought Wittgenstein to England to study the foundations of mathematics with Bertrand Russell. He completed his dissertation while serving in an artillery unit of the Austrian army during World War I. After the war, believing he had solved fundamental philosophical problems, Wittgenstein returned to Austria to teach in village schools until 1926. Over the next few years, conversations with members of the Vienna Circle led Wittgenstein to reconsider his early work. In 1929, he was back at Cambridge and he lectured there until 1946. He died of cancer in 1951.

Questions about the relationships between language, thought, and reality preoccupied Wittgenstein throughout his career. His project was critical. Like Kant, Wittgenstein sought to define the limits of thought. Unlike Kant, he took language as his starting point. In his early work, Wittgenstein argued that sentences "picture" the world by reflecting its logical structure, that is, the arrangement of simple objects in a state of affairs. According to the theory of meaning developed in this period, most traditional philosophical problems lie outside the limits of what can be sensibly said. Wittgenstein's

later work rejects the systematic aspirations of his early theory. A new understanding of language as first and foremost a product of social convention replaces the early realism. This new understanding of language in turn implies a new conception of meaning and philosophical method, both of which are perhaps most prominently displayed in what has come to be known as the private language argument.

Wittgenstein's major works are notoriously obscure and dense. His writing style is austere, almost epigrammatic. Two works in particular represent Wittgenstein's two distinct conceptions of philosophy. The *Tractatus*, Wittgenstein's dissertation, was the only book he published during his lifetime. He left instructions that his second major work, *Philosophical Investigations*, should be published after his death. The *Investigations* contains the core of Wittgenstein's refutation of his own early theory. In addition to these two authorized works, collections drawn from Wittgenstein's lectures and notebooks have been published by colleagues and friends.

Tractatus Logico-Philosophicas

The central feature of the *Tractatus* is the distinction Wittgenstein draws between "showing" and "saying." On the one hand, in a sequence of numbered sentences Wittgenstein develops his picture theory of meaning. This picture theory defines the limits of what can be said. But it is a consequence of the theory that the sentences of the *Tractatus* itself cannot sensibly be said. Instead, the limits they describe can only be shown. Wittgenstein's distinction between saying and showing turns the book from a treatise on the logical foundations of language to a work on metaphysics and, Wittgenstein himself claimed, ethics.

The basic intuition behind the *Tractatus* is Wittgenstein's conviction that all languages share a common logical form, a form they also share with the world. In fact, this shared form makes it possible for sentences to "say" something. What a sentence says *is* just the *logical picture* it presents of the world. It is the understanding that sentences are pictures that leads to the distinction between showing and saying. Sentences give pictures of the world, but they cannot give pictures of themselves. They show the logical form they share with the world, but they cannot say it. Sentences can only show their logical form, because trying to make them say it pushes language beyond the limits of sense.

When he wrote the *Tractatus*, Wittgenstein had a very particular understanding of what "sense" could be. As he saw it, language is made up of names arranged in sentences. The names have meaning because they stand for objects in the world. These names can be arranged in sentences in certain ways and the possible ways of arranging them define the limits of sense. For Wittgenstein, then, only a sentence has sense, and its sense is the arrangement of names that pictures a possible arrangement of elements in the world.

The problem, as Wittgenstein saw it, is that sentences lose their sense when they try to do more than picture a possible state of affairs in the world. Wittgenstein never gave an example of what he meant by a "name" or the kind of objects names stand for (sense data or ordinary objects, for instance) but a rough sketch of his ideas might go as follows:

That the world is as it is a purely contingent matter. "The cat is on the mat" describes one possibility. "The cat is not on the mat" describes another. To know which sentence is true, one would compare the picture with the world. But now consider the sentence "Either the cat is on the mat or the cat is not on the mat." This sentence is what logicians call a *tautology*. It is a special kind of sentence in that it must always be true; it cannot be false. The either-or sentence does not give a picture of the world. Instead, it tries to give a picture of the relationship between the sense, or form, of two sentences.

According to the *Tractatus*, sentences like tautologies are not really sentences at all. They are pseudo-sentences. Pseudo-sentences transgress the bounds of sense because instead of just showing their sense in a picture of a possible state of affairs, they try to say something necessary about the forms and limits of sense. But if sentences say something and have sense only by presenting pictures of the world, then pseudo-sentences, which do not present such pictures, say nothing. They are nonsense.

Like tautologies and contradictions, all of the sentences in the *Tractatus* lack sense. By describing the limits of what can be said, they go beyond them. Wittgenstein's attempt to describe the limits of language from within marks his project as Kantian. Wittgenstein recognized that there is no vantage point outside language from which to describe the limits of language, just as Kant had tried to show that there is no vantage point outside experience from which one can describe the limits of all possible experience. And just as Kant emphasized that reason constantly and inevitably seeks to transgress its limits, so Wittgenstein believed that we constantly try to say what cannot be said.

According to Wittgenstein's early view of sense and meaning, most philosophical theories, and in particular ethical discussions, come out as nonsense. It was for this reason that he thought he had solved philosophy's problems. However, calling them nonsense did not for Wittgenstein mean that they are unimportant. On the contrary, Wittgenstein thought that some nonsense, like the *Tractatus*, could be illuminating. This is the source of Wittgenstein's so-called "mysticism."

By 1929, when he returned to Cambridge, Wittgenstein had begun to revise his conception of meaning and language. He no longer thought that language primarily reflected the logical structure of the world. Instead, he now saw language as a product of social convention. There were several reasons for Wittgenstein's change of mind, one of the most important being his new sense of what is necessary to learn a word, or grasp a concept.

In the *Tractatus*, Wittgenstein argued that the meaning of a name is the object for which it stands. The intuition here is that the paradigm for learning the meaning of a word is ostensive definition—the teacher points at the object while saying the word and the student learns to associate the two together. But how does the student know what is being pointed to? For instance, if the teacher says "red" while pointing at an apple, how does the student know she means its color, and not its shape or taste?

Philosophical Investigations

The analogy of a chess game is often used to illustrate what Wittgenstein saw as the problem with thinking we learn a language by way of ostensive definitions. Someone who just knows that the king is the tallest piece on the board does not yet understand the meaning of the king. He does not understand even if he knows in addition how the king moves. To understand the meaning of the king is to understand its function in the game as a whole. Similarly, Wittgenstein argued in the *Investigations*, to grasp the meaning of a word is to know how to use it in a given context, that is, a particular "language game," a linguistic procedure. Meaning is use. Learning a language is like learning a game or, more accurately, a multitude of related games.

In the *Tractatus*, Wittgenstein asserted that the sentences of a language reflect the logical structure of the world in a kind of systematic unity. The *Investigations* rejects this view. Language is, instead, made up of interrelated language games that reflect "forms of life." It is not as though each game has definite boundaries and a distinct identity. It is not even possible to say precisely what a game is. Rather, language games are knit together by resemblances like those that mark the members of a family.

The rules of the games are embedded in the grammar of the language. By "grammar," Wittgenstein meant more than just how words are combined correctly in a sentence. He also meant to refer to the kinds of contexts in which certain words and sentences make sense. In the *Tractatus*, philosophical problems arise when language transgresses the limits of sense. In the *Investigations*, they arise when philosophers transgress the limits of grammar by confusing the limits of a language game. For instance, one speaks of having an understanding as though this were like having an apple, and one may then begin to wonder where the understanding is located (thus confusing the game of mental processes with that of material objects). In such situations, Wittgenstein claimed, meaning is lost, language is idling.

The new purpose of philosophy is to combat such confusion. The *Philosophical Investigations* is a kind of dialogue. The author speculates and raises questions designed to show an opponent where he or she has gone astray. This is nowhere more true than in the passages of the private language argument, where Wittgenstein argues against the sophist, who believes it is possible, and even unavoidable, to speak a language and live in a world of one's own. The author of the *Investigations* corrects the sophist of the *Tractatus*.

CONSTANCE CREEDE

Further Reading

Hacker, P. M. S. *Insight and Illusion: Wittgenstein on Philosophy and the Metaphysics of Experience.* Rev. ed. New York: Oxford University Press, 1987. A thorough and sophisticated study of the evolution of Wittgenstein's philosophy. The revised edition contains a response to Kripke's interpretation of the private language argument.

Janik, Allan, and Stephen Toulmin. *Wittgenstein's Vienna.* New York: Simon and Schuster, 1973. This work details the influence of the Austrian intellectual climate on the development of the *Tractatus*, correcting earlier, more narrow interpretations.

Kripke, Saul A. *Wittgenstein on Rules and Private Language.* Cambridge, Mass.: Harvard University Press, 1982. An original and provocative interpretation of the *Investigations'* private language argument.

Pears, David Francis. *Ludwig Wittgenstein.* New York: Viking Press, 1970. A clear and accessible introduction to Wittgenstein's philosophy.

ARNOLD TOYNBEE

Born: 1889, London, England
Died: 1975, York, England
Major Works: *A Study of History* (1934–61). *Civilization on Trial* (1948), *An Historian's Approach to Religion* (1956), *Change and Habit* (1966), *Cities on the Move* (1970)

Major Ideas

The proper study of history involves studying civilizations rather than nations or cultural periods.
Civilizations arise by the response of creative individuals to challenges presented by situations of special difficulty.
Progress in civilization consists in meeting difficulties by responding in creative ways that are internal and spiritual rather than external and material.
The breakdown of a society occurs when creative individuals fail to lead through the exercise of creative power, resulting in withdrawal of the allegiance of the majority and a subsequent loss of social unity.

Arnold Toynbee, British historian, earned a classical education at Oxford University and was a fellow and tutor there from 1912–15, after which he worked at the British Foreign Office and later served as a delegate to the Paris Peace Conference. In 1919 he became a professor of Byzantine and modern Greek studies at the University of London. He covered the Greco-Turkish war as a correspondent. Then, while holding several academic posts, he wrote his twelve-volume *A Study of History*, which occupied him from 1934–61. He wrote many other volumes on Western civilization, religions, classical history, and other subjects.

When an important figure dies, it is often appropriate to say that now that person belongs to the ages. For Toynbee, it might be said that during most of his life, the ages belonged to him. He was a researcher and author almost obsessed with facts—but not for their own sake. He saw them as clues to the nature and mystery of the universe in which every human person awakes to consciousness. He was a man trying to observe major patterns throughout history by studying the details of events not only in ancient Greece and Rome, medieval Europe, and Asian cultures but those of Eskimo, Sumeric, Osmanli, Shang, and Mayan civilizations as well.

What unveiled itself under Dr. Toynbee's keen analysis was what might be called the unity of humanity, which also led him to a rather ecumenical view of the presence of God in the world. Roland Stromberg referred to Toynbee as "the prophet of global unification." Toynbee's initial concentration was Greco-Roman history, which impressed him with its global rather than parochial outlook. In his volume *Civilization on Trial*, he emphasized his views by warning still-slumbering Westerners that "our neighbors' past is going to become a vital part of our Western future," a conclusion which more recent events seem to substantiate emphatically.

Implied in this is a call to responsible action. There are lessons from the past that we ignore only at our peril, insists the British historian. Our debt to the future cannot be overlooked, Toynbee reminds us in a number of publications, including *Change and Habit*, where we read that "our unborn potential successors cannot plead their own cause. Their plea to us has to be put to us by ourselves, since we, and only we, out of all those who have departed and all those who are still to come, are now alive and therefore now bear the responsibility of holding the trusteeship for the species of which we are the momentary representatives."

This sense of the interconnectedness of all of the dead, the living, and the as-yet unborn is rooted in Toynbee's sense of religious faith. Volume 6 of the work for which he will be longest remembered, *A Study of History*, ends with a highly religious tone. While he does not preach the dominance of a particular faith system, Toynbee indicates that the only way in which Western civilization will avoid annihilation will be by returning to its Christian heritage penitently and in humility. Elsewhere Toynbee wrote that the Christian impulse gave the West its great achievement: through God, to act not only for one's self but for all of humanity.

In his 1956 book, *An Historian's Approach to Religion*, the author shows a broader view of religion, an acknowledgment through an ecumenical approach of the complementariness of the various major faiths. A decade later he would write that "the higher religions have released Man from the social prison-house which he had inherited from his prehuman ancestors."

A good illustration of this overview perspective is found in *Cities on the Move*, wherein Toynbee tells how he became fascinated with Constantine Doxiadis's "Ekistics." The historian found the discipline "promising because 'Ekistics' is the common ground and natural meeting-place of a number of lives of study that have been pursued, till recently, more or less in isolation from each other. Architecture, town planning, the study of communications, economics, sociology, psychology, medicine, biology . . ." all contribute.

Some critics made harsh observations about Toynbee's comprehensive approach. Whatever he is doing, he is not uniting history, some of them complained. But the late Catholic historian Thomas P. Neill, who as a scholar seems to have understood Toynbee as well as anyone has, insisted that what the British historian was doing was writing *about history* but found the work to be a very effective scholarly effort. He concluded that Toynbee's work is "the first Christian philosophy of history of consequence since Bossuet." Neill then adds this commentary; "It reintroduces Providence into history, treats man as a free spiritual being created by God to enjoy the Beautific Vision. Moreover it is more truly a 'universal' history than Boussuet's or any earlier Christian's 'universal history,' for it sees the unity of mankind in creation and in destiny and it attempts to work out a theory of history to give all mankind a place. In this sense it is a richer and fuller inquiry into the meaning of history than previous Christian study."

But it would be an error to think that it was faith in the Christian God that originally prompted the young historian to pursue the career that he did. Late in his life, he explained that "my rejection of religion was sudden; my reconversion has been gradual, but it has been lasting." One impetus that motivated Toynbee's work all of his life was the death of his classmates in World War I. Here are just some of the illustrative quotations that have appeared throughout the author's writings, which cover over half a century: "Why am I still alive today, to be writing these lines? If, in 1914, I had been fit for active service, the chances are that, like so many of my school fellows, I should have been dead by 1916." "By the end of the First World War half my contemporaries had been killed. . . . I must work for the abolition of the wicked institution that was the cause of this criminal destruction. . . ." "I am now seventy-five. Half my contemporaries at school and at the university were killed before they were twenty-seven." And finally, from *A Study of History:* "In 1915 and 1916, about half the number of my school fellows were killed together with proportionate numbers of my contemporaries in other belligerent countries. The longer I live, the greater grows my grief and indignation at the wicked cutting short of all those lives. . . . The writing of this book has been one of my responses to the challenge that has been presented to me by the senseless criminality of human affairs."

"This book" is one of the publishing events of all time. *A Study of History* contains 3 million words, 332 pages of index, and some 19,000 footnotes. It is not for bulk, however, that the opus will be remembered. Rather it is the combination of great learning, method, and writing style that attracts readers. Toynbee chose to focus not on individuals, not on states, but on civilizations, defining them in spiritual terms that reflected in part, at least, the approach of mathematician-philosopher Alfred North Whitehead. A civilization "might be defined as an endeavor to create a state of society in which the whole of Mankind will be able to live together in harmony as members of a single, all-inclusive family."

According to Toynbee, civilizations arise not because of genetically superior individuals (there are none) nor because of a favorable geographical environment but because of a creative response by a minority of individuals to a situation of special difficulty. Among the challenging situations which serve as "stimuli" to creative individuals are "hard countries," that is, places where it is difficult (rather than easy) to survive; "new ground," where no effort to build a society has previously been made; "blows," defeats of one sort or another; the "pressures" of frontier conditions; and "penalizations," that is, coercive conditions and regulations imposed on one class or race by another.

A civilization grows and progresses, Toynbee argues, when the responses to external difficulties are internal and spiritual, rather than external and material. In general, the more severe the challenge posed by difficulties, the more creative and fruitful the response. The responses that promote growth are made by individuals who are so stimulated by challenging problems as to make original discoveries or come up with inspirations by which they transform the uncreative majority and encourage a new way of life. Toynbee calls this process "etherealization," and he uses the term "mimesis" to name the process of imitation by which the uncreative majority follows the creative minority.

A civilization breaks down and disintegrates, Toynbee argues, when the creative minority fails to exercise its creative power, leading to a withdrawal of the allegiance of the majority, a loss of social unity, and a failure of self-determination.

A society fails to determine itself in a positive way when the majority acts mechanically in its imitation of the creative spirit shown by its creative leaders or when the leaders themselves begin to act mechanically rather than creatively. Other causes of the failure of self-determination are the practice of using old social institutions as the vehicles for new social practices and the "idolization" of formerly creative but presently outmoded ideas, institutions, or techniques.

In *A Study of History*, Toynbee traces the fate of twenty-eight civilizations, not to everyone's satisfaction. Pitrim Sirokin, who finds Toynbee's contributions very significant, nevertheless sees the category of "civilizations" as invalid. Another critic says that the theory of challenge and response is too vague. Hugh Trevor-Roper charges his fellow countryman with "conjuring tricks," concluding that Toynbee's major study is a "terrible perversion of history."

One topic that has been among the most controversial for Toynbee is his view of Judaism, which he continually represents not as a living, vibrant higher religion but rather as a fossil of Syriac civilization. Lewis Mumford proclaims this a "major" lapse in Toynbee's thinking and Israel's Abba Eban reacted very strongly to this in an essay titled "The Toynbee Heresy." Even so sympathetic a commentator as Thomas P. Neill felt it necessary to label Toynbee both "harsh" and "unjust" on this topic.

Toynbee did have many contemporary admirers. Distinguished historian William McNeill believes that Toynbee "has opened vistas of history and put questions before me as no other single author has done." Here is how Tangye Lean ends his praise: "What remains astonishing is that we should have produced any individual of the size and strength to perform this creative act." Mumford predicts that "if our world civilization survives its threatened ordeals, *A Study of History* will stand out as a landmark, perhaps even as a turning point."

Arnold Toynbee was a compassionate person. His humanity was apparent in what he wrote. He discovered for himself the flaws of historical figures and he tried to understand them. But he refused to endorse those flaws; instead he attempted to learn from them and thus point to a better way to resolve history's problem. While not a member of any church, he considered himself to be an independent Christian. He wrote that "Christianity's fundamental tenet is, as I see it, a belief that self-sacrificing love is both the best and the most powerful of all spiritual impulses that are known to us."

HARRY JAMES CARGAS

Further Reading

McNeill, William H. *Arnold J. Toynbee: A Life.* New York: Oxford University Press, 1989. Highly regarded account of Toynbee as scholar and public figure, with some attention to his considerably turbulent private life.

Peper, Christian B., ed. *An Historian's Conscience: The Correspondence of Arnold J. Toynbee and Columba Cary-Elwes, Monk of Ampleforth.* Boston: Beacon, 1986. A meticulously edited exchange of letters that reveals the development of many of Toynbee's central ideas.

Toynbee, Arnold (with D. C. Somervell). *A Study of History, Abridgement of Volumes I-VI* and *A Study of History, Abridgement of Volumes VII-X.* New York and Oxford: Oxford University Press, 1946 (Vol. 1), 1957 (Vol. 2). A splendid abridgement by D. C. Somervell, a distinguished British scholar, who worked closely with Toynbee (who approved wholeheartedly of the result). The abridgement faithfully follows the plan of the original and throughout much of the abridged text contains Toynbee's words. An especially helpful feature is an abridgement of the abridgement, entitled simply "Argument," a 38-page summary of the entire work. Available in paperback.

Urban, G. R. *Toynbee on Toynbee.* New York: Oxford University Press, 1974. From a series of radio interviews in which the eighty-three-year-old historian reflects on and reconsiders his judgments on the history of civilizations.

MARTIN HEIDEGGER

Born: 1889, Messkirch, Baden, Germany
Died: 1976, Messkirch, Baden, Germany
Major Works: *Being and Time* (1927), *An Introduction to Metaphysics* (1953), *Poetry, Language, Thought* (1971), *On the Way to Language* (1959)

Major Ideas

Although the meaning of being is the basic issue for philosophy, its true nature has been forgotten and concealed.

Human beings are uniquely open to being but must be understood in terms of existential categories rather than traditional, objectifying categories.

Being must be understood in terms of temporality.

Being can be understood only through a meditative and poetic kind of thinking that is not calculative or objectifying.

Insofar as being can be conceptualized, it is that which enables beings to be revealed in a dynamic event that conceals even as it reveals.

Martin Heidegger is widely acknowledged to be one of the most significant philosophers of the twentieth century. Certainly he is one of the most influential philosophers, exerting an extraordinary impact upon many disciplines other than philosophy. This, however, does not mean that his thought is well understood. His most famous work, *Being and Time*, was a seminal text for the existentialist and phenomenological movements, but he himself refused his blessing to such developments of his work. He repeatedly claimed that every true thinker thinks only one thought, and his thought was that of the Being of beings. He was entranced with the classical question of ontology, "Why is there something rather than nothing?" *Being and Time*, with its anthropological and existentialist emphasis, was only a way station, as he himself later said, upon the route of contemplating being. Any treatment of Heidegger's thought therefore must take into consideration the early Heidegger, epitomized in *Being and Time*, and the later Heidegger, where his focus upon being is clearer.

Heidegger's early theological studies at Jesuit schools in preparation for the priesthood (1903–11) awakened his interest in hermeneutics and language. However, while studying and later teaching (1915–23) at the University of Freiburg, he fell under the spell of Edmund Husserl, the founder of phenomenology and for a decade regularly taught courses concerning phenomenology. He worked closely with Husserl until Heidegger left to become full professor at the University of Marburg in 1923. He returned to Freiburg to be the successor to Husserl's chair in 1928 and dedicated *Being and Time* to Husserl. At that time, though, the two had a serious disagreement about Heidegger's understanding of phenomenology as a method for ontology, which resulted in Heidegger's infrequent use of the term "phenomenology" in the rest of his work.

In 1933, Heidegger became rector of the University of Freiburg and enthusiastically supported the burgeoning National Socialist movement. Although he quickly withdrew from his rectorship in 1934 and from his avid support for the new regime, he was not allowed to teach for several years after the war. This problematic political involvement, coupled with the paucity of his publication in the intervening years, meant that Heidegger's fame centered for a long time on his earlier work *Being and Time*, often mediated through the works of existentialists such as Jean-Paul Sartre and theologians such as Rudolf Bultmann. A fuller understanding of Heidegger thus awaited the publication and translation of his later lectures and works.

In the meantime, Heidegger himself shifted away from the anthropological and phenomenological preoccupations of *Being and Time* toward more direct reflection on being. In the mid-thirties, he turned to a difficult, poetic mode of philosophizing, indeed, often reflecting on poetic texts themselves. In particular, he was stirred by the German poet Friedrich Hölderlin. *Being and Time*, however, continues to be indispensable for understanding his later work.

Being and Time

Against the prevailing characteristics of traditional philosophy, in *Being and Time* Heidegger inaugurated a dramatically different approach. He charged that the Western world is characterized by "a flight from thinking." Above all, he believed that the meaning of being has been forgotten and covered over by Western thought. Being has too often been understood as only the most abstract and therefore empty of categories, as a supreme being, as a first cause, or as simply the properties common to beings in general. This "ontotheological" approach to being, as he called it, continued the tradition of Western philosophy stemming from Plato in focusing on beings rather than on being as such. In Heidegger's terms, it ignored "the ontological difference" between the two. The prime concern of Heidegger's work, therefore, was to reorient the understanding of being, which Heidegger termed in *Being and Time* "fundamental ontology."

To complicate matters further, the nature of truth itself as well as that of being had to be rethought. "Truth" has been understood as the correspondence of the idea in a subject to an external object. This is an abstraction, Heidegger argued, based upon a more fundamental experience of truth as "unhiddenness," appealing, as he often did, to the etymology of the Greek word for truth, *aletheia*. Truth then is the dynamic disclosure or "presencing" of beings, made possible by being.

Heidegger's planned approach for *Being and Time* therefore consisted of two stages: One was through an existential analysis of human being to uncover a renewed understanding of time as the proper horizon for understanding being. The second was a "destruction" or "overcoming" of the history of philosophy to situate historically such a fundamental ontology. As the book stands, it is but a beginning. It contains the existential analysis, which is two-thirds of the first part of the total project. It omits a planned discussion of "time and being" as well as the entire historical second part.

Nevertheless, the existential anthropology contained in *Being and Time* remains as one of the small number of most significant works in the twentieth century. It represents a *tour de force* in providing a fresh framework for understanding human beings and, beyond that, Western philosophy in general. Despite the repeated emphasis in the book itself that his real concern was ontology, the foreshortened nature of *Being and Time* gave rise to the impression that Heidegger was an existentialist concerned primarily with human beings rather than with being. The reason for the preoccupation with persons evident in *Being and Time* was that human beings are unique manifestations of being. They are the only beings for whom being is an issue and, moreover, an inherently personal, or existential, issue. As Heidegger stated, one's being always has the character of "mineness." Thus, Heidegger argued that persons have a vague, preconceptual understanding of being, providing a starting point for ontology. More generally, he pointed out that being can never appear at all without the necessary awareness or "clearing" existing in human being.

The method for bringing this preconceptual understanding of being to light is that of hermeneutical phenomenology. Phenomenology directs one to a careful description of the lived experience of human being itself, apart from preoccupation with theories or common-sense ideas about such experience. As opposed to Husserl, however, Heidegger put this method in the service of revealing being and also realized that such an attempt to probe beneath what has been covered over is inevitably an act of interpretation. In this context, Heidegger reveals himself to be one of the premier advocates of the historicity of human beings, arguing that all understanding is inherently interpretive, or hermeneutical, in part due to the fact that people approach everything with preunderstandings shaped by their situation in history.

When Heidegger turned to a phenomenological description of persons, he saw that they are first immersed in the world before one can think of them as separate subjects or isolated egos, so he called human beings in this regard *Dasein*, literally, "being there." The preoccupation of modern philosophy with how the ego can validly know the external world is an example of not being able to discover the right answer because of having asked the wrong question. Heidegger's rich phenomenological description of *Dasein's* being-in-the-world therefore avoids traditional philosophical categories appropriate to subjects distinct from external objects. Rather, he intentionally seeks a language closer to human existence. As is already evident, he virtually has to create a new philosophical vocabulary to do so.

A major thesis is that human being's practical, everyday engagement with the world is in terms of practical tools that are "ready-to-hand," as opposed to inert objects for inspection and analysis that are simply "present-at-hand." Moreover, far from being isolated egos, everyday human being is always lived within the horizon of other persons, that is, in a "with-world."

Beginning with this more practical and more original relation to the world opens up an understanding of human being in dynamic categories, which Heidegger terms "existentials." The primary existential structures are temporally related. "State-of-being" or "facticity" refers to the givenness or thrownness of human life that stems from one's past, which is manifested in deep-seated moods, particularly the mood of anxiety. Heidegger calls the human orientation or projection toward the horizon of the future "understanding," which gives rise to "discourse" or speech in the present as an interpretation of how it stands with one's being. These three existentials, while separable for the purposes of analysis, in reality interpenetrate one another. The open-endedness of human projection into the future gave rise to Heidegger's paradoxical characterization of the essence of human beings as their existence, which in Jean-Paul Sartre's hands became the central maxim of the existentialist movement.

To these existentials Heidegger adds another that constantly accompanies average everydayness, namely, fallenness. This term refers to the way persons find themselves absorbed in an inauthentic way in the world, in the crowd, in anonymity. As Heidegger circles back again and again to view *Dasein* from yet another vantage point, he shows that authenticity occurs when one becomes aware of one's thrownness yet at the same time accepts one's responsibility for an open future and faces this contingency resolutely. This awareness he terms the call of conscience. It particularly occurs when anxiety reveals one's finite freedom in light of the confines of one's lifetime, in other words, in the light of the inevitable closure of one's death. *Dasein's* "being-towards-death" consequently is the entrée for the uncanny call of being to authenticity.

The Later Heidegger

The later Heidegger became convinced that even the novel approach of *Being and Time* was not radical enough; it partook too much of modern philosophy's Cartesian turn to the subject and search for foundational conditions of thought. Heidegger therefore shifted initiative away from *Dasein* to being itself. In several historical works, he argued that even ontology was hopelessly caught up in objectified ways of thinking, so he dropped his plea for a fundamental ontology. He presented Nietzsche as the culmination of Western philosophy, as an ironic "last metaphysician," whose subjective "will to power" is the end result of the turn in Plato from being to beings. Instead, he called for a return to earlier beginnings of philosophy, to pre-Socratics such as Parmenides and Heraclitus, to spur a new type of thinking at "the end of philosophy."

His dissatisfaction with traditional conceptualities to express the mystery of being was due to his conviction that they partake of the spirit of modern technology, which is but another way that the subject expresses its domination over a world of objects. Authentic thinking of being demands a meditative rather than calculative approach; it emphasizes "releasement" (*Gelassenheit*, or "letting be") rather than resoluteness. Questions are more important than answers. Additionally, the creative potential for thus evoking being lies in poetic language more than in the structure of human being. Despite the fact that Heidegger always thought that language was "worn out" and often merely "idle talk," he is a central figure in the linguistic turn that one finds throughout twentieth-century philosophy. As opposed to other emphases on logical analysis or on ordinary language, Heidegger sought to penetrate to the creative springs of language that he found best exemplified by certain poets and, enigmatically, in listening and silence as much as in verbalization. As this originating capacity for disclosure, language is "the house of Being." If being is to be revealed, it must be revealed through language. The ontological import of language for Heidegger is such that it is truer to say that language speaks us rather than to say that we speak language. So his later attempts to be "on the way to language," as the title of one of his books indicates, are one metaphorical foray after another in order to elicit an authentic thinking of being. This emphasis on the creative power of language has had great influence in the social sciences, aesthetics, and theology. A famous dialogue with a Buddhist priest in *On the Way to Language* also revealed much in common with mystical and Eastern ways of thought.

Although the later Heidegger indicated a more passive role for human being in relation to being, to thinking, and to language, he presupposed much of his earlier existential analytic. He continued to speak of "caring" *Dasein* as necessary for the appearing of being. He continued to emphasize that *Dasein* alone "stands out" ("ex-sists") from being in such a way that being can be revealed. The difference is that the later Heidegger prefers to speak of being itself rather than of *Dasein* as the "clearing"; being has the initiative. *Dasein*'s role in its receptive and nonmanipulative being at home with the things of its world is to be the "guardian" or "shepherd" of being.

Heidegger understood the actual disclosure of being as a temporal event, whose verbal nature may be captured by writing being as a verb, "be-ing." As "the shepherd of Being" therefore patiently carries out its task of "tending," be-ing may grant itself to human being as a gift. Thus the meditative thinking of being for which Heidegger appeals calls for "thanking." Nevertheless, in the light of being's initiative, *Dasein* can only wait for further disclosure of being. As time went on, Heidegger appeared to grow more pessimistic about the modern understanding of being. As he himself poetically put it in *Poetry, Language, Thought*, "We are too late for the gods and too early for Being." His understanding of the way being is always concealed even as it is revealed in beings and his insistence that authentic thinking always leads to what is unthinkable suggests that being will never be fully revealed. These emphases further underscore his thought as an anti-Cartesian philosophy characterized by fallibilism, finitude, and ambiguity.

Heidegger's groping attempts to think and to speak the mystery of being in ways that run counter to traditional thinking and speaking are seen by some as profound reminders of the depth of reality that is lost to modern alienated technological society. Others see it as mere wordplay, as a kind of "word magic" that is an extreme example of confusion in language. Others do not resonate with his search for being but find him of immense help in understanding human beings as existential, historical, linguistic creatures who largely create their own reality. Conversely, some see him as a covert theologian or mystic. Some look to the earlier Heidegger, while others prefer the later Heidegger. These diverse appraisals of Heidegger are probably the predictable effect of one who never saw himself as having arrived but as simply "on the way." "Everything," he once wrote, "is way." In many ways his concern was not so much to give answers as to ask the right questions. He summed up this attitude, often frustrating to interpreters, in *An Introduction to Metaphysics*: "To know how to question means to know how to wait, even a whole lifetime."

DAN R. STIVER

Further Reading

Caputo, John. *The Mystical Element in Heidegger's Thought*. Athens, Ohio: Ohio University Press, 1978. An original interpretation of Heidegger in light of the influence of the German mystic Meister Eckhart that is especially illuminating of the later Heidegger. While appreciative of Heidegger, Caputo appeals for a rejuvenation of philosophy between calculative thinking and meditative thinking.

Grene, Marjorie. *Martin Heidegger*. Studies in Modern European Literature and Thought. London: Bowes and Bowes, 1957. An introduction that is appreciative of the earlier, existentialist Heidegger but extremely critical of the later Heidegger.

Kockelmans, Joseph J. *Martin Heidegger: A First Introduction to His Philosophy*. Pittsburgh: Duquesne University Press, 1965. As the title indicates, this is an introduction with little critical analysis, but it is a helpful exposition, focusing on the earlier Heidegger, by one of the most able interpreters of continental phenomenological philosophy.

Langan, Thomas. *The Meaning of Heidegger: A Critical Study of an Existentialist Phenomenology*. New York: Columbia University Press, 1959. An early standard, Langan's book introduces Heidegger in the context of the existentialist and phenomenological movements.

Lovitt, William, and Harriet Brundage Lovitt. *Modern Technology in the Heideggerian Perspective*. Lewiston, N.Y.: The Edwin Mellen Press, 1991. Considers the theme of technology in the context of Heidegger's work. The authors argue convincingly that Heidegger maintains a single overarching perspective.

Macquarrie, John. *Martin Heidegger*. Makers of Contemporary Theology. Richmond: John Knox Press, 1968. A very concise (62 pages) introduction to the earlier Heidegger by one of the translators of *Being and Time*.

Okrent, Mark. *Heidegger's Pragmatism: Understanding, Being, and the Critique of Metaphysics*. Ithaca and London: Cornell University Press, 1988. An insightful critical analysis from the perspective of a philosopher in the analytic and pragmatic traditions, treating in detail both the earlier and later Heidegger.

Richardson, William J. *Heidegger: Through Phenomenology to Thought*. Preface by Martin Heidegger. 3d ed. The Hague: Martinus Nijhoff, 1974. An extensive exposition of the whole of Heidegger's thought that has become the standard, although Richardson tends to explain Heidegger by using Heidegger's own language rather than interpreting the language.

Sheehan, Thomas, ed. *Heidegger: The Man and Thinker*. Chicago: Precedent Publishing, 1981. A collection of essays on various aspects of Heidegger's thought, including a rare biographical piece as well as an extensive bibliography of English translations of Heidegger's work and of secondary works on Heidegger.

REINHOLD NIEBUHR

Born: 1892, Wright City, Missouri
Died: 1971, Stockbridge, Massachusetts
Major Works: *Moral Man and Immoral Society* (1932), *Beyond Tragedy* (1937), *The Nature and Destiny of Man* (1943), *Faith and History* (1949), *The Self and the Dramas of History* (1955)

Major Ideas

The nature of the human being is flawed in its inclination to pride and power, but it exists in freedom under the shadow of God, is endowed with moral capacity, and, in individual terms, can approach the ideal of Christian love.

God acts in history but is also hidden from history and cannot be known but by incomplete reason and completed faith.

The "self" struggles for spiritual authenticity, which can be located only in historical existence.

The moral endowment of the modern individual is thus destined to labor in a social context that, by its own very nature, both precludes any full realization of ideal possibility and makes social justice always a proximate affair.

Nonetheless, history—life in a world full of tragic potentiality—demands absolute seriousness as the "theater" of redemptive possibility, an ultimate "stage" whereon the highest measures of justice are to be sought.

The Christian vision, rooted in biblical revelation, is the only source and ground for a sense of life "beyond tragedy."

Reinhold Niebuhr spent a bold and varied career as the foremost public theologian in the United States during the first half of the twentieth century. Famous for his fiery declamations about the modern spiritual dilemma and his canny analyses of contemporary social problems, he was frequently called upon to advise national leaders impressed both by his grasp of fundamental social, economic, and political issues and by the way his "Christian realism" could be brought profoundly to bear on the problems of this tumultuous era. Indeed, during decades when many feared that religious life might suffer a final atrophy under the pressures of an urbanized, industrial existence and new international complexities, large numbers of Americans, trying to be true to their religious traditions, found in Niebuhr's voice a resonant power about the part and place of a Christian faith genuinely decisive for the times. Beyond the senses of crisis he was able to invoke, his theology met such people with a more credibly "Christian" understanding of the human and social situations than the most liberal religion-

ists wanted to muster and with a more actively "modern" Christianity than the neo-orthodox theologians sought to present.

In many respects, surely, Niebuhr's thought had its broad, public appeal not only by dint of its timely character but by virtue of what could be called his "nonproleptic" *way* of thinking. He did not begin in abstractions of reason or faith, devising theoretical notions to contain historical situations; his tactic, rather, was to plunge into the denser stuff of human sensations, trapped in the immediacies and ambiguities of historical situations, and to probe among these specificities for the meanings they might reveal. Whether musing about the situation of a biblical writer whose "myths" were made necessary because of the incomprehensible size of the truth he struggled to express, or about the social and psychological complexities of racial problems in modern American cities, Niebuhr wanted to lift up the human dimension of the matter as that which "mattered" most in theological reflection. This style of thought carried its own passions, addressing people in what they felt were their own situations, even as it had decided costs to the systematic character of his work.

Niebuhr himself followed an intellectual career that, in retrospect, reveals little fear of self-contradiction, much less of formal inconsistency, and naught of changes of mind. In fact, his own lineage and experience might well have contributed to his deep appreciation of paradox, irony, and ambiguity.

Reared in a German Evangelical synod of the American Midwest, young Reinhold found in the model of his minister father, Gustav, a strange combination. Embodied in this man, at once, was a heavy dosage of reformed "pietism" conjoined with an inveterate intellectual curiosity. He could be strenuously opposed to liberal dismissals of supernaturalist faith while simultaneously vigorous in his insistence on relating the gospel message to the realms of society and politics. However, even while steadfastly loyal to the German Reformed tradition, he gave no approval to any democratic socialism, committed instead to the progressivist ideals of the American capitalist system.

Reinhold's deep but deeply mingled intellectual inheritance—German/American, liberal/evangelical, pietist/intellectual—would be the source for him of many long struggles of the self, just as his indefatigable work habits would also bear Gustav's stamp. At Elmhurst College, entered early and specifically to prepare himself for the seminary, he apparently resisted the school's classical education and, under his father's instruction, pored over the more immediately liberal theological tradition. Later, at Eden Seminary (there to prepare himself for a pastorate in the evangelical context), he cultivated his oratorical and social skills, seeking to become more intellectually American in his outlooks and expression. At Yale Divinity School, entered to enhance his scholarly acumen, he veered away from liberal viewpoints, practiced more in the spirit of the scholarship of the Reformed tradition, and yet worried that scholarly study itself might deplete the life of genuinely religious devotion and action. When in 1915 he reached the Bethel Church

in Detroit, to which the synod had assigned him for his first full-time pastorate, Niebuhr charged the air with liberal theology and issued a call to activism for this suburban evangelical congregation. During his years on the faculty at Union Seminary in New York, beginning in 1928, he remained an activist but always chastened the school's liberal theological agenda with his own brand of theological orthodoxy and Christian realism.

If Niebuhr's intellectual bearings were disparate, his forms of theological expression tended to be "topical"—at least in the sense that he spoke and wrote virtually always in a way motivated by his attentiveness to particular problems, issues, and questions of modern historical experience as he believed they were to be illuminated by the wider light of Christian faith and addressed with a call to Christian practice. This analytical and interpretive reflexiveness in many respects characterized his work in the more formal, deliberative efforts of his Gifford Lectures, published as *The Nature and Destiny of Man*, quite as much as it animated the content, style, and purposes of the periodical *Christianity and Crisis*, for which Niebuhr was a founding editor and central writer.

Throughout all the years of his adult life, Niebuhr was a prolific writer of sermons, lectures, columns, editorials, scholarly articles, books, homiletical tracts, essays for large-circulation magazines, political position papers, and so on. He was continuously called upon to be a leader or spokesman for religious, social, and political groups whose causes might be informed and propelled by his prophetic voice and vision. In the latter roles, as liberal labor reformer, as a leader of Americans for Democratic Action, as ardent pro-Zionist, and many other "offices," Niebuhr fearlessly attached the overarching idea of the Kingdom of God to the dramas of the temporal realm.

Despite the diversity of occasions, the abundance of topics, the variety of styles, and the nonsystematic character of his thinking, certain major ideas and interpretations persist throughout the *body* of Niebuhr's writing. And these related and interpenetrating constellations of themes make Niebuhr's thought a unique and powerful presence in the traditions of Christian social thought.

History and the Kingdom of God

For Niebuhr, the ultimate meaning and fulfillment of history are to be expected only in faith stemming from revelation—in the Kingdom of God to appear "beyond history." But the sovereign God who stands over and apart from the historical realm is also in part revealed in the course and contours of the struggles of historical life. In books like *Faith and History* (1949) and *The Self and the Dramas of History* (1955), as well as in *The Nature and Destiny of Man* (1943), Niebuhr makes it clear that the central meanings of *human* history reside in Christ, that is, in the revelation both of God's judgment over history and of the law of love—the first of which places the final meaning of history beyond human comprehension, the latter of which provides to human existence a resource never to be completely realized in the finite realms of history. Within history, human beings must struggle to achieve God's purposes, must labor under the prospect of divine judgment, and must seek to bring to birth the transfigurations portended in Christ by the possibilities of love, but must do so without the vanity of believing that any or all of their efforts can be identified with the will of a God and without the pride of thinking they themselves can fully seize the promise of Christ's love. As Niebuhr argues in *The Children of Light and the Children of Darkness* (1944), the sons and daughters of the potential "goodnesses" of the democracies must recognize their own prideful complacency and naïveté as well as the brute malice and violence of the dark fascist forces. All human achievements, even the best intentioned and most gracious, are marred by human limitation, flawed by human finitude, capable of equations of exploitation and destruction.

Far from leading to any kind of pessimistic withdrawal from history into an "other-worldly" or "quietist" form of Christianity, this understanding of history, Niebuhr insists, calls for an absolute seriousness respecting the realm of human struggle because it emphasizes the human freedom to act, to aspire to the good, and to seek fulfillment. Biblical revelation proposes a world in which God acts and in which an economy of redemption operates, calling humankind to participate in the movement toward the Kingdom at the end of history. Although men and women can never equate their approximations of love and justice with divine love and justice, their spiritual endowment, however hindered by the stuff of finitude, pulls them toward depths of meaning in history that point beyond history. Thus, even their partial achievements have significance in the context of the coming Kingdom. If historical existence has its tragic potential—as people are caught in the throes of complicated situations of moral compromise—the spiritual self is saved from despair by that sense of life, rooted in biblical revelation, which assures that history can move "beyond tragedy."

So it is that Niebuhr brings revelation to bear on history and uses complex situations of social and historical existence to penetrate to the human element of biblical meaning. He was completely convinced that the messages of revelation could, with realism and reason, be profoundly applicable to opaque and contradictory aspects of the contemporary human situation, that the myths of biblical narrative present avenues into the depth dimension of current life. While the fundamentalists treat the myths as idols, confusing the form with the meaning, and while the liberals regard the myths as just so much prescientific folklore, Niebuhr suggests that the myths were the "deceptive" means utilized by the biblical writers, in their own localized lives, to get into human scale truths about God and history larger than human comprehension, then or now, can contain. Nothing they could say in any form could be adequate to render those meanings rooted in history that nevertheless point beyond history, and, yet, their experience of and faith in the mysterious depths of life, of the God in history who transcends history, required their struggle to tell the truth. In this way, the situation of the biblical writers is emblematic of the condition of modern people—called to be true to a truth larger than can be understood, deeper than can be told, yet warranted by their own faithful sense of life.

The Self and Social Existence

Niebuhr's interpretation of the salvific vista of history in relation to the Kingdom cannot be understood apart from his deep notion of the destiny of the individual human being. The single self, endowed with spirit and liberated to choose, could swerve away from the redemptive work to be done in "the dramas of history" or could seek the spiritual fulfillment, in the midst of tragic circumstances, to go beyond tragedy. But, as Niebuhr trained his attention on "the self" in works like *Moral Man and Immoral Society* (1932), *An Interpretation of Christian Ethics* (1935), and *The Self and the Dramas of History* (1955), it is also apparent that, for him, the "role" of the individual in the huge, unfolding story of the Kingdom has to be played out continuously, daily, on a smaller stage— mythic-sized meanings, perhaps, trapped in the smaller, gnarled stuff of living a life in an ambiguous and imperfect world. The fields of action for the human self, in short, have to be seen as complicated and constricted by the ineluctably social dimensions of historical existence wherein confident identifications of "darkness" and "light" are frequently problematical.

Niebuhr's theory of the self was first broadly announced in the passionate pages of *Moral Man and Immoral Society*, though he had no doubt been teaching himself for several years prior to that how questions of selfhood in modern industrial societies needed to be answered by Christian theology. In any event, by 1932, he had fashioned the fundaments at least of an interpretation of the self's nature, prospects, and limits that remained central to, and continuously modulated in, his subsequent thought. Rudimentary to his idea is the notion that men and women are in bondage to nature, conscious of their finitude and limitations, and yet freely capable of transcending the flawed natural order. This capacity stems from the human being's having been created in God's image, thus possessing the will,

the reason, and the spirit to enact the law of love. In this situation, the individual self, recognizing responsibility to and acknowledging dependence on God, could indeed, in close relationships, approach the moral ideal presented definitively in Christ. But, in freedom, the actions of virtue are always difficult: The self could also ignore the transcending course, surrendering to animal nature, or succumb to the pride of its own autonomy, refusing to accede to its dependence on God. Still, Niebuhr believed, consistently with his views on the requirements of historical existence, the moral endowment of the singular self could be potent in the movement toward the ideal of love to be realized in the coming Kingdom.

If Niebuhr's appraisal of the nature of the individual self is high, however, he could marshall no such understanding of human beings in their collectivity, and his urge for realism in Christian self-understanding stemmed from the perception that the nature of "immoral society" complicated every aspect of human moral endeavor. The sin of pride which might beset individuals is made manifold in the larger, more complex relationships of general social reality, wherein it is virtually inevitable. No matter how well intentioned, every action, every decision, every scheme in society opens to the possibilities of exploitation and dominance, to unanticipated equations of destruction, to vaunting self-interest and ambition, in group or national contexts. At its best, no program of social correction or progress should be thought other than a compromise, a choice among finite alternatives, undertaken perhaps with the aspirations of the rule of love but without any prideful illusion that it enacts God's will. While the rule of love might effectively obtain in personal life, Niebuhr argues, the impersonal and insentient character of all collectives renders such selfless love largely powerless in addressing social conflict and insufficient in meeting social evils. Realism dictates that, this side of the Kingdom, the rule of justice might be the highest form of spiritual striving— indeed, the responsible destiny of humankind.

Even given the ambiguity of social existence and the opaqueness of historical life, therefore, Niebuhr maintains throughout his work that Christians should make no withdrawal into quiescence—that, rather, men and women can find their spiritual authenticity only in trying to live out "the relevance of an impossible ethical ideal" of love in the modern social world. Without pride, without illusions, they should exert themselves to secure some approximations of justice. If this historical condition seems rife with tragic implication, the overarching Christian vision nonetheless infuses the call to human responsibility with a radiant principle of redemption in the coming Kingdom of God. If the imperative of love can never be fully realized, if moral endeavor is always anxious and uncertain, human beings can nonetheless be justified in the sight of God by that faith seeking righteousness in the ambiguous stuff of troubled finitude. That faith in God's saving grace, for Niebuhr, is the crucial thread in the complex fabric of self, society, history, and Kingdom woven by his lifelong thought.

In assessing the legacy of Reinhold Niebuhr, one has to own straightaway that, quite beyond the shifting fashions of Western culture with regard to what is intellectually palatable, several factors surely precluded the emergence of anything like a full-scale Niebuhrian school of thought. Perhaps foremost among these factors, given the volatility of the various theological fields in the second half of the twentieth century, is that Niebuhr's work finally lacks the kind of architectonic character that creates or entices those intellectual disciples who then "ply" the system in ever more elaborated ways. A second matter is the fact that his starting points for

reflection, grounded as they frequently were in the immediate issues of his day, make the arguments stemming from those bases seem slightly anachronistic in altered times and circumstances. Although controlled under broad themes and rubrics, Niebuhr's views and arguments are uniquely saturated with his sense of the age and its particular moral and religious demands. He could, for instance, quite innocently point to the liberal democracies as the best form for Christian society while in the very midst of an argument chastizing any social scheme or nationalism that presumed to consider itself more than a fallible, injust human construct. Another factor that serves to abridge any singular Niebuhrian movement, of course, is one substantive element of his own vision: his convictions about the tenuous, ambiguous, and "unfinished" nature of historical life lead to a realism that must have made him, and makes any potential follower, believe that any human conclusion must be radically premature—hardly the basis for any systemic closure.

Still, few can doubt Reinhold Niebuhr's influence in the Western traditions of religious thought. His ideas, if not his name, appear frequently, if not inevitably, as prophetic corrective whenever prideful religious communities display vaulting senses of superiority, whenever religious peoples retreat from difficult issues, whenever schemes of social progress proceed smugly toward "perfection," and indeed whenever anyone doubts that the theological imagination cannot engage the business of life in the world.

ROWLAND A. SHERRILL

Further Reading

Fox, Richard Wightman. *Reinhold Niebuhr: A Biography.* New York: Pantheon Books, 1985. In this considerable critical and intellectual biography, which places Niebuhr clearly and carefully in relation to the intellectual and socio-political currents of his time, Fox is especially acute in tracing the fluid and changeable nature of Niebuhr's mind.

Harland, Gordon. *The Thought of Reinhold Niebuhr.* New York: Oxford University Press, 1960. This book traces the development of Niebuhr's religious ideas but provides little sense of the connections of the ideas of Niebuhr's experience. This perhaps creates an overemphasis on the consistency of the various works.

Kegley, Charles W., and Robert W. Bretall, eds.

Reinhold Niebuhr: His Religious, Social, and Political Thought. New York: Macmillan, 1956. Over twenty essays, prepared by leading figures in several fields, explore specific aspects of Niebuhr's work, including contributions by Arthur Schlesinger, Jr., Hans Morganthau, and Paul Tillich.

Scott, Nathan A., Jr., ed. *The Legacy of Reinhold Niebuhr.* Chicago: University of Chicago Press, 1975. Appearing first as a special issue of the *Journal of Religion* (October, 1974), the essays in this collection, gathered shortly after Niebuhr's death, represent important early assessments of the cumulative character of Niebuhr's work from several perspectives.

Stone, Ronald. *Reinhold Niebuhr: Prophet to Politicians.* Nashville: Abingdon Press, 1972. As the subtitle suggests, Stone treats Niebuhr's powerful religious and cultural analyses of the political realm and his influence in that setting, giving sustained attention to Niebuhr's dealings with cold-war ideologies.

WERNER HEISENBERG

Born: 1901, Würzburg, Bavaria, Germany
Died: 1976, Munich, Germany
Major Works: Development of quantum mechanics (1925), the Heisenberg uncertainty principle (1927).

Major Ideas

Anomalous experimental results in microscopic physics can be explained through the use of matrices.

There is an unsurpassable limit to the accuracy with which certain properties (position and momentum) of subatomic particles can simultaneously be determined.

Every measurement of a subatomic entity necessarily involves the substantial interference of an observer, so physics must focus on describing the experimental setup, which includes a relationship between an observer and the object observed; hence, statistical descriptions are the most accurate possible descriptions for such systems.

Werner Heisenberg is largely responsible for the twentieth-century revolution in physics known as quantum mechanics. He is most famous for his development of the Heisenberg uncertainty principle (also called the "indeterminacy principle" or "uncertainty relations") and his espousal of radical philosophical conclusions drawn from it. Prior to the advent of quantum mechanics, the origination of which is often credited to Heisenberg, physical science was proceeding in the direction initiated by Isaac Newton, achieving greater and greater precision in the description of nature. It was the view of Newton and the majority of his followers that there was no theoretical reason why one could not approach an absolutely precise description of physical bodies and their motions. Many under Newton's influence were determinists in that they thought that sufficient knowledge of current physical conditions in the universe would enable the precise prediction of all future physical conditions. This Newtonian edifice was still standing when Werner Heisenberg was born in 1901 and it was weakened only slightly by the ideas of James Clerk Maxwell and Max Planck.

The foundations of Newton's idealized world were shaken by the work of Einstein in the years around 1905, but it was the work of Heisenberg and many of his peers that brought the walls crashing down. The Newtonian picture of a world of empty space filled with discrete, accurately representable physical bodies was shown by Heisenberg and

others to be a myth. He showed that precise mathematical description of individual microscopic bodies was impossible, not due solely to the limitations of contemporary experimental technique, but for all time.

Influenced by philosophers such as Plato, Aristotle, Kant, and the positivists, and physicists such as Planck, Einstein, Sommerfeld, and Bohr, Heisenberg began to elaborate the meaning of his discoveries for wider arenas of science and philosophy. His exposure to philosophy and the classics (his father was a university professor) allowed him to see very quickly that his ideas, when fully grasped, could send shock waves jolting through practically every area of human thought.

Heisenberg was recognized early in his life as a gifted mathematician and theoretician. He had a healthy dose of the theoretician's disdain for experimental work, a condition shared and encouraged by fellow student Wolfgang Pauli (to the dislike of their teacher Arnold Sommerfeld). Heisenberg received his Ph.D. in 1923 and proceeded to a number of teaching positions in theoretical physics. He won the 1932 Nobel Prize for his work in quantum mechanics. He helped found the Max Planck Institute for Physics in Göttingen in 1946 and directed the Planck Institute for Physics and Astrophysics in Munich for many years, working for its advance until he fell too ill to do so. He died in 1976.

Heisenberg was an amiable man, well liked by all who came in contact with him. Practically the only personal criticism directed toward him comes from those who lament his less-than-vociferous defiance of the Nazis during the 1930s and 1940s. Heisenberg was a sensitive but apolitical person and hence suffered inwardly for the millions who suffered more noticeably from the Nazi abuses.

The Discovery of Quantum Mechanics

Many things about the state of physics in the early 1920s disturbed the young Heisenberg. He particularly abhorred the conceptual model of the atom that described atoms joined to one another by means of hooks and eyes. If the structure of the atom is this complex, he thought, then there must be more fundamental units from which they are constructed. Heisenberg was familiar with the atomic theories of the ancient Greeks and found their mathematical and logical beauty compelling but could not tolerate their complete lack of experiential corroboration. Especially intriguing to him were the theories of Plato in the *Timaeus*. Plato's description of the ultimately small in terms of geometrically simple forms was aesthetically pleasing to Heisenberg, and even though he could find no physical reason to describe atoms in this way, Plato's description seemed more tenable than the hooks-and-eyes model. Heisenberg's inability to settle upon a satisfactory model for the portrayal of atoms would lead him to a description so abstract that it would befuddle and put off many of his peers.

In addition, there were myriad inexplicable experimental results that Heisenberg felt compelled to resolve. There were also several unusual theories, proposed by Niels Bohr, Wolfgang Pauli, and others, that matched experiments, though no one knew why. Poised in the background behind these questions was the older question concerning the nature of electromagnetic radiation (including light). The wave propagation of light and the absorption of light in discrete packets (quanta) were experimental facts that could not be explained away. Was this radiation ultimately wavelike or particlelike? All attempts to explain the situation in terms of models that made clear sense had failed.

By the time of Heisenberg's preoccupation with

these matters, in the period from 1923–25, Bohr, Heisenberg's mentor, was already developing his ideas on complementarity, the view that both kinds of descriptions (wave and particle) must be employed in the characterization of atomic phenomena. Any description of atomic phenomena that used exclusively the wave picture or the particle picture was doomed to fail, according to Bohr. Heisenberg saw that an entirely new conceptual scheme was called for. Bohr's freedom from restrictive thought pictures and Heisenberg's dissatisfaction with the same led to the first quantum mechanics, developed with the help of mathematical matrices.

In early 1925, no one had been able to find a mathematical tool that consistently accounted for the anomalies mentioned above. And Heisenberg had suffered a particularly severe attack of hay fever. He went to the island of Heligoland to recuperate and to ponder the numbers from the results of the perplexing experiments. Here it occurred to him that numbers handled in arrays, with their own mathematical peculiarities, sufficed to explain and to predict the hitherto befuddling experiments. It was pointed out to him that what he had used was matrix mathematics, whose properties had been known for several decades. A few physicists were adept at manipulating matrices, and with their help Heisenberg formulated the first consistent and widely applicable quantum theory. Max Born, Pascual Jordan, and Heisenberg collaborated on a paper that publicized these ideas. The paper was completed in mid-November of 1925 and became a crucial nail in the coffin of the classical (Newtonian) understanding of physical reality.

The ideas promulgated under the rubric "matrix mechanics" were very abstract, far removed from straightforward analyses of physical reality, and the language of matrices was largely unknown to the physicists of the day. To many it seemed quite absurd to describe physical particles in terms of an arcane branch of mathematics. Those close to the project were well aware of its rigor and precision, but it did not gain its widest acceptance until it became clear that Heisenberg's matrix mechanics was operationally equivalent to Schrödinger's wave mechanics, developed only a few months later. By then it was clear that quantum events, whether described by matrices or waves, did not behave anything like the classical particles they had been assumed to be. There remained a serious question concerning the application of the mathematical formalism created by Heisenberg to the physical reality that it somehow represented. These questions persist today. Physicists cannot say how subatomic particles, in themselves, behave, but Heisenberg was instrumental in defining just what physicists *can* say.

The Uncertainty Principle

Much of the reason that Heisenberg favored the matrix explanation of quantum events was his refusal to speculate about the existence or behavior of some ill-defined atomic "thing-in-itself." He had an ongoing dispute with Erwin Schrödinger over this very issue. Schrödinger insisted that there must be an underlying continuity and lawfulness in atomic processes even if such could not be observed in current experiments. Heisenberg thought it unbecoming of physics to ruminate over anything but observable quantities, and those observable quantities displayed discontinuities and apparent lawlessness.

This emphasis on the observable, along with certain peculiarities of matrix mathematics (noncommutativity), led Heisenberg to the formulation of his famous uncertainty principle. The seminal paper in which this principle was announced was published in the *Zeitschrift für Physik* in 1927. This publication assured Heisenberg's fame and provided him with a starting point from which much of his career would proceed. The principle, wrote Heisenberg three years later in "The Physical Principles of the Quantum Theory," centers around the fact that "the interaction between observer and object causes uncontrollable and large changes in the system being observed, because of the discontinuous changes characteristic of atomic processes." He continued by explaining the scope and significance of this discovery: "This lower limit to the accuracy with which certain variables can be known simul-

taneously may be postulated as a law of nature (in the form of the so-called uncertainty relations)." And further: "These uncertainty relations give us that measure of freedom from the limitations of classical concepts which is necessary for a consistent description of atomic processes."

The classical mechanics of Newton did recognize, of course, that the observer interfered in certain measurements and hence that there arose various means of compensating for this interference, which, when accomplished, would lead to results that were held to be true "objectively." It was assumed by most physicists that the refinement of experimental technique would eventually lead to greater precision of measurement and that the effect of the observer's interference could be minimized to the point of insignificance. Heisenberg's principle of uncertainty summarily demolished this Newtonian hope.

Heisenberg showed that it would be impossible to determine simultaneously both the position and momentum of an electron. Because of observer interference and the unpredictable behavior of individual quanta of radiation, there would always remain a haziness about either momentum or position, or both.

Specifically, Heisenberg showed that the greater the accuracy with which one determines the position of an electron (or other subatomic particle), the greater the inherent inaccuracy in the determination of its momentum, and vice versa. If one would measure precisely the momentum, then the position would be entirely unknown. Definite determination of the position produces inescapable and complete uncertainty about the momentum. More precisely, the uncertainty principle states that the product of the uncertainties regarding position and momentum must be greater than or equal to Planck's quantum of action divided by twice π (pi): If x is position, p is momentum, Δ is amount of indeterminacy, and $\hbar$ ("h bar") is Planck's constant divided by 2π, then the formula reads $\Delta x \Delta p \geq \hbar$.

Much of Heisenberg's theoretical work in this area was driven by his realization that Bohr's electron orbits were unobservable. Electrons were held by most thinkers to be classical particles, obeying

Newtonian laws of motion, but they were not directly observable (as classical particles were observable). The effects that *could* be seen painted a much more complicated picture. Heisenberg chose to focus on what could be observed and demonstrated the existence of permanent limits on the accuracy of that observation.

The accuracy of any measurement is always a function of the wavelength of the light used in the observation. Visible light has a wavelength much too long to allow the resolution of items as small as subatomic particles. Hence, if it were possible to observe individual electrons with visible light, then there would be a high degree of uncertainty in measurement. It might be suggested, Heisenberg postulated, that radiation of a shorter wavelength be used in order to arrive at more accurate measurements. Though this course of action may sound promising, Heisenberg indicates its inadequacy by proposing a thought experiment employing a gamma-ray microscope. Gamma radiation has a much shorter wavelength than visible light, so if a microscope could be constructed to utilize gamma radiation, the measurements it yielded should be more accurate. However, Heisenberg says, this smaller wavelength is necessarily accompanied by a higher energy. This increase in energy leads to a greater perturbation of the object under investigation, and an accurate measurement again becomes impossible. Any observation requires the exchange of at least one quantum (the smallest possible amount) of radiation between observer and object. For the low energy–large wavelength quantum, the observation cannot be precise due to poor resolving power. For the high energy–short wavelength quantum, the observation cannot be precise due to the increased interference affecting the observed object. Combine the notion of this perturbation with the fact that when the subatomic particle is disturbed it leaps discontinuously and unpredictably, and the result is a permanent and fateful inability to characterize accurately the behavior of microscopic phenomena. "Our knowledge then of this class of objects," says Heisenberg, "is limited to irreducible statistical distributions and correlations."

As the experimental prowess of modern physics approached analysis of the smallest particles of matter, where it seemed possible that physics would reach the precision of the classical ideal, Heisenberg pointed out the inherent impossibility of attaining the goal. This realization was bound to change not only the physicists' way of viewing nature but the very mind-set engendered by Newtonian successes, a mind-set shared by all persons educated in the nineteenth- and twentieth-century Western world. As Heisenberg himself said in a 1955 article, these changes in twentieth-century physics must "be considered as expressions of changes in our very existence and thus as affecting every realm of life."

Philosophical Interpretation of Uncertainty

Heisenberg spent untold amounts of time trying to fathom the full philosophical consequences of his uncertainty principle. In this effort he showed a degree of philosophical sophistication that outstripped most of his colleagues in the physical sciences. He began his career with very strong positivist leanings (believing that language has meaning only when it refers to potentially observable states of affairs) and later moved to a more highly nuanced Kantian-style rationalism (believing that certain *a priori* thought structures are prerequisite for the intelligible experience of nature).

Though he was originally opposed to both, Heisenberg eventually came to affirm the value of Schrödinger's wave mechanics and Bohr's principle of complementarity. These notions aided Heisenberg tremendously in his endeavor to develop a cogent philosophical understanding of his physical principles. Throughout the adjustments and refinements of his ideas, Heisenberg always held to what he and others have called the "Copenhagen interpretation" of quantum mechanics. This interpretation espoused the relative finality of the quantum mechanical description of the microscopic realm and forthrightly abandoned the classical notions of causality, determinism, and old-style materialism. Changes in atomic physics, says Heisenberg, "have made us abandon the world-view of ancient atomic philosophy. It has become clear that the desired objective reality of the elementary particles is too crude an oversimplification of what really happens, and that it must give way to very much more abstract conceptions."

Many physicists were vehemently opposed to the Copenhagen interpretation's dismissal of crucial explanatory notions such as causality and objective existence of physical bodies, but the experiments have vindicated Bohr, Heisenberg, and all the others who insisted that the statistical description of reality was the most complete description possible. The Copenhagen interpretation today is also called the orthodox interpretation.

This view, now so widely accepted in one form or another, was forged in an atmosphere of heated debate. Some of the most interesting literature in the history of science was born out of the correspondence between opponents and proponents of the Copenhagen interpretation. It seems wise to describe Heisenberg's understanding of certain elements of this position in light of some of the objections raised against it.

The Copenhagen interpretation as understood and spread by Heisenberg was essentially opposed to what he called the "ontology of materialism." He believed that this ontology, or ultimate understanding of existence, rested upon the illusion that concepts applicable to the everyday world of tangible and visible objects could be extrapolated into the world of the microscopic. As Heisenberg states in his 1958 monograph "Physics and Philosophy," the Copenhagen interpretation "starts from the fact that we describe our experiments in the terms of classical physics and at the same time from the knowledge that these concepts do not fit nature accurately. The tension between these two starting points is the root of the statistical character of quantum theory." This passage indicates many of the important features of the Copenhagen interpretation and indicates the abstract course that must be followed.

The statistical nature of the methods used to define quantum events calls into question perhaps the most revered principle of classical physics, the principle of causality. Heisenberg thinks that this is the most important of the traditional notions that must be abandoned. In quantum physics, one can make no sense of the idea that "natural phenomena obey exact laws." The principle of causality rests on the assumption that "it is possible to observe the phenomena without appreciably influencing them." So one element of the Copenhagen interpretation is an ineluctable subjectivity that renders inapplicable the traditional notion of complete causality. Subatomic reality, discontinuous and subject to uncontrollable observer-related perturbations, cannot be said to obey precise laws. This conclusion was anathema to many physicists, the most illustrious of whom were Planck, Einstein, and Schrödinger.

These three men, who have a minority following still, proposed that there is an underlying continuity in nature, that cause and effect are just as inexorable in the microscopic realm as they are at the level of the visible. They argued that the mere inability of humans to penetrate the mystery of elementary particles is no evidence in favor of the renunciation of causality.

Heisenberg's answer to these critics was twofold: First, no positive evidence has been produced in favor of such "hidden variables" (invisible causal connections); second, no experimental scheme has been devised in which the uncertainty principle can be shown to be anything but complete.

Heisenberg's opponents then created a series of thought experiments intended to illustrate a scenario in which Heisenberg's limits could be transcended. None of these thought experiments succeeded. Hidden-variables theories have not gained a substantial following, and various persons claim to have demonstrated their impossibility as consistent descriptors of microscopic nature. More advanced physical experiments in the 1970s and 1980s have served to corroborate further Heisenberg's contention that the quantum mechanical statistical description, involving the strange notions of acausality, complementarity, and subjectivity is the most complete that can be given (short of another scientific revolution akin to quantum mechanics in its impact).

Though Heisenberg's fame as a scientist and thinker is secure, there is still much controversy concerning the proper interpretation of his theories. He is accused of wavering between the view that the discontinuity and immeasurability of subatomic reality is subjective and the view that it is objective. A large amount of difficulty remains still surrounding this point, not the least of which surrounds the meaning of the terms "objective" and "subjective." For the early positivistic Heisenberg, questions about some unapproachable objective reality are meaningless. For the later, more rationalistic Heisenberg, it makes sense to speak of an objective world "out there," but its features are so far removed from the world of everyday experience that only metaphors suffice to point to it.

At least one thing cannot be doubted—quantum mechanics is an unqualified experimental and technological success. The electronic lifeblood of contemporary society is a fruit of the labor of many astute and daring quantum physicists. None from this group was more astute and daring than Werner Heisenberg.

D. BRIAN AUSTIN

Further Reading

Gribbin, John. *In Search of Schrödinger's Cat*. New York: Bantam Books, 1984. One of the better popularizations of quantum physics. Gribbin is as precise as possible given his nonmathematical presentation of the ideas. His writing is engaging and lucid.

Heelan, Patrick. *Quantum Mechanics and Objectivity: A Study in the Physical Philosophy of Werner Heisenberg*. The Hague: Martinus Nijhoff, 1965. A revised Ph.D. dissertation that includes a wealth of information on the conceptual foundations of Heisenberg's thought.

Jammer, Max. *The Conceptual Development of Quantum Mechanics*. New York: McGraw-Hill, 1966. An unparalleled historical source that recounts the theoretical development of quantum theory from its inception through the various debates about its proper interpretation.

———. *The Philosophy of Quantum Mechanics*. New York: John Wiley and Sons, 1974. An in-depth analysis of the philosophical interpretations and implications of quantum theory. The rigor is sustained by the author's refusal to shy away from the pertinent mathematics.

Mehra, Jagdish, and Helmut Rechenberg. *The Historical Development of Quantum Theory*. 5 vols. New York: Springer-Verlag, 1982. An exhaustive narration of the events leading to the development of quantum theory. The authors begin with an analysis of nineteenth-century physics and the difficulties that caused the twentieth century to begin on such a radical note. The final volume deals with the rise and interpretation of Schrödinger's wave mechanics.

Polkinghorne, J. C. *The Quantum World*. Princeton, N.J.: Princeton University Press, 1984. An excellent, brief popularization of quantum theory. His combination of a lively writing style and specific details of quantum theory is rare among such popularizations.

KARL RAHNER

Born: 1904, Freiberg, Germany
Died: 1984, Innsbruck, Austria
Major Works: *Spirit in the World* (1939), *Hearers of the Word* (1941), *Theological Investigations* (Selections from *Schriften zur Theologie*, 16 vols., (1938–85), *On Prayer* (1949), *The Dynamic Element in the Church* (1958), *Foundations of Christian Faith: An Introduction to the Idea of Christianity* (1976)

Major Ideas

In acts of knowledge and volition, a person experiences the inexhaustible depth and richness of the totality of being; this experience is an unthematic, nonconceptualized preapprehension of God as the end of all dynamic acts of the human spirit.

The triune God reveals his inner essence throughout the history of salvation and as such shows himself to be a God of absolute self-donation.

Symbols make the intangible present in the tangible, and the visible in the invisible; thus, they participate in what they symbolize and thereby serve as vehicles of self-realization.

In freedom, a person can distance the self from all other things and dispose the self toward all things: Freedom involves a fundamental option for or against God in all moral choices.

All human development depends on loving and being loved.

Karl Rahner, who taught at Münster, Munich, and Innsbruck, is considered one of the most important theologians of the twentieth century. His writings have had a great influence within the Roman Catholic church as it sought to present the ancient faith to the modern world at the Second Vatican Council (1962–65). The theological anthropology that emerges from his works has received wide notice outside the Catholic community. It seeks to address how it is possible to encounter the divine within contemporary secular experience. Rahner is noted for his attempts to retrieve the traditional teaching of Catholic Christianity in order to restate it in ways that speak to the depth of human experience. He once said of himself that as a theologian his obligation was simply to try to make Christianity credible to the modern age.

For sixty-two years of his life, Rahner was a member of the Jesuit order. In his studies for the priesthood, he received one of the finest philosophical and theological educations of the day. He possessed an awesome historical knowledge of patristic, scholastic, and modern authors. He was most conversant with Saint Thomas Aquinas (c. 1225–74) and was deeply influenced by modern interpreters of Thomism such as Pierre Rousselot

(1878–1915) and Joseph Maréchal (1878–1944). Rahner's many spiritual writings portray a genuine admiration for the Christian mystical tradition, especially as it was expressed by the founder of the Society of Jesus, Ignatius Loyola (c. 1495–1556). It was the mystics who saw the dimension of mystery in the ordinary events of life. For Karl Rahner, the Ignatian principle of finding God in all things was fundamental. This is the theme of the *Spiritual Exercises* of Saint Ignatius, the document at the core of Jesuit identity. In this text the focus is on discerning the will of God for the individual existing in this particular historical moment. Rather than an examination of the cosmos through the use of static, universal, and impersonal categories of thought, Rahner would focus much of his attention on the human person. His thought, like much of modern philosophy, is anthropocentric rather than cosmocentric. He grounds the basic paradigms of his theology not only on Scripture and tradition but also on human experience.

Transcendental Thomism

Rousselot, Maréchal, and Rahner are associated with a philosophical tradition known as transcendental Thomism. The term "transcendental" refers to the philosophy of Immanuel Kant (1724–1804), which focuses on the necessary conditions in the knowing subject that make knowledge possible. The term "Thomism" refers to the tradition of Saint Thomas Aquinas, which claims the primacy of *being* as the object of knowledge, of *perfection* over imperfection, of *activity* over potentiality.

Rahner's first major work, *Spirit in the World*, sought to articulate why Aquinas thought all knowledge was a return to one's own essence only after an experience of the creation, an experience that implicitly also offered the Creator. Kant had claimed that a knowledge of God was not possible by the activities of pure reason because judgments were always tied to the world of sense experiences. Transcendental Thomists, on the other hand, think that an analysis of the dynamics of the human spirit does offer a true experience of God because, as spirit, the person is dynamically oriented beyond the world of sense experiences.

To affirm this point, Rahner directs his attention to human knowing and willing. In knowledge, the person knows not only what is known but also that there is more to know. In willing a good for the self, the self realizes in desire that there is always more to desire. The mind is able to see that what is captured is only a truth, not all truth. The will experiences that it possesses a good, not all goods. This is why there continue to be questions and choices. To ask a question about a particular being implies that one knows the object of inquiry to be only a limited, finite being. To have this awareness, Rahner argues, one already has a preapprehension or pregrasp (*vorgriff*) of the unlimited, infinite horizon or total context of all being. The fact that a person knows that he or she is settling for less is already a recognition that there is more. Rahner puts it in the following way:

> In spite of the finiteness of his system man is always present to himself in his entirety. He can place everything in question. In his openness to everything and anything, whatever can come to expression can be at least a question for him. In the fact that he affirms the possi-bility of a merely finite horizon of questioning, this possibility is already surpassed, and man shows himself to be a being with an infinite horizon. (*Foundation of Christian Faith*)

Humanity is not submerged in a world of brute objects but is able to transcend all objects. No finite thing can satisfy infinite longings, nor can an endless series of finite goods. Human beings alone can ask whether every finite and limited good finally adds up to ultimate meaning, value, and coherence. Also, if the end of all knowing and willing is finally nothingness, then all human acts are to the core absurd, for any claim about a particular truth or a particular good would be a claim that it is grounded in the emptiness of being, not its fullness.

The Supernatural

To speak of a "supernatural existential" means that all persons are oriented not only to the natural but also to the supernatural. The very inability of the natural world to satisfy the deepest longings of the human spirit is evidenced by the *vorgriff* of the totality of being—a totality that is never capable of being completely conceptualized or grasped (*griff*). Hence the person remains a dynamic movement, one on the way toward absolute being.

This orientation toward God is the result of God's will to create humanity in a way that only God as absolute good can complete. God is seen not only as Creator but also as Perfector, one who is all-powerful and all-good. This offer of God to be humanity's end (*Woraufhin*) has left an intrinsic ontological effect on human nature. This "supernatural existential," Rahner writes in an essay on "Nature and Grace," is offered to every person and thus leaves the whole of humanity "within the open horizon of transcendence toward the God of the supernatural life." Here is the theological reason for all human longings for the good. This ideal would express itself in a genuine catholicity in Rahner's writings, where the universality of God's love is seen not only in events of salvation history but also at the core of all human beings.

Rahner's widely discussed idea of "anonymous Christianity" emerges from this line of thought. All persons by nature of their experience of unlimited rootedness in Absolute Being are experiencing in an unobjective, nonexplicit way the self-communication of the Trinity. God as the goal of humanity's spiritual transcendentality in knowledge and freedom is for Rahner the God of Christianity whether or not one explicitly affirms this in faith. Hence the universal salvific will of God made manifest on the cross is affirmed everywhere and always. God, as Saint Paul in the Epistle to Timothy puts it, ". . . desires all men to be saved and to come to the knowledge of the truth" (1 Timothy 2:4).

Grace

Humanity, although receptive by nature to God, must nevertheless wait in faith to hear God's word. No creature can lay claim upon the Creator; no finite being can control one who is infinite. Grace is the gift of God's personal presence in history and in the life of the individual. For Rahner, the full self-manifestation of God is in the actions of the Trinity. The way God is within himself, this Christian theologian argues, is how God manifests himself throughout salvation history (the immanent Trinity is the economic Trinity). Thus, the Father creates the world and humanity in such a way that he alone can be its source and goal; the Son, the person of Jesus, reveals the inner life of God in uttering the divine word (*Logos*); while the Spirit (*Pneuma*) is the very presence of God within the creation—sanctifying, healing, and elevating all things. For Rahner, one God in three persons is the primordial ground of all being. God offers his knowledge and his love in word and spirit in the gift of complete self-donation. The human person in transcendental openness to perfect knowledge and perfect love has the capacity to experience God's grace; as Rahner puts it, a "*potentia obedientialis*," that is, the potentiality to be obedient to God.

Symbol

All beings express themselves. The highest form of self-expression is the Trinity, which in Scripture is revealed as a plurality in unity. God, in his self-donation to the human through creation, word, and spirit, expresses himself in symbols that reveal and conceal, that contain the divine yet do not exhaust the divine. This divine love goes out of itself as *ecstasis*, a being outside itself. Just as the human body makes the soul present, a symbol reveals the invisible in the visible. Symbols are not arbitrary signs but true vehicles of the more in the less. The importance of symbols for Rahner's theology can easily be seen in the following famous passage from his essay on "Anonymous Christians":

> Man is that which happens when God expresses and divests himself. Man is . . . that which God becomes if he sets out to show himself in the region of the extra-divine. And conversely . . . man is he who realizes himself when he gives himself away into the incomprehensible mystery of God. Seeing in this way the incarnation of God is the uniquely supreme case of the actualization of man's nature in general.

Humanity, as Rahner puts it in *Sacramentum Mundi* (1968), is "the possible mode of existence of God if God exteriorizes Himself to what is other than himself; man is the potential brother of Christ."

Human persons express themselves in order to discover the self and to achieve perfection. To give the self away to the other is to experience self-discovery. Symbols in the form of words or actions are the vehicles of self-realization in the other. That is, the self-realization of the person always occurs through the mediation of the material. A human being is a "spirit in the world" and a "hearer of the word." Receptivity, humility, temptation, suffering, temporality, struggle, and death are therefore very important in Rahner's spiritual writings. Indeed, the whole of the created order is in a real sense the symbol of God, in that the divine is not only the inexhaustible horizon but also the inner-most core, the loving heart of the world. So we read in an essay on "The Theology of Symbols":

> . . . We must consider that the natural depth of the symbolic reality of all things (which in itself transcends to God in an inner worldly or purely natural way) has received, on-tologically, an infinite widening in that this reality has also become a determination or the environment of the logos itself. Each reality that originates from God . . . expresses much more than merely itself. Each one always indi-cates and resonates, in its own way, the totality of reality itself.

From this context throughout his career Rahner would consider the self-expression of God in the Church. The thrust of his ecclesiology was to see the Christian community as the vehicle of divine presence throughout history in its preaching, sacra-ments, saints, and structures.

Freedom and Love

In acts of self-possession, human beings can dis-tance themselves from the goods of creation. This transcendental freedom (*libertas transcendentalis*) is the ability to be over and above the creation. The radical openness to all being presents to the person the awareness that no finite element or any combi-nation of them is capable of finally and completely satisfying. For Rahner, the essence of freedom is the dynamic spirit of intellect and will that knows in its acts of self-presence that no limited good can absolutely determine.

All acts of self-determination are oriented in the direction of a person's final determination. Ulti-mately, the human being makes a "fundamental option" in the choices of life to either affirm the true good (God) or to repudiate it. Thus, freedom as a divine gift makes the individual. To do good is to become good; to do evil is to become evil. Freedom is thus linked to autonomy, responsibility, dignity, and sin. Free acts are not isolated, unrelated activ-ities but the very stance one takes toward the self, the other, and God. Hell is the absolute refusal to be open to the inexhaustible richness of being. The damned have, in the deification of the self, repudi-ated their true divine end. Therefore, for Rahner, the issue is not only freedom from limitation but also freedom for the Unlimited.

This divine end is love, for "God is love" (1 John 4:8). Only self-possessing persons can either give or refuse themselves to the other. Love is thus essen-tially linked with freedom and is to the core per-sonal: a gift and an event of wonder and grace. To dispose the self to the other and to allow the other access to the self is the most important factor in personal growth. All human success depends on loving and on being loved. In love, individuals con-struct themselves and their eternal destiny. In love, human beings remain open and receptive to the good. In that God is present in the neighbor (Mat-thew 25:31–46), to offer the self to another is si-multaneously an offer of the self to God. Thus the command to love God and the neighbor is nothing else than the command to become fully human by becoming what God already is. In love, an act that completely engages the person, there is the achieve-ment of self-realization in the process of self-donation.

LAWRENCE F. HUNDERSMARCK

Futher Reading

McCool, Gerald A. *A Rahner Reader.* New York: Seabury Press, 1975. An excellent anthology of Rahnerian thought from many diverse sources offered with learned introductions. This is the book to consult if one wishes a rich sampling of Rahner's own works and a sweeping overview of his major topics.

———. *From Unity to Pluralism: The Internal Evolution of Thomism.* New York: Fordham Uni-versity Press, 1989. While not specifically focused on Rahner, this is a survey of twentieth-century Thomism and as such serves to situate Rahner in the tradition of Rousselot and Maréchal in contrast to the Thomism of Maritain (1882–1973) and Gilson (1884–1978). For the uninitiated, this work could prove difficult due to its technical vocabulary; however, it has the value of showing the diversity of approach and issue for contemporary interpreters of Aquinas.

O'Donovan, Leo J. *A World of Grace: An Introduction to the Themes and Foundations of Karl Rahner's Theology.* New York: Seabury Press, 1980. An easy-to-read commentary on Rahner's *Foundations of Christian Faith.* While some essays are much stronger than others, the discussion questions and the suggestions for further reading are helpful to one who is approaching Rahner for the first time.

Tallon, Andrew. *Personal Becoming in Honor of Karl Rahner at 75.* Milwaukee: Marquette University Press, 1982. A clear and full discussion of the key elements of Rahner's philosophical anthropology disentangled from the theological implications and development; deals with such themes as matter, spirit, freedom, symbol, guilt, and love. This edition has the added benefit of offering an 846-item bibliography of secondary sources from the years 1939 to 1979.

Weger, Karl-Heinz. *Karl Rahner: An Introduction to His Theology.* New York: Seabury Press, 1980. This is a very clear, sympathetic presentation by a colleague at the University of Munich.

JEAN-PAUL SARTRE

Born: 1905, Paris, France
Died: 1980, Paris, France
Major Works: *Nausea* (1938), *Being and Nothingness* (1943), *Existentialism and Humanism* (1946)

Major Ideas

For human beings, "existence precedes essence"; we are defined by our choices and actions and not by a fixed "human nature."

The direction a person's life will take is always in question and a matter of contingency.

We exist in situations—typically these are interpersonal and social—and they affect us; but how we exist within them is decisively a matter of our choosing.

The radical freedom that permeates our lives makes us responsible for ourselves and for one another; it also means that a complete and final understanding of ourselves eludes us.

Our freedom confers immense responsibility, and thus people often live in "bad faith," evading responsibility for their lives by denying the reality of their own freedom.

Existentialism, a nineteenth- and twentieth-century philosophical movement that stresses the radical extent of human freedom and attempts to deal seriously with its consequences for people's day-to-day lives, is the tradition most frequently associated with Jean-Paul Sartre. Born in Paris, Sartre pursued university studies in literature and philosophy. He was teaching in Paris when World War II began. Sent to the front, he was captured by the Germans and imprisoned for nine months. When he was returned to France in 1941, he served in the Resistance. Sartre remained politically active after the war, often espousing Marxist causes. He was offered the Nobel Prize in literature in 1964 but refused to accept the honor.

Sartre's thought is distinctive partly because he developed his views in fictional forms—stories, novels, and plays—as well as in essays and theoretical books on subjects that ranged from literary theory to psychoanalysis and philosophy. As Sartre developed his version of existentialism, which he took to be optimistic even though many of its critics did not, there were accents on freedom, the difficulties it brings to human existence, and the chances we have to overcome them. These themes dominated his philosophical novel, *Nausea*, which appeared in 1938.

Nausea

Nausea's main character, a historian named Roquentin, is writing a biography, but he finds it increasingly difficult to carry out his project because he cannot be sure whether he is describing or creating the subject of his work. How much of the biography is a factual, objective account, and how much of it is really Roquentin's own construction? The answer is unclear, but Roquentin becomes convinced that his interpretations color everything he writes. Hence, he gives up the biography. At the novel's end, he considers trying his hand at fiction.

In the light of these issues, it is intriguing to note that in 1963 Sartre published *The Words*, the first volume of a projected two-volume autobiography. The second volume was abandoned, but late in his life, Sartre turned to biography and wrote a multivolume study of Gustave Flaubert, the famous French novelist. Be that as it may, Roquentin's shifting project reveals much more than a mere change of plans. As Sartre traces Roquentin's efforts to write a biography, he is recording our human struggle to cope with all existence. *Nausea* emerges as part of that struggle. As Sartre used the idea, nausea involves physical feeling, but nothing so tame as acid indigestion or motion sickness. The nausea

Sartre described is a condition that combines disorientation, queasiness, and even revulsion brought on by an awareness of the uncertainty that characterizes our basic situation in life. That situation is constituted by a fundamental freedom.

Roquentin discovered that his own interpretation influenced and formed everything he experienced. Why that should be the case, indeed, why anything should exist at all, he could not fathom. He found that the world is everywhere particularized. The tree one sees, for example, exists with its specific leaves and bark, colors, and textures. Reasons for this can be given, but none fully accounts for that particular thing. Existence seemed so definitely real and yet so unnecessary and inexplicable—especially Roquentin's own—that it made Roquentin nauseated.

As Roquentin came to realize, nausea resulted largely from his sense of freedom. Indeed, our existence condemns us to be free. Without having been consulted, we are thrown into life—it involves living with and for others—and we shape it by our choosing. Far from exulting in this freedom, however, Roquentin found it a heavy burden. Even if freedom allowed for creativity, he came to realize that the nausea caused by his struggle to cope with existence would never be far away. Even if controlled, repressed, or forgotten for a time, nausea would well up again and require him to define once more his relation to the choices before him.

Two Types of Being

If *Nausea* is Sartre's best-known fiction, *Being and Nothingness* (1943), which elaborates many of the themes in Roquentin's experience, remains the most important nonfictional expression of Sartre's existential philosophy. At one point in *Being and Nothingness*, Sartre states that "man is a useless passion." That remark might seem to counsel despair. But while Sartre did want his pronouncement to describe the human predicament, he also wanted it to challenge men and women to make an honest, humanistic response to it. Both the description and the challenge depend on human freedom. In fact, no

Western philosopher has gone further than Sartre in giving an emphatically affirmative answer to the question "Am I free to act?"

As Sartre explored human existence, he became intrigued by what he called "prereflective" experience. Such experience, he explained, is the kind we have prior to thinking about what we are doing or before we look back at what we have done. If you ski down a slope, for example, you are aware, but you probably are not thinking about skiiing or about yourself because you are just *doing* the skiing. Sartre noted that the prereflective experience, which comes before our thinking about experience, always has the quality of being *of* something. In short, it has content. That content, he affirmed, transcends and often resists our analysis. Sartre's general term for this "something" that we always encounter is "being-*in*-itself."

Of being-in-itself, Sartre concluded, we can only say that it exists and that it is different from "being-*for*-itself." His reason for this claim reflects Roquentin's dilemma in attempting to write an objective biography. "Being-for-itself," Sartre's technical term for consciousness, makes individual experience happen. As Sartre described the role played by consciousness, consciousness "negates" being-in-itself. In this way, being is broken apart into *this* and *not this*, into *that* and *not that*. Take away the negating power of consciousness and we are powerless to describe being-in-itself at all. Indeed, Sartre argued, apart from saying simply that being-in-itself is real, we cannot describe it directly. We can portray being as it is experienced, but what it is in itself remains hidden. Our consciousness, however, does alter being-in-itself, and we can observe the results of its discriminating activity.

Existence and Essence

"Existence," proclaimed Sartre, "precedes essence." This formula is basic for understanding his view of human existence and freedom. By emphasizing the negating power of consciousness in relation to being-in-itself, Sartre interpreted consciousness as a form of being that always seeks to transcend itself but never fully finishes its task. It seemed to Sartre that we humans move to leave behind what we have been and to become what we are not. We are always headed somewhere; we are never fixed, complete, and static. Short of death, there is a perpetual process of negation and a continuous movement into a future of possibility and uncertainty.

What one will become is indefinite until consciousness determines it. We are what we become more than we become what we are. In that sense, our existence precedes the formation of our essence. Sartre identified the negating power of consciousness with human freedom. The fact that we can move beyond what we are toward that which we are not, he argued, signifies freedom. Whenever we act freely, there is a sense in which we leave something behind. We negate what we have been to try to become what we are not. Hence, not only does existence precede essence but, Sartre claimed, "freedom is existence." According to Sartre, a person's life is characterized by freedom, by choosing what one will be and how one will see the world one inhabits. The determination of what one *is* results from our individual choices and not from a series of determined causes outside of or even within oneself.

Did Sartre go too far in describing the degree of freedom that men and women possess? Far from having lives permeated by freedom, most persons feel restricted on every side. Many cannot find enough food, shelter, or work to make a decent living. Sartre was aware of such difficulties. His account emphasizes that human existence is always situated in particular times and places, and it is specified further by the relationships we establish with other persons. Many of these situations are full of pain and tragedy. Yet Sartre contended that the structure of human freedom remains, because we keep seeking to make something of ourselves. We may be prevented from achieving what we want, but, in Sartre's view, any kind of human seeking fundamentally involves the freedom he has in mind.

Ultimately, Sartre argued, our seeking leads us to try to achieve a complete self-identity in which we comprehend ourselves totally and are no longer constantly at a distance from ourselves. To accomplish this task, he contended, would be to become God ("being-in-itself-for-itself"), but no person can succeed in this undertaking. In fact, Sartre claimed, the idea of God is contradictory (an outcome that makes his existentialism atheistic), for consciousness excludes self-identity, and self-identity also excludes consciousness. Consciousness always has the quality of being stretched out ahead of itself. If you became completely self-identical and unchanging, you would not be conscious any more. Where our drive to become self-identical is concerned, then, we are forever doomed to frustration. It is in this sense that human freedom makes our existence "a useless passion."

Responsibility and Bad Faith

Freedom goes hand-in-hand with consciousness, and our future projects leave us forever short of fulfillment. At the same time, freedom makes us thoroughly responsible for ourselves. Sartre thought it was not too much to say that we choose our own world and even our own birth. Such statements may seem excessive, but Sartre's point was that so long as we choose to live, we have in effect chosen to be born. Additionally, insofar as the world has significance, such significance is a result of consciousness. Our consciousness of being alive is what allows us to choose the goals and purposes we confront as we relate to other persons or project our own futures.

We are responsible, Sartre asserted, for making what we can of the world. Because such responsibility is awesome, our freedom can be dreadful, and we may try to flee from it. Sartre called that flight "bad faith." Unlike lying, a situation in which I know the truth and try to hide it from others, "in bad faith," said Sartre, "it is from myself that I am hiding the truth." Whenever we deny ourselves by ignoring or repressing the fact that our free decisions are crucial ingredients in determining the situations we are in, bad faith intrudes. In its place Sartre wanted to put honesty and responsibility. Even though he called human existence a useless passion because it is so radically free, that same freedom makes it possible for us to do the best we can with the lives we have.

It was Sartre's view that doing the best we can requires, first and foremost, an honest appraisal of the degree to which we are responsible for ourselves and for each other. We have to choose what will be good and what will be evil. Such norms are not fixed in advance. Wherever norms do exist, someone has chosen them to be authoritative. That realization does not mean that values are arbitrary or irrational. It does mean that we can and must decide what we ought to do. Responsibility for these uses of freedom is ours and ours alone.

JOHN K. ROTH

Further Reading

Aronson, Ronald. *Jean-Paul Sartre: Philosophy in the World*. London: Verso, 1980. A lucid, scholarly appraisal of Sartre's philosophy.

Brée, Germaine. *Camus and Sartre: Crisis and Commitment*. New York: Dell, 1972. This book does a thoughtful job of comparing and contrasting Sartre's philosophy with that of his French contemporary existentialist, Albert Camus.

Caws, Peter. *Sartre*. New York: Routledge, Chapman & Hall, 1984. Caws's treatment offers a solid critical overview of Sartre's life and thought.

Flynn, Thomas R. *Sartre and Marxist Existentialism: The Test Case of Collective Responsibility*. Chicago: University of Chicago Press, 1984. Flynn appraises the relationships among Sartre's philosophy, Marxist thought, and existentialism in general.

Gerassi, John. *Jean-Paul Sartre: Hated Conscience of His Century*. Chicago: University of Chicago Press, 1989. Gerassi provides a biography of Sartre.

Grene, Marjorie. *Sartre*. New York: New Viewpoints, 1973. A leading interpreter of twentieth-century existentialism, Grene provides a careful analysis of *Being and Nothingness* and other works by Sartre.

Manser, Anthony. *Sartre: A Philosophical Study*. New York: Oxford University Press, 1967. Manser's book opens with a chapter on Sartre's novel *Nausea*, and probes the philosophical argumentation that runs through the full range of Sartre's thought.

SIMONE DE BEAUVOIR

Born: 1908, Paris, France
Died: 1986, Paris, France
Major Works: *The Second Sex* (*Le deuxième sexe*, 1949), *The Mandarins* (*Les mandarins*, 1954), *Memoirs of a Dutiful Daughter* (*Mémoires d'une jeune fille rangée*, 1958)

Major Ideas

As human beings, we live in a tragically ambiguous condition, but we must assume responsibility for the direction of our lives.

Every person is originally free.

Woman is the "other"; she lives in a world in which men have compelled her to be the second sex.

Despite the historical and cultural conditions under which women have been oppressed, they must assume their human dignity as free and independent persons.

Ethics requires a definitive commitment through action; morality and politics are interrelated.

Simone de Beauvoir is known, even by those who are uninformed about the world of the intellect, as the lifelong companion of the philosopher and novelist Jean-Paul Sartre, as an imaginative advocate of the existentialism he so profoundly fashioned, and as the author of *The Second Sex*, a revolutionary work in the twentieth-century emergence of radical feminism.

The attachment to Sartre was both personally and intellectually gratifying, at least for the most part, to Beauvoir, but historically she has suffered from that alliance. She is regarded, because of her closeness to Sartre, as relying upon him for her ideas, her success as a writer, and even for encouragement in her effort to reveal the causes of woman's oppression and to call for a new courage in choosing a way of life for all women. The truth is that she had a mind that Sartre not only respected but with which he had to contend as exhibiting an intellectual power comparable to his own; her writing shows a vitality and creativeness that stems entirely from her own experience and genius, and the creative spirit that entered into her massive declaration of women's independence is a spirit that was fashioned in the course of the struggle she so eloquently describes: the struggle to be of significance on one's own, a person of dignity, showing in action the defining process of the new woman, a power to be reckoned with and admired, something far beyond the negative connotation of the "other" sex.

Simone de Beauvoir was born January 6, 1908, in Paris. She began her education at a private school, the Cours Désir, in 1913, and in 1917 she met Elizabeth Le Coin, a cynical and outspoken girl who profoundly influenced Simone's attitudes toward families and, in particular, mothers, toward woman's use of freedom, and toward death. (Elizabeth Le Coin, who died in 1929, was later called "ZaZa" in Beauvoir's autobiographical *Memoirs of a Dutiful Daughter*, 1958, which covers the years 1908–29.)

Beauvoir met Jean-Paul Sartre in the same year as ZaZa's death, 1929; she had been studying literature, Latin, mathematics, and philosophy, the latter at the Sorbonne since 1926. (She received her degree from the Sorbonne in 1927.) Sartre, like Beauvoir, was preparing for the *agrégation de philosophie* (a qualification for teaching) at the École Normale Supérieure. Their eventual relationship—intimate, intense, intellectual, moral, open, permissive, sometimes disturbing, but fundamentally and mutually supportive—was to pervade and affect their lives until Sartre's death in 1980 and her own in 1986.

Beauvoir held various teaching positions in Marseilles, Rouen, and Paris. In 1943, her first novel, *L'Invitée* (*She Came to Stay*) was published and was an immediate critical and financial success. (Sartre had joined the French armed forces when France declared war on Germany in 1939; in 1940 he was taken prisoner, and in 1941 he was released and returned to Paris.)

After the publication of several other books—and a four-year affair with Nelson Algren, which started during her visit to the United States in 1947—Beauvoir's most important book, _Le deuxième sexe_ (_The Second Sex_), started in 1946, was published in 1949.

Her affair with Algren ended in 1951; the following year she and the journalist Claude Lanzmann began to live together. Her most well-received novel, _Les mandarins_ (_The Mandarins_), which many persons regarded as being, at least in part, a _roman à clef_ (portraying her associations with Sartre, Algren, and Albert Camus, among others), was published in 1954. Although the novel is indeed a portrait of the society of French intellectuals of which she was a part, it is fundamentally a dramatization of the central ethical dilemmas of her times and of their existential resolutions. For this novel she received the prestigious Prix Goncourt.

She was committed to a socialist philosophy of government and was politically active, particularly in support of Algerian independence and North Vietnam. Her involvement in feminist activities intensified: She joined in marches calling for abortion on demand, cessation of discriminatory practices against women, and, in general, for the liberation of all women.

Her writing was extensive and influential; it ranged from short stories and moral essays through novels, social and political commentary, and autobiographical accounts.

By 1985 her health had deteriorated markedly, largely as a result of her years of heavy drinking. In April of 1986, after a period of hospitalization, she died in Paris.

Existentialism and Feminism

Simone de Beauvoir must be understood as a unique figure emerging from a literary–philosophical setting that persisted through two world wars. Out of the devastation of the Second World War, existentialism emerged as a dominant philosophy, por-

trayed as much in literature and plays as in prose works. Beauvoir, although not a major philosophical writer in the movement, was a major force in its application to social and political problems, that of feminism in particular.

It is interesting to explore the connections between existentialism and Beauvoir's perspective on the condition of women. Existentialism, which began with the work of Søren Kierkegaard in Denmark, stresses both the basic freedom of all human beings and the centrally trapped situation of most human beings because of the limiting conditions of their existence, conditions that tend to take away human dignity and to challenge human freedoms. Woman's situation is different from that of human beings in general, Beauvoir maintained, in that there are influences and constraints on woman that must be overcome through a kind of courageous and creative self-assertion that allows women to become free persons of significance in the world.

All existentialist thought centers on ethics and stresses the human responsibility to achieve and maintain human freedom, the source of human dignity. Beauvoir stressed, first of all, the "tragic ambiguity" of the human condition. Some philosophers, such as Descartes, had stressed the need to achieve clarity and distinctness of thought, but for Beauvoir, although science may aim at clarity, the human being, who must live without directives or definitive answers, cannot have any such goal. The burden, then, is upon human action and upon the human being, caught in an ambiguous situation, to choose in such a way as to fashion character and morality in the very act of choice. Action and response must be individual. Universal rules are of no help or, at least, are not sufficient alone to specify action for individuals in concrete situations.

We often think freedom comes to us if our situation is made clear and definite principles are applied. We can attempt that, but existentialists do not think it is a project that can succeed, nor is it the source of our freedom. When the rules for action are clear and obvious, no decision is called for by us. Where our situation is unclear, then action falls back on our decision, for resolution will not come except by individual determination. Our freedom is discovered only under stress and pressure.

We should not fight to dispel the ambiguity of our human situation but accept the task of realizing it; that is the meaning of our freedom. We should shun any absolutes; they are false to our condition. The question is not to be right in God's eyes but in our own. And our freedom, when we achieve and sustain it in our actions, never becomes a law valid for all. Beauvoir objects to Marxism because of its restraints on human will and freedom. "As for us, we believe in freedom," she says. In fact, there is no way *not* to be free; we are, as Sartre says, "condemned to be free." We are cast into the world. Patience, courage, and fidelity become the chief virtues in this ethical outlook.

We do not necessarily have a positive will. Just because an evil will is possible, "to will oneself free" has a meaning. Existentialism, like religion, gives a real role to evil. But our freedom is an occasion for anguish, so that freedom is the source of difficulty as well as good. But even in its difficulty, we cannot keep freedom to ourselves. To will oneself free is also to will that others be free.

Simone de Beauvoir has reflected existential thought in her literary work, but as a woman her final prominence came from her analysis of the ethical situation peculiar to women. Hers is a typical existential approach, since ethical principles cannot be determined in the abstract, but only by looking to the concrete conditions under which we live.

The Second Sex

The Second Sex is a monumental book both in scope and in size. As befits a philosophical approach, this is not so much a work of protest, as characterizes some feminist literature, but an attempt to achieve clarity and to understand woman's situation. She reviews history and myth and tries to bring them to bear on women's lives today. Her aim is to promote human liberation by understanding and promoting individual response.

Of course, what Beauvoir observes is that women to a greater degree than men fail to take a place of human dignity as free and independent beings. Yet "woman" for Beauvoir means more than being born female. Every woman must share in the mysterious and threatened reality known as "femininity." The different attitudes of many women today indicate that they are haunted by their femininity.

Humanity is male-dominated, and man defines woman not in herself but as relative to him: For the male, woman is the "other." The two sexes have never shared the world in equality. But since to decline to be the "other" is to lose all advantages, too, women have a special incentive to forgo liberty and to become a thing. Accordingly, many women are pleased with their role as "other" and make no attempt to revolt. But, Beauvoir writes, today things have changed: After centuries of delay, women are close to dethroning the myth of femininity.

Examining the data of biology, Beauvoir concludes that male and female can be distinguished, but that biology is not particularly determinative of social roles in itself. The real, experienced situation of woman is different. Nature does not define woman; woman defines herself in her emotional life. Sexuality is not genital and is difficult to define. Marxism attempts to reduce woman to her labor, but such a reduction slurs over the most important problems. Sexuality is, of course, at the center of the distinction between men and women, but it is impossible to bring the sexual instinct under a code of regulation.

When Beauvoir turns to history, she finds no neat separation of roles. Women have shared in warfare and with no less ferocity and cruelty than man. Women can claim to give life to others in birth, but Beauvoir balances this consideration by saying that it is not in giving life but in risking life that we are raised above the animals. And in maternity, woman is more bound to her body than man is.

Revolutions are not always liberating. Beauvoir cites the French Revolution: During the Revolution women enjoyed a liberty that was anarchic, but when society was reorganized, women were firmly enslaved again. So, Beauvoir writes, we must be careful not to think that any accomplished change is somehow permanent. We tend to achieve our freedom by enslaving others. As the motto says, the price of freedom is eternal vigilance. In romantic periods, women are glorified in the magic fertility of the land: Woman is fecund nature.

There is a "myth of women," which Beauvoir examines, but she is optimistic that, at last, the myth of women may be extinguished. She goes on to analyze and explain the myth of women in the writings of five authors: Montherlant, D. H. Lawrence, Claudel, Breton, and Stendhal. Man is often the actor; women exist on the emotional level. Despite the differences in the accounts of the authors, a collective myth about women may be found. However, all five authors use different forms of the myth, so there is no uniform image. Women are contingent, multiple, actual women, whereas the myths make them to be eternal, unique, and changeless. Clearly, Beauvoir reveals her existentialist background by siding with the contingent and unique images of women. She finds the various myths incompatible.

More important, Beauvoir finds many "typical" attributes of "women" present in men, too. The truth is, she concludes, there is mystery on both sides. Beauvoir finds human nature an enigma, but this enigma is present "in its most disturbing form" in women. One is not born a "woman"; one *becomes* a woman. Beauvoir goes on to trace childhood training, stressing the specific conditionings for the young girl due to her body. Beauvoir sees maternity as fulfilling women's psychological destiny. And woman is, to a much greater degree than man, bound up with her female functions. Her biological transitions from one stage to another are dangerously abrupt. Nevertheless, Beauvoir argues, women have never constituted a closed society.

In spite of all the advances, most women recognize that the world is masculine on the whole. Yet if women want liberation, it must be collective. First of all, there must be an economic revolution, which underlies all change. However, the problem is that Beauvoir finds women more subject than men to other influences. Despite the male sexual drive, love is more important for women, since only in love can women harmoniously reconcile their eroticism with their narcissism. But love has its transcendent aspect, Beauvoir claims, in that the sexuality of women in love is tinged with mysticism. Woman, when she directs her love toward a man, is often seeking God in him.

Beauvoir does not argue that man and woman are basically alike; on the contrary, she recognizes and appreciates the differences. Because men and women are different sexually, they are to some degree different in their sensuality and sensitivity and in their relations to childbearing and to children. Motherhood is not in itself oppressive or confining, but the institutions perpetuated by males have made motherhood a burden and a handicap. If in the concrete matters of everyday life men and women were equal, there would be some chance that the differences would enhance their interrelationships and that their common interests would be served by cooperative action.

Beauvoir argues against the perpetuation of femininity as the sole or principal device for woman in her effort to relate effectively to man. Men have enslaved women, she shows convincingly, and thus it is not surprising that femininity has been the preoccupation of women in the effort to secure some compensating power. If economic conditions are altered so as to guarantee to women the same rewards for their labor that men receive, some progress will have been made—but economic justice is not enough. There must be a recognition of the common humanity of men and women, and social practices must be built on that humanity and directed toward equality, freedom, and consequent mutual benefit.

"To emancipate woman," Beauvoir writes, "is to refuse to confine her to the relations she bears to man, not to deny them to her; let her have her independent existence and she will continue none the less to exist to him *also*; mutually recognizing each other as subject, each will yet remain for the other an *other*."

Beauvoir ends by directing women "toward liberation," more than ever possible today. "Obedience" is no longer a civic duty. Gainful employment has helped to guarantee woman's liberty. However, this gain affects only some, since the majority of women do not escape from the traditional feminine world. But for woman to renounce femininity itself is to renounce a part of her humanity. The independent woman will suffer.

On the positive side, men are beginning to reconcile themselves to the new status of women. Best of all, it is clear that a woman's destiny is not determined from all eternity. She can claim her freedom.

FREDERICK SONTAG

Further Reading

Appignanesi, Lisa. *Simone de Beauvoir*. London: Penguin Books, 1988. One of the volumes in the Penguin *Lives of Modern Women* series, this work provides a readable account of the most important of the various dimensions of Beauvoir as the dutiful daughter turned skeptic, rebel, and committed campaigner for women's rights.

Ascher, Carol A. *Simone de Beauvoir: A Life of Freedom*. Boston: Beacon Press, 1981. Ascher brings out the ambiguity of Beauvoir's own condition, her contradictions, her obsession with death, and her courage in forging a commitment born of the anguish of being a woman in a world that threatens freedom.

Bair, Deirdre. *Simone de Beauvoir: A Biography*. New York: Summit Books, 1990. The most exhaustive and entertaining biography yet written. Covers the entire span of Beauvoir's life, both public and private, and pays tribute to her as the philosophical and political champion of women's rights.

Cottrell, Robert D. *Simone de Beauvoir*. New York: Frederick Ungar, 1975. One of the volumes in the *Modern Literature Monographs* series, Cottrell's book emphasizes the development of Beauvoir's thought as that development is illuminated by her autobiographical writings and *The Second Sex*.

Fallaize, Elizabeth. *The Novels of Simone de Beauvoir*. London and New York: Routledge, 1988. A scholarly examination of Beauvoir's five novels and two collections of short stories.

Keefe, Terry. *Simone de Beauvoir: A Study of Her Writings*. Totowa, N.J.: Barnes & Noble Books, 1983. Keefe, senior lecturer in the French Department of the University of Leicester, concentrates on Beauvoir as a writer and discusses with critical perception Beauvoir's moral and sociopolitical essays and her fiction.

Madsen, Axel. *Hearts and Minds: The Common Journey of Simone de Beauvoir and Jean-Paul Sartre*. New York: William Morrow, 1977. Madsen focuses on the mutual creative influence of Beauvoir and Sartre on each other and shows the close relationship of the intellect to the heart in the lives of these two remarkable thinkers.

Okely, Judith. *Simone de Beauvoir*. New York and London: Pantheon Books and Virago Press, 1986. Okeley, who writes as a devotee of Beauvoir's feminist writings, undertakes a careful analysis of Beauvoir's works both as expressions of emotional commitment and as intellectual arguments.

Patterson, Yolanda Astirita. *Simone de Beauvoir and the Demystification of Motherhood*. Ann Arbor and London: UMI Research Press, 1989. A careful and engaging study of Beauvoir's attitudes toward motherhood, her relationship with her own mother, her portrayal of mothers in her fiction, and her ideas concerning motherhood as expressed in her writings.

Wenzel, Helene Vivienne, ed. *Simone de Beauvoir: Witness to a Century*. *Yale French Studies*, No. 72. New Haven and London: Yale University Press, 1986. A number of scholars discuss the accomplishments of Beauvoir in a series of essays reviewing and commenting critically on the "woman question," women's lives today, liberation and women writing about women, Beauvoir and Sartre. The contributors, in addition to the editor, include Judith Butler, Virgina M. Fichera, Martha N. Evans, Yolanda A. Patterson, Catherine Portuges, Dorothy Kaufmann, Isabelle de Courtivron, Deirdre Bair, Margaret A. Simons, and Elaine Marks.

Whitmarsh, Anne. *Simone de Beauvoir and the Limits of Commitment.* Cambridge: Cambridge University Press, 1981. Whitmarsh shows how

ethics and political action meet in the thought and life of Beauvoir.

Winegarten, Renee. *Simone de Beauvoir: A Critical View.* Oxford: Berg Publishers, 1988. A study of Beauvoir as, in her words, "a writer and a woman writer." One of the *Berg Women's Series.*

SIMONE WEIL

Born: 1909, Paris, France
Died: 1943, Ashford, Kent, England
Major Works: (in translation): *Waiting for God* (1951), *Intimations of Christianity Among the Ancient Greeks* (1957), *The Need for Roots* (1952), *The Notebooks of Simone Weil* (1956), *Oppression and Liberty* (1958)

Major Ideas

Thought is inextricably linked to action.
The person is a creation of natural and social forces and can be "decreated" by them.
Pure goodness for which the human aspires is found by God's direct descent and through the mediation of natural and social structures.
The suffering of Christ is the paradigm action for goodness.

Simone Weil was the second child born into a well-off family of Jewish lineage, although none of the family took much note of this heritage. While she did not share the prodigious mathematical gifts of her brother André, Simone Weil from an early age showed not only a rare intelligence but numerous personal qualities that marked even her adult life. She had a rare sort of moral courage and sense of moral purity that often led her on a harsh and demanding quest for "truth, beauty, virtue and every kind of goodness," even when that quest appeared headed toward her own hurt. She also showed a rare and deep compassion for others that could lead her to shed tears over the news of an earthquake halfway across the globe.

Her early schooling was eclectic, but in 1925 she enrolled in the Lycée Henri IV and came under the influence of the eminent philosopher Émile Chartier (Alain). He contributed greatly to Weil's topical, unsystematic style. His ideas concerning the bodily conditions of thinking were also to heavily influence her thought.

This intellectual influence is quite evident even in her first important essay, her diploma thesis at the École Normale Superieure, "Science and Perception in Descartes." In this thesis, she sought to undertake a sort of Cartesian meditation. Unlike Descartes, however, who located the human essence metaphysically in thought, Weil regarded the ability to act as primary. It was from this ability to act, especially when countered by other agents and forces, that Weil sought to find the basis of thought, which she claimed to have discovered in a sort of elementary "geometry" inherent in human action. By reflection on this geometry, she argued, we can give method, that is, reason, to our projects in the world. Human work that takes into consideration the opposing forces of the world not only grasps the reality of the world but exhibits humanity at its highest.

Weil's intent in this thesis was twofold. On the one hand, she was trying to find a way by which human thought could be employed in such a way that the world as thought is not lost in clouds of abstraction. On the other hand, she was also trying to avoid describing the human thinker abstractly, either by locating the human in a transcendental subject or by regarding thought itself as *a priori*. Unfortunately, this early attempt was flawed to the degree that it itself began with a subject divorced from the very real and formative social influences of human thought.

Two years later, in her "Lectures on Philosophy" (actually a set of complete notes taken by one of her philosophy students), she takes the role of language far more seriously, and suggests that distinctively human thought arises when through language we order the world that we are given; it is then, by means of that order, that we grasp necessity.

These philosophical investigations were reflected in Weil's own involvement in French leftist politics. While teaching philosophy in a number of *lycées*, Weil was active in the syndicalist labor movement, which sought to remove production from large enterprises and put it in the hands of smaller groups

of workers. Her activities on behalf of the syndical-
ists included teaching night courses (many of them
on Marx) for the unemployed, and even marching
with them against city hall, an action not looked
upon favorably by the bourgeois school authorities.
In addition, in 1932–33 she traveled to prewar Nazi
Germany and sent back to France a series of ten
articles of haunting prophecy describing workers'
conditions there. In 1936, she joined the anarchist
cause in the Spanish Civil War, until a clumsy
accident forced her evacuation.

Both her philosophical and political interests
came together in an important monograph she
wrote in 1934 titled "Reflections Concerning the
Causes of Liberty and Social Oppression." A masterful and yet sympathetic critique of Marx, it
charged him with failing to see the real implications
of his own analyses. Weil argued that Marx should
not have had much hope in the idea of revolution,
for even on his own materialistic basis all effective
change depends on being able to wield power; by
definition, then, the weak can never overpower the
strong. Revolutions by the weak in the past, she
argued, have only served to confirm a change that
had already taken place. The Marxists of her own
day had failed to see that a revolution of the weak
was especially ludicrous, as the economic system
had become so strong that individuals could no
longer control it, including the so-called capitalists.
Rather, the system controlled them; it was managed
by "technicians of management," who were coming to have the most real power in the contemporary world. But even in their cases, it was really
the enterprise that was all-important and all-
consuming. It subjected *everybody* in the end to its
force: This was oppression.

Not only had contemporary Marxists failed to see
this, by preaching a revolution whereby human beings would be freed from having to labor, they also
failed to see that the problem of oppression was
actually a question of means and ends having been
reversed. For oppression results when human beings, instead of using the forces of their own enterprises are used by them.

Given that human beings cannot escape necessity
entirely, Weil argued, dignity and freedom are not

marked by freedom *from* necessity but by a different
relationship between workers and their material than
is usually found in modern societies. Human dignity
and freedom could be achieved, she thought, by organizing work in such a way that the human mind
could grasp not only the physical necessity of labor
but also the logical necessity of its processes. If so
organized, humans could both consent to their labors
and find meaning in them, and thus find dignity and
freedom. This recognition of necessity and consent
to it was what marked the difference between human
beings and beasts of burdens.

Despite calling "Reflections" her masterpiece,
Weil obviously was not satisfied with it, since in
order to come into closer contact with the object of
her reflections she took a leave of absence from
teaching in 1934–35 to work in a number of Paris
factories as a common laborer.

Hoping to find the camaraderie of workers joined
in a common enterprise and the real significance of
labor, she instead found the phenomenon she called
"affliction" (*le malheur*). Affliction, as she described it, consisted not merely of physical pain
but, more importantly, is the destruction of individual workers as persons. Previously she had suggested that the human person is, in effect, a focus of
power, including social power. Now she realized
that when extreme force, especially the social forces
inherent in the factory system, was turned on a
person, that person could cease to exist, even if
physical life continued. She had discovered a kind
of case, unfortunately all too common in human
societies, especially in modern ones, where there is
no possibility of consenting to necessity to gain
dignity; affliction by its very nature is degrading
and not ennobling. This experience of affliction
wiped out the last vestiges of a metaphysical subject
behind an individual's specific acts and history.

The factory year left her, in her own words, "in
pieces, body and soul." However, during the next
couple of years she had three unexpected religious
experiences that began a new phase in her life and
thought. One was particularly important. In 1938,
while attending Holy Week services at the abbey of
Solesmes to hear the Gregorian chant, she met a
young Englishman who taught her George Herbert's

poem "Love." She constantly recited this to herself during the week, particularly while suffering from the migraines that continued to plague her all her life. At one point during such a recital, despite her suffering, she had a mystical experience of being possessed by Christ; she knew in its purity the goodness for which she had aspired so long. What was especially important about this experience was that by it she came to imagine how suffering and affliction need not be insuperable obstacles to pure goodness. She realized that in Christ's Passion, seemingly useless affliction might actually put the human being into contact with pure goodness.

After this experience, a period followed marked by Weil's important and unique religious writings, particularly during the years 1940–42 in Marseilles, to which she had fled with her parents from German-occupied Paris. One very important essay is "The Love of God and Affliction," in which she clearly defines affliction and then goes on to argue that Jesus himself was afflicted. What distinguished Jesus' affliction, undeserved and inexplicable as it was even to him, was that he both consented to it as the Father's will and that he continued to love and hope when there was nothing to love or to hope for. Thus, Weil argues, a perfect bond was formed between Jesus and the Father, a bond that affliction is used to create, for affliction effectively strips away all limited motives and false goods. Thus affliction, which is unwanted and inexplicable, is not an insuperable barrier to love and goodness, and can through God's love purify love.

Weil used this analysis of Christ's cross as a means to describe both creation and human spirituality. God created, she argued, not by an act of power but by an act of withdrawal and powerlessness. Ceasing to be all, God allowed something else to exist. But he did not exactly abandon creation for, she goes on to say, this withdrawal was accomplished by the Son's abandonment (which is historically seen in the cross) to the crushing forces of necessity that govern the world. By doing so, he gave creation a goodness and purpose it did not otherwise have. Necessity, while distant from good, can, in Plato's phrase, be persuaded to goodness. Using a musical analogy, she claimed that creation

and all the forces of necessity that make it up can be seen as the nodes, as it were, on a vibrating string, which binds God in the fullness of being to God at the pole of perfect nothingness and which harmonizes all existence.

In an analogous manner, human beings find perfect goodness not by acts of power and attempts at individual self-creation but by "decreation," that is, by ceasing to exercise power and domination. By accepting necessity, which obeys God and which sets their limits, they can be joined to perfect goodness and recreated in God's image. Weil shows this nowhere so clearly as in her "Forms of the Implicit Love of God." Here she argues that the ability to pay "attention," that is, to remove one's self from central stage when dealing with others or the natural world by letting them exist in their right and not simply as something useful to us is a form of both love for God and love by God, even when we are not explicitly aware of it. By paying attention to what exists outside ourselves, we begin to divest ourselves of self-interest and protection, thus "decreating" the empirical ego. It is at this point that we may be recreated in God's image.

Despite this seemingly mystical turn in her thinking, Weil formally remained outside the Church. She firmly resisted baptism until she received this sacrament shortly before her death at the nonordained hand of a friend. Much of her resistance was due to her belief that baptism would separate her from all who were outside the Church. Her concerns were not theological in either a narrow academic or ecclesiastical sense. This is confirmed by the fact that she continued to write and think on political questions. But from this point on, political and social analyses were never far from her religious concerns.

This dual focus on the political and the religious appears clearly in her last writings in London while working for the Free French. In 1942, she left Marseilles for New York, a place she did not like at all, and she felt that she had deserted the war effort. For six months she attempted to get back to France in order to institute a project for front-line nurses, which she thought would show that the Allies were fighting for something morally different from the goals of the Nazis. She managed to get as far as London, where she was set to work on writing numerous reports on the problems facing a legitimate government after the war.

While apparently on diverse subjects, these writings show a marked consistency and a mature synthesis of her earlier thinking. In them, she set out to provide an alternative to the poles of Marxism and liberalism, between which so much of Western political and ethical thinking oscillated. She was especially critical of liberal ideas of the person and personal "rights." Liberalism had provided a legal form of fairness, but it had hardly seen the real depths of justice for which human beings thirst, particularly the afflicted. Furthermore, the liberal emphasis on the right of the individual to protect and enhance an empirical personality not only prevented people from seeing these depths but also allowed them to be easily manipulated by national and economic structures, since people falsely came to believe that their social participation was a matter of simple choice.

Weil therefore sought to reenvision the relationship between persons and societies. In this she was aided by her theory of the *metaxu* (intermediaries) derived from her religious thought and her reading of Plato. By this theory, she dismissed both Marxist and capitalist visions of inexorable progression into an ever-better future and, instead, she tried to describe how nations and cultures could be of help to human beings seeking unshakable goodness—in short, how societies might be one of the nodes between the fullness of being and nothingness and be used as such by humans. She had two especially important elements in this redescription. The first was that of basing political and ethical thinking on obligations rather than rights. All human beings have an eternal obligation to respect other human beings. This respect, she argued, was shown by providing not only for the essential material needs but also for the various needs of soul. Chief among these needs, she claimed, was a "need for roots."

The idea of "rootedness" is the second crucial element in Weil's proposal. Much of what makes up each human being is due to his and her cultural and social relationships: his or her "roots." This is just

as true of moral strength and moral expectations as it is of food preferences. Weil meant by her remarks to describe how transcendent goodness can permeate limited, concrete life. The problem as such was one of trying to see how a culture or society can itself become rooted in the absolute good and there find the nourishment necessary for those who live within it. Weil thought such nourishment comes from a culture's having ordered its diverse elements around certain transcendent insights, transmitting them by moral habit and education.

When a society has no roots in anything of depth, it can hardly provide the necessary spiritual or moral nourishment, she argued. Particularly problematic is the modern nation-state, which has tried to set itself up as deserving ultimate allegiance; it tends to uproot persons from traditions that have grown from far better inspirations than those that give rise to national sovereignty and power. In Weil's redescription of how a society might become rooted, she points to ways by which the West might recover and interpret its most healthy traditions, especially those that have eschewed the adulation of power. Not only was Weil interested in such recoveries in the political realm, she was also interested in how the West might reconceive both the relations between science and religion and the spiritual place of physical labor.

Weil died in 1943, nine months after arriving in England. Although her death was called a suicide by the attending physician, it is evident that her death was in fact the consequence of overexertion while suffering from tuberculosis and refusing to eat any more food than she thought the people in occupied France were getting. Even while facing death, she had maintained her moral resolve.

At the time of her death, Weil was little known outside certain limited French circles, having published very little during her lifetime. However, after the war an impressive amount of material began to appear as the numerous manuscripts she had carefully entrusted to friends and family were published in various collections. The projected *Oeuvres completes*, currently being published, will run to fifteen volumes.

ERIC O. SPRINGSTED

Further Reading

Blum, Lawrence, and Victor Seidler. *A Truer Liberty: Simone Weil and Marxism.* New York: Routledge, 1989. Perhaps the best work on Weil's political thought, with the particular merit of providing her historical context. Not much discussion of *The Need for Roots.*

Little, Patricia. *Simone Weil: Waiting on Truth.* Oxford: Oxford University Press, 1988. A well-balanced and accurate introduction to Weil's thought as a whole.

Petrement, Simone. *Simone Weil: A Life.* New York: Pantheon Books, 1976. The "official" biography, condensed from two volumes in French. It is written by a close friend of Weil, herself a philosopher, which allows her to comment insightfully on Weil's thought.

Springsted, Eric O. *Christus Mediator: Platonic Mediation in the Thought of Simone Weil.* Chico, Calif.: Scholars Press, 1983. An examination of Weil's religious and philosophical thought, concentrating on its Christian platonism and Weil's theory of the *metaxu.*

————. *Simone Weil and the Suffering of Love.* Cambridge: Cowley Publications, 1986. A presentation of Weil's unique and demanding views on suffering, and their implications for contemporary thought and spirituality.

Winch, Peter. *Simone Weil: The Just Balance.* Cambridge: Cambridge University Press, 1989. A subtle and close reading of the development of Weil's philosophical thought, with helpful comparisons to Wittgenstein, by an eminent contemporary philosopher.

ALBERT CAMUS

Born: 1913, Mondovi, Algeria
Died: 1960, near Sens, France
Major Works: *The Stranger* (1942), *The Myth of Sisyphus* (1942), *The Plague* (1947), *The Rebel* (1951)

Major Ideas

Absurdity lies in the opposition between the human need for meaning, on the one hand, and the unconcerned and meaningless world, on the other.
The presence of the absurd makes the problem of suicide the most fundamental philosophical question.
The absurd does not dictate death; what gives life its value is the consciousness of the absurd together with the revolt that consists in a defiant heroism that resists injustice.
By rebelling against the absurd conditions that waste life—whether they be social, political, or personal—the rebel shows solidarity with other persons and encourages the struggle for a more human world.

Although Albert Camus was not fond of being called an existentialist, the writings that made him the 1957 Nobel laureate in literature did much to popularize that philosophical movement. Novelist, playwright, and essayist, Camus was born and educated in Algeria, where he founded a theater group for which he wrote and produced plays. In 1940, he moved to Paris, became active in the French Resistance against the Nazi occupation, and later practiced journalism. He was friendly with Jean-Paul Sartre, but the two had a falling out and became philosophical rivals, even though many of their views were similar.

Camus was not an academic philosopher. Living in difficult times when life could not be taken for granted, he set aside the technicalities of philosophical theory to appraise life's meaning. It seemed to Camus that traditional values and ways of life had collapsed. He dramatized that situation in plays and novels such as *The Stranger* (1942) and *The Plague* (1947) and reflected on it philosophically in essays that asked, "Does life make sense?" His demise leaves the answer in suspense, for Camus died suddenly. A lover of fast cars, he lost his life in a crash.

The Myth of Sisyphus

With its desire for scientific precision and mathematical clarity, much modern philosophy has tried to do away with mythical forms of expression. Yet few philosophical works in the twentieth century

have exerted greater popular appeal than Camus's *The Myth of Sisyphus* (1942). In this work, Camus adapted a theme from ancient tales about Greek gods and heroes. He was especially attracted to Sisyphus, a mortal who challenged fate. Sisyphus would not submit to the authoritarian gods, and the gods retaliated by requiring him throughout eternity to push a huge boulder up a hill only to see it roll down again. Endless repetitions of this task apparently gained him nothing, but he persisted in his task.

We have not progressed fundamentally beyond the mythical condition of Sisyphus, Camus argued. With that theme in mind, Camus begins *The Myth of Sisyphus* as follows: "There is but one truly serious philosophical problem, and that is suicide. Judging whether life is or is not worth living amounts to answering the fundamental question of philosophy." Camus did not think that God or religious faith can provide what we need to resolve this problem. His quest, Camus reports in a preface to the *Myth* written in 1955, is to live "without the aid of eternal values." He felt that an appeal to God and religion is no longer credible, for in our time "the absurd" has center stage.

Absurdity comes to us in a feeling that can strike a person, as Camus said, "at any streetcorner." One "feels alien, a stranger"—even to oneself. This feeling arises through an encounter between the world and the demands we make as rational beings. Specifically, Camus explained, absurdity arises from the confrontation between "human need and the unreasonable silence of the world." We ask a thousand "whys?" that lack answers. We want solutions, but we stir up absurdity, because no sooner does thought assert something than it seems to negate what is affirmed. "The absurd," wrote Camus, "depends as much on man as on the world." Thus, when we ask the question of life's meaning, we realize that our demand for an answer gives rise to the feeling of absurdity as much as any characteristic of the world itself. Nevertheless, even if it cannot be satisfied, the yearning for rational answers should not go away. Its reality makes us the human beings that we are.

If human awareness did not exist, the absurd would not exist, either, Camus asserts. But exist it does, and thus the meaning we take for granted can crumble almost before we know it. "It happens that the stage sets collapse," observed Camus. "Rising, streetcar, four hours in the office or the factory, meal, streetcar, four hours of work, sleep, and Monday Tuesday Wednesday Thursday Friday and Saturday according to the same rhythm—this path is easily followed most of the time. But one day the 'why' arises and everything begins in that weariness tinged with amazement." The feeling of absurdity, Camus went on to explain, is not "the notion of the absurd." That feeling comes to us because "the absurd is essentially a divorce." It is what results when human consciousness and the world collide and separate.

Convinced that he could not escape the absurd as long as he lived, Camus insisted that existence implies "a total absence of hope." He could see nothing that might make it possible for him to transcend the absurd. Death, however, would put an end to it. Hence, suicide is an option. Indeed, since absurdity infests existence so painfully, would it not make sense to say that the absurd invites us to die, even dictates that we should?

Camus's answer was emphatically "No!" Far from solving any problem, suicide is the ultimate retreat. In fact, it is the unforgivable existential sin: "It is essential to die unreconciled," insisted Camus, "and not of one's own free will." Suicide compounds the negation of meaning by making it

impossible to capitalize on the recognition that "the absurd has meaning only insofar as it is not agreed to." Absurdity will not go away if we say that we refuse to die. On the contrary, it will remain. But Camus thought we should let it remain in order to defy it. Paradoxically, he even advises that we should make a point of contemplating the absurd, because "life will be lived all the better if it has no meaning." Defiance of the absurd maximizes life's intensity in a way that would not be possible if some transcendent God guaranteed life's significance.

Camus contended that there is a logic that makes sense in the face of the absurd. "I want to know," he wrote, "whether I can live what I know and with that alone. . . . I don't know whether this world has a meaning that transcends it. But I know that I do not know that meaning and that it is impossible for me just now to know it." Thus, to hope that there is a way beyond the absurd in this life is philosophical suicide. One cannot remain honest if one has succumbed to the temptation offered by that hope. But at the same time, Camus understood that reason alone will not be enough to persuade us that he is right. Strength of will is required to draw the conclusions Camus wanted from his logic of the absurd. Among other things, we will have to decide what it means that "there is so much stubborn hope in the human heart."

Sisyphus is Camus's absurd hero. Sisyphus loves life and hates death. His passions have condemned him, but the grandeur of Sisyphus is that he never gives up and is never dishonest. He accepts his fate only to defy it. Thereby he gives meaning to existence, meaning that cannot negate absurdity but refuses to succumb to it. Sisyphus is a creator who makes sense in circumstances that apparently rob human life of significance.

Camus wanted us all to find a way to live like Sisyphus. He spoke at length about how artistic creativity, for example, can move us in that direction, but his point was that each individual must find his or her own way.

It is important to note the picture of Sisyphus with which Camus's *Myth* ends. Although it would be natural to focus on Sisyphus as he pushes his rock up the hill, Camus asks us to reflect on Sisyphus when he reaches the top. He knows the rock will roll down, and it does. But as Sisyphus heads down to retrieve it, he does not despair. He surmounts his fate by scorning it, and so, Camus concludes, "we must imagine Sisyphus happy." Sisyphus sees clearly; he has ceased to hope for release. Yet by giving up hope and facing absurdity squarely, he has created meaning—not only for himself but, by his example, for others as well. Although existence will never satisfy us, life has meaning if we make it so by our determination.

The Rebel

Camus drew three consequences from the existence of the absurd: "my revolt, my freedom, and my passion." Decision was his, and his love of life led him to defy the absurd. In *The Myth of Sisyphus*, Camus drew those consequences from a reflection on suicide. In its sequel, *The Rebel* (1951), Camus expanded on his earlier themes. This time, murder provoked him. The twentieth century was proving that history is a slaughter-bench, drenched with disease, injustice, and especially man-made death. The absurd does not dictate suicide, but, Camus wondered, does it legitimize murder?

Again, Camus answered emphatically "No!" If the absurd implies that everything is permitted, it does not follow that nothing is forbidden. Building on the insight that the most authentically human response to absurdity is to protest against it, Camus emphasized that such defiance is and should be fundamentally social and communal. Life is fundamentally lived with others. Absurdity enters existence not simply because one's private needs go unmet, but because so many conditions exist that destroy family and friends, waste our shared experience, and rob human relationships of significance.

Hence, far from dictating suicide or legitimating murder, the absurd should lead to rebellion in the name of justice and human solidarity. "I rebel," wrote Camus, "therefore we exist."

Here, like Sisyphus, we face an uphill climb, because the rebellion Camus advocated is characterized by moderation. By moderation, Camus did not mean to say that our actions should be hesitant, dispassionate, or weak. But he did not want the rebel to become the revolutionary who so often destroys life under the pretense of saving it. "The logic of the rebel," asserted Camus, "is to want to serve justice so as not to add to the injustice of the human condition, to insist on plain language so as not to increase the universal falsehood, and to wager, in spite of human misery, for happiness." Camus was no pacifist. He knew that at times the logic of the rebel might even require the rebel to kill. But Camus's true rebel will never say or do anything "to legitimize murder, because rebellion, in principle, is a protest against death."

As if the task of rebellion were not difficult enough, Camus once more reminds us that the rebel can never expect to escape the fate of Sisyphus: "Man can master in himself everything that should be mastered," he wrote. "He should rectify in creation everything that can be rectified. And after he has done so, children will still die unjustly even in a perfect society. Even by his greatest effort man can only propose to diminish arithmetically the sufferings of the world." Perhaps things would have been different if the world had been ours to create, but at least "man is not entirely to blame; it was not he who started history." On the other hand, Camus added, neither "is he entirely innocent, since he continues it." The task before us, Camus concluded, is "to learn to live and to die, and, in order to be a man, to refuse to be a god."

JOHN K. ROTH

Further Reading

Brée, Germaine. *Camus*. New Brunswick, N.J.: Rutgers University Press, 1959. Brée concentrates on Camus's novels but also greatly respects *The Myth of Sisyphus* and *The Rebel*.

————, ed. *Camus: A Collection of Critical Essays*. Englewood Cliffs, N.J.: Prentice-Hall, 1962. The essays in this volume, each by a well-qualified scholar, cover the full range of Camus's thought.

Lottman, Herbert R. *Albert Camus: A Biography*. Garden City, N.Y.: Doubleday & Company, 1979. Lottman offers a sensitive interpretation of Camus's life and times.

Masters, Brian. *Camus: A Study*. Totowa, N.J.: Rowman and Littlefield, 1974. Masters interprets Camus as a "stern moralist" who struggled to renew humane values that are under threat.

O'Brien, Conor Cruise. *Albert Camus of Europe and Africa*. New York: Viking Press, 1970. A distinguished scholar looks at Camus's background, thought, and lasting contributions.

Sprintzen, David. *Camus: A Critical Examination*. Philadelphia: Temple University Press, 1988. This book explores Camus's approach to and insights about human existence.

Tarrow, Susan. *Exile from the Kingdom: A Political Rereading of Albert Camus*. University: University of Alabama Press, 1985. A critical examination of Camus's political orientation and insight.

Wilhoite, Fred H., Jr. *Beyond Nihilism: Albert Camus's Contribution to Political Thought*. Baton Rouge: Louisiana State University Press, 1968. Wilhoite argues that political concerns were never far from Camus's attention, and he thinks Camus's reflections contribute significantly to twentieth-century social thought.

Woelfel, James W. *Camus: A Theological Perspective*. Nashville: Abingdon Press, 1975. This book explores the religious implications of Camus's philosophy.

BIBLIOGRAPHY

We acknowledge with appreciation the use of the following editions of classic works in the preparation of articles for *Great Thinkers of the Western World*.

Abelard, Peter. *The Story of My Misfortunes.* Translated by Henry Adams Bellows. New York: Macmillan, 1972.

Anselm of Canterbury, Saint. *Anselm of Canterbury.* Edited and translated by Jasper Hopkins and Herbert Richardson. Vols. 1–3. Toronto and New York: Edwin Mellen Press, 1974.

Aquinas, Saint Thomas. *On the Truth of the Catholic Faith: Summa contra gentiles.* Translated by Anton C. Pegis et al. 4 vols. Garden City, N.Y.: Doubleday Image Books, 1955.

————. *Summa theologica.* Translated by the Fathers of the English Dominican Province. New York: Benziger Brothers, 1947–48.

Archimedes. *Archimedis Opera Omnia.* Edited by J. L. Heiberg, 3 vols. Leipzig: Teubner, 1910, 1913, 1915.

Aristotle. *The Basic Works of Aristotle.* Edited and introduction by Richard McKeon. New York: Random House, 1941.

Augustine, Saint. *The City of God.* Translated by Demetrius B. Zema and Gerald G. Walsh. 3 vols. New York: Father of the Church, 1950–1954.

Bacon, Francis. *The Philosophical Works of Francis Bacon.* Edited by John M. Robertson. London: George Routledge & Sons, 1905.

Bayle, Pierre. *Historical and Critical Dictionary.* Translated with introduction and notes by Richard H. Popkin, with the assistance of Craig Bush. Indianapolis: Bobbs-Merrill, 1965.

Beauvoir, Simone de. *The Second Sex.* Translated and edited by H. M. Parshley. Introduction by Deirdre Bair. Vintage Books. New York: Random House, 1989.

Bentham, Jeremy. *An Introduction to the Principles of Morals and Legislation.* Edited by J. H. Burns and H. L. A. Hart. In *The Collected Works of Jeremy Bentham,* J. H. Burns, general editor. London: Athlone Press, 1970.

Bergson, Henri. *Creative Evolution.* Translated by A. Mitchell. New York: Henry Holt, 1911.

————. *Time and Free Will.* Translated by F. L. Pogson. London: George Allen & Unwin, 1910.

————. *Matter and Memory.* Translated by N. M. Paul and W. S. Palmer. London: George Allen & Unwin, 1911.

————. *Laughter.* Translated by C. Brerton and F. Rothwell. New York: Macmillan, 1911.

————. *An Introduction to Metaphysics.* Translated by T. E. Hulme. New York: Putnam's Sons, 1912.

————. *The Two Sources of Morality and Religion.* Translated by A. Audra and C. Brerton. London: Macmillan, 1935.

Berkeley, George. *Principles, Dialogues, and Philosophical Correspondence.* Edited by Colin Murray Turbayne. The Library of Liberal Arts. Indianapolis, New York, and Kansas City: Bobbs-Merrill, 1965.

Bernard of Clairvaux, Saint. *The Works of Saint Bernard of Clairvaux.* Translations by Michael Casey et al. Spencer, Mass., and Kalamazoo, Mich.: Cistercian Publications, 1969–.

Blake, William. *The Complete Poetry and Prose of William Blake.* Edited by David V. Erdman. Rev. ed. Commentary by Harold Bloom. Garden City, N.Y.: Anchor Press/Doubleday, 1982.

Boethius, Anicius Manlius Severinus. *The Consolation of Philosophy.* Translated by V. E. Watts. Baltimore: Penguin Books, 1969.

Bohr, Niels. *Atomic Theory and the Description of Nature.* Cambridge: Cambridge University Press, 1961.

————. *Atomic Physics and Human Knowledge.* New York: Wiley, 1958.

Bonaventure, Saint. *The Works of Saint Bonaventure.* Translated from the Latin by José de Winck. Paterson, N.J.: St. Anthony Guild Press, 1960–.

————. *The Soul's Journey into God, The Tree of Life, The Life of St. Francis.* Edited by Ewert Cousins. New York: Paulist Press, 1978.

Buber, Martin. *I and Thou.* Translated by Walter Kaufmann. New York: Charles Scribner's Sons, 1970.

Calvin, John. *Calvin: Institutes of the Christian Religion.* Edited by Colin Murray Turbayne. Translated by F. L. Battles. Library of Christian Classics. Vols. 20 and 21. Philadelphia: Westminster Press, 1960.

Camus, Albert. *The Myth of Sisyphus.* Translated by Justin O'Brien. New York: Vintage Books, Random House, and Alfred A. Knopf, 1955.

————. *The Rebel.* Translated by Anthony Bower. New York: Vintage Books, Random House, and Alfred A. Knopf, 1956.

Collingwood, Robin George. *An Autobiography.* Introduction by Stephen Toulmin. Oxford: Clarendon Press; New York: Oxford University Press, 1982.

————. *An Essay on Philosophical Method.* Oxford: Clarendon Press, 1933.

————. *Essays in the Philosophy of Art.* Edited by Alan Donegan. Bloomington: Indiana University Press, 1964.

————. *The Idea of History.* Oxford: Clarendon Press, 1946.

————. *The Principles of Art.* Oxford: Clarendon Press, 1938.

Comte, Auguste. *The Positive Philosophy.* Translated and condensed by Harriet Martineau. 2 vols. London: Paul, Trench, Trubner, 1853; New York: Calvin Blanchard, 1855.

————. *The System of Positive Polity.* Translated by J. H. Bridges, Frederick Harrison, et al. London: Longmans, Green & Co., 1875–77.

————. *The Catechism of Positive Religion.* Translated by Richard Congreve. London: Kegan Paul & Co., 1858; 3d ed., rev. corr., 1891.

Condorcet, Marquis de. *Sketch for a Historical Picture of the Progress of the Human Mind.* Translated by June Barraclough. London: Weidenfeld, 1955.

————. *Selected Writings.* Edited by Keith Michael Baker. Indianapolis: Bobbs-Merrill, 1976.

Copernicus, Nicolaus. *Complete Works.* London: Macmillan, 1972.

————. *Three Copernican Treatises.* Translated, with an introduction and notes by Edward Rosen. 2d ed. rev. New York: Dover Publications, 1959.

Croce, Benedetto. *Essays on Literature and Literary Criticism.* Translated and annotated with an introduction by M. E. Moss. New York: State University Press of New York, 1990.

————. *Historical Materialism and the Economics of Karl Marx.* Translated by C. M. Meredith, with an introduction by A. D. Lindsay. New York: Russell & Russell, 1966.

————. *History of Europe in the Nineteenth Century.* Translated by Henry Furst. New York: Harcourt Brace & Co., 1933.

————. *History of the Kingdom of Naples.* Translated by Frances Frenaye. Edited and with an introduction by H. Stuart Hughes. Chicago and London: University of Chicago Press, 1970.

————. *The Philosophy of Giambattista Vico.* Translated by R. G. Collingwood. London: H. Latimer, 1913.

————. *Philosophy, Poetry, History.* Translated by Cecil Sprigge. Oxford: Oxford University Press, 1966.

————. *Politics and Morals.* Translated by S. I. Castiglione. London: George Allen & Unwin, 1946.

————. *What is Living and What is Dead of the Philosophy of Hegel.* Translated by D. Ainslie. New York: Russell & Russell, 1969.

Cudworth, Ralph. *The True Intellectual System of the Universe.* London: Richard Royston, 1678.

Dante Alighieri. *The Inferno.* Translated by John Ciardi. New York: New American Library, 1954.

————. *The Purgatorio.* Translated by John Ciardi. New York: New American Library, 1957.

————. *The Paradiso.* Translated by John Ciardi. New York: New American Library, 1961.

Darwin, Charles. *On the Origin of Species by Means of Natural Selection.* Reprinted with an introduction by E. Mayr. Cambridge: Harvard University Press, 1964.

————. *The Descent of Man and Selection in Relation to Sex.* Reprint. New York: AMS Press, 1972.

Descartes, René. *The Philosophical Works of Descartes.* Translated and edited by E. S. Haldane and G. T. R. Ross. 2 vols. Cambridge: Cambridge University Press, 1911–12.

————. *Descartes' Philosophical Writings.* Translated and edited by Elizabeth Anscomb and Peter T. Geach. Indianapolis: Bobbs-Merrill, 1971.

Dewey, John. *The Collected Works of John Dewey.* Carbondale: Southern Illinois University Press, 1969–89.

Eckhart, Meister. *Meister Eckhart: A Modern Translation.* Translated by Raymond Blakney. New York: Harper Brothers, 1941.

————. *Meister Eckhart: The Essential Sermons, Commentaries, Treatises, and Defense.* Translation and introduction by Edmund Colledge and Bernard McGinn. Toronto: Paulist Press, 1981.

Edwards, Jonathan. *The Works of Jonathan Edwards.* New Haven: Yale University Press, 1957.

————. *Jonathan Edwards: Representative Selections.* Introduction and edited by Clarence H. Faust and Thomas H. Johnson. American Century Series. New York: Hill and Wang, 1962.

Einstein, Albert. *The Collected Papers of Albert Einstein.* 2 vols. (with more projected). Edited by John Stachel. Princeton, N.J.: Princeton University Press, 1987, 1989.

————. *The Principle of Relativity.* London: Methuen, 1923. Reprint. New York: Dover, 1954.

————. *Relativity: The Special and the General Theory: A Popular Exposition.* Translated by Robert W. Lawson. 15th ed., 1952. Reprint. New York: Crown Publishers, 1961.

————. *Ideas and Opinions.* New York: Crown Publishers, 1954.

————. See autobiography in *Albert Einstein, Philosopher-Scientist.* Edited by P. A. Schilpp. Evanston, Ill.: Library of Living Philosophers, 1949.

Emerson, Ralph Waldo. *The Complete Essays and Other Writings.* Edited by Brooks Atkinson. New York: Random House, 1940.

Epictetus. *Enchiridion.* Translated by Thomas W. Higginson, with an introduction by Albert Salomon. 2d ed. Indianapolis: Bobbs-Merrill, 1955.

————. *Moral Discourses.* Translated by Elizabeth Carter. Edited by W. H. D. Rouse. London: J. H. Dent; New York: E. P. Dutton, 1937.

Epicurus. *The Philosophy of Epicurus.* Translated with commentary by George K. Strodach. Evanston, Ill.: Northwestern University Press, 1963.

Erasmus, Desiderius. *The "Adages" of Erasmus.* Translated and edited by Margaret Mann Phillips. Cambridge: Cambridge University Press, 1964.

————. *The Enchiridion.* Translated and edited by Raymond Himeleck. Bloomington: University of Indiana Press, 1965.

————. *Praise of Folly.* Translated by Betty Radice. New York: Penguin Books, 1971.

Euclid. *The Thirteen Books of the Elements.* Translated with introduction and commentary by Sir Thomas L. Heath. Cambridge: Cambridge University Press, 1926; reprint, New York: Dover Publications, 1956.

Fox, George. *The Journal of George Fox.* Edited by John L. Nickalls. London: Religious Society of Friends, 1975.

————. *No More But My Love: Letters of George Fox, 1624–91.* Edited by Cecil W. Sharman. London: Quaker Home Service, 1980.

————. *Narrative Papers of George Fox.* Edited by Henry J. Cadbury. Richmond, Ind.: Friends United Press, 1972.

Freud, Sigmund. *The Standard Edition of the Complete Psychological Works of Sigmund Freud.* Translated by James Strachey, general editor, with Anna Freud, Alex Strachey, and Alan Tyson. 24 vols. London: Hogarth and The Institute of Psycho-analysis, 1953–74.

————. *The Concordance to the Standard Edition of the Complete Works of Sigmund Freud.* Edited by S. A. Guttman, R. L. Jones, and S. M. Parish. 6 vols. Madison: International Universities Press, 1984.

————. *The Freud Reader.* Edited by Peter Gay. New York: W. W. Norton, 1989.

Galileo Galilei. *Sidderius Nuncius, or the Sidereal Messenger.* Translated with introduction, conclusion, and notes by Albert Van Helden. Chicago: University of Chicago Press, 1989.

————. *The Controversy on the Comets of 1618.* Includes *The Assayer.* Translated by Stillman Drake. Philadelphia: University of Pennsylvania Press, 1960.

————. *Dialogue Concerning the Two Chief World Systems.* Translated by Stillman Drake. 2d ed. Berkeley: University of California Press, 1967.

————. *Two New Sciences.* Translated with introduction and notes by Stillman Drake. Madison: University of Wisconsin Press, 1974.

Gassendi, Pierre. *The Selected Works of Pierre Gassendi.* Edited and translated by Craig Brush. New York: Johnson Reprint, 1972.

Gauss, Carl F. *Disquisitiones Arithmeticae.* Translated by Arthur A. Clarke. New Haven: Yale University Press, 1966.

————. *General Investigations of Curved Surfaces.* Translated by Adam Hiltebeitel and James Morehead. New York: Raven Press, 1965.

————. *Inaugural Lecture on Astronomy and Papers on the Foundations of Mathematics.* Translated by G. Waldo Dunnington. Baton Rouge: Louisiana State University Press, 1937.

Godwin, William. *Caleb Williams.* Edited and with introduction by David McCracken. New York: W. W. Norton, 1977.

————. *An Enquiry Concerning Political Justice.* Abridged and edited by K. Codell Carter. Oxford: Clarendon Press, 1971.

————. *Essays Never Before Published.* Edited by C. Kegan Paul. London: Henry S. King, 1873.

————. *Memoirs of the Author of A Vindication of the Rights of Woman.* London: J. Johnson, 1798. Facsimile, New York: Garland, 1974.

————. *Uncollected Writings (1785–1822): Articles in Periodicals and Six Pamphlets.* Introduction by Jack W. Marken and Burton R. Pollin. Gainesville, Fl.: Scholars' Facsimiles & Reprints, 1968.

Hegel, G. W. F. *Phenomenology of Spirit.* Translated by A. V. Miller. Oxford: Oxford University Press, 1977.

————. *Science of Logic.* Translated by A. V. Miller. London: George Allen & Unwin, 1969.

————. *Logic.* Translated by William Wallace. Oxford: Clarendon Press, 1975.

————. *Philosophy of Nature.* Translated by A. V. Miller. Oxford: Clarendon Press, 1970.

————. *Philosophy of Mind.* Translated by William Wallace and A. V. Miller. Oxford: Clarendon Press, 1971.

————. *Philosophy of Right.* Translated by T. M. Knox. Oxford: Clarendon Press, 1962.

Heidegger, Martin. *Being and Time.* Translated by John Macquarrie and Edward Robinson. New York: Harper & Row, 1962.

————. *An Introduction to Metaphysics.* Translated by Ralph Manheim. New Haven: Yale University Press, 1959.

————. *On the Way to Language.* Translated by Peter D. Hertz. New York: Harper & Row, 1971.

————. *Poetry, Language and Thought.* Translated and with an introduction by Alfred Hofstadter. New York: Harper & Row, 1971.

Hippocrates. *Hippocrates.* Translated by W. H. S. Jones et al. 6 vols. The Loeb Classical Library. Cambridge, Mass.: Harvard University Press, 1923–88.

Hobbes, Thomas. *Leviathan, Parts I and II.* Edited by Herbert W. Schneider. The Library of Liberal Arts. Indianapolis and New York: Bobbs-Merrill, 1958.

Hume, David. *A Treatise of Human Nature.* Edited by L. A. Selby-Bigge and P. H. Nidditch. 2 ed. Oxford: Clarendon Press, 1978.

————. *Enquiries Concerning Human Understanding and Concerning the Principles of Morals.* Edited by L. A. Selby-Bigge. 3d ed. Oxford: Clarendon Press, 1975.

————. *Dialogues Concerning Natural Religion.*

Edited by N. K. Smith. Indianapolis: Bobbs-Merrill, n.d.

Husserl, Edmund. *Ideas: General Introduction to Pure Phenomenology.* Translated by W. R. Boyce Gibson. New York: Macmillan, 1931.

_____. *Transcendental Phenomenology.* Translated with an introduction by David Carr. Evanston, Ill.: Northwestern University Press, 1970.

James, William. *The Works of William James.* Edited by Frederick Burkhardt. (Includes *Pragmatism,* 1975; *The Principles of Psychology*, 3 vols., 1981; *The Varieties of Religious Experience*, 1985; *The Will to Believe*, 1979.) Cambridge, Mass.: Harvard University Press, 1975–88.

Jefferson, Thomas. *Writings.* New York: Literary Classics of the United States, 1984.

John of the Cross, Saint. *Ascent of Mount Carmel.* Translated by E. Allison Peers. New York: Doubleday, Image Books, 1958.

_____. *Dark Night of the Soul.* Translated by E. Allison Peers. New York: Doubleday, Image Books, 1959.

_____. *Spiritual Canticle.* Translated by E. Allison Peers. New York: Doubleday, Image Books, 1961.

_____. *Living Flame of Love.* Translated by E. Allison Peers. New York: Doubleday, Image Books, 1962.

Jung, Carl G. *The Collected Works of C. G. Jung.* Edited by Sir Herbert Read, Michael Fordham, and Gerhard Adler. London: Routledge & Kegan Paul, 1966–.

Kant, Immanuel. *Critique of Practical Reason and Other Writings in Moral Philosophy.* Translated by L. W. Beck. Chicago: University of Chicago Press, 1949.

_____. *Critique of Pure Reason.* Translated by Norman Kemp Smith. New York: Humanities Press, 1950.

_____. *Religion within the Limits of Reason Alone.* Translated by T. M. Greene and H. H. Hudson. 2d ed. La Salle: Open Court, 1960.

Kepler, Johannes. *Epitome* (books 4 and 5) and *Harmonice* (book 5) in *Great Books of the Western World.* Encyclopaedia Brittanica and the University of Chicago. Vol. 16. Chicago: W. Benton, 1952.

Kierkegaard, Søren. *Either/Or.* Translated by Walter Lowrie. 2 vols. Anchor Books. Garden City, N.Y.: Doubleday & Co., 1959.

_____. *Fear and Trembling* and *the Sickness unto Death.* Translated with an introduction and notes by Walter Lowrie. Princeton, N.J.: Princeton University Press, 1954.

_____. *Philosophical Fragments.* Translated by David Swenson. Introduction and commentary by Niels Thulstrup. Revised translation and commentary translated by Howard V. Hong. Princeton, N.J.: Princeton University Press, 1936, 1962.

Leibniz, Gottfried Wilhelm. *Monodology and Other Philosophical Essays.* Translated by Paul Schrecker and Anne Martin Schrecker. Indianapolis: Bobbs-Merrill, 1965.

_____. *New Essays Concerning Human Understanding.* Translated and edited by Peter Remnant and Jonathan Bennett. Cambridge: Cambridge University Press, 1981.

_____. *Philosophical Papers and Letters.* Translated and edited by Leroy E. Loemker. 2 vols. Chicago: University of Chicago Press, 1956.

_____. *Theodicy: Essays on the Goodness of God, the Freedom of Man, and the Origin of Evil.* Translated by E. M. Huggard. Introduction by Austin Farrer. London: Routledge & Kegan Paul, 1952.

Locke, John. *An Essay Concerning Human Understanding, Collated and Annotated, with Biographical, Critical, and Historical Prolegomena.* Edited by Alexander C. Fraser. New York: Dover Publications, 1959.

_____. *Two Treatises of Civil Government.* Edited by Peter Laslett. New York: Mentor Books, 1965.

_____. *The Second Treatise of Civil Government and a Letter Concerning Toleration.* Edited by J. W. Gough. Oxford: Basil Blackwell, 1948.

Luther, Martin. *Luther's Works.* Edited by J. Pelikan and H. T. Lehmann. St. Louis: Concordia, 1955–76.

_____. *What Luther Says: An Anthology.* 3 vols. Edited by E. Plass. St. Louis: Concordia, 1959.

Machiavelli, Niccolò. *Machiavelli: The Chief Works and*

Others. Translated by Allan Gilbert. 3 vols. Durham, N.C.: Duke University Press, 1965.

Maimonides, Moses. *Guide of the Perplexed*. Translated by Shlomo Pines. Chicago: University of Chicago Press, 1963.

Malebranche, Nicolas. *Dialogues on Metaphysics*. Translated by Willis Doney. New York: Abaris Books, 1980.

_____. *The Search after Truth and Elucidations of the Search after Truth*. Translated by Thomas M. Lennon and Paul J. Olscamp. Columbus: Ohio State University Press, 1980.

Malthus, Thomas Robert. *The Works of Robert Malthus*. Edited by E. A. Wrigley and D. Souden. 8 vols. London: Pickering and Chatto, 1986.

Marcus Aurelius Antoninus. *The Meditations*. Translated by G. M. A. Grube. Indianapolis: Hackett, 1983.

Marx, Karl. *Capital: A Critique of Political Economy*. Translated by Ben Fowkes. Introduction by Ernest Mandel. New York: Vintage Books, 1977.

_____, with Friedrich Engels. *Basic Writings on Politics and Literature*. Translated by Lewis S. Feuer. Garden City, N.Y.: Doubleday, 1959.

Maxwell, James Clerk. *A Treatise on Electricity and Magnetism*. 2 vols. Oxford, 1873. Reprint. New York: Dover, 1954.

_____. *Theory of Heat*. London, 1870. Reprint. Westport, Conn.: Greenwood Press, 1970.

_____. *The Scientific Papers of James Clerk Maxwell*. Edited by W. D. Niven. 2 vols. Cambridge, 1890. Reprint. New York: Dover, 1952.

Mendeleev, D. M. *The Principles of Chemistry*. 3d ed. London, 1905. Reprint, New York: Kraus Reprints, 1969.

Mill, John Stuart. *Collected Works of John Stuart Mill*. Toronto: University of Toronto Press; London: Routledge & Kegan Paul, 1965–.

Montaigne, Michel de. *The Complete Essays of Montaigne*. Translated by Donald M. Frame. Stanford: Stanford University Press, 1957.

More, Henry. *The Immortality of the Soul*. Dordrecht: Klüwer, 1988.

More, Thomas. *The Yale Edition of the Complete Works of Thomas More*. Edited by Richard Sylvester. New Haven and London: Yale University Press, 1963–.

Newman, John Henry. *Apologia pro vita sua*. Edited by David J. DeLaura. Norton Critical Editions. New York: W. W. Norton, 1968.

_____. *An Essay in Aid of a Grammar of Assent*. Edited with introduction and notes by I. T. Ker. Oxford: Clarendon Press, 1985.

_____. *The Idea of a University*. Edited with introduction and notes by I. T. Ker. Oxford: Clarendon Press, 1976.

Newton, Isaac. *Philosophiae naturalis principia mathematica*. Latin text of the 3d edition, 1726, with editorial comments in English. Edited by A. Koyre and I. B. Cohen. Cambridge: Harvard University Press, 1972.

_____. *Opticks*. 4th ed. London, 1730. Reprint. New York: Dover, 1952.

_____. *The Mathematical Papers of Isaac Newton*. 8 vols. Edited by D. T. Whiteside. Cambridge: Cambridge University Press, 1967–81.

_____. *Correspondence*. Edited by H. W. Turnbull. 7 vols. Cambridge: Cambridge University Press, 1959–77.

Niebuhr, Reinhold. *Moral Man and Immoral Society*. New York: Charles Scribner's Sons, 1932.

_____. *An Interpretation of Christian Ethics*. New York: Harper & Brothers, 1935.

_____. *Beyond Tragedy*. New York: Charles Scribner's Sons, 1937.

_____. *The Nature and Destiny of Man*. New York: Charles Scribner's Sons, 1943.

_____. *The Children of Light and the Children of Darkness*. New York: Charles Scribner's Sons, 1944.

_____. *Faith and History*. New York: Charles Scribner's Sons, 1949.

_____. *The Self and the Dramas of History*. New York: Charles Scribner's Sons, 1955.

_____. *Leaves from the Notebook of a Tamed Cynic.* New York: Doubleday & Company, 1957.

Nietzsche, Friedrich. *Beyond Good and Evil.* Translated by Walter Kaufmann. New York: Vintage Books, 1966.

_____. *The Gay Science.* Translated by Walter Kaufmann. New York: Vintage Books, 1974.

_____. *On the Genealogy of Morals.* Translated by Walter Kaufmann and R. J. Hollingdale. New York: Vintage Books, 1967.

_____. *Thus Spoke Zarathustra.* Translated by Walter Kaufmann. New York: Viking Press, 1966.

Ockham, William of. *Ockham's Philosophical Writings.* Translated by Philotheus Boehner. Edinburgh: Thomas Nelson, 1957.

_____. *Selections from Medieval Philosophers.* Translated by Richard McKeon. 2 vols. New York: Charles Scribner's Sons, 1930.

_____. *The De sacramento altaris' of William of Ockham.* Translated by Thomas Bruce Birch. Burlington, Iowa: Lutheran Literary Board, 1930.

_____. *Predestination, God's Foreknowledge and Future Contingents.* Translated by Marilyn McCord Adams and Norman Kretzmann. New York: Appleton-Century-Crofts, 1969.

_____. *Ockham Studies and Selections.* Edited by Stephen Chak Tornay. La Salle, Ill.: Open Court, 1938.

Origen. *On First Principles.* Translated by G. W. Butterworth. New York: Harper & Row, 1966.

Ortega y Gasset, José. *Meditations on Quixote.* Translated by Evelyn Rugg and Diego Marin. New York: W. W. Norton, 1963.

_____. *Invertebrate Spain.* Translated by Mildred Adams. New York: W. W. Norton, 1937.

_____. *The Revolt of the Masses.* Translated anonymously. London: George Allen & Unwin, 1932.

_____. *The Dehumanization of Art.* Translated by Helene Weyl. Princeton, N.J.: Princeton University Press, 1948.

Paine, Thomas. *The Complete Writings of Thomas Paine.* Edited by Philip S. Foner. 2 vols. New York: Citadel Press, 1945.

Parmenides. In Milton C. Nahm, ed., *Selections from Early Greek Philosophy.* 4th ed. New York: Appleton-Century-Crofts, 1964.

Pascal, Blaise. *Pensées and the Provincial Letters.* Translated by W. F. Trotter and Thomas M'Crie. New York: Modern Library, 1941.

_____. *Great Shorter Works of Pascal.* Translated by Emile Caillet and John C. Blankenagel. Westport, Conn.: Greenwood Press, 1974.

_____. *Pascal: Selections.* Edited by R. H. Popkin. New York: Macmillan, 1989.

Peirce, Charles Sanders. *The Collected Papers of Charles Sanders Peirce.* Edited by Charles Hartshorne and Paul Weiss. Vols. 1–6. Cambridge, Mass.: Harvard University Press, 1931–35. Edited by Arthur Burks. Vols. 7, 8. Cambridge, Mass.: Harvard University Press, 1958.

_____. *Philosophical Writings of Peirce.* Edited by Justus Buchler. New York: Dover Publications, 1955.

Planck, Max. *A Survey of Physical Theory.* Translated by R. Jones and D. H. Williams. 1920. Reprint. New York: Dover Publications, 1960.

_____. *The Philosophy of Physics.* Translated by W. H. Johnston. London: George Allen & Unwin, 1936.

_____. *Scientific Autobiography and Other Papers.* Translated by Frank Gaynor. New York: Philosophical Library, 1949.

Plato. *The Dialogues of Plato.* Edited by Benjamin Jowett. 4th ed., revised by D. J. Allan and H. E. Dole. 4 vols. London: Oxford University Press, 1953.

Plotinus. *Plotinus.* Translated by A. H. Armstrong. 7 vols. The Loeb Classical Library. Cambridge, Mass.: Harvard University Press, 1966–.

Protagoras of Abdera. In Kathleen Freeman, ed., *Ancilla to the Pre-Socratic Philosophers: A Complete Translation of the Fragments in Diels, "Fragmente der Vorsokratiker."* Cambridge, Mass.: Harvard University Press, 1983.

Ptolemy. *Ptolemy's Almagest.* London: Duckworth, 1984.

_____. *Tetrabiblos.* Edited and translated by F. E. Robbins. Cambridge, Mass.: Harvard University Press, 1940; reprint, 1980.

Rahner, Karl. *Foundations of Christian Faith: An Introduction to the Idea of Christianity.* Translated by W. Dych. New York: Seabury Press, 1978.

_____. *Sacramentum Mundi: An Encyclopedia of Theology.* 6 vols. New York: Herder & Herder, 1968.

_____. *Spirit in the World.* Translated by W. Dych. New York: Herder & Herder, 1968.

_____, with Herbert Vorgrimler. *Theological Dictionary.* Translated by Richard Strachan. New York: Herder & Herder, 1965.

_____. *Theological Investigations.* Translated with an introduction by Cornelius Ernst. 22 vols. Other translators of later volumes. Baltimore: Helicon Press; London: Darton, Longman & Todd; New York: Seabury Press, 1961–87.

Rousseau, Jean-Jacques. *Social Contract.* Translated and with introduction by Maurice Cranston. Baltimore: Penguin Books, 1968.

Russell, Bertrand. *Autobiography.* 3 vols. Boston: Little, Brown & Co., 1967–69.

_____. *Our Knowledge of the External World.* London: George Allen & Unwin, 1926.

Santayana, George. *The Works of George Santayana.* 15 vols. New York: Charles Scribner's Sons, Simon & Schuster, 1936–40.

Sartre, Jean-Paul. *Being and Nothingness.* Translated by Hazel E. Barnes. New York: Philosophical Library, 1956.

_____. *Existentialism and Humanism.* Translated by Philip Mairet. London: Methuen, 1970.

_____. *Nausea.* Translated by Lloyd Alexander. New York: New Directions, 1964.

Schopenhauer, Arthur. *The Works of Schopenhauer.* Abridged. Edited by Will Durant. Introduction by Thomas Mann. New York: Frederick Ungar, 1955.

_____. *The World as Will and Representation.* Translated by E. F. J. Payne. 2 vols. Indian Hills, Colo.: Falcon's Wing Press, 1958.

_____. *The Will to Live: Selected Writings of Arthur Schopenhauer.* Edited by Richard Taylor. Anchor Books. Garden City, N.Y.: Doubleday & Co., 1962.

Schrödinger, Erwin. *Collected Papers on Wave Mechanics.* London: Blackie and Son, 1928.

_____. *Science and Humanism: Physics in Our Times.* Cambridge: Cambridge University Press, 1951.

_____. *Nature and the Greeks.* Cambridge: Cambridge University Press, 1954.

_____. *Mind and Matter.* Cambridge: Cambridge University Press, 1958.

_____. *My View of the World.* Cambridge: Cambridge University Press, 1964.

Sextus Empiricus. *Sextus Empiricus.* Translated by R. G. Bury. 4 vols. Loeb Classical Library. London: Heinemann; and Cambridge, Mass.: Harvard University Press, 1933–49.

Smith, Adam. *An Inquiry into the Nature and Causes of the Wealth of Nations.* Edited by R. H. Campbell, A. S. Skinner, and W. B. Todd. Oxford: Clarendon Press, 1976.

_____. *The Theory of Moral Sentiments.* Edited by D. D. Raphael and A. L. Macfie. Oxford: Clarendon Press, 1976.

Spencer, Herbert. *An Autobiography.* New York: D. Appleton & Co., 1904.

_____. *First Principles.* New York: D. Appleton & Co., 1899.

Spinoza, Benedict. *The Chief Works of Benedict de Spinoza.* Translated by R. H. M. Elwes. 2 vols. Rev. ed., 1903. New York: Dover, 1951.

_____. *Earlier Philosophical Writings: The Cartesian Principles and Thoughts on Metaphysics.* Translated by Frank A. Hayes. Introduction by David Bidney. Indianapolis: Bobbs-Merrill, 1963.

_____. *Short Treatise on God, Man, and his Well-Being.* Translated by Lydia G. Robinson. Chicago: Open Court, 1909.

Teilhard de Chardin, Pierre. *Hymn of the Universe.* New York and Evanston: Harper & Row, 1965.

_____. *The Divine Milieu.* New York: Harper & Row, 1960.

————. *The Phenomenon of Man.* New York and Evanston: Harper & Row, 1959.

Teresa of Ávila, Saint. *The Life of Teresa of Jesus.* Translated by E. Allison Peers. Garden City, N.Y.: Doubleday, Image Books, 1960.

————. *Interior Castle.* Translated by E. Allison Peers. Garden City, N.Y.: Doubleday, Image Books, 1961.

Thoreau, Henry David. *The Writings of Henry David Thoreau.* Edited by Bradford Torrey. 20 vols. Boston: Houghton Mifflin & Co., 1906.

————. *Walden.* Edited by J. Lyndon Shanley. Princeton, N.J.: Princeton University Press, 1971.

Tillich, Paul. *Gesammelte Werke* (14 vols.) and *Erganzungsbande* (6 vols.). Stuttgart, Germany: Evangelisches Verlagswerk, 1959–62.

————. *The Interpretation of History.* New York: Charles Scribner's Sons, 1936.

————. *The Protestant Era.* Chicago: University of Chicago Press, 1948.

————. *Systematic Theology.* Chicago: University of Chicago Press, vol. 1, 1951; vol. 2, 1957; vol. 3, 1963.

————. *The Courage to Be.* New Haven: Yale University Press, 1952.

————. *Dynamics of Faith.* New York: Harper, Torchbook, 1958.

————. *A History of Christian Thought and Perspectives on Nineteenth and Twentieth Century Protestant Theology.* Edited by Carl E. Braaten. New York: Harper & Row, 1968.

Toynbee, Arnold. *A Study of History.* New edition revised and abridged by the author and June Caplan. London: Oxford University Press; Thames & Hudson, 1972.

————. *Change and Habit.* New York: Oxford University Press, 1966.

————. *Cities on the Move.* New York: Oxford University Press, 1956.

————. *Civilization on Trial.* New York: Oxford University Press, 1948.

————. *An Historian's Approach to Religion.* New York: Oxford University Press, 1956.

Unamuno y Jugo, Miguel de. *The Life of Don Quixote and Sancho.* Translated by Anthony Kerrigan. Princeton, N.J.: Princeton University Press, 1967.

————. *The Tragic Sense of Life.* Translated by J. E. Crawford Flitch. New York: Dover Publications, 1954.

————. *Abel Sanchez and Other Stories.* Translated by Anthony Kerrigan. Chicago: Henry Regnery Co., 1956.

Vico, Giambattista. *Autobiography.* Translated by Max Harold Fisch and Thomas Goddard Bergin. Ithaca, N.Y.: Great Seal Books, 1963.

————. *The New Science.* Translated from the 3d edition, 1744, by Thomas Goddard Bergin and Max Harold Fisch. Ithaca, N.Y.: Cornell University Press, 1948.

Voltaire (Françoise Marie Arouet de Voltaire). *Candide or Optimism.* Edited by Norman L. Torrey. New York: Appleton-Century-Crofts, 1946.

Weber, Max. *Economy and Society: An Outline of Interpretive Sociology.* Edited by Guenther Roth and Claus Wittich. Translated by Ephraim Fischoff et al. 2 vols. Berkeley: University of California Press, 1978.

————. *From Max Weber: Essays in Sociology.* Edited and translated by H. H. Gerth and C. Wright Mills. New York: Oxford University Press, 1976.

————. *The Methodology of the Social Sciences.* Edited and translated by Edward A. Shils and Henry A. Finch. New York: Free Press, 1949.

————. *The Protestant Ethic and the Spirit of Capitalism.* Translated by Talcott Parsons. New York: Charles Scribner's Sons, 1958.

————. *Weber: Selections in Translation.* Edited by W. G. Runciman. Translated by E. Matthews. Cambridge: Cambridge University Press, 1978.

Weil, Simone. *Waiting for God.* Translated by Emma Craufurd. Introduction by Leslie A. Fiedler. New York: Harper & Row, 1951.

Whitehead, Alfred North. *Process and Reality.* Corr. ed. Edited by David Ray Griffin and Donald W. Sherburne. New York: Macmillan, 1978.

Wittgenstein, Ludwig. *Philosophical Investigations.* Translated from 3d ed. by G. E. M. Anscombe. Oxford: B. Blackwell, 1963.

————. *Tractatus Logico-Philosophicus.* The German text with a new translation by D. F. Pears and B. F. McGuiness. Introduction by Bertrand Russell. New York: Humanities Press, 1961.

Wollstonecraft, Mary. *An Historical and Moral View of the Origin and Progress of the French Revolution and the Effect It Has Produced in Europe.* London: Joseph Johnson, 1795. Delmar, N.Y.: Scholars' Facsimiles & Reprints, 1975.

————. *Letters Written during a Short Residence in Sweden, Norway, and Denmark.* London: Joseph Johnson, 1796. Edited by Carol H. Poston. Lincoln: University of Nebraska, 1976.

————. *Mary, A Fiction* and *The Wrongs of Woman.* Edited by Gary Kelly. London: Oxford University Press, 1976.

————. *Original Stories from Real Life.* In *Classics of Children's Literature 1621–1932,* selected and arranged by Alison Lurie and Justin G. Schiller. Facsimile. New York: Garland, 1977.

————. *Thoughts on the Education of Daughters.* London: Joseph Johnson, 1787. Reprint. Clifton, N.J.: Augustus M. Kelley, 1972.

————. *A Vindication of the Rights of Men.* London: Joseph Johnson, 1790. Facsimile. Delmar, N.Y.: Scholars' Facsimiles & Reprints, 1975.

————. *A Vindication of the Rights of Woman.* London: Joseph Johnson, 1792. Edited by Carol H. Poston. 2d ed. New York: W. W. Norton, 1988.

Zeno of Elea. In John Burnet, ed., *Early Greek Philosophy.* Chapter 8, "The Younger Eleatics." 4th ed. London: Adam & Charles Black, 1930; reprint, 1963.

————. In W. D. Ross, ed., *Aristotle.* 5th ed. rev. London: Methuen, 1949.

————. In Aristotle: *Physics.* Translated by Philip H. Wicksteed and Francis M. Cornford. Cambridge, Mass., and London: Harvard University Press and William Heinemann, 1952.

THINKER INDEX